NATURAL MEDICINES
COMPREHENSIVE DATABASE
CONSUMER VERSION

Created by the Editors of:

NATURAL MEDICINES
COMPREHENSIVE DATABASE
PROFESSIONAL VERSION

Published by Therapeutic Research Faculty

3120 W. March Lane ◆ PO Box 8190 ◆ Stockton CA 95208
phone (209) 472-2244 ◆ fax (209) 472-2249
mail@naturaldatabaseconsumer.com
www.naturaldatabaseconsumer.com

Produced in cooperation with the Editors of:

PHARMACIST'S
LETTER

PRESCRIBER'S
LETTER

When referencing this *Database*, use the following format for the citation:

Jellin JM, Gregory PJ, et al. *Pharmacist's Letter/Prescriber's Letter Natural Medicines Comprehensive Database Consumer Version.* Stockton, CA: Therapeutic Research Faculty; 2006:pg xx-xx.

Errors, inaccuracies, or omissions are always possible in a work of this sort. The publisher assumes no responsibility for any adverse events, or any patient care based on the application of the information contained in the resource. Any person who uses this resource must rely on their own judgement before applying any of the information contained to any specific medical situation. People who are not health professionals should also not rely solely on the information contained in this resource and should seek appropriate professional guidance on the use of any medicinal or other agent before using it.

For information on obtaining additional copies of this Consumer Version, or the Professional Version, or access to the Web version or the PDA version of Natural Medicines Comprehensive Database, or a subscription to Prescriber's Letter or Pharmacist's Letter, see the last pages of this book, or contact: Therapeutic Research Faculty, 3120 W. March Lane, PO Box 8190, Stockton, CA 95208
TEL: 209-472-2244 • FAX: 209-472-2249
E-MAIL: mail@NaturalDatabaseConsumer.com
WEBSITE: www.therapeuticresearch.com

Printed in the United States of America
ISBN-10: 0-9788205-0-9
ISBN 13: 978-0-9788205-0-3

Table of Contents

Natural Medicines Comprehensive Database Consumer Version
About this Resource

Dear User:

There is both a Professional Version and a Consumer Version of this *Natural Medicines Comprehensive Database*. This is the Consumer Version. The Professional Version was created in the late 1990s and initially took two years to complete. Since then a full-time research and editorial staff consisting of pharmacists, physicians, and other healthcare professionals has continued to update the *Database* on a daily basis.

The *Database* developed due to the growth in use of natural medicines in North America during the 1990s. Healthcare providers needed practical, unbiased, and scientifically reliable information about natural medicines in order to better counsel their patients. But virtually no reliable information resources existed at the time.

When *Natural Medicines Comprehensive Database Professional Version* was launched, it filled a great need and was met with abundant praise from the medical community.

In a review in 2000, the *Journal of the American Medical Association* said, "This superb book...is highly recommended for all physicians, pharmacists, and others interested in the responsible use of natural medicines sold in North America."

U.S. News and World Report in a 2001 cover story, said the *Database* is "the scientific gold standard for medical professionals and avid users."

The *Journal of the American Pharmaceutical Association* reviewed several herbal medicine resources and proclaimed the *Database* the overall best, based on quality of information and cost.

Natural Medicines Comprehensive Database Professional Version continues to lead the way. In response to public demand, this Consumer Version of the *Database* has been created for people with an interest in natural medicines who want high quality, scientifically reliable information. It is written in easy-to-understand non-technical language and contains reliable information.

The Professional Version of the *Database* is also available to those who want more detailed and technical information. To find out more about the Professional Version, go to www.naturaldatabase.com. It provides sophisticated medical information, along with thousands of reference citations and links to the underlying medical research. It also provides various search functions to aid the user in finding information.

We hope you find the *Database* useful. If you have questions, comments, or suggestions, don't hesitate to contact us by phone: 209-472-2244, or by email: mail@NaturalDatabaseConsumer.com.

How to Use
Natural Medicines Comprehensive Database Consumer Version

Natural Medicines Comprehensive Database Consumer Version has four main sections. The first section provides users with chapters on general information related to natural medicines.

The next section provides useful charts and comparisons such as Effectiveness Ratings by Disease; Potential Interactions Between Drugs and Natural Medicines; Potential Interactions Between Natural Medicines and Drugs; Drug Influences on Nutrient Levels and Depletion.

The third section provides data on specific ingredients that are contained in natural medicines. For more sophisticated, detailed information and references see the *Natural Medicines Comprehensive Database Professional Version* at www.naturaldatabase.com.

The fourth section of this resource provides a general index for the data on natural medicines.

How to use Monographs

The third section consists of a collection of monographs. Each monograph contains the following:

What other names is this product known by?
Most natural medicines have several different names. There are common or colloquial names, and there are scientific names. The name of each monograph is usually the most commonly used name. This section lists all the other names the product is known by.

What is it?
This is a brief description of what the product is…a plant, herb, or other substance…and what is used to make the natural medicine.

Is it effective?
This section is one of the most useful sections for determining the scientific evidence to support the use of the product for a specific condition. In this section, each use is categorized based on a rating system. Natural medicines that have lots of positive supportive evidence for treating a certain condition might be rated Likely Effective. For other conditions where there is less supportive evidence, the natural medicine might be rated Possibly Effective. In many cases, there is not enough scientific research to give any effectiveness rating. This means that there is not enough scientific evidence currently known to prove whether the particular natural medicine is likely to be effective for the given condition.

Here is a breakdown of the specific meaning of each Effectiveness Rating:

EFFECTIVE = The product has passed a rigorous scientific review equivalent to a review by the FDA, Health Canada, or other governmental authority and has been found to be effective for a specific medical condition as an OTC drug, orphan drug, or prescription drug product.

LIKELY EFFECTIVE = Reputable references generally agree that the product is effective for the given condition, based on two or more high quality clinical studies involving several hundred to several thousand patients, giving positive results for relevant end-points and published in established journals.

POSSIBLY EFFECTIVE = Reputable references suggest that the product might work for the given condition based on one or more clinical studies giving positive results for clinically relevant end-points.

POSSIBLY INEFFECTIVE = Reputable references suggest that the product might not work for the given condition based on one clinical study giving negative results for clinically relevant end-points.

LIKELY INEFFECTIVE = Reputable references generally agree that the product is not effective for the given condition, based on two or more high quality clinical studies giving negative results for clinically relevant end-points and published in established journals.

INEFFECTIVE = Most reputable references agree that the product is not effective for the given condition, or multiple high-quality studies resulted in negative results; there are no equally reliable clinical studies offering convincing contradictory data.

How does it work?

This section briefly describes how the natural medicine might work in the body to treat a given condition.

Are there safety concerns?

The safety of a given natural medicine should be the first consideration before trying a product. Many products are safe, but some have unknown safety or might be unsafe. This section describes any potential safety concerns as well as lists potential side effects. It also indicates if people with certain conditions such as diabetes, high blood pressure, or other conditions should avoid the natural medicine.

This section also provides information as to whether the specific natural medicine is safe. Most natural medicines have not been tested in pregnant women or during breast-feeding. When there is not enough information, it is recommended that women NOT use the natural medicine.

Are there any interactions with medicines?

Many natural medicines are known to interact with regular medicines. This section provides information about which drugs the natural medicine might interact with. In many cases, there is not enough information to know if a natural medicine can interact with regular medicines. Therefore, it's always important to talk with a healthcare professional before taking any natural medicine, especially if you take any prescription or over-the-counter medicines.

Need-to-Know Information about Natural Medicines

Every country regulates the use of natural medicines in a different way. But just about every country considers natural medicines to be different than conventional prescription or over-the-counter (OTC) drugs. In general, regulations governing the testing and sales of natural medicines do not treat natural medicines as rigidly as over-the-counter or prescription drugs.

In the United States, natural medicines are referred to as "dietary supplements." These products are regulated under the Dietary Supplement Health and Education Act (DSHEA) of 1994. Under DSHEA, a dietary supplement includes any of the following:

- vitamin
- mineral
- herb or botanical
- amino acid
- dietary substance used to supplement the diet
- concentrate, metabolite, constituent, extract, or combination of any of the items listed above

There are a couple exceptions. Tobacco products are not considered a dietary supplement. Also, currently available prescription or over-the-counter drugs cannot also be considered a dietary supplement.

In 1994, when the DSHEA law was passed, the use of natural medicines exploded in the US. Since then, the dietary supplement industry has grown into a multi-billion dollar industry.

The DSHEA law allows dietary supplements on the market without the same testing for safety or effectiveness that is required of OTC or prescription drugs. Unlike prescription and over-the-counter drugs, dietary supplements do not have to be proven safe or effective before being marketed to the public. This means that companies can manufacturer and sell products without demonstrating that the product actually works for a given condition. The law also requires that these products not claim to treat or prevent any particular disease. For example, they are not permitted to say that they treat high blood pressure, prevent heart disease, or cure diabetes. Instead they are only permitted to make so-called "structure/function" claims. They can say things such as "helps promote good circulation," or "supports healthy blood sugar metabolism."

Upstanding manufacturers abide by these rules, however some supplement makers push the limits with product names and promotions materials that suggest effectiveness for a certain condition. Users must keep in mind that some dietary supplements that claim to work for a certain condition may or may not have the scientifically reliable evidence to support that claim.

Table. Regulations for Dietary Supplements compared to Conventional Medicines

	Dietary Supplements	Conventional Non-Prescription and Prescription Medicines
Proof of Effectiveness	Not required	Required
Proof of Safety	Manufacturers are not required to prove to the government that the ingredients are safe.	Ingredients are proven safe according to government regulations.
Burden of Proof	The government must prove that a product is NOT safe in order for the product to be removed from the market.	Manufacturers must prove to the government that a product is safe in order to put the product ON the market.

Manufacturers of dietary supplements also do not have to submit proof to the US Food and Drug Administration that a product is safe before putting the product on the market. If products are found to be unsafe after being sold on the market, then the Food and Drug Administration can remove those products from the market. This occurred with the product ephedra. Ephedra was sold in numerous supplements for weight loss and improving athletic performance. After several cases of death, heart attack, stroke, or seizure were reported in people who used these products, the Food and Drug Administration was able to remove ephedra products from the market.

It is important to keep in mind that "natural" does not always mean "safe." Some natural products, such as ephedra, can cause real, significant side effects.

Another important issue related to dietary supplements is how they are manufactured. Conventional prescription and over-the-counter drugs are required to meet manufacturing guidelines in order to be offered for sale. These same manufacturing guidelines are not currently required for dietary supplements. Over the years, there have been numerous concerns that some dietary supplement products do not always contain exactly what is stated on the label. Some products have either more or less of certain ingredients than the amounts stated on the label. In some cases, products have been found to be contaminated with heavy metals or even prescription drugs. Some dietary supplements have developed an excellent reputation for being very effective against certain conditions. However, upon examination it has been determined that some products actually contain certain amounts of a prescription drug. In these cases, it might make sense that the product is very effective, but there are also corresponding safety concerns related to using a prescription drug without realizing it.

Dietary supplements manufactured in the US in the future are likely to be manufactured under new guidelines developed by the Food and Drug Adminstration. Even as these new guidelines are being developed and turned into law, some independent organizations are working to verify the quality of various dietary supplements. One of the most trust organizations is the United States Pharmacopeia (USP).

USP Verified Products

USP now has a program to verify the ingredients in dietary supplements. Dietary supplements that are part of this program have followed stringent manufacturing guidelines and reliably contain the ingredients and the amounts of ingredients stated on the product label.

Natural Medicines Comprehensive Database consists of a listing of well over 14,000 brand name dietary supplements. Each product that is a part of the USP program and carries the *USP Verified* seal is identified in the *Database*. For the latest natural products that have the *USP Verified* designation, go to www.naturaldatabaseconsumer.com.

Homeopathy

There is often confusion about homeopathy. Many people think of homeopathy, natural medicine, alternative medicine, and holistic medicine to all be the same thing. But they are not.

Homeopathy is actually a distinct formal system of medicine. Homeopathy was started over 200 years ago by the German physician Samuel Hahnemann. The word "homeopathy" comes from Greek and literally means "similar disease."

Homeopathy is very controversial for several reasons. First, one of the key beliefs is that "like cures like." Practitioners of homeopathy believe that if a substance causes high blood pressure, then that same substance, in dilute form, can actually cure high blood pressure.

Related to this belief is that products that are MORE dilute are actually more powerful than products that are less dilute. Homeopathic products go through a special sequence of dilutions interspersed with vigorous shaking. Homeopathic practitioners believe that the process of diluting and shaking results in an "imprint" of the original substance in the water.

Homeopathic remedies have a special labeling system. Products marked with a 1X have a 1:10 dilution. Those with 2X are 1:100 dilutions. Products with marked with a 1C are also 1:100 dilutions. Those with a 3C are 1:1,000,000 dilutions. Products marked as 12c or 24X are so dilute that they no longer contain any detectable amount of original substance. These products basically contain just water. But from the homeopathic perspective, this means that they are super potent.

The homeopathic philosophy was developed before we had a solid understanding of physics and chemistry. Today, it is recognized that homeopathic beliefs do not fit with our understanding of chemistry, physics, or pharmacology. Because homeopathic products are often so dilute that they contain none of the original substance, conventional medical science would not expect them to have any beneficial effects or to cause any negative side effects.

Surprisingly, homeopathic products are regulated by the Food and Drug Administration and can be legally sold as homeopathic drugs in stores and pharmacies. This is due to old legislation originally passed in 1938. The legislation was sponsored by a senator who also happened to be a homeopathic physician. There is also confusion related to which products are truly homeopathic products. The reason for this is that brand name products consisting of homeopathic ingredients can legally be sold. In order for these products to meet the true and original intention of homeopathy, the products would need to be diluted. However, some modern day products consist of homeopathic ingredients but are not diluted. They are still sold as homeopathic products and fall under the law that allows the sale of homeopathic products, even though they are not diluted. Many times the undiluted ingredients are herbal ingredients that are listed in the Homeopathic Pharmacopeia.

Nutrient Depletion

Some conventional prescription and over-the-counter drugs can decrease the amount of certain vitamins and other nutrients in the body. For example, cholesterol-lowering drugs called "statins" can lower levels of the nutrient coenzyme Q10. Some sellers of dietary supplements use this information to promote the sale of a wide variety of vitamins. But the truth is, in most cases, taking a dietary supplement probably isn't necessary.

This book includes a detailed chart on this subject. The chart highlights which drugs might lower nutrient levels in the body. The chart also indicates when taking a dietary supplement might be necessary to prevent nutrient levels from going too low and causing problems. In many cases, there isn't enough information to know if taking a dietary supplement would be beneficial.

In all cases, before starting to take a new dietary supplement, especially if you take prescription medicine, talk with your pharmacist, physician, or other healthcare provider. One reason that this is important is because the ingredients in natural medicines can sometimes lead to interactions with certain conditions or with prescription or non-prescription drugs. Some herbal medicines can increase the body's bleeding time, especially when taken along with certain medications that cause the same effect. Other herbal medicines may change the blood sugar level in people with diabetes or have other effects that can interfere with treatments or conditions.

Natural Medicines Comprehensive Database
How the Consumer Version and Professional Version differ

There are two versions of the *Natural Medicines Comprehensive Database*. There is a Professional Version and a Consumer Version. This is the Consumer Version.

Natural Medicines Comprehensive Database Professional Version was created by Therapeutic Research Faculty at the Therapeutic Research Center to objectively answer inquiries from medical professionals about natural medicines. It was first launched in 1999. The *Natural Medicines Comprehensive Database Professional Version* was the first reliable, constantly updated, evidence-based comprehensive reference for physicians, pharmacists and other professionals seeking information about natural medicines. It became widely used in medical centers, doctors' offices, pharmacies, hospitals, drug information centers, and by government agencies around the world.

The ***Natural Medicines Comprehensive Database Professional Version*** is recognized as the scientific gold standard for evidence-based information on natural medicines. Leaders in conventional medicine as well as complementary, alternative, and integrative medicine recognize the ***Database*** as the most comprehensive and clinically relevant rescource on this subject. It gives medical professionals reliable information categorized as follows:

- Alternative Names
- Scientific Names
- Uses
- Safety
- Effectiveness
- Mechanism of Action
- Adverse Reactions
- Interactions with Herbs
- Interactions with Drugs
- Nutrient Depletion
- Interactions with Foods
- Interactions with Lab Tests
- Interactions with Diseases
- Dosage
- Brand Names
- Reference citations from scientific literature

The ***Database*** is updated daily with new findings including new interactions and safety concerns.

Natural Medicines Comprehensive Database Consumer Version was launched in 2004 so persons who are not medical professionals could also have access to reliable information about natural medicines. The ***Natural Medicines Comprehensive Database Consumer Version*** is based on the ***Natural Medicines Comprehensive Database Professional Version***. The original editors from Therapeutic Research Center created and update the Consumer Version to give consumers all the same scientific reliability in a format that is consumer-friendly to read and understand.

Natural Medicines Comprehensive Database is supported by the best available scientific evidence. This evidence is analyzed and evaluated using the same high standards the editors use to evaluate conventional pharmaceuticals. The researchers and editors at Therapeutic Research Center research and publish ***Prescriber's Letter*** and ***Pharmacist's Letter*** for physicians, nurse practitioners, physician assistants, pharmacists and other medical professionals. These publications are widely known for reliable scientific information and advice about conventional drug therapy. The editors apply the same rigorous analysis to the information published in ***Natural Medicines Comprehensive Database***. When evidence for natural medicines does not exist or is severely deficient for a particular product this deficiency is clearly acknowledged with a statement indicating a lack of data.

To gather the scientific data, editors, researchers, and contributors systematically review medical journals from around the world. Hundreds of articles are reviewed and analyzed. Reliable data providing clinically relevant information are added to the **Database**. This does not mean that only flawless studies are analyzed. But it does mean that the **Database** is based on is the best available data at the current time. The higher quality research data carry much more weight for addition to the *Database*.

Products receive a rating on effectiveness and on safety. Interactions are also noted. All statements in the **Database** are referenced to scientific studies and scientific reports. The **Natural Medicines Comprehensive Database Professional Version** is fully referenced, and the Consumer Version is not. Consumers who desire the reference citations or the very sophisticated medical information contained in the Professional Version may find it at www.naturaldatabase.com for a subscription fee.

Natural Medicines Comprehensive Database Team

Natural Medicines Comprehensive Database Team

SPECIAL CONSULTANTS

Karen Davidson, Pharm.D.
 Senior Associate Editor,
 Pharmacist's Letter and *Prescriber's Letter*
Kimberly Palacioz, Pharm.D.
 Associate Editor,
 Pharmacist's Letter and *Prescriber's Letter*
Crystal Amos, B.Sc.Pharm., ACPR
 Assistant Editor,
 Pharmacist's Letter and *Prescriber's Letter*
Melissa Blair, Pharm.D., BCPS, CDE
 Assistant Editor,
 Pharmacist's Letter and *Prescriber's Letter*
Kayla Dotson, Pharm.D.
 Assistant Editor,
 Pharmacist's Letter and *Prescriber's Letter*
Tanveer Khan, Pharm.D.
 Assistant Editor,
 Pharmacist's Letter and *Prescriber's Letter*
Tony Martin, Pharm.D., MBA
 Assistant Editor,
 Pharmacist's Letter and *Prescriber's Letter*
 Continuing Education Director
Kristin Weitzel, Pharm.D., CDE
 Assistant Editor,
 Pharmacist's Letter and *Prescriber's Letter*
Neeta O'Mara, Pharm.D., BCPS
 Drug Information Consultant,
 Pharmacist's Letter and *Prescriber's Letter*
Wan-Chi Tom, Pharm.D.
 Drug Information Consultant,
 Pharmacist's Letter and *Prescriber's Letter*
Karen Wilson
 Editorial Liaison,
 Pharmacist's Letter and *Prescriber's Letter*

EDITORIAL STAFF

Jocosa Bottemiller
Stephanie Feilzer
Rachel McGehee
Barbara Parnacott
Minda Paglinawan
Ryan Thomas

WEBSITE MANAGEMENT

Mike Acosta
Charles Callistro
Wes Johnson
David Prothero
Jon Rombough
Harold Sohrweide

STAFF

Georgene Albertini
Myleen Arcangel
Janna Foster
Jan Garr
Tillie Giovannetti
Sharon Gunishaw
Russ Johnson
Jessalyn Ka
Kasey Kaufman
Keith Marston
Julie McCloud
Linda McDonald
Darcy Meade
Ygraine Montgomery
Marji Mullins
Gemma Perez
Gloria Rios
Cessy Rios
Lisa Shawhan
Becky Thornburg
Neng Vang
Kathy Webb

Effectiveness Ratings by Disease

For more information on any of the natural medicines identified in this list, review the listing for that monograph in the database. Just because a product has a positive effectiveness rating does not mean it is appropriate for all patients. In some cases natural medicines that are rated effective might be unsafe for certain patients due to contraindications, drug interactions, or other reasons.

Aging

Aging skin
Possibly Effective
  DHEA
  Pyruvate
Eye conditions in the elderly (Age-related macular degeneration, AMD)
Possibly Effective
  Beta-Carotene
  DHA
  Lutein
  Vitamin C
  Vitamin E
  Zinc
Possibly Ineffective
  EPA
Eye conditions in the elderly (Age-related maculopathy)
Possibly Effective
  Fish Oil
Possibly Ineffective
  Lycopene
Fall prevention
Likely Effective
  Vitamin D
Low testosterone levels in the elderly (Age-related testosterone deficiency)
Possibly Effective
  Acetyl-L-Carnitine
  Propionyl-L-Carnitine
Memory and thinking problems caused by aging (Age-related cognitive impairment)
Possibly Effective
  Acetyl-L-Carnitine
  Citicoline
  Phosphatidylserine
Memory problems in the elderly (Age-related memory impairment)
Possibly Effective
  Ginkgo
Likely Ineffective
  Choline
Tooth retention in the elderly
Possibly Effective
  Calcium
Wrinkled skin
Likely Effective
  Alpha Hydroxy Acids
Possibly Effective
  Vitamin C

Bone, Muscle, and Joints

Athletic conditioning
Possibly Ineffective
  Androstenediol
  Boron
  Chromium
  Chrysin
Likely Ineffective
  Androstenedione
  Creatine
Athletic performance
Possibly Effective
  Caffeine
  Creatine
  Deanol
  Pycnogenol
Possibly Ineffective
  Bee Pollen
  Branched-Chain Amino Acids
  Choline
  Cordyceps
  Dimethylglycine
  Ginseng, Panax
  Ginseng, Siberian
  Glutamine
  L-Tryptophan
  Magnesium
  Ornithine
  Ornithine Ketoglutarate
  Pangamic Acid
  Puncture Vine
Likely Ineffective
  Coca
  Coenzyme Q-10
  Glycerol
  Inosine
  L-Carnitine
  Phosphate Salts
Back pain
Possibly Effective
  Devil's Claw
  Willow Bark
Bone Substitute
Likely Effective
  Coral
Fibromyalgia
Possibly Effective
  5-HTP
  Capsicum
  Gamma-Hydroxybutyrate (GHB)
  Magnesium
  SAMe
Inflammation caused by bone fractures
Possibly Effective
  Chymotrypsin

Muscle breakdown after injury or surgery
Possibly Effective
  Alpha-Ketoglutarate
Muscle breakdown during exercise
Possibly Effective
  Branched-Chain Amino Acids
Muscle cramps
Possibly Effective
  Zinc
Muscle soreness caused by exercise
Possibly Ineffective
  Bromelain
  Fish Oil
  Soy
Muscle strength in older adults
Possibly Ineffective
  DHEA
  Vitamin D
Osteoarthritis (OA)
Likely Effective
  Chondroitin Sulfate
  Glucosamine Sulfate
  SAMe
Possibly Effective
  Avocado
  Beta-Carotene
  Bovine Cartilage
  Bromelain
  Camphor
  Cat's Claw
  Cetylated Fatty Acids
  Devil's Claw
  Hyaluronic Acid
  MSM (Methylsulfonylmethane)
  Niacin And Niacinamide
  Rutin
  Soybean Oil
  Superoxide Dismutase
  Trypsin
  Vitamin C
Possibly Ineffective
  Bee Venom
  Cod Liver Oil
  Vitamin E
Osteoporosis
Likely Effective
  Calcium
  Ipriflavone
  Vitamin D
Possibly Effective
  DHEA
  Evening Primrose Oil
  Fish Oil
  Fluoride
  Magnesium
  Manganese
  Silicon

CONSUMER VERSION

Medical professionals should consult the Professional Version at www.NaturalDatabase.com.

Osteoporosis (Cont.)

Possibly Effective (Cont.)
  Soy
  Strontium
Possibly Ineffective
  Flaxseed
  Progesterone

Paget's disease

Possibly Effective
  Ipriflavone

Physical performance

Possibly Effective
  Beta-Carotene
  Vitamin C
  Vitamin E

Psoriatic arthritis

Possibly Ineffective
  Zinc

Rheumatoid arthritis (RA)

Possibly Effective
  Borage
  Bovine Cartilage
  Cat's Claw
  Fish Oil
  Olive
  Superoxide Dismutase
  Thunder God Vine
  Vitamin D
  Vitamin E
Possibly Ineffective
  Creatine
  Feverfew
  Flaxseed Oil
  Histidine
  New Zealand Green-Lipped
    Mussel
  Selenium
  Zinc

Weak and painful bones (Osteomalacia)

Effective
  Vitamin D

Brain, Nervous System, and Mental Health

Adjustment disorder with anxious mood

Possibly Effective
  Passionflower

Adrenoleukodystrophy

Possibly Effective
  Lorenzo's Oil

Adrenomyeloneuropathy

Possibly Ineffective
  Lorenzo's Oil

Alcoholism

Possibly Effective
  GHB

ALS, Lou Gehrig's disease (Amyotrophic lateral sclerosis)

Possibly Ineffective
  Creatine
  N-Acetyl Cysteine
  Threonine
  Transfer Factor
Likely Ineffective
  Branched-Chain Amino Acids

Alzheimer's disease (see also Dementia)

Possibly Effective
  Acetyl-L-Carnitine
  Idebenone
  Lemon Balm
  Niacin And Niacinamide
  Phosphatidylserine
  Sage
  Vitamin E
Possibly Ineffective
  Beta-Carotene
  Choline
  DHEA
  Inositol
  Pyridoxine
  Vitamin C
Likely Ineffective
  Deanol
  Lecithin
  N-Acetyl Cysteine

Anorexia nervosa

Possibly Effective
  Zinc

Anxiety

Likely Effective
  Kava
Possibly Effective
  Valerian

Attention deficit-hyperactivity disorder (ADHD)

Possibly Effective
  Lithium
  Zinc
Possibly Ineffective
  Caffeine
  DHA (Docosahexaenoic Acid)
  Evening Primrose Oil
  Phenylalanine
  Pycnogenol
  Tyrosine
  Vitamin C

Autism

Possibly Ineffective
  Dimethylglycine
  Inositol
  Pyridoxine
Likely Ineffective
  Secretin

Bipolar disorder

Effective
  Lithium
Possibly Effective
  Fish Oil

Carpal tunnel syndrome

Possibly Ineffective
  Vitamin B6

Cerebellar ataxia

Possibly Ineffective
  Choline

Cerebral palsy

Possibly Ineffective
  Magnesium

Chronic fatigue syndrome (CFS)

Possibly Effective
  Magnesium
Possibly Ineffective
  Folic Acid
  Melatonin
  Transfer Factor

Cluster headache

Possibly Effective
  Capsicum
  Magnesium
  Melatonin

Cognitive function

Possibly Effective
  Beer
  Brahmi
  Fish Oil
  Ginkgo
  Ginseng, Panax
  Huperzine A
  Iron
  Wine
Possibly Ineffective
  DHEA

Cognitive impairment

Possibly Effective
  Acetyl-L-Carnitine

Concentration, coordination, and endurance

Possibly Effective
  Schisandra

Dementia (see also Alzheimer's disease)

Possibly Effective
  Ginkgo
  Huperzine A
  Vinpocetine
  Vitamin E
Possibly Ineffective
  NADH

Depression

Likely Effective
  Lithium
  SAMe
  St. John's Wort
Possibly Effective
  5-HTP
  EPA (Eicosapentaenoic Acid)
  Fish Oil
  Folic Acid
  Saffron
Possibly Ineffective
  DHA (Docosahexaenoic Acid)
  Inositol
  Tyrosine

Natural Medicines Comprehensive Database Consumer Version

(209) 472-2244

Depression (Cont.)
Likely Ineffective
Melatonin
Difficulty learning and performing tasks (Dyspraxia)
Possibly Effective
Fish Oil
Vitamin E
Dyslexia
Possibly Effective
Fish Oil
Epilepsy/Seizure disorder
Possibly Effective
Medium Chain Triglycerides
N-Acetyl Cysteine
Possibly Ineffective
Dimethylglycine
Generalized anxiety disorder (GAD)
Possibly Effective
Passionflower
Headache
Effective
Caffeine
Possibly Ineffective
5-HTP
Hyperkinetic cerebral dysfunction syndrome
Possibly Effective
Pyridoxine
Mania
Possibly Effective
Branched-Chain Amino Acids
Mental alertness
Likely Effective
Black Tea
Caffeine
Coffee
Green Tea
Oolong Tea
Migraine headache
Effective
Caffeine
Possibly Effective
Butterbur
Coenzyme Q-10
Feverfew
Magnesium
Riboflavin
Possibly Ineffective
Fish Oil
Movement problems originating in the brain (Extrapyramidal disorders)
Likely Ineffective
Lecithin
Multiple sclerosis (MS)
Possibly Effective
Marijuana
Vitamin D
Possibly Ineffective
Bee Venom
Myasthenia gravis
Possibly Effective
Huperzine A

Nerve pain from herpes virus (Postherpetic neuralgia)
Possibly Effective
DMSO (Dimethylsulfoxide)
Nerve pain in the limbs (Peripheral neuropathy)
Possibly Effective
Alpha-Lipoic Acid
Nerve pain in several places (Polyneuropathy)
Possibly Ineffective
St. John's Wort
Obsessive-compulsive disorder (OCD)
Possibly Effective
Inositol
Panic disorder
Possibly Effective
Inositol
Parkinson's disease
Possibly Effective
Black Tea
Caffeine
Coenzyme Q-10
Coffee
Green Tea
Vitamin E
Pervasive developmental disorder
Likely Ineffective
Secretin
Reflex sympathetic dystrophy (RSD)
Possibly Effective
Vitamin C
Schizophrenia
Possibly Effective
DHEA
Glycine
Lithium
Possibly Ineffective
EPA (Eicosapentaenoic Acid)
Inositol
Likely Ineffective
Choline
Seasonal affective disorder (SAD)
Possibly Ineffective
Ginkgo
Somatization disorder
Possibly Effective
St. John's Wort
Spinal spasticity
Possibly Effective
Threonine
Tension Headache
Possibly Effective
Peppermint
Possibly Ineffective
5-HTP

Cancer

Bladder cancer
Possibly Effective
Green Tea
Vitamin E

Bladder cancer (Cont.)
Possibly Ineffective
Lycopene
Tomato
Bone pain due to cancer spread (Painful bony metastases)
Effective
Strontium
Breast cancer
Possibly Effective
Beta-Carotene
Folic Acid
Green Tea
Olive
Soy
Vitamin A
Possibly Ineffective
Black Tea
Coffee
Garlic
Likely Ineffective
Vitamin E
Breast cancer-related hot flashes
Possibly Ineffective
Vitamin E
Cancer prevention (General)
Possibly Effective
Vitamin C
Possibly Ineffective
Beer
Likely Ineffective
Beta-Carotene
Cancer treatment (General; used with other treatments)
Possibly Effective
Beta Glucans (As an injection)
Coriolus Mushroom (The PSK component has been used)
Likely Ineffective
DMSO (Dimethylsulfoxide)
European Mistletoe
Shark Cartilage
Ineffective
Apricot
Colorectal cancer
Possibly Effective
Coffee
Conjugated Linoleic Acid
Folic Acid
Garlic
Lutein
Olive
Possibly Ineffective
Barley
Green Tea
Hydrazine Sulfate
Lycopene
Oats
Rice Bran
Vitamin E
Wheat Bran

Medical professionals should consult the Professional Version at www.NaturalDatabase.com.

Colorectal non-cancerous tumor (Colorectal adenoma)
Possibly Ineffective
  Blond Psyllium
Digestive tract cancers
Possibly Ineffective
  Coffee
Endometrial cancer
Possibly Effective
  Fish Oil
Esophageal cancer
Possibly Effective
  Green Tea
Head and neck cancer
Possibly Ineffective
  Vitamin E
Likely Ineffective
  N-Acetyl Cysteine
  Vitamin A
Ill health and malnutrition related to cancer (Cachexia)
Possibly Effective
  Adenosine
  Fish Oil
  Medium Chain Triglycerides
    (MCT)
Lung cancer
Possibly Effective
  Lycopene
  Pyridoxine
Possibly Ineffective
  Garlic
  Selenium
  Transfer Factor
Likely Ineffective
  Beta-Carotene
  Hydrazine Sulfate
  N-Acetyl Cysteine
  Vitamin E
Nerve pain caused by cancer
Possibly Effective
  Magnesium
Ovarian cancer
Possibly Effective
  Beta-Carotene
  Black Tea
  Green Tea
  Lycopene
  Oolong Tea
Pancreatic cancer
Possibly Effective
  Folic Acid
  Green Tea
Possibly Ineffective
  Vitamin E
Pre-cancerous changes to the cervix (Cervical dysplasia)
Possibly Effective
  Green Tea
  Indole-3-Carbinol

Prostate cancer
Possibly Effective
  Lycopene
  Melatonin
  Selenium
  Strontium
  Tomato
Possibly Ineffective
  Beta-Carotene
  Shiitake Mushroom
Skin cancer
Possibly Ineffective
  Selenium
  Transfer Factor
Solid tumors
Possibly Effective
  Melatonin
Stomach (Gastric) cancer
Possibly Effective
  Barley
  Garlic
  Green Tea
  Oats
  Rice Bran
  Wheat Bran
Possibly Ineffective
  Black Tea
Thyroid cancer
Possibly Effective
  Tiratricol

Digestive, Mouth, Stomach, and Intestines

Anal fissures
Possibly Effective
  Bovine Cartilage
Cholera
Possibly Effective
  Niacin And Niacinamide
Colon spasm caused by barium enema
Possibly Effective
  Peppermint
Colostomy odor
Possibly Ineffective
  Chlorophyll
Constipation
Effective
  Black Psyllium
  Blond Psyllium
  Magnesium
Likely Effective
  Cascara
  European Buckthorn
  Glycerol
  Olive
  Senna
Possibly Effective
  Alder Buckthorn
  Aloe
  Castor
  Guar Gum
  Inulin
  Karaya Gum
  Sweet Almond

Constipation (Cont.)
Possibly Effective (Cont.)
  Wheat Bran
  Xanthan Gum
Crohn's disease
Possibly Ineffective
  Glutamine
  Lactobacillus
Decreased ability to taste (Hypogeusia)
Possibly Effective
  Zinc
Diarrhea
Likely Effective
  Zinc
Possibly Effective
  Blond Psyllium
  Guar Gum
  Lactobacillus
  Saccharomyces Boulardii
  Soy
  Yogurt
Possibly Ineffective
  Glutamine
Diarrhea caused by antibiotics
Possibly Effective
  Lactobacillus
  Saccharomyces Boulardii
  Yogurt
Diarrhea caused by Clostridium difficile bacteria
Possibly Effective
  Lactobacillus
  Saccharomyces Boulardii
Diarrhea caused by rotavirus
Likely Effective
  Lactobacillus
Possibly Effective
  Bifidobacteria
Diarrhea related to malnourishment
Possibly Ineffective
  Yogurt
Dry mouth
Possibly Effective
  Betaine Anhydrous
Fluorosis
Possibly Effective
  Calcium
Gingivitis
Possibly Effective
  Zinc
Possibly Ineffective
  Fish Oil
Grinding teeth (Bruxism)
Possibly Ineffective
  L-Tryptophan
Helicobacter pylori (H. pylori)
Possibly Effective
  Beer
  Bifidobacteria
  Lactobacillus
  Saccharomyces Boulardii
  Vitamin C
  Wine
  Yogurt

Helicobacter pylori (H. pylori) (Cont.)
Possibly Ineffective
  Fish Oil
  Garlic
Infectious diarrhea
Possibly Effective
  Colostrum
Inflammatory bowel disease (IBD)
Possibly Ineffective
  Zinc
Intestinal bacterial overgrowth
Possibly Ineffective
  Lactobacillus
Intestinal parasitic infection
Possibly Effective
  Oregano
Iron absorption
Likely Effective
  Vitamin C
Irritable bowel syndrome (IBS)
Possibly Effective
  Bifidobacteria
  Blond Psyllium
  Guar Gum
  Wheat Bran
Possibly Ineffective
  Brahmi
Jaw surgery (Sulcoplasty)
Possibly Effective
  Propolis
Lack of appetite (Anorexia)
Possibly Effective
  Branched-Chain Amino Acids
Lactose intolerance
Likely Effective
  Lactase
Possibly Effective
  Soy
  Yogurt
Possibly Ineffective
  Lactobacillus
Lactose intolerance, galactosemia, or hereditary lactase
Possibly Effective
  Soy
Mandibular alveolitis
Possibly Effective
  Bovine Cartilage
Motion sickness
Possibly Ineffective
  Ginger
Mouth sores (Oral mucosal lesions)
Possibly Ineffective
  Vitamin E
Necrotizing enterocolitis (NEC)
Possibly Effective
  Bifidobacteria
  L-Arginine
Periodontal disease
Likely Ineffective
  Coenzyme Q-10
Periodontitis
Possibly Effective
  Chitosan

Pouchitis
Possibly Effective
  Bifidobacteria
  Lactobacillus
Precancerous patches in the mouth (Oral leukoplakia)
Possibly Effective
  Beta-Carotene
  Blue-Green Algae
  Green Tea
Sensitive teeth (Dental hypersensitivity)
Effective
  Strontium
Temporomandibular joint (TMJ) arthritis
Possibly Effective
  Glucosamine Sulfate
Tooth decay (Dental caries)
Effective
  Fluoride
Likely Effective
  Xylitol
Traveler's diarrhea
Possibly Effective
  Bifidobacteria
  Lactobacillus
  Saccharomyces Boulardii
  Sangre De Grado
Possibly Ineffective
  Fructo-Oligosaccharides
Ulcerative colitis
Possibly Effective
  Bifidobacteria
  Blond Psyllium
  Lactobacillus
Ulcers in the stomach or intestines (Peptic ulcers)
Possibly Effective
  Zinc
Upset stomach (Dyspepsia)
Effective
  Calcium
  Magnesium
Possibly Effective
  Angelica
  Artichoke
  Caraway
  Clown's Mustard Plant
  German Chamomile
  Greater Celandine
  Lemon Balm
  Licorice
  Milk Thistle
  Peppermint
  Turmeric
Likely Ineffective
  Pancreatin
Wisdom tooth extraction
Possibly Ineffective
  Arnica

Eyes, Ears, Nose, and Throat

Cataracts
Effective
  Chymotrypsin
Likely Effective
  Hyaluronic Acid
Possibly Effective
  Fish Oil
  Lutein
  Niacin And Niacinamide
  Riboflavin
  Thiamine
  Tomato
  Vitamin A
Possibly Ineffective
  Beta-Carotene
  Zinc
Corneal calcium deposits
Possibly Effective
  EDTA
Dizziness (Vertigo)
Possibly Effective
  Ginger
  Ginkgo
Dry eyes
Possibly Effective
  Fish Oil
  Chondroitin Sulfate
Ear infection (Otitis media)
Possibly Effective
  Xylitol
Possibly Ineffective
  Olive
Earwax
Possibly Ineffective
  Olive
Eye conditions (Gyrate atrophy)
Possibly Effective
  Creatine
Eye conditions (Retinitis pigmentosa)
Possibly Ineffective
  Vitamin E
Eye conditions (Retinopathy)
Possibly Effective
  Bilberry
  Pycnogenol
Eye stress
Possibly Effective
  Grape
Eye surgery
Likely Effective
  Chondroitin Sulfate
Eye surgery recovery (Photoreactive keratectomy)
Possibly Effective
  Vitamin A
  Vitamin E
Glaucoma
Possibly Effective
  Ginkgo
  Marijuana

Medical professionals should consult the Professional Version at www.NaturalDatabase.com.

CONSUMER VERSION

Hearing loss
Possibly Effective
   Magnesium
Inflammation of the eye (Uveitis)
Possibly Effective
   Vitamin E
Night vision
Possibly Ineffective
   Bilberry
Ringing in the ears (Tinnitus)
Possibly Ineffective
   Ginkgo
   Zinc

Heart, Blood, and Circulation

Anemia
Possibly Effective
   Vitamin E
Possibly Ineffective
   Histidine
   Vitamin A
Anemia caused by long-term disease
Effective
   Iron
Angioplasty
Possibly Effective
   Fish Oil
Artery disease (Peripheral arterial disease)
Possibly Effective
   L-Arginine
   Mesoglycan
Possibly Ineffective
   Garlic
Bleeding conditions (Hemorrhagic disease)
Effective
   Vitamin K
Bleeding into the brain (Intracranial hemorrhage)
Possibly Effective
   Vitamin E
Blood clots in the veins (Deep vein thrombosis, DVT)
Possibly Ineffective
   Mesoglycan
Brain blood vessel disease (Cerebrovascular disease)
Possibly Effective
   Citicoline
   Mesoglycan
Chest pain (Angina)
Possibly Effective
   L-Arginine
   L-Carnitine
   N-Acetyl Cysteine
   Propionyl-L-Carnitine
   Terminalia
Possibly Ineffective
   Vitamin E
Chest pain (Vasospastic angina)
Possibly Effective
   Magnesium

Congestive heart failure (CHF)
Likely Effective
   Digitalis
Possibly Effective
   Beer
   Coenzyme Q-10
   Creatine
   Hawthorn
   L-Arginine
   L-Carnitine
   Propionyl-L-Carnitine
   Taurine
   Terminalia
   Wine
Possibly Ineffective
   Vitamin E
Coronary artery bypass
Possibly Effective
   Fish Oil
Coronary artery disease (CAD)
Possibly Effective
   DHA (Docosahexaenoic Acid)
   English Walnut
   EPA (Eicosapentaenoic Acid)
   Magnesium
   Ribose
Possibly Ineffective
   Folic Acid
   Lutein
Likely Ineffective
   EDTA
Damage caused by low oxygen supply to the heart (Ischemic reperfusion injury)
Possibly Effective
   Alpha-Ketoglutarate
   Coenzyme Q-10
Heart attack (Myocardial infarction, MI)
Possibly Effective
   Black Tea
   Coenzyme Q-10
   L-Carnitine
Possibly Ineffective
   L-Arginine
   Magnesium
Likely Ineffective
   Superoxide Dismutase
Heart condition (Idiopathic congestive cardiomyopathy)
Possibly Effective
   Forskolin
Heart disease
Likely Effective
   Beer
   Fish Oil
   Oats
   Wine
Possibly Effective
   Alpha-Linolenic Acid
   Niacin And Niacinamide
   Olive
   Tomato

Heart disease (Cont.)
Possibly Ineffective
   Lycopene
   Selenium
   Soy
Likely Ineffective
   Beta-Carotene
   Vitamin E
Heart stoppage (Cardiac arrest)
Possibly Ineffective
   Magnesium
Heart transplant
Possibly Effective
   Fish Oil
Heart valve conditions (Mitral valve prolapse)
Possibly Effective
   Magnesium
Hemodialysis grafts
Possibly Effective
   Fish Oil
Hemorrhoids
Possibly Effective
   Blond Psyllium
   Bovine Cartilage
   Diosmin
   Hesperidin
   Wheat Bran
   Witch Hazel
High blood lipids (Hyperlipidemia)
Effective
   Niacin And Niacinamide
Likely Effective
   Blond Psyllium
Possibly Effective
   Artichoke
   Garlic
   Green Tea
   Pantethine
   Soy
   Yogurt
Likely Ineffective
   Kefir
High blood pressure (Hypertension)
Possibly Effective
   Alpha-Linolenic Acid
   Blond Psyllium
   Calcium
   Cod Liver Oil
   Coenzyme Q-10
   Fish Oil
   Garlic
   Green Tea
   Magnesium
   Olive
   Oolong Tea
   Potassium
   Pycnogenol
   Stevia
   Sweet Orange
   Vitamin C
   Wheat Bran

       Natural Medicines Comprehensive Database Consumer Version   (209) 472-2244

High blood pressure (Hypertension) (Cont.)
Possibly Ineffective
    EPA (Eicosapentaenoic Acid)
    Gamma Linolenic Acid
    Oats
    Vitamin E
High cholesterol (Hypercholesterolemia)
Likely Effective
    Beta-Sitosterol
    Flaxseed
    Oats
    Red Yeast
    Sitostanol
Possibly Effective
    Alfalfa
    Avocado
    Barley
    Beta Glucans
    Black Psyllium
    Calcium
    English Walnut
    Guar Gum
    Jiaogulan
    Macadamia Nut
    Magnesium
    Olive
    Pectin
    Policosanol
    Rice Bran
    Safflower
    Soybean Oil
    Sweet Orange
Possibly Ineffective
    Acacia
    Amaranth
    Cod Liver Oil
    Guggul
    Inulin
    Lecithin
    Red Clover
High or abnormal blood lipids (Dyslipidemia)
Possibly Effective
    Fish Oil
    Gamma Oryzanol
High levels of homocysteine (Hyperhomocysteinemia)
Likely Effective
    Folic Acid
    Pyridoxine
    Vitamin B12
Possibly Effective
    N-Acetyl Cysteine
High triglycerides (Hypertriglyceridemia)
Effective
    Fish Oil
Likely Effective
    Cod Liver Oil
Possibly Effective
    Inulin
    Mesoglycan

Inflamed heart muscle (Myocarditis)
Possibly Effective
    L-Carnitine
Irregular heartbeat (Arrhythmias, general)
Possibly Effective
    Magnesium
Irregular heartbeat (Atrial fibrillation)
Likely Effective
    Digitalis
Irregular heartbeat (Paroxysmal supraventricular tachycardia)
Effective
    Adenosine
Irregular heartbeat (Torsades de pointes)
Likely Effective
    Magnesium
Low blood platelets (Thrombocytopenia)
Possibly Effective
    Melatonin
Low blood pressure (Hypotension)
Possibly Effective
    Black Tea
    Caffeine
    Coffee
    Green Tea
Multi-system organ failure
Likely Ineffective
    N-Acetyl Cysteine
Nerve damage in the heart (Cardiac autonomic neuropathy)
Possibly Ineffective
    Alpha-Lipoic Acid
Pain while walking due to clogged arteries (Intermittent claudication)
Possibly Effective
    Ginkgo
    Policosanol
    Propionyl-L-Carnitine
Possibly Ineffective
    Vitamin E
    Fish Oil
Pernicious anemia
Effective
    Vitamin B12
Plaque in the arteries (Atherosclerosis)
Possibly Effective
    Alpha-Linolenic Acid
    Black Tea
    Fish Oil
    Garlic
    Niacin And Niacinamide
    Vitamin C
Possibly Ineffective
    Vitamin E

Poor circulation (Chronic venous insufficiency)
Likely Effective
    Horse Chestnut
Possibly Effective
    Butcher's Broom
    Grape
    Gotu Kola
    Mesoglycan
    Pycnogenol
    Sweet Clover
Poor oxygen supply to the brain (Chronic cerebral ischemia)
Possibly Effective
    Acetyl-L-Carnitine
Poor oxygen supply to the heart (Chronic ischemic heart disease)
Possibly Effective
    Propionyl-L-Carnitine
Raynaud's syndrome
Possibly Effective
    Fish Oil
    Ginkgo
Sickle cell disease
Possibly Effective
    Zinc
Stroke
Possibly Effective
    Calcium
    Citicoline
    Fish Oil
    Glycine
    Magnesium
    Potassium
    Sweet Orange
Possibly Ineffective
    Beta-Carotene
    Folic Acid
    Mesoglycan
    Pyridoxine
    Vitamin B12
    Vitamin C
Likely Ineffective
    Glycerol
Vein disease (Peripheral vascular disease)
Possibly Effective
    Inositol Nicotinate
Vitamin K deficiency (Hypoprothrombinemia)
Effective
    Vitamin K

CONSUMER VERSION

Medical professionals should consult the Professional Version at www.NaturalDatabase.com.

Hormones, Glands, and Metabolism

Adrenal insufficiency
Possibly Effective
 DHEA
Bone loss caused by hyperparathyroidism
Possibly Effective
 Vitamin D
Diabetes
Possibly Effective
 Alpha-Lipoic Acid
 Beer
 Blond Psyllium
 Caffeine
 Coffee
 Ginseng, American
 Ginseng, Panax
 Glucomannan
 Guar Gum
 Magnesium
 Niacin And Niacinamide
 Oats
 Prickly Pear Cactus
 Soy
 Wine
 Xanthan Gum
Possibly Ineffective
 Beta-Carotene
 Cranberry
 DHA (Docosahexaenoic Acid)
 EPA (Eicosapentaenoic Acid)
 Garlic
 Jambolan
 Lutein
 Lycopene
 Tomato
 Vitamin C
 Wheat Bran
Likely Ineffective
 Fish Oil
Diabetic eye disease (Diabetic retinopathy)
Possibly Effective
 Ginkgo
Diabetic foot ulcers
Possibly Effective
 Iodine
Diabetic kidney disease (Diabetic nephropathy)
Possibly Effective
 Cod Liver Oil
 Fish Oil
 Soy
Diabetic nerve disease (Diabetic neuropathy)
Possibly Effective
 Acetyl-L-Carnitine
 Gamma Linolenic Acid
Likely Ineffective
 Inositol

Hyperparathyroidism
Likely Effective
 Calcium
Hyperthyroidism
Effective
 Iodine
Possibly Effective
 L-Carnitine
Hypoparathyroidism
Effective
 Vitamin D
Hypothyroidism
Possibly Effective
 Tiratricol
Metabolic disorders
Effective
 Thiamine
Metabolic syndrome
Possibly Effective
 Magnesium
Pituitary resistance to thyroid hormone (PRTH)
Likely Effective
 Tiratricol
Prediabetes (Impaired glucose tolerance)
Possibly Ineffective
 Chromium
Venous Stasis Ulcers
Possibly Effective
 Adenosine
 Diosmin
 Hesperidin
 Mesoglycan
Weight loss and obesity
Possibly Effective
 Caffeine
 Calcium
 Conjugated Linoleic Acid
 Diacylglycerol
 Ephedra
 Fish Oil
Possibly Ineffective
 Blue-Green Algae
 Garcinia
 Glycerol
 Guar Gum
 Inulin
Likely Ineffective
 Tiratricol

Inherited and Genetic Disorders

Acrodermatitis enteropathica
Possibly Effective
 Zinc
Beta-thalassemia
Possibly Effective
 Vitamin E
Cystinuria
Possibly Ineffective
 Glutamine
Duchenne muscular dystrophy
Possibly Ineffective
 Vitamin E

Erythropoietic protoporphyria (EPP)
Effective
 Beta-Carotene
Possibly Effective
 Canthaxanthin
Familial hypercholesterolemia
Possibly Effective
 Sitostanol
Possibly Ineffective
 Garlic
Familial hypophosphatemia
Effective
 Vitamin D
Fragile-X syndrome
Likely Ineffective
 Folic Acid
Genetic bone disorder (Osteogenesis imperfecta)
Possibly Effective
 Vitamin D
Glucose-6-phosphate dehydrogenase (G6PD) deficiency
Possibly Effective
 Vitamin E
Hereditary sideroblastic anemia
Effective
 Vitamin B6 (Pyridoxine)
Homocystinuria
Effective
 Betaine Anhydrous
Huntington's disease
Possibly Effective
 Coenzyme Q-10
 Vitamin E
Imerslund-Grasbeck disease
Effective
 Vitamin B12
McArdle's disease
Possibly Effective
 Creatine
Likely Ineffective
 Ribose
Mitochondrial encephalomyopathies
Likely Effective
 Coenzyme Q-10
Muscular dystrophy
Possibly Effective
 Coenzyme Q-10
 Creatine
Myoadenylate deaminase deficiency (MAD)
Possibly Effective
 Ribose
Myotonic dystrophy
Possibly Ineffective
 Vitamin E
Phenylketonuria (PKU)
Effective
 Tyrosine
Tyrosinemia
Likely Effective
 Vitamin C

Wilson's disease
Likely Effective
Zinc

Immune System and Allergies

AIDS
See HIV/AIDS
AIDS diarrhea-wasting syndrome
Possibly Ineffective
Zinc
AIDS-related myelopathy (Spinal cord disease in people with AIDS)
Possibly Effective
SAMe
Bee sting allergy
Likely Effective
Bee Venom
Excessive lymph fluid and swelling (Lymphedema)
Possibly Ineffective
Diosmin
Hesperidin
Food allergies
Possibly Effective
Thymus Extract
HIV transmission
Possibly Effective
Vitamin C
Possibly Ineffective
Vitamin A
HIV-related dementia
Possibly Ineffective
Alpha-Lipoic Acid
HIV/AIDS
Possibly Effective
Beta Glucans
Coenzyme Q-10
Lentinan
Red Yeast
Possibly Ineffective
St. John's Wort
HIV/AIDS-related diarrhea
Possibly Effective
Saccharomyces Boulardii
Sangre de Grado
Vitamin A
HIV/AIDS-related pregnancy complications
Possibly Ineffective
Zinc
HIV/AIDS-related wasting
Possibly Effective
Glutamine
HMB
L-Arginine
Possibly Ineffective
Medium Chain Triglycerides
HIV/AIDS-related weight loss
Possibly Effective
Marijuana
Whey Protein

Lupus (Systemic lupus erythematosus, SLE)
Possibly Effective
DHEA
Flaxseed
Possibly Ineffective
Copper
Nerve pain in people with HIV (HIV-associated peripheral neuropathy)
Possibly Ineffective
Capsicum
Sjogren's syndrome
Possibly Effective
Xanthan Gum

Kidney and Bladder

End-stage renal disease (ESRD)
Effective
L-Carnitine
Likely Effective
Folic Acid
Possibly Effective
N-Acetyl Cysteine
Possibly Ineffective
Blond Psyllium
Excess calcium in the urine (Hypercalciuria)
Possibly Effective
Potassium
Rice Bran
High calcium levels (Hypercalcemia)
Likely Effective
EDTA
Phosphate Salts
High potassium levels (Hyperkalemia)
Effective
Calcium
Inflammation of the bladder (Interstitial cystitis)
Effective
DMSO (Dimethylsulfoxide)
Possibly Effective
L-Arginine
Superoxide Dismutase
Inflammatory bladder disease
Possibly Effective
DMSO (Dimethylsulfoxide)
Kidney damage due to lab tests (Contrast agent-induced nephropathy)
Possibly Effective
N-Acetyl Cysteine
Vitamin C
Kidney dialysis
Possibly Ineffective
Phosphatidylcholine
Kidney disease
Possibly Effective
Soy
Kidney disease (IgA nephropathy)
Possibly Effective
Fish Oil

Kidney disease (Fanconi syndrome)
Effective
Vitamin D
Kidney failure
Effective
Calcium
Possibly Effective
Chitosan
Kidney stones (Nephrolithiasis)
Possibly Effective
Black Tea
IP-6
Magnesium
Phosphate Salts
Pyridoxine
Kidney transplant
Possibly Effective
L-Arginine
Kidney transplant-related bone loss
Possibly Ineffective
Vitamin D
Kidney-related bone disease (Osteodystrophy)
Effective
Vitamin D
Possibly Effective
Ipriflavone
Protein in the urine (Albuminuria)
Possibly Effective
Vitamin C
Scarring of kidney tissue (Glomerulosclerosis)
Possibly Effective
Vitamin E
Urinary tract infections (UTIs)
Possibly Effective
Cranberry
Urine odor
Possibly Effective
Cranberry
Possibly Ineffective
Chlorophyllin

Liver, Gallbladder, and Pancreas

Alcohol-related liver disease (see also Cirrhosis and Liver disease)
Possibly Ineffective
Alpha-Lipoic Acid
Brain disease caused by liver damage (Hepatic encephalopathy)
Possibly Effective
Branched-Chain Amino Acids
Likely Ineffective
Ornithine Ketoglutarate
Cirrhosis
Possibly Ineffective
Fish Oil
Fatty changes in the liver (Hepatic steatosis)
Likely Effective
Choline
Possibly Effective
Lecithin

Medical professionals should consult the Professional Version at www.NaturalDatabase.com.

CONSUMER VERSION

Medical professionals should consult the Professional Version at www.NaturalDatabase.com.

Gallbladder disease
Possibly Effective
Caffeine
Coffee
Vitamin C
Possibly Ineffective
Lecithin
Likely Ineffective
Beta-Sitosterol
Hepatitis (General)
Possibly Effective
Schisandra
Taurine
Hepatitis A
Possibly Ineffective
Phosphatidylcholine
Hepatitis B
Possibly Ineffective
Chanca Piedra
Hepatitis C
Possibly Effective
Lactoferrin
Phosphatidylcholine
Possibly Ineffective
St. John's Wort
Liver disease
Possibly Effective
SAMe
Pancreatic insufficiency
Effective
Lipase
Pancreatin
Pancreatitis
Possibly Effective
Chlorophyll

Lungs and Respiratory

Acute respiratory distress syndrome (ARDS) (see also Respiratory distress syndrome)
Possibly Effective
Borage
Altitude sickness
Possibly Ineffective
Ginkgo
Asthma
Possibly Effective
Caffeine
Choline
Fish Oil
Forskolin
Magnesium
Pycnogenol
Thymus Extract
Possibly Ineffective
EPA (Eicosapentaenoic Acid)
Picrorhiza
Yogurt
Bronchitis
Possibly Effective
English Ivy
N-Acetyl Cysteine
South African Geranium

Bronchitis (Cont.)
Possibly Ineffective
Vitamin C
Chronic obstructive pulmonary disease (COPD)
Possibly Effective
Beta-Carotene
Magnesium
N-Acetyl Cysteine
Possibly Ineffective
Pomegranate
Chronic runny nose (Perennial rhinitis)
Possibly Effective
Capsicum
Collapsed lung (Atelectasis)
Effective
N-Acetyl Cysteine
Common cold
Possibly Effective
Andrographis
Echinacea
Vitamin C
Zinc
Congestive lung conditions (Bronchopulmonary disorders)
Effective
N-Acetyl Cysteine
Possibly Effective
Superoxide Dismutase
Possibly Ineffective
Vitamin E
Cough
Effective
Camphor
Cystic fibrosis
Effective
N-Acetyl Cysteine
Possibly Ineffective
EPA (Eicosapentaenoic Acid)
Exercise-induced asthma
Possibly Effective
Beta-Carotene
Exercise-induced respiratory tract infections
Possibly Effective
Vitamin C
Flu (Influenza)
Possibly Effective
Elderberry
N-Acetyl Cysteine
Possibly Ineffective
Zinc
Hayfever (Allergic rhinitis)
Possibly Effective
Butterbur
Thymus Extract
Possibly Ineffective
EPA
Grape
Infant breathing problems (Neonatal apnea)
Possibly Effective
Caffeine

Inflammation and hardening of the lungs (Fibrosing alveolitis)
Possibly Effective
N-Acetyl Cysteine
Pharyngitis
Possibly Effective
Papain
Pneumonia
Possibly Effective
Alpha-Linolenic Acid
Possibly Ineffective
Fish Oil
Likely Ineffective
Vitamin A
Respiratory congestion
Effective
Iodine
Respiratory distress syndrome (see also Acute respiratory distress syndrome)
Possibly Effective
Inositol
Respiratory tract infections
Possibly Effective
Ginseng, American
Lactobacillus
Thymus Extract
Possibly Ineffective
Vitamin E
Sinus infection (Sinusitis)
Possibly Effective
Cowslip
Elderflower
Gentian
Sorrel
Verbena
Sore throat
Possibly Effective
Andrographis
Slippery Elm
South African Geranium
Tracheostomy care
Effective
N-Acetyl Cysteine
Tuberculosis
Possibly Ineffective
Beta-Sitosterol

Medication Complications

ACE inhibitor-associated cough
Possibly Effective
Iron
Acetaminophen (Tylenol) poisoning
Effective
N-Acetyl Cysteine
Possibly Effective
Methionine
Antidepressant-induced sexual dysfunction
Possibly Ineffective
Ginkgo

Chemotherapy burns (Extravasation)
Possibly Effective
　DMSO (Dimethylsulfoxide)
　Vitamin E
Chemotherapy toxicity
Possibly Effective
　Glutathione
Chemotherapy-induced gut side effects
Possibly Ineffective
　Vitamin A
Cisplatin-induced nerve damage
Possibly Effective
　Vitamin E
Cyclosporine-induced high blood pressure
Possibly Effective
　Fish Oil
Cyclosporine-induced kidney damage
Possibly Effective
　Fish Oil
Doxorubicin-induced heart damage
Possibly Ineffective
　N-Acetyl Cysteine
Ifosfamide (Ifex) toxicity
Possibly Effective
　N-Acetyl Cysteine
Interferon-related eye damage
Possibly Ineffective
　Vitamin C
Irregular heartbeat caused by heart medications (Cardiac glycoside-induced ventricular arrhythmias)
Likely Effective
　EDTA
Lithium-induced side effects
Possibly Effective
　Inositol
Lometrexol toxicity
Possibly Ineffective
　Folic Acid
Methotrexate toxicity
Likely Effective
　Folic Acid
Mouth sores caused by chemotherapy (Oral mucositis)
Likely Effective
　Hyaluronic Acid
Possibly Effective
　German Chamomile
　Glutamine
　Iodine
　Kaolin
Nitrate tolerance
Possibly Effective
　L-Arginine
　Vitamin C
　Vitamin E
Likely Ineffective
　N-Acetyl Cysteine
Orlistat (Xenical) side effects
Possibly Effective
　Blond Psyllium

Osteoporosis caused by taking steroids
Likely Effective
　Calcium
　Vitamin D
Phenytoin-related gum disease
Possibly Effective
　Folic Acid
Radiation emergency
Effective
　Iodine
Sedative withdrawal (Benzodiazepine withdrawal)
Possibly Effective
　Kava
　Melatonin
Possibly Ineffective
　Progesterone
Skin damage caused by radiation therapy (Radiation dermatitis)
Possibly Ineffective
　Pantothenic Acid
　Vitamin C
Movement problems caused by some medications (Tardive dyskinesia)
Possibly Effective
　Branched-Chain Amino Acids
　Melatonin
　Pyridoxine
　Vitamin E
Possibly Ineffective
　Phosphatidylcholine
Likely Ineffective
　Deanol
Tissue hardening caused by radiation therapy (Radiation-induced fibrosis)
Possibly Effective
　Vitamin E
Valproic acid-induced toxicities
Possibly Effective
　L-Carnitine
Warfarin anticoagulation
Effective
　Vitamin K

Men's Health

BPH (Benign prostatic hyperplasia)
Likely Effective
　Beta-Sitosterol
　Pygeum
　Saw Palmetto
Possibly Effective
　African Wild Potato
　Pumpkin
　Rye Grass
Possibly Ineffective
　Stinging Nettle
Erectile dysfunction (ED)
Possibly Effective
　DHEA
　Ginseng, Panax
　L-Arginine
　Melanotan-II
　Propionyl-L-Carnitine
　Yohimbe

Peyronie's disease
Possibly Effective
　Acetyl-L-Carnitine
　Propionyl-L-Carnitine
Premature ejaculation
Possibly Effective
　Angelica
　Cinnamon Bark
　Clove
　Dong Quai
　Ginseng, Panax
Prostatitis
Possibly Effective
　Quercetin

Pregnancy, Childbirth, and Lactation

Breast engorgement during lactation
Possibly Effective
　Cabbage
Eclampsia
Likely Effective
　Magnesium
Possibly Ineffective
　EPA (Eicosapentaenoic Acid)
Enhancing infant development
Possibly Ineffective
　Omega-6 Fatty Acids
Eye damage in premature infants
Possibly Effective
　Vitamin E
Fetal and early infant mortality
Possibly Ineffective
　Vitamin A
Fetal bone development
Likely Effective
　Calcium
Headache after an epidural (Postdural puncture headache)
Possibly Effective
　Caffeine
Itching caused by liver back up during pregnancy (Intrahepatic cholestasis)
Possibly Effective
　SAMe
Labor facilitation
Possibly Effective
　Castor
Possibly Ineffective
　Laminaria
　Red Raspberry
Low birth weight
Possibly Effective
　L-Carnitine
Morning sickness
Possibly Effective
　Ginger
Neural tube birth defects
Likely Effective
　Folic Acid
Possibly Effective
　Choline

Medical professionals should consult the Professional Version at www.NaturalDatabase.com.

Post-partum complications
Possibly Effective
Beta-Carotene
Vitamin A
Pre-eclampsia
Likely Effective
Magnesium
Possibly Effective
Vitamin C
Vitamin E
Possibly Ineffective
L-Arginine
Pregnancy-induced nausea and vomiting
Possibly Effective
Pyridoxine
Pregnancy-related complications
Possibly Effective
Beta-Carotene
Calcium
Vitamin A
Pregnancy-related gingivitis
Possibly Effective
Folic Acid
Pregnancy-related iron deficiency
Possibly Ineffective
Zinc
Pregnancy-related leg cramps
Possibly Effective
Magnesium
Prematurity
Possibly Effective
Borage

Reproductive Health

Abortion
Possibly Ineffective
Rosemary
Birth control (Contraception)
Possibly Effective
Castor
Gossypol
Genital warts (Condylomata acuminata)
Likely Effective
Podophyllum
Infertility
Likely Effective
Progesterone
Possibly Effective
Acetyl-L-Carnitine
L-Carnitine
Vitamin E
Intrauterine growth
Possibly Ineffective
EPA (Eicosapentaenoic Acid)
Miscarriage (Due to a rare autoimmune condition called Antiphospholipid syndrome)
Possibly Effective
Fish Oil
Sexual arousal
Possibly Ineffective
DHEA

Sexual desire
Possibly Effective
Maca
Sexual dysfunction
Possibly Effective
Yohimbe

Skin, Hair, and Nails

Acne
(see also Severe acne)
Possibly Effective
Alpha Hydroxy Acids
Bovine Cartilage
Saccharomyces Boulardii
Tea Tree Oil
Zinc
Acne scars
Possibly Effective
Alpha Hydroxy Acids
Allergic skin conditions (Atopic disease)
Possibly Effective
Lactobacillus
Whey Protein
Athlete's foot (Tinea pedis)
Possibly Effective
Bitter Orange
Garlic
Tea Tree Oil
Brittle nails
Possibly Effective
Biotin
Cold sores (Herpes labialis)
Possibly Effective
Lemon Balm
Lysine
Rhubarb
Sage
Possibly Ineffective
Tannic Acid
Tea Tree Oil
Dark discoloration of the skin (Melasma)
Possibly Effective
Alpha Hydroxy Acids
Diaper rash
Possibly Ineffective
Tannic Acid
Dry skin
Likely Effective
Alpha Hydroxy Acids
Lecithin
Eczema (Atopic dermatitis)
Possibly Effective
Bifidobacteria
Lactobacillus
Rice Bran
Possibly Ineffective
Borage
Evening Primrose Oil
Gamma Linolenic Acid
Zinc

Fungal infection (Cutaneous sporotrichosis)
Effective
Iodine
Fungal nail infection (Onychomycosis)
Possibly Effective
Tea Tree Oil
Granuloma annulare
Possibly Effective
Vitamin E
Hairloss (Alopecia areata)
Possibly Effective
Cedarwood Oil
Lavender
Rosemary
Possibly Ineffective
Zinc
Herpes simplex virus (HSV)
Possibly Effective
Sangre De Grado
Zinc
Possibly Ineffective
Echinacea
Herpes simplex virus type 2 (HSV-2)
Possibly Effective
Ginseng, Siberian
Propolis
Inflammation of the skin (Dermatitis)
Likely Effective
Lecithin
Possibly Ineffective
German Chamomile
Itching (Pruritus)
Effective
Camphor
Itchy lumps under the skin (Prurigo nodularis)
Possibly Effective
Capsicum
Jock itch (Tinea cruris)
Possibly Effective
Bitter Orange
Garlic
Leg ulcers
Possibly Effective
Glycine
Leprosy
Possibly Effective
Zinc
Lice
Effective
Pyrethrum
Possibly Effective
Quassia
Measles
Possibly Effective
Vitamin A
Minor bleeding
Possibly Effective
Witch Hazel
Mosquito repellent
Likely Effective
Lemon Eucalyptus
Soybean Oil

Mosquito repellent (Cont.)
Possibly Effective
Citronella Oil
Poison oak and poison ivy dermatitis
Possibly Effective
Bovine Cartilage
Prickly heat
Possibly Ineffective
Tannic Acid
Psoriasis
Effective
Vitamin D
Possibly Effective
Aloe
Bovine Cartilage
DHA (Docosahexaenoic Acid)
EPA (Eicosapentaenoic Acid)
Fish Oil
Oregon Grape
Possibly Ineffective
Zinc
Redness on the skin (Erythema)
Possibly Effective
Vitamin C
Ring worm (Tinea corporis)
Possibly Effective
Bitter Orange
Garlic
Scabies
Ineffective
Pyrethrum
Scaling of the skin (Scleroderma)
Possibly Ineffective
DMSO (Dimethylsulfoxide)
EDTA
Gamma Linolenic Acid
Para-Aminobenzoic Acid
(PABA)
Scarring
Possibly Ineffective
Vitamin E
Seborrheic dermatitis
Possibly Ineffective
Biotin
Severe acne (Nodulocystic acne)
Possibly Effective
Guggul
Shingles (Herpes zoster)
Possibly Effective
DMSO (Dimethylsulfoxide)
Papain
Transfer Factor
Skin infection
Effective
Iodine
Skin irritation
Possibly Effective
Sweet Almond
Witch Hazel
Sunburn
Effective
Para-Aminobenzoic Acid
(PABA)

Sunburn (Cont.)
Possibly Effective
Beta-Carotene
Melatonin
Vitamin C
Vitamin E
Tanning skin
Possibly Effective
Melanotan-II
Tick bites
Possibly Effective
Garlic
Tick repellent
Possibly Effective
Lemon Eucalyptus
Venous leg ulcers
Possibly Effective
Zinc
Vitiligo
Possibly Effective
Folic Acid
Phenylalanine
Picrorhiza
Wound healing
Possibly Effective
Trypsin

Sleep

Delayed sleep phase syndrome (DSPS)
Possibly Effective
Melatonin
Insomnia
Possibly Effective
Melatonin
Valerian
Jet lag
Possibly Effective
Melatonin
Narcolepsy
Possibly Effective
Gamma-Hydroxybutyrate
(GHB)
Shift work disorder
Possibly Ineffective
Melatonin
Sleep
Possibly Effective
Lemon Balm
Sleep deprivation
Possibly Effective
Tyrosine
Sleep disorders (Circadian rhythm)
Likely Effective
Melatonin
Possibly Ineffective
Vitamin B12
Sleep-wake cycle disturbances
Likely Effective
Melatonin

Surgery and Recovery

Anxiety after surgery
Possibly Effective
Melatonin

Headache after surgery
Effective
Caffeine
Infection after surgery
Possibly Effective
Beta Glucans
Plastic surgery
Possibly Effective
Chitosan
Recovering after surgery
Possibly Effective
L-Arginine
RNA And DNA
Surgery
Possibly Effective
EPA (Eicosapentaenoic Acid)
Glutamine
Swelling after surgery
Possibly Effective
Serrapeptase
Upset stomach and vomiting after surgery
Possibly Effective
Ginger
Possibly Ineffective
Peppermint

Vitamin Deficiency

Ataxia associated with vitamin E deficiency (AVED)
Effective
Vitamin E
Biotin deficiency
Likely Effective
Biotin
Coenzyme Q-10 deficiency
Likely Effective
Coenzyme Q-10
Condition caused by riboflavin (vitamin B2) deficiency (Ariboflavinosis)
Effective
Riboflavin
Copper deficiency
Likely Effective
Copper
Folate deficiency
Effective
Folic Acid
Iron deficiency anemia
Effective
Iron
L-carnitine deficiency
Effective
L-Carnitine
Low calcium levels (Hypocalcemia)
Effective
Calcium
Low magnesium levels (Hypomagnesemia)
Effective
Magnesium

CONSUMER VERSION

Medical professionals should consult the Professional Version at www.NaturalDatabase.com.

Low phosphate levels (Hypophosphatemia)
Effective
Phosphate Salts
Low potassium levels (Hypokalemia)
Effective
Potassium
Manganese deficiency
Effective
Manganese
Niacin deficiency and pellagra
Effective
Niacin And Niacinamide
Pantothenic acid deficiency
Effective
Pantothenic Acid
Pyridoxine deficiency
Effective
Pyridoxine
Pyridoxine-dependent seizures
Effective
Pyridoxine
Rickets
Effective
Vitamin D
Scurvy
Possibly Effective
Acerola
Thiamine deficiency
Effective
Thiamine
Vitamin A deficiency
Effective
Vitamin A
Possibly Effective
Palm Oil
Zinc
Vitamin B12 deficiency
Effective
Vitamin B12
Vitamin C deficiency
Effective
Vitamin C
Vitamin E deficiency
Effective
Vitamin E
Wernicke-Korsakoff syndrome (WKS)
Effective
Thiamine
Zinc deficiency
Effective
Zinc

Women's Health

Abnormal stopping of menstruation (Amenorrhea)
Likely Effective
Progesterone
Breast pain (Mastalgia)
Possibly Effective
Evening Primrose Oil
Possibly Ineffective
Fish Oil

Breast pain (Mastodynia)
Possibly Effective
Progesterone
Fibrocystic breast disease
Possibly Effective
Iodine
Hormone replacement therapy (HRT)
Likely Effective
Progesterone
Non-cancerous breast disease
Likely Ineffective
Vitamin E
Painful menstruation (Dysmenorrhea)
Possibly Effective
Fish Oil
Polycystic ovary syndrome
Possibly Effective
Inositol
Post-hysterectomy pain
Possibly Effective
Magnesium
Premenstrual dysphoric disorder (PMDD)
Possibly Effective
Chasteberry
L-Tryptophan
Premenstrual syndrome (PMS)
Likely Effective
Calcium
Possibly Effective
Brewer's Yeast
Chasteberry
Ginkgo
Magnesium
Pyridoxine
Vitamin E
Possibly Ineffective
Evening Primrose Oil
Progesterone
Thickening of the uterine lining (Endometrial hyperplasia)
Possibly Effective
Progesterone
Vulval lichen sclerosis
Possibly Ineffective
Progesterone
Yeast infection (Vaginal candidiasis)
Possibly Effective
Echinacea
Yogurt
Possibly Ineffective
Lactobacillus

Miscellaneous

Childhood poor coordination (Developmental disorder)
Possibly Effective
Fish Oil
Critical illness (Trauma)
Possibly Effective
Glutamine

Hangover
Possibly Effective
Prickly Pear Cactus
Possibly Ineffective
Artichoke
Elevated lead concentrations
Effective
EDTA
Possibly Effective
Vitamin C
Possibly Ineffective
Calcium
Malaria (Red blood cell infection)
Possibly Effective
Vitamin A
Possibly Ineffective
Palm Oil
Zinc
Nicotine withdrawal
Possibly Effective
Melatonin
Opiate withdrawal
Possibly Effective
Gamma-Hydroxybutyrate (GHB)
Passionflower
Pain
Effective
Camphor
Procaine
Likely Effective
Capsicum
Possibly Ineffective
Phenylalanine
Poisoning
Likely Effective
Activated Charcoal
Possibly Effective
Ipecac
Smoking cessation
Possibly Effective
L-Tryptophan
Likely Ineffective
Lobelia
Urine drug tests
Possibly Ineffective
Goldenseal
Water purification
Effective
Iodine

Natural Medicines Comprehensive Database Consumer Version
(209) 472-2244

Potential Interactions Between Drugs and Natural Medicines

For details on possible interactions between drugs and natural medicines, see the listing for the specific natural medicine in the body of this database. This chart does not contain all theoretical or unknown interactions.

Drug	Natural Medicine
ACENOCOUMAROL (*Sintrom*)	Acetyl-L-Carnitine • L-Carnitine • Propionyl-L-Carnitine
ACETAMINOPHEN (*Tylenol*, others)	Ambrette • Cabbage • Glucosamine Sulfate • Hibiscus • Vitamin C
ACTIVATED CHARCOAL	Ipecac • N-Acetyl Cysteine
ADENOSINE (*Adenocard*)	Black Tea • Caffeine • Cocoa • Coffee • Cola Nut • Green Tea • Guarana • Mate • Oolong Tea
ALCOHOL (Ethanol)	Activated Charcoal • Baikal Skullcap • Black Tea • Butanediol (BD) • Caffeine • Calcium D-Glucarate • Coca • Coffee • Cola Nut • Gamma Butyrolactone (GBL) • Gamma-Hydroxybutyrate (GHB) • Ginseng, Panax • Ginseng, Siberian • Green Tea • Guarana • Hops • Indian Snakeroot • Magnolia • Mate • Niacin and Niacinamide • Oolong Tea • Red Yeast • Ribose • Tansy • Valerian
ALENDRONATE (*Fosamax*)	Coffee • Whey Protein
ALLOPURINOL (*Zyloprim*)	Niacin and Niacinamide
ALPRAZOLAM (*Xanax*)	Ginkgo • Kava • St. John's Wort • Valerian
ALUMINUM	Cherokee Rosehip • Rose Hip • Vitamin C • Vitamin D
AMILORIDE (*Midamor*)	Zinc
AMINOLEVULINIC ACID	Procaine • St. John's Wort
AMIODARONE (*Cordarone*)	Iodine • Pyridoxine
AMITRIPTYLINE (*Elavil*)	St. John's Wort
AMOXICILLIN (*Amoxil, Trimox*)	Acacia • Bromelain
ANASTROZOLE (*Arimidex*)	DHEA
ANTACIDS Some drugs in this category include: Aluminum Hydroxide (*Amphojel*, others) • Calcium Carbonate (*Tums*, others) • Aluminum and Magnesium Hydroxide (*Maalox, Mylanta*)	Aletris • Alpinia • Black Mustard • Blessed Thistle • Calamus • Cinchona • Colombo • Cubebs • Devil's Claw • Northern Prickly Ash • Peppermint • Phosphate Salts • Quassia • Southern Prickly Ash • Yarrow
ANTIBIOTIC DRUGS (see also individual listings) Some drugs in this category include: <u>Fluoroquinolones:</u> Ciprofloxacin (*Cipro*) • Levofloxacin (*Levaquin*) • Norfloxacin (*Noroxin*) • Ofloxacin (*Floxin*) • Enoxacin (*Penetrex*) • Lomefloxacin (*Maxaquin*) • Trovafloxacin; Alatrofloxacin (*Trovan*) <u>Penicillins:</u> Penicillin (*Bicillin, Veetids*) • Nafcillin (*Unipen*) • Oxacillin (*Bactocill*) • Dicloxacillin (*Dynapen*) • Cloxacillin (*Cloxapen*) • Ampicillin (*Principen*) • Amoxicillin (*Amoxil*) • Amoxicillin;Potassium Clavulanate (*Augmentin*) • Ticarcillin (*Ticar*) • Ticarcillin;Clavulanate (*Timentin*) • Mezlocillin (*Mezlin*) • Piperacillin (*Pipracil*) • Piperacillin;Tazobactam (*Zosyn*) • Carbenicillin (*Geocillin*) <u>Macrolides:</u> Clarithromycin (*Biaxin*) • Azithromycin (*Zithromax*) • Dirithromycin (*Dynabac*) • Erythromycin Base (*E-Mycin, Ery-Tab*) • Erythromycin Ethylsuccinate (*E.E.S.*) Vancomycin (*Vancocin*) Clindamycin (*Cleocin*) <u>Aminoglycosides:</u> Tobramycin (*Nebcin*) • Amikacin (*Amikin*) • Kanamycin (*Kantrex*) • Gentamicin (*Garamycin*) (Continued on next page)	Bifidobacteria • Lactobacillus • Soy

Medical professionals should consult the Professional Version at www.NaturalDatabase.com.

Drug	Natural Medicine
ANTIBIOTIC DRUGS (Continued) (see also individual listings) Sulfadiazine • Sulfisoxazole • Sulfamethoxazole (*Gantanol*) • Sulfamethoxazole;Trimethoprim (*Bactrim*) Nitrofurantoin (*Macrodantin*) Tetracycline (*Sumycin*) • Doxycycline (*Vibramycin*) • Minocycline (*Minocin*) Cefpodoxime (*Vantin*) • Cefaclor (*Ceclor*) • Cephalexin (*Keflex*) • Cefadroxil (*Duricef*) • Cephradine (*Velosef*) • Loracarbef (*Lorabid*) • Cefprozil (*Cefzil*) • Cefitbuten (*Cedax*) • Cefdinir (*Omnicef*) • Cephapirin (*Cefadyl*) • Cefazolin (*Ancef*) • Cefoxitin (*Mefoxin*) • Cefuroxime (*Ceftin*) • Cefonicid (*Monocid*) • Ceftriaxone (*Rocephin*) • Cefixime (*Suprax*) • Cefoperazone (*Cefobid*) • Cefotaxime (*Claforan*) • Cefotetan (*Cefotan*) • Ceftazidime (*Fortaz*) • Cefamandole (*Mandol*) • Imipenem;Cilastatin (*Primaxin*) • Aztreonam (*Azactam*)	
ANTIBIOTICS (Aminoglycoside Antibiotics) Some drugs in this category include: Tobramycin (*Nebcin*) • Amikacin (*Amikin*) • Kanamycin (*Kantrex*) • Gentamicin (*Garamycin*)	Magnesium
ANTIBIOTICS (Macrolide Antibiotics) Some drugs in this category include: Clarithromycin (*Biaxin*) • Azithromycin (*Zithromax*) • Dirithromycin (*Dynabac*) • Erythromycin Base (*E-Mycin, Ery-Tab*) • Erythromycin Ethylsuccinate (*E.E.S.*)	Black Hellebore • Digitalis • Hedge Mustard • Lily-Of-The-Valley • Oleander • Swamp Milkweed • Uzara • Wahoo
ANTIBIOTICS (Quinolone Antibiotics) Some drugs in this category include: Ciprofloxacin (*Cipro*) • Gatifloxacin (*Tequin*) • Levofloxacin (*Levaquin*) • Moxifloxacin (*Avelox*) • Norfloxacin (*Noroxin*) • Ofloxacin (*Floxin*) • Trovafloxacin (*Trovan*)	Black Tea • Caffeine • Calcium • Cocoa • Coffee • Cola Nut • Colloidal Silver • Dandelion • Dolomite • Green Tea • Guarana • Iron • Magnesium • Manganese • Mate • Oolong Tea • Quercetin • Sweet Orange • Whey Protein • Zinc
ANTIBIOTICS (Sulfonamide Antibiotics) Some drugs in this category include: Sulfamethoxazole; Trimethoprim (*Bactrim*) • Sulfacetamide (*Sodium Sulamyd*) • Sulfisoxazole (*Gantrisin*)	Beer • Para-Aminobenzoic Acid (PABA) • Procaine • Wine
ANTIBIOTICS (Tetracycline Antibiotics) Some drugs in this category include: Demeclocycline (*Declomycin*) • Doxycycline (*Vibramycin*) • Minocycline (*Minocin*) • Tetracyline (*Achromycin, Sumycin*)	Black Hellebore • Bromelain • Calcium • Colloidal Silver • Digitalis • Dolomite • Hedge Mustard • Iron • Lily-Of-The-Valley • Magnesium • Manganese • Oleander • Pectin • Swamp Milkweed • Uzara • Vitamin A • Wahoo • Whey Protein • Yogurt • Zinc
ARTEMETHER (*Artenam, Paluther*)	Grapefruit
ACARBOSE (*Precose, Prandase*)	Pancreatin
AMPHETAMINES	Butanediol (BD) • Cola Nut • Gamma Butyrolactone (GBL) • Gamma Hydroxybutyrate (GHB) • Green Tea • Guarana • Mate • Oolong Tea
ASPIRIN	Beer • Cherokee Rosehip • Meadowsweet • Niacin and Niacinamide • Onion • Parsley • Ribose • Rose Hip • Tamarind • Vitamin C • Willow Bark • Wine • Wintergreen
BIRTH CONTROL PILLS (Contraceptive Drugs) Some drugs in this category include: Ethinyl Estradiol and Levonorgestrel (*Alesse, Levlen, Triphasil*, others) • Ethinyl Estradiol and Norethindrone (*Brevicon, Demulen, Loestrin, Ortho Novum*, others)	Alfalfa • Anise • Black Tea • Caffeine • Chasteberry • Cocoa • Coffee • Cola Nut • Fennel • Fish Oil • Garlic • German Chamomile • Green Tea • Guarana • Guggul • Kudzu • Mate • Melatonin • Oolong Tea • Red Clover • Saw Palmetto • St. John's Wort
BISPHOSPHONATES Some drugs in this category include: Alendronate (*Fosamax*) • Etidronate (*Didronel*) • Pamidronate (*Aredia*) • Risedronate (*Actonel*) • Tiludronate (*Skelid*)	Calcium • Dolomite • Iron • Magnesium
BUSPIRONE (*Buspar*)	Ginkgo • Grapefruit
CAFFEINE (*Excedrin, Anacin, Vivarin*, and others)	Bitter Orange • Creatine • Echinacea • Ginseng, Panax • Grapefruit • Melatonin • Bitter Orange

Potential Interactions: Drug/Natural Medicine   For additional data, refer to the database.

Drug	Natural Medicine
CALCIPOTRIENE (*Dovonex*)	Calcium • Vitamin D
CALCIUM SUPPLEMENTS (*Citracal, Caltrate, Os-Cal, Titrilac*)	Lily-Of-The-Valley • Lysine • Lysine • Oleander • Pheasant's Eye • Squill • Strophanthus • Wallflower
CARBAMAZEPINE (*Tegretol*)	Adenosine • Black Psyllium • Blond Psyllium • Cassia Auriculata • Cinchona • Grapefruit • Niacin and Niacinamide
CARBIDOPA (*Lodosyn*)	5-HTP
CARVEDILOL (*Coreg*)	Grapefruit
CEFAMANDOLE (*Mandol*)	Beer • Wine
CEFOPERAZONE (*Cefobid*)	Beer • Wine
CELIPROLOL (*Celicard*)	Sweet Orange
CHLORAL HYDRATE (*Aquachloral*)	Clary Sage • Lavender
CHLORAMPHENICOL	Dibencozide • Iron • Vitamin B12
CHLORPROPAMIDE (*Chloromycetin, Diabinese*)	Beer • Prickly Pear Cactus • Solomon's Seal • Wine
CHLORZOXAZONE (*Parafon Forte, Paraflex*)	Watercress
CHOLESTYRAMINE (*Questran*)	Phosphate Salts • Tiratricol
CHOLINE MAGNESIUM TRISALICYLATE (*Trilisate*)	Cherokee Rosehip • Meadowsweet • Ribose • Ribose • Rose Hip • Vitamin C • Willow Bark
CIMETIDINE (*Tagamet*)	Black Tea • Caffeine • Cocoa • Coffee • Cola Nut • Green Tea • Guarana • Mate • Oolong Tea • Vitamin D
CIPROFLOXACIN (*Cipro*)	Fennel • Yogurt
CISAPRIDE (*Propulsid*)	Beer • Grapefruit • Wine
CISPLATIN (*Platinol-AQ*)	Black Cohosh • Zinc
CLINDAMYCIN (*Cleocin*)	Kaolin
CLOMIPRAMINE (*Anafranil*)	Grapefruit
CLONIDINE (*Catapres*)	Niacin and Niacinamide • Yohimbe
CLOPIDOGREL (*Plavix*)	St. John's Wort
CLOZAPINE (*Clozaril*)	Black Tea • Caffeine • Cocoa • Coffee • Cola Nut • Glycine • Green Tea • Guarana • Hawaiian Baby Woodrose • Mate • Oolong Tea
COLCHICINE	Autumn Crocus
COLESTIPOL (*Colestid*)	Phosphate Salts
CORTISONE (*Cortisone Acetate*)	Para-Aminobenzoic Acid (PABA)
CYCLOPHOSPHAMIDE (*Cytoxan, Neosar*)	Astragalus • Cordyceps
CYCLOSPORINE (*Neoral, Sandimmune*)	Berberine • European Barberry • Garlic • Goldenseal • Goldthread • Grapefruit • Oregon Grape • Peppermint • Phellodendron • Red Yeast • St. John's Wort • Tree Turmeric • Vitamin E • Wine
CYPROHEPTADINE (*Periactin*)	Hawaiian Baby Woodrose
DAPSONE (*Avlosulfon*)	Para-Aminobenzoic Acid (PABA)
DEXAMETHASONE (*Decadron*)	Country Mallow • Ephedra
DEXTROMETHORPHAN (*Robitussin DM, and others*)	5-HTP • Bitter Orange • Ergot • Grapefruit • Hawaiian Baby Woodrose • Lithium • L-Tryptophan • SAMe • St. John's Wort
DIAZOXIDE (*Hyperstat, Proglycem*)	Branched-Chain Amino Acids

Drug	Natural Medicine
DIGOXIN (*Lanoxin*)	Alder Buckthorn • Aloe • Apple Cider Vinegar • Black Hellebore • Black Psyllium • Black Root • Blond Psyllium • Blue Flag • Butternut • Calcium • Calotropis • Canadian Hemp • Cascara • Cereus • Colocynth • Danshen • Digitalis • European Buckthorn • Fo-Ti • Gamboge • Ginseng, Siberian • Gossypol • Greater Bindweed • Guar Gum • Hawthorn • Hedge Mustard • Indian Snakeroot • Jalap • Kaolin • Khella • Laminaria • Licorice • Lily-Of-The-Valley • Manna • Mexican Scammony Root • Oleander • Pangamic Acid • Pectin • Pheasant's Eye • Pleurisy Root • Procaine • Quassia • Rhubarb • Sarsaparilla • Senna • Squill • St. John's Wort • Strophanthus • Swamp Milkweed • Uzara • Vitamin D • Wahoo • Wallflower • Wheat Bran • Yellow Dock
DILTIAZEM (*Cardizem, Dilacor, Tiazac*)	Calcium • Guggul • Vitamin D
DIPYRIDAMOLE (*Persantine*)	Adenosine • Black Tea • Caffeine • Cocoa • Coffee • Cola Nut • Green Tea • Guarana • Mate • Oolong Tea
DISULFIRAM (*Antabuse*)	Beer • Black Tea • Caffeine • Cocoa • Coffee • Cola Nut • Green Tea • Guarana • Kombucha Tea • Marijuana • Mate • Oolong Tea • Wine
DRYING MEDICATIONS (Anticholinergic Drugs) Some drugs in this category include: Amitriptyline (*Elavil*) • Diphenhydramine (*Benadryl*) • Cyproheptadine (*Periactin*) • Amantadine (*Symmetrel*) • Atropine;Belladonna;Scopolamine (*Donnatal*) • Clozapine (*Clozaril*) • Prochlorperazine (*Compazine*)	Angel's Trumpet • Areca • Belladonna • Calabar Bean • Chinese Club Moss • Deanol • European Mandrake • Henbane • Huperzine A • Iboga • Jimson Weed • Phosphatidylcholine • Phosphatidylserine • Riboflavin • Scopolia
EPHEDRINE (*Pretz-D*)	Black Tea • Caffeine • Coffee • Cola Nut • Green Tea • Guarana • Indian Snakeroot • Mate • Oolong Tea
ERGOT DERIVATIVES Some drugs in this category include: Bromocriptine (*Parlodel*) • Caffeine;Ergotamine (*Cafergot*) • Dihydroergotamine (*D.H.E.*) • Ergotamine (*Ergostat*) • Methylergonovine (*Methergine*) • Methysergide (*Sansert*)	Country Mallow • Ephedra • Ergot
ERGOTAMINE (*Ergomar*)	Cocoa
ERYTHROMYCIN (*E.E.S., E-Mycin, PCE*)	Beer • Grapefruit • Wine
ESTROGENS (*Estrace, Estratest, Ogen, Premarin*)	Acerola • Alfalfa • Androstenediol • Androstenedione • Anise • Black Tea • Boron • Caffeine • Calcium • Chasteberry • Cherokee Rosehip • Cocoa • Coffee • Cola Nut • Dolomite • Fennel • German Chamomile • Grapefruit • Green Tea • Guarana • Guggul • Hu Zhang • Kudzu • Licorice • Mate • Milk Thistle • Oolong Tea • Pleurisy Root • Pregnenolone • Progesterone • Red Clover • Rose Hip • Saw Palmetto • Soy • Vitamin C • Wild Carrot
ETHACRYNIC ACID (*Edecrin*)	Licorice
ETOPOSIDE (*Vepesid*)	Grapefruit
EXEMESTANE (*Aromasin*)	DHEA
EZETIMIBE (*Zetia*)	Beta-Sitosterol
FELODIPINE (*Plendil*)	Bitter Orange • Wine
FENFLURAMINE (*Pondimin*)	St. John's Wort
FEXOFENADINE (*Allegra*)	Apple • Grapefruit • St. John's Wort • Sweet Orange
FLUCONAZOLE (*Diflucan*)	Black Tea • Caffeine • Cocoa • Coffee • Cola Nut • Green Tea • Guarana • Mate • Oolong Tea
FLUMAZENIL (*Romazicon*)	Melatonin
FLUOXETINE (*Prozac*)	Ginkgo • Marijuana
FLUPHENAZINE (*Prolixin*)	Acerola • Cherokee Rosehip • Rose Hip • Vitamin C
FLUVOXAMINE (*Luvox*)	Black Tea • Caffeine • Coffee • Cola Nut • Green Tea • Guarana • Mate • Melatonin • Oolong Tea
FOSPHENYTOIN (*Cerebyx*)	Folic Acid

Natural Medicines Comprehensive Database Consumer Version   (209) 472-2244

Potential Interactions: Drug/Natural Medicine For additional data, refer to the database.

Drug	Natural Medicine
FULVESTRANT (*Faslodex*)	DHEA
FUROSEMIDE (*Lasix*)	Germanium • Ginseng, Panax • Licorice
GEMFIBROZIL (*Lopid*)	Red Yeast
GRISEOFULVIN (*Fulvicin*)	Beer • Wine
GUANABENZ (*Wytensin*)	Yohimbe
GUANETHIDINE (*Ismelin*)	Cowhage
HALOPERIDOL (*Haldol*)	Butanediol (BD) • Gamma Butyrolactone (GBL) • Gamma-Hydroxybutyrate (GHB) • Scotch Broom
HEPARIN	Vitamin D
HEXOBARBITAL	Greek Sage
HEXOBARBITONE	Clary Sage
IBUPROFEN (*Advil, Motrin,* others)	Ginkgo • Tamarind
IMATINIB (*Gleevec*)	St. John's Wort
INDINAVIR (*Crixivan*)	Bitter Orange
INSULIN	Apple Cider Vinegar • Chromium • DHEA • EDTA • Fig • Ginkgo • Ginseng, Panax • Gymnema • Ribose • Solomon's Seal
IRINOTECAN (*Camptosar*)	St. John's Wort
ISONIAZID (INH)	Hydrazine Sulfate
ITRACONAZOLE (*Sporanox*)	Grapefruit
IVERMECTIN (*Stromectol*)	Sweet Orange
KANAMYCIN (*Kanatrex*)	Calcium D-Glucarate
LACTULOSE	Glutamine
LETROZOLE (*Femara*)	DHEA
LEVODOPA	Branched-Chain Amino Acids • Indian Snakeroot • Iron • Kava • Phenylalanine • Pyridoxine • SAMe • Tyrosine • Whey Protein
LEVODOPA/CARBIDOPA (*Sinemet*)	Octacosanol
LEVOTHYROXINE (*Synthroid, Levothroid, Levoxyl,* and others)	Calcium • Celery • Colloidal Silver • Dolomite • Horseradish • Iron • Red Yeast
LITHIUM (*Eskalith, Lithobid*)	Black Psyllium • Black Tea • Blond Psyllium • Caffeine • Cocoa • Coffee • Cola Nut • Green Tea • Guarana • Iodine • Mate • Oolong Tea
LOSARTAN (*Cozaar*)	Grapefruit
LOVASTATIN (*Mevacor*)	Pectin
LOW MOLECULAR WEIGHT HEPARINS (LMWHs)	Vitamin D
MEDICATIONS APPLIED TO THE SKIN, EYES, OR EARS (Topical Drugs)	DMSO (Dimethylsulfoxide)
MEDICATIONS CHANGED BY THE BODY (Cytochrome P450 3A4 (CYP3A4) Substrates)	Echinacea
MEDICATIONS CHANGED BY THE LIVER (Cytochrome P450 1A1 (CYP1A1) Substrates) Some drugs in this category include: Chlorzoxazone • Theophylline • Bufuralol	Nutmeg and Mace
MEDICATIONS CHANGED BY THE LIVER (Cytochrome P450 1A2 (CYP1A2) Substrates) Some drugs in this category include: Clozapine (*Clozaril*) • Cyclobenzaprine (*Flexeril*) • Fluvoxamine (*Luvox*) • Haloperidol (*Haldol*) • Imipramine (*Tofranil*) • Mexiletine (*Mexitil*) • Olanzapine (*Zyprexa*) • Pentazocine (*Talwin*) • Propranolol (*Inderal*) • Tacrine (*Cognex*) • Theophylline • Zileuton (*Zyflo*) • Zolmitriptan (*Zomig*)	Cabbage • Chrysin • Dandelion • Diindolylmethane • Echinacea • Eucalyptus • Feverfew • Fo-Ti • German Chamomile • Ginkgo • Ginseng, Siberian • Grape • Grapefruit • Indole-3-Carbinol • Ipriflavone • Kava • Methoxylated Flavones • Nutmeg and Mace • Peppermint • Red Clover • St. John's Wort
MEDICATIONS CHANGED BY THE LIVER (Cytochrome P450 2B1 (CYP2B1) Substrates)	Nutmeg and Mace

Medical professionals should consult the Professional Version at www.NaturalDatabase.com.

Potential Interactions: Drug/Natural Medicine   For additional data, refer to the database.

Drug	Natural Medicine
MEDICATIONS CHANGED BY THE LIVER (**Cytochrome P450 2B2 (CYP2B2) Substrates**)	Nutmeg and Mace
MEDICATIONS CHANGED BY THE LIVER (**Cytochrome P450 2B6 (CYP2B6) Substrates**) Some drugs in this category include: Ketamine (*Ketalar*) • Phenobarbital (*Luminal*) • Orphenadrine (*Norflex*) • Secobarbital (*Seconal*) • Dexamethasone (*Decadron*)	Licorice
MEDICATIONS CHANGED BY THE LIVER (**Cytochrome P450 2C19 (CYP2C19) Substrates**) Some drugs in this category include: Amitriptyline (*Elavil*) • Clomipramine (*Anafranil*) • Cyclophosphamide (*Cytoxan*) • Diazepam (*Valium*) • Lanzoprazole (*Prevacid*) • Omeprazole (*Prilosec*) • Lansoprazole (*Protonix*) • Phenytoin (*Dilantin*) • Phenobarbital (*Luminal*)	Devil's Claw • Eucalyptus • Feverfew • Fo-Ti • Ginkgo • Grapefruit • Kava • Peppermint • Red Clover
MEDICATIONS CHANGED BY THE LIVER (**Cytochrome P450 2C9 (CYP2C9) Substrates**) Some drugs in this category include: Celecoxib (*Celebrex*) • Diclofenac (*Voltaren*) • Fluvastatin (*Lescol*) • Glipizide (*Glucotrol*) • Ibuprofen (*Advil, Motrin*) • Irbesartan (*Avapro*) • Losartan (*Cozaar*) • Phenytoin (*Dilantin*) • Piroxicam (*Feldene*) • Tamoxifen (*Nolvadex*) • Tolbutamide (*Tolinase*) • Torsemide (*Demadex*) • Warfarin (*Coumadin*)	Cranberry • Devil's Claw • Eucalyptus • Feverfew • Fo-Ti • Ginkgo • Ginseng, Siberian • Grapefruit • Ipriflavone • Kava • Limonene • Lycium • Milk Thistle • Peppermint • Red Clover • St. John's Wort
MEDICATIONS CHANGED BY THE LIVER (**Cytochrome P450 2D6 (CYP2D6) Substrates**) Some drugs in this category include: Amitriptyline (*Elavil*) • Codeine • Desipramine (*Norpramin*) • Flecainide (*Tambocor*) • Haloperidol (*Haldol*) • Imipramine (*Tofranil*) • Metoprolol (*Lopressor, Toprol XL*) • Ondansetron (*Zofran*) • Paroxetine (*Paxil*) • Risperidone (*Risperdal*) • Tramadol (*Ultram*) • Venlafaxine (*Effexor*)	Black Cohosh • Ginkgo • Ginseng, Panax • Ginseng, Siberian • Goldenseal • Kava • Pomegranate
MEDICATIONS CHANGED BY THE LIVER (**Cytochrome P450 2E1 (CYP2E1) Substrates**)	Garlic • Kava
MEDICATIONS CHANGED BY THE LIVER (**Cytochrome P450 3A4 (CYP3A4) Substrates**) Some drugs in this category include: Alprazolam (*Xanax*) • Amlodipine (*Norvasc*) • Clarithromycin (*Biaxin*) • Cyclosporine (*Sandimmune*) • Erythromycin • Lovastatin (*Mevacor*) • Ketoconazole (*Nizoral*) • Itraconazole (*Sporanox*) • Fexofenadine (*Allegra*) • Triazolam (*Halcion*) • Verapamil (*Calan, Isoptin*)	American Elder • Berberine • Bishop's Weed • Bitter Orange • Black Cohosh • Black Pepper and White Pepper • Cat's Claw • Devil's Claw • DHEA • Eucalyptus • European Barberry • Feverfew • Fo-Ti • Garlic • German Chamomile • Ginkgo • Ginseng, Siberian • Goldenseal • Goldthread • Grapefruit • Guggul • Kava • Licorice • Lime • Milk Thistle • Oregon Grape • Peppermint • Phellodendron • Pomegranate • Red Clover • Resveratrol • Schisandra • St. John's Wort • Tree Turmeric • Valerian • Vitamin E • Wild Cherry
MEDICATIONS CHANGED BY THE LIVER (**Glucuronidated Drugs**) Some drugs in this category include: Acetaminophen (*Tylenol*) • Estrogens (*Estrace, Premarin*, others) and Oral Contraceptives • Entacapone (*Comtan*) • Irinotecan (*Camptosar*) • Atorvastatin (*Lipitor*) • Diazepam (*Valium*) • Digoxin • Lamotrigine (*Lamictal*) • Lorazepam (*Ativan*) • Lovastatin (*Mevacor*) • Meprobamate • Morphine • Oxazepam (*Serax*)	Cabbage • Calcium D-Glucarate • Chrysin • Dandelion • Milk Thistle
MEDICATIONS FOR ALZHEIMER'S DISEASE (**Acetylcholinesterase (AChE) Inhibitors**) Some drugs in this category include: Donepezil (*Aricept*) • Galantamine (*Reminyl*) • Rivastigmine (*Exelon*) • Tacrine (*Cognex*)	Chinese Club Moss • Deanol • Huperzine A • Phosphatidylcholine • Phosphatidylserine
MEDICATIONS FOR AN OVERACTIVE THYROID (**Antithyroid Drugs**) Some drugs in this category include: Methimazole (*Tapazole*) • Potassium Iodide (*SSKI, Pima*) • Propylthiouracil; PTU	Bladderwrack • Iodine
MEDICATIONS FOR ASTHMA (**Beta-Adrenergic Agonists**) Some drugs in this category include: Albuterol (*Ventolin*) • Metaproterenol (*Alupent*) • Terbutaline (*Brethine*) • Isoproterenol (*Isuprel*)	Cocoa

    Natural Medicines Comprehensive Database Consumer Version   (209) 472-2244

Potential Interactions: Drug/Natural Medicine
For additional data, refer to the database.

Drug	Natural Medicine
MEDICATIONS FOR CANCER (Antimitotic Chemotherapy) Some drugs in this category include: Etoposide (*VePesid*) • Teniposide (*Vumon*) • Vinblastine (*Velban*) • Vincristine (*Oncovin*) • Vinorelbine (*Navelbine*)	Glucosamine Hydrochloride • Glucosamine Sulfate
MEDICATIONS FOR CANCER (Chemotherapy) Some drugs in this category include: Alkyl Sulfonates: Busulfan (*Myleran*) Triazines: Dacarbazine (*DTIC-Dome*) Nitrogen Mustards: Chlorambucil (*Leukeran*) • Cyclophosphamide (*Cytoxan*) • Ifosfamide (*Ifex*) • Melphalan (*Alkeran*) Nitrosoureas: Carmustine, BCNU (*Gliadel*) • Lomustine (*CeeNu*) • Streptozocin (*Zanosar*) Platinum Coordination Complex: Carboplatin (*Paraplatin*) • Cisplatin (*Platinol-AQ*) Antimetabolites: Hydroxyurea (*Hydrea*) Folic Acid Analogs: Methotrexate (*Rheumatrex*) Pyrimidine Analogs: Cytarabine ARA-C (*Cytosar-U*) • Fluorouracil, 5-FU (*Efudex*) • Gemcitabine (*Gemzar*) Purine Analogs: Cladribine (*Leustatin*) • Fludarabine (*Fludara*) • Mercaptopurine (*Purinethol*) • Pentostatin (*Nipent*) • Thioguanine Vinca Alkaloids: Vinblastine (*Velban*) • Vincristine (*Oncovin*) Taxoids: Paclitaxel (*Taxol*) • Docetaxel (*Taxotere*) Anthracyclines: Daunorubicin (*DaunoXome*) • Doxorubicin (*Adriamycin*) • Idarubicin (*Idamycin*) • Valrubicin (*Valstar*)	Alpha-Lipoic Acid • Coenzyme Q-10 • Glutamine • N-Acetyl Glucosamine • Vitamin E
MEDICATIONS FOR DEPRESSION (Antidepressant Drugs) Some drugs in this category include: Bupropion (*Wellbutrin*) Nefazodone (*Serzone*) Tetracyclics: Maprotiline (*Ludiomil*) • Mirtazapine (*Remeron*) Trazodone (*Desyrel*) Monoamine Oxidase Inhibitors: Phenelzine (*Nardil*) • Tranylcypromine (*Parnate*) • Isocarboxazid (*Marplan*) Selective Serotonin Reuptake Inhibitors: Citalopram (*Celexa*) • Fluoxetine (*Prozac*) • Fluvoxamine (*Luvox*) • Paroxetine (*Paxil*) • Sertraline (*Zoloft*) • Venlafaxine (*Effexor*) Tricyclics: Amitriptyline (*Elavil*) • Clomipramine (*Anafranil*) • Amoxapine (*Asendin*) • Desipramine (*Norpramin*) • Doxepin (*Sinequan*) • Imipramine (*Tofranil*) • Nortriptyline (*Pamelor*)	5-HTP • Ergot • Hawaiian Baby Woodrose • Lithium • L-Tryptophan • SAMe • St. John's Wort
MEDICATIONS FOR DEPRESSION (MAOIs) Some drugs in this category include: Phenelzine (*Nardil*) • Tranylcypromine (*Parnate*) • Isocarboxazid (*Marplan*)	5-HTP • Bitter Orange • Black Tea • Brewer's Yeast • Caffeine • Calamus • Cereus • Cocoa • Coffee • Cola Nut • Country Mallow • Cowhage • Ephedra • Ergot • Ginseng, American • Ginseng, Panax • Green Tea • Guarana • Hawaiian Baby Woodrose • Hydrazine Sulfate • Indian Snakeroot • Lithium • L-Tryptophan • Mate • Oolong Tea • Phenylalanine • SAMe • Scotch Broom • St. John's Wort • Wine • Yohimbe
MEDICATIONS FOR DEPRESSION (Tricyclic Antidepressants) Some drugs in this category include: Amitriptyline (*Elavil*) • Clomipramine (*Anafranil*) • Amoxapine (*Asendin*) • Desipramine (*Norpramin*) • Doxepin (*Sinequan*) • Imipramine (*Tofranil*) • Nortriptyline (*Pamelor*)	Black Tea • Coffee • Riboflavin • Yohimbe

Medical professionals should consult the Professional Version at www.NaturalDatabase.com.

Potential Interactions: Drug/Natural Medicine   For additional data, refer to the database.

Drug	Natural Medicine
MEDICATIONS FOR DIABETES Some drugs in this category include: Insulins: (*Humulin, Novolin, Lantus, Humalog, Novolog*) Biguanides: Metformin (*Glucophage*) Meglitinides: Repaglinide (*Prandin*) • Nateglinide (*Starlix*) Alpha-Glucosidase Inhibitors: Acarbose (*Precose*) • Miglitol (*Glyset*) Sulfonylureas: Chlorpropamide (*Diabinese*) • Glimepiride (*Amaryl*) • Glipizide (*Glucotrol*) • Glyburide (*DiaBeta, Glynase, Micronase*) • Tolbutamide (*Orinase*) Thiazolidinediones: Pioglitazone (*Actos*) • Rosiglitazone (*Avandia*)	Agrimony • Aloe • Alpha-Lipoic Acid • Annatto • Avocado Sugar Extract • Baikal Skullcap • Banaba • Barley • Bean Pod • Bilberry • Bitter Melon • Black Mulberry • Black Psyllium • Black Tea • Blond Psyllium • Blue Cohosh • Blueberry • Branched-Chain Amino Acids • Bugleweed • Caffeine • Capers • Caraway • Carqueja • Cassia Auriculata • Cassia Cinnamon • Chanca Piedra • Chinese Cucumber • Cinnamon Bark • Cocoa • Coffee • Cola Nut • Corn Silk • Country Mallow • Cowhage • Cumin • Damiana • Devil's Claw • Elderflower • Ephedra • Eucalyptus • Fenugreek • Fig • Flaxseed • Fo-Ti • Ginger • Ginseng, American • Ginseng, Panax • Ginseng, Siberian • Glucomannan • Glucosamine Hydrochloride • Glucosamine Sulfate • Goat's Rue • Green Tea • Guar Gum • Guarana • Gymnema • Horse Chestnut • Hydrazine Sulfate • Inositol Nicotinate • Ivy Gourd • Jambolan • Juniper • Kudzu • Lycium • Madagascar Periwinkle • Maitake Mushroom • Marshmallow • Mate • Melatonin • Myrrh • N-Acetyl Glucosamine • Neem • Niacin and Niacinamide • Olive • Onion • Oolong Tea • Puncture Vine • Ribose • Sage • Salacia • Solomon's Seal • Spinach • Stevia • Stinging Nettle • Tiratricol • Vanadium • Xanthan Gum
MEDICATIONS FOR DISSOLVING BLOOD CLOTS (Thrombolytic Drugs) (tPA, *Alteplase*)	Mesoglycan • Potato
MEDICATIONS FOR ESTROGEN SENSITIVE CANCERS (Aromatase Inhibitors) Some drugs in this category include: Anastrozole (*Arimidex*) • Exemestane (*Aromasin*) • Letrozole (*Femara*)	Chrysin
MEDICATIONS FOR FUNGAL INFECTIONS (Antifungals) Some drugs in this category include: Ciclopirox (*Loprox*) • Griseofulvin (*Grisactin, Gris-PEG*) • Terbinafine (*Lamisil*) • Clotrimazole (*Lotrimin, Mycelex*) • Fluconazole (*Diflucan*) • Itraconazole (*Sporanox*) • Ketoconazole (*Nizoral*) • Miconazole (*Desenex, Monistat*) • Terconazole (*Terazol*) • Amphotericin B (*Amphotec*) • Nystatin (*Mycostatin*)	Brewer's Yeast • Saccharomyces Boulardii
MEDICATIONS FOR GOUT (Antigout Drugs) Some drugs in this category include: Allopurinol (*Zyloprim*) • Probenecid (*Benemid*) • Colchicine	Niacin and Niacinamide • Adenosine
MEDICATIONS FOR HIGH BLOOD PRESSURE (ACE Inhibitors) Some drugs in this category include: Captopril (*Capoten*) • Enalapril (*Vasotec*) • Lisinopril (*Prinivil, Zestril*) • Fosinopril (*Monopril*) • Moexipril (*Univasc*) • Perindopril (*Aceon*) • Quinapril (*Accupril*) • Ramipril (*Altace*) • Spirapril (*Renormax*) • Trandolapril (*Mavik*)	Capsicum • Iodine • Laminaria • Lithium • Morinda • Pomegranate • Potassium
MEDICATIONS FOR HIGH BLOOD PRESSURE (Angiotensin Receptor Blockers (ARBs)) Some drugs in this category include: Candesartan (*Atacand*) • Eprosartan (*Teveten*) • Irbesartan (*Avapro*) • Losartan (*Cozaar*) • Telmisartan (*Micardis*) • Valsartan (*Diovan*)	Iodine • Morinda • Potassium

    Natural Medicines Comprehensive Database Consumer Version   (209) 472-2244

Potential Interactions: Drug/Natural Medicine   For additional data, refer to the database.

Drug	Natural Medicine
MEDICATIONS FOR HIGH BLOOD PRESSURE (Antihypertensive Drugs) Some drugs in this category include: Beta-Adrenergic Blockers: Atenolol (*Tenormin*) • Labetalol (*Normodyne*) • Metoprolol (*Lopressor*) • Nadolol (*Corgard*) • Propranolol (*Inderal*) Calcium Channel Blockers: Amlodipine (*Norvasc*) • Diltiazem (*Cardizem*) • Felodipine (*Plendil*) • Nifedipine (*Adalat, Procardia*) • Verapamil (*Calan*) Antiadrenergic Agents: Reserpine • Methyldopa (*Aldomet*) • Clonidine (*Catapres*) • Guanfacine (*Tenex*) • Guanabenz (*Wytensin*) Alpha-1 Adrenergic Blockers: Doxazosin (*Cardura*) • Prazosin (*Minipress*) • Terazosin (*Hytrin*) Angiotensin II Receptor Antagonists: Irbesartan (*Avapro*) • Losartan (*Cozaar*) • Valsartan (*Diovan*) Angiotensin-Converting Enzyme Inhibitors: Benazepril (*Lotensin*) • Captopril (*Capoten*) • Enalapril (*Vasotec*) • Fosinopril (*Monopril*) • Lisinopril (*Prinivil*) • Quinapril (*Accupril*) • Ramipril (*Altace*)	Andrographis • Asafoetida • Betony • Blue Cohosh • Carrageenan • Casein Peptides • Catechu • Cat's Claw • Cod Liver Oil • Coenzyme Q-10 • Coltsfoot • Corn Silk • Devil's Claw • DHA (Docosahexaenoic Acid) • EPA (Eicosapentaenoic Acid) • Epimedium • European Mistletoe • Fish Oil • Gentian • Japanese Persimmon • L-Arginine • Licorice • Lycium • Olive • Periwinkle • Pomegranate • Reishi Mushroom • Stevia • Stinging Nettle • Theanine • Wild Carrot • Yohimbe
MEDICATIONS FOR HIGH BLOOD PRESSURE (Alpha-Adrenergic Antagonists) Some drugs in this category include: Phenoxybenzamine (*Dibenzyline*) • Phentolamine (*Regitine*) • Tamsulosin (*Flomax*) • Terazosin (*Hytrin*) • Prazosin (*Minipress*) • Doxazosin (*Cardura*)	Butcher's Broom
MEDICATIONS FOR HIGH BLOOD PRESSURE (Beta-Blockers) Some drugs in this category include: Atenolol (*Tenormin*) • Metoprolol (*Lopressor, Toprol XL*) • Nadolol (*Corgard*) • Propranolol (*Inderal*)	Hawthorn
MEDICATIONS FOR HIGH BLOOD PRESSURE (Calcium Channel Blockers) Some drugs in this category include: Amlodipine (*Norvasc*) • Diltiazem (*Cardizem*) • Felodipine (*Plendil*) • Isradipine (*DynaCirc*) • Nicardipine (*Cardene*) • Nifedipine (*Procardia, Adalat*) • Nisoldipine (*Sular*) • Verapamil (*Calan*)	Calcium • Forskolin • Ginger • Grapefruit • Hawthorn • Lithium • Magnesium • Pangamic Acid • Stevia
MEDICATIONS FOR HIV/AIDS (Nonnucleoside Reverse Transcriptase Inhibitors (NNRTIs)) Some drugs in this category include: Nevirapine (*Viramune*) • Delavirdine (*Rescriptor*) • Efavirenz (*Sustiva*)	St. John's Wort
MEDICATIONS FOR HIV/AIDS (Protease Inhibitors) Some drugs in this category include: Indinavir (*Crixivan*) • Nelfinavir (*Viracept*) • Squinavir (*Invirase*)	St. John's Wort
MEDICATIONS FOR INFLAMMATION (Corticosteroids) Some drugs in this category include: Beclomethasone (*Beclovent, Celestone*) • Betamethasone (*Valisone*) • Budesonide (*Rhinocort*) • Cortisone (*Cortone*) • Dexamethasone (*Adrenocot, Decadron*) • Fludrocortisone (*Florinef*) • Flunisolide (*Aerobid*) • Fluocinonide (*Lidex*) • Fluticasone (*Flovent*) • Hydrocortisone (*Cortef*) • Methylprednisolone (*Medrol*) • Prednisolone (*Econopred, Orapred*) • Prednisone (*Orasone, Deltasone*) • Triamcinolone (*Kenalog*)	Alder Buckthorn • Branched-Chain Amino Acids • Butternut • Cascara • Cesium • Corn Silk • DHEA • Gamboge • Licorice • Lily-Of-The-Valley • Pheasant's Eye • Rhubarb • Squill • Strophanthus • Wallflower
MEDICATIONS FOR MALE SEXUAL DYSFUNCTION (Phosphodiesterase-5 Inhibitors) Some drugs in this category include: Sildenafil (*Viagra*) • Tadalafil (*Cialis*) • Vardenafil (*Levitra*)	Hawthorn

CONSUMER VERSION

Medical professionals should consult the Professional Version at www.NaturalDatabase.com.

Potential Interactions: Drug/Natural Medicine   For additional data, refer to the database.

Drug	Natural Medicine
MEDICATIONS FOR MENTAL CONDITIONS (Antipsychotic Drugs) Some drugs in this category include: Benzisoxazoles: Risperidone (*Risperdal*) Dibenzapines: Clozapine (*Clozaril*) • Loxapine (*Loxitane*) • Olanzapine (*Zyprexa*) • Quetiapine (*Seroquel*) • Ziprasidone (*Geodon*) Thioanthenes: Thiothixene (*Navane*) Phenylbutylpiperadines: Haloperidol (*Haldol*) Phenothiazines: Chlorpromazine (*Thorazine*) • Fluphenazine (*Prolixin*) • Mesoridazine (*Serentil*) • Perphenazine (*Trilafon*) • Thioridazine (*Mellaril*) • Trifluoperazine (*Stelazine*)	Butanediol (BD) • Chasteberry • Cowhage • Gamma Butyrolactone (GBL) • Gamma-Hydroxybutyrate (GHB) • Indian Snakeroot • Phenylalanine
MEDICATIONS FOR MIGRAINE HEADACHES ("Triptans") Some drugs in this category include: Eletriptan (*Relpax*) • Naratriptan (*Amerge*) • Rizatriptan (*Maxalt*) • Sumatriptan (*Imitrex*) • Zolmitriptan (*Zomig*)	St. John's Wort
MEDICATIONS FOR PAIN (Narcotic Drugs) Some drugs in this category include: Acetaminophen;Oxycodone (*Percocet*) • Acetaminophen;Propoxyphene (*Darvocet*) • Aspirin;Oxycodone (*Percodan*) • Fentanyl (*Duragesic*) • Hydromorphone (*Dilaudid*) • Meperidine (*Demerol*) • Methadone (*Methadose, Dolophine*) • Morphine (*MS Contin, Roxanol*) • Oxycodone (*OxyContin*) • Propoxyphene (*Darvon*) • Sufentanil (*Sufenta*)	Beer • Butanediol (BD) • Gamma Butyrolactone (GBL) • Gamma-Hydroxybutyrate (GHB) • Meadowsweet • St. John's Wort • Sweet Bay • Wine
MEDICATIONS FOR SKIN CONDITIONS (Retinoids) Some drugs in this category include: Adapelene (*Differin*) • Isotretinoin (*Isotrex*) • Tretinon (*Retin-A, Retinova*)	Vitamin A
MEDICATIONS GIVEN AS A SHOT (Injectable Drugs)	DMSO (Dimethylsulfoxide)
MEDICATIONS MOVED BY PUMPS IN CELLS (P-Glycoprotein Substrates) Some drugs in this category include: Etoposide (*VePesid*) • Paclitaxel (*Taxol*) • Vinblastine (*Velban*) • Vincristine (*Oncovin*) • Ketoconazole • Itraconazole • Amprenavir (*Agenerase*) • Indinavir (*Crixivan*) • Nelfinavir (*Viracept*) • Squinavir (*Fortovase, Invirase*) • Cimetidine • Ranitidine • Diltiazem • Verapamil • Corticosteroids • Erythromycin • Fexofenadine (*Allegra*) • Cyclosporine • Loperamide (*Imodium*) • Quinidine	Black Pepper and White Pepper • St. John's Wort
MEDICATIONS THAT CAN CAUSE AN IRREGULAR HEARTBEAT (QT Interval-Prolonging Drugs) Some drugs in this category include: • Amitriptyline • Clarithromycin (*Biaxin*) • Erythromycin • Quinidine • Sotalol (*Betapace*) • Thioridazine • Indapamide (*Lozol*) • Risperidone (*Risperdal*) • Moxifloxacin (*Avelox*) • Ziprasidone (*Geodon*)	Bitter Orange • Country Mallow • Ephedra
MEDICATIONS THAT CAN HARM THE KIDNEYS (Nephrotoxic Drugs) Some drugs in this category include: Carbamazepine (*Tegretol*) • Diclofenac (*Voltaren*) • Diflunisal (*Dolobid*) • Ganciclovir (*Cytovene*) • Gatifloxacin (*Tequin*) • Interferon • Meloxicam (*Mobic*) • Spironolactone (*Aldactone*) • Tacrolimus (*Prograf*) • Valacyclovir (*Valtrex*) • Amphotericin B (*Fungizone*) • Cisplatin (*Platinol*) • Cyclosporine (*Neoral*) • Enalapril (*Vasotec*) • Nafcillin (*Unipen*) • Tobramycin (*Nebcin*)	Creatine

Drug	Natural Medicine
MEDICATIONS THAT CAN HARM THE LIVER (Hepatotoxic Drugs) Some drugs in this category include: Amphotericin B (*Fungizone*) • Azathioprine (*Imuran*) • Carbamazepine (*Tegretol*) • Disulfiram (*Antabuse*) • Felbamate (*Felbatol*) • Flutamide (*Eulexin*) • Hydroxychloroquine (*Plaquenil*) • Indinavir (*Crixivan*) • Interferon (*Roferon, Intron, Wellferon*) • Itraconazole (*Sporanox*) • Leflunomide (*Arava*) • Methotrexate (*Rheumatrex*) • Procainamide (*Procan*) • Rosiglitazone (*Avandia*) • Stavudine, d4T (*Zerit*) • Tacrine (*Cognex*) • Terbinafine (*Lamisil*) • Ticlopidine (*Ticlid*) • Tolcapone (*Tasmar*) • Zalcitabine, ddC (*Hivid*)	Beer • Bishop's Weed • Black Cohosh • Boldo • Chaparral • Comfrey • Fo-Ti • Gotu Kola • Greater Celandine • Green Tea • Kava • Khella • Morinda • Sweet Clover • Vitamin A • Wine
MEDICATIONS THAT DECREASE STOMACH ACID (H2-Blockers) Some drugs in this category include: Famotidine (*Pepcid*) • Ranitidine (*Zantac*) • Nixatidine (*Axid*) • Cimetidine (*Tagamet*)	Aletris • Alpinia • Beer • Black Mustard • Blessed Thistle • Calamus • Cinchona • Colombo • Cubebs • Devil's Claw • Northern Prickly Ash • Peppermint • Quassia • Southern Prickly Ash • Wine • Yarrow
MEDICATIONS THAT DECREASE STOMACH ACID (Proton Pump Inhibitors) Some drugs in this category include: Esomeprazole (*Nexium*) • Lansoprazole (*Prevacid*) • Omeprazole (*Prilosec*) • Pantoprazole (*Protonix*) • Rabeprazole (*Aciphex*)	Aletris • Alpinia • Black Mustard • Blessed Thistle • Calamus • Cinchona • Colombo • Cubebs • Devil's Claw • Northern Prickly Ash • Peppermint • Quassia • Southern Prickly Ash • Yarrow
MEDICATIONS THAT DECREASE THE BREAK DOWN OF OTHER MEDICATIONS BY THE LIVER (Cytochrome P450 2C19 (CYP2C19) Inhibitors)	Limonene
MEDICATIONS THAT DECREASE THE BREAK DOWN OF OTHER MEDICATIONS BY THE LIVER (Cytochrome P450 2C9 (CYP2C9) Inhibitors)	Limonene
MEDICATIONS THAT DECREASE THE BREAKDOWN OF OTHER MEDICATIONS IN THE LIVER (Cytochrome P450 3A4 (CYP3A4) Inhibitors) Some drugs in this category include: Clarithromycin (*Biaxin*) • Erythromycin • Itraconazole • Ketoconazole • Cimetidine • Nefazodone (*Serzone*) • Indinavir (*Crixivan*) • Nelfinavir (*Viracept*) • Saquinavir (*Invirase*)	Ergot
MEDICATIONS THAT DECREASE THE IMMUNE SYSTEM (Immunosuppressants) Some drugs in this category include: Azathioprine (*Imuran*) • Basiliximab (*Simulect*) • Cyclosporine (*Neoral, Sandimmune*) • Daclizumab (*Zenapax*) • Muromonab-CD3 (*OKT3*) • Mycophenolate (*CellCept*) • Prednisone (*Orasone, Deltasone*) • Sirolimus (*Rapamune*) • Tacrolimus (*FK506, Prograf*)	Andrographis • Ashwagandha • Astragalus • Beta Glucans • Cat's Claw • Echinacea • Elderberry • European Mistletoe • Ginseng, Panax • Ipriflavone • Jiaogulan • Kefir • Lactobacillus • Larch Arabinogalactan • Melatonin • Neem • Picrorhiza • Pycnogenol • Thunder God Vine • Thymus Extract • Yogurt
MEDICATIONS THAT INCREASE BLOOD FLOW TO THE HEART (Nitrates) Some drugs in this category include: Isosorbide Dinitrate (*Isordil*) • Isosorbide Mononitrate (*Imdur*) • Nitroglycerin (*Nitrostat*)	Forskolin • Hawthorn • L-Arginine
MEDICATIONS THAT INCREASE SENSITIVITY TO SUNLIGHT (Photosensitizing Drugs) Some drugs in this category include: Acyclovir (*Zovirax*) • Amitriptyline (*Elavil*) • Azithromycin (*Zithromax*) • Captopril (*Capoten*) • Carbamazepine (*Tegretol*) • Chloroquine (*Aralen*) • Chlorthiazide (*Diuril*) • Chlorpromazine (*Thorazine*) • Ciprofloxacin (*Cipro*) • Dantrolene (*Dantrium*) • Dapsone • Divalproex (*Depakote*) • Oral Contraceptives • Felbamate (*Felbatol*) • Fluorouracil (*Efudex, Carac*) • Flutamide (*Eulexin*) • Furosemide (*Lasix*) • Glipizide (*Glucotrol*) • Glyburide (*Micronase*) • Hydroxychloroquine (*Plaquenil*) • Isotretinoin (*Accutane*) • Methoxsalen (*Oxsoralen*) • Minocycline (*Minocin*) • Phenobarbital • Promethazine (*Phenergan*) • Quinidine (*Quinidex*) • Sulfamethoxazole;Trimethoprim (*Bactrim, Septra*) • Tacrolimus (*Prograf*) • Tolbutamide (*Orinase*) • Trazodone (*Desyrel*) • Tretinoin (*Retin-A*) • Valproic Acid (*Depakene*)	Alfalfa • Arrach • Bergamot Oil • Bishop's Weed • Celery • Chenopodium Oil • Chlorophyll • Khella • Lime • Masterwort • Rue • St. John's Wort • Wild Carrot

CONSUMER VERSION

Medical professionals should consult the Professional Version at www.NaturalDatabase.com.

Potential Interactions: Drug/Natural Medicine

For additional data, refer to the database.

Drug	Natural Medicine
MEDICATIONS THAT INCREASE THE BREAK DOWN OF OTHER MEDICATIONS BY THE LIVER (Cytochrome P450 3A4 (CYP3A4) Inducers) Some drugs in this category include: Aminoglutethimide (*Cytadren*) • Aprepitant (*Emend*) • Carbamazepine (*Tegretol*) • Dexamethasone (*Dexone, Hexadrol*) • Efavirenz (*Sustiva*) • Ethosuximide (*Zarontin*) • Glucocorticoids • Glutethimide (*Doriden*) • Griseofulvin (*Fulvicin, Grisactin*) • Modafinil (*Provigil*) • Nafcillin (*Nallpen, Unipen*) • Nevirapine (*Viramune*) • Oxcarbazepine (*Trileptal*) • Phenobarbital (*Luminal*) • Phenytoin (*Dilantin, Phenytek*) • Primidone (*Mysoline*) • Rifabutin (*Mycobutin*) • Rifampin (*Rifadin, Rimactane*) • Rifapentine (*Priftin*)	Alkanna • Alpine Ragwort • Borage • Butterbur • Coltsfoot • Comfrey • Dusty Miller • Golden Ragwort • Gravel Root • Groundsel • Hemp Agrimony • Hound's Tongue • Tansy Ragwort
MEDICATIONS THAT INCREASE THE BREAK DOWN OF OTHER MEDICATIONS BY THE LIVER (Cytochrome P450 2C19 (CYP2C19) Inducers)	Limonene
MEDICATIONS THAT INCREASE THE BREAK DOWN OF OTHER MEDICATIONS BY THE LIVER (Cytochrome P450 2C9 (CYP2C9) Inducers)	Limonene
MEDICATIONS THAT INCREASE THE CHANCE OF HAVING A SEIZURE (Seizure Threshold Lowering Drugs) Some of the drugs in this category include: Anesthetics (*Propofol*, others) • Antiarrhythmics (*Mexiletine*) • Antibiotics (*Amphotericin, Penicillin, Cephalosporins, Imipenem*) • Antidepressants (*Bupropion*, others) • Antihistamines (*Cyproheptadine*, others) • Immunosuppressants (*Cyclosporin*) • Narcotics (*Fentanyl*, others) • Stimulants (*Methylphenidate*, others) • Theophylline	Ginkgo • Thuja
MEDICATIONS THAT SLOW BLOOD CLOTTING (Anticoagulant / Antiplatelet Drugs) Some drugs in this category include: Ardeparin (*Normiflo*) • Dalteparin (*Fragmin*) • Danaparoid (*Orgaran*) • Enoxaparin (*Lovenox*) Heparin Antithrombin III (*Thrombate III*) Lepirudin (*Refludan*) Warfarin (*Coumadin*) • Dicumarol • Clopidogrel (*Plavix*) • Cilostazol (*Pletal*) • Dipyridamole (*Persantine*) • Ticlopidine (*Ticlid*) • Tirofiban (*Aggrastat*) • Eptifibatide (*Integrilin*) • Abciximab (*ReoPro*) • Anagrelide (*Agrylin*)	Allspice • Andrographis • Arnica • Asafoetida • Bishop's Weed • Black Tea • Bladderwrack • Bogbean • Boldo • Borage • Bromelain • Buchu • Burdock • Caffeine • Capsicum • Carrageenan • Chinese Prickly Ash • Cinchona • Clove • Cod Liver Oil • Coffee • Coltsfoot • Danshen • Deertongue • DHA (Docosahexaenoic Acid) • Dong Quai • EPA (Eicosapentaenoic Acid) • Epimedium • Evening Primrose Oil • Fenugreek • Feverfew • Fish Oil • Flaxseed • Flaxseed Oil • Forskolin • Forsythia • Gamma Linolenic Acid • Garlic • Ginger • Ginkgo • Ginseng, Panax • Ginseng, Siberian • Green Tea • Guarana • Guggul • Holy Basil • Honeysuckle • Horse Chestnut • Inositol Nicotinate • IP-6 • Jiaogulan • Kudzu • Mate • Melatonin • Mesoglycan • Methoxylated Flavones • Nattokinase • Onion • Oolong Tea • Palm Oil • Pantethine • Pau D'arco • Peony • Policosanol • Red Clover • Reishi Mushroom • Resveratrol • Safflower • Saw Palmetto • Sea Buckthorn • Swallowroot • Sweet Clover • Sweet Vernal Grass • Thyme • Tiratricol • Tonka Bean • Turmeric • Vanadium • Vinpocetine • Vitamin E • Willow Bark • Yarrow
MEDICATIONS USED DURING SURGERY (Anesthesia) Some drugs in this category include: Thiopental Sodium (*Pentothal*) • Methohexital Sodium (*Brevital*) • Etomidate (*Amidate*) • Ketamine (*Ketalar*) • Propofol (*Diprivan*) • Nitrous Oxide • Enflurane (*Ethrane*) • Halothane (*Fluothane*) • Methoxyflurane (*Penthrane*) • Sevoflurane (*Ultane*) • Isoflurane (*Forane*) • Desflurane (*Suprane*)	Borage • Cowhage • Evening Primrose Oil • Fever Bark
MEDICATIONS USED FOR ALZHEIMER'S DISEASE (NMDA Antagonists) (Namenda)	Threonine
MEDICATIONS USED FOR DEPRESSION (Tricyclic Antidepressants) Some drugs in this category include: Amitriptyline (*Elavil*) • Clomipramine (*Anafranil*) • Desipramine (*Norpramin*) • Doxepin (*Sinequan*) • Imipramine (*Tofranil*) • Nortriptyline (*Pamelor*) • Protriptyline (*Vivactil*)	Cowhage • Indian Snakeroot • Scopolia

Potential Interactions: Drug/Natural Medicine   For additional data, refer to the database.

Drug	Natural Medicine
MEDICATIONS USED FOR HIV/AIDS (Non-Nucleoside Reverse Transcriptase Inhibitors (NNRTIs)) Some drugs in this category include: Nevirapine (*Viramune*) • Delavirdine (*Rescriptor*) • Efavirenz (*Sustiva*)	Garlic
MEDICATIONS USED FOR LOWERING CHOLESTEROL (Resins)	Niacin and Niacinamide (Vitamin B3)
MEDICATIONS USED FOR LOWERING CHOLESTEROL (Statins) Some drugs in this category include: Atorvastatin (*Lipitor*) • Fluvastatin (*Lescol*) • Lovastatin (*Mevacor*) • Pravastatin (*Pravachol*) • Simvastatin (*Zocor*)	Beta-Carotene • Grapefruit • Inositol Nicotinate • Niacin and Niacinamide (Vitamin B3) • Selenium • Vitamin E
MEDICATIONS USED FOR PARKINSON'S DISEASE (Dopamine Agonists) Some drugs in this category include: Bromocriptine (*Parlodel*) • Carbidopa (*Lodosyn*) • Carbidopa;Levodopa (*Sinemet*) • Pergolide (*Permax*) • Pramipexole (*Mirapex*) • Ropinirole (*Requip*)	Black Horehound • Chasteberry
MEDICATIONS USED TO PREVENT SEIZURES (Anticonvulsants) Some drugs in this category include: Carbamazepine (*Tegretol*) • Clonazepam (*Klonopin*) • Ethosuximide (*Zarontin*) • Gabapentin (*Neurontin*) • Lamotrigine (*Lamictal*) • Levetiracetam (*Keppra*) • Methsuximide (*Celontin*) • Oxcarbazepine (*Trileptal*) • Tiagabine (*Gabitril*) • Topiramate (*Topamax*) • Valproic Acid (*Depakote*) • Zonisamide (*Zonegran*)	Butanediol (BD) • Ephedra • Gamma Butyrolactone (GBL) • Gamma-Hydroxybutyrate (GHB) • Ginkgo • Glutamine • Lithium • Sage • Thuja • Wormwood
MEPERIDINE (*Demerol*)	5-HTP • Ergot • Hawaiian Baby Woodrose • Lithium • L-Tryptophan • SAMe • St. John's Wort
METFORMIN (*Glucophage*)	Beer • Guar Gum • Quillaia • Water Avens • Wine
METHOTREXATE (MTX, *Rheumatrex*)	Folic Acid • Kudzu
METHYLDOPA (*Aldomet*)	Cowhage • Iron • Lithium
METHYLPREDNISOLONE (*Adlone, A-Methapred, depMedalone, Depoject, Medrol, Solu-Medrol*)	Grapefruit
METHYLXANTHINES Some drugs in this category include: Caffeine (*NoDoz, Vivarin*) • Theophylline (*Slo-Bid, Theo-Dur, Theolair*)	Adenosine • Country Mallow • Ephedra • Lithium
METOCLOPRAMIDE (*Reglan*)	Chasteberry
METRONIDAZOLE (*Flagyl*)	Beer • Wine
MEXILETINE (*Mexitil*)	Black Tea • Caffeine • Cocoa • Coffee • Cola Nut • Green Tea • Guarana • Mate • Oolong Tea
MIDAZOLAM (*Versed*)	Bitter Orange • Echinacea
MUSCLE RELAXANTS	Butanediol (BD) • Gamma Butyrolactone (GBL) • Gamma-Hydroxybutyrate (GHB) • Lithium • Magnesium • Procaine
MYCOPHENOLATE MOFETIL (*Cellcept*)	Iron
NALOXONE (*Narcan*)	Butanediol (BD) • Fever Bark • Gamma Butyrolactone (GBL) • Gamma-Hydroxybutyrate (GHB) • Yohimbe
NEFAZODONE (*Serzone*)	St. John's Wort
NIACIN (*Niacor, Niaspan, Nicobid, Slo-Niacin*)	Beta-Carotene • Red Yeast • Selenium • Vitamin C (Ascorbic Acid) • Vitamin E
NICARDIPINE (*Cardene*)	Vitamin C (Ascorbic Acid)
NICOTINE (*Habitrol, Nicoderm, Nicorette, Nicotrol, Prestep*)	Blue Cohosh • Cola Nut • Green Tea • Guarana • Mate • Oolong Tea
NICOTINE PATCH (*Transdermal Nicotine*)	Inositol Nicotinate • Niacin and Niacinamide (Vitamin B3)
NIFEDIPINE (*Adalat, Procardia*)	Coca • Vitamin C (Ascorbic Acid)
NIFEDIPINE GITS (*Procardia XL*)	Melatonin
NITROGLYCERIN (*Minitran, Nitrek, Nitrostat*)	N-Acetyl Cysteine
NORTRIPTYLINE (*Pamelor, Aventyl*)	St. John's Wort

Potential Interactions: Drug/Natural Medicine   For additional data, refer to the database.

Drug	Natural Medicine
NSAIDs (Nonsteroidal Anti-Inflammatory Drugs) Some drugs in this category include: Diclofenac (*Voltaren*) • Etodolac (*Lodine*) • Flurbiprofen (*Ansaid*) • Ibuprofen (*Motrin*) • Indomethacin (*Indocin*) • Ketoprofen (*Orudis*) • Ketorolac (*Toradol*) • Meclofenamate; Mefenamic Acid (*Ponstel*) • Nabumetone (*Relafen*) • Naproxen (*Naprosyn*) • Oxaprozine (*Daypro*) • Piroxicam (*Feldene*) • Sulindac (*Clinoril*)	Beer • Borage • Chromium • Gossypol • Lithium • Wine
OMEPRAZOLE (*Prilosec*)	Ginkgo
OXAZEPAM (*Serax*)	Cabbage
PAROXETINE (*Paxil*)	St. John's Wort
PENICILLAMINE (*Cuprimine, Depen*)	Colloidal Silver • Copper • Iron • Zinc
PENICILLIN (*Penicillin VK, Pen VK, Veetids*)	Guar Gum
PENTAZOCINE (*Talwin*)	5-HTP • Ergot • Hawaiian Baby Woodrose • Lithium • L-Tryptophan • SAMe • St. John's Wort
PENTOBARBITAL (*Nembutal*)	Holy Basil • Black Tea • Caffeine • Coffee • Cola Nut • Green Tea • Guarana • Mate • Oolong Tea
PHENACETIN	Grape
PHENOBARBITAL (*Luminal*)	Cinchona • Folic Acid • Nutmeg and Mace • Pyridoxine • St. John's Wort
PHENOTHIAZINES Some drugs in this category include: Thioridazine (*Mellaril*) • Mesoridazine (*Serentil*) • Trifluoperazine (*Stelazine*) • Chlorpromazine (*Thorazine*) • Fluphenazine (*Prolixin*)	Black Tea • Coffee • Evening Primrose Oil • Fever Bark • Gamma Linolenic Acid • Lithium • L-Tryptophan • Yohimbe
PHENPROCOUMON	Ginger • St. John's Wort
PHENYLPROPANOLAMINE	Black Tea • Caffeine • Cocoa • Coffee • Cola Nut • Green Tea • Guarana • Mate • Oolong Tea
PHENYTOIN (*Dilantin*)	Beer • Black Pepper and White Pepper • Folic Acid • Indian Long Pepper • Peony • Pyridoxine • St. John's Wort • Wine
PRAVASTATIN (*Pravachol*)	Beta-Sitosterol • Sweet Orange
PRAZIQUANTEL (*Biltricide*)	Grapefruit
PREDNISOLONE	Cordyceps
PRIMIDONE (*Mysoline*)	Folic Acid • Niacin and Niacinamide
PROBENECID (*Benemid*)	Niacin and Niacinamide • Riboflavin
PROCYCLIDINE	Areca
PROGESTIN	Pregnenolone
PROPRANOLOL (*Inderal*)	Black Pepper and White Pepper • Guggul • Indian Long Pepper • Indian Snakeroot • Ribose
PYRIMETHAMINE (*Daraprim*)	Folic Acid
QUINIDINE (*Quinidex*)	Cinchona • Grapefruit • Kaolin • Pheasant's Eye • Scopolia • Scotch Broom • Squill • Strophanthus • Wallflower
QUININE	Black Hellebore • Cinchona • Digitalis • Hedge Mustard • Lily-Of-The-Valley • Oleander • Strophanthus • Swamp Milkweed • Uzara • Wahoo • Wallflower
RESERPINE	St. John's Wort
RIFAMPIN	Black Pepper and White Pepper
RILUZOLE (*Rilutek*)	Black Tea • Caffeine • Coffee • Cola Nut • Green Tea • Guarana • Mate • Oolong Tea
RISPERIDONE (*Risperdal*)	Hawaiian Baby Woodrose
RITONAVIR (*Norvir*)	Butanediol (BD) • Gamma Butyrolactone (GBL) • Gamma-Hydroxybutyrate (GHB)
SALSALATE (*Disalcid*)	Meadowsweet • Ribose • Rose Hip • Vitamin C • Willow Bark
SAQUINAVIR (*Fortovase, Invirase*)	Butanediol (BD) • Gamma Butyrolactone (GBL) • Gamma-Hydroxybutyrate (GHB) • Garlic • Grapefruit

   Natural Medicines Comprehensive Database Consumer Version   (209) 472-2244

Drug	Natural Medicine
SCOPOLAMINE (*Transderm Scop*)	Alpha-Gpc • Grapefruit
SEDATIVE MEDICATIONS (Barbiturates) Some drugs in this category include: Pentobarbital (*Nembutal*) • Phenobarbital • Primidone (*Mysoline*) • Secobarbital (*Seconal*)	Beer • Eastern Red Cedar • Indian Snakeroot • Lavender • Magnolia • Marijuana • St. John's Wort • Wine • Yarrow
SEDATIVE MEDICATIONS (Benzodiazepines) Some drugs in this category include: Alprazolam (*Xanax*) • Lorazepam (*Ativan*) • Clonazepam (*Klonopin*) • Clorazepate (*Tranxene*) • Chlordiazepoxide (*Librium*) • Diazepam (*Valium*) • Estazolam (*Prosom*) • Flurazepam (*Dalmane*) • Midazolam (*Versed*) • Oxazepam (*Serax*) • Quazepam (*Doral*) • Triazolam (*Halcion*) • Temazepam (*Restoril*)	Ashwagandha • Baikal Skullcap • Beer • Butanediol (BD) • California Poppy • Gamma Butyrolactone (GBL) • Gamma-Hydroxybutyrate (GHB) • German Chamomile • Grapefruit • L-Tryptophan • Magnolia • Melatonin • Valerian • Wine
SEDATIVE MEDICATIONS (CNS Depressants) Some drugs in this category include: Secobarbital (*Seconal*) • Pentobarbital (*Nembutal*) • Clonazepam (*Klonopin*) • Diazepam (*Valium*) • Midazolam (*Versed*) • Zolpidem (*Ambien*) • Zaleplon (*Sonata*) • Hydroxyzine (*Atarax*) • Temazepam (*Restoril*) • Flurazepam (*Dalmane*) • Triazolam (*Halcion*) • Lorazepam (*Ativan*) • Estazolam (*Prosom*) • Secobarbital (*Seconal*) • Phenobarbital (*Luminal*)	Ashwagandha • Baikal Skullcap • Beer • Bitter Almond • Butanediol (BD) • Calamus • Calendula • California Poppy • Catnip • Celery • Elecampane • Gamma Butyrolactone (GBL) • Gamma-Hydroxybutyrate (GHB) • German Chamomile • Ginseng, Siberian • Gotu Kola • Hops • Hydrazine Sulfate • Jamaican Dogwood • Kava • Lavender • Lemon Balm • L-Tryptophan • Magnolia • Marijuana • Marsh Tea • Melatonin • Motherwort • Passionflower • Sage • Sassafras • Shepherd's Purse • Stinging Nettle • Sweet Bay • Valerian • Wild Lettuce • Wine • Yerba Mansa
SERTRALINE (*Zoloft*)	St. John's Wort
SEVOFLURANE (*Ultane*)	Aloe
SILDENAFIL (*Viagra*)	Grapefruit • L-Arginine
SIMVASTATIN (*Zocor*)	St. John's Wort
SKELETAL MUSCLE RELAXANTS Some drugs in this category include: Baclofen (*Lioresal*) • Botulinum Toxin Type A (*Botox*) • Chlorzaoxazone (*Parafon Forte*) • Cyclobenzaprine (*Flexeril*) • Dantrolene (*Dantrium*) • Metaxalone (*Skelaxin*) • Orphenadrine (*Norflex*)	Butanediol (BD) • Gamma Butyrolactone (GBL) • Gamma-Hydroxybutyrate (GHB) • Lithium • Magnesium • Procaine
SOTALOL (*Betapace*)	Calcium • Dolomite • Iron
STIMULANT LAXATIVES Some drugs in this category include: Senna (*Senokot*) • Bisacodyl (*Dulcolax*)	Alder Buckthorn • Aloe • Black Hellebore • Butternut • Calotropis • Cascara • Digitalis • Fo-Ti • Gamboge • Gossypol • Hedge Mustard • Jalap • Lily-Of-The-Valley • Mexican Scammony Root • Oleander • Pheasant's Eye • Rhubarb • Squill • Strophanthus • Swamp Milkweed • Uzara • Wahoo • Wallflower
STIMULANT MEDICATIONS Some drugs in this category include: Pemoline (*Cylert*) • Methylphenidate (*Ritalin*) • Fenfluramine (*Pondimin*) • Dextroamphetamine (*Dexedrine*) • Dexfenfluramine (*Redux*) • Caffeine (*NoDoz*) • Pseudoephedrine	Bitter Orange • Black Tea • Caffeine • Coffee • Country Mallow • Ephedra • Ergot • Fever Bark • Giseng, Panax • Indian Snakeroot • Peyote • Theanine • Tiratricol • Yohimbe
STIMULANT MEDICATIONS (Alpha-Adrenergic Agonists) Some drugs in this category include: Pseudoephedrine (*Sudafed*, others) • Phenylephrine • Phenylpropanolamine	Butcher's Broom
SUCCINYLCHOLINE	Procaine
SULFINPYRAZONE (*Anturane*)	Niacin and Niacinamide
SYRUP OF IPECAC	Activated Charcoal
TACROLIMUS (*Prograf, Protopic*)	St. John's Wort
TAMOXIFEN (*Nolvadex*)	Anise • DHEA • Fennel • German Chamomile • Guggul • Kudzu • Red Clover • Soy
TERBINAFINE (*Lamisil*)	Black Tea • Caffeine • Coffee • Cola Nut • Green Tea • Guarana • Mate • Oolong Tea
TERFENADINE (*Seldane*)	Grapefruit
TESTOSTERONE	Androstenediol • Pregnenolone

CONSUMER VERSION

Medical professionals should consult the Professional Version at www.NaturalDatabase.com.

Drug	Natural Medicine
THEOPHYLLINE	Black Pepper and White Pepper • Black Tea • Caffeine • Capsicum • Cocoa • Coffee • Cola Nut • Gossypol • Grapefruit • Green Tea • Guarana • Indian Long Pepper • Ipriflavone • Marijuana • Mate • Oolong Tea • St. John's Wort
THYROID HORMONE Some drugs in this category include: Levothyroxine (*Synthroid, Levothroid, Levoxyl*)	Ashwagandha • Branched-Chain Amino Acids • Bugleweed • Guggul • Laminaria • L-Carnitine • Shepherd's Purse • Tiratricol • Tyrosine
TOLBUTAMIDE (*Orinase*)	Beer • Wine
TRAMADOL (*Ultram*)	5-HTP • Ergot • Hawaiian Baby Woodrose • Lithium • L-Tryptophan • SAMe • St. John's Wort
TRAZODONE (*Desyrel*)	Ginkgo
TRIAZOLAM (*Halcion*)	DHEA
TRIMETHOPRIM (*Proloprim*)	Kaolin
VARIOUS MEDICATIONS USED FOR GLAUCOMA, ALZHEIMER'S DISEASE, AND OTHER CONDITIONS (Cholinergic Drugs) Some drugs in this category include: Bethanechol (*Urecholine*) • Echothiophate (*Phospholine Iodide*) • Neostigmine (*Prostigmin*) • Physostigmine (*Antilirium*) • Pyridostigmine (*Mestinon*) • Succinylcholine (*Anectine*)	Areca • Chinese Club Moss • Deanol • Huperzine A • Iboga • Phosphatidylcholine • Phosphatidylserine
VERAPAMIL (*Calan, Covera, Isoptin, Verelan*)	Black Tea • Caffeine • Calcium • Cocoa • Coffee • Cola Nut • Green Tea • Guarana • Mate • Melatonin • Oolong Tea • Vitamin D
WARFARIN (*Coumadin*)	Acerola • Acetyl-L-Carnitine • Alfalfa • Avocado • Beer • Blond Psyllium • Boldo • Cabbage • Cherokee Rosehip • Chlorella • Chondroitin Sulfate • Coenzyme Q-10 • Corn Silk • Cranberry • Danshen • Devil's Claw • Dong Quai • EDTA • Fenugreek • Garlic • German Chamomile • Ginger • Ginkgo • Ginseng, American • Ginseng, Panax • Glucosamine Hydrochloride • Glucosamine Sulfate • Grape • Grapefruit • Great Plantain • Green Tea • L-Carnitine • Lycium • N-Acetyl Glucosamine • Papaya • Parsley • Propionyl-L-Carnitine • Rose Hip • Royal Jelly • Smartweed • Soy • Spinach • St. John's Wort • Stinging Nettle • Vinpocetine • Vitamin A • Vitamin C (Ascorbic Acid) • Vitamin E • Vitamin K • Watercress • Wine • Wintergreen
WATER PILLS (Diuretic Drugs) Some drugs in this category include: <u>Thiazides:</u> Indapamide (*Lozol*) • Chlorothiazide (*Diuril*) • Hydrochlorothiazide (*Esidrix, Hydrodiuril*, others) • Chlorthalidone (*Hygroton*) • Metolazone (*Zaroxolyn*) <u>Loop Diuretics:</u> Bumetanide (*Bumex*) • Ethacrynic Acid (*Edecrin*) • Furosemide (*Lasix*) • Torsemide (*Demadex*)	Alder Buckthorn • Aloe • Apple Cider Vinegar • Birch • Black Hellebore • Black Root • Blue Flag • Butternut • Calotropis • Canadian Hemp • Cascara • Castor • Cesium • Colocynth • Corn Silk • Digitalis • EDTA • European Buckthorn • Figwort • Fo-Ti • Gamboge • Goldenrod • Gossypol • Greater Bindweed • Hedge Mustard • Indian Snakeroot • Jalap • Juniper • Licorice • Lily-Of-The-Valley • Lovage • Manna • Mexican Scammony Root • Oleander • Parsley • Pheasant's Eye • Pleurisy Root • Quassia • Rhubarb • Senna • Squill • Stone Root • Strophanthus • Swamp Milkweed • Uzara • Wahoo • Wallflower • Yellow Dock
WATER PILLS (Loop Diuretics) Some drugs in this category include: Bumetanide (*Bumex*) • Ethacrynic Acid (*Edecrin*) • Furosemide (*Lasix*) • Torsemide (*Demadex*)	Lithium
WATER PILLS (Potassium-Sparing Diuretics) Some of the drugs in this category include: Amiloride (*Midamor*) • Triamterene (*Dyrenium*) • Spironolactone (*Aldacton*)	Dandelion • Dolomite • Iodine • Laminaria • Magnesium • Morinda • Potassium • Zinc
WATER PILLS (Thiazide Diuretics) Some drugs in this category include: Indapamide (*Lozol*) • Chlorothiazide (*Diuril*) • Hydrochlorothiazide (*Esidrix, Hydrodiuril*, others) • Chlorthalidone (*Hygroton*) • Metolazone (*Zaroxolyn*)	Calcium • Dolomite • Lithium • Pangamic Acid • Vitamin D • Zinc
ZIDOVUDINE (AZT, *Retrovir*)	Acetyl-L-Carnitine • L-Carnitine • Propionyl-L-Carnitine

Medical professionals should consult the Professional Version at www.NaturalDatabase.com.

   Natural Medicines Comprehensive Database Consumer Version   (209) 472-2244

Potential Interactions Between Natural Medicines and Drugs

For details on possible interactions between natural medicines and drugs, see the listing for the specific natural medicine in the body of this database. This chart does not contain all theoretical or unknown interactions.

Natural Medicine	Drug
5-HTP	Carbidopa (*Lodosyn*) • Dextromethorphan (*Robitussin DM*, and others) • Medications for depression (Antidepressant drugs) • Medications for depression (MAOIs) • Meperidine (*Demerol*) • Pentazocine (*Talwin*) • Tramadol (*Ultram*)
Acacia	Amoxicillin (*Amoxil, Trimox*)
Acerola	Estrogens • Fluphenazine (*Prolixin*) • Warfarin (*Coumadin*)
Acetyl-L-Carnitine	Acenocoumarol (*Sintrom*) • Warfarin (*Coumadin*) • Zidovudine (AZT, *Retrovir*)
Activated Charcoal	Alcohol (Ethanol) • Syrup of ipecac
Adenosine	Carbamazepine (*Tegretol*) • Dipyridamole (*Persantine*) • Medications for gout • Methylxanthines
Agrimony	Medications for diabetes (Antidiabetes drugs)
Alder Buckthorn	Digoxin (*Lanoxin*) • Medications for inflammation (Corticosteroids) • Stimulant laxatives • Water pills (Diuretic drugs)
Aletris	Antacids • Medications that decrease stomach acid (H2-blockers) • Medications that decrease stomach acid (Proton pump inhibitors)
Alfalfa	Birth control pills (Contraceptive drugs) • Estrogens • Medications that increase sensitivity to sunlight (Photosensitizing drugs) • Warfarin (*Coumadin*)
Alkanna	Medications that increase the breakdown of other medications by the liver (Cytochrome P450 3A4 (CYP3A4) inducers)
Allspice	Medications that slow blood clotting (Anticoagulant / Antiplatelet drugs)
Aloe	Digoxin (*Lanoxin*) • Medications for diabetes (Antidiabetes drugs) • Sevoflurane (*Ultane*) • Stimulant laxatives • Water pills (Diuretic drugs)
Alpha-GPC	Scopolamine (*Transderm Scop*)
Alpha-Lipoic Acid	Chemotherapy • Medications for diabetes (Antidiabetes drugs)
Alpine Ragwort	Medications that increase breakdown of other medications by the liver (Cytochrome P450 3A4 (CYP3A4) inducers)
Alpinia	Antacids
Ambrette	Acetaminophen (*Tylenol*, others)
American Elder	Medications changed by the liver (Cytochrome P450 3A4 (CYP3A4) substrates)
Andrographis	Medications for high blood pressure (Antihypertensive drugs) • Medications that decrease the immune system (Immunosuppressants) • Medications that slow blood clotting (Anticoagulant / Antiplatelet drugs)
Androstenediol	Estrogens • Testosterone
Androstenedione	Estrogens
Angel's Trumpet	Drying medications (Anticholinergic drugs)
Anise	Birth control pills (Contraceptive drugs) • Estrogens • Tamoxifen (*Nolvadex*)
Annatto	Medications for diabetes (Antidiabetes drugs)
Apple	Fexofenadine (*Allegra*)
Apple Cider Vinegar	Digoxin (*Lanoxin*) • Insulin • Water pills (Diuretic drugs)
Areca	Drying medications (Anticholinergic drugs) • Procyclidine • Various medications used for glaucoma, Alzheimer's disease, and other conditions (Cholinergic drugs)
Arnica	Medications that slow blood clotting (Anticoagulant / Antiplatelet drugs)
Arrach	Medications that increase sensitivity to sunlight (Photosensitizing drugs)
Asafoetida	Medications for high blood pressure (Antihypertensive drugs) • Medications that slow blood clotting (Anticoagulant / Antiplatelet drugs)

Potential Interactions: Natural Medicine/Drug
For additional data, refer to the database.

Natural Medicine	Drug
Ashwagandha	Medications that decrease the immune system (Immunosuppressants) • Sedative medications (Benzodiazepines) • Sedative medications (CNS depressants) • Thyroid hormone
Astragalus	Cyclophosphamide (*Cytoxan*, *Neosar*) • Medications that decrease the immune system (Immunosuppressants)
Autumn Crocus	Colchicine
Avocado	Warfarin (*Coumadin*)
Avocado Sugar Extract	Medications for diabetes (Antidiabetes drugs)
Baikal Skullcap	Alcohol • Medications for diabetes (Antidiabetes drugs) • Sedative medications (Benzodiazepines) • Sedative medications (CNS depressants)
Banaba	Medications for diabetes (Antidiabetes drugs)
Barley	Medications for diabetes (Antidiabetes drugs)
Bean Pod	Medications for diabetes (Antidiabetes drugs)
Beer	Antibiotics (Sulfonamide antibiotics) • Aspirin • Cefamandole (*Mandol*) • Cefoperazone (*Cefobid*) • Chlorpropamide (*Diabinese*) • Cisapride (*Propulsid*) • Disulfiram (*Antabuse*) • Erythromycin • Griseofulvin (*Fulvicin*) • Medications for pain (Narcotic drugs) • Medications that can harm the liver (Hepatotoxic drugs) • Medications that decrease stomach acid (H2-blockers) • Metformin (*Glucophage*) • Metronidazole (*Flagyl*) • NSAIDs (Nonsteroidal anti-inflammatory drugs) • Phenytoin (*Dilantin*) • Sedative medications (Barbiturates) • Sedative medications (Benzodiazepines) • Sedative medications (CNS depressants) • Tolbutamide (*Orinase*) • Warfarin (*Coumadin*)
Belladonna	Drying medications (Anticholinergic drugs)
Berberine	Cyclosporine (*Neoral*, *Sandimmune*) • Medications changed by the liver (Cytochrome P450 3A4 (CYP3A4) substrates)
Bergamot Oil	Medications that increase sensitivity to sunlight (Photosensitizing drugs)
Beta Glucans	Medications that decrease the immune system (Immunosuppressants)
Beta-Carotene	Medications used for lowering cholesterol (Statins) • Niacin
Beta-Sitosterol	Ezetimibe (*Zetia*) • Pravastatin (*Pravachol*)
Betony	Medications for high blood pressure (Antihypertensive drugs)
Bifidobacteria	Antibiotic drugs
Bilberry	Medications for diabetes (Antidiabetes drugs)
Birch	Water pills (Diuretic drugs)
Bishop's Weed	Medications changed by the liver (Cytochrome P450 3A4 (CYP3A4) substrates) • Medications that can harm the liver (Hepatotoxic drugs) • Medications that increase sensitivity to sunlight (Photosensitizing drugs) • Medications that slow blood clotting (Anticoagulant / Antiplatelet drugs)
Bitter Almond	Sedative medications (CNS depressants)
Bitter Melon	Medications for diabetes (Antidiabetes drugs)
Bitter Orange	Caffeine • Dextromethorphan (*Robitussin DM*, and others) • Felodipine (*Plendil*) • Indinavir (*Crixivan*) • Medications changed by the liver (Cytochrome P450 3A4 (CYP3A4) substrates) • Medications for depression (MAOIs) • Medications that can cause an irregular heartbeat (QT interval-prolonging drugs) • Midazolam (*Versed*) • Stimulant drugs
Black Cohosh	Cisplatin (*Platinol-AQ*) • Medications changed by the liver (Cytochrome P450 2D6 (CYP2D6) substrates) • Medications changed by the liver (Cytochrome P450 3A4 (CYP3A4) substrates) • Medications that can harm the liver (Hepatotoxic drugs)
Black Hellebore	Antibiotics (Macrolide antibiotics) • Antibiotics (Tetracycline antibiotics) • Digoxin (*Lanoxin*) • Quinine • Stimulant laxatives • Water pills (Diuretic drugs)
Black Horehound	Medications used for Parkinson's disease (Dopamine agonists)

   Natural Medicines Comprehensive Database Consumer Version   (209) 472-2244

Potential Interactions: Natural Medicine/Drug   For additional data, refer to the database.

Natural Medicine	Drug
Black Mulberry	Medications for diabetes (Antidiabetes drugs)
Black Mustard	Antacids • Medications that decrease stomach acid (H2-blockers) • Medications that decrease stomach acid (Proton pump inhibitors)
Black Pepper And White Pepper	Medications changed by the liver (Cytochrome P450 3A4 (CYP3A4) substrates) • Medications moved by pumps in cells (P-glycoprotein substrates) • Phenytoin (*Dilantin*) • Propranolol (*Inderal*) • Rifampin • Theophylline
Black Psyllium	Carbamazepine (*Tegretol*) • Digoxin (*Lanoxin*) • Lithium • Medications for diabetes (Antidiabetes drugs)
Black Root	Digoxin (*Lanoxin*) • Water pills (Diuretic drugs)
Black Tea	Adenosine (*Adenocard*) • Alcohol • Antibiotics (Quinolone antibiotics) • Birth control pills (Contraceptive drugs) • Cimetidine (*Tagamet*) • Clozapine (*Clozaril*) • Dipyridamole (*Persantine*) • Disulfiram (*Antabuse*) • Ephedrine • Estrogens • Fluconazole (*Diflucan*) • Fluvoxamine (*Luvox*) • Lithium • Medications for depression (MAOIs) • Medications for depression (Tricyclic antidepressants) • Medications for diabetes (Antidiabetes drugs) • Medications that slow blood clotting (Anticoagulant / Antiplatelet drugs) • Mexiletine (*Mexitil*) • Pentobarbital (*Nembutal*) • Phenothiazines • Phenylpropanolamine • Riluzole (*Rilutek*) • Stimulant drugs • Terbinafine (*Lamisil*) • Theophylline • Tricyclic antidepressants (TCAs) • Verapamil (*Calan, Covera, Isoptin, Verelan*)
Bladderwrack	Medications for an overactive thyroid (Antithyroid drugs) • Medications that slow blood clotting (Anticoagulant / Antiplatelet drugs)
Blessed Thistle	Antacids • Medications that decrease stomach acid (H2-blockers) • Medications that decrease stomach acid (Proton pump inhibitors)
Blond Psyllium	Carbamazepine (*Tegretol*) • Digoxin (*Lanoxin*) • Ethinyl estradiol • Lithium • Medications for diabetes (Antidiabetes drugs) • Warfarin (*Coumadin*)
Blue Cohosh	Medications for diabetes (Antidiabetes drugs) • Medications for high blood pressure (Antihypertensive drugs) • Nicotine
Blue Flag	Digoxin (*Lanoxin*) • Water pills (Diuretic drugs)
Blueberry	Medications for diabetes (Antidiabetes drugs)
Bogbean	Medications that slow blood clotting (Anticoagulant / Antiplatelet drugs)
Boldo	Medications that can harm the liver (Hepatotoxic drugs) • Medications that slow blood clotting (Anticoagulant / Antiplatelet drugs) • Warfarin (*Coumadin*)
Borage	Medications that increase the breakdown of other medications by the liver (Cytochrome P450 3A4 (CYP3A4) inducers) • Medications that slow blood clotting (Anticoagulant / Antiplatelet drugs) • Medications used during surgery (Anesthesia) • NSAIDs (Nonsteroidal anti-inflammatory drugs)
Boron	Estrogens
Branched-Chain Amino Acids	Diazoxide (*Hyperstat, Proglycem*) • Levodopa • Medications for diabetes (Antidiabetes drugs) • Medications for inflammation (Corticosteroids) • Thyroid hormone
Brewer's Yeast	Medications for depression (MAOIs) • Medications for fungal infections (Antifungals)
Bromelain	Amoxicillin • Antibiotics (Tetracycline antibiotics) • Medications that slow blood clotting (Anticoagulant / Antiplatelet drugs)
Buchu	Medications that slow blood clotting (Anticoagulant / Antiplatelet drugs)
Bugleweed	Medications for diabetes (Antidiabetes drugs) • Thyroid hormone
Burdock	Medications that slow blood clotting (Anticoagulant / Antiplatelet drugs)
Butanediol (BD)	Alcohol (Ethanol) • Amphetamines • Haloperidol (*Haldol*) • Medications for mental conditions (Antipsychotic drugs) • Medications for pain (Narcotic drugs) • Medications used to prevent seizures (Anticonvulsants) • Muscle relaxants • Naloxone (*Narcan*) • Ritonavir (*Norvir*) • Saquinavir (*Fortovase, Invirase*) • Sedative medications (Benzodiazepines) • Sedative medications (CNS depressants) • Skeletal muscle relaxants

Potential Interactions: Natural Medicine/Drug   For additional data, refer to the database.

Natural Medicine	Drug
Butcher's Broom	Medications used for high blood pressure (Alpha-adrenergic antagonists) • Stimulant medications (Alpha-adrenergic agonists)
Butterbur	Medications that increase breakdown of other medications by the liver (Cytochrome P450 3A4 (CYP3A4) inducers)
Butternut	Digoxin (*Lanoxin*) • Medications for inflammation (Corticosteroids) • Stimulant laxatives • Water pills (Diuretic drugs)
Cabbage	Acetaminophen (*Tylenol*, others) • Medications changed by the liver (Cytochrome P450 1A2 (CYP1A2) substrates) • Medications changed by the liver (Glucuronidated drugs) • Oxazepam (*Serax*) • Warfarin (*Coumadin*)
Caffeine	Adenosine (*Adenocard*) • Alcohol (Ethanol) • Antibiotics (Quinolone antibiotics) • Birth control pills (Contraceptive drugs) • Cimetidine (*Tagamet*) • Clozapine (*Clozaril*) • Dipyridamole (*Persantine*) • Disulfiram (*Antabuse*) • Ephedrine • Estrogens • Fluconazole (*Diflucan*) • Fluvoxamine (*Luvox*) • Lithium • Medications for depression (MAOIs) • Medications for diabetes (Antidiabetes drugs) • Medications that slow blood clotting (Anticoagulant / Antiplatelet drugs) • Mexiletine (*Mexitil*) • Pentobarbital (*Nembutal*) • Phenylpropanolamine • Riluzole (*Rilutek*) • Stimulant drugs • Terbinafine (*Lamisil*) • Theophylline • Verapamil (*Calan, Covera, Isoptin, Verelan*)
Calabar Bean	Drying medications (Anticholinergic drugs)
Calamus	Antacids • Medications for depression (MAOIs) • Medications that decrease stomach acid (H2-blockers) • Medications that decrease stomach acid (Proton pump inhibitors) • Sedative medications (CNS depressants)
Calcium	Antibiotics (Quinolone antibiotics) • Antibiotics (Tetracycline antibiotics) • Bisphosphonates • Calcipotriene (*Dovonex*) • Digoxin (*Lanoxin*) • Diltiazem (*Cardizem, Dilacor, Tiazac*) • Estrogens • Levothyroxine (*Synthroid, Levothroid, Levoxyl*, and others) • Medications for high blood pressure (Calcium channel blockers) • Sotalol (*Betapace*) • Verapamil (*Calan, Covera, Isoptin, Verelan*) • Water pills (Thiazide diuretics)
Calcium D-Glucarate	Alcohol (Ethanol) • Kanamycin • Medications changed by the liver (Glucuronidated drugs)
Calendula	Sedative medications (CNS depressants)
California Poppy	Sedative medications (Benzodiazepines) • Sedative medications (CNS depressants)
Calotropis	Digoxin (*Lanoxin*) • Stimulant laxatives • Water pills (Diuretic drugs)
Canadian Hemp	Digoxin (*Lanoxin*) • Water pills (Diuretic drugs)
Capers	Medications for diabetes (Antidiabetes drugs)
Capsicum	Medications for high blood pressure (ACE inhibitors) • Medications that slow blood clotting (Anticoagulant / Antiplatelet drugs) • Theophylline
Caraway	Medications for diabetes (Antidiabetes drugs)
Carqueja	Medications for diabetes (Antidiabetes drugs)
Carrageenan	Medications for high blood pressure (Antihypertensive drugs) • Medications that slow blood clotting (Anticoagulant / Antiplatelet drugs)
Cascara	Digoxin (*Lanoxin*) • Medications for inflammation (Corticosteroids) • Stimulant laxatives • Water pills (Diuretic drugs)
Casein Peptides	Medications for high blood pressure (Antihypertensive drugs)
Cassia Auriculata	Carbamazepine (*Tegretol*) • Medications for diabetes (Antidiabetes drugs)
Cassia Cinnamon	Medications for diabetes (Antidiabetes drugs)
Castor	Water pills (Diuretic drugs)
Catechu	Medications for high blood pressure (Antihypertensive drugs)
Catnip	Sedative medications (CNS depressants)

Natural Medicine	Drug
Cat's Claw	Medications changed by the liver (Cytochrome P450 3A4 (CYP3A4) substrates) • Medications for high blood pressure (Antihypertensive drugs) • Medications that decrease the immune system (Immunosuppressants)
Celery	Levothyroxine (*Synthroid, Levothroid, Levoxyl*, and others) • Medications that increase sensitivity to sunlight (Photosensitizing drugs) • Sedative medications (CNS depressants)
Cereus	Digoxin (*Lanoxin*) • Medications for depression (MAOIs)
Cesium	Medications for inflammation (Corticosteroids) • Water pills (Diuretic drugs)
Chanca Piedra	Medications for diabetes (Antidiabetes drugs)
Chaparral	Medications that can harm the liver (Hepatotoxic drugs)
Chasteberry	Birth control pills (Contraceptive drugs) • Estrogens • Medications for mental conditions (Antipsychotic drugs) • Medications used for Parkinson's disease (Dopamine agonists) • Metoclopramide (*Reglan*)
Chenopodium Oil	Medications that increase sensitivity to sunlight (Photosensitizing drugs)
Cherokee Rosehip	Aluminum • Aspirin • Choline Magnesium Trisalicylate (*Trilisate*) • Estrogens • Fluphenazine (*Prolixin*) • Warfarin (*Coumadin*)
Chinese Club Moss	Drying medications (Anticholinergic drugs) • Medications for Alzheimer's disease (Acetylcholinesterase (AChE) inhibitors) • Various medications used for glaucoma, Alzheimer's disease, and other conditions (Cholinergic drugs)
Chinese Cucumber	Medications for diabetes (Antidiabetes drugs)
Chinese Mallow	Medications for diabetes (Antidiabetes drugs)
Chinese Prickly Ash	Medications that slow blood clotting (Anticoagulant / Antiplatelet drugs)
Chlorella	Warfarin (*Coumadin*)
Chlorophyll	Medications that increase sensitivity to sunlight (Photosensitizing drugs)
Chondroitin Sulfate	Warfarin (*Coumadin*)
Chromium	Insulin • NSAIDs (Nonsteroidal anti-inflammatory drugs)
Chrysin	Medications changed by the liver (Cytochrome P450 1A2 (CYP1A2) substrates) • Medications changed by the liver (Glucuronidated drugs) • Medications for estrogen sensitive cancers (Aromatase inhibitors)
Cinchona	Antacids • Carbamazepine (*Tegretol*) • Medications that decrease stomach acid (H2-blockers) • Medications that decrease stomach acid (Proton pump inhibitors) • Medications that slow blood clotting (Anticoagulant / Antiplatelet drugs) • Phenobarbital (*Luminal*) • Quinidine • Quinine
Cinnamon Bark	Medications for diabetes (Antidiabetes drugs)
Clary Sage	Chloral Hydrate (*Aquachloral*) • Hexobarbitone
Clove	Medications that slow blood clotting (Anticoagulant / Antiplatelet drugs)
Coca	Alcohol • Nifedipine
Cocoa	Adenosine (*Adenocard*) • Antibiotics (Quinolone antibiotics) • Birth control pills (Contraceptive drugs) • Cimetidine (*Tagamet*) • Clozapine (*Clozaril*) • Dipyridamole (*Persantine*) • Disulfiram (*Antabuse*) • Ergotamine (*Ergomar*) • Estrogens • Fluconazole (*Diflucan*) • Lithium • Medications for asthma (Beta-adrenergic agonists) • Medications for depression (MAOIs) • Medications for diabetes (Antidiabetes drugs) • Mexiletine (*Mexitil*) • Phenylpropanolamine • Theophylline • Verapamil (*Calan, Covera, Isoptin, Verelan*)
Cod Liver Oil	Medications for high blood pressure (Antihypertensive drugs) • Medications that slow blood clotting (Anticoagulant / Antiplatelet drugs)
Coenzyme Q-10	Chemotherapy • Medications for high blood pressure (Antihypertensive drugs) • Warfarin (*Coumadin*)

Medical professionals should consult the Professional Version at www.NaturalDatabase.com.

Natural Medicine	Drug
Coffee	Adenosine (*Adenocard*) • Alcohol • Alendronate (*Fosamax*) • Antibiotics (Quinolone antibiotics) • Birth control pills (Contraceptive drugs) • Cimetidine (*Tagamet*) • Clozapine (*Clozaril*) • Dipyridamole (*Persantine*) • Disulfiram (*Antabuse*) • Ephedrine • Estrogens • Fluconazole (*Diflucan*) • Fluvoxamine (*Luvox*) • Lithium • Medications for depression (MAOIs) • Medications for depression (Tricyclic antidepressants) • Medications for diabetes (Antidiabetes drugs) • Medications that slow blood clotting (Anticoagulant / Antiplatelet drugs) • Mexiletine (*Mexitil*) • Pentobarbital (*Nembutal*) • Phenothiazines • Phenylpropanolamine • Riluzole (*Rilutek*) • Stimulant drugs • Terbinafine (*Lamisil*) • Theophylline • Verapamil (*Calan, Covera, Isoptin, Verelan*)
Cola Nut	Adenosine (*Adenocard*) • Alcohol (Ethanol) • Amphetamines • Antibiotics (Quinolone antibiotics) • Birth control pills (Contraceptive drugs) • Cimetidine (*Tagamet*) • Clozapine (*Clozaril*) • Dipyridamole (*Persantine*) • Disulfiram (*Antabuse*) • Ephedrine • Estrogens • Fluconazole (*Diflucan*) • Fluvoxamine (*Luvox*) • Lithium • Medications for depression (MAOIs) • Medications for diabetes (Antidiabetes drugs) • Mexiletine (*Mexitil*) • Nicotine • Pentobarbital (*Nembutal*) • Phenylpropanolamine • Riluzole (*Rilutek*) • Terbinafine (*Lamisil*) • Theophylline • Verapamil (*Calan, Covera, Isoptin, Verelan*)
Colloidal Silver	Antibiotics (Quinolone antibiotics) • Antibiotics (Tetracycline antibiotics) • Levothyroxine (*Synthroid, Levothroid, Levoxyl,* and others) • Penicillamine
Colocynth	Digoxin (*Lanoxin*) • Water pills (Diuretic drugs)
Colombo	Antacids • Medications that decrease stomach acid (H2-blockers) • Medications that decrease stomach acid (Proton pump inhibitors)
Coltsfoot	Medications for high blood pressure (Antihypertensive drugs) • Medications that increase breakdown of other medications by the liver (cytochrome P450 3A4 (CYP3A4) inducers) • Medications that slow blood clotting (Anticoagulant / Antiplatelet drugs)
Comfrey	Medications that can harm the liver (Hepatotoxic drugs) • Medications that increase the breakdown of other medications by the liver (Cytochrome P450 3A4 (CYP3A4) inducers)
Copper	Penicillamine
Cordyceps	Cyclophosphamide (*Cytoxan, Neosar*) • Prednisolone
Corn Silk	Medications for diabetes (Antidiabetes drugs) • Medications for high blood pressure (Antihypertensive drugs) • Medications for inflammation (Corticosteroids) • Warfarin (*Coumadin*) • Water pills (Diuretic drugs)
Country Mallow	Dexamethasone (*Decadron*) • Ergot Derivatives • Medications for depression (MAOIs) • Medications for diabetes (Antidiabetes drugs) • Medications that can cause an irregular heartbeat (QT interval-prolonging drugs) • Methylxanthines • Stimulant drugs
Cowhage	Anesthesia • Guanethidine (*Ismelin*) • Medications for depression (MAOIs) • Medications for diabetes (Antidiabetes drugs) • Medications for mental conditions (Antipsychotic drugs) • Medications used during surgery (Anesthesia) • Medications used for depression (Tricyclic antidepressants) • Methyldopa (*Aldomet*)
Cranberry	Medications changed by the liver (Cytochrome P450 2C9 (CYP2C9) substrates) • Warfarin (*Coumadin*)
Creatine	Medications that can harm the kidneys (Nephrotoxic drugs)
Cubebs	Antacids • Medications that decrease stomach acid (H2-blockers) • Medications that decrease stomach acid (Proton pump inhibitors)
Cumin	Medications for diabetes (Antidiabetes drugs)
Damiana	Medications for diabetes (Antidiabetes drugs)
Dandelion	Antibiotics (Quinolone antibiotics) • Medications changed by the liver (Cytochrome P450 1A2 (CYP1A2) substrates) • Medications changed by the liver (Glucuronidated drugs) • Water pills (Potassium-sparing diuretics)
Danshen	Digoxin (*Lanoxin*) • Medications that slow blood clotting (Anticoagulant / Antiplatelet drugs) • Warfarin (*Coumadin*)

Potential Interactions: Natural Medicine/Drug   For additional data, refer to the database.

Natural Medicine	Drug
Deanol	Drying medications (Anticholinergic drugs) • Medications for Alzheimer's disease (Acetylcholinesterase (AChE) inhibitors) • Various medications used for glaucoma, Alzheimer's disease, and other conditions (Cholinergic drugs)
Deertongue	Medications that slow blood clotting (Anticoagulant / Antiplatelet drugs)
Devil's Claw	Antacids • Medications changed by the liver (Cytochrome P450 2C19 (CYP2C19) substrates) • Medications changed by the liver (Cytochrome P450 2C9 (CYP2C9) substrates) • Medications changed by the liver (Cytochrome P450 3A4 (CYP3A4) substrates) • Medications for diabetes (Antidiabetes drugs) • Medications for high blood pressure (Antihypertensive drugs) • Medications that decrease stomach acid (H2-blockers) • Medications that decrease stomach acid (Proton pump inhibitors) • Warfarin (*Coumadin*)
DHA (Docosahexaenoic Acid)	Medications for high blood pressure (Antihypertensive drugs) • Medications that slow blood clotting (Anticoagulant / Antiplatelet drugs)
DHEA	Anastrozole (*Arimidex*) • Exemestane (*Aromasin*) • Fulvestrant (*Faslodex*) • Insulin • Letrozole (*Femara*) • Medications changed by the liver (Cytochrome P450 3A4 (CYP3A4) substrates) • Medications for inflammation (Corticosteroids) • Tamoxifen (*Nolvadex*) • Triazolam (*Halcion*)
Dibencozide	Chloramphenicol
Digitalis	Antibiotics (Macrolide antibiotics) • Antibiotics (Tetracycline antibiotics) • Digoxin (*Lanoxin*) • Quinine • Stimulant laxatives • Water pills (Diuretic drugs)
Diindolylmethane	Medications changed by the liver (Cytochrome P450 1A2 (CYP1A2) substrates)
DMSO (Dimethylsulfoxide)	Medications applied to the skin, eyes, or ears (Topical drugs) • Medications given as a shot (Injectable drugs)
Dolomite	Antibiotics (Quinolone antibiotics) • Antibiotics (Tetracycline antibiotics) • Bisphosphonates • Estrogens • Levothyroxine (*Synthroid, Levothroid, Levoxyl*, and others) • Sotalol (*Betapace*) • Water pills (Potassium-sparing diuretics) • Water pills (Thiazide diuretics)
Dong Quai	Medications that slow blood clotting (Anticoagulant / Antiplatelet drugs) • Warfarin (*Coumadin*)
Dusty Miller	Medications that increase breakdown of other medications by the liver (Cytochrome P450 3A4 (CYP3A4) inducers)
Eastern Red Cedar	Sedative medications (Barbiturates)
Echinacea	Medications changed by the body (Cytochrome P450 3A4 (CYP3A4) substrates) • Medications changed by the liver (Cytochrome P450 1A2 (CYP1A2) substrates) • Medications that decrease the immune system (Immunosuppressants) • Midazolam (*Versed*)
EDTA	Insulin • Warfarin (*Coumadin*) • Water pills (Diuretic drugs)
Elderberry	Medications that decrease the immune system (Immunosuppressants)
Elderflower	Medications for diabetes (Antidiabetes drugs)
Elecampane	Sedative medications (CNS depressants)
EPA (Eicosapentaenoic Acid)	Medications for high blood pressure (Antihypertensive drugs) • Medications that slow blood clotting (Anticoagulant / Antiplatelet drugs)
Ephedra	Dexamethasone (*Decadron*) • Ergot Derivatives • Medications for depression (MAOIs) • Medications for diabetes (Antidiabetes drugs) • Medications that can cause an irregular heartbeat (QT interval-prolonging drugs) • Medications used to prevent seizures (Anticonvulsants) • Methylxanthines • Stimulant drugs
Epimedium	Medications for high blood pressure (Antihypertensive drugs) • Medications that slow blood clotting (Anticoagulant / Antiplatelet drugs)
Ergot	Dextromethorphan (*Robitussin DM*, and others) • Ergot Derivatives • Medications for depression (Antidepressant drugs) • Medications for depression (MAOIs) • Medications that decrease the breakdown of other medications in the liver (Cytochrome P450 3A4 (CYP3A4) inhibitors) • Meperidine (*Demerol*) • Pentazocine (*Talwin*) • Stimulant drugs • Tramadol (*Ultram*)

Medical professionals should consult the Professional Version at www.NaturalDatabase.com.

Natural Medicine	Drug
Eucalyptus	Medications changed by the liver (Cytochrome P450 1A2 (CYP1A2) substrates) • Medications changed by the liver (Cytochrome P450 2C19 (CYP2C19) substrates) • Medications changed by the liver (Cytochrome P450 2C9 (CYP2C9) substrates) • Medications changed by the liver (Cytochrome P450 3A4 (CYP3A4) substrates) • Medications for diabetes (Antidiabetes drugs)
European Barberry	Cyclosporine (*Neoral, Sandimmune*) • Medications changed by the liver (Cytochrome P450 3A4 (CYP3A4) substrates)
European Buckthorn	Digoxin (*Lanoxin*) • Water pills (Diuretic drugs)
European Mandrake	Drying medications (Anticholinergic drugs)
European Mistletoe	Medications for high blood pressure (Antihypertensive drugs) • Medications that decrease the immune system (Immunosuppressants)
Evening Primrose Oil	Medications that slow blood clotting (Anticoagulant / Antiplatelet drugs) • Medications used during surgery (Anesthesia) • Phenothiazines
Fennel	Birth control pills (Contraceptive drugs) • Ciprofloxacin (*Cipro*) • Estrogens • Tamoxifen (*Nolvadex*)
Fenugreek	Medications for diabetes (Antidiabetes drugs) • Medications that slow blood clotting (Anticoagulant / Antiplatelet drugs) • Warfarin (*Coumadin*)
Fever Bark	Anesthesia • Medications used during surgery (Anesthesia) • Naloxone (*Narcan*) • Phenothiazines • Stimulant drugs
Feverfew	Medications changed by the liver (Cytochrome P450 1A2 (CYP1A2) substrates) • Medications changed by the liver (Cytochrome P450 2C19 (CYP2C19) substrates) • Medications changed by the liver (Cytochrome P450 2C9 (CYP2C9) substrates) • Medications changed by the liver (Cytochrome P450 3A4 (CYP3A4) substrates) • Medications that slow blood clotting (Anticoagulant / Antiplatelet drugs)
Fig	Insulin • Medications for diabetes (Antidiabetes drugs)
Figwort	Water pills (Diuretic drugs)
Fish Oil	Birth control pills (Contraceptive drugs) • Medications for high blood pressure (Antihypertensive drugs) • Medications that slow blood clotting (Anticoagulant / Antiplatelet drugs)
Flaxseed	Medications for diabetes (Antidiabetes drugs) • Medications that slow blood clotting (Anticoagulant / Antiplatelet drugs)
Flaxseed Oil	Medications that slow blood clotting (Anticoagulant / Antiplatelet drugs)
Folic Acid	Fosphenytoin (*Cerebyx*) • Methotrexate (MTX, *Rheumatrex*) • Phenobarbital (*Luminal*) • Phenytoin (*Dilantin*) • Primidone (*Mysoline*) • Pyrimethamine (*Daraprim*)
Forskolin	Medications for high blood pressure (Calcium channel blockers) • Medications that increase blood flow to the heart (Nitrates) • Medications that slow blood clotting (Anticoagulant / Antiplatelet drugs) • Nitrates
Forsythia	Medications that slow blood clotting (Anticoagulant / Antiplatelet drugs)
Fo-Ti	Digoxin (*Lanoxin*) • Medications changed by the liver (Cytochrome P450 1A2 (CYP1A2) substrates) • Medications changed by the liver (Cytochrome P450 2C19 (CYP2C19) substrates) • Medications changed by the liver (Cytochrome P450 2C9 (CYP2C9) substrates) • Medications changed by the liver (Cytochrome P450 3A4 (CYP3A4) substrates) • Medications for diabetes (Antidiabetes drugs) • Medications that can harm the liver (Hepatotoxic drugs) • Stimulant laxatives • Water pills (Diuretic drugs)
Gamboge	Digoxin (*Lanoxin*) • Medications for inflammation (Corticosteroids) • Stimulant laxatives • Water pills (Diuretic drugs)
Gamma Butyrolactone (GBL)	Alcohol (Ethanol) • Amphetamines • Haloperidol (*Haldol*) • Medications for mental conditions (Antipsychotic drugs) • Medications for pain (Narcotic drugs) • Medications used to prevent seizures (Anticonvulsants) • Muscle relaxants • Naloxone (*Narcan*) • Ritonavir (*Norvir*) • Saquinavir (*Fortovase, Invirase*) • Sedative medications (Benzodiazepines) • Sedative medications (CNS depressants)

Potential Interactions: Natural Medicine/Drug   For additional data, refer to the database.

Natural Medicine	Drug
Gamma Linolenic Acid	Medications that slow blood clotting (Anticoagulant / Antiplatelet drugs) • Phenothiazines
Gamma-Hydroxybutyrate (GHB)	Alcohol • Amphetamines • Haloperidol (*Haldol*) • Medications for mental conditions (Antipsychotic drugs) • Medications for pain (Narcotic drugs) • Medications used to prevent seizures (Anticonvulsants) • Muscle relaxants • Naloxone (*Narcan*) • Ritonavir (*Norvir*) • Saquinavir (*Fortovase, Invirase*) • Sedative medications (Benzodiazepines) • Sedative medications (CNS depressants)
Garlic	Birth control pills (Contraceptive drugs) • Cyclosporine (*Neoral, Sandimmune*) • Medications changed by the liver (Cytochrome P450 2E1 (CYP2E1) substrates) • Medications changed by the liver (Cytochrome P450 3A4 (CYP3A4) substrates) • Medications that slow blood clotting (Anticoagulant / Antiplatelet drugs) • Medications used for HIV/AIDS (Non-Nucleoside Reverse Transcriptase Inhibitors (NNRTIs)) • Saquinavir (*Fortovase, Invirase*) • Warfarin (*Coumadin*)
Gentian	Medications for high blood pressure (Antihypertensive drugs)
German Chamomile	Birth control pills (Contraceptive drugs) • Estrogens • Medications changed by the liver (Cytochrome P450 1A2 (CYP1A2) substrates) • Medications changed by the liver (Cytochrome P450 3A4 (CYP3A4) substrates) • Sedative medications (Benzodiazepines) • Sedative medications (CNS depressants) • Tamoxifen (*Nolvadex*) • Warfarin (*Coumadin*)
Germanium	Furosemide (*Lasix*)
Ginger	Medications for diabetes (Antidiabetes drugs) • Medications for high blood pressure (Calcium channel blockers) • Medications that slow blood clotting (Anticoagulant / Antiplatelet drugs) • Phenprocoumon • Warfarin (*Coumadin*)
Ginkgo	Alprazolam (*Xanax*) • Buspirone (*BuSpar*) • Fluoxetine (*Prozac*) • Ibuprofen • Insulin • Medications changed by the liver (Cytochrome P450 1A2 (CYP1A2) substrates) • Medications changed by the liver (Cytochrome P450 2C19 (CYP2C19) substrates) • Medications changed by the liver (Cytochrome P450 2C9 (CYP2C9) substrates) • Medications changed by the liver (Cytochrome P450 2D6 (CYP2D6) substrates) • Medications changed by the liver (Cytochrome P450 3A4 (CYP3A4) substrates) • Medications that increase the chance of having a seizure (Seizure threshold lowering drugs) • Medications that slow blood clotting (Anticoagulant / Antiplatelet drugs) • Medications used to prevent seizures (Anticonvulsants) • Omeprazole (*Prilosec*) • Trazodone (*Desyrel*) • Warfarin (*Coumadin*)
Ginseng, American	Medications for depression (MAOIs) • Medications for diabetes (Antidiabetes drugs) • Warfarin (*Coumadin*)
Ginseng, Panax	Alcohol (Ethanol) • Caffeine • Furosemide (*Lasix*) • Insulin • Medications changed by the liver (Cytochrome P450 2D6 (CYP2D6) substrates) • Medications for depression (MAOIs) • Medications for diabetes (Antidiabetes drugs) • Medications that decrease the immune system (Immunosuppressants) • Medications that slow blood clotting (Anticoagulant / Antiplatelet drugs) • Stimulant drugs • Warfarin (*Coumadin*)
Ginseng, Siberian	Alcohol • Digoxin (*Lanoxin*) • Medications changed by the liver (Cytochrome P450 1A2 (CYP1A2) substrates) • Medications changed by the liver (Cytochrome P450 2C9 (CYP2C9) substrates) • Medications changed by the liver (Cytochrome P450 2D6 (CYP2D6) substrates) • Medications changed by the liver (Cytochrome P450 3A4 (CYP3A4) substrates) • Medications for diabetes (Antidiabetes drugs) • Medications that slow blood clotting (Anticoagulant / Antiplatelet drugs) • Sedative medications (CNS depressants)
Glucomannan	Medications for diabetes (Antidiabetes drugs)
Glucosamine Hydrochloride	Chemotherapy (Antimitotic) • Medications for diabetes (Antidiabetes drugs) • Warfarin (*Coumadin*)
Glucosamine Sulfate	Acetaminophen (*Tylenol*, others) • Chemotherapy (Antimitotic) • Medications for diabetes (Antidiabetes drugs) • Warfarin (*Coumadin*)
Glutamine	Chemotherapy • Lactulose • Medications used to prevent seizures (Anticonvulsants)
Glycine	Clozapine (*Clozaril*)
Goat's Rue	Medications for diabetes (Antidiabetes drugs)

Medical professionals should consult the Professional Version at www.NaturalDatabase.com.

CONSUMER VERSION

Potential Interactions: Natural Medicine/Drug   For additional data, refer to the database.

Natural Medicine	Drug
Golden Ragwort	Medications that increase breakdown of other medications by the liver (Cytochrome P450 3A4 (CYP3A4) inducers)
Goldenrod	Water pills (Diuretic drugs)
Goldenseal	Cyclosporine (*Neoral, Sandimmune*) • Medications changed by the liver (Cytochrome P450 2D6 (CYP2D6) substrates) • Medications changed by the liver (Cytochrome P450 3A4 (CYP3A4) substrates)
Goldthread	Cyclosporine (*Neoral, Sandimmune*) • Medications changed by the liver (Cytochrome P450 3A4 (CYP3A4) substrates)
Gossypol	Digoxin (*Lanoxin*) • NSAIDs (Nonsteroidal anti-inflammatory drugs) • Stimulant laxatives • Theophylline • Water pills (Diuretic drugs)
Gotu Kola	Medications that can harm the liver (Hepatotoxic drugs) • Sedative medications (CNS depressants)
Grape	Medications changed by the liver (Cytochrome P450 1A2 (CYP1A2) substrates) • Phenacetin • Warfarin (*Coumadin*)
Grapefruit	Artemether (*Artenam, Paluther*) • Buspirone (*BuSpar*) • Caffeine • Carbamazepine (*Tegretol*) • Carvedilol (*Coreg*) • Cisapride (*Propulsid*) • Clomipramine (*Anafranil*) • Cyclosporine (*Neoral, Sandimmune*) • Dextromethorphan (*Robitussin DM*, and others) • Erythromycin • Estrogens • Etoposide (*VePesid*) • Fexofenadine (*Allegra*) • Itraconazole (*Sporanox*) • Losartan (*Cozaar*) • Medications changed by the liver (Cytochrome P450 1A2 (CYP1A2) substrates) • Medications changed by the liver (Cytochrome P450 2C19 (CYP2C19) substrates) • Medications changed by the liver (Cytochrome P450 2C9 (CYP2C9) substrates) • Medications changed by the liver (Cytochrome P450 3A4 (CYP3A4) substrates) • Medications for high blood pressure (Calcium channel blockers) • Medications used for lowering cholesterol (Statins) • Methylprednisolone • Praziquantel (*Biltricide*) • Quinidine • Saquinavir (*Fortovase, Invirase*) • Scopolamine (*Transderm Scop*) • Sedative medications (Benzodiazepines) • Sildenafil (*Viagra*) • Terfenadine (*Seldane*) • Theophylline • Warfarin (*Coumadin*)
Gravel Root	Medications that increase breakdown of other medications by the liver (Cytochrome P450 3A4 (CYP3A4) inducers)
Great Plantain	Warfarin (*Coumadin*)
Greater Bindweed	Digoxin (*Lanoxin*) • Water pills (Diuretic drugs)
Greater Celandine	Medications that can harm the liver (Hepatotoxic drugs)
Greek Sage	Hexobarbital
Green Tea	Adenosine (*Adenocard*) • Alcohol (Ethanol) • Amphetamines • Antibiotics (Quinolone antibiotics) • Birth control pills (Contraceptive drugs) • Cimetidine (*Tagamet*) • Clozapine (*Clozaril*) • Dipyridamole (*Persantine*) • Disulfiram (*Antabuse*) • Ephedrine • Estrogens • Fluconazole (*Diflucan*) • Fluvoxamine (*Luvox*) • Lithium • Medications for depression (MAOIs) • Medications for diabetes (Antidiabetes drugs) • Medications that can harm the liver (Hepatotoxic drugs) • Medications that slow blood clotting (Anticoagulant / Antiplatelet drugs) • Mexiletine (*Mexitil*) • Nicotine • Pentobarbital (*Nembutal*) • Phenylpropanolamine • Riluzole (*Rilutek*) • Terbinafine (*Lamisil*) • Theophylline • Verapamil (*Calan, Covera, Isoptin, Verelan*) • Warfarin (*Coumadin*)
Groundsel	Medications that increase breakdown of other medications by the liver (Cytochrome P450 3A4 (CYP3A4) inducers)
Guar Gum	Digoxin (*Lanoxin*) • Ethinyl estradiol • Medications for diabetes (Antidiabetes drugs) • Metformin (*Glucophage*) • Penicillin (*Penicillin VK, Pen VK, Veetids*)
Guarana	Adenosine (*Adenocard*) • Alcohol (Ethanol) • Amphetamines • Antibiotics (Quinolone antibiotics) • Birth control pills (Contraceptive drugs) • Cimetidine (*Tagamet*) • Clozapine (*Clozaril*) • Dipyridamole (*Persantine*) • Disulfiram (*Antabuse*) • Ephedrine • Estrogens • Fluconazole (*Diflucan*) • Fluvoxamine (*Luvox*) • Lithium • Medications for depression (MAOIs) • Medications for diabetes (Antidiabetes drugs) • Medications that slow blood clotting (Anticoagulant / Antiplatelet drugs) • Mexiletine (*Mexitil*) • Nicotine • Pentobarbital (*Nembutal*) • Phenylpropanolamine • Riluzole (*Rilutek*) • Terbinafine (*Lamisil*) • Theophylline • Verapamil (*Calan, Covera, Isoptin, Verelan*)

Potential Interactions: Natural Medicine/Drug   For additional data, refer to the database.

Natural Medicine	Drug
Guggul	Birth control pills (Contraceptive drugs) • Diltiazem (*Cardizem, Dilacor, Tiazac*) • Estrogens • Medications changed by the liver (Cytochrome P450 3A4 (CYP3A4) substrates) • Medications that slow blood clotting (Anticoagulant / Antiplatelet drugs) • Propranolol (*Inderal*) • Tamoxifen (*Nolvadex*) • Thyroid hormone
Gymnema	Insulin • Medications for diabetes (Antidiabetes drugs)
Hawaiian Baby Woodrose	Clozapine (*Clozaril*) • Cyproheptadine • Dextromethorphan (*Robitussin DM*, and others) • Medications for depression (Antidepressant drugs) • Medications for depression (MAOIs) • Meperidine (*Demerol*) • Pentazocine (*Talwin*) • Risperidone (*Risperdal*) • Tramadol (*Ultram*)
Hawthorn	Digoxin (*Lanoxin*) • Medications for high blood pressure (Beta-blockers) • Medications for high blood pressure (Calcium channel blockers) • Medications for male sexual dysfunction (Phosphodiesterase-5 inhibitors) • Medications that increase blood flow to the heart (Nitrates)
Hedge Mustard	Antibiotics (Macrolide antibiotics) • Antibiotics (Tetracycline antibiotics) • Digoxin (*Lanoxin*) • Quinine • Stimulant laxatives • Water pills (Diuretic drugs)
Hemp Agrimony	Medications that increase breakdown of other medications by the liver (Cytochrome P450 3A4 (CYP3A4) inducers)
Henbane	Drying medications (Anticholinergic drugs)
Hibiscus	Acetaminophen (*Tylenol*, others)
Holy Basil	Medications that slow blood clotting (Anticoagulant / Antiplatelet drugs) • Pentobarbital
Honeysuckle	Medications that slow blood clotting (Anticoagulant / Antiplatelet drugs)
Hops	Alcohol • Sedative medications (CNS depressants)
Horse Chestnut	Medications for diabetes (Antidiabetes drugs) • Medications that slow blood clotting (Anticoagulant / Antiplatelet drugs)
Horseradish	Levothyroxine (*Synthroid, Levothroid, Levoxyl*, and others)
Hound's Tongue	Medications that increase breakdown of other medications by the liver (Cytochrome P450 3A4 (CYP3A4) inducers)
Hu Zhang	Estrogens
Huperzine A	Drying medications (Anticholinergic drugs) • Medications for Alzheimer's disease (Acetylcholinesterase (AChE) inhibitors) • Various medications used for glaucoma, Alzheimer's disease, and other conditions (Cholinergic drugs)
Hydrazine Sulfate	Isoniazid (INH) • Medications for depression (MAOIs) • Medications for diabetes (Antidiabetes drugs) • Sedative medications (CNS depressants)
Iboga	Drying medications (Anticholinergic drugs) • Various medications used for glaucoma, Alzheimer's disease, and other conditions (Cholinergic drugs)
Indian Long Pepper	Phenytoin (*Dilantin*) • Propranolol (*Inderal*) • Theophylline
Indian Snakeroot	Alcohol (Ethanol) • Digoxin (*Lanoxin*) • Ephedrine • Levodopa • Medications for depression (MAOIs) • Medications for mental conditions (Antipsychotic drugs) • Medications used for depression (Tricyclic antidepressants) • Propranolol (*Inderal*) • Sedative medications (Barbiturates) • Stimulant drugs • Water pills (Diuretic drugs)
Indole-3-Carbinol	Medications changed by the liver (Cytochrome P450 1A2 (CYP1A2) substrates)
Inositol Nicotinate	Medications for diabetes (Antidiabetes drugs) • Medications that slow blood clotting (Anticoagulant / Antiplatelet drugs) • Medications used for lowering cholesterol (Statins) • Nicotine patch (Transdermal nicotine)
Iodine	Amiodarone (*Cordarone*) • Lithium • Medications for an overactive thyroid (Antithyroid drugs) • Medications for high blood pressure (ACE inhibitors) • Medications for high blood pressure (Angiotensin receptor blockers (ARBs)) • Water pills (Potassium-sparing diuretics)
IP-6	Medications that slow blood clotting (Anticoagulant / Antiplatelet drugs)
Ipecac	Activated charcoal

CONSUMER VERSION

Medical professionals should consult the Professional Version at www.NaturalDatabase.com.

Potential Interactions: Natural Medicine/Drug   For additional data, refer to the database.

Natural Medicine	Drug
Ipriflavone	Medications changed by the liver (Cytochrome P450 1A2 (CYP1A2) substrates) • Medications changed by the liver (Cytochrome P450 2C9 (CYP2C9) substrates) • Medications that decrease the immune system (Immunosuppressants) • Theophylline
Iron	Antibiotics (Quinolone antibiotics) • Antibiotics (Tetracycline antibiotics) • Bisphosphonates • Chloramphenicol • Levodopa • Levothyroxine (*Synthroid, Levothroid, Levoxyl*, and others) • Methyldopa (*Aldomet*) • Mycophenolate Mofetil (*CellCept*) • Penicillamine
Ivy Gourd	Medications for diabetes (Antidiabetes drugs)
Jalap	Digoxin (*Lanoxin*) • Stimulant laxatives • Water pills (Diuretic drugs)
Jamaican Dogwood	Sedative medications (CNS depressants)
Jambolan	Medications for diabetes (Antidiabetes drugs)
Japanese Apricot	Medications that slow blood clotting (Anticoagulant / Antiplatelet drugs)
Japanese Persimmon	Medications for high blood pressure (Antihypertensive drugs)
Jiaogulan	Medications that decrease the immune system (Immunosuppressants) • Medications that slow blood clotting (Anticoagulant / Antiplatelet drugs)
Jimson Weed	Drying medications (Anticholinergic drugs)
Juniper	Medications for diabetes (Antidiabetes drugs) • Water pills (Diuretic drugs)
Kaolin	Clindamycin (*Cleocin*) • Digoxin (*Lanoxin*) • Quinidine • Trimethoprim (*Proloprim*)
Kava	Alprazolam (*Xanax*) • Levodopa • Medications changed by the liver (Cytochrome P450 1A2 (CYP1A2) substrates) • Medications changed by the liver (Cytochrome P450 2C19 (CYP2C19) substrates) • Medications changed by the liver (Cytochrome P450 2C9 (CYP2C9) substrates) • Medications changed by the liver (Cytochrome P450 2D6 (CYP2D6) substrates) • Medications changed by the liver (Cytochrome P450 2E1 (CYP2E1) substrates) • Medications changed by the liver (Cytochrome P450 3A4 (CYP3A4) substrates) • Medications that can harm the liver (Hepatotoxic drugs) • Sedative medications (CNS depressants)
Kefir	Medications that decrease the immune system (Immunosuppressants)
Khella	Digoxin (*Lanoxin*) • Medications that can harm the liver (Hepatotoxic drugs) • Medications that increase sensitivity to sunlight (Photosensitizing drugs)
Kombucha Tea	Disulfiram (*Antabuse*)
Kudzu	Birth control pills (Contraceptive drugs) • Estrogens • Medications for diabetes (Antidiabetes drugs) • Medications that slow blood clotting (Anticoagulant / Antiplatelet drugs) • Methotrexate (MTX, *Rheumatrex*) • Tamoxifen (*Nolvadex*)
Lactobacillus	Antibiotic drugs • Medications that decrease the immune system (Immunosuppressants)
Laminaria	Digoxin (*Lanoxin*) • Medications for high blood pressure (ACE inhibitors) • Thyroid hormone • Water pills (Potassium-sparing diuretics)
Larch Arabinogalactan	Medications that decrease the immune system (Immunosuppressants)
L-Arginine	Medications for high blood pressure (Antihypertensive drugs) • Medications that increase blood flow to the heart (Nitrates) • Sildenafil (*Viagra*)
Lavender	Chloral Hydrate • Sedative medications (Barbiturates) • Sedative medications (CNS depressants)
L-Carnitine	Acenocoumarol (*Sintrom*) • Thyroid hormone • Warfarin (*Coumadin*) • Zidovudine (AZT, *Retrovir*)
Lemon Balm	Sedative medications (CNS depressants)
Licorice	Digoxin (*Lanoxin*) • Estrogens • Ethacrynic acid (*Edecrin*) • Furosemide (*Lasix*) • Medications changed by the liver (Cytochrome P450 2B6 (CYP2B6) substrates) • Medications changed by the liver (Cytochrome P450 3A4 (CYP3A4) substrates) • Medications for high blood pressure (Antihypertensive drugs) • Medications for inflammation (Corticosteroids) • Water pills (Diuretic drugs)

Potential Interactions: Natural Medicine/Drug
For additional data, refer to the database.

Natural Medicine	Drug
Lily-Of-The-Valley	Antibiotics (Macrolide antibiotics) • Antibiotics (Tetracycline antibiotics) • Digoxin (*Lanoxin*) • Medications for inflammation (Corticosteroids) • Quinine • Stimulant laxatives • Water pills (Diuretic drugs)
Lime	Medications changed by the liver (Cytochrome P450 3A4 (CYP3A4) substrates) • Medications that increase sensitivity to sunlight (Photosensitizing drugs)
Limonene	Medications changed by the liver (Cytochrome P450 2C9 (CYP2C9) substrates) • Medications that decrease the breakdown of other medications by the liver (Cytochrome P450 2C19 (CYP2C19) inhibitors) • Medications that decrease the breakdown of other medications by the liver (Cytochrome P450 2C9 (CYP2C9) inhibitors) • Medications that increase the breakdown of other medications by the liver (Cytochrome P450 2C19 (CYP2C19) inducers) • Medications that increase the breakdown of other medications by the liver (Cytochrome P450 2C9 (CYP2C9) inducers)
Lithium	Dextromethorphan (*Robitussin DM*, and others) • Medications for depression (Antidepressant drugs) • Medications for depression (MAOIs) • Medications for high blood pressure (ACE inhibitors) • Medications for high blood pressure (Calcium channel blockers) • Medications used to prevent seizures (Anticonvulsants) • Meperidine (*Demerol*) • Methyldopa (*Aldomet*) • Methylxanthines • Muscle relaxants • NSAIDs (Nonsteroidal anti-inflammatory drugs) • Pentazocine (*Talwin*) • Phenothiazines • Tramadol (*Ultram*) • Water pills (Loop diuretics) • Water pills (Thiazide diuretics)
Lovage	Water pills (Diuretic drugs)
L-Tryptophan	Dextromethorphan (*Robitussin DM*, and others) • Medications for depression (Antidepressant drugs) • Medications for depression (MAOIs) • Meperidine (*Demerol*) • Pentazocine (*Talwin*) • Phenothiazines • Sedative medications (Benzodiazepines) • Sedative medications (CNS depressants) • Tramadol (*Ultram*)
Lycium	Medications changed by the liver (Cytochrome P450 2C9 (CYP2C9) substrates) • Medications for diabetes (Antidiabetes drugs) • Medications for high blood pressure (Antihypertensive drugs) • Warfarin (*Coumadin*)
Madagascar Periwinkle	Medications for diabetes (Antidiabetes drugs)
Magnesium	Antibiotics (Aminoglycoside antibiotics) • Antibiotics (Quinolone antibiotics) • Antibiotics (Tetracycline antibiotics) • Bisphosphonates • Medications for high blood pressure (Calcium channel blockers) • Muscle relaxants • Water pills (Potassium-sparing diuretics)
Magnolia	Alcohol • Sedative medications (Barbiturates) • Sedative medications (Benzodiazepines) • Sedative medications (CNS depressants)
Maitake Mushroom	Medications for diabetes (Antidiabetes drugs)
Manganese	Antibiotics (Quinolone antibiotics) • Antibiotics (Tetracycline antibiotics)
Manna	Digoxin (*Lanoxin*) • Water pills (Diuretic drugs)
Marijuana	Disulfiram (*Antabuse*) • Fluoxetine (*Prozac*) • Sedative medications (Barbiturates) • Sedative medications (CNS depressants) • Theophylline
Marsh Tea	Sedative medications (CNS depressants)
Marshmallow	Medications for diabetes (Antidiabetes drugs)
Masterwort	Medications that increase sensitivity to sunlight (Photosensitizing drugs)
Mate	Adenosine (*Adenocard*) • Alcohol (Ethanol) • Amphetamines • Antibiotics (Quinolone antibiotics) • Birth control pills (Contraceptive drugs) • Cimetidine (*Tagamet*) • Clozapine (*Clozaril*) • Dipyridamole (*Persantine*) • Disulfiram (*Antabuse*) • Ephedrine • Estrogens • Fluconazole (*Diflucan*) • Fluvoxamine (*Luvox*) • Lithium • Medications for depression (MAOIs) • Medications for diabetes (Antidiabetes drugs) • Medications that slow blood clotting (Anticoagulant / Antiplatelet drugs) • Mexiletine (*Mexitil*) • Nicotine • Pentobarbital (*Nembutal*) • Phenylpropanolamine • Riluzole (*Rilutek*) • Terbinafine (*Lamisil*) • Theophylline • Verapamil (*Calan, Covera, Isoptin, Verelan*)
Meadowsweet	Aspirin • Choline magnesium trisalicylate (*Trilisate*) • Medications for pain (Narcotic drugs) • Salsalate (*Disalcid*)

CONSUMER VERSION

Medical professionals should consult the Professional Version at www.NaturalDatabase.com.

Potential Interactions: Natural Medicine/Drug   For additional data, refer to the database.

Natural Medicine	Drug
Melatonin	Birth control pills (Contraceptive drugs) • Caffeine • Flumazenil (*Romazicon*) • Fluvoxamine (*Luvox*) • Medications for diabetes (Antidiabetes drugs) • Medications that decrease the immune system (Immunosuppressants) • Medications that slow blood clotting (Anticoagulant / Antiplatelet drugs) • Nifedipine GITS (*Procardia XL*) • Sedative medications (Benzodiazepines) • Sedative medications (CNS depressants) • Verapamil (*Calan, Covera, Isoptin, Verelan*)
Mesoglycan	Medications for dissolving blood clots (Thrombolytic drugs) • Medications that slow blood clotting (Anticoagulant / Antiplatelet drugs)
Methoxylated Flavones	Medications changed by the liver (Cytochrome P450 1A2 (CYP1A2) substrates) • Medications that slow blood clotting (Anticoagulant / Antiplatelet drugs)
Mexican Scammony Root	Digoxin (*Lanoxin*) • Stimulant laxatives • Water pills (Diuretic drugs)
Milk Thistle	Estrogens • Medications changed by the liver (Cytochrome P450 2C9 (CYP2C9) substrates) • Medications changed by the liver (Cytochrome P450 3A4 (CYP3A4) substrates) • Medications changed by the liver (Glucuronidated drugs)
Morinda	Medications for high blood pressure (ACE inhibitors) • Medications for high blood pressure (Angiotensin receptor blockers (ARBs)) • Medications that can harm the liver (Hepatotoxic drugs) • Water pills (Potassium-sparing diuretics)
Motherwort	Sedative medications (CNS depressants)
N-Acetyl Cysteine	Activated charcoal • Nitroglycerin
N-Acetyl Glucosamine	Chemotherapy • Medications for diabetes (Antidiabetes drugs) • Warfarin (*Coumadin*)
Nattokinase	Medications that slow blood clotting (Anticoagulant / Antiplatelet drugs)
Neem	Medications for diabetes (Antidiabetes drugs) • Medications that decrease the immune system (Immunosuppressants)
Niacin And Niacinamide (Vitamin B3)	Alcohol (Ethanol) • Allopurinol (*Zyloprim*) • Aspirin • Bile acid sequestrants • Carbamazepine (*Tegretol*) • Clonidine (*Catapres*) • Medications for diabetes (Antidiabetes drugs) • Medications for gout • Medications used for lowering cholesterol (Resins) • Medications used for lowering cholesterol (Statins) • Nicotine patch (Transdermal nicotine) • Primidone (*Mysoline*) • Probenecid • Sulfinpyrazone (*Anturane*)
Northern Prickly Ash	Antacids • Medications that decrease stomach acid (H2-blockers) • Medications that decrease stomach acid (Proton pump inhibitors)
Nutmeg And Mace	Medications changed by the liver (Cytochrome P450 1A1 (CYP1A1) substrates) • Medications changed by the liver (Cytochrome P450 1A2 (CYP1A2) substrates) • Medications changed by the liver (Cytochrome P450 2B1 (CYP2B1) substrates) • Medications changed by the liver (Cytochrome P450 2B2 (CYP2B2) substrates) • Phenobarbital (*Luminal*)
Octacosanol	Levodopa/Carbidopa (*Sinemet*)
Oleander	Antibiotics (Macrolide antibiotics) • Antibiotics (Tetracycline antibiotics) • Digoxin (*Lanoxin*) • Quinine • Stimulant laxatives • Water pills (Diuretic drugs)
Olive	Medications for diabetes (Antidiabetes drugs) • Medications for high blood pressure (Antihypertensive drugs)
Onion	Aspirin • Medications for diabetes (Antidiabetes drugs) • Medications that slow blood clotting (Anticoagulant / Antiplatelet drugs)
Oolong Tea	Adenosine (*Adenocard*) • Alcohol (Ethanol) • Amphetamines • Antibiotics (Quinolone antibiotics) • Birth control pills (Contraceptive drugs) • Cimetidine (*Tagamet*) • Clozapine (*Clozaril*) • Dipyridamole (*Persantine*) • Disulfiram (*Antabuse*) • Ephedrine • Estrogens • Fluconazole (*Diflucan*) • Fluvoxamine (*Luvox*) • Lithium • Medications for depression (MAOIs) • Medications for diabetes (Antidiabetes drugs) • Medications that slow blood clotting (Anticoagulant / Antiplatelet drugs) • Mexiletine (*Mexitil*) • Nicotine • Pentobarbital (*Nembutal*) • Phenylpropanolamine • Riluzole (*Rilutek*) • Terbinafine (*Lamisil*) • Theophylline • Verapamil (*Calan, Covera, Isoptin, Verelan*)
Oregon Grape	Cyclosporine (Neoral, Sandimmune) • Medications changed by the liver (Cytochrome P450 3A4 (CYP3A4) substrates)
Palm Oil	Medications that slow blood clotting (Anticoagulant / Antiplatelet drugs)

    Natural Medicines Comprehensive Database Consumer Version   (209) 472-2244

Potential Interactions: Natural Medicine/Drug   For additional data, refer to the database.

Natural Medicine	Drug
Pancreatin	Acarbose (*Precose, Prandase*)
Pangamic Acid	Digoxin (*Lanoxin*) • Medications for high blood pressure (Calcium channel blockers) • Water pills (Thiazide diuretics)
Pantethine	Medications that slow blood clotting (Anticoagulant / Antiplatelet drugs)
Papaya	Warfarin (*Coumadin*)
Para-Aminobenzoic Acid (PABA)	Antibiotics (Sulfonamide antibiotics) • Cortisone (Cortisone Acetate) • Dapsone (*Avlosulfon*)
Parsley	Aspirin • Warfarin (*Coumadin*) • Water pills (Diuretic drugs)
Passionflower	Sedative medications (CNS depressants)
Pau D'arco	Medications that slow blood clotting (Anticoagulant / Antiplatelet drugs)
Pectin	Antibiotics (Tetracycline antibiotics) • Digoxin (*Lanoxin*) • Lovastatin (*Mevacor*)
Peony	Medications that slow blood clotting (Anticoagulant / Antiplatelet drugs) • Phenytoin (*Dilantin*)
Peppermint	Antacids • Cyclosporine (*Neoral, Sandimmune*) • Medications changed by the liver (Cytochrome P450 1A2 (CYP1A2) substrates) • Medications changed by the liver (Cytochrome P450 2C19 (CYP2C19) substrates) • Medications changed by the liver (Cytochrome P450 2C9 (CYP2C9) substrates) • Medications changed by the liver (Cytochrome P450 3A4 (CYP3A4) substrates) • Medications that decrease stomach acid (H2-blockers) • Medications that decrease stomach acid (Proton pump inhibitors)
Periwinkle	Medications for high blood pressure (Antihypertensive drugs)
Peyote	Stimulant drugs
Pheasant's Eye	Digoxin (*Lanoxin*) • Medications for inflammation (Corticosteroids) • Quinidine • Stimulant laxatives • Water pills (Diuretic drugs)
Phellodendron	Cyclosporine (*Neoral, Sandimmune*) • Medications changed by the liver (Cytochrome P450 3A4 (CYP3A4) substrates)
Phenylalanine	Levodopa • Medications for depression (MAOIs) • Medications for mental conditions (Antipsychotic drugs)
Phosphate Salts	Antacids • Cholestyramine (*Questran*) • Colestipol (*Colestid*)
Phosphatidylcholine	Drying medications (Anticholinergic drugs) • Medications for Alzheimer's disease (Acetylcholinesterase (AChE) inhibitors) • Various medications used for glaucoma, Alzheimer's disease, and other conditions (Cholinergic drugs)
Phosphatidylserine	Drying medications (Anticholinergic drugs) • Medications for Alzheimer's disease (Acetylcholinesterase (AChE) inhibitors) • Various medications used for glaucoma, Alzheimer's disease, and other conditions (Cholinergic drugs)
Picrorhiza	Medications that decrease the immune system (Immunosuppressants)
Pleurisy Root	Digoxin (*Lanoxin*) • Estrogens • Water pills (Diuretic drugs)
Policosanol	Medications that slow blood clotting (Anticoagulant / Antiplatelet drugs)
Pomegranate	Medications changed by the liver (Cytochrome P450 2D6 (CYP2D6) substrates) • Medications changed by the liver (Cytochrome P450 3A4 (CYP3A4) substrates) • Medications for high blood pressure (ACE inhibitors) • Medications for high blood pressure (Antihypertensive drugs)
Potassium	Medications for high blood pressure (ACE inhibitors) • Medications for high blood pressure (Angiotensin receptor blockers (ARBs)) • Water pills (Potassium-sparing diuretics)
Potato	Medications for dissolving blood clots (Thrombolytic drugs)
Pregnenolone	Estrogens • Progestin • Testosterone
Prickly Pear Cactus	Chlorpropamide (*Diabinese*)
Procaine	Aminosalicylic acid • Antibiotics (Sulfonamide antibiotics) • Digoxin (*Lanoxin*) • Muscle relaxants • Succinylcholine
Progesterone	Estrogens

Potential Interactions: Natural Medicine/Drug   For additional data, refer to the database.

Natural Medicine	Drug
Propionyl-L-Carnitine	Acenocoumarol (*Sintrom*) • Warfarin (*Coumadin*) • Zidovudine (AZT, *Retrovir*)
Puncture Vine	Medications for diabetes (Antidiabetes drugs)
Pycnogenol	Medications that decrease the immune system (Immunosuppressants)
Pyridoxine (Vitamin B6)	Amiodarone (*Cordarone*) • Levodopa • Phenobarbital (*Luminal*) • Phenytoin (*Dilantin*)
Quassia	Antacids • Digoxin (*Lanoxin*) • Medications that decrease stomach acid (H2-blockers) • Medications that decrease stomach acid (Proton pump inhibitors) • Water pills (Diuretic drugs)
Quercetin	Antibiotics (Quinolone antibiotics)
Quillaia	Metformin (*Glucophage*)
Red Clover	Birth control pills (Contraceptive drugs) • Estrogens • Medications changed by the liver (Cytochrome P450 1A2 (CYP1A2) substrates) • Medications changed by the liver (Cytochrome P450 2C19 (CYP2C19) substrates) • Medications changed by the liver (Cytochrome P450 2C9 (CYP2C9) substrates) • Medications changed by the liver (Cytochrome P450 3A4 (CYP3A4) substrates) • Medications that slow blood clotting (Anticoagulant / Antiplatelet drugs) • Tamoxifen (*Nolvadex*)
Red Yeast	Alcohol (Ethanol) • Cyclosporine (*Neoral, Sandimmune*) • Cytochrome P450 3A4 (CYP3A4) inhibitors • Gemfibrozil (*Lopid*) • HMG-CoA Reductase Inhibitors (Statins) • Levothyroxine (*Synthroid, Levothroid, Levoxyl*, and others)
Reishi Mushroom	Medications for high blood pressure (Antihypertensive drugs) • Medications that slow blood clotting (Anticoagulant / Antiplatelet drugs)
Resveratrol	Medications changed by the liver (Cytochrome P450 3A4 (CYP3A4) substrates) • Medications that slow blood clotting (Anticoagulant / Antiplatelet drugs)
Rhubarb	Digoxin (*Lanoxin*) • Medications for inflammation (Corticosteroids) • Stimulant laxatives • Water pills (Diuretic drugs)
Riboflavin (Vitamin B2)	Drying medications (Anticholinergic drugs) • Medications for depression (Tricyclic antidepressants) • Phenobarbital (*Luminal*) • Probenecid (*Benemid*)
Ribose	Alcohol • Aspirin • Choline magnesium trisalicylate (*Trilisate*) • Insulin • Medications for diabetes (Antidiabetes drugs) • Propranolol (*Inderal*) • Salsalate (*Disalcid*)
Rose Hip	Aluminum • Aspirin • Choline magnesium trisalicylate (*Trilisate*) • Estrogens • Fluphenazine (*Prolixin*) • Salsalate (*Disalcid*) • Warfarin (*Coumadin*)
Royal Jelly	Warfarin (*Coumadin*)
Rue	Medications that increase sensitivity to sunlight (Photosensitizing drugs)
Saccharomyces Boulardii	Medications for fungal infections (Antifungals)
Safflower	Medications that slow blood clotting (Anticoagulant / Antiplatelet drugs)
Sage	Medications for diabetes (Antidiabetes drugs) • Medications used to prevent seizures (Anticonvulsants) • Sedative medications (CNS depressants)
Salacia	Medications for diabetes (Antidiabetes drugs)
SAMe	Dextromethorphan (*Robitussin DM*, and others) • Levodopa • Medications for depression (Antidepressant drugs) • Medications for depression (MAOIs) • Meperidine (*Demerol*) • Pentazocine (*Talwin*) • Tramadol (*Ultram*)
Sarsaparilla	Digoxin (*Lanoxin*)
Sassafras	Sedative medications (CNS depressants)
Saw Palmetto	Birth control pills (Contraceptive drugs) • Estrogens • Medications that slow blood clotting (Anticoagulant / Antiplatelet drugs)
Schisandra	Medications changed by the liver (Cytochrome P450 3A4 (CYP3A4) substrates)
Scopolia	Drying medications (Anticholinergic drugs) • Medications used for depression (Tricyclic antidepressants) • Quinidine
Scotch Broom	Haloperidol (*Haldol*) • Medications for depression (MAOIs) • Quinidine
Sea Buckthorn	Medications that slow blood clotting (Anticoagulant / Antiplatelet drugs)

Potential Interactions: Natural Medicine/Drug   For additional data, refer to the database.

Natural Medicine	Drug
Selenium	Medications used for lowering cholesterol (Statins)
Senna	Digoxin (*Lanoxin*) • Water pills (Diuretic drugs)
Shepherd's Purse	Sedative medications (CNS depressants) • Thyroid hormone
Smartweed	Warfarin (*Coumadin*)
Solomon's Seal	Chlorpropamide (*Diabinese*) • Insulin • Medications for diabetes (Antidiabetes drugs)
Southern Prickly Ash	Antacids • Medications that decrease stomach acid (H2-blockers) • Medications that decrease stomach acid (Proton pump inhibitors)
Soy	Antibiotic drugs • Estrogens •Tamoxifen (*Nolvadex*) • Warfarin (*Coumadin*)
Spinach	Medications for diabetes (Antidiabetes drugs) • Warfarin (*Coumadin*)
Squill	Digoxin (*Lanoxin*) • Medications for inflammation (Corticosteroids) • Quinidine • Stimulant laxatives • Water pills (Diuretic drugs)
St. John's Wort	Alprazolam (*Xanax*) • Aminolevulinic acid • Amitriptyline (*Elavil*) • Birth control pills (Contraceptive drugs) • Clopidogrel (*Plavix*) • Cyclosporine (*Neoral, Sandimmune*) • Dextromethorphan (*Robitussin DM, and others*) • Digoxin (*Lanoxin*) • Fenfluramine (*Pondimin*) • Fexofenadine (*Allegra*) • Imatinib (*Gleevec*) • Irinotecan (*Camptosar*) • Medications changed by the liver (Cytochrome P450 1A2 (CYP1A2) substrates) • Medications changed by the liver (Cytochrome P450 2C9 (CYP2C9) substrates) • Medications changed by the liver (Cytochrome P450 3A4 (CYP3A4) substrates) • Medications for depression (Antidepressant drugs) • Medications for depression (MAOIs) • Medications for HIV/AIDS (Nonnucleoside Reverse Transcriptase Inhibitors (NNRTIs)) • Medications for HIV/AIDS (Protease Inhibitors) • Medications for migraine headaches ("Triptans") • Medications for pain (Narcotic drugs) • Medications moved by pumps in cells (P-glycoprotein substrates) • Medications that increase sensitivity to sunlight (Photosensitizing drugs) • Meperidine (*Demerol*) • Nefazodone (*Serzone*) • Nortriptyline (*Pamelor*) • Paroxetine (*Paxil*) • Pentazocine (*Talwin*) • Phenobarbital (*Luminal*) • Phenprocoumon • Phenytoin (*Dilantin*) • Reserpine • Sedative medications (Barbiturates) • Sertraline (*Zoloft*) • Simvastatin (*Zocor*) • Tacrolimus (*Prograf, Protopic*) • Theophylline • Tramadol (*Ultram*) • Warfarin (*Coumadin*)
Stevia	Medications for diabetes (Antidiabetes drugs) • Medications for high blood pressure (Antihypertensive drugs) • Medications for high blood pressure (Calcium channel blockers)
Stinging Nettle	Medications for diabetes (Antidiabetes drugs) • Medications for high blood pressure (Antihypertensive drugs) • Sedative medications (CNS depressants) • Warfarin (*Coumadin*)
Stone Root	Water pills (Diuretic drugs)
Strophanthus	Digoxin (*Lanoxin*) • Medications for inflammation (Corticosteroids) • Quinidine • Quinine • Stimulant laxatives • Water pills (Diuretic drugs)
Sulforaphane	Cytochrome P450 1A2 (CYP1A2) substrates
Swallowroot	Medications that slow blood clotting (Anticoagulant / Antiplatelet drugs)
Swamp Milkweed	Antibiotics (Macrolide antibiotics) • Antibiotics (Tetracycline antibiotics) • Digoxin (*Lanoxin*) • Quinine • Stimulant laxatives • Water pills (Diuretic drugs)
Sweet Bay	Medications for pain (Narcotic drugs) • Sedative medications (CNS depressants)
Sweet Clover	Medications that can harm the liver (Hepatotoxic drugs) • Medications that slow blood clotting (Anticoagulant / Antiplatelet drugs)
Sweet Orange	Antibiotics (Quinolone antibiotics) • Celiprolol (*Celicard*) • Fexofenadine (*Allegra*) • Ivermectin • Pravastatin (*Pravachol*)
Sweet Vernal Grass	Medications that slow blood clotting (Anticoagulant / Antiplatelet drugs)
Tamarind	Aspirin • Ibuprofen
Tansy	Alcohol (Ethanol)
Tansy Ragwort	Medications that increase breakdown of other medications by the liver (Cytochrome P450 3A4 (CYP3A4) inducers)

CONSUMER VERSION

Medical professionals should consult the Professional Version at www.NaturalDatabase.com.

Potential Interactions: Natural Medicine/Drug   For additional data, refer to the database.

Natural Medicine	Drug
Theanine	Medications for high blood pressure (Antihypertensive drugs) • Stimulant drugs
Threonine	Medications used for Alzheimer's disease (NMDA antagonists)
Thuja	Medications that increase the chance of having a seizure (Seizure threshold lowering drugs) • Medications used to prevent seizures (Anticonvulsants)
Thunder God Vine	Medications that decrease the immune system (Immunosuppressants)
Thyme	Medications that slow blood clotting (Anticoagulant / Antiplatelet drugs)
Thymus Extract	Medications that decrease the immune system (Immunosuppressants)
Tiratricol	Cholestyramine (*Questran*) • Medications for diabetes (Antidiabetes drugs) • Medications that slow blood clotting (Anticoagulant / Antiplatelet drugs) • Stimulant drugs • Thyroid hormone
Tonka Bean	Medications that slow blood clotting (Anticoagulant / antiplatelet drugs)
Tree Turmeric	Cyclosporine (*Neoral, Sandimmune*) • Medications changed by the liver (Cytochrome P450 3A4 (CYP3A4) substrates)
Turmeric	Medications that slow blood clotting (Anticoagulant / Antiplatelet drugs)
Tyrosine	Levodopa • Thyroid hormone
Uzara	Antibiotics (Macrolide antibiotics) • Antibiotics (Tetracycline antibiotics) • Digoxin (*Lanoxin*) • Quinine • Stimulant laxatives • Water pills (Diuretic drugs)
Valerian	Alcohol • Alprazolam (*Xanax*) • Medications changed by the liver (Cytochrome P450 3A4 (CYP3A4) substrates) • Sedative medications (Benzodiazepines) • Sedative medications (CNS depressants)
Vanadium	Medications for diabetes (Antidiabetes drugs) • Medications that slow blood clotting (Anticoagulant / Antiplatelet drugs)
Vinpocetine	Medications that slow blood clotting (Anticoagulant / Antiplatelet drugs) • Warfarin (*Coumadin*)
Vitamin A	Antibiotics (Tetracycline antibiotics) • Medications for skin conditions (Retinoids) • Medications that can harm the liver (Hepatotoxic drugs) • Warfarin (*Coumadin*)
Vitamin B12	Chloramphenicol
Vitamin C (Ascorbic Acid)	Acetaminophen (*Tylenol*, others) • Aspirin • Chemotherapy • Choline magnesium trisalicylate (*Trilisate*) • Estrogens • Fluphenazine (*Prolixin*) • HMG-CoA reductase inhibitors (Statins) • Nicardipine (*Cardene*) • Nifedipine • Protease inhibitors (PIs) • Salsalate (*Disalcid*) • Warfarin (*Coumadin*)
Vitamin D	Aluminum • Calcipotriene (*Dovonex*) • Cimetidine (*Tagamet*) • Digoxin (*Lanoxin*) • Diltiazem (*Cardizem, Dilacor, Tiazac*) • Heparin • Low molecular weight heparins (LMWHs) • Verapamil (*Calan, Covera, Isoptin, Verelan*) • Water pills (Thiazide diuretics)
Vitamin E	Chemotherapy • Cyclosporine (*Neoral, Sandimmune*) • Medications changed by the liver (Cytochrome P450 3A4 (CYP3A4) substrates) • Medications that slow blood clotting (Anticoagulant / Antiplatelet drugs) • Medications used for lowering cholesterol (Statins) • Niacin • Warfarin (*Coumadin*)
Vitamin K	Warfarin (*Coumadin*)
Wahoo	Antibiotics (Macrolide antibiotics) • Antibiotics (Tetracycline antibiotics) • Digoxin (*Lanoxin*) • Quinine • Stimulant laxatives • Water pills (Diuretic drugs)
Wallflower	Digoxin (*Lanoxin*) • Medications for inflammation (Corticosteroids) • Quinidine • Quinine • Stimulant laxatives • Water pills (Diuretic drugs)
Water Avens	Metformin (*Glucophage*)
Watercress	Chlorzoxazone (*Parafon Forte, Paraflex*) • Warfarin (*Coumadin*)
Wheat Bran	Digoxin (*Lanoxin*)
Whey Protein	Alendronate (*Fosamax*) • Antibiotics (Quinolone antibiotics) • Antibiotics (Tetracycline antibiotics) • Levodopa

Potential Interactions: Natural Medicine/Drug

For additional data, refer to the database.

Natural Medicine	Drug
Wild Carrot	Estrogens • Medications for high blood pressure (Antihypertensive drugs) • Medications that increase sensitivity to sunlight (Photosensitizing drugs)
Wild Cherry	Medications changed by the liver (Cytochrome P450 3A4 (CYP3A4) substrates)
Wild Lettuce	Sedative medications (CNS depressants)
Willow Bark	Aspirin • Choline Magnesium Trisalicylate (*Trilisate*) • Medications that slow blood clotting (Anticoagulant / Antiplatelet drugs) • Salsalate (*Disalcid*)
Wine	Antibiotics (Sulfonamide antibiotics) • Aspirin • Cefamandole (*Mandol*) • Cefoperazone (*Cefobid*) • Chlorpropamide (*Diabinese*) • Cisapride (*Propulsid*) • Cyclosporine (*Neoral, Sandimmune*) • Disulfiram (*Antabuse*) • Erythromycin • Felodipine (*Plendil*) • Griseofulvin (*Fulvicin*) • Medications for depression (MAOIs) • Medications for pain (Narcotic drugs) • Medications that can harm the liver (Hepatotoxic drugs) • Medications that decrease stomach acid (H2-blockers) • Metformin (*Glucophage*) • Metronidazole (*Flagyl*) • NSAIDs (Nonsteroidal anti-inflammatory drugs) • Phenytoin (Dilantin) • Sedative medications (Barbiturates) • Sedative medications (Benzodiazepines) • Sedative medications (CNS depressants) • Tolbutamide (*Orinase*) • Warfarin (*Coumadin*)
Wintergreen	Aspirin • Warfarin (*Coumadin*)
Wormwood	Medications used to prevent seizures (Anticonvulsants)
Xanthan Gum	Medications for diabetes (Antidiabetes drugs)
Yarrow	Antacids • Medications that decrease stomach acid (H2-blockers) • Medications that decrease stomach acid (Proton pump inhibitors) • Medications that slow blood clotting (Anticoagulant / Antiplatelet drugs) • Sedative medications (Barbiturates)
Yellow Dock	Digoxin (*Lanoxin*) • Water pills (Diuretic drugs)
Yerba Mansa	Sedative medications (CNS depressants)
Yogurt	Antibiotics (Tetracycline antibiotics) • Ciprofloxacin (*Cipro*) • Medications that decrease the immune system (Immunosuppressants)
Yohimbe	Clonidine (*Catapres*) • Guanabenz (*Wytensin*) • Medications for depression (MAOIs) • Medications for depression (Tricyclic antidepressants) • Medications for high blood pressure (Antihypertensive drugs) • Naloxone (*Narcan*) • Phenothiazines • Stimulant drugs
Zinc	Amiloride (*Midamor*) • Antibiotics (Quinolone antibiotics) • Antibiotics (Tetracycline antibiotics) • Cisplatin (*Platinol-AQ*) • Penicillamine • Water pills (Potassium-sparing diuretics) • Water pills (Thiazide diuretics)

Drug Influences on Nutrient Levels and Depletion

Some medications can affect the levels of certain nutrients in the body. There is considerable interest in using nutritional supplements to counteract these possible drug-induced "nutrient depletions." The chart below shows the current scientific understanding of these relationships, and suggested actions.

DRUGS (Includes some examples of US and Canadian drug names.)	NUTRIENT DECREASED IN THE BODY (DEPLETED)	WHAT HAPPENS?	COMMENTS
ANALGESICS / ANTI-INFLAMMATORIES (PAIN MEDICINES)			
Acetaminophen (*Tylenol*)	Glutathione	Acetaminophen can reduce the amount of glutathione in the body.	There is not enough information to know if this is a concern or if glutathione supplements are needed.
Aspirin and other salicylate drugs	Folic Acid	Taking aspirin might change how the body stores folic acid. It does not seem to reduce the amount of folic acid in the body.	Folic acid supplements do not seem to be necessary.
	Vitamin C	Taking large amounts of aspirin might decrease vitamin C in the body.	You are unlikely to need vitamin C supplements if you take low doses of aspirin. If you take high-doses of aspirin for long periods of time, you might need a vitamin C supplement.
ANTIMICROBIALS (DRUGS USED FOR INFECTIONS)			
Aminoglycosides: Amikacin (*Amikin*), Gentamicin (*Garamycin*), Kanamycin (*Kantrex*), Netilmicin (*Netromycin*), Tobramycin (*Nebcin*)	Magnesium Potassium	These antibiotics can damage the kidneys. The kidneys help control many substances in the body. Damaged kidneys can cause the body to lose potassium and magnesium in the urine.	Your healthcare provider can check your potassium and magnesium levels. If your levels are low, magnesium and potassium can be given.
Aminosalicylic Acid (Para-aminosalicylic Acid, *Paser*)	Folic Acid	Some people with tuberculosis have low levels of folic acid. Aminosalicylic acid can reduce the absorption of folic acid and possibly cause folic acid levels to go too low.	If you eat a diet that is low in folic acid and take aminosalicylic acid you might need to take a folic acid supplement. Your healthcare provider can check your folic acid levels with a lab test. Talk to your healthcare provider before taking any supplements, especially in large amounts, if you are being treated for tuberculosis.
	Iron	Aminosalicylic acid can reduce the absorption of iron. Low levels of iron can cause a condition called anemia.	Your healthcare provider can check your iron levels with a lab test, and if your levels are low you will need an iron supplement. Watch for signs of low iron such as being tired all the time and having pale skin and nails. Talk to your healthcare provider before taking any supplements, especially in large amounts, if you are being treated for tuberculosis.
	Dibencozide Vitamin B12	Aminosalicylic acid can reduce the absorption of vitamin B12.	If you need to take aminosalicylic acid more than one month, have your levels of vitamin B12 checked. Talk to your healthcare provider before taking any supplements, especially in large amounts, if you are being treated for tuberculosis.
Amphotericin B (*Abelcet, AmBisome, Amphocin, Amphotec, Fungizone*)	Magnesium Potassium	The kidneys help balance magnesium and potassium in the body. Amphotericin B can damage the kidneys and increase the amount of magnesium and potassium lost from the body in the urine.	Your healthcare provider can check your magnesium and potassium levels. If your levels are too low, magnesium or potassium can be given.

Medical professionals should consult the Professional Version at www.NaturalDatabase.com.

Drug Influences on Nutrient Levels and Depletion

Some medications can affect the levels of certain nutrients in the body. There is considerable interest in using nutritional supplements to counteract these possible drug-induced "nutrient depletions." The chart below shows the current scientific understanding of these relationships, and suggested actions.

DRUGS (Includes some examples of US and Canadian drug names.)	NUTRIENT DECREASED IN THE BODY (DEPLETED)	WHAT HAPPENS?	COMMENTS
ANTIMICROBIALS (DRUGS USED FOR INFECTIONS) (CONT.)			
Antibiotics - General	Biotin Dibencozide Folic Acid Pantothenic Acid (B5) Pyridoxine (B6) Riboflavin (B2) Thiamine (B1) Vitamin B12 Vitamin K	Friendly bacteria in the gut make a small amount of some vitamins. Antibiotics can kill these normal friendly bacteria in the gut as well as the harmful bacteria. Therefore, taking antibiotics might reduce levels of these vitamins in the body.	We get most of the vitamins we need from a healthy diet. The friendly bacteria in the gut only provide a small amount of vitamins. Supplements are usually not necessary.

You might need vitamin K supplements if you have low levels of vitamin K in your diet and need to take antibiotics for longer than 10 days. |
Cefditoren Pivoxil (*Spectracef*)	Acetyl-L-Carnitine L-Carnitine Propionyl-L-Carnitine	Taking cefditoren pivoxil for a long time might lead to carnitine deficiency.	If you need to take cefditoren pivoxil for a long time, you might need a carnitine supplement. But most people do not take this antibiotic long enough to need carnitine supplements.
Chloramphenicol (*Chloromycetin*)	Niacin / Niacinamide	Chloramphenicol might interfere with the actions of niacin or niacinamide in the body.	Chloramphenicol is usually used short-term. Short-term use is not likely to cause low levels of niacin or niacinamide.
Cycloserine (*Seromycin*)	Folic Acid	Cycloserine sometimes decreases folic acid levels. It might reduce folic acid absorption, or cause more to be broken down in the body.	If you eat a diet that is low in folic acid and take cycloserine, you might need a supplement. Talk to your healthcare provider before taking any supplements, especially in large amounts, if you are being treated for tuberculosis.
	Niacin / Niacinamide	Cycloserine might decrease the amount of niacin the body can make.	Niacin deficiency is not commonly caused by cycloserine unless you already do not get enough niacin in your diet, or you are also taking other medicines for tuberculosis. Talk to your healthcare provider before taking any supplements, especially in large amounts, if you are being treated for tuberculosis.
	Pyridoxine (B6)	Cycloserine can increase the breakdown of pyridoxine in the body and increase the loss of pyridoxine in the urine.	People taking cycloserine should take a pyridoxine supplement (150-300 mg daily). This will help prevent side effects such as nerve damage or seizures. Talk to your healthcare provider before taking any supplements, especially in large amounts, if you are being treated for tuberculosis.
Ethambutol (*Myambutol*)	Copper Zinc	Ethambutol binds copper and zinc and can remove them from some areas of the body.	Tell your healthcare provider if you have vision problems while taking ethambutol. This could be due to low copper and zinc levels in the eyes. There is not enough information to know if copper and zinc supplements are helpful. There is some concern that zinc supplements might make ethambutol less effective. Talk to your healthcare provider before taking any supplements, especially in large amounts, if you are being treated for tuberculosis.

Natural Medicines Comprehensive Database Consumer Version   (209) 472-2244

Drug Influences on Nutrient Levels and Depletion

Some medications can affect the levels of certain nutrients in the body. There is considerable interest in using nutritional supplements to counteract these possible drug-induced "nutrient depletions." The chart below shows the current scientific understanding of these relationships, and suggested actions.

DRUGS (Includes some examples of US and Canadian drug names.)	NUTRIENT DECREASED IN THE BODY (DEPLETED)	WHAT HAPPENS?	COMMENTS
ANTIMICROBIALS (DRUGS USED FOR INFECTIONS) (CONT.)			
Ethionamide (*Trecator-SC*)	Niacin / Niacinamide	Ethionamide might interfere with the ability of niacin to work in the body.	Deficiency is unlikely unless you don't get enough niacin in your diet, or you are also taking other medicines for tuberculosis. Talk to your healthcare provider before taking any supplements, especially in large amounts, if you are being treated for tuberculosis.
Fluconazole (*Diflucan*)	Potassium	Taking fluconazole might damage the kidneys in some people and increase the amount of potassium lost from the body in the urine.	If you need fluconazole for a long time your healthcare provider will check your potassium level. If your levels are too low, potassium can be given.
Foscarnet (*Foscavir*)	Magnesium	Foscarnet can decrease magnesium levels. It binds with magnesium and increases magnesium loss from the body in the urine.	Your healthcare provider will check your magnesium level if you take foscarnet. If your magnesium levels get too low, you might need to take a magnesium supplement.
Isoniazid (INH, *Laniazid*)	Pyridoxine (B6)	Isoniazid can increase the breakdown of pyridoxine in the body and increase the loss of pyridoxine in the urine. Low levels of pyridoxine can cause nerve damage.	Your healthcare provider may recommend a pyridoxine supplement, especially if you are taking a high dose of isoniazid. Talk to your healthcare provider before taking any supplements, especially in large amounts, if you are being treated for tuberculosis.
	Niacin / Niacinamide	Isoniazid might reduce how much niacin the body can make.	Niacin deficiency is not common unless you do not get enough niacin in your diet, or if you are also taking other medicines which interfere with niacin. Talk to your healthcare provider before taking any supplements, especially in large amounts, if you are being treated for tuberculosis.
Neomycin (*Mycifradin, Neo-Fradin*)	Beta-Carotene Dibencozide Vitamin A Vitamin B12	Large doses of neomycin can reduce the absorption of some vitamins and might cause a deficiency when taken for a long time.	Neomycin is usually used short-term. Short-term use is not likely to cause a deficiency in most people.
Penicillins: Carbenicillin (*Geocillin*), Mezlocillin (*Mezlin*), Penicillin G (*Pfizerpen*), Piperacillin (*Pipracil*), Ticarcillin (*Ticar*)	Potassium	The kidneys help balance sodium and potassium in the body. Some penicillins contain sodium. Taking penicillin with sodium can increase the amount of potassium lost from the body in the urine.	Your healthcare provider can check your potassium levels with a simple lab test. If your levels are low, you might need a potassium supplement or a different antibiotic.
Pentamidine (*NebuPent, Pentacarinat, Pentam 300*)	Folic Acid	The body converts folic acid from the diet to a form it can use. Pentamidine can prevent the body from converting folic acid in the diet to a form the body can use.	This is usually only a problem when pentamidine is given as an injection for a long time. Most people do not need folic acid supplements when taking pentamidine.
	Magnesium	Pentamidine can damage the kidneys and increase the amount of magnesium lost from the body in the urine.	Your healthcare provider will check your magnesium level. If your blood level is too low, magnesium can be given.
Pivampicillin (*Pondocillin*)	Acetyl-L-Carnitine L-Carnitine Propionyl-L-Carnitine	Taking pivampicillin for a long time might lead to carnitine deficiency.	If you need to take pivampicillin for a long time you might need a carnitine supplement. But most people do not take this antibiotic long enough to need a carnitine supplement.

Drug Influences on Nutrient Levels and Depletion

Some medications can affect the levels of certain nutrients in the body. There is considerable interest in using nutritional supplements to counteract these possible drug-induced "nutrient depletions." The chart below shows the current scientific understanding of these relationships, and suggested actions.

DRUGS (Includes some examples of US and Canadian drug names.)	NUTRIENT DECREASED IN THE BODY (DEPLETED)	WHAT HAPPENS?	COMMENTS
ANTIMICROBIALS (DRUGS USED FOR INFECTIONS) (CONT.)			
Pyrazinamide	Niacin / Niacinamide	Pyrazinamide might interfere with the ability of niacin to work in the body.	Niacin deficiency is unlikely unless you don't get enough niacin in your diet, or if you are also taking other medicines which interfere with niacin. Talk to your healthcare provider before taking any supplements, especially in large amounts, if you are being treated for tuberculosis.
Pyrimethamine (*Daraprim*)	Folic Acid	The body converts folic acid from the diet to an active form it can use. Pyrimethamine can decrease this change to the active form.	If you need large amounts of pyrimethamine, your healthcare provider may recommend that you take a special form of folic acid (called folinic acid or Leucovorin) to prevent folic acid deficiency. Avoid taking regular folic acid supplements because they can prevent pyrimethamine from working properly.
Tetracyclines: Doxycycline (*Doryx, Doxy Caps, Monodox, Periostat, Vibra-Tabs, Vibramycin*), Tetracycline (*Achromycin V*) Demeclocycline (*Declomycin*), Minocycline (*Dynacin*), Oxytetracycline (*Terramycin*), Erythromycin (*ERYC, Ery-Tab*)	Calcium Iron Magnesium Zinc	Tetracyclines can bind to these minerals in the gut. Taking tetracyclines at the same time as these minerals (in food, or as a supplement) can reduce the absorption of both the antibiotic and the mineral. However, the antibiotic doxycycline doesn't seem to affect zinc absorption.	Take these antibiotics 2 hours before, or 4-6 hours after anything containing these minerals. This will help prevent long-term deficiencies of the minerals and allow the antibiotic to be absorbed properly.
	Potassium	The kidneys balance potassium levels. Taking expired tetracycline antibiotics can damage the kidneys and increase the amount of potassium lost in the urine.	Don't take outdated or expired medications.
Rifampin (*Rifadin, Rimactane, Rofact*)	Vitamin D	Rifampin increases the breakdown of vitamin D.	Vitamin D deficiency is not common unless you need to take rifampin for more than one year, or if you don't get enough vitamin D in your diet. Your healthcare provider might recommend a vitamin D supplement. Talk to your healthcare provider before taking any supplements, especially in large amounts, if you are being treated for tuberculosis.
	Vitamin K	Rifampin might reduce vitamin K levels in some people. Rifampin might reduce the absorption of vitamin K from the gut, or decrease how well the body makes a usable form of vitamin K.	Most people do not need vitamin K supplements unless they have other problems, which also contribute to vitamin K deficiency such as a poor diet. Talk to your healthcare provider before taking any supplements, especially in large amounts, if you are being treated for tuberculosis.
Quinacrine (*Atarbrine*)	Riboflavin (B2)	The body converts riboflavin from the diet to an active form it can use. Quinacrine can decrease this change to the active form.	There is not enough information to know if this is a concern and if supplements are needed.

Medical professionals should consult the Professional Version at www.NaturalDatabase.com.

   Natural Medicines Comprehensive Database Consumer Version   (209) 472-2244

Drug Influences on Nutrient Levels and Depletion

Some medications can affect the levels of certain nutrients in the body. There is considerable interest in using nutritional supplements to counteract these possible drug-induced "nutrient depletions." The chart below shows the current scientific understanding of these relationships, and suggested actions.

DRUGS (Includes some examples of US and Canadian drug names.)	NUTRIENT DECREASED IN THE BODY (DEPLETED)	WHAT HAPPENS?	COMMENTS
ANTIMICROBIALS (DRUGS USED FOR INFECTIONS) (CONT.)			
Quinolones: Levofloxacin (*Levaquin*), Ciprofloxacin (*Cipro*), Gatifloxacin (*Tequin*), Lomefloxacin (*Maxaquin*), Moxifloxacin (*Avelox*), Norfloxacin (*Noroxin*), Ofloxacin (*Floxin*), Sparfloxacin (*Zagam*), Trovafloxacin (*Trovan*)	Calcium Iron Magnesium Zinc	Quinolones can bind these minerals in the gut. Taking these antibiotics at the same time as any of these minerals (in food, or as a supplement) can reduce the absorption of both the antibiotic and the mineral.	Take these antibiotics 2 hours before, or 4-6 hours after anything containing these minerals. This will prevent long-term deficiencies of the minerals and allow the antibiotic to be absorbed properly.
Zidovudine (AZT, *Retrovir*) Zidovudine / Lamivudine (*Combivir*)	Copper Dibencozide Vitamin B12 Zinc	Some people with HIV who take zidovudine can have low levels of copper, vitamin B12, and zinc. The reason is not clear.	There is not enough information to know if supplements are needed. Some research suggests that taking copper and zinc supplements could be harmful in some cases. Talk to your healthcare provider before taking any supplements, especially in large amounts, if you are being treated for HIV/AIDS.
CANCER DRUGS			
Aldesleukin (Interleukin-2, IL-2, *Proleukin*)	Magnesium	Aldesleukin might reduce magnesium levels in the blood. Aldesleukin causes magnesium to move from the blood to into the cells, but doesn't increase the amount lost from the body.	Taking a magnesium supplement is usually not needed. Magnesium blood levels return to normal when you finish taking aldesleukin.
Amifostine (*Ethyol*)	Magnesium	Amifostine increases the amount of magnesium lost from the body in the urine.	Magnesium levels usually return to normal within 24 hours after taking amifostine. Supplements are not necessary.
Busulfan (*Busulfex, Myleran*)	Vitamin E	Large doses of some drugs for cancer such as busulfan might reduce levels of vitamin E in the body. This probably happens because the body might use more vitamin E while taking this drug.	There is not enough information to know if vitamin E supplements are helpful.
Cisplatin (*Platinol-AQ*), Carboplatin (*Paraplatin*)	Magnesium	Cisplatin and carboplatin can damage the kidneys and increase the amount of magnesium lost from the body in the urine.	Your healthcare provider will check your magnesium level, especially when you need several courses of cisplatin or carboplatin. If your level is too low, magnesium can be given.
	Vitamin E	Large doses of some drugs used for cancer such as cisplatin or carboplatin may reduce levels of vitamin E. This probably happens because the body might use more vitamin E while taking this drug.	There is not enough information to know if vitamin E supplements are helpful.
	Zinc	Cisplatin increases the amount of zinc lost from the body in the urine.	Zinc levels usually return to normal within 24-48 hours after taking cisplatin. Supplements are usually not needed.
Cyclophosphamide (*Cytoxan, Neosar, Procytox*)	Vitamin E	Large amounts of some drugs used for cancer such as cyclophosphamide, may reduce levels of vitamin E in the body. This probably happens because the body might use more vitamin E while taking this.	There is not enough information to know if vitamin E supplements are helpful.

CONSUMER VERSION

Medical professionals should consult the Professional Version at www.NaturalDatabase.com.

Drug Influences on Nutrient Levels and Depletion

Some medications can affect the levels of certain nutrients in the body. There is considerable interest in using nutritional supplements to counteract these possible drug-induced "nutrient depletions." The chart below shows the current scientific understanding of these relationships, and suggested actions.

DRUGS (Includes some examples of US and Canadian drug names.)	NUTRIENT DECREASED IN THE BODY (DEPLETED)	WHAT HAPPENS?	COMMENTS
CANCER DRUGS (CONT.)			
Cytosine Arabinoside (Cytosar-U)	Vitamin E	Large amounts of some drugs used for cancer such as cytosine arabinoside may reduce the levels of vitamin E. This probably happens because the body might use more vitamin E while taking this drug.	There is not enough information to know if vitamin E supplements are helpful.
Doxorubicin (*Adriamycin, Rubex*) Liposomal Doxorubicin (*Doxil*)	Riboflavin (B2)	Doxorubicin might bind to riboflavin and increase the amount of riboflavin lost in the urine.	There is not enough information to know if riboflavin supplements are needed.
	Vitamin E	Large amounts of some drugs used for cancer such as doxorubicin may reduce the levels of vitamin E. This probably happens because the body might use more vitamin E while taking this drug.	There is not enough information to know if vitamin E supplements are helpful or if they reduce the effectiveness of doxorubicin.
Etoposide (*Etopophos, VePesid, Toposar*)	Vitamin E	Large doses of some drugs used for cancer such as etoposide may reduce levels of vitamin E in the body. This probably happens because the body might use more vitamin E while taking this drug.	There is not enough information to know if vitamin E supplements are helpful.
Fluorouracil (5-FU, *Adrucil*)	Niacin / Niacinamide	Fluorouracil might decrease the amount of niacin the body can make.	Supplements are only needed if you start to get symptoms of niacin deficiency.
	Thiamine (B1)	Fluorouracil might cause thiamine deficiency. It might decrease how well the body makes a form of thiamine that it can use or increase how fast the body breaks down thiamine.	There is not enough information to know if thiamine supplements are needed.
	Vitamin E	Large doses of some drugs used for cancer such as fluorouracil may reduce the levels of vitamin E. This probably happens because the body might use more vitamin E while taking this drug.	There is not enough information to know if vitamin E supplements are helpful.
Mercaptopurine (6-MP, *Purinethol*)	Niacin / Niacinamide	Mercaptopurine interferes with how well niacin works in the body.	A niacin supplement might be needed if you have to take high doses of mercaptopurine for long periods of time.
Methotrexate (*Folex, Rheumatrex*)	Vitamin E	Large doses of some drugs used for cancer such as methotrexate may reduce the levels of vitamin E. This probably happens because the body might use more vitamin E while taking this drug.	There is not enough information to know if vitamin E supplements are helpful.
	Folic Acid	Methotrexate prevents the body from turning folic acid into a form the body can use.	Folic acid supplements can interfere with how methotrexate treats cancer. If you are taking methotrexate for cancer, avoid folic acid supplements unless recommended by your healthcare provider.
Thiotepa (*Thioplex*)	Vitamin E	Large doses of some drugs used for cancer such as thiotepa may reduce the levels of vitamin E. This probably happens because the body might use more vitamin E while taking this drug.	There is not enough information to know if vitamin E supplements are helpful.

     Natural Medicines Comprehensive Database Consumer Version   (209) 472-2244

Drug Influences on Nutrient Levels and Depletion

Some medications can affect the levels of certain nutrients in the body. There is considerable interest in using nutritional supplements to counteract these possible drug-induced "nutrient depletions." The chart below shows the current scientific understanding of these relationships, and suggested actions.

DRUGS (Includes some examples of US and Canadian drug names.)	NUTRIENT DECREASED IN THE BODY (DEPLETED)	WHAT HAPPENS?	COMMENTS
DIABETES DRUGS			
Insulin	Magnesium	Insulin might increase how much magnesium your body loses in the urine.	There is not enough information to know if this is important. People with diabetes might already have low magnesium levels. Your healthcare provider can do a simple blood test to determine if you have low magnesium levels and if a magnesium supplement is needed.
Metformin (*Glucophage*)	Dibencozide Folic Acid Vitamin B12	Metformin can cause vitamin B12 deficiency and rarely folic acid deficiency. Metformin decreases the absorption of these vitamins.	Talk to your healthcare provider about having your vitamin B12 and folic acid levels checked, especially if you take metformin for several years. Also, try to eat a diet that is rich in vitamin B12 and folic acid.
	Thiamine (B1)	Metformin might block some of the actions of thiamine in the body. This might contribute to some side effects of metformin.	There is not enough information to know if this is a concern and if thiamine supplements are helpful.
ARTHRITIS & GOUT DRUGS			
Azathioprine (*Imuran*)	Niacin / Niacinamide	Azathioprine might decrease the activation of niacin and niacinamide in the body.	Niacin or niacinamide deficiency is rare. Supplements are usually not needed.
Colchicine	Beta-Carotene Dibencozide Vitamin B12	Colchicine can reduce absorption of these vitamins.	Taking colchicine in amounts less than 2 mg a day does not seem to cause deficiency of these vitamins. There is not enough information to know if supplements are needed when higher amounts of colchicine are taken.
Methotrexate (*Rheumatrex*)	Folic Acid	The body converts folic acid consumed in the diet to a form it can use. Methotrexate can decrease the body's ability to convert folic acid to this form.	Methotrexate is used in small amounts for conditions like rheumatoid arthritis (RA) and psoriasis. A folic acid supplement (1 mg daily) can help prevent side effects. Methotrexate is used in much larger amounts for cancer. If you are taking methotrexate for cancer, do not take a folic acid supplement unless recommended by your healthcare provider. Taking folic acid can decrease how methotrexate helps treat cancer.
Penicillamine (*Cuprimine, Depen*)	Copper Iron Magnesium Zinc	Penicillamine binds to copper, iron, magnesium, and zinc in the gut, reducing their absorption.	Supplements are probably not necessary for most people. If your healthcare provider recommends supplements of any of these minerals, take them at least 2 hours before or 2 hours after your penicillamine.
	Pyridoxine (B6)	Penicillamine can bind to and block the effects of pyridoxine in the body. Blocking the effects of pyridoxine in the body can lead to nerve problems such as tingling and numbness.	If you are taking penicillamine for a condition called Wilson's Disease, it is usually recommended that you also take pyridoxine 25 mg daily. If you are taking penicillamine for other conditions you should tell your healthcare provider if you develop any signs of nerve problems, such as numbness or tingling. If this happens you might need to take a pyridoxine supplement.

Drug Influences on Nutrient Levels and Depletion

Some medications can affect the levels of certain nutrients in the body. There is considerable interest in using nutritional supplements to counteract these possible drug-induced "nutrient depletions." The chart below shows the current scientific understanding of these relationships, and suggested actions.

DRUGS (Includes some examples of US and Canadian drug names.)	NUTRIENT DECREASED IN THE BODY (DEPLETED)	WHAT HAPPENS?	COMMENTS
CARDIOVASCULAR DRUGS (HEART MEDICINES)			
ANTIHYPERTENSIVES (BLOOD PRESSURE MEDICINES)			
Hydralazine (*Apresoline*)	Pyridoxine (B6)	Hydralazine can bind to and block the effects of pyridoxine in the body. Blocking the effects of pyridoxine in the body can lead to nerve problems such as tingling and numbness.	Tell your healthcare provider if you develop any signs of nerve problems, such as numbness or tingling. This may be a sign that you need to take a pyridoxine supplement.
Captopril (*Capoten*)	Zinc	Captopril may bind zinc and increase the amount lost from the body in the urine.	If you take more than 50 mg of captopril three times a day for a long time you might need a zinc supplement. Changes in your sense of taste might be a sign that you have a low zinc level.
CARDIAC GLYCOSIDES (HEART MEDICINES)			
Digoxin (*Lanoxicaps, Lanoxin*)	Magnesium	Digoxin increases the amount of magnesium lost in the urine.	Your healthcare provider will check your magnesium level with a simple blood test. If your level is too low you might need to take a supplement.
CHOLESTEROL-LOWERING DRUGS			
"Statins" (HMG CoA Reductase Inhibitors): Atorvastatin (*Lipitor*), Fluvastatin (*Lescol*), Lovastatin (*Mevacor*), Pravastatin (*Pravachol*), Rosuvastatin (*Crestor*), Simvastatin (*Zocor*)	Coenzyme Q-10	Drugs called "Statins" can lower blood levels of coenzyme Q-10 by blocking how much coenzyme Q-10 the body makes.	It seems that the "statins" only reduce levels of coenzyme Q-10 in the blood and not in other parts of the body. It is not known if this is important or if taking coenzyme Q-10 supplements is useful.
Drugs that bind bile (also called bile acid sequestrants): Cholestyramine (*LoCHOLEST, Questran*), Colestipol (*Colestid*)	Beta-Carotene Dibencozide Folic Acid Iron Vitamin A Vitamin B12 Vitamin D Vitamin E Vitamin K	Drugs that bind bile can also bind these vitamins and minerals in the gut and reduce the amount absorbed.	Deficiencies are rare. Supplements probably are not necessary unless you take large amounts of these medications for several years, or if you have an intestinal disease and also take these medications. If you take supplements of any of these vitamins or minerals, make sure the you take them at least 4 hours before or 4 hours after you take cholestyramine or colestipol.
Gemfibrozil (*Gen-Fibro, Lopid*)	Vitamin E	Gemfibrozil might reduce levels of vitamin E in the body.	There is not enough information to know if this occurs in everyone who takes gemfibrozil or if this interaction is a big concern.
DIURETICS ("WATER PILLS")			
Loop Diuretics: Bumetanide (*Bumex*), Ethacrynic acid (*Edecrin*), Furosemide (*Lasix, Uritol*), Torsemide (*Demadex*)	Calcium Magnesium Potassium	These diuretics increase how much calcium, magnesium, and potassium is lost from the body in the urine.	Your healthcare provider will check your calcium, magnesium, and potassium levels. If they get too low you may need to take supplements. This is more likely to occur if you take large amounts of these diuretics for long periods of time.
	Folic Acid	Diuretics might increase the loss of folic acid from the body in the urine.	There is not enough information to know if this is an important concern.
	Thiamine (B1)	Diuretics can increase the loss of thiamine from the body in the urine.	People over 60 years old who take large amounts of diuretics for long periods of time, and eat a poor diet might develop thiamine deficiency. Some people in this group have found thiamine supplements helpful, while others have not.

Drug Influences on Nutrient Levels and Depletion

Some medications can affect the levels of certain nutrients in the body. There is considerable interest in using nutritional supplements to counteract these possible drug-induced "nutrient depletions." The chart below shows the current scientific understanding of these relationships, and suggested actions.

DRUGS (Includes some examples of US and Canadian drug names.)	NUTRIENT DECREASED IN THE BODY (DEPLETED)	WHAT HAPPENS?	COMMENTS
CARDIOVASCULAR DRUGS (HEART MEDICINES)(CONT.)			
DIURETICS ("WATER PILLS")(CONT.)			
Thiazide diuretics: Bendroflumethiazide (*Naturetin*), Benzthiazide (*Exna*), Chlorothiazide (*Diuril*), Chlorthalidone (*Hygroton, Thalitone, Uridon*), Hydrochlorothiazide (*Esidrix, HydroDIURIL, Oretic*), Hydroflumethiazide (*Diucardin, Saluron*), Indapamide (*Lozide, Lozol*), Methyclothiazide (*Aquatensen, Enduron*), Metolazone (*Mykrox, Zaroxolyn*), Polythiazide (*Renese*), Quinethazone (*Hydromox*), Trichlormethiazide (*Metahydrin, Naqua, Trichlorex*)	Magnesium Potassium Zinc	Thiazide diuretics increase the loss of magnesium, potassium, and zinc from the body in the urine.	Your healthcare provider will check your magnesium, potassium, and zinc levels. If they get too low you may need to take supplements. This is more likely if you take large amounts of these diuretics for long periods of time.
	Folic Acid	Diuretics might increase the loss of folic acid from the body in the urine.	There is not enough information to know if this is an important concern.
	Thiamine (B1)	Diuretics can increase the loss of thiamine from the body in the urine.	People over 60 years old who take large amounts of diuretics for long periods of time and have poor diets might develop thiamine deficiency. Some people in this group have found thiamine supplements helpful, while others have not
Potassium-sparing diuretic: Triamterene (*Dyrenium*)	Folic Acid	Triamterene prevents the body from turning folic acid into a form it can use.	If you take triamterene for a long period of time and do not get plenty of folic acid in your diet, you may need to take a folic acid supplement.
CENTRAL NERVOUS SYSTEM DRUGS			
ANTICONVULSANTS (SEIZURE MEDICATIONS)			
Carbamazepine (*Atretol, Epitol, Tegretol*)	Biotin	Carbamazepine might reduce how much biotin the body can absorb. Carbamazepine can also increase how fast the body gets rid of biotin.	There is not enough information to know if this is an important concern or if biotin supplements are needed.
	Acetyl-L-Carnitine L-Carnitine Propionyl-L-Carnitine	Carbamazepine might reduce levels of carnitine in the body.	There is not enough information to know if this is an important concern or if carnitine supplements are needed.
	Folic Acid	Carbamazepine might reduce the amount of folic acid the body can absorb. Carbamazepine also increases how fast the body gets rid of folic acid.	Supplements are probably not necessary. Consult with your healthcare provider before you begin taking folic acid supplements, because they might increase the chance of having a seizure if you are taking carbamazepine.
	Calcium Vitamin D	The body uses vitamin D to help absorb calcium. Carbamazepine can reduce vitamin D levels, which might reduce calcium absorption.	If you take carbamazepine for 6 months or longer, you might need a calcium and vitamin D supplement.
	Vitamin K	Some children who take carbamazepine have low levels of vitamin E, possibly due to increased use of vitamin E in the body.	There is not enough information to know if this is a concern and if supplements would be helpful.
	Vitamin E	Phenytoin may reduce how much biotin the body absorbs. Phenytoin also increases how fast the body gets rid of biotin.	There is not enough information to know if this is an important concern or if biotin supplements are needed.

Medical professionals should consult the Professional Version at www.NaturalDatabase.com.

Drug Influences on Nutrient Levels and Depletion

Some medications can affect the levels of certain nutrients in the body. There is considerable interest in using nutritional supplements to counteract these possible drug-induced "nutrient depletions." The chart below shows the current scientific understanding of these relationships, and suggested actions.

Medical professionals should consult the Professional Version at www.NaturalDatabase.com.

DRUGS (Includes some examples of US and Canadian drug names.)	NUTRIENT DECREASED IN THE BODY (DEPLETED)	WHAT HAPPENS?	COMMENTS
CENTRAL NERVOUS SYSTEM DRUGS (CONT.)			
ANTICONVULSANTS (SEIZURE MEDICATIONS)(CONT.)			
Phenytoin (*Dilantin*), Fosphenytoin (*Cerebyx*)	Biotin	Phenytoin may reduce how much biotin the body absorbs. Phenytoin also increases how fast the body gets rid of biotin.	There is not enough information to know if this is an important concern or if biotin supplements are needed
	Folic Acid	Phenytoin can reduce folic acid levels in the body. Phenytoin may reduce how much folic acid the body absorbs. Phenytoin also increases how fast the body gets rid of folic acid.	Symptoms of folic acid deficiency sometimes occur in people who take phenytoin. However, you should consult your healthcare provider before taking folic acid supplements because they might increase the risk of having a seizure if you take phenytoin.
	Acetyl-L-Carnitine L-Carnitine Propionyl-L-Carnitine	Phenytoin may reduce levels of carnitine in the body.	There is not enough information to know if this is an important concern or if carnitine supplements are needed.
	Niacin / Niacinamide	Phenytoin might reduce niacin and niacinamide levels.	Niacin / niacinamide deficiency rarely occurs in people who take phenytoin. Supplements are usually not needed.
	Thiamine (B1)	Phenytoin might reduce thiamine levels.	There is not enough information to know if this is an important concern or if thiamine supplements are needed.
	Dibencozide Vitamin B12	Phenytoin decreases how much vitamin B12 the body can absorb.	Make sure you get enough vitamin B12 in your diet. If you develop symptoms of anemia such as feeling tired all the time, shortness of breath, or pale skin and nails your vitamin B12 levels should be checked to see if you need a supplement.
	Calcium Vitamin D	The body uses vitamin D to help absorb calcium. Phenytoin can reduce vitamin D levels, which might reduce calcium absorption.	If you take phenytoin for 6 months or longer you may need a calcium and vitamin D supplement.
	Vitamin E	Some children who take phenytoin have low levels of vitamin E, possibly due to increased use of vitamin E in the body.	There is not enough information to know if this is an important concern or if supplements would be helpful.
	Vitamin K	Phenytoin can increase how fast the body gets rid of vitamin K.	This isn't likely to be a problem in most people. Pregnant women who take phenytoin usually need to take a vitamin K supplement during the last month of pregnancy. The newborn baby will need a vitamin K shot immediately after birth.
	Zinc	Phenytoin can bind to zinc in the gut and might reduce how much the body absorbs.	This isn't likely to be an important concern. Supplements are probably not necessary.

 Natural Medicines Comprehensive Database Consumer Version (209) 472-2244

Drug Influences on Nutrient Levels and Depletion

Some medications can affect the levels of certain nutrients in the body. There is considerable interest in using nutritional supplements to counteract these possible drug-induced "nutrient depletions." The chart below shows the current scientific understanding of these relationships, and suggested actions.

DRUGS (Includes some examples of US and Canadian drug names.)	NUTRIENT DECREASED IN THE BODY (DEPLETED)	WHAT HAPPENS?	COMMENTS
CENTRAL NERVOUS SYSTEM DRUGS (CONT.)			
ANTICONVULSANTS (SEIZURE MEDICATIONS)(CONT.)			
Phenobarbital (*Ancalixir, Luminal, Solfoton*) Primidone (*Mysoline, Sertan*)	Biotin	Phenobarbital and primidone may reduce absorption of biotin, and increase how fast the body gets rid biotin.	There is not enough information to know if this is an important concern or if biotin supplements are needed.
	Folic Acid	Phenobarbital and primidone can reduce folic acid levels. These drugs might decrease how much folic acid the body can absorb, and increase how fast the body gets rid of folic acid.	Symptoms of folic acid deficiency sometimes occur in people who take phenobarbital or primidone. You should consult your healthcare provider before taking folic acid supplements because they can increase the chance of having a seizure if you take these drugs.
	Dibencozide Vitamin B12	Phenobarbital reduces absorption of vitamin B12.	Make sure you get enough vitamin B12 in your diet. If you develop symptoms of anemia such as feeling tired all the time, shortness of breath, and pale skin and nails your vitamin B12 levels should be checked to see if you need a supplement.
	Acetyl-L-Carnitine L-Carnitine Propionyl-L-Carnitine	Phenobarbital may reduce levels of carnitine in the body.	There is not enough information to know if this is an important concern or if carnitine supplements are needed.
	Vitamin E	Some children who take phenobarbital or primidone have low levels of vitamin E, possibly due to increased use of vitamin E in the body.	There is not enough information to know if this is an important concern or if supplements would be helpful.
	Calcium Vitamin D	The body uses vitamin D to help absorb calcium. Phenobarbital and primidone can reduce vitamin D levels, which can reduce calcium absorption.	If you take phenobarbital or primidone for 6 months or longer you may need a calcium and vitamin D supplement.
	Vitamin K	Phenobarbital and primidone can increase the breakdown of vitamin K in the body.	This isn't likely to be a problem in most people. Pregnant women who take phenobarbital or primidone usually need to take a vitamin K supplement during the last month of pregnancy. The baby will need a vitamin K shot immediately after birth.
Valproic Acid (*Depakene, Deproic*)	Folic Acid	Valproic acid may reduce levels of folic acid, but it is not clear how this occurs.	This isn't likely to be a problem in most people. Supplements probably are not necessary. You should talk to your healthcare provider before taking folic acid supplements because they can increase the risk of seizures if you take valproic aid.
	Acetyl-L-Carnitine L-Carnitine Propionyl-L-Carnitine	Valproic acid reduces levels of carnitine. It interferes with the production and breakdown of carnitine in the body.	Most people probably get enough carnitine from food and don't need carnitine supplements. Some people who are at risk for certain side effects from valproic acid, such as liver problems, might need a carnitine supplement. Discuss this with your healthcare provider.
	Niacin / Niacinamide	Niacin / niacinamide deficiency has been reported in people who take valproic acid.	Deficiency seems to be rare and most people do not need to take niacin supplements
	Zinc	Valproic acid might bind with zinc in the gut and reduce how much zinc the body absorbs.	Deficiency seems to be rare and most people do not need to take zinc supplements.

Drug Influences on Nutrient Levels and Depletion

Some medications can affect the levels of certain nutrients in the body. There is considerable interest in using nutritional supplements to counteract these possible drug-induced "nutrient depletions." The chart below shows the current scientific understanding of these relationships, and suggested actions.

Medical professionals should consult the Professional Version at www.NaturalDatabase.com.

DRUGS (Includes some examples of US and Canadian drug names.)	NUTRIENT DECREASED IN THE BODY (DEPLETED)	WHAT HAPPENS?	COMMENTS
CENTRAL NERVOUS SYSTEM DRUGS (CONT.)			
DOPAMINE AGONISTS (PARKINSON'S DISEASE MEDICINES)			
Levodopa (*Laradopa*)	Potassium	Taking levodopa increases potassium loss from the body in the urine.	Most people who take levodopa also take carbidopa (e.g., *Sinemet*), which prevents this loss of potassium. So this is probably not a big concern.
Levodopa / Carbidopa (*Sinemet*)	Niacin / Niacinamide	Carbidopa might reduce how much niacin the body can make.	Deficiency is unlikely and supplements do not seem to be necessary.
GASTROINTESTINAL MEDICINES			
ANTACIDS			
Aluminum Salts (*Amphojel, Alternajel, Basaljel*, etc), Magnesium Salts (*Mag-Ox, Milk of Magnesia*, etc) Aluminum Salt/Magnesium Salt mixtures (*Maalox*, etc)	Calcium Phosphate Salts	Aluminum salts bind phosphate and reduce the amount the body can absorb. Low phosphate levels in the body increase calcium loss from the bones into the urine .	Most people should avoid taking large amounts of aluminum salts for a long time. But some people with kidney problems have high phosphate levels and need to take aluminum salts for a long time to reduce phosphate.
	Chromium	Antacids that contain aluminum salts might decrease how much chromium the body absorbs.	This is probably not an important concern and supplements are not needed.
	Folic Acid	Antacids that contain aluminum salts can decrease how much folic acid the body absorbs.	This is only likely to be a concern if you take large amounts of antacids for a long time and do not get enough folic acid from your diet.
	Iron	Antacids can decrease how much iron the body absorbs.	This is not likely to cause iron deficiency in most people.
GASTROINTESTINAL ANTI-INFLAMMATORY DRUGS			
Sulfasalazine (*Azulfidine, Salazopyrin*)	Folic Acid	Sulfasalazine can decrease how much folic acid the body can absorb. It can also damage red blood cells and increase the need for folic acid to make new blood cells.	If you take more than 2 grams of sulfasalazine a day for a long time or if you have signs of anemia such as being tired all the time, shortness of breath, and pale nails and skin, you may need a folic acid supplement. Talk to your healthcare provider if you need to take sulfasalazine for a long time. A simple blood test can check for low folic acid levels.
H2-BLOCKERS, PROTON PUMP INHIBITORS (DRUGS THAT DECREASE STOMACH ACID)			
H2-blockers: Cimetidine (*Tagamet*), Famotidine (*Pepcid*), Nizatidine (*Axid*), Ranitidine (*Zantac*) Proton Pump Inhibitors (PPIs): Lansoprazole (*Prevacid*), Omeprazole (*Losec, Prilosec*), Rabeprazole (*AcipHex*), Pantoprazole (*Pantoloc, Protonix*)	Calcium	H2-blockers and PPIs can decrease how much calcium the body can absorb, especially from some supplements.	These drugs do not seem to cause calcium deficiency.
	Chromium Folic Acid	H2-blockers and PPIs might decrease how much chromium and folic acid the body can absorb.	This is unlikely to cause a deficiency unless your diet is very low in chromium and folic acid.
	Dibencozide Iron Vitamin B12	H2-blockers and PPIs can decrease how much iron and vitamin B12 the body can absorb.	Deficiency is unlikely if you get enough iron and vitamin B12 from your diet. If you take these drugs regularly for several years, watch for signs of anemia such as being very tired, shortness of breath, and pale skin and nails. Your healthcare provider can run simple lab tests to see if you have low levels of iron or vitamin B12.

Drug Influences on Nutrient Levels and Depletion

Some medications can affect the levels of certain nutrients in the body. There is considerable interest in using nutritional supplements to counteract these possible drug-induced "nutrient depletions." The chart below shows the current scientific understanding of these relationships, and suggested actions.

DRUGS (Includes some examples of US and Canadian drug names.)	NUTRIENT DECREASED IN THE BODY (DEPLETED)	WHAT HAPPENS?	COMMENTS
GASTROINTESTINAL MEDICINES (CONT.)			
LAXATIVES			
Mineral Oil	Beta-Carotene Calcium Vitamins A, D, E, K	Mineral oil interferes with absorption of beta-carotene, calcium, and vitamins A, D, E, and K.	Occasional use of mineral oil is unlikely to cause deficiencies. Avoid large amounts or prolonged use of mineral oil.
Sodium Phosphates (*Fleet Phospho-Soda*)	Magnesium Potassium	Sodium phosphates can cause excessive loss of magnesium and potassium from the body.	Avoid large amounts or frequent use of sodium phosphates to treat constipation. The chance of problems due to loss of magnesium and potassium is increased in elderly people and those with other health problems.
Stimulant laxatives: Senna (*Senexon, Senolax, Senokot, Senna-Gen, SenokotXTRA, Dr. Caldwell Senna, Fletcher's Castoria*), Bisacodyl tablets (*Biscolax, Correctol, Dulcolax, Feen-A-Mint, Fleet Laxative*)	Calcium Potassium Vitamin D	Stimulant laxatives can reduce absorption of calcium, potassium, and vitamin D.	Stimulant laxatives should be taken only for a short time.
PANCREATIC ENZYMES			
Pancreatin (*Donnazyme*) Pancrelipase (*Cotazym, Creon, Pancrease, Ultrase, Viokase*)	Folic Acid Iron	Pancreatic enzymes may bind with folic acid and iron, reducing how much the body can absorb.	If you need to take pancreatic enzymes for a long time talk to your healthcare provider about blood tests to check for deficiencies.
STEROIDS			
Corticosteroids: Prednisone (*Deltasone, Meticorten, Orasone, Panasol-S*) Dexamethasone (*Decadron, Dexameth, Dexone, Hexadrol*) Cortisone (*Cortone*) Hydrocortisone [Cortisol] (*Cortef, Hydrocortone*) Prednisolone (*Delta-Cortef, Pediapred, Prelone*) Triamcinolone (*Aristocort, Kenacort, Triamolone*) Methylprednisolone (*Medro, Solu-Medrol*) Betamethasone (*Celestone*)	Calcium Vitamin D	Corticosteroids reduce calcium absorption and increase calcium loss from the body in the urine.	Taking corticosteroids for long periods of time can cause bone problems, including osteoporosis. If you need to take corticosteroids on a daily basis talk with your healthcare provider about taking calcium and vitamin D supplements.
	Chromium	Corticosteroids can increase chromium loss from the body in the urine.	There is not enough information to know if this is an important concern or if supplements would be helpful.
	Magnesium	Taking corticosteroids for a long time seems to increase magnesium loss from the body in the urine.	Magnesium supplements probably are not necessary for most people.
	Potassium	Some corticosteroids increase the amount of potassium lost from the body in the urine.	If you need to take corticosteroids for a long time, talk to your healthcare provider about having your potassium levels checked.
	Strontium	Corticosteroids may increase strontium loss from the body in the urine.	There is not enough information to know if this is an important concern or if supplements are helpful.
	Zinc	Corticosteroids might cause zinc to move out of the blood and into the tissues. Corticosteroids might also increase the loss of zinc from the body in the urine.	Zinc supplements are probably not necessary for most people.

Medical professionals should consult the Professional Version at www.NaturalDatabase.com.

Drug Influences on Nutrient Levels and Depletion

Some medications can affect the levels of certain nutrients in the body. There is considerable interest in using nutritional supplements to counteract these possible drug-induced "nutrient depletions." The chart below shows the current scientific understanding of these relationships, and suggested actions.

Medical professionals should consult the Professional Version at www.NaturalDatabase.com.

DRUGS (Includes some examples of US and Canadian drug names.)	NUTRIENT DECREASED IN THE BODY (DEPLETED)	WHAT HAPPENS?	COMMENTS
HORMONES			
Estrogens: (*Alora, Cenestin, Climara, Estinyl, Estrace, Estraderm, Estralab, FemPatch, Menest, Ogen, Premarin, Prephase, Prempro, Vivelle*) Estrogen-containing oral contraceptives ("the pill")	Folic Acid	Estrogens may lower absorption of folic acid and increase folic acid loss from the body.	Most women taking estrogens probably do not need to take folic acid supplements.
	Magnesium	Estrogens can cause low levels of magnesium in the blood, possibly by causing magnesium to move into the tissues.	Supplements are not needed for most people. But this might cause problems if you eat a diet that is low in magnesium, or if you are at risk for low magnesium levels (hypomagnesemia). Ask your healthcare provider if you need to have your magnesium levels checked.
	Pyridoxine (B6)	Estrogens can interfere with how the body uses pyridoxine.	Some people think some of the side effects of oral contraceptives might be due to low pyridoxine levels. However, there is no proof that taking pyridoxine supplements help. Make sure you get plenty of pyridoxine in your diet.
	Riboflavin (B2)	Estrogens might reduce the absorption of riboflavin or interfere with how well the body converts it to a form that the body can use.	Lower riboflavin levels are found in women with a poor diet who and who take older, high-dose oral contraceptives. But most women taking oral contraceptives or other estrogens do not need riboflavin supplements.
	Vitamin A	The liver stores vitamin A. Estrogens might remove vitamin A from storage in the liver and result in increased amounts of vitamin A in the blood.	There is not enough information to know if low vitamin A levels in the liver are a big concern. Taking vitamin A supplements do not seem to be necessary.
	Dibencozide Vitamin B12	Estrogens might reduce vitamin B12 levels in the blood, but the vitamin B12 seems to move into the tissues and is not lost from the body.	Vitamin B12 supplements are not necessary.
	Vitamin C	Estrogens might reduce absorption of vitamin C or increase its breakdown in to body.	Vitamin C depletion is unlikely unless your intake of vitamin C from food is very low.
	Zinc	Estrogens might lower the amount of zinc carried in the blood and increase use of zinc in the tissues.	There is usually no increased loss of zinc from the body while taking estrogens, so supplements are probably not necessary.
Thyroid hormones: Levothyroxine (*Levothroid, Levoxyl, Synthroid, Unithroid*), Thyroid desiccated (*Armour Thyroid*), Liothyronine sodium (*Cytomel*)	Calcium	Thyroid hormones can cause calcium loss from the bones, which increases the loss of calcium from the body into urine.	This is more likely to be a problem when large amounts of thyroid hormone are taken. Have your thyroid function checked regularly to make sure you are taking the right amount of thyroid hormone. Make sure you are getting the recommended amounts of calcium and vitamin D from your food or from supplements. But if you take supplements, don't take them at the same time of day as your thyroid hormone.

 Natural Medicines Comprehensive Database Consumer Version (209) 472-2244

Drug Influences on Nutrient Levels and Depletion

Some medications can affect the levels of certain nutrients in the body. There is considerable interest in using nutritional supplements to counteract these possible drug-induced "nutrient depletions." The chart below shows the current scientific understanding of these relationships, and suggested actions.

DRUGS (Includes some examples of US and Canadian drug names.)	NUTRIENT DECREASED IN THE BODY (DEPLETED)	WHAT HAPPENS?	COMMENTS
RESPIRATORY DRUGS			
Beta-2-Agonists: Albuterol (salbutamol, *Proventil*, *Ventolin*), Bitolterol (*Tornalate*), Isoetharine (*Bronkometer*), Levalbuterol (*Xopenex*), Metaproterenol (*Alupent*), Pirbuterol (*Maxair*), Salmeterol (*Serevent*), Terbutaline (*Brethaire*)	Magnesium Potassium	Some drugs that help open up airways can cause magnesium and potassium to move out of the blood and into the tissues. They might also slightly increase loss of magnesium from the body into the urine.	This is most likely to be a problem when high doses of these medicines are needed for severe asthma attacks. Your healthcare provider will check your magnesium and potassium levels and give you supplements if needed.
Aminophylline (*Phyllocontin*), Oxtriphylline (*Choledyl SA*), Dyphylline (*Lufyllin*) Theophylline (*Slobid*, *Theo-SR*, *Theo-Dur*, *Theolair*)	Potassium	Theophylline and similar medicines can reduce potassium levels in the blood, possibly by increasing transfer of potassium to the tissues.	This is most likely to be a problem with large amounts of these medicines. Talk to your healthcare provider about having potassium level checked.
	Pyridoxine (B6)	Theophylline and similar medicines can decrease how well the body makes pyridoxine into a form that the body can use.	Low levels of pyridoxine might contribute to some of the side effects of these medicines. However, there is no proof that taking pyridoxine supplements helps.
MISCELLANEOUS DRUGS			
Cyclosporine (*Neoral*, *Sandimmune*)	Magnesium	The kidneys help control magnesium in the body. Cyclosporine can damage the kidneys and cause the body to lose magnesium in the urine.	Your healthcare provider will check your magnesium level. If your level is too low, you might need a supplement.
Deferoxamine (*Desferal*)	Zinc	Deferoxamine can increase the loss of zinc from the body in the urine	Zinc deficiency is rare and most people do not need zinc supplements.
Disulfuram (*Antabuse*)	Zinc	Disulfuram may bind zinc in the gut and decrease how much the body can absorb.	There is not enough information to know if this is an important concern or if supplements are needed.
EDTA	Zinc	EDTA combines with zinc and can prevent zinc from being absorbed.	If you take several courses of EDTA chelation therapy, discuss with your healthcare provider whether you need zinc supplements. Some people may have symptoms of a zinc deficiency with EDTA treatment. There is concern that zinc supplements might make EDTA less effective. Talk to your healthcare provider before taking zinc if you need to take EDTA.
Orlistat (*Xenical*)	Beta-Carotene Vitamin A Vitamin D Vitamin E Vitamin K	Orlistat can reduce the absorption of many vitamins.	If you take orlistat you should also take a multivitamin supplement. Make sure you take orlistat at least 2 hours before or 2 hours after the multivitamin.
Sunscreens	Vitamin D	Sunscreen can prevent the body from using sunlight to make active vitamin D.	This is not an important concern for most people. Make sure you get the recommended amount of vitamin D in your diet every day.
Tacrolimus (*Prograf*)	Magnesium	Tacrolimus increases the loss of magnesium from the body in the urine.	Your healthcare provider will check your magnesium levels. People taking tacrolimus commonly need magnesium supplements.

CONSUMER VERSION

Medical professionals should consult the Professional Version at www.NaturalDatabase.com.

5-HTP

What other names is the product known by?
5-hydroxytryptophan, L-5 HTP, L-5 hydroxytryptophan, Oxitriptan.

What is it?
5-HTP (5-Hydroxytryptophan) is a chemical by-product of the protein building block L-tryptophan. It is also produced commercially from the seeds of an African plant (Griffonia simplicfolia).

Is it Effective?
The effectiveness ratings for **5-HTP** are as follows:
Possibly Effective for... Depression • Fibromyalgia.
Possibly Ineffective for... Treating tension headaches.
Insufficient Evidence to Rate Effectiveness for... Alzheimer's disease, premenstrual syndrome (PMS), premenstrual dysphoric disorder (PMDD), weight loss and obesity, attention deficit-hyperactivity disorder (ADHD), sleep disorders, anxiety, and other conditions.

How does it work?
5-HTP works by increasing the production of the chemical serotonin. Serotonin can affect sleep, appetite, temperature, sexual behavior, and pain sensation.

Are there safety concerns?
5-HTP might be unsafe for use. There is concern that it can cause a serious side effect called eosinophilia myalgia syndrome. Some people think this side effect is only caused by a contaminant in some 5-HTP products. But there is not enough scientific evidence to know if it is caused by 5-HTP, a contaminant, or some other factor. Until more is known, 5-HTP should be avoided.

Other potential side effects of 5-HTP include heartburn, stomach pain, nausea, vomiting, diarrhea, drowsiness, sexual problems, and muscle problems.

Do not take 5-HTP if: You are pregnant or breast-feeding. • You have a condition called Down syndrome.

Are there any interactions with medications?
Carbidopa (Lodosyn). 5-HTP can affect the brain. Carbidopa (Lodosyn) can also affect the brain. Taking 5-HTP along with carbidopa can increase the risk of serious side effects including rapid speech, anxiety, aggressiveness, and others.

Dextromethorphan (Robitussin DM, and others). 5-HTP can affect a brain chemical called serotonin. Dextromethorphan (Robitussin DM, others) can also affect serotonin. Taking 5-HTP along with dextromethorphan (Robitussin DM, others) might cause too much serotonin in the brain and serious side effects including heart problems, shivering, and anxiety. Do not take 5-HTP if you are taking dextromethorphan (Robitussin DM, and others).

Medications for depression (Antidepressant drugs). 5-HTP increases a brain chemical called serotonin. Some medications for depression also increase serotonin. Taking 5-HTP along with these medications for depression might increase serotonin too much and cause serious side effects including heart problems, shivering, and anxiety. Do not take 5-HTP if you are taking medications for depression. Some of these medications for depression include fluoxetine (Prozac), paroxetine (Paxil), sertraline (Zoloft), amitriptyline (Elavil), clomipramine (Anafranil), imipramine (Tofranil), and others.

Medications for depression (MAOIs). 5-HTP increases a chemical in the brain. This chemical is called serotonin. Some medications used for depression also increase serotonin. Taking 5-HTP with these medications used for depression might cause there to be too much serotonin. This could cause serious side effects including heart problems, shivering, and anxiety. Some of these medications used for depression include phenelzine (Nardil), tranylcypromine (Parnate), and others.

Meperidine (Demerol). 5-HTP increases a chemical in the brain called serotonin. Meperidine (Demerol) can also increase serotonin in the brain. Taking 5-HTP along with meperidine (Demerol) might cause too much serotonin in the brain and serious side effects including heart problems, shivering, and anxiety.

Pentazocine (Talwin). 5-HTP increases a brain chemical called serotonin. Pentazocine (Talwin) also increases serotonin. Taking 5-HTP along with pentazocine (Talwin) might increase serotonin too much. This could cause serious side effects including heart problems, shivering, and anxiety. Do not take 5-HTP if you are taking pentazocine (Talwin).

Tramadol (Ultram). Tramadol (Ultram) can affect a chemical in the brain called serotonin. 5-HTP can also affect serotonin. Taking 5-HTP along with tramadol (Ultram) might cause too much serotonin in the brain and side effects including confusion, shivering, stiff muscles, and others.

7-ALPHA-HYDROXY-DHEA

What other names is the product known by?

7-alpha-hydroxy-dehydroepiandrosterone, 7-alpha-hydroxy-DHEA, 7-alpha-OH-DHEA, 7- hydroxy-dehydroepiandrosterone, 7-hydroxy DHEA, 7-OH-DHEA.

What is it?

7-alpha-hydroxy-DHEA is a by-product of dehydroepiandrosterone (DHEA) that is formed in the body. DHEA is a "parent hormone" produced by glands near the kidneys.

Is it Effective?

The effectiveness ratings for **7-ALPHA-HYDROXY-DHEA** are as follows:
Insufficient Evidence to Rate Effectiveness for... Weight loss and obesity, increasing lean body mass, building muscle, increasing immune system activity, boosting memory, and aging.

How does it work?

There isn't enough information to know how 7-alpha-hydroxy-DHEA might work.

Are there safety concerns?

There isn't enough information available to know if 7-alpha-hydroxy-DHEA is safe.

Do not use 7-alpha-hydroxy-DHEA if: You are pregnant or breast-feeding.

Are there any interactions with medications?

It is not known if 7-alpha-hydroxy-DHEA interacts with any medicines.
Before taking 7-alpha-hydroxy-DHEA, talk with your healthcare professional if you take any medications.

7-KETO-DHEA

What other names is the product known by?

3-acetyl-7-oxo-dehydroepiandrosterone; 3beta-acetoxy-androst-5-ene-7,17-dione; 5-androsten-3-beta-17-one-DHEA; 7-Keto; 7-keto dehydroepiandrosterone; 7-ketodehydroepiandrostenedione; 7-ODA; 7-oxo-dehydroepiandrosterone-3-acetate; 7-oxo-DHEA; 7-oxo-DHEA-acetate.

What is it?

7-keto-DHEA is a by-product of dehydroepiandrosterone (DHEA) that is formed in the body. DHEA is a "parent hormone" produced by glands near the kidneys.

Is it Effective?

The effectiveness ratings for **7-KETO-DHEA** are as follows:
Insufficient Evidence to Rate Effectiveness for... Promoting weight loss, improving lean body mass, building muscle, increasing activity of the thyroid gland and immune system, boosting memory, and aging.

How does it work?

7-keto-DHEA might promote weight loss by increasing the body's metabolism.

Are there safety concerns?

There isn't enough information available to know if 7-keto-DHEA is safe for use.

Do not use 7-keto-DHEA if: You are pregnant or breast-feeding.

Are there any interactions with medications?

It is not known if 7-keto-DHEA interacts with any medicines.
Before taking 7-keto-DHEA, talk with your healthcare professional if you take any medications.

ABSCESS ROOT

What other names is the product known by?
American Greek Valerian, Blue Bells, False Jacob's Ladder, Sweatroot, Polemonium Reptans.

What is it?
Abscess root is an herb. The ground root is used to make a tea.

Is it Effective?
The effectiveness ratings for **ABSCESS ROOT** are as follows:
Insufficient Evidence to Rate Effectiveness for... Fever, inflammation, cough, sweat stimulation, and as an astringent.

How does it work?
There isn't enough information to know how abscess root might work as a medicine.

Are there safety concerns?
There isn't enough information to know if abscess root is safe. It might cause side effects such as gastrointestinal upset, sneezing, and possibly others.

Do not take abscess root if: You are pregnant or breast-feeding.

Are there any interactions with medications?
It is not known if abscess root interacts with any medicines.
Before taking abscess root, talk with your healthcare professional if you take any medications.

ABUTA

What other names is the product known by?
Bejunco de Cerca, Butua, False Pareira, Pareira, Patacon, Velvetleaf. Cissampelos Pareira, Menispermaceae.

What is it?
Abuta is an herb. People use the bark as medicine.

Is it Effective?
The effectiveness ratings for **ABUTA** are as follows:
Insufficient Evidence to Rate Effectiveness for... Acne, asthma, diarrhea, fertility, high blood pressure, malaria, rabies, menstrual flow, wounds, nervous children, toothaches, and other conditions.

How does it work?
There isn't enough information to know how abuta might work.

Are there safety concerns?
It is not known if abuta is safe.

Do not take abuta if: You are pregnant or breast-feeding.

Are there any interactions with medications?
It is not known if abuta interacts with any medicines.
Before taking abuta, talk with your healthcare professional if you take any medications.

ACACIA

What other names is the product known by?
Gum Acacia, Gum Arabic, Bum Senegal, Bomme Arabique, Bomme de Senegal, Bummae Momosae, Kher, Acacia Senegal.

What is it?
Acacia is a gum. Acacia gum is used as medicine.

Medical professionals should consult the Professional Version at www.NaturalDatabase.com.

Is it Effective?
The effectiveness ratings for **ACACIA** are as follows:
Possibly Ineffective for... Lowering cholesterol levels.

How does it work?
There is not enough information to know how acacia might work as a medicine.

Are there safety concerns?
Acacia seems to be safe for most adults. It can cause gas, bloating, and loose stools. Some people can be allergic to acacia and have skin reactions or asthma attacks.

Do not take acacia if: You are pregnant or breast-feeding.

Are there any interactions with medications?
Amoxicillin (Amoxil, Trimox). Acacia can prevent the body from absorbing the antibiotic amoxicillin (Amoxil, Trimox). To prevent this interaction, take acacia at least four hours before or after taking amoxicillin (Amoxil, Trimox).

ACAI

What other names is the product known by?
Acai Berry, Acai Extract, Acai Fruit, Acai Palm, Amazon Acai, Amazon Acai Berry, Assai, Assai Palm, Cabbage Palm, Euterpe Oleracea.

What is it?
Acai is a palm tree. Its fruit is used to make medicine.

Is it Effective?
The effectiveness ratings for **ACAI** are as follows:
Insufficient Evidence to Rate Effectiveness for... Arthritis, high cholesterol, and improving general health.

How does it work?
Acai contains chemicals that are antioxidants.

Are there safety concerns?
There is not enough information to know if acai is safe.

Do not take acai if: You are pregnant or breast-feeding.

Are there any interactions with medications?
It is not known if acai interacts with any medicines.
Before taking acai, talk with your healthcare professional if you take any medications.

ACEROLA

What other names is the product known by?
Acerola Cherry, Barbados Cherry, Puerto Rican Cherry, West Indian Cherry. Malpighia glabra, Malpighia punicifolia.

What is it?
Acerola is a fruit.

Is it Effective?
The effectiveness ratings for **ACEROLA** are as follows:
Likely Effective for... As a source of Vitamin C to prevent scurvy.
Insufficient Evidence to Rate Effectiveness for... Preventing heart disease, treating the common cold, cancer prevention, tooth decay, depression, and other conditions.

How does it work?
Medicinal benefits of acerola are due to its vitamin C content.

Are there safety concerns?

Acerola is safe for most adults. It can cause some side effects including nausea, stomach cramps, sleepiness, and insomnia. Doses that are too high can cause diarrhea.

Do not take acerola if: You are pregnant or breast-feeding. • You have kidney stones or kidney disease. • You have gout.

Are there any interactions with medications?

Estrogens. Acerola contains a large amount of vitamin C. Vitamin C can increase how much estrogen the body absorbs. Increasing the absorption of estrogen can increase the effects and side effects of estrogens. Some estrogen pills include conjugated equine estrogens (Premarin), ethinyl estradiol, estradiol, and others.
Fluphenazine (Prolixin). Acerola contains vitamin C. Large amounts of vitamin C might decrease how much fluphenazine (Prolixin) is in the body. This might decrease how well fluphenazine works.
Warfarin (Coumadin). Warfarin (Coumadin) is used to slow blood clotting. Acerola contains vitamin C. Large amounts of vitamin C might decrease the effectiveness of warfarin (Coumadin). Decreasing the effectiveness of warfarin (Coumadin) might increase the risk of clotting. Be sure to have your blood checked regularly. The dose of your warfarin (Coumadin) might need to be changed.

ACETYL-L-CARNITINE

What other names is the product known by?

Acetyl L-Carnitine, Acetyl-Carnitine, Acetyl-Levocarnitine, Acetylcarnitine, ALC, Alcar, Carnitine Acetyl Ester, Gamma-Trimethyl-Beta-Acetylbutyrobetaine, L-acetylcarnitine, Levacecarnine, N-Acetyl-Carnitine, N-Acetyl-L-Carnitine, ST-200, Vitamin B(t) Acetate, 2-(acetyloxy)-3-carboxy-N,N,N-trimethyl-1-propanaminium inner salt; (3-carboxy-2-hydroxy-propyl)trimethylammonium hydroxide inner salt acetate.

What is it?

Acetyl-L-carnitine is an amino acid (a protein component) that is naturally produced in the body. It helps the body produce energy.

Is it Effective?

The effectiveness ratings for **ACETYL-L-CARNITINE** are as follows:
Possibly Effective for... Memory problems in elderly people • Improving thinking skills in people who have had a stroke • Neuropathy (nerve pain) caused by diabetes • Peyronie's disease • Treating male infertility caused by inflammation of some reproductive organs and tissues (prostate, seminal vesicles, and epididymis) • Treating symptoms of age-related testosterone deficiency ("male menopause") • Improving blood flow to the brain • Alzheimer's disease.
Insufficient Evidence to Rate Effectiveness for... Muscle weakness caused by medications taken for HIV disease, Down's syndrome, cognitive problems related to Lyme disease, cataracts, nerve problems including diabetic neuropathy, depression, and other conditions.

How does it work?

Acetyl-L-carnitine helps the body produce energy. It is important for heart and brain function, muscle movement, and many other body processes.

Are there safety concerns?

Acetyl-L-carnitine seems to be safe for most adults. It can cause some side effects including stomach upset, nausea, vomiting, and restlessness. It can cause a "fishy" odor of the urine, breath, and sweat.

Do not take acetyl-L-carnitine if: You are pregnant or breast-feeding. • You have had seizures. • You have thyroid problems.

Are there any interactions with medications?

Acenocoumarol (Sintrom). Acenocoumarol (Sintrom) is used to slow blood clotting. Acetyl-L-carnitine might increase the effectiveness of acenocoumarol (Sintrom). Increasing the effectiveness of acenocoumarol (Sintrom) might slow blood clotting too much. The dose of your acenocoumarol (Sintrom) might need to be changed.
Warfarin (Coumadin). Warfarin (Coumadin) is used to slow blood clotting. Acetyl-L-carnitine might increase the effects of warfarin (Coumadin) and increase the chances of bruising and bleeding. Be sure to have your blood checked regularly. The dose of your warfarin (Coumadin) might need to be changed.
Zidovudine (AZT, Retrovir). Zidovudine is used to treat HIV and AIDS infection. Zidovudine decreases how much L-carnitine is in muscles and might cause muscle weakness. More information is needed to know if taking acetyl-L-carnitine can decrease muscle weakness due to Zidovudine.

Medical professionals should consult the Professional Version at www.NaturalDatabase.com.

ACKEE

What other names is the product known by?
Akee, Aki, Anjye, Arbre Fricasse, Ishin, Seso Vegetal, Blighia Sapida, Cupania sapida.

What is it?
Ackee is a plant. The fruit is used to make medicine.

Is it Effective?
The effectiveness ratings for **ACKEE** are as follows:
Insufficient Evidence to Rate Effectiveness for... Colds, fever, water retention, and epilepsy.

How does it work?
There isn't enough information to know how ackee might work for medical purposes.

Are there safety concerns?
The ripe fruit of ackee seems to be safe, but the unripe fruit is UNSAFE. The unripe fruit contains liver toxins and can cause serious side effects including coma. Due to concerns about poisoning, ackee is illegal in the US.

Do not use ackee if: You are pregnant or breast-feeding.

Are there any interactions with medications?
It is not known if ackee interacts with any medicines.
Before taking ackee, talk with your healthcare professional if you take any medications.

ACONITE

What other names is the product known by?
Aconiti Tuber, Blue Monkshood Root, Monkshood, Monkshood Tuber, Wofsbane, Aconitum Napellus, Aconitum Species.

What is it?
Aconite is a plant. The root is used as medicine.

Is it Effective?
The effectiveness ratings for **ACONITE** are as follows:
Insufficient Evidence to Rate Effectiveness for... Nerve pain, facial paralysis, joint pain, gout, inflammation, wounds, heart problems, and other conditions.

How does it work?
Aconite root has chemicals that can adversely affect the heart, muscles, and nerves.

Are there safety concerns?
Aconite root is UNSAFE when taken by mouth. Do not use it. It contains a strong, fast-acting poison that causes severe side effects such as nausea, vomiting, weakness, sweating, heart problems, and death.

Some people use aconite in a cream or lotion that is applied to the skin. It is not known if aconite is safe when applied to the skin.

Are there any interactions with medications?
It is not known if aconite interacts with any medicines.
Before taking aconite, talk with your healthcare professional if you take any medications.

ACTIVATED CHARCOAL

What other names is the product known by?
Animal Charcoal, Carbon, Charcoal, Gas Black, Lamp Black, Medicinal Charcoal, Vegetable Carbon.

What is it?
Activated charcoal is similar to common charcoal, but is made specifically for use as a medicine.

Is it Effective?

The effectiveness ratings for **ACTIVATED CHARCOAL** are as follows:

Likely Effective for... Trapping chemicals to prevent poisoning.

Insufficient Evidence to Rate Effectiveness for... Lowering cholesterol levels, decreasing gas (flatulence), treating reduced bile flow (cholestasis) during pregnancy.

How does it work?

Activated charcoal is good at trapping chemicals and prevents their absorption.

Are there safety concerns?

Activated charcoal is safe for most adults when used short-term. Side effects of activated charcoal include constipation and black stools. More serious, but rare, side effects are a slowing or blockage of the intestinal tract, regurgitation into the lungs, and dehydration.

It might be safe when used short-term if you are pregnant or breast-feeding, but consult with your healthcare professional before using if you are pregnant.

Do not use activated charcoal if: You have a blockage in your intestinal tract.

Are there any interactions with medications?

Alcohol. Activated charcoal is sometimes used to prevent poisons from being absorbed into the body. Taking alcohol with activated charcoal might decrease how well activated charcoal works to prevent poison absorption.

Medications taken by mouth (Oral drugs). Activated charcoal absorbs substances in the stomach and intestines. Taking activated charcoal along with medications taken by mouth can decrease how much medicine your body absorbs, and decrease the effectiveness of your medication. To prevent this interaction, take activated charcoal at least one hour after medications you take by mouth.

Syrup of ipecac. Activated charcoal can bind up syrup of ipecac in the stomach. This decreases the effectiveness of syrup of ipecac.

ADENOSINE

What other names is the product known by?

Adenine Nucleoside, Adenine Riboside, Adenosine Phosphate, Adenosine; Adenosine Monophosphate (AMP); Adenosine-5-monophosphate (A5MP); Adenosine Diphosphate (ADP); Adenosine Triphosphate (ATP).

What is it?

Adenosine is a chemical that is present in all human cells. People use it for medicine.

Is it Effective?

The effectiveness ratings for **ADENOSINE** are as follows:

Effective for... Treating certain kinds of irregular heart beat (as a prescription-only intravenous medicine).

Possibly Effective for... Treating weight loss in people with advanced cancer • Varicose veins.

Insufficient Evidence to Rate Effectiveness for... Pain, shingles, lung cancer, and other conditions.

How does it work?

Adenosine blocks faulty circuitry in the heart, which causes irregular heart rhythm. Adenosine triphosphate (ATP) might prevent changes in energy metabolism that cause weight loss in people with advanced cancer.

Are there safety concerns?

Adenosine appears to be safe for most people when given by injection (shot) by qualified healthcare givers. It can cause breathing problems and chest pain, particularly when given at high doses. Headache, heart pounding, low blood pressure, nausea, sweating, flushing, lightheadedness, sleep problems, coughing, and anxiety can also occur.

Do not take adenosine if: You are pregnant or breast-feeding. • You have gout.

Are there any interactions with medications?

Carbamazepine (Tegretol). Adenosine can slow down the heart beat. Taking carbamazepine (Tegretol) with adenosine might cause the heart to beat too slowly. Do not take adenosine if you are taking carbamazepine (Tegretol).

Dipyridamole (Persantine). The body breaks down adenosine to get rid of it. Dipyridamole (Persantine) can decrease the break down of adenosine. Decreasing the breakdown of adenosine can cause heart problems. Do not take adenosine if you are taking dipyridamole (Persantine).

Medications for gout (Antigout drugs). Gout is caused by a build-up of uric acid crystals in the joints. Adenosine

Medical professionals should consult the Professional Version at www.NaturalDatabase.com.

CONSUMER VERSION

can increase uric acid in the body and might reduce the effectiveness of medications for gout.Some medications for gout include allopurinol (Zyloprim), colchicine, probenecid (Benemid), and others.

Methylxanthines. Methylxanthines might block the affects of adenosine. Adenosine is often used by doctors to do a test on the heart. This test is called a cardiac stress test. Stop drinking black tea or other caffeine containing products at least 24 hours before a cardiac stress test. Methylxanthines include aminophylline, caffeine, and theophylline.

ADRENAL EXTRACT

What other names is the product known by?
ACE, Adrenal, Adrenal Complex, Adrenal Concentrate, Adrenal Cortex Extract, Adrenal Factors, Adrenal Substance, Glandular, Whole Adrenal Extract.

What is it?
Adrenal extract is a chemical that is made from the adrenal glands of slaughtered cows, pigs, and sheep. People use the extract as a medicine.

Is it Effective?
The effectiveness ratings for **ADRENAL EXTRACT** are as follows:
Insufficient Evidence to Rate Effectiveness for... Low adrenal function, fatigue, stress, fighting off illness, allergies, asthma, skin conditions such as eczema and psoriasis, rheumatoid arthritis, depression, low blood pressure, low blood sugar, drug and alcohol withdrawal, and other conditions.

How does it work?
There isn't enough information to know how adrenal extract works.

Are there safety concerns?
Adrenal extract is unsafe when injected, and there is insufficient reliable information available about the safety of adrenal extract when taken by mouth. It can cause serious infections or diseases in people, if the adrenal extract is made from a sick farm animal.

Do not use adrenal extract from countries where a condition known as bovine spongiform encephalitis (BSE) has been reported, more commonly known as "mad cow disease." If you can't tell if the adrenal extract is from a country without BSE, don't use it.

Do not take adrenal extract if: You are pregnant or breast-feeding. • You have an immune system problem.

Are there any interactions with medications?
It is not known if adrenal extract interacts with any medicines.
Before taking adrenal extract, talk with your healthcare professional if you take any medications.

ADRUE

What other names is the product known by?
Chintul, Cyperus articulatus, Cyperus corymbosus, Guinea Rush, Jointed Flat Sedge, Piripiri.

What is it?
Adrue is a plant native to Turkey, Jamaica, and the Nile River region. The root is used to make medicine.

Is it Effective?
The effectiveness ratings for **ADRUE** are as follows:
Insufficient Evidence to Rate Effectiveness for... Vomiting, nausea, colic, gas, and a calming (sedative) effect.

How does it work?
There is insufficient reliable information available about how adrue works.

Are there safety concerns?
There is insufficient reliable information available about the safety of adrue.

Do not take adrue if: You are pregnant or breast-feeding.

Are there any interactions with medications?
It is not known if adrue interacts with any medicines.
Before taking adrue, talk with your healthcare professional if you take any medications.

AFRICAN WILD POTATO

What other names is the product known by?
African Potato, Bantu Tulip, Hypoxis Rooperi, South African Star Grass, Sterretjie.

What is it?
African wild potato is a plant. People use it to make medicine.

Is it Effective?
The effectiveness ratings for **AFRICAN WILD POTATO** are as follows:
Possibly Effective for... Trouble urinating because of an enlarged prostate, or "benign prostatic hyperplasia" (BPH).
Insufficient Evidence to Rate Effectiveness for... Lung cancer, bladder infections, cancer, lung disease, human immunodeficiency virus (HIV), tuberculosis (TB), arthritis, a skin condition called psoriasis, wound healing, and improving the immune system.

How does it work?
African wild potato contains chemicals that might decrease inflammation.

Are there safety concerns?
Some African wild potato products appear to be safe for most people. Side effects include nausea, indigestion, gas, diarrhea, or constipation, and possibly sexual side effects such as trouble getting an erection or less interest in sex. However, other African wild potato products have been associated with decreased production of blood cells and irregular heartbeat.

Do not take African wild potato if: You are pregnant or breast-feeding. • You have a rare inherited fat storage disease called "sitosterolemia."

Are there any interactions with medications?
It is not known if African wild potato interacts with any medicines.
Before taking African wild potato, talk with your healthcare professional if you take any medications.

AGA

What other names is the product known by?
Amanita Muscaria, Fly Agaric, Soma.

What is it?
Aga is a mushroom. People use the above ground mushroom parts to make medicine.

Is it Effective?
The effectiveness ratings for **AGA** are as follows:
Insufficient Evidence to Rate Effectiveness for... Nerve pain, joint pain, fever, anxiety, and alcohol poisoning.

How does it work?
Aga mushrooms have chemicals that cause the brain to misunderstand what the body is seeing, hearing, tasting, and feeling.

Are there safety concerns?
Aga is UNSAFE. It can cause side effects such as sleepiness, confusion, dizziness, delirium, and death.

Do not take aga if: You are pregnant or breast-feeding.

Are there any interactions with medications?
It is not known if aga interacts with any medicines.
Before taking aga, talk with your healthcare professional if you take any medications.

Medical professionals should consult the Professional Version at www.NaturalDatabase.com.

CONSUMER VERSION

Medical professionals should consult the Professional Version at www.NaturalDatabase.com.

AGAR

What other names is the product known by?

Agar-Agar, Agarweed, Chinese Gelatin, Colle du Japon, Garacilaria Confervoides, Gelidiella Acerosa, Gelidium Amanasii, Gelidium Cartilagineum, Gelidium Crinale, Gelidium Divaricatum, Gelidium Pacificum, Gelidium Vagum, Gelosa, Gelosae, Japanese Isinglas, , Kanten, Kanten Diet, Kanten Jelly, Kanten jellies, Kanten Plan, Layor Carang, Seaweed Gelatin, Vegetable Gelatin, Vegetarian Gelatin.

What is it?

Agar is a plant. People use it to make medicine.

Is it Effective?

The effectiveness ratings for **AGAR** are as follows:
Insufficient Evidence to Rate Effectiveness for... Constipation, diabetes, weight loss, and obesity.

How does it work?

Agar contains a gel-like substance, which bulks up in the gut and stimulates the intestines.

Are there safety concerns?

Agar seems safe for most adults when taken with at least one 8-ounce glass of water. If it is not taken with enough water, agar can swell and block the esophagus or bowel. Immediate medical attention is necessary if chest pain, vomiting, or difficulty swallowing or breathing occurs after taking agar. In some people, agar may also raise cholesterol.

Do not take agar if: You are pregnant or breast-feeding. • You have a blockage in your bowel. • You have trouble swallowing.

Are there any interactions with medications?

Medications taken by mouth (Oral drugs). Agar is a thick gel. Agar might stick to some medications in the stomach and intestines. Taking agar at the same time as medications that you take by mouth might decrease how much medication your body absorbs, and possibly decrease the effectiveness of your medication. To prevent this interaction, take agar at least one hour after medications you take by mouth.

AGRIMONY

What other names is the product known by?

Agromonia, Agrimoniae Herba, Ackerkraut, Cocklebur, Funffing, Funffingerkraut, Herba Agrimoniae, Herba Eupatoriae, Herbe d'Aigremoine, Herbe de Saint-Guillaume, Liverwort, Stickwort, Agrimonia Eupatoria, Agrimonia Procera.

What is it?

Agrimony is an herb. People use the dried, above-ground parts of the plant to make medicine.

Is it Effective?

The effectiveness ratings for **AGRIMONY** are as follows:
Insufficient Evidence to Rate Effectiveness for... Diarrhea, irritable bowel syndrome (IBS), sore throat, upset stomach, and other conditions.

How does it work?

Agrimony contains chemicals called tannins, which are thought to help conditions such as diarrhea.

Are there safety concerns?

Agrimony seems to be safe for most adults when used short-term. Agrimony can make some people's skin extra sensitive to sunlight and more likely to burn.

Do not take agrimony if: You are pregnant or breast-feeding.

Are there any interactions with medications?

Medications for diabetes (Antidiabetes drugs). Agrimony might decrease blood sugar. Diabetes medications are also used to lower blood sugar. Taking agrimony along with diabetes medications might cause your blood sugar to go too low. Monitor your blood sugar closely. The dose of your diabetes medication might need to be changed. Some medications used for diabetes include glimepiride (Amaryl), glyburide (DiaBeta, Glynase PresTab, Micronase), insulin, pioglitazone (Actos), rosiglitazone (Avandia), chlorpropamide (Diabinese), glipizide (Glucotrol), tolbutamide (Orinase), and others.

AHCC

What other names is the product known by?
Active hexose correlated compound, Basidiomycetes extract, Fungi extract.

What is it?
AHCC is a group of chemicals from fungus.

Is it Effective?
The effectiveness ratings for **AHCC** are as follows:
Insufficient Evidence to Rate Effectiveness for... Cancer, liver damage.

How does it work?
There isn't enough information to know how AHCC might work.

Are there safety concerns?
There is not enough known about AHCC to know if it is safe.

Are there any interactions with medications?
It is not known if AHCC interactions with any medicines.
Before using AHCC, talk to your health professional if you take any medications.

AJUGA NIPPONENSIS

What other names is the product known by?
Ajuga, Junihitoe.

What is it?
Ajuga nipponensis is an herb. The whole plant is used to make medicine.

Is it Effective?
The effectiveness ratings for **AJUGA NIPPONENSIS** are as follows:
Insufficient Evidence to Rate Effectiveness for... Cough, inflammation, liver disease, and other conditions.

How does it work?
Preliminary research suggests that chemicals in Ajuga nipponensis might help fight cancer and protect the liver.

Are there safety concerns?
It is not known if Ajuga nipponensis is safe. Side effects can include diarrhea, nausea, and vomiting.

Do not use Ajuga nipponensis if: You are pregnant or breast-feeding.

Are there any interactions with medications?
It is not known if Ajuga nipponensis interacts with any medicines.
Before taking Ajuga nipponensis, talk with your healthcare professional if you take any medications.

ALCHEMILLA

What other names is the product known by?
Feuilles d'Alchemille, Frauenmantelkraut, Lady's Mantle, Leontopodium, Lion's Foot, Marienmantel, Nine Hooks, Silerkraut, Stellaria, Alchemilla Xanthochlora, Alchemilla Vulgaris.

What is it?
Alchemilla is an herb. The above ground parts of alchemilla are used to make medicine.

Is it Effective?
The effectiveness ratings for **ALCHEMILLA** are as follows:
Insufficient Evidence to Rate Effectiveness for... Diarrhea, skin conditions such as ulcers, eczema, and rashes, diabetes, menstrual irregularities, bleeding and wound healing, stomach disorders, muscle spasms, and others.

How does it work?
Alchemilla contains chemicals called tannins, which might help diarrhea.

Are there safety concerns?
Alchemilla seems to be safe for most people. However, there is very little information available about the safety of alchemilla.

Do not take alchemilla if: You are pregnant or breast-feeding.

Are there any interactions with medications?
It is not known if alchemilla interacts with any medicines.
Before taking alchemilla, talk with your healthcare professional if you take any medications.

ALDER BUCKTHORN

What other names is the product known by?
Alder Dogwood, Arrow Wood, Black Dogwood, Buckthorn, Buckthorn Bark, Dog Wood, Frangula Alnus, Frangula Bark, Frangulae Cortex, Glossy Buckthorn, Rhamnus Frangula.

What is it?
Alder buckthorn is a plant. The bark of the plant is used to make medicine.

Is it Effective?
The effectiveness ratings for **ALDER BUCKTHORN** are as follows:
Possibly Effective for... Treating constipation.
Insufficient Evidence to Rate Effectiveness for... Treating cancer.

How does it work?
Alder buckthorn bark contains chemicals that work as a laxative by stimulating the intestines.

Are there safety concerns?
Alder buckthorn is safe for most adults when used for less than 8 days. Using alder buckthorn for more than 8 days can be unsafe because it might cause problems such as low potassium; heart problems; muscle weakness; and blood problems, including blood in the urine. Some people get uncomfortable cramps from alder buckthorn. If you experience diarrhea or watery stools while using alder buckthorn, stop taking it.

The fresh bark can cause severe vomiting. Make sure you are using a bark product that is at least one year old or has been heat processed.

Alder buckthorn is unsafe for children younger than 12 years of age.

Do not take alder buckthorn if: You are pregnant or breast-feeding. • You have a blockage in your intestine. • You have an intestine disorder such as appendicitis, Crohn's disease, irritable bowel syndrome (IBS), or ulcerative colitis. • You have stomach pain. • You have diarrhea.

Are there any interactions with medications?
Digoxin (Lanoxin). Alder buckthorn is a type of laxative called a stimulant laxative. Stimulant laxatives can decrease potassium levels in the body. Low potassium levels can increase the risk of side effects of digoxin (Lanoxin).
Medications for inflammation (Corticosteroids). Some medications for inflammation can decrease potassium in the body. Alder buckthorn is a type of laxative that might also decrease potassium in the body. Taking alder buckthorn along with some medications for inflammation might decrease potassium in the body too much. Some medications for inflammation include dexamethasone (Decadron), hydrocortisone (Cortef), methylprednisolone (Medrol), prednisone (Deltasone), and others.
Medications taken by mouth (Oral drugs). Alder buckthorn is a laxative. Laxatives can decrease how much medicine your body absorbs. Decreasing how much medicine your body absorbs can decrease the effectiveness of your medication.
Stimulant laxatives. Alder buckthorn is a type of laxative called a stimulant laxative. Stimulant laxatives speed up

Medical professionals should consult the Professional Version at www.NaturalDatabase.com.

Natural Medicines Comprehensive Database Consumer Version
(209) 472-2244

the bowels. Taking alder buckthorn along with other stimulant laxatives could speed up the bowels too much and cause dehydration and low minerals in the body. Some stimulant laxatives include bisacodyl (Correctol, Dulcolax), cascara, castor oil (Purge), senna (Senokot) and others.

Water pills (Diuretic drugs). Alder buckthorn is a laxative. Some laxatives can decrease potassium in the body. "Water pills" can also decrease potassium in the body. Taking alder buckthorn along with "water pills" might decrease potassium in the body too much. Some "water pills" that can decrease potassium include chlorothiazide (Diuril), chlorthalidone (Thalitone), furosemide (Lasix), hydrochlorothiazide (HCTZ, HydroDiuril, Microzide), and others.

ALETRIS

What other names is the product known by?
Ague Grass, Ague Root, Aletris Farinosa, Aloerot, Blazing Star, Colic Root, Crow Corn, Devil's-bit, Stargrass, Starwort, True Unicorn Root, Whitetube Stargrass.

What is it?
Aletris is a plant. The root is used to make medicine.

Is it Effective?
The effectiveness ratings for **ALETRIS** are as follows:
Insufficient Evidence to Rate Effectiveness for... Joint, muscle, and tendon pain; female disorders; constipation; gas; colic; diarrhea; menstrual disorders; and other conditions.

How does it work?
It is not known how aletris might work.

Are there safety concerns?
Aletris might be safe for most adults. Aletris can cause colic, dizziness, or confusion.

Do not use aletris if: You are pregnant or breast-feeding. • You have stomach or intestine problems. • You have a hormone-sensitive condition such as breast, uterine, and ovarian cancer; endometriosis; or uterine fibroids.

Are there any interactions with medications?
Antacids. Antacids are used to decrease stomach acid. Aletris may increase stomach acid. By increasing stomach acid, aletris might decrease the effectiveness of antacids. Some antacids include calcium carbonate (Tums, others), dihydroxyaluminum sodium carbonate (Rolaids, others), magaldrate (Riopan), magnesium sulfate (Bilagog), aluminum hydroxide (Amphojel), and others.

Medications that decrease stomach acid (H2-Blockers). Aletris might increase stomach acid. By increasing stomach acid, aletris might decrease the effectiveness of some medications that decrease stomach acid, called H2-Blockers. Some medications that decrease stomach acid include cimetidine (Tagamet), ranitidine (Zantac), nizatidine (Axid), and famotidine (Pepcid).

Medications that decrease stomach acid (Proton pump inhibitors). Aletris might increase stomach acid. By increasing stomach acid, aletris might decrease the effectiveness of medications that are used to decrease stomach acid, called proton pump inhibitors. Some medications that decrease stomach acid include omeprazole (Prilosec), lansoprazole (Prevacid), rabeprazole (Aciphex), pantoprazole (Protonix), and esomeprazole (Nexium).

ALFALFA

What other names is the product known by?
Feuille De Luzerne, Lucerne, Medicago, Purple Medick, Medicago Sativa.

What is it?
Alfalfa is an herb. People use the above ground parts of the plant to make medicine.

Is it Effective?
The effectiveness ratings for **ALFALFA** are as follows:
Possibly Effective for... Lowering cholesterol in people with high cholesterol.
Insufficient Evidence to Rate Effectiveness for... Kidney, bladder, and prostate problems; asthma; arthritis; diabetes; indigestion; and other conditions.

How does it work?
Alfalfa seems to prevent cholesterol absorption in the gut.

Medical professionals should consult the Professional Version at www.NaturalDatabase.com.

Are there safety concerns?

Alfalfa is safe for most adults. But alfalfa can make the skin extra sensitive to sunlight and might increase the chance of getting sunburn.

Do not take alfalfa if: You have lupus. • You have diabetes. • You have breast cancer. • You have uterine cancer. • You have ovarian cancer. • You have endometriosis. • You have uterine fibroids. • You have received a kidney transplant.

Are there any interactions with medications?

Birth control pills (Contraceptive drugs). Some birth control pills contain estrogen. Alfalfa might have some of the same effects as estrogen. But alfalfa isn't as strong as the estrogen in birth control pills. Taking alfalfa along with birth control pills might decrease the effectiveness of birth control pills. If you take birth control pills along with alfalfa, use an additional form of birth control such as a condom. Some birth control pills include ethinyl estradiol and levonorgestrel (Triphasil), ethinyl estradiol and norethindrone (Ortho-Novum 1/35, Ortho-Novum 7/7/7), and others.

Estrogens. Large amounts of alfalfa might have some of the same effects as estrogen. But even large amount of alfalfa aren't as strong as estrogen pills. Taking alfalfa along with estrogen pills might decrease the effects of estrogen pills. Some estrogen pills include conjugated equine estrogens (Premarin), ethinyl estradiol, estradiol, and others.

Medications that increase sensitivity to sunlight (Photosensitizing drugs). Some medications can increase sensitivity to sunlight. Large doses of alfalfa might also increase your sensitivity to sunlight. Taking alfalfa along with medication that increase sensitivity to sunlight could increase the chances of sunburn, blistering or rashes on areas of skin exposed to sunlight. Be sure to wear sunblock and protective clothing when spending time in the sun. Some drugs that cause photosensitivity include amitriptyline (Elavil), Ciprofloxacin (Cipro), norfloxacin (Noroxin), lomefloxacin (Maxaquin), ofloxacin (Floxin), levofloxacin (Levaquin), sparfloxacin (Zagam), gatifloxacin (Tequin), moxifloxacin (Avelox), trimethoprim/sulfamethoxazole (Septra), tetracycline, methoxsalen (8-methoxypsoralen, 8-MOP, Oxsoralen), and Trioxsalen (Trisoralen).

Warfarin (Coumadin). Alfalfa contains large amounts of vitamin K. Vitamin K is used by the body to help blood clot. Warfarin (Coumadin) is used to slow blood clotting. By helping the blood clot, alfalfa might decrease the effectiveness of warfarin (Coumadin). Be sure to have your blood checked regularly. The dose of your warfarin (Coumadin) might need to be changed.

ALGIN

What other names is the product known by?

Alginates, Ascophyllum Nodosum, Laminaria Digitata, Macrocystis Pyrifera, Pacific Kelp, Sodium Alginate.

What is it?

Algin is a chemical taken from brown seaweeds. It is used to make medicine.

Is it Effective?

The effectiveness ratings for **ALGIN** are as follows:

Insufficient Evidence to Rate Effectiveness for... Reducing cholesterol, reducing blood pressure, and decreasing the amount of the heavy chemicals taken up (absorption) by the body (strontium, barium, tin, cadmium, manganese, zinc).

How does it work?

Algin forms a gel that may lower cholesterol levels by reducing the amount of cholesterol entering the body.

Are there safety concerns?

It is not known if algin is safe.

Do not take algin if: You are pregnant or breast-feeding.

Are there any interactions with medications?

Medications taken by mouth (Oral drugs). Algin is a thick gel. Algin can stick to medications in the stomach and intestines. Taking algin at the same time as medications that you take by mouth can decrease how much medication your body absorbs, and decrease the effectiveness of your medication. To prevent this interaction, take algin at least one hour after medications you take by mouth.

ALKANNA

What other names is the product known by?
Alkanet, Alkanna Radix, Alkanna Tinctoria, Anchusa, Dyer's Bugloss, Henna, Orchanet, Radix Anchusae.

What is it?
Alkanna is a plant. The root is used to make medicine.

Is it Effective?
The effectiveness ratings for **ALKANNA** are as follows:
Insufficient Evidence to Rate Effectiveness for... Skin diseases, healing leg ulcer wounds, stomach ulcers, and diarrhea.

How does it work?
Alkanna might have antioxidant and anti-inflammatory activity.

Are there safety concerns?
Alkanna is UNSAFE when used directly on broken skin or when taken by mouth. There isn't enough information to know if alkanna is safe when applied to unbroken skin. Some alkanna products contain chemicals that can cause serious liver problems, blocked veins, and cancer.

Do not use alkanna if: You are pregnant or breast-feeding. • You have liver disease.

Are there any interactions with medications?
Medications that increase the breakdown of other medications by the liver (Cytochrome P450 3A4 (CYP3A4) inducers). Alkanna is broken down by the liver. Some chemicals that form when the liver breaks down alkanna can be harmful. Medications that cause the liver to break down alkanna might enhance the toxic effects of chemicals contained in alkanna. Some of these medicines include carbamazepine (Tegretol). Alkanna is broken down by the liver. Some chemicals that form when the liver breaks down alkanna can be harmful. Medications that cause the liver to break down alkanna might enhance the toxic effects of chemicals contained in alkanna. Some of these medicines include carbamazepine (Tegretol), phenobarbital, phenytoin (Dilantin), rifampin, rifabutin (Mycobutin), and others.

ALLSPICE

What other names is the product known by?
Clove Pepper, Eugenia Pimenta, Jamaica Pepper, Pimenta Dioica, Pimento, West Pimenta Officinalis.

What is it?
Allspice is a plant. The young fruit and leaves of the plant are used to make medicine.

Is it Effective?
The effectiveness ratings for **ALLSPICE** are as follows:
Insufficient Evidence to Rate Effectiveness for... Intestinal gas, stomachache, vomiting, diarrhea, purging the bowels, fever, flu, colds, heavy menstrual bleeding, and other conditions.

How does it work?
There isn't enough information available to know how allspice works. Allspice contains a chemical called eugenol, which is used in some dental products.

Are there safety concerns?
Allspice is safe for most adults when used as a spice. However, there is not enough information available to know if allspice is safe in medicinal amounts. When applied directly to the skin, allspice can cause allergic skin reactions in sensitive people.

Do not take allspice if: You are pregnant or breast-feeding, except as a spice in food.

Are there any interactions with medications?
Medications that slow blood clotting (Anticoagulant / Antiplatelet drugs). Allspice might slow blood clotting. Taking allspice along with medications that also slow clotting might increase the chances of bruising and bleeding. Allspice contains eugenol. Eugenol is the part of allspice that might slow blood clotting. Eugenol is very fragrant and gives allspice and cloves their distinctive smell. Some medications that slow blood clotting include aspirin,

clopidogrel (Plavix), diclofenac (Voltaren, Cataflam, others), ibuprofen (Advil, Motrin, others), naproxen (Anaprox, Naprosyn, others), dalteparin (Fragmin), enoxaparin (Lovenox), heparin, warfarin (Coumadin), and others.

ALOE

What other names is the product known by?

Aloe africana, Aloe arborescens Aloe barbadensis, Aloe capensis, Aloe Ferox, Aloe Gel, Aloe Latex, Aloe Leaf Gel, Aloe natalenis, Aloe Perfoliata, Aloe Perryi, Aloe spicata, Aloe Vera, Arborescens natalenis, Burn Plant, Cape Aloe, Elephant's Gall, Ghrita-Kumari, Hsiang-Dan, Kanya, Kumari, Lily of the Desert, Lu-Hui, Miracle Plant, Plant of Immortality.

What is it?

Aloe gel is the clear, jelly-like substance found in inner part of the aloe plant leaf. Aloe latex comes from just under the plant's skin and is yellow in color.

Is it Effective?

The effectiveness ratings for **ALOE** are as follows:
Possibly Effective for... Psoriasis, when applied to the skin • Constipation.
Insufficient Evidence to Rate Effectiveness for... Wound healing, healing skin sores, frostbite, burns, genital herpes, high cholesterol, skin problems caused by radiation used to treat cancer, arthritis, fever, ulcerative colitis, itching, stomach ulcers, diabetes, and asthma.

How does it work?

Aloe gel might cause changes in the skin that might help diseases like psoriasis. Aloe latex contains chemicals that work as a laxative.

Are there safety concerns?

Aloe appears to be safe for most people when taken by mouth or applied to the skin.
Taking large amounts of aloe latex by mouth is unsafe. Aloe latex can cause some side effects such as stomach pain and cramps. Long-term use of large amounts might cause diarrhea, kidney problems, blood in the urine, low potassium, muscle weakness, weight loss, and heart disturbances. Taking one gram per day for several days can be fatal.

Taking aloe by mouth might not be safe for children.

Do not use aloe if: You are pregnant or breast-feeding. • You have diabetes. • You have intestinal condition such as Crohn's disease, ulcerative colitis, or obstruction. • You have hemorrhoids. • You have kidney problems.

Are there any interactions with medications?

Digoxin (Lanoxin). When taken by mouth aloe latex is a type of laxative called a stimulant laxative. Stimulant laxatives can decrease potassium levels in the body. Low potassium levels can increase the risk of side effects of digoxin (Lanoxin).
Medications for diabetes (Antidiabetes drugs). Aloe gel might decrease blood sugar. Diabetes medications are also used to lower blood sugar. Taking aloe gel along with diabetes medications might cause your blood sugar to go too low. Monitor your blood sugar closely. The dose of your diabetes medication might need to be changed. Some medications used for diabetes include glimepiride (Amaryl), glyburide (DiaBeta, Glynase PresTab, Micronase), insulin, pioglitazone (Actos), rosiglitazone (Avandia), chlorpropamide (Diabinese), glipizide (Glucotrol), tolbutamide (Orinase), and others.
Medications taken by mouth (Oral drugs). When taken by mouth aloe latex is a laxative. Laxatives can decrease how much medicine your body absorbs. Taking aloe latex along with medications you take by mouth might decrease the effectiveness of your medication.
Stimulant laxatives. When taken orally aloe latex is a type of laxative called a stimulant laxative. Stimulant laxatives speed up the bowels. Taking aloe latex along with other stimulant laxatives could speed up the bowels too much and cause dehydration and low minerals in the body. Some stimulant laxatives include bisacodyl (Correctol, Dulcolax), cascara, castor oil (Purge), senna (Senokot), and others.
Sevoflurane (Ultane). Aloe might decrease clotting of the blood. Sevoflurane is used as anesthesia during surgery. Sevoflurane also decreases clotting of the blood. Taking aloe before surgery might cause increased bleeding during the surgical procedure. Do not take aloe by mouth if you are having surgery within 2 weeks.
Water pills (Diuretic drugs). When taken by mouth aloe latex is a laxative. Some laxatives can decrease potassium in the body. "Water pills" can also decrease potassium in the body. Taking aloe latex along with "water pills" might decrease potassium in the body too much. Some "water pills" that can decrease potassium

include chlorothiazide (Diuril), chlorthalidone (Thalitone), furosemide (Lasix), hydrochlorothiazide (HCTZ, HydroDIURIL, Microzide), and others.

ALPHA HYDROXY ACIDS

What other names is the product known by?

AHA, Apple Acid, Citric Acid, Dihydroxysuccinic Acid, Gluconolactone, Glycolic Acid, Hydroxyacetic Acid, Hydroxycaprylic Acid, Hydroxypropionic Acid, Hydroxysuccinic Acid, Lactic Acid, Malic Acid, Mixed Fruit Acid, Monohydroxysuccinic Acid, Tartaric Acid.

What is it?

Alpha hydroxy acids are a group of natural acids from foods. Some alpha hydroxy acids are gluconolactone; citric, glycolic, lactic, and malic acids; and others.

Is it Effective?

The effectiveness ratings for **ALPHA HYDROXY ACIDS** are as follows:

Likely Effective for... Treating sun damage when applied to the skin in a cream or lotion, but alpha hydroxy skin peels do not seem to work for this use • Treating dry skin when applied to the skin in a cream or lotion.

Possibly Effective for... Firming and smoothing skin when applied to the skin in a solution • Acne when applied to the skin in a cream or lotion • Acne scars when applied to the skin in a facial peel or lotion • Reducing the pigmentation associated with a skin disorder melasma • Wrinkled skin.

Insufficient Evidence to Rate Effectiveness for... Treating sun damaged skin when applied as a skin peel; and reducing pain and tenderness caused by fibromyalgia when a specific alpha hydroxy acid, called malic acid, is used in combination with magnesium.

How does it work?

Alpha hydroxy acids seem to work by removing the top layers of dead skin cells. They can also increase the thickness of deeper layers of skin, promoting firmness.

Are there safety concerns?

Alpha hydroxy acids at a concentration of 10% or less as a lotion or cream are generally safe for most people when applied to the skin appropriately and as directed. In some people, alpha hydroxy acids can make the skin extra sensitive to sunlight. Be sure to use a sunscreen while using alpha hydroxy acid products. Alpha hydroxy acids can also cause mild skin irritation, redness, swelling, itching, and skin discoloration. Facial peels, lotions, and creams with a concentration greater than 10% should only be used under the supervision of a dermatologist. Facial peels can cause moderate to severe skin irritation, redness, and burning. Facial peels left on the skin for periods longer than recommended can cause severe burns to the skin.

When taken by mouth, the alpha hydroxy acid called malic acid seems to be safe when used short-term. Some people can have side effects including diarrhea, nausea, and general stomach discomfort.

Do not take alpha hydroxy acids by mouth if: You are pregnant or breast-feeding.

Are there any interactions with medications?

It is not known if alpha hydroxy acids interact with any medicines.
Before taking alpha hydroxy acids, talk with your healthcare professional if you take any medications.

ALPHA-GPC

What other names is the product known by?

Alpha-glycerylphosphorylcholine, Choline alphoscerate, Glycerophosphorylcholine, Glycerophosphocholine, GPC, GroPCho, L-alpha-glycerylphosphorylcholine.

What is it?

Alpha-GPC is a chemical from a fatty acid found in soy.

Is it Effective?

The effectiveness ratings for **ALPHA-GPC** are as follows:

Insufficient Evidence to Rate Effectiveness for... Alzheimer's disease, vascular dementia, ischemic dementia, multi-infarct dementia, stroke, transient ischemic attack (TIA), improving memory and cognitive function, and learning.

How does it work?
Alpha-GPC seems to increase a chemical in the brain called acetylcholine. This brain chemical is important for memory and learning functions.

Are there safety concerns?
Alpha-GPC seems to be safe when used appropriately. It can cause side effects in some people including heartburn, headache, insomnia, dizziness, skin rash, and confusion.

Don't take alpha-GPC if: You are pregnant or breast-feeding.

Are there any interactions with medications?
Scopolamine (Transderm Scop). Alpha-GPC increases a chemical in the brain called acetylcholine. Scopolamine blocks this same chemical. But it's not known if alpha-GPC decreases the benefits of scopolamine.

ALPHA-KETOGLUTARATE

What other names is the product known by?
A-Ketoglutaric Acid, Alpha Ketoglutaric Acid, Alpha KG, AKG, 2-Oxoglutaric Acid, 2-Oxopentanedoicic Acid.

What is it?
Alpha-ketoglutarate is a chemical found in the body. People use it to make medicine.

Is it Effective?
The effectiveness ratings for **ALPHA-KETOGLUTARATE** are as follows:
Possibly Effective for... Preventing blood supply problems during heart surgery • Preventing muscle breakdown after surgery or trauma.
Insufficient Evidence to Rate Effectiveness for... Kidney disease, intestinal and stomach disorders, bacterial infections, yeast infections, improving athletic performance, improving protein usage in hemodialysis patients, and cataracts.

How does it work?
Alpha-ketoglutarate works in many pathways in the body, to help make muscle, and to help heal wounds.

Are there safety concerns?
Alpha-ketoglutarate appears to be safe for most adults.

Do not use alpha-ketoglutarate if: You are pregnant or breast-feeding.

Are there any interactions with medications?
It is not known if alpha-ketoglutarate interacts with any medicines.
Before taking alpha-ketoglutarate, talk with your healthcare professional if you take any medications.

ALPHA-LINOLENIC ACID

What other names is the product known by?
ALA, Essential Fatty Acid, LNA, n-3 Fatty Acid, n-3 Polyunsaturated Fatty Acid, Omega-3 Fatty Acid, Omega-3 Polyunsaturated Fatty Acid.

What is it?
Alpha-linolenic acid is an essential fatty acid, which means it is needed for normal human growth and development. Nuts such as walnuts are good sources of alpha-linolenic acid.

Is it Effective?
The effectiveness ratings for **ALPHA-LINOLENIC ACID** are as follows:
Possibly Effective for... Reducing the risk of heart disease and heart attacks • Reducing the risk of hardening of the arteries (atherosclerosis) • High blood pressure • Reducing the risk of pneumonia.
Insufficient Evidence to Rate Effectiveness for... Rheumatoid arthritis (RA), multiple sclerosis, lung infections in children, lupus, diabetes, high cholesterol, kidney disease, Crohn's disease, migraines, depression, skin diseases, preventing colds, and other conditions.

Medical professionals should consult the Professional Version at www.NaturalDatabase.com.

How does it work?

Alpha-linolenic acid is thought to decrease the risk of heart disease by helping to maintain normal heart rhythm and heart pumping. It might also reduce blood clots.

Are there safety concerns?

Alpha-linolenic acid is safe for most adults when used in amounts found in foods. There isn't enough information to know if it is safe in higher amounts. Alpha-linolenic acid from food sources is very well tolerated. However, it is high in calories and may cause weight gain if consumed in excess.

Do not use alpha-linolenic acid in amounts larger than found in foods if: You are pregnant or breast-feeding. • You have high blood triglyceride levels. • You have prostate cancer or are at high risk for prostate cancer (e.g., father or brother with prostate cancer).

Are there any interactions with medications?

It is not known if alpha-linolenic acid interacts with any medicines.
Before taking alpha-linolenic acid, talk with your healthcare professional if you take any medications.

ALPHA-LIPOIC ACID

What other names is the product known by?

Acetate Replacing Factor, a-Lipoic Acid, Alpha-Lipoic Acid Extract, ALA, Biletan, Lipoic Acid, Lipoicin, Thioctacid, Thioctan, Thioctic Acid, 1,2-dithiolane-3-pentanoic acid, 1,2-dithiolane-3-valeric acid, 6,8-dithiooctanoic acid, 6,8-thioctic acid, 5-(1,2-dithiolan-3-yl) valeric acid.

What is it?

Alpha-lipoic acid is a vitamin-like chemical called an antioxidant. Yeast, liver, kidney, spinach, broccoli, and potatoes are good sources of alpha-lipoic acid. It is also made in the laboratory for use as medicine.

Is it Effective?

The effectiveness ratings for **ALPHA-LIPOIC ACID** are as follows:
Possibly Effective for... Treating type 2 diabetes • Improving symptoms such as burning, pain, and numbness in the legs and arms of people with diabetes.
Possibly Ineffective for... Treating alcoholic liver disease • Treating HIV-related brain problems • Treating a heart related nerve problem called cardiac autonomic neuropathy.
Insufficient Evidence to Rate Effectiveness for... Dementia, eye problems, chronic fatigue syndrome (CFS), HIV/AIDS, cancer, Lyme disease, Wilson's disease, heart disease, Amanita mushroom poisoning, and other conditions.

How does it work?

Alpha-lipoic acid seems to help prevent certain kinds of cell damage in the body, and also restores vitamin levels such as vitamin E and vitamin C.

Are there safety concerns?

There is some scientific evidence that alpha-lipoic acid might be safe for most adults. People taking alpha-lipoic acid by mouth might get a rash. People at risk for thiamine deficiency should take a thiamine supplement.

Diabetics should be careful to check their blood sugar levels because alpha-lipoic acid might lower blood sugar.

Do not use alpha-lipoic acid if: You are pregnant or breast-feeding. • You use alcohol excessively. • You have thiamine deficiency. • You have thyroid disease.

Are there any interactions with medications?

Medications for cancer (Chemotherapy). Alpha-lipoic acid is an antioxidant. There is some concern that antioxidants might decrease the effectiveness of some medications used for cancers. But it is too soon to know if this interaction occurs.
Medications for diabetes (Antidiabetes drugs). Alpha-lipoic acid might decrease blood sugar. Diabetes medications are also used to lower blood sugar. Taking alpha-lipoic acid along with diabetes medications might cause your blood sugar to go too low. But more evidence is needed to know if this interaction is a big concern. Monitor your blood sugar closely. Some medications used for diabetes include glimepiride (Amaryl), glyburide (DiaBeta, Glynase PresTab, Micronase), insulin, pioglitazone (Actos), rosiglitazone (Avandia), chlorpropamide (Diabinese), glipizide (Glucotrol), tolbutamide (Orinase), and others.

ALPINE CRANBERRY

What other names is the product known by?

Cowberry, Dry Ground Cranberry, Foxberry, Lingen, Lingenberry, Lingon, Lingonberry, Lowbush Cranberry, Moss Cranberry, Partridgeberry, Red Bilberry, Redberries, Red Whortleberry, Rock Cranberry, Shore Cranberry, Vine of Mount Ida.

What is it?

Alpine Cranberry is a plant. The leaves and berries are used to make medicine.

Is it Effective?

The effectiveness ratings for **ALPINE CRANBERRY** are as follows:

Insufficient Evidence to Rate Effectiveness for... Urinary tract problems, gout, arthritis, kidney stones, increasing urine production (diuretic), viral infections, and other conditions.

How does it work?

Alpine cranberry has chemicals which might help disinfect the urine.

Are there safety concerns?

Alpine cranberry is unsafe to use when the preparations of the leaves are used long-term. There isn't enough information to know if alpine cranberry is safe for short-term use. It can cause some side effects including nausea and vomiting.

There is a concern that the same chemicals which make alpine cranberry a urine disinfectant can also cause liver damage and cancer.

Alpine cranberry is unsafe for children.

Do not take alpine cranberry if: You are pregnant or breast-feeding. • You have liver disease.

Are there any interactions with medications?

It is not known if alpine cranberry interacts with any medicines.
Before taking alpine cranberry, talk with your healthcare professional if you take any medications.

ALPINE LADY'S MANTLE

What other names is the product known by?

Alchemilla Alpina, Alchemillae Alpinae Herba, Alpine Ladys Mantle.

What is it?

Alpine lady's mantle is an herb. People use it to make medicine.

Is it Effective?

The effectiveness ratings for **ALPINE LADY'S MANTLE** are as follows:

Insufficient Evidence to Rate Effectiveness for... Female complaints, heart conditions, reducing spasms, and increasing urine production (diuretic).

How does it work?

It is not known how alpine lady's mantle might work for medicinal uses.

Are there safety concerns?

It is not known if alpine lady's mantle is safe.

Do not take alpine lady's mantle if: You are pregnant or breast-feeding.

Are there any interactions with medications?

It is not known if alpine lady's mantle interacts with any medicines.
Before taking alpine lady's mantle, talk with your healthcare professional if you take any medications.

ALPINE RAGWORT

What other names is the product known by?
Ragwort, Senecio Herb.

What is it?
Alpine ragwort is a plant. The above ground parts are used to make medicine.

Is it Effective?
The effectiveness ratings for **ALPINE RAGWORT** are as follows:
Insufficient Evidence to Rate Effectiveness for... Diabetes, high blood pressure, controlling bleeding, and other conditions.

How does it work?
There's not enough information to know how alpine ragwort might work.

Are there safety concerns?
Alpine ragwort is UNSAFE when taken by mouth. It has chemicals that can cause serious liver problems, blocked veins, and cancer.

Do not use alpine ragwort if: You are pregnant or breast-feeding. • You have liver disease.

Are there any interactions with medications?
Medications that increase break down of other medications by the liver (Cytochrome P450 3A4 (CYP3A4) inducers). Alpine ragwort is broken down by the liver. Some chemicals that form when the liver breaks down alpine ragwort can be harmful. Medications that cause the liver to break down alpine ragwort might enhance the toxic effects of chemicals contained in alpine ragwort. Some of these medicines include carbamazepine (Tegretol). Alpine ragwort is broken down by the liver. Some chemicals that form when the liver breaks down alpine ragwort can be harmful. Medications that cause the liver to break down alpine ragwort might enhance the toxic effects of chemicals contained in alpine ragwort. Some of these medicines include carbamazepine (Tegretol), phenobarbital, phenytoin (Dilantin), rifampin, rifabutin (Mycobutin), and others.

ALPINIA

What other names is the product known by?
Alpinia Officinarum, Catarrh Root, China Root, Chinese Ginger, Colic Root, East India Catarrh Root, East India Root, Galanga, Galangal, Galangal Officinal, Galgant, Gargaut, India Root, Lesser Galangal, Rasna, Rhizome Galangae.

What is it?
Alpinia is a plant related to ginger. The root-like stem is used to make medicine.

Is it Effective?
The effectiveness ratings for **ALPINIA** are as follows:
Insufficient Evidence to Rate Effectiveness for... Intestinal gas, infections, spasms, fever, reducing swelling (inflammation), and other conditions.

How does it work?
Alpinia contains chemicals which block certain steps in the swelling (inflammation) pathway.

Are there safety concerns?
Alpinia is safe for most adults.

Do not take alpinia if: You are pregnant or breast-feeding.

Are there any interactions with medications?
Antacids. Antacids are used to decrease stomach acid. Alpinia may increase stomach acid. By increasing stomach acid, alpinia might decrease the effectiveness of antacids. Some antacids include calcium carbonate (Tums, others), dihydroxyaluminum sodium carbonate (Rolaids, others), magaldrate (Riopan), magnesium sulfate (Bilagog), aluminum hydroxide (Amphojel), and others.
Medications that decrease stomach acid (H2-Blockers). Alpinia might increase stomach acid. By increasing stomach acid, alpinia might decrease the effectiveness of some medications that decrease stomach acid, called H2-

Medical professionals should consult the Professional Version at www.NaturalDatabase.com.

Blockers. Some medications that decrease stomach acid include cimetidine (Tagamet), ranitidine (Zantac), nizatidine (Axid), and famotidine (Pepcid).

Medications that decrease stomach acid (Proton pump inhibitors). Alpinia might increase stomach acid. By increasing stomach acid, alpinia might decrease the effectiveness of medications that are used to decrease stomach acid, called proton pump inhibitors. Some medications that decrease stomach acid include omeprazole (Prilosec), lansoprazole (Prevacid), rabeprazole (Aciphex), pantoprazole (Protonix), and esomeprazole (Nexium).

AMARANTH

What other names is the product known by?

Amaranthus frumentaceus, Amaranthus hypochondriacus, Amaranthus leucocarpus, Chua, Huantli, Lady Bleeding, Love-Lies-Bleeding, Lovely Bleeding, Pilewort, Prince's Feather, Red Cockscomb, Rhamdana, Velvet Flower.

What is it?

Amaranth is a plant. The leaf contains a small amount of vitamin C. People use the entire plant to make medicine.

Is it Effective?

The effectiveness ratings for **AMARANTH** are as follows:

Possibly Ineffective for... Lowering high cholesterol.

Insufficient Evidence to Rate Effectiveness for... Ulcers, diarrhea, swelling (inflammation) of the mouth and throat, and other conditions.

How does it work?

Amaranth might work for some conditions by reducing swelling (astringent).

Are there safety concerns?

It is not known if amaranth is safe.

Do not use amaranth if: You are pregnant or breast-feeding.

Are there any interactions with medications?

It is not known if amaranth interacts with any medicines.
Before taking amaranth, talk with your healthcare professional if you take any medications.

AMBRETTE

What other names is the product known by?

Abelmoschus Moschatus, Abelmosk, Ambretta, Egyptian Alcee, Gandapura, Kasturidana, Kasturilatika, Latakasthuri, Latakasturi, Lathakasthuri, Muskadana, Muskmallow, Musk Seed, Okra, Target-Leaved Hibiscus.

What is it?

Ambrette is a plant. The seed of the plant is used to make medicine.

Is it Effective?

The effectiveness ratings for **AMBRETTE** are as follows:

Insufficient Evidence to Rate Effectiveness for... Spasms, snakebites, stomach cramps, low appetite, headaches, stomach cancer, hysteria, gonorrhea, lung problems, and other conditions.

How does it work?

There isn't enough information to know how ambrette works.

Are there safety concerns?

Ambrette seems safe when used in amounts found in foods. It might also be safe when a small amount of the dilute oil is used on the skin. In some people, ambrette can cause skin irritation.

Do not use ambrette if: You are pregnant or breast-feeding.

Are there any interactions with medications?

Acetaminophen (Tylenol, others). Drinking an ambrette beverage before taking acetaminophen might increase how fast your body gets rid of acetaminophen. But more information is needed to know if this is a big concern.

AMERICAN ADDER'S TONGUE

What other names is the product known by?
American Adders Tongue, Dog's Tooth Violet, Dogs Tooth Voilet, Erythronium, Erythronium americanum, Lambs Tongue, Lamb's Tongue, Rattlesnake Violet, Serpents Tongue, Serpent's Tongue, Snake Leaf, Yellow Snakeleaf, Yellow Snowdrop.

What is it?
American adder's tongue is a plant. The leaves and stem-like parts are used to make medicine.

Is it Effective?
The effectiveness ratings for **AMERICAN ADDER'S TONGUE** are as follows:
Insufficient Evidence to Rate Effectiveness for... Skin ulcers.

How does it work?
When applied directly to the skin, the leaves of American adder's tongue help soothe and soften the skin.

Are there safety concerns?
It is not known if American adder's tongue is safe. People who are allergic to other plants, such as tulips and lilies, may also have an allergic reaction to American adder's tongue.

Do not use American adder's tongue if: You are pregnant or breast-feeding. • You are allergic to tulips, lilies, or any similar plants.

Are there any interactions with medications?
It is not known if American adder's tongue interacts with any medicines.
Before taking American adder's tongue, talk with your healthcare professional if you take any medications.

AMERICAN BITTERSWEET

What other names is the product known by?
Celastrus Scandens, False Bittersweet, Waxwork.

What is it?
American Bittersweet is a plant. The root and bark of the plant are used to make medicine.

Is it Effective?
The effectiveness ratings for **AMERICAN BITTERSWEET** are as follows:
Insufficient Evidence to Rate Effectiveness for... Arthritis, menstrual disorders, liver problems, and other conditions.

How does it work?
There isn't enough information to know how American bittersweet works.

Are there safety concerns?
It is not known if American bittersweet is safe.

Do not use American bittersweet if: You are pregnant or breast-feeding.

Are there any interactions with medications?
It is not known if American bittersweet interacts with any medicines.
Before taking American bittersweet, talk with your healthcare professional if you take any medications.

AMERICAN CHESTNUT

What other names is the product known by?
Castanea Americana, Castanea Dentate.

What is it?
American chestnut is a plant. The leaves and bark of the plant are used to make medicine.

Is it Effective?

The effectiveness ratings for **AMERICAN CHESTNUT** are as follows:

Insufficient Evidence to Rate Effectiveness for... Cough, arthritis-like pain, sore throat, sedation, reducing swelling (astringent), and other conditions.

How does it work?

American chestnut contains chemicals called tannins which help reduce swelling.

Are there safety concerns?

American chestnut is safe for most adults in the amounts found in food and beverages. It is not known if American chestnut is safe in larger amounts. American chestnut might cause some side effects such as stomach and intestinal problems, kidney and liver damage, and certain cancers.

Do not use American chestnut if: You are pregnant or breast-feeding.

Are there any interactions with medications?

Medications taken by mouth (Oral drugs). American chestnut contains a large amount of chemicals called tannins. Tannins absorb substances in the stomach and intestines. Taking American chestnut along with medications taken by mouth can decrease how much medicine your body absorbs, and decrease the effectiveness of your medicine. To prevent this interaction, take American chestnut at least 1 hour after medications you take by mouth.

AMERICAN DOGWOOD

What other names is the product known by?

Bitter Redberry, Box Tree, Boxwood, Budwood, Cornel, Cornelian tree, Cornus Florida Dog-Tree, Dogwood, False Box, Green Ozier, Osier, Rose Willow, Silky Cornel, Swamp Dogwood.

What is it?

American dogwood is a plant. The bark of the plant is used to make medicine.

Is it Effective?

The effectiveness ratings for **AMERICAN DOGWOOD** are as follows:

Insufficient Evidence to Rate Effectiveness for... Headaches, fatigue, weakness, fever, chronic diarrhea, loss of appetite, malaria, treating boils and wounds, and other conditions.

How does it work?

American dogwood might have some effects against malaria.

Are there safety concerns?

It is not known if American dogwood is safe.

Do not use American dogwood if: You are pregnant or breast-feeding.

Are there any interactions with medications?

It is not known if American dogwood interacts with any medicines.
Before taking American dogwood, talk with your healthcare professional if you take any medications.

AMERICAN ELDER

What other names is the product known by?

American Elderberry, Common Elderberry, Elderberry, Elder Flower, Sabugueiro, Sambucus, Sambucus Canadensis, Sweet Elder.

What is it?

American elder is a plant. The plant has lots of vitamin C. The flower and ripe fruit are used to make medicine.

Is it Effective?

The effectiveness ratings for **AMERICAN ELDER** are as follows:

Insufficient Evidence to Rate Effectiveness for... Asthma, bronchitis, bruises, cancer, intestinal gas, constipation, colds, water retention, epilepsy, fever, gout, headache, nerve problems, and other conditions.

How does it work?
American elder leaf might have some activity against bacteria, according to preliminary research.

Are there safety concerns?
American elder flowers or the ripe fruit are safe for most adults in the amounts found in foods. There is some scientific evidence that the flowers are safe when used in larger amounts. Some side effects might include nausea, vomiting, weakness, dizziness, numbness, and stupor.

The leaves, stems, or unripe fruit do not seem to be safe. If eaten, they can cause cyanide poisoning.

Do not use American elder in amounts greater than found in foods if: You are pregnant or breast-feeding.

Are there any interactions with medications?
Medications changed by the liver (Cytochrome P450 3A4 (CYP3A4) substrates). Some medications are changed and broken down by the liver. American elder might decrease how quickly the liver breaks down some medications. Taking American elder along with some medications that are broken down by the liver can increase the effects and side effects of some medications. Before taking American elder, talk to your healthcare provider if you are taking any medications that are changed by the liver. Some medications changed by the liver include lovastatin (Mevacor).

AMERICAN HELLEBORE

What other names is the product known by?
American Veratrum, American White Hellebore, Bugbane, Devil's Bite, Earth Gall, False Hellebore, Green Hellebore, Green Veratrum, Indian Poke, Itchweed, Tickleweed Veratro Verde, Veratrum viride.

What is it?
American hellebore is a plant. The bulb and root are used to make medicine.

Is it Effective?
The effectiveness ratings for **AMERICAN HELLEBORE** are as follows:
Insufficient Evidence to Rate Effectiveness for... Epilepsy, spasms, water-retention, nervousness, fever, high blood pressure, and other conditions.

How does it work?
American hellebore contains chemicals that can help reduce blood pressure, slow the heartbeat, and act as a sedative.

Are there safety concerns?
American Hellebore probably isn't safe for anyone. There are many possible side effects including irritation of the mouth and throat lining and slowing of the heartbeat.

Large doses can cause vomiting, diarrhea, trouble swallowing, nerve problems, blindness, convulsions, paralysis, trouble breathing, and death.

Do not use American hellebore if: You are pregnant or breast-feeding. • You have a heart condition. • You have a stomach or intestine condition.

Are there any interactions with medications?
It is not known if American hellebore interacts with any medicines.
Before taking American hellebore, talk with your healthcare professional if you take any medications.

Medical professionals should consult the Professional Version at www.NaturalDatabase.com.

Medical professionals should consult the Professional Version at www.NaturalDatabase.com.

AMERICAN IVY

What other names is the product known by?
American Woodbine, Creeper, False Grapes, Five Leaves, Ivy, Parthenocissus quinquefolia, Virginia Creeper, Wild Woodbine, Wild Woodvine, Woody Climber.

What is it?
American ivy is a plant. The bark of the plant is used to make medicine.

Is it Effective?
The effectiveness ratings for **AMERICAN IVY** are as follows:
Insufficient Evidence to Rate Effectiveness for... Digestive disorders, stimulating sweating, reducing swelling (astringent), and as a tonic.

How does it work?
There isn't enough information to know how American ivy might work.

Are there safety concerns?
There isn't enough information to know if American ivy is safe. The berries contain chemicals that are considered poisonous.

Do not use American ivy if: You are pregnant or breast-feeding.

Are there any interactions with medications?
It is not known if American ivy interacts with any medicines.
Before taking American ivy, talk with your healthcare professional if you take any medications.

AMERICAN MISTLETOE

What other names is the product known by?
Eastern Mistletoe, Mistletoe.

What is it?
American mistletoe is a plant. The flower, fruit, leaf, and stem are used as medicine.

Is it Effective?
The effectiveness ratings for **AMERICAN MISTLETOE** are as follows:
Insufficient Evidence to Rate Effectiveness for... Increasing muscle contractions, causing abortion, or any other uses.

How does it work?
Toxins in American mistletoe can adversely affect the heart.

Are there safety concerns?
American mistletoe is UNSAFE. Do not use it. It can cause nausea, vomiting, diarrhea, decreased heart rate, hallucinations, and heart problems.

Are there any interactions with medications?
It is not known if American mistletoe interacts with any medicines.
Before taking American mistletoe, talk with your healthcare professional if you take any medications.

AMERICAN PAWPAW

What other names is the product known by?
Annona triloba, Asimina triloba, Custard Apple, Dog-Banana, Pawpaw.

What is it?
American pawpaw is a plant. The bark, leaf, and seed are used to make medicine.

Is it Effective?
The effectiveness ratings for **AMERICAN PAWPAW** are as follows:
Insufficient Evidence to Rate Effectiveness for... Fever, vomiting, swelling of the mouth and throat, and other conditions.

How does it work?
American pawpaw has chemicals that might have activity against certain lung and breast cancers.

Are there safety concerns?
It is not known if American pawpaw is safe. It can cause some side effects such as nausea, rash, and itching.

Do not use American pawpaw if: You are pregnant or breast-feeding.

Are there any interactions with medications?
It is not known if American pawpaw interacts with any medicines.
Before taking American pawpaw, talk with your healthcare professional if you take any medications.

AMERICAN SPIKENARD

What other names is the product known by?
Aralia Racemosa, Indian Root, Life-of-Man, Life of Man, Old Man's Root, Pettymorell, Small Spikenard, Spignet.

What is it?
American spikenard is a plant. The root is used to make medicine.

Is it Effective?
The effectiveness ratings for **AMERICAN SPIKENARD** are as follows:
Insufficient Evidence to Rate Effectiveness for... Colds, coughs, asthma, arthritis, skin diseases, promoting sweating, and other conditions.

How does it work?
There isn't enough information to know how American spikenard works.

Are there safety concerns?
There isn't enough information to know if American spikenard is safe. If applied directly to the skin, it might be irritating.

Do not use American spikenard if: You are pregnant or breast-feeding.

Are there any interactions with medications?
It is not known if American spikenard interacts with any medicines.
Before taking American spikenard, talk with your healthcare professional if you take any medications.

AMERICAN WHITE POND LILY

What other names is the product known by?
Cow Cabbage, Nymphaea odorata, Pond Lily, Water Cabbage, Water Lily, Water Nymph.

What is it?
American white pond lily is a plant. The bulb and root are used to make medicine.

Is it Effective?
The effectiveness ratings for **AMERICAN WHITE POND LILY** are as follows:
Insufficient Evidence to Rate Effectiveness for... Chronic diarrhea, vaginal conditions, diseases of the throat and mouth, and healing burns and boils.

How does it work?
American white pond lily contains chemicals called tannins which probably help treat diarrhea by reducing swelling (inflammation). The tannins might also help kill some germs.

Are there safety concerns?

There isn't enough information to know if American white pond lily is safe.

Do not use American white pond lily if: You are pregnant or breast-feeding.

Are there any interactions with medications?

It is not known if American white pond lily interacts with any medicines.
Before taking American white pond lily, talk with your healthcare professional if you take any medications.

ANDIROBA

What other names is the product known by?

Andiroba-Saruba, Bastard Mahogany, Brazilian Mahogany, Carapa, Carapa guianensis, Cedro, Crabwood, Iandirova, Mahogany, Requia.

What is it?

Andiroba is a plant. The bark and leaf are used to make medicine.

Is it Effective?

The effectiveness ratings for **ANDIROBA** are as follows:
Insufficient Evidence to Rate Effectiveness for... Fevers, herpes, intestinal worms, coughs, skin conditions, sores, ulcers, removing ticks from the head, skin parasites, arthritis, muscle and joint aches and injuries, and other conditions.

How does it work?

There isn't enough information available to know how andiroba works.

Are there safety concerns?

There isn't enough information available to know if andiroba is safe to use.

Do not use andiroba if: You are pregnant or breast-feeding.

Are there any interactions with medications?

It is not known if andiroba interacts with any medicines.
Before taking andiroba, talk with your healthcare professional if you take any medications.

ANDRACHNE

What other names is the product known by?

Andrachne Aspera, Andrachne Cordifolia, Andrachne Phyllanthoides.

What is it?

Andrachne is a plant. In Yemen folklore, andrachne is used to make medicine.

Is it Effective?

The effectiveness ratings for **ANDRACHNE** are as follows:
Insufficient Evidence to Rate Effectiveness for... Eye swelling (inflammation).

How does it work?

There isn't enough information to know how andrachne works.

Are there safety concerns?

There isn't enough information to know if andrachne is safe.

Do not use andrachne if: You are pregnant or breast-feeding.

Are there any interactions with medications?

It is not known if andrachne interacts with any medicines.
Before taking andrachne, talk with your healthcare professional if you take any medications.

ANDROGRAPHIS

What other names is the product known by?

Andrographis Paniculata, Andrographolide, Bhunimba, Bidara, Carmantina, Chiretta, Chuan Xin Lian, Chuan Xin Lin, Creat, Fa Tha Lai Jone, Fa-Tha-Lai-Jone, Gubak, Indian Echinacea, Kalamegha, Kalmegha, Kariyat, King of Bitters, Kirta, Nabin Chanvandi, Poogiphalam, Sadilata, Sambilata, Shivaphala, Supari, Takila, Vizra Ufar, Yavatikta.

What is it?

Andrographis is a plant local to South Asian countries such as India and Sri Lanka. The leaf and underground stem are used to make medicine.

Is it Effective?

The effectiveness ratings for **ANDROGRAPHIS** are as follows:

Possibly Effective for... Treating the common cold • Reducing the fever and sore throat associated with tonsillitis.
Insufficient Evidence to Rate Effectiveness for... Familial Mediterranean fever, influenza, allergies, sinus infections, HIV/AIDS, anorexia, heart disease, liver problems, parasites, infections, skin diseases, ulcers, preventing the common cold, and other conditions.

How does it work?

Andrographis might stimulate the immune system. It may improve the blood cell counts in people with HIV, and help with allergies.

Are there safety concerns?

Andrographis is safe when used short-term in most adults. It might also be safe when used long-term.

It can cause side effects such as loss of appetite, diarrhea, vomiting, rash, headache, and fatigue.

When used in high doses or long-term, andrographis might cause swollen lymph glands, serious allergic reactions, elevations of liver enzymes, and other side effects.

Do not use andrographis if: You are pregnant or breast-feeding. • You have problems with infertility, or you are trying to get pregnant or father a child. • You have a bleeding disorder. • You have low blood pressure.

Are there any interactions with medications?

Medications that slow blood clotting (Anticoagulant / Antiplatelet drugs). Andrographis might slow blood clotting. Taking andrographis along with medications that also slow clotting might increase the chances of bruising and bleeding. Some medications that slow blood clotting include aspirin, clopidogrel (Plavix), diclofenac (Voltaren, Cataflam, others), ibuprofen (Advil, Motrin, others), naproxen (Anaprox, Naprosyn, others), dalteparin (Fragmin), enoxaparin (Lovenox), heparin, warfarin (Coumadin), and others.
Medications for high blood pressure (Antihypertensive drugs). Andrographis seems to decrease blood pressure. Taking andrographis along with medications for high blood pressure might cause your blood pressure to go too low. Some medications for high blood pressure include captopril (Capoten), enalapril (Vasotec), losartan (Cozaar), valsartan (Diovan), diltiazem (Cardizem), Amlodipine (Norvasc), hydrochlorothiazide (HydroDiuril), furosemide (Lasix), and many others.
Medications that decrease the immune system (Immunosuppressants). Andrographis increases the immune system. By increasing the immune system, andrographis might decrease the effectiveness of medications that decrease the immune system. Some medications that decrease the immune system include azathioprine (Imuran), basiliximab (Simulect), cyclosporine (Neoral, Sandimmune), daclizumab (Zenapax), muromonab-CD3 (OKT3, Orthoclone OKT3), mycophenolate (CellCept), tacrolimus (FK506, Prograf), sirolimus (Rapamune), prednisone (Deltasone, Orasone), corticosteroids (glucocorticoids), and others.

ANDROSTENEDIOL

What other names is the product known by?

Androdiol; 4-Androstenediol; 4-AD; 4-androstene-3beta,17beta-diol; 5-Androstenediol; 5-AD; 5-androstene-3beta,17beta-diol.

What is it?

Androstenediol is a steroid. It is used to make medicine.

Is it Effective?

The effectiveness ratings for **ANDROSTENEDIOL** are as follows:

Possibly Ineffective... Athletic conditioning. Androstenediol does not seem to help increase muscle size or strength.

Insufficient Evidence to Rate Effectiveness for... Increasing energy, improving body recovery and growth from exercise, heightening sexual arousal and function, increasing a sense of well being, and other conditions.

How does it work?

Androstenediol is a steroid hormone used by the body to make testosterone and estrogen.

Are there safety concerns?

Androstenediol seems to be unsafe. There is some concern that products can vary from what is listed on the label. Women might experience masculinization, which includes deepening of the voice, facial hair growth, acne, abnormal menstrual periods, male-pattern baldness, thickening of the skin, and depression. Androstenediol might also worsen breast or prostate cancers and other hormone-sensitive cancers. There is also concern that androstenediol might increase the risk for heart disease.

Do not use androstenediol if: You are pregnant or breast-feeding. • You have breast cancer. • You have a prostate condition known as benign prostate hypertrophy (BPH) or prostate cancer. • You have cancer of the uterus or ovaries or other hormone-sensitive cancers. • You have a hormone-sensitive condition such as endometriosis or uterine fibroids.

Are there any interactions with medications?

Estrogens. Androstenediol seems to increase estrogen levels in the body. Taking androstenediol along with estrogen pills might cause too much estrogen in the body. Some estrogen pills include conjugated equine estrogens (Premarin), ethinyl estradiol, estradiol, and others.

Testosterone. The body changes androstenediol into testosterone. Taking androstenediol with a testosterone pill might cause there to be too much testosterone in the body. This might increase the chance of testosterone side effects.

ANDROSTENEDIONE

What other names is the product known by?

Andro, Androstene, Androst-4-ene-3,17-dione, 4-androstene-3,17-dione.

What is it?

Androstenedione is a steroid. It is used to make medicine.

Is it Effective?

The effectiveness ratings for **ANDROSTENEDIONE** are as follows:

Likely Ineffective for... Improving muscle size or strength combined with weight lifting.

Insufficient Evidence to Rate Effectiveness for... Enhancing athletic performance, increasing energy, red blood cell health, heightening sexual arousal and function, and other conditions.

How does it work?

Androstenedione is a steroid hormone used by the body to make testosterone and estrogen.

Are there safety concerns?

Androstenedione probably isn't safe for anyone. Some side effects experienced by men include: reduced sperm production, shrunken testicles, painful or prolonged erections, breast development, behavioral changes, heart disease, and others. Women might experience masculinization, which includes deepening of the voice, facial hair growth, acne, abnormal menstrual periods, male-pattern baldness, coarsening of the skin, and depression. It can also increase the risk of cancers of the breast, prostate, or pancreas. Androstenedione is poisonous to the liver.

In children, androstenedione might stop bone growth and lead to decreased adult height, as well as early onset of puberty.

There is some concern that the strength and purity of androstenedione products can differ from the product labeling.

Do not take androstenedione if: You are pregnant or breast-feeding. • You have a hormone sensitive condition such as endometriosis or uterine fibroids. • You have a hormone sensitive cancer such as breast, uterine, ovarian, or prostate cancer. • You have liver disease.

Medical professionals should consult the Professional Version at www.NaturalDatabase.com.

Natural Medicines Comprehensive Database Consumer Version   (209) 472-2244

Are there any interactions with medications?

Estrogens. Androstenedione seems to increase estrogen levels in the body. Taking androstenedione along with estrogen pills might cause too much estrogen in the body. Some estrogen pills include conjugated equine estrogens (Premarin), ethinyl estradiol, estradiol, and others.

ANDROSTENETRIONE

What other names is the product known by?

4-androstene-3,6,17-trione, 6-Oxo, androst-4- ene-3,6,17-trione.

What is it?

Androstenetrione is a steroid.

Is it Effective?

The effectiveness ratings for **ANDROSTENETRIONE** are as follows:
Insufficient Evidence to Rate Effectiveness for... Improving athletic performance and other conditions.

How does it work?

Androstenetrione might make the body produce more testosterone and less estrogen.

Are there safety concerns?

Androstenetrione might increase testosterone in the body. Too much testosterone can cause serious side effects including liver problems, heart problems, and cancer. Avoid using androstenetrione.

Do not use androstenetrione if: You are pregnant or breast-feeding. • You have liver disease. • You have prostate cancer.

Are there any interactions with medications?

It is not known if androstentrione interacts with any medicines.
Before taking androstenetrione, talk with your healthcare professional if you take any medications.

ANGEL'S TRUMPET

What other names is the product known by?

Datura Sauveolens, Devil's Trumpet.

What is it?

Angel's trumpet is a plant. The leaves and flowers are used to make medicines.

Is it Effective?

The effectiveness ratings for **ANGEL'S TRUMPET** are as follows:
Insufficient Evidence to Rate Effectiveness for... Asthma, and causing euphoria and hallucinations.

How does it work?

Angel's trumpet contains chemicals which can cause euphoria and hallucinations.

Are there safety concerns?

Angel's trumpet is UNSAFE. It is poisonous. Some of the side effects include confusion, dilated pupils, intense thirst, dry skin, flushing, fever, high blood pressure, fast heartbeat, hallucinations, nervousness, loss of memory, convulsions, paralysis, coma, and death.

Severe poisoning has occurred in teenagers experimenting with angel's trumpet.

Do not use angel's trumpet if: You are pregnant or breast-feeding.

Are there any interactions with medications?

Drying medications (Anticholinergic drugs). Angel's trumpet contains chemicals that cause a drying effect. It also affects the brain and heart. Drying medications called anticholinergic drugs can also cause these effects. Taking angel's trumpet and drying medications together might cause side effects including dry skin, dizziness, low blood pressure, fast heartbeat, and other serious side effects. Some of these drying medications include atropine, scopolamine, and some medications used for allergies (antihistamines), and for depression (antidepressants).

Medical professionals should consult the Professional Version at www.NaturalDatabase.com.

ANGELICA

What other names is the product known by?

American Angelica, Angelica acutiloba, Angelica archangelica, Angelica atropurpurea, Angelica curtisi, Angelica Dahurica, Angelicae Fructus, Angelicae Herba, Angelicae Radix, Angelica sylvestris, Angelicae, Archangelica officinalis, Bai Zhi, Garden Angelica, European Angelica, Japanese Angelica, Root of the Holy Ghost, Wild Angelica, Wild Angelica.

What is it?

Angelica is a plant. The root, seed, and fruit are used to make medicine.

Is it Effective?

The effectiveness ratings for **ANGELICA** are as follows:
Possibly Effective for... Upset stomach (dyspepsia), when a combination of angelica and five other herbs is used (Iberogast, Enzymatic Therapy) • Premature ejaculation, when applied directly to the skin of the penis in combination with other medicines.
Insufficient Evidence to Rate Effectiveness for... Intestinal cramps and gas, nerve pain, arthritis-like pain, fluid retention, menstrual disorders, promoting sweating, and increasing urine production (diuretic).

How does it work?

Angelica root might work in premature ejaculation by increasing the threshold of vibrations and senses received by the penis.

Are there safety concerns?

Angelica is safe when used in foods. Angelica root seems to be safe for most adults when used as a cream. There is not enough information to know if angelica is safe when used as a medicine.

If you take angelica, wear sunblock outside, especially if you are light-skinned. Angelica might make your skin more sensitive to sunlight.

Do not use angelica root if: You are pregnant or breast-feeding.

Are there any interactions with medications?

It is not known if Angelica interacts with any medicines.
Before taking Angelica talk to you healthcare provider if you take any medications.

ANGOSTURA

What other names is the product known by?

Angustura, Angostura trifoliata, Bonplandia trifoliata, Carony Bark, Cusparia, Cusparia Bark, Cusparia febrifuga, Cusparia trifoliata, Galipea Officinalis, True Angostura.

What is it?

Angostura is a plant. The bark is used to make medicine.

Is it Effective?

The effectiveness ratings for **ANGOSTURA** are as follows:
Insufficient Evidence to Rate Effectiveness for... Fever, diarrhea, spasms, induce vomiting, preventing return of malaria, and purging the bowels.

How does it work?

Angostura has chemicals that help reduce spasms.

Are there safety concerns?

Angostura extract is safe for most adults when used in amounts commonly found in foods or drinks. There isn't enough information to know if angostura is safe in amounts greater than those found in foods or drinks. Large doses of angostura might cause nausea and vomiting.

Do not use angostura if: You are pregnant or breast-feeding.

Are there any interactions with medications?
It is not known if angostura interacts with any medicines.
Before taking angostura, talk with your healthcare professional if you take any medications.

ANISE

What other names is the product known by?
Aniseed, Anisi Fructus, Phystoestrogen, Pimpinella Anisum, Semen Anisi, Sweet Cumin.

What is it?
Anise is an herb. The seed (fruit) and oil, and less frequently the root and leaf, are used to make medicine.

Is it Effective?
The effectiveness ratings for **ANISE** are as follows:
Insufficient Evidence to Rate Effectiveness for... Head lice, upset stomach, intestinal gas, inducing menstrual periods, increasing breast milk, increasing libido, lice, scabies, psoriasis, as an expectorant for coughs, reducing spasms, and other conditions.

How does it work?
There are chemicals in anise that may have estrogen-like effects. Chemicals in anise may also act as insecticides.

Are there safety concerns?
Anise is safe in the amounts typically found in foods. It also appears to be safe when applied to the scalp in combination with other herbs. There isn't enough information available to know if anise is safe to take by mouth in medicinal amounts.
Do not use anise in amounts larger than those found in foods if: You are pregnant or breast-feeding. • You have a hormone-sensitive condition such as breast cancer, uterine cancer, ovarian cancer, endometriosis, or uterine fibroids.

Are there any interactions with medications?
Birth control pills (Contraceptive drugs). Some birth control pills contain estrogen. Anise might have some of the same effects as estrogen. But anise isn't as strong as the estrogen in birth control pills. Taking anise along with birth control pills might decrease the effectiveness of birth control pills. If you take birth control pills along with anise, use an additional form of birth control such as a condom. Some birth control pills include ethinyl estradiol and levonorgestrel (Triphasil), ethinyl estradiol and norethindrone (Ortho-Novum 1/35, Ortho-Novum 7/7/7), and others.
Estrogens. Large amounts of anise might have some of the same effects as estrogen. But large amounts of anise aren't as strong as estrogen pills. Taking anise along with estrogen pills might decrease the effects of estrogen pills. Some estrogen pills include conjugated equine estrogens (Premarin), ethinyl estradiol, estradiol, and others.
Tamoxifen (Nolvadex). Some types of cancer are affected by hormones in the body. Estrogen-sensitive cancers are cancers that are affected by estrogen levels in the body. Tamoxifen (Nolvadex) is used to help treat and prevent these types of cancer. Anise seems to also affect estrogen levels in the body. By affecting estrogen in the body, anise might decrease the effectiveness of tamoxifen (Nolvadex). Do not take anise if you are taking tamoxifen (Nolvadex).

ANNATTO

What other names is the product known by?
Achiote, Achiotillo, Annotta, Arnotta, Bija, Bixa orellana, Lipstick Tree, Roucou.

What is it?
Annatto is a plant. The seed and leaf are used to make medicine.

Is it Effective?
The effectiveness ratings for **ANNATTO** are as follows:
Insufficient Evidence to Rate Effectiveness for... Diarrhea, diabetes, fevers, hepatitis, sunburn, and other conditions.

How does it work?
There isn't enough information to know how annatto works.

Medical professionals should consult the Professional Version at www.NaturalDatabase.com.

Are there safety concerns?

Annatto is safe for most people when used in food amounts. It is not known if annatto is safe for use as a medicine.

Annatto might raise blood sugar levels. If you have diabetes, check your blood sugar levels.

Do not use annatto if: You are pregnant or breast-feeding.

Are there any interactions with medications?

Medications for diabetes (Antidiabetes drugs). Annatto might increase blood sugar. Diabetes medications are used to lower blood sugar. By increasing blood sugar, annatto might decrease the effectiveness of diabetes medications. Monitor your blood sugar closely. The dose of your diabetes medication might need to be changed. Some medications used for diabetes include glimepiride (Amaryl), glyburide (DiaBeta, Glynase PresTab, Micronase), insulin, pioglitazone (Actos), rosiglitazone (Avandia), chlorpropamide (Diabinese), glipizide (Glucotrol), tolbutamide (Orinase), and others.

APPLE

What other names is the product known by?

Apples, Malus Sylvestris.

What is it?

Apple the fruit from an apple tree. The fruit is used to make medicine.

Is it Effective?

The effectiveness ratings for **APPLE** are as follows:
Insufficient Evidence to Rate Effectiveness for... Cancer, diabetes, fever, heart problems, scurvy, warts, cleaning teeth, decreasing the risk of lung cancer, softening and passing gallstones, treating diarrhea, treating constipation, and other conditions.

How does it work?

Apples contain pectin, which helps bulk up the stool to treat diarrhea and constipation.

Are there safety concerns?

Apples are safe for most people when eaten without the seeds. No side effects are generally known or predicted to occur with apple fruit.

The apple seeds contain cyanide and are poisonous. If enough seeds are eaten, death can occur.

Do not use apple seeds if: You are pregnant or breast-feeding.

Are there any interactions with medications?

Fexofenadine (Allegra). Apple juice can decrease how much fexofenadine (Allegra) your body absorbs. Taking apple along with fexofenadine (Allegra) might decrease the effectiveness of fexofenadine (Allegra).

APPLE CIDER VINEGAR

What other names is the product known by?

Cider Vinegar.

What is it?

Apple cider vinegar is fermented juice from crushed apples. It contains vitamins and minerals such as vitamins B1, B2, B6, and C; folic acid; niacin; potassium; calcium; iron; magnesium; and many others. It is used to make medicine.

Is it Effective?

The effectiveness ratings for **APPLE CIDER VINEGAR** are as follows:
Insufficient Evidence to Rate Effectiveness for... Weight loss, leg cramps and pain, unsettled stomach, sore throats, sinus problems, high blood pressure, arthritis, infection, osteoporosis, lowering cholesterol, improving circulation, acne, sunburn, shingles, bites, dandruff, vaginitis, and other conditions.

 Natural Medicines Comprehensive Database Consumer Version (209) 472-2244

How does it work?
There isn't enough information to know how apple cider vinegar works.

Are there safety concerns?
It is not known if taking apple cider vinegar for medical uses is safe. Consuming 8 ounces of apple cider vinegar per day, long-term might lead to problems such as low potassium and osteoporosis.

Do not use apple cider vinegar if: You are pregnant or breast-feeding.

Are there any interactions with medications?
Digoxin (Lanoxin). Large amounts of apple cider vinegar can decrease potassium levels in the body. Low potassium levels can increase the side effects of digoxin (Lanoxin).
Insulin. Insulin might decrease potassium levels in the body. Large amounts of apple cider vinegar might also decrease potassium levels in the body. Taking apple cider vinegar along with insulin might cause potassium levels in the body to be too low. Avoid taking large amounts of apple cider vinegar if you take insulin.
Water pills (Diuretic drugs). Large amounts of apple cider vinegar can decrease potassium levels in the body. "Water pills" can also decrease potassium in the body. Taking apple cider vinegar along with "water pills" might decrease potassium in the body too much. Some "water pills" that can deplete potassium include chlorothiazide (Diuril), chlorthalidone (Thalitone), furosemide (Lasix), hydrochlorothiazide (HCTZ, HydroDiuril, Microzide), and others.

APRICOT

What other names is the product known by?
Amygdaloside, Apricots, Armeniaca, Chinese Almond, Laetrile, Madelonitrile, Vitamin B17.

What is it?
Apricot is the fruit from an apricot tree. The apricot seed and oil are sometimes used to make medicines.

Is it Effective?
The effectiveness ratings for **APRICOT** are as follows:
Ineffective for... Treating cancer.
Insufficient Evidence to Rate Effectiveness for... Asthma, cough, constipation, bleeding, and infertility.

How does it work?
Some people used to think that a chemical in apricot seeds called amygdalin could be used to fight cancer. This theory has been disproved. Amygdalin in apricot seeds is broken down into a dangerous chemical called hydrocyanic acid.

Are there safety concerns?
Apricot preparations that are applied to the skin seem to be safe, but don't take apricot preparations by mouth. They can contain a dangerous chemical that can cause serious side effects including dizziness, headache, nausea and vomiting, shortness of breath, irregular heartbeats, low blood pressure, seizures, paralysis, coma, and death.

Are there any interactions with medications?
It is not known if apricot interacts with any medicines.
Before taking apricot, talk with your healthcare professional if you take any medications.

ARECA

What other names is the product known by?
Areca catechu, Areca Nut, Betel Nut, Betel Quid, Gubak, Pinag, Pinlag, Poogiphalam, Puga, Supari, Tantusara.

What is it?
The nut part of the Areca plant is used to make medicine.

Is it Effective?
The effectiveness ratings for **ARECA** are as follows:
Insufficient Evidence to Rate Effectiveness for... Schizophrenia, glaucoma, or aiding in digestion.

Medical professionals should consult the Professional Version at www.NaturalDatabase.com.

CONSUMER VERSION

How does it work?
It is thought that areca affects chemicals in the brain and other parts of the central nervous system.

Are there safety concerns?
Areca is not considered safe when taken by mouth.

Chewing the areca nut can make your mouth, lips, and stool turn red. It can cause stimulant effects similar to caffeine and tobacco use. It can also cause more severe effects including vomiting, diarrhea, problems with the gums in the mouth, increased saliva, coma, and death.
Do not take areca if: You are pregnant or breast-feeding. • You have asthma.

Are there any interactions with medications?
Drying medications (Anticholinergic drugs). Areca contains chemicals that can affect the brain and heart. Some of these drying medications can also affect the brain and heart. But areca works differently than drying medications. Areca might decrease the effects of drying medications. Some of these drying medications include atropine, scopolamine, and some medications used for allergies (antihistamines), and for depression (antidepressants).
Procyclidine. Procyclidine can affect chemicals in the body. Areca can also affect chemicals in the body. But areca has the opposite effect of procyclidine. Taking areca along with procyclidine might decrease the effectiveness of procyclidine.
Various medications used for glaucoma, Alzheimer's disease, and other conditions (Cholinergic drugs). Areca contains a chemical that affects the body. This chemical is similar to some medications used for glaucoma, Alzheimer's disease, and other conditions. Taking areca with these medications might increase the chance of side effects. Some of these medications used for glaucoma, Alzheimer's disease, and other conditions include pilocarpine (Pilocar and others), donepezil (Aricept), tacrine (Cognex), and others.

ARENARIA RUBRA

What other names is the product known by?
Common Sandspurry, Sabline Rouge, Sandwort, Spergularia rubra.

What is it?
Arenaria rubra is an herb. The plant is used to make medicine.

Is it Effective?
The effectiveness ratings for **ARENARIA RUBRA** are as follows:
Insufficient Evidence to Rate Effectiveness for... Urinary tract problems.

How does it work?
Arenaria rubra might help increase urine production (diuretic).

Are there safety concerns?
There isn't enough information to know if arenaria rubra is safe.

Do not use arenaria rubra if: You are pregnant or breast-feeding.

Are there any interactions with medications?
It is not known if arenaria rubra interacts with any medicines.
Before taking arenaria rubra, talk with your healthcare professional if you take any medications.

ARISTOLOCHIA

What other names is the product known by?
Aristolochia Auricularia, Aristolochia Clematitis, Aristolochia Fangchi, Aristolochia Heterophylla, Aristolochia Kwangsiensis, Aristolochia Manshuriensis, Aristolochia Moupinensis, Aristolochia Reticulata, Aristolochia Serpentaria, Birthwort, Guang Fang Ji, Long Birthwort, Pelican Flower, Red River Snakeroot, Sangree Root, Sangrel, Serpentaria, Snakeroot, Snakeweed, Texas Snakeroot, Virginia Serpentary, Virginia Snakeroot.

What is it?
Aristolochia is a plant. The above ground parts and root of the plant are used to make medicine.

Is it Effective?

The effectiveness ratings for **ARISTOLOCHIA** are as follows:

Insufficient Evidence to Rate Effectiveness for... Sexual arousal, convulsions, immune stimulation, promoting menstruation, colic, gallbladder cramps, arthritis, gout, rheumatism, eczema, and wound treatment.

How does it work?

There isn't enough information to know how aristolochia works.

Are there safety concerns?

Aristolochia is UNSAFE. It contains aristolochic acid, which is toxic to the kidneys and causes cancer. Use of aristolochia can cause kidney damage leading to the need for kidney dialysis and kidney transplant. It also greatly increases the risk of bladder cancer and other urological tract cancers.

Due to safety concerns, aristolochia is banned in many countries.

Do not use aristolochia if: You are pregnant or breast-feeding. • You have kidney disease.

Are there any interactions with medications?

It is not known if aristolochia interacts with any medicines.

Before taking aristolochia, talk with your healthcare professional if you take any medications.

ARNICA

What other names is the product known by?

Arnica cordifolia, Arnica Flos, Arnica Flower, Arnica fulgens, Arnica latifolia, Arnica montana, Arnica sororia, Arnikabluten, Bergwohlverieih, Fleurs d'Arnica, Kraftwurz, Leopard's Bane, Mountain Tobacco, Wolf's Bane, Wundkraut.

What is it?

The flower of arnica is used to make medicine.

Is it Effective?

The effectiveness ratings for **ARNICA** are as follows:

Possibly Ineffective for... Reducing pain, swelling, and complications of wisdom tooth removal.

Insufficient Evidence to Rate Effectiveness for... Bruises, aches, sprains, insect bites, and sore throats.

How does it work?

The active chemicals in arnica may reduce swelling, decrease pain, and act as antibiotics.

Are there safety concerns?

Arnica products that are put on unbroken skin seem to be safe. Don't take arnica products by mouth. Don't apply it to broken or damaged skin.

Arnica is considered a poison. When taken by mouth it can cause irritation of the mouth and throat, stomach pain, vomiting, diarrhea, skin rashes, shortness of breath, a fast heartbeat, an increase in blood pressure, heart damage, coma, and death.

Do not use arnica if: You are pregnant or breast-feeding. • You are allergic to ragweed, chrysanthemums, marigolds, and daisies. • You have irritable bowel, ulcers, Chrohn's disease, or other stomach or intestinal conditions.

Are there any interactions with medications?

Medications that slow blood clotting (Anticoagulant / Antiplatelet drugs). Arnica might slow blood clotting. Taking arnica along with medications that also slow clotting might increase the chances of bruising and bleeding. Some medications that slow blood clotting include aspirin, clopidogrel (Plavix), diclofenac (Voltaren, Cataflam, others), ibuprofen (Advil, Motrin, others), naproxen (Anaprox, Naprosyn, others), dalteparin (Fragmin), enoxaparin (Lovenox), heparin, warfarin (Coumadin), and others.

Medical professionals should consult the Professional Version at www.NaturalDatabase.com.

ARRACH

What other names is the product known by?

Chenopodium vulvaria, Dog's Arrach, Goat's Arrach, Goosefoot, Netchweed, Oraches, Stinking Arrach, Stinking Goosefoot, Stinking Motherwort.

What is it?

Arrach is a plant. People use the whole flowering plant to make medicine.

Is it Effective?

The effectiveness ratings for **ARRACH** are as follows:
Insufficient Evidence to Rate Effectiveness for... Menstrual cramps and triggering menstrual flow.

How does it work?

There isn't enough information to know how arrach works.

Are there safety concerns?

There isn't enough information to know if arrach is safe. Arrach can cause skin to become extra sensitive to the sun. Wear sunblock outside, especially if you are light-skinned.

Do not use arrach if: You are pregnant or breast-feeding.

Are there any interactions with medications?

Medications that increase sensitivity to sunlight (Photosensitizing drugs). Some medications can increase sensitivity to sunlight. Arrach might also increase your sensitivity to sunlight. Taking arrach along with medication that increases sensitivity to sunlight could increase the chances of sunburn, blistering or rashes on areas of skin exposed to sunlight. Be sure to wear sunblock and protective clothing when spending time in the sun. Some drugs that cause photosensitivity include amitriptyline (Elavil), Ciprofloxacin (Cipro), norfloxacin (Noroxin), lomefloxacin (Maxaquin), ofloxacin (Floxin), levofloxacin (Levaquin), sparfloxacin (Zagam), gatifloxacin (Tequin), moxifloxacin (Avelox), trimethoprim/sulfamethoxazole (Septra), tetracycline, methoxsalen (8-methoxypsoralen, 8-MOP, Oxsoralen), and Trioxsalen (Trisoralen).

ARROWROOT

What other names is the product known by?

Maranta, Maranta arundinacea.

What is it?

Arrowroot is a plant. People use the root and rhizome (underground stem) to make medicine.

Is it Effective?

The effectiveness ratings for **ARROWROOT** are as follows:
Insufficient Evidence to Rate Effectiveness for... Stomach and intestine problems, including diarrhea. Soothing mucous membranes, such as the mouth and gum linings.

How does it work?

There is some scientific evidence that arrowroot may help get rid of cholesterol in the body. There isn't enough information to know how it works for stomach and intestine problems or for other uses.

Are there safety concerns?

Arrowroot is safe when the starch is used in foods. It might be safe when used as a medicine.

Do not use arrowroot if: You are pregnant or breast-feeding, except for amounts found in foods.

Are there any interactions with medications?

It is not known if arrowroot interacts with any medicines.
Before taking arrowroot, talk with your healthcare professional if you take any medications.

 Natural Medicines Comprehensive Database Consumer Version (209) 472-2244

ARTICHOKE

What other names is the product known by?

Alcachofa, Alcaucil, Artichaut Commun, Artichoke Extract, Artichoke Leaf, Artichoke Leaf Extract, Artischocke, Cardo, Cardo de Comer, Cardon d'Espagne, Cardoon, Cynara Cardunculus, Cynara Scolymus, Garden Artichoke, Gemuseartischocke, Globe Artichoke, Kardone, Tyosen-Azami.

What is it?

Artichoke is a plant. The leaf, stem, and root are used to make medicine.

Is it Effective?

The effectiveness ratings for **ARTICHOKE** are as follows:
Possibly Effective for... Upset stomach symptoms such as nausea, vomiting, flatulence (gas), and stomach pain • High cholesterol.
Possibly Ineffective for... Preventing alcohol-induced hangover.
Insufficient Evidence to Rate Effectiveness for... Irritable bowel syndrome, water retention, snakebites, kidney problems, anemia, arthritis, liver problems, preventing gallstones, high blood pressure, and other conditions.

How does it work?

Artichoke has chemicals that can reduce nausea and vomiting, spasms, and intestinal gas. These chemicals have also been shown to lower cholesterol.

Are there safety concerns?

Artichoke is safe in the amounts used in foods. It might be safe when used as a medicine. In some people, artichoke can cause some side effects such as intestinal gas and allergic reactions. People at the greatest risk of allergic reactions are those who are allergic to plants such as marigolds, daisies, and other similar herbs.

Do not use artichoke if: You are pregnant or breast-feeding, except in amounts found in foods. • You have a bile duct blockage. • You have gallstones. • You are allergic to marigolds, daisies, and other similar herbs.

Are there any interactions with medications?

It is not known if artichoke interacts with any medicines.
Before taking artichoke, talk with your healthcare professional if you take any medications.

ARUM

What other names is the product known by?

Adder's Root, Arum maculatum, Bobbins, Cocky Baby, Cuckoo Pint, Cypress Powder, Dragon Root, Friar's Cowl, Gaglee, Kings and Queens, Ladysmock, Lords and Ladies, Parson and Clerk, Portland Arrowroot, Quaker, Ramp, Starchwort, Wake Robin.

What is it?

Arum is a plant. The root is used to make medicine.

Is it Effective?

The effectiveness ratings for **ARUM** are as follows:
Insufficient Evidence to Rate Effectiveness for... Colds, throat swelling (inflammation), cough, and stimulating sweating.

How does it work?

There isn't enough information to know how arum works.

Are there safety concerns?

Arum is UNSAFE. The root has poisonous chemicals that can cause a swollen tongue and dangerous bleeding inside the body.

Are there any interactions with medications?

It is not known if arum interacts with any medicines.
Before taking arum, talk with your healthcare professional if you take any medications.

ASAFOETIDA

What other names is the product known by?

Asafetida, Asa Foetida, Assant, Devil's Dung, Ferula Assa-foetida, Ferula Foetida, Ferula Rubricaulis, Food of the Gods, Fum, Giant Fennel, Heeng.

What is it?

Asafoetida is a plant. People use the root to make medicine.

Is it Effective?

The effectiveness ratings for **ASAFOETIDA** are as follows:

Insufficient Evidence to Rate Effectiveness for... Bronchitis, asthma, pertussis or "whooping cough," hoarseness, hysteria, intestinal gas, stomach upset, irritable colon, convulsions, nerve disorders, menstrual problems, calluses, and other conditions.

How does it work?

There is some scientific evidence that the chemicals in asafoetida might help treat irritable bowel syndrome (IBS), and also protect against high cholesterol and high triglycerides. Chemicals called coumarins in asafoetida can thin the blood.

Are there safety concerns?

Asafoetida is safe for most people in the amounts typically found in foods. There is some evidence that it might be safe when used as medicine. In some people, asafoetida can cause swelling of the lips, burping, intestinal gas, diarrhea, headache, convulsions, blood disorders, and other side effects.

Asafoetida is unsafe for children due to the risk of blood disorders.

Do not use asafoetida if: You are pregnant or breast-feeding. • You have a bleeding disorder. • You have high or low blood pressure. • You have a stomach or intestine infection, or condition. • You have a history of convulsions or epilepsy.

Are there any interactions with medications?

Medications for high blood pressure (Antihypertensive drugs). Asafoetida seems to decrease blood pressure. Taking asafoetida along with medications for high blood pressure might cause your blood pressure to go too low. Some medications for high blood pressure include captopril (Capoten), enalapril (Vasotec), losartan (Cozaar), valsartan (Diovan), diltiazem (Cardizem), Amlodipine (Norvasc), hydrochlorothiazide (HydroDiuril), furosemide (Lasix), and many others.

Medications that slow blood clotting (Anticoagulant / Antiplatelet drugs). Asafoetida might slow blood clotting. Taking asafoetida along with medications that also slow clotting might increase the chances of bruising and bleeding. Some medications that slow blood clotting include aspirin, clopidogrel (Plavix), diclofenac (Voltaren, Cataflam, others), ibuprofen (Advil, Motrin, others), naproxen (Anaprox, Naprosyn, others), dalteparin (Fragmin), enoxaparin (Lovenox), heparin, warfarin (Coumadin), and others.

ASARABACCA

What other names is the product known by?

Asaroun, Asarum, Asarum europeaum, Azarum, False Coltsfoot, Hazelwort, Public House Plant, Snakeroot, Wild Ginger, Wild Nard.

What is it?

Asarabacca is a plant. The root is used to make medicine.

Is it Effective?

The effectiveness ratings for **ASARABACCA** are as follows:

Insufficient Evidence to Rate Effectiveness for... Asthma, angina, cough, pneumonia, migraine headaches, dehydration, liver diseases, bronchitis, and inducing vomiting.

How does it work?

The chemicals in asarabacca may have an effect on the lungs. Some people think that other chemicals in asarbacca cause vomiting.

Are there safety concerns?

Asarabacca is not safe to take by mouth. Many times it is contaminated with a chemical that can damage the kidneys or cause cancer. There is no way to know if the asarabacca you have is contaminated or not.

Asarabacca may cause nausea, vomiting, burning of the tongue, diarrhea, rash, and paralysis.

Do not take asarabacca if: You are pregnant or breast-feeding. • You have ulcers. • You have inflammatory bowel disease. • You have Crohn's disease.

Are there any interactions with medications?

It is not known if asarabacca interacts with any medicines.
Before taking asarabacca, talk with your healthcare professional if you take any medications.

ASH

What other names is the product known by?

Bird's Tongue, Common Ash, European Ash, Fraxinus Americana, Fraxinus Excelsior, Weeping Ash, White Ash.

What is it?

Ash is a plant. The bark and leaf are used to make medicine.

Is it Effective?

The effectiveness ratings for **ASH** are as follows:
Insufficient Evidence to Rate Effectiveness for... Fever, arthritis, gout, bladder complaints, constipation, increasing urine production (diuretic), and other conditions.

How does it work?

There isn't enough information to know how ash works.

Are there safety concerns?

There isn't enough information to know if ash is safe.

Do not use ash if: You are pregnant or breast-feeding.

Are there any interactions with medications?

It is not known if ash interacts with any medicines.
Before taking ash, talk with your healthcare professional if you take any medications.

ASHITABA

What other names is the product known by?

Angelica, Angelica keiskei, Japanese Ashitaba, Kenso, Leaves of Tomorrow.

What is it?

Ashitaba is an herb. Its root and stem are used to make medicine.

Is it Effective?

The effectiveness ratings for **ASHITABA** are as follows:
Insufficient Evidence to Rate Effectiveness for... Acid reflux, peptic ulcers, high blood pressure, high cholesterol, gout, constipation, allergies, cancer, small pox, food poisoning, and other conditions.

How does it work?

There is not enough information to know how it might work. Some chemicals in ashitaba seem to work as antioxidants. Other chemicals might block secretions of stomach acid.

Are there safety concerns?

There is not enough information available to know if ashitaba is safe.

Do not use ashitaba if: You are pregnant or breast-feeding.

Are there any interactions with medications?
There is not enough information available to know if ashitaba interacts with any medicines.
Talk to your healthcare professional before taking ashitaba if you take any medications.

ASHWAGANDHA

What other names is the product known by?
Ajagandha, Amangura, Amukkirag, Asgand, Ashvagandha, Ashwanga, Asundha, Asvagandha, Avarada, Ayurvedic Ginseng, Clustered Wintercherry, Indian Ginseng, Kanaje Hindi, Kuthmithi, Physalis somnifera, Samm Al Rerakh, Turangi-Ghanda, Winter Cherry, Withania, Withania somnifera, Withania Coagulans.

What is it?
Ashwagandha is a plant. The root and berry are used to make medicine.

Is it Effective?
The effectiveness ratings for **ASHWAGANDHA** are as follows:
Insufficient Evidence to Rate Effectiveness for... Tumors, tuberculosis, liver problems, swelling (inflammation), ulcerations, stress, inducing vomiting, altering immune function, improving aging effects, and other conditions.

How does it work?
Ashwagandha contains chemicals that might help calm the brain, reduce swelling (inflammation), lower blood pressure, and alter the immune system.

Are there safety concerns?
Ashwagandha seems to be safe when taken by mouth, short-term. The long-term safety of ashwagandha is not known. Large doses of ashwagandha might cause stomach upset, diarrhea, and vomiting.

Do not use ashwagandha if: You are pregnant or breast-feeding. • You have a stomach ulcer.

Are there any interactions with medications?
Medications that decrease the immune system (Immunosuppressants). Ashwagandha seems to increase the immune system. Taking ashwagandha along with medications that decrease the immune system might decrease the effectiveness of medications that decrease the immune system. Some medications that decrease the immune system include azathioprine (Imuran), basiliximab (Simulect), cyclosporine (Neoral, Sandimmune), daclizumab (Zenapax), muromonab-CD3 (OKT3, Orthoclone OKT3), mycophenolate (CellCept), tacrolimus (FK506, Prograf), sirolimus (Rapamune), prednisone (Deltasone, Orasone), corticosteroids (glucocorticoids), and others.
Sedative medications (Benzodiazepines). Ashwagandha might cause sleepiness and drowsiness. Drugs that cause sleepiness and drowsiness are called sedatives. Taking ashwagandha along with sedative medications might cause too much sleepiness. Some of these sedative medications include clonazepam (Klonopin), diazepam (Valium), lorazepam (Ativan), and others.
Sedative medications (CNS depressants). Ashwagandha might cause sleepiness and drowsiness. Medications that cause sleepiness are called sedatives. Taking ashwagandha along with sedative medications might cause too much sleepiness. Some sedative medications include clonazepam (Klonopin), lorazepam (Ativan), phenobarbital (Donnatal), zolpidem (Ambien), and others.
Thyroid hormone. The body naturally produces thyroid hormones. Ashwagandha might increase how much thyroid hormone the body produces. Taking ashwagandha with thyroid hormone pills might cause too much thyroid hormone in the body, and increase the effects and side effects of thyroid hormone.

ASPARAGUS

What other names is the product known by?
Asparagus officinalis, Asparagi Rhizoma Root, Asperge, Garden Asparagus, Sativari, Shatavari, Spargelkraut, Spargelwurzelstock, Sparrow Grass.

What is it?
Asparagus is a plant. It is a good source of vitamin E. The root and rhizome (underground stem) are used to make medicine.

Is it Effective?
The effectiveness ratings for **ASPARAGUS** are as follows:
Insufficient Evidence to Rate Effectiveness for... Urinary tract infections, bladder stones, arthritis-like joint pain

 Natural Medicines Comprehensive Database Consumer Version (209) 472-2244

and swelling, female hormone imbalances, dryness in the lungs and throat, AIDS, folic acid deficiency, constipation, nerve inflammation, parasitic diseases, cancer, acne, face cleaning, drying sores, swelling (inflammation) of the urinary tract, increasing urine production ("irrigation therapy") when taken with lots of water, preventing kidney stones and other conditions.

How does it work?

There is some scientific evidence that asparagus can increase urine production (diuretic). Fiber from the plant may help prevent cancer.

Are there safety concerns?

Asparagus is safe for most people when eaten in typical food amounts. There is some evidence that it might be safe when taken as a medicine. However, there isn't enough information to know if asparagus is safe when used on the skin. Asparagus can irritate the urinary tract and mucous membranes such as the mouth lining. It can also cause allergic reactions when used on the skin.

Do not use medicinal amounts of asparagus if: You are pregnant or breast-feeding. • You have kidney disease. • You have water retention from heart disease.

Are there any interactions with medications?

It is not known if asparagus interacts with any medicines.
Before taking asparagus, talk with your healthcare professional if you take any medications.

ASPARTATES

What other names is the product known by?

Asparatate Chelated Minerals, Aspartate Mineral Chelates, Aspartic Acid, L-Aspartic Acid, Mineral Aspartates.

What is it?

Aspartate is a vitamin-like substance called an amino acid. As a dietary supplement, it is available as copper aspartate, iron aspartate, magnesium aspartate, manganese aspartate, potassium aspartate, and zinc aspartate. People use it to make medicine.

Is it Effective?

The effectiveness ratings for **ASPARTATES** are as follows:
Insufficient Evidence to Rate Effectiveness for... Enhancing athletic performance, liver cirrhosis, and increasing mineral levels.

How does it work?

There isn't enough information to know how aspartates work.

Are there safety concerns?

It is not known if aspartates are safe.

Do not use aspartates if: You are pregnant or breast-feeding.

Are there any interactions with medications?

It is not known if aspartates interact with any medicines.
Before taking aspartates, talk with your healthcare professional if you take any medications.

ASPEN

What other names is the product known by?

American aspen, European Aspen, Populi cortex, Populi Cortex, Populi Folium, Populus Tremuloides, Populus tremula, Quaking Aspen, Zitter-Pappel.

What is it?

Aspen is a tree. The bark and leaf of the tree are used to make medicine.

Is it Effective?

The effectiveness ratings for **ASPEN** are as follows:
Insufficient Evidence to Rate Effectiveness for... Arthritis-like problems, prostate discomforts, back trouble, nerve pain, and bladder problems.

Medical professionals should consult the Professional Version at www.NaturalDatabase.com.

How does it work?

Aspen contains a chemical that is very similar to aspirin. This chemical, known as salicin, may help reduce swelling (inflammation).

Are there safety concerns?

There isn't enough information to know if aspen is safe. Skin reactions, such as rashes, can occur if aspen comes in contact with the skin.

Don't drink alcohol while taking aspen. Alcohol can also increase the risk and severity of bleeding in the stomach and intestines.

Do not use aspen if: You are pregnant or breast-feeding. • You are allergic to salicylates such as aspirin (Bayer). • You have an ulcer. • You have diabetes. • You have gout. • You have a blood disorder. • You have kidney or liver disease.

Are there any interactions with medications?

It is not known if aspen interacts with any medicines.
Before taking aspen, talk with your healthcare professional if you take any medications.

ASTAXANTHIN

What other names is the product known by?

Microalgae, Ovoester.

What is it?

Astaxanthin is a naturally occurring chemical that causes the pink or red color in seafood.

Is it Effective?

The effectiveness ratings for **ASTAXANTHIN** are as follows:
Insufficient Evidence to Rate Effectiveness for... Eye problems such as age-related macular degeneration (AMD), Alzheimer's disease, Parkinson's disease, improving recovery after stroke (brain attack), protecting against cancer, reducing cholesterol levels, reducing skin damage from ultraviolet (UV) light, and other conditions.

How does it work?

Astaxanthin is an antioxidant. This effect might protect cells from damage. Astaxanthin might also improve immune function.

Are there safety concerns?

Astaxanthin is safe when it is consumed in amounts found in food. The safety of astaxanthin supplements and astaxanthin in skin products is unknown.

Do not use astaxanthin supplements if: You are pregnant or breast-feeding.

Are there any interactions with medications?

It is not known if astaxanthin interacts with any medicines.
Before taking astaxanthin, talk with your healthcare professional if you take any medications.

ASTRAGALUS

What other names is the product known by?

Astragali, Astragalus membranaceus, Astragalus mongholicus Beg Kei, Bei Qi, Buck Qi, Huang Qi, Hwanggi, Membranous Milk Vetch, Milk Vetch, Mongolian Milk, Ogi, Phaca membranacea.

What is it?

Astragalus is an herb. The root is used to make medicine.

Is it Effective?

The effectiveness ratings for **ASTRAGALUS** are as follows:
Insufficient Evidence to Rate Effectiveness for... Common cold; chest pain; diabetes; chronic fatigue syndrome (CFS); hepatitis; HIV/AIDS; and cancer including breast cancer, lung cancer, and cervical cancer.

How does it work?
Astragalus seems to stimulate and increase the immune system.

Are there safety concerns?
Astragalus seems to be safe for most adults. The side effects of astragalus are not known.

Do not take astragalus if: You are pregnant or breast-feeding. • You have a condition called an auto-immune disorder. These conditions include rheumatoid arthritis, lupus, multiple sclerosis, and others. • You are an organ transplant recipient.

Are there any interactions with medications?
Cyclophosphamide (Cytoxan, Neosar). Cyclophosphamide (Cytoxan, Neosar) is used to decrease the immune system. Astragalus increases the immune system. Taking astragalus along with cyclophosphamide (Cytoxan, Neosar) might decrease the effectiveness of cyclophosphamide (Cytoxan, Neosar).
Medications that decrease the immune system (Immunosuppressants). Astragalus increases the immune system. Taking astragalus along with medications that decrease the immune system might decrease the effectiveness of medications that decrease the immune system. Some medications that decrease the immune system include azathioprine (Imuran), basiliximab (Simulect), cyclosporine (Neoral, Sandimmune), daclizumab (Zenapax), muromonab-CD3 (OKT3, Orthoclone OKT3), mycophenolate (CellCept), tacrolimus (FK506, Prograf), sirolimus (Rapamune), prednisone (Deltasone, Orasone), corticosteroids (glucocorticoids), and others.

ATLANTIC CEDAR

What other names is the product known by?
Atlantic Cedarwood Oil, Atlas Cedar, Cedarwood Oil, Cedrus atlantica.

What is it?
Atlantic cedar is a tree. The oil from the tree is used as a medicine.

Is it Effective?
The effectiveness ratings for **ATLANTIC CEDAR** are as follows:
Possibly Effective for... Hair loss when combined with other oils.
Insufficient Evidence to Rate Effectiveness for... Insect repellent.

How does it work?
There isn't enough information to know how Atlantic cedar might work.

Are there safety concerns?
Atlantic cedar oil appears to be safe for most people when applied to the skin. There isn't enough information to know if Atlantic cedar is safe when taken by mouth.

Do not use Atlantic cedar if: You are pregnant or breast-feeding.

Are there any interactions with medications?
It is not known if Atlantic cedar interacts with any medicines.
Before taking Atlantic cedar, talk to your healthcare professional if you take any medications.

ATRACTYLODES

What other names is the product known by?
Atractylis ovata, Atractylodes japonica, Atractylodes lancea, Atractylodes chinensis, Atractylodes japonica, Atractylodes macrocephala, Atractylodes ovata, Atractylodis Radix, Bai Zhu, Byaki-jutsu, Cang Zhu, Cangzhu, Chang Zhe, Jutsu, Paekch'ul, Red Atractylodes, So-jutsu, White Atractylodis.

What is it?
Atractylodes is a plant. People use the rhizome (underground stem) to make medicine.

Is it Effective?
The effectiveness ratings for **ATRACTYLODES** are as follows:
Insufficient Evidence to Rate Effectiveness for... Indigestion, stomach ache, bloating, edema, diarrhea, loss of appetite, rheumatism, and other conditions.

How does it work?

Chemicals in atractylodes might improve function of the digestive tract and reduce inflammation.

Are there safety concerns?

There isn't enough information to know if atractylodes might be safe. It can cause allergic reactions in people who are allergic to ragweed, marigolds, daisies, and other related herbs.

Do not take atractylodes if: You are pregnant or breast-feeding. • You are allergic to ragweed, marigolds, daisies, and other related herbs.

Are there any interactions with medications?

It is not known if atractylodes interacts with any medicines.
Before taking atractylodes, talk with your healthcare professional if you take any medications.

AUTUMN CROCUS

What other names is the product known by?

Colchicum, Colchicum Autumnale, Colchicum Speciosum, Colchicum Vernum, Crocus, Fall Crocus, Meadow Saffran, Meadow Saffron, Mysteria, Naked Ladies, Upstart, Vellorita, Wonder Bulb.

What is it?

Autumn crocus is a plant. The seed, bulb, and flower are used to make medicine.

Is it Effective?

The effectiveness ratings for **AUTUMN CROCUS** are as follows:
Insufficient Evidence to Rate Effectiveness for... Arthritis, gout, and Mediterranean fever.

How does it work?

The seeds of autumn crocus contain colchicine. This is the same active ingredient used in a prescription medication for gout and Mediterranean fever. Colchicine works by reducing the chemicals that cause joint swelling (inflammation) in people with these diseases.

Are there safety concerns?

Autumn crocus is UNSAFE. It is considered a poison, and can cause burning of the mouth and throat, vomiting, diarrhea, liver and kidney problems, blood disorders, nerve problems, shock, organ failure, and death.

If you have acute gout or familial Mediterranean fever, it is much safer to use colchicine prescribed by your healthcare provider. Prescription colchicine contains a set amount of medicine. The amount of colchicine in autumn crocus can vary from plant to plant.

Are there any interactions with medications?

Colchicine. Autumn crocus contains colchicine. Taking autumn crocus along with colchicine might increase the effects and side effects of colchicine.

AVENS

What other names is the product known by?

Benedict's Herb, Bennet's Root, Colewort, Geum, Geum Urbanum, Herb Bennet.

What is it?

Avens is a plant. The above ground parts are used to make medicine.

Is it Effective?

The effectiveness ratings for **AVENS** are as follows:
Insufficient Evidence to Rate Effectiveness for... Diarrhea, colitis, uterine bleeding, fevers, and other conditions.

How does it work?

Avens contains chemicals called tannins which help treat diarrhea by reducing swelling (inflammation).

Are there safety concerns?
Avens is safe when used in small amounts as a food flavoring. There isn't enough information to know if it is safe when used as a medicine.

Do not use avens if: You are pregnant or breast-feeding.

Are there any interactions with medications?
It is not known if avens interacts with any medicines.
Before taking avens, talk with your healthcare professional if you take any medications.

AVOCADO

What other names is the product known by?
Ahuacate, Alligator Pear, Laurus Persea, Persea Americana, Persea Gratissima.

What is it?
Avocado is a tree. The fruit is a good source of potassium and vitamin D. The fruit, leaves, and seeds are used to make medicine.

Is it Effective?
The effectiveness ratings for **AVOCADO** are as follows:
Possibly Effective for... Reducing "bad" cholesterol (LDL cholesterol) • Increasing "good" cholesterol (HDL cholesterol) • Treating osteoarthritis.
Insufficient Evidence to Rate Effectiveness for... Healing wounds, sclerosis, promoting hair growth, stimulating menstrual flow, diarrhea, toothache, and other conditions.

How does it work?
Avocado contains chemicals that might lower cholesterol and repair cartilage in joints damaged by osteoarthritis.

Are there safety concerns?
Avocado is safe for most people when the fruit is eaten in regular food amounts. Avocado is possibly safe when used as a medicine.

Avocado has a high fat calorie content. Keep this in mind while planning total daily calorie and fat intake.

Do not use avocado as a medicine if: You are pregnant or breast-feeding. • You are allergic to latex.

Are there any interactions with medications?
Warfarin (Coumadin). Warfarin (Coumadin) is used to slow blood clotting. Avocado has been reported to decrease the effectiveness of warfarin (Coumadin). Decreasing the effectiveness of warfarin (Coumadin) might increase the risk of clotting. It is unclear why this interaction might occur. Be sure to have your blood checked regularly. The dose of your warfarin (Coumadin) might need to be changed.

AVOCADO SUGAR EXTRACT

What other names is the product known by?
D-Mannoheptulose, Mannoheptulose, Manno-heptulose.

What is it?
Avocado sugar extract is a chemical from avocado fruit.

Is it Effective?
The effectiveness ratings for **AVOCADO SUGAR EXTRACT** are as follows:
Insufficient Evidence to Rate Effectiveness for... Weight loss and other conditions.

How does it work?
Preliminary research suggests avocado sugar extract might block the effects of insulin and prevent the break down of sugar (glucose).

Are there safety concerns?

It is not known if avocado sugar extract is safe.

Do not use avocado sugar extract if: You are pregnant or breast-feeding. • You have diabetes.

Are there any interactions with medications?

Medications for diabetes (Antidiabetes drugs). Avocado sugar extract might increase blood sugar. Diabetes medications are used to lower blood sugar. Taking avocado sugar extract along with diabetes medications might interfere with the blood sugar lowering effects of diabetes medications. Monitor your blood sugar closely. The dose of your diabetes medication might need to be changed. Some medications used for diabetes include glimepiride (Amaryl), glyburide (DiaBeta, Glynase PresTab, Micronase), insulin, pioglitazone (Actos), rosiglitazone (Avandia), chlorpropamide (Diabinese), glipizide (Glucotrol), tolbutamide (Orinase), and others.

Before taking avocado sugar extract, talk with your healthcare professional if you take these or any other medications.

BA JI TIAN

What other names is the product known by?

Bi Ji, Indian Mulberry, Morinda, Morinda Root, Morindae officinalis, Morindae radix, Noni.

What is it?

Ba ji tian is a plant. The root of the plant is used to make medicine.

Is it Effective?

The effectiveness ratings for **BA JI TIAN** are as follows:

Insufficient Evidence to Rate Effectiveness for... Cancer, gallbladder disorders, bedwetting, impotence and premature ejaculation, back pain, depression, kidney disorders, and other conditions.

How does it work?

Ba ji tian might help treat depression by increasing the effects of serotonin, a chemical found in the brain.

Are there safety concerns?

Ba ji tian is safe for most people.

Do not take ba ji tian: You are pregnant or breast-feeding. • You have difficulty urinating.

Are there any interactions with medications?

It is not known if ba ji tian interacts with any medicines.

Before taking ba ji tian, talk with your healthcare professional if you take any medications.

BAEL

What other names is the product known by?

Aegle Marmelos, Bel, Bengal Quince, Bilva, Bilwa, Indian Bael, Shivaphala.

What is it?

Bael is a plant. The unripe fruit, root, leaf, and branch are used to make medicine.

Is it Effective?

The effectiveness ratings for **BAEL** are as follows:

Insufficient Evidence to Rate Effectiveness for... Constipation and diarrhea.

How does it work?

Bael contains chemicals called tannins, which help treat diarrhea by reducing swelling (inflammation).

Are there safety concerns?

There isn't enough information to know if bael is safe. Large amounts may cause stomach upset and constipation.

Do not use bael if: You are pregnant or breast-feeding.

Are there any interactions with medications?

It is not known if bael interacts with any medicines.

Before taking bael, talk with your healthcare professional if you take any medications.

BAIKAL SKULLCAP

What other names is the product known by?
Baikal Scullcap, Baikal Skullcap Root, Chinese Skullcap, Huang Qin, Huangquin, Hwanggum, Ogon, Ou-gon, Scullcap, Scute, Skullcap, Wogon.

What is it?
Baikal skullcap is a plant. The root is used to make medicine.

Is it Effective?
The effectiveness ratings for **BAIKAL SKULLCAP** are as follows:
Insufficient Evidence to Rate Effectiveness for... Inflammation of small air passages in the lung (bronchiolitis) and other lung infections; kidney, stomach, and pelvic infections; hayfever; seizures; HIV/AIDS; nervous tension; hemorrhoids; prostate cancer; hepatitis; sores or swelling; osteoarthritis; fever; headache; red eyes; flushed face; and bitter taste in the mouth.

How does it work?
It is thought that the active chemicals in Baikal skullcap may be able to decrease inflammation, stop tumor growth, and prevent tumor cell reproduction.

Are there safety concerns?
Baikal skullcap seems to be safe for most people. It may cause drowsiness, fever, lung inflammation, and liver problems.

Do not take Baikal skullcap if: You are pregnant or breast-feeding. • You have diabetes. • You have been told you have problems with the function of your stomach or spleen.

Are there any interactions with medications?
Alcohol. Alcohol can cause sleepiness and drowsiness. Baikal skullcap might also cause sleepiness and drowsiness. Taking large amounts of baikal skullcap along with alcohol might cause too much sleepiness.
Medications for diabetes (Antidiabetes drugs). Baikal skullcap might decrease blood sugar. Diabetes medications are also used to lower blood sugar. Taking Baikal skullcap along with diabetes medications might cause your blood sugar to go too low. Monitor your blood sugar closely. The dose of your diabetes medication might need to be changed. Some medications used for diabetes include glimepiride (Amaryl), glyburide (DiaBeta, Glynase PresTab, Micronase), insulin, pioglitazone (Actos), rosiglitazone (Avandia), chlorpropamide (Diabinese), glipizide (Glucotrol), tolbutamide (Orinase), and others.
Sedative medications (Benzodiazepines). Baikal skullcap might cause sleepiness and drowsiness. Medications that cause sleepiness and drowsiness are called sedatives. Taking Baikal skullcap along with sedative medications might cause too much sleepiness. Some of these sedative medications include clonazepam (Klonopin), diazepam (Valium), lorazepam (Ativan), and others.
Sedative medications (CNS depressants). Baikal skullcap might cause sleepiness and drowsiness. Medications that cause sleepiness are called sedatives. Taking Baikal skullcap along with sedative medications might cause too much sleepiness. Some sedative medications include clonazepam (Klonopin), lorazepam (Ativan), phenobarbital (Donnatal), zolpidem (Ambien), and others.

BAMBOO

What other names is the product known by?
Arrow Bamboo, Arundinaria japonica, Pseudosasa japonica, Sasa japonica, Yadake.

What is it?
Bamboo is a plant. Juice from young bamboo shoots is used to make medicine.

Is it Effective?
The effectiveness ratings for **BAMBOO** are as follows:
Insufficient Evidence to Rate Effectiveness for... Asthma, cough, and gallbladder problems.

How does it work?
There isn't enough information to know how bamboo works.

Are there safety concerns?

There isn't enough information to know if bamboo is safe.

Do not use bamboo if: You are pregnant or breast-feeding.

Are there any interactions with medications?

It is not known if bamboo interacts with any medicines.
Before taking bamboo, talk with your healthcare professional if you take any medications.

BANABA

What other names is the product known by?

Banaba extract, Corosolic acid, Crape Myrtle, Crepe Myrtle, Lagerstroemia flos-reginae, Lagerstroemia speciosa, Munchausia speciosa, Pride-of-India, Pyinma, Queen's Crape Myrtle.

What is it?

Banaba is a tree. People use the leaves to make medicine.

Is it Effective?

The effectiveness ratings for **BANABA** are as follows:
Insufficient Evidence to Rate Effectiveness for... Diabetes and weight loss.

How does it work?

Banaba seems to lower blood glucose in people with type 2 diabetes, according to very preliminary research. It might help the body use insulin more efficiently.

Are there safety concerns?

Banaba seems to be safe for most people when taken by mouth on a short-term basis. The long-term safety is unknown.

Do not take banaba if: You are pregnant or breast-feeding.

Are there any interactions with medications?

Medications for diabetes (Antidiabetes drugs). Banaba might decrease blood sugar. Diabetes medications are also used to lower blood sugar. Taking banaba along with diabetes medications might cause your blood sugar to go too low. Monitor your blood sugar closely. The dose of your diabetes medication might need to be changed. Some medications used for diabetes include glimepiride (Amaryl), glyburide (DiaBeta, Glynase PresTab, Micronase), insulin, pioglitazone (Actos), rosiglitazone (Avandia), chlorpropamide (Diabinese), glipizide (Glucotrol), tolbutamide (Orinase), and others.

BARLEY

What other names is the product known by?

Dietary Fiber, Hordeum, Hordeum Distychum, Hordeum Vulgare, Mai Ya, Pearl Barley, Pot Barley, Scotch Barley.

What is it?

Barley is a plant. The grain of barley is used to make medicine.

Is it Effective?

The effectiveness ratings for **BARLEY** are as follows:
Possibly Effective for... High cholesterol • Preventing stomach cancer.
Possibly Ineffective for... Preventing cancer of the colon (bowels) or rectum.
Insufficient Evidence to Rate Effectiveness for... Bronchitis, cancer prevention, diarrhea, swelling (inflammation) of the stomach or bowel, boils, increasing strength and energy, weight loss, and other conditions.

How does it work?

The fiber in barley might lower cholesterol and blood pressure in people with high cholesterol. Barley may also reduce blood sugar and insulin levels. Barley seems to slow stomach emptying. This could help keep blood sugar stable and create a sensation of being full, which might suppress appetite.

Are there safety concerns?
Barley is safe for most people. Barley flour can sometimes cause asthma.

Pregnant women should not consume barley sprouts.

Do not use barley if: You have celiac disease or are sensitive to gluten.

Are there any interactions with medications?
Medications for diabetes (Antidiabetes drugs). Barley might decrease blood sugar by decreasing the absorption of sugars from food. Diabetes medications are also used to lower blood sugar. Taking barley with diabetes medications might cause your blood sugar to be too low. Monitor your blood sugar closely. The dose of your diabetes medication might need to be changed. Some medications used for diabetes include glimepiride (Amaryl), glyburide (DiaBeta, Glynase PresTab, Micronase), insulin, pioglitazone (Actos), rosiglitazone (Avandia), chlorpropamide (Diabinese), glipizide (Glucotrol), tolbutamide (Orinase), and others.
Medications taken by mouth (Oral drugs). Barley contains a large amount of fiber. Fiber can decrease how much medicine the body absorbs. Taking barley along with medicine you take by mouth can decrease the effectiveness of your medication. To prevent this interaction take barley at least 1 hour after medications you take by mouth.

BASIL

What other names is the product known by?
Basilici Herba, Basilici Herba, Common Basil, Garden Basil, Munjariki, St. Josephwort, Surasa, Sweet Basil, Vanatulasi, Varvara.

What is it?
Basil is an herb. The above ground plant parts of basil are used to make medicine.

Is it Effective?
The effectiveness ratings for **BASIL** are as follows:
Insufficient Evidence to Rate Effectiveness for... Head colds, loss of appetite, intestinal gas, stomach spasms, kidney disorders, blood circulation, worms, warts, snake and insect bites, and other conditions.

How does it work?
Basil contains many chemicals. These chemicals might help get rid of intestinal worms. Basil is a good source of vitamin C, calcium, magnesium, potassium, and iron.

Are there safety concerns?
Basil is safe for short-term use in most adults. In some people it can cause low blood sugar. Caution should be used in long-term treatment which may be unsafe for the liver and other organs.

Don't use basil oil. It isn't safe.

Basil is safe for children, and pregnant and breast-feeding women, when used in small amounts found in foods. However, it is unsafe when used in larger quantities as medicine.

Are there any interactions with medications?
It is not known if basil interacts with any medicines.
Before taking basil, talk with your healthcare professional if you take any medications.

BAYBERRY

What other names is the product known by?
Candleberry, Myrica, Myrica cerifera, Myrica pensylvanica, Southern Bayberry, Southern Wax Myrtle, Tallow Shrub, Vegetable Tallow, Waxberry.

What is it?
Bayberry is a plant. The root bark and berries are used to make medicine.

Medical professionals should consult the Professional Version at www.NaturalDatabase.com.

CONSUMER VERSION

Is it Effective?
The effectiveness ratings for **BAYBERRY** are as follows:
Insufficient Evidence to Rate Effectiveness for... Colds, diarrhea, fevers, and nausea.

How does it work?
The chemicals in bayberry have a drying effect on the skin.

Are there safety concerns?
Bayberry is not considered safe when taken by mouth. Bayberry can cause nausea, vomiting, and liver damage.

Do not take bayberry if: You are pregnant or breast-feeding. • You have high blood pressure or low blood pressure. • You have problems with retaining water.

Are there any interactions with medications?
It is not known if bayberry interacts with any medicines.
Before taking bayberry, talk with your healthcare professional if you take any medications.

BEAN POD

What other names is the product known by?
Cannelli Beans, Common Bean, Grean Bean, Navy Bean, Phaseoli Fructus, Phaseolus Vulgaris, Pinto Bean, Seed-Free Bean Pods, Sine Semine, Snap Bean, String Bean, Wax Bean, White Kidney Bean.

What is it?
Bean pod is a plant. Bean pods are used to make medicine.

Is it Effective?
The effectiveness ratings for **BEAN POD** are as follows:
Insufficient Evidence to Rate Effectiveness for... Lowering cholesterol, weight loss, urinary tract infections (UTIs), kidney stones, lung cancer, and diabetes.

How does it work?
Bean pods are a source of dietary fiber. Fiber might modestly lower cholesterol absorption and increase dietary fat elimination.

Are there safety concerns?
There is some evidence that bean pods might be safe for most adults. However, large amounts of fresh bean husks probably aren't safe. Raw husks contain chemicals that can cause stomach upset, vomiting and diarrhea.

Bean pod may lower blood sugar. If you have diabetes, monitor your blood sugar closely.

Do not use bean pod if: You are pregnant or breast-feeding.

Are there any interactions with medications?
Medications for diabetes (Antidiabetes drugs). Bean pod might decrease blood sugar. Diabetes medications are also used to lower blood sugar. Taking bean pod along with diabetes medications might cause your blood sugar to go too low. Monitor your blood sugar closely. The dose of your diabetes medication might need to be changed. Some medications used for diabetes include glimepiride (Amaryl), glyburide (DiaBeta, Glynase PresTab, Micronase), insulin, pioglitazone (Actos), rosiglitazone (Avandia), chlorpropamide (Diabinese), glipizide (Glucotrol), tolbutamide (Orinase), and others.

BEAR'S GARLIC

What other names is the product known by?
Allium Ursinum, Bears Garlic, Broad-Leaved Garlic, Ramsons, Wild Garlic.

What is it?
Bear's garlic is a plant. The leaf and bulb are used to make medicine.

     Natural Medicines Comprehensive Database Consumer Version   (209) 472-2244

Is it Effective?

The effectiveness ratings for **BEAR'S GARLIC** are as follows:

Insufficient Evidence to Rate Effectiveness for... Indigestion, intestinal gas, high blood pressure, heart disease, and skin rashes.

How does it work?

Bear's garlic has chemicals that might help protect against heart disease, by reducing blood platelet activity and lowering blood pressure.

Are there safety concerns?

There isn't enough information to know if bear's garlic is safe.

Do not use bear's garlic if: You are pregnant or breast-feeding.

Are there any interactions with medications?

It is not known if bear's garlic interacts with any medicines.
Before taking bear's garlic, talk with your healthcare professional if you take any medications.

BEE POLLEN

What other names is the product known by?

Bee Pollen Extract, Buckwheat Pollen, Honeybee Pollen, Maize Pollen, Pine Pollen, Pollen, Pollen D'Abeille.

What is it?

Bee pollen refers to the flower pollen that collects on the legs and bodies of worker bees. Pollens come from many plants.

Is it Effective?

The effectiveness ratings for **BEE POLLEN** are as follows:

Possibly Ineffective for... Increasing athletic performance and stamina.

Insufficient Evidence to Rate Effectiveness for... Appetite stimulation, premature aging, hayfever, premenstrual syndrome (PMS), mouth sores, joint pain, painful urination, prostate conditions, nosebleeds, menstrual problems, constipation, diarrhea, and colitis.

How does it work?

The enzymes in bee pollen are thought to act like medicines. However, these enzymes are broken down in the stomach, so it is unlikely that bee pollen has any effect.

Are there safety concerns?

Bee pollen seems to be safe for most people.

It can cause liver damage and allergic reactions including itching, swelling, problems with breathing, dizziness, and death in people allergic to pollen.

Do not take bee pollen if: You are pregnant or breast-feeding. • You are allergic to pollen. • You have a liver disease such as hepatitis.

Are there any interactions with medications?

It is not known if bee pollen interacts with any medicines.
Before taking bee pollen, talk with your healthcare professional if you take any medications.

BEE VENOM

What other names is the product known by?

Apis Mellifera, Apis Venenum Purum, Bald-faced Hornet, Bee Sting Venom, Bombus terrestis, Bumblebee Venom, Honeybee Benum, Mixed Vespids, Pure Bee Venom, Vespula Maculata, Wasp Venom, White-Faced Hornet, Yellow Hornet, Yellow-Jacket Venom.

What is it?

Bee venom is made by bees. This is the poison that makes bee stings painful. Bee venom is used to make medicine.

Medical professionals should consult the Professional Version at www.NaturalDatabase.com.

Is it Effective?

The effectiveness ratings for **BEE VENOM** are as follows:
Likely Effective for... Reducing the severity of allergic reactions to bee stings.
Possibly Ineffective for... Arthritis • Multiple sclerosis (MS).
Insufficient Evidence to Rate Effectiveness for... Nerve pain, tendonitis, and muscle swelling (inflammation).

How does it work?

Giving repeated and controlled injections of bee venom under the skin causes the immune system to get used to bee venom, and helps reduce the severity of an allergy to bee venom.

Are there safety concerns?

Bee venom is safe for most people when injected under the skin by a trained medical professional. Some people might get redness and swelling where the injection is given. Side effects include itching, anxiety, trouble breathing, chest tightness, heart palpitations, dizziness, nausea, vomiting, diarrhea, sleepiness, confusion, fainting, and low blood pressure.

Side effects are more common in people with the worst allergies to bee stings, in people treated with honeybee venom, and in women.

Do not use bee venom if: You are pregnant or breast-feeding, unless you are under the direct supervision of a trained medical professional.

Are there any interactions with medications?

It is not known if bee venom interacts with any medicines.
Before taking bee venom, talk with your healthcare professional if you take any medications.

BEER

What other names is the product known by?

Alcohol, Ethanol.

What is it?

Beer is an alcoholic drink.

Is it Effective?

The effectiveness ratings for **BEER** are as follows:
Likely Effective for... Preventing cardiovascular (heart and blood circulation) disease, such as heart attack, stroke, atherosclerosis (hardening of the arteries), and angina (heart pain) • Reducing the risk of dying from cardiovascular disease and other causes.
Possibly Effective for... Preventing diabetes (type 2), and heart disease in people with diabetes • Maintenance of intellectual function with aging • Preventing ulcers caused by the bacteria, Helicobacter pylori.
Possibly Ineffective for... Reducing the risk of death from cancer.
Insufficient Evidence to Rate Effectiveness for... Reducing the risk of Alzheimer's disease, anxiety, increasing bone density in women, gallstones, kidney stones, and stimulating appetite and digestion.

How does it work?

Beer is thought to help prevent heart disease by increasing high-density lipoprotein (HDL), also known as "good cholesterol." Also, the vitamin B6 (pyridoxine) contained in beer can help lower homocysteine levels, a chemical considered to be one of the risk factors for heart disease.

Are there safety concerns?

Beer seems to be safe for most people when used in moderation. This translates to two or fewer 12 ounce glasses a day. Drinking more than this at one sitting can cause a lot of side effects, including: flushing, confusion, trouble controlling emotions, blackouts, loss of coordination, seizures, drowsiness, trouble breathing, hypothermia, low blood sugar, vomiting, diarrhea, bleeding, irregular heart beat, and others.

Long-term use can lead to alcohol dependence and can cause many serious side effects, including: malnutrition, memory loss, mental problems, heart problems, liver failure, swelling (inflammation) of the pancreas, cancers of the digestive track, and others.

Do not use beer if: You are pregnant or breast-feeding. • You have a heart condition such as chest pain (angina) or congestive heart failure (CHF). • You have gout. • You have high blood pressure; 3 or more drinks a day can increase blood pressure. • You have high triglyceride levels. • You have a sleep disorder called insomnia. • You

CONSUMER VERSION

Medical professionals should consult the Professional Version at www.NaturalDatabase.com.

 Natural Medicines Comprehensive Database Consumer Version (209) 472-2244

have liver disease. • You have a pancreas condition called pancreatitis. • You have heartburn or a stomach ulcer. • You have blood disorder called porphyria. • You have a mental disorder.

Are there any interactions with medications?

Antibiotics (Sulfonamide antibiotics). The alcohol in beer can interact with some antibiotics. This can lead to upset stomach, vomiting, sweating, headache, and an increased heartbeat. Do not drink beer when taking antibiotics. Some antibiotics that interact with beer include sulfamethoxazole (Gantanol), sulfasalazine (Azulfidine), sulfisoxazole (Gantrisin), trimethoprim/sulfamethoxazole (Bactrim, Septra), and others.

Aspirin. Aspirin can sometimes damage the stomach and cause ulcers and bleeding. The alcohol in beer can also damage the stomach. Taking aspirin along with beer might increase the chance of ulcers and bleeding in the stomach. Avoid taking beer and aspirin together.

Cefamandole (Mandol). The alcohol in beer can interact with cefamandole (Mandol). This can lead to upset stomach, vomiting, sweating, headache, and an increased heartbeat. Do not drink beer while taking cefamandole (Mandol).

Cefoperazone (Cefobid). The alcohol in beer can interact with cefoperazone (Cefobid). This can lead to upset stomach, vomiting, sweating, headache, and an increased heartbeat. Do not drink beer while taking cefoperazone (Cefobid).

Chlorpropamide (Diabinese). The body breaks down the alcohol in beer to get rid of it. Chlorpropamide (Diabinese) might decrease how quickly the body breaks down alcohol. Drinking beer and taking chlorpropamide (Diabinese) might cause a headache, vomiting, flushing, and other unpleasant reactions. Don't drink beer if you are taking chlorpropamide (Diabinese).

Cisapride (Propulsid). Cisapride (Propulsid) might decrease how quickly the body gets rid of the alcohol in beer. Taking cisapride (Propulsid) along with beer might increase the effects and side effects of the alcohol in beer.

Disulfiram (Antabuse). The body breaks down the alcohol in beer to get rid of it. Disulfiram (Antabuse) decreases how fast the body breaks down alcohol. Drinking beer and taking disulfiram (Antabuse) can cause a pounding headache, vomiting, flushing, and other unpleasant reactions. Don't drink any alcohol if you are taking disulfiram (Antabuse).

Erythromycin. The body breaks down the alcohol in beer to get rid of it. Erythromycin can decrease how quickly the body gets rid of alcohol. Drinking beer and taking erythromycin might increase the effects and side effects of alcohol.

Griseofulvin (Fulvicin). The body breaks down the alcohol in beer to get rid of it. Griseofulvin (Fulvicin) decreases how quickly the body breaks down alcohol. Drinking beer and taking griseofulvin (Fulvicin) can cause a pounding headache, vomiting, flushing, and other unpleasant reactions. Don't drink any alcohol if you are taking griseofulvin (Fulvicin).

Medications that can harm the liver (Hepatotoxic drugs). The alcohol in beer can harm the liver. Drinking beer and taking medications that can harm the liver can increase the risk of liver damage. Do not drink beer if you are taking a medication that can harm the liver. Some medications that can harm the liver include acetaminophen (Tylenol and others), amiodarone (Cordarone), carbamazepine (Tegretol), isoniazid (INH), methotrexate (Rheumatrex), methyldopa (Aldomet), fluconazole (Diflucan), itraconazole (Sporanox), erythromycin (Erythrocin, Ilosone, others), phenytoin (Dilantin), lovastatin (Mevacor), pravastatin (Pravachol), simvastatin (Zocor), and many others.

Medications that decrease stomach acid (H2-Blockers). Some medications that decrease stomach acid might interact with the alcohol in beer. Drinking beer and taking some medications that decrease stomach acid might increase how much alcohol the body absorbs, and increase the risk of side effects of alcohol. Some medications that decrease stomach acid and might interact with alcohol include cimetidine (Tagamet), ranitidine (Zantac), nizatidine (Axid), and famotidine (Pepcid).

Medications for pain (Narcotic drugs). The body breaks down some medications for pain to get rid of them. The alcohol in beer might decrease how quickly the body gets rid of some medications for pain. Drinking beer and taking some medications for pain might increase the effects and side effects of some medications for pain. Some medications for pain that might interact with alcohol include meperidine (Demerol), hydrocodone, morphine, OxyContin, and many others.

Metformin (Glucophage). Metformin (Glucophage) is broken down by the body in the liver. The alcohol in beer is also broken down in the body by the liver. Drinking beer and taking metformin might cause serious side effects.

Metronidazole (Flagyl). The alcohol in beer can interact with metronidazole (Flagyl). This can lead to upset stomach, vomiting, sweating, headache, and an increased heartbeat. Do not drink beer while taking metronidazole (Flagyl).

NSAIDs (Nonsteroidal anti-inflammatory drugs). NSAIDs are anti-inflammatory medications used for decreasing pain and swelling. NSAIDs can sometimes damage the stomach and intestines and cause ulcers and bleeding. The alcohol in beer can also damage the stomach and intestines. Taking NSAIDs along with beer might increase the chance of ulcers and bleeding in the stomach and intestines. Avoid taking beer and NSAIDs together. Some NSAIDs include ibuprofen (Advil, Motrin, Nuprin, others), indomethacin (Indocin), naproxen (Aleve, Anaprox, Naprelan, Naprosyn), piroxicam (Feldene), aspirin, and others.

Phenytoin (Dilantin). The body breaks down phenytoin (Dilantin) to get rid of it. The alcohol in beer might increase how quickly the body breaks down phenytoin (Dilantin). Drinking beer and taking phenytoin (Dilantin) might decrease the effectiveness of phenytoin (Dilantin) and increase the possibility of seizures.

Sedative medications (Barbiturates). The alcohol in beer might cause sleepiness and drowsiness. Medications that cause sleepiness and drowsiness are called sedative medications. Taking beer along with sedative medications might cause too much sleepiness. Do not drink beer if you are taking sedative medications.

Sedative medications (Benzodiazepines). The alcohol in beer might cause sleepiness and drowsiness. Drugs that cause sleepiness and drowsiness are called sedative medications. Taking beer along with sedative medications might cause too much sleepiness. Do not drink beer if you are taking sedative medications. Some of these sedative medications include clonazepam (Klonopin), diazepam (Valium), lorazepam (Ativan), and others.

Sedative medications (CNS depressants). The alcohol in beer might cause sleepiness and drowsiness. Medications that cause sleepiness and drowsiness are called sedative medications. Drinking beer and taking sedative medications might cause too much sleepiness and other serious side effects. Some sedative medications include clonazepam (Klonopin), lorazepam (Ativan), phenobarbital (Donnatal), zolpidem (Ambien), and others.

Tolbutamide (Orinase). The body breaks down the alcohol in beer to get rid of it. Tolbutamide (Orinase) can decrease how quickly the body breaks down alcohol. Drinking beer and taking tolbutamide (Orinase) can cause a pounding headache, vomiting, flushing, and other unpleasant reactions. Don't drink beer if you are taking tolbutamide (Orinase).

Warfarin (Coumadin). Warfarin (Coumadin) is used to slow blood clotting. The alcohol in beer can interact with warfarin (Coumadin). Drinking large amounts of alcohol can change the effectiveness of warfarin (Coumadin). Be sure to have your blood checked regularly. The dose of your warfarin (Coumadin) might need to be changed.

BEESWAX

What other names is the product known by?
Apic Cerana, Apis Mellifera, Bees Wax, Bleached Beeswax, White Beeswax, White Wax, Yellow Beeswax, Yellow Wax.

What is it?
Beeswax is a product made from the honeycomb of the honeybee and other bees. It is used to make medicine.

Is it Effective?
The effectiveness ratings for **BEESWAX** are as follows:
Insufficient Evidence to Rate Effectiveness for... High cholesterol, ulcers, diarrhea, hiccups, and other conditions.

How does it work?
Beeswax has mild anti-swelling (anti-inflammatory) effects. There is also some evidence that it might help protect the stomach.

Are there safety concerns?
Beeswax is safe for most people.

Do not use beeswax in amounts larger than found in foods if: You are pregnant or breast-feeding.

Are there any interactions with medications?
It is not known if beeswax interacts with any medicines.
Before taking beeswax, talk with your healthcare professional if you take any medications.

BEET

What other names is the product known by?
Beta Vulgaris, Beets, Fodder Beet, Garden Beet, Mangel, Mangold, Red Beet, Sugarbeet, Yellow Beet.

What is it?
Beet is a plant. The root is used to make medicine.

Is it Effective?
The effectiveness ratings for **BEET** are as follows:
Insufficient Evidence to Rate Effectiveness for... Supportive therapy for fatty liver and other liver diseases.

How does it work?
There is some evidence that a chemical found in beets can help fight fat deposits in the liver.

Medical professionals should consult the Professional Version at www.NaturalDatabase.com.

 Natural Medicines Comprehensive Database Consumer Version (209) 472-2244

Are there safety concerns?

Beet is safe for most people when taken in the amounts typically found in foods. There isn't enough information to know if beet is safe when used as a medicine. Beets can cause low calcium levels and kidney damage.

Do not use beet as a medicine if: You are pregnant or breast-feeding. • You have kidney disease.

Are there any interactions with medications?

It is not known if beet interacts with any medicines.
Before taking beet, talk with your healthcare professional if you take any medications.

BELLADONNA

What other names is the product known by?

Atropa Belladonna, Atropa Belladonna Acuminata, Deadly Nightshade, Devil's Cherries, Devil's Herb, Divale, Dwale, Dwayberry, Great Morel, Naughty Man's Cherries, Poison Black Cherries.

What is it?

Belladonna is a plant. The leaf and root are used to make medicine.

Is it Effective?

The effectiveness ratings for **BELLADONNA** are as follows:
Insufficient Evidence to Rate Effectiveness for... Asthma, whooping cough, colds, hayfever, Parkinson's disease, motion sickness, arthritis-like pain, nerve problems, hemorrhoids, spasms and colic-like pain in the stomach and bile ducts, and other conditions.

How does it work?

Belladonna has chemicals that can block functions of the body's nervous system. Some of the bodily functions regulated by the nervous system include salivation, sweating, pupil size, urination, digestive functions, and others.

Are there safety concerns?

Prescription belladonna is probably safe for some people when used appropriately with the supervision of a trained medical professional.

Using belladonna in any other way is UNSAFE. Side effects of belladonna include dry mouth, enlarged pupils, blurred vision, red dry skin, hyperthermia, fast heartbeat, inability to urinate or sweat, hallucinations, spasms, mental problems, convulsions, and coma.

Belladonna is available as a prescription drug in the US Prescription belladonna is standardized, which means it contains a set dose of active chemicals.

Belladonna isn't safe when used in children six years and younger.

Do not use belladonna if: You are pregnant or breast-feeding. • You have congestive heart failure (CHF). • You have constipation. • You have Down syndrome. • You have heartburn. • You have a fever. • You have stomach ulcers or ulcerative colitis. • You have an infection or blockage of the stomach or intestines. • You have a hiatal hernia. • You have narrow-angle glaucoma. • You have an irregular heartbeat. • You have trouble urinating.

Are there any interactions with medications?

Drying medications (Anticholinergic drugs). Belladonna contains chemicals that cause a drying effect. It also affects the brain and heart. Drying medications called anticholinergic drugs can also cause these effects. Taking belladonna and drying medications together might cause side effects including dry skin, dizziness, low blood pressure, fast heart beat, and other serious side effects. Some of these drying medications include atropine, scopolamine, and some medications used for allergies (antihistamines), and for depression (antidepressants).

BENZOIN

What other names is the product known by?

Benzoe, Gum Benjamin, Gum Benzoin, Styrax Benzoin, Styrax Paralleloneurus, Sumatra Benzoin.

What is it?

Benzoin is a plant. The gum resin is used to make medicine.

Is it Effective?
The effectiveness ratings for **BENZOIN** are as follows:
Insufficient Evidence to Rate Effectiveness for... Chest congestion, swelling (inflammation) of the throat and airways, laryngitis, croup, skin cuts and ulcers, bedsores, cracked nipples, and other conditions.

How does it work?
There is some evidence that benzoin might act as a skin protectant, and also help to break up chest congestion by thinning mucous and making it easier to cough up (expectorant).

Are there safety concerns?
There is some evidence that benzoin might be safe for use as a medicine. People who are allergic to tincture of benzoin break out in a rash.

Do not use benzoin if: You are pregnant or breast-feeding.

Are there any interactions with medications?
It is not known if benzoin interacts with any medicines.
Before taking benzoin, talk with your healthcare professional if you take any medications.

BERBERINE

What other names is the product known by?
Berberine Alkaloid, Berberine Complex, Berberine Sulfate.

What is it?
Berberine is a chemical found in several plants.

Is it Effective?
The effectiveness ratings for **BERBERINE** are as follows:
Ineffective for... Heart failure, burns, trachoma (an eye infection that can cause blindness), and other conditions.

How does it work?
Berberine might cause stronger heart beats. It also might have antibacterial effects.

Are there safety concerns?
Berberine appears to be seems safe for most people for short term use when taken by mouth or applied to the skin.

Do not take berberine if: You are pregnant or breast-feeding.

Are there any interactions with medications?
Cyclosporin (Neoral, Sandimmune). The body breaks down cyclosporin (Neoral, Sandimmune) to get rid of it. Berberine might decrease how fast the body breaks down cyclosporin (Neoral, Sandimmune). This might cause there to be too much cyclosporin (Neoral, Sandimmune) in the body and potentially cause side effects.
Medications changed by the liver (Cytochrome P450 3A4 (CYP3A4) substrates). Some medications are changed and broken down by the liver. Berberine might decrease how quickly the liver breaks down some medications. Taking berberine along with some medications that are broken down by the liver can increase the effects and side effects of some medications. Before taking berberine, talk to your healthcare provider if you are taking any medications that are changed by the liver. Some medications changed by the liver include cyclosporin (Neoral, Sandimmune).

BERGAMOT OIL

What other names is the product known by?

Bergamot, Bergamot Orange, Bergamota, Bergamotier, Bergamoto, Bergamotte, Bergamotto Bigarade Orange, Citrus Bergamia, Citrus Aurantium Bergamia, Oleum Bergamotte.

What is it?

Bergamot is a plant. The oil of the plant is used to make medicine.

Is it Effective?

The effectiveness ratings for **BERGAMOT OIL** are as follows:

Insufficient Evidence to Rate Effectiveness for... Treating mycosis fungoides (a tumor under the skin due to a fungal infection) when combined with ultra-violet (UV) light, protecting the body against lice and other parasites, psoriasis, vitiligo (loss of the color pigment on the skin), anxiety during radiotherapy, and other conditions.

How does it work?

Bergamot oil has several active chemicals. These chemicals can make the skin sensitive to sunlight.

Are there safety concerns?

Bergamot oil is safe for most people in the small amounts found in food. It might not be safe when used on the skin (topically), because it can make the skin sensitive to the sun and more vulnerable to skin cancer. People who work with bergamot can develop skin problems including blisters, scabs, pigment spots, rashes, sensitivity to the sun, and cancerous changes.

Do not use bergamot oil in children. There have been serious side effects, including convulsion and death, in children who have taken large amounts of bergamot oil.

Do not use bergamot oil if: You are pregnant or breast-feeding.

Are there any interactions with medications?

Medications that increase sensitivity to sunlight (Photosensitizing drugs). Some medications can increase sensitivity to sunlight. Topical use of bergamot oil might also increase your sensitivity to sunlight. Using bergamot oil topically along with medication that increase sensitivity to sunlight could increase the chances of sunburn, blistering or rashes on areas of skin exposed to sunlight. Be sure to wear sunblock and protective clothing when spending time in the sun. Some drugs that cause photosensitivity include amitriptyline (Elavil), Ciprofloxacin (Cipro), norfloxacin (Noroxin), lomefloxacin (Maxaquin), ofloxacin (Floxin), levofloxacin (Levaquin), sparfloxacin (Zagam), gatifloxacin (Tequin), moxifloxacin (Avelox), trimethoprim/sulfamethoxazole (Septra), tetracycline, methoxsalen (8-methoxypsoralen, 8-MOP, Oxsoralen), and Trioxsalen (Trisoralen).

BETA GLUCANS

What other names is the product known by?

1-3,1-6-beta-glucan, beta-1,3-D-glucan, beta-1-6,1,3-beta-glucan, Beta Glucan, Beta Glycans, Grifolan (GRN), Lentinan, PGG Glucan, Poly-[1-6]-Beta-D-Glucopyranosyl-[1-3]-Beta-D-Glucopyranose, Schizophyllan (SPG), SSG, Yeast-Derived Beta Glucan.

What is it?

Beta glucans are sugars which are found in the cell walls of bacteria, fungi, yeasts, algae, lichens, and plants such as oats and barley. They are sometimes used as a medicine.

Is it Effective?

The effectiveness ratings for **BETA GLUCANS** are as follows:

Possibly Effective for... Lowering cholesterol levels when taken by mouth • Stimulating the immune system in people with AIDS or HIV infection, to increase survival in people with cancer, or to prevent infections in people who have had surgery or trauma when used by injection.

Insufficient Evidence to Rate Effectiveness for... Diabetes, cancer, HIV infection, AIDS, chronic fatigue syndrome, physical and emotional stress, colds, flu, allergies, liver problems, Lyme disease, asthma, ear infections, aging, ulcerative colitis and Crohn's disease, fibromyalgia, rheumatoid arthritis, multiple sclerosis, skin problems, wrinkles, bedsores, wounds, burns, diabetic ulcers, and radiation burns.

How does it work?

Beta glucans might lower blood cholesterol by preventing the absorption of cholesterol from food in the stomach and intestines, when it is taken by mouth. When given by injection, beta glucans might stimulate the immune system by increasing chemicals which prevent infections.

Medical professionals should consult the Professional Version at www.NaturalDatabase.com.

Are there safety concerns?

Beta glucans may be safe for most adults when taken by mouth or when the injectable solution is used for a short time period. Injections which have microparticles are not safe. There isn't enough information to know whether beta glucans are safe when applied to the skin.

The potential side effects of beta glucans, when taken by mouth, are not known. When used by injection, beta glucans can cause chills, fever, pain at the injection site, headache, back and joint pain, nausea, vomiting, diarrhea, dizziness, high or low blood pressure, flushing, rashes, decreased number of white blood cells, and increased urine. People with AIDS who take beta glucans have developed thickening of the skin of the hands and feet.

Do not take more than 15 grams per day by mouth and do not use it for longer than 8 weeks.

Do not use beta glucans if: You are pregnant or breast-feeding.

Are there any interactions with medications?

Medications that decrease the immune system (Immunosuppressants). Beta glucans increase the immune system. By increasing the immune system beta glucans might decrease the effectiveness of medications that decrease the immune system. Some medications that decrease the immune system include azathioprine (Imuran), basiliximab (Simulect), cyclosporine (Neoral, Sandimmune), daclizumab (Zenapax), muromonab-CD3 (OKT3, Orthoclone OKT3), mycophenolate (CellCept), tacrolimus (FK506, Prograf), sirolimus (Rapamune), prednisone (Deltasone, Orasone), corticosteroids (glucocorticoids), and others.

BETA-CAROTENE

What other names is the product known by?

A-Beta-Carotene, Beta Carotene, Carotenes, Carotenoids, Provitamin A.

What is it?

Beta-carotene is a dietary source of vitamin A. It can be found in fruits, vegetables, and whole grains. It can also be made in a laboratory.

Is it Effective?

The effectiveness ratings for **BETA-CAROTENE** are as follows:

Likely Effective for... Treating sun sensitivity in people who have a form of inherited blood disorder called "erythropoietic protoporphyria."

Possibly Effective for... Reducing the risk of breast cancer in women before menopause when beta-carotene is consumed in the diet from fruits and vegetables • Treating an eye disease called AMD (age-related macular degeneration) when used with other medicines • A tongue disease called oral leukoplakia • Preventing sunburn in people who are sun-sensitive. However, beta-carotene is unlikely to have much effect on sunburn risk in most people • Preventing a form of arthritis called osteoarthritis from getting worse • Reducing the risk of ovarian cancer in postmenopausal women • Reducing the risk of pregnancy-related death, night blindness, and postpartum diarrhea and fever in underfed women • Preventing exercise-induced asthma • Preventing bronchitis and difficulty breathing in smokers • Improving physical performance and strength in the elderly.

Possibly Ineffective for... Reducing the risk of stroke in male smokers • Reducing the risk of cataracts or preventing cataracts from getting worse • Reducing the risk of Alzheimer's disease • Reducing the risk of prostate cancer. • Diabetes.

Likely Ineffective for... Reducing the risk of heart disease • Reducing the risk of cancer of the uterus, cervix, thyroid, bladder, brain, pancreas, and blood and skin cancers • Reducing the risk of lung cancer in smokers.

Insufficient Evidence to Rate Effectiveness for...AIDS, alcoholism, chronic fatigue syndrome (CFS), colorectal cancer, esophageal cancer, depression, epilepsy, gastric cancer, headaches, heartburn, hypertension, infertility, pancreatic cancer, Parkinson's disease, psoriasis, rheumatoid arthritis, schizophrenia, side effects from chemotherapy, and other conditions.

How does it work?

Beta-carotene is converted to vitamin A, an essential nutrient. It has antioxidant activity, which helps to protect cells from damage.

Are there safety concerns?

Beta-carotene is safe for most people. In high doses, it can turn skin yellow or orange. High doses of beta-carotene, especially taken long-term, are not safe. This is particularly a concern for smokers, and for people who have been exposed to asbestos. Beta-carotene supplements may actually increase their risk of cancer.

The American Heart Association and other prominent organizations recommend obtaining beta-carotene from dietary sources rather than from supplements. Some authorities recommend limiting daily doses of beta-carotene supplements to 7 mg per day.

Do not take beta-carotene if: You are pregnant or breast-feeding. • You smoke. • You have been exposed to high-levels of asbestos. • You are going to have angioplasty, a heart procedure.

Are there any interactions with medications?
Medications used for lowering cholesterol (Statins). Taking beta-carotene, selenium, vitamin C, and vitamin E together might decrease the effectiveness of some medications used for lowering cholesterol. It is not known if beta-carotene alone decreases the effectiveness of some medications used for lowering cholesterol. Some medications used for lowering cholesterol include atorvastatin (Lipitor), fluvastatin (Lescol), lovastatin (Mevacor), and pravastatin (Pravachol).
Niacin. Taking beta-carotene along with vitamin E, vitamin C, and selenium might decrease some of the beneficial effects of niacin. Niacin can increase the good cholesterol. Taking beta-carotene along with these other vitamins might decrease the good cholesterol.

BETA-SITOSTEROL

What other names is the product known by?
Angelicin, B-sitosterol 3-B-D-glucoside, B-sitosterolin, Beta sitosterin, Beta-sitosterol glucoside, Beta-sitosterol glycoside, Cinchol, Cupreol, Phytosterols, Plant sterols, Quebrachol, Rhamnol, Sitosterin, Sitosterol, Sitosterolins, Sterinol, Sterolins, 3-beta-stigmast-5-en-3-ol, 22-23-dihydrostigmasterol, 24-beta-ethyl-delta-5-cholesten-3beta-ol, 24-ethyl-cholesterol.

What is it?
Beta-sitosterol is a substance derived from plants. It is found in fruits, vegetables, nuts, and seeds. It is used to make medicine.

Is it Effective?
The effectiveness ratings for **BETA-SITOSTEROL** are as follows:
Likely Effective for... High cholesterol • Trouble urinating from an enlarged prostate, or "benign prostatic hyperplasia" (BPH).
Possibly Ineffective for... Tuberculosis.
Likely Ineffective for... Gallstones.
Insufficient Evidence to Rate Effectiveness for... Burns, prostate infections, sexual dysfunction, preventing colon cancer, rheumatoid arthritis, psoriasis, allergies, cervical cancer, fibromyalgia, systemic lupus erythematosus (SLE), asthma, baldness, migraines, chronic fatigue syndrome, menopause, and other conditions.

How does it work?
Beta-sitosterol is a plant substance similar to cholesterol. It might help reduce cholesterol levels by limiting the amount of cholesterol that is able to enter the body. It can also bind to the prostate to help reduce swelling (inflammation).

Are there safety concerns?
Beta-sitosterol is safe for most people. It can cause some side effects, such as nausea, indigestion, gas, diarrhea, or constipation. Beta-sitosterol has also been linked to reports of erectile dysfunction and loss of libido.

Do not use beta-sitosterol if: You are pregnant or breast-feeding. • You have a rare inherited fat storage disease called "sitosterolemia."

Are there any interactions with medications?
Ezetimibe (Zetia). Taking ezetimibe (Zetia) can reduce of amount of beta-sitosterol the body absorbs. This might decrease the effectiveness of beta-sitosterol.
Pravastatin (Pravachol). Taking pravastatin (Pravachol) might decrease how much beta-sitosterol is in the body. This might decrease the effectiveness of beta-sitosterol.

Medical professionals should consult the Professional Version at www.NaturalDatabase.com.

CONSUMER VERSION

Medical professionals should consult the Professional Version at www.NaturalDatabase.com.

BETAINE ANHYDROUS

What other names is the product known by?
Betaine, Cystadane, Trimethyl Glycine, Trimethylglycine anhydrous, TMG.

What is it?
Betaine anhydrous occurs naturally in the body, and can be found in foods such as beets, spinach, cereals, seafood, and wine.

Is it Effective?
The effectiveness ratings for **BETAINE ANHYDROUS** are as follows:
Effective for... Homocystinuria, a rare but serious disease where homocystine levels are extremely high due to defective metabolism.
Possibly Effective for... Topical use in toothpaste to help with dry mouth.
Insufficient Evidence to Rate Effectiveness for... Reduction of homocysteine levels in people without homocystinuria, liver disease not due to alcohol.

How does it work?
Betaine anhydrous helps in the metabolism of homocysteine, a chemical involved in the normal function of many different parts of the body, including blood, bones, eyes, heart, nerves, and the brain. Betaine anhydrous prevents the buildup of homocysteine seen in people who have problems with its metabolism from birth.

Are there safety concerns?
Betaine anhydrous is safe for most people. It can cause some minor side effects. These include nausea, stomach upset, and diarrhea.

Betaine anhydrous is also available as a prescription drug in the US. Prescription betaine anhydrous is standardized which means it contains a set dose of active chemicals.

Do not use betaine anhydrous if: You are pregnant or breast-feeding.

Are there any interactions with medications?
It is not known if betaine anhydrous interacts with any medicines.
Before taking betaine anhydrous, talk with your healthcare professional if you take any medications.

BETAINE HYDROCHLORIDE

What other names is the product known by?
Betaine, Betaine HCl, Trimethylglycine, Trimethylglycine hydrochloride, TMG.

What is it?
Betaine hydrochloride is a chemical substance made in a laboratory. People use it as a medicine.

Is it Effective?
The effectiveness ratings for **BETAINE HYDROCHLORIDE** are as follows:
Insufficient Evidence to Rate Effectiveness for... Low potassium, hayfever, anemia, asthma, hardening of the arteries (atherosclerosis), yeast infection, diarrhea, food allergies, gallstones, inner ear infection, rheumatoid arthritis, protecting the liver, and thyroid disorders.

How does it work?
It isn't known how Betaine hydrochloride might work.

Are there safety concerns?
There isn't enough information to know if betaine hydrochloride is safe. It might cause heartburn.

Do not take betaine hydrochloride if: You are pregnant or breast-feeding. • You have a gastric or duodenal ulcer. Betaine hydrochloride might increase stomach acid, which could make these ulcers worse.

Are there any interactions with medications?
It is not known if betaine hydrochloride interacts with any medicines.
Before taking betaine hydrochloride, talk with your healthcare professional if you take any medications.

 Natural Medicines Comprehensive Database Consumer Version (209) 472-2244

BETH ROOT

What other names is the product known by?
Birthroot, Coughroot, Ground Lily, Harp Plant, Indian Shamrock, Jew's Indian Balm, Lamb's Quarters, Milk Ipecac, Pariswort, Rattlesnake Root, Snakebite, Stinking Benjamin, Three-Leafed Nightshade, Trillium Erectum, Wake Robin.

What is it?
Beth root is a plant. The root, root-like stem, and leaf are used to make medicine.

Is it Effective?
The effectiveness ratings for **BETH ROOT** are as follows:
Insufficient Evidence to Rate Effectiveness for... Heavy menstruation and pain, reducing swelling (astringent), breaking up chest congestion, varicose veins, ulcers, blood clots, and bleeding hemorrhoids.

How does it work?
There isn't enough information to know how beth root works.

Are there safety concerns?
Beth root might not be safe. It can cause irritation of the stomach and intestines, and vomiting. It might also cause skin irritation.

Do not use beth root if: You are pregnant or breast-feeding. • You have a heart condition. Beth root can have toxic effects on the heart.

Are there any interactions with medications?
It is not known if beth root interacts with any medicines.
Before taking beth root, talk with your healthcare professional if you take any medications.

BETONY

What other names is the product known by?
Betonica officinalis, Bishopswort, Hedge Nettles, Stachys officinalis, Wood Betony.

What is it?
Betony is a plant. The dried above ground parts are used to make medicine.

Is it Effective?
The effectiveness ratings for **BETONY** are as follows:
Insufficient Evidence to Rate Effectiveness for... Bronchitis, asthma, anxiety, epilepsy, heartburn, nerve pain, gout, bladder or kidney stones, bladder inflammation, headache, tension, facial pain, congestion, diarrhea, and as a mouth rinse or gargle for gum, mouth, and throat irritations (topical).

How does it work?
It is thought that the chemicals in betony act as a drying medicine when used topically. They may also decrease blood pressure, reduce anxiety, and decrease headaches.

Are there safety concerns?
There is not enough information about betony to know if it is safe to take. It might cause stomach upset in some people.

Do not take betony if: You are pregnant or breast-feeding.

Are there any interactions with medications?
Medications for high blood pressure (Antihypertensive drugs). Betony seems to decrease blood pressure. Taking betony along with medications for high blood pressure might cause your blood pressure to go too low. Some medications for high blood pressure include captopril (Capoten), enalapril (Vasotec), losartan (Cozaar), valsartan (Diovan), diltiazem (Cardizem), Amlodipine (Norvasc), hydrochlorothiazide (HydroDiuril), furosemide (Lasix), and many others.

Medical professionals should consult the Professional Version at www.NaturalDatabase.com.

BHT (BUTYLATED HYDROXYTOLUENE)

What other names is the product known by?
Butylated hydroxytoluene, butylhydroxytoluene, dibutylated hydroxytoluene.

What is it?
BHT is a synthetic chemical that is added to foods as a preservative.

Is it Effective?
The effectiveness ratings for **BHT (BUTYLATED HYDROXYTOLUENE)** are as follows:
Insufficient Evidence to Rate Effectiveness for... Cold sores caused by a type of virus called herpes, genital herpes, acquired immunodeficiency syndrome (AIDS).

How does it work?
BHT is an antioxidant. It may damage the protective outer layer of viral cells.

Are there safety concerns?
BHT is safe in the amounts found in processed foods.

There is not enough information to determine its safety when used in higher doses.

Do not use BHT as a dietary supplement if: You are pregnant or breast-feeding.

Are there any interactions with medications?
It is not known if BHT interacts with any medicines.
Before taking BHT, talk with your healthcare professional if you take any medications.

BIFIDOBACTERIA

What other names is the product known by?
B. Bifidum, Bifido, Bifidobacterium, Bifidobacterium adolescentis; Bifidobacterium animalis, Bifidobacterium bifidum; Bifidobacterium breve; Bifidobacterium infantis; Bifidobacterium lactis; Bifidobacterium longum, Bifidum, Bifidobacteria Bifidus, Probiotics.

What is it?
Bifidobacteria are a group of bacteria that normally live in the intestines. The bacteria are used as medicine.

Is it Effective?
The effectiveness ratings for **BIFIDOBACTERIA** are as follows:
Possibly Effective for... Prevention of diarrhea in infants, when used with another bacterium called Streptococcus thermophilus • Prevention of traveler's diarrhea, when used with other bacteria such as Lactobacillus acidophilus, Lactobacillus bulgaricus, or Streptococcus thermophilus • Treating a skin condition in infants called atopic eczema • Inflammation of the intestines in infants • Irritable bowel syndrome (IBS) • Preventing a complication after surgery for ulcerative colitis called pouchitis • Reducing side effects of treatment for the ulcer-causing bacterium Helicobacter pylori • Ulcerative colitis. Some research suggests that taking a specific combination product containing bifidobacteria, lactobacillus and streptococcus might help induce remission and prevent relapse.
Insufficient Evidence to Rate Effectiveness for... Common cold and flu (influenza); diarrhea caused by antibiotics; liver problems; high cholesterol; lactose intolerance; mastitis; mumps; cancer; stomach problems; replacing bacteria removed by diarrhea; chemotherapy; Lyme disease; preventing infections after exposure to radiation, aging, antibiotics, and other causes; and other conditions.

How does it work?
Bifidobacteria help decrease other organisms, such as the bacteria that cause diarrhea, from growing in the intestinal tract. Treatment with bifidobacteria seems to promote the correct balance of friendly bacteria and other organisms in the intestine.

Are there safety concerns?
Bifidobacteria are safe for most adults and children when used for up to one year. In some people, treatment with bifidobacteria might cause stomach and intestine upset including bloating and gas.

Bifidobacteria seem to be safe in children, including those under two years of age and critically ill infants, when used for up to 8 months.

Do not use bifidobacteria without medical advice if: You are pregnant or breast-feeding. • You have a weakened immune system.

Are there any interactions with medications?

Antibiotic drugs. Antibiotics are used to reduce harmful bacteria in the body. Antibiotics can also reduce friendly bacteria in the body. Bifidobacteria are a type of friendly bacteria. Taking antibiotics along with bifidobacteria might reduce the effectiveness of bifidobacteria. To avoid this interaction take bifidobacteria products at least two hours before or after antibiotics.

BILBERRY

What other names is the product known by?

Airelle, Bilberry Fruit, Bilberry Leaf, Black Whortles, Bleaberry, Blueberry, Burren Myrtle, Dwarf Bilberry, Dyeberry, Huckleberry, Hurtleberry, Myrtilli Fructus, Trackleberry, Vaccinium myrtillus, Whortleberry, Wineberry.

What is it?

Bilberry is a plant. The dried, ripe fruit and leaves are used to make medicine.

Is it Effective?

The effectiveness ratings for **BILBERRY** are as follows:
Possibly Effective for... Lesions in the eye (retina) in people with diabetes or high blood pressure.
Possibly Ineffective for... Improving night vision.
Insufficient Evidence to Rate Effectiveness for... Chest pain (angina), varicose veins, cataracts, hardening of the arteries (atherosclerosis), diabetes, arthritis (osteoarthritis), gout, skin problems, hemorrhoids, urinary tract problems, chronic fatigue syndrome, and other conditions.

How does it work?

Bilberry contains chemicals called tannins that can help improve diarrhea, and mouth and throat irritation by reducing swelling (inflammation). There is some evidence that the chemicals found in bilberry leaves can help lower blood sugar and cholesterol levels.

Are there safety concerns?

The dried, ripe fruit of bilberry is safe for most people when eaten in typical food amounts. There isn't enough information to know if it is safe when taken as a medicine. Bilberry leaf probably isn't safe for most people when taken in high doses or for a long time. If you have diabetes, keep in mind that bilberry leaf might lower blood sugar. Monitor your blood sugar closely.

Do not use bilberry in medicinal amounts if: You are pregnant or breast-feeding.

Are there any interactions with medications?

Medications for diabetes (Antidiabetes drugs). Bilberry leaves might decrease blood sugar. Diabetes medications are also used to lower blood sugar. Taking bilberry leaves along with diabetes medications might cause your blood sugar to go too low. Monitor your blood sugar closely. The dose of your diabetes medication might need to be changed. Some medications used for diabetes include glimepiride (Amaryl), glyburide (DiaBeta, Glynase PresTab, Micronase), insulin, pioglitazone (Actos), rosiglitazone (Avandia), chlorpropamide (Diabinese), glipizide (Glucotrol), tolbutamide (Orinase), and others.

BIOTIN

What other names is the product known by?

Coenzyme R, D-Biotin, Vitamin H, W Factor, Cis-hexahydro-2-oxo-1H-thieno[3,4-d]-imidazole-4-valeric Acid.

What is it?

Biotin is a vitamin.

Is it Effective?

The effectiveness ratings for **BIOTIN** are as follows:
Likely Effective for... Treating and preventing biotin deficiency.
Possibly Effective for... Brittle fingernails and toenails.
Possibly Ineffective for... Skin rash in infants.
Insufficient Evidence to Rate Effectiveness for... Hair loss, diabetes, diabetic nerve pain, and others.

How does it work?

Biotin is an important component of enzymes in the body that break down certain substances like fats, carbohydrates, and others.

Are there safety concerns?

Biotin is safe for most people.

Are there any interactions with medications?

It is not known if biotin interacts with any medicines.
Before taking biotin, talk with your healthcare professional if you take any medications.

BIRCH

What other names is the product known by?

Betula, Betulae Folium, Betula Pendula, Betula Verrucosa, Downy Birch, Silver Birch, White Birch.

What is it?

Birch is a tree. The leaves of the tree, which contain lots of vitamin C, are used to make medicine.

Is it Effective?

The effectiveness ratings for **BIRCH** are as follows:
Insufficient Evidence to Rate Effectiveness for... Arthritis, hair loss, rashes, conditions of the urinary tract (such as small kidney stones, when used with drinking lots of liquids), arthritis-like condition called rheumatism, and other conditions.

How does it work?

Birch leaves contain chemicals which increase water loss through the urine.

Are there safety concerns?

Birch seems to be safe for most adults. It can cause allergic reactions in some people. People who are sensitive to celery, wild carrot or mugwort are more likely to have an allergic reaction to birch.

Do not use birch if: You are pregnant or breast-feeding. • You have high blood pressure. • You have allergies to celery, wild carrot, or mugwort.

Are there any interactions with medications?

Water pills (Diuretic drugs). Birch seems to work like "water pills" by causing the body to lose water. Taking birch along with other "water pills" might cause the body to lose too much water. Losing too much water can cause you to be dizzy and your blood pressure to go too low. Some "water pills" include chlorothiazide (Diuril), chlorthalidone (Thalitone), furosemide (Lasix), hydrochlorothiazide (HCTZ, Hydrodiuril, Microzide), and others.

BISHOP'S WEED

What other names is the product known by?

Ajava Seeds, Ajowan, Ajowan Caraway, Ajowan Seed, Ajowanj, Ammi majus. Bishop's Flower, Bishops Weed, Bullwort, Carum, Flowering Ammi, Omum, Yavani.

What is it?

Bishop's weed is a plant. The seeds are used to make medicine.

Is it Effective?

The effectiveness ratings for **BISHOP'S WEED** are as follows:
Insufficient Evidence to Rate Effectiveness for... Skin conditions such as psoriasis and vitiligo, digestive problems, asthma, chest pain, kidney stones, and promoting water loss.

How does it work?

Bishop's weed contains several chemicals, including methoxsalen, a chemical used to make a prescription medication for the skin condition psoriasis.

Are there safety concerns?

There isn't enough information to know if bishop's weed is safe. When taken by mouth, bishop's weed might cause nausea, vomiting, and headache. Some people are allergic to bishop's weed. They can get a runny nose, rash, or hives. There is also some concern that bishop's weed might harm the liver or the retina of the eye.

Bishop's weed can cause skin to become extra sensitive to the sun. This might put you at greater risk for skin cancer. Wear sunblock outside, especially if you are light-skinned.

Do not use bishop's weed if: You are pregnant or breast-feeding. • You have liver disease.

Are there any interactions with medications?

Medications that slow blood clotting (Anticoagulant / Antiplatelet drugs). Bishop's weed might slow blood clotting. Taking bishop's weed along with medications that also slow clotting might increase the chances of bruising and bleeding. Some medications that slow blood clotting include aspirin, clopidogrel (Plavix), diclofenac (Voltaren, Cataflam, others), ibuprofen (Advil, Motrin, others), naproxen (Anaprox, Naprosyn, others), dalteparin (Fragmin), enoxaparin (Lovenox), heparin, warfarin (Coumadin), and others.

Medications changed by the liver (Cytochrome P450 3A4 (CYP3A4) substrates). Some medications are changed and broken down by the liver. Bishop's weed might decrease how quickly the liver breaks down some medications. Taking Bishop's weed along with some medications that are broken down by the liver can increase the effects and side effects of some medications. Before taking Bishop's weed, talk to your healthcare provider if you are taking any medications that are changed by the liver. Some medications changed by the liver include lovastatin (Mevacor), ketoconazole (Nizoral), itraconazole (Sporanox), fexofenadine (Allegra), triazolam (Halcion), and many others.

Medications that can harm the liver (Hepatotoxic drugs). Bishop's weed might harm the liver. Taking bishop's weed along with medication that might also harm the liver can increase the risk of liver damage. Do not take bishop's weed if you are taking a medication that can harm the liver. Some medications that can harm the liver include acetaminophen (Tylenol and others), amiodarone (Cordarone), carbamazepine (Tegretol), isoniazid (INH), methotrexate (Rheumatrex), methyldopa (Aldomet), fluconazole (Diflucan), itraconazole (Sporanox), erythromycin (Erythrocin, Ilosone, others), phenytoin (Dilantin), lovastatin (Mevacor), pravastatin (Pravachol), simvastatin (Zocor), and many others.

Medications that increase sensitivity to sunlight (Photosensitizing drugs). Some medications can increase sensitivity to sunlight. Bishop's weed might also increase your sensitivity to sunlight. Taking bishop's weed along with medication that increases sensitivity to sunlight could increase the chances of sunburn, blistering or rashes on areas of skin exposed to sunlight. Be sure to wear sunblock and protective clothing when spending time in the sun. Some drugs that cause photosensitivity include amitriptyline (Elavil), Ciprofloxacin (Cipro), norfloxacin (Noroxin), lomefloxacin (Maxaquin), ofloxacin (Floxin), levofloxacin (Levaquin), sparfloxacin (Zagam), gatifloxacin (Tequin), moxifloxacin (Avelox), trimethoprim/sulfamethoxazole (Septra), tetracycline, methoxsalen (8-methoxypsoralen, 8-MOP, Oxsoralen), and Trioxsalen (Trisoralen).

BISTORT

What other names is the product known by?

Adderwort, Dragonwort, Easter Giant, Easter Mangiant, Oderwort, Osterick, Patience Dock, Polygonum Bistorta, Red Legs, Snakeweed, Sweet Dock.

What is it?

Bistort is a plant. The root and root-like stem are used to make medicine.

Is it Effective?

The effectiveness ratings for **BISTORT** are as follows:
Insufficient Evidence to Rate Effectiveness for... Digestive disorders like diarrhea, mouth and throat infections, wounds, and other conditions.

How does it work?

Bistort contains chemicals called tannins that can help improve diarrhea and mouth and throat irritation by reducing swelling (inflammation).

Are there safety concerns?

There isn't enough information to know if bistort is safe.

Do not use bistort if: You are pregnant or breast-feeding.

CONSUMER VERSION

Medical professionals should consult the Professional Version at www.NaturalDatabase.com.

Are there any interactions with medications?

Medications taken by mouth (Oral drugs). Bistort contains a large amount of chemicals called tannins. Tannins absorb substances in the stomach and intestines. Taking bistort along with medications taken by mouth can decrease how much medicine your body absorbs, and decrease the effectiveness of your medicine. To prevent this interaction, take bistort at least 1 hour after medications you take by mouth.

BITTER ALMOND

What other names is the product known by?

Amygdala Amara, Badama, Bitter Almond Oil, Prunus Amygdalus Amara, Prunus Dulcis Amara, Vatadha, Vathada, Volatile Almond Oil.

What is it?

Bitter Almond is a plant. The bitter almond kernels are used to make medicine.

Is it Effective?

The effectiveness ratings for **BITTER ALMOND** are as follows:
Insufficient Evidence to Rate Effectiveness for... Spasms, pain, cough, itch, and other conditions.

How does it work?

The oil from bitter almond kernels contains a chemical that might act as a pain reliever.

Are there safety concerns?

Unprocessed bitter almond oil isn't safe in any amount. Bitter almond oil contains a poisonous chemical called hydrocyanic acid (HCN). Serious side effects can occur such as slowing of the nervous system, breathing problems, and death.

There is some evidence that bitter almond oil is safe in small amounts when processed to remove the hydrocyanic acid (HCN). However, even the processed oil isn't safe in large amounts.

Do not use bitter almond oil if: You are pregnant or breast-feeding.

Are there any interactions with medications?

Sedative medications (CNS depressants). Very large amounts of bitter almond might cause sleepiness and drowsiness. Medications that cause sleepiness are called sedatives. Taking bitter almond along with sedative medications might cause too much sleepiness. Some sedative medications include clonazepam (Klonopin), lorazepam (Ativan), phenobarbital (Donnatal), zolpidem (Ambien), and others.

BITTER MELON

What other names is the product known by?

African Cucumber, Balsam Pear, Balsam-Apple, Balsambirne, Balsamo, Bitter Apple, Bitter Cucumber, Bitter Gourd, Bittergurke, Carilla Gourd, Cerasee, Chinli-Chih, Cundeamor, Karavella, Kathilla, Karela, Kerala, Kuguazi, K'u-Kua, Lai Margose, Momordique, Pepino Montero, P'u-T'ao, Sorosi, Sushavi, Wild Cucumber.

What is it?

Bitter Melon is a plant. The fruit and seeds are used to make medicine.

Is it Effective?

The effectiveness ratings for **BITTER MELON** are as follows:
Insufficient Evidence to Rate Effectiveness for... Diabetes, a skin condition called psoriasis, HIV/AIDS, stomach and intestinal disorders such as ulcers and constipation, kidney stones, liver disease, and skin abscesses and wounds.

How does it work?

Bitter melon contains a chemical that acts like insulin to help reduce blood sugar levels.

Are there safety concerns?

There isn't enough information to know if bitter melon is safe. Bitter melon can lower blood sugar. If you have diabetes, check your blood sugar carefully.
Do not use bitter melon if: You are pregnant or breast-feeding.

Are there any interactions with medications?

Medications for diabetes (Antidiabetes drugs). Bitter melon can decrease blood sugar levels. Diabetes medications are also used to lower blood sugar. Taking bitter melon along with diabetes medications might cause your blood sugar to be too low. Monitor your blood sugar closely. The dose of your diabetes medication might need to be changed. Some medications used for diabetes include glimepiride (Amaryl), glyburide (DiaBeta, Glynase PresTab, Micronase), insulin, pioglitazone (Actos), rosiglitazone (Avandia), chlorpropamide (Diabinese), glipizide (Glucotrol), tolbutamide (Orinase), and others.

BITTER MILKWORT

What other names is the product known by?

European Bitter Polygala, European Senega, Evergreen Snakeroot, Flowering Wintergreen, Little Pollom, Polygala Amara, Snakeroot.

What is it?

Bitter milkwort is a plant. The flowering plant and root are used to make medicine.

Is it Effective?

The effectiveness ratings for **BITTER MILKWORT** are as follows:
Insufficient Evidence to Rate Effectiveness for... Breathing problems such as infections in the lungs, and cough.

How does it work?

Bitter milkwort has chemicals that help to break up chest congestion by thinning mucous and making it easier to cough up (expectorant).

Are there safety concerns?

There isn't enough information to know if bitter milkwort is safe.

Do not use bitter milkwort if: You are pregnant or breast-feeding.

Are there any interactions with medications?

It is not known if bitter milkwort interacts with any medicines.
Before taking bitter milkwort, talk with your healthcare professional if you take any medications.

BITTER ORANGE

What other names is the product known by?

Aurantii pericarpium, Bitter Orange Flower, Bitter Orange Peel, Citrus amara, Citrus aurantium, Citrus bigarradia, Citrus vulgaris, Fructus Aurantii, Green Orange, Kijitsu, Neroli Oil, Seville Orange, Shangzhou Zhiqiao, Sour Orange, Synephrine, Zhi Qiao, Zhi Shi.

What is it?

Bitter orange is a plant. The peel, flower, leaf, fruit, and fruit juice are used to make medicine.

Is it Effective?

The effectiveness ratings for **BITTER ORANGE** are as follows:
Possibly Effective for... Fungal skin infections such as ringworm, athlete's foot, and jock itch.
Insufficient Evidence to Rate Effectiveness for... Weight loss, nasal congestion, intestinal gas, cancer, stomach and intestinal upset, intestinal ulcers, regulating cholesterol, diabetes, chronic fatigue syndrome (CFS), liver and gallbladder problems, stimulation of the heart and circulation, eye swelling, colds, headaches, nerve and muscle pain, bruises, stimulating appetite, mild sleep problems (insomnia), and other conditions.

How does it work?

Bitter orange has many chemicals that affect the nervous system. These chemicals can constrict blood vessels, increase blood pressure, and cause the heart to beat faster.

Are there safety concerns?

Bitter orange is safe when consumed in the amounts found in foods. But there is concern that it might not be safe when used for medical purposes, such as in products promoted for weight loss. Bitter orange, particularly when taken with caffeine or caffeine-containing herbs, increases the risk for high blood pressure, fainting, heart attack, and stroke.

Medical professionals should consult the Professional Version at www.NaturalDatabase.com.

Bitter orange can cause sensitivity to the sun. Wear sunblock outside, especially if you are light-skinned.

Do not use bitter orange if: You are pregnant or breast-feeding. • You have high blood pressure. • You have glaucoma. • You have heart disease. • You have an irregular heartbeat or heart arrhythmia. • You have migraine or cluster headaches.

Are there any interactions with medications?

Caffeine (Excedrin, Anacin, Vivarin, and others). Bitter orange is a stimulant. Caffeine is also a stimulant. In combination, they can increase blood pressure and cause the heart to beat rapidly. This can cause serious adverse effects such as heat attack and stroke.

Dextromethorphan (Robitussin DM, and others). The body breaks down dextromethorphan (Robitussin DM, others) to get rid of it. Bitter orange might decrease how quickly the body breaks down dextromethorphan (Robitussin DM, others). Taking bitter orange along with dextromethorphan (Robitussin DM, others) might increase the effects and side effects of dextromethorphan (Robitussin DM, others).

Felodipine (Plendil). Felodipine (Plendil) is used to lower blood pressure. The body breaks down felodipine (Plendil) to get rid of it. Bitter orange might decrease how quickly the body gets rid of felodipine (Plendil). Taking bitter orange along with felodipine (Plendil) might increase the effects and side effects of felodipine (Plendil).

Indinavir (Crixivan). Indinavir (Crixivan) is used to treat HIV/AIDS. The body breaks down indinavir (Crixivan) to get rid of it. Bitter orange might decrease how quickly the body breaks down indinavir (Crixivan). Taking bitter orange along with indinavir (Crixivan) might increase the effects and side effects of indinavir (Crixivan).

Medications for depression (MAOIs). Bitter orange contains chemicals that stimulate the body. Some medications used for depression can increase these chemicals. Taking bitter orange with these medications used for depression might cause serious side effects including fast heartbeat, high blood pressure, seizures, nervousness, and others. Some of these medications used for depression include phenelzine (Nardil), tranylcypromine (Parnate), and others.

Medications changed by the liver (Cytochrome P450 3A4 (CYP3A4) substrates). Some medications are changed and broken down by the liver. Bitter orange might decrease how quickly the liver breaks down some medications. Taking bitter orange along with some medications that are broken down by the liver can increase the effects and side effects of some medications. Before taking bitter orange, talk to your healthcare provider if you are taking any medications that are changed by the liver. Some medications changed by the liver include lovastatin (Mevacor), ketoconazole (Nizoral), itraconazole (Sporanox), fexofenadine (Allegra), triazolam (Halcion), and many others.

Medications that can cause an irregular heartbeat (QT interval-prolonging drugs). Bitter orange might increase the speed of your heartbeat. Taking bitter orange along with medications that can cause an irregular heartbeat might cause serious side effects including heart arrhythmias. Some medications that can cause an irregular heartbeat include amiodarone (Cordarone), disopyramide (Norpace), dofetilide (Tikosyn), ibutilide (Corvert), procainamide (Pronestyl), quinidine, sotalol (Betapace), thioridazine (Mellaril), and many others.

Midazolam (Versed). The body breaks down midazolam (Versed) to get rid of it. Bitter orange can decrease how quickly the body breaks down midazolam (Versed). Taking bitter orange along with midazolam (Versed) might increase the effects and side effects of midazolam (Versed).

Stimulant drugs. Stimulant drugs speed up the nervous system. By speeding up the nervous system, stimulant medications can make you feel jittery and speed up your heartbeat. Bitter orange might also speed up the nervous system. Taking bitter orange along with stimulant drugs might cause serious problems including increased heart rate and high blood pressure. Avoid taking stimulant drugs along with bitter orange. Some stimulant drugs include diethylpropion (Tenuate), epinephrine, phentermine (Ionamin), pseudoephedrine (Sudafed), and many others.

BITTERSWEET NIGHTSHADE

What other names is the product known by?

Bitter Nightshade, Bittersweet, Blud Nightshade, Common Nightshade, Deadly Nightshade, Dulcamara, Fellen, Fellonwood, Felonwort, Fever Twig, Mortal, Scarlet Berry, Sanke Berry, Solanum Dulcamara, Staff Vine, Violet Bloom, Woody, Woody Nightshade.

What is it?

Bittersweet nightshade is a vine-like plant. It is in the same family as tomatoes and potatoes. The stem is used to make medicine.

    Natural Medicines Comprehensive Database Consumer Version   (209) 472-2244

Is it Effective?

The effectiveness ratings for **BITTERSWEET NIGHTSHADE** are as follows:
Insufficient Evidence to Rate Effectiveness for... Acne, itchy skin, boils, broken skin, warts, arthritis-like pain, nail bed swelling, eczema, promoting water loss (diuretic), pain relief, and calming nervous excitement.

How does it work?

It is not known how bittersweet nightshade might work.

Are there safety concerns?

The stem of bittersweet nightshade might be safe for most adults. The leaves or berries are UNSAFE, and are very poisonous. Symptoms of poisoning include: scratchy throat, headache, dizziness, enlarged eye pupils, trouble speaking, low body temperature, vomiting, diarrhea, bleeding in the stomach or intestines, convulsions, slowed blood circulation and breathing, and even death.

Bittersweet nightshade is UNSAFE for children. Some children have died from eating unripe bittersweet nightshade berries.

Do not use bittersweet nightshade if: You are pregnant or breast-feeding. • You have a stomach or intestine condition such as an ulcer or Irritable Bowel Syndrome (IBS).

Are there any interactions with medications?

It is not known if bittersweet nightshade interacts with any medicines.
Before taking bittersweet nightshade, talk with your healthcare professional if you take any medications.

BLACK ALDER

What other names is the product known by?

Alnus Glutinosa, Common Alder, Owler, Tag Alder.

What is it?

Black alder is a plant. The bark is used to make medicine.

Is it Effective?

The effectiveness ratings for **BLACK ALDER** are as follows:
Insufficient Evidence to Rate Effectiveness for... Sore throat, pharyngitis, and bleeding in the intestines.

How does it work?

There isn't enough information to know how black alder works.

Are there safety concerns?

There isn't enough information to know if black alder is safe.

Do not use black alder if: You are pregnant or breast-feeding.

Are there any interactions with medications?

It is not known if black alder interacts with any medicines.
Before taking black alder, talk with your healthcare professional if you take any medications.

BLACK BRYONY

What other names is the product known by?

Black Bindweed, Blackeye Root, Dioscorea communis, Lady's-Seal, Tamus communis, Tamus edulis.

What is it?

Black bryony is a plant. The root is used to make medicine.

Is it Effective?

The effectiveness ratings for **BLACK BRYONY** are as follows:
Insufficient Evidence to Rate Effectiveness for... Skin problems, bruises, strains, torn muscles, gout, arthritis-like pain, hair loss, improving blood flow to the scalp, and inducing vomiting.

How does it work?
Black bryony root can stimulate nerve endings by piercing the skin with tiny, needle like crystals.

Are there safety concerns?
Using black bryony on the skin might not be safe. It can cause severe skin irritation, rashes, swelling, pustules, and welts.

Black bryony root is UNSAFE for anyone when taken by mouth. It can cause serious side effects including severe irritation of the stomach and intestines, seizures, kidney failure, and dangerously slowed breathing.

Do not use black bryony if: You are pregnant or breast-feeding.

Are there any interactions with medications?
It is not known if black bryony interacts with any medicines.
Before taking black bryony, talk with your healthcare professional if you take any medications.

BLACK COHOSH

What other names is the product known by?
Actaea Macrotys, Actaea Racemosa, Baneberry, Black Snakeroot, Bugbane, Bugwort, Cimicifuga, Cimicifuga Racemosa, Phytoestrogen, Rattle Root, Rattle Snakeroot, Rattlesnake Root, Rattleweed, Squawroot.

What is it?
Black cohosh is an herb. The root is used to make medicine.

Is it Effective?
The effectiveness ratings for **BLACK COHOSH** are as follows:
Possibly Effective for... Menopausal symptoms such as hot flashes. It can take about a month of treatment before symptoms are relieved.
Insufficient Evidence to Rate Effectiveness for... Premenstrual syndrome (PMS), osteoporosis, painful menstruation, upset stomach, muscle pain, fever, sore throat, cough, repelling insects, acne, mole and wart removal, and other conditions.

How does it work?
Black cohosh seems to have effects like the hormone estrogen, but it is not known exactly how it works.

Are there safety concerns?
Black cohosh seems to be safe for most people. It might cause some mild side effects such as stomach upset, cramping, headache, rash, a feeling of heaviness, and weight gain.

Some reports have linked black cohosh to liver damage. It is not known for sure if black cohosh is the cause of liver damage in these cases. More information is needed. Until more is known, people who take black cohosh should watch for symptoms of liver damage such as yellowing of the skin and eyes (jaundice), unusual fatigue, or dark urine. If these symptoms develop, black cohosh should be stopped and medical attention should be sought. People who take black cohosh should also consider getting periodic blood tests to check for liver damage.

Do not use black cohosh if: You are pregnant or breast-feeding. • You have breast cancer. • You have uterine cancer. • You have ovarian cancer. • You have a condition called "endometriosis." • You have uterine "fibroids." • You have liver disease. • You have received a kidney transplant. • You have a condition called protein S deficiency.

Are there any interactions with medications?
Cisplatin (Platinol-AQ). Cisplatin is used to treat cancer. There is some concern that black cohosh might decrease how well cisplatin works for cancer. Do not take black cohosh if you are taking cisplatin.
Medications changed by the liver (Cytochrome P450 2D6 (CYP2D6) substrates). Some medications are changed and broken down by the liver. Black cohosh might decrease how quickly the liver breaks down some medications. Taking Black cohosh along with some medications that are change by the liver can increase the effects and side effects of your medication. Before taking black cohosh talk to your healthcare provider if you take any medications that are changed by the liver. Some medications that are changed by the liver include amitriptyline (Elavil), clozapine (Clozaril), codeine, desipramine (Norpramin), donepezil (Aricept), fentanyl (Duragesic), flecainide (Tambocor), fluoxetine (Prozac), meperidine (Demerol), methadone (Dolophine), metoprolol (Lopressor, Toprol XL), olanzapine (Zyprexa), ondansetron (Zofran), tramadol (Ultram), trazodone (Desyrel), and others.

Medications changed by the liver (Cytochrome P450 3A4 (CYP3A4) substrates). Some medications are changed and broken down by the liver. Black cohosh might decrease how quickly the liver breaks down some medications. Taking black cohosh along with some medications that are broken down by the liver can increase the effects and side effects of these medications. Before taking black cohosh, talk to your healthcare provider if you are taking any medications that are changed by the liver. Some medications changed by the liver include lovastatin (Mevacor), ketoconazole (Nizoral), itraconazole (Sporanox), fexofenadine (Allegra), triazolam (Halcion), and many others.

Medications that can harm the liver (Hepatotoxic drugs). Black cohosh might harm the liver. Taking black cohosh along with medication that might also harm the liver can increase the risk of liver damage. Do not take black cohosh if you are taking a medication that can harm the liver. Some medications that can harm the liver include acetaminophen (Tylenol and others), amiodarone (Cordarone), carbamazepine (Tegretol), isoniazid (INH), methotrexate (Rheumatrex), methyldopa (Aldomet), fluconazole (Diflucan), itraconazole (Sporanox), erythromycin (Erythrocin, Ilosone, others), phenytoin (Dilantin), lovastatin (Mevacor), pravastatin (Pravachol), simvastatin (Zocor), and many others.

BLACK CURRANT

What other names is the product known by?
Cassis, European Black Currant, Ribes Nigri Folium (Black Currant Leaf), Ribes Nero, Ribes Nigrum.

What is it?
Black currant is a plant. People use the seed oil, leaves, fruit, and flowers to make medicine.

Is it Effective?
The effectiveness ratings for **BLACK CURRANT** are as follows:
Insufficient Evidence to Rate Effectiveness for... Symptoms of menopause, premenstrual syndrome (PMS), painful menstrual periods, breast pain, improving immune response, arthritis, gout, Alzheimer's disease, diarrhea, liver problems, mouth and throat inflammation, coughs, colds, disinfecting the urine, fluid retention, bladder stones, wounds, insect bites, and other conditions.

How does it work?
Black currant seed oil contains a chemical called gamma-linolenic acid (GLA). Some research suggests that GLA might have a beneficial effect on the immune system. Black currant seed oil and leaves might also help decrease swelling.

Are there safety concerns?
Black currant seems to be safe. It is not known what the potential side effects might be.

Do not take black currant if: You are pregnant or breast-feeding.

Are there any interactions with medications?
It is not known if black currant interacts with any medicines.
Before taking black currant, talk with your healthcare professional if you take any medications.

BLACK HAW

What other names is the product known by?
Southern Black Haw, Stag Bush, Viburnum, Viburnum lentago, Viburnum prunifolium, Viburnum rufidulum.

What is it?
Black haw is a plant. People use the root bark and its extracts to make medicine.

Is it Effective?
The effectiveness ratings for **BLACK HAW** are as follows:
Insufficient Evidence to Rate Effectiveness for... Diarrhea, increasing urine, preventing miscarriage, asthma, menstrual cramps, spasms of the uterus (womb) following childbirth, and other conditions.

How does it work?
Black haw contains a chemical which might relax the uterus.

Are there safety concerns?

Black haw is safe for most people, but the potential side effects are not known.

Do not take black haw if: You are pregnant or breast-feeding. • You are allergic to aspirin. • You have had kidney stones.

Are there any interactions with medications?

It is not known if black haw interacts with any medicines.
Before taking black haw, talk with your healthcare professional if you take any medications.

BLACK HELLEBORE

What other names is the product known by?

Christe Herbe, Christmas Rose, Christmas Rose Plant, Helleborous niger, Melampode.

What is it?

Black hellebore is a plant. The leaves, root, and root-like stem ("rhizome") are used to make medicine. Be careful not to confuse black hellebore and white hellebore.

Is it Effective?

The effectiveness ratings for **BLACK HELLEBORE** are as follows:
Insufficient Evidence to Rate Effectiveness for... Nausea, worm infestations, regulating menstrual periods, kidney infections, colds, constipation, causing miscarriage in pregnancy, and other uses.

How does it work?

There isn't enough information to know how black hellebore might work for medicinal uses.

Are there safety concerns?

Black hellebore is UNSAFE. It contains chemicals similar to the prescription drug digoxin (Lanoxin) that can cause a dangerously irregular heartbeat. Black hellebore might cause miscarriage in pregnancy.

Do not take black hellebore if: You are pregnant or breast-feeding. • You have disorders of the digestive tract including stomach and intestines. • You have heart disease.

Are there any interactions with medications?

Antibiotics (Tetracycline antibiotics). Taking antibiotics along with black hellebore might increase the chance of side effects from black hellebore. Some antibiotics that interact with black hellebore include demeclocycline (Declomycin), minocycline (Minocin), and tetracycline (Achromycin).
Antibiotics (Macrolide antibiotics). Black hellebore can affect the heart. Some antibiotics might increase how much black hellebore the body absorbs. Taking black hellebore along with some antibiotics might increase the effects and side effects of black hellebore. Some of these antibiotics, called macrolide antibiotics, include erythromycin, azithromycin, and clarithromycin.
Digoxin (Lanoxin). Digoxin (Lanoxin) helps the heart beat more strongly. Black hellebore also seems to affect the heart. Taking black hellebore along with digoxin can increase the effects and the risk of side effects of digoxin and black hellebore. Do not take black hellebore if you are taking digoxin (Lanoxin) without talking to your healthcare professional.
Quinine. Black hellebore can affect the heart. Quinine can also affect the heart. Taking quinine along with black hellebore might cause serious heart problems.
Stimulant laxatives. Black hellebore can affect the heart. The heart uses potassium. Laxatives called stimulant laxatives can decrease potassium levels in the body. Low potassium levels can increase the chance of side effects from black hellebore. Some stimulant laxatives include bisacodyl (Correctol, Dulcolax), cascara, castor oil (Purge), senna (Senokot), and others.
Water pills (Diuretic drugs). Black hellebore might affect the heart. "Water pills" can decrease potassium in the body. Low potassium levels can also affect the heart and increase the risk of side effects from black hellebore. Some "water pills" that can deplete potassium include chlorothiazide (Diuril), chlorthalidone (Thalitone), furosemide (Lasix), hydrochlorothiazide (HCTZ, HydroDiuril, Microzide), and others.

 Natural Medicines Comprehensive Database Consumer Version (209) 472-2244

BLACK HOREHOUND

What other names is the product known by?
Ballota, Ballota nigra, Black Stinking Horehound.

What is it?
Black horehound is a plant. The above ground parts are used to make medicine.

Is it Effective?
The effectiveness ratings for **BLACK HOREHOUND** are as follows:
Insufficient Evidence to Rate Effectiveness for... Nausea, vomiting, nervous disorders, whooping cough, increasing bile flow, gout, intestinal worms, spasms, and other conditions.

How does it work?
Black horehound has chemicals which might have a variety of functions, such as helping to stop nausea, vomiting, spasms, and other effects.

Are there safety concerns?
Black horehound might be safe for most people when taken by mouth, but the potential side effects of black horehound are not known.

There isn't enough information to know if black horehound is safe when applied directly to the skin or what the side effects might be.

Do not take black horehound oil if: You are pregnant or breast-feeding. • You have Parkinson's disease. • You have a mental illness, such as schizophrenia or a psychotic disorder.

Are there any interactions with medications?
Medications used for Parkinson's Disease (Dopamine agonists). Black horehound contains chemicals that affect the brain. These chemicals affect the brain similarly to some medications used for Parkinson's disease. Taking black horehound with these medications might increase the effects and side effects of some medications used for Parkinson's disease. Some medications used for Parkinson's disease include bromocriptine (Parlodel), levodopa (Dopar, component of Sinemet), pramipexole (Mirapex), ropinirole (Requip), and others.

BLACK MULBERRY

What other names is the product known by?
Morus nigra, Mulberry, Purple Mulberry.

What is it?
Black mulberry is a plant. The ripe berry and root bark are used to make medicine.

Is it Effective?
The effectiveness ratings for **BLACK MULBERRY** are as follows:
Insufficient Evidence to Rate Effectiveness for... Constipation, rhinitis (runny nose), and other conditions.

How does it work?
Black mulberry fruit contains pectin, which might act as a laxative to help stool pass through the bowels.

Are there safety concerns?
It is not known if black mulberry is safe. Black mulberry might lower blood sugar. If you have diabetes, monitor your blood sugar levels closely.

Do not take black mulberry if: You are pregnant or breast-feeding.

Are there any interactions with medications?
Medications for diabetes (Antidiabetes drugs). Black mulberry leaves might decrease blood sugar. Diabetes medications are also used to lower blood sugar. Taking black mulberry leaves along with diabetes medications might cause your blood sugar to go too low. Monitor your blood sugar closely. The dose of your diabetes medication might need to be changed. Some medications used for diabetes include glimepiride (Amaryl), glyburide (DiaBeta, Glynase PresTab, Micronase), insulin, pioglitazone (Actos), rosiglitazone (Avandia), chlorpropamide (Diabinese), glipizide (Glucotrol), tolbutamide (Orinase), and others.

Medical professionals should consult the Professional Version at www.NaturalDatabase.com.

BLACK MUSTARD

What other names is the product known by?
Black Mustard Oil, Black Mustard Powder, Black Mustard Seed, Brassica Nigra, Mustard, Mustard Oil, Mustard Powder, Mustard Seed.

What is it?
Black mustard is a plant. The seed and oil from the seed are used to make medicine.

Is it Effective?
The effectiveness ratings for **BLACK MUSTARD** are as follows:
Insufficient Evidence to Rate Effectiveness for... Pneumonia, arthritis, aches, fluid retention, loss of appetite, causing vomiting, chest congestion, symptoms of the common cold, aching feet, and other conditions.

How does it work?
Black mustard contains chemicals that might help fight bacteria and fungi. When applied directly to the skin, black mustard seed preparations can cause redness and warmth which might help relieve pain.

Are there safety concerns?
Black mustard is safe for most people when applied to the skin and used less than 2 weeks. Black mustard can cause skin blisters and skin damage if left on the skin for more than 15 to 20 minutes.

When taken by mouth, black mustard seed is unsafe. It can damage the throat, especially if it causes vomiting. It can also cause other serious side effects including heart failure, diarrhea, drowsiness, breathing difficulties, coma, and death.

Do not use black mustard if: You are pregnant or breast-feeding. • You have asthma. • You have infections or inflammation of the digestive tract.

Are there any interactions with medications?
Antacids. Antacids are used to decrease stomach acid. Black mustard may increase stomach acid. By increasing stomach acid, black mustard might decrease the effectiveness of antacids. Some antacids include calcium carbonate (Tums, others) dihydroxyaluminum sodium carbonate (Rolaids, others), magaldrate (Riopan), magnesium sulfate (Bilagog), aluminum hydroxide (Amphojel), and others.
Medications that decrease stomach acid (H2-Blockers). Black mustard might increase stomach acid. By increasing stomach acid, black mustard might decrease the effectiveness of some medications that decrease stomach acid, called H2-Blockers. Some medications that decrease stomach acid include cimetidine (Tagamet), ranitidine (Zantac), nizatidine (Axid), and famotidine (Pepcid).
Medications that decrease stomach acid (Proton pump inhibitors). Black mustard might increase stomach acid. By increasing stomach acid, black mustard might decrease the effectiveness of medications that are used to decrease stomach acid, called proton pump inhibitors. Some medications that decrease stomach acid include omeprazole (Prilosec), lansoprazole (Prevacid), rabeprazole (Aciphex), pantoprazole (Protonix), and esomeprazole (Nexium).

BLACK NIGHTSHADE

What other names is the product known by?
Garden Nightshade, Houndsberry, Kakamachi, Petty Morel, Poisonberry, Solanum nigrum.

What is it?
Black nightshade is a plant. People use the whole plant, leaves, fruit, and root to make medicine.

Is it Effective?
The effectiveness ratings for **BLACK NIGHTSHADE** are as follows:
Insufficient Evidence to Rate Effectiveness for... Stomach problems, intestinal cramps, hemorrhoids, skin inflammation, burns, spasms, pain, and other conditions.

 Natural Medicines Comprehensive Database Consumer Version (209) 472-2244

How does it work?
There isn't enough information to know how black nightshade might work for medicinal uses.

Are there safety concerns?
Black nightshade is unsafe. It contains a toxic chemical called solanin. At lower doses, it can cause nausea, vomiting, headache, and other side effects. At higher doses, it can cause severe poisoning. Signs of poisoning include irregular heartbeat, trouble breathing, dizziness, drowsiness, twitching of the arms and legs, cramps, diarrhea, paralysis, coma, and death.

Do not take black nightshade if: You are pregnant or breast-feeding. It can harm the fetus.

Are there any interactions with medications?
It is not known if black nightshade interacts with any medicines.
Before taking black nightshade, talk with your healthcare professional if you take any medications.

BLACK PEPPER AND WHITE PEPPER

What other names is the product known by?
Black Pepper, Blanc Poivre, Kosho, Krishna, Maricha, Pepe, Pepper, Pepper Extract, Pepper Plant, Peppercorn, Pfeffer, Pimenta, Pimienta, Piper, Piperine, Poivre, Poivre Noir, Vellaja, White Pepper.

What is it?
Black and white pepper are made from the Piper nigrum plant. Black pepper is ground from dried, whole unripe fruit. White pepper is ground from dried, ripe fruit that has had the outer layer removed. The black pepper and white pepper powder is used to make medicine.

Is it Effective?
The effectiveness ratings for **BLACK PEPPER AND WHITE PEPPER** are as follows:
Insufficient Evidence to Rate Effectiveness for... Use of black pepper for airway inflammation, or "bronchitis." Use of white pepper for malaria and cholera. Use of black or white pepper for stomach upset, cancer, pain, scabies, and other conditions.

How does it work?
Black and white pepper might help fight germs (microbes) and cause the stomach to increase the flow of digestive juices. There is conflicting evidence about their role in cancer.

Are there safety concerns?
Black and white pepper might be safe for most people. It might have a burning aftertaste. Taking large amounts of black and white pepper by mouth, which can accidentally get into the lungs, has been reported to cause death. This is especially true in children.

Black and white pepper, when applied directly to the skin, is safe for most adults. However, there isn't enough information to know if use on the skin is safe for children. Black and white pepper may cause redness and burning if it gets into the eyes.

Do not take black or white pepper in amounts greater than typically found in foods if: You are pregnant or breast-feeding.

Are there any interactions with medications?
Medications changed by the liver (Cytochrome P450 3A4 (CYP3A4) substrates). Some medications are changed and broken down by the liver. Black and white pepper might decrease how quickly the liver breaks down some medications. Taking pepper along with some medications that are broken down by the liver can increase the chance of side effects from some medications. Before taking black or white pepper talk to your healthcare provider if you are taking any medications that are changed by the liver. Some medications changed by this liver include lovastatin (Mevacor), ketoconazole (Nizoral), itraconazole (Sporanox), fexofenadine (Allegra), triazolam (Halcion), and many others.
Medications moved by pumps in cells (P-Glycoprotein Substrates). Some medications are moved by pumps in cells. Black and white pepper might make these pumps less active and increase how much of some medications get absorbed by the body. This might cause more side effects from some medications. Some medications that are moved by these pumps include etoposide, paclitaxel, vinblastine, vincristine, vindesine, ketoconazole, itraconazole, amprenavir, indinavir, nelfinavir, saquinavir, cimetidine, ranitidine, diltiazem, verapamil, digoxin, corticosteroids, erythromycin, cisapride (Propulsid), fexofenadine (Allegra), cyclosporine, loperamide (Imodium), quinidine, and others.

Phenytoin (Dilantin). Black and white pepper might increase how much phenytoin (Dilantin) the body absorbs. Taking black and white pepper along with phenytoin (Dilantin) might increase the effects and side effects of phenytoin (Dilantin).

Propranolol (Inderal). Black and white pepper might increase how much propranolol (Inderal) the body absorbs. Taking black and white pepper along with propranolol (Inderal) might increase the effects and side effects of propranolol(Inderal).

Rifampin. Black and white pepper might increase how much rifampin the body absorbs. Taking black and white pepper along with rifampin might increase the effects and side effects of rifampin.

Theophylline. Black pepper and white pepper can increase how much theophylline the body can absorb. This might cause increased effects and side effects of theophylline.

BLACK PSYLLIUM

What other names is the product known by?
Brown Psyllium, Dietary Fiber, Fleaseed, Fleawort, French Psyllium, Plantago psyllium, Plantain, Psyllion, Psyllios, Psyllium afra, Psyllium arenaria, Psyllium indica, Psyllium Seed, Spanish Psyllium.

What is it?
Black psyllium is a plant. People use the seed to make medicine. Be careful not to confuse black psyllium with other forms of psyllium including blond psyllium.

Is it Effective?
The effectiveness ratings for **BLACK PSYLLIUM** are as follows:
Effective for... Constipation.
Possibly Effective for... Improving high cholesterol.
Insufficient Evidence to Rate Effectiveness for... Cancer, diarrhea, irritable bowel disease (IBS), and other conditions.

How does it work?
Black psyllium adds bulk to the stool which might help with constipation, diarrhea, and irritable bowel disease. It also increases the elimination of cholesterol from the body.

Are there safety concerns?
Black psyllium, when taken with enough water, is safe for most people. Mild side effects include bloating and gas. In some people, black psyllium can cause allergic reactions such as runny nose, red eyes, rash, and asthma. Black psyllium might lower blood sugar. If you have diabetes, check your blood sugar carefully.

Black psyllium should always be taken with water or other liquid. If taken without liquid, it can block the esophagus, throat, or intestine.

Black psyllium seeds contain a substance which can cause kidney damage. Commercial preparations of black psyllium usually have this substance removed. Do not use black psyliium seeds unless they have had special processing to make them less toxic.

Do not take black psyllium if: You have swallowing difficulties. • You have intestinal problems that might cause a blockage, such as intestinal narrowing or spastic bowel. • You have kidney problems.

Are there any interactions with medications?
Carbamazepine (Tegretol). Black psyllium contains large amounts of fiber. Fiber can decrease how much carbamazepine (Tegretol) the body absorbs. By decreasing how much carbamazepine (Tegretol) the body absorbs black psyllium might decrease the effectiveness of carbamazepine (Tegretol).

Digoxin (Lanoxin). Black psyllium is high in fiber. Fiber can decrease the absorption and decrease the effectiveness of digoxin (Lanoxin). As a general rule, any medications taken by mouth should be taken one hour before or four hours after black psyllium to prevent this interaction.

Lithium. Black psyllium contains large amounts of fiber. Fiber can decrease how much lithium the body absorbs. Taking lithium along with black psyllium might decrease the effectiveness of lithium. To avoid his interaction take black psyllium at least one hour after lithium.

Medications for diabetes (Antidiabetes drugs). Black psyllium might decrease blood sugar by decreasing how much sugar your body absorbs from foods. Diabetes medications are also used to lower blood sugar. Taking black psyllium with diabetes medications might cause your blood sugar to be too low. Monitor your blood sugar closely. The dose of your diabetes medication might need to be changed. Some medications used for diabetes include glimepiride (Amaryl), glyburide (DiaBeta, Glynase PresTab, Micronase), insulin, pioglitazone (Actos), rosiglitazone (Avandia), chlorpropamide (Diabinese), glipizide (Glucotrol), tolbutamide (Orinase), and others.

BLACK RASPBERRY

What other names is the product known by?
Blackcap, Rubus occidentalis, Thimbleberry, Virginia Raspberry.

What is it?
Black raspberry is a plant. The fruit (berry) and leaf are used to make medicine.

Is it Effective?
The effectiveness ratings for **BLACK RASPBERRY** are as follows:
Insufficient Evidence to Rate Effectiveness for... Stomach pain, bleeding, and preventing cancer.

How does it work?
Black raspberry contains chemicals that might protect from cancer by preventing changes to DNA and blocking the blood supply to tumors.

Are there safety concerns?
Black raspberry is safe when used as a food. There is not enough information to know if it is safe when taken as medicine.

Do not use black raspberry in medicinal amounts if: You are pregnant or breast-feeding.

Are there any interactions with medications?
It is not known if black raspberry interacts with any medicines.
Before taking black raspberry, talk with your healthcare professional if you take any medications.

BLACK ROOT

What other names is the product known by?
Beaumont Root, Bowman's Root, Culveris Root, Culvers, Culver's Physic, Culver's Root, Hini, Oxadoddy, Physic Root, Purple Leptandra, Leptandra virginica, Tall Speedwell, Tall Veronica, Veronicastrum Virginicum, Veronica Virginica Root, Whorlywort.

What is it?
Black root is a plant. People use the underground stem (rhizome) and the root as medicine.

Is it Effective?
The effectiveness ratings for **BLACK ROOT** are as follows:
Insufficient Evidence to Rate Effectiveness for... Constipation, liver and gallbladder problems, causing vomiting, and other conditions.

How does it work?
Black root might increase bile flow from the gallbladder into the intestine.

Are there safety concerns?
Dried black root might be safe for most people. Taking the fresh root may not be safe because it can be stronger and have more side effects. Black root can cause abdominal pain or cramps, changes in stool color or odor, drowsiness, headache, nausea, and vomiting. Large doses can cause liver damage.

Do not take black root if: You are pregnant or breast-feeding. It can damage the fetus or cause abortion. • You have gall stones or gall bladder problems. • You have inflammation of the stomach or intestines, such as colitis or Crohn's disease. • You have hemorrhoids. • You are having a menstrual period.

Are there any interactions with medications?
Digoxin (Lanoxin). Black root is high in fiber. Fiber can decrease the absorption and decrease the effectiveness of digoxin (Lanoxin). As a general rule, any medications taken by mouth should be taken one hour before or four hours after black root to prevent this interaction.
Water pills (Diuretic drugs). Black root is a laxative. Some laxatives can decrease potassium in the body. "Water pills" can also decrease potassium in the body. Taking black root along with "water pills" might decrease potassium in the body too much. Some "water pills" that can decrease potassium include chlorothiazide (Diuril), chlorthalidone (Thalitone), furosemide (Lasix), hydrochlorothiazide (HCTZ, Hydrodiuril, Microzide), and others.

Medical professionals should consult the Professional Version at www.NaturalDatabase.com.

BLACK SEED

What other names is the product known by?

Ajenuz, Arañuel, Baraka, Black Cumin, Black Caraway, Charnuska, Cominho Negro, Cominho-Negro, Fennel Flower, Fennel-Flower, Fitch, Kalajaji, Kalajira, Kalonji, Love in a Mist, Mugrela, Nigelle de Crète, Nutmeg Flower, Nutmeg-Flower, Roman-Coriander, Schwarzkümmel, Toute Épice.

What is it?

Black seed is a plant. People use the seed to make medicine.

Is it Effective?

The effectiveness ratings for **BLACK SEED** are as follows:

Insufficient Evidence to Rate Effectiveness for... Digestive problems including intestinal gas and diarrhea, asthma, allergies, cough, bronchitis, flu, congestion, high blood pressure, boosting the immune system, cancer prevention, birth control, menstrual disorders, increasing breast-milk flow, achy joints (rheumatism), headache, skin conditions, and many other uses.

How does it work?

There is some scientific evidence to suggest that black seed might help boost the immune system, fight cancer, prevent pregnancy, and lessen allergic reactions by acting as an antihistimine, but there isn't enough information in humans yet.

Are there safety concerns?

Black seed, when used in small quantities, such as a flavoring for foods, appears to be safe for most people. There isn't enough information to know if larger, medicinal quantities are safe. Black seed can cause allergic rashes when applied to the skin.

Do not take black seed in excess of amounts typically found in food if: You are pregnant or breast-feeding. Black seed can affect the uterus.

Are there any interactions with medications?

It is not known if black seed interacts with any medicines.
Before taking black seed, talk with your healthcare professional if you take any medications.

BLACK TEA

What other names is the product known by?

Black Leaf Tea, Camellia sinensis, Camellia thea, Camellia theifera, Chinese Tea, Tea, Thea bohea, Thea sinensis, Thea viridis.

What is it?

Black tea is a product made from the Camellia sinesis plant. The aged leaves and stems are used to make medicine. Green tea, which is made from fresh leaves of the same plant, has some different properties.

Is it Effective?

The effectiveness ratings for **BLACK TEA** are as follows:

Likely Effective for... Mental alertness.

Possibly Effective for... Preventing dizziness upon standing up (orthostatic hypotension) in older people • Reducing the risk of hardening of the arteries (atherosclerosis) • Reducing the risk of heart attacks • Reducing the risk of kidney stones • Reducing the risk of Parkinson's disease • Reducing the risk of ovarian cancer.

Possibly Ineffective for... Reducing the risk of stomach, colon, and rectal cancer • Reducing the risk of breast cancer.

Insufficient Evidence to Rate Effectiveness for... Osteoporosis, headache, stomach disorders, vomiting, diarrhea, preventing tooth decay, type 2 diabetes, lung cancer, reducing the risk of cancer, and promoting weight loss.

How does it work?

Black tea contains 2-4% caffeine, which affects thinking and alertness, increases urine output, and may reduce the symptoms of Parkinson's disease. It also contains antioxidants and other substances that might help protect the heart and blood vessels.

Medical professionals should consult the Professional Version at www.NaturalDatabase.com.

Are there safety concerns?

Black tea is safe for most adults. Too much black tea, such as more than five cups per day, can cause side effects because of the caffeine. These side effects can range from mild to serious and include headache, nervousness, sleep problems, vomiting, diarrhea, irritability, irregular heartbeat, tremor, heartburn, dizziness, ringing in the ears, convulsions, and confusion.

If you are pregnant or breast-feeding, black tea in small amounts is probably not harmful. However, do not drink more than 3 cups a day of black tea. Too much caffeine might cause premature delivery, low birth weight, and harm to the baby.

Caffeine is probably safe in children in amounts commonly found in foods.

Do not take black tea if: You have a heart condition (arrhythmia). • You have severe anemia. • You have breast, uterine, or ovarian cancer. • You have endometriosis or uterine fibroids. • You have high blood pressure. Small amounts of black tea taken regularly do not seem to raise blood pressure, but the caffeine in black tea can affect blood pressure in someone who consumes caffeinated drinks infrequently.

Are there any interactions with medications?

Adenosine (Adenocard). Black tea contains caffeine. The caffeine in black tea might block the affects of adenosine (Adenocard). Adenosine (Adenocard) is often used by doctors to do a test on the heart. This test is called a cardiac stress test. Stop drinking black tea or other caffeine-containing products at least 24 hours before a cardiac stress test.

Alcohol. The body breaks down the caffeine in black tea to get rid of it. Alcohol can decrease how quickly the body breaks down caffeine. Taking black tea along with alcohol might cause too much caffeine in the bloodstream and caffeine side effects including jitteriness, headache, and fast heartbeat.

Antibiotics (Quinolone antibiotics). The body breaks down caffeine to get rid of it. Some antibiotics might decrease how quickly the body breaks down caffeine. Taking these antibiotics along with black tea can increase the risk of side effects including jitteriness, headache, increased heart rate, and other side effects. Some antibiotics that decrease how quickly the body breaks down caffeine include ciprofloxacin (Cipro), enoxacin (Penetrex), norfloxacin (Chibroxin, Noroxin), sparfloxacin (Zagam), trovafloxacin (Trovan), and grepafloxacin (Raxar).

Birth control pills (Contraceptive drugs). The body breaks down the caffeine in black tea to get rid of it. Birth control pills can decrease how quickly the body breaks down caffeine. Taking black tea along with birth control pills can cause jitteriness, headache, fast heartbeat, and other side effects. Some birth control pills include ethinyl estradiol and levonorgestrel (Triphasil), ethinyl estradiol and norethindrone (Ortho-Novum 1/35, Ortho-Novum 7/7/7), and others.

Cimetidine (Tagamet). Black tea contains caffeine. The body breaks down caffeine to get rid of it. Cimetidine (Tagamet) can decrease how quickly your body breaks down caffeine. Taking cimetidine (Tagamet) along with black tea might increase the chance of caffeine side effects including jitteriness, headache, fast heartbeat, and others.

Clozapine (Clozaril). The body breaks down clozapine (Clozaril) to get rid of it. The caffeine in black tea seems to decrease how quickly the body breaks down clozapine (Clozaril). Taking black tea along with clozapine (Clozaril) can increase the effects and side effects of clozapine (Clozaril).

Dipyridamole (Persantine). Black tea contains caffeine. The caffeine in black tea might block the affects of dipyridamole (Persantine). Dipyridamole (Persantine) is often used by doctors to do a test on the heart. This test is called a cardiac stress test. Stop drinking black tea or other caffeine containing products at least 24 hours before a cardiac stress test.

Disulfiram (Antabuse). The body breaks down caffeine to get rid of it. Disulfiram (Antabuse) can decrease how quickly the body gets rid of caffeine. Taking black tea (which contains caffeine) along with disulfiram (Antabuse) might increase the effects and side effects of caffeine including jitteriness, hyperactivity, irritability, and others.

Ephedrine. Stimulant drugs speed up the nervous system. Black tea contains caffeine. Caffeine and ephedrine are both stimulant drugs. Taking black tea along with ephedrine might cause too much stimulation and sometimes serious side effects and heart problems. Do not take caffeine containing products and ephedrine at the same time.

Estrogens. The body breaks down the caffeine in black tea to get rid of it. Estrogens can decrease how quickly the body breaks down caffeine. Taking estrogen pills and drinking black tea can cause jitteriness, headache, fast heartbeat, and other side effects. If you take estrogen pills limit your caffeine intake. Some estrogen pills include conjugated equine estrogens (Premarin), ethinyl estradiol, estradiol, and others.

Fluconazole (Diflucan). Black tea contains caffeine. The body breaks down caffeine to get rid of it. Fluconazole (Diflucan) might decrease how quickly the body gets rid of caffeine. This could cause caffeine to stay in to body too long and increase the risk of side effects such as nervousness, anxiety, and insomnia.

Fluvoxamine (Luvox). The body breaks down the caffeine in black tea to get rid of it. Fluvoxamine (Luvox) can decrease how quickly the body breaks down caffeine. Taking caffeine along with fluvoxamine (Luvox) might cause too much caffeine in the body, and increase the effects and side effects of caffeine.

Lithium. Your body naturally gets rid of lithium. The caffeine in black tea can increase how quickly your body gets rid of lithium. If you take products that contain caffeine and you take lithium, stop taking caffeine products slowly. Stopping caffeine too quickly can increase the side effects of lithium.

Medications for depression (MAOIs). The caffeine in black tea can stimulate the body. Some medications used for depression can also stimulate the body. Drinking black tea and taking some medications for depression might cause too much stimulation of the body and serious side effects including fast heartbeat, high blood pressure, nervousness, and others. Some of these medications used for depression include phenelzine (Nardil), tranylcypromine (Parnate), and others.

Medications for depression (Tricyclic Antidepressants). Coffee contains chemicals called tannins. Tannins can bind to many medications and decrease how much medicine the body absorbs. To avoid this interaction avoid coffee 1 hour before and 2 hours after taking medications for depression called tricyclic antidepressants. Some medications for depression include amitriptyline (Elavil) or imipramine (Tofranil, Janimine).

Medications for diabetes (Antidiabetes drugs). Black tea might increase blood sugar. Diabetes medications are used to lower blood sugar. By increasing blood sugar, black tea might decrease the effectiveness of diabetes medications. Monitor your blood sugar closely. The dose of your diabetes medication might need to be changed. Some medications used for diabetes include glimepiride (Amaryl), glyburide (DiaBeta, Glynase PresTab, Micronase), insulin, pioglitazone (Actos), rosiglitazone (Avandia), chlorpropamide (Diabinese), glipizide (Glucotrol), tolbutamide (Orinase), and others.

Medications that slow blood clotting (Anticoagulant / Antiplatelet drugs). Black tea might slow blood clotting. Taking black tea along with medications that also slow clotting might increase the chances of bruising and bleeding. Some medications that slow blood clotting include aspirin, clopidogrel (Plavix), diclofenac (Voltaren, Cataflam, others), ibuprofen (Advil, Motrin, others), naproxen (Anaprox, Naprosyn, others), dalteparin (Fragmin), enoxaparin (Lovenox), heparin, warfarin (Coumadin), and others.

Mexiletine (Mexitil). Black tea contains caffeine. The body breaks down caffeine to get rid of it. Mexiletine (Mexitil) can decrease how quickly the body breaks down caffeine. Taking Mexiletine (Mexitil) along with black tea might increase the caffeine effects and side effects of black tea.

Phenothiazines. Black tea contains chemicals called tannins. Tannins can bind to many medications and decrease how much medicine the body absorbs. To avoid this interaction avoid coffee 1 hour before and 2 hours after taking phenothiazine medications. Some phenothiazine medications include fluphenazine (Permitil, Prolixin), chlorpromazine (Thorazine), haloperidol (Haldol), prochlorperazine (Compazine), thioridazine (Mellaril), and trifluoperazine (Stelazine).

Phenylpropanolamine. The caffeine in black tea can stimulate the body. Phenylpropanolamine can also stimulate the body. Taking caffeine and phenylpropanolamine together might cause too much stimulation and increase heartbeat, blood pressure, and cause nervousness.

Pentobarbital (Nembutal). The stimulant effects of the caffeine in black tea can block the sleep-producing effects of pentobarbital.

Riluzole (Rilutek). The body breaks down riluzole (Rilutek) to get rid of it. Drinking black tea can decrease how quickly the body breaks down riluzole (Rilutek) and increase the effects and side effects of riluzole.

Stimulant drugs. Stimulant drugs speed up the nervous system. By speeding up the nervous system, stimulant medications can make you feel jittery and speed up your heartbeat. The caffeine in black tea can also speed up the nervous system. Drinking black tea along with stimulant drugs might cause serious problems including increased heart rate and high blood pressure. Avoid taking stimulant drugs along with black tea. Some stimulant drugs include diethylpropion (Tenuate), epinephrine, phentermine (Ionamin), pseudoephedrine (Sudafed), and many others.

Terbinafine (Lamisil). The body breaks down the caffeine in black tea to get rid of it. Terbinafine (Lamisil) can decrease how quickly the body gets rid of caffeine and increase the risk of side effects including jitteriness, headache, increased heartbeat, and other effects.

Theophylline. Black tea contains caffeine. Caffeine works similarly to theophylline. Caffeine can also decrease how quickly the body gets rid of theophylline. This might cause increased effects and side effects of theophylline.

Verapamil (Calan, Covera, Isoptin, Verelan). The body breaks down the caffeine in black tea to get rid of it. Verapamil (Calan, Covera, Isoptin, Verelan) can decrease how quickly the body gets rid of caffeine. Drinking black tea and taking verapamil (Calan, Covera, Isoptin, Verelan) can increase the risk of side effects for caffeine including jitteriness, headache, and an increased heartbeat.

     Natural Medicines Comprehensive Database Consumer Version   (209) 472-2244

BLACK WALNUT

What other names is the product known by?
Juglans nigra, Nogal Americano, Nogueira-preta, Noyer Noir, Schwarze Walnuss, Walnut.

What is it?
Black walnut is a tree. People use the hull of the nuts to make medicine.

Is it Effective?
The effectiveness ratings for **BLACK WALNUT** are as follows:
Insufficient Evidence to Rate Effectiveness for... Leukemia and infections such as diphtheria, syphilis, intestinal worms; use as a gargle; and skin wounds.

How does it work?
Black walnut contains high concentrations of tannins, which can reduce inflammation and body fluids such as mucous.

Are there safety concerns?
Black walnut might be safe for most people when used short-term. It is not known what the potential side effects from short-term use might be.

Black walnut might be unsafe for long-term use. It contains a chemical which might cause tongue or lip cancer.

Do not take black walnut if: You are pregnant or breast-feeding.

Are there any interactions with medications?
Medications taken by mouth (Oral drugs). Black walnut hulls contains a large amount of chemicals called tannins. Tannins absorb substances in the stomach and intestines. Taking black walnut along with medications taken by mouth can decrease how much medicine your body absorbs, and decrease the effectiveness of your medicine. To prevent this interaction, take black walnut at least one hour after medications you take by mouth.

BLACKBERRY

What other names is the product known by?
Black Berry, Bramble, Dewberry, Goutberry, Rubi Fruticosi Folium, Rubi Fruticosi Radix, Rubus affinis, Rubus canadensis, Rubus fruticosus, Rubus laciniatus, Rubus plicatus, Thimbleberry.

What is it?
Blackberry is a plant. The leaf, root, and fruit (berry) are used to make medicine.

Is it Effective?
The effectiveness ratings for **BLACKBERRY** are as follows:
Insufficient Evidence to Rate Effectiveness for... Fluid retention, diarrhea, and other conditions.

How does it work?
Blackberry contains chemicals that might have antioxidant effects. It also contains chemicals that might protect against cancer.

Are there safety concerns?
Blackberry is safe in amounts used as food. There isn't enough information available to know if blackberry is safe for medicinal use.

Do not take blackberry in amounts greater than those found in foods if: You are pregnant or breast-feeding.

Are there any interactions with medications?
It is not known if blackberry interacts with any medicines.
Before taking blackberry, talk with your healthcare professional if you take any medications.

CONSUMER VERSION

Medical professionals should consult the Professional Version at www.NaturalDatabase.com.

BLACKTHORN

What other names is the product known by?
Blacthorn Berry, Blackthorn Flower, Blackthorn Fruit, Pruni Spinosae Fructus, Pruni Spinosae Flos, Prunus spinosa, Sloe, Sloe Berry, Sloe Flower, Wild Plum Flower.

What is it?
Blackthorn is a plant. People use the berry and dried flower as medicine.

Is it Effective?
The effectiveness ratings for **BLACKTHORN** are as follows:
Insufficient Evidence to Rate Effectiveness for... Indigestion, purging the bowels, fluid retention, sore mouth or throat, colds, coughs, breathing problems, general exhaustion, indigestion, constipation, kidney and bladder ailments, stomach spasms, fluid retention, promoting sweating, "blood cleansing," rashes, and other conditions.

How does it work?
Blackthorn berries contain chemicals called tannins which might reduce inflammation.

Are there safety concerns?
Blackthorn might not be safe when swallowed. It contains toxic chemicals.

Do not take blackthorn if: You are pregnant or breast-feeding.

Are there any interactions with medications?
It is not known if blackthorn interacts with any medicines.
Before taking blackthorn, talk with your healthcare professional if you take any medications.

BLADDERWORT

What other names is the product known by?
Utricularia vulgaris.

What is it?
Bladderwort is a plant. People use the dried leaves to make a medicinal tea.

Is it Effective?
The effectiveness ratings for **BLADDERWORT** are as follows:
Insufficient Evidence to Rate Effectiveness for... Urinary tract infections, kidney stones, fluid retention, weight loss, inflammation, spasms, burns, and other uses.

How does it work?
There isn't enough information to know how bladderwort works.

Are there safety concerns?
There isn't enough information to know if bladderwort is safe or what the potential side effects might be.

Do not take bladderwort if: You are pregnant or breast-feeding.

Are there any interactions with medications?
It is not known if bladderwort interacts with any medicines.
Before taking bladderwort, talk with your healthcare professional if you take any medications.

BLADDERWRACK

What other names is the product known by?
Ascophyllum nodosum, Black Tang, Bladder Fucus, Bladder Wrack, Blasentang, Cutweed, Fucus, Fucus vesiculosis, Kelp, Kelpware, Kelp-Ware, Knotted Wrack, Marine Oak, Meereiche, Quercus Marina, Rockweed, Rockwrack, Schweintang, Seawrack, Tang, Varech.

What is it?
Bladderwrack is a type of seaweed. People use the whole plant to make medicine.

 Natural Medicines Comprehensive Database Consumer Version (209) 472-2244

Is it Effective?

The effectiveness ratings for **BLADDERWRACK** are as follows:

Insufficient Evidence to Rate Effectiveness for... Thyroid problems including an over-sized thyroid gland (goiter), iodine deficiency, obesity, arthritis, achy joints (rheumatism), hardening of the arteries (arteriosclerosis), digestive problems, "blood cleansing," constipation, and other conditions.

How does it work?

Bladderwrack, like many sea plants, contains varying amounts of iodine, which is used to prevent or treat some thyroid disorders. Bladderwrack products may contain varying amounts of iodine, which makes it an inconsistent source of iodine. Bladderwrack also contains algin, which can act as a laxative to help stool pass through the bowels.

Are there safety concerns?

Bladderwrack appears to be UNSAFE. It may contain high concentrations of iodine, which could cause or worsen some thyroid problems. Prolonged, high intake of dietary iodine is associated with goiter and increased risk of thyroid cancer. Treatment of thyroid problems should not be attempted without medical supervision.

Like other sea plants, bladderwrack can concentrate toxic heavy metals, such as arsenic, from the water in which it lives.

Do not take bladderwrack if: You are pregnant or breast-feeding. • You have a thyroid problem known as hyperthyroidism (too much thyroid hormone), or hypothyroidism (too little thyroid hormone). • You are allergic to iodine. • You are trying to become pregnant.

Are there any interactions with medications?

Medications that slow blood clotting (Anticoagulant / Antiplatelet drugs). Bladderwrack might slow blood clotting. Taking bladderwrack along with medications that also slow clotting might increase the chances of bruising and bleeding. Some medications that slow blood clotting include aspirin, clopidogrel (Plavix), diclofenac (Voltaren, Cataflam, others), ibuprofen (Advil, Motrin, others), naproxen (Anaprox, Naprosyn, others), dalteparin (Fragmin), enoxaparin (Lovenox), heparin, warfarin (Coumadin), and others.

Medications for an overactive thyroid (Antithyroid drugs). Bladderwrack can contains significant amounts of iodine. Iodine can affect the thyroid. Taking iodine along with medications for an overactive thyroid might decrease the thyroid too much. Do not take bladderwrack if you are taking medications for an overactive thyroid. Some of these medications include methenamine mandelate (Methimazole), methimazole (Tapazole), potassium iodide (Thyro-Block), and others.

BLESSED THISTLE

What other names is the product known by?

Carbenia benedicta, Cardo Santo, Carduus, Carduus benedictus, Cnici Benedicti Herba, Cnicus, Cnicus benedictus, Holy Thistle, Spotted Thistle, St. Benedict Thistle.

What is it?

Blessed thistle is a plant. People use the flowering tops, leaves, and upper stems to make medicine.

Is it Effective?

The effectiveness ratings for **BLESSED THISTLE** are as follows:

Insufficient Evidence to Rate Effectiveness for... Diarrhea, coughs, infections, and to promote milk flow in breast-feeding mothers, boils, wounds, and other conditions.

How does it work?

Blessed thistle contains tannins which might help diarrhea, coughs, and inflammation. However, there isn't enough information to know how well blessed thistle might work for many of its uses.

Are there safety concerns?

Blessed thistle might be safe for most people. In high doses, such as more than 5 grams per cup of tea, blessed thistle can cause stomach irritation and vomiting.

Do not take blessed thistle if: You are pregnant or breast-feeding. • You are allergic to ragweed, chrysanthemums, marigolds, daisies, or other members of this plant family (Asteraceae/Compositae). • You have stomach or intestinal problems such as infections, Crohn's disease, and other inflammatory conditions.

Are there any interactions with medications?

Antacids. Antacids are used to decrease stomach acid. Blessed thistle may increase stomach acid. By increasing stomach acid, blessed thistle might decrease the effectiveness of antacids. Some antacids include calcium carbonate (Tums, others) dihydroxyaluminum sodium carbonate (Rolaids, others), magaldrate (Riopan), magnesium sulfate (Bilagog), aluminum hydroxide (Amphojel), and others.

Medications that decrease stomach acid (H2-Blockers). Blessed thistle might increase stomach acid. By increasing stomach acid, blessed thistle might decrease the effectiveness of some medications that decrease stomach acid, called H2-Blockers. Some medications that decrease stomach acid include cimetidine (Tagamet), ranitidine (Zantac), nizatidine (Axid), and famotidine (Pepcid).

Medications that decrease stomach acid (Proton pump inhibitors). Blessed thistle might increase stomach acid. By increasing stomach acid, blessed thistle might decrease the effectiveness of medications that are used to decrease stomach acid, called proton pump inhibitors. Some medications that decrease stomach acid include omeprazole (Prilosec), lansoprazole (Prevacid), rabeprazole (Aciphex), pantoprazole (Protonix), and esomeprazole (Nexium).

BLOND PSYLLIUM

What other names is the product known by?

Blond Plantago, Blonde Psyllium, Che Qian Zi, Dietary Fiber, Englishman's Foot, Indian Plantago, Ispagol, Pale Psyllium, Plantaginis Ovatae Semen, Plantaginis Ovatae Testa, Plantago decumbens, Plantago fastigiata, Plantago insularis, Plantago ispaghula, Plantago ovata, Ispaghula, Psyllium, Sand Plantain, Spogel.

What is it?

Blond psyllium is an herb. The seed and the seed husk are used to make medicine.

Is it Effective?

The effectiveness ratings for **BLOND PSYLLIUM** are as follows:

Effective for... Relieving constipation and softening stools.

Likely Effective for... Lowering cholesterol in people with high cholesterol.

Possibly Effective for... Diarrhea • Irritable bowel syndrome (IBS) • Lowering blood sugar after eating a meal in people with diabetes (type 2) • Preventing the relapse of ulcerative colitis • High blood pressure • Hemorrhoids • Treating side effects of a drug called Orlistat (Xenical).

Possibly Ineffective for... Serious kidney disease • Skin growths in the large intestine and rectum (colorectal adenoma).

Insufficient Evidence to Rate Effectiveness for... Preventing fat redistribution syndrome in people with HIV disease, some types of cancer and skin conditions, and other conditions.

How does it work?

The husks of the psyllium seed absorb water and form a large mass. In people with constipation, this mass stimulates the bowel to move. In people with diarrhea, it can slow down the bowel and reduce bowel movements.

Are there safety concerns?

Blond psyllium is safe for most people when taken with plenty of fluids. Drink at least 8 ounces of fluids for every 3-5 grams of husk or 7 grams of seed. In some people, blond psyllium might cause gas, stomach pain, diarrhea, constipation, and nausea. It has also been linked to reports of headache, backache, runny nose, cough, and sinus problems.

Some people can have an allergic response to blond psyllium with symptoms such as inflamed nasal passages, sneezing, inflamed mucous membranes of the eyelids, hives, and asthma. Some people can also become sensitized to psyllium through occupational exposure or repeated ingestion of psyllium. Discontinue using blond psyllium and seek medical attention immediately if you develop symptoms such as flushing, severe itching, shortness of breath, wheezing, swelling of the face or body, chest and throat tightness, or loss of consciousness.

Do not take blond psyllium if: You have difficulty swallowing. • You have bowel or intestinal problems such as impaction, obstruction, spasms, or other bowel problems.

Are there any interactions with medications?

Carbamazepine (Tegretol). Blond psyllium contains large amounts of fiber. Fiber can decrease how much carbamazepine (Tegretol) the body absorbs. By decreasing how much carbamazepine (Tegretol) the body absorbs blond psyllium might decrease the effectiveness of carbamazepine (Tegretol).

Digoxin (Lanoxin). Blond psyllium is high in fiber. Fiber can decrease the absorption and decrease the effectiveness of digoxin (Lanoxin). As a general rule, any medications taken by mouth should be taken one hour before or four hours after black psyllium to prevent this interaction.

     Natural Medicines Comprehensive Database Consumer Version   (209) 472-2244

Ethinyl estradiol. Ethinyl estradiol is a form of estrogen that's in some estrogen products and birth control pills. Some people worry that psyllium can decrease how much ethinyl estradiol the body absorbs. But it is unlikely that psyllium will significantly affect ethinyl estradiol absorption.

Lithium. Blond psyllium contains large amounts of fiber. Fiber can decrease how much lithium the body absorbs. Taking lithium along with blond psyllium might decrease the effectiveness of lithium. To avoid his interaction take blond psyllium at least one hour after lithium.

Medications for diabetes (Antidiabetes drugs). Blond psyllium might decrease blood sugar by decreasing the absorption of sugars from food. Diabetes medications are also used to lower blood sugar. Taking blond psyllium with diabetes medications might cause your blood sugar to be too low. Monitor your blood sugar closely. The dose of your diabetes medication might need to be changed. Some medications used for diabetes include glimepiride (Amaryl), glyburide (DiaBeta, Glynase PresTab, Micronase), insulin, pioglitazone (Actos), rosiglitazone (Avandia), chlorpropamide (Diabinese), glipizide (Glucotrol), tolbutamide (Orinase), and others.

Warfarin (Coumadin). Warfarin (Coumadin) is used to slow blood clotting. Some people worry that blond psyllium may decrease warfarin (Coumadin) absorption and its effectiveness, which could increase the risk of clotting. But blond psyllium does NOT seem to affect warfarin (Coumadin) absorption or effectiveness.

BLOODROOT

What other names is the product known by?

Blood Root, Bloodwort, Coon Root, Indian Plant, Indian Red Paint, Pauson, Red Indian Paint, Red Puccoon, Red Root, Sanguinaria, Sanguinaria canadensis, Snakebite, Sweet Slumber, Tetterwort.

What is it?

Bloodroot is a plant. People use the underground stem (rhizome) to make medicine.

Is it Effective?

The effectiveness ratings for **BLOODROOT** are as follows:

Possibly Effective for... Preventing dental plaque, when used in dental products.

Insufficient Evidence to Rate Effectiveness for... Coughs, spasms, purging the bowel, causing vomiting, wound cleaning, skin cancers of the nose and ear when applied directly to the skin, and other conditions.

How does it work?

Bloodroot contains chemicals that might help fight bacteria, inflammation, and plaque.

Are there safety concerns?

Bloodroot might be safe for most people, when used short-term. Side effects include nausea, vomiting, drowsiness, and grogginess. Skin contact with the fresh plant can cause a rash.

Long-terms or high doses of bloodroot could be unsafe. At high doses it can cause low blood pressure, shock, coma, and glaucoma.

Do not take bloodroot if: You are pregnant or breast-feeding. • You have stomach or intestinal problems, such as infections, Crohn's disease, or other inflammatory conditions. • You have glaucoma, an eye disease.

Are there any interactions with medications?

It is not known if bloodroot interacts with any medicines.
Before taking bloodroot, talk with your healthcare professional if you take any medications.

BLUE COHOSH

What other names is the product known by?

Blue Ginseng, Caulophyllum, Caulophyllum thalictroides Papoose Root, Squaw Root, Yellow Ginseng.

What is it?

Blue cohosh is a plant. The plant is used to make medicine.

Is it Effective?

The effectiveness ratings for **BLUE COHOSH** are as follows:

Insufficient Evidence to Rate Effectiveness for... Inducing labor and menstruation, use as a laxative, stomach cramps, sore throat, hiccups, and seizures.

How does it work?
It is thought that blue cohosh might have effects similar to the hormone estrogen. It also may narrow the vessels that carry blood to the heart that can decrease oxygen in the heart.

Are there safety concerns?
Blue cohosh is not safe for adults or children.

It can cause diarrhea, stomach cramps, chest pain, increased blood pressure, increased blood sugar, and other severe side effects. When taken by the mother late in pregnancy, blue cohosh can cause severe heart problems in the newborn baby.

Do not take blue cohosh if: You are pregnant or breast-feeding. • You have heart disease such as angina or high blood pressure. • You have diabetes. • You have diarrhea. • You have breast, uterine, or ovarian cancer. • You have endometriosis or uterine fibroids.

Are there any interactions with medications?
Medications for high blood pressure (Antihypertensive drugs). Blue cohosh seems to increase blood pressure. By increasing blood pressure blue cohosh might decrease the effectiveness of medications for high blood pressure. Some medications for high blood pressure include captopril (Capoten), enalapril (Vasotec), losartan (Cozaar), valsartan (Diovan), diltiazem (Cardizem), amlodipine (Norvasc), hydrochlorothiazide (HydroDiuril), furosemide (Lasix), and many others.
Medications for diabetes (Antidiabetes drugs). Blue cohosh might increase blood sugar. Diabetes medications are used to lower blood sugar. By increasing blood sugar, blue cohosh might decrease the effectiveness of diabetes medications. Monitor your blood sugar closely. The dose of your diabetes medication might need to be changed. Some medications used for diabetes include glimepiride (Amaryl), glyburide (DiaBeta, Glynase PresTab, Micronase), insulin, pioglitazone (Actos), rosiglitazone (Avandia), chlorpropamide (Diabinese), glipizide (Glucotrol), tolbutamide (Orinase), and others.
Nicotine. Blue cohosh contains chemicals that work similarly to nicotine. Taking blue cohosh with nicotine might increase the effects and side effects of nicotine.

BLUE FLAG

What other names is the product known by?
Iris, Iris caroliniana, Iris versicolor, Iris virginica, Sweet Flag.

What is it?
Blue flag is a plant. People use the root-like stem (rhizome) to make medicine.

Is it Effective?
The effectiveness ratings for **BLUE FLAG** are as follows:
Insufficient Evidence to Rate Effectiveness for... Constipation, fluid retention, increasing bile flow, liver problems, vomiting, skin rashes, and other conditions.

How does it work?
There isn't enough information to know how blue flag works.

Are there safety concerns?
Blue flag is UNSAFE. It can cause nausea and vomiting, and the fresh root can irritate the mouth, throat, digestive tract, and skin. Blue flag can also cause headache and swollen, watery eyes.

Do not take blue flag if: You are pregnant or breast-feeding. • You have stomach or intestinal problems such as infections, ulcerative colitis, Crohn's disease, and other conditions.

Are there any interactions with medications?
Digoxin (Lanoxin). Blue flag is a type of laxative called a stimulant laxative. Stimulant laxatives can decrease potassium levels in the body. Low potassium levels can increase the risk of side effects of digoxin (Lanoxin).
Water pills (Diuretic drugs). Blue flag is a laxative. Some laxatives can decrease potassium in the body. "Water pills" can also decrease potassium in the body. Taking blue flag along with "water pills" might decrease potassium in the body too much. Some "water pills" that can decrease potassium include chlorothiazide (Diuril), chlorthalidone (Thalitone), furosemide (Lasix), hydrochlorothiazide (HCTZ, Hydrodiuril, Microzide), and others.

BLUE-GREEN ALGAE

What other names is the product known by?
AFA, Anabaena, Aphanizomenon flos-aquae, BGA, Blue-Green Micro-Algae, Cyanobacteria, Dihe, Klamath, Lyngbya wollei, Microcystis aeruginosa, Microcystis wesenbergii, Nostoc ellipsosporum, Spirulina maxima, Spirulina platensis, Spirulina pacifica, Tecuitlatl.

What is it?
Blue-green algae is a plant found in salt water and some large fresh water lakes.

Is it Effective?
The effectiveness ratings for **BLUE-GREEN ALGAE** are as follows:
Possibly Effective for... Treating precancerous mouth lesions.
Possibly Ineffective for... Weight loss.
Insufficient Evidence to Rate Effectiveness for... Attention deficit-hyperactivity disorder (ADHD), premenstrual syndrome, diabetes, to stimulate the immune system, fatigue, anxiety, depression, memory, energy, high cholesterol, heart disease, wound healing, digestion, and as a source of dietary protein, vitamin B12, and iron.

How does it work?
Blue-green algae has a high protein, iron, and other mineral content which is absorbed when taken orally. It is not known how it might work for precancerous mouth lesions.

Are there safety concerns?
Blue-green algae that is free of contaminants such as liver-damaging substances called mycrocystins, toxic metals, and bacteria seems to be safe for most people.

It is UNSAFE for children.

Contaminated blue-green algae can cause liver damage, stomach pain, nausea, vomiting, weakness, thirst, rapid heartbeat, shock, and death. Purchase only products that have been tested for mycrocystins and contamination with foreign substances.

Do not take blue-green algae if: You are pregnant or breast-feeding. • You have been told you have phenylketonuria. • You have a skin condition called pemphigus vulgaris.

Are there any interactions with medications?
It is not known if blue-green algae interacts with any medicines.
Before taking blue-green algae, talk with your healthcare professional if you take any medications.

BLUEBERRY

What other names is the product known by?
Blueberries, Highbush Blueberry, Hillside Blueberry, Lowbush Blueberry, Rabbiteye Blueberry, Vaccinium altomontanum, Vaccinium amoenum, Vaccinium angustifolium, Vaccinium ashei, Vaccinium brittonii, Vaccinium constablaei, Vaccinium corymbosum, Vaccinium lamarckii, Vaccinium pallidum, Vaccinium pensylvanicum, Vaccinium vacillans, Vaccinium virgatum.

What is it?
Blueberry is a plant. People use the fruit and leaves to make medicine. Be careful not to confuse blueberry with bilberry. Outside of the United States, the name blueberry may be used for a plant called bilberry in the US.

Is it Effective?
The effectiveness ratings for **BLUEBERRY** are as follows:
Insufficient Evidence to Rate Effectiveness for... Preventing cataracts and glaucoma, ulcers, urinary tract infections (UTIs), multiple sclerosis (MS), chronic fatigue syndrome (CFS), fever, sore throat, varicose veins, hemorrhoids, bad circulation, diarrhea, constipation, labor pains, and other conditions.

How does it work?
Blueberry, like its relative the cranberry, might help prevent bladder infections by stopping bacteria from attaching to the walls of the bladder. Blueberry fruit is high in fiber which could help normal digestive function. It also contains vitamin C and other antioxidants.

Medical professionals should consult the Professional Version at www.NaturalDatabase.com.

Are there safety concerns?

Blueberry is safe for most people. There is some concern that blueberry might lower blood sugar levels. If you have diabetes, check your blood sugar carefully.

Do not take blueberry in amounts greater than typically consumed as food if: You are pregnant or breast-feeding.

Are there any interactions with medications?

Medications for diabetes (Antidiabetes drugs). Blueberry leaves might decrease blood sugar. Diabetes medications are also used to lower blood sugar. Taking blueberry leaves along with diabetes medications might cause your blood sugar to go too low. Monitor your blood sugar closely. The dose of your diabetes medication might need to be changed. Some medications used for diabetes include glimepiride (Amaryl), glyburide (DiaBeta, Glynase PresTab, Micronase), insulin, pioglitazone (Actos), rosiglitazone (Avandia), chlorpropamide (Diabinese), glipizide (Glucotrol), tolbutamide (Orinase), and others.

BOG BILBERRY

What other names is the product known by?

Moosbeere, Vaccinium uliginosum, Western-Huckleberry.

What is it?

Bog bilberry is a plant. People use the dried, ripe fruit to make medicine. Be careful not to confuse bog bilberry with bilberry fruit or bilberry leaf.

Is it Effective?

The effectiveness ratings for **BOG BILBERRY** are as follows:
Insufficient Evidence to Rate Effectiveness for... Inflammation of the stomach and intestines, diarrhea, bladder problems, and other conditions.

How does it work?

Bog bilberry contains tannins which might help reduce inflammation and diarrhea.

Are there safety concerns?

Bog bilberry might not be safe. Poisonings have occurred in people who took large quantities of potentially fungus-infested bog bilberry. Signs of poisoning include vomiting, mental changes, weakness, changes in vision, and other symptoms.

Do not take bog bilberry if: You are pregnant or breast-feeding.

Are there any interactions with medications?

It is not known if bog bilberry interacts with any medicines.
Before taking bog bilberry, talk with your healthcare professional if you take any medications.

BOGBEAN

What other names is the product known by?

Buckbean, Marsh Trefoil, Menyanthes, Menyanthes trifoliata, Water Shamrock.

What is it?

Bogbean is a plant. People use the leaf to make medicine.

Is it Effective?

The effectiveness ratings for **BOGBEAN** are as follows:
Insufficient Evidence to Rate Effectiveness for... Achy joints (rheumatism), rheumatoid arthritis, indigestion, loss of appetite, and other uses.

How does it work?

Bogbean contains bitter chemicals that can increase the flow of saliva and stomach juices. This might help stimulate the appetite or relieve indigestion.

Are there safety concerns?
Bogbean might be safe for most people when used in medicinal amounts. It might not be safe in large quantities. Bogbean can irritate the stomach and intestines and cause diarrhea, pain, nausea, and vomiting.

Do not take bogbean if: You are pregnant or breast-feeding. • You are at risk for bleeding. • You have stomach or intestinal problems such as diarrhea, colitis, or Crohn's disease.

Are there any interactions with medications?
Medications that slow blood clotting (Anticoagulant / Antiplatelet drugs). Bogbean might slow blood clotting. Taking bogbean along with medications that also slow clotting might increase the chances of bruising and bleeding. Some medications that slow blood clotting include aspirin, clopidogrel (Plavix), diclofenac (Voltaren, Cataflam, others), ibuprofen (Advil, Motrin, others), naproxen (Anaprox, Naprosyn, others), dalteparin (Fragmin), enoxaparin (Lovenox), heparin, warfarin (Coumadin), and others.

BOIS DE ROSE OIL

What other names is the product known by?
Aniba rosaeodora, Cayenne Rosewood Oil, Distilled Oil from Aniba Rosaeodora Wood, Rosewood Oil.

What is it?
Bois de rose oil is a plant product. People use the wood from the Aniba rosaeodora tree to make Bois de rose oil. It is used in perfume and in food as flavoring.

Is it Effective?
The effectiveness ratings for **BOIS DE ROSE OIL** are as follows:
Insufficient Evidence to Rate Effectiveness for... Sore muscles and stress.

How does it work?
Bois de rose oil might have some anti-seizure and antibiotic activity in mice, but there isn't enough information to know how bois de rose oil might work in people.

Are there safety concerns?
Bois de rose oil is safe when used in small amounts in foods or when applied directly to the skin, but the potential side effects of bois de rose oil are not known.

Do not use bois de rose oil if: You are pregnant or breast-feeding.

Are there any interactions with medications?
It is not known if bois de rose oil interacts with any medicines.
Before taking bois de rose oil, talk with your healthcare professional if you take any medications.

BOLDO

What other names is the product known by?
Boldea fragrans, Boldine, Boldoak Boldea, Boldo Folium, Boldus, Boldus Boldus, Peumus boldus, Peumus fragrans.

What is it?
Boldo is a plant. People use the leaf to make medicine.

Is it Effective?
The effectiveness ratings for **BOLDO** are as follows:
Insufficient Evidence to Rate Effectiveness for... Gallstones, achy joints (rheumatism), bladder infections, liver disease, anxiety, gonorrhea, fluid retention, constipation or flushing out of the bowels, mild stomach or intestinal spasms, and other conditions.

How does it work?
Boldo contains chemicals that might increase urine output, fight bacterial growth in the urine, and stimulate the stomach.

Medical professionals should consult the Professional Version at www.NaturalDatabase.com.

CONSUMER VERSION

Are there safety concerns?

Boldo might be unsafe when used for medicinal purposes. Poisoning by ascaridole, a chemical that occurs naturally in boldo, has occurred in people taking boldo. Boldo might cause liver damage when taken by mouth. When applied to the skin, boldo can cause irritation.

Do not take boldo if: You are pregnant or breast-feeding. • You have liver disease. • You have gallstones or gall bladder disease.

Are there any interactions with medications?

Medications that can harm the liver (Hepatotoxic drugs). Boldo might harm the liver. Taking boldo along with medication that might also harm the liver can increase the risk of liver damage. Do not take boldo if you are taking a medication that can harm the liver. Some medications that can harm the liver include acetaminophen (Tylenol and others), amiodarone (Cordarone), carbamazepine (Tegretol), isoniazid (INH), methotrexate (Rheumatrex), methyldopa (Aldomet), fluconazole (Diflucan), itraconazole (Sporanox), erythromycin (Erythrocin, Ilosone, others), phenytoin (Dilantin), lovastatin (Mevacor), pravastatin (Pravachol), simvastatin (Zocor), and many others.
Medications that slow blood clotting (Anticoagulant / Antiplatelet drugs). Boldo might slow blood clotting. Taking boldo along with medications that also slow clotting might increase the chances of bruising and bleeding. Some medications that slow blood clotting include aspirin, clopidogrel (Plavix), diclofenac (Voltaren, Cataflam, others), ibuprofen (Advil, Motrin, others), naproxen (Anaprox, Naprosyn, others), dalteparin (Fragmin), enoxaparin (Lovenox), heparin, warfarin (Coumadin), and others.
Warfarin (Coumadin). Warfarin (Coumadin) is used to slow blood clotting. Boldo might also slow blood clotting. Taking boldo along with warfarin (Coumadin) might increase the chances of bruising and bleeding. Be sure to have your blood checked regularly. The dose of your warfarin (Coumadin) might need to be changed.

BONESET

What other names is the product known by?

Agueweed, Crosswort, Eupatorium perfoliatum, Feverwort, Indian Sage, Sweating Plant, Teasel, Thoroughwort, Vegetable Antimony.

What is it?

Boneset is a plant. The dried leaf and flowers are used to make medicine.

Is it Effective?

The effectiveness ratings for **BONESET** are as follows:
Insufficient Evidence to Rate Effectiveness for... Constipation, causing vomiting, fluid retention, aching muscles, reducing inflammation, and stimulating the immune system.

How does it work?

Boneset contains chemicals that might work like anti-cancer medications. It also might have some mild activity against bacteria.

Are there safety concerns?

Boneset is not considered safe when taken orally in excessive amounts. Some plants in the same botanical family as boneset contain chemicals called pyrrolizidine alkaloids that might damage the liver. It is not known if boneset contains these chemicals.

Boneset can cause an allergic reaction in people who are allergic to ragweed, chrysanthemums, marigolds, daisies, and many other herbs.

Do not take boneset if: You are pregnant or breast-feeding. • You are allergic to ragweed, chrysanthemums, marigolds, or daisies.

Are there any interactions with medications?

It is not known if boneset interacts with any medicines.
Before taking boneset, talk with your healthcare professional if you take any medications.

 Natural Medicines Comprehensive Database Consumer Version (209) 472-2244

BORAGE

What other names is the product known by?

Bee Plant, Beebread, Borage Flower, Borage Leaf, Borage Oil, Borage Seed Oil, Borago, Borago Officinalis, Burage, Burrage, Common Borage, Common Bugloss, Cool Tankard, Huile De Bourrache, Ox's Tongue, Talewort, Starflower.

What is it?

Borage is a plant. The flowers, leaves, and seed oil from borage are used as medicine.

Is it Effective?

The effectiveness ratings for **BORAGE** are as follows:

Possibly Effective for... Improving symptoms of rheumatoid arthritis when used with other anti-inflammatory medications • Improving the function of the lungs in critically ill patients • Improving growth and development in premature infants.

Possibly Ineffective for... Atopic dermatitis (eczema).

Insufficient Evidence to Rate Effectiveness for... Premenstrual syndrome (PMS), diabetes, attention-deficit hyperactivity disorder (ADHD), alcoholism, heart disease, stroke, skin conditions in infants, fever, cough, depression, dry skin, arthritis, pain relief, inflamed veins (phlebitis), menopausal disorders, fluid retention, and other conditions.

How does it work?

Borage seed oil contains a fatty acid called gamma-linolenic acid (GLA). GLA seems to have anti-inflammatory effects. Borage flower might have an antioxidant effect.

Are there safety concerns?

Borage seed oil seems to be safe for most adults. Some borage seed oil products can contain dangerous chemicals called pyrrolizidine alkaloids (PAs), which can damage the liver or cause cancer, especially when used in high doses or for a long time. Only use products that are certified and labeled PA-free.

Do not take borage if: You are pregnant or breast-feeding. • You have liver disease. • You have a bleeding disorder.

Are there any interactions with medications?

Medications that slow blood clotting (Anticoagulant / Antiplatelet drugs). Borage seed oil might slow blood clotting. Taking borage seed oil along with medications that also slow clotting might increase the chances of bruising and bleeding. Borage seed oil contains GLA (gamma linolenic acid). GLA is the part of borage seed oil that might slow blood clotting. Some medications that slow blood clotting include aspirin, clopidogrel (Plavix), diclofenac (Voltaren, Cataflam, others), ibuprofen (Advil, Motrin, others), naproxen (Anaprox, Naprosyn, others), dalteparin (Fragmin), enoxaparin (Lovenox), heparin, warfarin (Coumadin), and others.

Medications used during surgery (Anesthesia). Borage seed oil might interact with medications used during surgery. Be sure to tell your doctor what natural products you are taking before having surgery. To be on the safe side, you should stop taking borage seed oil at least two weeks before surgery.

Medications that increase the break down of other medications by the liver (Cytochrome P450 3A4 (CYP3A4) inducers). Borage is broken down by the liver. Some chemicals that form when the liver breaks down borage seed oil can be harmful. Medications that cause the liver to break down borage seed oil might enhance the toxic effects of chemicals contained in borage seed oil. Some of these medicines include carbamazepine (Tegretol), phenobarbital, phenytoin (Dilantin), rifampin, rifabutin (Mycobutin), and others.

NSAIDs (Nonsteroidal anti-inflammatory drugs). NSAIDs are anti-inflammatory medications used to decrease pain and swelling. Borage seed oil is also used as an anti-inflammatory medication. Sometimes NSAIDs and borage seed oil are used together for rheumatoid arthritis. But borage seed oil seems to work in a different way than NSAIDs. Some scientists think that taking NSAIDs along with borage seed oil might decrease the effectiveness of borage seed oil. But it is too soon to know if this is true. Some NSAIDs include ibuprofen (Advil, Motrin, Nuprin, others), indomethacin (Indocin), naproxen (Aleve, Anaprox, Naprelan, Naprosyn), piroxicam (Feldene), aspirin, and others.

Medical professionals should consult the Professional Version at www.NaturalDatabase.com.

BORON

What other names is the product known by?
Atomic number 5, B (chemical symbol), Borate, Borates, Boric Acid, Boric Anhydride, Boric Tartrate, Sodium Borate.

What is it?
Boron is a mineral. Boron is found in food and in the environment. People take boron supplements as medicine.

Is it Effective?
The effectiveness ratings for **BORON** are as follows:
Possibly Ineffective for... Body building.
Insufficient Evidence to Rate Effectiveness for... Bone loss (osteoporosis), improving thinking and coordination in older people, and increasing testosterone.

How does it work?
Boron seems to affect the way the body handles other minerals such as magnesium and phosphorus. It also seems to increase estrogen levels in post-menopausal women and healthy men. Estrogen is thought to be helpful in maintaining healthy bones and mental function.

Are there safety concerns?
Boron is safe for most people when used in doses less than 20 mg per day. Doses less than 10 mg per day are unlikely to cause adverse effects in adults.

Large quantities can cause poisoning. Signs of poisoning include skin inflammation and peeling, irritability, tremors, convulsions, weakness, headaches, depression, diarrhea, vomiting, and other symptoms.
Boron is safe for pregnant and lactating women age 19-50 when used in doses less that 20 mg per day. Pregnant and lactating women age 14 to 18 should not take more then 17 mg per day. Higher amounts can be harmful.

Do not take boron if: You have kidney disease. • You have a hormone sensitive cancer such as breast, uterine, or ovarian cancer. • You have a hormone sensitive condition such as endometriosis (irregular uterine lining), uterine fibroids (fibrous growths in the uterus), or other conditions.

Are there any interactions with medications?
Estrogens. Boron might increase estrogen levels in the body. Taking boron along with estrogens might cause too much estrogen in the body.

BOVINE CARTILAGE

What other names is the product known by?
Antitumor Angiogenesis Factor (anti-TAF), Bovine Tracheal Cartilage (BTC), Catrix, Catrix-S, Processed Bovine Cartilage, Psoriacin, Psoriacin-T, Rumalon.

What is it?
Bovine cartilage comes from cows (bovine). Cartilage is a substance in the body that provides structure support. People sometimes use cow (bovine) cartilage as medicine.

Is it Effective?
The effectiveness ratings for **BOVINE CARTILAGE** are as follows:
Possibly Effective for... Treating poison oak and poison ivy • Treating acne • Treating skin conditions such as psoriasis • Treating hemorrhoids, rectal tears, and anal itching • Treating osteoarthritis when given under the skin • Treating rheumatoid arthritis • Treating "dry socket" after tooth extraction.
Possibly Ineffective for... Treating osteoarthritis when given in the muscle.
Insufficient Evidence to Rate Effectiveness for... Ulcerative colitis, cancer, and other conditions.

How does it work?
Bovine cartilage might work by providing components to support the rebuilding of cartilage in people with osteoarthritis. It might also help reduce swelling and help wounds heal more effectively.

Are there safety concerns?
Bovine cartilage seems safe for use as a medicine. It can cause side effects such as diarrhea, nausea, swelling, local redness, and itching.

There is some concern about the possibility of catching "mad cow disease" (bovine spongiform encephalitis, BSE) or other diseases from products that come from animals. "Mad cow disease" does not appear to be transmitted through cartilage products, but it is probably wise to avoid animal products from countries where mad cow disease has been found.

Do not use bovine cartilage if: You are pregnant or breast-feeding.

Are there any interactions with medications?
It is not known if bovine cartilage interacts with any medicines.
Before taking bovine cartilage, talk with your healthcare professional if you take any medications.

BOXWOOD

What other names is the product known by?
Boxwood Extract, Bush Tree, Buxaceae, Buxus, Buxus sempervirens, Dudgeon, SPV 30.

What is it?
Boxwood is a plant. People use the leaf to make medicine.

Is it Effective?
The effectiveness ratings for **BOXWOOD** are as follows:
Insufficient Evidence to Rate Effectiveness for... Treating HIV/AIDS, stimulating the immune system, arthritis, detoxifying the blood, and other uses.

How does it work?
Boxwood might stop viruses from reproducing, but there isn't enough scientific evidence to support this theory.

Are there safety concerns?
Boxwood extract (SPV 30) appears to be safe for most people when taken up to 16 months. It sometimes causes diarrhea or stomach cramps.

Do not use whole boxwood leaf. It has serious side effects that the leaf extract doesn't seem to have. Whole boxwood leaf can cause poisoning, including life threatening side effects such as seizures, paralysis, and death.

Do not take boxwood if: You are pregnant or breast-feeding.

Are there any interactions with medications?
It is not known if boxwood interacts with any medicines.
Before taking boxwood, talk with your healthcare professional if you take any medications.

BRAHMI

What other names is the product known by?
Bacopa monniera, Bacopa monnieri, Herpestis monniera, Jalanimba, Jalnaveri, Nira-Brahmi, Moniera cuneifolia, Sambrani Chettu, Thyme-Leave Gratiola, Water Hyssop.

What is it?
Brahmi is a plant. People use the above ground parts for medicine. Be careful not to confuse brahmi (Bacopa monnieri) with gotu kola and other natural medicines which are also sometimes called brahmi.

Is it Effective?
The effectiveness ratings for **BRAHMI** are as follows:
Possibly Effective for... Aiding learning and memory improvement.
Possibly Ineffective for... Irritable bowel syndrome (IBS).
Insufficient Evidence to Rate Effectiveness for... Asthma, backache, hoarseness, mental illness, epilepsy, rheumatism, sexual problems, fluid retention, and other conditions.

How does it work?
Brahmi contains chemicals that might enhance thinking and learning. There is some evidence to suggest that it might relax muscles in the blood vessels, airways, and the small intestine. It might also have activity as a tranquilizer and pain reliever.

CONSUMER VERSION

Medical professionals should consult the Professional Version at www.NaturalDatabase.com.

Are there safety concerns?

Brahmi seems safe for most people when used short-term and appropriately. Side effects include nausea, dry mouth, and fatigue.

Do not take brahmi if: You are pregnant or breast-feeding.

Are there any interactions with medications?

It is not known if brahmi interacts with any medicines.
Before taking brahmi, talk with your healthcare professional if you take any medications.

BRANCHED-CHAIN AMINO ACIDS

What other names is the product known by?

BCAA, BCAAs, Isoleucine, Leucine, L-Isoleucine, L-Leucine, L-Valine, Valine.

What is it?

Branched-chain amino acids are essential nutrients that the body obtains from proteins found in food. People use branched-chain amino acids for medicine.

Is it Effective?

The effectiveness ratings for **BRANCHED-CHAIN AMINO ACIDS** are as follows:
Possibly Effective for... Improving muscle control and mental function in people with advanced liver disease (latent hepatic encephalopathy) • Reducing muscle breakdown during exercise • Decreasing symptoms associated with mania • Reducing movements associated with tardive dyskinesia, a disorder associated with the use of antipsychotic medications • Reducing loss of appetite and improving nutrition in elderly patients on hemodialysis.
Possibly Ineffective for... Enhancing exercise or athletic performance.
Likely Ineffective for... Amyotrophic lateral sclerosis (ALS, Lou Gehrig's disease).
Insufficient Evidence to Rate Effectiveness for... Treating a disease of the spine called spinocerebellar degeneration (SCD), preventing fatigue, improving concentration, restoring appetite in cancer patients, preventing muscle wasting in people confined to bed, and other uses.

How does it work?

Branched-chain amino acids stimulate the building of protein in muscle and possibly reduce muscle breakdown. Branched-chain amino acids seem to prevent faulty message transmission in the brain cells of people with advanced liver disease, mania, tardive dyskinesia, and anorexia.

Are there safety concerns?

Branched-chain amino acids appear to be safe for most people when used for up to 6 months. Some side effects are known to occur, such as fatigue and loss of coordination. Branched-chain amino acids should be used cautiously before or during activities where performance depends on motor coordination, such as driving.

Do not take branched-chain amino acids if: You are pregnant or breast-feeding. • You drink alcohol excessively. • You have amyotrophic lateral sclerosis (ALS, Lou Gehrig's disease). Use of branched-chain amino acids has led to lung failure and higher death rates in people with ALS. • You have a disorder known as branched-chain keto aciduria. Use of branched-chain amino acids have been known to cause seizures and other mental effects in people with this disorder. • You have diabetes.

Are there any interactions with medications?

Diazoxide (Hyperstat, Proglycem). Branched-chain amino acids are used to help make proteins in the body. Taking Diazoxide along with branched-chain amino acids might decrease the effects of branched-chain amino acids on proteins. More information is needed about this interaction.
Medications for inflammation (Corticosteroids). Branched-chain amino acids are used to help make proteins in the body. Taking drugs called glucocorticoids along with branched-chain amino acids might decrease the effects of branched-chain amino acids on proteins. More information is needed about this interaction.
Levodopa. Branched-chain amino acids might decrease how much levodopa the body absorbs. By decreasing how much levodopa the body absorbs, branched-chain amino acids might decrease the effectiveness of levodopa. Do not take branched-chain amino acids and levodopa at the same time.
Medications for diabetes (Antidiabetes drugs). Branched-chain amino acids might decrease blood sugar. Diabetes medications are also used to lower blood sugar. Taking branched-chain amino acids along with diabetes medications might cause your blood sugar to go too low. Monitor your blood sugar closely. The dose of your diabetes medication might need to be changed. Some medications used for diabetes include glimepiride (Amaryl), glyburide (DiaBeta, Glynase PresTab, Micronase), insulin, pioglitazone (Actos), rosiglitazone (Avandia),

chlorpropamide (Diabinese), glipizide (Glucotrol), tolbutamide (Orinase), and others.
Thyroid hormone. Branched-chain amino acids help the body make proteins. Some thyroid hormone medications can decrease how fast the body breaks down branched-chain amino acids. However, more information is needed to know the significance of this interaction.

BREWER'S YEAST

What other names is the product known by?
Baker's Yeast, Brewers Yeast, Faex Medicinalis, Levure De Biere, Medicinal Yeast, Saccharomyces cerevisiae.

What is it?
Brewer's yeast is a microscopic plant that is a by-product of brewing beer. People use it to make medicine.

Is it Effective?
The effectiveness ratings for **BREWER'S YEAST** are as follows:
Possibly Effective for... Premenstrual syndrome when taken with vitamins and minerals.
Insufficient Evidence to Rate Effectiveness for... Diarrhea, loss of appetite, acne, boils, and diabetes.

How does it work?
Brewer's yeast seems to stimulate intestinal enzymes that could help relieve diarrhea. It also might help fight bacteria that cause infections in the intestine. Brewer's yeast is a source of B vitamins and protein.

Are there safety concerns?
Brewer's yeast seems safe for most people when used short-term. It can cause headache, stomach discomfort, and gas (flatulence). People who are allergic or sensitive to brewer's yeast might also experience itching and swelling.

Brewer's yeast seems safe for children to use short-term, with the approval of a healthcare professional.

Do not take brewer's yeast if: You are pregnant or breast-feeding. • You are allergic to yeast. • You have Crohn's disease.

Are there any interactions with medications?
Medications for depression (MAOIs). Brewer's yeast contains a chemical called tyramine. Large amounts of tyramine can cause high blood pressure. But the body naturally breaks down tyramine to get rid of it. This usually prevents the tyramine from causing high blood pressure. Some medications used for depression stop the body from breaking down tyramine. This can cause too much tyramine in the body and dangerously high blood pressure. Some of these medications used for depression include phenelzine (Nardil), tranylcypromine (Parnate), and others.
Medications for fungal infections (Antifungals). Brewer's yeast is a fungus. Medications for fungal infections help reduce fungus in and on the body. Taking brewer's yeast with medications for fungal infections can reduce the effectiveness of brewer's yeast. Some medications for fungal infection include fluconazole (Diflucan), terbinafine (Lamisil), itraconazole (Sporanox), and others.

BRICKELLIA

What other names is the product known by?
Brickellia arguta, Brickellia glutinosa, Brickellia veronicaefolia, Hierba Dorada.

What is it?
Brickellia is a shrub. The leaf is used to make medicine.

Is it Effective?
The effectiveness ratings for **BRICKELLIA** are as follows:
Insufficient Evidence to Rate Effectiveness for... Diabetes, diarrhea, stomach pain, gallbladder disease, and other conditions.

How does it work?
Preliminary research suggests brickellia might have antioxidant and antidiabetic effects.

Are there safety concerns?
It is not known if brickellia is safe or what potential side effects it might cause.

Do not use brickellia if: You are pregnant or breast-feeding.

Are there any interactions with medications?

It is not known if brickellia interacts with any medicines.
Before taking brickellia, talk with your healthcare professional if you take any medications.

BROCCOLI

What other names is the product known by?

Brassica Oleracea Italica Group, Brassica oleracea var. italica, Calabrese, Purple Sprouting Broccoli.

What is it?

Broccoli is a vegetable. The above ground parts are used to make medicine.

Is it Effective?

The effectiveness ratings for **BROCCOLI** are as follows:
Insufficient Evidence to Rate Effectiveness for... Preventing prostate, breast, colon, rectal, and stomach cancer.

How does it work?

Chemicals in broccoli might have cancer-preventing and antioxidant effects.

Are there safety concerns?

Broccoli is safe when consumed in food amounts. There's not enough information to know if broccoli is safe when taken as medicine. When applied to the skin, broccoli can cause an allergic rash in hypersensitive people.

Do not use broccoli as medicine if: You are pregnant or breast-feeding.

Are there any interactions with medications?

It is not known if broccoli interacts with any medicines.
Before taking broccoli, talk with your healthcare professional if you take any medications.

BROMELAIN

What other names is the product known by?

Ananus ananus, Ananus duckei, Ananas comosus, Ananas sativus, Bromelains, Bromelainum, Bromelia ananus, Bromelia comosa, Bromelin, Pineapple, Pineapple enzyme, Plant Protease Concentrate.

What is it?

Bromelain is an enzyme found in pineapple juice and in the pinapple stem. People use it for medicine.

Is it Effective?

The effectiveness ratings for **BROMELAIN** are as follows:
Possibly Effective for... Arthritis (osteoarthritis) when used in combination with trypsin and rutin.
Possibly Ineffective for... Preventing muscle soreness after exercise.
Insufficient Evidence to Rate Effectiveness for... Knee pain, severe burns, inflammation, reducing swelling after surgery or injury, improving antibiotic absorption, hayfever, preventing cancer, shortening of labor, making it easier to get rid of fats, ulcerative colitis, and other conditions.

How does it work?

Bromelain seems to cause the body to produce substances that fight inflammation.

Are there safety concerns?

Bromelain seems to be safe for most people when taken in appropriate amounts. Bromelain may cause some side effects, such as diarrhea and stomach and intestinal discomfort. Bromelain may also cause allergic reactions, especially in people who have other allergies. If you have allergies, be sure to check with your healthcare professional before taking bromelain.

Do not take bromelain if: You are pregnant or breast-feeding. • You are allergic to pineapple, wheat, celery, papain, carrot, fennel, cypress pollen, or grass pollen. • You are allergic to ragweed, mums, daisies, or similar plants.

Medical professionals should consult the Professional Version at www.NaturalDatabase.com.

Natural Medicines Comprehensive Database Consumer Version
(209) 472-2244

CONSUMER VERSION

Are there any interactions with medications?

Amoxicillin. Taking bromelain might increase how much amoxicillin is in the body. Taking bromelain along with amoxicillin might increase effects and side effects of amoxicillin.

Antibiotics (Tetracycline antibiotics). Taking bromelain might increase how much antibiotic the body absorbs. Taking bromelain along with some antibiotics might increase effects and side effects of some antibiotics called tetracyclines. Some tetracyclines include demeclocycline (Declomycin), minocycline (Minocin), and tetracycline (Achromycin).

Medications that slow blood clotting (Anticoagulant / Antiplatelet drugs). Bromelain might slow blood clotting. Taking bromelain along with medications that also slow clotting might increase the chances of bruising and bleeding. Some medications that slow blood clotting include aspirin, clopidogrel (Plavix), diclofenac (Voltaren, Cataflam, others), ibuprofen (Advil, Motrin, others), naproxen (Anaprox, Naprosyn, others), dalteparin (Fragmin), enoxaparin (Lovenox), heparin, warfarin (Coumadin), and others.

BROOKLIME

What other names is the product known by?

Beccabunga, Mouth-Smart, Neckweed, Speedwell, Veronica beccabunga, Water Pimpernel, Water Purslane.

What is it?

Brooklime is a plant. The juice of the plant is used as medicine.

Is it Effective?

The effectiveness ratings for **BROOKLIME** are as follows:

Insufficient Evidence to Rate Effectiveness for... Reducing urine, constipation, liver complaints, dysentery, lung infection, bleeding gums, and other uses.

How does it work?

There isn't enough information to know how brooklime might work.

Are there safety concerns?

It is not known if brooklime is safe or what the potential side effects might be.

Do not take brooklime if: You are pregnant or breast-feeding.

Are there any interactions with medications?

It is not known if brooklime interacts with any medicines.
Before taking brooklime, talk with your healthcare professional if you take any medications.

BROOM CORN

What other names is the product known by?

Darri, Durri, Guinea Corn, Sorghum, Sorghum vulgare.

What is it?

Broom corn is a plant. People use the seed for medicine.

Is it Effective?

The effectiveness ratings for **BROOM CORN** are as follows:
Insufficient Evidence to Rate Effectiveness for... Digestive disorders and other uses.

How does it work?

Broom corn is thought to have a soothing effect on the digestive system.

Are there safety concerns?

It is not known if broom corn is safe in amounts greater than that found in foods or what the potential side effects might be.

Do not take broom corn if: You are pregnant or breast-feeding.

Medical professionals should consult the Professional Version at www.NaturalDatabase.com.

CONSUMER VERSION

Are there any interactions with medications?

It is not known if broom corn interacts with any medicines.
Before taking broom corn, talk with your healthcare professional if you take any medications.

BROWN RICE

What other names is the product known by?

Genmai, Oryza sativa.

What is it?

Brown rice is "unpolished" white rice. It is eaten as food and taken as medicine.

Is it Effective?

The effectiveness ratings for **BROWN RICE** are as follows:
Insufficient Evidence to Rate Effectiveness for... Diarrhea, dyspepsia, jaundice, nausea, stomach ailments inflammation, paralysis, hemorrhoids, psoriasis, skin ailments, and other conditions.

How does it work?

It is not known how brown rice might work for medical conditions. Preliminary research suggests brown rice might have cancer-fighting and antidiabetic effects. But there isn't enough information to know if it has these effects when consumed by people.

Are there safety concerns?

Brown rice is safe for most people when consumed in amounts commonly found in foods.

The safety of brown rice when used as medicine is unknown.

Do not use brown rice as medicine if: You are pregnant or breast-feeding.

Are there any interactions with medications?

It is not known if brown rice interacts with any medicines.
Before taking brown rice, talk with your healthcare professional if you take any medications.

BRYONIA

What other names is the product known by?

Bryonia Alba, Bryonia Cretica, Bryoniae Radix, Devil's Turnip, English Mandrake, Ladies' Seal, Tamus, Tetterberry, White Bryony, Wild Hops, Wild Nep, Wild Vine, Wood Vine.

What is it?

Bryonia is a plant. People use the root for medicine.

Is it Effective?

The effectiveness ratings for **BRYONIA** are as follows:
Insufficient Evidence to Rate Effectiveness for... Stomach or intestinal diseases, lung diseases, arthritis, liver disease, metabolic disorders, preventing infections, causing vomiting, fluid retention, and other conditions.

How does it work?

Bryonia root contains a resin that has a strong laxative effect to purge the contents of the bowels.

Are there safety concerns?

Bryonia is not safe to use for anyone. It can cause many side effects including dizziness, vomiting, convulsions, colic, bloody diarrhea, abortion, nervous excitement, and kidney damage at fairly low doses. Larger doses may cause fatal poisoning in adults and children. Just touching fresh bryonia can cause skin irritation.

Are there any interactions with medications?

It is not known if bryonia interacts with any medicines.
Before taking bryonia, talk with your healthcare professional if you take any medications.

 Natural Medicines Comprehensive Database Consumer Version (209) 472-2244

BUCHU

What other names is the product known by?
Agathosma betulina, Barosma betulina, Barosma crenulata, Barosmae folium, Barosma serratifolia, Bookoo, Bucco, Bucku, Diosma, Round Buchu, and Short Buch.

What is it?
Buchu is a plant. The leaf is used to make medicine.

Is it Effective?
The effectiveness ratings for **BUCHU** are as follows:
Insufficient Evidence to Rate Effectiveness for... Urinary tract infections, kidney infections, and sexually transmitted diseases.

How does it work?
It is thought that the active chemicals in buchu may act as an antiseptic and decrease fluid retention.

Are there safety concerns?
Buchu may be unsafe when used as a medicine. It may cause liver damage, irritate the stomach and kidneys, increase menstrual flow, and cause abortions in pregnant women.

Do not take buchu if: You are pregnant or breast-feeding. • You have a kidney infection. • You have a urinary tract inflammation.

Are there any interactions with medications?
Medications that slow blood clotting (Anticoagulant / Antiplatelet drugs). Buchu might slow blood clotting. Taking buchu along with medications that also slow clotting might increase the chances of bruising and bleeding. Some medications that slow blood clotting include aspirin, clopidogrel (Plavix), diclofenac (Voltaren, Cataflam, others), ibuprofen (Advil, Motrin, others), naproxen (Anaprox, Naprosyn, others), dalteparin (Fragmin), enoxaparin (Lovenox), heparin, warfarin (Coumadin), and others.

BUCKHORN PLANTAIN

What other names is the product known by?
Buckhorn, Chimney-Sweeps, English Plantain, Headsman, Hoary Plantain, Plantago lanceolata, Plantaginis lanceolatae herba, Plantain, Ribgrass, Ribwort, Ribwort Plantain, Ripplegrass, Soldier's Herb, Spitzwegerichkraut.

What is it?
Buckhorn plantain is a plant. People use the above ground parts for medicine.

Is it Effective?
The effectiveness ratings for **BUCKHORN PLANTAIN** are as follows:
Insufficient Evidence to Rate Effectiveness for... The common cold, cough, fevers, bleeding, inflammation of breathing passages such as bronchitis, sore mouth, sore throat, inflamed skin when applied directly to the irritated area, and other conditions.

How does it work?
Buckhorn plantain contains tannins and mucous-like substances that might help soothe inflamed areas.

Are there safety concerns?
Buckhorn plantain might be safe for most people in medicinal doses. It can trigger allergies in sensitive people.

Do not take buckhorn plantain if: You are pregnant or breast-feeding.

Are there any interactions with medications?
It is not known if buckhorn plantain interacts with any medicines.
Before taking buckhorn plantain, talk with your healthcare professional if you take any medications.

BUCKWHEAT

What other names is the product known by?
Buchweizen, Fagopyrum esculentum, Fagopyrum sagittatum, Fagopyrum vulgare, Grano Turco, Sarrasin, Silverhull Buckwheat.

What is it?
Buckwheat is a plant. People use the leaves and flowers for medicine.

Is it Effective?
The effectiveness ratings for **BUCKWHEAT** are as follows:
Insufficient Evidence to Rate Effectiveness for... Improving blood flow, varicose veins and poor blood circulation in the legs, diabetes, preventing hardening of the arteries, and other conditions.

How does it work?
Buckwheat might help people with diabetes by improving how well the body deals with blood sugar.

Are there safety concerns?
Buckwheat seems to be safe for adults. Some side effects are known to occur such as increased sensitivity to the sun.

Do not take buckwheat if: You are pregnant or breast-feeding. • You are allergic to buckwheat.

Are there any interactions with medications?
It is not known if buckwheat interacts with any medicines.
Before taking buckwheat, talk with your healthcare professional if you take any medications.

BUGLE

What other names is the product known by?
Ajuga reptans, Bugula, Carpenter's Herb, Middle Comfrey, Middle Confound, Sicklewort.

What is it?
Bugle is a plant. People use the above ground parts for medicine.

Is it Effective?
The effectiveness ratings for **BUGLE** are as follows:
Insufficient Evidence to Rate Effectiveness for... Gallbladder and stomach disorders, inflammation of the mouth and throat, wounds, and other uses.

How does it work?
There isn't enough information to know how bugle might work.

Are there safety concerns?
There isn't enough information to know if bugle is safe or what the potential side effects might be.

Do not take bugle if: You are pregnant or breast-feeding.

Are there any interactions with medications?
It is not known if bugle interacts with any medicines.
Before taking bugle, talk with your healthcare professional if you take any medications.

BUGLEWEED

What other names is the product known by?
Archangle, Ashangee, Green Wolf's Foot, Gypsy Weed, Gypsywort, Hoarhound, Lycopi Herba, Lycopus americanus, Lycopus europaeus, Lycopus virginicus, Paul's Betony, Sweet Bugle, Water Bugle, Water Hoarhound, Water Horehound, Virginia Water Horehound, Wolfstrapp.

What is it?
Bugleweed is a plant. People use the above ground parts for medicine.

Is it Effective?

The effectiveness ratings for **BUGLEWEED** are as follows:

Insufficient Evidence to Rate Effectiveness for... Premenstrual syndrome (PMS), nervousness, trouble sleeping (insomnia), bleeding, high levels of thyroid hormones (hyperthyroidism), breast pain, and other conditions.

How does it work?

Bugleweed might reduce the body's production of thyroid hormone. Bugleweed also seems to reduce the secretion of the hormone prolactin, which might help relieve breast pain.

Are there safety concerns?

Bugleweed might be safe for most people, but thyroid disease should not be self-treated due to possible complications. Long-term use of bugleweed can cause an enlarged thyroid gland. Discontinuing bugleweed abruptly can result in high levels of thyroid and prolactin, which might cause physical symptoms.

Bugleweed might lower blood sugar. If you have diabetes, use bugleweed cautiously, watch for symptoms of low blood sugar, and check your blood sugar carefully. The dose of your diabetes medications may need to be adjusted.

Do not take bugleweed if: You are pregnant or breast-feeding. • You have certain types of thyroid disease such as an enlarged thyroid, your thyroid doesn't function fully (thyroid hypofunction), or you are taking other thyroid treatments.

Are there any interactions with medications?

Medications for diabetes (Antidiabetes drugs). Bugleweed might decrease blood sugar. Diabetes medications are also used to lower blood sugar. Taking bugleweed along with diabetes medications might cause your blood sugar to go too low. Monitor your blood sugar closely. The dose of your diabetes medication might need to be changed. Some medications used for diabetes include glimepiride (Amaryl), glyburide (DiaBeta, Glynase PresTab, Micronase), insulin, pioglitazone (Actos), rosiglitazone (Avandia), chlorpropamide (Diabinese), glipizide (Glucotrol), tolbutamide (Orinase), and others.

Thyroid hormone. Taking bugleweed might decrease how well thyroid hormone pills work. Don't take bugleweed if you take thyroid pills.

BULBOUS BUTTERCUP

What other names is the product known by?

Crowfoot, Cuckoo Buds, Frogsfoot, Frogwort, Goldcup, King's Cup, Meadowbloom, Pilewort, Ranunculus bulbosus, St. Anthony's Turnip.

What is it?

Bulbous buttercup is a plant. People use the whole flowering plant to make medicine. Be careful not to confuse bulbous buttercup with buttercup and poisonous buttercup.

Is it Effective?

The effectiveness ratings for **BULBOUS BUTTERCUP** are as follows:

Insufficient Evidence to Rate Effectiveness for... Skin diseases, arthritis, gout, nerve pain, flu (influenza), meningitis, and other uses.

How does it work?

There is not enough information to know how bulbous buttercup might work.

Are there safety concerns?

Bulbous buttercup is unsafe. It is very irritating to the lining of the urinary and digestive tract, causing stomach pain and diarrhea. When applied to the skin, it can also cause hard-to-heal skin blisters and burns.

Do not take bulbous buttercup if: You are pregnant or breast-feeding.

Are there any interactions with medications?

It is not known if bulbous buttercup interacts with any medicines.
Before taking bulbous buttercup, talk with your healthcare professional if you take any medications.

BUPLEURUM

What other names is the product known by?
Bei Chai Hu, Bupleurum chinense, Bupleurum exaltatum, Bupleurum falcatum, Bupleurum fruticosum, Bupleurum longifolium, Bupleurum multinerve, Bupleurum octoradiatum, Bupleurum rotundifolium, Bupleurum scorzonerifolium, Chi Hu, Chinese Thoroughwax, Hare's Ear Root, Sho-saiko-to, Shrubby Hare's-ear, Sickle-leaf Hare's-ear, Thoroughwax, Xiao Chai Hu Tang.

What is it?
Bupleurum is a plant. People use the root for medicine.

Is it Effective?
The effectiveness ratings for **BUPLEURUM** are as follows:
Insufficient Evidence to Rate Effectiveness for... Fevers, flu, the common cold, cough, fatigue, headache, ringing in the ears, liver disorders, blood disorders, stimulating the immune system, and many other uses.

How does it work?
Bupleurum might stimulate the cells of the immune system to work harder. It might also have other effects, but none of these are proven in humans.

Are there safety concerns?
There isn't enough information to know if bupleurum is safe. However, some side effects are known to occur such as increased bowel movements, intestinal gas, and drowsiness. In combination with other herbs, such as in the Japanese herbal formula called Sho-saiko-to, it has caused serious lung and breathing problems.

Do not take bupleurum if: You are pregnant or breast-feeding.

Are there any interactions with medications?
It is not known if bupleurum interacts with any medicines.
Before taking bupleurum, talk with your healthcare professional if you take any medications.

BURDOCK

What other names is the product known by?
Arctium, Arctium lappa, Arctium minus, Arctium tomentosum, Bardana, Bardana-minor, Bardanae Radix, Bardane, Beggar's Buttons, Burr Seed, Clotbur, Cocklebur, Cockle Buttons, Edible Burdock, Fox's Clote, Great Bur, Great Burdocks, Happy Major, Hardock, Harebur, Lappa, Love Leaves, Niu Bang Zi, Orelha-de-gigante, Personata, Philanthropium, Thorny Burr.

What is it?
Burdock is a plant. The root, leaf, and seed are used to make medicine.

Is it Effective?
The effectiveness ratings for **BURDOCK** are as follows:
Insufficient Evidence to Rate Effectiveness for... Fluid retention, fever, anorexia, stomach conditions, gout, acne, severely dry skin, and psoriasis.

How does it work?
Burdock contains chemicals that might have activity against bacteria and inflammation.

Are there safety concerns?
Burdock is safely used as a food in Asia. There's not enough information to know if burdock is safe when taken in medicinal doses.

It may cause an allergic reaction in people sensitive to certain flowers and herbs. When applied to the skin, it can cause a rash.

Do not take burdock if: You are pregnant or breast-feeding. • You are allergic to ragweed, chrysanthemums, marigolds, and daisies.

 Natural Medicines Comprehensive Database Consumer Version (209) 472-2244

Are there any interactions with medications?

Medications that slow blood clotting (Anticoagulant / Antiplatelet drugs). Burdock might slow blood clotting. Taking burdock along with medications that also slow clotting might increase the chances of bruising and bleeding. Some medications that slow blood clotting include aspirin, clopidogrel (Plavix), diclofenac (Voltaren, Cataflam, others), ibuprofen (Advil, Motrin, others), naproxen (Anaprox, Naprosyn, others), dalteparin (Fragmin), enoxaparin (Lovenox), heparin, warfarin (Coumadin), and others.

BURNING BUSH

What other names is the product known by?

Adiptam, Burnet Saxifrage, Burning Bush leaf, Dictamnus albus, Dictamnus caucasicus, Dictamnus fraxinellus, Dictamo Blanco, Dittany, Fraxinella, Gas Plant, Herba Dictamni Herba.

What is it?

Burning bush is a plant. People use the leaves and roots for medicine.

Is it Effective?

The effectiveness ratings for **BURNING BUSH** are as follows:
Insufficient Evidence to Rate Effectiveness for... Digestive problems, urinary and genital tract disorders, spasms, arthritis, fever, hepatitis, promoting hair growth, skin disorders such as eczema and inflammation, bacterial skin infections (impetigo), scabies (lice-like insects), worms, and other conditions.

How does it work?

There isn't enough information about burning bush to know how it might work.

Are there safety concerns?

There isn't enough information to know if burning bush is safe. Some side-effects are known to occur such as an increased risk of sunburn if burning bush comes in contact with the skin.

Do not take burning bush if: You are pregnant or breast-feeding.

Are there any interactions with medications?

It is not known if burning bush interacts with any medicines.
Before taking burning bush, talk with your healthcare professional if you take any medications.

BURR MARIGOLD

What other names is the product known by?

Bidens tripartita, Water Agrimony.

What is it?

Burr marigold is a plant. People use the above ground parts for medicine.

Is it Effective?

The effectiveness ratings for **BURR MARIGOLD** are as follows:
Insufficient Evidence to Rate Effectiveness for... Hair loss, colitis, gout, fluid retention, promoting sweating, and other uses.

How does it work?

There isn't enough information about burr marigold to know how it might work.

Are there safety concerns?

There isn't enough information about burr marigold to know if it is safe for most people. Burr marigold can cause allergic reactions in sensitive people, especially in people who are allergic to plants such as ragweed, chrysanthemums, marigolds, or daisies.
Do not take burr marigold if: You are pregnant or breast-feeding. • You are allergic to ragweed, mums, daisies, or similar plants.

Are there any interactions with medications?

It is not known if burr marigold interacts with any medicines.
Before taking burr marigold, talk with your healthcare professional if you take any medications.

BUTANEDIOL (BD)

What other names is the product known by?
Butylene glycol, Tetramethylene glycol.

What is it?
Butanediol is a chemical that is used to make floor stripper, paint thinner, and other solvent products. It's illegal to sell butanediol for use as medicine, but it is sometimes used as a substitute for other illegal substances such as gamma butyrolactone (GBL) and gamma hydroxybutyrate (GHB).

Is it Effective?
The effectiveness ratings for **BUTANEDIOL (BD)** are as follows:
Insufficient Evidence to Rate Effectiveness for... Stimulating growth hormone production and muscle growth, bodybuilding, weight loss, insomnia, and other uses.

How does it work?
Butanediol is converted to gamma hydroxybutyrate (GHB) in the body. GHB slows down the brain, which can cause loss of consciousness along with dangerous slowing of breathing and other vital functions. It also stimulates growth hormone secretion.

Are there safety concerns?
Butanediol is UNSAFE. It has caused serious illness and death. Some side effects of butanediol are breathing problems, coma, amnesia, combativeness, confusion, agitation, vomiting, seizures, and very slow heartbeat. People who use butanediol on a regular basis and then stop may experience withdrawal symptoms such as insomnia, tremor, and anxiety.

While butanediol isn't safe for anyone, some people are at even greater risk for serious side effects. Be especially careful not to take butanediol if: You are pregnant or breast-feeding. • You have high blood pressure. • Your heart beats irregularly. • You have epilepsy.

Are there any interactions with medications?
Alcohol. Alcohol can cause sleepiness and drowsiness. Taking butanediol along with alcohol might greatly increase sleepiness and drowsiness caused by alcohol. Taking butanediol along with alcohol can lead to serious side effects. Do not take butanediol if you have been drinking.

Amphetamines. Amphetamines are drugs that can speed up your nervous system. Butanediol is changed in the body to GHB (gamma hydroxybutyrate). GHB can slow down your nervous system. Taking butanediol along with amphetamines can lead to serious side effects.

Haloperidol (Haldol). Butanediol can affect the brain. Haloperidol (Haldol) can also affect the brain. Taking haloperidol (Haldol) along with butanediol might cause serious side effects.

Medications for mental conditions (Antipsychotic drugs). Butanediol can affect the brain. Medications for mental conditions also affect the brain. Taking butanediol along with medications for mental conditions might increase the effects and serious side effects of butanediol. Do not take butanediol if you are taking medications for a mental condition. Some of these medications include fluphenazine (Permitil, Prolixin), haloperidol (Haldol), chlorpromazine (Thorazine), prochlorperazine (Compazine), thioridazine (Mellaril), trifluoperazine (Stelazine), and others.

Medications for pain (Narcotic drugs). Some medications for pain can cause sleepiness and drowsiness. Butanediol might also cause sleepiness and drowsiness. Taking butanediol along with some medications for pain might cause severe side effects. Do not take butanediol if you are taking medications for pain. Some medications for pain include meperidine (Demerol), hydrocodone, morphine, OxyContin, and many others.

Medications used to prevent seizures (Anticonvulsants). Medications used to prevent seizures affect chemicals in the brain. Butanediol is changed in the body to one of these brain chemicals called GABA. Taking butanediol along with medications used to prevent seizures might decrease the effects of butanediol. Some medications used to prevent seizures include phenobarbital, primidone (Mysoline), valproic acid (Depakene), gabapentin (Neurontin), carbamazepine (Tegretol), phenytoin (Dilantin), and others.

Muscle relaxants. Muscle relaxants can cause drowsiness. Butanediol can also cause drowsiness. Taking butanediol along with muscle relaxants might cause too much drowsiness and serious side effects. Do not take butanediol if you are taking muscle relaxants. Some of these muscle relaxants include carisoprodol (Soma), pipecuronium (Arduan), orphenadrine (Banflex, Disipal), cyclobenzaprine, gallamine (Flaxedil), atracurium (Tracrium), pancuronium (Pavulon), succinylcholine (Anectine), and others.

Naloxone (Narcan). Butanediol is changed by the body to another chemical. This chemical is called GHB. GHB can affect the brain. Taking naloxone (Narcan) along with butanediol might decrease the effects of butanediol on the brain.

Ritonavir (Norvir). Ritonavir (Norvir) and saquinavir (Fortovase, Invirase) are commonly used together for HIV/AIDS. Taking both these medications plus butanediol might decrease how quickly the body gets rid of

Medical professionals should consult the Professional Version at www.NaturalDatabase.com.

CONSUMER VERSION

 Natural Medicines Comprehensive Database Consumer Version (209) 472-2244

butanediol. This could cause serious side effects.

Saquinavir (Fortovase, Invirase). Saquinavir (Fortovase, Invirase) and ritonavir (Norvir) are commonly used together for HIV/AIDS. Taking both these medications plus butanediol might decrease how fast the body gets rid of butanediol. This could cause serious side effects.

Sedative medications (CNS depressants). Butanediol might cause sleepiness and drowsiness. Medications that cause sleepiness are called sedatives. Taking butanediol along with sedative medications might cause serious side effects. Do not take butanediol if you are taking sedative medications. Some sedative medications include clonazepam (Klonopin), lorazepam (Ativan), phenobarbital (Donnatal), zolpidem (Ambien), and others.

Sedative medications (Benzodiazepines). Butanediol might cause sleepiness and drowsiness. Medications that cause sleepiness and drowsiness are called sedatives. Taking butanediol along with sedative medications might cause serious side effects. Do not take butanediol if you are taking sedative medications. Some of these sedative medications include clonazepam (Klonopin), diazepam (Valium), lorazepam (Ativan), and others.

BUTCHER'S BROOM

What other names is the product known by?
Box Holly, Jew's Myrtle, Kneeholm, Knee Holly, Pettigree, Sweet Broom, Rusci Aculeati, Rusci Aculeati Rhizoma, Ruscus Aculeatus.

What is it?
Butcher's broom is a plant. The root is used to make medicine.

Is it Effective?
The effectiveness ratings for **BUTCHER'S BROOM** are as follows:
Possibly Effective for... Poor circulation in the legs including pain, heaviness, leg cramps, itching, and swelling.
Insufficient Evidence to Rate Effectiveness for... Low blood pressure when getting up, constipation, hemorrhoids, fluid retention, broken bones, circulation diseases, and other conditions.

How does it work?
The chemicals in butcher's broom might cause the blood vessels to narrow or constrict. Butcher's broom might improve blood circulation in the legs by preventing blood from "pooling" in the veins.

Are there safety concerns?
Butcher's broom is considered safe for most people.

It may cause stomach upset and nausea.

Do not take butcher's broom if: You are pregnant or breast-feeding.

Are there any interactions with medications?
Medications used for high blood pressure (Alpha-adrenergic antagonists). Butcher's broom might speed up the nervous system, increase blood pressure, and make the heart beat fast. By increasing blood pressure, butcher's broom might decrease the effectiveness of some medications used for high blood pressure. Some of these medications used for high blood pressure include doxazosin (Cardura), terazosin (Hytrin), and others.
Stimulant Medications (Alpha-adrenergic agonists). Butcher's broom might speed up the nervous system, increase blood pressure, and make the heart beat fast. Stimulant medications can also speed up the nervous system, increase blood pressure, and make the heart beat fast. Taking butcher's broom with stimulant medications might cause too much stimulation. This might make the blood pressure go too high or the heart beat too fast. Some of these stimulant medications include pseudoephedrine (Sudafed, others), ephedrine, phenylpropanolamine, and others.

BUTTERBUR

What other names is the product known by?
Blatterdock, Bog Rhubarb, Bogshorns, Butter Bur, Butterburr, Butter-Dock, Butterfly Dock, Capdockin, Exwort, Flapperdock, Langwort, Petasites, Petasites flower, Petasites hybridus, Petasites officinalis Petasites leaf, Petasites rhizome, Petasites root, Petasitidis folium, Petasitidis rhizoma, Petasitidis hybridus, Plague Root, Tussilago hybrida, Umbrella Leaves.

What is it?
Butterbur is an herb. People use the leaf, root, and bulb to make medicine.

Is it Effective?

The effectiveness ratings for **BUTTERBUR** are as follows:

Possibly Effective for... Preventing migraine headaches • Hayfever caused by grass pollen.

Insufficient Evidence to Rate Effectiveness for... Pain, colic, cough, asthma, irritable bladder, urinary tract spasms, wounds, and other conditions.

How does it work?

Butterbur contains chemicals that might relieve spasms and decrease swelling (inflammation).

Are there safety concerns?

Butterbur products that have been chemically processed to remove chemicals called pyrrolizidine alkaloids (PAs) that can damage the liver seem safe for most people when used for up to four months. Butterbur can cause some side effects including burping, stomach upset, diarrhea, fatigue, itching, and possibly other side effects.

Butterbur products that contain the pyrrolizidine alkaloids are UNSAFE. These chemicals can damage the liver, lungs, and blood circulation, and possibly cause cancer. Do not use butterbur products unless they are certified and labeled as free of PAs that cause liver damage.

Butterbur products theoretically might cause allergic reactions in people who are allergic to ragweed, marigolds, daisies, and other related herbs.

Do not take butterbur if: You are pregnant or breast-feeding. • You are allergic to ragweed, marigolds, daisies, and other related herbs. • You have liver disease.

Are there any interactions with medications?

Medications that increase break down of other medications by the liver (Cytochrome P450 3A4 (CYP3A4) inducers). Butterbur is broken down by the liver. Some chemicals that form when the liver breaks down butterbur can be harmful. Medications that cause the liver to break down butterbur might enhance the toxic effects of chemicals contained in butterbur. Some of these medicines include carbamazepine (Tegretol), phenobarbital, phenytoin (Dilantin), rifampin, rifabutin (Mycobutin), and others.

BUTTERCUP

What other names is the product known by?

Acrid Crowfoot, Batchelor's Buttons, Blisterweed, Burrwort, Globe Amaranth, Gold Cup, Meadowbloom, Meadow Buttercup, Ranunculus acris, Ranunculus friesianus, Tall Buttercup, Yellows, Yellowweed.

What is it?

Buttercup is a plant. People use the above ground parts for medicine.

Is it Effective?

The effectiveness ratings for **BUTTERCUP** are as follows:

Insufficient Evidence to Rate Effectiveness for... Arthritis, blisters, bronchitis, chronic skin problems, nerve pain, and other conditions.

How does it work?

Buttercup contains toxins which are very irritating to the skin and the lining of the mouth, stomach, and intestines. There is not enough information to know how buttercup might work for medicinal uses.

Are there safety concerns?

Fresh buttercup is UNSAFE. It may cause severe irritation of the digestive tract, with colic and diarrhea. Irritation of the bladder and urinary tract can also occur. Skin contact may cause blisters and burns that are difficult to heal. It can also increase the risk of sunburn.

Some of the toxins in fresh buttercup might be destroyed in the drying process, but there isn't enough information to know if dried buttercup might be safe.

Do not take buttercup if: You are pregnant or breast-feeding.

Are there any interactions with medications?

It is not known if buttercup interacts with any medicines.

Before taking buttercup, talk with your healthcare professional if you take any medications.

BUTTERNUT

What other names is the product known by?
Butternussbaum, Juglans cinerea, Lemon Walnut, Oil Nut, White Walnut, Nogal Ceniciento, Noyer Cerdré.

What is it?
Butternut is a plant. People use the bark for medicine.

Is it Effective?
The effectiveness ratings for **BUTTERNUT** are as follows:
Insufficient Evidence to Rate Effectiveness for... Gallbladder disorders, hemorrhoids, skin diseases, constipation, cancer, infections, restoring body function, and other uses.

How does it work?
Butternut bark might work as a laxative to help stool move through the intestine.

Are there safety concerns?
Butternut appears to be safe for most people, but it can cause diarrhea and irritation of the stomach and intestines.

Do not take butternut if: You are pregnant or breast-feeding.

Are there any interactions with medications?
Digoxin (Lanoxin). Butternut is a type of laxative called a stimulant laxative. Stimulant laxatives can decrease potassium levels in the body. Low potassium levels can increase the risk of side effects of digoxin (Lanoxin).
Medications for inflammation (Corticosteroids). Some medications for inflammation can decrease potassium in the body. Butternut is a type of laxative that might also decrease potassium in the body. Taking butternut along with some medications for inflammation might decrease potassium in the body too much. Some medications for inflammation include dexamethasone (Decadron), hydrocortisone (Cortef), methylprednisolone (Medrol), prednisone (Deltasone), and others.
Medications taken by mouth (Oral drugs). Butternut is a laxative. Laxatives can decrease how much medicine your body absorbs. Decreasing how much medicine your body absorbs can decrease the effectiveness of your medication.
Stimulant laxatives. Butternut is a type of laxative called a stimulant laxative. Stimulant laxatives speed up the bowels. Taking butternut along with other stimulant laxatives could speed up the bowels too much and cause dehydration and low minerals in the body. Some stimulant laxatives include bisacodyl (Correctol, Dulcolax), cascara, castor oil (Purge), senna (Senokot), and others.
Water pills (Diuretic drugs). Butternut is a laxative. Some laxatives can decrease potassium in the body. "Water pills" can also decrease potassium in the body. Taking butternut along with "water pills" might decrease potassium in the body too much. Some "water pills" that can decrease potassium include chlorothiazide (Diuril), chlorthalidone (Thalitone), furosemide (Lasix), hydrochlorothiazide (HCTZ, HydroDiuril, Microzide), and others.

CABBAGE

What other names is the product known by?
Brassica oleracea, Colewort, Kale, Red Cabbage, White Cabbage.

What is it?
Cabbage is a plant. People use the leaves for medicine.

Is it Effective?
The effectiveness ratings for **CABBAGE** are as follows:
Possibly Effective for... Relieving breast engorgement (hard, painful breasts) in breast-feeding women, when applied to the skin of the breasts.
Insufficient Evidence to Rate Effectiveness for... Stomach pain, stomach and intestinal ulcers, excess stomach acid, asthma, morning sickness, preventing osteoporosis and cancer, and other uses.

How does it work?
Cabbage might change the way estrogen is used in the body. It contains lots of potentially active substances, but it isn't well-understood how they might work for medicinal uses.

Medical professionals should consult the Professional Version at www.NaturalDatabase.com.

Are there safety concerns?

Cabbage in medicinal doses appears to be safe for most people when taken by mouth or used on the skin. There isn't much evidence about potential side effects.

When applied directly to the skin of women who are breast-feeding, cabbage seems to be safe for short-term use. However, women who are breast-feeding should avoid taking cabbage by mouth as food or medicine. Nursing infants of women who eat cabbage as little as once per week seem to suffer from colic.

Do not take cabbage if: You have low thyroid (hypothyroidism).

Are there any interactions with medications?

Acetaminophen (Tylenol, others). The body breaks down acetaminophen (Tylenol, others) to a get rid of it. Cabbage might increase the breakdown of acetaminophen (Tylenol, others). Taking cabbage along with acetaminophen (Tylenol, others) might decrease the effectiveness of acetaminophen (Tylenol, others).

Medications changed by the liver (Cytochrome P450 1A2 (CYP1A2) substrates). Some medications are changed and broken down by the liver. Cabbage might increase how quickly the liver breaks down some medications. Taking cabbage along with some medications that are changed by the liver can decrease the effectiveness of some medications. Before taking cabbage talk to your healthcare provider if you take any medications that are changed by the liver. Some of these medications that are changed by the liver include clozapine (Clozaril), cyclobenzaprine (Flexeril), fluvoxamine (Luvox), haloperidol (Haldol), imipramine (Tofranil), mexiletine (Mexitil), olanzapine (Zyprexa), pentazocine (Talwin), propranolol (Inderal), tacrine (Cognex), theophylline, zileuton (Zyflo), zolmitriptan (Zomig), and others.

Medications changed by the liver (Glucuronidated Drugs). The liver helps the body break down and change some medications. The body breaks down some medications to get rid of them. Cabbage might increase how quickly the body breaks down some medications changed by the liver. Taking cabbage along with these medications changed by the liver might decrease the effectiveness of some medications change by the liver. Some of these medications changed by the liver include acetaminophen, atorvastatin (Lipitor), diazepam (Valium), digoxin, entacapone (Comtan), estrogen, irinotecan (Camptosar), lamotrigine (Lamictal), lorazepam (Ativan), lovastatin (Mevacor), meprobamate, morphine, oxazepam (Serax), and others.

Oxazepam (Serax). The body breaks down oxazepam (Serax) to get rid of it. Cabbage can increase how quickly the body gets rid of oxazepam (Serax). Taking cabbage along with oxazepam (Serax) might decrease the effectiveness of oxazepam (Serax).

Warfarin (Coumadin). Cabbage contains large amounts of vitamin K. Vitamin K is used by the body to help blood clot. Warfarin (Coumadin) is used to slow blood clotting. By helping the blood clot, cabbage might decrease the effectiveness of warfarin (Coumadin). Be sure to have your blood checked regularly. The dose of your warfarin (Coumadin) might need to be changed.

CADE OIL

What other names is the product known by?

Alquitran de Enebro, Goudron de Cade, Juniper Tar, Juniper Tar Oil, Juniperus oxycedrus, Kadeol, Oil of Cade, Oil of Juniper Tar, Oleum Cadinum, Oleum Juniperi Empyreumaticum, Pix Cadi, Pix Juniper, Pix Oxycedri, Pyroleum Juniperi, Pyroleum Oxycedri, Wacholderteer.

What is it?

Cade is a plant. The oil from the wood is used for medicine.

Is it Effective?

The effectiveness ratings for **CADE OIL** are as follows:

Insufficient Evidence to Rate Effectiveness for... Itching, pain, psoriasis, eczema, skin infections caused by parasites, wounds, scalp conditions, dandruff, hair loss, and cancers.

How does it work?

Cade oil contains chemicals which might relieve itching and kill bacteria.

Are there safety concerns?

There is not enough information to know if cade oil is safe.

Do not use cade oil if: You are pregnant or breast-feeding.

Are there any interactions with medications?

It is not known if cade oil interacts with any medicines.
Before taking cade oil, talk with your healthcare professional if you take any medications.

CAFFEINE

What other names is the product known by?
1,3,7-trimethylxanthine, Anhydrous Caffeine, Caffeine and Sodium Benzoate, Caffeine Anhydrous, Caffeine Citrate, Citrated Caffeine, Methylxanthine.

What is it?
Caffeine is a chemical. Caffeine containing products include coffee, tea, cola, guarana, mate, and other sources.

Is it Effective?
The effectiveness ratings for **CAFFEINE** are as follows:
Effective for... Headache, including migraine and headache following surgery.
Likely Effective for... Mental alertness.
Possibly Effective for... Improving athletic performance • Preventing dizziness on standing up (orthostatic hypotension) in older people • Delaying the onset of Parkinson's disease • Asthma • Preventing type 2 diabetes when consumed from coffee or tea • Breathing problems in infants • Preventing gallstones • Weight loss when given with other drugs • Headache after epidural anesthesia.
Possibly Ineffective for... Treating attention deficit-hyperactivity disorder (ADHD) in children.
Insufficient Evidence to Rate Effectiveness for... Skin irritation, redness, and itching; improvement of exercise endurance; overdose; and other conditions.

How does it work?
Caffeine works by stimulating the central nervous system (CNS), heart, and muscles. Caffeine also seems to improve the effectiveness of pain-relievers such as acetaminophen (Tylenol) and aspirin. Caffeine also works as a "water pill" to promote fluid loss.

Are there safety concerns?
Caffeine is safe for most adults. Caffeine can cause insomnia, nervousness and restlessness, stomach irritation, nausea and vomiting, increased heart rate and respiration, and other side effects. Caffeine can make sleep disorders in patients with acquired immunodeficiency syndrome (AIDS) worse. Larger doses might cause headache, anxiety, agitation, chest pain, and ringing in the ears. Large doses may be UNSAFE and can cause irregular heartbeats and even death. Weight-loss products that contain bitter orange (and formerly ephedra, before the FDA removed it from the market) in combination with caffeine can further increase the risk of serious adverse effects such as heart attack and stroke.

Caffeine is probably safe in pregnant or breast-feeding women in daily amounts of less than 200 mg. This is about the amount in 1-2 cups of coffee.

Caffeine is also probably safe in children in amounts commonly found in foods.

Do not take caffeine if: You have a heart condition. • You have diabetes. • You have anxiety. • You have a condition called bipolar disorder. • You have an eye disease called glaucoma. • You have high blood pressure. • You have osteoporosis. • You have a bleeding condition.

Are there any interactions with medications?
Adenosine (Adenocard). Caffeine might block the effects of adenosine (Adenocard). Adenosine (Adenocard) is often used by doctors to do a test on the heart. This test is called a cardiac stress test. Stop consuming caffeine-containing products at least 24 hours before a cardiac stress test.
Alcohol. The body breaks down caffeine to get rid of it. Alcohol can decrease how quickly the body breaks down caffeine. Taking caffeine along with alcohol might cause too much caffeine in the bloodstream and caffeine side effects including jitteriness, headache, and fast heartbeat.
Antibiotics (Quinolone antibiotics). The body breaks down caffeine to get rid of it. Some antibiotics might decrease how quickly the body breaks down caffeine. Taking these antibiotics along with caffeine can increase the risk of side effects including jitteriness, headache, increased heart rate, and other side effects. Some antibiotics that decrease how quickly the body breaks down caffeine include ciprofloxacin (Cipro), enoxacin (Penetrex), norfloxacin (Chibroxin, Noroxin), sparfloxacin (Zagam), trovafloxacin (Trovan), and grepafloxacin (Raxar).
Birth control pills (Contraceptive drugs). The body breaks down caffeine to get rid of it. Birth control pills can decrease how quickly the body breaks down caffeine. Taking caffeine along with birth control pills can cause jitteriness, headache, fast heartbeat, and other side effects. Some birth control pills include ethinyl estradiol and levonorgestrel (Triphasil), ethinyl estradiol and norethindrone (Ortho-Novum 1/35, Ortho-Novum 7/7/7), and others.
Cimetidine (Tagamet). The body breaks down caffeine to get rid of it. Cimetidine (Tagamet) can decrease how quickly your body breaks down caffeine. Taking cimetidine (Tagamet) along with caffeine might

Medical professionals should consult the Professional Version at www.NaturalDatabase.com.

CONSUMER VERSION

increase the chance of caffeine side effects including jitteriness, headache, fast heartbeat, and others.

Clozapine (Clozaril). The body breaks down clozapine (Clozaril) to get rid of it. Caffeine seems to decrease how quickly the body breaks down clozapine (Clozaril). Taking caffeine along with clozapine (Clozaril) can increase the effects and side effects of clozapine (Clozaril).

Dipyridamole (Persantine). Caffeine might block the affects of dipyridamole (Persantine). Dipyridamole (Persantine) is often used by doctors to do a test on the heart. This test is called a cardiac stress test. Stop consuming caffeine-containing products at least 24 hours before a cardiac stress test.

Disulfiram (Antabuse). The body breaks down caffeine to get rid of it. Disulfiram (Antabuse) can decrease how quickly the body gets rid of caffeine. Taking caffeine along with disulfiram (Antabuse) might increase the effects and side effects of caffeine including jitteriness, hyperactivity, irritability, and others.

Ephedrine. Stimulant drugs speed up the nervous system. Caffeine and ephedrine are both stimulant drugs. Taking caffeine along with ephedrine might cause too much stimulation and sometimes serious side effects and heart problems. Do not take caffeine-containing products and ephedrine at the same time.

Estrogens. The body breaks down caffeine to get rid of it. Estrogens can decrease how quickly the body breaks down caffeine. Taking caffeine along with estrogens might cause jitteriness, headache, fast heartbeat, and other side effects. If you take estrogens limit your caffeine intake. Some estrogen pills include conjugated equine estrogens (Premarin), ethinyl estradiol, estradiol, and others.

Fluconazole (Diflucan). The body breaks down caffeine to get rid of it. Fluconazole (Diflucan) might decrease how quickly the body gets rid of caffeine. Taking caffeine along with fluconazole (Diflucan) might cause caffeine to stay in to body too long and increase the risk of side effects such as nervousness, anxiety, and insomnia.

Fluvoxamine (Luvox). The body breaks down caffeine to get rid of it. Fluvoxamine (Luvox) can decrease how quickly the body breaks down caffeine. Taking caffeine along with fluvoxamine (Luvox) might cause too much caffeine in the body, and increase the effects and side effects of caffeine.

Lithium. You body naturally gets rid of lithium. Caffeine can increase how quickly your body gets rid of lithium. If you take products that contain caffeine and you take lithium, stop taking caffeine products slowly. Stopping caffeine too quickly can increase the side effects of lithium.

Medications that slow blood clotting (Anticoagulant / Antiplatelet drugs). Caffeine might slow blood clotting. Taking caffeine along with medications that also slow clotting might increase the chances of bruising and bleeding. Some medications that slow blood clotting include aspirin, clopidogrel (Plavix), diclofenac (Voltaren, Cataflam, others), ibuprofen (Advil, Motrin, others), naproxen (Anaprox, Naprosyn, others), dalteparin (Fragmin), enoxaparin (Lovenox), heparin, warfarin (Coumadin), and others.

Medications for diabetes (Antidiabetes drugs). Caffeine might increase blood sugar. Diabetes medications are used to lower blood sugar. Taking some medications for diabetes along with caffeine might decrease the effectiveness of diabetes medications. Monitor your blood sugar closely. The dose of your diabetes medication might need to be changed. Some medications used for diabetes include glimepiride (Amaryl), glyburide (DiaBeta, Glynase PresTab, Micronase), insulin, pioglitazone (Actos), rosiglitazone (Avandia), chlorpropamide (Diabinese), glipizide (Glucotrol), tolbutamide (Orinase), and others.

Medications for depression (MAOIs). Caffeine can stimulate the body. Some medications used for depression can also stimulate the body. Taking caffeine along with some medications for depression might cause serious side effects including fast heartbeat, high blood pressure, nervousness, and others. Some of these medications used for depression include phenelzine (Nardil), tranylcypromine (Parnate), and others.

Mexiletine (Mexitil). The body breaks down caffeine to get rid of it. Mexiletine (Mexitil) can decrease how quickly the body breaks down caffeine. Taking Mexiletine (Mexitil) along with caffeine might increase the effects and side effects of caffeine.

Phenylpropanolamine. Caffeine can stimulate the body. Phenylpropanolamine can also stimulate the body. Taking caffeine along with phenylpropanolamine might cause too much stimulation and increase heartbeat, blood pressure, and cause nervousness.

Pentobarbital (Nembutal). The stimulant effects of caffeine can block the sleep-producing effects of pentobarbital.

Riluzole (Rilutek). The body breaks down riluzole (Rilutek) to get rid of it. Taking caffeine along with riluzole (Rilutek) might decrease how fast the body breaks down riluzole (Rilutek) and increase the effects and side effects of riluzole (Rilutek).

Stimulant drugs. Stimulant drugs speed up the nervous system. By speeding up the nervous system, stimulant medications can make you feel jittery and speed up your heart rate. Caffeine might also speed up the nervous system. Taking caffeine along with stimulant drugs might cause serious problems including increased heart rate and high blood pressure. Avoid taking stimulant drugs along with caffeine. Some stimulant drugs include diethylpropion (Tenuate), epinephrine, phentermine (Ionamin), pseudoephedrine (Sudafed), and many others.

Terbinafine (Lamisil). The body breaks down caffeine to get rid of it. Terbinafine (Lamisil) can decrease how fast the body gets rid of caffeine. Taking caffeine along with terbinafine (Lamisil) can increase the risk of caffeine side effects including jitteriness, headache, increased heartbeat, and other effects.

Theophylline. Caffeine works similarly to theophylline. Caffeine can also decrease how quickly the body gets rid of theophylline. Taking theophylline along with caffeine might increase the effects and side effects of theophylline.

Verapamil (Calan, Covera, Isoptin, Verelan). The body breaks down caffeine to get rid of it. Verapamil (Calan,

Covera, Isoptin, Verelan) can decrease how quickly the body gets rid of caffeine. Taking caffeine along with verapamil (Calan, Covera, Isoptin, Verelan) can increase the risk of side effects for caffeine including jitteriness, headache, and an increased heartbeat.

CAJEPUT OIL

What other names is the product known by?
Cajeputi Aetheroleum, Cajuput, Melaleuca leucodendra, Melaleuca leucodendron, Melaleuca quinquenervia, Paperbark Tree Oil, Punk Tree.

What is it?
Cajeput is a plant. People use the oil made from the leaves and twigs for medicine.

Is it Effective?
The effectiveness ratings for **CAJEPUT OIL** are as follows:
Insufficient Evidence to Rate Effectiveness for... Toothache, colds, headaches, tumors, use as a tonic, thinning mucous (congestion) and making it easier to cough up, arthritis and rheumatism, and other uses.

How does it work?
Cajeput oil contains a chemical called cineole. When applied to the skin, cineole can cause surface warmth and irritation, which relieves pain beneath the skin.

Are there safety concerns?
Low concentrations of cajeput oil might to be safe for most people when applied in medicinal amounts to unbroken skin, but it can cause allergic reactions. It should not be inhaled or applied to the faces of children because it can cause serious breathing problems.
Very small amounts of cajeput oil are likely safe when added to food as flavoring, but the concentrated oil is unsafe when taken by mouth.
Do not take cajeput oil if: You are pregnant or breast-feeding. • You have asthma.

Are there any interactions with medications?
It is not known if cajeput oil interacts with any medicines.
Before taking cajeput oil, talk with your healthcare professional if you take any medications.

CALABAR BEAN

What other names is the product known by?
Chop Nut, Esere Nut, Faba Calabarica, Ordeal Bean, Physotigma, Physostigma venenosum.

What is it?
Calabar is a plant. The bean is used for medicines.

Is it Effective?
The effectiveness ratings for **CALABAR BEAN** are as follows:
Insufficient Evidence to Rate Effectiveness for... Eye problems, reversing anesthesia, treating poisonings, constipation, epilepsy, cholera, and tetanus.

How does it work?
Calabar bean contains a chemical that affects signals between muscles and nerves. This chemical affects many parts of the body.

Are there safety concerns?
Calabar bean is UNSAFE.

Calabar bean can cause excessive saliva and sweating, small pupils of the eye, nausea, vomiting, diarrhea, irregular heartbeat, blood pressure changes, confusion, seizures, coma, severe muscle weakness, paralysis, and death.

Do not take calabar bean if: You are pregnant or breast-feeding. • You have Parkinson's disease. • You have heart disease or slow heartbeat. • You have asthma. • You have diabetes. • You have blockage of the intestinal tract. • You have blockage of the urinary tract.

Medical professionals should consult the Professional Version at www.NaturalDatabase.com.

Are there any interactions with medications?

Drying medications (Anticholinergic drugs). Calabar bean contains chemicals that can affect the brain and heart. Some of these drying medications called anticholinergic drugs can also affect the brain and heart. But calabar bean works differently than drying medications. Calabar bean might decrease the effects of drying medications. Some of these drying medications include atropine, scopolamine, and some medications used for allergies (antihistamines), and for depression (antidepressants).

CALAMINT

What other names is the product known by?

Basil Thyme, Lesser Calamint, Calamintha nepeta, Mill Mint, Mountain Balm, Mountain Mint.

What is it?

Calamint is a plant. The above ground parts are used to make medicine.

Is it Effective?

The effectiveness ratings for **CALAMINT** are as follows:
Insufficient Evidence to Rate Effectiveness for... Colds, fever, breathing problems, and chest congestion.

How does it work?

There isn't enough information to know how calamint works.

Are there safety concerns?

There isn't enough information to know if calamint is safe.

Do not use calamint if: You are pregnant or breast-feeding.

Are there any interactions with medications?

It is not known if calamint interacts with any medicines.
Before taking calamint, talk with your healthcare professional if you take any medications.

CALAMUS

What other names is the product known by?

Acorus americanus, Acorus calamus, Acorus gramineus, Acorus sp., Bach, Cinnamon Sedge, Flagroot, Gladdon, Grass Myrtle, Kalmus, Myrtle Flag, Myrtle Sedge, Sadgrantha, Sweet Cane, Sweet Cinnamon, Sweet Calamus, Sweet Flag, Sweet Grass, Sweet Myrtle, Sweet Root, Sweet Rush, Sweet Sedge, Ugragandha, Vacha, Vayambur.

What is it?

Calamus is a plant. The root-like part is used to make medicine.

Is it Effective?

The effectiveness ratings for **CALAMUS** are as follows:
Insufficient Evidence to Rate Effectiveness for... Ulcers, gas, upset stomach, appetite stimulation, arthritis, strokes, and skin disorders.

How does it work?

It is thought that chemicals in calamus cause muscle relaxation and sedation.

Are there safety concerns?

Calamus is not safe when taken by mouth. It can cause kidney damage, shaking, and seizures.

Do not take calamus if: You are pregnant or breast-feeding.

Are there any interactions with medications?

Antacids. Antacids are used to decrease stomach acid. Calamus may increase stomach acid. By increasing stomach acid, calamus might decrease the effectiveness of antacids. Some antacids include calcium carbonate (Tums, others), dihydroxyaluminum sodium carbonate (Rolaids, others), magaldrate (Riopan), magnesium sulfate (Bilagog), aluminum hydroxide (Amphojel), and others.
Medications that decrease stomach acid (H2-Blockers). Calamus might increase stomach acid. By increasing stomach acid, calamus might decrease the effectiveness of some medications that decrease stomach acid, called

H2-Blockers. Some medications that decrease stomach acid include cimetidine (Tagamet), ranitidine (Zantac), nizatidine (Axid), and famotidine (Pepcid).

Medications that decrease stomach acid (Proton pump inhibitors). Calamus might increase stomach acid. By increasing stomach acid, calamus might decrease the effectiveness of medications that are used to decrease stomach acid, called proton pump inhibitors. Some medications that decrease stomach acid include omeprazole (Prilosec), lansoprazole (Prevacid), rabeprazole (Aciphex), pantoprazole (Protonix), and esomeprazole (Nexium).

Medications for depression (MAOIs). Calamus contains a chemical that affects the body. This chemical might increase the side effects of some medications used for depression. Some of these medications used for depression include phenelzine (Nardil), tranylcypromine (Parnate), and others.

Sedative medications (CNS depressants). Calamus might cause sleepiness and drowsiness. Medications that cause sleepiness are called sedatives. Taking calamus along with sedative medications might cause too much sleepiness. Some sedative medications include clonazepam (Klonopin), lorazepam (Ativan), Phenobarbital (Donnatal), zolpidem (Ambien), and others.

CALCIUM

What other names is the product known by?
Bone Meal, Calcium Acetate, Calcium Aspartate, Calcium Carbonate, Calcium Chelate, Calcium Chloride, Calcium Citrate, Calcium Citrate Malate, Calcium Gluconate, Calcium Lactate, Calcium Lactogluconate, Calcium Orotate, Calcium Phosphate, Dicalcium Phosphate, Di-calcium Phosphate, Heated Oyster Shell-Seaweed Calcium, Hydroxyapatite, Oyster Shell Calcium, Tricalcium Phosphate.

What is it?
Calcium is a mineral that is an essential part of bones and teeth. The heart, nerves, and blood clotting systems also need calcium to work.

Is it Effective?
The effectiveness ratings for **CALCIUM** are as follows:

Effective for... Raising calcium levels in people who have low calcium • Preventing low calcium levels • Use as an antacid as calcium carbonate • Reducing phosphate levels in people with kidney disease.

Likely Effective for... Preventing bone loss caused by insufficient calcium in the diet. This can reduce the risk of breaking bones • Reducing bone loss in people taking drugs called corticosteroids • Treating osteoporosis (weak bones) • Reducing symptoms of premenstrual syndrome (PMS), especially mood swings, bloating, food cravings, and pain • Increasing fetal bone density in pregnant women with low calcium intake • Reducing thyroid hormone levels in people with kidney failure.

Possibly Effective for... Lowering high blood pressure • Reducing tooth loss in elderly people • Reducing pregnancy-related leg cramps • Reducing cholesterol when used with a low fat diet • Preventing fluoride poisoning in children when taken with vitamin C and D • Preventing stroke • Reducing weight and body fat while dieting.

Possibly Ineffective for... Reducing lead levels in breast-feeding women.

Insufficient Evidence to Rate Effectiveness for... Colorectal cancer, preventing seizures, preventing falls, metabolic syndrome, diabetes, Lyme disease, and other conditions.

How does it work?
Bones are always breaking down and rebuilding, and calcium is needed for this process. Taking extra calcium helps the bones rebuild properly and stay strong.

Are there safety concerns?
Calcium seems to be safe for most people. Calcium can cause some minor side effects such as belching or gas. Taking too much calcium (over 2500 mg/day) might increase the risk of side effects.

Some people shouldn't take calcium unless it is prescribed by their healthcare provider. Calcium should be avoided or used carefully in people who have conditions that cause too much calcium in the blood, such as parathyroid gland disorders and sarcoidosis.

Are there any interactions with medications?
Antibiotics (Quinolone antibiotics). Calcium might decrease how much antibiotic your body absorbs. Taking calcium along with some antibiotics might decrease the effectiveness of some antibiotics. To avoid this interaction, take calcium supplements at least 1 hour after antibiotics. Some of these antibiotics that might interact with calcium include ciprofloxacin (Cipro), enoxacin (Penetrex), norfloxacin (Chibroxin, Noroxin), sparfloxacin (Zagam), and trovafloxacin (Trovan).

Antibiotics (Tetracycline antibiotics). Calcium can attach to some antibiotics called tetracyclines in the stomach. This decreases the amount of tetracyclines that can be absorbed. Taking calcium with tetracyclines might decrease the effectiveness of tetracyclines. To avoid this interaction take calcium 2 hours before or 4 hours after taking tetracyclines. Some tetracyclines include demeclocycline (Declomycin), minocycline (Minocin), and tetracycline (Achromycin, and others).

Bisphosphonates. Calcium can decrease how much bisphosphate your body absorbs. Taking calcium along with bisphosphates can decrease the effectiveness of bisphosphate. To avoid this interaction, take bisphosphonate at least 30 minutes before calcium or later in the day. Some bisphosphonates include alendronate (Fosamax), etidronate (Didronel), risedronate (Actonel), tiludronate (Skelid), and others.

Calcipotriene (Dovonex). Calcipotriene (Dovonex) is a drug that is similar to vitamin D. Vitamin D helps your body absorb calcium. Taking calcium supplements along with calcipotriene (Dovonex) might cause the body to have too much calcium.

Digoxin (Lanoxin). Calcium can affect your heart. Digoxin (Lanoxin) is used to help your heart beat stronger. Taking calcium along with digoxin (Lanoxin) might increase the effects of digoxin (Lanoxin) and lead to an irregular heartbeat. If you are taking digoxin (Lanoxin), talk to your doctor before taking calcium supplements.

Diltiazem (Cardizem, Dilacor, Tiazac). Calcium can affect your heart. Diltiazem (Cardizem, Dilacor, Tiazac) can also affect your heart. Taking large amounts of calcium along with diltiazem (Cardizem, Dilacor, Tiazac) might decrease the effectiveness of diltiazem (Cardizem, Dilacor, Tiazac).

Estrogens. Estrogen helps your body absorb calcium. Taking estrogen pills along with large amounts of calcium might increase calcium in the body too much. Estrogen pills include conjugated equine estrogens (Premarin), ethinyl estradiol, estradiol, and others.

Levothyroxine. Levothyroxine is used for low thyroid function. Calcium can decrease how much levothyroxine your body absorbs. Taking calcium along with levothyroxine might decrease the effectiveness of levothyroxine. Levothyroxine and calcium should be taken at least 4 hours apart. Some brands that contain levothyroxine include Armour Thyroid, Eltroxin, Estre, Euthyrox, Levo-T, Levothroid, Levoxyl, Synthroid, Unithroid, and others.

Medications for high blood pressure (Calcium channel blockers). Some medications for high blood pressure affect calcium in your body. These medications are called calcium channel blockers. Getting calcium injections might decrease the effectiveness of these medications for high blood pressure. Some medications for high blood pressure include nifedipine (Adalat, Procardia), verapamil (Calan, Isoptin, Verelan), diltiazem (Cardizem), isradipine (DynaCirc), felodipine (Plendil), amlodipine (Norvasc), and others.

Sotalol (Betapace). Taking calcium with sotalol (Betapace) can decrease how much sotalol (Betapace) your body absorbs. Taking calcium along with sotalol (Betapace) might decrease the effectiveness of sotalol (Betapace). To avoid this interaction, take calcium at least 2 hours before or 4 hours after taking sotalol (Betapace).

Water pills (Thiazide diuretics). Some water pills increase the amount of calcium in your body. Taking large amounts of calcium with some water pills might cause there to be too much calcium in the body. This could cause serious side effects, including kidney problems. Some of these water pills include chlorothiazide (Diuril), hydrochlorothiazide (HydroDIURIL, Esidrix), indapamide (Lozol), metolazone (Zaroxolyn), and chlorthalidone (Hygroton).

Verapamil (Calan, Covera, Isoptin, Verelan). Calcium can affect your heart. Verapamil (Calan, Covera, Isoptin, Verelan) can also affect your heart. Do not take large amounts of calcium if you are taking verapamil (Calan, Covera, Isoptin, Verelan).

CALCIUM D-GLUCARATE

What other names is the product known by?

Calcium Glucarate, D-Glucarate (GA).

What is it?

Calcium D-glucarate is a chemical. It is similar to a naturally occurring chemical called glucaric acid. Glucaric acid is found in our bodies as well as in fruits and vegetables such as oranges, apples, brussels sprouts, broccoli, and cabbage. Calcium D-glucarate is made by combining glucaric acid with calcium to make supplements which people use for medicine.

Is it Effective?

The effectiveness ratings for **CALCIUM D-GLUCARATE** are as follows:

Insufficient Evidence to Rate Effectiveness for... Preventing breast, prostate, and colon cancer; and for detoxifying the body of carcinogens, toxins, and steroid hormones.

How does it work?

Calcium D-glucarate might lower estrogen levels, which is thought to be helpful in some people with hormone-dependent cancers. There isn't enough evidence to support the use of calcium D-glucarate for preventing cancer in humans.

 (209) 472-2244

Are there safety concerns?

There isn't not enough information to know if calcium D-glucarate is safe or what the potential side effects might be.

Do not take calcium D-glucarate if: You are pregnant or breast-feeding.

Are there any interactions with medications?

Alcohol. The body breaks down calcium D-glucarate to get rid of it. Alcohol might increase how fast the body gets rid of calcium D-glucarate. By increasing how fast the body gets rid of calcium D-glucarate, alcohol might decrease the effectiveness of calcium D-glucarate.

Kanamycin. Kanamycin is an antibiotic. The body breaks down kanamycin to get rid of it. Calcium D-glucarate might increase how quickly the body gets rid of kanamycin. Taking calcium-D-glucarate along with kanamycin might decrease the effectiveness of kanamycin.

Medications changed by the liver (Glucuronidated drugs). The body breaks down some medications to get rid of them. The liver helps break down these medications. Calcium D-glucarate might increase how quickly some medications are broken down by the liver. Taking calcium-D glucarate along with medications changed by the liver might decrease the effectiveness of these medications. Some of these medications changed by the liver include acetaminophen (Tylenol, others), atorvastatin (Lipitor), diazepam (Valium), digoxin, entacapone (Comtan), estrogen, irinotecan (Camptosar), lamotrigine (Lamictal), lorazepam (Ativan), lovastatin (Mevacor), meprobamate, morphine, oxazepam (Serax), and others.

CALENDULA

What other names is the product known by?

Calendula officinalis, Garden Marigold, Gold-Bloom, Holligold, Marigold, Marybud, Pot Marigold, Zergul.

What is it?

Calendula is a plant. The flower is used to make medicine.

Is it Effective?

The effectiveness ratings for **CALENDULA** are as follows:
Insufficient Evidence to Rate Effectiveness for... Muscle spasms, fever, cancer, nosebleeds, varicose veins, hemorrhoids, promoting menstruation, treating mouth and throat soreness, wounds, leg ulcers, and other conditions.

How does it work?

It is thought that the chemicals in calendula help new tissue to grow in wounds and decrease swelling in the mouth and throat.

Are there safety concerns?

Calendula seems to be safe for most people.

Calendula can cause an allergic reaction in individuals allergic to ragweed, chrysanthemums, marigolds, daisies, and many other herbs.

Do not take calendula if: You are pregnant or breast-feeding. • You are allergic to ragweed, chrysanthemums, marigolds, or daisies.

Are there any interactions with medications?

Sedative medications (CNS depressants). Calendula might cause sleepiness and drowsiness. Medications that cause sleepiness are called sedatives. Taking calendula along with sedative medications might cause too much sleepiness. Some sedative medications include clonazepam (Klonopin), lorazepam (Ativan), Phenobarbital (Donnatal), zolpidem (Ambien), and others.

CALIFORNIA POPPY

What other names is the product known by?

Eschscholzia californica, Eschscholtzia californica, Poppy California, Yellow Poppy.

What is it?

California poppy is a plant. People use the dried above ground parts for medicine.

Is it Effective?

The effectiveness ratings for **CALIFORNIA POPPY** are as follows:

Insufficient Evidence to Rate Effectiveness for... Anxiety, trouble sleeping (insomnia), aches, bedwetting, diseases of the bladder and liver, and other conditions.

How does it work?

California poppy contains chemicals which might have sedative effects.

Are there safety concerns?

California poppy appears to be safe for most people when taken appropriately by mouth for three months or less. There isn't enough information to know if California poppy is safe for long-term use.

Do not take California poppy if: You are pregnant or breast-feeding.

Are there any interactions with medications?

Sedative medications (CNS depressants). California poppy might cause sleepiness and drowsiness. Medications that cause sleepiness are called sedatives. Taking California poppy along with sedative medications might cause too much sleepiness. Some sedative medications include clonazepam (Klonopin), lorazepam (Ativan), phenobarbital (Donnatal), zolpidem (Ambien), and others.

Sedative medications (Benzodiazepines). California poppy might cause sleepiness and drowsiness. Drugs that cause sleepiness and drowsiness are called sedatives. Taking California poppy along with sedative medications might cause too much sleepiness. Some of these sedative medications include clonazepam (Klonopin), diazepam (Valium), lorazepam (Ativan), and others.

CALOTROPIS

What other names is the product known by?

Calotropis procera, Ak, Akada, Alarka, Arka, Mudar Bark, Muder Yercum, Sodom-Apple.

What is it?

Calotropis is a plant. People use the bark and root bark for medicine.

Is it Effective?

The effectiveness ratings for **CALOTROPIS** are as follows:

Insufficient Evidence to Rate Effectiveness for... Toothache, syphilis, cough, asthma, digestive disorders, diarrhea, boils, cancer, inflammation, joint pain, ulcers, and other conditions.

How does it work?

Calotropis contains chemicals that might help thin mucous and make it easier to cough up. In studies in animals, calotropis has shown some activity against pain, inflammation, bacteria, fever, and ulcers caused by alcohol and medications such as aspirin, indomethacin (Indocin), and others.

Are there safety concerns?

Calotropis is UNSAFE. It contains chemicals that can interfere with heart function, particularly at high doses. It can cause serious side effects including vomiting, diarrhea, slow heartbeat, convulsions, and death.

Do not take calotropis if: You are pregnant or breast-feeding.

Are there any interactions with medications?

Digoxin (Lanoxin). Digoxin (Lanoxin) helps the heart beat more strongly. Calotropis also seems to affect the heart. Taking calotropis along with digoxin can increase the effects of digoxin and increase the risk of side effects. Do not take calotropis if you are taking digoxin (Lanoxin) without talking to your healthcare professional.

Stimulant laxatives. Calotropis can affect the heart. The heart uses potassium. Laxatives called stimulant laxatives can decrease potassium levels in the body. Low potassium levels can increase the chance of side effects from calotropis. Some stimulant laxatives include bisacodyl (Correctol, Dulcolax), cascara, castor oil (Purge), senna (Senokot), and others.

Water pills (Diuretic drugs). Calotropis might affect the heart. "Water pills" can decrease potassium in the body. Low potassium levels can also affect the heart and increase the risk of side effects from calotropis. Some "water pills" that can deplete potassium include chlorothiazide (Diuril), chlorthalidone (Thalitone), furosemide (Lasix), hydrochlorothiazide (HCTZ, HydroDiuril, Microzide), and others.

Medical professionals should consult the Professional Version at www.NaturalDatabase.com.

CAMPHOR

What other names is the product known by?
Camphora, Camphor Tree, Cemphire, Cinnamomum Camphora, Gum Camphor, Karpoora, Laurel Camphor, Laurus camphora.

What is it?
Camphor was formerly obtained by distilling the bark and wood of the camphor tree. Today, camphor is chemically manufactured from turpentine oil. It is used in products such as Vicks VapoRub.

Is it Effective?
The effectiveness ratings for **CAMPHOR** are as follows:
Effective for... Skin itching or irritation, when applied to affected areas • Pain, when applied to the skin over the area of pain • Cough, when applied as a chest rub.
Possibly Effective for... Osteoarthritis, when a cream containing camphor is applied to the skin over the stiff joints.
Insufficient Evidence to Rate Effectiveness for..."Toe nail fungus," warts, hemorrhoids, and other conditions.

How does it work?
Camphor seems to stimulate nerve endings that relieve symptoms such as pain and itching when applied to the skin. Camphor is also active against fungi that cause infections in the toenails.

Are there safety concerns?
Camphor is safe for most adults when applied to the skin in a cream or lotion. Camphor can cause some minor side effects such as skin redness and irritation. Don't use undiluted camphor products or products containing more than 11% camphor. These can be irritating and unsafe. Also, don't apply camphor containing products to broken or injured skin.

Camphor is also safe for most adults when inhaled as vapor in small amounts as a part of aromatherapy. Don't use more than 1 tablespoon camphor solution per quart of water. Do not heat camphor-containing products (Vick's VapoRub, BenGay, Heet, many others) in the microwave. The product can explode and cause severe burns.

Don't take camphor products by mouth. Ingesting camphor can cause severe side effects, including death.

Do not use camphor on children. They tend to be more sensitive to the side effects. Keep camphor-containing products away from children. Seizures and death can occur if these products are eaten.

Do not use camphor if: You are pregnant or breast-feeding.

Are there any interactions with medications?
It is not known if camphor interacts with any medicines.
Before taking camphor, talk with your healthcare professional if you take any medications.

CANADA BALSAM

What other names is the product known by?
Abies balsamea, Balm of Gilead, Balsam Canada, Balsam, Balsam Fir, Balsam Fir Canada, Balsam of Fir, Canada Turpentine, Canadian Balsam, Eastern Fir.

What is it?
Canada balsam is a plant. People use it for medicine.

Is it Effective?
The effectiveness ratings for **CANADA BALSAM** are as follows:
Insufficient Evidence to Rate Effectiveness for... Hemorrhoids, burns, sores, cuts, tumors, chest pains, cancer, inflammation, use in dental products, and other conditions.

How does it work?
There isn't enough information to know how Canada balsam might work.

Are there safety concerns?
Canada balsam might be safe for most people when applied to the skin. Canada balsam needles and twigs are used to make food flavoring, but there isn't enough information to know if it's safe in amounts greater than those

CONSUMER VERSION

Medical professionals should consult the Professional Version at www.NaturalDatabase.com.

typically found in foods. There aren't any known adverse effects of Canada balsam, but it hasn't been well-researched by scientists.

Do not take Canada balsam if: You are pregnant or breast-feeding.

Are there any interactions with medications?
It is not known if Canada balsam interacts with any medicines.
Before taking Canada balsam, talk with your healthcare professional if you take any medications.

CANADIAN FLEABANE

What other names is the product known by?
Butterweed, Canadian Horseweed, Canadian-Fleabane, Canadian Trailing Arbutus, Coltstail, Conyza canadensis, Erigeron canadensis, Flea Wort, Hogweed, Horsewood, Prideweed.

What is it?
Canadian fleabane is a plant. The above ground parts are used for medicine.

Is it Effective?
The effectiveness ratings for **CANADIAN FLEABANE** are as follows:
Insufficient Evidence to Rate Effectiveness for... Bronchitis, diarrhea, dysentery, worms, fever, inflammation, swelling, bleeding from the uterus, sore throat, urinary tract infections (UTIs), and tumors.

How does it work?
There is not enough information about Canadian fleabane to know how it might work.

Are there safety concerns?
It is not known if Canadian fleabane is safe.

Canadian fleabane can cause allergic reactions in people who are allergic to ragweed, chrysanthemums, marigolds, daisies, and other members of the Asteraceae/Compositae plant family.

Do not take Canadian fleabane if: You are pregnant or breast-feeding.

Are there any interactions with medications?
It is not known if Canadian fleabane interacts with any medicines.
Before taking Canadian fleabane, talk with your healthcare professional if you take any medications.

CANADIAN HEMP

What other names is the product known by?
Apocynum cannabinum, Bitter Root, Catchfly, Dogbane, Fly-Trap, Honeybloom, Indian-Hemp, Indian Physic, Milk Ipecac, Milkweed, Wallflower, Wild Cotton.

What is it?
Canadian hemp is an herb. The root is used for medicine.

Is it Effective?
The effectiveness ratings for **CANADIAN HEMP** are as follows:
Insufficient Evidence to Rate Effectiveness for... Warts, heart problems, increasing urine, asthma, coughs, swelling, and syphilis.

How does it work?
Canadian hemp contains chemicals that may slow the heartbeat, lower blood pressure, increase the strength of the heartbeat, and increase urine. It may work similarly to the prescription drug digoxin (Lanoxin), but is less effective and causes more side effects.

Are there safety concerns?
Canadian hemp is UNSAFE because of its effects on the heart and other side effects.
Canadian hemp is irritating to the throat, stomach, and intestines, and can cause nausea and vomiting. It can slow the rate of the heartbeat, which can cause the body to release substances that cause the blood pressure to increase.
Do not take Canadian hemp if: You are pregnant or breast-feeding.

Are there any interactions with medications?

Digoxin (Lanoxin). Digoxin (Lanoxin) helps the heart beat more strongly. Canadian hemp also seems to affect the heart. Taking Canadian hemp along with digoxin can increase the effects of digoxin and increase the risk of side effects. Do not take Canadian hemp if you are taking digoxin (Lanoxin) without talking to your healthcare professional.

Water pills (Diuretic drugs). Canadian hemp might affect the heart. "Water pills" can decrease potassium in the body. Low potassium levels can also affect the heart and increase the risk of side effects from Canadian hemp. Some "water pills" that can deplete potassium include chlorothiazide (Diuril), chlorthalidone (Thalitone), furosemide (Lasix), hydrochlorothiazide (HCTZ, HydroDiuril, Microzide), and others.

CANAIGRE

What other names is the product known by?

Red American Ginseng, Rumex hymenosepalus, Wild Red American Ginseng, Wild Red Desert Ginseng.

What is it?

Canaigre is a plant. The root is used to make medicine.

Is it Effective?

The effectiveness ratings for **CANAIGRE** are as follows:
Insufficient Evidence to Rate Effectiveness for... Improving physical stamina and mental concentration, depression, fluid retention, and soothing irritated skin.

How does it work?

The chemicals in canaigre act as a drying medicine.

Are there safety concerns?

Canaigre seems to be safe for most people, but taking excessive amounts might be unsafe.

Do not take canaigre if: You are pregnant or breast-feeding.

Are there any interactions with medications?

It is not known if canaigre interacts with any medicines.
Before taking canaigre, talk with your healthcare professional if you take any medications.

CANANGA OIL

What other names is the product known by?

Cananga odorata forma. macrophylla, canangium odoratum forma. macrophylla.

What is it?

Cananga is a plant. The distilled oil of the cananga flower is used primarily as an ingredient in foods and cosmetics.

Is it Effective?

The effectiveness ratings for **CANANGA OIL** are as follows:
Insufficient Evidence to Rate Effectiveness for... Any medicinal use.

How does it work?

There isn't enough information to know how cananga oil might work.

Are there safety concerns?

Cananga oil appears to be safe for most people when applied to the skin in concentrations up to 0.8%. Cananga oil can cause allergic skin reactions in sensitive people.

There isn't enough information to know if cananga oil is safe to take by mouth in amounts higher than those typically used for food flavoring.

Do not take cananga oil in amounts exceeding those in foods and cosmetics if: You are pregnant or breast-feeding.

Medical professionals should consult the Professional Version at www.NaturalDatabase.com.

Are there any interactions with medications?

It is not known if cananga oil interacts with any medicines.
Before taking cananga oil, talk with your healthcare professional if you take any medications.

CANELLA

What other names is the product known by?

Barbasco, Curbana, Macambo, Canella alba, Canella winteriana, Laurus winteriana, White Cinnamon, White Wood, Wild Cinnamon, and Winterana canella.

What is it?

Canella is an herb. The ground bark is used as a flavoring for food and as medicine.

Is it Effective?

The effectiveness ratings for **CANELLA** are as follows:
Insufficient Evidence to Rate Effectiveness for... Colds, poor circulation, and other conditions.

How does it work?

Canella might have stimulant, tonic, or antibacterial effects.

Are there safety concerns?

It is not known if canella is safe or what the potential side effects might be.

Do not take canella if: You are pregnant or breast-feeding.

Are there any interactions with medications?

It is not known if canella interacts with any medicines.
Before taking canella, talk with your healthcare professional if you take any medications.

CANTHAXANTHIN

What other names is the product known by?

Canthaxanthine, Carophyll Red, CI Food Orange 8, Colour Index No. 40850, E161, Roxanthin Red 10.

What is it?

Canthaxanthin is a chemical that occurs naturally. It can also be made in a laboratory. People use it for medicine.

Is it Effective?

The effectiveness ratings for **CANTHAXANTHIN** are as follows:
Possibly Effective for... Sensitivity to sunlight (photosensitivity) associated with erythropoietic protoporphyria (EPP), a genetic disorder.
Insufficient Evidence to Rate Effectiveness for... Medication-induced sun sensitivity, itching caused by the sun, artificial sun tanning, and other conditions.

How does it work?

Canthaxanthin is a dye similar to the carotenes in vegetables such as carrots. It deposits in the skin to produce an artificial "tan." It might protect against sun sensitivity through antioxidant activity.

Are there safety concerns?

Canthaxanthin appears to be UNSAFE. It can cause damage to the eyes when taken at doses used for tanning or medicinal uses. At high doses, it has caused a serious, potentially fatal blood disorder called aplastic anemia. It can also cause diarrhea, nausea, stomach cramps, dry and itchy skin, hives, orange or red body secretions, and other side effects.

Do not take canthaxanthin if: You are pregnant or breast-feeding. • You are allergic to vitamin A or carotenoids.

Are there any interactions with medications?

It is not known if canthaxanthin interacts with any medicines.
Before taking canthaxanthin, talk with your healthcare professional if you take any medications.

CAPERS

What other names is the product known by?
Capparis spinosa, Cabra, Cappero, Himsra.

What is it?
The caper is a plant. The unopened flower bud and above ground parts are used for medicine.

Is it Effective?
The effectiveness ratings for **CAPERS** are as follows:
Insufficient Evidence to Rate Effectiveness for... Diabetes, skin disorders, improving the function of enlarged capillaries, and dry skin.

How does it work?
Capers contain chemicals that might help control blood sugar. It might also have antioxidant activity.

Are there safety concerns?
Capers are safe for most people when eaten as a food. There is not enough information available to know if capers are safe in medicinal doses.
Capers can cause skin rash and irritation.

Do not use capers if: You are pregnant or breast-feeding.

Are there any interactions with medications?
Medications for diabetes (Antidiabetes drugs). Capers might decrease blood sugar. Diabetes medications are also used to lower blood sugar. Taking capers along with diabetes medications might cause your blood sugar to go too low. Monitor your blood sugar closely. The dose of your diabetes medication might need to be changed. Some medications used for diabetes include glimepiride (Amaryl), glyburide (DiaBeta, Glynase PresTab, Micronase), insulin, pioglitazone (Actos), rosiglitazone (Avandia), chlorpropamide (Diabinese), glipizide (Glucotrol), tolbutamide (Orinase), and others.

CAPSICUM

What other names is the product known by?
African Chillies, African Pepper, Bird Pepper, Capsaicin, Capsicum annuum, Capsicum baccatum, Capsicum chinense, Capsicum frutescens, Capsicum pubscens, Cayenne, Chili Pepper, Cis-capsaicin, Garden Pepper, Goat's Pod, Grains Of Paradise, Green Chili Pepper, Green Pepper, Hot Pepper, Hungarian Pepper, Ici Fructus, Katuvira, Louisiana Long Pepper, Louisiana Sport Pepper, Mexican Chilies, Mirchi, Oleoresin capsicum, Paprika, Pimento, Red Pepper, Sweet Pepper, Tabasco Pepper, trans-capsaicin, Zanzibar Pepper, Zucapsaicin.

What is it?
Capsicum is an herb. The fruit of the capsicum plant is used to make medicine.

Is it Effective?
The effectiveness ratings for **CAPSICUM** are as follows:
Likely Effective for... Arthritis pain when applied to the skin • Pain from shingles when applied to the skin • Nerve pain (neuropathy) in people with diabetes when applied to the skin.
Possibly Effective for... Reducing painful tender points in people with fibromyalgia when applied to the skin • Relieving symptoms of prurigo nodularis, a skin disease • Cluster headache, when used nasally.
Possibly Ineffective for... Nerve pain related to HIV or AIDS when applied to the skin.
Insufficient Evidence to Rate Effectiveness for... Colic, cramps, toothache, blood clots, fever, nausea, high cholesterol, heart disease, stomach ulcers, heartburn, irritable bowel syndrome, migraine headache, allergic rhinitis, perennial rhinitis, nasal polyps, muscle spasms, laryngitis, swallowing dysfunction, and other conditions.

How does it work?
The fruit of the capsicum plant contains a chemical called capsaicin. Capsaicin seems to reduce pain sensations when applied to the skin.

Are there safety concerns?
Capsicum extract-containing lotion or cream is safe for most adults when applied to the skin. Side effects can include skin irritation, burning, and itching. Capsicum can also be extremely irritating to the eyes, nose, and throat. Don't use capsicum on sensitive skin or around the eyes.

Medical professionals should consult the Professional Version at www.NaturalDatabase.com.

Capsicum extract seems to be safe for most adults when taken by mouth, short-term. Side effects can include stomach irritation and upset, sweating, flushing, and runny nose. Don't take capsicum by mouth in large doses or for long periods of time. In rare cases, this can lead to more serious side effects like liver or kidney damage.

Capsicum extract seems to be safe when used nasally. No serious side effects have been reported, but application in the nose can be very painful. Nasal application can cause burning pain, sneezing, watery eyes, and runny nose.

These side effects tend to decrease and go away after 5 or more days of repeated use.

Do not apply capsicum cream or lotion to children under two years old.

Do not apply capsicum to the skin if: You have a pepper allergy. • You have damaged or broken skin.

Do not take capsicum by mouth if: You are pregnant or breast-feeding. • You have a pepper allergy.

Are there any interactions with medications?

Cocaine. Cocaine has many dangerous side effects. Using capsicum along with cocaine might increase the side effects of cocaine including heart attack and death.

Medications that slow blood clotting (Anticoagulant / Antiplatelet drugs). Capsicum might slow blood clotting. Taking capsicum along with medications that also slow clotting might increase the chances of bruising and bleeding. Some medications that slow blood clotting include aspirin, clopidogrel (Plavix), diclofenac (Voltaren, Cataflam, others), ibuprofen (Advil, Motrin, others), naproxen (Anaprox, Naprosyn, others), dalteparin (Fragmin), enoxaparin (Lovenox), heparin, warfarin (Coumadin), and others.

Medications for high blood pressure (ACE inhibitors). Some medications for high blood pressure might cause a cough. There is one report of someone whose cough worsened when using a cream with capsicum along with these medications for high blood pressure. But is it not clear if this interaction is a big concern. Some medications for high blood pressure include captopril (Capoten), enalapril (Vasotec), lisinopril (Prinivil, Zestril), ramipril (Altace), and others.

Theophylline. Capsicum can increase how much theophylline the body can absorb. Taking capsicum along with theophylline might increase the effects and side effects of theophylline.

CARAWAY

What other names is the product known by?

Anis des Vosges, Apium carvi, Carvi Fructus, Cumin des Pres, Haravi, Krishan Jeeraka, Krishnajiraka, Kummel, Kummich, Roman Cumin, Semen Cumini Pratensis, Semences de Carvi, Wiesen-Feldkummel, Wild Cumin.

What is it?

Caraway is a plant. People use the oil, fruit, and seeds as medicine.

Is it Effective?

The effectiveness ratings for **CARAWAY** are as follows:

Possibly Effective for... Stomach upset, when used in combination with other herbs.

Insufficient Evidence to Rate Effectiveness for... Indigestion. appetite stimulation, increasing digestive juices, constipation, gas, bloating, spasms of stomach and intestines, infection, inducing menstruation, relieving menstrual cramps, increasing milk flow in nursing mothers, improving blood flow, and other conditions.

How does it work?

Caraway oil might improve digestion and relieve spasms in the stomach and intestines.

Are there safety concerns?

Caraway seems to be safe for most people. The oil can cause belching, heartburn, and nausea when used with peppermint oil. It can cause skin rashes and itching in sensitive people when applied to the skin.

Do not take caraway if: You are pregnant or breast-feeding.

Are there any interactions with medications?

Medications for diabetes (Antidiabetes drugs). Caraway might decrease blood sugar. Diabetes medications are also used to lower blood sugar. Taking caraway along with diabetes medications might cause your blood sugar to go too low. Monitor your blood sugar closely. The dose of your diabetes medication might need to be changed. Some medications used for diabetes include glimepiride (Amaryl), glyburide (DiaBeta, Glynase PresTab, Micronase), insulin, pioglitazone (Actos), rosiglitazone (Avandia), chlorpropamide (Diabinese), glipizide (Glucotrol), tolbutamide (Orinase), and others. Before taking caraway, talk with your healthcare professional if you take any medications.

CARDAMOM

What other names is the product known by?
Amomum cardamomum, Bai Dou Kou, Cardamon, Cardomomi Fructus, Ela, Elettaria cardamomum.

What is it?
Cardamom is an herb. The seeds are used to make medicine.

Is it Effective?
The effectiveness ratings for **CARDAMOM** are as follows:
Insufficient Evidence to Rate Effectiveness for... Intestinal spasms, heartburn, irritable bowel syndrome (IBS), cold, cough, bronchitis, inflammation of the mouth and throat, liver and gallbladder problems, loss of appetite, preventing infections, gas, constipation, and urinary problems.

How does it work?
Cardamom contains chemicals that appear to treat stomach and intestinal spasms and gas, and increase the movement of food through the intestine.

Are there safety concerns?
Cardamom is safe for most people but the potential side effects of cardamom are not known.

Do not take cardamom in amounts greater than those typically found in food if: You are pregnant or breast-feeding.
• You have gallstones.

Are there any interactions with medications?
It is not known if cardamom interacts with any medicines.
Before taking cardamom, talk with your healthcare professional if you take any medications.

CARLINA

What other names is the product known by?
Carlina acaulis, Carlinae Radix, Dwarf Carline, Eberwurz, Ground Thistle, Racine de Carline Acaule, Radix Cardopatiae, Radix Chamaeleontis Albae, Silberdistelwurz, Stemless Carlina Root, Southernwood Root.

What is it?
Carlina is an herb. The extracts of the roots are used for medicine.

Is it Effective?
The effectiveness ratings for **CARLINA** are as follows:
Insufficient Evidence to Rate Effectiveness for... Gallbladder disease; poor digestion; spasms of the esophagus, stomach, and intestines; skin problems; wounds; cancer of the tongue; herpes; toothache; causing sweating; and use as a diuretic, tonic, or gargle.

How does it work?
Some extracts of carlina might work by killing bacteria.

Are there safety concerns?
There isn't enough information to know if carlina is safe.

Carlina can cause allergic reactions in people who are allergic to ragweed, chrysanthemums, marigolds, daisies, and other members of the Asteraceae/Compositae plant family.

Do not take carlina if: You are pregnant or breast-feeding.

Are there any interactions with medications?
It is not known if carlina interacts with any medicines.
Before taking carlina, talk with your healthcare professional if you take any medications.

CARNOSINE

What other names is the product known by?
B-alanyl-L-histidine, B-alanyl histidine, Beta-alanyl-L-histidine, L-carnosine.

What is it?
Carnosine is a protein building block that is naturally produced in the body.

Is it Effective?
The effectiveness ratings for **CARNOSINE** are as follows:
Insufficient Evidence to Rate Effectiveness for... Preventing or treating complications of diabetes such as nerve damage, eye disorders, and kidney damage.

How does it work?
Carnosine is important for many normal bodily functions including the proper function and development of the muscles, heart, liver, kidneys, brain, and many other organs.

Are there safety concerns?
There isn't enough information available to know if carnosine is safe.

Do not use carnosine if: You are pregnant or breast-feeding.

Are there any interactions with medications?
It is not known if carnosine interacts with any medicines.
Before taking carnosine, talk with your healthcare professional if you take any medications.

CAROB

What other names is the product known by?
Ceratonia siliqua, Locust Bean, Locust Pods, St. John's Bread, Sugar Pods.

What is it?
Carob is an herb. People use the fruit for medicine and in foods.

Is it Effective?
The effectiveness ratings for **CAROB** are as follows:
Insufficient Evidence to Rate Effectiveness for... Nutritional disorders, celiac disease, obesity, diarrhea, heartburn, intestinal inflammation, and vomiting during pregnancy.

How does it work?
Carob contains chemicals called tannins which inhibit digestive enzymes. It might cause weight loss, reduce blood glucose and insulin levels, and lower cholesterol levels.

Are there safety concerns?
Carob is safe for most people. There aren't any known adverse effects of carob.

Do not take carob in amounts greater than those typically found in food if: You are pregnant or breast-feeding. • You are diabetic.

Are there any interactions with medications?
It is not known if carob interacts with any medicines.
Before taking carob talk with your healthcare professional if you take any medications.

CARQUEJA

What other names is the product known by?

Baccharis trimera, Baccharis genistelloides, Baccharis triptera, Baccharis trinervis, Baccharis cylindrica, Baccharis myriocephala, Baccharis milleflora, Baccharis crispa, Baccharis gaudichaudiana, Bqacanta, Cacalia Amara, Caclia Doce, Cacalia-Amarga, Cacalia-Amargosa, Cacliadoce, Carqueja Amara, Carqueja-Amargosa, Carqueja-Do-Mato, Carquejilla, Carquejinha, Chinchimani, Chirca Melosa, Condamina, Cuchi-Cuchi, Quimsa-Kuchu, Quina-De-Condamiana, Quinsu-Cucho, Tiririca-De-Balaio, Tres-Espigas, Vassoura.

What is it?

Carqueja is an herb. People use the dried above ground parts to make medicine.

Is it Effective?

The effectiveness ratings for **CARQUEJA** are as follows:
Insufficient Evidence to Rate Effectiveness for... Protecting the liver, diabetes, heart pain (angina), improving circulation, and other conditions.

How does it work?

Carqueja contains chemicals that might relieve inflammation (swelling) and improve blood flow.

Are there safety concerns?

There is not enough information to know if carqueja is safe. Theoretically, carqueja might cause allergic reactions, especially in people who are allergic to ragweed, mums, marigolds, or daisies. If you have allergies, be sure to check with your healthcare provider before taking carqueja.

Do not take carqueja if: You are pregnant or breast-feeding.

Are there any interactions with medications?

Medications for diabetes (Antidiabetes drugs). Carqueja can decrease blood sugar levels. Diabetes medications are also used to lower blood sugar. Taking carqueja along with diabetes medications might cause your blood sugar to be too low. Monitor your blood sugar closely. The dose of your diabetes medication might need to be changed. Some medications used for diabetes include glimepiride (Amaryl), glyburide (DiaBeta, Glynase PresTab, Micronase), insulin, pioglitazone (Actos), rosiglitazone (Avandia), chlorpropamide (Diabinese), glipizide (Glucotrol), tolbutamide (Orinase), and others.

CARRAGEENAN

What other names is the product known by?

Carrageenin, Carragheenan, Chondrus crispus, Chondrus Extract, Euchema species, Gigartina mamillosa, Irish Moss Extract, Mousse D'Irlande.

What is it?

Carrageenan is made from parts of various red algae or seaweeds and is used for medicine.

Is it Effective?

The effectiveness ratings for **CARRAGEENAN** are as follows:
Insufficient Evidence to Rate Effectiveness for... Cough, bronchitis, tuberculosis, weight loss, laxative, peptic ulcers, and intestinal problems.

How does it work?

Carrageenan contains chemicals that seem to decrease stomach and intestinal secretions. It also might decrease inflammation.

Are there safety concerns?

Carrageenan is safe for most people in food amounts. There is a chemically altered form of carrageenan that is available in France to treat peptic ulcers. This form might be UNSAFE because there's some evidence that it might cause cancer.

Do not take carrageenan in amounts larger than those typically found in food if: You are pregnant or breast-feeding.

Are there any interactions with medications?

Medications that slow blood clotting (Anticoagulant / Antiplatelet drugs). Carrageenan might slow blood clotting. Taking carrageenan along with medications that also slow clotting might increase the chances of bruising and bleeding. Some medications that slow blood clotting include aspirin, clopidogrel (Plavix), diclofenac (Voltaren, Cataflam, others), ibuprofen (Advil, Motrin, others), naproxen (Anaprox, Naprosyn, others), dalteparin (Fragmin), enoxaparin (Lovenox), heparin, warfarin (Coumadin), and others.

Medications for high blood pressure (Antihypertensive drugs). Carrageenan seems to decrease blood pressure. Taking carrageenan along with medications for high blood pressure might cause your blood pressure to go too low. Some medications for high blood pressure include captopril (Capoten), enalapril (Vasotec), losartan (Cozaar), valsartan (Diovan), diltiazem (Cardizem), Amlodipine (Norvasc), hydrochlorothiazide (HydroDiuril), furosemide (Lasix), and many others.

Medications taken by mouth (Oral drugs). Carrageenan is a thick gel. Carrageenan can stick to medications in the stomach and intestines. Taking carrageenan at the same time as medications that you take by mouth can decrease how much medication your body absorbs, and decrease the effectiveness of your medication. To prevent this interaction, take carrageenan at least one hour after medications you take by mouth.

CASCARA

What other names is the product known by?

Bitter Bark, Buckthorn, California Buckthorn, Cascara Sagrada, Chittem Bark, Dogwood Bark, Frangula purshiana, Purshiana Bark, Rhamni Purshianae Cortex, Rhamnus purshiana, Sacred Bark, Sagrada Bark, Yellow Bark.

What is it?

Cascara is a shrub. The dried bark is used to make medicine.

Is it Effective?

The effectiveness ratings for **CASCARA** are as follows:
Likely Effective for... Use as a laxative in people with constipation.
Insufficient Evidence to Rate Effectiveness for... Gallstones, liver disease, and cancer.

How does it work?

Cascara contains chemicals that stimulate the bowel and have a laxative effect.

Are there safety concerns?

Cascara seems safe for most adults when used short-term. Side effects include stomach discomfort and cramps. Don't use cascara for more than one to two weeks. Long-term use can cause more serious side effects including dehydration, low electrolytes, heart problems, muscle weakness, and others.
Do not use cascara in children.

Do not take cascara if: You are pregnant or breast-feeding. • You have stomach pain or intestinal disorder. • You have Crohn's disease. • You have ulcerative colitis. • You have appendicitis. • You have stomach ulcers.

Are there any interactions with medications?

Digoxin (Lanoxin). Cascara is a type of laxative called a stimulant laxative. Stimulant laxatives can decrease potassium levels in the body. Low potassium levels can increase the risk of side effects of digoxin (Lanoxin).
Medications for inflammation (Corticosteroids). Some medications for inflammation can decrease potassium in the body. Cascara is a type of laxative that might also decrease potassium in the body. Taking cascara along with some medications for inflammation might decrease potassium in the body too much. Some medications for inflammation include dexamethasone (Decadron), hydrocortisone (Cortef), methylprednisolone (Medrol), prednisone (Deltasone), and others.
Medications taken by mouth (Oral drugs). Cascara is a laxative. Laxatives can decrease how much medicine your body absorbs. Decreasing how much medicine your body absorbs can decrease the effectiveness of your medication.
Stimulant laxatives. Cascara is a type of laxative called a stimulant laxative. Stimulant laxatives speed up the bowels. Taking cascara along with other stimulant laxatives could speed up the bowels too much and cause dehydration and low minerals in the body. Some stimulant laxatives include bisacodyl (Correctol, Dulcolax), castor oil (Purge), senna (Senokot), and others.
Water pills (Diuretic drugs). Cascara is a laxative. Some laxatives can decrease potassium in the body. "Water pills" can also decrease potassium in the body. Taking cascara along with "water pills" might decrease potassium in the body too much. Some "water pills" that can decrease potassium include chlorothiazide (Diuril), chlorthalidone (Thalitone), furosemide (Lasix), hydrochlorothiazide (HCTZ, HydroDiuril, Microzide), and others.

CASCARILLA

What other names is the product known by?
Bahama Cascarilla, Croton eluteria, Sweet Bark, Sweet Wood Bark.

What is it?
Cascarilla is a plant. People use the bark for medicine.

Is it Effective?
The effectiveness ratings for **CASCARILLA** are as follows:
Insufficient Evidence to Rate Effectiveness for... Digestive disorders, diarrhea, vomiting, and other uses.

How does it work?
There isn't enough information to know how cascarilla might work for medicinal uses.

Are there safety concerns?
There isn't enough information to know if cascarilla is safe or what the potential side effects might be.

Do not take cascarilla if: You are pregnant or breast-feeding.

Are there any interactions with medications?
It is not known if cascarilla interacts with any medicines.
Before taking cascarilla, talk with your healthcare professional if you take any medications.

CASEIN PEPTIDES

What other names is the product known by?
Bovine casein hydrosylate, C12, C12 peptide, Casein decapeptide, Casein-derived peptide, Casein hydrosylate, Casein peptide, Casein phosphopeptide, Casein protein extract, Casein protein hydrosylate, Casein tripeptide, Hydrolyzed casein, Hypotensive peptides, Milk protein extract, Milk protein hydrosylate, Sour milk extract, Sour milk peptides.

What is it?
Casein peptides are byproducts of milk proteins.

Is it Effective?
The effectiveness ratings for **CASEIN PEPTIDES** are as follows:
Insufficient Evidence to Rate Effectiveness for... High blood pressure, high cholesterol, anxiety, fatigue, epilepsy, intestinal disorders, cancer prevention, and reducing stress.

How does it work?
Some casein peptides are thought to cause blood vessels to dilate and therefore lower blood pressure.

Are there safety concerns?
Casein peptides are normally consumed in the diet from milk products. But there isn't enough information to know if casein peptides in dietary supplements are safe.

Do not take casein peptides if: You are pregnant or breast-feeding. • You are allergic to milk or dairy products.

Are there any interactions with medications?
Medications for high blood pressure (Antihypertensive drugs). Some casein peptides might decrease blood pressure. Taking casein peptides along with medications for high blood pressure might cause your blood pressure to go too low. Some medications for high blood pressure include captopril (Capoten), enalapril (Vasotec), losartan (Cozaar), valsartan (Diovan), diltiazem (Cardizem), Amlodipine (Norvasc), hydrochlorothiazide (HydroDiuril), furosemide (Lasix), and many others.

CASHEW

What other names is the product known by?
Anacardium occidentale, East Indian Almond.

What is it?
Cashew is a nut. People use it to make medicine.

Is it Effective?
The effectiveness ratings for **CASHEW** are as follows:
Insufficient Evidence to Rate Effectiveness for... Stomach and intestinal disorders, skin ulcers, warts, and corns.

How does it work?
Cashew contains chemicals that might work against certain bacteria.

Are there safety concerns?
Cashew is safe in normal food amounts. There isn't enough information to know if cashew is safe for use as a medicine. Unroasted cashew can irritate the skin and cause redness and blisters.

Do not take cashew in amounts greater than normal food amounts if: You are pregnant or breast-feeding.

Are there any interactions with medications?
It is not known if cashew interacts with any medicines.
Before taking cashew, talk with your healthcare professional if you take any medications.

CASSIA AURICULATA

What other names is the product known by?
Asplenium scolopendrium, Buttonhole, God's-Hair, Hind's Tongue, Horse Tongue, Scolopendrium vulgare.

What is it?
Cassia auriculata is a shrub. The flower, leaves, stem, root, and unripe fruit are used to make medicine.

Is it Effective?
The effectiveness ratings for **CASSIA AURICULATA** are as follows:
Insufficient Evidence to Rate Effectiveness for... Diabetes, digestive disorders, conjunctivitis, urinary tract diseases, and other conditions.

How does it work?
Cassia auriculata might increase the body's production of insulin.

Are there safety concerns?
There isn't enough information available to know if Cassia auriculata is safe.

Do not use Cassia auriculata if: You are pregnant or breast-feeding.

Are there any interactions with medications?
Medications for diabetes (Antidiabetes drugs). Cassia auriculata might decrease blood sugar. Diabetes medications are also used to lower blood sugar. Taking Cassia auriculata along with diabetes medications might cause your blood sugar to go too low. Monitor your blood sugar closely. The dose of your diabetes medication might need to be changed. Some medications used for diabetes include glimepiride (Amaryl), glyburide (DiaBeta, Glynase PresTab, Micronase), insulin, pioglitazone (Actos), rosiglitazone (Avandia), chlorpropamide (Diabinese), glipizide (Glucotrol), tolbutamide (Orinase), and others.
Carbamazepine (Tegretol). Cassia auriculata might increase how much carbamazepine (Tegretol) is in the body. Taking Cassia auriculata with carbamazepine (Tegretol) might increase the effects and side effects of carbamazepine (Tegretol).

CONSUMER VERSION

CASSIA CINNAMON

What other names is the product known by?

Bastard Cinnamon, Canton Cassia, Cassia, Cassia Aromaticum, Cassia Bark, Cassia Lignea, Chinese Cinnamon, Cinnamon Flos, Cinnamomi cassiae cortex, Cinnamomum, Cinnamomum aromaticum, Cinnamomum cassia, Cortex Cinnamomi, Cinnamon, False Cinnamon, Gui Zhi, Keishi, Nees, Rou Gui, Sthula Tvak, Taja, Zimbluten.

What is it?

Cassia cinnamon is a plant. People use the bark and flower for medicine.

Is it Effective?

The effectiveness ratings for **CASSIA CINNAMON** are as follows:
Insufficient Evidence to Rate Effectiveness for... Type 2 diabetes, loss of appetite, muscle and stomach spasms, bloating, intestinal gas, vomiting, diarrhea, common cold, impotence, bed wetting, menstrual complaints, chest pain, high blood pressure, kidney problems, cancer, and other conditions.

How does it work?

Cassia cinnamon might lower blood sugar in people with type 2 diabetes. Cassia cinnamon also contains the chemical cinnamaldehyde, which might have activity against bacteria and fungi.

Are there safety concerns?

Cassia cinnamon is safe when used in amounts commonly found in foods and in medicinal doses. It appears to be UNSAFE when applied to the skin in high (>0.2%) concentrations. Cassia cinnamon can cause skin irritation and allergic skin reactions.

Cassia cinnamon also might DECREASE blood sugar. If you have diabetes, check your blood sugar carefully.

Do not take cassia cinnamon in amounts greater than those typically found in food if: You are pregnant or breast-feeding. • You are allergic to cassia cinnamon.

Are there any interactions with medications?

Medications for diabetes (Antidiabetes drugs). Cassia cinnamon might decrease blood sugar. Diabetes medications are also used to lower blood sugar. Taking cassia cinnamon along with diabetes medications might cause your blood sugar to go too low. Monitor your blood sugar closely. The dose of your diabetes medication might need to be changed. Some medications used for diabetes include glimepiride (Amaryl), glyburide (DiaBeta, Glynase PresTab, Micronase), insulin, pioglitazone (Actos), rosiglitazone (Avandia), chlorpropamide (Diabinese), glipizide (Glucotrol), tolbutamide (Orinase), and others.

CASSIE ABSOLUTE

What other names is the product known by?

Acacia farnesiana, Huisache, Mimosa farnesiana, Popinac Absolute, Sweet Acacia.

What is it?

Cassie absolute is an extract of the flower of Acacia farnesiana. It is used for medicine.

Is it Effective?

The effectiveness ratings for **CASSIE ABSOLUTE** are as follows:
Insufficient Evidence to Rate Effectiveness for... Spasms, diarrhea, fever, insecticide, aphrodisiac, stimulant, rheumatoid arthritis, tuberculosis, gonorrhea, sore throat, and stomach cancer.

How does it work?

Cassie absolute contains chemicals called glycosides that may decrease inflammation and open the airways in the respiratory tract.

Are there safety concerns?

It is not known if cassie absolute is safe in amounts greater than found in food or what the potential side effects might be.

Do not take cassie absolute in amounts greater than those typically found in food if: You are pregnant or breast-feeding.

Are there any interactions with medications?
It is not known if cassie absolute interacts with any medicines.
Before taking cassie absolute, talk with your healthcare professional if you take any medications.

CASTOR

What other names is the product known by?
African Coffee Tree, Bofareira, Castorbean, Castor Bean, Castor Bean Plant, Castor Oil, Castor Oil Plant, Castor Seed, Eranda, Gandharva Hasta, Mexico Weed, Palma Christi, Ricin, Ricinus communis, Ricinus Sanguines, Tangantangan Oil Plant, Wonder Tree.

What is it?
Castor is a bean. People use the oil from castor as medicine.

Is it Effective?
The effectiveness ratings for **CASTOR** are as follows:
Possibly Effective for... Constipation • Birth control • Stimulating full-term labor in pregnant women.
Insufficient Evidence to Rate Effectiveness for... Syphilis; arthritis; skin disorders; boils; blisters; swelling (inflammation) of the middle ear; migraines; softening cysts, warts, bunions and corns; promoting the flow of breast milk; and other conditions.

How does it work?
Castor seed is used to make castor oil, which is a strong laxative. In pregnancy, castor oil might induce labor by stimulating the uterus.

Are there safety concerns?
Castor oil seems to be safe for most people when used short-term. In some people, castor oil can cause stomach discomfort, cramping, nausea, and faintness. Castor oil might also cause fluid and potassium loss from the body, especially when used for more than a week or in doses more than 15-60 mL per day.

Although castor oil might be safe when used for inducing labor in pregnant women at term, it should not be used without the supervision of a healthcare professional. It is not safe to use in pregnant women who are not at term.

The whole seed is unsafe to take by mouth. The outer coating of the castor bean contains a deadly poison. This outer coating can cause nausea; vomiting; diarrhea; abdominal pain; dehydration; shock; blood cell destruction; severe fluid and electrolyte disturbances; liver, kidney, and pancreas damage; and death.

Do not take castor if: You are pregnant or breast-feeding. • You have bowel obstruction. • You have gallbladder problems.

Are there any interactions with medications?
Water pills (Diuretic drugs). Castor oil is a laxative. Some laxatives can decrease potassium in the body. "Water pills" can also decrease potassium in the body. Taking castor oil along with "water pills" might decrease potassium in the body too much. Some "water pills" that can decrease potassium include chlorothiazide (Diuril), chlorthalidone (Thalitone), furosemide (Lasix), hydrochlorothiazide (HCTZ, HydroDIURIL, Microzide), and others.

CASTOREUM

What other names is the product known by?
Canadian Beaver, Castor Canadensis, Castor Fiber, European Beaver, Siberian Beaver.

What is it?
Castoreum is a secretion collected from the glands of Canadian, European, and Siberian beavers.

Is it Effective?
The effectiveness ratings for **CASTOREUM** are as follows:
Insufficient Evidence to Rate Effectiveness for... Menstrual abnormalities, anxiety, sleeping disorders, and other conditions.

How does it work?
Castoreum seems to have calming and soothing effects.

Are there safety concerns?
Castoreum seems safe for most people when applied directly to the skin.

Do not take castoreum if: You are pregnant or breast-feeding.

Are there any interactions with medications?
It is not known if castoreum interacts with any medicines.
Before taking castoreum, talk with your healthcare professional if you take any medications.

CAT'S CLAW

What other names is the product known by?
Griffe Du Chat, Life-giving Vine of Peru, Samento, Una De Gato, Uncaria guianensis, Uncaria tomentosa.

What is it?
Cat's claw is a plant. People use the root and bark for medicine. Be careful not to confuse cat's claw with cat's foot.

Is it Effective?
The effectiveness ratings for **CAT'S CLAW** are as follows:
Possibly Effective for... Reducing pain from a kind of arthritis called osteoarthritis • Improving symptoms of a kind of arthritis called rheumatoid arthritis when used with regular rheumatoid arthritis medications.
Insufficient Evidence to Rate Effectiveness for... Stomach or intestinal ulcers, inflammation of the digestive tract including colitis and diverticulitis, hemorrhoids, parasites, leaky bowel syndrome, shingles, chronic fatigue syndrome (CFS), chicken pox, mouth or genital herpes, human immunodeficiency virus (HIV), wounds, arthritis, asthma, hayfever, cancer, glioblastoma, gonorrhea, birth control, bone pains, and other conditions.

How does it work?
Cat's claw contains chemicals that might stimulate the immune system, kill cancer cells, and fight viruses.

Are there safety concerns?
Cat's claw seems safe for most people, when taken short-term. Cat's claw can cause headache, dizziness, and vomiting in some people.

Do not take cat's claw if: You are pregnant or breast-feeding. • You have low blood pressure. • You have an immune system disease such as multiple sclerosis, lupus erythematosus, or other auto-immune diseases.

Are there any interactions with medications?
Medications for high blood pressure (Antihypertensive drugs). Cat's claw seems to decrease blood pressure. Taking cat's claw along with medications for high blood pressure might cause your blood pressure to go too low. Some medications for high blood pressure include captopril (Capoten), enalapril (Vasotec), losartan (Cozaar), valsartan (Diovan), diltiazem (Cardizem), Amlodipine (Norvasc), hydrochlorothiazide (HydroDiuril), furosemide (Lasix), and many others.
Medications that decrease the immune system (Immunosuppressants). Cat's claw might increase the immune system. By increasing the immune system cat's claw might decrease the effectiveness of medications that decrease the immune system. Some medications that decrease the immune system include azathioprine (Imuran), basiliximab (Simulect), cyclosporine (Neoral, Sandimmune), daclizumab (Zenapax), muromonab-CD3 (OKT3, Orthoclone OKT3), mycophenolate (CellCept), tacrolimus (FK506, Prograf), sirolimus (Rapamune), prednisone (Deltasone, Orasone), corticosteroids (glucocorticoids), and others.
Medications changed by the liver (Cytochrome P450 3A4 (CYP3A4) substrates). Some medications are changed and broken down by the liver. Cat's claw might decrease how quickly the liver breaks down some medications. Taking cat's claw along with some medications that are broken down by the liver can increase the effects and side effects of some medications. Before taking cat's claw, talk to your healthcare provider if you are taking any medications that are changed by the liver. Some medications changed by the liver include lovastatin (Mevacor), ketoconazole (Nizoral), itraconazole (Sporanox), fexofenadine (Allegra), triazolam (Halcion), and many others.

Medical professionals should consult the Professional Version at www.NaturalDatabase.com.

CAT'S FOOT

What other names is the product known by?
Antennaria Dioica, Antennariase Dioicae Flos, Cat's Ear Flower, Cudweed, Katsenpfotchenbluten, Life Everlasting, Mountain Everlasting.

What is it?
Cat's foot is a plant. People use the fresh or dried flowers to make medicine. Be careful not to confuse cat's foot with cat's claw.

Is it Effective?
The effectiveness ratings for **CAT'S FOOT** are as follows:
Insufficient Evidence to Rate Effectiveness for... Intestinal disease, fluid retention, and other conditions.

How does it work?
There is some evidence from animal experiments that cat's foot might relieve intestinal spasms and increase bile flow. However, there isn't enough information to know how it might work in people.

Are there safety concerns?
There isn't enough information to know if cat's foot is safe. It can cause allergic reactions in people who are allergic to ragweed, chrysanthemums, marigolds, daisies, and other members of the Asteraceae/Compositae plant family.

Do not take cat's foot if: You are pregnant or breast-feeding. • You are allergic to ragweed, chrysanthemums, marigolds, daisies, or related plants.

Are there any interactions with medications?
It is not known if cat's foot interacts with any medicines.
Before taking cat's foot, talk with your healthcare professional if you take any medications.

CATECHU

What other names is the product known by?
Black Catechu: Acacia catechu, Acacia Catechu Heartwood Extract, Black Cutch, Cachou, Cashou, Catechu nigrum, Cutch, Dark Catechu, Khair, Khadira, Pegu Catechu.

Pale Catechu: Cube Gambir, Gambier, Gambir, Gambir Catechu, Terra Japonica, Uncaria gambier, Uncaria Gambier Leaf/Twig Extract.

What is it?
Catechu is an herb. The leaves, shoots, and wood are used to make medicine.

Is it Effective?
The effectiveness ratings for **CATECHU** are as follows:
Insufficient Evidence to Rate Effectiveness for... Diarrhea, swelling of the nose and throat, swelling in the colon, bleeding, cancer, skin diseases, hemorrhoids, osteoarthritis, and injuries.

How does it work?
It is thought that catechu may contain chemicals that can decrease inflammation and kill bacteria.

Are there safety concerns?
Catechu is safe in amounts found in food, but there's not enough information to know if it's safe in amounts used as medicine.

Do not take catechu if: You are pregnant or breast-feeding. • You have low blood pressure (hypotension).

Are there any interactions with medications?
Medications for high blood pressure (Antihypertensive drugs). Catechu might decrease blood pressure. Taking catechu along with medications used for high blood pressure might cause your blood pressure to go too low. Some medications for high blood pressure include captopril (Capoten), enalapril (Vasotec), losartan (Cozaar), valsartan (Diovan), diltiazem (Cardizem), Amlodipine (Norvasc), hydrochlorothiazide (HydroDIURIL), furosemide (Lasix), and many others.

CATNIP

What other names is the product known by?
Catmint, Catnep, Catswort, Field Balm, Menta De Gato, Nepeta cataria.

What is it?
Catnip is a plant. The flowering tops are used to make medicine.

Is it Effective?
The effectiveness ratings for **CATNIP** are as follows:
Insufficient Evidence to Rate Effectiveness for... Difficulty sleeping, migraine headaches, colds, flu, fever, hives, stomach upset, gas, anxiety, arthritis, increasing urination, treatment of worms, stimulating menstruation in girls, and hemorrhoids.

How does it work?
It is thought that the chemicals in catnip have a calming effect.

Are there safety concerns?
Catnip seems to be safe for most adults. It is UNSAFE when smoked, when taken by mouth in high doses, or when used in children.

It can cause headaches, vomiting, and an ill feeling.

Do not take catnip if: You are pregnant or breast-feeding. • You have been told you have a condition called pelvic inflammatory disease (PID). • You have very heavy periods.

Are there any interactions with medications?
Sedative medications (CNS depressants). Catnip might cause sleepiness and drowsiness. Medications that cause sleepiness are called sedatives. Taking catnip along with sedative medications might cause too much sleepiness. Some sedative medications include clonazepam (Klonopin), lorazepam (Ativan), Phenobarbital (Donnatal), zolpidem (Ambien), and others.

CATUABA

What other names is the product known by?
Caramuru, Catuaba Casca, Chuchuhuasha, Erythroxylum catuaba, Golden Trumpet, Pau De Reposta, Piratancara, Tatuaba.

What is it?
Catuaba is an herb. People use the bark to make medicine.

Is it Effective?
The effectiveness ratings for **CATUABA** are as follows:
Insufficient Evidence to Rate Effectiveness for... Male sexual problems, anxiety, exhaustion, fatigue, sleeplessness, nervousness, poor memory or forgetfulness, skin cancer, and other conditions.

How does it work?
Catuaba contains chemicals that might work against certain bacteria and viruses.

Are there safety concerns?
There isn't enough information available to know if catuaba is safe.

Do not take catuaba if: You are pregnant or breast-feeding.

Are there any interactions with medications?
It is not known if catuaba interacts with any medicines.
Before taking catuaba, talk with your healthcare professional if you take any medications.

Medical professionals should consult the Professional Version at www.NaturalDatabase.com.

Medical professionals should consult the Professional Version at www.NaturalDatabase.com.

CELERY

What other names is the product known by?
Aches des Marais, Ajamoda, Apii Frutus, Apium graveolens, Celery Fruit, Celery Seed, Fruit de Celeri, Smallage, Selleriefruchte, Selleriesamen.

What is it?
Celery is a plant. The fruit and seeds are used to make medicine.

Is it Effective?
The effectiveness ratings for **CELERY** are as follows:
Insufficient Evidence to Rate Effectiveness for... Muscle and joint aches and pains, gout, nervousness, headache, appetite stimulation, exhaustion, fluid retention, regulating bowel movements, use as a sleeping sedative, gas, stimulating menstruation, breast milk reduction, and aiding digestion.

How does it work?
It is thought that the chemicals in celery act to cause sleepiness, increase urine to decrease fluid retention, decrease arthritis symptoms, decrease blood pressure, decrease blood sugar, decrease blood clotting, and muscle relaxation.

Are there safety concerns?
Celery seems to be safe for most people.

It may cause skin inflammation and sensitivity to the sun.

Do not take celery if: You are pregnant or breast-feeding. • You have been told you have a kidney condition. • You are allergic to carrots, dandelions, and other related herbs.

Are there any interactions with medications?
Medications that increase sensitivity to sunlight (Photosensitizing drugs). Some medications can increase sensitivity to sunlight. Celery might also increase your sensitivity to sunlight. Taking celery along with medications that increase sensitivity to sunlight could increase the chances of sunburn, blistering or rashes on areas of skin exposed to sunlight. Be sure to wear sunblock and protective clothing when spending time in the sun. Some drugs that cause photosensitivity include amitriptyline (Elavil), Ciprofloxacin (Cipro), norfloxacin (Noroxin), lomefloxacin (Maxaquin), ofloxacin (Floxin), levofloxacin (Levaquin), sparfloxacin (Zagam), gatifloxacin (Tequin), moxifloxacin (Avelox), trimethoprim/sulfamethoxazole (Septra), tetracycline, methoxsalen (8-methoxypsoralen, 8-MOP, Oxsoralen), and Trioxsalen (Trisoralen).
Sedative medications (CNS depressants). Celery might cause sleepiness and drowsiness. Medications that cause sleepiness are called sedatives. Taking celery along with sedative medications might cause too much sleepiness. Some sedative medications include clonazepam (Klonopin), lorazepam (Ativan), phenobarbital (Donnatal), zolpidem (Ambien), and others.
Levothyroxine. Levothyroxine is used for low thyroid function. Taking celery seed along with levothyroxine might decrease the effectiveness of levothyroxine. But it is not clear why this interaction might occur, or if it is a big concern. Some brands that contain levothyroxine include Armour Thyroid, Eltroxin, Estre, Euthyrox, Levo-T, Levothroid, Levoxyl, Synthroid, Unithroid, and others.

CENTAURY

What other names is the product known by?
Bitter Herb, Centaurium erythraea, Centaurium minus, Centaurium umbellatum, Common Centaury, Drug Centaurium, Erythraea centaurium, Lesser Centauru, Minor Centaury.

What is it?
Centaury is an herb. People use the dried above ground parts to make medicine.

Is it Effective?
The effectiveness ratings for **CENTAURY** are as follows:
Insufficient Evidence to Rate Effectiveness for... Loss of appetite and stomach discomfort.

How does it work?
Centaury contains chemicals that might help stimulate the appetite.

Are there safety concerns?

Centaury seems safe for most people.

Do not take centaury in amounts greater than normal food amounts if: You are pregnant or breast-feeding.

Are there any interactions with medications?

It is not known if centaury interacts with any medicines.
Before taking centaury, talk with your healthcare professional if you take any medications.

CEREUS

What other names is the product known by?

Cactus grandiflorus, Cereus grandiflorus, Night Blooming Cereus, Selenicereus grandiflorus, Sweet Scented Cactus.

What is it?

Cereus is an herb. People use the flower, stem, and young shoots for medicine.

Is it Effective?

The effectiveness ratings for **CEREUS** are as follows:
Insufficient Evidence to Rate Effectiveness for... Chest pain, heart failure, heavy menstrual pain and bleeding, hemorrhage, arthritis-like pain, and other conditions.

How does it work?

Cereus contains chemicals that can stimulate and strengthen the heart.

Are there safety concerns?

Cereus seems safe for most people, when used under the direct supervision of a healthcare professional. The fresh juice may cause burning of the mouth, nausea, vomiting, and diarrhea. It can cause itching and skin blisters when applied to the skin.

Do not take cereus if: You are pregnant or breast-feeding. • You have heart problems.

Are there any interactions with medications?

Digoxin (Lanoxin). Digoxin (Lanoxin) helps the heart beat more strongly. Cereus also seems to affect the heart. Taking cereus along with digoxin can increase the effects of digoxin and increase the risk of side effects. Do not take cereus if you are taking digoxin (Lanoxin) without talking to your healthcare professional.
Medications for depression (MAOIs). Cereus contains a chemical called tyramine. Large amounts of tyramine can cause high blood pressure. But the body naturally breaks down tyramine to get rid of it. This usually prevents the tyramine from causing high blood pressure. Some medications used for depression stop the body from breaking down tyramine. This can cause there to be too much tyramine and lead to dangerously high blood pressure. Some of these medications used for depression include phenelzine (Nardil), tranylcypromine (Parnate), and others.

CESIUM

What other names is the product known by?

Caesium, Cesium-137, Cesium Chloride, Cs, CsCl, High pH Therapy.

What is it?

Cesium is an element. People use it for medicine.

Is it Effective?

The effectiveness ratings for **CESIUM** are as follows:
Insufficient Evidence to Rate Effectiveness for... Cancer, depession, and other conditions.

How does it work?

There isn't enough information to know how cesium might work. Some proponents say cesium affects the pH (acidity) of cancer cells, but there's no scientific research to support this claim.

Medical professionals should consult the Professional Version at www.NaturalDatabase.com.

Are there safety concerns?

High doses of cesium might be UNSAFE. There is one report of severe life-threatening low blood pressure and irregular heartbeat in someone who took cesium 3 grams/day for several weeks. There isn't enough information to know if lower doses of cesium are safe. Some people who take cesium by mouth can have nausea, diarrhea, and loss of appetite. Tingling of the lips, hands, and feet may also occur.

Do not take cesium if: You are pregnant or breast-feeding.

Are there any interactions with medications?

Medications for inflammation (Corticosteroids). Some medications for inflammation can decrease potassium in the body. Cesium might also decrease potassium levels in the body. Taking cesium along with some medications for inflammation might decrease potassium in the body too much. Some medications for inflammation include dexamethasone (Decadron), hydrocortisone (Cortef), methylprednisolone (Medrol), prednisone (Deltasone), and others.

Water pills (Diuretic drugs). Large amounts of cesium can decrease potassium levels in the body. "Water pills" can also decrease potassium in the body. Taking cesium along with "water pills" might decrease potassium in the body too much. Some "water pills" that can deplete potassium include chlorothiazide (Diuril), chlorthalidone (Thalitone), furosemide (Lasix), hydrochlorothiazide (HCTZ, Hydrodiuril, Microzide), and others.

CETYLATED FATTY ACIDS

What other names is the product known by?

Cerasomal-cis-9-cetylmyristoleate, Cetyl Laureate, Cetyl Myristate, Cetyl Myristoleate, Cetyl Oleate, Cetyl Palmitate, Cetyl Palmitoleate, Cetylated Monounsaturated Fatty Acids, Cetylmyristoleate, CM, CMO.

What is it?

Cetylated fatty acids are a kind of fat.

Is it Effective?

The effectiveness ratings for **CETYLATED FATTY ACIDS** are as follows:
Possibly Effective for...A type of arthritis called osteoarthritis, when taken by mouth or applied to the skin over the affected joint.
Insufficient Evidence to Rate Effectiveness for... Rheumatoid arthritis, lupus, multiple sclerosis, Reiter's syndrome, Behcet's syndrome, Sjogren's syndrome, psoriasis, fibromyalgia, emphysema, benign prostate hyperplasia (BPH), silicone breast disease, leukemia and other cancers, and various types of back pain.

How does it work?

Cetylated fatty acids might help lubricate joints and muscles, soften tissues, and increase flexibility. It also might help the immune system and reduce inflammation (swelling).

Are there safety concerns?

Cetylated fatty acids seem to be safe when taken by mouth or applied to the skin, short-term. Side effects have not been reported. But there is not much information available about the safety of long-term use.

Do not take cetylated fatty acids if: You are pregnant or breast-feeding.

Are there any interactions with medications?

It is not known if cetylated fatty acids interact with any medicines.
Before taking cetylated fatty acids, talk with your healthcare professional if you take any medications.

CHA DE BUGRE

What other names is the product known by?

Boid d'inde, Bois d'ine, Brazlian Diet Pill, Bugrinho, Cafezinho, Cafe de Bugre, Cafe do Mato, Cha-de-Negro-Mina, Cha de Frade, Claraiba, Coffee of the Woods, Coquelicot, Cordia Ecalyculata, Cordia Salicifolia, Grao-do-Porco, Laranjeira-do-Mato, Louro-Salgueiro, Louro-Mole, Porangaba, Rabugem.

What is it?

Cha de bugre is a Brazilian tree. The fruit and leaves are used to make tea and medicine.

 (209) 472-2244

Is it Effective?

The effectiveness ratings for **CHA DE BUGRE** are as follows:

Insufficient Evidence to Rate Effectiveness for... Weight loss and obesity, reducing cellulite, cough, edema, gout, cancer, herpes, viral infections, fever, heart disease, and wound healing.

How does it work?

Some people think cha de bugre decreases appetite, but there is not scientific evidence that this is true. There is not enough known about cha de bugre to know how it might work for any medical use.

Are there safety concerns?

There is not enough known about cha de bugre to know if there are any safety concerns or if it is safe to take.

Do not take cha de bugre if: You are pregnant or breast-feeding.

Are there any interactions with medications?

It is not known if cha de bugre interacts with any medicines.
Before taking cha de bugre, talk to your healthcare professional if you take any medications.

CHANCA PIEDRA

What other names is the product known by?

Chancapiedra, Chanca-Piedra Blanca, Child Pick-a-Back, Derriere Dos, Derrière-Dos, Des Dos, Dukong Anak, Feuilles la Fievre, Memeniran, Meniran, Niruri, Phyllanthus niruri, Pitirishi, Quebra Pedra, Quebrapedra, Quinina Criolla, Quinine Créole, Rami Buah, Sacha Foster, Sasha Foster, Seed on the Leaf, Shatter Stone, Stone Breaker, Stonebreaker, Tamalaka, Turi Hutan.

What is it?

Chanca piedra is an herb. The whole plant is used to make medicine.

Is it Effective?

The effectiveness ratings for **CHANCA PIEDRA** are as follows:

Possibly Ineffective for... Hepatitis B infection.

Insufficient Evidence to Rate Effectiveness for... Urinary tract infections and inflammation, kidney stones, increasing urine, intestinal gas, stimulating the appetite, use as a liver tonic and blood purifier, diabetes, gallstones, colic, stomachache, indigestion, intestinal infections, constipation, dysentery, flu, jaundice, abdominal tumors, fever, pain, syphilis, gonorrhea, malaria, tumors, caterpillar stings, cough, swelling, itching, miscarriage, rectal inflammation, tremors, typhoid, infections of the vagina, anemia, asthma, bronchitis, thirst, tuberculosis, or dizziness.

How does it work?

It is thought that chanca piedra contains chemicals that might relieve spasms and fever, increase urine, and have activity against bacteria and viruses. It might also lower blood sugar.

Are there safety concerns?

It is not known if chanca piedra is safe or what the possible side effects might be.

Do not take chanca piedra if: You are pregnant or breast-feeding. • You have diabetes.

Are there any interactions with medications?

Medications for diabetes (Antidiabetes drugs). Chanca piedra might decrease blood sugar. Diabetes medications are also used to lower blood sugar. Taking chanca piedra along with diabetes medications might cause your blood sugar to go too low. Monitor your blood sugar closely. The dose of your diabetes medication might need to be changed. Some medications used for diabetes include glimepiride (Amaryl), glyburide (DiaBeta, Glynase PresTab, Micronase), insulin, pioglitazone (Actos), rosiglitazone (Avandia), chlorpropamide (Diabinese), glipizide (Glucotrol), tolbutamide (Orinase), and others.

Medical professionals should consult the Professional Version at www.NaturalDatabase.com.

CHAPARRAL

What other names is the product known by?
Creosote Bush, Greasewood, Hediondilla, Larrea tridentata, Larrea divaricata.

What is it?
Chaparral is a plant. It is used to make medicine.

Is it Effective?
The effectiveness ratings for **CHAPARRAL** are as follows:

Insufficient Evidence to Rate Effectiveness for... Arthritis, cancer, sexually transmitted diseases, tuberculosis, colds, skin conditions, stomach ailments (cramps, gas), weight loss, urinary and respiratory infections, and chicken pox.

How does it work?
The chemicals in chaparral are thought to work as antioxidants.

Are there safety concerns?
Chaparral is UNSAFE.

Chaparral can cause side effects including stomach pain, nausea, diarrhea, weight loss, fever, and liver and kidney damage. Putting chaparral on the skin can cause skin reactions including rash and itching.

Do not take chaparral if: You are pregnant or breast-feeding. • You have been told you have kidney or liver problems.

Are there any interactions with medications?
Medications that can harm the liver (Hepatotoxic drugs). Chaparral might harm the liver. Taking chaparral along with medication that might also harm the liver can increase the risk of liver damage. Do not take chaparral if you are taking a medication that can harm the liver. Some medications that can harm the liver include acetaminophen (Tylenol and others), amiodarone (Cordarone), carbamazepine (Tegretol), isoniazid (INH), methotrexate (Rheumatrex), methyldopa (Aldomet), fluconazole (Diflucan), itraconazole (Sporanox), erythromycin (Erythrocin, Ilosone, others), phenytoin (Dilantin), lovastatin (Mevacor), pravastatin (Pravachol), simvastatin (Zocor), and many others.

CHASTEBERRY

What other names is the product known by?
Agnolyt, Agnus-Castus, Chaste Berry, Chaste Tree Berry, Chastetree, Chinese Vitex, Gattilier, Hemp Tree, Mang Jing Zi, Monk's Pepper, Vitex, Vitex agnus-castus, Vitex rotundifolia, Vitex trifolia, Viticis Fructus.

What is it?
Chasteberry is the fruit of the chaste tree. The fruit and seed are used to make medicine.

Is it Effective?
The effectiveness ratings for **CHASTEBERRY** are as follows:

Possibly Effective for... Premenstrual syndrome (PMS) • Premenstrual dysphoric disorder (PMDD).

Insufficient Evidence to Rate Effectiveness for... Infertility in women, menopausal symptoms, cyclical breast pain, prevention of miscarriage, enlarged prostate, increasing lactation, insect repellent, and other conditions.

How does it work?
Chasteberry seems to affect many hormones that regulate women's reproductive cycles.

Are there safety concerns?
Chasteberry seems to be safe for most people. Uncommon side effects include upset stomach, nausea, itching, rash, headaches, acne, trouble sleeping, and weight gain. Some women notice a change in menstrual flow when they start taking chasteberry.

Do not take chasteberry if: You are pregnant or breast-feeding. • You have a hormone-sensitive condition such as endometriosis; uterine fibroids; or cancer of the breast, uterus, or ovaries. • You are trying to get pregnant using in-vitro fertilization.

     Natural Medicines Comprehensive Database Consumer Version   (209) 472-2244

Are there any interactions with medications?

Birth control pills (Contraceptive drugs). Chasteberry seems to change hormone levels in the body. Birth control pills contain hormones. Taking chasteberry along with birth control pills might decrease the effectiveness of birth control pills. If you take birth control pills along with chasteberry, use an additional form of birth control such as a condom. Some birth control pills include ethinyl estradiol and levonorgestrel (Triphasil), ethinyl estradiol and norethindrone (Ortho-Novum 1/35, Ortho-Novum 7/7/7), and others.

Estrogens. Chasteberry seems to change hormone levels in the body. Taking chasteberry along with estrogen pills might decrease the effects of estrogen pills. Some estrogen pills include conjugated equine estrogens (Premarin), ethinyl estradiol, estradiol, and others.

Medications for mental conditions (Antipsychotic drugs). Chasteberry seems to affect a chemical in the brain called dopamine. Some medications for mental disorders help to decrease dopamine. Taking chasteberry along with medications for mental conditions might decrease the effectiveness of some medications for mental conditions. Some medications for mental conditions include chlorpromazine (Thorazine), clozapine (Clozaril), fluphenazine (Prolixin), haloperidol (Haldol), olanzapine (Zyprexa), perphenazine (Trilafon), prochlorperazine (Compazine), quetiapine (Seroquel), risperidone (Risperdal), thioridazine (Mellaril), thiothixene (Navane), and others.

Medications used for Parkinson's disease (Dopamine agonists). Chasteberry contains chemicals that affect the brain. These chemicals affect the brain similarly to some medications used for Parkinson's disease. Taking chasteberry with these medications might increase the effects and side effects of some medications used for Parkinson's disease. Some medications used for Parkinson's disease include bromocriptine (Parlodel), levodopa (Dopar, component of Sinemet), pramipexole (Mirapex), ropinirole (Requip), and others.

Metoclopramide (Reglan). Chasteberry seems to affect a certain brain chemical. This chemical is called dopamine. Metoclopramide (Reglan) also affects dopamine. Taking chasteberry along with metoclopramide might decrease the effectiveness of metoclopramide (Reglan).

CHAULMOOGRA

What other names is the product known by?

Hydnocarp, Hydnocarpus anthelminthicus, Hydnocarpus kurzii, Gynocardia Oil, Oleum Chaulmoograe, Taraktogenos kurzii.

What is it?

Chaulmoogra is an herb. People use the seed to make medicine.

Is it Effective?

The effectiveness ratings for **CHAULMOOGRA** are as follows:
Insufficient Evidence to Rate Effectiveness for... Skin disorders, psoriasis, eczema, and leprosy.

How does it work?

Chaulmoogra might have calming and fever reducing properties. It might also have activity against skin disorders, including the bacterium that causes leprosy.

Are there safety concerns?

Chaulmoogra is UNSAFE because of its potential to cause cyanide poisoning. It can cause cough, difficulty breathing, throat spasms, kidney damage, visual disorders, head and muscle pain, and paralysis. It can cause irritation when applied to the skin.

Do not take chaulmoogra if: You are pregnant or breast-feeding.

Are there any interactions with medications?

It is not known if chaulmoogra interacts with any medicines.
Before taking chaulmoogra, talk with your healthcare professional if you take any medications.

CHEKEN

What other names is the product known by?

Arryan, Chekan, Eugenia chequen, Luma chequen, Myrtus, Myrtus chequen.

What is it?

Cheken is an herb. People use the dried leaves and leaf oil to make medicine.

Is it Effective?

The effectiveness ratings for **CHEKEN** are as follows:
Insufficient Evidence to Rate Effectiveness for... Cough, high cholesterol, diarrhea, fever, gout, high blood pressure, and other conditions.

How does it work?

Cheken leaf oil might affect the way the body breaks down fat and could be useful to help lower cholesterol.

Are there safety concerns?

There isn't enough information available to know if cheken is safe.

Do not take cheken if: You are pregnant or breast-feeding.

Are there any interactions with medications?

It is not known if cheken interacts with any medicines.
Before taking cheken, talk with your healthcare professional if you take any medications.

CHELATED MINERALS

What other names is the product known by?

Chelated Boron, Chelated Calcium, Chelated Chromium, Chelated Cobalt, Chelated Copper, Chelated Iron, Chelated Magnesium, Chelated Manganese, Chelated Molybdenum, Chelated Potassium, Chelated Selenium, Chelated Trace Minerals, Chelated Vanadium, Chelated Zinc, Mineral-amino acid complex.

What is it?

Chelated minerals are complexes of minerals and amino acids.

Is it Effective?

The effectiveness ratings for **CHELATED MINERALS** are as follows:
Insufficient Evidence to Rate Effectiveness for... Use as a dietary mineral supplement, improving immune system function, and building strong muscles and bones.

How does it work?

Minerals are required for the proper growth and maintenance of the body. There is no evidence to support the claim that chelated minerals can be used by the body better than non-chelated minerals.

Are there safety concerns?

There isn't enough information available to know if chelated minerals are safe.

Do not take chelated minerals if: You are pregnant or breast-feeding

Are there any interactions with medications?

It is not known if chelated minerals interact with any medicines.
Before taking chelated minerals, talk with your healthcare professional if you take any medications.

CHENOPODIUM OIL

What other names is the product known by?

Chenopodium ambrosioides, Chenopodium ambrosioides anthelminticum, Epazote, Jesuit Tea, and Mexican Tea.

What is it?

Chenopodium is an herb. The oil of fresh, above ground, flowering, and fruiting parts or seed oil are used for medicine.

Is it Effective?

The effectiveness ratings for **CHENOPODIUM OIL** are as follows:
Insufficient Evidence to Rate Effectiveness for... Treating intestinal worms.

How does it work?

Chenopodium oil appears to work by paralyzing worms in the intestine.

Are there safety concerns?

Chenopodium oil is UNSAFE.

Chenopodium oil contains the chemical ascaridole, which is very toxic. It can irritate the skin, mouth, throat, and lining of the stomach and intestines, and cause vomiting, headache, vertigo/dizziness, kidney and liver damage, temporary deafness, convulsions, paralysis, and death. Chenopodium oil can explode if heated or mixed with acids.

Do not take chenopodium oil if: You are pregnant or breast-feeding.

Are there any interactions with medications?

Medications that increase sensitivity to sunlight (Photosensitizing drugs). Some medications can increase sensitivity to sunlight. Chenopodium oil might also increase your sensitivity to sunlight. Taking chenopodium oil along with medications that increase sensitivity to sunlight could increase the chances of sunburn, blistering or rashes on areas of skin exposed to sunlight. Be sure to wear sunblock and protective clothing when spending time in the sun. Some drugs that cause photosensitivity include amitriptyline (Elavil), Ciprofloxacin (Cipro), norfloxacin (Noroxin), lomefloxacin (Maxaquin), ofloxacin (Floxin), levofloxacin (Levaquin), sparfloxacin (Zagam), gatifloxacin (Tequin), moxifloxacin (Avelox), trimethoprim/sulfamethoxazole (Septra), tetracycline, methoxsalen (8-methoxypsoralen, 8-MOP, Oxsoralen), and Trioxsalen (Trisoralen).

CHEROKEE ROSEHIP

What other names is the product known by?

Chinese Rosehip, Fructus Rosae Laevigatae, Jinyingzi, Rosa camellia, Rosa cherokensis, Rosa laevigata, Rosa nivea, Rosa sinica, Rosa ternata.

What is it?

Cherokee rosehip is an herb. People use the fruit to make medicine.

Is it Effective?

The effectiveness ratings for **CHEROKEE ROSEHIP** are as follows:
Insufficient Evidence to Rate Effectiveness for... Male sexual dysfunction, gynecologic problems, night sweats, frequent urination, bedwetting, chronic cough, high blood pressure, diarrhea, intestinal swelling (inflammation), and other conditions.

How does it work?

Cherokee rosehip contains vitamin C. It seems to have an anti-diarrheal effect.

Are there safety concerns?

Cherokee rosehip appears to be safe for most people when taken at recommended doses. It can cause nausea, stomach cramps, fatigue, and sleeplessness.

Large doses (67 grams of Cherokee rosehip or more per day) can cause diarrhea and symptoms of vitamin C poisoning, such as kidney and urinary problems.

Do not take Cherokee rosehip if: You are pregnant or breast-feeding. • You have gout. • You have a history of kidney stones. • You are diabetic.

Are there any interactions with medications?

Aluminum. Aluminum is found in most antacids. Cherokee rosehips contain vitamin C. Vitamin C can increase how much aluminum the body absorbs. But it isn't clear if this interaction is a big concern. Take Cherokee rosehip two hours before, or four hours after antacids.
Aspirin. The body breaks down aspirin to get rid of it. Cherokee rosehip contains large amounts of vitamin C. Large amounts of vitamin C might decrease the breakdown of aspirin. Taking Cherokee rosehip along with aspirin might increase the effects and side effects of aspirin. Do not take large amounts of vitamin C if you take large amounts of aspirin.
Choline Magnesium Trisalicylate (Trilisate). Rosehip contains vitamin C. Vitamin C might decrease how quickly the body gets rid of choline magnesium trisalicylate (Trilisate). But it is not clear if this interaction is a big concern.
Estrogens. Cherokee rosehip contains a large amount of vitamin C. Vitamin C can increase how much estrogen the body absorbs. Taking Cherokee rosehip along with estrogens can increase the effects and side effects of estrogens. Some estrogen pills include conjugated equine estrogens (Premarin), ethinyl estradiol, estradiol, and others.
Fluphenazine (Prolixin). Cherokee rosehip contains vitamin C. Large amounts of vitamin C might increase how quickly the body gets rid of fluphenazine (Prolixin). Taking Cherokee rosehip along with this might decrease how

well fluphenazine works.

Warfarin (Coumadin). Warfarin (Coumadin) is used to slow blood clotting. Cherokee rosehip contains vitamin C. Large amounts of vitamin C might decrease the effectiveness of warfarin (Coumadin). Decreasing the effectiveness of warfarin (Coumadin) might increase the risk of clotting. Be sure to have your blood checked regularly. The dose of your warfarin (Coumadin) might need to be changed.

CHERRY LAUREL WATER

What other names is the product known by?
Common Cherry Laurel, Laurocerasus Leaves, Prunus laurocerasus, Laurocerasus officinalis.

What is it?
Cherry laurel water is produced by water distillation of cherry laurel (Prunus laurocerasus) leaves. People use the water as medicine.

Is it Effective?
The effectiveness ratings for **CHERRY LAUREL WATER** are as follows:
Insufficient Evidence to Rate Effectiveness for... Pain relief, muscle spasms, cough, colds, sleeplessness, stomach and intestinal spasms, vomiting, and cancer.

How does it work?
There isn't enough information available to know how cherry laurel water works.

Are there safety concerns?
Cherry laurel water seems safe for use, when used in small amounts (up to about 1 and 1\2 teaspoonfuls). Large amounts, or overdoses, can cause poisoning and death.

Do not use cherry laurel water if: You are pregnant or breast-feeding.

Are there any interactions with medications?
It is not known if cherry laurel water interacts with any medicines.
Before taking cherry laurel water, talk with your healthcare professional if you take any medications.

CHERVIL

What other names is the product known by?
Anthriscus cerefolium, Anthriscus longirostris, Garden Chervil, Salad Chervil.

What is it?
Chervil is an herb. People use the leaves and dried flowering parts to make medicine.

Is it Effective?
The effectiveness ratings for **CHERVIL** are as follows:
Insufficient Evidence to Rate Effectiveness for... Cough, digestive disorders, high blood pressure, eczema, gout, abscesses, and other conditions.

How does it work?
Chervil is a good source of calcium and potassium. There isn't enough information available to understand how chervil works.

Are there safety concerns?
There isn't enough information to know if chervil is safe for use as a medicine.

Do not take chervil in amounts greater than those typically found in foods if: You are pregnant or breast-feeding.

Are there any interactions with medications?
It is not known if chervil interacts with any medicines.
Before taking chervil, talk with your healthcare professional if you take any medications.

CHICKEN COLLAGEN

What other names is the product known by?
Chicken Collagen Type II, Type II Collagen.

What is it?
Collagen is a protein that is part of cartilage, bone, and other tissues in animals and humans. People use collagen from chickens for medicine.

Is it Effective?
The effectiveness ratings for **CHICKEN COLLAGEN** are as follows:
Insufficient Evidence to Rate Effectiveness for... Pain associated with many types of arthritis, post-surgical joint pain, post-traumatic pain, and back and neck pain.

How does it work?
Chicken collagen is said to work by causing the body to produce substances that fight inflammation, but this is unproven. Chicken collagen also contains the chemicals chondroitin and glucosamine, which might help rebuild cartilage.

Are there safety concerns?
There isn't enough information to know if chicken collagen is safe or what the side effects might be. Other collagen products, such as bovine collagen and gelatin, have caused allergic reactions. Since chicken collagen contains chondroitin and glucosamine, large doses might lead to the same side effect as those seen with chondroitin and glucosamine supplements. These side effects include nausea, heartburn, diarrhea and constipation, drowsiness, skin reactions, and headache.

Do not take chicken collagen if: You are pregnant or breast-feeding. • You are allergic to chicken or eggs.

Are there any interactions with medications?
It is not known if chicken collagen interacts with any medicines.
Before taking chicken collagen, talk with your healthcare professional if you take any medications.

CHICKWEED

What other names is the product known by?
Alsine media, Star Chickweed, Starweed, Stellaria media.

What is it?
Chickweed is a plant. The leaf is used to make medicine.

Is it Effective?
The effectiveness ratings for **CHICKWEED** are as follows:
Insufficient Evidence to Rate Effectiveness for... Constipation; asthma; stomach problems; obesity; psoriasis; muscle and joint pain; and skin conditions including boils, abscesses, and ulcers.

How does it work?
There isn't enough information to know how chickweed might work.

Are there safety concerns?
Chickweed is considered safe for most adults when taken by mouth, but the potential side effects are not known. It is not known if applying chickweed to the skin is safe or what the potential side effects might be.

Do not take chickweed if: You are pregnant or breast-feeding.

Are there any interactions with medications?
It is not known if chickweed interacts with any medicines.
Before taking chickweed, talk with your healthcare professional if you take any medications.

CONSUMER VERSION

Medical professionals should consult the Professional Version at www.NaturalDatabase.com.

Medical professionals should consult the Professional Version at www.NaturalDatabase.com.

CHICORY

What other names is the product known by?

Blue Sailors, Cichorii Herba, Cichorium Intybus, Cichorii Radix, Common Chicory Root, Hendibeh, Kasani, Succory, Wild Chicory.

What is it?

Chicory is a plant. The roots and dried, above ground parts of chicory are used to make medicine.

Is it Effective?

The effectiveness ratings for **CHICORY** are as follows:
Insufficient Evidence to Rate Effectiveness for... Constipation, liver and gallbladder disorders, cancer, skin inflammation, loss of appetite, upset stomach, and other conditions.

How does it work?

Chicory root has a mild laxative effect, increases bile from the gallbladder, and decreases swelling. Chicory is a rich source of beta-carotene.

Are there safety concerns?

Chicory is safe for most adults. Handling the chicory plant might cause skin irritation. Chicory might also cause an allergic reaction in people who are sensitive to the Asteraceae/Compositae family.

Do not take chicory if: You are pregnant or breast-feeding. • You have gallstones. • You are sensitive to the Asteraceae/Compositae family. Some of these plants include ragweed, chrysanthemums, marigolds, daisies, and more.

Are there any interactions with medications?

It is not known if chicory interacts with any medicines.
Before taking chicory, talk with your healthcare professional if you take any medications.

CHINESE CLUB MOSS

What other names is the product known by?

Huperzia serrata, Huperazon, Qian Ceng Ta.

What is it?

Chinese club moss is an herb. People use it to make medicine.

Is it Effective?

The effectiveness ratings for **CHINESE CLUB MOSS** are as follows:
Insufficient Evidence to Rate Effectiveness for... Alzheimer's disease and other memory disorders.

How does it work?

Chinese club moss might help increase the level of a brain chemical that is low in patients with memory disorders. It may also protect brain cells against certain poisons.

Are there safety concerns?

There isn't enough information available to know if Chinese club moss is safe. It might cause side effects such as dizziness, nausea, and sweating.

Do not use Chinese club moss if: You are pregnant or breast-feeding. • You have asthma or chronic obstructive pulmonary disease (COPD). • You have heart disease. • You have an obstruction of the intestinal or urinary tracts. • You have stomach or intestinal ulcers. • You have seizures.

Are there any interactions with medications?

Drying medications (Anticholinergic drugs). Chinese club moss contains chemicals that can affect the brain and heart. Some of these drying medications called anticholinergic drugs can also affect the brain and heart. But Chinese club moss works differently than drying medications. Chinese club moss might decrease the effects of drying medications. Some of these drying medications include atropine, scopolamine, and some medications used for allergies (antihistamines), and for depression (antidepressants).
Medications for Alzheimer's disease (Acetylcholinesterase (AChE) inhibitors). Chinese club moss contains a chemical that affects the brain. Medications for Alzheimer's also affect the brain. Taking Chinese club moss along

with medications for Alzheimer's disease might increase effects and side effects of medications for Alzheimer's disease.

Various medications used for glaucoma, Alzheimer's disease, and other conditions (Cholinergic drugs). Chinese club moss contains a chemical that affects the brain. Medications for Alzheimer's also affect the brain. Taking Chinese club moss along with medications for Alzheimer's disease might increase effects and side effects of medications for Alzheimer's disease.

Various medications used for glaucoma, Alzheimer's disease, and other conditions (Cholinergic drugs). Chinese club moss contains a chemical that affects the body. This chemical is similar to some medications used for glaucoma, Alzheimer's disease and other conditions. Taking Chinese club moss with these medications might increase the chance of side effects. Some of these medications used for glaucoma, Alzheimer's disease and other conditions include pilocarpine (Pilocar and others), donepezil (Aricept), tacrine (Cognex), and others.

CHINESE CUCUMBER

What other names is the product known by?
Chinese Cucumber Fruit, Chinese Cucumber Root, Chinese Cucumber Seed, Chinese Snake Gourd, Compound Q, Gua Lou, Gua Luo Ren, Tian Hua Fen, Trichosanthes, Trichosanthes Fruit Peel, Trichosanthes Japonica, Trichosanthes Kirilowii.

What is it?
Chinese cucumber is an herb. People use the fruit, seed, and root to make medicine.

Is it Effective?
The effectiveness ratings for **CHINESE CUCUMBER** are as follows:
Insufficient Evidence to Rate Effectiveness for...HIV infection, inducing abortion, cough, fever, tumors, diabetes, and other conditions.

How does it work?
Chinese cucumber ROOT contains a chemical that might cause abortions when injected during the first trimester of pregnancy. Chinese cucumber SEED might help decrease pain and swelling (inflammation). The FRUIT might also help protect against stomach ulcers.

Are there safety concerns?
Chinese cucumber ROOT is UNSAFE. Chinese cucumber root injections can cause severe side effects, including allergic reactions, seizures, fever, fluid build-up in the lungs and brain, bleeding in the brain, heart damage, and death.

Chinese cucumber FRUIT and SEED seem to be safe for most people. They can cause some mild side effects such as diarrhea and upset stomach.

Do not use Chinese cucumber if: You are pregnant or breast-feeding. • You have diabetes.

Are there any interactions with medications?
Medications for diabetes (Antidiabetes drugs). Chinese cucumber root might decrease blood sugar. Diabetes medications are also used to lower blood sugar. Taking Chinese cucumber root along with diabetes medications might cause your blood sugar to go too low. Monitor your blood sugar closely. The dose of your diabetes medication might need to be changed. Some medications used for diabetes include glimepiride (Amaryl), glyburide (DiaBeta, Glynase PresTab, Micronase), insulin, pioglitazone (Actos), rosiglitazone (Avandia), chlorpropamide (Diabinese), glipizide (Glucotrol), tolbutamide (Orinase), and others.

CHINESE MALLOW

What other names is the product known by?
Cluster Malva, Malva, Malva verticillata.

What is it?
Chinese mallow is an herb. The seed is used to make medicine.

Is it Effective?
The effectiveness ratings for **CHINESE MALLOW** are as follows:
Insufficient Evidence to Rate Effectiveness for... Kidney disorders, stimulating breast milk flow, constipation, and other conditions.

How does it work?
Chinese mallow might lower blood sugar and affect immune system function, according to preliminary research.

Are there safety concerns?
There isn't enough information available to know if Chinese mallow is safe.

Do not use Chinese mallow if: You are pregnant or breast-feeding. • You have diabetes.

Are there any interactions with medications?
Medications for diabetes (Antidiabetes drugs). Chinese mallow extract might decrease blood sugar. Diabetes medications are also used to lower blood sugar. Taking Chinese mallow extract along with diabetes medications might cause your blood sugar to go too low. Monitor your blood sugar closely. The dose of your diabetes medication might need to be changed. Some medications used for diabetes include glimepiride (Amaryl), glyburide (DiaBeta, Glynase PresTab, Micronase), insulin, pioglitazone (Actos), rosiglitazone (Avandia), chlorpropamide (Diabinese), glipizide (Glucotrol), tolbutamide (Orinase), and others.

CHINESE PRICKLY ASH

What other names is the product known by?
Chinese Pepper, Flatspine Prickly Ash, Sansho, Szechwan Pepper, Szechuan Peppercorn, Zanthoxylum bungeanum, Zanthoxylum bungei, Zanthoxylum simulans.

What is it?
Chinese prickly ash is a plant. The bark and berry are used to make medicine. Be careful not to confuse Chinese prickly ash with ash, or northern or southern prickly ash.

Is it Effective?
The effectiveness ratings for **CHINESE PRICKLY ASH** are as follows:
Insufficient Evidence to Rate Effectiveness for... Pain, vomiting, diarrhea, abdominal pain, snakebite, skin diseases, and other conditions.

How does it work?
It is not known how Chinese prickly ash might work.

Are there safety concerns?
There isn't enough information to know if Chinese prickly ash is safe for use as a medicine.

Do not use Chinese prickly ash if: You are pregnant or breast-feeding.

Are there any interactions with medications?
Medications that slow blood clotting (Anticoagulant / Antiplatelet drugs). Chinese prickly ash might slow blood clotting. Taking Chinese prickly ash along with medications that also slow clotting might increase the chances of bruising and bleeding. Some medications that slow blood clotting include aspirin, clopidogrel (Plavix), diclofenac (Voltaren, Cataflam, others), ibuprofen (Advil, Motrin, others), naproxen (Anaprox, Naprosyn, others), dalteparin (Fragmin), enoxaparin (Lovenox), heparin, warfarin (Coumadin), and others.

CHIRATA

What other names is the product known by?
Bitter Stick, Chirayta, Chiretta, East Indian Balmony, Gentiana chirata, Gentiana chirayita, Indian Bolonong, Indian Gentian, Kairata, Kirata, Swertia chirata, Swertia chirayita, Yin Du Zhang Ya Cai.

What is it?
Chirata is an herb. People use the above ground parts to make medicine.

Is it Effective?
The effectiveness ratings for **CHIRATA** are as follows:
Insufficient Evidence to Rate Effectiveness for... Fever, malaria, constipation, worm infestations, upset stomach, loss of appetite, skin diseases, and cancer.

 Natural Medicines Comprehensive Database Consumer Version (209) 472-2244

How does it work?

Chirata contains a chemical that may help reduce swelling (inflammation) and might also have activity against malaria.

Are there safety concerns?

Chirata is safe when taken in the amounts found in beverages; however, there isn't enough information available to know if chirata is safe for use as a medicine.

Do not use chirata if: You are pregnant or breast-feeding. • You have a duodenal (intestine) ulcer.

Are there any interactions with medications?

It is not known if chirata interacts with any medicines.
Before taking chirata, talk with your healthcare professional if you take any medications.

CHITOSAN

What other names is the product known by?

Chitosan Ascorbate; Deacetylated chitosan, Enzymatic polychitosamine hydrolisat, HEP-30; N-Carboxybutyl Chitosan; N,O-Sulfated Chitosan; O-Sulfated N-Acetylchitosan; Sulfated N-Carboxymethylchitosan; Sulfated O-Carboxymethylchitosan.

What is it?

Chitosan is an indigestible sugar. It is obtained from the hard outer skeleton of shellfish, including crab, lobster, and shrimp.

Is it Effective?

The effectiveness ratings for **CHITOSAN** are as follows:
Possibly Effective for... Patients with kidney failure who are on chronic hemodialysis. When ingested by these patients, chitosan may reduce high cholesterol; improve anemia; and improve physical strength, appetite, and sleep • Treating periodontitis, a dental condition • Helping to remake tissue after plastic surgery.
Insufficient Evidence to Rate Effectiveness for... Weight loss and obesity, high cholesterol, Crohn's disease (an intestinal disorder), and other conditions.

How does it work?

Chitosan is extracted from the shells of shrimp, lobster, and crabs. It is a fibrous substance that might block absorption of dietary fat and cholesterol.

Are there safety concerns?

Chitosan seems to be safe for most people. It might cause mild stomach upset, constipation, or gas.

Chitin is extracted from the shells of shellfish. People with shellfish allergies might be allergic to chitosan.

Do not use chitosan if: You are pregnant or breast-feeding. • You have a shellfish allergy.

Are there any interactions with medications?

It is not known if chitosan interacts with any medicines.
Before taking chitosan, talk with your healthcare professional if you take any medications.

CHIVE

What other names is the product known by?

Allium schoenoprasum, Cives.

What is it?

Chive is an herb. People use the above ground plant parts to make medicine.

Is it Effective?

The effectiveness ratings for **CHIVE** are as follows:
Insufficient Evidence to Rate Effectiveness for... Removing parasitic worms.

How does it work?
There isn't enough information available to know how chives work.

Are there safety concerns?
Chives are safe for most people in food amounts. They also seem to be safe when used in larger amounts. Chives can cause an upset stomach when used in large amounts.

Do not use chives in amounts larger than food amounts if: You are pregnant or breast-feeding.

Are there any interactions with medications?
It is not known if chives interact with any medicines.
Before taking chives, talk with your healthcare professional if you take any medications.

CHLORELLA

What other names is the product known by?
Chlorella Vulgaris, Chlorella pyrenoidosa.

What is it?
Chlorella is a freshwater algae. The whole plant is used to make medicine.

Is it Effective?
The effectiveness ratings for **CHLORELLA** are as follows:
Insufficient Evidence to Rate Effectiveness for... Cancer prevention, radiation or chemotherapy side-effects, fibromyalgia, colds, Crohn's disease, ulcerative colitis, ulcers, constipation, bad breath, high blood pressure, high cholesterol, and other conditions.

How does it work?
Chlorella is a good source of protein, fats, carbohydrates, fiber, chlorophyll, vitamins, and minerals. The cell wall of chlorella must be broken down before people can digest it.

Are there safety concerns?
Chlorella seems to be safe for most people when used as a food supplement. The most common side effects include diarrhea, nausea, gas (flatulence), green discoloration of the stools, and stomach cramping, especially in the first week it is used.

Chlorella has caused serious allergic reactions, including asthma and other dangerous breathing problems, especially in people allergic to iodine or seafood.

Chlorella can cause skin to become extra sensitive to the sun. Wear sunblock outside, especially if you are light-skinned.

Do not use chlorella if: You are pregnant or breast-feeding. • You have an iodine sensitivity. • You are allergic to seafood. • You have a disease that causes a weak immune system.

Are there any interactions with medications?
Warfarin (Coumadin). Chlorella contains large amounts of vitamin K. Vitamin K is used by the body to help blood clot. Warfarin (Coumadin) is used to slow blood clotting. By helping the blood clot, chlorella might decrease the effectiveness of warfarin (Coumadin). Be sure to have your blood checked regularly. The dose of your warfarin (Coumadin) might need to be changed.

CHLOROPHYLL

What other names is the product known by?
Chlorophyll a, Chlorophyll b, Chlorophyll c, Chlorophyll d.

What is it?
Chlorophyll is a green pigment found in plants. It helps plants make food. People use it as medicine.

Medical professionals should consult the Professional Version at www.NaturalDatabase.com.

Is it Effective?

The effectiveness ratings for **CHLOROPHYLL** are as follows:

Possibly Effective for... Pancreatitis.

Possibly Ineffective for... Reducing colostomy odor.

Insufficient Evidence to Rate Effectiveness for... Bad breath, constipation, and wounds.

How does it work?

There isn't enough information available to know how chlorophyll works.

Are there safety concerns?

Chlorophyll seems to be safe for most people when taken by mouth. It should not be used by injection without the supervision of a trained medical professional.

Chlorophyll can cause skin to become extra sensitive to the sun. Wear sunblock outside, especially if you are light-skinned.

Do not use chlorophyll if: You are pregnant or breast-feeding, without the supervision of a trained medical professional.

Are there any interactions with medications?

Medications that increase sensitivity to sunlight (Photosensitizing drugs). Some medications can increase sensitivity to sunlight. Chlorophyll might also increase your sensitivity to sunlight. Taking chlorophyll along with medication that increase sensitivity to sunlight could increase the chances of sunburn, blistering or rashes on areas of skin exposed to sunlight. Be sure to wear sunblock and protective clothing when spending time in the sun. Some drugs that cause photosensitivity include amitriptyline (Elavil), Ciprofloxacin (Cipro), norfloxacin (Noroxin), lomefloxacin (Maxaquin), ofloxacin (Floxin), levofloxacin (Levaquin), sparfloxacin (Zagam), gatifloxacin (Tequin), moxifloxacin (Avelox), trimethoprim/sulfamethoxazole (Septra), tetracycline, methoxsalen (8-methoxypsoralen, 8-MOP, Oxsoralen), and Trioxsalen (Trisoralen).

CHLOROPHYLLIN

What other names is the product known by?

None.

What is it?

Chlorophyllin is a chemical that is derived from chlorophyll. People use it as medicine.

Is it Effective?

The effectiveness ratings for **CHLOROPHYLLIN** are as follows:

Possibly Ineffective for... Controlling urinary odor in older patients who can't hold their urine and have a catheter.

Insufficient Evidence to Rate Effectiveness for... Reducing body and fecal odors, treating constipation and gas (flatulence), and other conditions.

How does it work?

There isn't enough information available to know how chlorophyllin works.

Are there safety concerns?

Chlorophyllin seems to be safe for most people.

Do not use chlorophyllin if: You are pregnant or breast-feeding.

Are there any interactions with medications?

It is not known if chlorophyllin interacts with any medicines.

Before taking chlorophyllin, talk with your healthcare professional if you take any medications.

CHOLINE

What other names is the product known by?

Choline Bitartrate, Choline Chloride, Choline Citrate, Intrachol, Lipotropic Factor, Methylated Phosphatidylethanolamine, Trimethylethanolamine, (beta-hydroxyethyl) Trimethylammonium hydroxide.

What is it?

Choline is a nutrient made in the human body. Foods that supply large amounts of choline include liver, muscle meats, fish, nuts, beans, peas, and eggs.

Is it Effective?

The effectiveness ratings for **CHOLINE** are as follows:

Likely Effective for... Liver disease caused by exclusive feeding by vein (parenteral nutrition).

Possibly Effective for... Asthma • Preventing neural tube defects, when taken by a mother around the time of conception.

Possibly Ineffective for...A brain condition called cerebellar ataxia • Alzheimer's disease • Delaying fatigue in endurance sports.

Likely Ineffective for... Memory loss due to age • Schizophrenia.

Insufficient Evidence to Rate Effectiveness for... Hepatitis and other liver disorders, depression, high cholesterol, seizures, Huntington's chorea, and Tourette's syndrome.

How does it work?

Choline is thought to help patients with asthma by decreasing swelling (inflammation). Also, a chemical necessary for normal brain function is made from choline.

Are there safety concerns?

Choline seems to be safe for most adults when used orally in doses of 3.5 grams or less per day. Higher doses are more likely to cause side effects. Choline should not be used intravenously (IV) without the supervision of a medical professional. Side effects caused by choline include sweating, a fishy body odor, gastrointestinal distress, and vomiting. Large doses can cause diarrhea.

Choline is safe for use in pregnant and breast-feeding women. It is also safe for children, if the dose is appropriately adjusted.

Are there any interactions with medications?

It is not known if choline interacts with any medicines.

Before taking choline, talk with your healthcare professional if you take any medications.

CHONDROITIN SULFATE

What other names is the product known by?

CDS, Chondroitin, Chondroitin Polysulfate, Chondroitin Polysulphate, Chondroitin Sulfate A, Chondroitin Sulfates, Chondroitin Sulfate B, Chondroitin Sulfate C, Chondroitin Sulphates, Chondroitin Sulphate A Sodium, Condroitin, CS, CPS, CSA, CSC, GAG, Galactosaminoglucuronoglycan Sulfate, Chondroitin 4-sulfate, Chondroitin 4- and 6-sulfate.

What is it?

Chondroitin sulfate is a chemical that is normally found in cartilage around joints in the body. Chondroitin sulfate is manufactured from animal sources such as cow cartilage.

Is it Effective?

The effectiveness ratings for **CHONDROITIN SULFATE** are as follows:

Likely Effective for... Reducing pain from a kind of arthritis called osteoarthritis • Eye surgery as an FDA-approved prescription eye drop.

Possibly Effective for... Dry eyes as an eye drop.

Insufficient Evidence to Rate Effectiveness for... Heart disease, osteoporosis (weak bones), high cholesterol, and other conditions.

How does it work?

In osteoarthritis, the cartilage in the joints breaks down. Taking chondroitin sulfate, one of the building blocks of cartilage, might slow this breakdown.

 Natural Medicines Comprehensive Database Consumer Version (209) 472-2244

Are there safety concerns?

Chondroitin sulfate seems to be safe for most people. It can cause some mild stomach pain and nausea. Other side effects that have been reported are diarrhea, constipation, swollen eyelids, leg swelling, hair loss, and irregular heartbeat.

There is some concern about the safety of chondroitin sulfate because it comes from animal sources. Some people are worried that unsafe manufacturing practices might lead to contamination of chondroitin products with diseased animal tissues including those that might transmit bovine spongiform encephalopathy (mad cow disease). So far, there are no reports of chondroitin causing disease in humans, and the risk is thought to be low.

Some chondroitin products contain excess amounts of manganese. Ask your healthcare professional about reliable brands.

Do not use chondroitin sulfate if: You are pregnant or breast-feeding. • You have asthma. • You have prostate cancer or an increased risk for prostate cancer.

Are there any interactions with medications?

Warfarin (Coumadin). Warfarin (Coumadin) is used to slow blood clotting. There is one report of someone taking very large amounts of glucosamine and chondroitin and having blood that was too "thin." Blood that is too "thin" can cause bruising and bleeding. But there is not enough information to know if this interaction is a big concern or if it can happen with normal amounts of glucosamine and chondroitin.

CHROMIUM

What other names is the product known by?

Atomic Number 24, Chromic Chloride, Chromium Chloride, Chromium Nicotinate, Chromium Picolinate, Cr.

What is it?

Chromium is a metal. It is called an "essential trace element" because very small amounts of chromium are necessary for human health.

Is it Effective?

The effectiveness ratings for **CHROMIUM** are as follows:
Possibly Ineffective for... Athletic conditioning • Prediabetes.
Insufficient Evidence to Rate Effectiveness for... Diabetes, improving athletic performance, low blood sugar (hypoglycemia), obesity and weight loss, depression, preventing a heart attack, Turner's syndrome (a genetic disorder that has a high risk of diabetes), and other conditions.

How does it work?

Chromium might help keep blood sugar levels normal by improving the way our bodies use insulin.

Are there safety concerns?

Chromium is safe for most adults when used appropriately for 6 months or less. Chromium also seems to be safe for most people when used for longer periods of time. Some people experience side effects such as skin irritation, headaches, dizziness, nausea, mood changes and impaired thinking, judgment, and coordination. High doses have been linked to more serious side effects including blood disorders, liver or kidney damage, and other problems. But it is not known if chromium is the actual cause of these side effects.

Do not take chromium supplements if: You are pregnant or breast-feeding. • You have kidney problems. • You have a chromate allergy. • You have a behavioral or psychiatric condition such as depression, anxiety, or schizophrenia. • You have liver disease.

Are there any interactions with medications?

Insulin. Chromium might decrease blood sugar. Insulin is also used to decrease blood sugar. Taking chromium along with insulin might cause your blood sugar to be too low. Monitor your blood sugar closely. The dose of your insulin might need to be changed.
NSAIDs (Nonsteroidal anti-inflammatory drugs). NSAIDs are anti-inflammatory medications used for decreasing pain and swelling. NSAIDs might increase chromium levels in the body and increase the risk of adverse effects. Avoid taking chromium supplements and NSAIDs at the same time. Some NSAIDs include ibuprofen (Advil, Motrin, Nuprin, others), indomethacin (Indocin), naproxen (Aleve, Anaprox, Naprelan, Naprosyn), piroxicam (Feldene), aspirin, and others.

CHRYSANTHEMUM

What other names is the product known by?
Anthemis grandiflorum, Anthemis stipulacea, Chrysanthemum sinense, Chrysanthemum stipulaceum, Chrysanthemum morifolium, Dendranthema grandiflorum, Dendranthema morifolium, Florist's Chrysanthemum, Ju Hua, Matricaria morifolia, Mum.

What is it?
Chrysanthemum is a plant. People use the flowers to make medicine.

Is it Effective?
The effectiveness ratings for **CHRYSANTHEMUM** are as follows:
Insufficient Evidence to Rate Effectiveness for... Angina, high blood pressure, diabetes, fevers, headache, dizziness, prostate cancer, and other conditions.

How does it work?
Chrysanthemum may increase blood flow to the heart. It may also increase sensitivity to insulin.

Are there safety concerns?
There isn't enough information to know if chrysanthemum is safe. Chrysanthemum can cause skin to become extra sensitive to the sun. Wear sunblock outside, especially if you are light-skinned. It can also cause an allergic reaction in people sensitive to marigolds, daisies, and related herbs.

Do not use chrysanthemum if: You are pregnant or breast-feeding. • You are allergic to marigolds, daisies, and related herbs.

Are there any interactions with medications?
It is not known if chrysanthemum interacts with any medicines.
Before taking chrysanthemum, talk with your healthcare professional if you take any medications.

CHRYSIN

What other names is the product known by?
5,7-Chrysin, 5,7-Dihydroxyflavone, Flavone X, Flavonoid, Galangin Flavanone.

What is it?
Chrysin is a substance called a flavonoid that occurs naturally in plants such as the passionflower, silver linden, and some geranium species; and in honey and bee propolis (glue).

Is it Effective?
The effectiveness ratings for **CHRYSIN** are as follows:
Possibly Ineffective for... Improving resistance training (bodybuilding) in athletes (in combination with other supplements).
Insufficient Evidence to Rate Effectiveness for... Anxiety, inflammation, gout, HIV infection/AIDS, impotence, baldness, or preventing cancer.

How does it work?
Laboratory research suggested that chrysin might increase the male hormone called testosterone and increase bodybuilding effects, but research in humans hasn't found any effect on testosterone levels. The amount of chrysin that is absorbed from the gut may be very small, which would make therapeutic effects unlikely.

Are there safety concerns?
Chrysin is possibly safe for most adults when used appropriately for up to 8 weeks. No adverse effects have been reported.

Do not use chrysin if: You are pregnant or breast-feeding.

Are there any interactions with medications?
Medications for estrogen sensitive cancers (Aromatase inhibitors). Some types of cancer are affected by hormones in the body. Estrogen sensitive cancers are cancers that are affected by estrogen levels in the body. Medications for estrogen sensitive cancers help decrease estrogen in the body. Chrysin might also decrease estrogen in the body. Taking chrysin along with medications for estrogen sensitive cancers might decrease estrogen

 Natural Medicines Comprehensive Database Consumer Version (209) 472-2244

in the body too much. Some medications for estrogen sensitive cancers include aminoglutethimide (Cytadren), anastrozole (Arimidex), exemestane (Aromasin), letrozole (Femara), and others.

Medications changed by the liver (Glucuronidated Drugs). The body breaks down some medications to get rid of them. The liver helps break down these medications. Chrysin might increase how quickly some medications are changed by the liver. This could decrease how well some of these medications work. Some of these medications changed by the liver include acetaminophen, atorvastatin (Lipitor), diazepam (Valium), digoxin, entacapone (Comtan), estrogen, irinotecan (Camptosar), lamotrigine (Lamictal), lorazepam (Ativan), lovastatin (Mevacor), meprobamate, morphine, oxazepam (Serax), and others.

Medications changed by the liver (Cytochrome P450 1A2 (CYP1A2) substrates). Some medications are changed and broken down by the liver. Chrysin might decrease how quickly the liver breaks down some medications. Taking chrysin along with some medications that are changed by the liver might increase the effects and side effects of some medications. Before taking chrysin talk to your healthcare provider if you take any medications that are changed by the liver. Some of these medications that are changed by the liver include clozapine (Clozaril), cyclobenzaprine (Flexeril), fluvoxamine (Luvox), haloperidol (Haldol), imipramine (Tofranil), mexiletine (Mexitil), olanzapine (Zyprexa), pentazocine (Talwin), propranolol (Inderal), tacrine (Cognex), theophylline, zileuton (Zyflo), zolmitriptan (Zomig), and others.

CHYMOTRYPSIN

What other names is the product known by?

A-Chymotrypsin, Alpha-Chymotrypsin, Chymotrypsin A, Chymotrypsin B, Chymotrypsinum, Quimotripsina.

What is it?

Chymotrypsin is an enzyme. People use it to make medicine.

Is it Effective?

The effectiveness ratings for **CHYMOTRYPSIN** are as follows:

Effective for... Cataract surgery, when used by a healthcare professional.

Possibly Effective for... Fluid retention and swelling (inflammation) associated with a broken hand and burns.

Insufficient Evidence to Rate Effectiveness for... Asthma, bronchitis, lung diseases, sinusitis, and other conditions.

How does it work?

Chymotrypsin has ingredients that reduce swelling (inflammation) and tissue destruction.

Are there safety concerns?

Chymotrypsin is safe when used in the eye by a healthcare professional. Chymotrypsin can cause side effects when used in the eye, including an increase in pressure in the eye and other eye conditions such as uveitis, paralysis of the iris, and keratitis.

It also seems to be safe for most people to apply directly to the skin.

Rarely, chymotrypsin might cause an allergic reaction when taken by mouth. Symptoms include itching, shortness of breath, swelling of the lips or throat, shock, loss of consciousness, and death.

Do not use chymotrypsin if: You are pregnant or breast-feeding.

Are there any interactions with medications?

It is not known if chymotrypsin interacts with any medicines.

Before taking chymotrypsin, talk with your healthcare professional if you take any medications.

CIGUATERA

What other names is the product known by?
Gambierdiscus toxicus.

What is it?
Ciguatera is a poison. It can be ingested by eating contaminated fish.

Is it Effective?
The effectiveness ratings for **CIGUATERA** are as follows:
Insufficient Evidence to Rate Effectiveness for... Ciguatera does not have any medicinal uses.

How does it work?
Ciguatera interferes with the normal function of nerve cells.

Are there safety concerns?
Ciguatera is UNSAFE. One bite of contaminated fish can be enough to cause symptoms. The most common symptoms include stomach cramps, nausea, vomiting, and diarrhea. Other symptoms include itching; numbness of lips, tongue, and throat; blurred vision; low blood pressure; slowed heart rate; alternating hot and cold sensations; and coma. In severe cases, shock, muscular paralysis, and death can occur.

Ciguatera poisoning can be caused by eating normally safe, bottom-feeding, coral-reef fish that have collected a poison from the food chain. It is common in areas of disturbed reef, including waterfront construction. Over 400 normally safe fish species may contain toxin, with the red snapper, barracuda, and grouper most often involved. Florida and Hawaii have the greatest incidence of ciguatera poisoning. These fish appear normal, including smell and taste. There are no good "rules of thumb" for detecting poisonous fish.

Do not use ciguatera if: You are pregnant or breast-feeding.

Are there any interactions with medications?
It is not known if ciguatera interacts with any medicines.
Before taking ciguatera, talk with your healthcare professional if you take any medications.

CINCHONA

What other names is the product known by?
Cinchona calisaya, Cinchona ledgeriana, Cinchona pubescens, Cinchona succirubra, Chinarinde, Ecorce de Quina, Fieberrinde, Jesuit's Bark, Peruvian Bark, Quinine, Red Cinchona Bark.

What is it?
Cinchona is a tree. People use the bark to make medicine.

Is it Effective?
The effectiveness ratings for **CINCHONA** are as follows:
Insufficient Evidence to Rate Effectiveness for... Hemorrhoids, varicose veins, colds, leg cramps, influenza, malaria, fever, cancer, mouth and throat diseases, enlarged spleen, muscle cramps, loss of appetite, and stomach discomforts such as bloating and fullness.

How does it work?
Cinchona bark stimulates saliva and stomach (gastric) juice secretion.

Are there safety concerns?
Cinchona bark seems to be safe for most people. In large amounts, cinchona is UNSAFE and can be deadly. Symptoms of overdose include ringing of the ears, headache, nausea, diarrhea, and vision disturbances. Cinchona can also cause bleeding and allergic reactions, including hives and fever.

Do not use cinchona if: You are pregnant or breast-feeding. • You have stomach (gastric) or intestinal (duodenal) ulcers.

Are there any interactions with medications?
Antacids. Antacids are used to decrease stomach acid. Cinchona may increase stomach acid. By increasing stomach acid, cinchona might decrease the effectiveness of antacids. Some antacids include calcium carbonate

Medical professionals should consult the Professional Version at www.NaturalDatabase.com.

(Tums, others), dihydroxyaluminum sodium carbonate (Rolaids, others), magaldrate (Riopan), magnesium sulfate (Bilagog), aluminum hydroxide (Amphojel), and others.

Medications that decrease stomach acid (H2-Blockers). Cinchona might increase stomach acid. By increasing stomach acid, cinchona might decrease the effectiveness of some medications that decrease stomach acid, called H2-Blockers. Some medications that decrease stomach acid include cimetidine (Tagamet), ranitidine (Zantac), nizatidine (Axid), and famotidine (Pepcid).

Medications that decrease stomach acid (Proton pump inhibitors). Cinchona might increase stomach acid. By increasing stomach acid, cinchona might decrease the effectiveness of medications that are used to decrease stomach acid, called proton pump inhibitors. Some medications that decrease stomach acid include omeprazole (Prilosec), lansoprazole (Prevacid), rabeprazole (Aciphex), pantoprazole (Protonix), and esomeprazole (Nexium).

Medications that slow blood clotting (Anticoagulant / Antiplatelet drugs). Cinchona might slow blood clotting. Taking cinchona along with medications that also slow clotting might increase the chances of bruising and bleeding. Some medications that slow blood clotting include aspirin, clopidogrel (Plavix), diclofenac (Voltaren, Cataflam, others), ibuprofen (Advil, Motrin, others), naproxen (Anaprox, Naprosyn, others), dalteparin (Fragmin), enoxaparin (Lovenox), heparin, warfarin (Coumadin), and others.

Phenobarbital (Luminal). Cinchona contains quinine. Quinine might increase how much phenobarbital (Luminal) is in the body. Taking cinchona with phenobarbital might increase the effects and side effects of phenobarbital.

Carbamazepine (Tegretol). The body breaks down carbamazepine to get rid of it. Cinchona contains quinine. Quinine can cause the body to break down carbamazepine (Tegretol) too quickly. Taking cinchona along with carbamazepine (Tegretol) can decrease the effectiveness of carbamazepine (Tegretol).

Quinidine. Cinchona contains quinidine. Taking quinidine along with cinchona can increase the effects and side effects of quinidine and cause heart problems. Do not take cinchona if you are taking quinidine.

Quinine. Cinchona contains quinine. Taking quinidine along with cinchona can increase the effects and side effects of quinine and cause heart problems. Do not take cinchona if you are taking quinine.

CINNAMON bark

What other names is the product known by?

Batavia Cassia, Batavia Cinnamon, Cannelier de Ceylan, Ceylon Cinnamon, Ceylonzimt, Ceylonzimtbaum, Cinnamomum verum, Cinnamomum zeylanicum, Laurus cinnamomum, Madagascar Cinnamon, Padang-Cassia, Panang Cinnamon, Saigon Cassia, Saigon Cinnamon, Sri Lanka Cinnamon, Thwak, Tvak.

What is it?

Cinnamon comes from a tree. People use the bark to make medicine.

Is it Effective?

The effectiveness ratings for **CINNAMON bark** are as follows:

Possibly Effective for... Premature ejaculation. Some evidence suggests that a specific cream containing cinnamon and many other ingredients might prevent premature ejaculation.

Insufficient Evidence to Rate Effectiveness for... Diabetes, diarrhea, infections, worm infestations, the common cold, influenza, upset stomach, gas (flatulence), spasms, appetite stimulation, and menstrual discomfort.

How does it work?

The oils found in cinnamon bark are thought to reduce spasms, reduce gas (flatulence), and stimulate the appetite. Cinnamon might also increase blood flow. Cinnamon bark also contains a chemical that might work like insulin to lower blood sugar.

Are there safety concerns?

Consuming cinnamon bark in food amounts is safe. Cinnamon bark seems to be safe for most people, in amounts slightly higher than those found in foods. It is unsafe when taken in large amounts. Ingesting cinnamon oil might not be safe. The oil can be irritating to the skin and mucous membranes, including the stomach, intestine, and urinary tract. It can cause side effects such as diarrhea, vomiting, dizziness, sedation, and others.

Do not use cinnamon in amounts greater than those found in food if: You are pregnant or breast-feeding. • You have diabetes. Cinnamon might lower blood sugar.

Are there any interactions with medications?

Medications for diabetes (Antidiabetes drugs). Cinnamon bark might decrease blood sugar. Diabetes medications are also used to lower blood sugar. Taking cinnamon bark along with diabetes medications might cause your blood sugar to go too low. Monitor your blood sugar closely. The dose of your diabetes medication might need to be changed. Some medications used for diabetes include glimepiride (Amaryl), glyburide (DiaBeta, Glynase PresTab, Micronase), insulin, pioglitazone (Actos), rosiglitazone (Avandia), chlorpropamide (Diabinese), glipizide (Glucotrol), tolbutamide (Orinase), and others.

Medical professionals should consult the Professional Version at www.NaturalDatabase.com.

Medical professionals should consult the Professional Version at www.NaturalDatabase.com.

CITICOLINE

What other names is the product known by?
CDPC, CDP Choline, CDP-Choline, Citicholine, Cytidine 5-diphosphocholine, Cytidine 5'-diphosphocholine, Cytidine (5') diphosphocholine, Cytidine diphosphate choline, Cytidine Diphosphocholine, Cytidinediphosphocholine.

What is it?
Citicoline is a brain chemical that occurs naturally in the body. People use citicoline supplements as medicine.

Is it Effective?
The effectiveness ratings for **CITICOLINE** are as follows:
Possibly Effective for... Age-related memory problems • Stroke.
Insufficient Evidence to Rate Effectiveness for... Alzheimer's disease and other types of dementia, head trauma, Parkinson's disease, and glaucoma.

How does it work?
Citicoline seems to increase a brain chemical called phosphatidylcholine. This brain chemical is important for brain function. Citicoline might also decrease brain tissue damage when the brain is injured.

Are there safety concerns?
Citicoline seems to be safe when taken short-term. The safety of long-term use is not known. Most people who take citicoline don't experience problematic side effects. But some people can have side effects such as insomnia, headache, diarrhea, low or high blood pressure, nausea, blurred vision, chest pains, and others.

Do not take citicoline if: You are pregnant or breast-feeding.

Are there any interactions with medications?
It is not known if citicoline interacts with any medicines.
Talk to your healthcare provider before taking citicoline if you are currently taking any medications.

CITRONELLA OIL

What other names is the product known by?
Andropogon nardus, Ceylon Citronella, Cymbopogon nardus, Cymbopogon winterianus, Java Citronella.

What is it?
Citronella is an herb. People use the oil to make medicine.

Is it Effective?
The effectiveness ratings for **CITRONELLA OIL** are as follows:
Possibly Effective for... Preventing mosquito bites when applied to the skin. Citronella oil is an ingredient in some commercial mosquito repellents. It seems to prevent mosquito bites for a very short amount of time. Other mosquito repellents, such as those containing DEET, are usually preferred because these repellents last much longer.
Insufficient Evidence to Rate Effectiveness for... Worm infestations, fluid retention, spasms, and other conditions.

How does it work?
There isn't enough information available to know how citronella oil works.

Are there safety concerns?
Citronella seems to be safe for most people when used in the amounts found in foods. There isn't enough information to know if citronella oil is safe for any medical conditions.

When applied to the skin, it might cause skin irritation. If it is inhaled, it can cause severe irritation of the lungs.

Keep out of the reach of children. Death has occurred in a child following the ingestion of citronella oil in insect repellents.

Do not use citronella oil if: You are pregnant or breast-feeding.

Are there any interactions with medications?
It is not known if citronella oil interacts with any medicines.
Before taking citronella oil, talk with your healthcare professional if you take any medications.

CIVET

What other names is the product known by?
African Civet, Civettictis civetta, Large Indian Civet, Viverra civetta, Viverra zibetha, Zibeth.

What is it?
Civet is a secretion from the glands of an African mammal. It is used to make medicine.

Is it Effective?
The effectiveness ratings for **CIVET** are as follows:
Insufficient Evidence to Rate Effectiveness for... Pain relief and sleeplessness.

How does it work?
There isn't enough information available to know how civet works.

Are there safety concerns?
Civet seems to be safe for most people when used in the amounts found in foods. There isn't enough information to know if civet is safe for any medical conditions.

Do not use civet if: You are pregnant or breast-feeding.

Are there any interactions with medications?
It is not known if civet interacts with any medicines.
Before taking civet, talk with your healthcare professional if you take any medications.

CLARY SAGE

What other names is the product known by?
Clary, Clary Wort, Clear Eye, Eyebright, Muscatel Sage, Salvia sclarea, See Bright.

What is it?
Clary sage is an herb. The flowers and leaves are used to make medicine.

Is it Effective?
The effectiveness ratings for **CLARY SAGE** are as follows:
Insufficient Evidence to Rate Effectiveness for... Upset stomach, digestive disorders, kidney diseases, tumors, and other conditions.

How does it work?
The oil found in clary sage might help reduce seizure activity. Because the oil is thick and sticky, it might also help pull objects from under the eyelid and from the skin.

Are there safety concerns?
Clary sage is safe when used in amounts found in foods. There isn't enough information to know if it is safe when used in medicinal amounts.

Do not take clary sage if: You are pregnant or breast-feeding.

Are there any interactions with medications?
Chloral Hydrate. Chloral hydrate causes sleepiness and drowsiness. Clary sage seems to increase the effects of choral hydrate. Taking clary sage along with chloral hydrate might cause too much sleepiness.
Hexobarbitone. Hexobarbitone can cause sleepiness and drowsiness. Clary sage seems to increase the effects of hexobarbitone. Taking clary sage along with hexobarbitone might cause too much sleepiness.

CLEMATIS

What other names is the product known by?
Clematis recta, Upright Virgin's Bower.

What is it?
Clematis is an herb. People use the above ground parts to make medicine.

Is it Effective?
The effectiveness ratings for **CLEMATIS** are as follows:
Insufficient Evidence to Rate Effectiveness for... Arthritis-like pain, headache, varicose veins, syphilis, gout, bone disorders, skin conditions, fluid retention, blisters, wounds, and ulcers.

How does it work?
The crushed fresh clematis plant contains a chemical that causes skin and mucous membrane irritation. This chemical becomes less effective as the plant dries.

Are there safety concerns?
Clematis is UNSAFE. It can cause colic, diarrhea, and severe irritation to the gastrointestinal and urinary tracts when taken by mouth. With extended skin contact, the fresh plant can cause slow healing blisters and burns.

Are there any interactions with medications?
It is not known if clematis interacts with any medicines.
Before taking clematis, talk with your healthcare professional if you take any medications.

CLIVERS

What other names is the product known by?
Barweed, Bedstraw, Catchweed, Cleavers, Cleaverwort, Coachweed, Eriffe, Everlasting Friendship, Galium aparine, Goose Grass, Goosebill, Gosling Weed, Grip Grass, Hayriffe, Hayruff, Hedge-Burs, Hedgeheriff, Love-Man, Mutton Chops, Robin-Run-in-the-Grass, Scratchweed, Stick-a-Back, Sweethearts.

What is it?
Clivers is an herb. People use the above ground parts to make medicine.

Is it Effective?
The effectiveness ratings for **CLIVERS** are as follows:
Insufficient Evidence to Rate Effectiveness for... Fluid retention, painful urination, psoriasis, enlarged lymph nodes, skin ulcers, breast lumps, and skin rashes.

How does it work?
Clivers contains chemicals called tannins that might help reduce skin inflammation and have a drying (astringent) effect on the tissues.

Are there safety concerns?
Clivers seems to be safe for most people.

Do not use clivers if: You are pregnant or breast-feeding. • You have diabetes.

Are there any interactions with medications?
It is not known if clivers interacts with any medicines.
Before taking clivers, talk with your healthcare professional if you take any medications.

 Natural Medicines Comprehensive Database Consumer Version (209) 472-2244

CLOVE

What other names is the product known by?

Caryophylli Flos, Caryophyllum, Caryophyllus aromaticus, Clous de Girolfe, Clove Flower, Clove Flowerbud, Clove Leaf, Clove Oil, Clove Stem, Cloves, Eugenia Aromatica, Eugenia Caryophyllata, Eugenia Caryophyllus, Flores Caryophylli, Flores Caryophyllum, Gewurznelken Nagelein, Kreteks, Lavanga, Syzygium aromaticum.

What is it?

Clove is an herb. People use the oils, dried flower buds, leaves, and stems to make medicine.

Is it Effective?

The effectiveness ratings for **CLOVE** are as follows:

Possibly Effective for... Premature ejaculation when applied directly to the skin of the penis in combination with other medicines.

Insufficient Evidence to Rate Effectiveness for... Toothache, "dry socket" following tooth extraction, vomiting, upset stomach, nausea, gas (flatulence), diarrhea, hernia, mouth and throat swelling (inflammation), cough, and other conditions.

How does it work?

Clove oil contains a chemical that may decrease pain.

Are there safety concerns?

Clove seems safe for most people when taken by mouth or applied to the skin. Prolonged use of clove oil in the mouth can cause damage to the gums, tooth pulp, skin, and mucous membranes.

Clove oil is UNSAFE to take by mouth. As little as one teaspoonful can cause severe side effects such as seizures, liver damage, and fluid imbalances.

Inhalation of the smoke from clove cigarettes is UNSAFE and can cause side effects such as breathing problems and lung infections. Dried clove can also cause mouth sensitivity and irritation, and damage to dental tissues.

Clove, mixed with other ingredients for impotence, also seems to be safe when applied to the penis and removed after one hour. It might cause mild pain, irritation or a burning sensation, and delayed ejaculation. It is not known if this cream is safe for repeated, long-term use.

Do not use clove in medicinal amounts if: You are pregnant or breast-feeding. • You have a bleeding disorder.

Are there any interactions with medications?

Medications that slow blood clotting (Anticoagulant / Antiplatelet drugs). Clove might slow blood clotting. Taking clove oil along with medications that also slow clotting might increase the chances of bruising and bleeding. Clove contains eugenol. Eugenol is the part of clove that might slow blood clotting. Eugenol is very fragrant and gives allspice and clove their distinctive smell. Some medications that slow blood clotting include aspirin, clopidogrel (Plavix), diclofenac (Voltaren, Cataflam, others), ibuprofen (Advil, Motrin, others), naproxen (Anaprox, Naprosyn, others), dalteparin (Fragmin), enoxaparin (Lovenox), heparin, warfarin (Coumadin), and others.

CLOWN'S MUSTARD PLANT

What other names is the product known by?

Bitter Candytuft, Candytuft, Iberis Amara.

What is it?

Clown's mustard plant is an herb. People use the leaves, stem, roots, and seeds to make medicine.

Is it Effective?

The effectiveness ratings for **CLOWN'S MUSTARD PLANT** are as follows:

Possibly Effective for... Upset stomach (dyspepsia), when a combination of clown's mustard plant and several other herbs is used.

Insufficient Evidence to Rate Effectiveness for... Irritable bowel syndrome (IBS), gastritis, bloating, gout, muscular aches and pains (rheumatism), rapid heart rate, asthma, bronchitis, and other conditions.

How does it work?
Preliminary research suggests clown's mustard plant might increase contractions in the small intestine, which helps move food through the digestive tract.

Are there safety concerns?
Clown's mustard plant seems to be safe for most people when used for up to eight weeks. It can cause side effects in some people, including nausea, diarrhea, and skin rashes.

Do not take clown's mustard plant if: You are pregnant or breast-feeding.

Are there any interactions with medications?
It is not known if clown's mustard plant interacts with any medicines.
Before taking clown's mustard plant, talk with your healthcare professional if you take any medications.

CLUB MOSS

What other names is the product known by?
Lycopodium clavatum, Stags Horn, Vegetable Sulfur, Witch Meal, Wolfs Claw.

What is it?
Club moss is an herb. People use the whole plant to make medicine.

Is it Effective?
The effectiveness ratings for **CLUB MOSS** are as follows:
Insufficient Evidence to Rate Effectiveness for... Bladder and kidney disorders.

How does it work?
There isn't enough information available to know how club moss works.

Are there safety concerns?
Club moss seems unsafe for use because it contains several poisonous chemicals.

Do not use club moss if: You are pregnant or breast-feeding.

Are there any interactions with medications?
It is not known if club moss interacts with any medicines.
Before taking club moss, talk with your healthcare professional if you take any medications.

CNIDIUM

What other names is the product known by?
Cnidium Extract, Cnidium Fruit, Cnidium Fruit Extract, Cnidium monnier, Cnidium monnieri fructus, Cnidium Seeds, Monnier's Snowparsley, Selinum monnieri, She Chuang Zi.

What is it?
Cnidium is a plant native to China. The fruit, seed, and other plant parts are used as medicine.

Is it Effective?
The effectiveness ratings for **CNIDIUM** are as follows:
Insufficient Evidence to Rate Effectiveness for... Increasing sexual performance and libido, erectile dysfunction, infertility, body building, increasing energy, cancer, osteoporosis, infections, itchy skin, rashes, eczema, and ringworm.

How does it work?
Chemicals in cnidium might decrease itching.

Are there safety concerns?
There is not enough known about the safety of cnidium.

Do not use cnidium if: You are pregnant or breast-feeding.

Are there any interactions with medications?
It is not known if cnidium interacts with any medicines.
Before taking cnidium, talk with your healthcare professional if you are taking any medications.

COCA

What other names is the product known by?
Bolivian Coca, Cocaine Plant, Erythroxylum coca, Erythroxylum novogranatense, Health Inca Tea, Huanuco Coca, Inca Health Tea, Inca Tea, Java Coca, Mate de Coca, Peruvian Coca, Spadic, Truxillo Coca.

What is it?
Coca is a plant. Cocaine is the major component found in the coca plant. People use the leaf to make medicine.

Is it Effective?
The effectiveness ratings for **COCA** are as follows:
Likely Ineffective for... Improving physical performance.
Insufficient Evidence to Rate Effectiveness for... Stimulation of stomach function, asthma, colds, and other conditions.

How does it work?
The cocaine found in coca can cause an increase in brain activity and have numbing (anesthetic) effects. Cocaine is highly addictive.

Are there safety concerns?
Coca leaf without the cocaine (decocainized) is safe for most people when used in normal food amounts. The component cocaine is safe for use on the eye or skin under the supervision of a medical professional.

Cocaine is UNSAFE and illegal for either medicinal or recreational self-use. Cocaine can cause hyperactivity, restlessness, excitement, migraine headaches, seizures, strokes, heart attacks, aneurysms, high blood pressure, and liver and kidney failure.
As little as 1/4 of a teaspoon of cocaine can be deadly. Cocaine is highly addictive.

Do not use coca if: You are pregnant or breast-feeding. • You have asthma. • You have a heart condition or high blood pressure. • You have a history of strokes or are at risk for strokes. • You have a condition called plasma pseudocholinesterase deficiency (PPD).

Are there any interactions with medications?
Alcohol. Coca contains cocaine. Cocaine can affect your thinking. Alcohol can also affect your thinking. Do not take coca if you have been drinking alcohol.
Nifedipine. Coca contains cocaine. Taking cocaine with nifedipine increases the risk of serious side effects such as seizure.

COCILLANA

What other names is the product known by?
Grape Bark, Guapi, Guarea rusbyi, Sycocarpus rusbyi, Trompillo, Upas.

What is it?
Cocillana is an herb. People use the bark to make medicine.

Is it Effective?
The effectiveness ratings for **COCILLANA** are as follows:
Insufficient Evidence to Rate Effectiveness for... Coughs and skin tumors.

How does it work?
There isn't enough information currently available to know how cocillana works.

Are there safety concerns?
There isn't enough information currently available to know if cocillana is safe.

Do not use cocillana if: You are pregnant or breast-feeding.

Medical professionals should consult the Professional Version at www.NaturalDatabase.com.

CONSUMER VERSION

Are there any interactions with medications?

It is not known if cocillana interacts with any medicines.

Before taking cocillana, talk with your healthcare professional if you take any medications.

COCOA

What other names is the product known by?

Cacao, Chocolate, Cocoa Bean, Cocoa Butter, Cocoa Oleum, Cocoa Seed, Cocoa Semen, Cocoa Testae, Theobroma, Theobromine.

What is it?

Cocoa is the plant from which chocolate is made. People use the seed to make medicine.

Is it Effective?

The effectiveness ratings for **COCOA** are as follows:

Insufficient Evidence to Rate Effectiveness for... High blood pressure, intestinal diseases, diarrhea, asthma, bronchitis, lung congestion, liver, bladder and kidney ailments, diabetes, preventing heart disease, wrinkles, and stretch marks during pregnancy.

How does it work?

Cocoa contains a variety of chemicals, including antioxidants called flavonoids. It is not clear how these might work in the body, but they appear to cause relaxation of veins. This could lead to lower blood pressure.

Are there safety concerns?

Consuming cocoa is safe for most people. Cocoa contains caffeine and related chemicals. Consuming large amounts might cause caffeine-related side effects such as nervousness, sleeplessness, and a fast heartbeat. Cocoa butter used on the skin appears to be safe for most people.

Do not use cocoa in large doses if: You are pregnant or breast-feeding. • You have a history of anxiety attacks. • You have acid reflux disease. • You have migraine headaches. • You have diabetes. • You have a rapid heartbeat known as an arrhythmia.

Are there any interactions with medications?

Adenosine (Adenocard). Cocoa contains caffeine. The caffeine in cocoa might block the affects of adenosine (Adenocard). Adenosine (Adenocard) is often used by doctors to do a test on the heart. This test is called a cardiac stress test. Stop taking cocoa or other caffeine-containing products at least 24 hours before a cardiac stress test.

Antibiotics (Quinolone antibiotics). The body breaks down caffeine to get rid of it. Some antibiotics might decrease how quickly the body breaks down caffeine. Taking these antibiotics along with cocoa can increase the risk of side effects including jitteriness, headache, increased heart rate, and other side effects. Some antibiotics that decrease how quickly the body breaks down caffeine include ciprofloxacin (Cipro), enoxacin (Penetrex), norfloxacin (Chibroxin, Noroxin), sparfloxacin (Zagam), trovafloxacin (Trovan), and grepafloxacin (Raxar).

Birth control pills (Contraceptive drugs). The body breaks down the caffeine in cocoa to get rid of it. Birth control pills can decrease how quickly the body breaks down caffeine. Taking cocoa along with birth control pills can cause jitteriness, headache, fast heartbeat, and other side effects. Some birth control pills include ethinyl estradiol and levonorgestrel (Triphasil), ethinyl estradiol and norethindrone (Ortho-Novum 1/35, Ortho-Novum 7/7/7), and others.

Cimetidine (Tagamet). Cocoa contains caffeine. The body breaks down caffeine to get rid of it. Cimetidine (Tagamet) can decrease how quickly your body breaks down caffeine. Taking cimetidine (Tagamet) along with cocoa might increase the chance of caffeine side effects including jitteriness, headache, fast heartbeat, and others.

Clozapine (Clozaril). The body breaks down clozapine (Clozaril) to get rid of it. The caffeine in cocoa seems to decrease how quickly the body breaks down clozapine (Clozaril). Taking cocoa along with clozapine (Clozaril) can increase the effects and side effects of clozapine (Clozaril).

Dipyridamole (Persantine). Cocoa contains caffeine. The caffeine in cocoa might block the affects of dipyridamole (Persantine). Dipyridamole (Persantine) is often used by doctors to do a test on the heart. This test is called a cardiac stress test. Stop drinking cocoa or other caffeine-containing products at least 24 hours before a cardiac stress test.

Disulfiram (Antabuse). The body breaks down caffeine to get rid of it. Disulfiram (Antabuse) can decrease how quickly the body gets rid of caffeine. Taking cocoa (which contains caffeine) along with disulfiram (Antabuse) might increase the effects and side effects of caffeine including jitteriness, hyperactivity, irritability, and others.

Ergotamine (Ergomar). Cocoa contains caffeine. Caffeine can increase how much ergotamine (Ergomar) the body absorbs. Taking cocoa along with ergotamine (Ergomar) might increase the effects and side effects of ergotamine.

Estrogens. The body breaks down the caffeine in cocoa to get rid of it. Estrogens can decrease how quickly the body breaks down caffeine. Taking caffeine along with estrogens might cause jitteriness, headache, fast heartbeat, and other side effects. If you take estrogens limit your caffeine intake. Some estrogen pills include conjugated equine estrogens (Premarin), ethinyl estradiol, estradiol, and others.

Fluconazole (Diflucan). Cocoa contains caffeine. The body breaks down caffeine to get rid of it. Fluconazole (Diflucan) might decrease how quickly the body gets rid of caffeine. Fluconazole (Diflucan) might cause caffeine to stay in the body too long. Taking cocoa along with fluconazole (Diflucan) might increase the risk of caffeine side effects such as nervousness, anxiety, and insomnia.

Lithium. You body naturally gets rid of lithium. The caffeine in cocoa can increase how quickly your body gets rid of lithium. If you take products that contain caffeine and you take lithium, stop taking caffeine products slowly. Stopping caffeine too quickly can increase the side effects of lithium.

Medications for asthma (Beta-adrenergic agonists). Cocoa contains caffeine. Caffeine can stimulate the heart. Some medications for asthma can also stimulate the heart. Taking caffeine with some medications for asthma might cause too much stimulation and cause heart problems. Some medications for asthma include albuterol (Proventil, Ventolin, Volmax), metaproterenol (Alupent), terbutaline (Bricanyl, Brethine), and isoproterenol (Isuprel).

Medications for depression (MAOIs). Cocoa contains caffeine. Caffeine can stimulate the body. Some medications used for depression can also stimulate the body. Consuming cocoa with these medications used for depression might cause too much stimulation. This could cause serious side effects including fast heartbeat, high blood pressure, nervousness, and others. Some of these medications used for depression include phenelzine (Nardil), tranylcypromine (Parnate), and others.

Medications for diabetes (Antidiabetes drugs). Cocoa might increase blood sugar. Diabetes medications are used to lower blood sugar. By increasing blood sugar, cocoa might decrease the effectiveness of diabetes medications. Monitor your blood sugar closely. The dose of your diabetes medication might need to be changed. Some medications used for diabetes include glimepiride (Amaryl), glyburide (DiaBeta, Glynase PresTab, Micronase), insulin, pioglitazone (Actos), rosiglitazone (Avandia), chlorpropamide (Diabinese), glipizide (Glucotrol), tolbutamide (Orinase), and others.

Mexiletine (Mexitil). Cocoa contains caffeine. The body breaks down caffeine to get rid of it. Mexiletine (Mexitil) can decrease how quickly the body breaks down caffeine. Taking Mexiletine (Mexitil) along with cocoa might increase the caffeine effects and side effects of cocoa.

Phenylpropanolamine. The caffeine in cocoa can stimulate the body. Phenylpropanolamine can also stimulate the body. Taking cocoa along with phenylpropanolamine might cause too much stimulation and increase heartbeat, blood pressure, and cause nervousness.

Theophylline. Cocoa contains caffeine. Caffeine works in similar ways in the body as theophylline. Caffeine can also decrease how quickly the body gets rid of theophylline. Taking cocoa along with theophylline might increase the effects and side effects of theophylline.

Verapamil (Calan, Covera, Isoptin, Verelan). The body breaks down the caffeine in cocoa to get rid of it. Verapamil (Calan, Covera, Isoptin, Verelan) can decrease how quickly the body gets rid of caffeine. Taking caffeine along with verapamil (Calan, Covera, Isoptin, Verelan) can increase the risk of caffeine side effects including jitteriness, headache, and an increased heartbeat.

COCONUT OIL

What other names is the product known by?
Coconut Palm, Coco Palm, Coconut, Cocos nucifera, Cold Pressed Coconut Oil, Fermented Coconut Oil, Virgin Coconut Oil.

What is it?
Coconut is the fruit of the coconut palm tree. The oil of the nut (fruit) is used to make medicine.

Is it Effective?
The effectiveness ratings for **COCONUT OIL** are as follows:
Insufficient Evidence to Rate Effectiveness for... Head lice, psoriasis, weight loss, heart disease, hypercholesterolemia, diabetes, chronic fatigue, Crohn's disease, irritable bowel syndrome, thyroid conditions, and other conditions.

How does it work?
Coconut oil is high in saturated fat and can increase cholesterol. When applied to the skin, it has a moisturizing effect.

Are there safety concerns?
Coconut oil is safe for most people if used in amounts commonly found in foods. It also appears to be safe when applied to the scalp in combination with other herbs. Its high saturated fat content can cause weight gain and increase cholesterol.

Natural Medicines Comprehensive Database Consumer Version (209) 472-2244

Medical professionals should consult the Professional Version at www.NaturalDatabase.com.

The safety of coconut oil used in medicinal amounts is unknown.

Do not use coconut oil in amounts greater than those found in food if: You are pregnant or breast-feeding. • You have high cholesterol.

Are there any interactions with medications?
It is not known if coconut oil interacts with any medicines.
Before taking coconut oil, talk with your healthcare professional if you take any medications.

COD LIVER OIL

What other names is the product known by?
Cod Oil, Fish Oil, Liver Oil, n-3 Fatty Acids, Omega-3 Fatty Acids, Omega-3 Fatty Acid, Polyunsaturated Fatty Acids.

What is it?
Cod liver oil can be obtained from eating fresh cod liver or by taking supplements.

Is it Effective?
The effectiveness ratings for **COD LIVER OIL** are as follows:
Likely Effective for... Lowering fats called triglycerides.
Possibly Effective for... High blood pressure • Kidney disease in people with type 2 diabetes.
Possibly Ineffective for... Osteoarthritis • Cholesterol disease that runs in families (familial hypercholesterolemia).
Insufficient Evidence to Rate Effectiveness for... Heart disease, systemic lupus erythematosus (SLE), wound healing, glaucoma, preventing an irregular heartbeat in people with heart disease, and preventing ear infections in young children.

How does it work?
Cod liver oil contains certain "fatty acids" that prevent the blood from clotting easily. These fatty acids also reduce pain and swelling.

Are there safety concerns?
Cod liver oil is safe for most people. It can cause side effects including belching, bad breath, heartburn, and nosebleeds. Taking cod liver oil with meals can often decrease these side effects.

High doses might keep blood from clotting and can increase the chance of bleeding. Vitamin A and vitamin D levels might also become too high with high doses of cod liver oil. High doses might also cause nausea and loose stools.

Do not take cod liver oil if: You are pregnant or breast-feeding. • You are sensitive to aspirin. Cod liver oil might affect your breathing.

Are there any interactions with medications?
Medications that slow blood clotting (Anticoagulant / Antiplatelet drugs). Cod liver oil might slow blood clotting. Taking cod liver oil along with medications that also slow clotting might increase the chances of bruising and bleeding. Some medications that slow blood clotting include aspirin, clopidogrel (Plavix), diclofenac (Voltaren, Cataflam, others), ibuprofen (Advil, Motrin, others), naproxen (Anaprox, Naprosyn, others), dalteparin (Fragmin), enoxaparin (Lovenox), heparin, warfarin (Coumadin), and others.
Medications for high blood pressure (Antihypertensive drugs). Cod liver oil seems to decrease blood pressure. Taking cod liver oil along with medications for high blood pressure might cause your blood pressure to go too low. Some medications for high blood pressure include captopril (Capoten), enalapril (Vasotec), losartan (Cozaar), valsartan (Diovan), diltiazem (Cardizem), Amlodipine (Norvasc), hydrochlorothiazide (HydroDiuril), furosemide (Lasix), and many others.

CODONOPSIS

What other names is the product known by?
Bastard Ginseng, Bellflower, Bonnet Bellflower, Codonopsis pilosula, Codonopsis tangshen, Codonopsis tubulosa, Dangshen, Radix Codonopsis.

What is it?
Codonopsis is an herb. People use the root of the herb to make medicine.

   Natural Medicines Comprehensive Database Consumer Version   (209) 472-2244

Is it Effective?
The effectiveness ratings for **CODONOPSIS** are as follows:
Insufficient Evidence to Rate Effectiveness for...HIV infection, protection against radiotherapy in cancer treatment, brain disorders, anorexia, diarrhea, asthma, cough, diabetes, and other conditions.

How does it work?
Codonopsis seems to promote weight gain and increase endurance. It also seems to increase red and white blood cells counts and promote blood circulation.

Are there safety concerns?
Codonopsis seems to be safe for most people.

Do not use codonopsis if: You are pregnant or breast-feeding.

Are there any interactions with medications?
It is not known if codonopsis interacts with any medicines.
Before taking codonopsis, talk with your healthcare professional if you take any medications.

COENZYME Q-10

What other names is the product known by?
CoQ, CoQ-10, Mitoquinone, Ubidecarenone, Ubiquinol, Ubiquinone, Q10.

What is it?
Coenzyme Q-10 (CoQ-10) is a vitamin-like substance found throughout the body, but especially in the heart, liver, kidney, and pancreas. It is eaten in small amounts in meats and seafood. Coenzyme Q-10 can also be made in a laboratory. It is used as medicine.

Is it Effective?
The effectiveness ratings for **COENZYME Q-10** are as follows:
Likely Effective for... Coenzyme Q-10 deficiency (very rare) • Mitochondrial disorders, inherited or acquired disorders that limit energy production in the cells of the body.
Possibly Effective for... Congestive heart failure (CHF), in combination with other medications • Decreasing the risk of additional heart problems in people who have had a recent heart attack (myocardial infarction) • Huntington's disease • Preventing blood vessel complications caused by heart bypass surgery • High blood pressure (hypertension) in combination with other medications • Preventing migraine headache • Parkinson's disease • Improving the immune system of people with HIV/AIDS • Muscular dystrophy, an inherited disorder involving muscle wasting.
Likely Ineffective for... Improving exercise performance • Dental (periodontal) disease, when applied directly to the teeth and gums.
Insufficient Evidence to Rate Effectiveness for... Improving blood sugar control in people with diabetes, breast cancer, fatigue, Lyme disease, male infertility, chest pain (angina), a muscle condition called "statin-induced myopathy," cardiomyopathy in children and adults, and other conditions.

How does it work?
Coenzyme Q-10 is an important vitamin-like substance required for the proper function of many organs and chemical reactions in the body. It helps provide energy to cells. Coenzyme Q-10 also seems to have antioxidant activity. People with certain diseases, such as congestive heart failure, high blood pressure, periodontal disease, Parkinson's disease, certain muscular diseases, and AIDS, might have lower levels of coenzyme Q-10.

Are there safety concerns?
Coenzyme Q-10 is safe for most adults. While most people tolerate coenzyme Q-10 well, it can cause some mild side effects including stomach upset, loss of appetite, nausea, vomiting, and diarrhea. It can cause allergic skin rashes in some people. It also might lower blood pressure, so check your blood pressure carefully if you have very low blood pressure. Dividing the total daily dose by taking smaller amounts two or three times a day instead of a large amount all at once can help reduce side effects.

Coenzyme Q-10 also seems to be safe for most children. But coenzyme Q-10 should not be used in children without medical supervision.

Do not use coenzyme Q-10 if: You are pregnant or breast-feeding.

Medical professionals should consult the Professional Version at www.NaturalDatabase.com.

Are there any interactions with medications?

Medications for high blood pressure (Antihypertensive drugs). Coenzyme Q-10 seems to decrease blood pressure. Taking coenzyme Q-10 along with medications for high blood pressure might cause your blood pressure to go too low. Some medications for high blood pressure include captopril (Capoten), enalapril (Vasotec), losartan (Cozaar), valsartan (Diovan), diltiazem (Cardizem), Amlodipine (Norvasc), hydrochlorothiazide (HydroDiuril), furosemide (Lasix), and many others.

Medications for cancer (Chemotherapy). Coenzyme Q-10 is an antioxidant. There is some concern that antioxidants might decrease the effectiveness of some medications used for cancers. But it is too soon to know if the interaction occurs.

Warfarin (Coumadin). Warfarin (Coumadin) is used to slow blood clotting. Coenzyme Q-10 might help the blood clot. By helping the blood clot, coenzyme Q-10 might decrease the effectiveness of warfarin (Coumadin). Decreasing the effectiveness of warfarin (Coumadin) might increase the risk of clotting. Be sure to have your blood checked regularly. The dose of your warfarin (Coumadin) might need to be changed.

COFFEE

What other names is the product known by?

Cafe, Caffea, Coffea arabica, Coffea canephora, Coffea liberica, Coffea robusta, Espresso, Java, Mocha.

What is it?

Coffee is a drink made from coffee beans. Coffee beans are the roasted fruit of the Coffea arabica bush.

Is it Effective?

The effectiveness ratings for **COFFEE** are as follows:

Likely Effective for... Mental alertness.

Possibly Effective for... Reducing the risk of colorectal cancer • Preventing dizziness on standing up (orthostatic hypotension) in older people • Preventing or delaying Parkinson's disease • Preventing gallstones • Reducing the risk of type 2 diabetes.

Possibly Ineffective for... Reducing the risk of esophageal, stomach, and colon cancers • Reducing the risk of breast cancer.

Insufficient Evidence to Rate Effectiveness for... Lung cancer and improving thinking.

How does it work?

Coffee contains caffeine. Caffeine works by stimulating the central nervous system (CNS), heart, and muscles.

Are there safety concerns?

Coffee is safe for most adults. Drinking more than 6 cups/day might cause "caffeinism" and cause symptoms such as anxiety or agitation.

Coffee containing caffeine can cause insomnia, nervousness and restlessness, stomach upset, nausea and vomiting, increased heart and breathing rate, and other side effects. Consuming large amounts of coffee might also cause headache, anxiety, agitation, ringing in the ears, and irregular heartbeats.

Coffee might also increase the loss of calcium and magnesium from the body. It can also increase total cholesterol, low-density lipoprotein (LDL), and triglyceride levels, which might increase the risk of heart disease. Using coffee filters helps to reduce these effects on cholesterol.

There is some concern that consuming more than 5 cups/day of coffee might not be safe for people with heart disease. But for people who don't have heart disease, consuming several cups daily does not seem to increase the change of developing a heart problem.

Coffee containing caffeine is probably safe for pregnant women in amounts of 3 cups/day or less. This amount of coffee provides about 300 mg of caffeine.

Avoid caffeinated coffee if: You are pregnant or breast-feeding. • You have a heart condition. • You have diabetes. • You have high blood pressure. Small amounts of coffee taken regularly do not seem to raise blood pressure, but the caffeine in coffee can affect blood pressure in someone who consumes caffeinated drinks infrequently. • You have osteoporosis. • You have high cholesterol. • You have glaucoma. • You have a bleeding disorder. • You have anxiety.

Are there any interactions with medications?

Adenosine (Adenocard). The caffeine in coffee might block the affects of adenosine (Adenocard). Adenosine (Adenocard) is often used by doctors to do a test on the heart. This test is called a cardiac stress test. Stop consuming coffee or other caffeine-containing products at least 24 hours before a cardiac stress test.

Alcohol. The body breaks down the caffeine in coffee to get rid of it. Alcohol can decrease how quickly the body breaks down caffeine. Taking coffee along with alcohol might cause too much caffeine in the bloodstream and caffeine side effects including jitteriness, headache, and fast heartbeat.

Alendronate (Fosamax). Coffee can decrease how much alendronate (Fosamax) the body absorbs. Taking coffee and alendronate (Fosamax) at the same time can decrease the effectiveness of alendronate (Fosamax). Don't drink coffee within two hours of taking alendronate (Fosamax).

Antibiotics (Quinolone antibiotics). The body breaks down caffeine to get rid of it. Some antibiotics might decrease how quickly the body breaks down caffeine. Taking these antibiotics along with coffee can increase the risk of side effects including jitteriness, headache, increased heart rate, and other side effects. Some antibiotics that decrease how quickly the body breaks down caffeine include ciprofloxacin (Cipro), enoxacin (Penetrex), norfloxacin (Chibroxin, Noroxin), sparfloxacin (Zagam), trovafloxacin (Trovan), and grepafloxacin (Raxar).

Birth control pills (Contraceptive drugs). The body breaks down the caffeine in coffee to get rid of it. Birth control pills can decrease how quickly the body breaks down caffeine. Taking coffee along with birth control pills can cause jitteriness, headache, fast heartbeat, and other side effects. Some birth control pills include ethinyl estradiol and levonorgestrel (Triphasil), ethinyl estradiol and norethindrone (Ortho-Novum 1/35, Ortho-Novum 7/7/7), and others.

Cimetidine (Tagamet). The body breaks down the caffeine in coffee to get rid of it. Cimetidine (Tagamet) can decrease how quickly your body breaks down caffeine. Taking cimetidine (Tagamet) along with coffee might increase the chance of caffeine side effects including jitteriness, headache, fast heartbeat, and others.

Clozapine (Clozaril). The body breaks down clozapine (Clozaril) to get rid of it. The caffeine in coffee might decrease how fast the body breaks down clozapine (Clozaril). Taking coffee along with clozapine (Clozaril) can increase the effects and side effects of clozapine (Clozaril).

Dipyridamole (Persantine). The caffeine in coffee might block the affects of dipyridamole (Persantine). Dipyridamole (Persantine) is often used by doctors to do a test on the heart. This test is called a cardiac stress test. Stop drinking coffee or other caffeine-containing products at least 24 hours before a cardiac stress test.

Disulfiram (Antabuse). The body breaks down the caffeine in coffee to get rid of it. Disulfiram (Antabuse) can decrease how quickly the body gets rid of caffeine. Taking coffee along with disulfiram (Antabuse) might increase the effects and side effects of coffee including jitteriness, hyperactivity, irritability, and others.

Ephedrine. Stimulant drugs speed up the nervous system. The caffeine in coffee and ephedrine are both stimulant drugs. Drinking coffee and taking ephedrine might cause too much stimulation and sometimes serious side effects and heart problems. Do not take caffeine-containing products and ephedrine at the same time.

Estrogens. The body breaks down the caffeine in coffee to get rid of it. Estrogens can decrease how quickly the body breaks down caffeine. Taking estrogen pills and drinking coffee can cause jitteriness, headache, fast heartbeat, and other side effects. If you take estrogen pills limit your caffeine intake. Some estrogen pills include conjugated equine estrogens (Premarin), ethinyl estradiol, estradiol, and others.

Fluconazole (Diflucan). The body breaks down the caffeine in coffee to get rid of it. Fluconazole (Diflucan) might decrease how quickly the body gets rid of caffeine. Taking fluconazole (Diflucan) and drinking coffee might increase the effects and side effects of coffee including nervousness, anxiety, and insomnia.

Fluvoxamine (Luvox). The body breaks down the caffeine in coffee to get rid of it. Fluvoxamine (Luvox) can decrease how quickly the body breaks down caffeine. Taking caffeine along with fluvoxamine (Luvox) might cause too much caffeine in the body, and increase the effects and side effects of caffeine.

Lithium. You body naturally gets rid of lithium. The caffeine in coffee can increase how quickly your body gets rid of lithium. If you take products that contain caffeine and you take lithium, stop taking caffeine products slowly. Stopping caffeine too quickly can increase the side effects of lithium.

Medications for depression (MAOIs). The caffeine in coffee can stimulate the body. Some medications used for depression can also stimulate the body. Drinking coffee and taking some medications for depression might cause too much stimulation and serious side effects including fast heartbeat, high blood pressure, nervousness, and others. Some of these medications used for depression include phenelzine (Nardil), tranylcypromine (Parnate), and others.

Medications for diabetes (Antidiabetes drugs). Coffee might increase blood sugar. Diabetes medications are used to lower blood sugar. By increasing blood sugar, coffee might decrease the effectiveness of diabetes medications. Monitor your blood sugar closely. The dose of your diabetes medication might need to be changed. Some medications used for diabetes include glimepiride (Amaryl), glyburide (DiaBeta, Glynase PresTab, Micronase), insulin, pioglitazone (Actos), rosiglitazone (Avandia), chlorpropamide (Diabinese), glipizide (Glucotrol), tolbutamide (Orinase), and others.

Medications that slow blood clotting (Anticoagulant / Antiplatelet drugs). Coffee might slow blood clotting. Taking coffee along with medications that also slow clotting might increase the chances of bruising and bleeding. Some medications that slow blood clotting include aspirin, clopidogrel (Plavix), diclofenac (Voltaren, Cataflam, others), ibuprofen (Advil, Motrin, others), naproxen (Anaprox, Naprosyn, others), dalteparin (Fragmin), enoxaparin (Lovenox), heparin, warfarin (Coumadin), and others.

Medications for depression (Tricyclic Antidepressants). Coffee contains chemicals called tannins. Tannins can bind to many medications and decrease how much medicine the body absorbs. To avoid this interaction avoid coffee one hour before and two hours after taking medications for depression called tricyclic antidepressants. Some medications for depression include amitriptyline (Elavil) or imipramine (Tofranil, Janimine).

Mexiletine (Mexitil). Coffee contains caffeine. The body breaks down caffeine to get rid of it. Mexiletine (Mexitil) can decrease how quickly the body breaks down caffeine. Taking Mexiletine (Mexitil) along with coffee might increase the caffeine effects and side effects of coffee.

Pentobarbital (Nembutal). The stimulant effects of the caffeine in coffee can block the sleep-producing effects of pentobarbital.

Phenothiazines. Coffee contains chemicals called tannins. Tannins can bind to many medications and decrease how much medicine the body absorbs. To avoid this interaction avoid coffee one hour before and two hours after taking phenothiazine medications. Some phenothiazine medications include fluphenazine (Permitil, Prolixin), chlorpromazine (Thorazine), haloperidol (Haldol), prochlorperazine (Compazine), thioridazine (Mellaril), and trifluoperazine (Stelazine).

Phenylpropanolamine. The caffeine in coffee can stimulate the body. Phenylpropanolamine can also stimulate the body. Taking caffeine and phenylpropanolamine together might cause too much stimulation and increase heartbeat, blood pressure, and cause nervousness.

Riluzole (Rilutek). The body breaks down riluzole (Rilutek) to get rid of it. Drinking coffee can decrease how fast the body breaks down riluzole (Rilutek) and increase the effects and side effects of riluzole.

Stimulant drugs. Stimulant drugs speed up the nervous system. By speeding up the nervous system, stimulant medications can make you feel jittery and speed up your heartbeat. The caffeine in coffee can also speed up the nervous system. Drinking coffee along with stimulant drugs might cause serious problems including increased heart rate and high blood pressure. Avoid taking stimulant drugs along with coffee. Some stimulant drugs include diethylpropion (Tenuate), epinephrine, phentermine (Ionamin), pseudoephedrine (Sudafed), and many others.

Terbinafine (Lamisil). The body breaks down the caffeine in coffee to get rid of it. Terbinafine (Lamisil) can decrease how fast the body gets rid of caffeine and increase the risk of side effects including jitteriness, headache, increased heartbeat, and other effects.

Theophylline. The caffeine in coffee works similarly to theophylline. Caffeine can also decrease how quickly the body gets rid of theophylline. Drinking coffee and taking theophylline might increase the effects and side effects of theophylline.

Verapamil (Calan, Covera, Isoptin, Verelan). The body breaks down the caffeine in coffee to get rid of it. Verapamil (Calan, Covera, Isoptin, Verelan) can decrease how quickly the body gets rid of caffeine. Drinking coffee and taking verapamil (Calan, Covera, Isoptin, Verelan) can increase the risk of side effects for coffee including jitteriness, headache, and an increased heartbeat.

COFFEE CHARCOAL

What other names is the product known by?
Coffea arabica, Coffea canephora, Coffea liberica.

What is it?
Coffee charcoal is an herb. It is produced by roasting the outer portion of coffee beans until blackened or charred.

Is it Effective?
The effectiveness ratings for **COFFEE CHARCOAL** are as follows:
Insufficient Evidence to Rate Effectiveness for... Diarrhea, mouth and throat swelling (inflammation).

How does it work?
Coffee charcoal might help reduce inflammation, and have a drying (astringent) effect on the tissues.

Are there safety concerns?
Coffee charcoal seems to be safe for most people.

Do not use coffee charcoal if: You are pregnant or breast-feeding.

Are there any interactions with medications?
Medications taken by mouth (Oral drugs). Coffee charcoal absorbs substances in the stomach and intestines. Taking coffee charcoal along with medications taken by mouth can decrease how much medicine your body absorbs, and decrease the effectiveness of your medication. To prevent this interaction, take coffee charcoal at least one hour after medications you take by mouth.

COLA NUT

What other names is the product known by?
Bissy Nut, Cola acuminata, Cola nitida, Guru Nut, Gworo, Kola Nut, Soudan Coffee, Sterculia acuminata.

What is it?
Cola nut is the seed of the cola nut plant. People use it to make medicine.

Is it Effective?
The effectiveness ratings for **COLA NUT** are as follows:
Insufficient Evidence to Rate Effectiveness for... Weight loss, depression, exhaustion, chronic fatigue syndrome (CFS), dysentery, diarrhea, anorexia, migraines, mental and physical fatigue, and other conditions.

How does it work?
Cola nut contains caffeine. Caffeine works by stimulating the central nervous system (CNS), heart, and muscles.

Are there safety concerns?
Cola nut seems to be safe for most people in amounts found in foods. If used medicinally in larger amounts or for a long period of time, it may be unsafe. The caffeine in cola nut can cause insomnia, nervousness and restlessness, stomach irritation, nausea and vomiting, increased heart rate and respiration, and other side effects. Large amounts might cause headache, anxiety, agitation, ringing in the ears, and irregular heartbeats. The abrupt discontinuance can sometimes result in headaches, irritation, nervousness, anxiety, and dizziness.

Do not use cola nut if: You have a heart condition. • You have high blood pressure. • You have anxiety. • You have an eye disease called glaucoma. • You have osteoporosis. • You have a bleeding condition.

Are there any interactions with medications?
Adenosine (Adenocard). Cola nut contains caffeine. The caffeine in cola nut might block the affects of adenosine (Adenocard). Adenosine (Adenocard) is often used by doctors to do a test on the heart. This test is called a cardiac stress test. Stop consuming cola nut or other caffeine-containing products at least 24 hours before a cardiac stress test.

Alcohol. The body breaks down the caffeine in cola nut to get rid of it. Alcohol can decrease how quickly the body breaks down caffeine. Taking cola nut along with alcohol might cause too much caffeine in the bloodstream and caffeine side effects including jitteriness, headache, and fast heartbeat.

Amphetamines. Stimulant drugs such as amphetamines speed up the nervous system. By speeding up the nervous system, stimulant medications can make you feel jittery and increase your heart rate. The caffeine in cola nut might also speed up the nervous system. Taking caffeine along with stimulant drugs might cause serious problems including increased heart rate and high blood pressure. Avoid taking stimulant drugs along with caffeine.

Antibiotics (Quinolone antibiotics). The body breaks down the caffeine in cola nut to get rid of it. Some antibiotics might decrease how quickly the body breaks down caffeine. Taking these antibiotics along with cola nut can increase the risk of side effects including jitteriness, headache, increased heart rate, and other side effects. Some antibiotics that decrease how quickly the body breaks down caffeine include ciprofloxacin (Cipro), enoxacin (Penetrex), norfloxacin (Chibroxin, Noroxin), sparfloxacin (Zagam), trovafloxacin (Trovan), and grepafloxacin (Raxar).

Birth control pills (Contraceptive drugs). The body breaks down the caffeine in cola nut to get rid of it. Birth control pills can decrease how quickly the body breaks down caffeine. Taking cola nut along with birth control pills can cause jitteriness, headache, fast heartbeat, and other side effects. Some birth control pills include ethinyl estradiol and levonorgestrel (Triphasil), ethinyl estradiol and norethindrone (Ortho-Novum 1/35, Ortho-Novum 7/7/7), and others.

Cimetidine (Tagamet). The body breaks down the caffeine in cola nut to get rid of it. Cimetidine (Tagamet) can decrease how quickly your body breaks down caffeine. Taking cimetidine (Tagamet) along with cola nut might increase the chance of caffeine side effects including jitteriness, headache, fast heartbeat, and others.

Clozapine (Clozaril). The body breaks down clozapine (Clozaril) to get rid of it. The caffeine in cola nut seems to decrease how quickly the body breaks down clozapine (Clozaril). Taking cola nut along with clozapine (Clozaril) can increase the effects and side effects of clozapine (Clozaril).

Cocaine. Stimulant drugs such as cocaine speed up the nervous system. By speeding up the nervous system, stimulant medications can make you feel jittery and increase your heart rate. The caffeine in cola nut might also speed up the nervous system. Taking caffeine along with stimulant drugs might cause serious problems including increased heart rate and high blood pressure. Avoid taking stimulant drugs along with cola nut.

Dipyridamole (Persantine). Cola nut contains caffeine. The caffeine in cola nut might block the affects of dipyridamole (Persantine). Dipyridamole (Persantine) is often used by doctors to do a test on the heart. This test is called a cardiac stress test. Stop consuming cola nut or other caffeine-containing products at least 24 hours before a cardiac stress test.

Disulfiram (Antabuse). The body breaks down the caffeine in cola nut to get rid of it. Disulfiram (Antabuse) can

Medical professionals should consult the Professional Version at www.NaturalDatabase.com.

decrease how quickly the body gets rid of caffeine. Taking cola nut along with disulfiram (Antabuse) might increase the effects and side effects of caffeine including jitteriness, hyperactivity, irritability, and others.

Ephedrine. Stimulant drugs speed up the nervous system. The caffeine in cola nut and ephedrine are both stimulant drugs. Taking caffeine along with ephedrine might cause too much stimulation and sometimes serious side effects and heart problems. Do not take caffeine-containing products and ephedrine at the same time.

Estrogens. The body breaks down the caffeine in cola nut to get rid of it. Estrogens can decrease how quickly the body breaks down caffeine. Taking estrogens along with cola nut can cause jitteriness, headache, fast heartbeat, and other side effects. If you take estrogens limit your caffeine intake. Some estrogen pills include conjugated equine estrogens (Premarin), ethinyl estradiol, estradiol, and others.

Fluconazole (Diflucan) Cola nut contains caffeine. The body breaks down caffeine to get rid of it. Fluconazole (Diflucan) might decrease how quickly the body gets rid of caffeine. This could cause caffeine to stay in to body too long and increase the risk of side effects such as nervousness, anxiety, and insomnia.

Fluvoxamine (Luvox). The body breaks down the caffeine in cola nut to get rid of it. Fluvoxamine (Luvox) can decrease how quickly the body breaks down caffeine. Taking caffeine along with fluvoxamine (Luvox) might cause too much caffeine in the body, and increase the effects and side effects of caffeine.

Lithium. You body naturally gets rid of lithium. The caffeine in cola nut can increase how quickly your body gets rid of lithium. If you take products that contain caffeine and you take lithium, stop taking caffeine products slowly. Stopping caffeine too quickly can increase the side effects of lithium.

Medications for depression (MAOIs). Cola nut contains caffeine. Caffeine can stimulate the body. Some medications used for depression can also stimulate the body. Taking cola nut with these medications used for depression might cause too much stimulation. This could cause serious side effects including fast heartbeat, high blood pressure, nervousness, and others. Some of these medications used for depression include phenelzine (Nardil), tranylcypromine (Parnate), and others.

Medications for diabetes (Antidiabetes drugs). Cola nut might increase blood sugar. Diabetes medications are used to lower blood sugar. By increasing blood sugar, cola nut might decrease the effectiveness of diabetes medications. Monitor your blood sugar closely. The dose of your diabetes medication might need to be changed. Some medications used for diabetes include glimepiride (Amaryl), glyburide (DiaBeta, Glynase PresTab, Micronase), insulin, pioglitazone (Actos), rosiglitazone (Avandia), chlorpropamide (Diabinese), glipizide (Glucotrol), tolbutamide (Orinase), and others.

Mexiletine (Mexitil). Cola nut contains caffeine. The body breaks down caffeine to get rid of it. Mexiletine (Mexitil) can decrease how quickly the body breaks down caffeine. Taking cola nut along with mexiletine (Mexitil) might increase the effects and side effects of caffeine.

Nicotine. Stimulant drugs such as nicotine speed up the nervous system. By speeding up the nervous system, stimulant medications can make you feel jittery and increase your heart rate. The caffeine in cola nut might also speed up the nervous system. Taking caffeine along with stimulant drugs might cause serious problems including increased heart rate and high blood pressure. Avoid taking stimulant drugs along with caffeine.

Pentobarbital (Nembutal). The stimulant effects of the caffeine in cola nut can block the sleep-producing effects of pentobarbital.

Phenylpropanolamine. The caffeine in cola nut can stimulate the body. Phenylpropanolamine can also stimulate the body. Taking cola nut along with phenylpropanolamine might cause too much stimulation and increase heartbeat, blood pressure, and cause nervousness.

Riluzole (Rilutek). The body breaks down riluzole (Rilutek) to get rid of it. Taking cola nut can decrease how fast the body breaks down riluzole (Rilutek) and increase the effects and side effects of riluzole.

Terbinafine (Lamisil). Cola nut contains caffeine. The body breaks down the caffeine in cola nut to get rid of it. Terbinafine (Lamisil) can decrease how fast the body gets rid of caffeine. Taking cola nut along with terbinafine (Lamisil) can increase the risk of caffeine side effects including jitteriness, headache, and an increased heartbeat.

Theophylline. Cola nut contains caffeine. Caffeine works similarly to theophylline. Caffeine can also decrease how quickly the body gets rid of theophylline. Taking cola nut along with theophylline might increase the effects and side effects of theophylline.

Verapamil (Calan, Covera, Isoptin, Verelan). The body breaks down the caffeine in cola nut to get rid of it. Verapamil (Calan, Covera, Isoptin, Verelan) can decrease how fast the body gets rid of caffeine. Taking cola nut along with verapamil (Calan, Covera, Isoptin, Verelan) can increase the risk of side effects from caffeine including jitteriness, headache, and an increased heartbeat.

COLLOIDAL MINERALS

What other names is the product known by?

Anhydrous aluminum silicates, Bioelectrical Minerals, Clay Suspension Products, Humic Shale, Plant-Derived Liquid Minerals.

What is it?

Colloidal minerals are derived from clay or shale deposits. People use them for medicine.

Is it Effective?
The effectiveness ratings for **COLLOIDAL MINERALS** are as follows:
Insufficient Evidence to Rate Effectiveness for... Mineral deficiencies, low energy, diabetes, arthritis, reducing blood cell clumping, reversing early cataracts, turning gray hair dark again, flushing poisonous heavy metals from the body, improving general well being, reducing aches and pains, and other conditions.

How does it work?
There isn't enough information to know how colloidal minerals might work. Despite claims that colloidal minerals are more usable by the body than other minerals, there isn't any evidence to support this idea.

Are there safety concerns?
Colloidal minerals are possibly unsafe for use. These products contain varying amounts of potentially unsafe radioactive metals. These metals include aluminum, arsenic, lead, barium, nickel, and titanium.

Do not take colloidal minerals if: You are pregnant or breast-feeding. • You have hemochromatosis (iron overload). • You have Wilson's disease.

Are there any interactions with medications?
It is not known if colloidal minerals interact with any medicines.
Before taking colloidal minerals, talk with your healthcare professional if you take any medications.

COLLOIDAL SILVER

What other names is the product known by?
Colloidal Silver Protein, Silver in suspending agent, Silver Protein.

What is it?
Colloidal silver is a mineral.

Is it Effective?
The effectiveness ratings for **COLLOIDAL SILVER** are as follows:
Insufficient Evidence to Rate Effectiveness for... Ear infections, emphysema, bronchitis, fungal infections, Lyme disease, rosacea, sinus infections, stomach ulcers, yeast infections, chronic fatigue syndrome, AIDS, tuberculosis, food poisoning, gum disease, digestion, preventing flu and colds, and other conditions.

How does it work?
Colloidal silver can kill certain germs by binding to and destroying proteins.

Are there safety concerns?
Colloidal silver is LIKELY UNSAFE for use. The silver in colloidal silver products gets deposited in vital organs such as the skin, liver, spleen, kidney, muscle, and brain. This can lead to an irreversible bluish skin discoloration that first appears in the gums. It can also stimulate melanin production in skin, and areas exposed to the sun will become increasingly discolored.

Do not use colloidal silver if: You are pregnant or breast-feeding.

Are there any interactions with medications?
Antibiotics (Tetracycline antibiotics). Colloidal silver might decrease how much tetracycline antibiotics the body can absorb. Taking colloidal silver with tetracycline antibiotics might decrease the effectiveness of tetracycline antibiotics. To avoid this interaction take colloidal silver two hours before or four hours after taking tetracyclines. Some tetracyclines include demeclocycline (Declomycin), minocycline (Minocin), and tetracycline (Achromycin).
Antibiotics (Quinolone antibiotics). Colloidal silver might decrease how much antibiotic the body absorbs. Taking colloidal silver along with antibiotics might decrease the effectiveness of some antibiotics. Some antibiotics that might interact with colloidal silver include ciprofloxacin (Cipro), enoxacin (Penetrex), norfloxacin (Chibroxin, Noroxin), sparfloxacin (Zagam), trovafloxacin (Trovan), and grepafloxacin (Raxar).
Penicillamine. Penicillamine is used for Wilson's disease and rheumatoid arthritis. Colloidal silver might decrease how much penicillamine your body absorbs and decrease the effectiveness of penicillamine.
Levothyroxine. Colloidal silver might decrease how much levothyroxine the body absorbs. Taking levothyroxine along with colloidal silver might decrease the effectiveness of thyroxine.

Medical professionals should consult the Professional Version at www.NaturalDatabase.com.

COLOCYNTH

What other names is the product known by?
Alhandal, Bitter Apple, Bitter Cucumber, Citrullus colocynthis, Colocynthis vulgaris, Cucumis colocynthis, Colocynth Pulp, Colocynthidis Fructus, Koloquinthen, Tumba, Vine-of-Sodom, Wild Gourd.

What is it?
Colocynth is an herb. The ripe fruit is used as a medicine.

Is it Effective?
The effectiveness ratings for **COLOCYNTH** are as follows:
Insufficient Evidence to Rate Effectiveness for... Constipation and liver and gallbladder problems.

How does it work?
Colocynth contains the chemical cucurbitacin, which is extremely irritating to the mucous membranes, including the mucous membranes in the stomach and intestines.

Are there safety concerns?
Colocynth is UNSAFE for use. It was banned by the Food and Drug Administration (FDA) in 1991.

Ingestion of even very small amounts of colocynth can cause severe irritation of the stomach and intestine lining, bloody diarrhea, kidney damage, bloody urine, and inability to urinate. Other side effects include convulsions, paralysis, and death.

Are there any interactions with medications?
Digoxin (Lanoxin). Colocynth is a type of laxative called a stimulant laxative. Stimulant laxatives can decrease potassium levels in the body. Low potassium levels can increase the risk of side effects of digoxin (Lanoxin).
Water pills (Diuretic drugs). Colocynth is a laxative. Some laxatives can decrease potassium in the body. "Water pills" can also decrease potassium in the body. Taking colocynth along with "water pills" might decrease potassium in the body too much. Some "water pills" that can decrease potassium include chlorothiazide (Diuril), chlorthalidone (Thalitone), furosemide (Lasix), hydrochlorothiazide (HCTZ, Hydrodiuril, Microzide), and others.

COLOMBO

What other names is the product known by?
Calomba Root, Calumba, Calumbo Root, Cocculus palmatus, Jateorhiza columba, Jateorhiza miersii, Jateorhiza palmate, Menispermum columba, Menispermum palmatum, Wateorhiza palmate.

What is it?
Colombo is an herb. People use the root of the plant to make medicine.

Is it Effective?
The effectiveness ratings for **COLOMBO** are as follows:
Insufficient Evidence to Rate Effectiveness for... Upset stomach, heartburn, intestinal disorders, and diarrhea.

How does it work?
Colombo can help relax the muscles in the intestinal tract. It might also increase stomach acid secretions.

Are there safety concerns?
There isn't enough information available to know if colombo is safe. Large amounts of colombo may cause vomiting and stomach pain.

An overdose of colombo can lead to paralysis and unconsciousness.

Do not use colombo if: You are pregnant or breast-feeding.

Are there any interactions with medications?
Antacids. Antacids are used to decrease stomach acid. Colombo may increase stomach acid. By increasing stomach acid, colombo might decrease the effectiveness of antacids. Some antacids include calcium carbonate (Tums, others), dihydroxyaluminum sodium carbonate (Rolaids, others), magaldrate (Riopan), magnesium sulfate (Bilagog), aluminum hydroxide (Amphojel), and others.
Medications that decrease stomach acid (H2-Blockers). Colombo might increase stomach acid. By increasing

stomach acid, colombo might decrease the effectiveness of some medications that decrease stomach acid, called H2-blockers. Some medications that decrease stomach acid include cimetidine (Tagamet), ranitidine (Zantac), nizatidine (Axid), and famotidine (Pepcid).

Medications that decrease stomach acid (Proton pump inhibitors). Colombo might increase stomach acid. By increasing stomach acid, colombo might decrease the effectiveness of medications that are used to decrease stomach acid, called proton pump inhibitors. Some medications that decrease stomach acid include omeprazole (Prilosec), lansoprazole (Prevacid), rabeprazole (Aciphex), pantoprazole (Protonix), and esomeprazole (Nexium).

COLOSTRUM

What other names is the product known by?
Bovine Colostrum, Bovine Immunoglobulin, Cow Milk Colostrum, Goat Colostrum, Hyperimmune Bovine Colostrum.

What is it?
Colostrum is a milky fluid that comes from the breasts of humans, cows, and other mammals the first few days after giving birth before true milk appears. It contains proteins, carbohydrates, fats, vitamins, minerals, and antibodies. People sometimes use cow (bovine) colostrum as medicine.

Is it Effective?
The effectiveness ratings for **COLOSTRUM** are as follows:
Possibly Effective for... Infectious diarrhea.
Insufficient Evidence to Rate Effectiveness for... Inflammation of the colon, stimulating the immune system, healing injuries, repairing nervous system damage, burning fat, building lean muscle, increasing stamina and vitality, elevating mood and sense of well being, slowing and reversing aging, bacterial and fungal infections, and other conditions.

How does it work?
Colostrum is collected from cows that have been vaccinated to produce antibodies that fight the bacteria that cause diarrheal disease. These antibodies appear in the colostrum that is collected as medicine. Though the hope is that these cow antibodies will help fight human disease, the cow antibodies do not seem to be very active in humans.

Are there safety concerns?
Bovine colostrum is safe for most people. While most people don't experience any side effects from bovine colostrum, there have been isolated reports of problems in HIV+ patients such as nausea, vomiting, abnormal liver function tests, and decreased red blood cells.

There is some concern about the possibility of catching "mad cow disease" (bovine spongiform encephalitis, BSE) or other diseases from products that come from animals. "Mad cow disease" does not appear to be transmitted through milk products, but it is probably wise to avoid animal products from countries where mad cow disease has been found.

Do not take bovine colostrum if: You are pregnant or breast-feeding. • You are allergic to cow's milk or milk products.

Are there any interactions with medications?
It is not known if bovine colostrum interacts with any medicines.
Before taking bovine colostrum, talk with your healthcare professional if you take any medications.

COLTSFOOT

What other names is the product known by?
Ass's Foot, Brandlattich, British Tobacco, Bullsfoot, Coughwort, Farfarae Folium Leaf, Fieldhove, Filuis Ante Patrem, Flower Velure, Foal's Foot, Foalswort, Guflatich, Hallfoot, Horsefoot, Horsehoof, Kuandong Hua, Kwandong Hwa, Pas Diane, Pas d'Ane, Pferdefut, Tussilage, Tussilago Farfara.

What is it?
Coltsfoot is a plant. The leaf is used to make medicine.

Medical professionals should consult the Professional Version at www.NaturalDatabase.com.

Is it Effective?

The effectiveness ratings for **COLTSFOOT** are as follows:

Insufficient Evidence to Rate Effectiveness for... Asthma, sore throat, cough, bronchitis, hoarseness, wheezing, and laryngitis.

How does it work?

The chemicals in coltsfoot might fight inflammation.

Are there safety concerns?

Coltsfoot is considered UNSAFE.

Coltsfoot can damage the liver or cause cancer, especially when used in high doses or for a long time.

Do not take coltsfoot if: You are pregnant or breast-feeding. • You have high blood pressure. • You have heart disease. • You have liver disease. • You are allergic to ragweed, chrysanthemums, marigolds, or daisies.

Are there any interactions with medications?

Medications that slow blood clotting (Anticoagulant / Antiplatelet drugs). Coltsfoot might slow blood clotting. Taking coltsfoot along with medications that also slow clotting might increase the chances of bruising and bleeding. Some medications that slow blood clotting include aspirin, clopidogrel (Plavix), diclofenac (Voltaren, Cataflam, others), ibuprofen (Advil, Motrin, others), naproxen (Anaprox, Naprosyn, others), dalteparin (Fragmin), enoxaparin (Lovenox), heparin, warfarin (Coumadin), and others.

Medications for high blood pressure (Antihypertensive drugs). Excessive doses of coltsfoot seem to increase blood pressure. By increasing blood pressure coltsfoot might decrease the effectiveness of medications for high blood pressure. Some medications for high blood pressure include captopril (Capoten), enalapril (Vasotec), losartan (Cozaar), valsartan (Diovan), diltiazem (Cardizem), amlodipine (Norvasc), hydrochlorothiazide (HydroDiuril), furosemide (Lasix), and many others.

Medications that increase break down of other medications by the liver (Cytochrome P450 3A4 (CYP3A4) inducers). Coltsfoot is broken down by the liver. Some chemicals that form when the liver breaks down coltsfoot can be harmful. Medications that cause the liver to break down coltsfoot might enhance the toxic effects of chemicals contained in coltsfoot. Some of these medicines include carbamazepine (Tegretol), phenobarbital, phenytoin (Dilantin), rifampin, rifabutin (Mycobutin), and others.

COLUMBINE

What other names is the product known by?

Aquilegia vulgaris, Culverwort.

What is it?

Columbine is an herb. People use the above ground parts to make medicine.

Is it Effective?

The effectiveness ratings for **COLUMBINE** are as follows:

Insufficient Evidence to Rate Effectiveness for... Stomach and intestine problems, gallbladder disorders, scurvy, jaundice, and other conditions.

How does it work?

There isn't enough information currently available to know how columbine works.

Are there safety concerns?

There isn't enough information to know if columbine is safe for use as a medicine.

Do not use columbine if: You are pregnant or breast-feeding.

Are there any interactions with medications?

It is not known if columbine interacts with any medicines.
Before taking columbine, talk with your healthcare professional if you take any medications.

COMFREY

What other names is the product known by?

Black Root, Blackwort, Bruisewort, Common Comfrey, Consolidae Radix, Consound, Gum Plant, Healing Herb, Knitback, Knitbone, Salsify, Slippery Root, Symphytum Radix, Symphytum officinale, Wallwort.

What is it?

Comfrey is a plant. The leaf, root, and root-like stem (rhizome) are used to make medicine.

Is it Effective?

The effectiveness ratings for **COMFREY** are as follows:

Insufficient Evidence to Rate Effectiveness for... Skin ulcers, wounds, broken bones, heavy periods, diarrhea, cough, sore throat, gum disease, joint pain, chest pain, cancer, bruises, inflammation (swelling) and sprains when applied to the skin, and other conditions.

How does it work?

The chemicals in comfrey might have a healing effect and reduce inflammation when applied to the skin. However, comfrey contains toxic chemicals that can be absorbed through the skin.

Are there safety concerns?

Comfrey is UNSAFE for anyone when taken by mouth. It contains chemicals which can cause liver damage and cancer. Comfrey seems to be safe for most people when applied to unbroken skin for less than 10 days in small amounts.

Do not use comfrey if: You are pregnant or breast-feeding. • You have broken or damaged skin. • You have liver disease.

Are there any interactions with medications?

Medications that can harm the liver (Hepatotoxic drugs). Comfrey might harm the liver. Taking comfrey along with medication that might also harm the liver can increase the risk of liver damage. Do not take comfrey if you are taking a medication that can harm the liver. Some medications that can harm the liver include acetaminophen (Tylenol and others), amiodarone (Cordarone), carbamazepine (Tegretol), isoniazid (INH), methotrexate (Rheumatrex), methyldopa (Aldomet), fluconazole (Diflucan), itraconazole (Sporanox), erythromycin (Erythrocin, Ilosone, others), phenytoin (Dilantin), lovastatin (Mevacor), pravastatin (Pravachol), simvastatin (Zocor), and many others.

Medications that increase the breakdown of other medications by the liver (Cytochrome P450 3A4 (CYP3A4) inducers). Comfrey is broken down by the liver. Some chemicals that form when the liver breaks down comfrey can be harmful. Medications that cause the liver to break down comfrey might enhance the toxic effects of chemicals contained in comfrey. Some of these medicines include carbamazepine (Tegretol), phenobarbital, phenytoin (Dilantin), rifampin, rifabutin (Mycobutin), and others.

COMMON STONECROP

What other names is the product known by?

Bird Bread, Creeping Tom, Gold Chain, Golden Moss, Jack-of-the-Buttery, Mousetail, Prick Madam, Sedum acre, Wall Ginger, Wallpepper.

What is it?

Common stonecrop is an herb. People use the above ground parts to make medicine.

Is it Effective?

The effectiveness ratings for **COMMON STONECROP** are as follows:

Insufficient Evidence to Rate Effectiveness for... High blood pressure, coughs, wounds, burns, hemorrhoids, warts, eczema, and mouth ulcers.

How does it work?

There isn't enough information currently available to know how common stonecrop works.

Are there safety concerns?

There isn't enough information to know if common stonecrop is safe for use as a medicine. Large amounts can cause vomiting and diarrhea.

Medical professionals should consult the Professional Version at www.NaturalDatabase.com.

Do not use common stonecrop if: You are pregnant or breast-feeding. • You have swelling (inflammation) of the gastrointestinal or urinary tract.

Are there any interactions with medications?
It is not known if common stonecrop interacts with any medicines.
Before taking common stonecrop, talk with your healthcare professional if you take any medications.

CONDURANGO

What other names is the product known by?
Common Condorvine, Condurango Cortex, Eagle-Vine Bark, Gonolobus cundurango, Marsdenia condurango, Marsdenia reichenbachii.

What is it?
Condurango is an herb. People use the bark to make medicine.

Is it Effective?
The effectiveness ratings for **CONDURANGO** are as follows:
Insufficient Evidence to Rate Effectiveness for... Increasing (stimulating) the appetite, indigestion, heartburn, and stomach cancer.

How does it work?
Condurango contains a substance that stimulates salivation and stomach juices.

Are there safety concerns?
Condurango seems safe for most people. Some people can develop severe allergic reactions from using condurango, especially individuals allergic to natural rubber latex.

Do not use condurango if: You are pregnant or breast-feeding. • You are allergic to latex.

Are there any interactions with medications?
It is not known if condurango interacts with any medicines.
Before taking condurango, talk with your healthcare professional if you take any medications.

CONJUGATED LINOLEIC ACID

What other names is the product known by?
Cis-9,trans-11 conjugated linoleic acid; CLA; linoleic; trans-10,cis-12 conjugated linoleic acid.

What is it?
Conjugated linoleic acid (CLA) refers to a group of chemicals found in the fatty acid linoleic acid. Dairy products and beef are the major dietary sources.

Is it Effective?
The effectiveness ratings for **CONJUGATED LINOLEIC ACID** are as follows:
Possibly Effective for... Colon and rectal cancer. Some research suggests that a diet high in conjugated linoleic acid might reduce the risk of cancer of the colon and rectum in women • Obesity. Conjugated linoleic acid might help decrease body fat, but it does not seem to decrease body weight.
Insufficient Evidence to Rate Effectiveness for... Cancer, bodybuilding, reducing cholesterol levels, and other conditions.

How does it work?
Conjugated linoleic acid might help reduce body fat deposits and improve immune function.

Are there safety concerns?
Conjugated linoleic acid is safe when used in amounts found in foods and seems safe for use in medicinal amounts. It might cause side effects such as stomach upset, diarrhea, nausea, and fatigue.

Do not use medicinal amounts of conjugated linoleic acid if: You are pregnant or breast-feeding. • You have diabetes. There are concerns that taking conjugated linoleic acid can worsen diabetes. • You have a condition called metabolic syndrome. There are concerns that taking conjugated linoleic acid can increase the risk of getting diabetes.

Are there any interactions with medications?

It is not known if conjugated linoleic acid interacts with any medicines.

Before taking conjugated linoleic acid, talk with your healthcare professional if you take any medications.

CONTRAYERVA

What other names is the product known by?

Contrayerba, Dorstenia contrajerva Dorstenia contrayerva, Herbe-Chapeau.

What is it?

Contrayerva is an herb. People use the root to make medicine.

Is it Effective?

The effectiveness ratings for **CONTRAYERVA** are as follows:

Insufficient Evidence to Rate Effectiveness for... Treating snakebites and increasing energy (stamina).

How does it work?

Contrayerva might work by acting as a stimulant and inducing sweating.

Are there safety concerns?

Contrayerva seems unsafe for use. It can cause heart problems and might also increase sensitivity to ultraviolet (UV) radiation, such as sunlight.

Do not use contrayerva if: You are pregnant or breast-feeding.

Are there any interactions with medications?

It is not known if contrayerva interacts with any medicines.

Before taking contrayerva, talk with your healthcare professional if you take any medications.

COOLWORT

What other names is the product known by?

Foam Flower, Mitrewort, Tiarella cordifolia.

What is it?

Coolwort is an herb. People use the herb to make medicine.

Is it Effective?

The effectiveness ratings for **COOLWORT** are as follows:

Insufficient Evidence to Rate Effectiveness for... Urinary tract and digestive disorders, bladder diseases and stones, indigestion, and heartburn.

How does it work?

Coolwort might work by increasing the amount of urine made by the body (diuretic).

Are there safety concerns?

There isn't enough information to know if coolwort is safe for use as a medicine.

Do not use coolwort if: You are pregnant or breast-feeding.

Are there any interactions with medications?

It is not known if coolwort interacts with any medicines.

Before taking coolwort, talk with your healthcare professional if you take any medications.

Medical professionals should consult the Professional Version at www.NaturalDatabase.com.

COPAIBA BALSAM

What other names is the product known by?
Copaifera langsdorfii, Copaifera officinalis, Copaifera reticulata, Copaiva, Jesuit's Balsam.

What is it?
Copaiba balsam is an herb. People use the oil and sap-like substance (oleoresin) to make medicine.

Is it Effective?
The effectiveness ratings for **COPAIBA BALSAM** are as follows:
Insufficient Evidence to Rate Effectiveness for... Hemorrhoids, diarrhea, urinary tract infections (UTIs), constipation, bronchitis, and other conditions.

How does it work?
Copaiba balsam oil might help kill germs, decrease swelling (inflammation), and increase the production of urine (diuretic).

Are there safety concerns?
Copaiba balsam seems safe for most people when consumed in normal food amounts. However, it seems UNSAFE for use as a medicine. Copaiba balsam can cause side effects such as stomach pains, vomiting, diarrhea, rash, tremor, groin pain, and sleeplessness (insomnia). When used on the skin, it can cause redness, itching, and a rash that might leave brown spots after healing.

Do not use copaiba balsam if: You are pregnant or breast-feeding.

Are there any interactions with medications?
It is not known if copaiba balsam interacts with any medicines.
Before taking copaiba balsam, talk with your healthcare professional if you take any medications.

COPPER

What other names is the product known by?
Atomic number 29, Cu, Cuivre, Cupric Oxide, Elemental Copper.

What is it?
Copper is a mineral.

Is it Effective?
The effectiveness ratings for **COPPER** are as follows:
Likely Effective for... Copper deficiency • Anemia due to copper deficiency.
Possibly Ineffective for... Systemic lupus erythematosus (SLE).
Insufficient Evidence to Rate Effectiveness for... Wound healing, arthritis, and osteoporosis.

How does it work?
Copper is necessary for producing and storing iron.

Are there safety concerns?
Copper is safe when it is used to treat a copper deficiency. It is unsafe when used in large amounts. Symptoms of copper overdose include nausea, vomiting, bloody diarrhea, fever, stomach pain, low blood pressure, anemia, and heart problems.

Adults should consume no more than 10 mg of copper per day. Kidney failure and death can occur with as little as 1 gram of copper sulfate.

Pregnant or breast-feeding women should consume no more than 8 mg per day if they are 14 to 18 years old, and no more than 10 mg per day if they are 19 or older. Higher amounts can be dangerous.

Do not use copper if: You have Wilson's disease.

Are there any interactions with medications?
Penicillamine. Penicillamine is used for Wilson's disease and rheumatoid arthritis. Copper might decrease how much penicillamine your body absorbs and decrease the effectiveness of penicillamine.

 Natural Medicines Comprehensive Database Consumer Version (209) 472-2244

CORAL

What other names is the product known by?
Calcium Carbonate Matrix, Coral Calcium, Coralline Hydroxyapatite, Goniopora species, Madrepora species, Porites species, Sea Coral.

What is it?
Coral is the skeletal structure of a marine animal. It makes up coral reefs.

Is it Effective?
The effectiveness ratings for **CORAL** are as follows:
Possibly Effective for... As a surgical replacement for bone in orthopedic (bone), neurosurgical (head), periodontal (dental), and other kinds of surgery.
Insufficient Evidence to Rate Effectiveness for... Calcium supplement; treating multiple sclerosis; treating and preventing cancer, heart disease, and other chronic health problems.

How does it work?
Surgeons use coral as a replacement for bone. It seems to allow the body to grow new bone in its place.

Are there safety concerns?
Coral used in surgery seems safe for most people. There is not enough information to know if coral taken by mouth is safe. Some oral coral products contain lead.

Do not use coral if: You are pregnant or breast-feeding.

Are there any interactions with medications?
It is not known if coral interacts with any medicines.
Before taking coral, talk with your healthcare professional if you take any medications.

CORAL ROOT

What other names is the product known by?
Chicken Toe, Corallorhiza odontorhiza, Crawley, Crawley Root, Cymbidium odontorhizum, Fever Root, Scaley Dragon's Claw, Turkey Claw.

What is it?
Coral root is an herb. People use the bulb or root to make medicine.

Is it Effective?
The effectiveness ratings for **CORAL ROOT** are as follows:
Insufficient Evidence to Rate Effectiveness for... Colds and inducing sweating (perspiration).

How does it work?
Coral root might help induce sweating, reduce fever, and cause drowsiness.

Are there safety concerns?
There isn't enough information to know if coral root is safe for use as a medicine.

Do not use coral root if: You are pregnant or breast-feeding.

Are there any interactions with medications?
It is not known if coral root interacts with any medicines.
Before taking coral root, talk with your healthcare professional if you take any medications.

Medical professionals should consult the Professional Version at www.NaturalDatabase.com.

CORDYCEPS

What other names is the product known by?

Caterpillar Fungus, Cs-4, Cordyceps sinensis, Dong Chong Xia Cao, Dong Chong Zia Cao, Hsia Ts'Ao Tung Ch'Ung, Tochukaso, Vegetable Caterpillar.

What is it?

Cordyceps is a fungus that lives on certain Chinese caterpillars.

Is it Effective?

The effectiveness ratings for **CORDYCEPS** are as follows:
Possibly Ineffective for... Improving athletic performance.
Insufficient Evidence to Rate Effectiveness for... Promoting longevity, decreasing fatigue, cough, bronchitis, breathing disorders, kidney disorders, male sexual dysfunction, anemia, heart arrhythmias, high cholesterol, liver disorders, kidney disorders, dizziness, weakness, ringing in the ears, improving quality of life after cancer chemotherapy, improving immune system function after cancer chemotherapy, improving liver function in people with hepatitis B, and other conditions.

How does it work?

Cordyceps might improve immunity by stimulating cells and specific chemicals in the immune system. It may also have activity against cancer cells and may shrink tumor size, particularly with lung or skin cancers.

Are there safety concerns?

Cordyceps seems to be safe for most people.

Do not use cordyceps if: You are pregnant or breast-feeding.

Are there any interactions with medications?

Cyclophosphamide (Cytoxan, Neosar). Cyclophosphamide (Cytoxan, Neosar) is used to decrease the immune system. Cordyceps seems to increase the immune system. Taking cordyceps along with cyclophosphamide (Cytoxan, Neosar) might decrease the effectiveness of cyclophosphamide (Cytoxan, Neosar).
Prednisolone. Prednisolone is sometimes used to decrease the immune system. Taking cordyceps might make prednisolone less effective for decreasing the immune system.

CORIANDER

What other names is the product known by?

Chinese Parsley, Cilantro, Coriandri Fructus, Coriandrum sativum, Dhanyaka, Koriander, Kustumburi.

What is it?

Coriander is a plant. People use the seed for medicine.

Is it Effective?

The effectiveness ratings for **CORIANDER** are as follows:
Insufficient Evidence to Rate Effectiveness for... Stomach upset, loss of appetite, spasms, intestinal gas (flatulence), diarrhea, bacterial or fungal infections, measles, hemorrhoids, toothaches, nausea, painful hernia, worms, joint pain, and other conditions.

How does it work?

Coriander may lower blood sugar and help kill some parasites, but there currently isn't enough information to know how coriander might work for medicinal uses.

Are there safety concerns?

Coriander is possibly safe for most people when taken by mouth in medicinal amounts. Coriander can cause some side effects, including allergic reactions and increased sensitivity to the sun. Increased sensitivity to the sun might put you at greater risk for sunburns and skin cancer. Avoid sunlight. Wear sunblock and protective clothing outside, especially if you are light-skinned.

When coriander comes in contact with the skin, it can cause skin irritation and inflammation.

Do not use coriander if: You are pregnant or breast-feeding. • You are allergic to other plants in the carrot family.

 Natural Medicines Comprehensive Database Consumer Version (209) 472-2244

Are there any interactions with medications?
It is not known if coriander interacts with any medicines.
Before taking coriander, talk with your healthcare professional if you take any medications.

CORIOLUS MUSHROOM

What other names is the product known by?
Boletus Versicolor, Coriolus versicolor, Kawaratake, Krestin, Polyporus Versicolor, Polysaccharide Peptide, Polysaccharide-K, Polystictus Versicolor, PSK, PSP, Trametes versicolor, Turkey Tail, Yun-Zhi (cloud mushroom).

What is it?
Coriolus mushroom is a fungus. People use the fruiting body and other parts for medicine.

Is it Effective?
The effectiveness ratings for **CORIOLUS MUSHROOM** are as follows:
Possibly Effective for... Cancer when used with chemotherapy regimens (when PSK products isolated from coriolus mushroom are used).
Insufficient Evidence to Rate Effectiveness for... Boosting immune function, herpes, chronic fatigue syndrome, hepatitis, lung disorders, body building, ringworm, skin infections (impetigo), urinary and digestive tract infections, poor appetite, and other uses.

How does it work?
Coriolus contains polysaccharide peptide (PSP) and polysaccharide-K (PSK, krestin), which may have antitumor and immune stimulating effects.

Are there safety concerns?
Coriolus mushroom is possibly safe for most people. There are no reported side effects of coriolus mushroom. However, people who have received chemotherapy and PSK (which is isolated from coriolus mushroom) experienced nausea, low white blood cell counts, and liver problems. It is unclear if these side effects were due to the chemotherapy or PSK.

Do not use coriolus mushroom if: You are pregnant or breast-feeding.

Are there any interactions with medications?
It is not known if coriolus mushroom interacts with any medicines.
Before taking coriolus mushroom, talk with your healthcare professional if you take any medications.

CORKWOOD TREE

What other names is the product known by?
Duboisia myoporoides, Pituri.

What is it?
Corkwood tree is a plant. The cured and rolled leaves are used to make medicine.

Is it Effective?
The effectiveness ratings for **CORKWOOD TREE** are as follows:
Insufficient Evidence to Rate Effectiveness for... Hunger, pain, tiredness, and other conditions.

How does it work?
Corkwood tree is a plant. People use the leaf of the tree to make medicine.

Are there safety concerns?
Corkwood tree is UNSAFE when taken by mouth.

Corkwood tree can cause many side effects including dry mouth, decreased perspiration, dilation of pupils, blurred vision, red, dry skin, increased body temperature, increased heart rate, difficulty urinating, hallucinations, spasms, acute psychosis, convulsions, and coma. Overdose poisoning symptoms include sleepiness followed by restlessness, hallucinations, delirium, and manic episodes followed by exhaustion and sleep. Corkwood tree can cause death.

Medical professionals should consult the Professional Version at www.NaturalDatabase.com.

Medical professionals should consult the
Professional Version at www.NaturalDatabase.com.

Do not use corkwood tree if: You are pregnant or breast-feeding. • You have Down's syndrome. • You have congestive heart failure. • You have a digestive condition, such as gastroesophageal reflux disease (GERD), hiatal hernia, stomach and intestine disease, or peptic ulcer disease. • You have constipation, an intestinal infection, ulcerative colitis, or Crohn's disease. • You have a fever. • You have narrow-angle glaucoma. • You have heart arrhythmias. • You have urinary retention.

Are there any interactions with medications?
It is not known if corkwood tree interacts with any medicines.
Before taking corkwood tree, talk with your healthcare professional if you take any medications.

CORN COCKLE

What other names is the product known by?
Agrostemma githago, Cockle, Corn Campion, Corn Rose, Crown-of-the-Field, Purple Cockle.

What is it?
Corn cockle is an herb. People use the root and seed to make medicine.

Is it Effective?
The effectiveness ratings for **CORN COCKLE** are as follows:
Insufficient Evidence to Rate Effectiveness for... Cancers, tumors, warts, swelling of the uterus, swelling of the eye (conjunctiva and cornea), skin conditions, hemorrhoids, coughs, menstrual disorders, worms, jaundice, and other conditions.

How does it work?
There isn't enough information available to know how corn cockle works.

Are there safety concerns?
Corn cockle is UNSAFE for use. Several chemicals found in it are considered poisonous. Poisoning symptoms include diarrhea, drooling, dizziness, vomiting, paralysis, breathing difficulty, and coma.

Do not use corn cockle if: You are pregnant or breast-feeding.

Are there any interactions with medications?
It is not known if corn cockle interacts with any medicines.
Before taking corn cockle, talk with your healthcare professional if you take any medications.

CORN POPPY

What other names is the product known by?
Copperose, Corn Rose, Cup-Puppy, Headache, Headwark, Rakta-Posta, Rakta Khakasa, Red Poppy, Rhoeados Flos.

What is it?
Corn poppy is an herb. People use the flower to make medicine.

Is it Effective?
The effectiveness ratings for **CORN POPPY** are as follows:
Insufficient Evidence to Rate Effectiveness for... Lung diseases and disorders, disturbed sleep, and pain.

How does it work?
There isn't enough information available to know how corn poppy works.

Are there safety concerns?
Corn poppy seems safe for most adults to use.

The fresh leaves and blossoms seem UNSAFE for use in children. They might cause side effects such as vomiting and stomach pain.

Do not use corn poppy if: You are pregnant or breast-feeding.

Are there any interactions with medications?
It is not known if corn poppy interacts with any medicines.
Before taking corn poppy, talk with your healthcare professional if you take any medications.

CORN SILK

What other names is the product known by?
Indian Corn, Maidis Stigma, Maize Silk, Stigma Maydis, Zea mays.

What is it?
Corn silk is from the corn plant. The silk from the top of an ear of corn is used as a medicine.

Is it Effective?
The effectiveness ratings for **CORN SILK** are as follows:
Insufficient Evidence to Rate Effectiveness for... Bedwetting, inflammation of the prostate, inflammation of the urinary system, congestive heart failure, diabetes, and high blood pressure.

How does it work?
Corn silk contains tannins, which act as drying agents. It also contains cryptoxanthin, which acts like vitamin A.

Are there safety concerns?
Corn silk seems to be safe for most people.

Corn silk can decrease potassium levels in the blood and can cause skin rashes, itching, and allergies.

Do not take corn silk if: You are pregnant or breast-feeding. • You have diabetes. • You have low or high blood pressure. • You have low potassium levels. • You are allergic to corn.

Are there any interactions with medications?
Medications for diabetes (Antidiabetes drugs). Corn silk might decrease blood sugar. Diabetes medications are also used to lower blood sugar. Taking corn silk along with diabetes medications might cause your blood sugar to go too low. Monitor your blood sugar closely. The dose of your diabetes medication might need to be changed. Some medications used for diabetes include glimepiride (Amaryl), glyburide (DiaBeta, Glynase PresTab, Micronase), insulin, pioglitazone (Actos), rosiglitazone (Avandia), chlorpropamide (Diabinese), glipizide (Glucotrol), tolbutamide (Orinase), and others.

Medications for high blood pressure (Antihypertensive drugs). Large amounts of corn silk seem to decrease blood pressure. Taking corn silk along with medications for high blood pressure might cause your blood pressure to go too low. Some medications for high blood pressure include captopril (Capoten), enalapril (Vasotec), losartan (Cozaar), valsartan (Diovan), diltiazem (Cardizem), Amlodipine (Norvasc), hydrochlorothiazide (HydroDiuril), furosemide (Lasix), and many others.

Medications for inflammation (Corticosteroids). Some medications for inflammation can decrease potassium in the body. Corn silk might also decrease potassium in the body. Taking corn silk along with some medications for inflammation might decrease potassium in the body too much. Some medications for inflammation include dexamethasone (Decadron), hydrocortisone (Cortef), methylprednisolone (Medrol), prednisone (Deltasone), and others.

Water pills (Diuretic drugs). Corn silk seems to work like "water pills." Corn silk and "water pills" might cause the body to get rid of potassium along with water. Taking corn silk along with "water pills" might decrease potassium in the body too much. Some "water pills" that can deplete potassium include chlorothiazide (Diuril), chlorthalidone (Thalitone), furosemide (Lasix), hydrochlorothiazide (HCTZ, HydroDiuril, Microzide), and others.

Warfarin (Coumadin). Corn silk contains large amounts of vitamin K. Vitamin K is used by the body to help blood clot. Warfarin (Coumadin) is used to slow blood clotting. By helping the blood clot, corn silk might decrease the effectiveness of warfarin (Coumadin). Be sure to have your blood checked regularly. The dose of your warfarin (Coumadin) might need to be changed.

Medical professionals should consult the Professional Version at www.NaturalDatabase.com.

CORNFLOWER

What other names is the product known by?

Batchelor's Buttons, Bluebonnet, Bluebottle, Bluebow, Blue Cap, Blue Centaury, Centaurea cyanus, Centaurea segetum, Cyani Blossoms, Cyani Flos, Cyani Flower, Cyani Petals, Hurtsickle.

What is it?

Cornflower is an herb. People use the flowers to make medicine.

Is it Effective?

The effectiveness ratings for **CORNFLOWER** are as follows:

Insufficient Evidence to Rate Effectiveness for... Fever, menstrual disorders, yeast infections, constipation, coughs, liver and gallbladder disorders, eye irritation, and other conditions.

How does it work?

There isn't enough information available to know how cornflower works.

Are there safety concerns?

There isn't enough information to know if cornflower is safe for use as a medicine. It may cause an allergic reaction in individuals sensitive to ragweed, marigolds, daisies, and similar herbs.

Do not use cornflower if: You are pregnant or breast-feeding. • You are allergic to ragweed, marigolds, daisies, and similar plants.

Are there any interactions with medications?

It is not known if cornflower interacts with any medicines.
Before taking cornflower, talk with your healthcare professional if you take any medications.

CORYDALIS

What other names is the product known by?

Corydalis cava, Early Fumitory, Squirrel Corn.

What is it?

Corydalis is a plant. People use the tuber and root for medicine.

Is it Effective?

The effectiveness ratings for **CORYDALIS** are as follows:

Insufficient Evidence to Rate Effectiveness for... Mild depression, neuroses and emotional disturbances, severe nerve damage, tremors, insomnia, high blood pressure, intestinal spasms, and other uses.

How does it work?

There isn't enough information to know how corydalis might work.

Are there safety concerns?

It is not known if using corydalis is safe. When too much is taken, corydalis can cause rhythmic spasms and muscle tremors.

Do not use corydalis if: You are pregnant or breast-feeding.

Are there any interactions with medications?

It is not known if corydalis interacts with any medicines.
Before taking corydalis, talk with your healthcare professional if you take any medications.

Natural Medicines Comprehensive Database Consumer Version (209) 472-2244

COSTUS

What other names is the product known by?

Aucklandia Costus, Aucklandia Lappa, Costus Oil, Costus Root, Kushta, Kushtha, Kuth, Mokko, Mokkou, Mu Xiang, Saussurea Costus, Saussurea Lappa, Saussureae Radix, Yun Mu Xiang.

What is it?

Costus is an herb. The root and oil from the root are used to make medicine.

Is it Effective?

The effectiveness ratings for **COSTUS** are as follows:

Insufficient Evidence to Rate Effectiveness for... Worm (nematode) infections, digestive problems, gas, asthma, cough, dysentery, and cholera.

How does it work?

Costus root contains chemicals that seem to kill nematodes (worms). Some researchers think that the chemicals in costus oil might prevent the airways from constricting and lower blood pressure.

Are there safety concerns?

Costus seems to be safe for most people. However, costus often contains a contaminant called aristocholic acid. Aristocholic acid damages the kidneys and causes cancer.

Allergic reactions to costus root have occurred in people who are allergic to other plants and herbs in the Asteraceae/Compositae family. Members of this family include daisies, ragweed, chrysanthemums, marigolds, and many other herbs.

Do not use costus if: You are pregnant or breast-feeding.

Are there any interactions with medications?

It is not known if costus interacts with any medicines.
Before taking costus, check with your healthcare professional if you take any medications.

COTTON

What other names is the product known by?

Cotton root, Gossypium herbaceum, Gossypium hirsutum, Karpasa.

What is it?

Cotton is a plant. People use the bark of the root to make medicine.

Is it Effective?

The effectiveness ratings for **COTTON** are as follows:

Insufficient Evidence to Rate Effectiveness for... Menstrual disorders, menopausal symptoms, nausea, fever, headache, diarrhea, kidney and bladder conditions, inducing labor and delivery, male contraception, and other conditions.

How does it work?

Cotton root bark might help stimulate menstrual flow, induce labor and delivery, and act as a male contraceptive.

Are there safety concerns?

Cotton seems safe for most people to use short-term.

Do not use cotton if: You are pregnant or breast-feeding. • You have a bladder condition. • You have a kidney condition. • You have a genital condition.

Are there any interactions with medications?

It is not known if cotton interacts with any medicines.
Before taking cotton, talk with your healthcare professional if you take any medications.

Medical professionals should consult the Professional Version at www.NaturalDatabase.com.

COUNTRY MALLOW

What other names is the product known by?

Bala, Bariar, Heartleaf, Khareti, Malva-Branca, Malva-Branca-Sedosa, Sida Cordifolia, Silky White Mallow, Vatya, White Mallow.

What is it?

Country mallow is a plant. The seeds and root are used to make medicine.

Is it Effective?

The effectiveness ratings for **COUNTRY MALLOW** are as follows:

Insufficient Evidence to Rate Effectiveness for... Weight loss, fatigue, impotence, asthma and bronchitis, cold, flu, chills, lack of perspiration, headache, nasal congestion, and many other conditions.

How does it work?

Country mallow plant contains ephedrine, which is an amphetamine-like stimulant. It is unknown how country mallow might work for other medicinal uses.

Are there safety concerns?

Country mallow is UNSAFE for any use. Country mallow contains ephedrine. Country mallow is banned in the US due to safety concerns. Another herb that contains ephedrine called ephedra is linked to high blood pressure, heart attacks, muscle disorders, seizures, strokes, irregular heartbeat, loss of consciousness, and death. Country mallow might also cause these side effects.

Country mallow might also cause dizziness, restlessness, irritability, insomnia, headache, lack of appetite, nausea, vomiting, flushing, tingling, difficulty urinating, and heart palpitations.

Do not use country mallow with other stimulants such as caffeine. This might increase the chance of having side effects, including life-threatening ones. Sources of caffeine include coffee, tea, kola nut, guarana, and mate.

Do not use country mallow if: You are pregnant or breast-feeding. • You have chest pains. • You feel anxious. • You have diabetes. • You have glaucoma. • You have heart disease or irregular heartbeat. • You have thyroid problems. • You have high blood pressure. • You have tremors. • You have kidney stones. • You have a condition called pheochromocytoma.

Are there any interactions with medications?

Dexamethasone (Decadron). The body breaks down dexamethasone (Decadron) to get rid of it. Country mallow might increase how quickly the body breaks down dexamethasone (Decadron). By increasing how quickly the body breaks down dexamethasone (Decadron) country mallow might decrease the effectiveness of dexamethasone (Decadron).

Ergot Derivatives. Country mallow can increase blood pressure. Ergot derivatives can also increase blood pressure. Taking country mallow with ergot derivatives might increase blood pressure too much. Some of these ergot derivatives include bromocriptine (Parlodel), dihydroergotamine (Migranal, DHE-45), ergotamine (Cafergot), and pergolide (Permax).

Medications for depression (MAOIs). Country mallow contains chemicals that stimulate the body. Some medications used for depression can increase these chemicals. Taking country mallow with these medications used for depression might cause too much stimulation. This could cause serious side effects including fast heartbeat, high blood pressure, seizures, nervousness, and others. Some of these medications used for depression include phenelzine (Nardil), tranylcypromine (Parnate), and others.

Medications for diabetes (Antidiabetes drugs). Country mallow might increase blood sugar. Diabetes medications are used to lower blood sugar. By increasing blood sugar, country mallow might decrease the effectiveness of diabetes medications. Monitor your blood sugar closely. The dose of your diabetes medication might need to be changed. Some medications used for diabetes include glimepiride (Amaryl), glyburide (DiaBeta, Glynase PresTab, Micronase), insulin, pioglitazone (Actos), rosiglitazone (Avandia), chlorpropamide (Diabinese), glipizide (Glucotrol), tolbutamide (Orinase), and others.

Medications that can cause an irregular heartbeat (QT interval-prolonging drugs). Country mallow can increase the speed of your heartbeat. Taking country mallow along with medications that can cause an irregular heartbeat might cause serious side effects including heart attack. Some medications that can cause an irregular heartbeat include amiodarone (Cordarone), disopyramide (Norpace), dofetilide (Tikosyn), ibutilide (Corvert), procainamide (Pronestyl), quinidine, sotalol (Betapace), thioridazine (Mellaril), and many others.

Methylxanthines. Country mallow can simulate the body. Methylxanthines also stimulate the body. Taking country mallow with methylxanthines might cause side effects such as jitteriness, nervousness, a fast heartbeat, high blood pressure, and anxiety. Methylxanthines include aminophylline, caffeine, and theophylline.

Stimulant drugs. Stimulant drugs speed up the nervous system and can make you feel jittery and speed up your

 Natural Medicines Comprehensive Database Consumer Version (209) 472-2244

heartbeat. Country mallow can also speed up the nervous system. Taking country mallow along with stimulant drugs might cause serious problems including increased heart rate and high blood pressure. Avoid taking stimulant drugs along with country mallow. Some stimulant drugs include diethylpropion (Tenuate), epinephrine, phentermine (Ionamin), pseudoephedrine (Sudafed), and many others.

COWHAGE

What other names is the product known by?
Atmagupta, Couhage, Cowitch, Feijao macaco, HP 200, HP-200, Kapikachchhu, Kaunch, Kawanch, Kiwach, Macuna, Mucuna pruriens, Pica Pica, Stizolobium pruriens, Velvet Bean.

What is it?
Cowhage is a plant. The bean, seed, and hair of the bean pod are used to make medicine.

Is it Effective?
The effectiveness ratings for **COWHAGE** are as follows:
Insufficient Evidence to Rate Effectiveness for... Worm infestations, bone and joint conditions, muscle pain, Parkinson's disease, and to stimulate surface blood flow in conditions that involve paralysis.

How does it work?
Cowhage contains levodopa (L-dopa), which is used to treat Parkinson's disease. L-dopa is changed to the chemical dopamine in the brain. Symptoms of Parkinson's disease occur in patients due to low levels of dopamine in the brain. Unfortunately, most L-dopa is broken down in the body before it ever reaches the brain unless special chemicals are used with levodopa. These chemicals are not present in cowhage.

Are there safety concerns?
The cowhage bean wall formulation called HP-200 seems to be safe for most people. The hair of the cowhage bean pod is not safe for use.

The most common side effects include nausea and a sensation of abdominal bloating. Less frequently reported side effects include vomiting, abnormal body movements, and insomnia. Cowhage bean can also cause headache, palpitations, and symptoms of psychosis including confusion, agitation, hallucinations, and delusions. The hair of the cowhage bean pod is a strong irritant and can cause severe itching, burning, and swelling.

Do not use cowhage if: You are pregnant or breast-feeding. • You have cardiovascular disease. • You have diabetes. • You have hypoglycemia. • You have melanoma. • You have liver disease. • You have peptic ulcer disease. • You have a psychiatric condition.

Are there any interactions with medications?
Guanethidine (Ismelin). Cowhage can decrease blood pressure. Guanethidine (Ismelin) can also decrease blood pressure. Taking cowhage and guanethidine together might cause blood pressure to go too low.
Medications for depression (MAOIs). Cowhage contains chemicals that stimulate the body. Some medications used for depression can increase these chemicals. Taking cowhage along with these medications used for depression might cause serious side effects including fast heartbeat, high blood pressure, seizures, nervousness, and others. Some of these medications used for depression include phenelzine (Nardil), tranylcypromine (Parnate), and others.
Medications used for depression (Tricyclic antidepressants). Some medications used for depression can slow down the stomach and intestines. This might decrease how much cowhage is absorbed. Taking some medications used for depression might decrease the effects of cowhage.
Medications for diabetes (Antidiabetes drugs). Cowhage might decrease blood sugar. Diabetes medications are also used to lower blood sugar. Taking cowhage along with diabetes medications might cause your blood sugar to go too low. Monitor your blood sugar closely. The dose of your diabetes medication might need to be changed. Some medications used for diabetes include glimepiride (Amaryl), glyburide (DiaBeta, Glynase PresTab, Micronase), insulin, pioglitazone (Actos), rosiglitazone (Avandia), chlorpropamide (Diabinese), glipizide (Glucotrol), tolbutamide (Orinase), and others.
Medications for mental conditions (Antipsychotic drugs). Cowhage seems to increase a chemical in the brain called dopamine. Some medications for mental conditions help to decrease dopamine. Taking cowhage along with some medications for mental conditions might decrease the effectiveness of some medications for mental conditions. Some medications for mental conditions include chlorpromazine (Thorazine), clozapine (Clozaril), fluphenazine (Prolixin), haloperidol (Haldol), olanzapine (Zyprexa), perphenazine (Trilafon), prochlorperazine (Compazine), quetiapine (Seroquel), risperidone (Risperdal), thioridazine (Mellaril), thiothixene (Navane), and others.
Medications used during surgery (Anesthesia). Cowhage contains a chemical called L-dopa (levodopa). Taking

L-dopa along with medications used for surgery can cause heart problems. Be sure to tell your doctor what natural products you are taking before having surgery. You should stop taking cowhage at least two weeks before surgery. **Methyldopa (Aldomet).** Cowhage can lower blood pressure. Methyldopa (Aldomet) can also lower blood pressure. Taking cowhage and methyldopa together might lower blood pressure too much. Some of these medicines used for depression include amitriptyline (Elavil), imipramine (Tofranil), and others.

COWSLIP

What other names is the product known by?
Artetyke, Arthritica, Buckels, Butter Rose, Crewel, Drelip, English Cowslip, Fairy Caps, Herb Perter, Key Flower, Key of Heaven, Mayflower, Our Lady's Keys, Paigle, Paigle Peggle, Palsywort, Password, Peagle, Peagles, Petty Mulleins, Plumrocks, Primrose, Primula, Primula elatior, Primula officinalis, Primula veris.

What is it?
Cowslip is a plant. The flower and root are used to make medicine.

Is it Effective?
The effectiveness ratings for **COWSLIP** are as follows:
Possibly Effective for... Inflamed nasal passages or sinusitis when taken with gentian root, European elder flower, verbena, and cowslip flower (SinuComp, Sinupret).
Insufficient Evidence to Rate Effectiveness for... Bronchitis, in combination with thyme; cough; whooping cough; insomnia; nervous excitability; headache; hysteria; nerve pain; tremors; fluid retention; spasms; asthma; gout; neurologic complaints; and other conditions.

How does it work?
Cowslip contains chemicals that might thin and loosen mucus.

Are there safety concerns?
Cowslip seems to be safe for most people when used in small amounts as part of a combination product containing gentian root, European elder flower, verbena, and sorrel (SinuComp, Sinupret). There isn't enough information to know if cowslip is safe when used in medicinal amounts other than as part of the combination product. The combination product can cause digestive system upset and occasionally allergic skin rash.

Do not use cowslip if: You are pregnant or breast-feeding.

Are there any interactions with medications?
It is not known if cowslip interacts with any medicines.
Before taking cowslip, talk with your healthcare professional if you take any medications.

CRAMP BARK

What other names is the product known by?
Common Guelder-Rose, Crampbark, Cranberry bush, European Cranberry-Bush, Guelder Rose, High Bush Cranberry, High-bush Cranberry, Snowball Bush, Viburnum opulus.

What is it?
Cramp bark is a plant. The bark and root bark are used to make medicine.

Is it Effective?
The effectiveness ratings for **CRAMP BARK** are as follows:
Insufficient Evidence to Rate Effectiveness for... Cramps, muscle spasms, menstrual cramps, cramps during pregnancy, as a kidney stimulant in urinary conditions which involve pain or spasms, cancer, hysteria, nervous disorders, and many other conditions.

How does it work?
Chemicals in cramp bark seem to decrease muscle spasms. These chemicals might also lower blood pressure and decrease heart rate.

Are there safety concerns?
There isn't enough information to know if cramp bark is safe.

Do not use cramp bark if: You are pregnant or breast-feeding.

Are there any interactions with medications?
It is not known if cramp bark interacts with any medicines.
Before taking cramp bark, talk with your healthcare professional if you take any medications.

CRANBERRY

What other names is the product known by?
American Cranberry, Arandano Americano, Arandano Trepador, European Cranberry, Grosse Moosbeere, Kranbeere, Moosebeere, Mossberry, Ronce d'Amerique, Trailing Swamp Cranberry, Tsuru-kokemomo, Vaccinium Macrocarpon, Oxycoccus Macrocarpos, Vaccinium oxycoccos, Oxycoccus Hagerupii, Oxycoccus Microcarpus, Oxycoccus Palustris, Oxycoccus Quadripetalus, Vaccinium Hagerupii, Vaccinium Microcarpum, Vaccinium Palustre.

What is it?
Cranberry is a fruit. The fruit is used to make medicine.

Is it Effective?
The effectiveness ratings for **CRANBERRY** are as follows:
Possibly Effective for...PREVENTING urinary tract infections (UTIs) • Reducing urinary odor in older people.
Possibly Ineffective for...TREATING urinary tract infections (UTIs) • PREVENTING UTIs in people with a bladder disease called neurogenic bladder • Treating type 2 diabetes.
Insufficient Evidence to Rate Effectiveness for... Skin healing, pleurisy, cancer, chronic fatigue syndrome (CFS), and other conditions.

How does it work?
Cranberries contain certain chemicals that prevent bacteria from growing in the urinary tract.

Are there safety concerns?
Cranberry is safe for most people, but drinking too much cranberry juice can cause some side effects such as mild stomach upset and diarrhea. Drinking more than 1 liter per day for a long period of time might increase the chance of getting kidney stones.

Some cranberry juice products are sweetened with extra sugar. If you have diabetes, stick with cranberry products that are sweetened with artificial sweeteners.

Cranberries and cranberry juice are safe to consume during pregnancy and breast-feeding. But don't use dietary supplements that contain cranberry products. It is not known if these are safe to use during pregnancy and breast-feeding.

Cranberries, like many other fruits and berries, contain significant amounts of salicylic acid. Salicylic acid is similar to aspirin. Avoid drinking large quantities of cranberry juice if you are allergic to aspirin.

Are there any interactions with medications?
Medications changed by the liver (Cytochrome P450 2C9 (CYP2C9) substrates). Some medications are changed and broken down by the liver. Cranberry might decrease how quickly the liver breaks down some medications. Taking cranberry along with some medications that are broken down by the liver can increase the effects and side effects of some medications. Before taking cranberry, talk to your healthcare provider if you take any medications that are changed by the liver. Some medications that are changed by the liver include amitriptyline (Elavil), diazepam (Valium), zileuton (Zyflo), celecoxib (Celebrex), diclofenac (Voltaren), fluvastatin (Lescol), glipizide (Glucotrol), ibuprofen (Advil, Motrin), irbesartan (Avapro), losartan (Cozaar), phenytoin (Dilantin), piroxicam (Feldene), tamoxifen (Nolvadex), tolbutamide (Tolinase), torsemide (Demadex), warfarin (Coumadin), and others.
Warfarin (Coumadin). Warfarin (Coumadin) is used to slow blood clotting. Cranberry might increase how long warfarin (Coumadin) is in the body, and increase the chances of bruising and bleeding. Be sure to have your blood checked regularly. The dose of your warfarin (Coumadin) might need to be changed.

Medical professionals should consult the Professional Version at www.NaturalDatabase.com.

CONSUMER VERSION

Medical professionals should consult the
Professional Version at www.NaturalDatabase.com.

CREATINE

What other names is the product known by?

Cr, Creatine Monohydrate, Creatin Pyruvate, N-amidinosarcosine; N-(aminoiminomethyl)-N Methyl Glycine.

What is it?

Creatine is a chemical that is normally found in the body, mostly in muscles. Creatine can also be made in the laboratory.

Is it Effective?

The effectiveness ratings for **CREATINE** are as follows:

Possibly Effective for... Improving the athletic performance of young, healthy people during brief, high-intensity exercise such as sprinting. However, it does not seem to help highly trained athletes. It also does not help increase muscle strength • Increasing strength and endurance in patients with heart failure • Increasing strength in people with muscle diseases such as muscular dystrophy • Slowing an eye disease called Gyrate Atrophy.

Possibly Ineffective for... Rheumatoid arthritis (RA) • Amyotrophic lateral sclerosis (ALS, Lou Gehrig's disease).

Insufficient Evidence to Rate Effectiveness for... High cholesterol, rheumatoid arthritis, various muscle diseases, and other conditions.

How does it work?

Creatine is involved in making the energy muscles need to work.

Are there safety concerns?

Creatine seems to be safe for most people when used at recommended doses. Creatine can cause stomach pain, nausea, diarrhea, and muscle cramping.

Creatine causes muscles to draw water from the rest of your body. Be sure to drink extra water to make up for this. Also, if you are taking creatine, don't exercise in the heat. It might cause you to become dehydrated.

Many people who use creatine gain weight. This is because creatine causes the muscles to hold water, not because it actually builds muscle.

There is some concern that combining creatine with caffeine and the herb ephedra (also called Ma Huang) might increase the chance of having serious side effects such as stroke.

There is concern that creatine might cause heart arrhythmia in some people. But more information is needed to know if creatine can cause this problem.

Do not use creatine if: You are pregnant or breast-feeding. • You have kidney disease. • You have diabetes, because you might have a higher chance of developing kidney disease.

Are there any interactions with medications?

Medications that can harm the kidneys (Nephrotoxic Drugs). Taking high doses of creatine might harm the kidneys. Some medications can also harm the kidneys. Taking creatine with medications that can harm the kidneys might increase the chance of kidney damage. Some of these medications that can harm the kidneys include cyclosporine (Neoral, Sandimmune); aminoglycosides including amikacin (Amikin), gentamicin (Garamycin, Gentak, others), and tobramycin (Nebcin, others); nonsteroidal anti-inflammatory drugs (NSAIDs) including ibuprofen (Advil, Motrin, Nuprin, others), indomethacin (Indocin), naproxen (Aleve, Anaprox, Naprelan, Naprosyn), piroxicam (Feldene); and numerous others.

CROTON SEEDS

What other names is the product known by?

Croton, Croton tiglium, Tiglium, Tiglium Seeds.

What is it?

Croton is a plant. The oil from the seeds is used to make medicine.

Is it Effective?

The effectiveness ratings for **CROTON SEEDS** are as follows:

Insufficient Evidence to Rate Effectiveness for... Gallbladder problems, obstruction of the intestines, malaria, joint pain, gout, nerve pain, bronchitis, and emptying and cleansing the stomach and intestines.

How does it work?
Croton seeds contain chemicals that have a powerful irritating effect on the stomach and intestines.

Are there safety concerns?
Croton seeds are UNSAFE when taken by mouth or put on the skin.

Croton seeds can cause burning of the mouth, vomiting, dizziness, stupor, painful bowel movements, abortions in pregnant women, and collapse when taken by mouth. If it is put on the skin, croton seed oil can cause itching, burning, and blistering of skin.

One drop of croton seed oil can cause side effects, and 20 drops of oil can cause death.

Do not use croton seeds if: You are pregnant or breast-feeding.

Are there any interactions with medications?
It is not known if croton seeds interact with any medicines.
Before taking croton seeds, talk with your healthcare professional if you take any medications.

CUBEBS

What other names is the product known by?
Cubeb Berries, Cubeba, Cubeba officinalis, Java Pepper, Piper cubeba, Tailed Chubebs, Tailed Pepper.

What is it?
Cubebs is an herb. The dried, fully grown but unripe fruit is used to make medicine.

Is it Effective?
The effectiveness ratings for **CUBEBS** are as follows:
Insufficient Evidence to Rate Effectiveness for... Increasing urination, amoebic dysentery, gas, gonorrhea, loosening of mucous, and cancer.

How does it work?
Cubebs contains cubebic acid which might have an effect on the urinary and respiratory tracts.

Are there safety concerns?
Cubebs seems to be safe when taken by mouth for most people, but the potential side effects are not known.

Do not use cubebs if: You are pregnant or breast-feeding. • You have an infection or inflammation of the stomach or intestines. • You have any kidney diseases.

Are there any interactions with medications?
Antacids. Antacids are used to decrease stomach acid. Cubebs may increase stomach acid. By increasing stomach acid, cubebs might decrease the effectiveness of antacids. Some antacids include calcium carbonate (Tums, others), dihydroxyaluminum sodium carbonate (Rolaids, others), magaldrate (Riopan), magnesium sulfate (Bilagog), aluminum hydroxide (Amphojel), and others.
Medications that decrease stomach acid (H2-Blockers). Cubebs might increase stomach acid. By increasing stomach acid, cubebs might decrease the effectiveness of some medications that decrease stomach acid, called H2-blockers. Some medications that decrease stomach acid include cimetidine (Tagamet), ranitidine (Zantac), nizatidine (Axid), and famotidine (Pepcid).
Medications that decrease stomach acid (Proton pump inhibitors). Cubebs might increase stomach acid. By increasing stomach acid, cubebs might decrease the effectiveness of medications that are used to decrease stomach acid called proton pump inhibitors. Some medications that decrease stomach acid include omeprazole (Prilosec), lansoprazole (Prevacid), rabeprazole (Aciphex), pantoprazole (Protonix), and esomeprazole (Nexium).

Medical professionals should consult the Professional Version at www.NaturalDatabase.com.

CUDWEED

What other names is the product known by?
Cotton Dawes, Cotton Weed, Dysentery Weed, Everlasting, Filaginella uliginosa, Gnaphalium uliginosum, Mouse Ear, Wartwort.

What is it?
Cudweed is an herb. The parts above the ground are used to make medicine. Avoid confusion with cat's foot (Antennaria dioica), which is also known as cudweed, and with Pilosella officinarum, which is also known as mouse ear.

Is it Effective?
The effectiveness ratings for **CUDWEED** are as follows:
Insufficient Evidence to Rate Effectiveness for...A gargle or rinse for diseases of the mouth or throat.

How does it work?
There isn't enough information to know how cudweed might work.

Are there safety concerns?
It is not known if cudweed is safe or what the potential side effects might be. But allergic reactions have occurred in people who are allergic to other plants and herbs in the Asteraceae/Compositae family. Members of this family include daisies, ragweed, chrysanthemums, marigolds, and many other herbs.

Do not use cudweed if: You are pregnant or breast-feeding. • You are allergic to other plants in the Asteraceae/Compositae family, such as daisies, chrysanthemums, or ragweed.

Are there any interactions with medications?
It is not known if cudweed interacts with any medicines.
Before taking cudweed, talk with your healthcare professional if you take any medications.

CUMIN

What other names is the product known by?
Cummin, Cuminum cyminum, Cuminum odorum, Jeeraka, Svetajiraka, Zira.

What is it?
Cumin is an herb. The seeds of the plant are used to make medicine.

Is it Effective?
The effectiveness ratings for **CUMIN** are as follows:
Insufficient Evidence to Rate Effectiveness for... Diarrhea, colic, gas, bowel spasms, and others.

How does it work?
It's not known how cumin might work on the conditions for which people use it.

Are there safety concerns?
Cumin seems to be safe for most adults. The side effects of cumin are not known.

Do not take cumin if: You are pregnant or breast-feeding.

Are there any interactions with medications?
Medications for diabetes (Antidiabetes drugs). Cumin might decrease blood sugar. Diabetes medications are also used to lower blood sugar. Taking cumin along with diabetes medications might cause your blood sugar to go too low. Monitor your blood sugar closely. The dose of your diabetes medication might need to be changed. Some medications used for diabetes include glimepiride (Amaryl), glyburide (DiaBeta, Glynase PresTab, Micronase), insulin, pioglitazone (Actos), rosiglitazone (Avandia), chlorpropamide (Diabinese), glipizide (Glucotrol), tolbutamide (Orinase), and others.

CUP PLANT

What other names is the product known by?
Indian Gum, Pilot Plant, Polar Plant, Prairie Dock, Ragged Cup, Rosinweed, Silphium perfoliatum, Turpentine Weed.

What is it?
Cup plant is an herb. The root is used to make medicine.

Is it Effective?
The effectiveness ratings for **CUP PLANT** are as follows:
Insufficient Evidence to Rate Effectiveness for... Digestive disorders.

How does it work?
It is not known how cup plant might work for medicinal uses.

Are there safety concerns?
It is not known if cup plant is safe or what the potential side effects might be.

Do not use cup plant if: You are pregnant or breast-feeding.

Are there any interactions with medications?
It is not known if cup plant interacts with any medicines.
Before taking cup plant, talk with your healthcare professional if you take any medications.

CUPMOSS

What other names is the product known by?
Chin Cups, Cladonia pyxidata.

What is it?
Cupmoss is an herb. It is used to make medicine.

Is it Effective?
The effectiveness ratings for **CUPMOSS** are as follows:
Insufficient Evidence to Rate Effectiveness for... Coughs, bronchitis, and whooping cough.

How does it work?
There isn't enough information to know how cupmoss might work.

Are there safety concerns?
It is not known if cupmoss is safe or what the potential side effects might be.

Do not use cupmoss if: You are pregnant or breast-feeding.

Are there any interactions with medications?
It is not known if cupmoss interacts with any medicines.
Before taking cupmoss, talk with your healthcare professional if you take any medications.

CYCLAMEN

What other names is the product known by?
Cyclamen europaeum, Groundbread, Ivy-Leafed Cyclamen, Sowbread, Swinebread.

What is it?
Cyclamen is a plant. People use the root and root-like stem (rhizome) for medicine.

Is it Effective?
The effectiveness ratings for **CYCLAMEN** are as follows:
Insufficient Evidence to Rate Effectiveness for... Menstrual complaints, "nervous emotional states," and digestive problems.

How does it work?

There isn't enough information to know how cyclamen might work.

Are there safety concerns?

Cyclamen is UNSAFE for use. Poisoning with cyclamen has been reported with doses as low as 300 mg. Symptoms of poisoning include stomach pain, nausea, vomiting, and diarrhea. High doses can cause severe poisoning which can cause symptoms including spasms and serious breathing problems.

Do not use cyclamen if: You are pregnant or breast-feeding.

Are there any interactions with medications?

It is not known if cyclamen interacts with any medicines.
Before taking cyclamen, talk with your healthcare professional if you take any medications.

CYPRESS

What other names is the product known by?

Cupressus sempervirens.

What is it?

Cypress is a plant. People use the branch, cone, and oil for medicine.

Is it Effective?

The effectiveness ratings for **CYPRESS** are as follows:
Insufficient Evidence to Rate Effectiveness for... Head colds, cough, bronchitis, and other uses.

How does it work?

There isn't enough information to know how cypress might work.

Are there safety concerns?

It is not known if cypress is safe, but cypress can cause kidney irritation.

Do not use cypress if: You are pregnant or breast-feeding.

Are there any interactions with medications?

It is not known if cypress interacts with any medicines.
Before taking cypress, talk with your healthcare professional if you take any medications.

CYPRESS SPURGE

What other names is the product known by?

Euphorbia cyparissias.

What is it?

Cypress spurge is a plant. The flowering plant and root are used to make medicine.

Is it Effective?

The effectiveness ratings for **CYPRESS SPURGE** are as follows:
Insufficient Evidence to Rate Effectiveness for... Breathing disorders, diarrhea, or skin diseases.

How does it work?

It is not known how cypress spurge might work for medicinal uses.

Are there safety concerns?

Cypress spurge is UNSAFE. The plant contains poisonous white milky liquid and chemicals that can cause cancer. Both the fresh and dried products are unsafe.
Cypress spurge can cause nausea, vomiting, diarrhea, burning of the mouth, dilation of the pupils, dizziness, painful bowel movements, stupor, irregular heartbeat, and collapse. Cypress spurge can also cause rash, reddening, itching, burning, and blisters if it is put on the skin. Getting cypress spurge in the eye can cause eyelid and eye swelling and damage.
Do not use cypress spurge if: You are pregnant or breast-feeding.

   Natural Medicines Comprehensive Database Consumer Version   (209) 472-2244

Are there any interactions with medications?

It is not known if cypress spurge interacts with any medicines.

Before taking cypress spurge, talk with your healthcare professional if you take any medications.

D-MANNOSE

What other names is the product known by?

Carubinose, Mannose, Seminose.

What is it?

D-mannose is a kind of sugar, related to glucose.

Is it Effective?

The effectiveness ratings for **D-MANNOSE** are as follows:

Insufficient Evidence to Rate Effectiveness for... Carbohydrate-deficient glycoprotein syndrome type 1b (a rare genetic disorder) and preventing urinary tract infections.

How does it work?

D-mannose might treat the deficiency caused by a genetic defect that causes abnormal breakdown and production of mannose. D-mannose might prevent certain kinds of bacteria from sticking to the walls of the urinary tract and causing infection.

Are there safety concerns?

D-mannose appears to be safe for when used orally and appropriately. D-mannose can cause loose stools and bloating. In high doses, it might harm the kidneys.

Do not use d-mannose if: You are pregnant or breast-feeding. • You have diabetes.

Are there any interactions with medications?

It is not known if d-mannose interacts with any medicines.

Before taking d-mannose, talk with your healthcare professional if you take any medications.

DAFFODIL

What other names is the product known by?

Lent Lily, Narcissus pseudonarcissus.

What is it?

Daffodil is a plant. People use the bulb, leaf, and flower to make medicine.

Is it Effective?

The effectiveness ratings for **DAFFODIL** are as follows:

Insufficient Evidence to Rate Effectiveness for... Whooping cough, colds, asthma, wounds, burns, strains, joint pain, and other conditions.

How does it work?

Daffodil contains chemicals that help reduce pain. It is also being investigated for use in the treatment of Alzheimer's disease.

Are there safety concerns?

Daffodil is unsafe for use. It can cause irritation and swelling of the mouth, tongue and throat. Daffodil can also cause vomiting, salivation, diarrhea, brain and nerve disorders, lung collapse, and death.

People who handle daffodil plants or bulbs can have skin swelling and irritation.

Do not use daffodil if: You are pregnant or breast-feeding.

Are there any interactions with medications?

It is not known if daffodil interacts with any medicines.

Before taking daffodil, talk with your healthcare professional if you take any medications.

Medical professionals should consult the Professional Version at www.NaturalDatabase.com.

DAMIANA

What other names is the product known by?

Damiana aphrodisiaca, Herba de la Pastora, Mexican Damiana, Mizibcoc, Old Woman's Broom, Rosemary, Turnera diffusa, Turnerae diffusae folium, Turnerae diffusae herba, Turnera microphyllia.

What is it?

Damiana is a plant. The stem and leaf are used to make medicine.

Is it Effective?

The effectiveness ratings for **DAMIANA** are as follows:
Insufficient Evidence to Rate Effectiveness for... Headaches, bedwetting, depression, nervous stomach, constipation, sexual problems, boosting mental and physical stamina, and other conditions.

How does it work?

Damiana contains chemicals which may affect the brain and nervous system.

Are there safety concerns?

Damiana might be safe when taken for medicinal uses, but there have been serious side effects. Convulsions and other symptoms similar to rabies or strychnine poisoning have been reported after taking 200 grams of damiana extract.

Do not take damiana if: You are pregnant or breast-feeding. • You have diabetes.

Are there any interactions with medications?

Medications for diabetes (Antidiabetes drugs). Damiana might decrease blood sugar. Diabetes medications are also used to lower blood sugar. Taking damiana along with diabetes medications might cause your blood sugar to go too low. Monitor your blood sugar closely. The dose of your diabetes medication might need to be changed. Some medications used for diabetes include glimepiride (Amaryl), glyburide (DiaBeta, Glynase PresTab, Micronase), insulin, pioglitazone (Actos), rosiglitazone (Avandia), chlorpropamide (Diabinese), glipizide (Glucotrol), tolbutamide (Orinase), and others.

DANDELION

What other names is the product known by?

Blowball, Cankerwort, Common Dandelion, Dandelion Herb, Leontodon taracum, Lion's Teeth, Lion's Tooth, Pissenlit, Priest's Crown, Swine Snout, Taraxaci herba, Taraxacum officinale, Taraxacum vulgare, Wild Endive.

What is it?

Dandelion is an herb. People use the above ground parts and root to make medicine.

Is it Effective?

The effectiveness ratings for **DANDELION** are as follows:
Insufficient Evidence to Rate Effectiveness for... Preventing urinary tract infection (UTI), loss of appetite, upset stomach, gas (flatulence), constipation, arthritis-like pain, and other conditions.

How does it work?

Dandelion contains chemicals that may increase urine production and decrease swelling (inflammation).

Are there safety concerns?

Dandelion seems to be safe for most people. It can cause allergic reactions when taken by mouth or applied to the skin of sensitive people.

Do not use dandelion if: You are pregnant or breast-feeding. • You are allergic to other plants such as daisies or ragweed.

Are there any interactions with medications?

Antibiotics (Quinolone antibiotics). Dandelion might decrease how much antibiotic the body absorbs. Taking dandelion along with antibiotics might decrease the effectiveness of some antibiotics. Some antibiotics that might interact with dandelion include ciprofloxacin (Cipro), enoxacin (Penetrex), norfloxacin (Chibroxin, Noroxin), sparfloxacin (Zagam), trovafloxacin (Trovan), and grepafloxacin (Raxar).
Medications changed by the liver (Cytochrome P450 1A2 (CYP1A2) substrates). Some medications are

changed and broken down by the liver. Dandelion might decrease how quickly the liver breaks down some medications. Taking dandelion along with some medications that are broken down by the liver can increase the effects and side effects of some medications. Before taking dandelion, talk to your healthcare provider if you take any medications that are changed by the liver. Some medications that are changed by the liver include amitriptyline (Elavil), haloperidol (Haldol), ondansetron (Zofran), propranolol (Inderal), theophylline (Theo-Dur, others), verapamil (Calan, Isoptin, others), and others.

Medications changed by the liver (Glucuronidated Drugs). The body breaks down some medications to get rid of them. The liver helps break down these medications. Dandelion might increase how quickly some medications are changed by the liver. This could decrease how well some of these medications work. Some of these medications changed by the liver include acetaminophen, atorvastatin (Lipitor), diazepam (Valium), digoxin, entacapone (Comtan), estrogen, irinotecan (Camptosar), lamotrigine (Lamictal), lorazepam (Ativan), lovastatin (Mevacor), meprobamate, morphine, oxazepam (Serax), and others.

Water pills (Potassium-sparing diuretics). Dandelion contains significant amounts of potassium. Some "water pills" can also increase potassium levels in the body. Taking some "water pills" along with dandelion might cause too much potassium to be in the body. Some "water pills" that increase potassium in the body include amiloride (Midamor), spironolactone (Aldactone), and triamterene (Dyrenium).

DANSHEN

What other names is the product known by?

Ch'ih Shen, Chinese Salvia, Dan-Shen, Huang Ken, Pin-Ma Ts'ao, Red Rooted Sage, Red Sage, Salvia bowelyana, Salvia miltiorrhiza, Salvia przewalskii, Salvia przewalskii mandarinorum, Salvia yunnanensis, Shu-Wei Ts'ao, Tan-Shen, Tzu Tan-Ken.

What is it?

Danshen is an herb. People use the root to make medicine.

Is it Effective?

The effectiveness ratings for **DANSHEN** are as follows:

Insufficient Evidence to Rate Effectiveness for... Blood circulation problems, stroke, chest pain and other heart diseases, menstrual problems, abdominal masses, sleeplessness (insomnia) due to chest complaints, acne, skin conditions, bruising, chronic liver inflammation (hepatitis), and wound healing.

How does it work?

Danshen appears to thin the blood by preventing platelet and blood clotting.

Are there safety concerns?

Danshen seems to be safe for most people. It can cause some mild side effects, including itching, upset stomach, and reduced appetite.

Do not use danshen if: You are pregnant or breast-feeding. • You have a bleeding disorder.

Are there any interactions with medications?

Digoxin (Lanoxin). Digoxin (Lanoxin) helps the heart beat more strongly. Danshen also seems to affect the heart. Taking danshen along with digoxin can increase the effects of digoxin and increase the risk of side effects. Do not take danshen if you are taking digoxin (Lanoxin) without talking to your healthcare professional.

Medications that slow blood clotting (Anticoagulant / Antiplatelet drugs). Danshen might slow blood clotting. Taking danshen along with medications that also slow clotting might increase the chances of bruising and bleeding. Some medications that slow blood clotting include aspirin, clopidogrel (Plavix), diclofenac (Voltaren, Cataflam, others), ibuprofen (Advil, Motrin, others), naproxen (Anaprox, Naprosyn, others), dalteparin (Fragmin), enoxaparin (Lovenox), heparin, warfarin (Coumadin), and others.

Warfarin (Coumadin). Warfarin (Coumadin) is used to slow blood clotting. Danshen might increase how long warfarin (Coumadin) is in the body, and increase the chances of bruising and bleeding. Be sure to have your blood checked regularly. The dose of your warfarin (Coumadin) might need to be changed.

Medical professionals should consult the Professional Version at www.NaturalDatabase.com.

CONSUMER VERSION

DATE PALM

What other names is the product known by?

Dade, Date, Dattel, Datter, Dattero, Dattier, Datil, Edible date, Kharjura, Phoenix dactylifera, Tamera.

What is it?

Date palm is a plant. The fruit is used to make medicine.

Is it Effective?

The effectiveness ratings for **DATE PALM** are as follows:
Insufficient Evidence to Rate Effectiveness for... Coughs and other breathing problems.

How does it work?

There isn't enough information to know how date palm might work.

Are there safety concerns?

Date palm fruit seems to be safe for most people when taken in amounts found in foods. There isn't enough information to know if larger amounts of date palm are safe or what the potential side effects might be.

Do not use date palm in amounts more than those found in foods if: You are pregnant or breast-feeding.

Are there any interactions with medications?

It is not known if date palm interacts with any medicines.
Before taking date palm, talk with your healthcare professional if you take any medications.

DEANOL

What other names is the product known by?

Deanol aceglumate, Deanol acetamidobenzoate, Deanol benzilate, Deanol bisorcate, Deanol cyclohexylpropionate, Deanol hemisuccinate, Deanol pidolate, Deanol tartrate, Dimethylaminoethanol, 2-Dimethyl Aminoethanol, 2-Dimethylaminoethanol, Dimethylethanolamine, DMAE, DMAE Bitartrate.

What is it?

Deanol is a precursor to choline, a chemical in the body used to make the chemical acetylcholine, which is found in the brain and other areas of the body.

Is it Effective?

The effectiveness ratings for **DEANOL** are as follows:
Likely Effective for... Improving exercise performance (when used with ginseng, vitamins, and minerals).
Possibly Ineffective for... Alzheimer's disease • Unwanted movements of the face and mouth (tardive dyskinesia).
Insufficient Evidence to Rate Effectiveness for... Any other medical condition, including attention deficit-hyperactivity disorder (ADHD), aging skin, declining memory and mood, improving intelligence and physical energy, preventing aging or liver spots, improving red blood cell function, improving muscle reflexes, increasing oxygen efficiency, extending life span, and treating autism.

How does it work?

Deanol is a precursor to the chemical choline and might increase the production of acetylcholine.

Are there safety concerns?

Deanol seems to be safe for most people when taken by mouth or applied to the skin.

When taken by mouth, deanol can cause constipation, itching, headache, drowsiness, insomnia, overstimulation, vivid dreams, confusion, depression, increased blood pressure, an increase in schizophrenia symptoms, and unwanted movements of the face and mouth.

Do not use deanol if: You are pregnant or breast-feeding. • You have schizophrenia. • You have depression. • You have a seizure disorder.

Are there any interactions with medications?

Drying medications (Anticholinergic drugs). Some drying medications are called anticholinergic drugs. Deanol might increase chemicals that can decrease the effects of these drying medications. Some drying medications include atropine, scopolamine, and some medications used for allergies (antihistamines), and for depression (antidepressants).

Medications for Alzheimer's disease (Acetylcholinesterase (AChE) inhibitors). Deanol might increase a chemical in the body called acetylcholine. Medications for Alzheimer's called acetylcholinesterase inhibitors also increase the chemical acetylcholine. Taking deanol along with medications for Alzheimer's disease might increase effects and side effects of medications for Alzheimer's disease. Some medications called acetylcholinesterase inhibitors include donepezil (Aricept). Deanol might increase a chemical in the body called acetylcholine. Medications for Alzheimer's called acetylcholinesterase inhibitors also increase the chemical acetylcholine. Taking deanol along with medications for Alzheimer's disease might increase effects and side effects of medications for Alzheimer's disease. Some medications called acetylcholinesterase inhibitors include donepezil (Aricept), tacrine (Cognex), rivastigmine (Exelon), and galantamine (Reminyl, Razadyne).

Various medications used for glaucoma, Alzheimer's disease, and other conditions (Cholinergic drugs). Deanol might increase a chemical in the body called acetylcholine. This chemical is similar to some medications used for glaucoma, Alzheimer's disease, and other conditions. Taking deanol with these medications might increase the chance of side effects. Some of these medications used for glaucoma, Alzheimer's disease, and other conditions include pilocarpine (Pilocar and others), and others.

DEER VELVET

What other names is the product known by?
Cervus elaphus, Cervus Nippon, Cornu Cervi Parvum, Deer Antler, Deer Antler Velvet, Elk Antler, Elk Antler Velvet, Horns of Gold, Lu Rong, Nokyong, Rokujo, Velvet Antler, Velvet of Young Deer Horn.

What is it?
Deer velvet covers the growing bone and cartilage that develops into deer antlers. People use deer velvet as medicine.

Is it Effective?
The effectiveness ratings for **DEER VELVET** are as follows:
Insufficient Evidence to Rate Effectiveness for... Boosting strength and endurance, muscle aches and pains, use as an aphrodisiac and for sexual problems, improving immune system function, high cholesterol, high blood pressure, asthma, indigestion, acne, cancer, and many other uses.

How does it work?
Deer velvet contains multiple substances including the female sex hormones estrone and estradiol. It also contains substances which may help cells grow and function.

Are there safety concerns?
It is not known if deer velvet is safe or what the potential side effects might be.

Do not use deer velvet if: You are pregnant or breast-feeding. • You have an estrogen-sensitive condition, such as a history of breast or cervical cancer.

Are there any interactions with medications?
It is not known if deer velvet interacts with any medicines.
Before taking deer velvet, talk with your healthcare professional if you take any medications.

DEERTONGUE

What other names is the product known by?
Carolina Vanilla, Carphephorus odoratissimus, Deer's Tongue, Hound's Tongue, Trilisa odoratissima, Vanilla Leaf, Vanilla Plant, Vanilla Trilisa, Wild Vanilla.

What is it?
Deertongue is a plant. People use the dried leaf to make medicine.

Is it Effective?
The effectiveness ratings for **DEERTONGUE** are as follows:
Insufficient Evidence to Rate Effectiveness for... Malaria.

How does it work?
Deertongue contains coumarins, which may thin the blood and cause liver damage. It is not known how deertongue might work for medicinal uses.

Are there safety concerns?

Deertongue is UNSAFE for use. It can cause liver injury and bleeding.

Do not use deertongue if: You are pregnant or breast-feeding. • You are allergic to other plants in the Asteraceae/Compositae family, such as ragweed, daisies, chrysanthemums, marigolds, and many others. • You have a blood clotting disorder.

Are there any interactions with medications?

Medications that slow blood clotting (Anticoagulant / Antiplatelet drugs). Deertongue might slow blood clotting. Taking deertongue along with medications that also slow clotting might increase the chances of bruising and bleeding. Some medications that slow blood clotting include aspirin, clopidogrel (Plavix), diclofenac (Voltaren, Cataflam, others), ibuprofen (Advil, Motrin, others), naproxen (Anaprox, Naprosyn, others), dalteparin (Fragmin), enoxaparin (Lovenox), heparin, warfarin (Coumadin), and others.

DELPHINIUM

What other names is the product known by?

Delphinii Flos, Delphinium consolida, Knight's Spur, Lark Heel, Lark's Claw, Larkspur, Lark's Toe, Ritterspornblüten, Staggerweed.

What is it?

Delphinium is an herb. People use the flower to make medicine.

Is it Effective?

The effectiveness ratings for **DELPHINIUM** are as follows:
Insufficient Evidence to Rate Effectiveness for... Worm infestations, water retention, sleeplessness (insomnia), and lack of appetite.

How does it work?

There currently isn't enough information available to know how delphinium works.

Are there safety concerns?

Delphinium is UNSAFE for use as a medicine. Delphinium can cause slowing of the heart rate, low blood pressure, and lung failure.

Do not use delphinium if: You are pregnant or breast-feeding.

Are there any interactions with medications?

It is not known if delphinium interacts with any medicines.
Before taking delphinium, talk with your healthcare professional if you take any medications.

DEVIL'S CLAW

What other names is the product known by?

Devils Claw, Devil's Claw Root, Grapple Plant, Griffe Du Diable, Harpagophyti Radix, Harpagophytum, Wood Spider, Harpagophytum Procumbens, Harpagophytum zeyheri.

What is it?

Devil's claw is an herb. The roots and tubers of the plant are used to make medicine.

Is it Effective?

The effectiveness ratings for **DEVIL'S CLAW** are as follows:
Possibly Effective for... Decreasing pain from a kind of arthritis called osteoarthritis • Back pain.
Insufficient Evidence to Rate Effectiveness for... Upset stomach, loss of appetite, high cholesterol, gout, rheumatoid arthritis, muscle pain, migraine headache, skin injuries and conditions, and other conditions.

How does it work?

Devil's claw contains chemicals that might decrease inflammation and swelling.

Are there safety concerns?

Devil's claw seems to be safe for most adults when used short-term. Side effects can include diarrhea, nausea, vomiting, abdominal pain, headaches, ringing in the ears, loss of appetite, and loss of taste. It can also cause allergic skin reactions, menstrual problems, and changes in blood pressure.

Do not take devil's claw if: You are pregnant or breast-feeding. • You have high blood pressure or low blood pressure. • You have diabetes. • You have a stomach ulcer. • You have gallstones. • You have a heart condition or disorder.

Are there any interactions with medications?

Antacids. Antacids are used to decrease stomach acid. Devil's claw may increase stomach acid. By increasing stomach acid, devil's claw might decrease the effectiveness of antacids. Some antacids include calcium carbonate (Tums, others) dihydroxyaluminum sodium carbonate (Rolaids, others), magaldrate (Riopan), magnesium sulfate (Bilagog), aluminum hydroxide (Amphojel), and others.

Medications for high blood pressure (Antihypertensive drugs). Devil's claw seems to decrease blood pressure. Taking devil's claw along with medications for high blood pressure might cause your blood pressure to go too low. Some medications for high blood pressure include captopril (Capoten), enalapril (Vasotec), losartan (Cozaar), valsartan (Diovan), diltiazem (Cardizem), Amlodipine (Norvasc), hydrochlorothiazide (HydroDiuril), furosemide (Lasix), and many others.

Medications for diabetes (Antidiabetes drugs). Devil's claw might decrease blood sugar. Diabetes medications are also used to lower blood sugar. Taking devil's claw along with diabetes medications might cause your blood sugar to go too low. Monitor your blood sugar closely. The dose of your diabetes medication might need to be changed. Some medications used for diabetes include glimepiride (Amaryl), glyburide (DiaBeta, Glynase PresTab, Micronase), insulin, pioglitazone (Actos), rosiglitazone (Avandia), chlorpropamide (Diabinese), glipizide (Glucotrol), tolbutamide (Orinase), and others.

Medications that decrease stomach acid (H2-Blockers). Devil's claw might increase stomach acid. By increasing stomach acid, devil's claw might decrease the effectiveness of some medications that decrease stomach acid, called H2-Blockers. Some medications that decrease stomach acid include cimetidine (Tagamet), ranitidine (Zantac), nizatidine (Axid), and famotidine (Pepcid).

Medications that decrease stomach acid (Proton pump inhibitors). Devil's claw might increase stomach acid. By increasing stomach acid, devil's claw might decrease the effectiveness of medications that are used to decrease stomach acid, called proton pump inhibitors. Some medications that decrease stomach acid include omeprazole (Prilosec), lansoprazole (Prevacid), rabeprazole (Aciphex), pantoprazole (Protonix), and esomeprazole (Nexium).

Medications changed by the liver (Cytochrome P450 2C9 (CYP2C9) substrates). Some medications are changed and broken down by the liver. Devil's claw might decrease how quickly the liver breaks down some medications. Taking devil's claw along with some medications that are broken down by the liver can increase the effects and side effects of some medications. Before taking devil's claw talk to your healthcare provider if you take any medications that are changed by the liver. Some medications that are changed by the liver include diclofenac (Cataflam, Voltaren), ibuprofen (Motrin), meloxicam (Mobic), and piroxicam (Feldene); celecoxib (Celebrex); amitriptyline (Elavil); warfarin (Coumadin); glipizide (Glucotrol); losartan (Cozaar); and others.

Medications changed by the liver (Cytochrome P450 2C19 (CYP2C19) substrates). Some medications are changed and broken down by the liver. Devil's claw might decrease how quickly the liver breaks down some medications. Taking devil's claw along with some medications that are broken down by the liver can increase the effects and side effects of some medications. Before taking devil's claw talk to your healthcare provider if you take any medications that are changed by the liver. Some medications that are changed by the liver include omeprazole (Prilosec), lansoprazole (Prevacid), and pantoprazole (Protonix); diazepam (Valium); carisoprodol (Soma); nelfinavir (Viracept); and others.

Medications changed by the liver (Cytochrome P450 3A4 (CYP3A4) substrates). Some medications are changed and broken down by the liver. Devil's claw might decrease how quickly the liver breaks down some medications. Taking devil's claw along with some medications that are broken down by the liver can increase the effects and side effects of some medications. Before taking devil's claw, talk to your healthcare provider if you are taking any medications that are changed by the liver. Some medications changed by the liver include lovastatin (Mevacor), ketoconazole (Nizoral), itraconazole (Sporanox), fexofenadine (Allegra), triazolam (Halcion), and many others.

Warfarin (Coumadin). Warfarin (Coumadin) is used to slow blood clotting. Devil's claw might increase the effects of warfarin (Coumadin) and increase the chances of bruising and bleeding. Be sure to have your blood checked regularly. The dose of your warfarin (Coumadin) might need to be changed.

Medical professionals should consult the Professional Version at www.NaturalDatabase.com.

DEVIL'S CLUB

What other names is the product known by?
Cukilanarpak, Devils Club, Devil's Root, Echinopanax horridus, Fatsia, Fatsia horrida, Oplopanax horridus, Panax horridum.

What is it?
Devil's club is a plant. People use the root bark for medicine.

Is it Effective?
The effectiveness ratings for **DEVIL'S CLUB** are as follows:
Insufficient Evidence to Rate Effectiveness for... Arthritis, purging the bowels, causing vomiting, wound healing, fever, tuberculosis, stomach trouble, coughs, colds, pneumonia, swollen glands, boils, sores, skin infections, diabetes, hypoglycemia, and other uses.

How does it work?
Devil's club contains chemicals that might fight some bacteria, fungi, and viruses.

Are there safety concerns?
There isn't enough information to know if devil's club is safe or what the potential side effects might be.

Do not use devil's club if: You are pregnant or breast-feeding.

Are there any interactions with medications?
It is not known if devil's club interacts with any medicines.
Before taking devil's club, talk with your healthcare professional if you take any medications.

DHA (DOCOSAHEXAENOIC ACID)

What other names is the product known by?
Fish Oil Fatty Acid, N-3 Fatty Acid, Neuromins, Omega 3, Omega Fatty Acid, Omega-3 Fatty Acids, Omega-3 Fatty Acid, W-3 Fatty Acid.

What is it?
DHA is a fatty acid found in the flesh of cold-water fish, including mackerel, herring, tuna, halibut, salmon, cod liver, whale blubber, and seal blubber.

Is it Effective?
The effectiveness ratings for **DHA (DOCOSAHEXAENOIC ACID)** are as follows:
Possibly Effective for... Reducing the risk of death in people with coronary artery disease, when DHA is consumed as part of the diet • Preventing an eye disease called AMD (age-related macular degeneration), when DHA is consumed as part of the diet • Psoriasis.
Possibly Ineffective for... Attention deficit-hyperactivity disorder (ADHD) • Depression • Type 2 diabetes.
Insufficient Evidence to Rate Effectiveness for... Preventing depression, reducing symptoms of dementia, improving vision, reducing aggressive behavior in people under stressful situations, improving visual attention when given to preterm infants, improving brain development and growth up to 18 months of age (used as a supplement in infant formula), improving night vision in children with dyslexia, improving movement disorders in children, and other conditions.

How does it work?
DHA plays a key role in the development of eye and nerve tissues. DHA may also reduce the risk of heart and circulatory disease by decreasing the thickness of the blood and lowering blood levels of high-density lipoprotein (HDL) cholesterol ("good" cholesterol).

Are there safety concerns?
DHA is safe for most people in low to moderate doses. DHA can cause nausea, flatulence, bruising, and prolonged bleeding. Fish oils containing DHA can cause fishy taste, belching, nosebleeds, nausea, and loose stools. Taking DHA with meals can often decrease these side effects.

When used in amounts greater than 3 grams per day, fish oils containing DHA can thin the blood and increase the risk for bleeding.

Do not use DHA if: You are sensitive to aspirin. DHA might affect your breathing.

     Natural Medicines Comprehensive Database Consumer Version   (209) 472-2244

Are there any interactions with medications?

Medications that slow blood clotting (Anticoagulant / Antiplatelet drugs). DHA (docosahexaenoic acid) is often combined with EPA (eicosapentaenoic acid). EPA might slow blood clotting. Taking DHA (docosahexaenoic acid) along with medications that also slow clotting might increase the chances of bruising and bleeding. Some medications that slow blood clotting include aspirin, clopidogrel (Plavix), diclofenac (Voltaren, Cataflam, others), ibuprofen (Advil, Motrin, others), naproxen (Anaprox, Naprosyn, others), dalteparin (Fragmin), enoxaparin (Lovenox), heparin, warfarin (Coumadin), and others.

Medications for high blood pressure (Antihypertensive drugs). DHA can decrease blood pressure. Taking DHA along with medications for high blood pressure might cause you blood pressure to go too low. Some medications for high blood pressure include captopril (Capoten), enalapril (Vasotec), losartan (Cozaar), valsartan (Diovan), diltiazem (Cardizem), Amlodipine (Norvasc), hydrochlorothiazide (HydroDiuril), furosemide (Lasix), and many others.

DHEA

What other names is the product known by?

Dehydroepiandrosterone, GL701, Prasterone.

What is it?

DHEA is a "parent hormone" produced by glands near the kidneys. It is changed in the body to a hormone called androstenedione. Androstenedione is then changed into the major male and female hormones.

DHEA can be made in the laboratory from chemicals found in wild yam and soy, but the human body cannot make DHEA from these chemicals. So simply eating wild yam or soy will not increase DHEA levels.

Is it Effective?

The effectiveness ratings for **DHEA** are as follows:

Possibly Effective for... Schizophrenia • Improving the appearance of older people's skin • Improving ability to achieve an erection in men with sexual dysfunction • Improving symptoms of lupus • Treating male hormone (androgen) deficiency in women with thyroid disease • Menopausal symptoms • Osteoporosis.

Possibly Ineffective for... Alzheimer's disease • Improving thinking in healthy older people • Improving sexual arousal in healthy women • Improving muscle strength in elderly people.

Insufficient Evidence to Rate Effectiveness for... Heart disease, breast cancer, diabetes, weight loss, metabolic syndrome, depression, aging, HIV/AIDS, Parkinson's disease, Addison's disease, chronic fatigue syndrome, and improving growth and maturation in girls with hormone deficiency.

How does it work?

The body normally makes DHEA. DHEA levels seem to go down as people get older. DHEA levels also seem to be lower in people with certain conditions like depression. Some researchers think that replacing DHEA with supplements might prevent some diseases and conditions.

Are there safety concerns?

DHEA seems to be safe for most people when used for just a few months. It can cause some side effects including acne, hair loss, stomach upset, and high blood pressure. Some women can have changes in menstrual cycle, facial hair growth, and a deeper voice after taking DHEA.

Do not use DHEA in doses higher than 50-100 mg a day or for a long period of time. Using higher doses or long-term use of DHEA can increase the chance of side effects.

Do not take DHEA if: You are pregnant or breast-feeding. • You have a hormone-sensitive cancer such as breast cancer, prostate cancer, cancer of the uterus, or cancer of the ovaries. • You have polycystic ovary syndrome. • You have diabetes. • You have a liver disease. • You have depression or a mood disorder, unless you have discussed DHEA with your healthcare professional. Some people with these conditions feel worse when they take DHEA.

Are there any interactions with medications?

Anastrozole (Arimidex). The body changes DHEA to estrogen in the body. Anastrozole (Arimidex) is used to help decrease estrogen in the body. Taking DHEA along with anastrozole (Arimidex) might decrease the effectiveness of anastrozole (Arimidex). Do not take DHEA if you are taking anastrozole (Arimidex).

Exemestane (Aromasin). The body changes DHEA to estrogen in the body. Exemestane (Aromasin) is used to help decrease estrogen in the body. Taking DHEA along with exemestane (Aromasin) might decrease the effectiveness of exemestane (Aromasin). Do not take DHEA if you are taking exemestane (Aromasin).

Fulvestrant (Faslodex). Some types of cancer are affected by hormones in the body. Estrogen-sensitive cancers are cancers that are affected by estrogen levels in the body. Fulvestrant (Faslodex) is used for this type of estrogen cancer. DHEA might increase estrogen in the body and decrease the effectiveness of fulvestrant for treating cancer. Do not take DHEA if you are taking fulvestrant.

Insulin. Insulin is used to decrease blood sugar. Insulin can also decrease the amount of DHEA in the body. By decreasing DHEA in the body insulin might decrease the effectiveness of DHEA supplements.

Letrozole (Femara). Some types of cancer are affected by hormones in the body. Estrogen-sensitive cancers are cancers that are affected by estrogen levels in the body. Letrozole (Femara) is used for this type of estrogen cancer. DHEA might increase estrogen in the body and decrease the effectiveness of letrozole (Femara) for treating cancer. Do not take DHEA if you are taking letrozole (Femara).

Medications for inflammation (Corticosteroids). The body naturally makes DHEA. Some medications for inflammation might decrease how much DHEA the body makes. Taking some medications for inflammation might decrease the effects of taking DHEA pills. Some medications for inflammation include dexamethasone (Decadron), hydrocortisone (Cortef), methylprednisolone (Medrol), prednisone (Deltasone), and others.

Medications changed by the liver (Cytochrome P450 3A4 (CYP3A4) substrates). Some medications are changed and broken down by the liver. DHEA might decrease how quickly the liver breaks down some medications. Taking DHEA along with some medications that are broken down by the liver can increase the effects and side effects of some medications. Before taking DHEA, talk to your healthcare provider if you are taking any medications that are changed by the liver. Some medications changed by the liver include lovastatin (Mevacor), ketoconazole (Nizoral), itraconazole (Sporanox), fexofenadine (Allegra), triazolam (Halcion), and many others.

Tamoxifen (Nolvadex). Some types of cancer are affected by hormones in the body. Estrogen-sensitive cancers are cancers that are affected by estrogen levels in the body. Tamoxifen (Nolvadex) is used to help treat and prevent these types of cancer. DHEA increases estrogen levels in the body. By increasing estrogen in the body, DHEA might decrease the effectiveness of tamoxifen (Nolvadex). Do not take DHEA if you are taking tamoxifen (Nolvadex).

Triazolam (Halcion). The body breaks down triazolam (Halcion) to get rid of it. DHEA might decrease how quickly the body breaks down triazolam (Halcion). Taking DHEA along with triazolam (Halcion) might increase the effects and side effects of triazolam (Halcion).

DIACYLGLYCEROL

What other names is the product known by?
DAG, Diglyceride, Diacylglycerol Oil.

What is it?
Diacylglycerol is a minor component of plant oils. In its concentrated form, it is used to replace fats in the diet.

Is it Effective?
The effectiveness ratings for **DIACYLGLYCEROL** are as follows:
Possibly Effective for... Weight loss and reduction of body fat.
Insufficient Evidence to Rate Effectiveness for... Type 2 diabetes and high blood levels of fat (triglyceride).

How does it work?
Diacylglycerol might work by increasing energy use and the breakdown of fat.

Are there safety concerns?
Diacylglycerol appears to be safe for most people. It can cause digestive tract upset, headache, taste changes, acne, and rash.

Do not take diacylglycerol if: You are pregnant or breast-feeding.

Are there any interactions with medications?
It is not known if diacylglycerol interacts with any medicines.
Before taking diacylglycerol, talk with your healthcare professional if you take any medications.

DIBENCOZIDE

What other names is the product known by?
Adenosylcobalamin, Cobalamin Enzyme, Cobamamide, Coenzyme B-12, Co-Enzyme B-12.

What is it?
Dibencozide is a form of vitamin B12. People use it as medicine.

   Natural Medicines Comprehensive Database Consumer Version (209) 472-2244

Is it Effective?

The effectiveness ratings for **DIBENCOZIDE** are as follows:

Insufficient Evidence to Rate Effectiveness for... Use in people without vitamin B12 deficiency, stimulating protein metabolism, increasing muscle mass and strength, increasing mental concentration, depression, anxiety, panic attacks, and other uses.

How does it work?

Dibencozide is a form of vitamin B12. Vitamin B12 is important in chemical reactions throughout the body. However, dibencozide is not as stable as cyanocobalamin, the form of vitamin B12 most often found in vitamin tablets, and may break down during storage.

Are there safety concerns?

Dibencozide seems to be safe for most people. There are no reported side effects.

Do not use dibencozide if: You are pregnant or breast-feeding.

Are there any interactions with medications?

Chloramphenicol. Dibencozide is a form of vitamin B12. Vitamin B12 is important for producing new blood cells. Chloramphenicol might decrease new blood cells. Taking chloramphenicol for a long time might decrease the effects of dibencozide on new blood cells. But most people only take chloramphenicol for a short time so this interaction isn't a big problem.

DIGITALIS

What other names is the product known by?

Dead Man's Bells, Digitalis lanata, Digitalis purpurea, Fairy Cap, Fairy Finger, Foxglove, Lady's Thimble, Lion's Mouth, Purple Foxglove, Scotch Mercury, Throatwort, Witch's Bells, Wolly Foxglove.

What is it?

Digitalis is a plant. People use the above ground parts for medicine.

Is it Effective?

The effectiveness ratings for **DIGITALIS** are as follows:

Likely Effective for... Irregular heart rhythms, such as atrial fibrillation or flutter • Congestive heart failure (CHF).

Insufficient Evidence to Rate Effectiveness for... Asthma, promoting vomiting, epilepsy, tuberculosis, constipation, headache, spasm, wound and burn healing, and other conditions.

How does it work?

Digitalis contains chemicals from which the prescription medication digoxin (Lanoxin) is made. These chemicals can increase the strength of heart muscle contractions, change heart rate, and increase heart blood output.

Are there safety concerns?

Digitalis is UNSAFE for self-medication without the advice and care of a healthcare professional. Digitalis can cause irregular heart function and death. Signs of digitalis poisoning include stomach upset, small eye pupils, blurred vision, strong slow pulse, nausea, vomiting, dizziness, excessive urination, fatigue, muscle weakness and tremors, stupor, confusion, convulsions, abnormal heartbeats, and death. Long-term use of digitalis can lead to symptoms of toxicity, including visual halos, yellow-green vision, and stomach upset.

Digitalis isn't safe for anyone to use without the advice and care of a healthcare professional. Some people are especially sensitive to the toxic side effects of digitalis and should be extra careful to avoid use.

Do not use digitalis if: You are pregnant or breast-feeding. • You have heart disease. • You have kidney disease.

Are there any interactions with medications?

Antibiotics (Macrolide antibiotics). Digitalis can affect the heart. Some antibiotics might increase how much digitalis the body absorbs. Increasing how much digitalis the body absorbs might increase the effects and side effects of digitalis. Some antibiotics called macrolide antibiotics include erythromycin, azithromycin, and clarithromycin.

Antibiotics (Tetracycline antibiotics). Taking some antibiotics called tetracyclines with digitalis might increase the chance of side effects from digitalis. Some tetracyclines include demeclocycline (Declomycin), minocycline (Minocin), and tetracycline (Achromycin).

Digoxin (Lanoxin). Digoxin (Lanoxin) helps the heart beat more strongly. Digitalis also seems to affect the heart. Taking digitalis along with digoxin can increase the effects of digoxin and increase the risk of side effects. Do not

Medical professionals should consult the Professional Version at www.NaturalDatabase.com.

take digitalis if you are taking digoxin (Lanoxin) without talking to your healthcare professional.

Quinine. Digitalis can affect the heart. Quinine can also affect the heart. Taking quinine along with digitalis might cause serious heart problems.

Stimulant laxatives. Digitalis can affect the heart. The heart uses potassium. Laxatives called stimulant laxatives can decrease potassium levels in the body. Low potassium levels can increase the chance of side effects from digitalis. Some stimulant laxatives include bisacodyl (Correctol, Dulcolax), cascara, castor oil (Purge), senna (Senokot), and others.

Water pills (Diuretic drugs). Digitalis might affect the heart. "Water pills" can decrease potassium in the body. Low potassium levels can also affect the heart and increase the risk of side effects from digitalis. Some "water pills" that can deplete potassium include chlorothiazide (Diuril), chlorthalidone (Thalitone), furosemide (Lasix), hydrochlorothiazide (HCTZ, HydroDiuril, Microzide), and others.

DIINDOLYLMETHANE

What other names is the product known by?
DIM; 3,3'-Diindolylmethane.

What is it?
Diindolylmethane is formed in the body from plant substances contained in vegetables such as cabbage, Brussels sprouts, cauliflower, and broccoli.

Is it Effective?
The effectiveness ratings for **DIINDOLYLMETHANE** are as follows:
Insufficient Evidence to Rate Effectiveness for... Preventing breast cancer, uterine cancer, colon cancer, preventing prostate enlargement (benign prostatic hypertrophy, BPH), and treating premenstrual syndrome (PMS).

How does it work?
Diindolylmethane might have some effects which are similar to estrogens in the body, and some effects which block estrogen effects.

Are there safety concerns?
Diindolylmethane is safe when consumed in the small amounts found in foods. There isn't enough information to know if supplements containing diindolylmethane are safe.

Do not use diindolylmethane supplements if: You are pregnant or breast-feeding.

Are there any interactions with medications?
Medications changed by the liver (Cytochrome P450 1A2 (CYP1A2) substrates). Some medications are changed and broken down by the liver. Diindolylmethane might increase how quickly the liver breaks down some medications. Taking diindolylmethane along with some medications that are changed by the liver can decrease the effectiveness of some medications. Before taking diindolylmethane talk to your healthcare provider if you take any medications that are changed by the liver. Some of these medications that are changed by the liver include clozapine (Clozaril), cyclobenzaprine (Flexeril), fluvoxamine (Luvox), haloperidol (Haldol), imipramine (Tofranil), mexiletine (Mexitil), olanzapine (Zyprexa), pentazocine (Talwin), propranolol (Inderal), tacrine (Cognex), theophylline, zileuton (Zyflo), zolmitriptan (Zomig), and others.

DIIODOTHYRONINE

What other names is the product known by?
3,5 diiodothyronine; 3,5-diiodo-L-thyronine; 3,5-L-diiodothyronine; 3,5-T2; T2; T-2.

What is it?
Diiodothyronine is a hormone.

Is it Effective?
The effectiveness ratings for **DIIODOTHYRONINE** are as follows:
Insufficient Evidence to Rate Effectiveness for... Weight loss, high cholesterol, and improving athletic ability.

How does it work?
Diiodothyronine might speed up metabolism and reduce fat storage. But there is no reliable research in humans about the effects of diiodothyronine.

 Natural Medicines Comprehensive Database Consumer Version   (209) 472-2244

Are there safety concerns?

There isn't enough information to know if diiodothyronine is safe.

Do not use diiodothyronine if: You are pregnant or breast-feeding.

Are there any interactions with medications?

It is not known if diiodothyronine interacts with any medicines.
Before taking diiodothyronine, talk with your healthcare professional if you take any medications.

DILL

What other names is the product known by?

American Dill, Anethum Graveolens, Anethum Sowa, Anethi Herba, Dill Herb, Dill Oil, Dill Weed, Dillweed, Dilly, European Dill, Madhura, Peucedanum Graveolens, Satahva, Sotapa, Sowa.

What is it?

Dill is a plant. People use the seeds and above ground plant parts as medicine.

Is it Effective?

The effectiveness ratings for **DILL** are as follows:
Insufficient Evidence to Rate Effectiveness for... Loss of appetite, infections, digestive and urinary tract problems, spasms, intestinal gas (flatulence), sleep disorders, fever and colds, cough, bronchitis, liver and gallbladder problems, mouth and throat inflammation, and other conditions.

How does it work?

Chemicals contained in dill seed might help relax muscles, but more information is needed.

Are there safety concerns?

Dill is safe when consumed as a food. Dill also seems to be safe for most people when taken by mouth for medicinal purposes.

When applied to the skin, dill can sometimes cause skin irritation. Fresh dill juice can also cause the skin to become extra sensitive to the sun. This might put you at greater risk for sunburns and skin cancer. Avoid sunlight. Wear sunblock and protective clothing outside, especially if you are light-skinned.

Do not use dill if: You are pregnant or breast-feeding. • You are allergic to plants in the carrot family such as asafoetida, caraway, celery, coriander, fennel, and other related plants.

Are there any interactions with medications?

It is not known if dill interacts with any medicines.
Before taking dill, talk with your healthcare professional if you take any medications.

DIMETHYLGLYCINE

What other names is the product known by?

Dimethyl Glycine, (Dimethylamino)acetic Acid, DMG, N,N-dimethylaminoacetic Acid, N,N-dimethylglycine, N-methylsarcosine.

What is it?

Dimethylglycine is an amino acid that is found in the body in very small amounts. People use dimethylglycine to make medicine.

Is it Effective?

The effectiveness ratings for **DIMETHYLGLYCINE** are as follows:
Possibly Effective for... Athletic performance.
Possibly Ineffective for... Treating epilepsy • Treating autism.
Insufficient Evidence to Rate Effectiveness for... Attention deficit-hyperactivity disorder (ADHD), cancer, chronic fatigue syndrome (CFS), stress, allergies, breathing problems, alcoholism, drug addiction, high blood pressure, high cholesterol, improving the body's immune system, and other conditions.

Medical professionals should consult the Professional Version at www.NaturalDatabase.com.

How does it work?
Dimethylglycine might help improve the way the body's immune system works.

Are there safety concerns?
Dimethylglycine might be safe to use short-term. The safety of long-term use is unknown.

Do not use dimethylglycine if: You are pregnant or breast-feeding.

Are there any interactions with medications?
It is not known if dimethylglycine interacts with any medicines.
Before taking dimethylglycine, talk with your healthcare professional if you take any medications.

DIOSMIN

What other names is the product known by?
Citrus Bioflavonoid, Citrus Bioflavonoids, Diosmetin.

What is it?
Diosmin is a type of plant chemical found mainly in citrus fruits. People use diosmin to make medicine.

Is it Effective?
The effectiveness ratings for **DIOSMIN** are as follows:
Possibly Effective for... Treating hemorrhoids • Treating leg ulcers caused by poor circulation, when used in combination with hesperidin.
Possibly Ineffective for... Treating swelling of the arms following surgery for breast cancer.
Insufficient Evidence to Rate Effectiveness for... Varicose veins, bleeding (hemorrhage) in the eye, bleeding gums, and preventing damage to the liver.

How does it work?
Diosmin might help treat hemorrhoids by reducing swelling (inflammation), and restoring normal vein function.

Are there safety concerns?
Diosmin is safe for most people when used short-term for up to three months. It can cause some side effects such as stomach and abdominal pain, diarrhea, and headache.

Do not take disomin for more than three months without medical supervision.

Do not take diosmin if: You are pregnant or breast-feeding.

Are there any interactions with medications?
It is not known if diosmin interacts with any medicines.
Before taking diosmin, talk with your healthcare professional if you take any medications.

DIVI-DIVI

What other names is the product known by?
Caesalpinia bonducella, Nichol Seeds, Nikkar Nuts, Putikaranja, Udakiryaka.

What is it?
Divi-divi is an herb. Its seeds are ground or roasted to make medicine.

Is it Effective?
The effectiveness ratings for **DIVI-DIVI** are as follows:
Insufficient Evidence to Rate Effectiveness for... Fever and diabetes.

How does it work?
There isn't enough information to know how divi-divi works.

Are there safety concerns?
There isn't enough information to know if divi-divi is safe.

Do not take divi-divi if: You are pregnant or breast-feeding.

Are there any interactions with medications?
It is not known if divi-divi interacts with any medicines.
Before taking divi-divi, talk with your healthcare professional if you take any medications.

DIVINER'S SAGE

What other names is the product known by?
Divine Mexican Mint, Diviner's Mint, Divinorin, Divinorin A, Herb-of-the-Virgin, Herba de María, Hierba de la Virgen, Hojas de la Pastora, La Hembra, Leaves of the Virgin Shepherdess, Mexican Sage, Mexican Sage Incense, Pipiltzintzintli, Sadi, Salvia, Salvia divinorum, Salvinorin, Salvinorin A, Sage of the Seers, Ska Maria, Ska Maria Pastora, Yerba de Maria.

What is it?
Diviner's sage is an herb. The leaves are used to make medicine.

Is it Effective?
The effectiveness ratings for **DIVINER'S SAGE** are as follows:
Insufficient Evidence to Rate Effectiveness for... Producing hallucinations, diarrhea, headache, rheumatism, bloating, regulating urine and feces, or use as a tonic.

How does it work?
There isn't enough information to know how diviner's sage might work.

Are there safety concerns?
There isn't enough information to know if diviner's sage is safe.

It can cause nausea, dizziness, slurred speech, confusion, and hallucinations.

Do not use diviner's sage if: You are pregnant or breast-feeding.

Are there any interactions with medications?
It is not known if diviner's sage interacts with any medicines.
Before taking diviner's sage, talk with your healthcare professional if you take any medications.

DMSO (DIMETHYLSULFOXIDE)

What other names is the product known by?
Dimethylis Sulfoxidum, Dimethyl Sulfoxide, Dimethyl Sulphoxide, Methyl Sulphoxide, NSC-763, SQ-9453, Sulphinybismethane.

What is it?
DMSO is a prescription medicine and dietary supplement. It is also used as an industrial solvent.

Is it Effective?
The effectiveness ratings for **DMSO (DIMETHYLSULFOXIDE)** are as follows:
Effective for... Interstitial cystitis when used as an FDA-approved product.
Possibly Effective for... Decreasing pain caused by the herpes zoster virus (shingles) when used with a drug called idoxuridine • Inflammatory bladder disease .
Possibly Ineffective for...A skin condition called scleroderma.
Likely Ineffective for... Cancer.
Insufficient Evidence to Rate Effectiveness for... Headaches, arthritis, eye problems, gallstones, a condition called amyloidosis, muscle problems, high blood pressure in the brain, helping skin heal after surgery, asthma, skin problems such as calluses, and other conditions.

How does it work?
DMSO helps medicines get through the skin and can affect proteins, carbohydrates, fats, and water in the body.

Are there safety concerns?
DMSO is safe when used as a prescription medication. Don't use products that are not prescribed by your health professional. There is concern that some non-prescription DMSO products are not intended for human use. They can contain impurities that can cause side effects.

Medical professionals should consult the Professional Version at www.NaturalDatabase.com.

CONSUMER VERSION

Some side effects of taking DMSO by mouth or applying it to the skin include skin reactions, dry skin, headache, dizziness, drowsiness, nausea, vomiting, diarrhea, constipation, breathing problems, vision problems, blood problems, and allergic reactions. DMSO also causes a garlic-like taste, and breath and body odor.

Do not use DMSO if: You are pregnant or breast-feeding. • You have liver problems. • You have kidney problems. • You have eye problems. • You have diabetes. • You have headaches. • You have urinary tract cancer.

Are there any interactions with medications?
Medications taken by mouth (Oral drugs). DMSO (dimethylsulfoxide) might increase how much medicine your body absorbs. Taking DMSO along with medications taken by mouth might increase how much medicine your body absorbs. Increasing how much medicine your body absorbs can increase the effects and side effects of your medicines.
Medications applied to the skin, eyes, or ears (Topical drugs). DMSO can sometimes increase how much medicine the body absorbs. Applying DMSO along with medications you put on the skin or in the eyes or ears can increase how much medicine your body absorbs. Increasing how much medicine your body absorbs might increase the effects and side effects of the medicine.
Medications given as a shot (Injectable drugs). DMSO (dimethylsulfoxide) might help the body absorb some medicines. Using DMSO and getting a shot might increase how much medicine the body absorbs and increase the effects and side effects of medications given as a shot.

DODDER

What other names is the product known by?
Beggarweed, Cuscuta chinensis, Cuscuta epithymum, Cuscutae, Devil's Guts, Dodder Of Thyme, Hellweed, Lesser Dodder, Scaldweed, Strangle Tare, Tu Si Zi, Tu Sizi.

What is it?
Dodder is an herb. People use the above ground parts to make medicine.

Is it Effective?
The effectiveness ratings for **DODDER** are as follows:
Insufficient Evidence to Rate Effectiveness for... Bladder, liver, and spleen problems.

How does it work?
Dodder might have laxative effects.

Are there safety concerns?
There isn't enough information available to know if dodder is safe. Dodder might cause stomach pain in some people.

Do not use dodder if: You are pregnant or breast-feeding.

Are there any interactions with medications?
It is not known if dodder interacts with any medicines.
Before taking dodder, talk with your healthcare professional if you take any medications.

DOLOMITE

What other names is the product known by?
Dolomitic limestone.

What is it?
Dolomite is a type of mineral supplement called limestone.

Is it Effective?
The effectiveness ratings for **DOLOMITE** are as follows:
Insufficient Evidence to Rate Effectiveness for... Use as a source of calcium and magnesium.

How does it work?
Dolomite might be a good source of calcium carbonate and magnesium.

Are there safety concerns?

Dolomite is safe for most adults. Dolomite can cause stomach irritation, constipation, nausea, vomiting, and diarrhea. Some dolomite products might be contaminated with heavy metals like aluminum, arsenic, lead, mercury, and nickel.

Don't take dolomite in large amounts for long periods or in combination with other calcium or magnesium supplements.

Don't use dolomite in children because they are more sensitive to contaminants like lead.

Do not use dolomite if: You are pregnant or breast-feeding. • You have epilepsy. Contaminants can cause seizures. • You have a thyroid condition. • You have kidney problems. • You have a condition known as sarcoidosis. • You have a heart condition known as heart block.

Are there any interactions with medications?

Antibiotics (Tetracycline antibiotics). Dolomite contains calcium. The calcium in dolomite can attach to some antibiotics called tetracyclines in the stomach. This decreases the amount of tetracyclines that the body can absorb. Taking dolomite along with tetracyclines might decrease the effectiveness of tetracyclines. To avoid this interaction take dolomite two hours before or four hours after taking tetracyclines. Some tetracycline antibiotics include demeclocycline (Declomycin), minocycline (Minocin), and tetracycline (Achromycin).

Antibiotics (Quinolone antibiotics). Dolomite might decrease how much antibiotic the body absorbs. Taking dolomite along with some antibiotics called quinolone antibiotics might decrease the effectiveness of these antibiotics. To avoid this interaction take dolomite supplements at least one hour after antibiotics. Some of these quinolone antibiotics that might interact with dolomite include ciprofloxacin (Cipro), enoxacin (Penetrex), norfloxacin (Chibroxin, Noroxin), sparfloxacin (Zagam), trovafloxacin (Trovan), and grepafloxacin (Raxar).

Bisphosphonates. Dolomite can decrease how much bisphosphate the body absorbs. Taking dolomite along with bisphosphates can decrease the effectiveness of bisphosphate. To avoid this interaction take bisphosphonate at least 30 minutes before dolomite or later in the day. Some bisphosphonates include alendronate (Fosamax), etidronate (Didronel), risedronate (Actonel), tiludronate (Skelid), and others.

Estrogens. Dolomite contains calcium. Estrogens help the body absorb calcium. Taking estrogens along with large amounts of calcium might increase calcium in the body too much.

Levothyroxine. Levothyroxine is used for low thyroid function. Dolomite can decrease how much levothyroxine the body absorbs. Taking dolomite along with levothyroxine might decrease the effectiveness of levothyroxine. Some brands that contain levothyroxine include Armour Thyroid, Eltroxin, Estre, Euthyrox, Levo-T, Levothroid, Levoxyl, Synthroid, Unithroid, and others.

Sotalol (Betapace). Dolomite contains calcium. Taking calcium with sotalol (Betapace) can decrease how much sotalol the body absorbs. This could decrease the effectiveness of sotalol. Take dolomite at least two hours before or four hours after taking sotalol.

Water pills (Potassium-sparing diuretics). Dolomite contains magnesium. Some "water pills" can increase magnesium levels in the body. Taking some "water pills" along with dolomite might cause too much magnesium to be in the body. Some "water pills" that increase magnesium in the body include amiloride (Midamor), spironolactone (Aldactone), and triamterene (Dyrenium).

Water pills (Thiazide Diuretics). Dolomite contains calcium. Some "water pills" increase the amount of calcium in the body. Taking large amounts of calcium with some "water pills" might cause there to be too much calcium in the body. This could cause serious side effects including kidney problems. Some of these "water pills" include chlorothiazide (Diuril), hydrochlorothiazide (HydroDiuril, Esidrix), indapamide (Lozol), metolazone (Zaroxolyn), and chlorthalidone (Hygroton).

DONG QUAI

What other names is the product known by?

Angelica Sinensis, Angelica Polymorpha Var. Sinensis, Angelicae Gigantis Radix, Chinese Angelica, Dang Gui, Danggui, Ligustilides, Radix Angelicae Gigantis, Tang Kuei, Tan Kue Bai Zhi.

What is it?

Dong quai is a plant. People use the root to make medicine.

Is it Effective?

The effectiveness ratings for **DONG QUAI** are as follows:

Possibly Effective for... Premature ejaculation, when applied directly to the skin of the penis in combination with other medicines.

Possibly Ineffective for... Menopausal symptoms.

Insufficient Evidence to Rate Effectiveness for... Menstrual problems (dysmenorrhea), premenstrual syndrome (PMS), high blood pressure, joint aches and pains, ulcers, anemia, constipation, skin discoloration and psoriasis, the prevention and treatment of allergic problems, and other conditions.

How does it work?
Dong quai root has been shown to affect estrogen and other hormones in animals. It is not known if these same effects happen in humans.

Are there safety concerns?
Dong quai is safe for most adults. Dong quai can cause skin to become extra sensitive to the sun. This might put you at greater risk for skin cancer. Wear sunblock outside, especially if you are light-skinned.

There is some concern that dong quai might increase the risk for cancer even without sun exposure, especially when taken in large amounts.

Do not take dong quai if: You are pregnant or breast-feeding. It can affect the uterus. • You have hormone sensitive cancers such as breast, uterine, or ovarian cancer. • You have hormone sensitive diseases such as endometriosis or uterine fibroids. • You have a condition called protein S deficiency.

Are there any interactions with medications?
Medications that slow blood clotting (Anticoagulant / Antiplatelet drugs). Dong quai might slow blood clotting. Taking dong quai along with medications that also slow clotting might increase the chances of bruising and bleeding. Some medications that slow blood clotting include aspirin, clopidogrel (Plavix), diclofenac (Voltaren, Cataflam, others), ibuprofen (Advil, Motrin, others), naproxen (Anaprox, Naprosyn, others), dalteparin (Fragmin), enoxaparin (Lovenox), heparin, warfarin (Coumadin), and others.
Warfarin (Coumadin). Warfarin (Coumadin) is used to slow blood clotting. Dong quai can also slow blood clotting. Taking dong quai along with warfarin (Coumadin) can increase the chances of bruising and bleeding. Be sure to have your blood checked regularly. The dose of your warfarin (Coumadin) might need to be changed.

DRAGON'S BLOOD

What other names is the product known by?
Calamus draco, Daemonorops draco, Draconis Resina, Dracorubin, Dragon's-blood Palm, Sanguis Draconis, Xue Jie.

What is it?
Dragon's blood is a red substance removed from the fruit of a tree.

Is it Effective?
The effectiveness ratings for **DRAGON'S BLOOD** are as follows:
Insufficient Evidence to Rate Effectiveness for... Diarrhea and digestive problems.

How does it work?
There isn't enough information available to know how dragon's blood works.

Are there safety concerns?
Dragon's blood appears to be safe for most adults.

Do not use dragon's blood if: You are pregnant or breast-feeding.

Are there any interactions with medications?
It is not known if dragon's blood interacts with any medicines.
Before taking dragon's blood, talk with your healthcare professional if you take any medications.

DUCKWEED

What other names is the product known by?
Lemna minor.

What is it?
Duckweed is an herb. The whole fresh plant is used to make medicine.

 Natural Medicines Comprehensive Database Consumer Version (209) 472-2244

Is it Effective?

The effectiveness ratings for **DUCKWEED** are as follows:
Insufficient Evidence to Rate Effectiveness for... Lung problems, jaundice, and arthritis.

How does it work?

There isn't enough information available to know how duckweed works.

Are there safety concerns?

There isn't enough information available to know if duckweed is safe.

Do not use duckweed if: You are pregnant or breast-feeding.

Are there any interactions with medications?

It is not known if duckweed interacts with any medicines.
Before taking duckweed, talk with your healthcare professional if you take any medications.

DUSTY MILLER

What other names is the product known by?

Cineraria maritima, Senecio cineraria, Silver Ragwort.

What is it?

Dusty miller is an herb. The above ground parts are used to make medicine.

Is it Effective?

The effectiveness ratings for **DUSTY MILLER** are as follows:
Insufficient Evidence to Rate Effectiveness for... Migraine headache, vision problems, and improving menstrual flow.

How does it work?

There isn't enough information available to know how dusty miller works.

Are there safety concerns?

Dusty miller is unsafe for people to use. It contains chemicals which can cause blood circulation problems, liver damage, lung damage, and cancer.

It can also cause allergic reactions in people sensitive to plants like ragweed, marigolds, and daisies.

Do not use dusty miller if: You are pregnant or breast-feeding. • You have liver disease.

Are there any interactions with medications?

Medications that increase break down of other medications by the liver (Cytochrome P450 3A4 (CYP3A4) inducers). Dusty miller is broken down by the liver. Some chemicals that form when the liver breaks down dusty miller can be harmful. Medications that cause the liver to break down dusty miller might enhance the toxic effects of chemicals contained in dusty miller. Some of these medicines include carbamazepine (Tegretol), phenobarbital, phenytoin (Dilantin), rifampin, rifabutin (Mycobutin), and others.

DWARF ELDER

What other names is the product known by?

Blood Elder, Blood Hilder, Danewort, Sambucus ebulus, Walewort.

What is it?

Dwarf elder is an herb. The fruit, dried leaves, and dried roots are used to make medicine.

Is it Effective?

The effectiveness ratings for **DWARF ELDER** are as follows:
Insufficient Evidence to Rate Effectiveness for... Arthritis, weight reduction, and increasing urine production (diuretic).

How does it work?

There isn't enough information to know how dwarf elder works.

Medical professionals should consult the Professional Version at www.NaturalDatabase.com.

CONSUMER VERSION

Medical professionals should consult the
Professional Version at www.NaturalDatabase.com.

Are there safety concerns?

Using dwarf elder in large amounts is unsafe. It can cause vomiting, bloody diarrhea, dizziness, and headache. It can also cause breathing problems, unconsciousness, and death.

It isn't known whether small amounts of dwarf elder can be used safely.

Do not use dwarf elder if: You are pregnant or breast-feeding.

Are there any interactions with medications?

It is not known if dwarf elder interacts with any medicines.
Before taking dwarf elder, talk with your healthcare professional if you take any medications.

DWARF PINE NEEDLE

What other names is the product known by?

Pinus mugo, Pinus montana, Pinus pumilio, Pinus mugo pumilio.

What is it?

Dwarf pine is a tree. Oil from the needles and twigs is used to make medicine.

Is it Effective?

The effectiveness ratings for **DWARF PINE NEEDLE** are as follows:
Insufficient Evidence to Rate Effectiveness for... Preventing skin infections and clearing mucus from the lungs.

How does it work?

There isn't enough information available to know how dwarf pine needle oil works.

Are there safety concerns?

Dwarf pine needle oil is safe for most people when used in amounts found in foods. It seems to be safe when applied directly to the skin. Some people experience irritation if they apply dwarf pine needle oil to the skin, and some people are allergic to it.

Do not use dwarf pine needle oil if: You are pregnant or breast-feeding. • You are allergic to pine oil.

Are there any interactions with medications?

It is not known if dwarf pine needle interacts with any medicines.
Before taking dwarf pine needle, talk with your healthcare professional if you take any medications.

DYER'S BROOM

What other names is the product known by?

Broom Flower, Dyers Broom, Dyer's Greenwood, Dyer's Weed, Dyer's Whin, Furze, Genista tinctoria, Green Broom, Greenweed, Wood Waxen.

What is it?

Dyer's broom is an herb. The whole plant is used to make medicine.

Is it Effective?

The effectiveness ratings for **DYER'S BROOM** are as follows:
Insufficient Evidence to Rate Effectiveness for... Digestive disorders, gout, back pain, bladder stones, increasing heart rate, and kidney and lung conditions.

How does it work?

There isn't enough information to know how dyer's broom works.

Are there safety concerns?

Dyer's broom might be unsafe when taken orally. It can cause nausea, vomiting, and diarrhea.

Do not use dyer's broom if: You are pregnant or breast-feeding.

Are there any interactions with medications?

It is not known if dyer's broom interacts with any medicines.
Before taking dyer's broom, talk with your healthcare professional if you take any medications.

EASTERN RED CEDAR

What other names is the product known by?

Ashe Juniper, Cedar, Juniperus virginiana, Red Cedar, Red Cedarwood, Red Juniper, Texas Cedarwood, Virginia Cedarwood.

What is it?

Eastern red cedar is a tree. The bark, berries, leaves, seeds, and twigs are used for medicine.

Is it Effective?

The effectiveness ratings for **EASTERN RED CEDAR** are as follows:
Insufficient Evidence to Rate Effectiveness for... Cough, bronchitis, rheumatism, venereal warts, and skin rash.

How does it work?

There isn't enough information to know how Eastern red cedar might work for medicinal uses.

Are there safety concerns?

There is not enough information to know if Eastern red cedar is safe.

Do not take Eastern red cedar if: You are pregnant or breast-feeding.

Are there any interactions with medications?

Sedative medications (Barbiturates). Medications that cause sleepiness and drowsiness are called sedatives. Eastern red cedar seems to decrease the effectiveness of some sedative medications. But is it not clear why this interaction occurs. Some sedative medications include clonazepam (Klonopin), lorazepam (Ativan), phenobarbital (Donnatal), zolpidem (Ambien), and others.

ECDYSTERONE

What other names is the product known by?

Alfa-ecdysone, Beta-ecdysone, Ecdisten, Ecdysone, Hydroxyecdysterone, Isoinokosterone, Suma.

What is it?

Ecdysterone is a chemical found in insects, some animals that live in water, and some plants.

Is it Effective?

The effectiveness ratings for **ECDYSTERONE** are as follows:
Insufficient Evidence to Rate Effectiveness for... Muscle building and improving athletic performance.

How does it work?

Ecdysterone is similar in structure to testosterone, but there's no evidence that it has masculinizing effects in humans.

Are there safety concerns?

There isn't enough reliable information available about ecdysterone to know if it is safe.

Are there any interactions with medications?

It is not known if ecdysterone interacts with any medicines.
Before taking ecdysterone, talk to your healthcare professional if you take any medications.

Medical professionals should consult the Professional Version at www.NaturalDatabase.com.

ECHINACEA

What other names is the product known by?

American Cone Flower, Black Sampson, Black Susans, Brauneria Angustifolia, Brauneria Pallida, Comb Flower, Coneflower, Echinacea Angustifolia, Echinacea Pallida, Echinacea Purpurea, Echinaceawurzel, Hedgehog, Igelkopfwurzel, Indian Head, Kansas Snakeroot, Narrow-Leaved Purple Cone Flower, Pale Coneflower, Purple Cone Flower, Purpursonnenhutkraut, Purpursonnenhutwurzel, Racine d'echininacea, Red Sunflower, Rock-Up-Hat, Roter Sonnenhut, Schmallblaettrige Kegelblumenwurzel, Schmallblaettriger Sonnenhut, Scurvy Root, Snakeroot, Sonnenhutwurzel.

What is it?

Echinacea is an herb. Several species of the echinacea plant are used to make medicine from its leaves, flower, and root.

Is it Effective?

The effectiveness ratings for **ECHINACEA** are as follows:

Possibly Effective for...TREATING a common cold. Many scientific studies say that taking echinacea when cold symptoms are first noticed can modestly reduce symptoms of the common cold in adults. But some scientific studies show no benefit. The problem is that scientific studies have used different types of echinacea plants and different methods of preparation. Since the studies have not been consistent, it is not surprising that different studies show different results. If it helps for treating a cold, the benefit will likely be modest at best.

Keep in mind that TREATING a common cold is different than PREVENTING a common cold. Taking echinacea does not seem to PREVENT a cold from starting • Preventing vaginal yeast infections when used with a medicated cream called econazole (Spectazole).

Possibly Ineffective for... Preventing recurrent genital herpes.

Insufficient Evidence to Rate Effectiveness for... Urinary tract infections (UTIs), migraine headaches, chronic fatigue syndrome (CFS), eczema, hayfever, allergies, bee stings, attention deficit-hyperactivity disorder (ADHD), influenza (flu), and other conditions.

How does it work?

Echinacea seems to activate chemicals in the body that decrease inflammation, which might reduce cold and flu symptoms. Laboratory research suggests that echinacea can stimulate the body's immune system, but there's no evidence that this occurs in people. Echinacea also seems to contain some chemicals that can attack yeast and other kinds of fungus directly.

Are there safety concerns?

Echinacea seems to be safe for most people when used short-term. There is not enough information to know if echinacea is safe for long-term use. Some side effects have been reported such as fever, nausea, vomiting, unpleasant taste, stomach pain, diarrhea, sore throat, dry mouth, headache, numbness of the tongue, dizziness, insomnia, disorientation, and joint and muscle aches.

Echinacea can also cause allergic reactions, especially in people who are allergic to ragweed, mums, marigolds, or daisies. If you have allergies, be sure to check with your healthcare professional before taking echinacea.

Applying echinacea to the skin can cause redness, itchiness, or a rash.

Do not take echinacea if: You are pregnant or breast-feeding. • You have a skin condition called pemphigus vulgaris.

Are there any interactions with medications?

Caffeine. The body breaks down caffeine to get rid of it. Echinacea might decrease how quickly the body breaks down caffeine. Taking echinacea along with caffeine might cause too much caffeine in the bloodstream and increase the risk of side effects. Common side effects include jitteriness, headache, and fast heartbeat.

Medications that decrease the immune system (Immunosuppressants). Echinacea can increase the immune system. Taking echinacea along with some medications that decrease the immune system might decrease the effectiveness of medications that decrease the immune system. Some medications that decrease the immune system include azathioprine (Imuran), basiliximab (Simulect), cyclosporine (Neoral, Sandimmune), daclizumab (Zenapax), muromonab-CD3 (OKT3, Orthoclone OKT3), mycophenolate (CellCept), tacrolimus (FK506, Prograf), sirolimus (Rapamune), prednisone (Deltasone, Orasone), corticosteroids (glucocorticoids), and others.

Medications changed by the liver (Cytochrome P450 1A2 (CYP1A2) substrates). Some medications are changed and broken down by the liver. Echinacea might decrease how quickly the liver breaks down some medications. Taking echinacea along with some medications might increase the effects and side effects of some medications. Before taking echinacea, talk to your healthcare provider if you are taking any medications that are changed by the liver. Some of the medications that are changed by the liver include clozapine (Clozaril),

 Natural Medicines Comprehensive Database Consumer Version (209) 472-2244

cyclobenzaprine (Flexeril), fluvoxamine (Luvox), haloperidol (Haldol), imipramine (Tofranil), mexiletine (Mexitil), olanzapine (Zyprexa), pentazocine (Talwin), propranolol (Inderal), tacrine (Cognex), theophylline, zileuton (Zyflo), zolmitriptan (Zomig), and others.

Medications changed by the body (Cytochrome P450 3A4 (CYP3A4) substrates). Some medications are changed and broken down by the body. Echinacea might change how the body breaks down some medications. Taking echinacea along with some medications might increase the effects and side effects of some medications. Before taking echinacea, talk to your healthcare provider if you are taking any medications that are changed by the body. Some medications changed by the body include lovastatin (Mevacor), clarithromycin (Biaxin), cyclosporine (Neoral, Sandimmune), diltiazem (Cardizem), estrogens, indinavir (Crixivan), triazolam (Halcion), and many others.

Midazolam (Versed). Taking midazolam with echinacea increases how much midazolam the body absorbs. This might increase the effects and side effects of midazolam, but more information is needed.

EDTA

What other names is the product known by?

Calcium Disodium Edathamil, Calcium Disodium EDTA, Calcium Disodium Edetate, Calcium Disodium Versenate, Calcium Edetate, Calcium EDTA, Disodium Edathamil, Disodium Edetate, Disodium EDTA, Disodium ethylenediamine tetraacetic acid, Disodium Tetraacetate, Ethylenediamine tetraacetic acid, Iron EDTA, Sodium Edetate, Trisodium ethylenediamine tetraacetic acid.

What is it?

EDTA is a prescription medicine, given by injection.

Is it Effective?

The effectiveness ratings for **EDTA** are as follows:

Effective for... Treating lead poisoning.

Likely Effective for... Emergency treatment of life-threatening high calcium levels (hypercalcemia) • Treating heart rhythm problems caused by drugs such as digoxin (Lanoxin).

Possibly Effective for... Treating corneal (eye) calcium deposits.

Possibly Ineffective for... Hardened skin (scleroderma).

Likely Ineffective for... Treating coronary heart disease (CHD) or peripheral arterial occlusive disease.

Insufficient Evidence to Rate Effectiveness for... Poisoning by radioactive products, Wilson's disease, atherosclerosis (hardening of the arteries), high cholesterol, high blood pressure, Raynaud's syndrome, gangrene, cancer, arthritis, vision problems, diabetes, Alzheimer's disease, multiple sclerosis, Parkinson's disease, psoriasis, angina, and other conditions.

How does it work?

EDTA is a chemical that binds and holds on to minerals and metals such as chromium, iron, mercury, copper, aluminum, nickel, zinc, calcium, cobalt, manganese, and magnesium. When they are bound they can't have any effects on the body and they are removed from the body.

Are there safety concerns?

EDTA is safe when used as a prescription medicine and in small amounts as a preservative in foods. EDTA can cause abdominal cramps, nausea, vomiting, diarrhea, headache, low blood pressure, skin problems, and fever.

It is UNSAFE to use more than 3 grams of EDTA per day, or to take it longer than 5 to 7 days. Too much can cause kidney damage, dangerously low calcium levels, and death.

Do not use EDTA in amounts greater than those commonly found in foods if: You are pregnant or breast-feeding. • You have heart rhythm problems. • You have diabetes. • You have low levels of calcium, potassium, or magnesium (known as hypocalcemia, hypokalemia, and hypomagnesemia, respectively). • You have liver problems. • You have kidney problems. • You have epilepsy (seizures). • You have tuberculosis (TB).

Are there any interactions with medications?

Insulin. EDTA can decrease blood sugar. Insulin is also used to decrease blood sugar. Taking EDTA along with insulin can cause serious decreases in your blood sugar. Monitor your blood sugar closely. The dose of your insulin might need to be changed.

Water pills (Diuretic drugs). Large amounts of EDTA can decrease potassium levels in the body. "Water pills" can also decrease potassium in the body. Taking EDTA along with "water pills" might decrease potassium in the body too much. Some "water pills" that can deplete potassium include chlorothiazide (Diuril), chlorthalidone (Thalitone), furosemide (Lasix), hydrochlorothiazide (HCTZ, HydroDiuril, Microzide), and others.

Medical professionals should consult the Professional Version at www.NaturalDatabase.com.

CONSUMER VERSION

Warfarin (Coumadin). Warfarin (Coumadin) is used to slow blood clotting. EDTA has been reported to decrease the effectiveness of warfarin (Coumadin). Decreasing the effectiveness of warfarin (Coumadin) might increase the risk of clotting. It is unclear why this interaction might occur. Be sure to have your blood checked regularly. The dose of your warfarin (Coumadin) might need to be changed.

ELDERBERRY

What other names is the product known by?

Baccae, Baises De Sureau, Black-Berried Alder, Black Elder, Black Elderberry, Boor Tree, Bountry, Elder, Ellanwood, Ellhorn, European Alder, European Elder Fruit, European Elderberry, Holunderbeeren, Sambuci Sambucus, Sambucus nigra.

What is it?

Elderberry is a plant. The flowers and the berries are used to make medicine.
Do not confuse elderberry with American elder.

Is it Effective?

The effectiveness ratings for **ELDERBERRY** are as follows:
Possibly Effective for..."The flu," also called influenza.
Insufficient Evidence to Rate Effectiveness for... Cancer, constipation, nerve pain, chronic fatigue syndrome (CFS), hayfever, HIV/AIDS, and other conditions.

How does it work?

Elderberry might affect the immune system. Elderberry seems to have activity against viruses including the flu, and might reduce inflammation.

Are there safety concerns?

Taking an elderberry juice extract seems to be safe when used for up to five days. It's not known if taking elderberry juice extract is safe when used for long periods of time. The cooked elderberry fruit seems to be safe. But raw and unripe fruit might cause nausea, vomiting, or severe diarrhea.

Do not take elderberry if: You are pregnant or breast-feeding. • You have an autoimmune disease such as multiple sclerosis (MS), systemic lupus erythematosus (SLE), or rheumatoid arthritis (RA).

Are there any interactions with medications?

Medications that decrease the immune system (Immunosuppressants). Elderberry can increase the immune system. Taking elderberry along with some medications that decrease the immune system might decrease the effectiveness of medications that decrease the immune system. Some medications that decrease the immune system include azathioprine (Imuran), basiliximab (Simulect), cyclosporine (Neoral, Sandimmune), daclizumab (Zenapax), muromonab-CD3 (OKT3, Orthoclone OKT3), mycophenolate (CellCept), tacrolimus (FK506, Prograf), sirolimus (Rapamune), prednisone (Deltasone, Orasone), corticosteroids (glucocorticoids), and others.

ELDERFLOWER

What other names is the product known by?

Black-Berried Alder, Black Elder, Boor Tree, Bountry, Common Elder, Ellanwood, Ellhorn, European Alder, European Elder Flower, Sambucus, Sambucus nigra, Sweet Elder.

What is it?

Elderflower is the flower of a tree. An extract of the flower is used to make medicine.

Is it Effective?

The effectiveness ratings for **ELDERFLOWER** are as follows:
Possibly Effective for... Treating sinusitis when taken with gentian root, verbena, cowslip flower, and sorrel.
Insufficient Evidence to Rate Effectiveness for... Bronchitis, cold, flu, cough, laryngitis, diabetes, arthritis-like pain, constipation, and swelling (inflammation).

How does it work?

Elderflower might work like insulin to lower blood sugar.

CONSUMER VERSION

Medical professionals should consult the Professional Version at www.NaturalDatabase.com.

 © Copyright 2006, Therapeutic Research Faculty.

Are there safety concerns?

Elderflower seems to be safe for most people when used in small amounts as part of a combination product containing elderflower, sorrel, gentian root, verbena, and cowslip flower (SinuComp, Sinupret). There isn't enough information to know if elderflower is safe when used in medicinal amounts other than as part of the combination product. The combination product can cause digestive system upset and occasionally allergic skin rash.

Do not take elderflower if: You are pregnant or breast-feeding. • You have diabetes.

Are there any interactions with medications?

Medications for diabetes (Antidiabetes drugs). Elderflower can decrease blood sugar levels. Diabetes medications are also used to lower blood sugar. Taking elderflower along with diabetes medications might cause your blood sugar to be too low. Monitor your blood sugar closely. The dose of your diabetes medication might need to be changed. Some medications used for diabetes include glimepiride (Amaryl), glyburide (DiaBeta, Glynase PresTab, Micronase), insulin, pioglitazone (Actos), rosiglitazone (Avandia), chlorpropamide (Diabinese), glipizide (Glucotrol), tolbutamide (Orinase), and others.

ELECAMPANE

What other names is the product known by?

Alant, Aster helenium, Aster officinalis, Elfdock, Elfwort, Helenium grandiflorum, Horse-Elder, Horseheal, Inula helenium, Scabwort, Velvet Dock, Wild Sunflower, Yellow Starwort.

What is it?

Elecampane is an herb. The root is used to make medicine.

Is it Effective?

The effectiveness ratings for **ELECAMPANE** are as follows:
Insufficient Evidence to Rate Effectiveness for... Coughs, asthma, bronchitis, nausea, diarrhea, worms which infest the gut (hookworm, roundworm, threadworm, and whipworm), and other conditions.

How does it work?

Elecampane contains chemicals which can kill worms that infest the gut.

Are there safety concerns?

Elecampane seems to be safe for most adults. Large amounts can cause vomiting, diarrhea, spasms, and paralysis.

If elecampane is applied to the skin, it can cause allergic reactions.

Do not use elecampane if: You are pregnant or breast-feeding. • You have diabetes. • You have high or low blood pressure (hypertension or hypotension). • You are allergic to plants such as ragweed, marigolds, or daisies.

Are there any interactions with medications?

Sedative medications (CNS depressants). Elecampane might cause sleepiness and drowsiness. Medications that cause sleepiness are called sedatives. Taking elecampane along with sedative medications might cause too much sleepiness. Some sedative medications include clonazepam (Klonopin), lorazepam (Ativan), Phenobarbital (Donnatal), zolpidem (Ambien), and others.

ELEMI

What other names is the product known by?

Canarium commune, Canarium luzonicum, Elemi Oleoresin, Elemi Resin, Manila Elemi.

What is it?

Elemi is a tree. The resin (gum) and oil from the elemi tree are used to make medicine.

Is it Effective?

The effectiveness ratings for **ELEMI** are as follows:
Insufficient Evidence to Rate Effectiveness for... Stomach conditions and coughs.

How does it work?

There isn't enough information to know how elemi works.

Are there safety concerns?

Elemi is safe for most people in the amounts found in foods. There isn't enough information to know if elemi is safe for use in larger amounts.

Do not use elemi if: You are pregnant or breast-feeding.

Are there any interactions with medications?

It is not known if elemi interacts with any medicines.
Before taking elemi, talk with your healthcare professional if you take any medications.

ELLAGIC ACID

What other names is the product known by?

None.

What is it?

Ellagic acid is a naturally occurring substance. The best sources of ellagic acid in the diet are strawberries, raspberries, blackberries, and walnuts.

Is it Effective?

The effectiveness ratings for **ELLAGIC ACID** are as follows:
Insufficient Evidence to Rate Effectiveness for... Preventing cancer, treating viral infections, and treating bacterial infections.

How does it work?

Ellagic acid may bind to chemicals that cause cancer and it may inhibit the growth of cancer cells.

Are there safety concerns?

There isn't enough reliable information available about ellagic acid to know if it is safe.

Are there any interactions with medications?

It is not known if ellagic acid interacts with any medicines.
Before taking ellagic acid, talk to your healthcare professional if you take any medications.

ELM BARK

What other names is the product known by?

Smooth-Leaved Elm, Ulmus minor.

What is it?

Elm bark is the bark of a tree. People use the bark to make medicine.

Is it Effective?

The effectiveness ratings for **ELM BARK** are as follows:
Insufficient Evidence to Rate Effectiveness for... Digestive disorders, diarrhea, increasing urine production (diuretic), and wounds.

How does it work?

There isn't enough information available to know how elm bark works.

Are there safety concerns?

There isn't enough information available to know if elm bark is safe.

Are there any interactions with medications?

It is not known if elm bark interacts with any medicines.
Before taking elm bark, talk with your healthcare professional if you take any medications.

EMU OIL

What other names is the product known by?
Dromiceius nova-hollandiae, Emu.

What is it?
Emu oil is taken from the fat of a bird during processing. It is used to make medicine.

Is it Effective?
The effectiveness ratings for **EMU OIL** are as follows:
Insufficient Evidence to Rate Effectiveness for... Headaches, reducing cholesterol, weight loss, coughs, skin and hair conditions, burns, wounds, muscle and joint problems, earaches, eye irritation, shingles, hemorrhoids, insect bites, diabetic nerve problems, and other conditions.

How does it work?
Emu oil contains chemicals called fatty acids which might reduce swelling (inflammation).

Are there safety concerns?
It is not known if emu oil is safe.

Do not use emu oil if: You are pregnant or breast-feeding.

Are there any interactions with medications?
It is not known if emu oil interacts with any medicines.
Before taking emu oil, talk with your healthcare professional if you take any medications.

ENGLISH ADDER'S TONGUE

What other names is the product known by?
Christs Spear, Christ's Spear, Green Oil of Charity, Ophioglossum vulgatum, Serpent's Tongue.

What is it?
English adder's tongue is an herb. The root and leaf are used to make medicine.

Is it Effective?
The effectiveness ratings for **ENGLISH ADDER'S TONGUE** are as follows:
Insufficient Evidence to Rate Effectiveness for... Treating skin ulcers.

How does it work?
There isn't enough information to know how English adder's tongue works.

Are there safety concerns?
There isn't enough information to know whether English adder's tongue is safe.

Do not use English adder's tongue if: You are pregnant or breast-feeding.

Are there any interactions with medications?
It is not known if English adder's tongue interacts with any medicines.
Before taking English adder's tongue, talk with your healthcare professional if you take any medications.

ENGLISH HORSEMINT

What other names is the product known by?
Biblical Mint, Mentha longifolia, Wild Mint.

What is it?
English horsemint is an herb. The above ground parts are used to make medicine.

Is it Effective?
The effectiveness ratings for **ENGLISH HORSEMINT** are as follows:
Insufficient Evidence to Rate Effectiveness for... Digestive disorders such as gas (flatulence), pain, and headaches.

How does it work?
There isn't enough information to know how English horsemint might work.

Are there safety concerns?
There isn't enough information available to know if English horsemint is safe.

Do not use English horsemint if: You are pregnant or breast-feeding.

Are there any interactions with medications?
It is not known if English horsemint interacts with any medicines.
Before taking English horsemint, talk with your healthcare professional if you take any medications.

ENGLISH IVY

What other names is the product known by?
Gum Ivy, Hederae helicis folium, Hedera helix, Ivy, True Ivy, Woodbind.

What is it?
English ivy is an herb. The leaves are used to make medicine.

Is it Effective?
The effectiveness ratings for **ENGLISH IVY** are as follows:
Possibly Effective for... Chronic bronchitis.
Insufficient Evidence to Rate Effectiveness for... Coughs; spasms; gout; arthritis-like pain; diseases of the liver, spleen, and gallbladder; burns; calluses; nerve pain; and ulcers.

How does it work?
English ivy seems to help breathing in children with chronic bronchitis.

Are there safety concerns?
English ivy taken by mouth appears to be safe for most adults. It can have a bitter taste.

There isn't enough information to know if English ivy is safe to apply directly to the skin. Fresh leaves can irritate the skin.

Do not use English ivy if: You are pregnant or breast-feeding.

Are there any interactions with medications?
It is not known if English ivy interacts with any medicines.
Before taking English ivy, talk with your healthcare professional if you take any medications.

ENGLISH WALNUT

What other names is the product known by?
Akschota, ructus Cortex, Juglans, Juglandis, Juglandis Folium, Juglans regia, Nogal, Walnussblätter, Walnussfrüchtschalen, Walnut, Walnut Fruit, Walnut Hull, Walnut Leaf.

What is it?
English walnut is a food.

Is it Effective?
The effectiveness ratings for **ENGLISH WALNUT** are as follows:
Possibly Effective for... Reducing the risk of heart disease • Lowering cholesterol, as part of a special diet • Preventing heart disease when walnuts are eaten.

 Natural Medicines Comprehensive Database Consumer Version (209) 472-2244

Insufficient Evidence to Rate Effectiveness for... Diarrhea, diabetes, anemia, acne, eczema, ulcers, treating swelling (inflammation) of the skin, treating excessive sweating (perspiration) of the hands and feet, and other conditions.

How does it work?
English walnut fruit contains chemicals called fatty acids, which might be useful as part of a cholesterol lowering diet. It also contains chemicals that can dilate blood vessels, possibly improving heart and circulatory function.

Are there safety concerns?
English walnut fruit is safe for most people in the amounts used for food. There isn't enough information to know if larger amounts are safe to use. The fruit can cause softening of the stools and bloating. English walnuts can cause weight gain unless they're substituted for other fats in the diet. English walnut may cause allergic reactions in people who are sensitive to it.

Do not use English walnut in medicinal amounts if: You are pregnant or breast-feeding.

Are there any interactions with medications?
It is not known if English walnut interacts with any medicines.
Before taking English walnut, talk with your healthcare professional if you take any medications.

EPA (EICOSAPENTAENOIC ACID)

What other names is the product known by?
Eicosapentaenoic Acid, Ethyl Eicosapentaenoic Acid, Fish Oil Fatty Acid, N-3 Fatty Acid, Omega Fatty Acid, Omega-3 Fatty Acid, Omega-3 Fatty Acids, W-3 Fatty Acid.

What is it?
EPA (Eicosapentaenoic Acid) is a fatty acid found in the flesh of cold water fish, including mackerel, herring, tuna, halibut, salmon, cod liver, whale blubber, or seal blubber.

Is it Effective?
The effectiveness ratings for **EPA (EICOSAPENTAENOIC ACID)** are as follows:
Possibly Effective for... Treating depression, when used with conventional antidepressants • Wound healing, when used with RNA and L-arginine following surgery • Treating borderline personality disorder, a mood disorder • Reducing the risk of death in people with coronary artery disease, when EPA is consumed as part of the diet • Psoriasis.
Possibly Ineffective for... Treating the mental disorder schizophrenia, when combined with standard medications • Treatment of type 2 diabetes • Treating symptoms of cystic fibrosis • Pregnancy-related high blood pressure • High blood pressure • Treating asthma • Relieving hayfever symptoms including wheezing, cough, and nasal symptoms • Preventing an eye disease called AMD (age-related macular degeneration), when EPA is consumed as part of the diet • Reducing growths in the uterus.
Insufficient Evidence to Rate Effectiveness for... Cancer, menstrual disorders, lung diseases, lupus, and other conditions.

How does it work?
EPA can prevent the blood from clotting easily. These fatty acids also reduce pain and swelling.

Are there safety concerns?
EPA seems to be safe for most people in low to moderate doses. There are no reported side effects for EPA used alone. However, for fish oils containing EPA, side effects can include fishy taste, belching, nosebleeds, nausea, and loose stools. Taking EPA with meals can often decrease these side effects.

When used in amounts greater than 3 grams per day, EPA can thin the blood and increase the risk for bleeding.

Do not use EPA if: You are pregnant or breast-feeding. • You are sensitive to aspirin. It might affect your breathing.

Are there any interactions with medications?
Medications for high blood pressure (Antihypertensive drugs). EPA can decrease blood pressure. Taking EPA along with medications for high blood pressure might cause you blood pressure to go too low. Some medications for high blood pressure include captopril (Capoten), enalapril (Vasotec), losartan (Cozaar), valsartan (Diovan), diltiazem (Cardizem), Amlodipine (Norvasc), hydrochlorothiazide (HydroDiuril), furosemide (Lasix), and many others.

Medical professionals should consult the Professional Version at www.NaturalDatabase.com.

Medications that slow blood clotting (Anticoagulant / Antiplatelet drugs). EPA (eicosapentaenoic acid) might slow blood clotting. Taking EPA (eicosapentaenoic acid) along with medications that also slow clotting might increase the chances of bruising and bleeding. Some medications that slow blood clotting include aspirin, clopidogrel (Plavix), diclofenac (Voltaren, Cataflam, others), ibuprofen (Advil, Motrin, others), naproxen (Anaprox, Naprosyn, others), dalteparin (Fragmin), enoxaparin (Lovenox), heparin, warfarin (Coumadin), and others.

EPHEDRA

What other names is the product known by?
Cao Mahuang, Desert Herb, Ephedra Distachya, Ephedra Equisetina, Ephedra Gerardiana, Ephedra Intermedia, Ephedra Shennungiana, Ephedra Sinensis, Ephedra Sinica, Ephedra vulgaris, Ephedrae Herba, Herbal Ecstasy, Joint Fir, Ma Huang, Ma-Huang, Mahuang, Mahuanggen (ma huang root), Muzei Mahuang, Popotillo, Sea Grape, Teamster's Tea, Yellow Astringent, Yellow Horse, Zhong Mahuang.

What is it?
Ephedra is an herb. Usually, the branches and tops are used to make medicine, but the root or whole plant can also be used.

Is it Effective?
The effectiveness ratings for **EPHEDRA** are as follows:
Possibly Effective for... Weight loss. Ephedra can produce modest weight loss when used with exercise and a low fat diet, but it can cause serious side effects, even in healthy people who follow product dosage directions.
Insufficient Evidence to Rate Effectiveness for... Improving athletic performance, allergies, asthma and other breathing disorders, nasal congestion, colds, flu, fever, and other conditions.

How does it work?
Ephedra contains a chemical called ephedrine. Ephedrine stimulates the heart, the lungs, and the nervous system.

Are there safety concerns?
Ephedra is banned in the US due to safety concerns. Ephedra use is linked to high blood pressure, heart attacks, muscle disorders, seizures, strokes, irregular heartbeat, loss of consciousness, and death. These side effects might be more likely if ephedra is used in high doses or long-term. Doses greater than 32 mg per day might more than triple the risk for bleeding within the brain (hemorrhagic stroke). The risk for serious side effects seems to be greater than any potential benefit.

Ephedra can also cause less serious side effects including dizziness, restlessness, anxiety, irritability, heart pounding, headache, loss of appetite, nausea, vomiting, and others.
Do not use ephedra with other stimulants such as caffeine. This might increase the chance of having side effects, including life-threatening ones. Sources of caffeine include coffee, tea, kola nut, guarana, and mate.

Do not use ephedra if: You are pregnant or breast-feeding. • You have chest pains. • You feel anxious. • You have diabetes. • You have glaucoma. • You have rapid or irregular heartbeat. • You have thyroid problems. • You have high blood pressure. • You have tremors. • You have kidney stones. • You have a condition called pheochromocytoma. • You have a seizure disorder.

Are there any interactions with medications?
Dexamethasone (Decadron). The body breaks down dexamethasone (Decadron) to get rid of it. Ephedra might increase how quickly the body breaks down dexamethasone (Decadron). Taking ephedra along with dexamethasone (Decadron) might decrease the effectiveness of dexamethasone (Decadron).
Ergot Derivatives. Ephedra can increase blood pressure. Ergot derivatives can also increase blood pressure. Taking ephedra with ergot derivatives might increase blood pressure too much. Some of these ergot derivatives include bromocriptine (Parlodel), dihydroergotamine (Migranal, DHE-45), ergotamine (Cafergot), and pergolide (Permax).
Medications for depression (MAOIs). Ephedra contains chemicals that stimulate the body. Some medications used for depression can increase these chemicals. Taking ephedra with these medications used for depression might cause serious side effects including fast heartbeat, high blood pressure, seizures, nervousness, and others. Some of these medications used for depression include phenelzine (Nardil), tranylcypromine (Parnate), and others.
Medications for diabetes (Antidiabetes drugs). Ephedra might increase blood sugar. Diabetes medications are used to lower blood sugar. By increasing blood sugar, ephedra might decrease the effectiveness of diabetes medications. Monitor your blood sugar closely. The dose of your diabetes medication might need to be changed. Some medications used for diabetes include glimepiride (Amaryl), glyburide (DiaBeta, Glynase PresTab, Micronase), insulin, pioglitazone (Actos), rosiglitazone (Avandia), chlorpropamide (Diabinese), glipizide

 Natural Medicines Comprehensive Database Consumer Version (209) 472-2244

(Glucotrol), tolbutamide (Orinase), and others.

Medications that can cause an irregular heartbeat (QT interval-prolonging drugs). Ephedra can increase the speed of your heartbeat. Taking ephedra along with medications that can cause an irregular heartbeat might cause serious side effects including heart attack. Some medications that can cause an irregular heartbeat include amiodarone (Cordarone), disopyramide (Norpace), dofetilide (Tikosyn), ibutilide (Corvert), procainamide (Pronestyl), quinidine, sotalol (Betapace), thioridazine (Mellaril), and many others.

Methylxanthines. Ephedra can simulate the body. Methylxanthines also stimulate the body. Taking ephedra along with methylxanthines might cause side effects such as jitteriness, nervousness, a fast heartbeat, high blood pressure, and anxiety. Methylxanthines include aminophylline, caffeine, and theophylline.

Medications used to prevent seizures (Anticonvulsants). Medications used to prevent seizures affect chemicals in the brain. Ephedra may also affect chemicals in the brain. By affecting chemicals in the brain, ephedra may decrease the effectiveness of medications used to prevent seizures. Some medications used to prevent seizures include phenobarbital, primidone (Mysoline), valproic acid (Depakene), gabapentin (Neurontin), carbamazepine (Tegretol), phenytoin (Dilantin), and others.

Stimulant drugs. Stimulant drugs speed up the nervous system and can make you feel jittery and speed up your heartbeat. Ephedra can also speed up the nervous system. Taking ephedra along with stimulant drugs might cause serious problems including increased heart rate and high blood pressure. Avoid taking stimulant drugs along with ephedra. Some stimulant drugs include diethylpropion (Tenuate), epinephrine, phentermine (Ionamin), pseudoephedrine (Sudafed), and many others.

EPIMEDIUM

What other names is the product known by?
Barrenwort, Epimedium acuminatum, Epimedium brevicornum, Epimedium grandiflorum, Epimedium koreanum, Epimedium pubescens, Epimedium sagittatum, Epimedium wushanese, Herba Epimedii, Horny Goat Weed, Japanese Epimedium, Xian Ling Pi, Yin Yang Huo.

What is it?
Epimedium is an herb. The leaves are used to make medicine.

Is it Effective?
The effectiveness ratings for **EPIMEDIUM** are as follows:

Insufficient Evidence to Rate Effectiveness for... Impotence, ejaculation problems, sexual dysfunction, fatigue, memory loss, high blood pressure, heart disease, liver disease, bronchitis, joint pain, HIV/AIDS, and other conditions.

How does it work?
Epimedium contains chemicals which might help increase blood flow and improve sexual function.

Are there safety concerns?
Epimedium does not seem to be safe. Long-term use of epimedium might cause dizziness, vomiting, dry mouth, thirst, and nosebleed. Taking large amounts of epimedium might cause spasms and severe breathing problems.

Do not use epimedium if: You are pregnant or breast-feeding. • You have low blood pressure (hypotension).

Are there any interactions with medications?
Medications that slow blood clotting (Anticoagulant / Antiplatelet drugs). Epimedium might slow blood clotting. Taking epimedium along with medications that also slow clotting might increase the chances of bruising and bleeding. Some medications that slow blood clotting include aspirin, clopidogrel (Plavix), diclofenac (Voltaren, Cataflam, others), ibuprofen (Advil, Motrin, others), naproxen (Anaprox, Naprosyn, others), dalteparin (Fragmin), enoxaparin (Lovenox), heparin, warfarin (Coumadin), and others.

Medications for high blood pressure (Antihypertensive drugs). Epimedium seems to decrease blood pressure. Taking epimedium along with medications for high blood pressure might cause your blood pressure to go too low. Some medications for high blood pressure include captopril (Capoten), enalapril (Vasotec), losartan (Cozaar), valsartan (Diovan), diltiazem (Cardizem), Amlodipine (Norvasc), hydrochlorothiazide (HydroDiuril), furosemide (Lasix), and many others.

Medical professionals should consult the Professional Version at www.NaturalDatabase.com.

CONSUMER VERSION

ERGOT

What other names is the product known by?

Cockspur Rye, Hornseed, Mother of Rye, Secale cornutum, Smut Rye, Spurred Rye.

What is it?

Ergot is a fungus that occurs on rye. Ergot derivatives are available in a standardized form in prescription medicines.

Is it Effective?

The effectiveness ratings for **ERGOT** are as follows:

Insufficient Evidence to Rate Effectiveness for... Reducing bleeding in childbirth, assisting delivery, menstrual pain, and other conditions.

How does it work?

Ergot contains chemicals that can help reduce bleeding by causing a narrowing of the blood vessels.

Are there safety concerns?

Ergot is UNSAFE. There is a high risk of poisoning, and it can be fatal. Early symptoms include nausea, vomiting, muscle pain and weakness, numbness, itching, and rapid or slow heartbeat. It can progress to gangrene, vision problems, confusion, spasms, convulsions, unconsciousness, and death.

Do not use ergot if: You are pregnant or breast-feeding.

Are there any interactions with medications?

Ergot Derivatives. Ergot contains the same chemicals as ergot derivatives in prescription medications. Taking ergot supplements with prescription ergot derivatives can increase the effects and side effects of ergot. Some of these ergot derivatives include bromocriptine (Parlodel), dihydroergotamine (Migranal, DHE-45), ergotamine (Cafergot), and pergolide (Permax).

Dextromethorphan (Robitussin DM, and others). Ergot can affect a brain chemical called serotonin. Dextromethorphan (Robitussin DM, others) can also affect serotonin. Taking ergot along with dextromethorphan (Robitussin DM, others) might cause too much serotonin in the brain and serious side effects including heart problems, shivering, and anxiety. Do not take ergot if you are taking dextromethorphan (Robitussin DM, and others).

Medications that decrease the breakdown of other medications in the liver (Cytochrome P450 3A4 (CYP3A4) inhibitors). Some medications are changed and broken down by the liver. Some medications might decrease how quickly the liver breaks down ergot. Taking ergot along with some medications that decrease the break-down of other medications in the liver can increase the effects and side effects of ergot. Before taking ergot, talk to your healthcare provider if you are taking any medications that are changed by the liver. Some medications that might decrease how quickly the liver breaks down ergot include amiodarone (Cordarone), clarithromycin (Biaxin), diltiazem (Cardizem), erythromycin (E-mycin, Erythrocin), indinavir (Crixivan), ritonavir (Norvir), saquinavir (Fortovase, Invirase), and many others.

Medications for depression (Antidepressant drugs). Ergot increases a brain chemical called serotonin. Some medications for depression also increase the brain chemical serotonin. Taking ergot along with these medications for depression might increase serotonin too much and cause serious side effects including heart problems, shivering, and anxiety. Do not take ergot if you are taking medications for depression. Some of these medications for depression include fluoxetine (Prozac), paroxetine (Paxil), sertraline (Zoloft), amitriptyline (Elavil), clomipramine (Anafranil), imipramine (Tofranil), and others.

Medications for depression (MAOIs). Ergot increases a chemical in the brain. This chemical is called serotonin. Some medications used for depression also increase serotonin. Taking ergot with these medications used for depression might cause serious side effects including heart problems, shivering, and anxiety. Some of these medications used for depression include phenelzine (Nardil), tranylcypromine (Parnate), and others.

Meperidine (Demerol). Ergot increases a chemical in the brain called serotonin. Meperidine (Demerol) can also increase serotonin in the brain. Taking ergot along with meperidine (Demerol) might cause too much serotonin in the brain and serious side effects including heart problems, shivering, and anxiety.

Pentazocine (Talwin). Ergot increases a brain chemical called serotonin. Pentazocine (Talwin) also increases serotonin. Taking ergot along with pentazocine (Talwin) might increase serotonin too much. Too much serotonin can cause serious side effects including heart problems, shivering, and anxiety. Do not take ergot if you are taking pentazocine (Talwin).

Stimulant drugs. Stimulant drugs speed up the nervous system. Speeding up the nervous system can make you feel jittery and speed up your heartbeat. Ergot might also speed up the nervous system. Taking ergot along with stimulant drugs might cause serious problems including increased heart rate and high blood pressure. Avoid taking stimulant drugs along with ergot. Some stimulant drugs include diethylpropion (Tenuate), epinephrine, phentermine (Ionamin), pseudoephedrine (Sudafed), and many others.

     Natural Medicines Comprehensive Database Consumer Version   (209) 472-2244

Tramadol (Ultram). Tramadol (Ultram) can affect a chemical in the brain called serotonin. Ergot can also affect serotonin. Taking ergot along with tramadol (Ultram) might cause too much serotonin in the brain and side effects including confusion, shivering, stiff muscles, and other side effects.

ERYNGO

What other names is the product known by?
Eringo, Eryngii Herba, Eryngii Radix, Eryngo Root, Eryngium Campestre, Eryngium Maritimum, Eyrnigium Planum, Eryngium Yuccifolium, Sea Holly, Sea Holme, Sea Hulver.

What is it?
Eryngo is an herb. The above ground parts and root are used to make medicine.

Is it Effective?
The effectiveness ratings for **ERYNGO** are as follows:
Insufficient Evidence to Rate Effectiveness for... Urinary tract infections (UTIs), prostate problems, cough, bronchitis, kidney and bladder stones, kidney pain and swelling, fluid retention, problems urinating, skin problems, and other conditions.

How does it work?
Eryngo above ground parts might increase urine production. Eryngo root might reduce spasms and help break up chest congestion by thinning mucus and making it easier to cough up (expectorant).

Are there safety concerns?
There is not enough information available to know if eryngo is safe.

Do not take eryngo if: You are pregnant or breast-feeding. • You are allergic to celery, fennel, dill, or other plants in the Apiaceae family.

Are there any interactions with medications?
It is not known if eryngo interacts with any medicines.
Before taking eryngo, talk with your healthcare professional if you take any medications.

EUCALYPTUS

What other names is the product known by?
Blue Gum, Blue Mallee, Blue Mallee Oil, Eucalypti Folium, Eucalyptus blatter, Eucalyptus bicostata, Eucalyptus fructicetorum, Eucalyptus globulus, Eucalyptus leaf, Eucalyptus odorata, Eucalyptus oil, Eucalyptus polybractea, Eucalyptus smithii, Fever Tree, Fieberbaumblatter, Gully Gum, Gully Gum Oil, Gum Tree, Red Gum, Stringy Bark Tree, Sugandhapatra, Tailapatra, Tasmanian Blue Gum.

What is it?
Eucalyptus is a tree. The dried leaves and oil are used to make medicine.

Is it Effective?
The effectiveness ratings for **EUCALYPTUS** are as follows:
Insufficient Evidence to Rate Effectiveness for... Asthma, cough, reducing swelling (inflammation) of the upper airway tract, stuffy nose, wounds, burns, ulcers, acne, bleeding gums, bladder diseases, diabetes, fever, flu, liver and gallbladder complaints, loss of appetite, arthritis pain, and other conditions.

How does it work?
Eucalyptus leaf contains chemicals that might help control blood sugar. It also contains chemicals that might have activity against bacteria and fungi. Eucalyptus oil contains chemicals that might help pain and inflammation. It might also block chemicals that cause asthma.

Are there safety concerns?
Eucalyptus is safe in amounts found in foods. Eucalyptol, a chemical in eucalyptus oil, appears to be safe when taken by mouth for up to 12 weeks.

Eucalyptus oil can cause nausea, vomiting, and diarrhea. Signs of eucalyptus poisoning might include stomach pain and burning, dizziness, muscle weakness, small eye pupils, feelings of suffocation, and some others.

CONSUMER VERSION

Medical professionals should consult the Professional Version at www.NaturalDatabase.com.

The oil is UNSAFE when it is either taken by mouth or applied directly to the skin without first being diluted. Taking 3.5 mL of undiluted oil can be fatal.

Eucalyptus oil is safe for pregnant and breast-feeding women only when used in amounts found in foods.

Eucalyptus oil is unsafe for children.

Do not use eucalyptus if: You are pregnant or breast-feeding, except in amounts found in foods. • You have diabetes.

Are there any interactions with medications?

Medications for diabetes (Antidiabetes drugs). Eucalyptus leaf extract might decrease blood sugar. Diabetes medications are also used to lower blood sugar. Taking eucalyptus leaf extract along with diabetes medications might cause your blood sugar to go too low. Monitor your blood sugar closely. The dose of your diabetes medication might need to be changed. Some medications used for diabetes include glimepiride (Amaryl), glyburide (DiaBeta, Glynase PresTab, Micronase), insulin, pioglitazone (Actos), rosiglitazone (Avandia), chlorpropamide (Diabinese), glipizide (Glucotrol), tolbutamide (Orinase), and others.

Medications changed by the liver (Cytochrome P450 1A2 (CYP1A2) substrates). Some medications are changed and broken down by the liver. Eucalyptus oil might decrease how quickly the liver breaks down some medications. Taking eucalyptus oil along with some medications that are broken down by the liver can increase the effects and side effects of some medications. Before taking eucalyptus oil, talk to your healthcare provider if you take any medications that are changed by the liver. Some medications that are changed by the liver include amitriptyline (Elavil), haloperidol (Haldol), ondansetron (Zofran), propranolol (Inderal), theophylline (Theo-Dur, others), verapamil (Calan, Isoptin, others), and others.

Medications changed by the liver (Cytochrome P450 2C19 (CYP2C19) substrates). Some medications are changed and broken down by the liver. Eucalyptus oil might decrease how quickly the liver breaks down some medications. Taking eucalyptus oil along with some medications that are broken down by the liver can increase the effects and side effects of some medications. Before taking eucalyptus oil, talk to your healthcare provider if you take any medications that are changed by the liver. Some medications that are changed by the liver include omeprazole (Prilosec), lansoprazole (Prevacid), and pantoprazole (Protonix); diazepam (Valium); carisoprodol (Soma); nelfinavir (Viracept); and others.

Medications changed by the liver (Cytochrome P450 2C9 (CYP2C9) substrates). Some medications are changed and broken down by the liver. Eucalyptus oil might decrease how quickly the liver breaks down some medications. Taking eucalyptus oil along with some medications that are broken down by the liver can increase the effects and side effects of some medications. Before taking eucalyptus oil, talk to your healthcare provider if you take any medications that are changed by the liver. Some medications that are changed by the liver include diclofenac (Cataflam, Voltaren), ibuprofen (Motrin), meloxicam (Mobic), and piroxicam (Feldene); celecoxib (Celebrex); amitriptyline (Elavil); warfarin (Coumadin); glipizide (Glucotrol); losartan (Cozaar); and others.

Medications changed by the liver (Cytochrome P450 3A4 (CYP3A4) substrates). Some medications are changed and broken down by the liver. Eucalyptus oil might decrease how quickly the liver breaks down some medications. Taking eucalyptus oil along with some medications that are broken down by the liver can increase the effects and side effects of some medications. Before taking eucalyptus oil, talk to your healthcare provider if you are taking any medications that are changed by the liver. Some medications changed by the liver include lovastatin (Mevacor), ketoconazole (Nizoral), itraconazole (Sporanox), fexofenadine (Allegra), triazolam (Halcion), and many others.

EUPHORBIA

What other names is the product known by?
Asthmaplant, Euphorbia hirta, Euphorbia capitulata, Euphorbia pilulifera, Pillbearing Spurge, Snakeweed.

What is it?
Euphorbia is an herb. The above ground parts are used to make medicine.

Is it Effective?
The effectiveness ratings for **EUPHORBIA** are as follows:
Insufficient Evidence to Rate Effectiveness for... Asthma, bronchitis, coughs, hayfever, tumors, digestive problems, intestinal worms, gonorrhea, and other conditions.

How does it work?
There isn't enough information to know how euphorbia works.

 Natural Medicines Comprehensive Database Consumer Version (209) 472-2244

Are there safety concerns?

There isn't enough information available to know if euphorbia is safe. It can cause some side effects such as nausea and vomiting.

Avoid contact with the fresh herb which can cause skin irritation or allergic reactions.

Do not use euphorbia if: You are pregnant or breast-feeding. • You have stomach or intestinal problems.

Are there any interactions with medications?

It is not known if euphorbia interacts with any medicines.
Before taking euphorbia, talk with your healthcare professional if you take any medications.

EUROPEAN BARBERRY

What other names is the product known by?

Agracejo, Berberidis cortex, Berberidis fructus, Berberidis radicis cortex, Berberidis radix, Berberis vulgaris, Berberitze, Berberry, Berbis, Common Barberry, Épine-Vinette, Espino Cambrón, Jaundice Berry, Mountain Grape, Oregon Grape, Pipperidge, Piprage, Sauerdorn, Sow Berry, Vinettier.

What is it?

European barberry is an herb. The fruit, bark, and roots are used to make medicine.

Is it Effective?

The effectiveness ratings for **EUROPEAN BARBERRY** are as follows:
Insufficient Evidence to Rate Effectiveness for... Kidney problems, bladder problems, heartburn, stomach cramps, constipation, diarrhea, liver problems, spleen problems, lung problems, heart and circulation problems, fever, gout, arthritis, and other conditions.

How does it work?

European barberry contains chemicals that might cause stronger heartbeat. It also might help fight inflammation.

Are there safety concerns?

The fruit of European barberry is safe when consumed in food amounts. There is not enough information to know if European barberry is safe in medicinal amounts. European barberry is UNSAFE in newborn infants.

Do not use European barberry in medicinal amounts if: You are pregnant or breast-feeding.

Are there any interactions with medications?

Cyclosporin (Neoral, Sandimmune). The body breaks down cyclosporin (Neoral, Sandimmune) to get rid of it. European barberry might decrease how fast the body breaks down cyclosporin (Neoral, Sandimmune). This might cause there to be too much cyclosporin (Neoral, Sandimmune) in the body and potentially cause side effects.
Medications changed by the liver (Cytochrome P450 3A4 (CYP3A4) substrates). Some medications are changed and broken down by the liver. European barberry might decrease how quickly the liver breaks down some medications. Taking European barberry along with some medications that are broken down by the liver can increase the effects and side effects of some medications. Before taking European barberry, talk to your healthcare provider if you are taking any medications that are changed by the liver. Some medications changed by the liver include cyclosporin (Neoral, Sandimmune), lovastatin (Mevacor), clarithromycin (Biaxin), indinavir (Crixivan), sildenafil (Viagra), triazolam (Halcion), and many others.

EUROPEAN BUCKTHORN

What other names is the product known by?

Buckthorn, Buckthorn Berry, Hartshorn, Highwaythorn, Kreuzdornbeeren, Ramsthorn, Rhamni cathartica fructus, Rhamnus catharticus, Waythorn.

What is it?

European buckthorn is an herb. The berries are used to make medicine.

Is it Effective?

The effectiveness ratings for **EUROPEAN BUCKTHORN** are as follows:
Likely Effective for... Relieving constipation.

CONSUMER VERSION

Medical professionals should consult the Professional Version at www.NaturalDatabase.com.

How does it work?

European buckthorn contains chemicals that stimulate the gut to relieve constipation.

Are there safety concerns?

Standardized preparations of European buckthorn are probably safe for most adults when used short-term, for less than eight to ten days. Avoid non-standardized preparations. European buckthorn can cause some side effects such as stomach cramps, watery diarrhea, discolored urine, muscle weakness, heart problems, and blood in the urine.

Do not give European buckthorn to children younger than 12 years of age.

Do not use European buckthorn if: You are pregnant or breast-feeding. • You have stomach pain. • You have intestinal problems such as Crohn's disease, irritable bowel syndrome, or ulcerative colitis.

Are there any interactions with medications?

Digoxin (Lanoxin). European buckthorn is high in fiber. Fiber can decrease the absorption and decrease the effectiveness of digoxin (Lanoxin). As a general rule, any medications taken by mouth should be taken one hour before or four hours after European buckthorn to prevent this interaction.
Medications taken by mouth (Oral drugs). European buckthorn is a laxative. Laxatives can decrease how much medicine your body absorbs. Decreasing how much medicine your body absorbs can decrease the effectiveness of your medication.
Water pills (Diuretic drugs). European buckthorn is a laxative. Some laxatives can decrease potassium in the body. "Water pills" can also decrease potassium in the body. Taking European buckthorn along with "water pills" might decrease potassium in the body too much. Some "water pills" that can decrease potassium include chlorothiazide (Diuril), chlorthalidone (Thalitone), furosemide (Lasix), hydrochlorothiazide (HCTZ, HydroDiuril, Microzide), and others.

EUROPEAN CHESTNUT

What other names is the product known by?

Castaneae Folium, Castanea sativa, Castanea vesca, Castanea vulgaris, Fagus castanea, Fagus procera, Husked Nut, Jupiter's Nut, Kastanienblaetter, Sardian Nut, Spanish Chestnut, Sweet Chestnut.

What is it?

European chestnut is a tree. The leaves are used to make medicine.

Is it Effective?

The effectiveness ratings for **EUROPEAN CHESTNUT** are as follows:
Insufficient Evidence to Rate Effectiveness for... Bronchitis, whooping cough, nausea, diarrhea, stomach problems, circulation problems, fever, infections, kidney disorders, muscle pain, sore throat, wounds, and other conditions.

How does it work?

European chestnut contains chemicals called tannins that might help reduce skin inflammation and have a drying (astringent) effect on the tissues.

Are there safety concerns?

European chestnut is probably safe for most adults.

Do not use European chestnut if: You are pregnant or breast-feeding.

Are there any interactions with medications?

Medications taken by mouth (Oral drugs). European chestnut contains a large amount of chemicals called tannins. Tannins absorb substances in the stomach and intestines. Taking European chestnut along with medications taken by mouth can decrease how much medicine your body absorbs, and decrease the effectiveness of your medicine. To prevent this interaction, take European chestnut at least one hour after medications you take by mouth.

EUROPEAN FIVE-FINGER GRASS

What other names is the product known by?
Cinquefoil, European five finger grass, Five-Finger Blossom, Five Fingers, Potentilla reptans, Sunkfield, Synkfoyle.

What is it?
European five-finger grass is an herb. The dried plant is used to make medicine.

Is it Effective?
The effectiveness ratings for **EUROPEAN FIVE-FINGER GRASS** are as follows:
Insufficient Evidence to Rate Effectiveness for... Diarrhea, fever, toothache, heartburn, wounds, and other conditions.

How does it work?
European fiver-finger grass contains chemicals called tannins that might help reduce skin inflammation and have a drying (astringent) effect on the tissues.

Are there safety concerns?
There isn't enough information available to know if European five-finger grass is safe.

Do not use European five-finger grass if: You are pregnant or breast-feeding.

Are there any interactions with medications?
It is not known if European five-finger grass interacts with any medicines.
Before taking European five-finger grass, talk with your healthcare professional if you take any medications.

EUROPEAN MANDRAKE

What other names is the product known by?
Alraunwurzel, Mandrake, Mandragora, Mandragora officinarum, Mandragora vernalis, Mandragore, Satan's Apple.

What is it?
European mandrake is an herb. The root and leaves are used to make medicine.

Is it Effective?
The effectiveness ratings for **EUROPEAN MANDRAKE** are as follows:
Insufficient Evidence to Rate Effectiveness for... Pain, sedation, stomach ulcers, constipation, colic, asthma, hayfever, convulsions, arthritis-like pain, whooping cough, skin ulcers, and other conditions.

How does it work?
European mandrake can reduce the actions of certain chemicals which can affect many body systems, including the eyes, bladder, lungs, bowels, and mouth.

Are there safety concerns?
European mandrake is probably unsafe and should be avoided. It can cause many side effects, including confusion, drowsiness, dry mouth, heart problems, vision problems, overheating, problems with urination, and hallucinations. Large doses can be fatal.

Do not give European mandrake to children, people with Down Syndrome, or elderly people. They are very sensitive to the side effects.

Do not use European mandrake if: You are pregnant or breast-feeding. • You have heart problems or high blood pressure. • You have disorders of the esophagus, stomach, or intestines. • You have glaucoma. • You have urinary problems. • You have a condition called myasthenia gravis. • You have kidney problems. • You have liver problems. • You have prostate problems. • You have thyroid problems.

Are there any interactions with medications?
Drying medications (Anticholinergic drugs). European mandrake contains chemicals that cause a drying effect. It also affects the brain and heart. Drying medications called anticholinergic drugs can also cause these effects. Taking European mandrake and drying medications together might cause side effects including dry skin, dizziness, low blood pressure, fast heartbeat, and other serious side effects. Some of these drying medications include

CONSUMER VERSION

Medical professionals should consult the Professional Version at www.NaturalDatabase.com.

atropine, scopolamine, and some medications used for allergies (antihistamines), and for depression (antidepressants).

Medications taken by mouth (Oral drugs). European mandrake seems to slow down the bowels. Taking European mandrake along with medications taken by mouth might increase how much medicine your body absorbs. Increasing how much medicine your body absorbs can increase the effects and side effects of your medicines.

EUROPEAN MISTLETOE

What other names is the product known by?

All-Heal, Birdlime Mistletoe, Devil's Fuge, Drudenfuss, Eurixor, Helixor, Hexenbesen, Iscador, Isorel, Leimmistel, Mistlekraut, Mistletein, Mistletoe, Mystyldene, Visci, Visci albi folia, Visci albi fructus, Visci albi herba, Visci albi stipites, Vogelmistel, Vysorel, Viscum album.

What is it?

European mistletoe is a plant that grows on several different trees. The berries, leaf, and stem of European mistletoe are used to make medicine.

Is it Effective?

The effectiveness ratings for **EUROPEAN MISTLETOE** are as follows:

Likely Ineffective for... Some cancers, including pancreatic cancer, kidney cancer, lung cancer, and melanoma.

Insufficient Evidence to Rate Effectiveness for... Reducing the side effects of chemotherapy and radiation therapy, high blood pressure, internal bleeding, hemorrhoids, seizures, high cholesterol, gout, depression, sleep disorders, headache, menstrual disorders, and many other conditions.

How does it work?

European mistletoe has several active chemicals. It might stimulate the immune system and kill certain cancer cells in a test tube, but it doesn't seem to work in people.

Are there safety concerns?

European mistletoe might be safe when used in appropriate amounts. Taking three berries or two leaves or less by mouth does not seem to cause serious side effects, but larger amounts can be unsafe and cause serious side effects. European mistletoe can cause vomiting, diarrhea, cramping, and other side effects. Some people inject European mistletoe products. This can cause fever, chills, allergic reactions, and other side effects. Because the correct amount is sometimes hard to determine, do not take European mistletoe without the advice of your healthcare professional.

Do not take European mistletoe if: You are pregnant or breast-feeding. • You are an organ transplant recipient. • You have heart disease.

Are there any interactions with medications?

Medications for high blood pressure (Antihypertensive drugs). European mistletoe seems to decrease blood pressure. Taking European mistletoe along with medications for high blood pressure might cause your blood pressure to go too low. Some medications for high blood pressure include captopril (Capoten), enalapril (Vasotec), losartan (Cozaar), valsartan (Diovan), diltiazem (Cardizem), Amlodipine (Norvasc), hydrochlorothiazide (HydroDiuril), furosemide (Lasix), and many others.

Medications that decrease the immune system (Immunosuppressants). European mistletoe seems to increase the immune system. By increasing the immune system European mistletoe might decrease the effectiveness of medications that decrease the immune system. Some medications that decrease the immune system include azathioprine (Imuran), basiliximab (Simulect), cyclosporine (Neoral, Sandimmune), daclizumab (Zenapax), muromonab-CD3 (OKT3, Orthoclone OKT3), mycophenolate (CellCept), tacrolimus (FK506, Prograf), sirolimus (Rapamune), prednisone (Deltasone, Orasone), corticosteroids (glucocorticoids), and others.

EURYCOMA LONGIFOLIA

What other names is the product known by?

Ali's Walking Stick, Eurycoma, E. longifolia, Eurycoma Longifolia, Longjack, Malaysian Ginseng, Tongkat Ali.

What is it?

Eurycoma longifolia is a shrub. The root and bark are used to make medicine.

Is it Effective?

The effectiveness ratings for **EURYCOMA LONGIFOLIA** are as follows:

Insufficient Evidence to Rate Effectiveness for... Erectile dysfunction, impotence, infertility, increasing libido, fever, malaria, ulcers, hypertension, tuberculosis, bone pain, cough, diarrhea, headache, syphilis, and cancer.

How does it work?

There is not enough information to know how Eurycoma longifolia might work.

Are there safety concerns?

There is not enough information to know if Eurycoma longifolia is safe.

Do not take Eurycoma longifolia if: You are pregnant or breast-feeding.

Are there any interactions with medications?

There is not enough information to know if Eurycoma longifolia interacts with any medicines. Talk to your health professional before taking Eurycoma longifolia if you take any medications.

EVENING PRIMROSE OIL

What other names is the product known by?

EPO, Evening Primrose, Fever Plant, Huile D'Onagre, King's Cureall, Night Willow-Herb, Primrose, Oenothera biennis, Oenothera muricata, Oenothera purpurata, Oenothera rubricaulis, Oenothera suaveolens, Onagra biennis, Scabish, Sun Drop.

What is it?

Evening primrose oil is the oil from the seed of the evening primrose plant.

Is it Effective?

The effectiveness ratings for **EVENING PRIMROSE OIL** are as follows:

Possibly Effective for... Breast pain • Osteoporosis, when used in combination with calcium and fish oils.

Possibly Ineffective for... Symptoms of premenstrual syndrome (PMS) • Attention deficit-hyperactivity disorder (ADHD) • Reducing symptoms of a kind of skin disorder called atopic dermatitis (eczema) • Hot flashes due to menopause.

Insufficient Evidence to Rate Effectiveness for... High blood pressure due to pregnancy (pre-eclampsia), shortening labor in pregnant women, chronic fatigue syndrome, acne, multiple sclerosis (MS), rheumatoid arthritis, Sjogren's syndrome, cancer, heart disease, high cholesterol, Alzheimer's disease, and other conditions.

How does it work?

Evening primrose oil contains "fatty acids." Some women with breast pain might not have high enough levels of certain "fatty acids." Fatty acids also seem to help decrease inflammation related to conditions such as arthritis and eczema.

Are there safety concerns?

Evening primrose oil is safe for most people. It can sometimes cause mild side effects including upset stomach, nausea, diarrhea, and headache.

There is some concern that evening primrose oil might increase the chance of problems during pregnancy and delivery.

Do not use evening primrose oil if: You are pregnant or breast-feeding. • You have a bleeding disorder. • You have epilepsy or another seizure disorder. • You have schizophrenia.

Are there any interactions with medications?

Medications that slow blood clotting (Anticoagulant / Antiplatelet drugs). Evening primrose oil might slow blood clotting. Taking evening primrose oil along with medications that also slow clotting might increase the chances of bruising and bleeding. Evening primrose oil contains GLA (gamma-linolenic acid). GLA is the part of evening primrose oil that might slow blood clotting. Some medications that slow blood clotting include aspirin, clopidogrel (Plavix), diclofenac (Voltaren, Cataflam, others), ibuprofen (Advil, Motrin, others), naproxen (Anaprox, Naprosyn, others), dalteparin (Fragmin), enoxaparin (Lovenox), heparin, warfarin (Coumadin), and others.

Medications used during surgery (Anesthesia). Evening primrose oil might interact with medications used during surgery. One person who was taking evening primrose oil and other medications had a seizure during surgery. But there isn't enough information to know if evening primrose oil or the other medications caused the

Medical professionals should consult the Professional Version at www.NaturalDatabase.com.

seizure. Be sure to tell your doctor what natural products you are taking before having surgery. To be on the safe side, you should stop taking evening primrose oil at least 2 weeks before surgery.

Phenothiazines. Taking evening primrose oil with phenothiazines might increase the risk of having a seizure in some people. Some phenothiazines include chlorpromazine (Thorazine), fluphenazine (Prolixin), trifluoperazine (Stelazine), thioridazine (Mellaril), and others.

EYEBRIGHT

What other names is the product known by?

Augentrostkraut, Euphraisiae herba, Euphrasia, Euphrasia officinalis. Eurphrasia rostkoviana, Herbed Euphraise.

What is it?

Eyebright is a plant. The above ground parts are used to make medicine.

Is it Effective?

The effectiveness ratings for **EYEBRIGHT** are as follows:

Insufficient Evidence to Rate Effectiveness for... Inflamed nasal passages, inflamed sinuses (sinusitis), colds, allergies, coughs, earaches, headache, and many other uses. Use directly on the eye for eye conditions, including fatigue, inflammation, infections, and other conditions.

How does it work?

The chemicals in eyebright might act as astringents and kill bacteria.

Are there safety concerns?

Eyebright might be safe for most people when taken by mouth. Eyebright, when used directly on the eye, may not be safe and is not recommended. It can be contaminated and cause eye infections. Side effects of eyebright tincture include confusion, headache, tearing, itching, redness, vision problems, sneezing, nausea, toothache, constipation, cough, trouble breathing, trouble sleeping (insomnia), sweating, and others.

Do not take eyebright if: You are pregnant or breast-feeding.

Are there any interactions with medications?

It is not known if eyebright interacts with any medicines.
Before taking eyebright, talk with your healthcare professional if you take any medications.

FALSE UNICORN

What other names is the product known by?

Blazing Star, Chamaelirium luteum, Chamaelirium carolianum, Fairywand, Helonias, Helonias dioica, Helonias lutea, Starwort, Veratrum luteum.

What is it?

False unicorn is an herb. The rhizome and root are used to make medicine.

Is it Effective?

The effectiveness ratings for **FALSE UNICORN** are as follows:

Insufficient Evidence to Rate Effectiveness for... Ovarian cysts, menstrual problems, menopause, vomiting, digestive problems, water retention, intestinal worms, and other conditions.

How does it work?

False unicorn might contain chemicals which stimulate the uterus and kill intestinal worms. It might also increase the production of urine (diuretic).

Are there safety concerns?

False unicorn seems to be safe for most adults. Large doses can cause nausea and vomiting.

Do not take false unicorn if: You are pregnant or breast-feeding. • You have stomach or intestinal disorders.

Are there any interactions with medications?

It is not known if false unicorn interacts with any medicines.
Before taking false unicorn, talk with your healthcare professional if you take any medications.

 Natural Medicines Comprehensive Database Consumer Version (209) 472-2244

FENNEL

What other names is the product known by?
Anethum Foeniculum, Bari-Sanuf, Bitter Fennel, Carosella, Common Fennel, Fennel Oil, Fennel Seed, Finnochio, Florence Fennel, Foeniculi Antheroleum, Foeniculum Officinale, Foeniculum Capillaceum, Foeniculum Vulgare, Garden Fennel, Large Fennel, Sanuf, Shatapuspha, Sweet Fennel, Wild Fennel.

What is it?
Fennel is an herb. The dried, ripe seeds and oil are used to make medicine.

Is it Effective?
The effectiveness ratings for **FENNEL** are as follows:
Insufficient Evidence to Rate Effectiveness for... Stomach upset and indigestion, airway inflammation, bronchitis, cough, mild spasms of the stomach and intestines, gas (flatulence), bloating (feeling of fullness), upper airway tract infection, and other conditions.

How does it work?
Fennel might relax the colon and decrease respiratory tract secretions.

Are there safety concerns?
Fennel seems to be safe for short-term use, but don't use it for extended periods. There is some concern that long-term use might not be safe.

Some people can have allergic skin reactions to fennel. People who are allergic to plants such as celery, carrot, and mugwort are more likely to also be allergic to fennel. Fennel can also make skin extra sensitive to sunlight and make it easier to get a sunburn.

Do not take fennel if: You are pregnant or breast-feeding. • You are allergic to carrots, celery, mugwort, or other plants in the Apiaceae family. • You have breast cancer. • You have uterine cancer. • You have ovarian cancer. • You have endometriosis. • You have uterine fibroids.

Are there any interactions with medications?
Birth control pills (Contraceptive drugs). Some birth control pills contain estrogen. Fennel might have some of the same effects as estrogen. But fennel isn't as strong as the estrogen in birth control pills. Taking fennel along with birth control pills might decrease the effectiveness of birth control pills. If you take birth control pills along with fennel, use an additional form of birth control such as a condom. Some birth control pills include ethinyl estradiol and levonorgestrel (Triphasil), ethinyl estradiol and norethindrone (Ortho-Novum 1/35, Ortho-Novum 7/7/7), and others.
Ciprofloxacin (Cipro). Ciprofloxacin (Cipro) is an antibiotic. Fennel might decrease how much ciprofloxacin (Cipro) the body absorbs. Taking fennel along with ciprofloxacin (Cipro) might decrease the effectiveness of ciprofloxacin (Cipro). To avoid this interaction take fennel at least one hour after ciprofloxacin (Cipro).
Estrogens. Large amounts of fennel might have some of the same effects as estrogen. But fennel isn't as strong as estrogen pills. Taking fennel along with estrogen pills might decrease the effects of estrogen pills. Some estrogen pills include conjugated equine estrogens (Premarin), ethinyl estradiol, estradiol, and others.
Tamoxifen (Nolvadex). Some types of cancer are affected by hormones in the body. Estrogen-sensitive cancers are cancers that are affected by estrogen levels in the body. Tamoxifen (Nolvadex) is used to help treat and prevent these types of cancer. Fennel seems to also affect estrogen levels in the body. Taking fennel along with tamoxifen might decrease the effectiveness of tamoxifen (Nolvadex). Do not take fennel if you are taking tamoxifen (Nolvadex).

FENUGREEK

What other names is the product known by?
Alholva, Bird's Foot, Bockshornklee, Bockshornsame, Chandrika, Foenugraeci Semen, Foenugreek, Greek Clover, Greek Hay, Greek Hay Seed, Hu Lu Ba, Medhika, Methi, Trigonella, Trigonella foenum-graecum.

What is it?
Fenugreek is a plant. The seed is used to make medicine.

Medical professionals should consult the Professional Version at www.NaturalDatabase.com.

Is it Effective?

The effectiveness ratings for **FENUGREEK** are as follows:

Insufficient Evidence to Rate Effectiveness for... Diabetes, high cholesterol, high triglycerides, stomach upset, decreased appetite, constipation, hardening of the arteries (atherosclerosis), gout, sexual problems (impotence), fever, baldness, and other conditions.

How does it work?

Fenugreek appears to slow absorption of sugars in the stomach and stimulate insulin. Both of these effects lower blood sugar in people with diabetes.

Are there safety concerns?

Fenugreek might be safe for most people when taken by mouth for medicinal purposes. Side effects include diarrhea, stomach upset, bloating, gas, and a "maple syrup" odor in urine. Fenugreek can cause nasal congestion, coughing, wheezing, facial swelling, and severe allergic reactions in hypersensitive people. Fenugreek might lower blood sugar. People with diabetes should watch for signs of low blood sugar (hypoglycemia) and check their blood sugars carefully.

Fenugreek might be unsafe for children. Some reports have linked fenugreek tea to loss of consciousness in children.

Do not use fenugreek if: You are pregnant or breast-feeding. • You are allergic to chickpeas, peanuts, soybeans, or green peas.

Are there any interactions with medications?

Medications that slow blood clotting (Anticoagulant / Antiplatelet drugs). Fenugreek might slow blood clotting. Taking fenugreek along with medications that also slow clotting might increase the chances of bruising and bleeding. Some medications that slow blood clotting include aspirin, clopidogrel (Plavix), diclofenac (Voltaren, Cataflam, others), ibuprofen (Advil, Motrin, others), naproxen (Anaprox, Naprosyn, others), dalteparin (Fragmin), enoxaparin (Lovenox), heparin, warfarin (Coumadin), and others.

Medications for diabetes (Antidiabetes drugs). Fenugreek might decrease blood sugar. Diabetes medications are also used to lower blood sugar. Taking fenugreek along with diabetes medications might cause your blood sugar to go too low. Monitor your blood sugar closely. The dose of your diabetes medication might need to be changed. Some medications used for diabetes include glimepiride (Amaryl), glyburide (DiaBeta, Glynase PresTab, Micronase), insulin, pioglitazone (Actos), rosiglitazone (Avandia), chlorpropamide (Diabinese), glipizide (Glucotrol), tolbutamide (Orinase), and others.

Warfarin (Coumadin). Warfarin (Coumadin) is used to slow blood clotting. Fenugreek might also slow blood clotting. Taking fenugreek along with warfarin (Coumadin) might increase the chances of bruising and bleeding. Be sure to have your blood checked regularly. The dose of your warfarin (Coumadin) might need to be changed.

FEVER BARK

What other names is the product known by?

Alstonia Bark, Alstonia constricta, Australian Febrifuge, Australian Fever Bush, Australian Quinine, Bitterbark, Devil's Bit, Devil Tree, Dita Bark, Pale Mara, Pali-Mara.

What is it?

Fever bark is the bark of a tree. A tea made from the bark is used as medicine.

Is it Effective?

The effectiveness ratings for **FEVER BARK** are as follows:

Insufficient Evidence to Rate Effectiveness for... Fever, hypertension, diarrhea, malaria, and arthritis-like pain (rheumatism).

How does it work?

Fever bark contains chemicals that can lower blood pressure.

Are there safety concerns?

Fever bark seems to be UNSAFE. It contains chemicals that can cause side effects such as nasal stuffiness, irritability, allergic reactions, eye problems, kidney problems, depression, and psychotic reactions. Large doses can cause heart problems and death.

Do not use fever bark if: You are pregnant or breast-feeding. • You have schizophrenia. • You have depression. • You have stomach ulcers.

Are there any interactions with medications?

Medications used during surgery (Anesthesia). Fever bark contains a chemical called reserpine. Taking reserpine along with medications used for surgery can cause heart problems. Be sure to tell your doctor what natural products you are taking before having surgery. You should stop taking fever bark at least two weeks before surgery.

Naloxone (Narcan). Fever bark contains a chemical that can affect the brain. This chemical is called yohimbine. Naloxone also affects the brain. Taking naloxone with yohimbine might increase the chance of side effects such as anxiety, nervousness, trembling, and hot flashes.

Phenothiazines. Fever bark contains a chemical called yohimbine. Some phenothiazines have effects similar to yohimbine. Taking fever bark and phenothiazines together might increase the effects and side effects of yohimbine. Some phenothiazines include chlorpromazine (Thorazine), fluphenazine (Prolixin), trifluoperazine (Stelazine), thioridazine (Mellaril), and others.

Stimulant drugs. Stimulant drugs speed up the nervous system. By speeding up the nervous system, stimulant medications can make you feel jittery and speed up your heartbeat. Fever bark might also speed up the nervous system. Taking fever bark along with stimulant drugs might cause serious problems including increased heart rate and high blood pressure. Avoid taking stimulant drugs along with fever bark. Some stimulant drugs include diethylpropion (Tenuate), epinephrine, phentermine (Ionamin), pseudoephedrine (Sudafed), and many others.

FEVERFEW

What other names is the product known by?

Altamisa, Bachelor's Buttons, Featerfoiul, Featherfew, Featherfoil, Flirtwort Midsummer Daisy, Matricaria eximia, Matricaria parthenium, Santa Maria, Tanaceti Parthenii, Tanacetum Parthenium, Chrysanthemum Parthenium, Leucanthemum Parthenium, Pyrethrum Parthenium.

What is it?

Feverfew is an herb. The leaves are used to make medicine.

Is it Effective?

The effectiveness ratings for **FEVERFEW** are as follows:

Possibly Effective for... Preventing migraine headache.

Possibly Ineffective for... Rheumatoid arthritis.

Insufficient Evidence to Rate Effectiveness for... Fever, menstrual irregularities, arthritis, psoriasis, allergies, asthma, dizziness, nausea, vomiting, earache, cancer, common cold, and many other conditions.

How does it work?

Feverfew leaves contain many different chemicals, including one called parthenolide. Parthenolide or other chemicals decrease factors in the body that might cause migraine headaches.

Are there safety concerns?

Feverfew is safe for most people when used short-term. Side effects might include upset stomach, heartburn, diarrhea, constipation, bloating, flatulence, nausea, and vomiting. Other reported side effects include nervousness, dizziness, headache, insomnia, joint stiffness, tiredness, menstrual changes, rash, palpitations, and weight gain.

The safety of feverfew beyond 4-months' use has not been studied.

Feverfew can also cause allergic reactions, especially in people who are allergic to ragweed, mums, marigolds, or daisies. If you have allergies, be sure to check with your healthcare provider before taking feverfew.

Some people chew feverfew instead of swallowing it in a pill. Chewing fresh feverfew leaves can cause mouth sores; swelling of the mouth, tongue, and lips; and loss of taste.

Do not take feverfew if: You are pregnant or breast-feeding.

Are there any interactions with medications?

Medications changed by the liver (Cytochrome P450 1A2 (CYP1A2) substrates). Some medications are changed and broken down by the liver. Feverfew might decrease how quickly the liver breaks down some medications. Taking feverfew along with some medications that are broken down by the liver can increase the effects and side effects of some medications. Before taking feverfew, talk to your healthcare provider if you take any medications that are changed by the liver. Some medications that are changed by the liver include amitriptyline (Elavil), haloperidol (Haldol), ondansetron (Zofran), propranolol (Inderal), theophylline (Theo-Dur, others), verapamil (Calan, Isoptin, others), and others.

Medications changed by the liver (Cytochrome P450 2C19 (CYP2C19) substrates). Some medications are changed and broken down by the liver. Feverfew might decrease how quickly the liver breaks down some medications. Taking feverfew along with some medications that are broken down by the liver can increase the effects and side effects of some medications. Before taking feverfew, talk to your healthcare provider if you take any medications that are changed by the liver. Some medications that are changed by the liver include omeprazole (Prilosec), lansoprazole (Prevacid), and pantoprazole (Protonix); diazepam (Valium); carisoprodol (Soma); nelfinavir (Viracept); and others.

Medications changed by the liver (Cytochrome P450 2C9 (CYP2C9) substrates). Some medications are changed and broken down by the liver. Feverfew might decrease how quickly the liver breaks down some medications. Taking feverfew along with some medications that are broken down by the liver can increase the effects and side effects of some medications. Before taking feverfew, talk to your healthcare provider if you take any medications that are changed by the liver. Some medications that are changed by the liver include diclofenac (Cataflam, Voltaren), ibuprofen (Motrin), meloxicam (Mobic), and piroxicam (Feldene); celecoxib (Celebrex); amitriptyline (Elavil); warfarin (Coumadin); glipizide (Glucotrol); losartan (Cozaar); and others.

Medications changed by the liver (Cytochrome P450 3A4 (CYP3A4) substrates). Some medications are changed and broken down by the liver. Feverfew might decrease how quickly the liver breaks down some medications. Taking feverfew along with some medications that are broken down by the liver can increase the effects and side effects of some medications. Before taking feverfew, talk to your healthcare provider if you are taking any medications that are changed by the liver. Some medications changed by the liver include lovastatin (Mevacor), ketoconazole (Nizoral), itraconazole (Sporanox), fexofenadine (Allegra), triazolam (Halcion), and many others.

Medications that slow blood clotting (Anticoagulant / Antiplatelet drugs). Feverfew might slow blood clotting. Taking feverfew along with medications that also slow clotting might increase the chances of bruising and bleeding. Some medications that slow blood clotting include aspirin, clopidogrel (Plavix), diclofenac (Voltaren, Cataflam, others), ibuprofen (Advil, Motrin, others), naproxen (Anaprox, Naprosyn, others), dalteparin (Fragmin), enoxaparin (Lovenox), heparin, warfarin (Coumadin), and others.

FICIN

What other names is the product known by?
Doctor Oje, Ficus insipida, Ficus anthelmintica, Ficus glabrata, Ficus laurfolia, Leche de Higueron, Leche de Oje, Oje.

What is it?
Ficin is a latex substance from the trunk of a tree.

Is it Effective?
The effectiveness ratings for **FICIN** are as follows:
Insufficient Evidence to Rate Effectiveness for... Treating worms and intestinal problems.

How does it work?
Ficin contains chemicals that might help break down proteins, and kill intestinal worms.

Are there safety concerns?
There isn't enough information to know if ficin is safe to take by mouth. Large amounts can cause severe diarrhea.

Don't use ficin on the skin. It can cause bleeding and allergic reactions.

Do not use ficin if: You are pregnant or breast-feeding.

Are there any interactions with medications?
It is not known if ficin interacts with any medicines.
Before taking ficin, talk with your healthcare professional if you take any medications.

FIELD SCABIOUS

What other names is the product known by?
Bluebuttons, Gypsy's-Rose, Knautia arvensis, Scabiosa arvensis.

What is it?
Field scabious is an herb. The above ground parts are used to make medicine.

Is it Effective?

The effectiveness ratings for **FIELD SCABIOUS** are as follows:
Insufficient Evidence to Rate Effectiveness for... Cough, sore throat, bruises, skin ulcers, eczema, anal fissures and itching, scabies, and roundworm.

How does it work?

Field scabious has chemicals that help to break up chest congestion by thinning mucous and making it easier to cough up (expectorant). It also has a drying effect on the skin.

Are there safety concerns?

There isn't enough information to know if field scabious is safe.

Do not use field scabious if: You are pregnant or breast-feeding.

Are there any interactions with medications?

It is not known if field scabious interacts with any medicines.
Before taking field scabious, talk with your healthcare professional if you take any medications.

FIG

What other names is the product known by?

Caricae Fructus, Feigen, Ficus carica.

What is it?

Fig is a tree. The fruit and leaves are used to make medicine.

Is it Effective?

The effectiveness ratings for **FIG** are as follows:
Insufficient Evidence to Rate Effectiveness for... Constipation, diabetes, and other conditions.

How does it work?

Fig leaf contains chemicals that might help people with type 1 diabetes use insulin more efficiently.

Are there safety concerns?

Fresh or dried fig fruit is safe for most people when used in food amounts. Fig leaf appears to be safe for most people when used short-term. In high doses fig latex, the waxy coating on the leaf, might cause bleeding in the digestive tract in some people.

Avoid excessive sun exposure when taking fig leaf because it can cause skin to become extra sensitive to the sun. Wear sunblock outside, especially if you are light-skinned. Fig fruit is unlikely to cause sun sensitivity. Skin contact with fig fruit or leaves can cause rash in sensitive people.

Do not use fig leaf or fig fruit in amounts larger than those found in food if: You are pregnant or breast-feeding.

Are there any interactions with medications?

Insulin. Fig leaf might decrease blood sugar. Insulin is also used to decrease blood sugar. Taking fig leaf along with insulin might cause your blood sugar to be too low. Monitor your blood sugar closely. The dose of your insulin might need to be changed.
Medications for diabetes (Antidiabetes drugs). Fig leaf supplements seem to lower blood sugar in people with diabetes. Diabetes medications are also used to lower blood sugar. Taking fig leaf along with diabetes medications might cause your blood sugar to go too low. Monitor your blood sugar closely. The dose of your diabetes medication might need to be changed. Some medications used for diabetes include glimepiride (Amaryl), glyburide (DiaBeta, Glynase PresTab, Micronase), insulin, pioglitazone (Actos), rosiglitazone (Avandia), chlorpropamide (Diabinese), glipizide (Glucotrol), tolbutamide (Orinase), and others.

CONSUMER VERSION

Medical professionals should consult the Professional Version at www.NaturalDatabase.com.

FIGWORT

What other names is the product known by?
Carpenter's Square, Common Figwort, Heal-all, Rosenoble, Scrophularia, Scrophularia mailandica, Scrophularia nodosa, Scrophula Plant, Throatwort.

What is it?
Figwort is an herb. The whole plant is used to make medicine.

Is it Effective?
The effectiveness ratings for **FIGWORT** are as follows:
Insufficient Evidence to Rate Effectiveness for... Eczema, itching, psoriasis, and hemorrhoids.

How does it work?
Figwort might contain substances which decrease swelling (inflammation).

Are there safety concerns?
There isn't enough information to know if figwort is safe.

Do not use figwort if: You are pregnant or breast-feeding. • You have diabetes. • You have a heart condition called ventricular tachycardia.

Are there any interactions with medications?
Water pills (Diuretic drugs). Figwort seems to work like "water pills." Figwort and "water pills" might cause the body to get rid of potassium along with water. Taking figwort along with "water pills" might decrease potassium in the body too much. Some "water pills" that can deplete potassium include chlorothiazide (Diuril), chlorthalidone (Thalitone), furosemide (Lasix), hydrochlorothiazide (HCTZ, Hydrodiuril, Microzide), and others.

FIR

What other names is the product known by?
Abies alba, Abies pectinata, Fir Tree, Norway Spruce, Picea abies, Picea excelsa, Piceae turiones recentes, Spruce, Spruce Fir.

What is it?
Fir is a plant. People use the shoot for medicine.

Is it Effective?
The effectiveness ratings for **FIR** are as follows:
Insufficient Evidence to Rate Effectiveness for... Colds, cough, bronchitis, fever, inflammation of the mouth and throat, nerve and muscle pain, tuberculosis, and other conditions.

How does it work?
Fir shoot may reduce mucus production in the airways and act as a mild antiseptic. The essential oil, when applied to the skin, increases blood flow to the area, causes redness, and creates a sensation of warmth which can help relieve pain in the tissue underneath.

Are there safety concerns?
Fir is possibly safe for most people. The potential side effects of fir are not known.

Do not use fir if: You are pregnant or breast-feeding. • You have asthma. • You have whooping cough.
Do not use fir on your skin (or added to bath water) if: You have skin injuries or skin diseases. • You have a fever. • You have an infection. • You have heart problems. • You have a condition of your muscles or arteries called hypertonia.

Are there any interactions with medications?
It is not known if fir interacts with any medicines.
Before taking fir, talk with your healthcare professional if you take any medications.

FIREWEED

What other names is the product known by?

Blood Vine, Blooming Sally, Chamaenerion angustifolium, Chamerion angustifolium, Epilobium angustifolium, Epilobium spicatum, Flowering Willow, French Willow, Great Willowherb, Persian Willow, Purple Rocket, Rosebay Willow, Tame Withy, Wickup, Wicopy, Willow Herb.

What is it?

Fireweed is an herb. The above ground parts of the plant are used to make medicine.

Is it Effective?

The effectiveness ratings for **FIREWEED** are as follows:
Insufficient Evidence to Rate Effectiveness for... Fevers, tumors, and wounds.

How does it work?

Fireweed might contain substances which reduce swelling (inflammation).

Are there safety concerns?

Fireweed seems to be safe for most adults.
Do not use fireweed if: You are pregnant or breast-feeding.

Are there any interactions with medications?

It is not known if fireweed interacts with any medicines.
Before taking fireweed, talk with your healthcare professional if you take any medications.

FISH OIL

What other names is the product known by?

Cod Liver Oil, Fish Oil Fatty Acids, Fish Body Oil, Fish Oils, Fish Liver Oil, Fish Liver Oils, Marine Oils, Menhaden Oil, N-3 Fatty Acids, N3-polyunsaturated Fatty Acids, Omega Fatty Acids, Omega-3 Fatty Acids, Omega-3 Fatty Acid, PUFA, Salmon Oil, W-3 Fatty Acids.

What is it?

Fish oils can be obtained from eating fish or by taking supplements. Fish oil supplements are usually made from mackerel, herring, tuna, halibut, salmon, cod liver, whale blubber, or seal blubber.

Is it Effective?

The effectiveness ratings for **FISH OIL** are as follows:
Effective for... Lowering fats called triglycerides.
Likely Effective for... Preventing heart disease and heart attacks.
Possibly Effective for... High blood pressure • Reducing stiffness in a kind of arthritis called rheumatoid arthritis • Menstrual pain (dysmenorrhea) • Abnormal sensitivity to cold (Raynaud's syndrome) • Preventing stroke. Moderate fish consumption (once or twice a week) seems to lower stroke risk, but very high fish consumption might increase stroke risk • Osteoporosis, alone or in combination with calcium and evening primrose oil • Preventing hardening of the arteries (atherosclerosis) • Improving night vision in children with a disorder called dyslexia • Preventing kidney problems • Bipolar disorder • Depression, when taken with conventional antidepressant medications • Promoting weight loss • Preventing endometrial cancer • Preventing eye disease (age-related maculopathy) • Reducing the risk of blood vessel re-blockage after heart bypass surgery or "balloon" catheterization (balloon angioplasty) • Preventing recurrent miscarriage in pregnant women with antiphospholipid syndrome • Preventing high blood pressure and kidney problems after heart transplant • Preventing damage to the kidneys and high blood pressure caused by taking a drug called cyclosporine • Improving movement disorders in children, in combination with evening primrose oil, thyme oil, and vitamin E (Efalex) • Preventing blockage of grafts used in kidney dialysis • Preventing age-related mental decline • Psoriasis when used intravenously • Lowering cholesterol • Slowing weight loss in patients with advanced cancer • Asthma in children • Developmental coordination disorder • Dry eye syndrome • Preventing cataracts.
Possibly Ineffective for... Gum infection (gingivitis) • Liver disease • Leg pain due to blood flow problems (claudication) • Preventing migraine headaches • Preventing muscle soreness caused by physical exercise • Breast pain • Skin rashes caused by allergic reactions • Stomach ulcers • Loss of appetite in people with advanced cancer.
Likely Ineffective for... Type 2 diabetes.
Insufficient Evidence to Rate Effectiveness for... Lung disease; pneumonia; hayfever; cystic fibrosis; chronic fatigue syndrome; attention deficit-hyperactivity disorder (ADHD); decreased kidney function; inflammatory bowel disease; complications during pregnancy; glaucoma; eczema in infants; schizophrenia; Lyme disease;

Natural Medicines Comprehensive Database Consumer Version   (209) 472-2244   **309**

CONSUMER VERSION

Medical professionals should consult the Professional Version at www.NaturalDatabase.com.

systemic lupus erythematosus (an immune system disorder); "prediabetes"; irregular heartbeat; preventing cancers such as oral and pharyngeal cancer, esophageal cancer, colon cancer, rectal cancer, breast cancer, prostate cancer, and ovarian cancer; and other conditions.

How does it work?
Fish oils contain certain "fatty acids" that reduce pain and swelling. These fatty acids also prevent the blood from clotting easily. This might make fish oils helpful for some heart conditions.

Are there safety concerns?
Fish oils are safe for most people. They can cause side effects including belching, bad breath, heartburn, nausea, loose stools, rash, and nosebleeds. Taking fish oil supplements with meals or freezing them can often decrease these side effects. Some fish meats are contaminated with mercury and other industrial and environmental chemicals. Fish oil supplements typically do not contain these contaminants.

High doses might keep blood from clotting and can INCREASE the chance of bleeding.

Do not take fish oils if: You have liver disease. • You are allergic to fish or seafood. • You have a condition called bipolar disorder. • You have an implantable defibrillator (a surgically placed device to prevent irregular heartbeat).

Are there any interactions with medications?
Birth control pills (Contraceptive drugs). Fish oils seem to help reduce some fat levels in the blood. These fats are called triglycerides. Birth control pills might decrease the effectiveness of fish oils by reducing these fat levels in the blood. Some birth control pills include ethinyl estradiol and levonorgestrel (Triphasil), ethinyl estradiol and norethindrone (Ortho-Novum 1/35, Ortho-Novum 7/7/7), and others.
Medications that slow blood clotting (Anticoagulant / Antiplatelet drugs). Fish oils might slow blood clotting. Taking fish oils along with medications that also slow clotting might increase the chances of bruising and bleeding. Some medications that slow blood clotting include aspirin, clopidogrel (Plavix), diclofenac (Voltaren, Cataflam, others), ibuprofen (Advil, Motrin, others), naproxen (Anaprox, Naprosyn, others), dalteparin (Fragmin), enoxaparin (Lovenox), heparin, warfarin (Coumadin), and others.
Medications for high blood pressure (Antihypertensive drugs). Fish oils seem to decrease blood pressure. Taking fish oils along with medications for high blood pressure might cause your blood pressure to go too low. Some medications for high blood pressure include captopril (Capoten), enalapril (Vasotec), losartan (Cozaar), valsartan (Diovan), diltiazem (Cardizem), Amlodipine (Norvasc), hydrochlorothiazide (HydroDiuril), furosemide (Lasix), and many others.

FLAXSEED

What other names is the product known by?
Atasi, Flax Seed, Graine De Lin, Leinsamen, Lini Semen, Linseed, Lint Bells, Linum, Linum usitatissimum, Winterlien.

What is it?
Flaxseed is the seed from the plant Linum usitatissimum. The seed or the seed oil is used to make medicine. The information on this page concerns medicine made from the seed only.

Is it Effective?
The effectiveness ratings for **FLAXSEED** are as follows:
Likely Effective for... Lowering cholesterol levels in people with high cholesterol.
Possibly Effective for... Improving kidney function in people with lupus • Relieving mild menopausal symptoms.
Possibly Ineffective for... Osteoporosis.
Insufficient Evidence to Rate Effectiveness for... Prostate cancer, diverticulitis, irritable bowel syndrome (IBS), constipation, stomach upset, bladder inflammation, lung cancer, breast cancer, skin irritation, attention deficit-hyperactivity disorder (ADHD), and other conditions.

How does it work?
Flaxseed binds with cholesterol in the gut and prevents it from being absorbed. Flaxseed is also a source of dietary fiber.

Are there safety concerns?
Flaxseed is safe for most people. Taking flaxseed might INCREASE the number of bowel movements each day. It might also cause bloating, gas, abdominal pain, constipation, diarrhea, stomachache, and nausea.

Flaxseed should be taken with plenty of water to prevent blockage in the gut.

Natural Medicines Comprehensive Database Consumer Version (209) 472-2244

Medical professionals should consult the Professional Version at www.NaturalDatabase.com.

Flaxseed might be safe to use while pregnant or breast-feeding, but talk to your healthcare professional before using it.

Do not take flaxseed if: You have a bleeding disorder. • You have high triglyceride levels. • You have bowel obstruction. • You have esophageal stricture. • You have intestinal inflammation. • You have breast cancer. • You have uterine cancer. • You have ovarian cancer. • You have endometriosis. • You have uterine fibroids.

Are there any interactions with medications?

Medications that slow blood clotting (Anticoagulant / Antiplatelet drugs). Flaxseed might slow blood clotting. Taking flaxseed along with medications that also slow clotting might increase the chances of bruising and bleeding. Some medications that slow blood clotting include aspirin, clopidogrel (Plavix), diclofenac (Voltaren, Cataflam, others), ibuprofen (Advil, Motrin, others), naproxen (Anaprox, Naprosyn, others), dalteparin (Fragmin), enoxaparin (Lovenox), heparin, warfarin (Coumadin), and others.

Medications for diabetes (Antidiabetes drugs). Flaxseed can decrease blood sugar levels. Diabetes medications are also used to lower blood sugar. Taking flaxseed along with diabetes medications might cause your blood sugar to be too low. Monitor your blood sugar closely. The dose of your diabetes medication might need to be changed. Some medications used for diabetes include glimepiride (Amaryl), glyburide (DiaBeta, Glynase PresTab, Micronase), insulin, pioglitazone (Actos), rosiglitazone (Avandia), chlorpropamide (Diabinese), glipizide (Glucotrol), tolbutamide (Orinase), and others.

FLAXSEED OIL

What other names is the product known by?
Atasi, Flax Oil, Graine De Lin, Linoleic Acid, Linseed Oil, Linum usitatissimum.

What is it?
Flaxseed is the seed from the plant Linum usitatissimum. The seed oil is used to make medicine.

Is it Effective?
The effectiveness ratings for **FLAXSEED OIL** are as follows:
Possibly Ineffective for... Rheumatoid arthritis.
Insufficient Evidence to Rate Effectiveness for... Constipation, cancer, anxiety, prostate problems, vaginal problems, weight loss, high cholesterol levels, and heart attack prevention.

How does it work?
Flaxseed oil is used for rheumatoid arthritis because it might help decrease swelling (inflammation).

Are there safety concerns?
Flaxseed oil is safe in the amounts found in foods. Medicinal amounts are probably safe for most adults, when used for 3 months or less. Large doses of 30 grams per day and higher can cause diarrhea.

Allergic reactions have occurred while taking flaxseed oil, and also in workers processing flaxseed products.

Do not use flaxseed oil as a medicine if: You are pregnant or breast-feeding. • You have a condition which makes you more likely to bleed.

Are there any interactions with medications?
Medications that slow blood clotting (Anticoagulant / Antiplatelet drugs). Flaxseed oil might slow blood clotting. Taking flaxseed oil along with medications that also slow clotting might increase the chances of bruising and bleeding. Some medications that slow blood clotting include aspirin, clopidogrel (Plavix), diclofenac (Voltaren, Cataflam, others), ibuprofen (Advil, Motrin, others), naproxen (Anaprox, Naprosyn, others), dalteparin (Fragmin), enoxaparin (Lovenox), heparin, warfarin (Coumadin), and others.

FLUORIDE

What other names is the product known by?
Acidulated Phosphate Fluoride, Fluorophosphate, Hydrogen Fluoride, Monofluorophosphate, MFP, Sodium Fluoride, Sodium Monofluorophosphate, Stannous Fluoride.

What is it?
Fluoride is a form of the chemical element fluorine. People use it for medicine.

Medical professionals should consult the Professional Version at www.NaturalDatabase.com.

Is it Effective?

The effectiveness ratings for **FLUORIDE** are as follows:

Effective for... Preventing tooth decay.

Possibly Effective for... Treating osteoporosis (bone loss).

Insufficient Evidence to Rate Effectiveness for... Preventing bone loss in people with rheumatoid arthritis and Crohn's disease (an intestinal disorder).

How does it work?

Fluoride protects teeth from the bacteria in plaque. It also promotes new bone formation.

Are there safety concerns?

Fluoride is safe for most people when consumed in amounts added to public water supplies and used in toothpastes, mouthwashes, and other dental products. Low doses (up to 20 mg per day of elemental fluoride) of supplemental fluoride taken by mouth appear to be safe for most people. High doses are unsafe and can weaken bones and ligaments, and cause muscle weakness and nervous system problems. High doses of fluoride in children before their permanent teeth come through the gums can cause tooth discoloration.

Are there any interactions with medications?

It is not known if fluoride interacts with any medicines.

Before taking fluoride, talk with your healthcare professional if you take any medications.

FO-TI

What other names is the product known by?

Chinese Cornbind, Chinese Knotweed, Climbing Knotweed, Flowery Knotweed, Fo-Ti-Tient, He Shou Wu, Ho Shou Wu, Multiflora Preparata, Poligonum, Poligonum multiflorum, Polygonum, Polygonum multiflorum, Radix Polygoni Multiflori, Radix Polygoni Shen Min, Shen Min, Shou Wu, Shou Wu Pian, Zhihe Shou Wu, Zi Shou Wu.

What is it?

Fo-ti is an herb. The processed (cured) root of the plant is used to make medicine.

Is it Effective?

The effectiveness ratings for **FO-TI** are as follows:

Insufficient Evidence to Rate Effectiveness for... Liver and kidney problems, high cholesterol, insomnia, lower back and knee soreness, premature graying, dizziness, and other conditions.

How does it work?

Fo-ti cured root might affect the levels of various chemicals in the body which have been suggested to have anti-aging effects.

Are there safety concerns?

Fo-ti might be unsafe to take by mouth due to concerns that it might cause liver damage in both adults and children. Fo-ti has been linked to liver damage in several reports.

There isn't enough information available to know if fo-ti is safe when applied topically.

Do not use fo-ti if: You are pregnant or breast-feeding. • You have liver disease.

Are there any interactions with medications?

Digoxin (Lanoxin). Fo-ti is a type of laxative called a stimulant laxative. Stimulant laxatives can decrease potassium levels in the body. Low potassium levels can increase the risk of side effects of digoxin (Lanoxin).

Medications changed by the liver (Cytochrome P450 1A2 (CYP1A2) substrates). Some medications are changed and broken down by the liver. Fo-ti might decrease how quickly the liver breaks down some medications. Taking fo-ti along with some medications that are broken down by the liver can increase the effects and side effects of some medications. Before taking fo-ti, talk to your healthcare provider if you take any medications that are changed by the liver. Some medications that are changed by the liver include amitriptyline (Elavil), haloperidol (Haldol), ondansetron (Zofran), propranolol (Inderal), theophylline (Theo-Dur, others), verapamil (Calan, Isoptin, others), and others.

Medications changed by the liver (Cytochrome P450 2C19 (CYP2C19) substrates). Some medications are changed and broken down by the liver. Fo-ti might decrease how quickly the liver breaks down some medications. Taking fo-ti along with some medications that are broken down by the liver can increase the effects and side effects of some medications. Before taking fo-ti, talk to your healthcare provider if you take any medications that are changed by the liver. Some medications that are changed by the liver include omeprazole (Prilosec), lansoprazole (Prevacid), and pantoprazole (Protonix); diazepam (Valium); carisoprodol (Soma); nelfinavir (Viracept); and others.

Medications changed by the liver (Cytochrome P450 2C9 (CYP2C9) substrates). Some medications are changed and broken down by the liver. Fo-ti might decrease how quickly the liver breaks down some medications. Taking fo-ti along with some medications that are broken down by the liver can increase the effects and side effects of some medications. Before taking fo-ti, talk to your healthcare provider if you take any medications that are changed by the liver. Some medications that are changed by the liver include diclofenac (Cataflam, Voltaren), ibuprofen (Motrin), meloxicam (Mobic), and piroxicam (Feldene); celecoxib (Celebrex); amitriptyline (Elavil); warfarin (Coumadin); glipizide (Glucotrol); losartan (Cozaar); and others.

Medications changed by the liver (Cytochrome P450 3A4 (CYP3A4) substrates). Some medications are changed and broken down by the liver. Fo-ti might decrease how quickly the liver breaks down some medications. Taking fo-ti along with some medications that are broken down by the liver can increase the effects and side effects of some medications. Before taking fo-ti, talk to your healthcare provider if you are taking any medications that are changed by the liver. Some medications changed by the liver include lovastatin (Mevacor), ketoconazole (Nizoral), itraconazole (Sporanox), fexofenadine (Allegra), triazolam (Halcion), and many others.

Medications that can harm the liver (Hepatotoxic drugs). Fo-ti might harm the liver. Taking fo-ti along with medication that might also harm the liver can increase the risk of liver damage. Do not take fo-ti if you are taking a medication that can harm the liver. Some medications that can harm the liver include acetaminophen (Tylenol and others), amiodarone (Cordarone), carbamazepine (Tegretol), isoniazid (INH), methotrexate (Rheumatrex), methyldopa (Aldomet), fluconazole (Diflucan), itraconazole (Sporanox), erythromycin (Erythrocin, Ilosone, others), phenytoin (Dilantin) , lovastatin (Mevacor), pravastatin (Pravachol), simvastatin (Zocor), and many others.

Medications for diabetes (Antidiabetes drugs). Fo-ti might decrease blood sugar. Diabetes medications are also used to lower blood sugar. Taking fo-ti along with diabetes medications might cause your blood sugar to go too low. Monitor your blood sugar closely. The dose of your diabetes medication might need to be changed. Some medications used for diabetes include glimepiride (Amaryl), glyburide (DiaBeta, Glynase PresTab, Micronase), insulin, pioglitazone (Actos), rosiglitazone (Avandia), chlorpropamide (Diabinese), glipizide (Glucotrol), tolbutamide (Orinase), and others.

Stimulant laxatives. Fo-ti is a type of laxative called a stimulant laxative. Stimulant laxatives speed up the bowels. Taking fo-ti along with other stimulant laxatives could speed up the bowels too much and cause dehydration and low minerals in the body. Some stimulant laxatives include bisacodyl (Correctol, Dulcolax), cascara, castor oil (Purge), senna (Senokot), and others.

Water pills (Diuretic drugs). Fo-ti is a laxative. Some laxatives can decrease potassium in the body. "Water pills" can also decrease potassium in the body. Taking fo-ti along with "water pills" might decrease potassium in the body too much. Some "water pills" that can decrease potassium include chlorothiazide (Diuril), chlorthalidone (Thalitone), furosemide (Lasix), hydrochlorothiazide (HCTZ, HydroDIURIL, Microzide), and others.

FOLIC ACID

What other names is the product known by?

B Complex Vitamin, Folacin, Folate, L-methylfoldate, Methylfolate, Vitamin B9, Pteroylglutamic Acid, Pteroylmonoglutamic Acid, Pteroylpolyglutamate.

What is it?

Folic acid is a water-soluble vitamin that is often added to cold cereals, flour, breads, pasta, bakery items, cookies, and crackers. Some foods that are naturally high in folic acid include spinach, okra, asparagus, beans, beef liver, and orange and tomato juice.

Is it Effective?

The effectiveness ratings for **FOLIC ACID** are as follows:

Effective for... Treating and preventing folic acid deficiency.

Likely Effective for... Lowering homocysteine levels in people with kidney disease • Lowering homocysteine levels ("hyperhomocysteinemia") in people with high amounts of homocysteine in their blood. High levels of homocysteine have been linked to heart disease and stroke • Reducing harmful effects of a medicine called methotrexate • Decreasing the risk of certain birth defects when taken by pregnant women • Kidney problems,

Possibly Effective for... Reducing the risk of getting colorectal cancer. Increasing consumption of dietary folate and supplemental folic acid seems to lower the chances of developing colon cancer, but does not seem to help people who already have colon cancer • Reducing the risk of pancreatic cancer • Reducing the risk of breast cancer • Depression, when used with conventional antidepressant medicines • Treating a skin disease called vitiligo • Gum problems due to a drug called phenytoin when applied to the gums • Treating gum disease during pregnancy, when used in mouthwash.

Possibly Ineffective for... Reducing the risk of heart attack, stroke, and other related conditions in people with coronary heart disease • Reducing the possibility of another stroke • Reducing harmful effects of a medicine called lometrexol • Chronic fatigue syndrome • Improving thinking and memory in people aged 65 and older, when used in combination with vitamin B6 and vitamin B12.

Likely Ineffective for... Treating an inherited disease called Fragile-X syndrome.

Insufficient Evidence to Rate Effectiveness for... Preventing re-blockage of blood vessels after angioplasty, liver disease, alcoholism, Alzheimer's disease, preventing pregnancy loss, preventing cervical cancer, infertility, lung cancer, restless leg syndrome (RLS), sickle cell disease, cancer due to a disease called ulcerative colitis, osteoporosis (brittle bones), and other conditions.

How does it work?

Folic acid is needed for the proper development of the human body. It is involved in producing the genetic material called DNA and in numerous other bodily functions.

Are there safety concerns?

Folic acid is safe for most people. Most adults do not experience any side effects when consuming the recommended amount each day, which is 400 mcg. Don't take more than 400 mcg per day unless directed by your healthcare professional. High doses of folic acid might cause abdominal cramps, diarrhea, rash, sleep disorders, irritability, confusion, nausea, stomach upset, behavior changes, skin reactions, seizures, gas, excitability, and other side effects. Preliminary research suggests it might increase the risk of heart attack in people who have heart problems. Other preliminary research suggests high doses might increase the risk of cancer.

When used in recommended amounts, folic acid is safe for pregnant or breast-feeding women. For pregnant women, 600 mcg per day is recommended. For breast-feeding women, 500 mcg per day is recommended. Do not use folic acid in doses greater than 400 mcg per day without medical advice if: You have anemia. • You have epilepsy or a seizure disorder. • You have a psychiatric condition such as schizophrenia. • You have a heart condition. • You have cancer or have had cancer.

Are there any interactions with medications?

Fosphenytoin (Cerebyx). Fosphenytoin (Cerebyx) is used for seizures. The body breaks down fosphenytoin (Cerebyx) to get rid of it. Folic acid can increase how quickly the body breaks down fosphenytoin (Cerebyx). Taking folic acid along with fosphenytoin (Cerebyx) might decrease the effectiveness of fosphenytoin (Cerebyx) for preventing seizures.

Methotrexate (MTX, Rheumatrex). Methotrexate (MTX, Rheumatrex) works by decreasing the effects of folic acid in the body's cells. Taking folic acid pills along with methotrexate might decrease the effectiveness of methotrexate (MTX, Rheumatrex).

Phenobarbital (Luminal). Phenobarbital (Luminal) is used for seizures. Taking folic acid can decrease how well phenobarbital (Luminal) works for preventing seizures.

Phenytoin (Dilantin). The body breaks down phenytoin (Dilantin) to get rid of it. Folic acid might increase how quickly the body breaks down phenytoin (Dilantin). Taking folic acid and taking phenytoin (Dilantin) might decrease the effectiveness of phenytoin (Dilantin) and increase the possibility of seizures.

Primidone (Mysoline). Primidone (Mysoline) is used for seizures. Folic acid might cause seizure in some people. Taking folic acid can along with primidone (Mysoline) might decrease how well primidone works for preventing seizures.

Pyrimethamine (Daraprim). Pyrimethamine (Daraprim) is used to treat parasite infections. Folic acid might decrease the effectiveness of pyrimethamine (Daraprim) for treating parasite infections.

FOOL'S PARSLEY

What other names is the product known by?

Aethusa cynapium, Dog Parsley, Dog Poison, Fool's-Cicely, Lesser Hemlock, Small Hemlock.

What is it?

Fool's parsley is an herb. The above ground parts are used to make medicine.

Is it Effective?

The effectiveness ratings for **FOOL'S PARSLEY** are as follows:
Insufficient Evidence to Rate Effectiveness for... Stomach and intestinal complaints, diarrhea, and convulsions.

How does it work?

There isn't enough information available to know how fool's parsley works.

Are there safety concerns?

Fool's parsley is UNSAFE. Avoid using it. It might cause serious, potentially life-threatening poisonings.
Fool's parsley got its name because it looks a lot like young garden parsley. Be careful not to confuse the two, since fool's parsley is poisonous.
Do not use fool's parsley if: You are pregnant or breast-feeding.

Are there any interactions with medications?

It is not known if fool's parsley interacts with any medicines.
Before taking fool's parsley, talk with your healthcare professional if you take any medications.

FORGET-ME-NOT

What other names is the product known by?

Field Scorpion-Grass, Myosotis arvensis.

What is it?

Forget-me-not is an herb. The whole plant is used to make medicine.

Is it Effective?

The effectiveness ratings for **FORGET-ME-NOT** are as follows:
Insufficient Evidence to Rate Effectiveness for... Lung problems and nosebleeds.

How does it work?

There isn't enough information available to know how forget-me-not works.

Are there safety concerns?

Forget-me-not might be UNSAFE. Avoid using. It belongs to a plant family that contains chemicals that can cause severe liver damage and cancer.

Do not use forget-me-not if: You are pregnant or breast-feeding.

Are there any interactions with medications?

It is not known if forget-me-not interacts with any medicines.
Before taking forget-me-not, talk with your healthcare professional if you take any medications.

FORSKOLIN

What other names is the product known by?

17beta-acetoxy-8,13-epoxy-1alpha, 6beta,9alpha-trihydroxylabd-14-en-11-one, Borforsin, Coleus barbatus, Coleus forskolii, Coleus forskohlii, Colforsin, Forskohlii, Forskolin, HL-362, L-75-1362B, Plectranthus barbatus.

What is it?

Forskolin is extracted from the roots of the plant Plectranthus barbatus (Coleus forskohlii).

Is it Effective?

The effectiveness ratings for **FORSKOLIN** are as follows:
Possibly Effective for... Use by injection for a heart condition called idiopathic congestive cardiomyopathy • Asthma, when inhaled (breathed in).
Insufficient Evidence to Rate Effectiveness for... Use by mouth for asthma, allergies, skin conditions such as eczema or psoriasis, obesity, dysmenorrhea (period pains), irritable bowel syndrome (IBS), urinary tract infections (UTIs) and bladder infections, high blood pressure, angina (chest pain), cancer, thrombosis (blood clots), insomnia, sexual problems in men, or convulsions. Use by injection for congestive heart failure (CHF). Use as eye drops for glaucoma (increased pressure in the eyes).

How does it work?

Forskolin works on muscles in the heart and in the walls of the blood vessels. It produces a more powerful heartbeat and widening of the blood vessels, which lowers blood pressure.

Are there safety concerns?

Forskolin is possibly safe for most adults when used appropriately by injection, inhalation (breathing in), or as eye drops.

Medical professionals should consult the Professional Version at www.NaturalDatabase.com.

When given by injection, forskolin can cause flushing and low blood pressure. When inhaled (breathed in), forskolin can cause throat irritation, cough, tremor, and restlessness. Eye drops containing forskolin can cause stinging.

Do not use forskolin if: You are pregnant or breast-feeding. • You have heart or blood pressure problems. • You have any condition which makes you more likely to bleed.

Are there any interactions with medications?

Medications that slow blood clotting (Anticoagulant / Antiplatelet drugs). Forskolin might slow blood clotting. Taking forskolin along with medications that also slow clotting might increase the chances of bruising and bleeding. Some medications that slow blood clotting include aspirin, clopidogrel (Plavix), diclofenac (Voltaren, Cataflam, others), ibuprofen (Advil, Motrin, others), naproxen (Anaprox, Naprosyn, others), dalteparin (Fragmin), enoxaparin (Lovenox), heparin, warfarin (Coumadin), and others.

Medications for high blood pressure (Calcium channel blockers). Forskolin might decrease blood pressure. Taking forskolin with medication for high blood pressure might cause your blood pressure to go too low. Some medications for high blood pressure include nifedipine (Adalat, Procardia), verapamil (Calan, Isoptin, Verelan), diltiazem (Cardizem), isradipine (DynaCirc), felodipine (Plendil), amlodipine (Norvasc), and others.

Medications that increase blood flow to the heart (Nitrates). Forskolin increases blood flow. Taking forskolin with medications that increase blood flow to the heart might increase the chance of dizziness and lightheadedness. Some of these medications that increase blood flow to the heart include nitroglycerin (Nitro-Bid, Nitro-Dur, Nitrostat) and isosorbide (Imdur, Isordil, Sorbitrate).

FORSYTHIA

What other names is the product known by?

Forsythia Fructus, Forsythia koreana, Forsythia suspensa, Forsythia Suspensa Fructus, Syringa suspensa, Forsythia viridissima, Golden Bell, Lian Qiao, Lien Chiao, Rengyo, Weeping Golden Bell.

What is it?

Forsythia is a plant. The fruit is used for medicine.

Is it Effective?

The effectiveness ratings for **FORSYTHIA** are as follows:

Insufficient Evidence to Rate Effectiveness for... Inflammation of small air passages in the lung (bronchiolitis), tonsillitis, pharyngitis, fever, gonorrhea, and inflammation.

How does it work?

Forsythia might decrease inflammation. However, more information is needed to determine how forsythia might work.

Are there safety concerns?

It is not known if forsythia is safe when taken by mouth. There is some information that an injectable form might be safe when used in children.

Do not use forsythia if: You are pregnant or breast-feeding.

Are there any interactions with medications?

Medications that slow blood clotting (Anticoagulant / Antiplatelet drugs). Forsythia might slow blood clotting. Taking forsythia along with medications that also slow clotting might increase the chances of bruising and bleeding. Some medications that slow blood clotting include aspirin, clopidogrel (Plavix), diclofenac (Voltaren, Cataflam, others), ibuprofen (Advil, Motrin, others), naproxen (Anaprox, Naprosyn, others), dalteparin (Fragmin), enoxaparin (Lovenox), heparin, warfarin (Coumadin), and others.

FRANKINCENSE

What other names is the product known by?

Bible Frankincense, Boswellia carteri, Boswellia sacra, Olibanum.

What is it?

Frankincense is the hardened gum-like material (resin) that comes from cuts made in the trunk of the Boswellia carteri tree. People use it to make medicine.

Is it Effective?

The effectiveness ratings for **FRANKINCENSE** are as follows:
Insufficient Evidence to Rate Effectiveness for... Colic, intestinal gas (flatulence), and other conditions.

How does it work?

There isn't enough information available to know how frankincense works.

Are there safety concerns?

Frankincense seems safe for use by most adults. It might cause irritation when applied to the skin.

Do not use frankincense if: You are pregnant or breast-feeding.

Are there any interactions with medications?

It is not known if frankincense interacts with any medicines.
Before taking frankincense, talk with your healthcare professional if you take any medications.

FRINGETREE

What other names is the product known by?

Chionanthus virginicus, Gray Beard Tree, Old Man's Beard, Poison Ash, Snowdrop Tree, Snowflower, White Fringe.

What is it?

Fringetree is a small tree or shrub. The dried root and bark are used to make medicine.

Is it Effective?

The effectiveness ratings for **FRINGETREE** are as follows:
Insufficient Evidence to Rate Effectiveness for... Liver problems, gallstones, water retention, and other conditions.

How does it work?

There isn't enough information available to know how fringetree works.

Are there safety concerns?

There isn't enough information to know if fringetree is safe. It has a very bitter taste.

Do not use fringetree if: You are pregnant or breast-feeding.

Are there any interactions with medications?

It is not known if fringetree interacts with any medicines.
Before taking fringetree, talk with your healthcare professional if you take any medications.

FROSTWORT

What other names is the product known by?

Frost Plant, Frostweed, Helianthemum canadense, Rock-Rose, Sun Rose.

What is it?

Frostwort is an herb. The above ground parts are used to make medicine.

Is it Effective?

The effectiveness ratings for **FROSTWORT** are as follows:
Insufficient Evidence to Rate Effectiveness for... Digestive problems and ulcers.

How does it work?

Frostwort might help reduce skin inflammation and have a drying (astringent) effect on the tissues.

Are there safety concerns?

There isn't enough information to know if frostwort is safe.

Do not use frostwort if: You are pregnant or breast-feeding.

Medical professionals should consult the Professional Version at www.NaturalDatabase.com.

Medical professionals should consult the Professional Version at www.NaturalDatabase.com.

Are there any interactions with medications?

It is not known if frostwort interacts with any medicines.

Before taking frostwort, talk with your healthcare professional if you take any medications.

FRUCTO-OLIGOSACCHARIDES

What other names is the product known by?

Beta-D-fructofuranosidase, Chicory Inulin Hydrolysate, FOS, Fructo Oligo Saccharides, Fructooligosaccharides, Inulin Hydrolysate, Oligofructose, Oligosaccharides, Prebiotic, SC-FOS, Short Chain Fructo-Oligosaccharides.

What is it?

Fructo-oligosaccharides are made up of plant sugars linked in chains. People use the sugars to make medicine.

Is it Effective?

The effectiveness ratings for **FRUCTO-OLIGOSACCHARIDES** are as follows:

Possibly Ineffective for... Preventing traveler's diarrhea.

Insufficient Evidence to Rate Effectiveness for... Promoting growth of bacteria in the gut, high cholesterol levels, and constipation.

How does it work?

Fructo-oligosaccharides pass undigested into the colon where they increase bowel mass and promote growth of certain bacteria that are thought to be beneficial.

Are there safety concerns?

Fructo-oligosaccharides can cause intestinal gas (flatulence), intestinal noises, bloating, stomach cramps, and diarrhea. These effects are usually mild if the dose is less than 10 grams per day.

Do not use fructo-oligosaccharides if: You are pregnant or breast-feeding.

Are there any interactions with medications?

It is not known if fructo-oligosaccharides interact with any medicines.

Before taking fructo-oligosaccharides, talk with your healthcare professional if you take any medications.

FUMITORY

What other names is the product known by?

Beggary, Earth Smoke, Fumaria officinalis, Fumiterry, Fumus, Hedge Fumitory, Herba fumariae, Vapor, Wax Dolls.

What is it?

Fumitory is a shrub. The above ground parts are used to make medicine.

Is it Effective?

The effectiveness ratings for **FUMITORY** are as follows:

Insufficient Evidence to Rate Effectiveness for... Spasms of the gut, skin conditions, eye irritation, heart problems, bile (a fluid secreted from the liver) disorders, and other conditions.

How does it work?

Fumitory contains a substance that may reduce spasms of the bile duct or gut.

Are there safety concerns?

Fumitory seems safe for most adults when used in the recommended amounts. Large amounts can cause trembling, convulsions, and death.

Don't use eye drop preparations of fumitory that haven't been commercially sterilized.

Do not use fumitory if: You are pregnant or breast-feeding.

Are there any interactions with medications?

It is not known if fumitory interacts with any medicines.

Before taking fumitory, talk with your healthcare professional if you take any medications.

GABA (GAMMA-AMINOBUTYRIC ACID)

What other names is the product known by?
GABA, Gamma Amino Butyric Acid.

What is it?
GABA is a chemical that is made in the brain.

Is it Effective?
The effectiveness ratings for **GABA (GAMMA-AMINOBUTYRIC ACID)** are as follows:
Insufficient Evidence to Rate Effectiveness for... Relieving anxiety, elevating mood, relieving premenstrual syndrome (PMS), treating attention deficit-hyperactivity disorder (ADHD), promoting lean muscle growth, burning fat, stabilizing blood pressure, and relieving pain.

How does it work?
GABA works by blocking brain signals (neurotransmissions).

Are there safety concerns?
There isn't enough information available to know if GABA is safe for use.

Do not use GABA if: You are pregnant or breast-feeding.

Are there any interactions with medications?
It is not known if GABA interacts with any medicines.
Before taking GABA, talk with your healthcare professional if you take any medications.

GALBANUM

What other names is the product known by?
Ferula gummosa, Galbanum Gum, Galbanum Gum Resin, Galbanum Oleogum Resin, Galbanum Oleoresin.

What is it?
Galbanum is a gum-like material (resin) from the roots and trunk of a tree. It is used to make medicine.

Is it Effective?
The effectiveness ratings for **GALBANUM** are as follows:
Insufficient Evidence to Rate Effectiveness for... Digestive problems, intestinal gas (flatulence), reducing spasms, coughs, healing wounds, and other conditions.

How does it work?
Galbanum might help get rid of certain types of bacteria.

Are there safety concerns?
Galbanum seems safe for use when applied directly to the skin. There isn't enough information available to know if it is safe to take by mouth as a medicine.

Do not use galbanum in amounts larger than typically found in foods if: You are pregnant or breast-feeding.

Are there any interactions with medications?
It is not known if galbanum interacts with any medicines.
Before taking galbanum, talk with your healthcare professional if you take any medications.

GAMBOGE

What other names is the product known by?
Camboge, Gambodia, Garcinia hanburyi, Gummigutta, Gutta Cambodia, Gutta Gamba, Tom Rong.

What is it?
Gamboge is a gum-like substance (resin) from the trunk of a tree.

CONSUMER VERSION

Medical professionals should consult the Professional Version at www.NaturalDatabase.com.

Is it Effective?

The effectiveness ratings for **GAMBOGE** are as follows:
Insufficient Evidence to Rate Effectiveness for... Constipation or intestinal worms.

How does it work?

Gamboge has a strong laxative effect.

Are there safety concerns?

Gamboge seems to be UNSAFE. It can cause stomach pain and vomiting.

Large amounts are poisonous and may cause death.

Do not use gamboge if: You are pregnant or breast-feeding. • You have heart problems. • You have nausea or vomiting. • You have stomach pain, ulcers, or obstruction. • You have Crohn's disease, ulcerative colitis, or appendicitis.

Are there any interactions with medications?

Digoxin (Lanoxin). Gamboge is a type of laxative called a stimulant laxative. Stimulant laxatives can decrease potassium levels in the body. Low potassium levels can increase the risk of side effects of digoxin (Lanoxin).
Medications for inflammation (Corticosteroids). Some medications for inflammation can decrease potassium in the body. Gamboge is a type of laxative that might also decrease potassium in the body. Taking gamboge along with some medications for inflammation might decrease potassium in the body too much. Some medications for inflammation include dexamethasone (Decadron), hydrocortisone (Cortef), methylprednisolone (Medrol), prednisone (Deltasone), and others.
Stimulant laxatives. Gamboge is a type of laxative called a stimulant laxative. Stimulant laxatives speed up the bowels. Taking gamboge along with other stimulant laxatives could speed up the bowels too much and cause dehydration and low minerals in the body. Some stimulant laxatives include bisacodyl (Correctol, Dulcolax), cascara, castor oil (Purge), senna (Senokot), and others.
Water pills (Diuretic drugs). Gamboge is a laxative. Some laxatives can decrease potassium in the body. "Water pills" can also decrease potassium in the body. Taking gamboge along with "water pills" might decrease potassium in the body too much. Some "water pills" that can decrease potassium include chlorothiazide (Diuril), chlorthalidone (Thalitone), furosemide (Lasix), hydrochlorothiazide (HCTZ, HydroDiuril, Microzide), and others.

GAMMA BUTYROLACTONE (GBL)

What other names is the product known by?

1,2-Butanolide, 2,3-dihydro furanone, 2(3H)-Furanone Dihydro, 3-Hydroxybutyric Acid Lactone, 4-Butanolide, 4-Butyrolactone, 4-Hydroxybutanoic Acid Lactone, Butyrolactone, Butyrolactone Gamma, Dihydro-2(3H)-Furanone, Gamma Butyrolactone, Gamma Hydroxybutyric Acid Lactone, Tetrahydro-2-Furanone.

What is it?

Gamma butyrolactone is a chemical. People use it as medicine. Be careful not to confuse gamma butyrolactone (GBL) with gamma hydroxybutyrate (GHB).

Is it Effective?

The effectiveness ratings for **GAMMA BUTYROLACTONE (GBL)** are as follows:
Insufficient Evidence to Rate Effectiveness for... Relaxation, calming, increased mental clarity, fat loss, use as a body or muscle "builder," recreational drug use, releasing growth hormone, improving athletic performance, trouble sleeping (insomnia), relieving depression and stress, prolonging life, improving sexual performance and pleasure, and other conditions.

How does it work?

Gamma butyrolactone is converted in the body to gamma hydroxybutyrate (GHB) which affects several nerve pathways in the brain.

Are there safety concerns?

Gamma butyrolactone (GBL) is UNSAFE. It is illegal to manufacture or sell GBL. Use of GBL, or the closely related gamma hydroxybutyrate (GHB) and butanediol (BD), has been linked to deaths and cases of serious side effects. These serious side effects include bowel incontinence, vomiting, mental changes, sedation, agitation, combativeness, memory loss, serious breathing and heart problems, fainting, seizures, coma, and death. The effects can be made worse by alcohol or narcotics (opiates such as morphine, heroin, and others). Long-term use may lead to withdrawal symptoms including insomnia, tremor, and anxiety.
GBL is UNSAFE and should not be taken by anyone. Certain people are at even more risk for side effects.

Medical professionals should consult the Professional Version at www.NaturalDatabase.com.

Do not take GBL if: You are pregnant or breast-feeding. • You have epilepsy or a seizure disorder. • You have high blood pressure. • You have an irregular heartbeat.

Are there any interactions with medications?

Alcohol. Alcohol can cause sleepiness and drowsiness. Taking GBL along with alcohol might greatly increase sleepiness and drowsiness caused by alcohol. Taking GBL along with alcohol can lead to serious side effects. Do not take GBL if you have been drinking.

Amphetamines. Amphetamines are drugs that can speed up your nervous system. GBL is changed in the body to GHB (gamma hydroxybutyrate). GHB can slow down your nervous system. Taking GBL along with amphetamines can lead to serious side effects.

Haloperidol (Haldol). GBL can affect the brain. Haloperidol (Haldol) can also affect the brain. Taking haloperidol (Haldol) along with GBL might cause serious side effects.

Medications for mental conditions (Antipsychotic drugs). GBL can affect the brain. Medications for mental conditions also affect the brain. Taking GBL along with medications for mental conditions might increase the effects and serious side effects of GBL. Do not take GBL if you are taking medications for a mental condition. Some of these medications include fluphenazine (Permitil, Prolixin), haloperidol (Haldol), chlorpromazine (Thorazine), prochlorperazine (Compazine), thioridazine (Mellaril), trifluoperazine (Stelazine), and others.

Medications for pain (Narcotic drugs). Some medications for pain can cause sleepiness and drowsiness. GBL might also cause sleepiness and drowsiness. Taking GBL along with some medications for pain might cause severe side effects. Do not take GBL if you are taking medications for pain. Some medications for pain include meperidine (Demerol), hydrocodone, morphine, OxyContin, and many others.

Medications used to prevent seizures (Anticonvulsants). Medications used to prevent seizures affect chemicals in the brain. GBL is changed in the body to one of these brain chemicals called GABA. Taking GBL along with medications used to prevent seizures might decrease the effects of GBL. Some medications used to prevent seizures include phenobarbital, primidone (Mysoline), valproic acid (Depakene), gabapentin (Neurontin), carbamazepine (Tegretol), phenytoin (Dilantin), and others.

Muscle relaxants. Muscle relaxants can cause drowsiness. GBL can also cause drowsiness. Taking GBL along with muscle relaxants might cause too much drowsiness and serious side effects. Do not take GBL if you are taking muscle relaxants. Some of these muscle relaxants include carisoprodol (Soma), pipecuronium (Arduan), orphenadrine (Banflex, Disipal), cyclobenzaprine, gallamine (Flaxedil), atracurium (Tracrium), pancuronium (Pavulon), succinylcholine (Anectine), and others.

Naloxone (Narcan). GBL is changed by the body to another chemical. This chemical is called GHB. GHB can affect the brain. Taking naloxone (Narcan) along with GBL might decrease the effects of GBL on the brain.

Ritonavir (Norvir). Ritonavir (Norvir) and saquinavir (Fortovase, Invirase) are commonly used together for HIV/AIDS. Taking both of these medications plus GBL might decrease how quickly the body gets rid of GBL. This could cause serious side effects.

Saquinavir (Fortovase, Invirase). Saquinavir (Fortovase, Invirase) and ritonavir (Norvir) are commonly used together for HIV/AIDS. Taking both these medications plus GBL might decrease how fast the body gets rid of GBL. This could cause serious side effects.

Sedative medications (CNS depressants). GBL might cause sleepiness and drowsiness. Medications that cause sleepiness are called sedatives. Taking GBL along with sedative medications might cause serious side effects. Do not take GBL if you are taking sedative medications. Some sedative medications include clonazepam (Klonopin), lorazepam (Ativan), phenobarbital (Donnatal), zolpidem (Ambien), and others.

Sedative medications (Benzodiazepines). GBL might cause sleepiness and drowsiness. Medications that cause sleepiness and drowsiness are called sedatives. Taking GBL along with sedative medications might cause serious side effects. Do not take GBL if you are taking sedative medications. Some of these sedative medications include clonazepam (Klonopin), diazepam (Valium), lorazepam (Ativan), and others.

GAMMA LINOLENIC ACID

What other names is the product known by?

Gamolenic Acid, GLA, Gammalinolenic Acid, (Z,Z,Z)-Octadeca-6,9,12-trienoic acid.

What is it?

Gamma linolenic acid is a fatty substance found in various plant seed oils such as borage oil and evening primrose oil. People use it as medicine.

Is it Effective?

The effectiveness ratings for **GAMMA LINOLENIC ACID** are as follows:

Possibly Effective for... Rheumatoid arthritis (RA) • Nerve problems due to diabetes (diabetic neuropathy).

Possibly Ineffective for... Allergic skin conditions (atopic dermatitis) • High blood pressure • Systemic sclerosis, a condition in which skin hardens.

Insufficient Evidence to Rate Effectiveness for... Breast cancer, oral polyps, hyperlipidemia (high cholesterol and blood fat levels), heart disease, cancer prevention, attention deficit-hyperactivity disorder (ADHD), depression, chronic fatigue syndrome, hayfever, psoriasis, eczema, and other conditions.

How does it work?
Gamma linolenic acid is an omega-6 fatty acid, which the body can convert to substances that reduce inflammation and cell growth.

Are there safety concerns?
Gamma linolenic acid appears to be safe for most adults. It can cause digestive tract side effects, such as soft stools, diarrhea, belching, and intestinal gas. It can also cause a longer than normal time for bleeding to stop.

Do not use gamma linolenic acid if: You are pregnant or breast-feeding. • You have any condition that makes you more likely to bleed.

Are there any interactions with medications?
Medications that slow blood clotting (Anticoagulant / Antiplatelet drugs). Gamma linolenic acid might slow blood clotting. Taking gamma linolenic acid along with medications that also slow clotting might increase the chances of bruising and bleeding. Some medications that slow blood clotting include aspirin, clopidogrel (Plavix), diclofenac (Voltaren, Cataflam, others), ibuprofen (Advil, Motrin, others), naproxen (Anaprox, Naprosyn, others), dalteparin (Fragmin), enoxaparin (Lovenox), heparin, warfarin (Coumadin), and others.
Phenothiazines. Taking gamma linolenic acid with phenothiazines might increase the risk of having a seizure in some people. Some phenothiazines include chlorpromazine (Thorazine), fluphenazine (Prolixin), trifluoperazine (Stelazine), thioridazine (Mellaril), and others.

GAMMA ORYZANOL

What other names is the product known by?
Gamma-OZ, Oryzanol.

What is it?
Gamma oryzanol is a substance extracted from rice bran oil. It is also found in wheat bran and some fruits and vegetables. People use it as medicine.

Is it Effective?
The effectiveness ratings for **GAMMA ORYZANOL** are as follows:
Possibly Effective for... Lowering cholesterol levels.
Insufficient Evidence to Rate Effectiveness for... Increasing testosterone and human growth hormone levels, improving strength during resistance exercise training, treating symptoms associated with menopause and aging, and other uses.

How does it work?
Gamma oryzanol might reduce cholesterol levels by reducing absorption of cholesterol from foods.

Are there safety concerns?
Gamma oryzanol is possibly safe for most adults. However, the potential side effects of gamma oryzanol are not known.

Do not use gamma oryzanol if: You are pregnant or breast-feeding. • You have low thyroid (hypothyroidism). Gamma oryzanol might lower thyroid function.

Are there any interactions with medications?
It is not known if gamma oryzanol interacts with any medicines.
Before taking gamma oryzanol, talk with your healthcare professional if you take any medications.

GAMMA-HYDROXYBUTYRATE (GHB)

What other names is the product known by?

4-Hydroxy Butyrate, 4-hydroxybutyric acid, Gamma Hydrate, Gamma Hydroxybutyrate Sodium, Gamma Hydroxybutyric Acid, Gamma-OH, Sodium 4-hydroxybutyrate, Sodium gamma-hydroxybutyrate, Sodium Oxybate, Sodium Oxybutyrate.

What is it?

Gamma hydroxybutyrate (GHB) is a chemical found in the brain and other areas of the body. It can also be made in a laboratory. People use it as medicine.

Is it Effective?

The effectiveness ratings for **GAMMA-HYDROXYBUTYRATE (GHB)** are as follows:

Possibly Effective for... Pain, fatigue, and sleep problems associated with a condition called fibromyalgia • Alcohol dependence and withdrawal • Treatment of loss of muscle control and weakness associated with a condition called narcolepsy • Withdrawal from heroin, opium, morphine, and other opiate drugs.

Insufficient Evidence to Rate Effectiveness for... Reducing weight, enhancing muscle growth, use as an aphrodisiac, reducing pressure in the brain caused by head injury, and other conditions.

How does it work?

The natural function of GHB in the body might be to slow down brain activity during sleep. Gamma hydroxybutyrate affects several nerve pathways in the brain, including activating the body's pain-killing (opioid) system and raising levels of growth hormone.

Are there safety concerns?

The prescription medication Gamma hydroxybutyrate (sodium oxybate) is possibly safe for adults who are taking it for symptoms of a condition called narcolepsy, under close medical supervision.

Gamma hydroxybutyrate (GHB) is UNSAFE and illegal for use as a dietary supplement. Use of GHB, or the closely related gamma butyrolactone (GBL) and butanediol (BD), has been linked to at least three deaths and 122 cases of serious side effects. GHB can cause many serious side effects including headaches, hallucinations, dizziness, confusion, nausea, vomiting, drowsiness, agitation, diarrhea, sexual arousal, numbing of legs, vision problems, tightness of chest, mental changes, combativeness, memory loss, serious breathing and heart problems, seizures, coma, and death. Long-term use may lead to withdrawal symptoms.

Do not use gamma hydroxybutyrate if: You are pregnant or breast-feeding. • You have epilepsy or a seizure disorder. • You have high blood pressure or an irregular heartbeat.

Are there any interactions with medications?

Alcohol. Alcohol can cause sleepiness and drowsiness. Taking GHB along with alcohol might greatly increase sleepiness and drowsiness caused by alcohol. Taking GHB along with alcohol can lead to serious side effects. Do not take GHB if you have been drinking.

Amphetamines. Amphetamines are drugs that can speed up your nervous system. GHB can slow down your nervous system. Taking GHB along with amphetamines can lead to serious side effects.

Haloperidol (Haldol). GHB can affect the brain. Haloperidol (Haldol) can also affect the brain. Taking haloperidol (Haldol) along with GHB might cause serious side effects.

Medications for mental conditions (Antipsychotic drugs). GHB can affect the brain. Medications for mental conditions also affect the brain. Taking GHB along with medications for mental conditions might increase the effects and serious side effects of GHB. Do not take GHB if you are taking medications for a mental condition. Some of these medications include fluphenazine (Permitil, Prolixin), haloperidol (Haldol), chlorpromazine (Thorazine), prochlorperazine (Compazine), thioridazine (Mellaril), trifluoperazine (Stelazine), and others.

Medications for pain (Narcotic drugs). Some medications for pain can cause sleepiness and drowsiness. GHB might also cause sleepiness and drowsiness. Taking GHB along with some medications for pain might cause severe side effects. Do not take GHB if you are taking medications for pain. Some medications for pain include meperidine (Demerol), hydrocodone, morphine, OxyContin, and many others.

Medications used to prevent seizures (Anticonvulsants). Medications used to prevent seizures affect chemicals in the brain. GHB is changed in the body to one of these brain chemicals called GABA. Taking GHB along with medications used to prevent seizures might decrease the effects of GHB. Some medications used to prevent seizures include phenobarbital, primidone (Mysoline), valproic acid (Depakene), gabapentin (Neurontin), carbamazepine (Tegretol), phenytoin (Dilantin), and others.

Muscle relaxants. Muscle relaxants can cause drowsiness. GHB can also cause drowsiness. Taking GHB along with muscle relaxants might cause too much drowsiness and serious side effects. Do not take GHB if you are taking muscle relaxants. Some of these muscle relaxants include carisoprodol (Soma), pipecuronium (Arduan), orphenadrine (Banflex, Disipal), cyclobenzaprine, gallamine (Flaxedil), atracurium (Tracrium), pancuronium

Medical professionals should consult the Professional Version at www.NaturalDatabase.com.

(Pavulon), succinylcholine (Anectine), and others.

Naloxone (Narcan). GHB can affect the brain. Taking naloxone (Narcan) along with GHB might decrease the effects of GHB on the brain.

Ritonavir (Norvir). Ritonavir (Norvir) and saquinavir (Fortovase, Invirase) are commonly used together for HIV/AIDS. Taking both of these medications plus GHB might decrease how quickly the body gets rid of GHB. This could cause serious side effects.

Saquinavir (Fortovase, Invirase). Saquinavir (Fortovase, Invirase) and ritonavir (Norvir) are commonly used together for HIV/AIDS. Taking both these medications plus GHB might decrease how fast the body gets rid of GHB. This could cause serious side effects.

Sedative medications (CNS depressants). GHB might cause sleepiness and drowsiness. Medications that cause sleepiness are called sedatives. Taking GHB along with sedative medications might cause serious side effects. Do not take GHB if you are taking sedative medications. Some sedative medications include clonazepam (Klonopin), lorazepam (Ativan), phenobarbital (Donnatal), zolpidem (Ambien), and others.

Sedative medications (Benzodiazepines). GHB (BD) might cause sleepiness and drowsiness. Medications that cause sleepiness and drowsiness are called sedatives. Taking GHB along with sedative medications might cause serious side effects. Do not take GHB if you are taking sedative medications. Some of these sedative medications include clonazepam (Klonopin), diazepam (Valium), lorazepam (Ativan), and others.

GARCINIA

What other names is the product known by?
Brindal Berry, Brindall Berry, Brindle Berry, Garcinia Cambogi, Garcinia Cambogia, Gorikapuli, Hydroxycitrate, Hydroxycitric Acid, HCA, Kankusta, Malabar Tamarind, Vrikshamla.

What is it?
Garcinia is a plant. The fruit rind is used to make medicine.

Is it Effective?
The effectiveness ratings for **GARCINIA** are as follows:
Possibly Ineffective for... Weight loss.
Insufficient Evidence to Rate Effectiveness for... Treating worms and parasites, purging the bowels, severe diarrhea (dysentery), and other conditions.

How does it work?
Preliminary research suggests that garcinia might prevent fat storage and suppress hunger; however, whether these effects occur in humans is unclear.

Are there safety concerns?
Garcinia appears to be safe for most people when used for 12 weeks or less. Long-term safety is unknown. Garcinia can cause nausea, digestive tract discomfort, and headache.

Do not use garcinia if: You are pregnant or breast-feeding.

Are there any interactions with medications?
It is not known if garcinia interacts with any medicines.
Before taking garcinia, talk with your healthcare professional if you take any medications.

GARDEN CRESS

What other names is the product known by?
Lepidium sativum.

What is it?
Garden cress is a plant. The above ground parts are used to make medicine.

Is it Effective?
The effectiveness ratings for **GARDEN CRESS** are as follows:
Insufficient Evidence to Rate Effectiveness for... Coughs, vitamin C deficiency, constipation, poor immunity, water retention, and other uses.

How does it work?
Garden cress might help fight some bacteria and viruses, but there isn't enough information to know if it works in humans.

Are there safety concerns?
There isn't enough information to know whether garden cress is safe to use as a medicine. Large amounts might cause irritation of the gut.

Do not use garden cress if: You are pregnant or breast-feeding.

Are there any interactions with medications?
It is not known if garden cress interacts with any medicines.
Before taking garden cress, talk with your healthcare professional if you take any medications.

GARDEN VIOLET

What other names is the product known by?
Viola odorata.

What is it?
Garden violet is a plant. The plant and an oil extracted from the leaves are used to make medicine. Be careful not to confuse garden violet with sweet violet.

Is it Effective?
The effectiveness ratings for **GARDEN VIOLET** are as follows:
Insufficient Evidence to Rate Effectiveness for... Bronchitis, asthma, coughs, colds and other lung problems; trouble sleeping (insomnia); hysteria; skin diseases; and other uses.

How does it work?
There isn't enough information to know how garden violet might work.

Are there safety concerns?
There isn't enough information to know whether garden violet is safe or what the potential side effects might be.

Do not use garden violet if: You are pregnant or breast-feeding.

Are there any interactions with medications?
It is not known if garden violet interacts with any medicines.
Before taking garden violet, talk with your healthcare professional if you take any medications.

GARLIC

What other names is the product known by?
Aged Garlic Extract, Ail, Ajo, Allii Sativi Bulbus, Allium, Allium sativum, Camphor of the Poor, Clove Garlic, Garlic Clove, Lasuna, Nectar of the Gods, Poor Man's Treacle, Rust Treacle, Stinking Rose.

What is it?
Garlic is an herb. The fresh clove or supplements made from the clove are used for medicine.

Is it Effective?
The effectiveness ratings for **GARLIC** are as follows:
Possibly Effective for... High cholesterol • High blood pressure • Hardening of the arteries (atherosclerosis) • Preventing colon cancer, rectal cancer, stomach cancer • Preventing tick bites • Fungal infections on the skin.
Possibly Ineffective for... Diabetes • Treating a bacteria called H. pylori that can cause ulcers • High cholesterol in children • Breast cancer • Lung cancer • Treating peripheral arterial occlusive disease (a disease that makes walking painful).
Insufficient Evidence to Rate Effectiveness for... Treating a special condition involving high cholesterol in people with HIV/AIDS, common cold, benign prostatic hyperplasia (BPH), earaches, arthritis, allergies, colds, flu, traveler's diarrhea, urinary tract problems in men, preventing prostate cancer, chronic fatigue syndrome (CFS), and other conditions.

Medical professionals should consult the Professional Version at www.NaturalDatabase.com.

How does it work?

Garlic produces a chemical called allicin. This is what seems to make garlic work for certain conditions. Allicin also makes garlic smell. Some products are made "odorless" by aging the garlic, but this process can also make the garlic less effective. It's a good idea to look for supplements that are coated (enteric coating) so they will dissolve in the intestine and not in the stomach.

Are there safety concerns?

Garlic is safe for most people. Garlic can cause bad breath, a burning sensation in the mouth or stomach, heartburn, gas, nausea, vomiting, body odor, and diarrhea. These side effects are often worse with raw garlic. When used on the skin as a thick paste, garlic can cause damage to the skin that is similar to a burn.

Do not take garlic if: You are pregnant or breast-feeding. • You have a bleeding disorder. • You are scheduled for surgery within two weeks. • You have stomach or digestion problems. • You are being treated for HIV/AIDS.

Are there any interactions with medications?

Birth control pills (Contraceptive drugs). Some birth control pills contain estrogen. The body breaks down the estrogen in birth control pills to get rid of it. Garlic might increase the breakdown of estrogen. Taking garlic along with birth control pills might decrease the effectiveness of birth control pills. If you take birth control pills along with garlic, use an additional form of birth control such as a condom. Some birth control pills include ethinyl estradiol and levonorgestrel (Triphasil), ethinyl estradiol and norethindrone (Ortho-Novum 1/35, Ortho-Novum 7/7/7), and others.

Cyclosporine (Neoral, Sandimmune). The body breaks down cyclosporine (Neoral, Sandimmune) to get rid of it. Garlic might increase how quickly the body breaks down cyclosporine (Neoral, Sandimmune). Taking garlic along with cyclosporine (Neoral, Sandimmune) might decrease the effectiveness of cyclosporine (Neoral, Sandimmune). Do not take garlic if you are taking cyclosporine (Neoral, Sandimmune).

Medications changed by the liver (Cytochrome P450 2E1 (CYP2E1) substrates). Some medications are changed and broken down by the liver. Garlic oil might decrease how quickly the liver breaks down some medications. Taking garlic oil along with some medications that are changed by the liver can increase the effects and side effects of your medication. Before taking garlic oil talk to your healthcare provider if you take any medications that are changed by the liver. Some medications that are changed by the liver include acetaminophen, chlorzoxazone (Parafon Forte), ethanol, theophylline, and drugs used for anesthesia during surgery such as enflurane (Ethrane), halothane (Fluothane), isoflurane (Forane), and methoxyflurane (Penthrane).

Medications changed by the liver (Cytochrome P450 3A4 (CYP3A4) substrates). Some medications are changed and broken down by the liver. Garlic might increase how quickly the liver breaks down some medications. Taking garlic along with some medications that are broken down by the liver can decrease the effectiveness of some medications. Before taking garlic talk to your healthcare provider if you are taking any medications that are changed by the liver. Some medications changed by this liver include lovastatin (Mevacor), ketoconazole (Nizoral), itraconazole (Sporanox), fexofenadine (Allegra), triazolam (Halcion), and many others.

Medications that slow blood clotting (Anticoagulant / Antiplatelet drugs). Garlic might slow blood clotting. Taking garlic along with medications that also slow clotting might increase the chances of bruising and bleeding. Some medications that slow blood clotting include aspirin, clopidogrel (Plavix), diclofenac (Voltaren, Cataflam, others), ibuprofen (Advil, Motrin, others), naproxen (Anaprox, Naprosyn, others), dalteparin (Fragmin), enoxaparin (Lovenox), heparin, warfarin (Coumadin), and others.

Medications used for HIV/AIDS (Non-Nucleoside Reverse Transcriptase Inhibitors (NNRTIs)). The body breaks down medications used for HIV/AIDS to get rid of them. Garlic can increase how fast the body breaks down some medication for HIV/AIDS. Taking garlic along with some medications used for HIV/AIDS might decrease the effectiveness of some medications used for HIV/AIDS. Some of these medications used for HIV/AIDS include nevirapine (Viramune), delavirdine (Rescriptor), and efavirenz (Sustiva).

Saquinavir (Fortovase, Invirase). The body breaks down saquinavir (Fortovase, Invirase) to get rid of it. Garlic might increase how quickly the body breaks down saquinavir. Taking garlic along with saquinavir (Fortovase, Invirase) might decrease the effectiveness of saquinavir (Fortovase, Invirase).

Warfarin (Coumadin). Warfarin (Coumadin) is used to slow blood clotting. Garlic might increase the effectiveness of warfarin (Coumadin). Taking garlic along with warfarin (Coumadin) might increase the chances of bruising and bleeding. Be sure to have your blood checked regularly. The dose of your warfarin (Coumadin) might need to be changed.

GELATIN

What other names is the product known by?

Collagen hydrolysate, denatured collagen, gelatine, hydrolyzed collagen protein, hydrolyzed gelatin.

What is it?

Gelatin is a protein made from animal products. Gelatin is also used for preparation of foods, cosmetics, and medicines.

Is it Effective?

The effectiveness ratings for **GELATIN** are as follows:

Insufficient Evidence to Rate Effectiveness for...A kind of arthritis called osteoarthritis, osteoporosis (brittle bones), strengthening bones and joints, strengthening fingernails, improving hair quality, weight loss, shortening recovery after exercise and sports-related injury, and other conditions.

How does it work?

Gelatin contains collagen, a normal component of cartilage and bone, so some people think it might help for arthritis and other joint conditions.

Are there safety concerns?

Gelatin appears to be safe for most people. Gelatin can cause an unpleasant taste, sensation of heaviness in the stomach, bloating, heartburn, and belching. Gelatin can cause allergic reactions in some people.

There is some concern about the safety of gelatin because it comes from animal sources. Some people are worried that unsafe manufacturing practices might lead to contamination of gelatin products with diseased animal tissues including those that might transmit bovine spongiform encephalopathy (mad cow disease). Although this risk seems to be low, many experts advise against using animal-derived supplements like gelatin.

Do not take gelatin in amounts higher than those typically found in foods if: You are pregnant or breast-feeding.

Are there any interactions with medications?

It is not known if gelatin interacts with any medicines.
Before taking gelatin, talk with your healthcare professional if you take any medications.

GELSEMIUM

What other names is the product known by?

Bignonia sempervirens, Caroline Jasmine, Evening Trumpet Flower, False Jasmine, Gelsemii Rhizoma, Gelsemin, Gelsemium nitidum, Gelsemium sempervirens, Gelsemiumwurzelstock Jessamine, Trumpet Flower, Woodbine, Yellow Jasmine, Yellow Jessamine Root.

What is it?

Gelsemium is a plant. The root and underground stem (rhizome) are used to make medicine. Be careful not to confuse gelsemium with American ivy or honeysuckle, which are also known as woodbine.

Is it Effective?

The effectiveness ratings for **GELSEMIUM** are as follows:

Insufficient Evidence to Rate Effectiveness for... Asthma, pain due to migraine headaches, pain due to a condition of facial nerves called trigeminal neuralgia, and other uses.

How does it work?

Gelsemium contains substances which might act in the brain to reduce pain.

Are there safety concerns?

Gelsemium is UNSAFE. Relatively small amounts can cause serious toxicity, including death. Symptoms of poisoning include headache, vision problems, difficulty swallowing, dizziness, muscle problems, seizures, breathing problems, slowing of the heart, and others.

Do not give gelsemium to children. It can poison them, even in very small amounts.

Do not use gelsemium if: You are pregnant or breast-feeding. • You have heart disease.

Medical professionals should consult the Professional Version at www.NaturalDatabase.com.

Are there any interactions with medications?
It is not known if gelsemium interacts with any medicines.
Before taking gelsemium, talk with your healthcare professional if you take any medications.

GENISTEIN COMBINED POLYSACCHARIDE

What other names is the product known by?
Basidiomycetes Polysaccharide, Fermented Genistein, Fermented Isoflavone, GCP, Genistein Polysaccharide, Isoflavone Combined Polysaccharide, Soy Isoflavone Polysaccharide.

What is it?
Genistein combined polysaccharide is an extract of fermented soy.

Is it Effective?
The effectiveness ratings for **GENISTEIN COMBINED POLYSACCHARIDE** are as follows:
Insufficient Evidence to Rate Effectiveness for... Prostate cancer, breast cancer, and other conditions.

How does it work?
Genistein combined polysaccharide might work for some forms of cancer by decreasing certain hormones.

Are there safety concerns?
There isn't enough information to know if genistein combined polysaccharide is safe.

Do not use genistein combined polysaccharide if: You are pregnant or breast-feeding. • You have breast cancer. • You have uterine cancer. • You have ovarian cancer. • You have endometriosis. • You have uterine fibroids.

Are there any interactions with medications?
It is not known if genistein combined polysaccharide interacts with any medicines.
Before taking genistein combined polysaccharide, talk with your healthcare professional if you take any medications.

GENTIAN

What other names is the product known by?
Bitter Root, Bitterwort, Gall Weed, Gentianae Radix, Pale Gentian, Stemless Gentian, Yellow Gentian, Wild Gentian, Gentiana Lutea, Gentiana Acaulis.

What is it?
Gentian is an herb. The root of the plant and less commonly, the bark, are used to make medicine.

Is it Effective?
The effectiveness ratings for **GENTIAN** are as follows:
Possibly Effective for... Symptoms of sinus infection (sinusitis) when combined with other herbs including elderflower, verbena, cowslip flower, and sorrel.
Insufficient Evidence to Rate Effectiveness for... Stomach disorders, high blood pressure, diarrhea, fever, heartburn, vomiting, menstrual disorders, cancer, and other conditions.

How does it work?
Gentian contains a chemical that might dilate blood vessels.

Are there safety concerns?
Gentian seems to be safe for most people when used in small amounts as part of a combination product containing gentian root, elderflower, verbena, and cowslip flower (SinuComp, Sinupret). There isn't enough information to know if gentian is safe when used in medicinal amounts other than as part of the combination product. The combination product can cause digestive system upset and occasionally allergic skin rash.

The highly toxic white hellebore (Veratrum album) can be mistaken for gentian and has caused accidental poisoning when used in home-made preparations.

Do not take gentian if: You are pregnant or breast-feeding. • You have low blood pressure.

Are there any interactions with medications?

Medications for high blood pressure (Antihypertensive drugs). Theoretically, gentian might decrease blood pressure. Taking gentian along with medications for high blood pressure might cause your blood pressure to go too low. Some medications for high blood pressure include captopril (Capoten), enalapril (Vasotec), losartan (Cozaar), valsartan (Diovan), diltiazem (Cardizem), Amlodipine (Norvasc), hydrochlorothiazide (HydroDiuril), furosemide (Lasix), and many others.

GERMAN CHAMOMILE

What other names is the product known by?

Blue Chamomile, Chamomile, Camomilla, Camomille Allemande, Chamomilla recutita, Echte Kamille, Feldkamille, Fleur de Camomile, Hungarian Chamomile, Kamillen, Kleine Kamille, Manzanilla, Matricaire, Matricaria chamomilla, Matricaria recutita, Matricariae Flos, Pin Heads, Sweet False Chamomile, True Chamomile, Wild Chamomile.

What is it?

German chamomile is an herb. People use the flower head of the plant to make medicine.

Is it Effective?

The effectiveness ratings for **GERMAN CHAMOMILE** are as follows:

Possibly Effective for... Treating or preventing swelling and deterioration (mucositis) of the mouth lining caused by radiation therapy and some types of chemotherapy • Upset stomach (dyspepsia), when a combination of German chamomile and five other herbs is used.

Possibly Ineffective for... Preventing skin irritation caused by radiation used to treat cancer.

Insufficient Evidence to Rate Effectiveness for... Intestinal gas, travel sickness, nasal swelling (inflammation), hayfever, diarrhea, restlessness, sleeplessness, attention deficit-hyperactivity disorder (ADHD), stomach and intestinal disorders, menstrual cramps, and other conditions.

How does it work?

German chamomile contains chemicals that might have relaxant and anti-inflammatory effects.

Are there safety concerns?

German chamomile seems safe when taken by mouth for short periods of time. The long-term safety of German chamomile is unknown. German chamomile can cause allergic reactions in some people. It is in the same plant family as ragweed, marigolds, daisies, and other related herbs.

When applied topically, German chamomile can cause allergic skin reactions. When applied near the eyes, German chamomile may cause eye irritation.

Do not take German chamomile in medicinal amounts if: You are pregnant or breast-feeding. • You are allergic to ragweed or related plants. • You have a hormone-sensitive condition such as breast cancer, uterine cancer, ovarian cancer, endometriosis, or uterine fibroids.

Are there any interactions with medications?

Birth control pills (Contraceptive drugs). Some birth control pills contain estrogen. German chamomile might have some of the same effects as estrogen. But German chamomile isn't as strong as the estrogen in birth control pills. Taking German chamomile along with birth control pills might decrease the effectiveness of birth control pills. If you take birth control pills along with German chamomile, use an additional form of birth control such as a condom. Some birth control pills include ethinyl estradiol and levonorgestrel (Triphasil), ethinyl estradiol and norethindrone (Ortho-Novum 1/35, Ortho-Novum 7/7/7), and others.

Estrogens. Large amounts of German chamomile might have some of the same effects as estrogen. But large amounts of German chamomile aren't as strong as estrogen pills. Taking German chamomile along with estrogen pills might decrease the effects of estrogen pills. Some estrogen pills include conjugated equine estrogens (Premarin), ethinyl estradiol, estradiol, and others.

Medications changed by the liver (Cytochrome P450 1A2 (CYP1A2) substrates). Some medications are changed and broken down by the liver. German chamomile might decrease how quickly the liver breaks down some medications. Taking German chamomile along with some medications that are broken down by the liver can increase the effects and side effects of these medications. Before taking German chamomile, talk to your healthcare provider if you take any medications that are changed by the liver. Some medications that are changed by the liver include amitriptyline (Elavil), haloperidol (Haldol), ondansetron (Zofran), propranolol (Inderal), theophylline (Theo-Dur, others), verapamil (Calan, Isoptin, others), and others.

Medications changed by the liver (Cytochrome P450 3A4 (CYP3A4) substrates). Some medications are changed and broken down by the liver. German chamomile might decrease how quickly the liver breaks down

Medical professionals should consult the Professional Version at www.NaturalDatabase.com.

some medications. Taking German chamomile along with some medications that are broken down by the liver can increase the effects and side effects of some medications. Before taking German chamomile, talk to your healthcare provider if you are taking any medications that are changed by the liver. Some medications changed by the liver include lovastatin (Mevacor), ketoconazole (Nizoral), itraconazole (Sporanox), fexofenadine (Allegra), triazolam (Halcion), and many others.

Sedative medications (Benzodiazepines). German chamomile might cause sleepiness and drowsiness. Drugs that cause sleepiness and drowsiness are called sedatives. Taking German chamomile along with sedative medications might cause too much sleepiness. Some of these sedative medications include alprazolam (Xanax), clonazepam (Klonopin), diazepam (Valium), lorazepam (Ativan), midazolam (Versed), temazepam (Restoril), triazolam (Halcion), and others.

Sedative medications (CNS depressants). German chamomile might cause sleepiness and drowsiness. Medications that cause sleepiness are called sedatives. Taking German chamomile along with sedative medications might cause too much sleepiness. Some sedative medications include pentobarbital (Nembutal), phenobarbital (Luminal), secobarbital (Seconal), fentanyl (Duragesic, Sublimaze), morphine, zolpidem (Ambien), and others.

Tamoxifen (Nolvadex). Some types of cancer are affected by hormones in the body. Estrogen-sensitive cancers are cancers that are affected by estrogen levels in the body. Tamoxifen (Nolvadex) is used to help treat and prevent these types of cancer. German chamomile seems to also affect estrogen levels in the body. By affecting estrogen in the body, German chamomile might decrease the effectiveness of tamoxifen (Nolvadex). Do not take German chamomile if you are taking tamoxifen (Nolvadex).

Warfarin (Coumadin). Warfarin (Coumadin) is used to slow blood clotting. German chamomile might increase the effects of warfarin (Coumadin). Taking German chamomile and warfarin (Coumadin) together might slow blood clotting too much and cause bruising and bleeding. Be sure to have your blood checked regularly. The dose of your warfarin (Coumadin) might need to be changed.

GERMAN IPECAC

What other names is the product known by?
Cynanchum vincetoxicum, Swallow Wort.

What is it?
German ipecac is a plant. The leaf, root, and underground stem (rhizome) are used to make medicine.

Is it Effective?
The effectiveness ratings for **GERMAN IPECAC** are as follows:
Insufficient Evidence to Rate Effectiveness for... Digestive problems, kidney problems, difficult and painful menstrual periods, snake bite, fluid retention, swelling and bruising, and other uses.

How does it work?
There isn't enough information to know how German ipecac might work.

Are there safety concerns?
German ipecac is UNSAFE. It can cause vomiting, breathing problems, paralysis, heart stoppage, and other problems.

Do not use German ipecac if: You are pregnant or breast-feeding.

Are there any interactions with medications?
It is not known if German ipecac interacts with any medicines.
Before taking German ipecac, talk with your healthcare professional if you take any medications.

GERMAN SARSAPARILLA

What other names is the product known by?
Carex arenaria, Caricis rhizoma, Red Couchgrass, Red Sage, Sandriedgraswurzelstock, Sand Sedge, Sea Sedge.

What is it?
German sarsaparilla is a plant. The underground stems are used to make medicine. Be careful not to confuse German sarsaparilla with other forms of sarsaparilla.

Natural Medicines Comprehensive Database Consumer Version   (209) 472-2244

Is it Effective?

The effectiveness ratings for **GERMAN SARSAPARILLA** are as follows:

Insufficient Evidence to Rate Effectiveness for... Preventing gout, inducing sweating, arthritis, skin problems, fluid retention, sexually transmitted diseases (STD, VD), intestinal gas, colic, liver problems, diabetes, tuberculosis, lack of menstruation (periods), and other conditions.

How does it work?

German sarsaparilla contains many chemicals including salicylates, which are similar to aspirin.

Are there safety concerns?

There isn't enough information to know whether German sarsaparilla is safe. It may cause irritation when it comes in contact with skin, nose, eyes, or the digestive tract.

Do not use German sarsaparilla if: You are pregnant or breast-feeding. • You have asthma. • You have an allergy to aspirin.

Are there any interactions with medications?

It is not known if German sarsaparilla interacts with any medicines.
Before taking German sarsaparilla, talk with your healthcare professional if you take any medications.

GERMANDER

What other names is the product known by?

Teucrium chamaedrys, Wall Germander, Wild Germander.

What is it?

Germander is a plant. The above ground parts are used to make medicine.

Is it Effective?

The effectiveness ratings for **GERMANDER** are as follows:
Insufficient Evidence to Rate Effectiveness for... Gallbladder conditions, fever, gout, stomachache, diarrhea, weight loss, use as an antiseptic, use as a mouthwash, and other uses.

How does it work?

There isn't enough information to know how germander might work.

Are there safety concerns?

Germander is UNSAFE. Germander has caused several cases of hepatitis (liver disease) and death. Germander shouldn't be used by anyone. Some people may be at even higher risk of side effects.

Do not use germander if: You are pregnant or breast-feeding.

Are there any interactions with medications?

It is not known if germander interacts with any medicines.
Before taking germander, talk with your healthcare professional if you take any medications.

GERMANIUM

What other names is the product known by?

Bis-Carboxyethyl Germanium Sesquioxide, Carboxyethylgermanium Sesquioxide, Ge, Ge-132, Ge-Oxy 132, Germanium Lactate Citrate, Inorganic Germanium, Organic Germanium.

What is it?

Germanium is a chemical element. People use it as medicine.

Is it Effective?

The effectiveness ratings for **GERMANIUM** are as follows:
Insufficient Evidence to Rate Effectiveness for... Arthritis, pain relief, osteoporosis (weak bones), low energy, AIDS, cancer, high blood pressure, high cholesterol, heart disease, glaucoma, cataracts, depression, liver problems, food allergies, yeast infections, ongoing viral infections, heavy metal poisoning, increasing circulation of blood to the brain, supporting the immune system, use as an antioxidant, or other uses.

Medical professionals should consult the Professional Version at www.NaturalDatabase.com.

Medical professionals should consult the Professional Version at www.NaturalDatabase.com.

How does it work?

Germanium might act against inflammation. It might also have antioxidant properties and affect the immune system.

Are there safety concerns?

Germanium is unsafe. There have been more than 30 reports of kidney failure and death associated with use of germanium. It builds up in the body and can damage vital organs such as the kidneys. It can also cause anemia, muscle weakness, nerve problems, and other side effects.

Do not use germanium if: You are pregnant or breast-feeding.

Are there any interactions with medications?

Furosemide (Lasix). Some scientists think that germanium might decrease how well furosemide (Lasix) works. But there isn't enough information to know if this is a big concern.

GINGER

What other names is the product known by?

Amomum Zingiber, African Ginger, Black Ginger, Cochin Ginger, Gingembre, Ginger Root, Imber, Jamaica Ginger, Jiang, Kankyo, Kanshokyo, Race Ginger, Sheng Jiang, Shoga, Shokyo, Sunthi, Zingiber Officinale, Zingiberis Rhizoma, Zinzeberis.

What is it?

Ginger is an herb. The rhizome (underground stem) is used to make medicine.

Is it Effective?

The effectiveness ratings for **GINGER** are as follows:
Possibly Effective for... Preventing dizziness • Preventing morning sickness, after discussing the possible risks with your healthcare provider. Nausea and vomiting following surgery.
Possibly Ineffective for... Preventing motion sickness and seasickness.
Insufficient Evidence to Rate Effectiveness for... Rheumatoid arthritis, osteoarthritis, loss of appetite, colds, flu, migraine headache, preventing nausea caused by chemotherapy, and other conditions.

How does it work?

Ginger contains chemicals that may reduce nausea and inflammation.

Are there safety concerns?

Ginger is safe for most people. Some people can have mild side effects including heartburn, diarrhea, and general stomach discomfort. When applied to the skin, ginger may cause irritation.

Do not take ginger if: You are pregnant or breast-feeding, unless prescribed by your healthcare provider. • You have a bleeding disorder. • You have diabetes. • You have a heart condition.

Are there any interactions with medications?

Medications that slow blood clotting (Anticoagulant / Antiplatelet drugs). Ginger might slow blood clotting. Taking ginger along with medications that also slow clotting might increase the chances of bruising and bleeding. Some medications that slow blood clotting include aspirin, clopidogrel (Plavix), diclofenac (Voltaren, Cataflam, others), ibuprofen (Advil, Motrin, others), naproxen (Anaprox, Naprosyn, others), dalteparin (Fragmin), enoxaparin (Lovenox), heparin, warfarin (Coumadin), phenprocoumon (an anticlotting medicine available outside the US), and others.
Phenprocoumon. Phenprocoumon is used in Europe to slow blood clotting. Ginger can also slow blood clotting. Taking ginger along with phenprocoumon might increase the chances of bruising and bleeding. Be sure to have your blood checked regularly. The dose of your phenprocoumon might need to be changed.
Warfarin (Coumadin). Warfarin (Coumadin) is used to slow blood clotting. Ginger can also slow blood clotting. Taking ginger along with warfarin (Coumadin) might increase the chances of bruising and bleeding. Be sure to have your blood checked regularly. The dose of your warfarin (Coumadin) might need to be changed.
Medications for high blood pressure (Calcium channel blockers). Ginger might reduce blood pressure in a way that is similar to some medications for blood pressure and heart disease. Taking ginger along with these medications might cause your blood pressure to drop too low or an irregular heartbeat. Some medications for high blood pressure and heart disease include nifedipine (Adalat, Procardia), verapamil (Calan, Isoptin, Verelan), diltiazem (Cardizem), isradipine (DynaCirc), felodipine (Plendil), amlodipine (Norvasc), and others.
Medications for diabetes (Antidiabetes drugs). Ginger might decrease blood sugar. Diabetes medications are also used to lower blood sugar. Taking ginger along with diabetes medications might cause your blood sugar to go

too low. Monitor your blood sugar closely. The dose of your diabetes medication might need to be changed. Some medications used for diabetes include glimepiride (Amaryl), glyburide (DiaBeta, Glynase PresTab, Micronase), insulin, pioglitazone (Actos), rosiglitazone (Avandia), chlorpropamide (Diabinese), glipizide (Glucotrol), tolbutamide (Orinase), and others.

GINKGO

What other names is the product known by?

Adiantifolia, Bai Guo Ye, Baiguo, Fossil Tree, Ginkgo biloba, Ginkgo Extract, Ginkgo Folium, Ginkgo Leaf Extact, Ginkgo Seed, Japanese Silver Apricot, Kew Tree, Maidenhair Tree, Salisburia Adiantifolia, Yinhsing.

What is it?

Ginkgo is an herb. The leaves are generally used to make medicine. However, a few medicines are made from the seed, but these are not well studied.

Is it Effective?

The effectiveness ratings for **GINKGO** are as follows:

Possibly Effective for... Alzheimer's disease and other forms of dementia • Improving thinking problems caused by old age • Improving thinking in young people • Raynaud's syndrome (a painful response to cold especially in the fingers and toes) • Leg pain when walking due to poor blood flow (claudication) • Vertigo and dizziness • Premenstrual syndrome (PMS) • Improving color vision in people with diabetes • Treating some kinds of eye diseases (glaucoma and eye damage caused by diabetes).

Possibly Ineffective for... Ringing in the ears (tinnitus) • Winter depression in people with seasonal affective disorder (SAD) • Sexual problems related to antidepressant medicines • Preventing symptoms of mountain or altitude sickness in climbers.

Insufficient Evidence to Rate Effectiveness for... Age-related macular degeneration (AMD), attention deficit-hyperactivity disorder (ADHD), blood clots, heart disease, high cholesterol, "hardening" of the arteries (atherosclerosis), advanced colon and rectal cancer, hearing loss, and other conditions when the extract is used. Coughs, asthma, bronchitis, urinary problems, cognitive problems related to Lyme disease, digestion disorders, chronic fatigue syndrome (CFS), scabies, and skin sores when the seeds are used.

How does it work?

Ginkgo seems to improve blood circulation, which might help the brain, eyes, ears, and legs function better. It may slow down Alzheimer's disease by interfering with the changes in the brain that interfere with thinking.

Ginkgo seeds contain substances that might kill bacteria and fungi which cause infections in the body. The seeds also contain a toxin that can cause side effects like seizure and loss of consciousness.

Are there safety concerns?

Ginkgo seems to be safe for most people. It can cause some minor side effects such as stomach upset, headache, dizziness, constipation, forceful heartbeat, and allergic skin reactions.

There is some concern that ginkgo might increase the risk of bruising and bleeding. Ginkgo thins the blood and decreases its ability to form clots. A few people taking ginkgo have had bleeding into the eye and into the brain, and excessive bleeding following surgery.

Ginkgo seeds might not be safe. Long-term use or use of medical amounts can cause serious side effects including stomach ache, nausea, diarrhea, vomiting, restlessness, difficulty breathing, weak pulse, shock, seizures, loss of consciousness, and death.

Do not take ginkgo if: You are pregnant or breast-feeding. • You are scheduled for surgery in the next two weeks. It might increase the risk of bleeding. • You have a bleeding problem. • You have seizures, convulsions, or epilepsy. • You are trying to get pregnant or father a child.
Use ginkgo cautiously if: You have diabetes.

Are there any interactions with medications?

Alprazolam (Xanax). Taking Ginkgo along with alprazolam might decrease the effects of alprazolam.
Buspirone (BuSpar). Ginkgo seems to affect the brain. Buspirone (BuSpar) also affects the brain. One person felt hyper and overexcited when taking ginkgo, buspirone (BuSpar), and other medications. It is unclear if this interaction was caused by ginkgo or the other medications.
Fluoxetine (Prozac). Taking ginkgo along with St. John's wort, other herbs and fluoxetine (Prozac) might cause you to feel irritated, nervous, jittery, and excited. This is called hypomania. It's not known if this is a concern when just ginkgo is taken with fluoxetine (Prozac).

Natural Medicines Comprehensive Database Consumer Version (209) 472-2244 **333**

Medical professionals should consult the Professional Version at www.NaturalDatabase.com.

Medical professionals should consult the Professional Version at www.NaturalDatabase.com.

Ibuprofen. Ginkgo can slow blood clotting. Ibuprofen can also slow blood clotting. Taking ginkgo with ibuprofen can slow blood clotting too much and increase the chance of bruising and bleeding.

Insulin. Ginkgo might change how much insulin your body makes. By changing how much insulin your body makes ginkgo might change how much insulin you need to inject. Monitor your blood sugar closely. The dose of your insulin might need to be changed.

Medications that slow blood clotting (Anticoagulant / Antiplatelet drugs). Ginkgo can slow blood clotting. Taking ginkgo along with medications that also slow clotting might increase the chances of bruising and bleeding. Some medications that slow blood clotting include aspirin, clopidogrel (Plavix), diclofenac (Voltaren, Cataflam, others), ibuprofen (Advil, Motrin, others), naproxen (Anaprox, Naprosyn, others), dalteparin (Fragmin), enoxaparin (Lovenox), heparin, warfarin (Coumadin), and others.

Medications changed by the liver (Cytochrome P450 1A2 (CYP1A2) substrates). Some medications are changed and broken down by the liver. Ginkgo might decrease how quickly the liver breaks down some medications. Taking ginkgo along with some medications that are changed by the liver might increase the effects and side effects of some medications. Before taking ginkgo talk to your healthcare provider if you take any medications that are changed by the liver. Some of these medications that are changed by the liver include clozapine (Clozaril), cyclobenzaprine (Flexeril), fluvoxamine (Luvox), haloperidol (Haldol), imipramine (Tofranil), mexiletine (Mexitil), olanzapine (Zyprexa), pentazocine (Talwin), propranolol (Inderal), tacrine (Cognex), theophylline, zileuton (Zyflo), zolmitriptan (Zomig), and others.

Medications changed by the liver (Cytochrome P450 2C9 (CYP2C9) substrates). Some medications are changed and broken down by the liver. Ginkgo might decrease how quickly the liver breaks down some medications. Taking ginkgo along with these medications that are change by the liver might increase the effects and side effects of your medication. Before taking ginkgo talk to your healthcare provider if you take any medications that are changed by the liver. Some medications that are changed by this liver include amitriptyline (Elavil), diazepam (Valium), zileuton (Zyflo), celecoxib (Celebrex), diclofenac (Voltaren), fluvastatin (Lescol), glipizide (Glucotrol), ibuprofen (Advil, Motrin), irbesartan (Avapro), losartan (Cozaar), phenytoin (Dilantin), piroxicam (Feldene), tamoxifen (Nolvadex), tolbutamide (Tolinase), torsemide (Demadex), warfarin (Coumadin), and others.

Medications changed by the liver (Cytochrome P450 2C19 (CYP2C19) substrates). Some medications are changed and broken down by the liver. Ginkgo might increase how quickly the liver breaks down some medications. Taking ginkgo with these medications might decrease how well the medication works. Before taking ginkgo, talk to your healthcare provider if you take any medications that are changed by the liver. Some of these medications that are changed by the liver include amitriptyline (Elavil), carisoprodol (Soma), citalopram (Celexa), diazepam (Valium), lansoprazole (Prevacid), omeprazole (Prilosec), phenytoin (Dilantin), warfarin (Coumadin), and many others.

Medications changed by the liver (Cytochrome P450 2D6 (CYP2D6) substrates). Some medications are changed and broken down by the liver. Ginkgo might decrease how quickly the liver breaks down some medications. Taking ginkgo along with some medications that are change by the liver can increase the effects and side effects of your medication. Before taking ginkgo talk to your healthcare provider if you take any medications that are changed by the liver. Some medications that are changed by the liver include amitriptyline (Elavil), clozapine (Clozaril), codeine, desipramine (Norpramin), donepezil (Aricept), fentanyl (Duragesic), flecainide (Tambocor), fluoxetine (Prozac), meperidine (Demerol), methadone (Dolophine), metoprolol (Lopressor, Toprol XL), olanzapine (Zyprexa), ondansetron (Zofran), tramadol (Ultram), trazodone (Desyrel), and others.

Medications changed by the liver (Cytochrome P450 3A4 (CYP3A4) substrates). Some medications are changed and broken down by the liver. Ginkgo might affect how quickly the liver breaks down some medications, and lead to a variety of effects and side effects. Before taking ginkgo talk to your healthcare provider if you are taking any medications that are changed by the liver. Some medications changed by the liver include lovastatin (Mevacor), clarithromycin (Biaxin), cyclosporine (Neoral, Sandimmune), diltiazem (Cardizem), estrogens, indinavir (Crixivan), triazolam (Halcion), and others.

Medications that increase the chance of having a seizure (Seizure threshold lowering drugs). Some medications increase the chance of having a seizure. Taking ginkgo might cause seizures in some people. Taking medications that increase the chance of having a seizure along with ginkgo might greatly increase the risk of having a seizure. Do not take ginkgo with medications that increase the chance of having a seizure. Some medications that increase the chance of having a seizure include anesthesia (propofol, others), antiarrhythmics (mexiletine), antibiotics (amphotericin, penicillin, cephalosporins, imipenem), antidepressants (bupropion, others), antihistamines (cyproheptadine, others), immunosuppressants (cyclosporine), narcotics (fentanyl, others), stimulants (methylphenidate), theophylline, and others.

Medications used to prevent seizures (Anticonvulsants). Medications used to prevent seizures affect chemicals in the brain. Ginkgo can also affect chemicals in the brain. By affecting chemicals in the brain, ginkgo might decrease the effectiveness of medications used to prevent seizures. Some medications used to prevent seizures include phenobarbital, primidone (Mysoline), valproic acid (Depakene), gabapentin (Neurontin), carbamazepine (Tegretol), phenytoin (Dilantin), and others.

Omeprazole (Prilosec). Omeprazole (Prilosec) is changed and broken down by the liver. Ginkgo might increase how fast the liver breaks down omeprazole (Prilosec). Taking ginkgo with omeprazole (Prilosec) might decrease how well omeprazole (Prilosec) works.

Natural Medicines Comprehensive Database Consumer Version   (209) 472-2244

Trazodone (Desyrel). Trazodone (Desyrel) affects chemicals in the brain. Ginkgo can also affect chemicals in the brain. Taking trazodone (Desyrel) along with ginkgo might cause serious side effects in the brain. One person taking trazodone and ginkgo went into a coma. Do not take ginkgo if you are taking trazodone (Desyrel).

Warfarin (Coumadin). Warfarin (Coumadin) is used to slow blood clotting. Ginkgo might also slow blood clotting. Taking ginkgo along with warfarin (Coumadin) might increase the chances of bruising and bleeding. Be sure to have your blood checked regularly. The dose of your warfarin (Coumadin) might need to be changed.

GINSENG, AMERICAN

What other names is the product known by?

American Ginseng, Anchi Ginseng, Canadian Ginseng, Ginseng, Ginseng Root, North American Ginseng, Occidental Ginseng, Ontario Ginseng, Panax quinquefolium, Panax quinquefolius, Red Berry, Ren Shen, Sang, Shang, Wisconsin Ginseng, Xi Yang Shen.

What is it?

American ginseng is an herb. The root is used to make medicine.

Is it Effective?

The effectiveness ratings for **GINSENG, AMERICAN** are as follows:

Possibly Effective for... Lowering blood sugar after a meal in people with type 2 diabetes • Preventing respiratory tract infections such as the common cold or influenza in adults.

Insufficient Evidence to Rate Effectiveness for... Stress, anemia, insomnia, gastritis, impotence, fever, attention deficit-hyperactivity disorder (ADHD), HIV/AIDS, and other conditions.

How does it work?

American ginseng contains chemicals called ginsenosides that seem to affect insulin levels in the body and lower blood sugar. Other chemicals, called polysaccharides might affect the immune system.

Are there safety concerns?

American ginseng seems to be safe when used short-term. It can cause some side effects including diarrhea, itching, insomnia, headache, and nervousness. In some people, American ginseng might also cause rapid heartbeat, increased blood pressure, breast tenderness, vaginal bleeding in women, and other side effects. Uncommon side effects that have been reported include severe rash called Stevens-Johnson syndrome, liver damage, and severe allergic reactions. American ginseng may not be safe in pregnancy. One of the chemicals in Panax ginseng, a plant related to American ginseng, has been linked to possible birth defects.

Do not take American ginseng if: You are pregnant or breast-feeding. • You have diabetes. • You have insomnia. • You have a psychiatric condition called schizophrenia. • You have breast cancer. • You have uterine cancer. • You have ovarian cancer. • You have endometriosis. • You have uterine fibroids.

Are there any interactions with medications?

Medications for diabetes (Antidiabetes drugs). American ginseng might decrease blood sugar. Diabetes medications are also used to lower blood sugar. Taking American ginseng along with diabetes medications might cause your blood sugar to go too low. Monitor your blood sugar closely. The dose of your diabetes medication might need to be changed. Some medications used for diabetes include glimepiride (Amaryl), glyburide (DiaBeta, Glynase PresTab, Micronase), insulin, pioglitazone (Actos), rosiglitazone (Avandia), chlorpropamide (Diabinese), glipizide (Glucotrol), tolbutamide (Orinase), and others.

Medications for depression (MAOIs). American ginseng might stimulate the body. Some medications used for depression can also stimulate the body. Taking American ginseng along with these medications used for depression might cause side effects such as anxiousness, headache, restlessness, and insomnia. Some of these medications used for depression include phenelzine (Nardil), tranylcypromine (Parnate), and others.

Warfarin (Coumadin). Warfarin (Coumadin) is used to slow blood clotting. American ginseng has been reported to decrease the effectiveness of warfarin (Coumadin). Decreasing the effectiveness of warfarin (Coumadin) might increase the risk of clotting. It is unclear why this interaction might occur. To avoid this interaction do not take American ginseng if you take warfarin (Coumadin).

Medical professionals should consult the Professional Version at www.NaturalDatabase.com.

Medical professionals should consult the
Professional Version at www.NaturalDatabase.com.

GINSENG, PANAX

What other names is the product known by?

Asian Ginseng, Asiatic Ginseng, Chinese Ginseng, Ginseng, Ginseng Asiatique, Ginseng Radix Alba, Ginseng Root, Guigai, Hong Shen, Japanese Ginseng, Jen-Shen, Jinsao, Jintsam, Insam, Korean Ginseng, Korean Panax Ginseng, Korean Red Ginseng, Ninjin, Oriental Ginseng, Panax schinseng, Radix Ginseng Rubra, Red Ginseng, Ren Shen, Renshen, Renxian, Sang, Seng, Sheng Shai Shen, White Ginseng.

What is it?

Panax ginseng is a plant. People use the root to make medicine. Do not confuse Panax ginseng with American Ginseng, Siberian Ginseng, or Panax Pseudoginseng.

Is it Effective?

The effectiveness ratings for **GINSENG, PANAX** are as follows:

Possibly Effective for... Thinking and memory • Diabetes • Cancer prevention • Male impotence (erectile dysfunction) • Premature ejaculation when a cream containing ginseng and other ingredients is applied directly to the skin of the penis.

Possibly Ineffective for... Improving athletic performance • Improving mood and sense of well-being • Hot flashes associated with menopause.

Insufficient Evidence to Rate Effectiveness for... Depression, anemia, fluid retention, stomach inflammation and other digestive problems, chronic fatigue syndrome (CFS), fever, bronchitis, cancer, common cold, influenza, and other conditions.

How does it work?

Panax ginseng contains many active substances. It is often referred to as a general well-being medication, because it affects many different systems of the body.

Are there safety concerns?

Panax ginseng is safe when taken by mouth for most adults when used for less than 3 months. The most common side effect is trouble sleeping. Less commonly people have menstrual problems, breast pain, increased heart rate, high or low blood pressure, headache, loss of appetite, diarrhea, itching, rash, dizziness, mood changes, vaginal bleeding, and many others. Uncommon side effects that have been reported include severe rash called Stevens-Johnson syndrome, liver damage, and severe allergic reactions.

Panax ginseng cream, made with other ingredients for impotence, seems to be safe when applied to the penis and removed after one hour. It might cause mild pain, irritation or a burning sensation, and delayed ejaculation. It is not known if this cream is safe with repeated, long-term use.

Panax ginseng is UNSAFE for infants and children. It may not be safe in pregnancy. One of the chemicals in Panax ginseng has been linked to possible birth defects.

Do not take Panax ginseng if: You are pregnant or breast-feeding. • You have a bleeding disorder. • You have a heart condition. • You have low or unstable blood pressure. • You have diabetes. • You have hormone sensitive cancers such as breast, uterine, or ovarian cancer. • You have hormone sensitive conditions such as endometriosis or uterine fibroids. • You have insomnia or difficulty sleeping. • You have had an organ transplant. • You have a mental condition called schizophrenia.

Are there any interactions with medications?

Alcohol. The body breaks down alcohol to get rid of it. Taking Panax ginseng might increase how fast your body gets rid of alcohol.

Caffeine. Caffeine can speed up the nervous system. By speeding up the nervous system, caffeine can make you feel jittery and speed up your heartbeat. Panax ginseng might also speed up the nervous system. Taking Panax ginseng along with caffeine might cause serious problems including increased heart rate and high blood pressure. Avoid taking caffeine along with Panax ginseng.

Furosemide (Lasix). Some scientists think that Panax ginseng might decrease how well furosemide (Lasix) works. But there isn't enough information to know if this is a big concern.

Insulin. Panax ginseng might decrease blood sugar. Insulin is also used to decrease blood sugar. Taking Panax ginseng along with insulin might cause your blood sugar to be too low. Monitor your blood sugar closely. The dose of your insulin might need to be changed.

Medications that slow blood clotting (Anticoagulant / Antiplatelet drugs). Panax ginseng might slow blood clotting. Taking Panax ginseng along with medications that also slow clotting might increase the chances of bruising and bleeding. Some medications that slow blood clotting include aspirin, clopidogrel (Plavix), diclofenac (Voltaren, Cataflam, others), ibuprofen (Advil, Motrin, others), naproxen (Anaprox, Naprosyn, others), dalteparin (Fragmin), enoxaparin (Lovenox), heparin, warfarin (Coumadin), and others.

Medications for diabetes (Antidiabetes drugs). Panax ginseng might decrease blood sugar. Diabetes medications are also used to lower blood sugar. Taking Panax ginseng along with diabetes medications might cause your blood sugar to go too low. Monitor your blood sugar closely. The dose of your diabetes medication might need to be changed. Some medications used for diabetes include glimepiride (Amaryl), glyburide (DiaBeta, Glynase PresTab, Micronase), insulin, pioglitazone (Actos), rosiglitazone (Avandia), chlorpropamide (Diabinese), glipizide (Glucotrol), tolbutamide (Orinase), and others.

Medications changed by the liver (Cytochrome P450 2D6 (CYP2D6) substrates). Some medications are changed and broken down by the liver. Panax ginseng might decrease how quickly the liver breaks down some medications. Taking Panax ginseng along with some medications that are changed by the liver can increase the effects and side effects of your medication. Before taking Panax ginseng talk to your healthcare provider if you take any medications that are changed by the liver. Some medications that are changed by the liver include amitriptyline (Elavil), clozapine (Clozaril), codeine, desipramine (Norpramin), donepezil (Aricept), fentanyl (Duragesic), flecainide (Tambocor), fluoxetine (Prozac), meperidine (Demerol), methadone (Dolophine), metoprolol (Lopressor, Toprol XL), olanzapine (Zyprexa), ondansetron (Zofran), tramadol (Ultram), trazodone (Desyrel), and others.

Medications that decrease the immune system (Immunosuppressants). Panax ginseng increases the immune system. By increasing the immune system, Panax ginseng might decrease the effectiveness of medications that decrease the immune system. Some medications that decrease the immune system include azathioprine (Imuran), basiliximab (Simulect), cyclosporine (Neoral, Sandimmune), daclizumab (Zenapax), muromonab-CD3 (OKT3, Orthoclone OKT3), mycophenolate (CellCept), tacrolimus (FK506, Prograf), sirolimus (Rapamune), prednisone (Deltasone, Orasone), corticosteroids (glucocorticoids), and others.

Medications for depression (MAOIs). Panax ginseng might stimulate the body. Some medications used for depression can also stimulate the body. Taking Panax ginseng with these medications used for depression might cause too much stimulation. This might cause side effects such as anxiousness, headache, restlessness, and insomnia. Some of these medications used for depression include phenelzine (Nardil), tranylcypromine (Parnate), and others.

Stimulant drugs. Stimulant drugs speed up the nervous system. By speeding up the nervous system, stimulant medications can make you feel jittery and speed up your heartbeat. Panax ginseng might also speed up the nervous system. Taking Panax ginseng along with stimulant drugs might cause serious problems including increased heart rate and high blood pressure. Avoid taking stimulant drugs along with Panax ginseng. Some stimulant drugs include diethylpropion (Tenuate), epinephrine, phentermine (Ionamin), pseudoephedrine (Sudafed), and many others.

Warfarin (Coumadin). Warfarin (Coumadin) is used to slow blood clotting. There is some concern that Panax ginseng might decrease the effectiveness of warfarin (Coumadin). But it's not clear if this interaction is a big problem. Be sure to have your blood checked regularly. The dose of your warfarin (Coumadin) might need to be changed.

GINSENG, SIBERIAN

What other names is the product known by?
Acanthopanax senticosus, Ci Wu Jia, Ciwujia, Devil's Bush, Devil's Shrub, Eleuthera, Eleuthero, Eleutherococc, Eleutherococci radix, Eleutherococcus senticosus, Ginseng Root, Hedera senticosa, Pepperbrush, Prickly Eleutherococc, Shigoka, Touch-Me-Not, Ussuri, Ussurian Thorny, Wild Pepper, Wu Jia Pi.

What is it?
Siberian ginseng is a plant. People use the root of the plant to make medicine.

Other herbs are often confused with Siberian ginseng. Be careful about which product you choose. Siberian ginseng is not the same herb as American or Panax ginseng.

Is it Effective?
The effectiveness ratings for **GINSENG, SIBERIAN** are as follows:
Possibly Effective for...A viral infection called herpes simplex 2.
Possibly Ineffective for... Increasing the speed, quality, and ability to do physical work.
Insufficient Evidence to Rate Effectiveness for... Improving memory, stroke, heart disease, kidney problems, Alzheimer's disease, attention deficit-hyperactivity disorder (ADHD), chronic fatigue syndrome, high cholesterol, fatigue, fibromyalgia, flu, chemotherapy side effects, bronchitis, tuberculosis, low oxygen levels, motion sickness, and other conditions.

How does it work?
Siberian ginseng contains many chemicals that affect the brain, immune system, and certain hormones. It might also contain chemicals that have activity against some bacteria and viruses.

Medical professionals should consult the Professional Version at www.NaturalDatabase.com.

Are there safety concerns?

Siberian ginseng is safe for most adults when used short-term. While side effects are rare, some people can have drowsiness, changes in heart rhythm, melancholy, anxiety, muscle spasms, and other side effects. In high doses, increased blood pressure might occur.

Do not take Siberian ginseng if: You are pregnant or breast-feeding. • You have a heart condition or high blood pressure. • You have breast, uterine, or ovarian cancer. • You have endometriosis or uterine fibroids. • You have diabetes. • You have a psychiatric condition such as mania or schizophrenia.

Are there any interactions with medications?

Alcohol. Alcohol can cause sleepiness and drowsiness. Siberian ginseng might also cause sleepiness and drowsiness. Taking large amounts of Siberian ginseng along with alcohol might cause too much sleepiness.

Digoxin (Lanoxin). Digoxin (Lanoxin) helps the heart beat more strongly. One person had too much digoxin in their system while taking a natural product that might have had Siberian ginseng in it. But it is unclear if Siberian ginseng or other herbs in the supplement were the cause.

Medications that slow blood clotting (Anticoagulant / Antiplatelet drugs). Siberian ginseng might slow blood clotting. Taking Siberian ginseng along with medications that also slow clotting might increase the chances of bruising and bleeding. Some medications that slow blood clotting include aspirin, clopidogrel (Plavix), diclofenac (Voltaren, Cataflam, others), ibuprofen (Advil, Motrin, others), naproxen (Anaprox, Naprosyn, others), dalteparin (Fragmin), enoxaparin (Lovenox), heparin, warfarin (Coumadin), and others.

Medications for diabetes (Antidiabetes drugs). Siberian ginseng might affect blood sugar, either lowering or increasing blood sugar levels. Diabetes medications are also used to lower blood sugar. Taking Siberian ginseng along with diabetes medications might cause your blood sugar to go too low or cause your diabetes medication to be less effective. Monitor your blood sugar closely. The dose of your diabetes medication might need to be changed. Some medications used for diabetes include glimepiride (Amaryl), glyburide (DiaBeta, Glynase PresTab, Micronase), insulin, pioglitazone (Actos), rosiglitazone (Avandia), chlorpropamide (Diabinese), glipizide (Glucotrol), tolbutamide (Orinase), and others.

Medications changed by the liver (Cytochrome P450 1A2 (CYP1A2) substrates). Some medications are changed and broken down by the liver. Siberian ginseng might decrease how quickly the liver breaks down some medications. Taking Siberian ginseng along with some medications that are changed by the liver might increase the effects and side effects of some medications. Before taking Siberian ginseng talk to your healthcare provider if you take any medications that are changed by the liver. Some of these medications that are changed by the liver include clozapine (Clozaril), cyclobenzaprine (Flexeril), fluvoxamine (Luvox), haloperidol (Haldol), imipramine (Tofranil), mexiletine (Mexitil), olanzapine (Zyprexa), pentazocine (Talwin), propranolol (Inderal), tacrine (Cognex), theophylline, zileuton (Zyflo), zolmitriptan (Zomig), and others.

Medications changed by the liver (Cytochrome P450 2C9 (CYP2C9) substrates). Some medications are changed and broken down by the liver. Siberian ginseng might decrease how quickly the liver breaks down some medications. Taking Siberian ginseng along with some medications that are broken down by the liver can increase the effects and side effects of some medications. Before taking Siberian ginseng talk to your healthcare provider if you take any medications that are changed by the liver. Some medications that are changed by the liver include amitriptyline (Elavil), diazepam (Valium), zileuton (Zyflo), celecoxib (Celebrex), diclofenac (Voltaren), fluvastatin (Lescol), glipizide (Glucotrol), ibuprofen (Advil, Motrin), irbesartan (Avapro), losartan (Cozaar), phenytoin (Dilantin), piroxicam (Feldene), tamoxifen (Nolvadex), tolbutamide (Tolinase), torsemide (Demadex), warfarin (Coumadin), and others.

Medications changed by the liver (Cytochrome P450 2D6 (CYP2D6) substrates). Some medications are changed and broken down by the liver. Siberian ginseng might decrease how quickly the liver breaks down some medications. Taking Siberian ginseng along with some medications that are change by the liver can increase the effects and side effects of your medication. Before taking Siberian ginseng talk to your healthcare provider if you take any medications that are changed by the liver. Some medications that are changed by the liver include amitriptyline (Elavil), clozapine (Clozaril), codeine, desipramine (Norpramin), donepezil (Aricept), fentanyl (Duragesic), flecainide (Tambocor), fluoxetine (Prozac), meperidine (Demerol), methadone (Dolophine), metoprolol (Lopressor, Toprol XL), olanzapine (Zyprexa), ondansetron (Zofran), tramadol (Ultram), trazodone (Desyrel), and others.

Medications changed by the liver (Cytochrome P450 3A4 (CYP3A4) substrates). Some medications are changed and broken down by the liver. Siberian ginseng might decrease how quickly the liver breaks down some medications. Taking Siberian ginseng along with some medications that are broken down by the liver can increase the effects and side effects of some medications. Before taking Siberian ginseng, talk to your healthcare provider if you are taking any medications that are changed by the liver. Some medications changed by the liver include lovastatin (Mevacor), ketoconazole (Nizoral), itraconazole (Sporanox), fexofenadine (Allegra), triazolam (Halcion), and many others.

Sedative medications (CNS depressants). Siberian ginseng might cause sleepiness and drowsiness. Medications that cause sleepiness are called sedatives. Taking Siberian ginseng along with sedative medications might cause too much sleepiness. Some sedative medications include clonazepam (Klonopin), lorazepam (Ativan), phenobarbital (Donnatal), zolpidem (Ambien), and others.

GLOBE FLOWER

What other names is the product known by?
Globe Crowfoot, Globe Ranunculus, Globe Trollius, Trollius europaeus.

What is it?
Globe flower is a plant. The whole fresh plant is used to make medicine.

Is it Effective?
The effectiveness ratings for **GLOBE FLOWER** are as follows:
Insufficient Evidence to Rate Effectiveness for... Scurvy (vitamin C deficiency) and other uses.

How does it work?
There isn't enough information to know how globe flower might work.

Are there safety concerns?
Fresh globe flower plant is UNSAFE. Fresh globe flower contains substances which are very irritating to the digestive tract, causing stomach pain and diarrhea. It can also irritate the urinary system, which includes the kidney and bladder. Skin contact can cause blisters and burns that are difficult to heal.

There isn't enough information to know whether the dried plant might be safe or what the potential side effects might be.

Do not use globe flower if: You are pregnant or breast-feeding.

Are there any interactions with medications?
It is not known if globe flower interacts with any medicines.
Before taking globe flower, talk with your healthcare professional if you take any medications.

GLOSSY PRIVET

What other names is the product known by?
Chinese Privet, Dongqingzi, Joteishi, Ligustro, Ligustrum, Ligustrum Fruit, Ligustrum lucidum, Nu Zhen, Nu Zhen Zi, Nuzhenzi, Privet, To-Nezumimochi, Troène De Chine, Trueno, White Waxtree, Yojungja.

What is it?
Glossy privet is a plant. The ripe fruit is used to make medicine. Be careful not to confuse glossy privet (Ligustrum lucidum) with other species of privet such as Japanese privet, border privet, Chinese privet, common privet, golden privet, and others.

Is it Effective?
The effectiveness ratings for **GLOSSY PRIVET** are as follows:
Insufficient Evidence to Rate Effectiveness for... Promoting growth and darkening of hair, reducing dark spots on the face, heart palpitations, rheumatism, swelling, tumors, vertigo, common cold, congestion, constipation, fever, headache, chronic fatigue syndrome (CFS), liver problems, trouble sleeping (insomnia), improving immune function, reducing the side effects of cancer treatment, and many other uses.

How does it work?
It is not well-understood how glossy privet might work. There is some evidence that it may stimulate the immune system and help fight cancer.

Are there safety concerns?
Glossy privet is possibly safe for most adults when used appropriately. Some people may have allergic reactions such as a runny nose and asthma.

Do not use glossy privet if: You are pregnant or breast-feeding. • You are allergic to the pollen of related plants such as common privet, olive, ash, or lilac.

Are there any interactions with medications?
It is not known if glossy privet interacts with any medicines.
Before taking glossy privet, talk with your healthcare professional if you take any medications.

Medical professionals should consult the Professional Version at www.NaturalDatabase.com.

CONSUMER VERSION

GLUCOMANNAN

What other names is the product known by?
Amorphophallus konjac, Konjac, Konjac Mannan.

What is it?
Glucomannan is a sugar made from the root of the konjac plant (Amorphophallus konjac).

Is it Effective?
The effectiveness ratings for **GLUCOMANNAN** are as follows:
Possibly Effective for... Reducing cholesterol levels in people with diabetes • Helping control type 2 diabetes.
Insufficient Evidence to Rate Effectiveness for... Constipation, weight loss, and high cholesterol when used with chitosan.

How does it work?
Glucomannan might work in the stomach and intestines by absorbing water to form a bulky fiber which treats constipation. It may also slow the absorption of glucose (sugar) and cholesterol from the gut, helping to control sugar levels in diabetes, and reducing cholesterol levels.

Are there safety concerns?
Glucomannan powder or flour in enriched foods such as noodles is safe. Glucomannan powder and capsules seem to be safe for most adults and children. Avoid using solid tablets containing glucomannan. These can sometimes cause blockages of the throat or intestines.

Do not use glucomannan if: You are pregnant or breast-feeding.

Are there any interactions with medications?
Medications for diabetes (Antidiabetes drugs). Glucomannan can decrease blood sugar in people with type 2 diabetes. Diabetes medications are also used to lower blood sugar. Taking glucomannan along with diabetes medications might cause your blood sugar to go too low. Monitor your blood sugar closely. The dose of your diabetes medication might need to be changed. Some medications used for diabetes include glimepiride (Amaryl), glyburide (DiaBeta, Glynase PresTab, Micronase), insulin, pioglitazone (Actos), rosiglitazone (Avandia), chlorpropamide (Diabinese), glipizide (Glucotrol), tolbutamide (Orinase), and others.
Medications taken by mouth (Oral drugs). Glucomannan absorbs substances in the stomach and intestines. Taking glucomannan along with medications taken by mouth can decrease how much medicine your body absorbs, and decrease the effectiveness of your medication. To prevent this interaction, take glucomannan at least one hour after medications you take by mouth.

GLUCOSAMINE HYDROCHLORIDE

What other names is the product known by?
2-amino-2-deoxyglucose hydrochloride, 2-amino-2-deoxyglucose hydrochloride, Glucosamine, Glucosamine HCL, Glucosamine KCL.

What is it?
Glucosamine is usually made from seashells, or it can be made in the laboratory. Glucosamine hydrochloride is a salt form of glucosamine.

Is it Effective?
The effectiveness ratings for **GLUCOSAMINE HYDROCHLORIDE** are as follows:
Insufficient Evidence to Rate Effectiveness for... Osteoarthritis, joint pain, back pain, and glaucoma.

How does it work?
Glucosamine in the body is used to make a "cushion" that surrounds the joints. In osteoarthritis, this cushion becomes thinner and stiff. Taking glucosamine hydrochloride as a supplement might help to supply the materials needed to rebuild the cushion.

Are there safety concerns?
Glucosamine hydrochloride seems to be safe for most adults. Glucosamine hydrochloride can cause gas, bloating, and cramps.
Some glucosamine products do not contain the labeled amount of glucosamine or contain excessive amounts of manganese. Ask your healthcare professional about reliable brands.

Some preliminary research suggests that glucosamine might raise blood sugar in people with diabetes. However, glucosamine doesn't seem to significantly affect blood sugar control in people with diabetes. Glucosamine with routine blood sugar monitoring appears to be safe for most people with diabetes.

There is some concern that glucosamine products might cause allergic reactions in people who are sensitive to shellfish. Glucosamine is produced from the shells of shrimp, lobster, and crabs. But allergic reactions in people with shellfish allergy are caused by the meat of shellfish, not the shell. There are no reports of allergic reactions to glucosamine in people who are allergic to shellfish. There is also some information that people with shellfish allergy can safely take glucosamine products.

Do not use glucosamine hydrochloride if: You are pregnant or breast-feeding. • You have asthma.

Are there any interactions with medications?

Medications for cancer (Antimitotic chemotherapy). Some medications for cancer work by decreasing how fast cancer cells can copy themselves. Some scientists think that glucosamine might increase how fast tumor cells can copy themselves. Taking glucosamine along with some medications for cancer might decrease the effectiveness of these medications.

Medications for diabetes (Antidiabetes drugs). Glucosamine hydrochloride might increase blood sugar in some people. Diabetes medications are used to lower blood sugar. By increasing blood sugar, glucosamine hydrochloride might decrease the effectiveness of diabetes medications. But some people with diabetes can take glucosamine hydrochloride without any blood sugar problems. If you take glucosamine hydrochloride and have diabetes, monitor your blood sugar closely. The dose of your diabetes medication might need to be changed. Some medications used for diabetes include glimepiride (Amaryl), glyburide (DiaBeta, Glynase PresTab, Micronase), insulin, pioglitazone (Actos), rosiglitazone (Avandia), chlorpropamide (Diabinese), glipizide (Glucotrol), tolbutamide (Orinase), and others.

Warfarin (Coumadin). Warfarin (Coumadin) is used to slow blood clotting. There is one report of someone taking very large amounts of glucosamine and chondroitin and having blood that was too "thin." Blood that is too "thin" can cause bruising and bleeding. But there is not enough information to know if this interaction is a big concern or if it can happen with normal amounts of glucosamine and chondroitin.

GLUCOSAMINE SULFATE

What other names is the product known by?

D-Glucosamine, Glucosamine, Glucosamine Sulphate, Glucosamine Sulfate HCL, Glucosamine SO4.

What is it?

Glucosamine sulfate is a chemical compound found in the fluid around joints. It can also be taken from natural sources such as seashells, or it can be made in the laboratory.

Don't confuse glucosamine sulfate with other forms such as glucosamine hydrochloride or N-acetyl-glucosamine. They may not have the same effects.

Is it Effective?

The effectiveness ratings for **GLUCOSAMINE SULFATE** are as follows:

Likely Effective for... Osteoarthritis when taken by mouth.

Possibly Effective for... Temporomandibular joint (TMJ) arthritis.

Insufficient Evidence to Rate Effectiveness for... Glaucoma and weight loss.

How does it work?

Glucosamine in the body is used to make cartilage, a "cushion" that surrounds joints. In osteoarthritis, this cushion becomes thinner and stiff. Taking glucosamine sulfate as a supplement might help to supply the materials needed to rebuild cartilage.

Are there safety concerns?

Glucosamine sulfate seems to be safe for most people. It can cause some mild side effects including nausea, heartburn, diarrhea, and constipation. Uncommon side effects are drowsiness, skin reactions, and headache. Some glucosamine products do not contain the labeled amount of glucosamine or contain excessive amounts of manganese. Ask your healthcare professional about reliable brands.

Some preliminary research suggests that glucosamine sulfate might raise blood sugar in people with diabetes. However, more reliable research indicates that glucosamine sulfate does not seem to significantly affect blood sugar control in people with type 2 diabetes. Glucosamine with routine blood sugar monitoring appears to be safe for most people with diabetes.

There is some concern that glucosamine products might cause allergic reactions in people who are sensitive to shellfish. Glucosamine is produced from the shells of shrimp, lobster, and crabs. But allergic reactions in people with shellfish allergy are caused by the meat of shellfish, not the shell. There are no reports of allergic reactions to glucosamine in people who are allergic to shellfish. There is also some information that people with shellfish allergy can safely take glucosamine products.

Do not take glucosamine if: You are pregnant or breast-feeding. • You have asthma.

Are there any interactions with medications?

Acetaminophen (Tylenol, others). Glucosamine sulfate and acetaminophen (Tylenol, others) might decrease each other's effectiveness. But more information is needed to know if this interaction is a big concern.

Medications for cancer (Antimitotic chemotherapy). Some medications for cancer work by decreasing how fast cancer cells can copy themselves. Some scientists think that glucosamine might increase how fast tumor cells can copy themselves. Taking glucosamine along with some medications for cancer might decrease the effectiveness of these medications for cancer.

Medications for diabetes (Antidiabetes drugs). Glucosamine sulfate might increase blood sugar in some people. Diabetes medications are used to lower blood sugar. By increasing blood sugar, glucosamine sulfate might decrease the effectiveness of diabetes medications. But some people with diabetes can take glucosamine sulfate without any blood sugar problems. If you take glucosamine sulfate and have diabetes, monitor your blood sugar closely. The dose of your diabetes medication might need to be changed. Some medications used for diabetes include glimepiride (Amaryl), glyburide (DiaBeta, Glynase PresTab, Micronase), insulin, pioglitazone (Actos), rosiglitazone (Avandia), chlorpropamide (Diabinese), glipizide (Glucotrol), tolbutamide (Orinase), and others.

Warfarin (Coumadin). Warfarin (Coumadin) is used to slow blood clotting. There is one report of someone taking very large amounts of glucosamine and chondroitin and having blood that was too "thin." Blood that is too "thin" can cause bruising and bleeding. But there is not enough information to know if this interaction is a big concern or if it can happen with normal amounts of glucosamine and chondroitin.

GLUTAMINE

What other names is the product known by?

GLN, Glutamate, Glutamic Acid, Glutaminate, Levoglutamide, Levoglutamine, L-(+)-2-Aminoglutaramic acid, L-Glutamic Acid, L-Glutamic Acid 5-Amide, L-Glutamine, Q.

What is it?

Glutamine is an amino acid (a building block for proteins), found naturally in the body.

Is it Effective?

The effectiveness ratings for **GLUTAMINE** are as follows:

Possibly Effective for... Improving recovery after surgery • Soreness and swelling inside the mouth, caused by chemotherapy treatments for cancer • Improving well-being in people with traumatic injuries • Treating weight loss and intestinal problems in people with HIV disease (AIDS).

Possibly Ineffective for...A urinary problem called cystinuria • An intestinal condition called Crohn's disease • Improving exercise performance • Rehydrating infants with severe diarrhea.

Insufficient Evidence to Rate Effectiveness for... Nutrition problems after major gut surgery (short bowel syndrome), depression, moodiness, irritability, anxiety, attention deficit-hyperactivity disorder (ADHD), insomnia, stomach ulcers, ulcerative colitis, sickle cell anemia, muscle and joint pains caused by the drug paclitaxel (Taxol, used to treat cancer), treating alcoholism, reducing damage to the immune system during cancer treatment, and other conditions.

How does it work?

Glutamine is an amino acid that might help gut function, the immune system, and other essential processes in the body, especially in times of stress. It is also important for providing "fuel" to many different cells in the body. Glutamine is needed to make other chemicals in the body.

Are there safety concerns?

Glutamine seems safe for most adults and children when taken by mouth, but the potential side effects of glutamine are not known.

Avoid using more than 40 grams of glutamine daily.

Do not use glutamine if: You are pregnant or breast-feeding. • You have severe liver disease with difficulty thinking or confusion. • You are allergic to monosodium glutamate (MSG), also known as "Chinese restaurant syndrome." • You have mania, a mental disorder. • You have seizures.

Are there any interactions with medications?

Lactulose. Lactulose helps decrease ammonia in the body. Glutamine is changed into ammonia in the body. Taking glutamine along with lactulose might decrease the effectiveness of lactulose.

Medications for cancer (Chemotherapy). There is some concern that glutamine might decrease the effectiveness of some medications for cancer. But it is too soon to know if this interaction occurs.

Medications used to prevent seizures (Anticonvulsants). Medications used to prevent seizures affect chemicals in the brain. Glutamine may also affect chemicals in the brain. By affecting chemicals in the brain, glutamine may decrease the effectiveness of medications used to prevent seizures. Some medications used to prevent seizures include phenobarbital, primidone (Mysoline), valproic acid (Depakene), gabapentin (Neurontin), carbamazepine (Tegretol), phenytoin (Dilantin), and others.

GLUTATHIONE

What other names is the product known by?

Gamma-Glutamylcysteinylglycine, Gamma-L-Glutamyl-L-Cysteinylglycine, L-Glutathione, GSH, N-(N-L-gamma-Glutamyl-L-cysteinyl)glycine.

What is it?

Glutathione is a substance produced naturally by the liver. It is also present in fruits, vegetables, and meats.

Is it Effective?

The effectiveness ratings for **GLUTATHIONE** are as follows:

Possibly Effective for... Reducing side effects of chemotherapy treatments for cancer, when given by injection into the veins.

Insufficient Evidence to Rate Effectiveness for... Treating lung diseases by inhaling (breathing in) glutathione, use as an injection into the veins to treat infertility in men, Parkinson's disease, diabetes, anemia in people on hemodialysis, or clogging of the arteries (atherosclerosis). When taken by mouth for cataracts, glaucoma, preventing aging, treating or preventing alcoholism, asthma, cancer, heart disease, high cholesterol levels, liver problems, AIDS, chronic fatigue syndrome, memory loss, Alzheimer's disease, osteoarthritis, or Parkinson's disease.

How does it work?

Glutathione is involved in many processes in the body, including tissue building and repair, making chemicals and proteins needed in the body, and for the immune system.

Are there safety concerns?

Glutathione may be safe for most adults, but the potential side effects are not known.

Do not use glutathione if: You are pregnant or breast-feeding. • You have asthma (do not inhale glutathione).

Are there any interactions with medications?

It is not known if glutathione interacts with any medicines.
Before taking glutathione, talk with your healthcare professional if you take any medications.

GLYCEROL

What other names is the product known by?

1,2,3-propanetriol, Glicerol, Glucerite, Glycerin, Glycerine, Glycerolum, Glyceryl Alcohol.

What is it?

Glycerol is a naturally occurring chemical. People use it as a medicine. Some uses and dosage forms have been approved by the Food and Drug Administration (FDA).

Is it Effective?

The effectiveness ratings for **GLYCEROL** are as follows:

Likely Effective for... Constipation, when used rectally as a suppository.

Possibly Ineffective for... Helping with weight loss, when taken by mouth.

Likely Ineffective for... Improving exercise performance when taken by mouth • Treating stroke when used intravenously.

Insufficient Evidence to Rate Effectiveness for... Helping maintain the body's water levels (hydration) in athletes and people with intestinal problems, and other conditions.

CONSUMER VERSION

Medical professionals should consult the Professional Version at www.NaturalDatabase.com.

How does it work?
Glycerol attracts water into the gut, softening stools and relieving constipation.

Are there safety concerns?
Glycerol is safe for most adults. It may not be safe when preparations of glycerol are used which have not been reviewed for safety and efficacy by the FDA. When taken by mouth, glycerol can cause side effects including headaches, dizziness, bloating, nausea, vomiting, thirst, and diarrhea.

Glycerol may not be safe when injected intravenously (I.V. use). Red blood cells might get seriously damaged.

Do not use glycerol if: You are pregnant or breast-feeding.

Are there any interactions with medications?
It is not known if glycerol interacts with any medicines.
Before taking glycerol, talk with your healthcare professional if you take any medications.

GLYCINE

What other names is the product known by?
Athenon, G Salt, Free Base Glycine, Glycocoll, Glycosthene, Iconyl, L-Glycine, Monazol.

What is it?
Glycine is an amino acid that the body makes and also obtains from food.

Is it Effective?
The effectiveness ratings for **GLYCINE** are as follows:
Possibly Effective for... Treating schizophrenia, when used with other medicine • Treating leg ulcers • Treating strokes.
Insufficient Evidence to Rate Effectiveness for... Memory enhancement, benign prostatic hypertrophy, and other uses.

How does it work?
The body uses glycine to make proteins. Glycine is also involved in the transmission of chemical signals in the brain.

Are there safety concerns?
Glycine is usually well-tolerated. Rarely nausea, vomiting, and stomach upset have been reported.

Do not use glycine if: You are pregnant or breast-feeding.

Are there any interactions with medications?
Clozapine (Clozaril). Clozapine (Clozaril) is used to help treat schizophrenia. Taking glycine along with clozapine (Clozaril) might decrease the effectiveness of clozapine (Clozaril). It is not clear why this interaction occurs yet.
Do not take glycine if you are taking clozapine (Clozaril).

GOA POWDER

What other names is the product known by?
Andira araroba, Araoba, Bahia Powder, Brazil Powder, Chrysatobine, Crude Chrysarobin, Ringworm Powder.

What is it?
Goa powder is the dried, powdered latex from a Brazilian tree. People use it as medicine.

Is it Effective?
The effectiveness ratings for **GOA POWDER** are as follows:
Insufficient Evidence to Rate Effectiveness for... Psoriasis or fungal infections, when applied to the skin.

How does it work?

Goa powder contains chemicals that resemble some prescription medications used for psoriasis.

Are there safety concerns?

Goa powder is possibly unsafe. When used on the skin, it is very irritating and can cause side effects including redness, swelling and pustules. It can also be absorbed through the skin to cause vomiting, diarrhea and kidney problems.

Do not use goa powder if: You are pregnant or breast-feeding.

Are there any interactions with medications?

It is not known if goa powder interacts with any medicines.
Before taking goa powder, talk with your healthcare professional if you take any medications.

GOAT'S RUE

What other names is the product known by?

French Honeysuckle, French Lilac, Galega officinalis, Galega bicolor, Galega patula, Galegae officinalis herba, Geissrautenkraut, Goat's Rue Herb, Italian Fitch.

What is it?

Goat's rue is a plant. The above ground parts are used to make medicine. Be careful not to confuse goat's rue (galega officinalis) with rue (ruta graveolens).

Is it Effective?

The effectiveness ratings for **GOAT'S RUE** are as follows:
Insufficient Evidence to Rate Effectiveness for... Diabetes, blood purification, digestive problems, and other uses.

How does it work?

Goat's rue contains a chemical that may lower blood sugar when isolated from the rest of the plant. It is unclear if goat's rue has this effect when taken by people.

Are there safety concerns?

There isn't enough information to know whether goat's rue is safe. No adverse effects have been reported in humans, but fatal poisoning has occurred in grazing animals that ate large quantities of goat's rue.

Do not use goat's rue if: You are pregnant or breast-feeding. • You have diabetes.

Are there any interactions with medications?

Medications for diabetes (Antidiabetes drugs). Goat's rue might decrease blood sugar. Diabetes medications are also used to lower blood sugar. Taking goat's rue along with diabetes medications might cause your blood sugar to go too low. Monitor your blood sugar closely. The dose of your diabetes medication might need to be changed. Some medications used for diabetes include glimepiride (Amaryl), glyburide (DiaBeta, Glynase PresTab, Micronase), insulin, pioglitazone (Actos), rosiglitazone (Avandia), chlorpropamide (Diabinese), glipizide (Glucotrol), tolbutamide (Orinase), and others.

GOLDEN RAGWORT

What other names is the product known by?

Cocash Weed, Coughweed, False Valerian, Female Regulator, Golden Groundsel, Golden Senecio, Grundy Swallow, Life Root, Ragwort, Senecio aureus, Squaw Weed.

What is it?

Golden ragwort is a plant. It is used to make medicine. Be careful not to confuse golden ragwort (Senecio aureus) with other species of ragwort such as alpine ragwort and tansy ragwort.

Is it Effective?

The effectiveness ratings for **GOLDEN RAGWORT** are as follows:
Insufficient Evidence to Rate Effectiveness for... Diabetes, high blood pressure, spasms, fluid retention, bleeding, irregular or painful menstrual periods, and other uses.

Medical professionals should consult the Professional Version at www.NaturalDatabase.com.

How does it work?
There isn't enough information to know how golden ragwort might work.

Are there safety concerns?
Golden ragwort is considered UNSAFE when used by mouth or directly on the skin. Golden ragwort contains substances which cause serious toxicities including liver damage, increased risk for cancer, and circulation problems.

Golden ragwort can cause allergic reactions. People at the greatest risk of allergic reactions are those who are allergic to plants such as ragweed, chrysanthemums, marigolds, daisies, and many others.

Do not use golden ragwort if: You are pregnant or breast-feeding. • You have liver disease. • You are allergic to the plant family Asteraceae/Compositae which includes ragweed, chrysanthemums, marigolds, and daisies.

Are there any interactions with medications?
Medications that increase break down of other medications by the liver (Cytochrome P450 3A4 (CYP3A4) inducers). Golden ragwort is broken down by the liver. Some chemicals that form when the liver breaks down golden ragwort can be harmful. Medications that cause the liver to break down golden ragwort might enhance the toxic effects of chemicals contained in golden ragwort. Some of these medicines include carbamazepine (Tegretol), phenobarbital, phenytoin (Dilantin), rifampin, rifabutin (Mycobutin), and others.

GOLDENROD

What other names is the product known by?
Aaron's Rod, European Goldenrod, Solidago canadensis, Solidago gigantea, Solidago longifolia, Solidago serotina, Solidago virgaurea, Woundwort.

What is it?
Goldenrod is an herb. People use the above ground plant parts for medicine.

Is it Effective?
The effectiveness ratings for **GOLDENROD** are as follows:
Insufficient Evidence to Rate Effectiveness for... Spasms; swelling (inflammation) of the mouth, throat, and lower urinary tract; wounds; gout; arthritis; kidney stones; skin conditions; tuberculosis; diabetes; enlargement of the liver; hemorrhoids; internal bleeding; asthma; hayfever; and prostate enlargement.

How does it work?
Goldenrod contains chemicals that increase urine flow and have anti-swelling (anti-inflammatory) effects.

Are there safety concerns?
There is not enough information available to know if goldenrod is safe.

It may cause an allergic reaction in people sensitive to plants such as daisies or ragweed.

Do not use goldenrod if: You are pregnant or breast-feeding. • You are allergic to plants such as daisies or ragweed. • You have fluid retention due to heart or kidney disease. • You have high blood pressure. • You have a urinary tract infection.

Are there any interactions with medications?
Water pills (Diuretic drugs). Goldenrod seems to work like "water pills" by causing the body to lose water. Taking goldenrod along with other "water pills" might cause the body to lose too much water. Losing too much water can cause you to be dizzy and your blood pressure to go too low. Some "water pills" include chlorothiazide (Diuril), chlorthalidone (Thalitone), furosemide (Lasix), hydrochlorothiazide (HCTZ, Hydrodiuril, Microzide), and others.

GOLDENSEAL

What other names is the product known by?

Eye Balm, Eye Root, Goldenroot, Goldsiegel, Ground Raspberry, Indian Dye, Indian Plant, Indian Tumeric, Jaundice Root, Orange Root, Sceau D'Or, Turmeric Root, Warnera, Wild Curcuma, Yellow Indian Paint, Yellow Puccoon, Yellow Root, Hydrastis Canadensis.

What is it?

Goldenseal is an herb. The dried root is used to make medicine.

Is it Effective?

The effectiveness ratings for **GOLDENSEAL** are as follows:

Possibly Ineffective for... Causing false-negative test results for urine drug tests.

Insufficient Evidence to Rate Effectiveness for... Urinary tract infections (UTIs), hemorrhoids, stomach upset, anorexia, stomach ulcers, colitis, menstrual irregularities, chronic fatigue syndrome (CFS), conjunctivitis, nasal congestion, hayfever, and many other conditions.

How does it work?

Goldenseal contains the chemical berberine, which might prevent the bacteria Escherichia coli (E. coli) from binding to urinary tract walls.

Are there safety concerns?

Goldenseal seems to be safe when used as a single dose. There is not enough reliable information to know if goldenseal is safe for long-term use.

Don't use goldenseal in newborn babies. It is unsafe for them.

Do not take goldenseal if: You are pregnant or breast-feeding.

Are there any interactions with medications?

Cyclosporin (Neoral, Sandimmune). The body breaks down cyclosporin (Neoral, Sandimmune) to get rid of it. Goldenseal might decrease how fast the body breaks down cyclosporin (Neoral, Sandimmune). This might cause there to be too much cyclosporin (Neoral, Sandimmune) in the body and potentially cause side effects.

Medications changed by the liver (Cytochrome P450 2D6 (CYP2D6) substrates). Some medications are changed and broken down by the liver. Goldenseal might decrease how quickly the liver breaks down some medications. Taking goldenseal along with some medications that are changed by the liver can increase the effects and side effects of your medication. Before taking goldenseal talk to your healthcare provider if you take any medications that are changed by the liver. Some medications that are changed by the liver include amitriptyline (Elavil), clozapine (Clozaril), codeine, desipramine (Norpramin), donepezil (Aricept), fentanyl (Duragesic), flecainide (Tambocor), fluoxetine (Prozac), meperidine (Demerol), methadone (Dolophine), metoprolol (Lopressor, Toprol XL), olanzapine (Zyprexa), ondansetron (Zofran), tramadol (Ultram), trazodone (Desyrel), and others.

Medications changed by the liver (Cytochrome P450 3A4 (CYP3A4) substrates). Some medications are changed and broken down by the liver. Goldenseal might decrease how quickly the liver breaks down some medications. Taking goldenseal along with some medications that are broken down by the liver can increase the effects and side effects of some medications. Before taking goldenseal, talk to your healthcare provider if you are taking any medications that are changed by the liver. Some medications changed by the liver include lovastatin (Mevacor), ketoconazole (Nizoral), itraconazole (Sporanox), fexofenadine (Allegra), triazolam (Halcion), and many others.

GOLDTHREAD

What other names is the product known by?

Cankerroot, Chinese Goldthread, Coptide, Coptis, Coptis Chinesis, Coptis deltoidea, Coptis teetoides, Coptis trifolia, Coptis groenlandica, Goldenthread, Huang Lian, Mouth Root, Yellowroot.

What is it?

Goldthread is a plant. The underground stem (rhizome) is used to make medicine.

Is it Effective?

The effectiveness ratings for **GOLDTHREAD** are as follows:

Insufficient Evidence to Rate Effectiveness for... Digestive problems and other uses.

Medical professionals should consult the Professional Version at www.NaturalDatabase.com.

How does it work?
Goldthread might decrease acid in the stomach. It also appears to have antibacterial effects.

Are there safety concerns?
There is not enough information to know if goldthread is safe in medicinal amounts. Goldthread is unsafe in newborn infants.

Do not use goldthread if: You are pregnant or breast-feeding.

Are there any interactions with medications?
Cyclosporin (Neoral, Sandimmune). The body breaks down cyclosporin (Neoral, Sandimmune) to get rid of it. Goldthread might decrease how fast the body breaks down cyclosporin (Neoral, Sandimmune). This might cause there to be too much cyclosporin (Neoral, Sandimmune) in the body and potentially cause side effects.
Medications changed by the liver (Cytochrome P450 3A4 (CYP3A4) substrates). Some medications are changed and broken down by the liver. Goldthread might decrease how quickly the liver breaks down some medications. Taking goldthread along with some medications that are broken down by the liver can increase the effects and side effects of some medications. Before taking goldthread, talk to your healthcare provider if you are taking any medications that are changed by the liver. Some medications changed by the liver include cyclosporin (Neoral, Sandimmune), lovastatin (Mevacor), clarithromycin (Biaxin), indinavir (Crixivan), sildenafil (Viagra), triazolam (Halcion), and many others.

GOSSYPOL

What other names is the product known by?
Cottonseed Oil, Gossypium herbaceum, Gossypium hirsutum, Karpasa.

What is it?
Gossypol is a substance found in the cotton plant. It is extracted commercially from the seeds and used for medicine.

Is it Effective?
The effectiveness ratings for **GOSSYPOL** are as follows:
Possibly Effective for... Male contraception (birth control), when taken by mouth.
Insufficient Evidence to Rate Effectiveness for... Use as a vaginal spermicide, problems of the uterus (womb) and ovaries, HIV/AIDS, cancer, and other conditions.

How does it work?
Gossypol interferes with sperm development and function.

Are there safety concerns?
Gossypol might be UNSAFE for use without close supervision by a healthcare professional. When men take gossypol by mouth, the effects on sperm are unpredictable and might cause sterility with long-term use. When women take gossypol by mouth, it might be toxic to cells lining the uterus and could prevent normal function of the ovaries. Gossypol can also cause loss of energy, changes in appetite, decreased sexual desire (libido), changes in body potassium levels, and digestive tract problems. High doses of gossypol (100 times the dose used for contraception) can cause changes in hair color, malnutrition, blood circulation problems, heart failure, and other problems.

There isn't enough information to know whether gossypol is safe to use directly on the skin. It can cause a burning sensation.

Do not use gossypol if: You are pregnant or breast-feeding. • You have low potassium levels (hypokalemia). • You have irritation or sensitivity of your urinary system. • You have a stomach or intestinal disorder. • You are trying to conceive a child.

Are there any interactions with medications?
Digoxin (Lanoxin). Large amounts of gossypol can decrease potassium levels in the body. Low potassium levels can increase the side effects of digoxin (Lanoxin).
NSAIDs (Nonsteroidal anti-inflammatory drugs). NSAIDs are anti-inflammatory medications used for decreasing pain and swelling. NSAIDs can cause irritation to the stomach and intestines. Gossypol can also cause irritation to the stomach and intestines. Taking NSAIDs along with gossypol might increase the chances of adverse effects. Avoid taking NSAIDs and gossypol together. Some NSAIDs include ibuprofen (Advil, Motrin, Nuprin,

others), indomethacin (Indocin), naproxen (Aleve, Anaprox, Naprelan, Naprosyn), piroxicam (Feldene), aspirin, and others.

Stimulant laxatives. Stimulant laxatives speed up the bowels. Overuse of stimulant laxatives can cause low minerals in the body. Gossypol can also decrease minerals in the body. Do not take gossypol along with stimulant laxatives.

Theophylline. Theophylline might decrease some of the effects of gossypol.

Water pills (Diuretic drugs). Large amounts of gossypol can decrease potassium levels in the body. "Water pills" can also decrease potassium in the body. Taking gossypol along with "water pills" might decrease potassium in the body too much. Some "water pills" that can deplete potassium include chlorothiazide (Diuril), chlorthalidone (Thalitone), furosemide (Lasix), hydrochlorothiazide (HCTZ, HydroDiuril, Microzide), and others.

GOTU KOLA

What other names is the product known by?

Brahma-Buti, Brahma-Manduki, Centellase, Centella Asiatica, Centella Coriacea, Gota Kola, Hydrocotyle Asiatica, Indischer Wassernabel, Indian Pennywort, Indian Water Navelwort, Luei Gong Gen, Madecassol, Mandukaparni, Manduk Parani, Marsh Penny, TTFCA, Talepetrako, Thick-Leaved Pennywort, Tsubo-kusa, Tungchian, White Rot.

What is it?

Gotu kola is an herb. The above ground parts are used to make medicine.

Is it Effective?

The effectiveness ratings for **GOTU KOLA** are as follows:

Possibly Effective for... Decreased return of blood from the feet and legs back to the heart called venous insufficiency • Preventing blood clots in the legs while flying.

Insufficient Evidence to Rate Effectiveness for... Fatigue, anxiety, increasing circulation in people with diabetes, atherosclerosis, stretch marks associated with pregnancy, common cold and flu, sunstroke, tonsillitis, urinary tract infection (UTI), schistosomiasis, hepatitis, jaundice, diarrhea, indigestion, improving wound healing when applied to the skin, a skin condition called psoriasis, and other conditions.

How does it work?

Gotu kola contains certain chemicals that seem to decrease inflammation and also decrease blood pressure in veins. Gotu kola also boosts production of the substance collagen, which is important for wound healing.

Are there safety concerns?

Gotu kola might not be safe when taken by mouth. Gotu kola might cause liver damage in some people. It can also cause other side effects including stomach upset, nausea, and itching. Too much gotu kola might also cause drowsiness.

Do not take gotu kola if: You are pregnant or breast-feeding. • You have liver disease.

Are there any interactions with medications?

Medications that can harm the liver (Hepatotoxic drugs). Gotu kola might harm the liver. Taking gotu kola along with medication that might also harm the liver can increase the risk of liver damage. Some medications that can harm the liver include acetaminophen (Tylenol and others), amiodarone (Cordarone), carbamazepine (Tegretol), isoniazid (INH), methotrexate (Rheumatrex), methyldopa (Aldomet), fluconazole (Diflucan), itraconazole (Sporanox), erythromycin (Erythrocin, Ilosone, others), phenytoin (Dilantin), lovastatin (Mevacor), pravastatin (Pravachol), simvastatin (Zocor), and many others.

Sedative medications (CNS depressants). Large amounts of gotu kola might cause sleepiness and drowsiness. Medications that cause sleepiness are called sedatives. Taking gotu kola along with sedative medications might cause too much sleepiness. Some sedative medications include clonazepam (Klonopin), lorazepam (Ativan), phenobarbital (Donnatal), zolpidem (Ambien), and others.

GOUTWEED

What other names is the product known by?
Achweed, Aegopodium podagraria, Ashweed, Bishop's Elder, Bishopsweed, Bishopswort, Eltroot, English Goatweed, Gout Herb, Goutwort, Ground Elder, Herb Gerard, Jack-Jump-About, Masterwort, Pigweed, Weyl Ash, White Ash.

What is it?
Goutweed is a plant. People use the above ground parts for medicine.

Is it Effective?
The effectiveness ratings for **GOUTWEED** are as follows:
Insufficient Evidence to Rate Effectiveness for... Gout; rheumatic disease; hemorrhoids; kidney, bladder, and intestinal disorders; and other uses.

How does it work?
There isn't enough information to know how goutweed might work.

Are there safety concerns?
There isn't enough information to know if goutweed is safe or what the potential side effects might be.

Do not use goutweed if: You are pregnant or breast-feeding.

Are there any interactions with medications?
It is not known if goutweed interacts with any medicines.
Before taking goutweed, talk with your healthcare professional if you take any medications.

GRAINS OF PARADISE

What other names is the product known by?
Aframomum melegueta, Amomum melegueta, Guinea Grains, Mallaguetta Pepper, Melegueta Pepper.

What is it?
Grains of paradise are the fruit and seeds of the Aframomum melegueta plant. They are used as medicine. Be careful not to confuse grains of paradise with capsicum; both are known as grains of paradise.

Is it Effective?
The effectiveness ratings for **GRAINS OF PARADISE** are as follows:
Insufficient Evidence to Rate Effectiveness for... Use as a stimulant.

How does it work?
There isn't enough information to know how grains of paradise might work.

Are there safety concerns?
Grains of paradise are possibly safe for most adults. They might cause irritation of the stomach, intestine, and urinary system.

Do not use grains of paradise if: You are pregnant or breast-feeding.

Are there any interactions with medications?
It is not known if grains of paradise interact with any medicines.
Before taking grains of paradise, talk with your healthcare professional if you take any medications.

GRAPE

What other names is the product known by?

Activin, Black Grape Raisins, Calzin, Draksha, Enocianina, Extrait De Pepins De Raisin, Flame Seedless, Folia Vitis Viniferae, Grape Fruit, Grape Fruit Skin, Grape Juice, Grape Leaf, Grape Leaf Extract, Grape Seed Extract, Grape Seed Oil, Grape Skin, Grape Skin Extract, Grapeseed, Leucoanthocyanin, Muskat, Oligomeric Proanthocyanidins, Oligomeric Procyanidins, OPC, OPCs, PCO, PCOs, Petite Sirah, Proanthodyn, Procyanidolic Oligomers, Raisins, Red Globe, Red Malaga, Red Vine Leaf AS 195, Red Vine Leaf Extract, Sultanas, Table Grapes, Thompson Seedless, Wine Grapes, Vitis vinifera.

What is it?

Grapes are the fruit of a vine (Vitis vinifera). The whole fruit, skin, leaves and seed of the grape plant are used as medicine. Be careful not to confuse grape with grapefruit, and other similar sounding medicines.

Is it Effective?

The effectiveness ratings for **GRAPE** are as follows:

Possibly Effective for... Circulation problems, such as chronic venous insufficiency that can cause the legs to swell • Decreasing certain types of eye stress.

Possibly Ineffective for... Hayfever and seasonal nasal allergies.

Insufficient Evidence to Rate Effectiveness for... Preventing heart disease, treating varicose veins, hemorrhoids, constipation, cough, attention deficit hyperactivity disorder (ADHD), chronic fatigue syndrome (CFS), diarrhea, heavy menstrual bleeding (periods), age-related macular degeneration (ARMD), canker sores, poor night vision, liver damage, high cholesterol levels, and other conditions.

How does it work?

Grape contains antioxidants which might help to prevent heart disease and have other potentially beneficial effects.

Grape leaf might reduce inflammation and have astringent effects, which could help stop bleeding and diarrhea.

Are there safety concerns?

Grape is safe for most people. Eating large quantities of grapes, dried grapes, raisins, or sultanas might cause diarrhea. Some people have allergic reactions to grapes and grape products.

Some other potential side effects include stomach upset, indigestion, diarrhea, nausea, vomiting, cough, dry mouth, sore throat, infections, headache, and muscular problems.

Do not use medicinal amounts of grape if: You are pregnant or breast-feeding.

Are there any interactions with medications?

Medications changed by the liver (Cytochrome P450 1A2 (CYP1A2) substrates). Some medications are changed and broken down by the liver. Grape juice might increase how quickly the liver breaks down some medications. Taking grape along with some medications that are changed by the liver can decrease the effectiveness of some medications. Before taking grape talk to your healthcare provider if you take any medications that are changed by the liver. Some of these medications that are changed by the liver include clozapine (Clozaril), cyclobenzaprine (Flexeril), fluvoxamine (Luvox), haloperidol (Haldol), imipramine (Tofranil), mexiletine (Mexitil), olanzapine (Zyprexa), pentazocine (Talwin), propranolol (Inderal), tacrine (Cognex), theophylline, zileuton (Zyflo), zolmitriptan (Zomig), and others.

Phenacetin. The body breaks down phenacetin to get rid of it. Drinking grape juice might increase how quickly the body breaks down phenacetin. Taking phenacetin along with grape juice might decrease the effectiveness of phenacetin.

Warfarin (Coumadin). Warfarin (Coumadin) is used to slow blood clotting. Grape seed might also slow blood clotting. Taking grape seed along with warfarin (Coumadin) might increase the chances of bruising and bleeding. Be sure to have your blood checked regularly. The dose of your warfarin (Coumadin) might need to be changed.

GRAPEFRUIT

What other names is the product known by?
Bioflavonoid Concentrate, Citrus Decumana, Citrus Grandis Extract, Citrus Maxima, Citrus Paradisi, Citrus Seed Extract, Cold-Pressed Grapefruit Oil, CSE, Expressed Grapefruit Oil, Grapefruit Extract, Grapefruit Oil, Grapefruit Seed Extract, Grapefruit Seed Glycerate, GSE, Paradisapfel, Pomelo, Shaddock Oil, Standardized Extract of Grapefruit, Toronja.

What is it?
Grapefruit is a citrus fruit. People use the fruit, oil from the peel, and extracts from the seed as medicine.

Is it Effective?
The effectiveness ratings for **GRAPEFRUIT** are as follows:
Insufficient Evidence to Rate Effectiveness for... Asthma, lowering cholesterol, hardening of the arteries (atherosclerosis), preventing cancer, weight loss, psoriasis, muscle fatigue, promoting hair growth, toning the skin, reducing acne and oily skin, treating headaches, stress, depression, infections, digestive complaints in people with eczema, yeast infections (as a vaginal douche), and other conditions.

How does it work?
Grapefruit is a source of vitamin C, fiber, potassium, pectin, and other nutrients. Some components might have antioxidant effects that might help protect cells from damage or reduce cholesterol.
It is not clear how the oil might work for medicinal uses.

Are there safety concerns?
Grapefruit is safe in the amounts normally used as food. There isn't enough information to know whether grapefruit is safe in larger, medicinal amounts (e.g. four or more glasses of juice per day). Grapefruit might cause some side effects including low blood pressure (hypotension) and a reduction in the number of cells in the blood (hematocrit).

Avoid taking grapefruit seed extract products by mouth if they contain preservatives. These can cause serious side effects such as vomiting, seizures, collapse, and coma.

Applying grapefruit oil to the skin might increase the risk of sunburn. Avoid getting grapefruit seed extract in the eyes, nose, genitals, or anus because it can cause irritation.

Do not use medicinal amounts of grapefruit products if: You are pregnant or breast-feeding.

Are there any interactions with medications?
Artemether (Artenam, Paluther). The body breaks down artemether (Artenam, Paluther) to get rid of it. Grapefruit juice can decrease how quickly the body breaks down artemether (Artenam, Paluther). Drinking grapefruit juice while taking artemether (Artenam, Paluther) might increase the effects and side effects of artemether (Artenam, Paluther). Do not drink grapefruit juice if you are taking artemether (Artenam, Paluther).
Buspirone (BuSpar). Grapefruit juice might increase how much buspirone (BuSpar) the body absorbs. Drinking grapefruit juice while taking buspirone (BuSpar) might increase the effects and side effects of buspirone (BuSpar).
Caffeine. The body breaks down caffeine to get rid of it. Grapefruit might decease how quickly the body gets rid of caffeine. Drinking grapefruit while taking caffeine might increase the side effects of caffeine including jitteriness, headache, and a fast heartbeat.
Carbamazepine (Tegretol). Grapefruit juice might increase how much carbamazepine (Tegretol) the body absorbs. Drinking grapefruit juice while taking carbamazepine (Tegretol) might increase the effects and side effects of carbamazepine (Tegretol).
Carvedilol (Coreg). The body breaks down carvedilol (Coreg) to get rid of it. Grapefruit juice seems to decrease how quickly the body breaks down carvedilol (Coreg). Drinking grapefruit juice while taking carvedilol (Coreg) might increase the effects and side effects of carvedilol (Coreg).
Cisapride (Propulsid). Grapefruit juice might decrease how quickly the body gets rid of cisapride (Propulsid). Drinking grapefruit juice while taking cisapride (Propulsid) might increase the effects and side effects of cisapride (Propulsid).
Clomipramine (Anafranil). The body breaks down clomipramine (Anafranil) to get rid of it. Grapefruit juice might decrease how quickly the body gets rid of clomipramine (Anafranil). Taking grapefruit juice along with clomipramine (Anafranil) might increase the effects and side effects of clomipramine (Anafranil).
Cyclosporine (Neoral, Sandimmune). Grapefruit might increase how much cyclosporine (Neoral, Sandimmune) the body absorbs. Drinking grapefruit juice while taking cyclosporine (Neoral, Sandimmune) might increase the side effects of cyclosporine.
Dextromethorphan (Robitussin DM, and others). The body breaks down dextromethorphan (Robitussin DM, others) to get rid of it. Grapefruit might decrease how quickly the body breaks down dextromethorphan (Robitussin

 Natural Medicines Comprehensive Database Consumer Version (209) 472-2244

DM, others). Drinking grapefruit juice while taking dextromethorphan (Robitussin DM, others) might increase the effects and side effects of dextromethorphan (Robitussin DM, others).

Erythromycin. The body breaks down erythromycin to get rid of it. Grapefruit can decrease how quickly the body gets rid of erythromycin. Taking grapefruit juice along with erythromycin might increase the effects and side effects of erythromycin.

Estrogens. The body breaks down estrogens to get rid of them. Grapefruit juice seems to decrease how quickly the body breaks down estrogens. Drinking grapefruit juice while taking estrogens might increase estrogen in the body too much. Some estrogen pills include conjugated equine estrogens (Premarin), ethinyl estradiol, estradiol, and others.

Etoposide (VePesid). Grapefruit might decrease how much etoposide (VePesid) the body absorbs. Drinking grapefruit juice while taking etoposide (VePesid) might decrease the effectiveness of etoposide (VePesid).

Fexofenadine (Allegra). Grapefruit might decrease how much fexofenadine (Allegra) the body absorbs. Drinking grapefruit juice while taking fexofenadine (Allegra) might decrease the effectiveness of fexofenadine (Allegra).

Itraconazole (Sporanox). Itraconazole (Sporanox) is used to treat fungal infections. Grapefruit juice might decrease how much itraconazole (Sporanox) the body absorbs. Drinking grapefruit juice while taking itraconazole (Sporanox) might decrease the effectiveness of Itraconazole (Sporanox). Do not drink grapefruit juice if you are taking Itraconazole (Sporanox).

Losartan (Cozaar). The liver activates losartan (Cozaar) to make it work. Grapefruit juice might decrease how quickly the body activates losartan (Cozaar). Drinking grapefruit juice while taking losartan (Cozaar) might decrease the effectiveness of losartan.

Medications changed by the liver (Cytochrome P450 1A2 (CYP1A2) substrates). Some medications are changed and broken down by the liver. Grapefruit juice might decrease how quickly the liver breaks down some medications. Taking grapefruit juice along with some medications that are broken down by the liver can increase the effects and side effects of some medications. Before taking grapefruit juice talk to your healthcare provider if you take any medications that are changed by the liver. Some medications that are changed by the liver include amitriptyline (Elavil), haloperidol (Haldol), ondansetron (Zofran), propranolol (Inderal), theophylline (Theo-Dur, others), verapamil (Calan, Isoptin, others), and others.

Medications changed by the liver (Cytochrome P450 2C9 (CYP2C9) substrates). Some medications are changed and broken down by the liver. Grapefruit juice might decrease how quickly the liver breaks down some medications. Taking grapefruit juice along with some medications that are broken down by the liver can increase the effects and side effects of some medications. Before taking grapefruit juice talk to your healthcare provider if you take any medications that are changed by the liver. Some medications that are changed by the liver include diclofenac (Cataflam, Voltaren), ibuprofen (Motrin), meloxicam (Mobic), and piroxicam (Feldene); celecoxib (Celebrex); amitriptyline (Elavil); warfarin (Coumadin); glipizide (Glucotrol); losartan (Cozaar); and others.

Medications changed by the liver (Cytochrome P450 2C19 (CYP2C19) substrates). Some medications are changed and broken down by the liver. Grapefruit juice might decrease how quickly the liver breaks down some medications. Taking grapefruit juice along with some medications that are broken down by the liver can increase the effects and side effects of some medications. Before taking grapefruit juice talk to your healthcare provider if you take any medications that are changed by the liver. Some medications that are changed by the liver include omeprazole (Prilosec), lansoprazole (Prevacid), and pantoprazole (Protonix); diazepam (Valium); carisoprodol (Soma); nelfinavir (Viracept); and others.

Medications changed by the liver (Cytochrome P450 3A4 (CYP3A4) substrates). Some medications are changed and broken down by the liver. Grapefruit juice might decrease how quickly the liver breaks down some medications. Drinking grapefruit juice while taking some medications that are broken down by the liver can increase the effects and side effects of some medications. Before taking grapefruit, talk to your healthcare provider if you are taking any medications that are changed by the liver. Some medications changed by the liver include lovastatin (Mevacor), ketoconazole (Nizoral), itraconazole (Sporanox), fexofenadine (Allegra), triazolam (Halcion), and many others.

Medications for high blood pressure (Calcium channel blockers). Grapefruit juice might increase how much medication for high blood pressure the body absorbs. Drinking grapefruit juice while taking some medications for high blood pressure might cause your blood pressure to go too low. Some medications for high blood pressure include nifedipine (Adalat, Procardia), verapamil (Calan, Isoptin, Verelan), diltiazem (Cardizem), isradipine (DynaCirc), felodipine (Plendil), amlodipine (Norvasc), and others.

Medications used for lowering cholesterol (Statins). The body breaks down some medications used for lowering cholesterol to get rid of them. Grapefruit juice might decrease how quickly the body breaks down some medications used for lowering cholesterol. Drinking grapefruit juice while taking some medications used for lowering cholesterol might increase the effects and side effects of these medications. Some medications used for high cholesterol include lovastatin (Mevacor) simvastatin (Zocor), atorvastatin (Lipitor), cerivastatin (Baycol), and others. However, grapefruit juice doesn't seem to affect pravastatin (Pravachol).

Methylprednisolone. The body breaks down methylprednisolone to get rid of it. Grapefruit juice can decrease how quickly the body gets rid of methylprednisolone. Drinking grapefruit juice while taking methylprednisolone might increase the effects and side effects of methylprednisolone.

Praziquantel (Biltricide). The body breaks down praziquantel (Biltricide) to get rid of it. Grapefruit juice can decrease how quickly the body breaks down praziquantel (Biltricide). Drinking grapefruit juice while taking praziquantel (Biltricide) might increase the effects and side effects of praziquantel (Biltricide).

Quinidine. The body breaks down quinidine to get rid of it. Grapefruit juice might decrease how fast the body gets rid of quinidine. Drinking grapefruit juice while taking quinidine might increase the chance of side effects.

Saquinavir (Fortovase, Invirase). Drinking grapefruit juice can increase how much saquinavir (Fortovase, Invirase) the body absorbs. Drinking grapefruit juice while taking saquinavir (Fortovase, Invirase) might increase the effects and side effects of saquinavir.

Scopolamine (Transderm Scop). The body breaks down scopolamine to get rid of it. Grapefruit juice can decrease how fast the body breaks down scopolamine. Drinking grapefruit juice while taking scopolamine might increase the effects and side effects of scopolamine.

Sedative medications (Benzodiazepines). Sedative medications can cause sleepiness and drowsiness. Grapefruit juice can decrease how quickly the body breaks down some medications. Drinking grapefruit juice while taking some sedative medications can increase the effects and side effects of some sedative medications. Some sedative medications that might interact with grapefruit juice include clonazepam (Klonopin), diazepam (Valium), lorazepam (Ativan), and others.

Sildenafil (Viagra). The body breaks down sildenafil (Viagra) to get rid of it. Grapefruit can decrease how quickly the body breaks down sildenafil (Viagra). Drinking grapefruit juice while taking sildenafil (Viagra) can increase the effects and side effects of sildenafil.

Terfenadine (Seldane). Grapefruit can increase how much terfenadine (Seldane) that the body absorbs. Drinking grapefruit juice while taking terfenadine (Seldane) might increase the effects and side effects of terfenadine (Seldane).

Theophylline. Drinking grapefruit juice might decrease the effects of theophylline. There's not enough information to know if this is a big concern.

Warfarin (Coumadin). Warfarin (Coumadin) is used to slow blood clotting. Drinking grapefruit juice might increase the effects of warfarin (Coumadin) and increase the chances of bruising and bleeding. Be sure to have your blood checked regularly. The dose of your warfarin (Coumadin) might need to be changed.

GRAVEL ROOT

What other names is the product known by?
Eupatorium purpureum, Joe-Pye Weed, Kidney Root, Purple Boneset, Queen of the Meadow, Roter Wasserhanf, Trumpet Weed.

What is it?
Gravel root is an herb. The above ground parts, bulb, and root are used to make medicine.

Is it Effective?
The effectiveness ratings for **GRAVEL ROOT** are as follows:
Insufficient Evidence to Rate Effectiveness for... Urinary and kidney stones, arthritis-like pain, gout, malaria, and other conditions.

How does it work?
Gravel root might work for certain conditions by reducing swelling (inflammation).

Are there safety concerns?
Gravel root is UNSAFE for use. It might cause side effects such as stomach pain, liver problems, blood circulation disorders, and cancer.

Do not use gravel root if: You are pregnant or breast-feeding. • You have liver disease. • You are allergic to ragweed, marigolds, daisies, and related herbs.

Are there any interactions with medications?
Medications that increase break down of other medications by the liver (Cytochrome P450 3A4 (CYP3A4) inducers). Gravel root is broken down by the liver. Some chemicals that form when the liver breaks down gravel root can be harmful. Medications that cause the liver to break down gravel root might enhance the toxic effects of chemicals contained in gravel root. Some of these medicines include carbamazepine (Tegretol), phenobarbital, phenytoin (Dilantin), rifampin, rifabutin (Mycobutin), and others.

   Natural Medicines Comprehensive Database Consumer Version   (209) 472-2244

GRAVIOLA

What other names is the product known by?
Brazilian Cherimoya, Brazilian Paw Paw, Corossolier, Durian Benggala, Guanabana, Guanavana, Nangka Blanda, Nangka Londa, Soursop, Sour Sop, Toge-Banreisi.

What is it?
Graviola is a small evergreen tree. The leaves, fruit, seeds, and stem are used to make medicine.

Is it Effective?
The effectiveness ratings for **GRAVIOLA** are as follows:
Insufficient Evidence to Rate Effectiveness for... Use as an antibiotic, sedative, antiparasitic, cathartic, emetic; and for coughs, inflammation of the nose and throat, herpes, leishmaniasis (an infection caused by sand flies), cancer, and other conditions.

How does it work?
Graviola contains many chemicals that may have antimicrobial and anticancer effects.

Are there safety concerns?
Graviola is UNSAFE. It can kill nerve cells in the brain and other parts of the body. It should NOT be used.

Do not use graviola if: You have Parkinson's disease or another condition involving nerve function. • You are pregnant or breast-feeding.

Are there any interactions with medications?
It is not known if graviola interacts with any medicines.
Before taking graviola, talk with your healthcare professional if you take any medications.

GREAT PLANTAIN

What other names is the product known by?
Common Plantain, Erva-De-Orelha, General Plantain, Greater Plantain, Plantago major, Tanchagem.

What is it?
Great plantain is a plant. The leaves and seed are used to make medicine. Be careful not to confuse great plantain with buckhorn plantain, water plantain, or other similar sounding medicines.

Is it Effective?
The effectiveness ratings for **GREAT PLANTAIN** are as follows:
Insufficient Evidence to Rate Effectiveness for... Common cold, ongoing (chronic) bronchitis, bladder infections, hemorrhoids, skin conditions, eye irritation, and other conditions.

How does it work?
Great plantain contains substances which might help decrease inflammation, decrease mucous (phlegm) production, and open airways. It might also have activity against bacteria and fungi.

Are there safety concerns?
Great plantain is possibly safe when taken by mouth by most adults. It may cause some side effects including diarrhea and low blood pressure.

Avoid using great plantain on the skin. It can cause allergic skin reactions.

Do not use great plantain if: You are pregnant or breast-feeding. • You are allergic to plantains or melon.

Are there any interactions with medications?
Warfarin (Coumadin). Great plantain contains large amounts of vitamin K. Vitamin K is used by the body to help blood clot. Warfarin (Coumadin) is used to slow blood clotting. By helping the blood clot, great plantain might decrease the effectiveness of warfarin (Coumadin). Be sure to have your blood checked regularly. The dose of your warfarin (Coumadin) might need to be changed.

Medical professionals should consult the Professional Version at www.NaturalDatabase.com.

GREATER BINDWEED

What other names is the product known by?

Bearbind, Bear's-Bind, Calystegia sepium, Devil's Vine, Hedge Bindweed, Hedge Convolvulus, Hedge Lily, Lady's Nightcap, Old Man's Night Cap, Rutland Beauty.

What is it?

Greater bindweed is a plant. The powdered root and whole flowering plant are used to make medicine.

Is it Effective?

The effectiveness ratings for **GREATER BINDWEED** are as follows:
Insufficient Evidence to Rate Effectiveness for... Fever, urinary tract diseases, constipation, increasing bile production, and other conditions.

How does it work?

Greater bindweed contains substances which can soften stools and increase gut muscle contractions, which helps stool move through the digestive tract to produce a laxative effect.

Are there safety concerns?

Greater bindweed may be unsafe due to its strong laxative effects. Large amounts can cause stomach pain.

Do not use greater bindweed if: You have stomach pain or intestinal conditions such as obstruction, appendicitis, colitis, Crohn's disease, or irritable bowel syndrome (IBS). • You are pregnant or breast-feeding.

Are there any interactions with medications?

Digoxin (Lanoxin). Greater bindweed is a type of laxative called a stimulant laxative. Stimulant laxatives can decrease potassium levels in the body. Low potassium levels can increase the risk of side effects of digoxin (Lanoxin).
Water pills (Diuretic drugs). Greater bindweed is a laxative. Some laxatives can decrease potassium in the body. "Water pills" can also decrease potassium in the body. Taking greater bindweed along with "water pills" might decrease potassium in the body too much. Some "water pills" that can decrease potassium include chlorothiazide (Diuril), chlorthalidone (Thalitone), furosemide (Lasix), hydrochlorothiazide (HCTZ, Hydrodiuril, Microzide), and others.

GREATER BURNET

What other names is the product known by?

Garden Burnet, Sanguisorba, Sanguisorba officinalis.

What is it?

Greater burnet is a plant. The flowering above ground parts are used to make medicine.

Is it Effective?

The effectiveness ratings for **GREATER BURNET** are as follows:
Insufficient Evidence to Rate Effectiveness for... Taking by mouth for heavy menstrual flow during menopause, hot flashes, irregular menstrual (period) flow, diarrhea, ulcerative colitis, hemorrhoids, bladder problems, varicose veins, and other uses. Applying to the skin as a plaster for wounds and boils.

How does it work?

There is some information that greater burnet might work as an astringent to help stop bleeding.

Are there safety concerns?

It is not known if greater burnet is safe or what the potential side effects might be.

Do not use greater burnet if: You are pregnant or breast-feeding.

Are there any interactions with medications?

It is not known if greater burnet interacts with any medicines.
Before taking greater burnet, talk with your healthcare professional if you take any medications.

GREATER CELANDINE

What other names is the product known by?
Bai Qu Cai, Celandine, Celandine Herb, Celandine Root, Chelidonii, Chelidonii Herba, Chelidonium Majus, Greater Celandine Above Ground Parts, Greater Celandine Rhizome, Greater Celandine Root, Schollkraut, Tetterwort, Verruguera.

What is it?
Greater celandine is a plant. The dried above ground parts, root, and rhizome (underground stem) are used to make medicine.

Is it Effective?
The effectiveness ratings for **GREATER CELANDINE** are as follows:
Possibly Effective for... Upset stomach (dyspepsia), when a combination of greater celandine and several other herbs is used.
Insufficient Evidence to Rate Effectiveness for... Cancer, warts, blister rashes, scabies, pain and swelling, loss of appetite, stomach flu, high blood pressure, gout, arthritis, spasms in the digestive tract, irregular menstrual periods, toothache, and other conditions.

How does it work?
The chemicals in greater celandine might slow the growth of cancer cells, but might also be harmful to normal cells. Preliminary research suggests greater celandine might increase the flow of bile. Greater celandine might also have some pain-relieving properties.

Are there safety concerns?
Greater celandine might not be safe when taken by mouth. It can cause serious liver problems. When applied to the skin, greater celandine can cause allergic skin rash.

Do not take greater celandine if: You are pregnant or breast-feeding. • You have liver problems, including hepatitis. • You have a blockage of your bile duct (bile duct obstruction).

Are there any interactions with medications?
Medications that can harm the liver (Hepatotoxic drugs). Greater celandine might harm the liver. Taking greater celandine along with medication that might also harm the liver can increase the risk of liver damage. Do not take greater celandine if you are taking a medication that can harm the liver. Some medications that can harm the liver include acetaminophen (Tylenol and others), amiodarone (Cordarone), carbamazepine (Tegretol), isoniazid (INH), methotrexate (Rheumatrex), methyldopa (Aldomet), fluconazole (Diflucan), itraconazole (Sporanox), erythromycin (Erythrocin, Ilosone, others), phenytoin (Dilantin) , lovastatin (Mevacor), pravastatin (Pravachol), simvastatin (Zocor), and many others. Before taking greater celandine, talk with your healthcare professional if you take any medications.

GREEK SAGE

What other names is the product known by?
Greek Oregano, Salvia fruticosa, Salvia triloba, Three-Lobe Sage.

What is it?
Greek sage is a plant. The leaves are used to make a medicinal tea.

Is it Effective?
The effectiveness ratings for **GREEK SAGE** are as follows:
Insufficient Evidence to Rate Effectiveness for... Inflammation of the mouth and throat and other conditions.

How does it work?
There isn't enough information to know how Greek sage might work.

Are there safety concerns?
It is not known if Greek sage is safe or what the potential side effects might be.

Do not use Greek sage if: You are pregnant or breast-feeding.

Medical professionals should consult the Professional Version at www.NaturalDatabase.com.

Are there any interactions with medications?

Hexobarbital. Hexobarbital can cause sleepiness and drowsiness. Greek sage might increase the effects of hexobarbital. Taking Greek sage along with hexobarbital might cause too much sleepiness.

GREEN TEA

What other names is the product known by?

Camellia sinensis, Camellia thea, Camellia theifera, EGCG, Epigallo Catechin Gallate, Epigallocatechin Gallate, Thea bohea, Thea sinensis, Thea viridis, Tea Green.

What is it?

Green tea is a product made from the Camellia sinensis plant. The fresh leaves are used to make medicine.

Is it Effective?

The effectiveness ratings for **GREEN TEA** are as follows:

Likely Effective for... Increasing mental alertness, due to the caffeine content of green tea.

Possibly Effective for... Preventing dizziness upon standing up (orthostatic hypotension) in older people • Preventing bladder, esophageal, ovarian, stomach, pancreatic, breast, and mouth cancers • Reducing the risk of Parkinson's disease • Decreasing high levels of fat in the blood (hyperlipidemia) • Reducing abnormal development and growth of cells of the cervix (cervical dysplasia) caused by human papilloma virus infection • Preventing high blood pressure • Low blood pressure. Green tea might help in elderly people who have low blood pressure after eating.

Possibly Ineffective for... Preventing colon cancer.

Insufficient Evidence to Rate Effectiveness for... Weight loss, heart disease prevention, type 2 diabetes, lung cancer, dental cavities, gingivitis, kidney stones, prostate cancer, diarrhea, chronic fatigue syndrome (CFS), and other conditions.

How does it work?

Green tea contains 2 to 4% caffeine which affects thinking and alertness, increases urine output, and may improve the function of brain messengers important in Parkinson's disease. It also contains antioxidants and other substances that might help protect the heart and blood vessels.

Are there safety concerns?

Green tea is safe for most adults. Green tea extract seems to be safe for most people for short-term use. In some people, green tea can cause stomach upset and constipation. Green tea extracts have been reported to cause liver problems.

Too much green tea, such as more than five cups per day, can cause side effects because of the caffeine. These side effects can range from mild to serious and include headache, nervousness, sleep problems, vomiting, diarrhea, irritability, irregular heartbeat, tremor, heartburn, dizziness, ringing in the ears, convulsions, and confusion. Green tea seems to reduce the absorption of iron from food.

If you are pregnant or breast-feeding, green tea in small amounts is probably not harmful. Do not drink more than 3 cups a day of green tea. Too much caffeine might cause premature delivery, low birth weight, and harm to the baby.

Caffeine is probably safe in children in amounts commonly found in foods.

Do not take green tea if: You have a heart condition. • You have a liver disease. • You have severe anemia. • You have high blood pressure. Small amounts of green tea taken regularly do not seem to raise blood pressure, but blood pressure can be affected in someone who isn't used to the caffeine in green tea. • You have glaucoma. • You have anxiety disorder.

Are there any interactions with medications?

Adenosine (Adenocard). Green tea contains caffeine. The caffeine in green tea might block the affects of adenosine (Adenocard). Adenosine (Adenocard) is often used by doctors to do a test on the heart. This test is called a cardiac stress test. Stop consuming green tea or other caffeine-containing products at least 24 hours before a cardiac stress test.

Alcohol. The body breaks down the caffeine in green tea to get rid of it. Alcohol can decrease how quickly the body breaks down caffeine. Taking green tea along with alcohol might cause too much caffeine in the bloodstream and caffeine side effects including jitteriness, headache, and fast heartbeat.

Amphetamines. Stimulant drugs such as amphetamines speed up the nervous system. By speeding up the nervous system, stimulant medications can make you feel jittery and increase your heart rate. The caffeine in green tea might also speed up the nervous system. Taking green tea along with stimulant drugs might cause serious problems including increased heart rate and high blood pressure. Avoid taking stimulant drugs along with caffeine.

Antibiotics (Quinolone antibiotics). The body breaks down caffeine to get rid of it. Some antibiotics might decrease how quickly the body breaks down caffeine. Taking these antibiotics along with green tea can increase the risk of side effects including jitteriness, headache, increased heart rate, and other side effects. Some antibiotics that decrease how quickly the body breaks down caffeine include ciprofloxacin (Cipro), enoxacin (Penetrex), norfloxacin (Chibroxin, Noroxin), sparfloxacin (Zagam), trovafloxacin (Trovan), and grepafloxacin (Raxar).

Birth control pills (Contraceptive drugs). The body breaks down the caffeine in green tea to get rid of it. Birth control pills can decrease how quickly the body breaks down caffeine. Taking green tea along with birth control pills can cause jitteriness, headache, fast heartbeat, and other side effects. Some birth control pills include ethinyl estradiol and levonorgestrel (Triphasil), ethinyl estradiol and norethindrone (Ortho-Novum 1/35, Ortho-Novum 7/7/7), and others.

Cimetidine (Tagamet). Green tea contains caffeine. The body breaks down caffeine to get rid of it. Cimetidine (Tagamet) can decrease how quickly your body breaks down caffeine. Taking cimetidine (Tagamet) along with green tea might increase the chance of caffeine side effects including jitteriness, headache, fast heartbeat, and others.

Clozapine (Clozaril). The body breaks down clozapine (Clozaril) to get rid of it. The caffeine in green tea seems to decrease how quickly the body breaks down clozapine (Clozaril). Taking green tea along with clozapine (Clozaril) can increase the effects and side effects of clozapine (Clozaril).

Cocaine. Stimulant drugs such as cocaine speed up the nervous system. By speeding up the nervous system, stimulant medications can make you feel jittery and increase your heart rate. The caffeine in green tea might also speed up the nervous system. Taking green tea along with stimulant drugs might cause serious problems including increased heart rate and high blood pressure. Avoid taking stimulant drugs along with caffeine.

Dipyridamole (Persantine). Green tea contains caffeine. The caffeine in green tea might block the affects of dipyridamole (Persantine). Dipyridamole (Persantine) is often used by doctors to do a test on the heart. This test is called a cardiac stress test. Stop drinking green tea or other caffeine-containing products at least 24 hours before a cardiac stress test.

Disulfiram (Antabuse). The body breaks down caffeine to get rid of it. Disulfiram (Antabuse) can decrease how quickly the body gets rid of caffeine. Taking green tea (which contains caffeine) along with disulfiram (Antabuse) might increase the effects and side effects of caffeine including jitteriness, hyperactivity, irritability, and others.

Ephedrine. Stimulant drugs speed up the nervous system. Caffeine (contained in green tea) and ephedrine are both stimulant drugs. Taking green tea along with ephedrine might cause too much stimulation and sometimes serious side effects and heart problems. Do not take caffeine-containing products and ephedrine at the same time.

Estrogens. The body breaks down the caffeine in green tea to get rid of it. Estrogens can decrease how quickly the body breaks down caffeine. Taking estrogen pills and drinking green tea can cause jitteriness, headache, fast heartbeat, and other side effects. If you take estrogen pills limit your caffeine intake. Some estrogen pills include conjugated equine estrogens (Premarin), ethinyl estradiol, estradiol, and others.

Fluconazole (Diflucan). Green tea contains caffeine. The body breaks down caffeine to get rid of it. Fluconazole (Diflucan) might decrease how quickly the body gets rid of caffeine and cause caffeine to stay in the body too long. Taking fluconazole (Diflucan) along with green tea might increase the risk of caffein side effects such as nervousness, anxiety, and insomnia.

Fluvoxamine (Luvox). The body breaks down the caffeine in green tea to get rid of it. Fluvoxamine (Luvox) can decrease how quickly the body breaks down caffeine. Taking green tea along with fluvoxamine (Luvox) might cause too much caffeine in the body, and increase the effects and side effects of caffeine.

Lithium. Your body naturally gets rid of lithium. The caffeine in green tea can increase how quickly your body gets rid of lithium. If you take products that contain caffeine and you take lithium, stop taking caffeine products slowly. Stopping caffeine too quickly can increase the side effects of lithium.

Medications for depression (MAOIs). The caffeine in green tea can stimulate the body. Some medications used for depression can also stimulate the body. Drinking green tea and taking some medications for depression might cause too much stimulation of the body and serious side effects including fast heartbeat, high blood pressure, nervousness, and others. Some of these medications used for depression include phenelzine (Nardil), tranylcypromine (Parnate), and others.

Medications for diabetes (Antidiabetes drugs). Green tea contains caffeine. Caffeine might increase blood sugar. Diabetes medications are used to lower blood sugar. Taking some medications for diabetes along with caffeine might decrease the effectiveness of diabetes medications. Monitor your blood sugar closely. The dose of your diabetes medication might need to be changed. Some medications used for diabetes include glimepiride (Amaryl), glyburide (DiaBeta, Glynase PresTab, Micronase), insulin, pioglitazone (Actos), rosiglitazone (Avandia), chlorpropamide (Diabinese), glipizide (Glucotrol), tolbutamide (Orinase), and others.

Mexiletine (Mexitil). Green tea contains caffeine. The body breaks down caffeine to get rid of it. Mexiletine (Mexitil) can decrease how quickly the body breaks down caffeine. Taking mexiletine (Mexitil) along with green tea might increase the caffeine effects and side effects of green tea.

Medications that can harm the liver (Hepatotoxic drugs). Green tea extracts might harm the liver. Taking green tea extracts along with medication that might also harm the liver can increase the risk of liver damage. Do not take green tea extracts if you are taking a medication that can harm the liver. Some medications that can harm the liver include acetaminophen (Tylenol and others), amiodarone (Cordarone), carbamazepine (Tegretol), isoniazid (INH),

Medical professionals should consult the Professional Version at www.NaturalDatabase.com.

CONSUMER VERSION

methotrexate (Rheumatrex), methyldopa (Aldomet), fluconazole (Diflucan), itraconazole (Sporanox), erythromycin (Erythrocin, Ilosone, others), phenytoin (Dilantin), lovastatin (Mevacor), pravastatin (Pravachol), simvastatin (Zocor), and many others.

Medications that slow blood clotting (Anticoagulant / Antiplatelet drugs). Green tea might slow blood clotting. Taking green tea along with medications that also slow clotting might increase the chances of bruising and bleeding. Some medications that slow blood clotting include aspirin, clopidogrel (Plavix), diclofenac (Voltaren, Cataflam, others), ibuprofen (Advil, Motrin, others), naproxen (Anaprox, Naprosyn, others), dalteparin (Fragmin), enoxaparin (Lovenox), heparin, warfarin (Coumadin), and others.

Nicotine. Stimulant drugs such as nicotine speed up the nervous system. By speeding up the nervous system, stimulant medications can make you feel jittery and increase your heart rate. The caffeine in green tea might also speed up the nervous system. Taking green tea along with stimulant drugs might cause serious problems including increased heart rate and high blood pressure. Avoid taking stimulant drugs along with caffeine.

Phenylpropanolamine. Green tea contains caffeine. Caffeine can stimulate the body. Phenylpropanolamine can also stimulate the body. Taking green tea and phenylpropanolamine together might cause too much stimulation and increase heartbeat, blood pressure, and cause nervousness.

Pentobarbital (Nembutal). The stimulant effects of the caffeine in green tea can block the sleep-producing effects of pentobarbital.

Riluzole (Rilutek). The body breaks down riluzole (Rilutek) to get rid of it. Drinking green tea can decrease how quickly the body breaks down riluzole (Rilutek) and increase the effects and side effects of riluzole.

Terbinafine (Lamisil). The body breaks down the caffeine in green tea to get rid of it. Terbinafine (Lamisil) can decrease how fast the body gets rid of caffeine. Taking green tea along with terbinafine (Lamisil) can increase the risk of caffeine side effects including jitteriness, headache, increased heartbeat, and other effects.

Theophylline. Green tea contains caffeine. Caffeine works similarly to theophylline. Caffeine can also decrease how quickly the body gets rid of theophylline. Taking green tea along with theophylline might increase the effects and side effects of theophylline.

Verapamil (Calan, Covera, Isoptin, Verelan). The body breaks down the caffeine in green tea to get rid of it. Verapamil (Calan, Covera, Isoptin, Verelan) can decrease how quickly the body gets rid of caffeine. Drinking green tea and taking verapamil (Calan, Covera, Isoptin, Verelan) can increase the risk of side effects for caffeine including jitteriness, headache, and an increased heartbeat.

Warfarin (Coumadin). Warfarin (Coumadin) is used to slow blood clotting. Large amounts of green tea have been reported to decrease the effectiveness of warfarin (Coumadin). Decreasing the effectiveness of warfarin (Coumadin) might increase the risk of clotting. It is unclear why this interaction might occur. Be sure to have your blood checked regularly. The dose of your warfarin (Coumadin) might need to be changed.

GROUND IVY

What other names is the product known by?
Alehoof, Catsfoot, Cat's-Paw, Creeping Charlie, Gill-Go-By-The-Hedge, Gill-Go-Over-The-Ground, Glechoma hederacea, Haymaids, Hedgemaids, Lizzy-Run-Up-The-Hedge, Nepeta hederacea, Robin-Run-In-The-Hedge, Tun-Hoof, Turnhoof.

What is it?
Ground ivy is a plant. The dried plant and crushed leaves are used to make medicine.

Is it Effective?
The effectiveness ratings for **GROUND IVY** are as follows:

Insufficient Evidence to Rate Effectiveness for... Mild lung problems, coughs, arthritis, rheumatism, menstrual (period) problems, diarrhea, hemorrhoids, stomach problems, bladder or kidney stones, wounds or other skin conditions, and other uses.

How does it work?
Ground ivy might work as an astringent to dry out body fluids such as mucous and to help stop bleeding.

Are there safety concerns?
Ground ivy is possibly safe in the amounts used to flavor foods and in small doses as medicine. However, it is known to contain substances which can damage the liver and also cause miscarriages. Larger amounts can irritate the stomach, intestines, and kidneys, and have toxic effects on the liver.

Do not use ground ivy if: You are pregnant or breast-feeding. • You have liver problems. • You have kidney problems. • You have epilepsy or seizures.

Medical professionals should consult the Professional Version at www.NaturalDatabase.com.

Are there any interactions with medications?
It is not known if ground ivy interacts with any medicines.
Before taking ground ivy, talk with your healthcare professional if you take any medications.

GROUND PINE

What other names is the product known by?
Ajuga chamaepitys, Bugle, Yellow Bugle.

What is it?
Ground pine is a plant. The above ground parts are used to make medicine.

Is it Effective?
The effectiveness ratings for **GROUND PINE** are as follows:
Insufficient Evidence to Rate Effectiveness for... Stimulating menstrual (or "period") flow, gout, rheumatism, malaria, fluid retention (edema), causing sweating, wound healing, use as a tonic, and other uses.

How does it work?
There isn't enough information to know how ground pine might work.

Are there safety concerns?
It is not known if ground pine is safe or what the potential side effects might be.

Do not use ground pine if: You are pregnant or breast-feeding.

Are there any interactions with medications?
It is not known if ground pine interacts with any medicines.
Before taking ground pine, talk with your healthcare professional if you take any medications.

GROUNDSEL

What other names is the product known by?
Common Groundsel, Ground Glutton, Grundy Swallow, Senecio vulgaris, Simson.

What is it?
Groundsel is a plant. The whole flowering plant is used to make medicine.

Is it Effective?
The effectiveness ratings for **GROUNDSEL** are as follows:
Insufficient Evidence to Rate Effectiveness for... Colic, worms, epilepsy, irregular or painful menstrual periods (dysmenorrhea), stopping dental bleeding, and other conditions.

How does it work?
There isn't enough information to know how groundsel might work.

Are there safety concerns?
Groundsel is UNSAFE for anyone to use. Groundsel can cause liver problems and cancer. It can also cause a serious problem called "veno-occlusive disease" with symptoms such as nausea, vomiting, loss of appetite and energy, swollen and aching belly, and death. Some people might have allergic reactions to groundsel, especially if they are allergic to the Asteraceae/Compositae family which includes ragweed and other plants.

Do not use groundsel if: You are pregnant or breast-feeding. • You are allergic to ragweed, chrysanthemums, marigolds, daisies, or similar plants. • You have liver problems.

Are there any interactions with medications?
Medications that increase break down of other medications by the liver (Cytochrome P450 3A4 (CYP3A4) inducers). Groundsel is broken down by the liver. Some chemicals that form when the liver breaks down groundsel can be harmful. Medications that cause the liver to break down groundsel might enhance the toxic effects of chemicals contained in groundsel. Some of these medicines include carbamazepine (Tegretol), phenobarbital, phenytoin (Dilantin), rifampin, rifabutin (Mycobutin), and others.

Medical professionals should consult the Professional Version at www.NaturalDatabase.com.

GUAIAC WOOD resin, wood

What other names is the product known by?
Guaiac, Guaiac Heartwood, Guaiacum, Guaiacum officinale, Guaiacum sanctum, Guajaci Lignum, Lingum Vitae, Pockwood.

What is it?
Guaiac is a tree. The wood and wood resin are used to prepare medicinal extracts. Be careful not to confuse guaiac wood resin or wood with guaiac wood oil.

Is it Effective?
The effectiveness ratings for **GUAIAC WOOD resin, wood** are as follows:
Insufficient Evidence to Rate Effectiveness for... Rheumatism, gout, lung problems, skin problems, syphilis, use in mouthwashes, and other conditions.

How does it work?
There isn't enough information to know how guaiac wood or wood resin might work.

Are there safety concerns?
Guaiac wood resin or wood are possibly safe for most adults in the amounts found in foods and in small medicinal doses. Higher doses can cause some side effects including diarrhea and stomach and intestinal problems. Guaiac wood resin or wood can also cause skin rashes.

Do not use guaiac wood resin or wood if: You are pregnant or breast-feeding. • You have any swelling or inflammation.

Are there any interactions with medications?
It is not known if guaiac wood resin and wood interacts with any medicines.
Before taking guaiac wood resin and wood, talk with your healthcare professional if you take any medications.

GUAR GUM

What other names is the product known by?
Cyamopsis psoraloides, Cyamopsis tetragonoloba, Dolichos psoraloides, Cyamopsis psoralioides, Cyamopsis tetragonolobus, Dietary Fiber, Guar Flour, Indian Guar Plant, Jaguar Gum, Psoralea tetragonoloba.

What is it?
Guar gum is a fiber from the seed of a plant.

Is it Effective?
The effectiveness ratings for **GUAR GUM** are as follows:
Possibly Effective for... Diarrhea • Constipation • Irritable bowel syndrome (IBS) • High cholesterol • Diabetes.
Possibly Ineffective for... Weight loss.
Insufficient Evidence to Rate Effectiveness for... Hardening of the arteries (atherosclerosis).

How does it work?
Guar gum is a fiber that normalizes the moisture content of the stool, absorbing excess liquid in diarrhea, and softening the stool in constipation. It also might help decrease the amount of cholesterol and glucose that is absorbed in the stomach and intestines.

Are there safety concerns?
Guar gum seems to be safe for most people when taken with at least 8 ounces of liquid.

Side effects include increased gas production, diarrhea, and loose stools. These side effects usually decrease or disappear after several days of use. High doses of guar gum or not drinking enough fluid with the dose of guar gum can cause blockage of the esophagus and the intestines.

Do not use guar gum if: You are breast-feeding. • You have diabetes. • You have a condition causing obstruction or narrowing of your esophagus or intestine. • You have difficulty swallowing.

Natural Medicines Comprehensive Database Consumer Version   (209) 472-2244

Are there any interactions with medications?

Medications for diabetes (Antidiabetes drugs). Guar gum might decrease blood sugar. Diabetes medications are also used to lower blood sugar. Taking guar gum along with diabetes medications might cause your blood sugar to go too low. Monitor your blood sugar closely. The dose of your diabetes medication might need to be changed. Some medications used for diabetes include glimepiride (Amaryl), glyburide (DiaBeta, Glynase PresTab, Micronase), insulin, pioglitazone (Actos), rosiglitazone (Avandia), chlorpropamide (Diabinese), glipizide (Glucotrol), tolbutamide (Orinase), and others.

Digoxin (Lanoxin). Some people worry that guar gum can decrease how much digoxin the body absorbs. But it is unlikely that guar gum will significantly affect digoxin absorption.

Ethinyl estradiol. Ethinyl estradiol is a form of estrogen that's in some estrogen products and birth control pills. Guar gum can decrease how much ethinyl estradiol the body absorbs. Taking guar gum along with estrogen-containing medicines might decrease the effectiveness of estrogen.

Metformin (Glucophage). Guar gum can decrease how much metformin the body absorbs. Taking guar gum along with metformin can decrease the effectiveness of metformin.

Penicillin (Penicillin VK, Pen VK, Veetids). Guar gum can decrease how much penicillin the body absorbs. Taking guar gum along with penicillin can decrease the ability of penicillin to fight infection.

GUARANA

What other names is the product known by?

Brazilian Cocoa, Guarana Bread, Guarana Gum, Guarana Seed Paste, Paullinia Cupana, Paullinia Sorbilis, Zoom.

What is it?

Guarana is a plant. The seeds are used to make medicine.

Is it Effective?

The effectiveness ratings for **GUARANA** are as follows:

Insufficient Evidence to Rate Effectiveness for... Malaria, diarrhea, fever, headaches, heart problems, improvement of exercise endurance, improvement of short-term, high-intensity performance and power, increased mental alertness, increasing blood pressure in people who have low blood pressure, chronic fatigue syndrome (CFS), joint pain, fluid retention, weight loss, and other conditions.

How does it work?

Guarana contains caffeine. Caffeine works by stimulating the central nervous system (CNS), heart, and muscles. Guarana also contains theophylline and theobromine, which are chemicals similar to caffeine.

Are there safety concerns?

Guarana is safe for most adults. The caffeine in guarana can cause insomnia, nervousness and restlessness, stomach irritation, nausea, vomiting, increased heart rate and blood pressure, rapid breathing, tremors, delirium, diuresis, and other side effects. Large guarana doses might cause headache, anxiety, agitation, ringing in the ears, pain when urinating, stomach cramps, and irregular heartbeats. People who take guarana regularly may experience caffeine withdrawal symptoms if they reduce their usual amount.

Do not take guarana if: You are pregnant or breast-feeding. Large amounts of guarana might not be safe. • You have a heart condition. • You have high blood pressure. • You have anxiety. • You have an eye disease called glaucoma. • You have osteoporosis. • You have a bleeding condition.

Are there any interactions with medications?

Adenosine (Adenocard). Guarana contains caffeine. The caffeine in guarana might block the affects of adenosine (Adenocard). Adenosine (Adenocard) is often used by doctors to do a test on the heart. This test is called a cardiac stress test. Stop consuming guarana or other caffeine-containing products at least 24 hours before a cardiac stress test.

Alcohol. The body breaks down the caffeine in guarana to get rid of it. Alcohol can decrease how quickly the body breaks down caffeine. Taking guarana along with alcohol might cause too much caffeine in the bloodstream and caffeine side effects including jitteriness, headache, and fast heartbeat.

Amphetamines. Stimulant drugs such as amphetamines speed up the nervous system. By speeding up the nervous system, stimulant medications can make you feel jittery and increase your heart rate. The caffeine in guarana might also speed up the nervous system. Taking guarana along with stimulant drugs might cause serious problems including increased heart rate and high blood pressure. Avoid taking stimulant drugs along with caffeine.

Antibiotics (Quinolone antibiotics). The body breaks down caffeine to get rid of it. Some antibiotics might decrease how quickly the body breaks down caffeine. Taking these antibiotics along with guarana can increase the risk of side effects including jitteriness, headache, increased heart rate, and other side effects. Some antibiotics that decrease how quickly the body breaks down caffeine include ciprofloxacin (Cipro), enoxacin (Penetrex),

Medical professionals should consult the Professional Version at www.NaturalDatabase.com.

norfloxacin (Chibroxin, Noroxin), sparfloxacin (Zagam), trovafloxacin (Trovan), and grepafloxacin (Raxar).

Birth control pills (Contraceptive drugs). The body breaks down the caffeine in guarana to get rid of it. Birth control pills can decrease how quickly the body breaks down caffeine. Taking guarana along with birth control pills can cause jitteriness, headache, fast heartbeat, and other side effects. Some birth control pills include ethinyl estradiol and levonorgestrel (Triphasil), ethinyl estradiol and norethindrone (Ortho-Novum 1/35, Ortho-Novum 7/7/7), and others.

Cimetidine (Tagamet). Guarana contains caffeine. The body breaks down caffeine to get rid of it. Cimetidine (Tagamet) can decrease how quickly your body breaks down caffeine. Taking cimetidine (Tagamet) along with guarana might increase the chance of caffeine side effects including jitteriness, headache, fast heartbeat, and others.

Clozapine (Clozaril). The body breaks down clozapine (Clozaril) to get rid of it. The caffeine in guarana seems to decrease how quickly the body breaks down clozapine (Clozaril). Taking guarana along with clozapine (Clozaril) can increase the effects and side effects of clozapine (Clozaril).

Cocaine. Stimulant drugs such as cocaine speed up the nervous system. By speeding up the nervous system, stimulant medications can make you feel jittery and increase your heart rate. The caffeine in guarana might also speed up the nervous system. Taking guarana along with stimulant drugs might cause serious problems including increased heart rate and high blood pressure. Avoid taking stimulant drugs along with caffeine.

Dipyridamole (Persantine). Guarana contains caffeine. The caffeine in guarana might block the affects of dipyridamole (Persantine). Dipyridamole (Persantine) is often used by doctors to do a test on the heart. This test is called a cardiac stress test. Stop consuming guarana or other caffeine-containing products at least 24 hours before a cardiac stress test.

Disulfiram (Antabuse). The body breaks down caffeine to get rid of it. Disulfiram (Antabuse) can decrease how quickly the body gets rid of caffeine. Taking guarana (which contains caffeine) along with disulfiram (Antabuse) might increase the effects and side effects of caffeine including jitteriness, hyperactivity, irritability, and others.

Ephedrine. Stimulant drugs speed up the nervous system. Caffeine (contained in guarana) and ephedrine are both stimulant drugs. Taking guarana along with ephedrine might cause too much stimulation and sometimes serious side effects and heart problems. Do not take caffeine-containing products and ephedrine at the same time.

Estrogens. The body breaks down the caffeine in guarana to get rid of it. Estrogens can decrease how quickly the body breaks down caffeine. Taking guarana along with estrogens can cause jitteriness, headache, fast heartbeat, and other side effects. If you take estrogens limit your caffeine intake. Some estrogen pills include conjugated equine estrogens (Premarin), ethinyl estradiol, estradiol, and others.

Fluconazole (Diflucan). Guarana contains caffeine. The body breaks down caffeine to get rid of it. Fluconazole (Diflucan) might decrease how quickly the body gets rid of caffeine. Taking guarana along with fluconazole (Diflucan) might increase the risk of caffeine side effects such as nervousness, anxiety, and insomnia.

Fluvoxamine (Luvox). The body breaks down the caffeine in guarana to get rid of it. Fluvoxamine (Luvox) can decrease how quickly the body breaks down caffeine. Taking guarana along with fluvoxamine (Luvox) might cause too much caffeine in the body, and increase the effects and side effects of caffeine.

Lithium. You body naturally gets rid of lithium. The caffeine in guarana can increase how quickly your body gets rid of lithium. If you take products that contain caffeine and you take lithium, stop taking caffeine products slowly. Stopping caffeine too quickly can increase the side effects of lithium.

Medications that slow blood clotting (Anticoagulant / Antiplatelet drugs). Guarana contains caffeine. Caffeine might slow blood clotting. Taking guarana along with medications that also slow clotting might increase the chances of bruising and bleeding. Some medications that slow blood clotting include aspirin, clopidogrel (Plavix), diclofenac (Voltaren, Cataflam, others), ibuprofen (Advil, Motrin, others), naproxen (Anaprox, Naprosyn, others), dalteparin (Fragmin), enoxaparin (Lovenox), heparin, warfarin (Coumadin), and others.

Medications for depression (MAOIs). Guarana contains caffeine. Caffeine can stimulate the body. Some medications used for depression can also stimulate the body. Taking guarana with these medications used for depression might cause serious side effects including fast heartbeat, high blood pressure, nervousness, and others. Some of these medications used for depression include phenelzine (Nardil), tranylcypromine (Parnate), and others.

Medications for diabetes (Antidiabetes drugs). Guarana might increase blood sugar. Diabetes medications are used to lower blood sugar. By increasing blood sugar, guarana might decrease the effectiveness of diabetes medications. Monitor your blood sugar closely. The dose of your diabetes medication might need to be changed. Some medications used for diabetes include glimepiride (Amaryl), glyburide (DiaBeta, Glynase PresTab, Micronase), insulin, pioglitazone (Actos), rosiglitazone (Avandia), chlorpropamide (Diabinese), glipizide (Glucotrol), tolbutamide (Orinase), and others.

Mexiletine (Mexitil). Guarana contains caffeine. The body breaks down caffeine to get rid of it. Mexiletine (Mexitil) can decrease how quickly the body breaks down caffeine. Taking mexiletine (Mexitil) along with guarana might increase the caffeine effects and side effects of guarana.

Nicotine. Stimulant drugs such as nicotine speed up the nervous system. By speeding up the nervous system, stimulant medications can make you feel jittery and increase your heart rate. The caffeine in guarana might also speed up the nervous system. Taking caffeine along with stimulant drugs might cause serious problems including increased heart rate and high blood pressure. Avoid taking stimulant drugs along with caffeine.

Pentobarbital (Nembutal). The stimulant effects of the caffeine in guarana can block the sleep-producing effects of pentobarbital.

Phenylpropanolamine. The caffeine in guarana can stimulate the body. Phenylpropanolamine can also stimulate the body. Taking guarana along with phenylpropanolamine might cause too much stimulation and increase heartbeat, blood pressure and cause nervousness.

Riluzole (Rilutek). The body breaks down riluzole (Rilutek) to get rid of it. Taking guarana can decrease how fast the body breaks down riluzole (Rilutek) and increase the effects and side effects of riluzole.

Terbinafine (Lamisil). The body breaks down caffeine (contained in guarana) to get rid of it. Terbinafine (Lamisil) can decrease how fast the body gets rid of caffeine and increase the risk of side effects including jitteriness, headache, increased heartbeat, and other effects.

Theophylline. Guarana contains caffeine. Caffeine works similarly to theophylline. Caffeine can also decrease how quickly the body gets rid of theophylline. Taking guarana along with theophylline might increase the effects and side effects of theophylline.

Verapamil (Calan, Covera, Isoptin, Verelan). The body breaks down the caffeine in guarana to get rid of it. Verapamil (Calan, Covera, Isoptin, Verelan) can decrease how quickly the body gets rid of caffeine. Taking guarana along with verapamil (Calan, Covera, Isoptin, Verelan) can increase the risk of caffeine side effects including jitteriness, headache, and an increased heartbeat.

GUAVA

What other names is the product known by?

Brazilian Guava, Brazilian Red Guava, Guajava, Guava Leaf, Guava Leaves, Guava Peel, Guava Pulp, Guava Seed, Guava Seed Protein, Guavas, Psidium, Psidium Guajava, Red guava.

What is it?

Guava is a tropical fruit. The fruit, leaves, and juice are used as medicine.

Is it Effective?

The effectiveness ratings for **GUAVA** are as follows:

Insufficient Evidence to Rate Effectiveness for... Colic, diarrhea, diabetes, cough, cataracts, high cholesterol, heart disease, cancer, and other conditions.

How does it work?

The guava fruit is a source of vitamin C, fiber and other components with antioxidant effects. Guava leaves also contain components with antioxidant and other effects. It is not known how guava works for medical conditions.

Are there safety concerns?

Guava fruit is safe when consumed as a food. There is not enough information to know if guava is safe when used for medical purposes.

Are there any interactions with medications?

There is not enough information to know if guava interacts with any medicines.

Talk to your health care professional before using guava in medicinal amounts if you are taking any medications.

GUGGUL

What other names is the product known by?

Balsamodendrum wightii, Balsamodendrum mukul, Commiphora mukul, Commiphora wightii, Guggal, Guggul Gum Resin, Guggulipid, Guggulu, Guggulu Suddha, Guggulsterones, Gum Guggal, Gum Guggulu, Indian Bdellium-Tree, Mukul Myrrh Tree.

What is it?

Guggul is the gum resin of a tree native to India. The gum resin in the plant is used to make medicine.

Is it Effective?

The effectiveness ratings for **GUGGUL** are as follows:

Possibly Effective for... Treating some types of acne.

Possibly Ineffective for... Lowering cholesterol and triglycerides in the blood of people eating a Western diet.

Insufficient Evidence to Rate Effectiveness for... Arthritis and weight loss.

How does it work?

Guggul contains substances that lower cholesterol and triglycerides. One of these substances also decreases the redness and swelling that occurs in some types of acne.

Medical professionals should consult the Professional Version at www.NaturalDatabase.com.

Are there safety concerns?

Guggul seems to be safe for most people.

It can cause side effects such as stomach upset, headaches, nausea, vomiting, loose stools, diarrhea, belching, and hiccups. Guggul can also cause allergic reactions such as rash and itching. Guggul can also cause skin rash and itching that is not related to allergy. These adverse reactions are more common with higher doses, such as 6000 mg per day.

Do not use guggul if: You are pregnant or breast-feeding. • You have a thyroid disorder (hypothyroidism or hyperthyroidism). • You have breast cancer. • You have uterine cancer. • You have ovarian cancer. • You have endometriosis. • You have uterine fibroids.

Are there any interactions with medications?

Birth control pills (Contraceptive drugs). Some birth control pills contain estrogen. Guggul might theoretically increase the side effects of birth control pills. Some birth control pills include ethinyl estradiol and levonorgestrel (Triphasil), ethinyl estradiol and norethindrone (Ortho-Novum 1/35, Ortho-Novum 7/7/7), and others.

Estrogens. Large amounts of guggul might theoretically increase the side effects of estrogen. Some estrogen pills include conjugated equine estrogens (Premarin), ethinyl estradiol, estradiol, and others.

Diltiazem (Cardizem, Dilacor, Tiazac). Taking guggul can decrease how much diltiazem (Cardizem) that the body absorbs. Taking guggul along with diltiazem (Cardizem) might decrease the effectiveness of diltiazem (Cardizem).

Medications changed by the liver (Cytochrome P450 3A4 (CYP3A4) substrates). Some medications are changed and broken down by the liver. Guggul might increase how quickly the liver breaks down some medications. Taking guggul along with some medications that are broken down by the liver can decrease the effectiveness of some medications. Before taking guggul talk to your healthcare provider if you are taking any medications that are changed by the liver. Some medications changed by the liver include lovastatin (Mevacor), atorvastatin (Lipitor), ketoconazole (Nizoral), itraconazole (Sporanox), fexofenadine (Allegra), triazolam (Halcion), and many others.

Medications that slow blood clotting (Anticoagulant / Antiplatelet drugs). Guggul might slow blood clotting. Taking guggul along with medications that also slow clotting might increase the chances of bruising and bleeding. Some medications that slow blood clotting include aspirin, clopidogrel (Plavix), diclofenac (Voltaren, Cataflam, others), ibuprofen (Advil, Motrin, others), naproxen (Anaprox, Naprosyn, others), dalteparin (Fragmin), enoxaparin (Lovenox), heparin, warfarin (Coumadin), and others.

Propranolol (Inderal). Guggul might decrease how much propranolol (Inderal) the body absorbs. Taking guggul along with propranolol (Inderal) might decrease the effectiveness of propranolol (Inderal).

Tamoxifen (Nolvadex). Some types of cancer are affected by hormones in the body. Estrogen-sensitive cancers are cancers that are affected by estrogen levels in the body. Tamoxifen (Nolvadex) is used to help treat and prevent these types of cancer. Guggul could theoretically affect estrogen levels in the body. By affecting estrogen in the body, guggul might decrease the effectiveness of tamoxifen (Nolvadex). Do not take guggul if you are taking tamoxifen (Nolvadex).

Thyroid hormone. Guggul might increase thyroid hormone in the body. Taking guggul along with thyroid hormone pills might increase the effects and side effects of thyroid hormones.

GUMWEED

What other names is the product known by?

August flower, Grindelia, Grindeliae herba, Grindelia robusta, Grinelia squarrosa, Gum Weed, Gumweed Herb, Rosin Weed, Tar Weed.

What is it?

Gumweed is an herb. People use the leaves and top of the plant to make medicine.

Is it Effective?

The effectiveness ratings for **GUMWEED** are as follows:
Insufficient Evidence to Rate Effectiveness for... Cough; bronchitis; and treating swelling (inflammation) of the nose, sinuses, and throat.

How does it work?

Gumweed might help prevent bacterial growth.

Are there safety concerns?

Gumweed seems safe for most people. It can cause some side effects such as stomach upset and diarrhea.

Do not use gumweed if: You are pregnant or breast-feeding. • You are allergic to ragweed, marigolds, daisies, and other related plants.

Are there any interactions with medications?

It is not known if gumweed interacts with any medicines.
Before taking gumweed, talk with your healthcare professional if you take any medications.

GYMNEMA

What other names is the product known by?

Gemnema melicida, Gur-Mar, Gurmar, Gurmarbooti, Gymnema sylvestre, Merasingi, Meshashringi, Miracle Plant, Periploca sylvestris, Vishani.

What is it?

Gymnema is a plant. The leaves are used to make medicine.

Is it Effective?

The effectiveness ratings for **GYMNEMA** are as follows:
Insufficient Evidence to Rate Effectiveness for... Diabetes, controlling metabolism, stimulating digestion, malaria, coughs, snake bites, softening the stool (laxative), and increasing urine excretion (diuretic).

How does it work?

Gymnema contains substances that decrease the absorption of sugar from the intestine. Gymnema may also increase the amount of insulin in the body and increase the growth of cells in the pancreas, which is the place in the body where insulin is made.

Are there safety concerns?

There isn't enough information to know if gymnema is safe.

Gymnema can affect blood sugar control and lower blood glucose levels.

Do not use gymnema if: You are pregnant or breast-feeding.

Are there any interactions with medications?

Insulin. Gymnema might decrease blood sugar. Insulin is also used to decrease blood sugar. Taking gymnema along with insulin might cause your blood sugar to be too low. Monitor your blood sugar closely. The dose of your insulin might need to be changed.
Medications for diabetes (Antidiabetes drugs). Gymnema supplements seem to lower blood sugar in people with diabetes. Diabetes medications are also used to lower blood sugar. Taking gymnema along with diabetes medications might cause your blood sugar to go too low. Monitor your blood sugar closely. The dose of your diabetes medication might need to be changed. Some medications used for diabetes include glimepiride (Amaryl), glyburide (DiaBeta, Glynase PresTab, Micronase), insulin, pioglitazone (Actos), rosiglitazone (Avandia), chlorpropamide (Diabinese), glipizide (Glucotrol), tolbutamide (Orinase), and others.

HARONGA

What other names is the product known by?

Harongabladder leaf, Haronga madagascariensis, Harongarinde bark, Harungana madagascariensis, Harunganae madagascariensis cortex bark, Harunganae madagascariensis folium leaf.

What is it?

Haronga is a plant. The bark and leaves are used to make medicine.

Is it Effective?

The effectiveness ratings for **HARONGA** are as follows:
Insufficient Evidence to Rate Effectiveness for... Liver and gallbladder complaints, loss of appetite, upset stomach (dyspepsia), problems of the pancreas, and other conditions.

Medical professionals should consult the Professional Version at www.NaturalDatabase.com.

CONSUMER VERSION

How does it work?
Haronga might stimulate the gallbladder, pancreas, and stomach to produce more digestive juices.

Are there safety concerns?
Haronga is possibly safe for most people if used for a short time. The recommended maximum safe duration of use is two months. In can cause increased sensitivity to sunlight (photosensitivity), especially in fair skinned people.

Do not use haronga if: You are pregnant or breast-feeding. • You have inflammation of the pancreas (pancreatitis). • You have liver problems. • You have gallbladder problems, including gallstones. • You have blockage of your bile duct (biliary obstruction). • You have a blockage of your bowels (bowel obstruction).

Are there any interactions with medications?
It is not known if haronga interacts with any medicines.
Before taking haronga, talk with your healthcare professional if you take any medications.

HARTSTONGUE

What other names is the product known by?
Asplenium scolopendrium, Buttonhole, God's-Hair, Hind's Tongue, Horse Tongue, Scolopendrium vulgare.

What is it?
Hartstongue is a fern. The leaves, stem, and flower are used to make medicine.

Is it Effective?
The effectiveness ratings for **HARTSTONGUE** are as follows:
Insufficient Evidence to Rate Effectiveness for... Digestive disorders and urinary tract diseases.

How does it work?
Hartstongue might help increase urine production, soften the stool, and stimulate the bowel to contract and empty.

Are there safety concerns?
There isn't enough information available to know if hartstongue is safe.

Do not use hartstongue if: You are pregnant or breast-feeding.

Are there any interactions with medications?
It is not known if hartstongue interacts with any medicines.
Before taking hartstongue, talk with your healthcare professional if you take any medications.

HAWAIIAN BABY WOODROSE

What other names is the product known by?
Argyreia nervosa, Argyreia speciosa, Baby Hawaiian Woodrose, Baby Woodrose, Convolvulus nervosus, Convolvulus speciosus, Elephant-Climber, Elephant Creeper, Lettsomia nervosa, Silver-Morning-Glory, Vidhara, Vriddadaru, Wood-Rose, Woolly Morning Glory, Woolly-Morning-Glory.

What is it?
Hawaiian baby woodrose is a plant. The seeds are used to make medicine.

Is it Effective?
The effectiveness ratings for **HAWAIIAN BABY WOODROSE** are as follows:
Insufficient Evidence to Rate Effectiveness for... Pain relief and promoting sweating.

How does it work?
There isn't enough information to know how Hawaiian baby woodrose works as a medicine.

Are there safety concerns?
Hawaiian baby woodrose is UNSAFE. It can cause side effects such as nausea, vomiting, dizziness, hallucinations, blurred vision, dilated pupils, rapid movement of eyeballs, sweating, fast heart rate, and increased blood pressure.

Do not use Hawaiian baby woodrose if: You are pregnant breast-feeding. • You have a mood disorder.

Are there any interactions with medications?

Clozapine (Clozaril). Clozapine (Clozaril) affects the brain. Hawaiian baby woodrose also affects the brain. Taking clozapine (Clozaril) along with Hawaiian baby woodrose might decrease the effects of Hawaiian baby woodrose.

Cyproheptadine. Cyproheptadine can affect the brain. Hawaiian baby woodrose might also affect the brain. But cyproheptadine affects the brain differently than Hawaiian baby woodrose. Taking cyproheptadine along with Hawaiian baby woodrose might decrease the effects of Hawaiian baby woodrose.

Dextromethorphan (Robitussin DM, and others). Hawaiian baby woodrose can affect a brain chemical called serotonin. Dextromethorphan (Robitussin DM, others) can also affect serotonin. Taking Hawaiian baby woodrose along with dextromethorphan (Robitussin DM, others) might cause too much serotonin in the brain and serious side effects including heart problems, shivering, and anxiety. Do not take Hawaiian baby woodrose if you are taking dextromethorphan (Robitussin DM, and others).

Medications for depression (Antidepressant drugs). Hawaiian baby woodrose increases a brain chemical called serotonin. Some medications for depression also increase the brain chemical serotonin. Taking Hawaiian baby woodrose along with these medications for depression might increase serotonin too much and cause serious side effects including heart problems, shivering, and anxiety. Do not take Hawaiian baby woodrose if you are taking medications for depression. Some of these medications for depression include fluoxetine (Prozac), paroxetine (Paxil), sertraline (Zoloft), amitriptyline (Elavil), clomipramine (Anafranil), imipramine (Tofranil), and others.

Medications for depression (MAOIs). Hawaiian baby woodrose increases a chemical in the brain. This chemical is called serotonin. Some medications used for depression also increase serotonin. Taking Hawaiian baby woodrose with these medications used for depression might cause there to be too much serotonin. This could cause serious side effects including heart problems, shivering, and anxiety. Some of these medications used for depression include phenelzine (Nardil), tranylcypromine (Parnate), and others.

Meperidine (Demerol). Hawaiian baby woodrose increases a chemical in the brain called serotonin. Meperidine (Demerol) can also increase serotonin in the brain. Taking Hawaiian baby woodrose along with meperidine (Demerol) might cause too much serotonin in the brain and serious side effects including heart problems, shivering, and anxiety.

Pentazocine (Talwin). Hawaiian baby woodrose increases a brain chemical called serotonin. Pentazocine (Talwin) also increases serotonin. Taking Hawaiian baby woodrose along with pentazocine (Talwin) might increase serotonin too much. This could cause serious side effects including heart problems, shivering, and anxiety. Do not take Hawaiian baby woodrose if you are taking pentazocine (Talwin).

Risperidone (Risperdal). Taking risperidone (Risperdal) along with Hawaiian baby woodrose might decrease the effects of Hawaiian baby woodrose.

Tramadol (Ultram). Tramadol (Ultram) can affect a chemical in the brain called serotonin. Hawaiian baby woodrose can also affect serotonin. Taking Hawaiian baby woodrose along with tramadol (Ultram) might cause too much serotonin in the brain and side effects including confusion, shivering, stiff muscles, and other side effects.

HAWTHORN

What other names is the product known by?

Aubepine, Bianco Spino, Crataegi Fructus, Crataegus cuneata, Crataegus laevigata, Crataegus oxyacantha, Crataegus monogyna, Crataegus pinnatifida, English Hawthorn, Epine Blanche, Epine de Mai, Haagdorn, Hagedorn, Harthorne, Haw, Hawthrone, Hedgethorn, May, Maybush, Maythorn, Mehlbeebaum, Meidorn, Nan Shanzha, Oneseed Hawthorn, Shanzha, Weissdorn, Whitehorn.

What is it?

Hawthorn is a plant. The leaves, berries, and flowers of hawthorn are used to make medicine.

Is it Effective?

The effectiveness ratings for **HAWTHORN** are as follows:

Possibly Effective for... Treating heart failure symptoms when a standard form (LI132 Faros or WS 1442 Crataegutt) is used.

Insufficient Evidence to Rate Effectiveness for... Decreased heart function, blood circulation problems, heart disease, abnormal heartbeat rhythms (arrhythmias), high blood pressure, low blood pressure, high cholesterol, muscle spasms, anxiety, sedation, and other conditions.

How does it work?

Hawthorn can help improve the amount of blood pumped out of the heart during contractions, widen the blood vessels, and increase the transmission of nerve signals.

Are there safety concerns?

Hawthorn seems safe for most adults when a standard form (LI132 Faros or WS 1442 Crataegutt) is used short-term. In some people, it can cause nausea, stomach upset, fatigue, sweating, headache, dizziness, palpitations, nosebleeds, insomnia, agitation, and other problems.

Do not use hawthorn if: You are pregnant or breast-feeding. • You have a heart condition, without the help of a healthcare provider.

Are there any interactions with medications?

Digoxin (Lanoxin). Digoxin (Lanoxin) helps the heart beat more strongly. Hawthorn also seems to affect the heart. Taking hawthorn along with digoxin (Lanoxin) might increase the effects of digoxin and increase the risk of side effects. Do not take hawthorn if you are taking digoxin (Lanoxin) without talking to your healthcare professional.
Medications that increase blood flow to the heart (Nitrates). Hawthorn increases blood flow. Taking hawthorn with medications that also increase blood flow to the heart might increase the chance of dizziness and lightheadedness. Some of these medications that increase blood flow to the heart include nitroglycerin (Nitro-Bid, Nitro-Dur, Nitrostat) and isosorbide (Imdur, Isordil, Sorbitrate).
Medications for high blood pressure (Beta-blockers). Hawthorn might decrease blood pressure. Taking hawthorn along with medication for high blood pressure might cause your blood pressure to go too low. Some medications for high blood pressure include atenolol (Tenormin), metoprolol (Lopressor, Toprol XL), nadolol (Corgard), propranolol (Inderal), and others.
Medications for high blood pressure (Calcium channel blockers). Hawthorn might decrease blood pressure. Taking hawthorn along with medication for high blood pressure might cause your blood pressure to go too low. Some medications for high blood pressure include nifedipine (Adalat, Procardia), verapamil (Calan, Isoptin, Verelan), diltiazem (Cardizem), isradipine (DynaCirc), felodipine (Plendil), amlodipine (Norvasc), and others.
Medications for male sexual dysfunction (Phosphodiesterase-5 Inhibitors). Hawthorn might decrease blood pressure. Some medications for male sexual dysfunction can also decrease blood pressure. Taking hawthorn along with medications for male sexual dysfunction might cause your blood pressure to go too low. Some medications for male sexual dysfunction include sildenafil (Viagra), tadalafil (Cialis), and vardenafil (Levitra).

HAZELNUT

What other names is the product known by?

Aveleira, Avelinier, Avellano, Cobnut, Corylus avellana, Corylus heterophylla, Coudrier, European filbert, European Hazel, Haselnuss, Haselstrauch, Hazel, Hazel Nut, Noisetier.

What is it?

Hazelnut is the nut from the hazel tree. People use it as medicine.

Is it Effective?

The effectiveness ratings for **HAZELNUT** are as follows:
Insufficient Evidence to Rate Effectiveness for... High cholesterol, use as an antioxidant, and other conditions.

How does it work?

Hazelnut contains oil, protein, and fiber. There isn't enough information to know how hazelnut might work for medicinal uses.

Are there safety concerns?

Hazelnut seems to be safe for most people in food amounts. But some people are allergic to hazelnuts and have had serious allergic reactions including life-threatening breathing problems (anaphylaxis). Hazelnuts have also been associated with one reported outbreak of botulism from contaminated yogurt.

Are there any interactions with medications?

It is not known if hazelnut interacts with any medicines.
Before taking hazelnut, talk with your healthcare professional if you take any medications.

HEART'S EASE

What other names is the product known by?

European Wild Pansy, Field Pansy, Johnny-Jump-Up, Ladies Delight, Pansy, Pensee Sauvage, Viola, Violae Tricoloris Herba, Viola tricolor, Wild Pansy.

What is it?

Heart's ease is a plant. The above ground parts are used to make medicine.

Is it Effective?

The effectiveness ratings for **HEART'S EASE** are as follows:

Insufficient Evidence to Rate Effectiveness for... Promoting metabolism, soothing sore throats and whooping cough, warts, skin conditions, reducing swelling in dry and scaly skin (seborrhea), and other conditions.

How does it work?

Heart's ease might decrease inflammation and have antioxidant properties.

Are there safety concerns?

Heart's ease is possibly safe for most people, but the potential side effects of heart's ease are not known.

Do not use heart's ease if: You are pregnant or breast-feeding.

Are there any interactions with medications?

It is not known if heart's ease interacts with any medicines.
Before taking heart's ease, talk with your healthcare professional if you take any medications.

HEATHER

What other names is the product known by?

Callunae vulgaris herba, Calluna vulgaris, Calluna vulgaris flos, Erica vulgaris, Ling, Scotch Heather.

What is it?

Heather is a plant. The flower, leaf, and plant top are used to make medicine.

Is it Effective?

The effectiveness ratings for **HEATHER** are as follows:

Insufficient Evidence to Rate Effectiveness for... Ailments of the kidney and lower urinary tract, prostate enlargement, fluid retention, digestive disorders such as diarrhea and spasms, colic (stomach pain), diseases of the liver and gallbladder, gout, arthritis, wounds, inflamed eyes, and many other uses.

How does it work?

There isn't enough information to know how heather might work.

Are there safety concerns?

Heather is possibly safe for most people, but the potential side effects are not known.

Do not use heather if: You are pregnant or breast-feeding.

Are there any interactions with medications?

It is not known if heather interacts with any medicines.
Before taking heather, talk with your healthcare professional if you take any medications.

Medical professionals should consult the Professional Version at www.NaturalDatabase.com.

HEDGE MUSTARD

What other names is the product known by?

English Watercress, Erysimum, Erysimum officinale, St. Barbara's Hedge Mustard, Singer's Plant, Sisymbrium officinale, Thalictroc.

What is it?

Hedge mustard is a plant. The leaves, stems, and flowers are used to make medicine. Be careful not to confuse hedge mustard with other types of mustards such as black mustard, brown mustard, white mustard, Indian mustard, and Chinese mustard.

Is it Effective?

The effectiveness ratings for **HEDGE MUSTARD** are as follows:

Insufficient Evidence to Rate Effectiveness for... Urinary tract diseases, coughs, chronic bronchitis, inflammation of the gallbladder, use as a gargle or mouthwash, and other conditions.

How does it work?

Hedge mustard contains vitamin C and mustard oil. There isn't enough information to know how hedge mustard might work for medicinal uses.

Are there safety concerns?

The flowering, above ground parts of hedge mustard are considered unsafe. Hedge mustard can cause serious side effects including vomiting, diarrhea, headache, and heart rhythm disorders.

While hedge mustard isn't safe for anyone, be especially careful not to use hedge mustard if: You are pregnant or breast-feeding. • You have heart disease. Hedge mustard may worsen existing heart conditions.

Are there any interactions with medications?

Antibiotics (Macrolide antibiotics). Hedge mustard can affect the heart. Some antibiotics might increase how much hedge mustard the body absorbs. Taking hedge mustard along with some antibiotics might increase the effects and side effects of hedge mustard. Some antibiotics called macrolide antibiotics include erythromycin, azithromycin, and clarithromycin.

Antibiotics (Tetracycline antibiotics). Taking tetracyclines with hedge mustard might increase the chance of side effects from hedge mustard. Some tetracyclines include demeclocycline (Declomycin), minocycline (Minocin), and tetracycline (Achromycin).

Digoxin (Lanoxin). Digoxin (Lanoxin) helps the heart beat more strongly. Hedge mustard also seems to affect the heart. Taking hedge mustard along with digoxin (Lanoxin) can increase the effects and side effects of digoxin (Lanoxin). Do not take hedge mustard if you are taking digoxin (Lanoxin) without talking to your health care professional.

Quinine. Hedge mustard can affect the heart. Quinine can also affect the heart. Taking quinine along with hedge mustard might cause serious heart problems.

Stimulant laxatives. Hedge mustard can affect the heart. The heart uses potassium. Laxatives called stimulant laxatives can decrease potassium levels in the body. Low potassium levels can increase the chance of side effects from hedge mustard. Some stimulant laxatives include bisacodyl (Correctol, Dulcolax), cascara, castor oil (Purge), senna (Senokot), and others.

Water pills (Diuretic drugs). Hedge mustard might affect the heart. "Water pills" can decrease potassium in the body. Low potassium levels can also affect the heart and increase the risk of side effects from hedge mustard. Some "water pills" that can deplete potassium include chlorothiazide (Diuril), chlorthalidone (Thalitone), furosemide (Lasix), hydrochlorothiazide (HCTZ, HydroDiuril, Microzide), and others.

HEDGE-HYSSOP

What other names is the product known by?

Gratiola, Gratiola officinalis.

What is it?

Hedge-hyssop is a plant. The above ground parts are used to make medicine.

Is it Effective?

The effectiveness ratings for **HEDGE-HYSSOP** are as follows:

Insufficient Evidence to Rate Effectiveness for... Liver disorders, heart conditions, parasites in the intestines, purging the bowels, increasing urination, and other conditions.

     Natural Medicines Comprehensive Database Consumer Version   (209) 472-2244

How does it work?
It is not known how hedge-hyssop might work.

Are there safety concerns?
Hedge-hyssop is considered to be unsafe. It is poisonous if too much is taken. Side effects and toxicities include vomiting, bloody diarrhea, stomach pain, increased urine followed by the inability to urinate, spasms, paralysis, blood circulation failure (circulatory collapse), and death.

Hedge-hyssop is unsafe for anyone to take. Some people are especially sensitive to the toxic effects.

Do not use hedge-hyssop if: You are pregnant or breast-feeding.

Are there any interactions with medications?
It is not known if hedge-hyssop interacts with any medicines.
Before taking hedge-hyssop, talk with your healthcare professional if you take any medications.

HEMLOCK

What other names is the product known by?
California Fern, Carrot Weed, Conium, Conium maculata, Conium maculatum, Nebraska Fern, Poison Fool's Parsley, Poison-Hemlock, Spotted Hemlock, Wild Carrot.

What is it?
Hemlock is a poisonous plant. Its leaves, root, and seeds are used to make medicine.

Is it Effective?
The effectiveness ratings for **HEMLOCK** are as follows:
Insufficient Evidence to Rate Effectiveness for... Anxiety, muscle spasms, teething in children, cramps, mania, bronchitis, whooping cough, asthma, and other conditions.

How does it work?
Hemlock contains poisons that affect the transmission of nerve impulses to muscle.

Are there safety concerns?
All parts of hemlock, including seeds, flowers, and fruits, are UNSAFE and poisonous. It can cause death. If someone takes hemlock, they should get prompt medical attention. Side effects and toxicities include increased saliva, burning of the digestive tract, drowsiness, muscle pain, rapid swelling and stiffening of muscles, rapid heart rate followed by a decreased heart rate, loss of speech, paralysis, unconsciousness, heart and lung failure, and death.

Are there any interactions with medications?
It is not known if hemlock interacts with any medicines.
Before taking hemlock, talk with your healthcare professional if you take any medications.

HEMLOCK SPRUCE

What other names is the product known by?
Abies excelsa, Balm of Gilead Fir, Balsam Fir, Canada Balsam, Fir Tree, Fir Needle Oil, Norway Pine, Norway Spruce, Picea abies, Picea aetheroleum, Picea excelsa, Picea turiones recentes, Spruce, Spruce Fir.

What is it?
Hemlock spruce is a plant. People use the needles and the oil distilled from the needles, branch tips, or branches of fresh fir shoots for medicine.

Is it Effective?
The effectiveness ratings for **HEMLOCK SPRUCE** are as follows:
Insufficient Evidence to Rate Effectiveness for... Coughs, the common cold, bronchitis, fevers, inflammation of the mouth and throat, muscular and nerve pain, arthritis, bacterial infection, arthritis pain, nerve pain, muscle pain, tuberculosis, and other conditions.

Medical professionals should consult the Professional Version at www.NaturalDatabase.com.

How does it work?
There isn't enough information to know how hemlock spruce might work.

Are there safety concerns?
It is not known if hemlock spruce is safe or what the potential side effects might be.

Do not use hemlock spruce if: You are pregnant or breast-feeding. • You have asthma. • You have whooping cough. • You have skin injuries or skin diseases. • You have heart problems.

Are there any interactions with medications?
It is not known if hemlock spruce interacts with any medicines.
Before taking hemlock spruce, talk with your healthcare professional if you take any medications.

HEMLOCK WATER DROPWORT

What other names is the product known by?
Dead Tongue, Five-Fingered Root, Horsebane, Oenanthe crocata, Yellow Water Dropwort.

What is it?
Hemlock water dropwort is a plant. The root is used to make medicine. Be careful not to confuse hemlock water dropwort with similar sounding plants such as water hemlock and hemlock. Also be careful not to mistake the extremely poisonous hemlock water dropwort with other similar looking plants, such as wild parsnip, sweet flag, or pignut.

Is it Effective?
The effectiveness ratings for **HEMLOCK WATER DROPWORT** are as follows:
Insufficient Evidence to Rate Effectiveness for... Use as a poultice for allergic skin reactions.

How does it work?
Hemlock water dropwort contains a poison that might decrease nerve signals to the brain.

Are there safety concerns?
Hemlock water dropwort is UNSAFE and poisonous. Swallowing even very small amounts of root may be fatal. Get medical attention immediately if hemlock water dropwort is taken by mouth. Signs of poisoning include nausea, dizziness, stomach pain, vomiting, sweating, drooling, blood in the urine, weakness, confusion, slurred speech, muscle spasm, increased breathing rate, turning blue, exhaustion, seizure, convulsions, unconsciousness, and death.

It is not known if hemlock water dropwort is safe for use on the skin or what the side effects might be. But since it is known to be poisonous if accidentally swallowed, especially to children, it is a dangerous substance to handle and use should be avoided.

Hemlock water dropwort isn't safe for anyone to use. Some people are especially sensitive to the poisonous effects and should be especially careful to avoid use.

Do not use hemlock water dropwort if: You are pregnant or breast-feeding.

Are there any interactions with medications?
It is not known if hemlock water dropwort interacts with any medicines.
Before taking hemlock water dropwort, talk with your healthcare professional if you take any medications.

HEMP AGRIMONY

What other names is the product known by?
Alpenkraut, Chanvrin, Donnerkraut, Dostenkraut, Drachenkraut, Dutch Agrimony, Dutch Eupatoire Commune, Eupatorium cannabinum, Gemeiner Wasswedost, Herbe de Sainte Cunegonde, Hirshklee, Holy Rope, Kunigundendraut, Leberkraut, Origan De Marais, St. John's Herb, Sweet Mandulin, Sweet-Smelling Trefoil, Thoroughwort, Wasshanf, Waterhemp, Water Maudlin.

What is it?
Hemp agrimony is an herb. The flowering parts of the plant are used to make medicine.

Is it Effective?

The effectiveness ratings for **HEMP AGRIMONY** are as follows:
Insufficient Evidence to Rate Effectiveness for... Liver and gallbladder disorders, colds, and fever.

How does it work?

There isn't enough information available to know how hemp agrimony works.

Are there safety concerns?

Hemp agrimony is unsafe for use. It might cause side effects such as stomach pain, liver problems, blood circulation disorders, and cancer.

Do not use hemp agrimony if: You are pregnant or breast-feeding. • You are allergic to ragweed, marigolds, daisies, and related herbs. • You have liver problems.

Are there any interactions with medications?

Medications that increase break down of other medications by the liver (Cytochrome P450 3A4 (CYP3A4) inducers). Hemp agrimony is broken down by the liver. Some chemicals that form when the liver breaks down hemp agrimony can be harmful. Medications that cause the liver to break down hemp agrimony might enhance the toxic effects of chemicals contained in hemp agrimony. Some of these medicines include carbamazepine (Tegretol), phenobarbital, phenytoin (Dilantin), rifampin, rifabutin (Mycobutin), and others.

HEMPNETTLE

What other names is the product known by?

Galeopsidis Herba, Galeopsis segetum, Galeopsis ochroleuca.

What is it?

Hempnettle is a plant. The leaves, stems, and flowers are used to make medicine.

Is it Effective?

The effectiveness ratings for **HEMPNETTLE** are as follows:
Insufficient Evidence to Rate Effectiveness for... Cough, bronchitis, lung diseases, mild swelling of the respiratory (breathing) tract, and use as a medicine to increase excretion of urine (diuretic).

How does it work?

Hempnettle increases the coughing up and spitting up of mucous from the lungs, bronchi, and wind pipe (expectorant) and shrinks body tissues (astringent effects).

Are there safety concerns?

Hempnettle seems to be safe when taken by mouth for most people, but the potential side effects are not known.

Do not use hempnettle if: You are pregnant or breast-feeding.

Are there any interactions with medications?

It is not known if hempnettle interacts with any medicines.
Before taking hempnettle, talk with your healthcare professional if you take any medications.

HENBANE

What other names is the product known by?

Devil's Eye, Fetid Nightshade, Hen Bell, Hog Bean, Hyoscyami Folium, Hyoscyamus niger, Jupiter's Bean, Khurasani-Ajavayan, Parasigaya, Poison Tobacco, Stinking Nightshade.

What is it?

Henbane is a plant. The leaf is used to make medicine.

Is it Effective?

The effectiveness ratings for **HENBANE** are as follows:
Insufficient Evidence to Rate Effectiveness for... Treating scar tissue, when the leaf oil is used on the skin. Spasms of the digestive tract, including the stomach and intestines.

Medical professionals should consult the Professional Version at www.NaturalDatabase.com.

Medical professionals should consult the Professional Version at www.NaturalDatabase.com.

How does it work?

Henbane contains chemicals, such as hyoscyamine and scopolamine, that might relax the muscles lining the digestive tract. Henbane might also relieve muscle tremors and have a calming effect.

Are there safety concerns?

Henbane is possibly safe for most people when used for a short time with the help of a healthcare professional. Side effects include dry mouth, red skin, constipation, overheating, reduced sweating, vision disturbances, increased heart rate, difficulty with urinating, drowsiness, restlessness, hallucinations, delirium, manic episodes, and death.

Henbane is unsafe when used for self-medication. Since henbane can be very toxic, the dose must be carefully chosen and side effects checked by a healthcare professional. Too much henbane can cause poisoning and death.

Do not use henbane if: You are pregnant or breast-feeding. • You have a heart condition such as heart failure or an abnormal heartbeat. Henbane may increase the heart rate and worsen heart failure. • You have a condition called Down syndrome. People with Down syndrome might be extremely sensitive to the effects of henbane. • You have a fever. • You have narrow-angle glaucoma. • You have trouble urinating (urinary retention). • You have a problem in your digestive tract, such as heartburn or "gastroesophageal reflux disease" (GERD), a hiatal hernia, an infection, constipation, a blockage, ulcerative colitis, a serious condition called toxic megacolon, or other disorders.

Are there any interactions with medications?

Drying medications (Anticholinergic drugs). Henbane contains chemicals that cause a drying effect. It also affects the brain and heart. Drying medications called anticholinergic drugs can also cause these effects. Taking henbane and drying medications together might cause side effects including dry skin, dizziness, low blood pressure, fast heartbeat, and other serious side effects. Some of these drying medications include atropine, scopolamine, and some medications used for allergies (antihistamines), and for depression (antidepressants).

HENNA

What other names is the product known by?

Alcanna, Egyptian Privet, Hennae folium, Henne, Jamaica Mignonette, Lawsonia alba, Lawsonia inermis, Mehndi, Mendee, Mignonette Tree, Reseda, Smooth Lawsonia.

What is it?

Henna is a plant. The leaf is used to make medicine.

Is it Effective?

The effectiveness ratings for **HENNA** are as follows:
Insufficient Evidence to Rate Effectiveness for... Ulcers in the stomach or intestines, dandruff, skin conditions, severe diarrhea caused by amoebas (amoebic dysentery), cancer, enlarged spleen, headache, yellow skin (jaundice), and other conditions.

How does it work?

Henna contains substances that might help fight certain infections. There is also some information that henna might decrease the growth of tumors, prevent or reduce spasms, decrease inflammation, and relieve pain.

Are there safety concerns?

Henna seems to be safe for most people when used on the skin or hair. It can cause some side effects such as inflammation of the skin (dermatitis), including redness, itching, burning, swelling, scaling, broken skin, blisters, and scarring of the skin. Rarely, allergic reactions can occur such as hives, runny nose, wheezing, and asthma.

Henna is considered to be unsafe when taken by mouth. Accidentally swallowing henna requires prompt medical attention. It can cause stomach upset and other side effects.

Henna is considered unsafe for use in children, especially in infants. There have been cases of serious side effects, including blood disorders, when henna was applied to the skin of infants.

Do not use henna if: You are pregnant or breast-feeding. • You have a disorder known as glucose-6-phosphate deficiency. Use of henna in infants with glucose-6-phosphate deficiency has been reported to cause red blood cells to burst (hemolysis).

 Natural Medicines Comprehensive Database Consumer Version (209) 472-2244

Are there any interactions with medications?
It is not known if henna interacts with any medicines.
Before taking henna, talk with your healthcare professional if you take any medications.

HERB PARIS

What other names is the product known by?
Einbeere, Herb-Paris, One Berry, Paris quadrifolia, Tilki Uzumu, Uva De Raposa, Wang Sun.

What is it?
Herb Paris is a plant. The plant and its fruit are used to make medicine.

Is it Effective?
The effectiveness ratings for **HERB PARIS** are as follows:
Insufficient Evidence to Rate Effectiveness for... Headache; living longer; nerve pain; sore and painful muscles and joints; genital tumors; rapid fluttering or throbbing of the heart; muscle spasms; use as a medicine to cause vomiting, or cleansing and emptying the intestinal tract.

How does it work?
Herb Paris contains a chemical that causes the pupil of the eye to get smaller and it can also affect breathing.

Are there safety concerns?
Herb Paris is unsafe when taken by mouth. Side effects of Herb Paris include nausea, vomiting, diarrhea, headache, small pupils, paralysis of the breathing muscles, and death.

Do not use Herb Paris if: You are pregnant or breast-feeding.

Are there any interactions with medications?
It is not known if Herb Paris interacts with any medicines.
Before taking Herb Paris, talk with your healthcare professional if you take any medications.

HERB ROBERT

What other names is the product known by?
Dragon's Blood, Geranium robertianum, Mountain Geranium, Stinky Bob, Storkbill, Wild Crane's-Bill.

What is it?
Herb Robert is a plant. The leaves, stems, and flowers are used to make medicine.

Is it Effective?
The effectiveness ratings for **HERB ROBERT** are as follows:
Insufficient Evidence to Rate Effectiveness for... Diarrhea, liver and kidney conditions, bladder and gallbladder conditions, and the prevention of stones forming in the kidney, bladder, or gallbladder.

How does it work?
An extract of Herb Robert may inhibit the growth of bacteria and viruses.

Are there safety concerns?
There isn't enough information available to know if Herb Robert is safe.

Do not use Herb Robert if: You are pregnant or breast-feeding.

Are there any interactions with medications?
It is not known if Herb Robert interacts with any medicines.
Before taking Herb Robert, talk with your healthcare professional if you take any medications.

HESPERIDIN

What other names is the product known by?
Citrus Bioflavonoid, Citrus Bioflavonoids.

What is it?
Hesperidin is a chemical compound called a bioflavonoid. It is found primarily in citrus fruits. People use it as medicine.

Is it Effective?
The effectiveness ratings for **HESPERIDIN** are as follows:
Possibly Effective for... Internal hemorrhoids, when used in combination with diosmin • Treating leg ulcers caused by poor circulation, when used in combination with diosmin.
Possibly Ineffective for... Treating swelling of the arms following surgery for breast cancer.
Insufficient Evidence to Rate Effectiveness for... Varicose veins and other conditions.

How does it work?
Hesperidin may reduce inflammation and pain and help blood vessels function better.

Are there safety concerns?
Hesperidin is possibly safe for most people when used for less than three months. Side effects include stomach pain and upset, diarrhea, and headache.

Do not use hesperidin if: You are pregnant or breast-feeding.

Are there any interactions with medications?
It is not known if hesperidin interacts with any medicines.
Before taking hesperidin, talk with your healthcare professional if you take any medications.

HIBISCUS

What other names is the product known by?
Guinea Sorrel, Hibiscus sabdariffa, Jamaica Sorrel, Karkade, Red Tea, Roselle, Sudanese Tea.

What is it?
Hibiscus is a plant. The flowers are used to make medicine.

Is it Effective?
The effectiveness ratings for **HIBISCUS** are as follows:
Insufficient Evidence to Rate Effectiveness for... Loss of appetite, colds, constipation, irritated stomach, fluid retention, heart disease, and nerve disease.

How does it work?
The fruit acids in hibiscus may work like a laxative. Some researchers think that other chemicals in hibiscus might be able to lower blood pressure; decrease spasms in the stomach, intestines, and uterus; and work like antibiotics to kill bacteria and worms.

Are there safety concerns?
Hibiscus seems to be safe for most people, but the potential side effects of hibiscus are not known.

Do not take hibiscus if: You are pregnant or breast-feeding.

Are there any interactions with medications?
Acetaminophen (Tylenol, others). Drinking a hibiscus beverage before taking acetaminophen might increase how fast your body gets rid of acetaminophen. But more information is needed to know if this is a big concern.

     Natural Medicines Comprehensive Database Consumer Version   (209) 472-2244

HISTIDINE

What other names is the product known by?
Alpha-amino-4-imidazole propanoic acid, L-2-Amino-3-(1H-imidazol-4-yl) proprionic acid, L-Histidine, Levo-Histidine.

What is it?
Histidine is an amino acid. Amino acids are the building blocks of protein in our bodies. People use histidine as medicine.

Is it Effective?
The effectiveness ratings for **HISTIDINE** are as follows:
Possibly Ineffective for... Rheumatoid arthritis • Anemia associated with kidney failure or kidney dialysis.
Insufficient Evidence to Rate Effectiveness for... Allergic diseases, ulcers, and other conditions.

How does it work?
Histidine is involved in a wide range of metabolic processes in the body.

Are there safety concerns?
Histidine is possibly safe for most people, but the potential side effects are not known.

Do not use histidine if: You are pregnant or breast-feeding. • You have low folic acid (folic acid deficiency).

Are there any interactions with medications?
It is not known if histidine interacts with any medicines.
Before taking histidine, talk with your healthcare professional if you take any medications.

HOLLY

What other names is the product known by?
Christ's Thorn, Holm, Holme Chase, Holy Tree, Hulm, Hulver Bush, Hulver Tree.

What is it?
Holly is a plant. The leaf and berry are used to make medicine.

Is it Effective?
The effectiveness ratings for **HOLLY** are as follows:
Insufficient Evidence to Rate Effectiveness for... Coughs, digestive disorders, liver disorders, arthritis-like pain, heart disease, dizziness, blood pressure, and other conditions.

How does it work?
There isn't enough information available to know how holly works.

Are there safety concerns?
Holly berries are poisonous and unsafe for use. Accidental ingestion of the berries may be deadly, in both children and adults.

There isn't enough information available to know if holly leaves are safe for use. The leaves can cause side effects such as diarrhea, nausea, vomiting, and stomach and intestinal problems. Ingestion of holly leaf spines may tear or puncture skin or mucous membranes.

Do not use holly if: You are pregnant or breast-feeding. • You are dehydrated. • You have a fluid (electrolyte) imbalance.

Are there any interactions with medications?
It is not known if holly interacts with any medicines.
Before taking holly, talk with your healthcare professional if you take any medications.

HOLLYHOCK

What other names is the product known by?

Alcea rosea, Althaea rosea, Althea Rose, Hollyhock Flower, Malvae arboreae flos, Malva, Malva Flower, Rose Mallow.

What is it?

Hollyhock is a plant. The flower is used to make medicine.

Is it Effective?

The effectiveness ratings for **HOLLYHOCK** are as follows:

Insufficient Evidence to Rate Effectiveness for... Breathing disorders, digestive tract problems, skin inflammation, skin ulcers, and other conditions.

How does it work?

There isn't enough information to know how hollyhock might work.

Are there safety concerns?

Hollyhock is possibly safe for most people, but the potential side effects aren't known.

Do not use hollyhock if: You are pregnant or breast-feeding.

Are there any interactions with medications?

It is not known if hollyhock interacts with any medicines.
Before taking hollyhock, talk with your healthcare professional if you take any medications.

HOLY BASIL

What other names is the product known by?

Bai Gkaprow, Green Holy Basil, Hot Basil, Indian Basil, Kemangen, Krishna Tulsi, Ocimum tenuiflorum, Ocimum sanctum, Rama Tulsi, Red Holy Basil, Sacred Basil, Sacred Purple Basil, Shyama Tulsi, Tulsi, Tulasi.

What is it?

Holy basil is a plant. Medicine is made from the leaves, stems, and seeds.

Is it Effective?

The effectiveness ratings for **HOLY BASIL** are as follows:

Insufficient Evidence to Rate Effectiveness for... Diabetes, common cold, influenza ("the flu"), asthma, bronchitis, earache, headache, stomach upset, heart disease, fever, viral hepatitis, malaria, tuberculosis, mercury poisoning, use as an antidote to snake and scorpion bites, or ringworm.

How does it work?

Chemicals in holy basil are thought to decrease inflammation. Other chemicals might lower blood sugar in people with diabetes.

Are there safety concerns?

Holy basil might be safe when used for short periods of time, up to four weeks. It's not known if long-term use is safe.

Do not take holy basil if: You are pregnant or breast-feeding.

Are there any interactions with medications?

Medications that slow blood clotting (Anticoagulant / Antiplatelet drugs). Holy basil might slow blood clotting. Taking holy basil along with medications that also slow clotting might increase the chances of bruising and bleeding. But there isn't enough information to know if this is a big concern. Some medications that slow blood clotting include include aspirin, clopidogrel (Plavix), dalteparin (Fragmin), enoxaparin (Lovenox), heparin, ticlopidine (Ticlid), warfarin (Coumadin), and others.

Pentobarbital. Pentobarbital causes drowsiness. There is some concern that taking holy basil seed oil with pentobarbital might cause too much drowsiness. But there isn't enough information to know if this is a big concern.

 Natural Medicines Comprehensive Database Consumer Version   (209) 472-2244

HONEY

What other names is the product known by?
Apis mellifera, Clarified Honey, Honig, Mel, Miel Blanc, Purified Honey, Strained Honey.

What is it?
Honey is a substance produced by bees from the nectar of plants. The honey is used as a medicine.

Is it Effective?
The effectiveness ratings for **HONEY** are as follows:
Possibly Effective for... Burns.
Insufficient Evidence to Rate Effectiveness for... Cough, wound healing, sunburn, foot ulcers caused by diabetes, asthma, allergies, breaking up thick mucus secretions, diarrhea, digestive tract ulcers, and cataracts.

How does it work?
Some of the chemicals in honey may work like an antibiotic or antifungal medicine by killing bacteria and fungus. When applied to the skin, honey may serve as a barrier to moisture and improve wound healing.

Are there safety concerns?
Honey seems to be safe for most adults and older children when applied to the skin. Honey is considered safe in women who are pregnant or breast-feeding.

Do not use raw honey in infants and young children under 12 months of age due to the chance of botulism poisoning.

Do not use honey if: You have pollen allergies due to the chance of allergic reactions.

Are there any interactions with medications?
It is not known if honey interacts with any medicines.
Before taking honey, talk with your healthcare professional if you take any medications.

HONEYSUCKLE

What other names is the product known by?
Goat's Leaf, Honey Suckle, Jin Yin Hua, Jinyinhua, Lonicera, Lonicera aureoreticulata, Lonicera bournei, Lonicera caprifolia, Lonicera japonica, Woodbine.

What is it?
Honeysuckle is a plant. The flower, seed, and leaves are used for medicine. Be careful not to confuse honeysuckle with other plants which are also known as woodbine, such as American ivy or gelsemium.

Is it Effective?
The effectiveness ratings for **HONEYSUCKLE** are as follows:
Insufficient Evidence to Rate Effectiveness for... Inflammation of small air passages in the lung (bronchiolitis), digestive disorders, cancerous tumors, constipation, skin inflammation, itching, colds, fever, swelling, boils, sores, bacterial or viral infections, promoting sweating, and other conditions.

How does it work?
Honeysuckle might decrease inflammation. However, more information is needed to determine how honeysuckle might work.

Are there safety concerns?
It is not known if honeysuckle is safe. Skin contact with honeysuckle can cause rash in allergic people.

Do not use honeysuckle if: You are pregnant or breast-feeding.

Are there any interactions with medications?
Medications that slow blood clotting (Anticoagulant / Antiplatelet drugs). Honeysuckle might slow blood clotting. Taking honeysuckle along with medications that also slow clotting might increase the chances of bruising and bleeding. Some medications that slow blood clotting include aspirin, clopidogrel (Plavix), diclofenac (Voltaren, Cataflam, others), ibuprofen (Advil, Motrin, others), naproxen (Anaprox, Naprosyn, others), dalteparin (Fragmin), enoxaparin (Lovenox), heparin, warfarin (Coumadin), and others.

HOODIA

What other names is the product known by?

Hoodia Cactus, Hoodia Extract, Hoodia Gordonii, Hoodia Gordonii Cactus, Hoodia P57, Kalahari Cactus, Kalahari Diet, P57, Xhoba.

What is it?

Hoodia is a succulent from the Kalahari dessert.

Is it Effective?

The effectiveness ratings for **HOODIA** are as follows:
Insufficient Evidence to Rate Effectiveness for... Suppressing appetite or weight loss.

How does it work?

A chemical in hoodia called P57 is thought to decrease feelings of hunger. But it is not known if hoodia has this effect when used in people.

Are there safety concerns?

There isn't enough information to know if hoodia is safe.

Do not take hoodia if: You are pregnant or breast-feeding.

Are there any interactions with medications?

It's not known if hoodia interacts with any medicines.
Before taking hoodia, talk with your healthcare professional if you take any medications.

HOPS

What other names is the product known by?

Common Hops, European Hops, Hopfenzapfen, Hop Strobile, Houblon, Humulus lupulus, Lupuli Strobulus.

What is it?

Hops is a plant. The dried, flowering part of the plant is used to make medicine.

Is it Effective?

The effectiveness ratings for **HOPS** are as follows:
Insufficient Evidence to Rate Effectiveness for... Anxiety, inability to sleep, tenseness, attention deficit-hyperactivity disorder (ADHD), improving appetite, indigestion, intestinal cramps, leg ulcers, tuberculosis, inflammation of the bladder, nerve pain, and other conditions.

How does it work?

The chemicals in hops seem to have weak estrogen effects.

Are there safety concerns?

Hops are considered safe for most people.

Do not take hops if: You are pregnant or breast-feeding. • You have been diagnosed with depression.

Are there any interactions with medications?

Alcohol. Alcohol can cause sleepiness and drowsiness. Hops might also cause sleepiness and drowsiness. Taking large amounts of hops along with alcohol might cause too much sleepiness.
Sedative medications (CNS depressants). Hops might cause sleepiness and drowsiness. Medications that cause sleepiness are called sedatives. Taking hops along with sedative medications might cause too much sleepiness. Some sedative medications include clonazepam (Klonopin), lorazepam (Ativan), Phenobarbital (Donnatal), zolpidem (Ambien), and others.

HORSE CHESTNUT

What other names is the product known by?

Aesculus hippocastanum, Buckeye, Castaño de Indias, Chestnut, Escine, Hippocastani Cortex, Hippocastani Flos, Hippocastani folium, Hippocastani Semen, Marron Europeen, Marronnier, Spanish Chestnut, Venastat, Venostasin Retard, Venostat.

What is it?

Horse chestnut is a plant. The seed, bark, flower, and leaves of the plant are used to make medicine. Be careful not to confuse aesculus hippocastanum (Horse chestnut) with aesculus californica (California buckeye) or aesculus glabra (Ohio buckeye). All three may be called horse chestnut. This sheet refers to aesculus hippocastanum (Horse chestnut).

Is it Effective?

The effectiveness ratings for **HORSE CHESTNUT** are as follows:

Likely Effective for... Varicose veins and other circulatory problems (chronic venous insufficiency) • Pain, tiredness, tension, swelling in the legs, itching, and water retention (edema).

Insufficient Evidence to Rate Effectiveness for... Hemorrhoids, diarrhea, fever, cough, enlarged prostate, eczema, menstrual pain, soft tissue swelling from bone fracture and sprains, arthritis, rheumatism, and other conditions.

How does it work?

Horse chestnut contains a substance that thins the blood. It also makes it harder for fluid to leak out of veins and capillaries and weakly promotes fluid loss through the urine to help prevent water retention (edema).

Are there safety concerns?

Horse chestnut seems to be safe for most people when a standardized seed extract product is used short-term. Standardized products have been tested to contain exact amounts of a verified chemical. Look for products which have had the toxic substance esculin removed. Horse chestnut products can sometimes cause side effects such as dizziness, headache, stomach upset, and itching.

Pollen from the horse chestnut flower can cause allergic reactions. Rectal (suppository) use of horse chestnut may cause inflammation and itching in the anal area. Intravenous injection (IV) of horse chestnut seed extracts has caused kidney and liver damage.

Raw horse chestnut seed, bark, flower, and leaf are unsafe and poisonous when taken by mouth. Death can occur. Signs of poisoning include stomach upset, kidney problems, muscle twitching, weakness, loss of coordination, enlarged eye pupils, vomiting, diarrhea, depression, paralysis, and stupor. Accidental ingestion of horse chestnut requires prompt medical attention. Children have been poisoned by drinking a tea made from the leaves and twigs or eating seeds.

Horse chestnut might lower blood sugar. If you have diabetes, watch for signs of too low blood sugar (hypoglycemia) and check your blood sugar carefully.

Do not take horse chestnut if: You are pregnant or breast-feeding. • You have a latex allergy. • You have a kidney disease. • You have a liver disease.

Are there any interactions with medications?

Medications that slow blood clotting (Anticoagulant / Antiplatelet drugs). Horse chestnut seed might slow blood clotting. Taking horse chestnut seed along with medications that also slow clotting might increase the chances of bruising and bleeding. Some medications that slow blood clotting include aspirin, clopidogrel (Plavix), diclofenac (Voltaren, Cataflam, others), ibuprofen (Advil, Motrin, others), naproxen (Anaprox, Naprosyn, others), dalteparin (Fragmin), enoxaparin (Lovenox), heparin, warfarin (Coumadin), and others.

Medications for diabetes (Antidiabetes drugs). Horse chestnut might decrease blood sugar. Diabetes medications are also used to lower blood sugar. Taking horse chestnut along with diabetes medications might cause your blood sugar to go too low. Monitor your blood sugar closely. The dose of your diabetes medication might need to be changed. Some medications used for diabetes include glimepiride (Amaryl), glyburide (DiaBeta, Glynase PresTab, Micronase), insulin, pioglitazone (Actos), rosiglitazone (Avandia), chlorpropamide (Diabinese), glipizide (Glucotrol), tolbutamide (Orinase), and others.

Medical professionals should consult the Professional Version at www.NaturalDatabase.com.

HORSEMINT

What other names is the product known by?
Monarda lutea, Monarda punctata, Spotted monarda, Wild Bergamot.

What is it?
Horsemint is a plant. The leaves are used to make medicine.

Is it Effective?
The effectiveness ratings for **HORSEMINT** are as follows:
Insufficient Evidence to Rate Effectiveness for... Digestive disorders, intestinal gas (flatulence), painful or abnormal menstruation (dysmenorrhea), or other uses.

How does it work?
There isn't enough information to know how horsemint might work.

Are there safety concerns?
It is not known if horsemint is safe or what the potential side effects might be.

Do not use horsemint if: You are pregnant or breast-feeding.

Are there any interactions with medications?
It is not known if horsemint interacts with any medicines.
Before taking horsemint, talk with your healthcare professional if you take any medications.

HORSERADISH

What other names is the product known by?
Amoraciae Rusticanae Radix, Armoracia lopathifolia, Armoracia Rusticana, Cochlearia Armoracia, Great Raifort, Meerrettich, Mountain Radish, Nasturtium Armoracia, Pepperrot, Red Cole, Roripa Armoracia.

What is it?
Horseradish is a plant. The roots are used to make medicine.

Is it Effective?
The effectiveness ratings for **HORSERADISH** are as follows:
Insufficient Evidence to Rate Effectiveness for... Urinary tract problems, fluid retention (edema), cough, bronchitis, achy joints and muscles, gout, gallbladder disorders, sciatic nerve pain, colic, intestinal worms in children, and other conditions.

How does it work?
Horseradish might help fight bacteria and stop spasms.

Are there safety concerns?
Horseradish is possibly safe for most people when used by mouth in medicinal amounts, but it contains substances that are extremely irritating to the lining of the mouth, throat, nose, digestive system, and urinary tract. Horseradish can cause side effects including stomach upset, bloody vomiting and diarrhea, and low thyroid.

When used on the skin, horseradish is possibly safe when preparations containing 2% mustard oil or less are used, but it can cause skin irritation and allergic reactions.

Horseradish is unsafe when used in children less than four years of age or in pregnant or breast-feeding women.

Do not use horseradish if: You have a kidney disorder. • You have low thyroid (hypothyroidism). • You have a digestive tract problem such as stomach or intestinal ulcers, inflammatory bowel disease, infections, or other conditions.

Are there any interactions with medications?
Levothyroxine. Levothyroxine is used for low thyroid function. Horseradish seems to decrease the thyroid. Taking horseradish along with levothyroxine might decrease the effects of levothyroxine. Some brands that contain levothyroxine include Armour Thyroid, Eltroxin, Estre, Euthyrox, Levo-T, Levothroid, Levoxyl, Synthroid, Unithroid, and others.

HORSETAIL

What other names is the product known by?

Bottle Brush, Cavalinha, Coda Cavallina, Common Horsetail, Corn Horsetail, Dutch Rushes, Equiseti Herba, Equisetum, Equisetum arvense, Equisetum Telmateia, Field Horsetail, Horse Herb, Horsetail, Horsetail Grass, Horsetail Rush, Horsetail Grass, Horsetail Rush, Horse Willow, Paddock-Pipes, Pewterwort, Prele, Scouring Rush, Souring Rush, Shave Grass, Shavegrass, and Toadpipe.

What is it?

Horsetail is a plant. The above ground parts are used to make medicine.

Is it Effective?

The effectiveness ratings for **HORSETAIL** are as follows:

Insufficient Evidence to Rate Effectiveness for... Kidney and bladder stones, weight loss, hair loss, gout, frostbite, heavy periods, fluid retention, urinary tract infections, incontinence, and use on the skin for wound healing.

How does it work?

The chemicals in horsetail may have antioxidant and anti-inflammatory effects. Plants related to horsetail contain chemicals that work like "water pills" (diuretics) and increase urine output. But it isn't clear whether horsetail has this effect.

Are there safety concerns?

Horsetail might not be safe. It contains a chemical called thiaminase that breaks down the vitamin thiamine. Some products are labeled "thiaminase-free," but there's not enough information available to know if these products are safe.

Do not take horsetail if: You are pregnant or breast-feeding. • You have thiamine deficiency. • You have diabetes. • You have heart problems. • You have kidney problems.

Are there any interactions with medications?

It is not known if horsetail interacts with any medicines.
Before taking horsetail, talk with your healthcare professional if you take any medications.

HOUND'S TONGUE

What other names is the product known by?

Cynoglossi Herba, Cynoglossi Radix, Cynoglossum Officinale, Dog-Bur, Dog's Tongue, Gypsy Flower, Hounds Tongue, Sheep-Lice, Woolmat.

What is it?

Hound's tongue is a plant. People use it as medicine.

Is it Effective?

The effectiveness ratings for **HOUND'S TONGUE** are as follows:

Insufficient Evidence to Rate Effectiveness for... Diarrhea and other digestive tract problems, skin diseases, bronchitis, pain, cough, wounds, and other conditions.

How does it work?

There isn't enough information available to know how hound's tongue works.

Are there safety concerns?

Hound's tongue is unsafe and poisonous. Hound's tongue contains significant amounts of substances that are known to cause liver damage and cancer. Regular use of hound's tongue can cause a liver disorder known as veno-occlusive disease. Symptoms of veno-occlusive disease include a painful, swollen belly and decreased urine production.

Hound's tongue isn't safe for anyone to use. Some people may be extra-sensitive to the toxic effects and should be particularly careful to avoid use.

Do not use hound's tongue if: You are pregnant or breast-feeding. • You have a liver disorder.

Medical professionals should consult the
Professional Version at www.NaturalDatabase.com.

Are there any interactions with medications?

Medications that increase break down of other medications by the liver (Cytochrome P450 3A4 (CYP3A4) inducers). Hound's tongue is broken down by the liver. Some chemicals that form when the liver breaks down hound's tongue can be harmful. Medications that cause the liver to break down hound's tongue might enhance the toxic effects of chemicals contained in hound's tongue. Some of these medicines include carbamazepine (Tegretol), phenobarbital, phenytoin (Dilantin), rifampin, rifabutin (Mycobutin), and others.

HOUSELEEK

What other names is the product known by?

Aaron's Rod, Ayegreen, Ayron, Bullock's Eye, Hens and Chickens, Jupiter's Beard, Jupiter's Eye, Liveforever, Sempervivum tectorum, Sengreen, Thor's Beard, Thunder Plant.

What is it?

Houseleek is a plant. The leaf of the nonflowering plant is used to make medicine.

Is it Effective?

The effectiveness ratings for **HOUSELEEK** are as follows:
Insufficient Evidence to Rate Effectiveness for... Severe diarrhea; ulcers in the mouth; burns; skin ulcers; warts; itchy, burning skin; and swelling from insect bites.

How does it work?

There isn't enough information to know how houseleek might work.

Are there safety concerns?

There isn't enough information to know if houseleek is safe when taken by mouth or put on the skin or what the potential side effects might be.

Do not use houseleek if: You are pregnant or breast-feeding.

Are there any interactions with medications?

It is not known if houseleek interacts with any medicines.
Before taking houseleek, talk with your healthcare professional if you take any medications.

HU ZHANG

What other names is the product known by?

Fallopia Japonica, Fleece Flower, He Shou Wu, Hu Zhang Extract, Hu Zhang Root, Japanese Bamboo, Japanese Knotweed, Mexican Bamboo, PCWE, Polygoni Multiflora, Polygonum Cuspidatum, Polygonum Cuspidatum Water Extract, Reynoutria Japonica.

What is it?

Hu zhang is a plant. The root is used as medicine.

Is it Effective?

The effectiveness ratings for **HU ZHANG** are as follows:
Insufficient Evidence to Rate Effectiveness for... Constipation, menstrual problems, hot flashes, heart disease, high cholesterol, cancer, skin burns, liver disease, gout, and gallstones.

How does it work?

There is not enough known about how hu zhang might work. Some chemicals in hu zhang might decrease how fast some cells grow.

Are there safety concerns?

There is not enough known about hu zhang to know if it is safe.

Are there any interactions with medications?

Estrogens. Hu zhang seems to have some of the same effects as estrogen. Taking hu zhang along with estrogens might decrease the effects of estrogens. Some estrogen pills include conjugated equine estrogens (Premarin), ethinyl estradiol, estradiol, and others.

HUMIC ACID

What other names is the product known by?
Humate.

What is it?
Humic acid is a chemical produced by decaying plants. People use it to make medicine.

Is it Effective?
The effectiveness ratings for **HUMIC ACID** are as follows:
Insufficient Evidence to Rate Effectiveness for... Preventing the flu, stimulating the immune system, treating viral diseases, and other conditions.

How does it work?
There isn't enough information to know how humic acid works.

Are there safety concerns?
There isn't enough reliable information about the safety of humic acid for people. Laboratory research and population research has associated humic acid with joint disease, circulatory disease, and thyroid disease.

Do not take humic acid if: You are pregnant or breast-feeding.

Are there any interactions with medications?
It is not known if humic acid interacts with any medicines.
Before taking humic acid, talk with your healthcare professional if you take any medications.

HUPERZINE A

What other names is the product known by?
HupA, Huperzine, Huperzine A, Selagine.

What is it?
Huperzine A is a substance purified from a plant called Chinese club moss. People use it as medicine. Be careful not to confuse huperzine A, which is also called selagine with similar sounding medications such as selegiline (Eldepryl). Also be careful not to confuse one of the brand names for huperizine A (Cerebra) with the brand names for unrelated prescription drugs such as celecoxib (Celebrex), citalopram (Celexa), and fosphenytoin (Cerebyx).

Is it Effective?
The effectiveness ratings for **HUPERZINE A** are as follows:
Possibly Effective for... Improving memory, mental function, and behavior in people with dementia from certain conditions such as Alzheimer's disease, multi-infarct dementia, or senile dementia • Improving memory in healthy adolescents • Use by injection to prevent muscle weakness due to the muscular disorder myasthenia gravis.
Insufficient Evidence to Rate Effectiveness for... Age-related memory loss, increasing alertness and energy, protection from agents poisonous to nerves, and other conditions.

How does it work?
Huperzine A is thought to be beneficial for problems with memory, loss of mental abilities (dementia), and the muscular disorder myasthenia gravis because it causes an increase in the levels of acetylcholine. Acetylcholine is one of the chemicals that our nerves use to communicate in the brain, muscles, and other areas.

Are there safety concerns?
Huperzine A seems to be safe when used for a short time, such as less than one month. It can cause some side effects including nausea, diarrhea, vomiting, sweating, blurred vision, slurred speech, restlessness, loss of appetite (anorexia), contraction and twitching of muscle fibers (fasciculations), cramping, increased saliva and urine, inability to control urination (incontinence), high blood pressure, and slowed heart rate (bradycardia).

Do not use huperzine A if: You are pregnant or breast-feeding. • You have a heart condition. • You have a seizure disorder called epilepsy. • You have a blockage, or "obstruction," in your digestive tract. • You have a stomach or intestinal ulcer. • You have a lung condition such as asthma or chronic pulmonary obstructive disease (COPD). • You have a blockage of your urinary or reproductive systems.

Medical professionals should consult the Professional Version at www.NaturalDatabase.com.

Are there any interactions with medications?

Drying medications (Anticholinergic drugs). Huperzine A contains chemicals that can affect the brain and heart. Some of these drying medications called anticholinergic drugs can also affect the brain and heart. But huperzine A works differently than drying medications. Huperzine A might decrease the effects of drying medications. Some of these drying medications include atropine, scopolamine, and some medications used for allergies (antihistamines), and for depression (antidepressants).

Medications for Alzheimer's disease (Acetylcholinesterase (AChE) inhibitors). Huperzine A contains a chemical that affects the brain. Medications for Alzheimer's disease also affect the brain. Taking Huperzine A along with medications for Alzheimer's disease might increase effects and side effects of medications for Alzheimer's disease.

Various medications used for glaucoma, Alzheimer's disease, and other conditions (Cholinergic drugs). Huperzine A contains a chemical that affects the body. This chemical is similar to some medications used for glaucoma, Alzheimer's disease and other conditions. Taking Huperzine A with these medications might increase the chance of side effects. Some of these medications used for glaucoma, Alzheimer's disease, and other conditions include pilocarpine (Pilocar and others), donepezil (Aricept), tacrine (Cognex), and others.

HYALURONIC ACID

What other names is the product known by?

Hyaluran, Hyaluronan, Hyaluronate Sodium, Sodium Hyaluronate.

What is it?

Hyaluronic acid is a substance that is present in the human body naturally, in the highest concentrations in fluids in eyes and joints.

Is it Effective?

The effectiveness ratings for **HYALURONIC ACID** are as follows:
Likely Effective for... Sores in the mouth • Eye surgery and corneal transplant, when injected by an eye surgeon.
Possibly Effective for... Osteoarthritis, when injected into the joint.
Insufficient Evidence to Rate Effectiveness for... Healing skin wounds and burns, and preventing aging.

How does it work?

Hyaluronic acid works by acting as a cushion and lubricant in the joints and other tissues. In addition, it might affect the inflammatory response of the body.

Are there safety concerns?

Prescription forms of hyaluronic acid are safe for most people. There isn't enough information about hyaluronic acid to know if it is safe when taken by mouth. Sometimes hyaluronic acid can cause pain and redness where it is injected. Increased pressure in the eye may occur after hyaluronic acid is used for eye surgery. Rarely, hyaluronic acid may cause allergic reactions.

Do not take hyaluronic acid unless administered by a healthcare professional if: You are pregnant or breast-feeding.

Are there any interactions with medications?

It is not known if hyaluronic acid interacts with any medicines.
Before taking hyaluronic acid, talk with your healthcare professional if you take any medications.

HYDRANGEA

What other names is the product known by?

Hydrangea arborscens, Mountain Hydrangea, Seven Barks, Smooth Hydrangea, Viburnum alnifolium, Viburnum americanum, Wild Hydrangea.

What is it?

Hydrangea is a plant. The root and rhizome (underground stem) are used to make medicine.

Is it Effective?

The effectiveness ratings for **HYDRANGEA** are as follows:
Insufficient Evidence to Rate Effectiveness for... Enlarged prostate, prostate and bladder infections, kidney stones, and hayfever.

How does it work?
The chemicals in hydrangea may cause increased urine output, which could help some urinary tract problems.

Are there safety concerns?
Hydrangea is safe for most people when used only for a few days.

Side effects include nausea, vomiting, diarrhea, dizziness, and chest tightness.

Do not use more than two grams at a time or for a long period of time.

Do not take hydrangea if: You are pregnant or breast-feeding.

Are there any interactions with medications?
It is not known if hydrangea interacts with any medicines.
Before taking hydrangea, talk with your healthcare professional if you take any medications.

HYDRAZINE SULFATE

What other names is the product known by?
Hydrazine, sehydrin.

What is it?
Hydrazine sulfate is a chemical used in industry. Some people use it as medicine.

Is it Effective?
The effectiveness ratings for **HYDRAZINE SULFATE** are as follows:
Possibly Ineffective for... Colon and rectal cancer that has spread (metastatic colorectal cancer).
Likely Ineffective for... Use with chemotherapy for non-small cell lung cancer.
Insufficient Evidence to Rate Effectiveness for... General weight loss and wasting associated with cancer, brain cancer (neuroblastoma), Hodgkin's disease (lymph cancer), and other kinds of cancer.

How does it work?
Hydrazine sulfate may block enzymes in the body that might lead to malnutrition and muscle wasting associated with cancer.

Are there safety concerns?
Hydrazine sulfate is possibly UNSAFE. Some research suggests it can damage the liver. It can cause some side effects including nausea, vomiting, dizziness, drowsiness, nerve problems, violent behavior, restlessness, seizures, coma, confusion, mood stimulation, excitement, weakness, irregular breathing, abnormal blood sugar levels, rash, and kidney damage.

Do not use hydrazine sulfate if: You are pregnant or breast-feeding. • You have diabetes. • You have liver disease.

Are there any interactions with medications?
Medications for depression (MAOIs). Hydrazine sulfate contains a chemical that affects the body. This chemical might increase the side effects of some medications used for depression. Some of these medications used for depression include phenelzine (Nardil), tranylcypromine (Parnate), and others.
Medications for diabetes (Antidiabetes drugs). Hydrazine sulfate might decrease blood sugar. Diabetes medications are also used to lower blood sugar. Taking hydrazine sulfate along with diabetes medications might cause your blood sugar to go too low. Monitor your blood sugar closely. The dose of your diabetes medication might need to be changed. Some medications used for diabetes include glimepiride (Amaryl), glyburide (DiaBeta, Glynase PresTab, Micronase), insulin, pioglitazone (Actos), rosiglitazone (Avandia), chlorpropamide (Diabinese), glipizide (Glucotrol), tolbutamide (Orinase), and others.
Sedative medications (CNS depressants). Hydrazine sulfate might cause sleepiness and drowsiness. Medications that cause sleepiness are called sedatives. Taking hydrazine sulfate along with sedative medications might cause too much sleepiness. Some sedative medications include clonazepam (Klonopin), lorazepam (Ativan), phenobarbital (Donnatal), zolpidem (Ambien), and others.
Isoniazid (INH). Isoniazid is a drug used for tuberculosis. The body breaks isoniazid down to hydrazine. Using both isoniazid and hydrazine might increase the risk of liver damage.

HYDROXYMETHYLBUTYRATE (HMB)

What other names is the product known by?
Beta-hydroxy-beta-methylbutyrate, B-Hydroxy B-Methylbutyrate Monohydreate, Beta-Hydroxy-Beta-Methylbutyric Acid, Hydroxymethyl Butyrate.

What is it?
HMB is a byproduct of the chemical (amino acid) leucine. People use HMB to make medicine.

Is it Effective?
The effectiveness ratings for **HYDROXYMETHYLBUTYRATE (HMB)** are as follows:
Possibly Effective for... Increasing body weight and muscle in people with AIDS.
Insufficient Evidence to Rate Effectiveness for... Heart and blood vessel disease (cardiovascular disease), muscle building, lowering blood pressure, and lowering high cholesterol.

How does it work?
HMB might promote muscle growth. It seems to reduce the destructive breakdown of muscle in people with AIDS.

Are there safety concerns?
HMB seems to be safe for most people when used short-term. Doses of three grams per day or less for up to eight weeks seem to be safe.

Do not use HMB if: You are pregnant or breast-feeding.

Are there any interactions with medications?
It is not known if HMB interacts with any medicines.
Before taking HMB, talk with your healthcare professional if you take any medications.

HYPERIMMUNE EGG

What other names is the product known by?
Egcel, Egg Extract, Egg Powder with Immune Components, HEY, Hyperimmune Egg Powder, Hyperimmune Hen Egg, Hyperimmunized Egg Yolk, IgY, Immune Egg, Immunoglobulin Egg Extract, Immunoglobulin IgY, Yolk Immunoglobulin.

What is it?
Hyperimmune egg is an egg from a hen that has been vaccinated against certain infectious diseases. Antibodies from the egg are used to treat human diseases.

Is it Effective?
The effectiveness ratings for **HYPERIMMUNE EGG** are as follows:
Insufficient Evidence to Rate Effectiveness for... Rotaviral diarrhea, infectious diarrhea, arthritis including osteoarthritis and rheumatoid arthritis, and high cholesterol.

How does it work?
Antibodies contained in hyperimmune egg are thought to stimulate the immune system and help the body fight disease.

Are there safety concerns?
Hyperimmune egg seems to be safe when used appropriately. Some side effects include diarrhea, gas, and bloating.

Do not use hyperimmune egg if: You are pregnant or breast-feeding. • You are allergic to eggs.

Are there any interactions with medications?
It is not known if hyperimmune egg interacts with any medicines.
Before taking hyperimmune egg, talk to your healthcare professional if you take any medications.

HYSSOP

What other names is the product known by?
Hissopo, Hyssopus officinalis, Hysope Officinale, Jufa, Rabo De Gato, Ysop.

What is it?
Hyssop is a plant. The above ground parts are used to make medicine.

Is it Effective?
The effectiveness ratings for **HYSSOP** are as follows:
Insufficient Evidence to Rate Effectiveness for... Liver and gallbladder problems, intestinal problems, the common cold, sore throat, asthma, urinary tract infection (UTI), gas, colic, decreased appetite, poor circulation, skin conditions (bruises, rashes, burns, frostbite), HIV/AIDS, and menstrual cramps.

How does it work?
The chemicals in hyssop may affect the heart and may increase secretions in the lungs.

Are there safety concerns?
Hyssop is considered safe for most people. Do not use the oil product.

The potential side effects of hyssop are not known, but the hyssop oil has caused seizures in some people.

Do not use hyssop if: You are pregnant or breast-feeding. • You have seizures.

Are there any interactions with medications?
It is not known if hyssop interacts with any medicines.
Before taking hyssop, talk with your healthcare professional if you take any medications.

IBOGA

What other names is the product known by?
Tabernanthe iboga.

What is it?
Iboga is an herb. People use the root of the plant to make medicine.

Is it Effective?
The effectiveness ratings for **IBOGA** are as follows:
Insufficient Evidence to Rate Effectiveness for... Fever, flu, high blood pressure, nerve disorders, preventing fatigue and drowsiness, and other conditions.

How does it work?
Iboga contains chemicals that can cause brain stimulation.

Are there safety concerns?
There isn't enough information to know if iboga is safe for use. Iboga can cause side effects such as low blood pressure, slow heart rate, seizures, paralysis, difficulty breathing, anxiety, and hallucinations.

Do not take iboga if: You are pregnant or breast-feeding.

Are there any interactions with medications?
Drying medications (Anticholinergic drugs). Iboga contains chemicals that can affect the brain and heart. Some of these drying medications called anticholinergic drugs can also affect the brain and heart. But iboga works differently than drying medications. Iboga might decrease the effects of drying medications. Some of these drying medications include atropine, scopolamine, and some medications used for allergies (antihistamines), and for depression (antidepressants).
Various medications used for glaucoma, Alzheimer's disease, and other conditions (Cholinergic drugs). Iboga contains a chemical that affects the body. This chemical is similar to some medications used for glaucoma, Alzheimer's disease, and other conditions. Taking iboga with these medications might increase the chance of side effects. Some of these medications used for glaucoma, Alzheimer's disease, and other conditions include pilocarpine (Pilocar and others), donepezil (Aricept), tacrine (Cognex), and others.

Medical professionals should consult the Professional Version at www.NaturalDatabase.com.

CONSUMER VERSION

ICELAND MOSS

What other names is the product known by?
Centraria, Cetraria islandica, Eryngo-leaved Liverwort, Iceland Lichen, Lichen Islandicus.

What is it?
Iceland moss is an algae and a fungus growing together. The entire plant is used to make medicine.

Is it Effective?
The effectiveness ratings for **ICELAND MOSS** are as follows:
Insufficient Evidence to Rate Effectiveness for... Dry cough, loss of appetite, common cold, bronchitis, indigestion, fevers, lung disease, kidney and bladder complaints, wound healing, irritation or swelling (inflammation) of mucous membranes in the mouth or throat, and other conditions.

How does it work?
Iceland moss seems to have a soothing action. It might also reduce the growth of bacteria.

Are there safety concerns?
Iceland moss seems safe for most people when taken short-term. It is unsafe when used in large amounts because lead contamination can occur in the plant.

Iceland moss is regulated in the United States, and is allowed only as a flavoring agent in alcoholic beverages.

Do not use Iceland moss if: You are pregnant or breast-feeding. • You have an ulcer in the stomach. • You have an ulcer in the small intestine.

Are there any interactions with medications?
Medications taken by mouth (Oral drugs). Iceland moss contains a type of soft fiber called mucilage. Mucilage can decrease how much medicine the body absorbs. Taking Iceland moss at the same time you take medications by mouth can decrease the effectiveness of your medication. To prevent this interaction take Iceland moss at least one hour after medications you take by mouth.

IDEBENONE

What other names is the product known by?
Hydroxydecyl benzoquinone.

What is it?
Idebenone is a man-made product similar to coenzyme Q-10.

Is it Effective?
The effectiveness ratings for **IDEBENONE** are as follows:
Possibly Effective for... Treating Alzheimer's disease.
Insufficient Evidence to Rate Effectiveness for... Friedreich's ataxia (a condition of heart failure, breathing difficulty, and muscle weakness), and mitochondrial encephalomyopathies (a condition of stroke-like conditions and brain damage).

How does it work?
Idebenone seems to have antioxidant activity, and appears to protect a wide variety of cells from oxidative damage.

Are there safety concerns?
Idebenone seems safe for most people.

Do not use idebenone if: You are pregnant or breast-feeding.

Are there any interactions with medications?
It is not known if idebenone interacts with any medicines.
Before taking idebenone, talk with your healthcare professional if you take any medications.

© Copyright 2006, Therapeutic Research Faculty.   Natural Medicines Comprehensive Database Consumer Version   (209) 472-2244

IGNATIUS BEAN

What other names is the product known by?
Lu Song Guo, Saint Ignatius-beans, Strychnos ignatii, Strychnos tieute.

What is it?
Ignatius bean is gathered from the Strychnos ignatii plant. The bean is used to make medicine.

Is it Effective?
The effectiveness ratings for **IGNATIUS BEAN** are as follows:
Insufficient Evidence to Rate Effectiveness for... Faintness, use as a tonic, and other uses.

How does it work?
Ignatius bean contains the poisons strychnine and brucine which affect the transmission of nerve impulses to muscle.

Are there safety concerns?
Ignatius bean is UNSAFE. It is poisonous. Side effects and toxicities include restlessness, feelings of anxiety, heightened sense perception, enhanced reflexes, dizziness, painful neck and back stiffness, twitching, jaw and neck spasms, painful convulsions of the entire body, increased muscle tension, difficulty in breathing, seizures, renal failure, and death.

Long-term use of Ignatius bean can cause liver damage and be fatal. If you already have liver damage, you are especially at risk for toxicity.

Since Ignatius bean is poisonous, be especially careful not to take it if: You are pregnant or breast-feeding. It can harm you and the baby.

Are there any interactions with medications?
It is not known if Ignatius bean interacts with any medicines.
Before taking Ignatius bean, talk with your healthcare professional if you take any medications.

IMMORTELLE

What other names is the product known by?
Common Shrubby Everlasting, Eternal Flower, Goldilocks, Helichrysum arenarium, Yellow Chaste Weed.

What is it?
Immortelle is a plant. The dried flower is used to make medicine.

Is it Effective?
The effectiveness ratings for **IMMORTELLE** are as follows:
Insufficient Evidence to Rate Effectiveness for... Gallstones and gallbladder disorders, liver disorders, stomach upset (dyspepsia), loss of appetite, stimulating bile flow, fighting bacteria, and other conditions.

How does it work?
There isn't enough information to know how immortelle might work.

Are there safety concerns?
There isn't enough information to know if immortelle is safe. It may cause colic (stomach cramps) in people with gallstones. Immortelle can cause allergic reactions, especially in people who are allergic to ragweed, chrysanthemums, marigolds, daisies, and related plants.

Do not use immortelle if: You are pregnant or breast-feeding. • You have a condition where your bile duct is blocked or obstructed. • You are allergic to any plants in the Asteraceae/Compositae family such as ragweed, chrysanthemums, marigolds, daisies, and many other plants.

Are there any interactions with medications?
It is not known if immortelle interacts with any medicines.
Before taking immortelle, talk with your healthcare professional if you take any medications.

Medical professionals should consult the Professional Version at www.NaturalDatabase.com.

INDIAN FRANKINCENSE

What other names is the product known by?
Boswellia, Boswellia serrata, Boswellin, Boswellin Serrata Resin, Gajabhakshya, Indian Olibanum, Salai Guggal, Sallaki Guggul, Shallaki.

What is it?
Indian frankincense is a plant. The resin in the plant is used to make medicine.

Is it Effective?
The effectiveness ratings for **INDIAN FRANKINCENSE** are as follows:
Insufficient Evidence to Rate Effectiveness for... Asthma, arthritis, colitis, Crohn's disease, and other conditions.

How does it work?
The resin of Indian frankincense contains substances that may decrease inflammation.

Are there safety concerns?
Indian frankincense seems to be safe for most people. It can cause side effects such as abdominal pain, nausea, and diarrhea. When applied to the skin, it can cause allergic rash.

Do not use Indian frankincense in amounts greater than those found in foods if: You are pregnant or breast-feeding.

Are there any interactions with medications?
It is not known if Indian frankincense interacts with any medicines.
Before taking Indian frankincense, talk with your healthcare professional if you take any medications.

INDIAN GOOSEBERRY

What other names is the product known by?
Aamalaki, Amalaki, Amblabaum, Amla, Aonla, Emblic, Emblica officinalis, Emblic Myrobalan, Groseillier de Ceylan, Mirobalano, Myrobalan Emblic, Mirobalanus embilica, Neli, Phyllanthus emblica.

What is it?
Indian gooseberry is a tree. People use the fruit of the tree to make medicine.

Is it Effective?
The effectiveness ratings for **INDIAN GOOSEBERRY** are as follows:
Insufficient Evidence to Rate Effectiveness for... Lowering cholesterol and triglyceride levels, cancer, indigestion, eye problems, joint pain, diarrhea, obesity, diabetes, and other conditions.

How does it work?
Indian gooseberry seems to work by reducing total cholesterol levels, including the fatty acids called triglycerides, without affecting the "good cholesterol" called high-density lipoprotein (HDL).

Are there safety concerns?
Indian gooseberry seems safe for most people when consumed in amounts found in foods. There isn't enough information to know if it is safe for use as a medicine.

Do not use Indian gooseberry in medicinal amounts if: You are pregnant or breast-feeding.

Are there any interactions with medications?
It is not known if Indian gooseberry interacts with any medicines.
Before taking Indian gooseberry, talk with your healthcare professional if you take any medications.

INDIAN LONG PEPPER

What other names is the product known by?
Bi Bo, Jaborandi Pepper, Kana, Langer Pfeffer, Long Pepper, Magadhi, Pimenta-Longa, Piper longum, Pippali, Poivre Long, Ushana.

What is it?
Indian long pepper is a plant. The fruit of the plant is used to make medicine.

Is it Effective?
The effectiveness ratings for **INDIAN LONG PEPPER** are as follows:
Insufficient Evidence to Rate Effectiveness for... Headache, toothache, asthma, bronchitis, cholera, coma, cough, diarrhea, epilepsy, fever, stomachache, stroke, indigestion, menstrual disorders, and other conditions.

How does it work?
Indian long pepper may have activity against certain parasite infections.

Are there safety concerns?
Indian long pepper seems safe for most people when used in amounts found in foods. There isn't enough information to know if Indian long pepper is safe for use as a medicine.

Do not use Indian long pepper if: You are pregnant or breast-feeding.

Are there any interactions with medications?
Phenytoin (Dilantin). Indian long pepper might increase how much phenytoin (Dilantin) the body absorbs. Taking Indian long pepper along with phenytoin (Dilantin) might increase the effects and side effects of phenytoin (Dilantin).
Propranolol (Inderal). Indian long pepper might increase how much propranolol (Inderal) the body absorbs. Taking Indian long pepper along with propranolol (Inderal) might increase the effects and side effects of propranolol (Inderal).
Theophylline. Indian long pepper can increase how much theophylline the body absorbs. Taking theophylline along with Indian long pepper might increase the effects and side effects of theophylline.

INDIAN PHYSIC

What other names is the product known by?
American Ipecacuanha, Bowman's Root, Gillenia, Gillenia trifoliate, Indian Hippo.

What is it?
Indian physic is a plant. The dried root and root bark is used to make medicine. Be careful not to confuse Indian physic (Gillenia trifoliata) with Canadian hemp (apocynum cannabinum) as both are known as Indian physic. Also be careful not to confuse Indian physic (Gillenia trifoliata) with black root (Leptandra virginica) as both are known as bowman's root.

Is it Effective?
The effectiveness ratings for **INDIAN PHYSIC** are as follows:
Insufficient Evidence to Rate Effectiveness for... Digestive disorders, causing vomiting (emetic), and other uses.

How does it work?
There isn't enough information to know how Indian physic might work.

Are there safety concerns?
It is not known if Indian physic is safe or what the potential side effects might be.

Do not use Indian physic if: You are pregnant or breast-feeding.

Are there any interactions with medications?
It is not known if Indian physic interacts with any medicines.
Before taking Indian physic, talk with your healthcare professional if you take any medications.

Medical professionals should consult the Professional Version at www.NaturalDatabase.com.

CONSUMER VERSION

INDIAN SNAKEROOT

What other names is the product known by?

Chandrika, Chota-Chand, Covanamilpori, Dhanburua, Pagla-Ka-Dawa, Patalagandhi, Rauwolfae radix, Rauwolfia, Rauwolfia Serpentina, Rauwolfiawurzel, Rauvolfia serpentina, Sarpagandha.

What is it?

Indian snakeroot is a plant. The root is used to make medicine.

Is it Effective?

The effectiveness ratings for **INDIAN SNAKEROOT** are as follows:

Insufficient Evidence to Rate Effectiveness for... Nervousness, trouble sleeping (insomnia), mental disorders such as schizophrenia, constipation, fever, liver problems, joint pain, spasms in the legs due to poor circulation, mild high blood pressure, and other conditions.

How does it work?

Indian snakeroot contains chemicals such as reserpine that decrease heart rate and blood pressure.

Are there safety concerns?

Indian snakeroot is possibly safe when a standardized extract is used under the supervision of a healthcare professional trained in its use. Standardized Indian snakeroot contains a set amount of medicine. The amount of reserpine and other chemicals in Indian snakeroot can vary from plant to plant. Since the reserpine and other chemicals in Indian snakeroot can be very toxic, the dose must be accurate and the side effects monitored by a trained healthcare professional. Self-medication is UNSAFE. Side effects can range from mild to serious and include nasal congestion, stomach cramps, diarrhea, nausea, vomiting, loss of appetite, drowsiness, convulsions, Parkinson's-like symptoms, and coma. Indian snakeroot can slow reaction times and should not be used when driving or operating heavy machinery.

Do not take Indian snakeroot if: You are pregnant or breast-feeding. • You have ulcers or ulcerative colitis. • You have a history of gall stones. • You receive ECT (electroconvulsive therapy). • You have depression. • You have pheochromocytoma, a tumor in your adrenal glands which causes dangerously high blood pressure. • You are sensitive to reserpine or similar medicines known as rauwolfia alkaloids.

Are there any interactions with medications?

Alcohol. Alcohol can cause sleepiness and drowsiness. Indian snakeroot might also cause sleepiness and drowsiness. Taking large amounts of Indian snakeroot along with alcohol might cause too much sleepiness.

Digoxin (Lanoxin). Digoxin (Lanoxin) helps the heart beat more strongly. Indian snakeroot seems to slow the heartbeat. Taking Indian snakeroot along with digoxin might decrease the effectiveness of digoxin. Do not take Indian snakeroot if you are taking digoxin (Lanoxin).

Ephedrine. Ephedrine can speed up the nervous system and make you feel jittery. Indian snakeroot can calm you down and make you sleepy. Taking Indian snakeroot along with ephedrine can decrease the effects of ephedrine.

Levodopa. Levodopa is used for Parkinson's disease. Taking Indian snakeroot along with levodopa might decrease the effectiveness of levodopa. It is not clear why this interaction might occur. To be on the safe side, do not take Indian snakeroot if you are taking levodopa.

Medications for depression (MAOIs). Indian snakeroot contains a chemical that affects the body. This chemical might increase the side effects of some medications used for depression. Some of these medications used for depression include phenelzine (Nardil), tranylcypromine (Parnate), and others.

Medications used for depression (Tricyclic antidepressants). Taking some medications used for depression might decrease the effects of Indian snakeroot. Some of these medicines used for depression include amitriptyline (Elavil), imipramine (Tofranil), and others.

Medications for mental conditions (Antipsychotic drugs). Indian snakeroot seems to have a calming effect. Medications for mental conditions also help calm you down. Taking Indian snakeroot along with some medications for mental conditions might increase the risk of side effects of medications for mental conditions. Some of these medications include chlorpromazine (Thorazine), clozapine (Clozaril), fluphenazine (Prolixin), haloperidol (Haldol), olanzapine (Zyprexa), perphenazine (Trilafon), prochlorperazine (Compazine), quetiapine (Seroquel), risperidone (Risperdal), thioridazine (Mellaril), thiothixene (Navane), and others.

Propranolol (Inderal). Propanolol (Inderal) is used to decrease blood pressure. Indian snakeroot also seems to reduce blood pressure. Taking Indian snakeroot along with propanolol (Inderal) might cause your blood pressure to go too low.

Sedative medications (Barbiturates). Indian snakeroot might cause sleepiness and drowsiness. Medications that cause sleepiness are called sedatives. Taking Indian snakeroot along with sedative medications might cause too much sleepiness.

Stimulant drugs. Stimulant drugs speed up the nervous system. By speeding up the nervous system, stimulant medications can make you feel jittery and speed up your heartbeat. Indian snakeroot might also speed up the nervous system. Taking Indian snakeroot along with stimulant drugs might cause serious problems including increased heart rate and high blood pressure. Avoid taking stimulant drugs along with Indian snakeroot. Some stimulant drugs include diethylpropion (Tenuate), epinephrine, phentermine (Ionamin), pseudoephedrine (Sudafed), and many others.

Water pills (Diuretic drugs). Indian snakeroot might affect the heart. "Water pills" can decrease potassium in the body. Low potassium levels can also affect the heart and increase the risk of side effects from Indian snakeroot. Some "water pills" that can deplete potassium include chlorothiazide (Diuril), chlorthalidone (Thalitone), furosemide (Lasix), hydrochlorothiazide (HCTZ, HydroDuril, Microzide), and others.

INDOLE-3-CARBINOL

What other names is the product known by?
3-Hydroxymethyl Indole, I3C, Indole 3 Carbinol, 3-(hydroxymethyl), 3-Indolylcarbinol, 3-Indolylmethanol, Indole, Indole 3 Carbinol, Indole-3-methanol.

What is it?
Indole-3-Carbinol is a substance found in vegetables such as broccoli, Brussels sprouts, cabbage, collards, cauliflower, kale, mustard greens, turnips, and rutabagas.

Is it Effective?
The effectiveness ratings for **INDOLE-3-CARBINOL** are as follows:
Possibly Effective for... Abnormal development and growth of cells of the cervix (cervical dysplasia).
Insufficient Evidence to Rate Effectiveness for... Prevention of breast cancer, colon cancer, fibromyalgia, systemic lupus erythematosus (SLE), hormone imbalances, and other conditions.

How does it work?
Indole-3-carbinol might be one of several substances in vegetables that are cancer protective. Diets with higher amounts of fruit and vegetable consumption are associated with a decreased risk of developing cancer.

Are there safety concerns?
Indole-3-carbinol is likely safe for most people when used in amounts typically found in the diet. It seems to be safe for most people when used in medicinal amounts, under proper medical supervision. It can cause side effects such as skin rashes and small increases in liver enzymes.
In very high doses, indole-3-carbinol can cause equilibrium imbalances, tremor, and nausea.

Do not use indole-3-carbinol in amounts greater than found in foods if: You are pregnant or breast-feeding.

Are there any interactions with medications?
Medications changed by the liver (Cytochrome P450 1A2 (CYP1A2) substrates). Some medications are changed and broken down by the liver. Indole-3-carbinol might increase how quickly the liver breaks down some medications. Taking indole-3-carbinol along with some medications that are changed by the liver can decrease the effectiveness of some medications. Before taking indole-3-carbinol talk to your healthcare provider if you take any medications that are changed by the liver. Some of these medications that are changed by the liver include clozapine (Clozaril), cyclobenzaprine (Flexeril), fluvoxamine (Luvox), haloperidol (Haldol), imipramine (Tofranil), mexiletine (Mexitil), olanzapine (Zyprexa), pentazocine (Talwin), propranolol (Inderal), tacrine (Cognex), theophylline, zileuton (Zyflo), zolmitriptan (Zomig), and others.

INOSINE

What other names is the product known by?
Hypoxanthine Riboside, Hypoxanthosine, 2,3-Diphosphoglycerate, 6-9 Dihydro-9-B-D-ribofuranosyl-1H-puin-6-one, 9-B-D-ribofuranosylhypoxanthine.

What is it?
Inosine is a chemical. It can be made in a laboratory. People use it to make medicine.

Is it Effective?
The effectiveness ratings for **INOSINE** are as follows:
Likely Ineffective for... Improving athletic performance.

Medical professionals should consult the Professional Version at www.NaturalDatabase.com.

How does it work?
There is information that suggests inosine might stimulate the growth of branches (axons) from healthy to injured nerve cells in the brain and spinal cord.

Are there safety concerns?
It is not known if inosine is safe or what the potential side effects might be.

Do not use inosine if: You are pregnant or breast-feeding. • You have gout.

Are there any interactions with medications?
It is not known if inosine interacts with any medicines.
Before taking inosine, talk with your healthcare professional if you take any medications.

INOSITOL

What other names is the product known by?
Antialopecia Factor, Cyclohexitol, Dambrose, Hexahydroxycyclohexane, Inose, Inosite, Inositol Monophosphate, Lipositol, Meso-inositol, Mouse Antialopecia Factor, Myo-inositol, Vitamin B8.

What is it?
Inositol is a vitamin-like substance. It is found in many plants and animals. It can also be made in a laboratory.

Is it Effective?
The effectiveness ratings for **INOSITOL** are as follows:
Possibly Effective for... Panic disorder • Obsessive-compulsive disorder (OCD) • An ovary disorder known as "polycystic ovary syndrome" • Problems breathing in premature infants known as "acute respiratory distress syndrome" • Psoriasis brought on or made worse by lithium drug therapy. Inositol doesn't seem to help psoriasis in people not taking lithium.
Possibly Ineffective for... Schizophrenia • Alzheimer's disease • Autism • Depression.
Likely Ineffective for... Diabetic nerve problems.
Insufficient Evidence to Rate Effectiveness for... Problems metabolizing fat, high cholesterol, inability to sleep, attention deficit-hyperactivity disorder (ADHD), cancer, hair growth, and other conditions.

How does it work?
Inositol might balance certain chemicals in the body to possibly help with conditions such as panic disorder, depression, obsessive-compulsive disorder, and "polycystic ovary syndrome."

Are there safety concerns?
Inositol seems to be safe for most adults. It can cause nausea, tiredness, headache, and dizziness.

Inositol might be safe when used in the hospital for premature infants with acute respiratory distress syndrome.

Do not take inositol if: You are pregnant or breast-feeding. • You have a condition called bipolar disorder.

Are there any interactions with medications?
It is not known if inositol interacts with any medicines.
Before taking inositol, talk with your healthcare professional if you take any medications.

INOSITOL NICOTINATE

What other names is the product known by?
Hexanicotinyl cis-1,2,3-5-trans-4,6-cyclohexane, Hexanicotinoyl Inositol, Inositol Hexaniacinate, Inositol Hexanicotinate, Inositol Niacnate, Meso-Inositol Hexanicotinate, Myo-inositol hexa-3-pyridine-carboxyalte, No-Flush Niacin.

What is it?
Inositol nicotinate is a compound made of niacin (vitamin B3) and inositol.

Is it Effective?
The effectiveness ratings for **INOSITOL NICOTINATE** are as follows:
Possibly Effective for... Improving intermittent claudication (cramping pain and weakness in the legs) • Improving

 Natural Medicines Comprehensive Database Consumer Version (209) 472-2244

Raynaud's disease (spasms of the blood capillaries) • Treating high cholesterol.
Insufficient Evidence to Rate Effectiveness for... Blood disorders of the brain, migraine headaches, a disorder of fibrous connective tissue deposits in the skin and organs (scleroderma), sleeplessness (insomnia), lowering blood pressure, restless leg syndrome, acne, skin inflammation (dermatitis), inflammation of the tongue (exfoliative glossitis), psoriasis, schizophrenia, and other conditions.

How does it work?

Inositol nicotinate can widen blood vessels, lower blood levels of fats such as cholesterol, and break up a protein needed for the clotting of blood.

Are there safety concerns?

Inositol nicotinate seems to be safe for most people. It can cause some side effects such as stomach upset, headache, nausea, burping, and hiccups. It might also cause liver damage like other niacin products in some people.

Some inositol nicotinate products are promoted as "no-flush" niacin because some people think they don't cause as much flushing as regular niacin. But this potential benefit has not been proven in studies.

Do not use inositol nicotinate if: You are pregnant or breast-feeding. • You have allergies. • You have a bleeding disorder. • You have coronary (heart) artery disease. • You have chest pain (angina). • You have diabetes. • You have gallbladder disorders. • You have gout. • You have low blood pressure (hypotension). • You have kidney disorders. • You are allergic to niacin. • You have a disorder causing ulcers in the stomach or intestines (peptic ulcer disease).

Are there any interactions with medications?

Medications that slow blood clotting (Anticoagulant / Antiplatelet drugs). Inositol nicotinate might slow blood clotting. Taking inositol nicotinate along with medications that also slow clotting might increase the chances of bruising and bleeding. Some medications that slow blood clotting include aspirin, clopidogrel (Plavix), diclofenac (Voltaren, Cataflam, others), ibuprofen (Advil, Motrin, others), naproxen (Anaprox, Naprosyn, others), dalteparin (Fragmin), enoxaparin (Lovenox), heparin, warfarin (Coumadin), and others.
Medications used for lowering cholesterol (Statins). Inositol nicotinate is changed in the body to niacin. Niacin can affect the muscles. Some medication used for lowering cholesterol can also affect the muscles. Taking niacin along with some medications used for lowering high cholesterol might increase the risk of muscle problems. Some medications used for high cholesterol include cerivastatin (Baycol), atorvastatin (Lipitor), lovastatin (Mevacor), pravastatin (Pravachol), simvastatin (Zocor), and others.
Medications for diabetes (Antidiabetes drugs). Chronic use of inositol nicotinate might increase blood sugar. Diabetes medications are used to lower blood sugar. By increasing blood sugar, inositol nicotinate might decrease the effectiveness of diabetes medications. Monitor your blood sugar closely. The dose of your diabetes medication might need to be changed. Some medications used for diabetes include glimepiride (Amaryl), glyburide (DiaBeta, Glynase PresTab, Micronase), insulin, pioglitazone (Actos), rosiglitazone (Avandia), chlorpropamide (Diabinese), glipizide (Glucotrol), tolbutamide (Orinase), and others.
Nicotine patch (Transdermal nicotine). Inositol nicotinate is broken down in the body to niacin. Niacin can sometimes cause flushing and dizziness. The nicotine patch can also cause flushing and dizziness. Taking inositol nicotinate and using a nicotine patch can increase the possibility of becoming flushed and dizzy.

INULIN

What other names is the product known by?

Beta(2-1)fructans, Chicory Extract, Chicory Inulin, Dahlia Extract, Dahlia Inulin, Fructo-Oligosaccharides, Fructooligosaccharides, Long-chain Oligosaccharides, Oligosaccharides, Prebiotic.

What is it?

Inulin is a starchy substance found in a wide variety of fruits, vegetables, and herbs. It is most commonly obtained by soaking chicory roots in hot water.

Is it Effective?

The effectiveness ratings for **INULIN** are as follows:
Possibly Effective for... Lowering high levels of a kind of fat called triglycerides • Constipation.
Possibly Ineffective for... Weight loss • High cholesterol levels.

How does it work?

Inulin is not digested or absorbed in the stomach. It goes to the bowels where bacteria are able to use it to grow. It supports the growth of a special kind of bacteria that are associated with improving bowel function and general health. Inulin decreases the body's ability to make certain kinds of fats.

Are there safety concerns?

Inulin seems to be safe when used appropriately. The most common side effects occur in the stomach. Using too much inulin causes more stomach problems.

Do not use inulin if: You are pregnant or breast-feeding.

Are there any interactions with medications?

It is not known if inulin interacts with any medicines.
Before taking inulin, talk with your healthcare professional if you take any medications.

IODINE

What other names is the product known by?

Atomic number 53, Potassium Iodide, Povidone Iodine.

What is it?

Iodine is a chemical element. People use it as medicine.

Is it Effective?

The effectiveness ratings for **IODINE** are as follows:
Effective for... Conditions related to too much thyroid gland activity (hyperthyroidism) • Radiation emergency associated with the use of radioactive iodides • Skin infection caused by the fungus Sporothrix (cutaneous sporotrichosis) • Use as an antiseptic • Water purification • Respiratory congestion.
Possibly Effective for... Painful, fibrous breast tissue (fibrocystic breast disease) • Preventing soreness and swelling inside the mouth, caused by chemotherapy treatments for cancer • Foot ulcers associated with diabetes.

How does it work?

Iodine reduces thyroid hormone and can kill fungus, bacteria, and other microorganisms such as amoebas. A specific kind of iodine called potassium iodide is also used to treat (but not prevent) the effects of a radioactive accident.

Are there safety concerns?

Iodine seems to be safe for most people. It can cause side effects including swelling of the lips and face (angioedema), severe bleeding and bruising, fever, joint pain, lymph node enlargement, allergic reactions including hives, and death. Large amounts or long-term use can cause metallic taste, soreness of teeth and gums, burning in mouth and throat, increased saliva, throat inflammation, stomach upset, diarrhea, anorexia, depression, skin problems, and many other side effects.

When iodine is used directly on the skin, it can cause skin irritation, stains, allergic reactions, and other side effects. Be careful not to bandage or tightly cover areas that have been treated with iodine to avoid iodine burn.

Do not use iodine if: You are pregnant or breast-feeding. • You have a thyroid disorder such as too little thyroid function (hypothyroidism), an enlarged thyroid gland (goiter), or a thyroid tumor.

Are there any interactions with medications?

Amiodarone (Cordarone). Amiodarone (Cordarone) contains iodine. Taking iodine supplements along with amiodarone (Cordarone) might cause too much iodine in the blood. Too much iodine in the blood can cause side effects that affect the thyroid.
Lithium. Large amounts of iodine can decrease thyroid function. Lithium can increase iodine's effects on the thyroid. Taking iodine along with lithium might decrease the thyroid function too much. Do not take large amounts of iodine if you are taking lithium.
Medications for high blood pressure (Angiotensin receptor blockers (ARBs)). Some medications for high blood pressure might decrease how quickly the body gets rid of potassium. Most iodine supplements contain potassium. Taking potassium iodide along with some medications for high blood pressure might cause too much potassium in the body. Do not take potassium iodide if you are taking medications for high blood pressure. The ARBs include losartan (Cozaar), valsartan (Diovan), irbesartan (Avapro), candesartan (Atacand), telmisartan (Micardis), and eprosartan (Teveten).
Medications for high blood pressure (ACE inhibitors). Some medications for high blood pressure might decrease how quickly the body gets rid of potassium. Most iodide supplements contain potassium. Taking potassium iodide along with some medications for high blood pressure might cause too much potassium in the body. Do not take potassium iodide if you are taking medications for high blood pressure. Some medications for high blood pressure include captopril (Capoten), enalapril (Vasotec), lisinopril (Prinivil, Zestril), ramipril (Altace), and others.

   Natural Medicines Comprehensive Database Consumer Version   (209) 472-2244

Medications for an overactive thyroid (Antithyroid drugs). Iodine can affect the thyroid. Taking iodine along with medications for an overactive thyroid might decrease the thyroid too much. Do not take iodine supplements if you are taking medications for an overactive thyroid. Some of these medications include methenamine mandelate (Methimazole), methimazole (Tapazole), potassium iodide (Thyro-Block), and others.

Water pills (Potassium-sparing diuretics). Most iodine supplements contain potassium. Some "water pills" might also increase potassium in the body. Taking potassium iodide along with some "water pills" might cause too much potassium to be in the body. Do not take potassium iodide if you are taking "water pills" that increase potassium in the body. Some "water-pills" that increase potassium in the body include spironolactone (Aldactone), triamterene (Dyrenium), and amiloride (Midamor).

IP-6

What other names is the product known by?
Fytic Acid, Inositol Hexaphosphate, Phytic Acid.

What is it?
IP-6, inositol hexaphosphate, is a vitamin-like substance. It is found in many plants and animals. It can also be made in a laboratory.

Is it Effective?
The effectiveness ratings for **IP-6** are as follows:

Possibly Effective for... Preventing kidney stones, when IP-6 is consumed in the diet.

Insufficient Evidence to Rate Effectiveness for... Treating and preventing cancer, preventing heart attacks, preventing and treating kidney stones, and other conditions.

How does it work?
IP-6 might help treat and prevent cancer by slowing down the production of cancer cells. It might also bind to certain minerals, decreasing the risk of colon cancer.

Are there safety concerns?
IP-6 is safe when used in amounts found in foods. There isn't enough information to know if it is safe when used in medicinal amounts.

Do not take IP-6 in medicinal amounts if: You are pregnant or breast-feeding. • You have a low iron condition called iron-deficiency anemia. • You have a bone condition called osteoporosis or osteopenia.

Are there any interactions with medications?
Medications that slow blood clotting (Anticoagulant / Antiplatelet drugs). IP-6 nicotinate might slow blood clotting. Taking IP-6 along with medications that also slow clotting might increase the chances of bruising and bleeding. Some medications that slow blood clotting include aspirin, clopidogrel (Plavix), diclofenac (Voltaren, Cataflam, others), ibuprofen (Advil, Motrin, others), naproxen (Anaprox, Naprosyn, others), dalteparin (Fragmin), enoxaparin (Lovenox), heparin, warfarin (Coumadin), and others.

IPECAC

What other names is the product known by?
Brazilian Ipecac, Brazil Root, Cartagena Ipecac, Cephaelis acuminata, Cephaelis ipecacuanha, Ipecacuanha, Matto Grosso Ipecac, Nicaragua Ipecac, Panama Ipecac, Psychotria ipecacuanha, Rio Ipecac, Uragoga granatensis, Uragoga ipecacuanha.

What is it?
Ipecac is a plant. It is used to make medicine.

Is it Effective?
The effectiveness ratings for **IPECAC** are as follows:

Possibly Effective for... Causing vomiting (emetic).

Insufficient Evidence to Rate Effectiveness for... Thinning mucous to make coughing easier, bronchitis associated with croup, hepatitis, amoebic dysentery, loss of appetite, cancer, and other conditions.

How does it work?
Ipecac contains chemicals that irritate the digestive tract and trigger the brain to cause vomiting.

Are there safety concerns?

Ipecac might be safe for most people when taken by mouth and used for a short time. It can cause nausea, vomiting, stomach irritation, dizziness, low blood pressure, shortness of breath, and a fast heartbeat.

Ipecac is UNSAFE when used long-term, in large amounts, and in children under the age of one. Children are more sensitive than adults to the side effects of ipecac. Misuse of ipecac can lead to serious poisoning, heart damage, and death. Signs of poisoning include difficulty breathing, digestive tract problems, abnormal heart rates, blood in the urine, convulsions, shock, coma, and death.

Ipecac seems to be safe for children when used appropriately as a prescription product to induce vomiting (emesis). However, the American Academy of Pediatrics' recommendation to keep a 1-ounce bottle of syrup of ipecac at home has recently been reversed. The new statement reads, "Syrup of ipecac should no longer be routinely used as a poison treatment intervention in the home." Talk with your healthcare provider or poison control center about how to use ipecac correctly in cases of poisoning in children.

Ipecac should not be used in people who are unconscious or have been poisoned with certain chemicals including corrosives, petroleum products, strychnine, and others. Talk to your healthcare provider or poison control center about whether ipecac is appropriate to use in each case of suspected poisoning. If ipecac is used incorrectly, serious complications can arise including damage of the esophagus, pneumonia, and convulsions.

Ipecac is UNSAFE when inhaled or used on the skin. It can cause breathing problems and irritate the skin.

Do not use ipecac if: You are pregnant or breast-feeding. • You have heart disease. • You have digestive tract problems including ulcers, infections, or Crohn's disease.

Are there any interactions with medications?

Activated charcoal. Activated charcoal can bind up syrup of ipecac in the stomach. This decreases the effectiveness of syrup of ipecac.

IPORURU

What other names is the product known by?

Alchornea castaneifolia, Iporoni, Iporuro, Ipurosa, Macochihua, Niando.

What is it?

Iporuru is a plant. The bark, leaves, and root are used to make medicine.

Is it Effective?

The effectiveness ratings for **IPORURU** are as follows:
Insufficient Evidence to Rate Effectiveness for... Coughs, problems with erections (impotence), diabetes, diarrhea, headache, toothache, snakebite, bronchitis, chancre sores, chills, eye inflammation (conjunctivitis), severe diarrhea (dysentery), painful or abnormal menstrual periods, arthritis, colds, and many other uses.

How does it work?

There isn't enough information to know how iporuru might work.

Are there safety concerns?

It is not known if iporuru is safe or what the potential side effects might be.

Do not use iporuru if: You are pregnant or breast-feeding.

Are there any interactions with medications?

It is not known if iporuru interacts with any medicines.
Before taking iporuru, talk with your healthcare professional if you take any medications.

IPRIFLAVONE

What other names is the product known by?
FL-113, 7-Isopropoxy-Isoflavone, TC-80.

What is it?
Ipriflavone is a substance man-made in the laboratory from another substance (daidzein) that is derived from soy.

Is it Effective?
The effectiveness ratings for **IPRIFLAVONE** are as follows:
Likely Effective for... Treating and preventing osteoporosis (low bone mass) in postmenopausal women.
Possibly Effective for... Bone pain in people with Paget's disease • Bone disease due to chronic kidney disease (renal osteodystrophy).
Insufficient Evidence to Rate Effectiveness for... Increasing metabolism in bodybuilders.

How does it work?
Ipriflavone may prevent bone density loss, and help improve the effects of estrogen in preventing osteoporosis. When used in combination with estrogens, it might allow lower estrogen doses to be used in postmenopausal women.

Are there safety concerns?
Ipriflavone is likely safe for most people when used with proper medical supervision. It can cause side effects such as stomach pain, diarrhea, or dizziness.

There is some concern that ipriflavone can cause a decreased white cell count (lymphocytopenia) in people taking it for greater than six months. White cell counts should be monitored, especially in people taking ipriflavone long-term.

Do not use ipriflavone if: You are pregnant or breast-feeding. • You have decreased immune function. Ipriflavone may worsen this condition. • You have low white cell counts. Ipriflavone may worsen this condition.

Are there any interactions with medications?
Medications that decrease the immune system (Immunosuppressants). Ipriflavone might decrease the immune system. Taking ipriflavone along with other medications that decrease the immune system might decrease the immune system too much. Avoid taking ipriflavone with medications that decrease the immune system. Some medications that decrease the immune system include azathioprine (Imuran), basiliximab (Simulect), cyclosporine (Neoral, Sandimmune), daclizumab (Zenapax), muromonab-CD3 (OKT3, Orthoclone OKT3), mycophenolate (CellCept), tacrolimus (FK506, Prograf), sirolimus (Rapamune), prednisone (Deltasone, Orasone), corticosteroids (glucocorticoids), and others.

Medications changed by the liver (Cytochrome P450 1A2 (CYP1A2) substrates). Some medications are changed and broken down by the liver. Ipriflavone might decrease how quickly the liver breaks down some medications. Taking ipriflavone along with some medications that are changed by the liver might increase the effects and side effects of some medications. Before taking ipriflavone talk to your healthcare provider if you take any medications that are changed by the liver. Some of these medications that are changed by the liver include clozapine (Clozaril), cyclobenzaprine (Flexeril), fluvoxamine (Luvox), haloperidol (Haldol), imipramine (Tofranil), mexiletine (Mexitil), olanzapine (Zyprexa), pentazocine (Talwin), propranolol (Inderal), tacrine (Cognex), theophylline, zileuton (Zyflo), zolmitriptan (Zomig), and others.

Medications changed by the liver (Cytochrome P450 2C9 (CYP2C9) substrates). Some medications are changed and broken down by the liver. Ipriflavone might decrease how quickly the liver breaks down some medications. Taking ipriflavone along with some medications that are broken down by the liver can increase the effects and side effects of some medications. Before taking ipriflavone talk to your healthcare provider if you take any medications that are changed by the liver. Some medications that are changed by the liver include amitriptyline (Elavil), diazepam (Valium), zileuton (Zyflo), celecoxib (Celebrex), diclofenac (Voltaren), fluvastatin (Lescol), glipizide (Glucotrol), ibuprofen (Advil, Motrin), irbesartan (Avapro), losartan (Cozaar), phenytoin (Dilantin), piroxicam (Feldene), tamoxifen (Nolvadex), tolbutamide (Tolinase), torsemide (Demadex), warfarin (Coumadin), and others.

Theophylline. The body breaks down theophylline to get rid of it. Ipriflavone might decrease how quickly the body gets rid of theophylline. Taking ipriflavone along with theophylline might increase the effects and side effects of theophylline.

Medical professionals should consult the Professional Version at www.NaturalDatabase.com.

IRON

What other names is the product known by?

Atomic number 26, Elemental Iron, Fe, Fer, Ferrous Carbonate Anhydrous, Ferrous Fumarate, Ferrous Gluconate, Ferrous Pyrophosphate, Ferrous Sulfate.

What is it?

Iron is a mineral.

Is it Effective?

The effectiveness ratings for **IRON** are as follows:

Effective for... Anemia from low levels of iron in the blood (iron deficiency anemia) • Improving the effectiveness of medicines such as epoetin alfa (erythropoietin, EPO, Epogen, Procrit) for building red blood cells in people treated with kidney dialysis or chemotherapy.

Possibly Effective for... Improving thinking, learning, and memory in iron-deficient children • Coughs which are caused by certain medications used for high blood pressure called angiotensin converting enzyme (ACE) inhibitors. These medications include captopril (Capoten), enalapril (Vasotec), lisinopril (Prinivil, Zestril), and many others.

Insufficient Evidence to Rate Effectiveness for... Attention deficit-hyperactivity disorder (ADHD), improving athletic performance, canker sores, a digestive tract disease called Crohn's disease, depression, fatigue, female infertility, heavy menstrual bleeding, and other conditions.

How does it work?

Iron helps red blood cells deliver oxygen from the lungs to cells all over the body. Once the oxygen is delivered, iron then helps red blood cells carry carbon dioxide waste back to the lungs to be exhaled. Iron also plays a role in many important chemical reactions in the body.

Are there safety concerns?

Iron is safe for most people when it is used correctly. However, it can cause some side effects including stomach upset and pain, constipation or diarrhea, nausea, and vomiting. Liquid iron supplements may blacken teeth.

High doses of iron are not safe, especially for children. Iron poisoning can cause many serious problems including stomach and intestinal distress, liver failure, dangerously low blood pressure, and death. If you suspect an adult or child has taken more than the recommended amount of iron, call your healthcare professional or the nearest poison control center immediately.

Do not take iron if: You have stomach or intestinal ulcers. • You have intestinal inflammation, such as ulcerative colitis or Crohn's disease. • You have a disease, such as thalassemia, which affects a component of blood called hemoglobin.

Are there any interactions with medications?

Antibiotics (Tetracycline antibiotics). Iron can attach to tetracycline antibiotics in the stomach and decrease how much tetracycline antibiotics the body can absorb. Taking iron along with tetracycline antibiotics might decrease the effectiveness of tetracycline antibiotics. To avoid this interaction take iron two hours before or four hours after taking tetracyclines. Some tetracycline antibiotics include demeclocycline (Declomycin), minocycline (Minocin), and tetracycline (Achromycin).

Antibiotics (Quinolone antibiotics). Iron might decrease how much antibiotic the body absorbs. Taking iron along with some antibiotics might decrease the effectiveness of some antibiotics. To avoid this interaction take iron two hours before or two hours after taking antibiotics. Some of these antibiotics that might interact with iron include ciprofloxacin (Cipro), enoxacin (Penetrex), norfloxacin (Chibroxin, Noroxin), sparfloxacin (Zagam), trovafloxacin (Trovan), and grepafloxacin (Raxar).

Bisphosphonates. Iron can decrease how much bisphosphate the body absorbs. Taking iron along with bisphosphates can decrease the effectiveness of bisphosphates. To avoid this interaction take bisphosphonate at least two hours before iron or later in the day. Some bisphosphonates include alendronate (Fosamax), etidronate (Didronel), risedronate (Actonel), tiludronate (Skelid), and others.

Chloramphenicol. Iron is important for producing new blood cells. Chloramphenicol might decrease new blood cells. Taking chloramphenicol for a long time might decrease the effects of iron on new blood cells. But most people only take chloramphenicol for a short time so this interaction isn't a big problem.

Levodopa. Iron might decrease how much levodopa the body absorbs. Taking iron along with levodopa might decrease the effectiveness of levodopa. Do not take iron and levodopa at the same time.

Levothyroxine. Levothyroxine is used for low thyroid function. Iron can decrease how much levothyroxine the body absorbs. Taking iron along with levothyroxine might decrease the effectiveness of levothyroxine. Some brands that contain levothyroxine include Armour Thyroid, Eltroxin, Estre, Euthyrox, Levo-T, Levothroid, Levoxyl, Synthroid, Unithroid, and others.

Methyldopa (Aldomet). Iron can decrease how much methyldopa (Aldomet) the body absorbs. Taking iron along with methyldopa (Aldomet) might decrease the effectiveness of methyldopa (Aldomet). To prevent this interaction take iron at least two hours before or after taking methyldopa (Aldomet).

Mycophenolate Mofetil (CellCept). Iron might decrease how much mycophenolate mofetil (CellCept) the body absorbs. Taking iron along with mycophenolate mofetil (CellCept) might decrease the effectiveness of mycophenolate mofetil (CellCept). To avoid this interaction take iron at least two hours after mycophenolate mofetil (CellCept).

Penicillamine. Penicillamine is used for Wilson's disease and rheumatoid arthritis. Iron might decrease how much penicillamine your body absorbs and decrease the effectiveness of penicillamine. To avoid this interaction take iron two hours before or two hours after taking penicillamine.

ISATIS

What other names is the product known by?

Ban Lan Gen, Ban Lang Gen, Chinese Indigo, Da Qing Ye, Da Quing Ye, Dyer's Woad, Farberwaid (Färberwaid), Folium Isatidis, Hierba Pastel, Indigo, Indigo Woad, Isatis indigotica, Isatis tinctoria, Pastel Des Teinturiers, Qing Dai, Quing Dai, Radix Isatidis, Woad.

What is it?

Isatis is an herb. The dried leaf and root are used to make medicine.

Is it Effective?

The effectiveness ratings for **ISATIS** are as follows:

Insufficient Evidence to Rate Effectiveness for... Prostate cancer, upper respiratory infections, inflammation in the brain, hepatitis, lung abscess, diarrhea, and HIV.

How does it work?

Isatis might have antibacterial and antiviral activity, as well as fever-reducing, anti-inflammatory, and cancer-fighting activity.

Are there safety concerns?

There isn't enough information to know if isatis is safe.

Do not use isatis if: You are pregnant or breast-feeding. • You are allergic to aspirin.

Are there any interactions with medications?

It is not known if isatis interacts with any medicines.
Before taking isatis, talk with your healthcare professional if you take any medications.

IVY GOURD

What other names is the product known by?

Coccinia grandis, Coccinia indica, Coccinia ordifolia, Kovai, Little Gourd, Tela Kucha.

What is it?

Ivy gourd is a plant. The leaves, root, and fruit are used to make medicine.

Is it Effective?

The effectiveness ratings for **IVY GOURD** are as follows:
Insufficient Evidence to Rate Effectiveness for... Diabetes, gonorrhea, constipation, and skin abscesses.

How does it work?

Ivy gourd contains chemicals that may reduce blood sugar levels.

Are there safety concerns?

Ivy gourd appears to be safe for most people when taken by mouth for up to six weeks. There isn't enough information to know if ivy gourd is safe for longer-term use. Ivy gourd can lower blood sugar. If you have diabetes, check your blood sugar carefully.

Do not use ivy gourd if: You are pregnant or breast-feeding.

CONSUMER VERSION

Medical professionals should consult the Professional Version at www.NaturalDatabase.com.

Are there any interactions with medications?

Medications for diabetes (Antidiabetes drugs). Ivy gourd can decrease blood sugar levels. Diabetes medications are also used to lower blood sugar. Taking ivy gourd along with diabetes medications might cause your blood sugar to be too low. Monitor your blood sugar closely. The dose of your diabetes medication might need to be changed. Some medications used for diabetes include glimepiride (Amaryl), glyburide (DiaBeta, Glynase PresTab, Micronase), insulin, pioglitazone (Actos), rosiglitazone (Avandia), chlorpropamide (Diabinese), glipizide (Glucotrol), tolbutamide (Orinase), and others.

JABORANDI

What other names is the product known by?

Arruda Bravam, Arruda Do Mato, Jamguarandi, Juarandi, Maranhao Jaborandi, Pilocarpus microphyllus.

What is it?

Jaborandi is an herb. The leaves are used to make medicine.

Is it Effective?

The effectiveness ratings for **JABORANDI** are as follows:
Insufficient Evidence to Rate Effectiveness for... Diarrhea, eye problems, causing sweating, and other conditions.

How does it work?

It is not known how Jaborandi might work. It might stimulate saliva production, sweat, and muscle contractions in the stomach and intestines.

Are there safety concerns?

Jaborandi is UNSAFE for use as a medicinal herb. It is, however, used in the production of pilocarpine, an FDA approved prescription medication.

Do not use jaborandi if: You are pregnant or breast-feeding.

Are there any interactions with medications?

It is not known if jaborandi interacts with any medicines.
Before taking jaborandi, talk with your healthcare professional if you take any medications.

JACOB'S LADDER

What other names is the product known by?

Charity, English Green Valerian, Polemonium caeruleum.

What is it?

Jacob's ladder is a plant. The above ground parts are used to make medicine.

Is it Effective?

The effectiveness ratings for **JACOB'S LADDER** are as follows:
Insufficient Evidence to Rate Effectiveness for... Fever, inflammation, promoting sweating, and other conditions.

How does it work?

There isn't enough information to know how Jacob's ladder might work.

Are there safety concerns?

It is not known if Jacob's ladder is safe or what the potential side effects might be.

Do not use Jacob's ladder if: You are pregnant or breast-feeding.

Are there any interactions with medications?

It is not known if Jacob's ladder interacts with any medicines.
Before taking Jacob's ladder, talk with your healthcare professional if you take any medications.

JALAP

What other names is the product known by?
Convolvulus purga, Exogonium purga, Ipomoea purga, Jalapa, Jalape, Mechoacan.

What is it?
Jalap is a plant. The root is used to make medicine.

Is it Effective?
The effectiveness ratings for **JALAP** are as follows:
Insufficient Evidence to Rate Effectiveness for... Emptying and cleansing the bowels (cathartic, purgative), increasing body water loss (diuretic), and other uses.

How does it work?
Jalap contains substances that increase water loss and cause contractions of bowel muscles to push out stool.

Are there safety concerns?
Jalap is UNSAFE. It has potent effects on the bowel which might cause irritation of the digestive tract, including diarrhea and vomiting and a loss of electrolytes such as potassium.

While jalap isn't safe for anyone to use, some people should be especially careful to avoid it.
Do not use jalap if: You are pregnant or breast-feeding. Jalap can stimulate menstruation. • You have digestive tract problems, such as ulcers, Crohn's disease, or other conditions. • You have symptoms of appendicitis (abdominal pain, nausea, and vomiting).

Are there any interactions with medications?
Digoxin (Lanoxin). Jalap is a type of laxative called a stimulant laxative. Stimulant laxatives can decrease potassium levels in the body. Low potassium levels can increase the risk of side effects of digoxin (Lanoxin).
Medications taken by mouth (Oral drugs). Jalap is a laxative. Laxatives can decrease how much medicine your body absorbs. Decreasing how much medicine your body absorbs can decrease the effectiveness of your medication.
Stimulant laxatives. Jalap is a type of laxative called a stimulant laxative. Stimulant laxatives speed up the bowels. Taking jalap along with other stimulant laxatives could speed up the bowels too much and cause dehydration and low minerals in the body. Some stimulant laxatives include bisacodyl (Correctol, Dulcolax), cascara, castor oil (Purge), senna (Senokot), and others.
Water pills (Diuretic drugs). Jalap is a laxative. Some laxatives can decrease potassium in the body. "Water pills" can also decrease potassium in the body. Taking jalap along with "water pills" might decrease potassium in the body too much. Some "water pills" that can decrease potassium include chlorothiazide (Diuril), chlorthalidone (Thalitone), furosemide (Lasix), hydrochlorothiazide (HCTZ, HydroDiuril, Microzide), and others.

JAMAICAN DOGWOOD

What other names is the product known by?
Fishfudle, Fish Poison Bark, Fish-Poison Tree, Ichthyomethia piscipula, Jamaica Dogwood, Piscidia communis, Piscidia erythrina, Piscidia piscipula, West Indian Dogwood.

What is it?
Jamaican dogwood is a plant. The root bark is used to make medicine. Be careful not to confuse Jamaican dogwood and American dogwood.

Is it Effective?
The effectiveness ratings for **JAMAICAN DOGWOOD** are as follows:
Insufficient Evidence to Rate Effectiveness for... Anxiety, fear, nerve pain, migraines, insomnia, abnormal or painful menstruation, and other uses.

How does it work?
Jamaican dogwood might have sedative effects, decrease inflammation, and decrease muscle spasms in internal organs.

Are there safety concerns?
Jamaican dogwood is UNSAFE and poisonous when used for self-medication. Jamaican dogwood is an irritant and can cause numbness, tremors, salivation, and sweating.

While Jamaican dogwood is UNSAFE for anyone to use, some people are particularly sensitive to the toxic effects and should avoid use. Do not give Jamaican dogwood to children.

Do not use Jamaican dogwood if: You are pregnant or breast-feeding. • You are elderly.

Are there any interactions with medications?

Sedative medications (CNS depressants). Jamaican dogwood might cause sleepiness and drowsiness. Medications that cause sleepiness are called sedatives. Taking Jamaican dogwood along with sedative medications might cause too much sleepiness. Some sedative medications include clonazepam (Klonopin), lorazepam (Ativan), phenobarbital (Donnatal), zolpidem (Ambien), and others.

JAMBOLAN

What other names is the product known by?

Badijamun, Black Plum, Duhat, Indian Blackberry, Jaman, Jambolan, Jambolan Plum, Jambolao, Eugenia cumini, Eugenia jambolana, Jambu, Jambul, Jamelonguier, Jamum, Java Plum, Jumbul, Kavika Ni India, Mahajambu, Mesegerak, Phadena, Plum, Rajajambu, Rose Apple, Syxygii cumini cortex, Syzygium cumini, Syzygium jambolanum.

What is it?

Jambolan is a tree. The seed, leaf, bark, and fruit are used to make medicine.

Is it Effective?

The effectiveness ratings for **JAMBOLAN** are as follows:
Possibly Ineffective for... Diabetes (jambolan leaf).
Insufficient Evidence to Rate Effectiveness for... Bronchitis, asthma, severe diarrhea (dysentery), skin ulcers, sore mouth and throat, skin inflammation (swelling), intestinal gas (flatulence), spasms, stomach problems, increasing sexual desire (aphrodisiac), constipation, exhaustion, and other conditions.

How does it work?

Jambolan seed and bark contains chemicals that might lower blood sugar, but extracts from jambolan leaf and fruit don't seem to affect blood sugar. Jambolan also contains chemicals that might have antioxidant and anti-inflammatory effects.

Are there safety concerns?

Jambolan is possibly safe for most people, but the potential side effects are not known.

Do not use jambolan if: You are pregnant or breast-feeding.

Are there any interactions with medications?

Medications for diabetes (Antidiabetes drugs). Jambolan seed and bark extracts might decrease blood sugar levels. Diabetes medications are also used to lower blood sugar. Taking jambolan seed or bark along with diabetes medications might cause your blood sugar to be too low. Monitor your blood sugar closely. The dose of your diabetes medication might need to be changed. Some medications used for diabetes include glimepiride (Amaryl), glyburide (DiaBeta, Glynase PresTab, Micronase), insulin, pioglitazone (Actos), rosiglitazone (Avandia), chlorpropamide (Diabinese), glipizide (Glucotrol), tolbutamide (Orinase), and others.

JAPANESE APRICOT

What other names is the product known by?

Armeniaca mume, Apricot tree, Beni chidori, Beni-chidori, Japanese flowering apricot, Mae-sil-na-moo, Mei, Pickled ume, Prunus mume, Ume brandy, Wu-mei juice.

What is it?

Japanese apricot is a fruit tree. The fruit, branches, and flowers are used to make medicine.

Is it Effective?

The effectiveness ratings for **JAPANESE APRICOT** are as follows:
Insufficient Evidence to Rate Effectiveness for... Fever, cough, stomach disorders, insomnia, menopausal symptoms, cancer, prevention of heart disease, and other uses.

     Natural Medicines Comprehensive Database Consumer Version   (209) 472-2244

How does it work?

There is not enough information to know how Japanese apricot might work for any medical condition.

Are there safety concerns?

The processed fruit is safe for food consumption. But the raw fruit is dangerous to consume because it contains toxic chemicals. Only processed fruit products should be consumed.

There is not enough information about other forms of Japanese apricot to know if they are safe.

Do not take Japanese apricot if: You are pregnant or breast feeding.

Are there any interactions with medications?

Medications that slow blood clotting (Anticoagulant / Antiplatelet drugs). Japanese apricot flower extract might slow blood clotting. Taking Japanese apricot flower extracts along with medications that also slow clotting might increase the chances of bruising and bleeding. Some medications that slow blood clotting include aspirin, clopidogrel (Plavix), diclofenac (Voltaren, Cataflam, others), ibuprofen (Advil, Motrin, others), naproxen (Anaprox, Naprosyn, others), dalteparin (Fragmin), enoxaparin (Lovenox), heparin, warfarin (Coumadin), and others.

JAPANESE MINT

What other names is the product known by?

American Corn Mint, Brook Mint, Canadian Mint, Chinese Mint, Chinese Mint Oil, Corn Mint, Cornmint Oil, Field Mint Oil, Mentha arvensis aetheroleum, Mentha arvensis piperascens, Mentha canadensis, Mint Oil, Minzol, Poleo, Pudina, Putiha.

What is it?

Japanese mint is a plant. The oil is distilled from the above ground parts and used to make medicine.

Is it Effective?

The effectiveness ratings for **JAPANESE MINT** are as follows:

Insufficient Evidence to Rate Effectiveness for... Irritable bowel syndrome, itching, hives, mouth inflammation, rheumatic conditions, common cold, cough, fever, tendency to infection, nausea, sore throat, diarrhea, headaches, toothaches, cramps, earache, tumors, sores, cancer, cardiac complaints, sensitivity to weather changes, intestinal gas (flatulence), inflammation of the airways such as bronchitis, muscular pain (myalgia), ailments associated with nerve pain, and other uses.

How does it work?

Japanese mint oil is thought to prevent intestinal gas, stimulate bile flow, and fight infections.

Are there safety concerns?

Japanese mint oil is possibly safe for most people. It can cause some side effects such as stomach upset when taken by mouth. It can cause allergic skin reactions when used directly on the skin. If applied directly on the face or inhaled, it can worsen asthma, cause vocal cord spasms, and serious breathing problems. It can also cause flushing, headache, and allergic reactions.

Japanese mint oil is unsafe for use in infants and children, especially when applied around the nose, since it can trigger serious breathing problems.

Do not use Japanese mint oil if: You are pregnant or breast-feeding. • You have liver disease or damage. • You have a gallbladder condition such as inflammation, gallstones, or a blocked bile duct. • You have asthma.

Are there any interactions with medications?

It is not known if Japanese mint interacts with any medicines.
Before taking Japanese mint, talk with your healthcare professional if you take any medications.

Medical professionals should consult the Professional Version at www.NaturalDatabase.com.

JAPANESE PERSIMMON

What other names is the product known by?
Chinese Persimmon, Chinese Plum, Diospyros Kaki, Diospyroskaki, Dried Persimmon, Fuyu, Hachiya, Hachiya Persimmon, Hanagosho, Jiro, Kaki, Kaki Persimmon, Korean Persimmon, Oriental Persimmon, Persimmon, Persimmon Fruit, Persimmon Juice, Persimmon Punch, Sharon Fruit.

What is it?
Japanese persimmon is a plant. People use the fruit and leaf for medicine.

Is it Effective?
The effectiveness ratings for **JAPANESE PERSIMMON** are as follows:
Insufficient Evidence to Rate Effectiveness for... High blood pressure, constipation, hiccough, stroke, excessive fluid, improving blood flow, and reducing body temperature.

How does it work?
Japanese persimmon contains chemicals that might lower blood pressure and body temperature, along with other effects.

Are there safety concerns?
There isn't enough information available to know if Japanese persimmon is safe for medicinal use. The fruit, eaten as food, rarely causes allergic reactions.

Do not take Japanese persimmon if: You are pregnant or breast-feeding. • You have low blood pressure.

Are there any interactions with medications?
Medications for high blood pressure (Antihypertensive drugs). Japanese persimmon seems to decrease blood pressure. Taking Japanese persimmon along with medications for high blood pressure might cause your blood pressure to go too low. Some medications for high blood pressure include captopril (Capoten), enalapril (Vasotec), losartan (Cozaar), valsartan (Diovan), diltiazem (Cardizem), amlodipine (Norvasc), hydrochlorothiazide (HydroDiuril), furosemide (Lasix), and many others.

JASMINE

What other names is the product known by?
Catalonina Jasmine, Common Jasmine, Italian Jasmine, Jasminum grandiflorum, Jasminum officinale, Jati, Poet's Jessamine, Royal Jasmine, Spanish Jasmine.

What is it?
Jasmine is a plant. The flower is used to make medicine.

Is it Effective?
The effectiveness ratings for **JASMINE** are as follows:
Insufficient Evidence to Rate Effectiveness for... Liver problems such as hepatitis and cirrhosis, stomach pain due to severe diarrhea (dysentery), increasing sexual desire (aphrodisiac), cancer treatment, use as a sedative, and other uses.

How does it work?
There isn't enough information to know how jasmine might work.

Are there safety concerns?
Jasmine seems to be safe for most people in food amounts. It is not known if jasmine is safe when used as a medicine. Jasmine may cause allergic reactions.

Do not use jasmine in amounts greater than what is used for food if: You are pregnant or breast-feeding.

Are there any interactions with medications?
It is not known if jasmine interacts with any medicines.
Before taking jasmine, talk with your healthcare professional if you take any medications.

JAVA TEA

What other names is the product known by?
Orthosiphon, Orthosiphonis folium, Orthosiphon spicatus, Orthosiphon stamineus.

What is it?
Java tea is a plant. The leaves and stem tips are used to make medicine.

Is it Effective?
The effectiveness ratings for **JAVA TEA** are as follows:
Insufficient Evidence to Rate Effectiveness for... Liver complaints, bladder and kidney disorders, gallstones, gout, rheumatism, and other conditions.

How does it work?
Java tea might increase the loss of body water through the urine (diuretic effect), stop spasms, and help fight microbes such as bacteria.

Are there safety concerns?
There isn't enough information available to know if java tea is safe.

Do not use java tea if: You are pregnant or breast-feeding. • You are swollen and retaining water (edema) due to decreased kidney or heart function.

Are there any interactions with medications?
It is not known if java tea interacts with any medicines.
Before taking java tea, talk with your healthcare professional if you take any medications.

JAVANESE TURMERIC

What other names is the product known by?
Curcuma, Curcuma xanthorrhiza, Curcumae xanthorrhizae rhizoma, Temu Lawak, Temu Lawas, Tewon Lawa.

What is it?
Javanese turmeric is a plant. The root and rhizome (underground stem) are used to make medicine. Be careful not to confuse Javanese turmeric with turmeric.

Is it Effective?
The effectiveness ratings for **JAVANESE TURMERIC** are as follows:
Insufficient Evidence to Rate Effectiveness for... Stomach and digestive disorders and other uses.

How does it work?
Javanese turmeric contains substances that might stimulate the production of bile.

Are there safety concerns?
Javanese turmeric is possibly safe for most people when used for a short time. Javanese turmeric is possibly unsafe when used in large amounts or for prolonged periods of time. It may cause stomach irritation and nausea.

Do not use Javanese turmeric if: You are pregnant or breast-feeding. • You have a liver or gallbladder disorder.

Are there any interactions with medications?
It is not known if Javanese turmeric interacts with any medicines.
Before taking Javanese turmeric, talk with your healthcare professional if you take any medications.

JEWELWEED

What other names is the product known by?

Balsam-Weed, Garden Balsam, Impatiens balsamina, Impatiens biflora, Impatiens capensis, Impatiens pallida, Jewel Balsam Weed, Jewel Weed, Quick-In-The-Hand, Silverweed, Slipper Weed, Speckled Jewels, Spotted Touch-Me-Not, Touch-Me-Not, Wild Balsam, Wild Celandine, Wild Lady's Slipper.

What is it?

Jewelweed is a plant. The above ground parts are used to make medicine. Be careful not to confuse jewelweed with potentilla as both are known as silverweed.

Is it Effective?

The effectiveness ratings for **JEWELWEED** are as follows:
Insufficient Evidence to Rate Effectiveness for... Mild digestive disorders, rash from poison ivy, and other conditions.

How does it work?

Jewelweed is said to aid digestion and increase the loss of body water through the urine (diuretic effect), but there isn't scientific information to back these claims. It is not known how jewelweed might work for medicinal uses.

Are there safety concerns?

Jewelweed is possibly safe for most people when taken by mouth or used on the skin. It is not known what the potential side effects might be.

Do not use jewelweed if: You are pregnant or breast-feeding.

Are there any interactions with medications?

It is not known if jewelweed interacts with any medicines.
Before taking jewelweed, talk with your healthcare professional if you take any medications.

JIAOGULAN

What other names is the product known by?

Amachazuru, Dungkulcha, Fairy Herb, Gynostemma pedatum, Gynostemma pentaphyllum, Miracle Grass, Penta Tea, Southern Ginseng, Vitis pentaphylla.

What is it?

Jiaogulan is a plant. The leaves are used to make medicine.

Is it Effective?

The effectiveness ratings for **JIAOGULAN** are as follows:
Possibly Effective for... Reducing cholesterol levels.
Insufficient Evidence to Rate Effectiveness for... Regulating blood pressure, bronchitis, stomach disorders, ulcers, constipation, gallstones, obesity, cancer, diabetes, sleeplessness (insomnia), backache, pain, improving memory, improving heart function, and other conditions.

How does it work?

Jiaogulan contains substances that might help reduce cholesterol levels.

Are there safety concerns?

There isn't enough information available to know if jiaogulan is safe. It can cause some side effects such as severe nausea and increased bowel movements.
Jiaogulan may be UNSAFE in pregnancy. One of the chemicals in jiaogulan has been linked to possible birth defects.

Do not use jiaogulan if: You are pregnant or breast-feeding. • You have a bleeding disorder.

Are there any interactions with medications?

Medications that slow blood clotting (Anticoagulant / Antiplatelet drugs). Jiaogulan might slow blood clotting. Taking jiaogulan along with medications that also slow clotting might increase the chances of bruising and bleeding. Some medications that slow blood clotting include aspirin, clopidogrel (Plavix), diclofenac (Voltaren, Cataflam, others), ibuprofen (Advil, Motrin, others), naproxen (Anaprox, Naprosyn, others), dalteparin (Fragmin), enoxaparin (Lovenox), heparin, warfarin (Coumadin), and others.

Medications that decrease the immune system (Immunosuppressants). Jiaogulan increases the immune system. By increasing the immune system jiaogulan might decrease the effectiveness of medications that decrease the immune system. Some medications that decrease the immune system include azathioprine (Imuran), basiliximab (Simulect), cyclosporine (Neoral, Sandimmune), daclizumab (Zenapax), muromonab-CD3 (OKT3, Orthoclone OKT3), mycophenolate (CellCept), tacrolimus (FK506, Prograf), sirolimus (Rapamune), prednisone (Deltasone, Orasone), corticosteroids (glucocorticoids), and others.

JIMSON WEED

What other names is the product known by?
Angel Tulip, Datura, Datura inermis Datura stramonium, Datura tatula, Devil's Apple, Devil's Trumpet, Jamestown Weed, Locoweed, Mad-apple, Nightshade, Peru-apple, Stinkweed, Stinkwort, Stramonium, Thorn-apple.

What is it?
Jimson weed is a plant. The leaves and seeds are used to make medicine.

Is it Effective?
The effectiveness ratings for **JIMSON WEED** are as follows:
Insufficient Evidence to Rate Effectiveness for... Asthma, cough, nerve diseases, causing hallucinations and elevated mood (euphoria), and other uses.

How does it work?
Jimson weed contains substances such as atropine, hyoscyamine, and scopolamine which interfere with one of the chemical messengers (acetylcholine) in the brain and nerves.

Are there safety concerns?
Jimson weed is UNSAFE. It is poisonous and can cause many toxic effects including dry mouth and extreme thirst, vision problems, nausea and vomiting, fast heart rate, hallucinations, high temperature, seizures, confusion, loss of consciousness, breathing problems, and death.

Do not give jimson weed to children. They are more sensitive than adults to the toxic effects of jimson weed. Even a small amount can kill them.

No one should take jimson weed, but certain people are especially at risk for toxic side effects.
Do not use jimson weed if: You are pregnant or breast-feeding. • You have congestive heart failure (CHF). • You have a fast heartbeat (palpitations, arrhythmias). • You have Down syndrome. • You have a type of heartburn called esophageal reflux disease (GERD). • You have a high temperature (fever). • You have stomach or intestinal problems including ulcers, hiatal hernia, toxic megacolon, obstruction, infection, constipation, or ulcerative colitis. • You have, or are prone to having, problems passing urine (urinary retention). • You have an eye condition called narrow-angle glaucoma.

Are there any interactions with medications?
Drying medications (Anticholinergic drugs). Jimson weed contains chemicals that cause a drying effect. It also affects the brain and heart. Drying medications called anticholinergic drugs can also cause these effects. Taking jimson weed and drying medications together might cause side effects including dry skin, dizziness, low blood pressure, fast heartbeat, and other serious side effects. Some of these drying medications include atropine, scopolamine, and some medications used for allergies (antihistamines), and for depression (antidepressants).

JOJOBA

What other names is the product known by?
Buxus chinensis, Deernut, Goatnut, Pignut, Simmondsia califlornica, Simmondsia chinensis.

What is it?
Jojoba is a plant. The seed and oil are used to make medicine.

Is it Effective?
The effectiveness ratings for **JOJOBA** are as follows:
Insufficient Evidence to Rate Effectiveness for... Acne, psoriasis, sunburn, chapped skin, hair loss, and other uses.

Medical professionals should consult the Professional Version at www.NaturalDatabase.com.

How does it work?

Jojoba, when applied to the skin, is an emollient which soothes skin and unclogs hair follicles.

Are there safety concerns?

Jojoba is considered safe for most people when used on the skin. It can cause some side effects such as a rash and allergic reactions.

Jojoba is unsafe for anyone when taken by mouth. It can cause serious side effects such as heart damage.

While jojoba is not safe for anyone when taken by mouth, some people should be especially careful to avoid it.

Do not take jojoba by mouth if: You are pregnant or breast-feeding.

Are there any interactions with medications?

It is not known if jojoba interacts with any medicines.
Before taking jojoba, talk with your healthcare professional if you take any medications.

JUJUBE

What other names is the product known by?

Black Date, Chinese Date, Chinese Jujube, Da Zao, Hei Zao, Hong Zao, Jujube Plum, Jujubi, Red Date, Rhamnus zizyphus, Zao, Suan Zao Ren, Ziziphus jujuba, synonyms Ziziphus sativa, Ziziphus spinosa, Ziziphus vulgaris, Ziziphus zizyphus, Zizyphus, Zyzyphus jujube.

What is it?

Jujube is a shrub or small tree. The fruit is used to make medicine.

Is it Effective?

The effectiveness ratings for **JUJUBE** are as follows:
Insufficient Evidence to Rate Effectiveness for... Liver disease, muscular conditions, ulcers, dry skin, wounds, diarrhea, fatigue, and other conditions.

How does it work?

Jujube might help protect the body against certain types of liver damage. It might also help increase body weight.

Are there safety concerns?

There isn't enough information available to know if jujube is safe.

Do not use jujube if: You are pregnant or breast-feeding.

Are there any interactions with medications?

It is not known if jujube interacts with any medicines.
Before taking jujube, talk with your healthcare professional if you take any medications.

JUNIPER

What other names is the product known by?

Common Juniper, Common Juniper Berry, Juniper Berry Oil, Enebro, Extract of Juniper, Genievre, Ginepro, Juniper berry, Juniper extract, Juniper oil, Juniperi fructus, Juniperus communis Oil, Oil of Juniper, Wacholderbeeren, Zimbro.

What is it?

Juniper is an herb. People use the juniper berry to make medicine.

Is it Effective?

The effectiveness ratings for **JUNIPER** are as follows:
Insufficient Evidence to Rate Effectiveness for... Upset stomach, heartburn, bloating, loss of appetite, urinary tract infections (UTIs), kidney and bladder stones, joint and muscle pain, wounds, and other conditions.

How does it work?

Juniper berries contain chemicals that might decrease inflammation and gas. It might also have some antibacterial and antiviral effects. Juniper might also have a diuretic effect and increase the need to urinate.

Are there safety concerns?

Juniper seems to be safe for most adults when taken short-term, but don't use for longer than four weeks. Long-term use can cause kidney problems, seizures, and other serious side-effects.

Juniper seems to be safe when applied to the skin in small areas. Using juniper on the skin can cause some side effects including irritation, burning, redness, and swelling.

Do not use juniper if: You are pregnant or breast-feeding. • You have blood pressure problems. • You have diabetes. • You have kidney disease. • You have seizures. • You have heart problems. • You have skin disease or skin wounds. • You have a stomach disorder.

Are there any interactions with medications?

Medications for diabetes (Antidiabetes drugs). Juniper might decrease blood sugar. Diabetes medications are also used to lower blood sugar. Taking juniper along with diabetes medications might cause your blood sugar to go too low. Monitor your blood sugar closely. The dose of your diabetes medication might need to be changed. Some medications used for diabetes include glimepiride (Amaryl), glyburide (DiaBeta, Glynase PresTab, Micronase), insulin, pioglitazone (Actos), rosiglitazone (Avandia), chlorpropamide (Diabinese), glipizide (Glucotrol), tolbutamide (Orinase), and others.

Water pills (Diuretic drugs). Juniper seems to work like "water pills" by causing the body to lose water. Taking juniper along with other "water pills" might cause the body to lose too much water. Losing too much water can cause you to be dizzy and your blood pressure to go too low. Some "water pills" include chlorothiazide (Diuril), chlorthalidone (Thalitone), furosemide (Lasix), hydrochlorothiazide (HCTZ, Hydrodiuril, Microzide), and others.

KAMALA

What other names is the product known by?

Kamcela, Kameela, Mallotus philippensis, Rottiera Tinctoria, Spoonwood.

What is it?

Kamala is a plant. The gland and hair of the fruit are used to make medicine.

Is it Effective?

The effectiveness ratings for **KAMALA** are as follows:
Insufficient Evidence to Rate Effectiveness for... Tapeworm and other conditions.

How does it work?

Kamala contains substances that might get rid of parasitic worms and purge the bowels.

Are there safety concerns?

There isn't enough information to know if kamala is safe or what the potential side effects might be.

Do not use kamala if: You are pregnant or breast-feeding. • You have appendicitis or symptoms of appendicitis such as stomach pain, nausea, and vomiting.

Are there any interactions with medications?

It is not known if kamala interacts with any medicines.
Before taking kamala, talk with your healthcare professional if you take any medications.

KAOLIN

What other names is the product known by?

Argilla, Bolus Alba, China Clay, Heavy Kaolin, Hydrated aluminum silicate, Light Kaolin, Porcelain Clay, White Bole.

What is it?

Kaolin is a type of clay found in nature. It can also be made in a laboratory. People use it to make medicine.

Medical professionals should consult the Professional Version at www.NaturalDatabase.com.

Is it Effective?

The effectiveness ratings for **KAOLIN** are as follows:

Possibly Effective for... Soreness and swelling inside the mouth, caused by radiation treatments.

Insufficient Evidence to Rate Effectiveness for... Diarrhea, ulcers and inflammation in the colon (chronic ulcerative colitis), and other conditions.

How does it work?

Kaolin acts as a protective coating for the digestive tract to decrease pain associated with radiation-induced damage. Kaolin was formerly used for diarrhea as an ingredient in products such as Kaopectate. But the Food and Drug Administration (FDA) could not find sufficient research to support its use for diarrhea. Kaopectate and similar products no longer contain kaolin.

Are there safety concerns?

Kaolin seems to be safe for most people. It can cause some side effects including constipation, particularly in children and the elderly.

Do not inhale kaolin. It can cause lung problems.

Are there any interactions with medications?

Clindamycin (Cleocin). Kaolin might decrease how quickly the body absorbs of clindamycin (Cleocin), an antibiotic. But it probably doesn't decrease the amount of clindamycin (Cleocin) that is absorbed.

Digoxin (Lanoxin). Kaolin might decrease the absorption and decrease the effectiveness of digoxin (Lanoxin), a heart medication. To avoid a potential interaction, separate digoxin (Lanoxin) and kaolin doses by at least two hours.

Quinidine. Kaolin might decrease the absorption and decrease the effectiveness of quinidine (Quinidex), a heart medication. To avoid a potential interaction, separate quinidine (Quinidex) and kaolin doses by at least two hours.

Trimethoprim (Proloprim). Kaolin might decrease the absorption and decrease the effectiveness of trimethoprim (Proloprim), an antibiotic. To avoid a potential interaction, separate trimethoprim (Proloprim) and kaolin doses by at least two hours.

KARAYA GUM

What other names is the product known by?

Bassora Tragacanth, Indian Tragacanth, Kadaya, Kadira, Katila, Kullo, Mucara, Sterculia Gum, Sterculia tragacanth, Sterculia urens, Sterculia villosa.

What is it?

Karaya gum is a sap-like material from a tree. People use it to make medicine.

Is it Effective?

The effectiveness ratings for **KARAYA GUM** are as follows:

Possibly Effective for... Use as a bulk-forming laxative to treat constipation.

Insufficient Evidence to Rate Effectiveness for... Stimulating sexual desire (aphrodisia).

How does it work?

Karaya gum swells in the intestine, which stimulates the digestive tract to push stool through.

Are there safety concerns?

Karaya gum seems safe for most people when taken with plenty of fluids. It can block the intestines if you do not drink enough fluid.

Do not use karaya gum if: You are pregnant or breast-feeding. • You have a blockage in your bowel.

Are there any interactions with medications?

Medications taken by mouth (Oral drugs). Karaya contains a type of soft fiber called mucilage. Mucilage can decrease how much medicine the body absorbs. Taking karaya at the same time you take medications by mouth can decrease the effectiveness of your medication. To prevent this interaction take karaya at least one hour after medications you take by mouth.

KAVA

What other names is the product known by?
Ava, Awa, Intoxicating Pepper, Kava Kava, Kava-kava, Kava Pepper, Kava Root, Kawa, Kawa Kawa, Kawa-Kawa, Kew, Piper methysticum, Rauschpfeffer, Sakau, Tonga, Wurzelstock, Yagona.

What is it?
Kava is a plant native to the South Pacific. The root is used for medicine.

Is it Effective?
The effectiveness ratings for **KAVA** are as follows:
Likely Effective for... Anxiety.
Possibly Effective for... Reducing withdrawal symptoms in people who need to stop taking anti-anxiety and sleep medicines called benzodiazepines • Anxiety in women going through menopause.
Insufficient Evidence to Rate Effectiveness for... Stress, insomnia, restlessness, social anxiety, attention deficit-hyperactivity disorder (ADHD), epilepsy, psychosis, depression, chronic fatigue syndrome (CFS), headaches, colds, respiratory tract infections, tuberculosis, rheumatism, chronic bladder infections, sexually transmitted diseases, menstrual problems, cancer prevention, and other conditions.

How does it work?
Kava affects the brain and other parts of the central nervous system. The kava-lactones in kava are believed to be responsible for its effects.

Are there safety concerns?
Kava may be unsafe; avoid using it. Serious illness, including liver damage, has occurred even with short-term use of normal doses.

Early symptoms of liver damage include yellowed eyes and skin (jaundice), fatigue, and dark urine.

Do not take kava if: You are pregnant or breast-feeding. • You have been told by your healthcare professional that you are depressed. • You have a liver disease such as hepatitis. • Using kava can make you unable to drive or operate machinery safely. Do not take kava before you plan on driving. "Driving-under-the-influence" citations have been issued to people driving erratically after drinking large amounts of kava tea.

Are there any interactions with medications?
Alprazolam (Xanax). Kava can cause drowsiness. Alprazolam (Xanax) can also cause drowsiness. Taking kava along with alprazolam (Xanax) may cause too much drowsiness. Avoid taking kava and alprazolam (Xanax) together.
Levodopa. Levodopa affects the brain by increasing a brain chemical called dopamine. Kava might decrease dopamine in the brain. Taking kava along with levodopa might decrease the effectiveness of levodopa.
Medications changed by the liver (Cytochrome P450 1A2 (CYP1A2) substrates). Some medications are changed and broken down by the liver. Kava might decrease how quickly the liver breaks down some medications. Taking kava along with some medications that are changed by the liver might increase the effects and side effects of some medications. Before taking kava talk to your healthcare provider if you take any medications that are changed by the liver. Some of these medications that are changed by the liver include clozapine (Clozaril), cyclobenzaprine (Flexeril), fluvoxamine (Luvox), haloperidol (Haldol), imipramine (Tofranil), mexiletine (Mexitil), olanzapine (Zyprexa), pentazocine (Talwin), propranolol (Inderal), tacrine (Cognex), theophylline, zileuton (Zyflo), zolmitriptan (Zomig), and others.
Medications changed by the liver (Cytochrome P450 2C19 (CYP2C19) substrates). Some medications are changed and broken down by the liver. Kava might decrease how quickly the liver breaks down some medications. Taking kava along with some medications that are broken down by the liver can increase the effects and side effects of your medication. Before taking Kava talk to your healthcare provider if you take any medications that are changed by the liver. Some of these medications changed by the liver include amitriptyline (Elavil), clomipramine (Anafranil), cyclophosphamide (Cytoxan), diazepam (Valium), lansoprazole (Prevacid), omeprazole (Prilosec), lansoprazole (Protonix), phenytoin (Dilantin), phenobarbital (Luminal), progesterone, and others.
Medications changed by the liver (Cytochrome P450 2C9 (CYP2C9) substrates). Some medications are changed and broken down by the liver. Kava might decrease how quickly the liver breaks down some medications. Taking kava along with some medications that are broken down by the liver can increase the effects and side effects of some medications. Before taking kava talk to your healthcare provider if you take any medications that are changed by the liver. Some medications that are changed by the liver include amitriptyline (Elavil), diazepam (Valium), zileuton (Zyflo), celecoxib (Celebrex), diclofenac (Voltaren), fluvastatin (Lescol), glipizide (Glucotrol), ibuprofen (Advil, Motrin), irbesartan (Avapro), losartan (Cozaar), phenytoin (Dilantin), piroxicam (Feldene), tamoxifen (Nolvadex), tolbutamide (Tolinase), torsemide (Demadex), warfarin (Coumadin), and others.
Medications changed by the liver (Cytochrome P450 2D6 (CYP2D6) substrates). Some medications are

Medical professionals should consult the Professional Version at www.NaturalDatabase.com.

changed and broken down by the liver. Kava might decrease how quickly the liver breaks down some medications. Taking Kava along with some medications that are change by the liver can increase the effects and side effects of your medication. Before taking kava talk to your healthcare provider if you take any medications that are changed by the liver. Some medications that are changed by the liver include amitriptyline (Elavil), clozapine (Clozaril), codeine, desipramine (Norpramin), donepezil (Aricept), fentanyl (Duragesic), flecainide (Tambocor), fluoxetine (Prozac), meperidine (Demerol), methadone (Dolophine), metoprolol (Lopressor, Toprol XL), olanzapine (Zyprexa), ondansetron (Zofran), tramadol (Ultram), trazodone (Desyrel), and others.

Medications changed by the liver (Cytochrome P450 2E1 (CYP2E1) substrates). Some medications are changed and broken down by the liver. Kava might decrease how quickly the liver breaks down some medications. Taking kava along with some medications that are change by the liver can increase the effects and side effects of your medication. Before taking kava talk to your healthcare provider if you take any medications that are changed by the liver. Some medications that are changed by the liver include acetaminophen, chlorzoxazone (Parafon Forte), ethanol, theophylline, and drugs used for anesthesia during surgery such as enflurane (Ethrane), halothane (Fluothane), isoflurane (Forane), and methoxyflurane (Penthrane).

Medications changed by the liver (Cytochrome P450 3A4 (CYP3A4) substrates). Some medications are changed and broken down by the liver. Kava might decrease how quickly the liver breaks down some medications. Taking kava along with some medications that are broken down by the liver can increase the effects and side effects of some medications. Before taking kava, talk to your healthcare provider if you are taking any medications that are changed by the liver. Some medications changed by the liver include lovastatin (Mevacor), ketoconazole (Nizoral), itraconazole (Sporanox), fexofenadine (Allegra), triazolam (Halcion), and many others.

Medications that can harm the liver (Hepatotoxic drugs). Kava might harm the liver. Taking kava along with medication that might also harm the liver can increase the risk of liver damage. Do not take kava if you are taking a medication that can harm the liver. Some medications that can harm the liver include acetaminophen (Tylenol and others), amiodarone (Cordarone), carbamazepine (Tegretol), isoniazid (INH), methotrexate (Rheumatrex), methyldopa (Aldomet), fluconazole (Diflucan), itraconazole (Sporanox), erythromycin (Erythrocin, Ilosone, others), phenytoin (Dilantin), lovastatin (Mevacor), pravastatin (Pravachol), simvastatin (Zocor), and many others.

Sedative medications (CNS depressants). Kava might cause sleepiness and drowsiness. Medications that cause sleepiness are called sedatives. Taking kava along with sedative medications might cause too much sleepiness. Some sedative medications include clonazepam (Klonopin), lorazepam (Ativan), Phenobarbital (Donnatal), zolpidem (Ambien), and others.

KEFIR

What other names is the product known by?

Fermented Dairy Product, Fermented Milk, Kefir Cheese, Kefir Grains, Kefir Yogurt.

What is it?

Kefir is a fermentation product of milk.

Is it Effective?

The effectiveness ratings for **KEFIR** are as follows:

Likely Ineffective for... Lowering serum cholesterol.

Insufficient Evidence to Rate Effectiveness for... Lactose intolerance, improving digestion.

How does it work?

Kefir contains actively growing bacteria and yeast. Their effect on milk results in production of enzymes and chemicals that affect the way food is digested.

Are there safety concerns?

Kefir appears to be safe for most people. Kefir can cause intestinal cramping and constipation, especially with initial use.

Do not use if: You are pregnant or breast-feeding. • You have any condition that might reduce your immune function.

Are there any interactions with medications?

Medications that decrease the immune system (Immunosuppressants). Kefir contains live bacteria and yeast. The immune system usually controls bacteria and yeast in the body to prevent infections. Medications that decrease the immune system can increase your chances of getting sick from bacteria and yeast. Taking kefir along with medications that decrease the immune system might increase the chances of getting sick. Some medications that decrease the immune system include azathioprine (Imuran), basiliximab (Simulect), cyclosporine (Neoral, Sandimmune), daclizumab (Zenapax), muromonab-CD3 (OKT3, Orthoclone OKT3), mycophenolate (CellCept), tacrolimus (FK506, Prograf), sirolimus (Rapamune), prednisone (Deltasone, Orasone), corticosteroids (glucocorticoids), and others.

KHAT

What other names is the product known by?

Abyssinian Tea, Arabian-Tea, Catha edulis, Celastrus edulis, Chaat, Gat, Kat, Kus es Salahin, Qut, Miraa, Tchaad, Tohai, Tohat, Tschut.

What is it?

Khat is a plant. People use the leaf and stem for medicine.

Is it Effective?

The effectiveness ratings for **KHAT** are as follows:
Insufficient Evidence to Rate Effectiveness for... Depression, fatigue, obesity, stomach ulcers, elevating mood, and other uses.

How does it work?

Khat contains stimulants similar to amphetamines.

Are there safety concerns?

Khat is possibly unsafe for use. Although it isn't associated with physical addiction, it can cause psychological dependence. It can cause many side effects including mood changes, increased alertness, excessive talkativeness, hyperactivity, excitement, aggressiveness, anxiety, elevated blood pressure, manic behavior, paranoia, and psychoses. Trouble sleeping (insomnia), loss of energy (malaise), and lack of concentration usually follow. Other effects include rapid heart rate, heart palpitations, increased blood pressure, faster breathing rates, increased body temperature, sweating, eye changes, mouth ulcers, inflammation of the esophagus and stomach, gum disease, jaw problems (TMJ), and constipation. Regular use in young people is linked to high blood pressure. Severe side effects include migraine, bleeding in the brain, heart attack, lung problems, liver damage, changes in sex drive, and inability to get an erection (impotence). Chewing khat leaves has lead to infections that can cause problems such as pain below the ribs, changes in white blood cells, and an enlarged liver.

Do not use khat if: You are pregnant or breast-feeding. • You have diabetes.

Are there any interactions with medications?

It is not known if khat interacts with any medicines.
Before taking khat, talk with your healthcare professional if you take any medications.

KHELLA

What other names is the product known by?

Ammi, Ammi daucoides, Ammi visnaga, Bischofskrautfruchte, Bishop's Weed, Bishops Weed Fruit, Daucus visagna, Fruits De Khella Fruit, Khellin, Toothpick Ammi, Toothpick Plant, Visnaga, Visnagae, Visnagafruchte, Visnaga Fruit, Visgagin.

What is it?

Khella is a plant. The dried, ripe fruit is used to make medicine.

Is it Effective?

The effectiveness ratings for **KHELLA** are as follows:
Insufficient Evidence to Rate Effectiveness for... Stomach cramps, kidney stones, menstrual (period) pain, premenstrual syndrome (PMS), asthma, bronchitis, cough, whooping cough, high blood pressure (hypertension), abnormal rhythm of the heartbeat (arrhythmias), congestive heart failure (CHF), chest pain (angina), hardening of the arteries (atherosclerosis), high cholesterol (hypercholesterolemia), skin problems, and other uses.

How does it work?

Khella contains substances that seem to relax and widen blood vessels; decrease heart contraction; open up the lungs; increase "good cholesterol" (HDL, high-density lipoprotein); and fight bacteria, viruses, and fungi.

Are there safety concerns?

Khella is possibly unsafe when taken in high doses. It can cause side effects including nausea, dizziness, constipation, lack of appetite, headache, itching, trouble sleeping, skin sensitivity to sunlight (photosensitization), liver problems, and other side effects.

Do not use khella if: You are pregnant or breast-feeding. • You have liver disease.

Are there any interactions with medications?

Digoxin (Lanoxin). Digoxin (Lanoxin) helps the heart beat more strongly. Khella seems to slow the heartbeat. Taking khella along with digoxin might decrease the effectiveness of digoxin. Do not take khella if you are taking digoxin (Lanoxin).

Medications that can harm the liver (Hepatotoxic drugs). Khella might harm the liver. Taking khella along with medication that might also harm the liver can increase the risk of liver damage. Do not take khella if you are taking a medication that can harm the liver. Some medications that can harm the liver include acetaminophen (Tylenol and others), amiodarone (Cordarone), carbamazepine (Tegretol), isoniazid (INH), methotrexate (Rheumatrex), methyldopa (Aldomet), fluconazole (Diflucan), itraconazole (Sporanox), erythromycin (Erythrocin, Ilosone, others), phenytoin (Dilantin), lovastatin (Mevacor), pravastatin (Pravachol), simvastatin (Zocor), and many others.

Medications that increase sensitivity to sunlight (Photosensitizing drugs). Some medications can increase sensitivity to sunlight. Khella might also increase your sensitivity to sunlight. Taking khella along with medication that increase sensitivity to sunlight could increase the chances of sunburn, blistering or rashes on areas of skin exposed to sunlight. Be sure to wear sunblock and protective clothing when spending time in the sun. Some drugs that cause photosensitivity include amitriptyline (Elavil), Ciprofloxacin (Cipro), norfloxacin (Noroxin), lomefloxacin (Maxaquin), ofloxacin (Floxin), levofloxacin (Levaquin), sparfloxacin (Zagam), gatifloxacin (Tequin), moxifloxacin (Avelox), trimethoprim/sulfamethoxazole (Septra), tetracycline, methoxsalen (8-methoxypsoralen, 8-MOP, Oxsoralen), and Trioxsalen (Trisoralen).

KINETIN

What other names is the product known by?

Kinerase, Kinetase, Kn, N-(2-furanylmethyl)-1H-purin-6-amine, N(6)furfuryladenine, 6-furfurylaminopurine.

What is it?

Kinetin is a cytokinin. Cytokinins are compounds that stimulate plants to grow. Kinetin is used to make medicine.

Is it Effective?

The effectiveness ratings for **KINETIN** are as follows:

Insufficient Evidence to Rate Effectiveness for... Reducing the signs of skin aging, skin roughness, fine wrinkles, and other skin imperfections.

How does it work?

Kinetin prevents green plant leaves from turning brown. There is some information that suggests kinetin might prevent age-related changes in human skin by protecting the DNA in skin cells from damage (antioxidant effects) and decreasing skin water loss.

Are there safety concerns?

There isn't enough information available to know if kinetin is safe.
Do not use kinetin if: You are pregnant or breast-feeding.

Are there any interactions with medications?

It is not known if kinetin interacts with any medicines.
Before taking kinetin, talk with your healthcare professional if you take any medications.

KIWI

What other names is the product known by?

Actinidia chinensis, China Gooseberry, Chinese Gooseberry, Kiwi Fruit.

What is it?

Kiwi is a plant. The fruit is used as medicine.

Is it Effective?

The effectiveness ratings for **KIWI** are as follows:

Insufficient Evidence to Rate Effectiveness for... Improving lung function in people with asthma and other conditions.

How does it work?

There is information that suggests the antioxidant effects of vitamin C or other compounds that are found in high concentrations in kiwi might benefit people with asthma.

 (209) 472-2244

Are there safety concerns?
Kiwi seems to be safe for most people when used in food amounts. In people who are allergic to kiwi, it can cause allergic reactions such as trouble swallowing (dysphagia), vomiting, and hives.

Do not take kiwi if: You are allergic to latex.

Are there any interactions with medications?
It is not known if kiwi interacts with any medicines.
Before taking kiwi, talk with your healthcare professional if you take any medications.

KNOTWEED

What other names is the product known by?
Allseed Nine-Joints, Armstrong, Beggarweed, Bird's Tongue, Birdweed, Centinode, Cow Grass, Crawlgrass, Doorweed, Hogweed, Knot Grass, Knotweed Herb, Mexican Sanguinaria, Ninety-Knot, Pigrush, Pigweed, Polygoni Avicularis Herba, Polygonum aviculare, Red Robin, Sparrow Tongue, Swine Grass, Swynel Grass, Vogelknoeterichkraut.

What is it?
Knotweed is an herb. The whole flowering plant is used to make medicine.

Is it Effective?
The effectiveness ratings for **KNOTWEED** are as follows:
Insufficient Evidence to Rate Effectiveness for... Bronchitis; cough; lung diseases; skin diseases; decreasing sweating with tuberculosis; increasing urine; redness, swelling, and bleeding of the gums, mouth, and throat; and preventing or stopping bleeding.

How does it work?
Knotweed might have astringent and anti-inflammatory properties. It might also prevent plaque from building up on teeth.

Are there safety concerns?
Knotweed may be safe for most people, but the potential side effects of knotweed are not known.

Do not use knotweed if: You are pregnant or breast-feeding.

Are there any interactions with medications?
It is not known if knotweed interacts with any medicines.
Before taking knotweed, talk with your healthcare professional if you take any medications.

KOMBUCHA TEA

What other names is the product known by?
Champagne Of Life, Combucha Tea, Mushroom Infusion, Fungus Japonicus, Kargasok Tea, Kombucha Mushroom Tea, Kwassan, Manchurian Fungus, Manchurian Mushroom Tea, Spumonto, T'Chai from the Sea, Tschambucco.

What is it?
Kombucha is derived from the fermentation of yeast and bacteria with black tea, sugar, and other ingredients. The resulting liquid is called kombucha tea. People use it as medicine.

Is it Effective?
The effectiveness ratings for **KOMBUCHA TEA** are as follows:
Insufficient Evidence to Rate Effectiveness for... Memory loss, premenstrual syndrome (PMS), rheumatism, aging, anorexia, AIDS, cancer, high blood pressure, increasing white cell (T-cell) counts, strengthening the immune system and metabolism, constipation, arthritis, hair growth, pain, and other uses.

How does it work?
Kombucha tea contains alcohol, vinegar, B vitamins, caffeine, sugar, and other substances. However, there isn't enough evidence to know how kombucha tea might work for medicinal uses.

Medical professionals should consult the Professional Version at www.NaturalDatabase.com.

Are there safety concerns?

Kombucha tea is possibly unsafe for most adults. It can cause side effects including stomach problems, yeast infections, allergic reactions, yellow skin (jaundice), nausea, vomiting, head and neck pain, and possibly death.

Kombucha tea can be contaminated with disease-causing fungus (Aspergillus) and bacteria (anthrax). Kombucha tea is particularly unsafe in people with weakened immune systems, such as people with HIV/AIDS, who are more susceptible to infections. Also, lead poisoning has been reported from kombucha tea that was prepared in a lead-glazed ceramic pot.

Do not use kombucha tea if: You are pregnant or breast-feeding. • You are recovering from alcoholism. The alcohol content of the tea could worsen this condition. • You have an immune disorder. Kombucha tea can harbor organisms that can cause a serious infection.

Are there any interactions with medications?

Disulfiram (Antabuse). Kombucha tea contains alcohol. The body breaks down alcohol to get rid of it. Disulfiram (Antabuse) decreases the break-down of alcohol. Taking kombucha tea along with disulfiram (Antabuse) can cause a pounding headache, vomiting, flushing, and other unpleasant reactions. Don't drink any alcohol if you are taking disulfiram (Antabuse).

KOUSSO

What other names is the product known by?

Brayera anthelmintica, Cossoo, Hagenia abyssinica, Kooso, Kosso.

What is it?

Kousso is a plant. The leaves, fruit, and flowers are used to make medicine.

Is it Effective?

The effectiveness ratings for **KOUSSO** are as follows:
Insufficient Evidence to Rate Effectiveness for... Tapeworm and other conditions.

How does it work?

There isn't enough information to know how kousso might work.

Are there safety concerns?

Kousso is UNSAFE. It can cause side effects including irritation of the stomach and intestines, stomach pain, increased salivation, headache, weakness, unconsciousness, vision disorders, spasms, and shock.

While taking kousso isn't safe for anyone, some people should be especially careful to avoid it.

Do not use kousso if: You are pregnant or breast-feeding. • You have a stomach or intestinal problem.

Are there any interactions with medications?

It is not known if kousso interacts with any medicines.
Before taking kousso, talk with your healthcare professional if you take any medications.

KUDZU

What other names is the product known by?

Daidzein, Dolichos lobatus, Fen Ke, Fenge, Gange, Ge Gen, Gegen, Isoflavone, Isoflavones, Japanese Arrowroot, Kakkon, Kudsu, Kudzu Vine, Kwaao Khruea, Mealy Kudzu, Pueraria, Pueraria lobata, Pueraria mirifica, Pueraria Montana, Pueraria pseudohirsuta, Pueraria Root, Pueraria thomsonii, Pueraria thunbergiana, Pueraria tuberosa, Radix Puerariae, Yege.

What is it?

Kudzu is a plant. The root, flower, and leaf are used to make medicine.

Is it Effective?

The effectiveness ratings for **KUDZU** are as follows:
Insufficient Evidence to Rate Effectiveness for... Symptoms of alcohol hangover (headache, upset stomach, dizziness and vomiting), chest pains, treatment of alcoholism, menopause, muscle pain, measles, dysentery,

CONSUMER VERSION

stomach inflammation (gastritis), fever, diarrhea, thirst, cold, flu, neck stiffness, promoting sweating (diaphoretic), high blood pressure, abnormal heart rate and rhythm, and other conditions.

How does it work?
There is information that suggests kudzu contains ingredients that counteract alcohol. It might also have effects like estrogen. Chemicals in kudzu might also increase blood circulation in the heart.

Are there safety concerns?
Kudzu might be safe for most people when used appropriately. Kudzu may lower blood sugar. If you have diabetes, watch for signs of low blood sugar (hypoglycemia) and check your blood sugar carefully.

Do not use kudzu if: You are pregnant or breast-feeding. • You have a heart disorder. • You have a bleeding or blood clotting disorder. • You have breast cancer. • You have uterine cancer. • You have ovarian cancer. • You have endometriosis. • You have uterine fibroids.

Are there any interactions with medications?
Birth control pills (Contraceptive drugs). Some birth control pills contain estrogen. Kudzu might have some of the same effects as estrogen. But kudzu isn't as strong as the estrogen in birth control pills. Taking kudzu along with birth control pills might decrease the effectiveness of birth control pills. If you take birth control pills along with kudzu, use an additional form of birth control such as a condom. Some birth control pills include ethinyl estradiol and levonorgestrel (Triphasil), ethinyl estradiol and norethindrone (Ortho-Novum 1/35, Ortho-Novum 7/7/7), and others.

Estrogens. The body breaks down caffeine (contained in kudzu) to get rid of it. Estrogens can decrease how quickly the body breaks down caffeine. Decreasing the break-down of caffeine can cause jitteriness, headache, fast heartbeat, and other side effects. If you take estrogens, limit your caffeine intake. Some estrogen pills include conjugated equine estrogens (Premarin), ethinyl estradiol, estradiol, and others.

Medications that slow blood clotting (Anticoagulant / Antiplatelet drugs). Kudzu might slow blood clotting. Taking kudzu along with medications that also slow clotting might increase the chances of bruising and bleeding. Some medications that slow blood clotting include aspirin, clopidogrel (Plavix), diclofenac (Voltaren, Cataflam, others), ibuprofen (Advil, Motrin, others), naproxen (Anaprox, Naprosyn, others), dalteparin (Fragmin), enoxaparin (Lovenox), heparin, warfarin (Coumadin), and others.

Medications for diabetes (Antidiabetes drugs). Kudzu might decrease blood sugar. Diabetes medications are also used to lower blood sugar. Taking kudzu along with diabetes medications might cause your blood sugar to go too low. Monitor your blood sugar closely. The dose of your diabetes medication might need to be changed. Some medications used for diabetes include glimepiride (Amaryl), glyburide (DiaBeta, Glynase PresTab, Micronase), insulin, pioglitazone (Actos), rosiglitazone (Avandia), chlorpropamide (Diabinese), glipizide (Glucotrol), tolbutamide (Orinase), and others.

Methotrexate (MTX, Rheumatrex). Kudzu might decrease how fast the body gets rid of methotrexate (Rheumatrex). This might increase the risk of methotrexate side effects.

Tamoxifen (Nolvadex). Some types of cancer are affected by hormones in the body. Estrogen-sensitive cancers are cancers that are affected by estrogen levels in the body. Tamoxifen (Nolvadex) is used to help treat and prevent these types of cancer. Kudzu seems to also affect estrogen levels in the body. By affecting estrogen in the body, kudzu might decrease the effectiveness of tamoxifen (Nolvadex). Do not take kudzu if you are taking tamoxifen (Nolvadex).

L-ARGININE

What other names is the product known by?
Arg, Arginine, Arginine HCl, Arginine Hydrochloride, L-Arginine HCl, L-Arginine Hydrochloride.

What is it?
L-arginine is an amino acid that is obtained from the diet and is necessary for the body to make proteins. It is found in red meat, poultry, fish, and dairy products. It can also be made in a laboratory and used as medicine.

Is it Effective?
The effectiveness ratings for **L-ARGININE** are as follows:
Possibly Effective for... Congestive heart failure • Chest pain associated with coronary artery disease (angina pectoris) • Preventing loss of effect of nitroglycerin in people with angina pectoris • Problems with erections of the penis (erectile dysfunction) • Improving kidney function in kidney transplant patients taking cyclosporine • Bladder inflammation • Cramping pain and weakness in the legs associated with blocked arteries (intermittent claudication) • Wasting and weight loss in people with HIV/AIDS, when used with hydroxymethylbutyrate (HMB) • Preventing inflammation of the digestive tract in premature infants. • Improving recovery after surgery.
Possibly Ineffective for... Heart attack. Taking L-arginine does not seem to help prevent a heart attack. L-arginine

Medical professionals should consult the Professional Version at www.NaturalDatabase.com.

also does not seem to be beneficial for treating a heart attack after it has occurred. In fact, there is concern that L-arginine might be harmful for people who have had a recent heart attack. Don't take L-arginine if you have had a recent heart attack. • Pre-eclamspia. An increase in blood pressure during pregnancy.

Insufficient Evidence to Rate Effectiveness for... Male infertility, prevention of the common cold, migraine headache, decreased mental function in the elderly, improving athletic performance, increase in blood pressure during pregnancy (pre-eclampsia), breast cancer when used in combination with chemotherapy, wound healing, female sexual problems, sickle cell disease, and improving the immune system in people with head and neck cancer.

How does it work?

L-arginine is converted in the body into a chemical called nitric oxide. Nitric oxide causes blood vessels to open wider for improved blood flow. L-arginine also stimulates the release of growth hormone, insulin, and other substances in the body.

Are there safety concerns?

L-arginine is safe for most people when taken appropriately by mouth. It can cause some side effects such as abdominal pain, bloating, diarrhea, gout, blood abnormalities, allergies, airway inflammation, worsening of asthma, and low blood pressure.

Do not use L-arginine if: You are pregnant or breast-feeding. • You have allergies or asthma. • You have cirrhosis of the liver. • You have herpes. • You have low blood pressure. • You have recently had a heart attack.

Are there any interactions with medications?

Medications that increase blood flow to the heart (Nitrates). L-Arginine increases blood flow. Taking L-arginine with medications that increase blood flow to the heart might increase the chance of dizziness and lightheadedness. Some of these medications that increase blood flow to the heart include nitroglycerin (Nitro-Bid, Nitro-Dur, Nitrostat), and isosorbide (Imdur, Isordil, Sorbitrate).

Medications for high blood pressure (Antihypertensive drugs). L-arginine seems to decrease blood pressure. Taking L-arginine along with medications for high blood pressure might cause your blood pressure to go too low. Some medications for high blood pressure include captopril (Capoten), enalapril (Vasotec), losartan (Cozaar), valsartan (Diovan), diltiazem (Cardizem), Amlodipine (Norvasc), hydrochlorothiazide (HydroDiuril), furosemide (Lasix), and many others.

Sildenafil (Viagra). Sildenafil (Viagra) can lower blood pressure. L-arginine can also lower blood pressure. Taking sildenafil and L-arginine together might cause the blood pressure to go too low. Blood pressure that is too low can cause dizziness and other side effects.

L-CARNITINE

What other names is the product known by?

B(t) Factor, Carnitine, Carnitor, D-Carnitine, DL-Carnitine, Levocarnitine, Vitacarn, Vitamin B(t), beta-hydroxy-gamma-trimethylammonium butyrate.

What is it?

L-carnitine is an amino acid (a protein component) that is naturally produced in the body.

Is it Effective?

The effectiveness ratings for **L-CARNITINE** are as follows:

Effective for... Treating and preventing L-carnitine deficiency • Increasing red blood cell count in people with serious kidney disease.

Possibly Effective for... Improving low birth weight • Preventing side effects caused by valproic acid (Depacon, Depakene, Depakote, VPA), a seizure medication • Improving symptoms and complications of heart disease and heart failure (chest pain, heart attack, and others) • Symptoms of high thyroid hormone levels • Treating male infertility caused by inflammation of some reproductive organs and tissues (prostate, seminal vesicles, and epididymis).

Likely Ineffective for... Improving athletic ability.

Insufficient Evidence to Rate Effectiveness for... Eating disorders, chronic fatigue syndrome, diabetes, high cholesterol, blood disorders, circulatory problems in the legs, leg ulcers, attention deficit-hyperactivity disorder (ADHD), Lyme disease, autism, Rett syndrome, and other conditions.

How does it work?

L-carnitine helps the body produce energy. It is important for heart and brain function, muscle movement, and many other body processes.

Medical professionals should consult the Professional Version at www.NaturalDatabase.com.

Are there safety concerns?

L-carnitine is safe for most people when taken by mouth. It is also safe when used as an injection, with the approval of a healthcare provider. It can cause side effects such as nausea, vomiting, stomach upset, heartburn, diarrhea, and seizures. It can also cause a "fishy" odor of the urine, breath, and sweat.

L-carnitine seems safe for most breast-feeding women when taken in the amounts recommended. The effects of large doses taken by a breast-feeding mother are unknown.

Do not take L-carnitine if: You are pregnant. • You have seizures or a history of seizures. • You have thyroid problems.

Are there any interactions with medications?

Acenocoumarol (Sintrom). Acenocoumarol (Sintrom) is used to slow blood clotting. L-carnitine might increase the effectiveness of acenocoumarol (Sintrom). Increasing the effectiveness of acenocoumarol (Sintrom) might slow blood clotting too much. The dose of your acenocoumarol (Sintrom) might need to be changed.

Thyroid hormone. L-carnitine seems to decrease how well thyroid hormone works in the body. Taking L-carnitine with thyroid hormone might decrease the effectiveness of the thyroid hormone.

Warfarin (Coumadin). Warfarin (Coumadin) is used to slow blood clotting. L-carnitine might increase the effects of warfarin (Coumadin) and increase the chances of bruising and bleeding. Be sure to have your blood checked regularly. The dose of your warfarin (Coumadin) might need to be changed.

Zidovudine (AZT, Retrovir). Zidovudine is used to treat HIV and AIDS infection. Zidovudine decreases how much L-carnitine is in muscles and might cause muscle weakness. More information is needed to know if taking L-carnitine can decrease muscle weakness due to Zidovudine.

L-TRYPTOPHAN

What other names is the product known by?

L-trypt, Tryptophan, L-2-amino-3-(indole-3-yl) propionic acid.

What is it?

L-tryptophan is a protein building block that can be found in many plant and animal proteins.

Is it Effective?

The effectiveness ratings for **L-TRYPTOPHAN** are as follows:
Possibly Effective for... Treating premenstrual dysphoric disorder (PMDD) • Smoking cessation (helping people quit smoking).
Possibly Ineffective for... Treating teeth grinding • Treating facial pain • Improving athletic ability.
Insufficient Evidence to Rate Effectiveness for... Depression, anxiety, seasonal affective disorder, attention deficit-hyperactivity disorder (ADHD), treating sleep disorders, and other conditions.

How does it work?

L-tryptophan is important for many normal bodily functions including the proper function and development of the brain and other organs throughout the body.

Are there safety concerns?

L-tryptophan is LIKELY UNSAFE for use. It can cause side effects such as heartburn, stomach pain, belching and gas, nausea, vomiting, diarrhea, and loss of appetite. It can also cause headache, lightheadedness, drowsiness, dry mouth, visual blurring, muscle weakness, and sexual problems. Impurities in L-tryptophan may cause swelling (inflammation) of the joints, skin, lungs, heart, and liver and other side effects, including death.

Do not take L-tryptophan if: You are pregnant or breast-feeding. • You have a kidney disorder. • You have a liver disorder. • You have a white blood cell disorder.

Are there any interactions with medications?

Dextromethorphan (Robitussin DM, and others). L-Tryptophan can affect a brain chemical called serotonin. Dextromethorphan (Robitussin DM, others) can also affect serotonin. Taking L-tryptophan along with dextromethorphan (Robitussin DM, others), might cause there to be too much serotonin in the brain and serious side effects including heart problems, shivering and anxiety could occur. Do not take L-tryptophan if you are taking dextromethorphan (Robitussin DM, others).

Medications for depression (Antidepressant drugs). L-tryptophan increases a brain chemical called serotonin. Some medications for depression also increase the brain chemical serotonin. Taking L-tryptophan along with these medications for depression might increase serotonin too much and cause serious side effects including heart problems, shivering, and anxiety. Do not take L-tryptophan if you are taking medications for depression. Some of

Medical professionals should consult the Professional Version at www.NaturalDatabase.com.

these medications for depression include fluoxetine (Prozac), paroxetine (Paxil), sertraline (Zoloft), amitriptyline (Elavil), clomipramine (Anafranil), imipramine (Tofranil), and others.

Medications for depression (MAOIs). L-tryptophan increases a chemical in the brain. This chemical is called serotonin. Some medications used for depression also increase serotonin. Taking L-tryptophan with these medications used for depression might cause there to be too much serotonin. This could cause serious side effects including heart problems, shivering, and anxiety. Some of these medications used for depression include phenelzine (Nardil), tranylcypromine (Parnate), and others.

Meperidine (Demerol). L-tryptophan increases a chemical in the brain called serotonin. Meperidine (Demerol) can also increase serotonin in the brain. Taking L-tryptophan along with meperidine (Demerol) might cause too much serotonin in the brain and serious side effects including heart problems, shivering, and anxiety.

Pentazocine (Talwin). L-tryptophan increases a brain chemical called serotonin. Pentazocine (Talwin) also increases serotonin. Taking L-tryptophan along with pentazocine (Talwin) might cause serious side effects including heart problems, shivering, and anxiety. Do not take L-tryptophan if you are taking pentazocine (Talwin).

Phenothiazines. Taking L-tryptophan with phenothiazines can cause serious side effects including movement disorders. Some phenothiazines include chlorpromazine (Thorazine), fluphenazine (Prolixin), trifluoperazine (Stelazine), thioridazine (Mellaril), and others.

Sedative medications (Benzodiazepines). Sedative medications can affect the nervous system. L-tryptophan can also affect the nervous system. Taking L-tryptophan along with sedative medications can cause serious side effects. Do not take L-tryptophan if you are taking sedative medications. Some of these sedative medications include clonazepam (Klonopin), diazepam (Valium), lorazepam (Ativan), and others.

Sedative medications (CNS depressants). L-tryptophan might cause sleepiness and drowsiness. Medications that cause sleepiness are called sedatives. Taking L-tryptophan along with sedative medications might cause too much sleepiness. Some sedative medications include clonazepam (Klonopin), lorazepam (Ativan), phenobarbital (Donnatal), zolpidem (Ambien), and others.

Tramadol (Ultram). Tramadol (Ultram) can affect a chemical in the brain called serotonin. L-tryptophan can also affect serotonin. Taking L-tryptophan along with tramadol (Ultram) might cause too much serotonin in the brain and side effects including confusion, shivering, and stiff muscles could result.

LABDANUM

What other names is the product known by?

Ambreine, Ciste, Cistus incanus, Cistus ladanifer, Cistus ladaniferus, Cistus polymorphus, Cistus villosus, Cyste, Rockrose.

What is it?

Labdanum is a plant. The leaves, stems, and flowers are used to make medicine.

Is it Effective?

The effectiveness ratings for **LABDANUM** are as follows:

Insufficient Evidence to Rate Effectiveness for... Bronchitis, diarrhea, edema, hernia, leprosy, hardening of the spleen, expelling mucus from the chest, use as a stimulant, emptying and cleansing the bowel, stopping or preventing bleeding, and other uses.

How does it work?

Labdanum contains substances that might kill bacteria and fungi.

Are there safety concerns?

Labdanum may be safe when used on the skin. It is not known if using labdanum by mouth is safe or what the possible side effects might be.

Do not use labdanum if: You are pregnant or breast-feeding.

Are there any interactions with medications?

It is not known if labdanum interacts with any medicines.
Before taking labdanum, talk with your healthcare professional if you take any medications.

LABRADOR TEA

What other names is the product known by?
Continental Tea, Ledum groenlandicum, Ledum latifolium, St. James's Tea.

What is it?
Labrador tea is a plant. The leaves and flowering shoots are used to make medicine.

Is it Effective?
The effectiveness ratings for **LABRADOR TEA** are as follows:
Insufficient Evidence to Rate Effectiveness for... Cough, causing abortion, "female disorders," sore throat, lung infections, chest ailments, diarrhea, kidney problems, rheumatism, headache, cancer, skin problems, and other uses.

How does it work?
Labrador tea might thin mucus to make it easier to cough. There isn't enough information to know how labrador tea might work for other medicinal uses.

Are there safety concerns?
Labrador tea is possibly safe for most people when used as a weak tea or in small amounts. Labrador tea is likely unsafe when used in concentrated solutions or in large amounts and requires prompt medical attention. It can cause side effects such as vomiting, inflammation of the lining in the stomach and the intestines (gastroenteritis), diarrhea, delirium, spasms, paralysis, and death.

Do not use labrador tea if: You are pregnant or breast-feeding.

Are there any interactions with medications?
It is not known if labrador tea interacts with any medicines.
Before taking labrador tea, talk with your healthcare professional if you take any medications.

LABURNUM

What other names is the product known by?
Bean Trifoil, Cytisus laburnum, Golden Chain, Legume, Pea Tree.

What is it?
Laburnum is a plant. The seed is used to make medicine.

Be careful not to confuse laburnum and labdanum. They are very different plants.

Is it Effective?
The effectiveness ratings for **LABURNUM** are as follows:
Insufficient Evidence to Rate Effectiveness for... Inducing vomiting.

How does it work?
There isn't enough information to know how laburnum might work.

Are there safety concerns?
Laburnum is UNSAFE. All parts, including the seeds and berries, are unsafe and poisonous. Death has resulted after taking laburnum. Accidentally taking laburnum requires immediate medical attention.
Laburnum can cause side effects such as nausea, dizziness, salivation, mouth, throat, and stomach pain, sweating, headache, vomiting, vomiting with blood, spasms, paralysis, decreased urine excretion, decreased breathing, and death.

Do not use laburnum if: You are pregnant or breast-feeding.

Are there any interactions with medications?
It is not known if laburnum interacts with any medicines.
Before taking laburnum, talk with your healthcare professional if you take any medications.

LACTASE

What other names is the product known by?
Beta-galactosidase.

What is it?
Lactase is an enzyme.

Is it Effective?
The effectiveness ratings for **LACTASE** are as follows:
Likely Effective for... Preventing symptoms of lactose intolerance, such as cramps, diarrhea and gas, when milk products or lactose are taken by people with lactose intolerance.

How does it work?
People who are lactose intolerant have trouble digesting the milk sugar lactose. Lactase is an enzyme that splits the milk sugar lactose, to produce the sugars glucose and galactose.

Are there safety concerns?
Lactase seems to be safe for most people. There are no reported side effects.

Do not use lactase if: You are pregnant or breast-feeding.

Are there any interactions with medications?
It is not known if lactase interacts with any medicines.
Before taking lactase, talk with your healthcare professional if you take any medications.

LACTOBACILLUS

What other names is the product known by?
Acidophilus, L. Acidophilus, L. amylovorus, L. brevis, L. bulgaricus, L. casei, L. crispatus, L. delbrueckii, L. fermentum, L. gallinarum, L. johnsonii, L. johnsonii LC-1, L. plantarum, L. reuteri, L. salivarius, L. sporogenes, LC-1, Lacto Bacillus, Lactobacilli, Lactobacillus acidophilus, Lactobacillus amylovorus, Lactobacillus brevis, Lactobacillus bulgaricus, Lactobacillus casei sp. Rhamnosus, Lactobacillus crispatus, Lactobacillus delbrueckii, Lactobacillus fermentum, Lactobacillus gallinarum, Lactobacillus GG, Lactobacillus johnsonii, Lactobacillus paracasei, Lactobacillus plantarum, Lactobacillus reuteri, Lactobacillus rhamnosus, Lactobacillus rhamnosus GG, Lactobacillus salivarius, LC-1 L. johnsonii, Lactobacillus sporogenes, Probiotics.

What is it?
Lactobacillus is a type of bacteria. There are lots of different species of lactobacillus. These are "friendly" bacteria that normally live in our digestive, urinary, and genital systems without causing disease. It is also in some fermented foods like yogurt and in dietary supplements.

Is it Effective?
The effectiveness ratings for **LACTOBACILLUS** are as follows:
Likely Effective for... Diarrhea in children caused by certain viruses.
Possibly Effective for... Preventing diarrhea in children caused by antibiotics or hospitalization • Treating diarrhea caused by the bacterium Clostridium difficile • Treating and preventing eczema (atopic dermatitis) in infants and children • Helping prescription medications treat Helicobacter pylori (H pylori) infection • Lung infections in children • Preventing diarrhea due to traveling • Ulcerative colitis. Some research suggests that taking a specific combination product containing lactobacillus, bifidobacteria, and streptococcus might help induce remission and prevent relapse.
Possibly Ineffective for... Crohn's disease • Lactose intolerance • Reducing symptoms of too much bacteria in the intestines • Yeast infections after taking antibiotics.
Insufficient Evidence to Rate Effectiveness for... Irritable bowel syndrome (IBS), urinary tract infections (UTIs), general digestion problems, yeast infections, bacterial vaginal infections, high cholesterol, Lyme disease, hives, fever blisters, canker sores, acne, cancer, stimulating the immune system, and other conditions.

How does it work?
Many bacteria and other organisms live in our bodies normally. "Friendly" bacteria such as lactobacillus can help us break down food, absorb nutrients, and fight off "unfriendly" organisms that might cause diseases such as diarrhea.

    Natural Medicines Comprehensive Database Consumer Version   (209) 472-2244

Are there safety concerns?

Lactobacillus is safe for most people, including babies and children. Side effects are usually mild and most often include intestinal gas.

There is some concern that people with weakened immune systems, such as people with HIV/AIDS or organ transplant recipients, might have an overgrowth of lactobacillus from taking supplements containing live bacteria. Lactobacillus has caused disease (rarely) in people with weakened immune systems. To be on the safe side, if you have a weakened immune system, avoid taking supplements containing live bacteria without advice from your healthcare giver.

Some products labeled to contain certain Lactobacillus species have not contained what was claimed. In fact, some have been contaminated with potentially disease-causing bacteria.

Do not take lactobacillus without guidance from your healthcare provider if: Your immune system is weakened by diseases such as HIV/AIDS or medicines to prevent organ transplant rejection. • You have a condition called short bowel syndrome.

Are there any interactions with medications?

Antibiotic drugs. Antibiotics are used to reduce harmful bacteria in the body. Antibiotics can also reduce friendly bacteria in the body. Lactobacillus is a type of friendly bacteria. Taking antibiotics along with lactobacillus can reduce the effectiveness of lactobacillus. To avoid this interaction take lactobacillus products at least 2 hours before or after antibiotics.

Medications that decrease the immune system (Immunosuppressants). Lactobacillus contains live bacteria and yeast. The immune system usually controls bacteria and yeast in the body to prevent infections. Medications that decrease the immune system can increase your chances of getting sick from bacteria and yeast. Taking lactobacillus along with medications that decrease the immune system might increase the chances of getting sick. Some medications that decrease the immune system include azathioprine (Imuran), basiliximab (Simulect), cyclosporine (Neoral, Sandimmune), daclizumab (Zenapax), muromonab-CD3 (OKT3, Orthoclone OKT3), mycophenolate (CellCept), tacrolimus (FK506, Prograf), sirolimus (Rapamune), prednisone (Deltasone, Orasone), corticosteroids (glucocorticoids), and others.

LACTOFERRIN

What other names is the product known by?

Bovine lactoferrin, human lactoferrin, lactoferrins, recombinant human lactoferrin.

What is it?

Lactoferrin is a protein found in animal and human milk.

Is it Effective?

The effectiveness ratings for **LACTOFERRIN** are as follows:

Possibly Effective for... Hepatitis C.

Insufficient Evidence to Rate Effectiveness for... Helicobacter pylori infection (an ulcer-causing bacterial infection), stimulating the immune system, preventing damage related to aging, promoting healthy bacteria in the intestine, regulating iron metabolism, fighting bacteria and viruses (antibacterial and antiviral agent), use as an antioxidant, and other conditions.

How does it work?

Lactoferrin seems to have antibacterial, antiviral, and antifungal activity. It might prevent growth of bacteria by depriving them of essential nutrients or kill bacterial by destroying the bacterial cell wall.

Are there safety concerns?

Lactoferrin is safe in amounts consumed in food. Consuming higher amounts of lactoferrin from cow's milk might also be safe for up to a year. Human lactoferrin that is biochemically synthesized appears to be safe for up to 14 days. Lactoferrin can cause diarrhea. In very high doses, skin rash, loss of appetite, fatigue, chills, and constipation have been reported.

Do not use lactoferrin if: You are pregnant or breast-feeding.

Are there any interactions with medications?

It is not known if lactoferrin interacts with any medicines.
Before taking lactoferrin, talk with your healthcare professional if you take any medications.

Medical professionals should consult the Professional Version at www.NaturalDatabase.com.

LADY FERN

What other names is the product known by?
Athyrium filix-femina, Brake Root, Common Polypod, Oak Fern, Polypodium filix-femina, Rock Brake, Rock of Polypody.

What is it?
Lady fern is a plant. The root and root-like stem are used to make medicine.

Is it Effective?
The effectiveness ratings for **LADY FERN** are as follows:
Insufficient Evidence to Rate Effectiveness for... Lung and breathing problems, cough, digestive tract illnesses, and other conditions.

How does it work?
There isn't enough information to know how lady fern might work.

Are there safety concerns?
There isn't enough information to know if lady fern is safe or what the potential side effects might be.

Do not use lady fern if: You are pregnant or breast-feeding.

Are there any interactions with medications?
It is not known if lady fern interacts with any medicines.
Before taking lady fern, talk with your healthcare professional if you take any medications.

LADY'S BEDSTRAW

What other names is the product known by?
Cheese Rennet, Cheese Renning, Curdwort, Galium verum, Ladys Bedstraw, Maid's Hair, Petty Mugget, Yellow Cleavers, Yellow Galium.

What is it?
Lady's bedstraw is a plant. The leaves, stems, and flowers are used to make medicine.

Is it Effective?
The effectiveness ratings for **LADY'S BEDSTRAW** are as follows:
Insufficient Evidence to Rate Effectiveness for... Swollen ankles, increasing urine, cancer, epilepsy, hysteria, spasms, tumors, relief of chest and lung ailments, causing sweating, use as a tonic, increasing the appetite, use as an aphrodisiac, use as an astringent, stimulating and emptying the bowels, poorly healing wounds, and stopping bleeding.

How does it work?
There isn't enough information to know how lady's bedstraw might work.

Are there safety concerns?
It is not known if lady's bedstraw is safe or what the potential side effects might be.
Do not use lady's bedstraw if: You are pregnant or breast-feeding.

Are there any interactions with medications?
It is not known if lady's bedstraw interacts with any medicines.
Before taking lady's bedstraw, talk with your healthcare professional if you take any medications.

LAMINARIA

What other names is the product known by?
Brown Algae, Kelp, Kombu, Laminaria digitata, Laminaria japonica, Makombu Thallus, Sea Girdles, Seagirdle Thallus.

What is it?
Laminaria is a plant, a Japanese seaweed. It is used to make medicine.

   Natural Medicines Comprehensive Database Consumer Version   (209) 472-2244

Is it Effective?

The effectiveness ratings for **LAMINARIA** are as follows:

Possibly Ineffective for... Preparation ("ripening") of the cervix in women, such as during childbirth or procedures.
Insufficient Evidence to Rate Effectiveness for... Weight loss, high blood pressure, cancer prevention, heartburn, and other conditions.

How does it work?

Laminaria contains iodide, but it isn't known how it might work.

Are there safety concerns?

Laminaria does not appear to be safe. It contains significant amounts of iodine and might adversely affect the thyroid gland when taken by mouth. Some laminaria products also contain significant amounts of arsenic.

The use of laminaria directly on the cervix during pregnancy or childbirth is unsafe. It can cause serious side effects for both mother and child including infection, rupture of the cervix, and infant death.

Do not use laminaria if: You are pregnant or breast-feeding. • You have problems with your kidneys. It might cause dangerously high potassium levels. • You have thyroid gland disease.

Are there any interactions with medications?

Digoxin (Lanoxin). Laminaria contains large amounts of potassium. Large amounts of potassium can increase the effects and side effects of digoxin (Lanoxin). Do not take laminaria if you are taking digoxin (Lanoxin).
Medications for high blood pressure (ACE inhibitors). Laminaria contains large amounts of potassium. Some medications for high blood pressure can increase potassium levels in the blood. Taking laminaria along with some medications for high blood pressure might cause too much potassium in the blood. Some medications for high blood pressure include captopril (Capoten), enalapril (Vasotec), lisinopril (Prinivil, Zestril), ramipril (Altace), and others.
Potassium supplements. Laminaria contains large amounts of potassium. Taking potassium supplements along with laminaria might cause too much potassium to be in the body. Do not take laminaria if you are taking potassium supplements.
Thyroid hormone. The body naturally produces thyroid hormones. Laminaria might increase how much thyroid hormone the body produces. Taking laminaria along with thyroid hormone pills might increase the effects and side effects of thyroid hormones.
Water pills (Potassium-sparing diuretics). Laminaria contains large amounts of potassium. Some "water pills" can also increase potassium levels in the body. Taking some "water pills" along with laminaria might cause too much potassium to be in the body. Some "water pills" that increase potassium in the body include amiloride (Midamor), spironolactone (Aldactone), triamterene (Dyrenium), and others.

LARCH ARABINOGALACTAN

What other names is the product known by?

AG, Ara-6, Arabinogalactan, Dietary Fiber, Larch, Larch Gum, Larix, Larix dahurica, Larix occidentalis, Mongolian Larch, Mongolian Larchwood, Stractan, Western Larch, Wood Gum, Wood Sugar.

What is it?

Larch arabinogalactan is a carbohydrate produced from the bark of the Larch tree. It is used to make medicine.

Is it Effective?

The effectiveness ratings for **LARCH ARABINOGALACTAN** are as follows:

Insufficient Evidence to Rate Effectiveness for... Common cold, flu, liver disease, earache (otitis media), HIV/AIDS, cancer treatment, dietary fiber supplementation, stimulating the immune system, inflammation, and other uses.

How does it work?

Larch arabinogalactan is a fibrous product. It might increase gut bacteria, such as Lactobacillus, and have other effects that could be beneficial to digestive tract health. There is also information that suggests larch arabinogalactan might stimulate the immune system and help prevent cancer cells in the liver from growing.

Are there safety concerns?

Larch arabinogalactan is possibly safe when used short-term and appropriately for medicinal purposes. It can cause side effects such as bloating and intestinal gas (flatulence).

Medical professionals should consult the Professional Version at www.NaturalDatabase.com.

Do not use larch arabinogalactan if: You are pregnant or breast-feeding. • You are a recipient of an organ transplant. Larch arabinogalactan might increase the risk of organ transplant rejection.

Are there any interactions with medications?
Medications that decrease the immune system (Immunosuppressants). Larch arabinogalactan increases the immune system. By increasing the immune system larch arabinogalactan might decrease the effectiveness of medications that decrease the immune system. Some medications that decrease the immune system include azathioprine (Imuran), basiliximab (Simulect), cyclosporine (Neoral, Sandimmune), daclizumab (Zenapax), muromonab-CD3 (OKT3, Orthoclone OKT3), mycophenolate (CellCept), tacrolimus (FK506, Prograf), sirolimus (Rapamune), prednisone (Deltasone, Orasone), corticosteroids (glucocorticoids), and others.
Medications taken by mouth (Oral drugs). Larch arabinogalactan might absorb substances in the stomach and intestines. Taking larch arabinogalactan along with medications taken by mouth can decrease how much medicine your body absorbs, and decrease the effectiveness of your medication. To prevent this interaction, take larch arabinogalactan at least one hour after medications you take by mouth.

LARCH TURPENTINE

What other names is the product known by?
Larix decidua, Terebinthina Laricina, Terebinthina Veneta, Venetian Turpentine.

What is it?
Larch turpentine is an oily substance from the trunk of a tree.

Is it Effective?
The effectiveness ratings for **LARCH TURPENTINE** are as follows:
Insufficient Evidence to Rate Effectiveness for... Nerve pain, arthritis-like pain, bronchitis, boils, fevers, colds, cough, blood pressure problems, and swelling (inflammation) of the mouth and throat.

How does it work?
When applied to the skin, larch turpentine can increase blood flow and prevent the growth of bacteria.

Are there safety concerns?
Larch turpentine seems safe when used on intact skin. It might be unsafe when taken by mouth, applied to damaged or broken skin, or inhaled. When used improperly, larch turpentine can cause side effects such as allergic skin reactions, kidney problems, nerve system damage, or lung problems.

Do not use larch turpentine if: You are pregnant or breast-feeding. • You have bronchitis. Inhalation of larch turpentine may worsen this condition.

Are there any interactions with medications?
It is not known if larch turpentine interacts with any medicines.
Before taking larch turpentine, talk with your healthcare professional if you take any medications.

LATHYRUS

What other names is the product known by?
Caley Pea, Chickling Vetch, Chick-Pea, Everlasting Pea, Flat-Podded Vetch, Lathyrus cicera, Lathyrus clymenu, Lathyrus hirsutus, Lathyrus incanus, Lathyrus odoratus, Lathyrus pusillus, Lathyrus sativus, Lathyrus sylvestris, Singletary Pea, Spanish Vetchling, Sweet Pea, Wild Pea.

What is it?
Lathyrus is a plant. The seeds are used to make medicine.

Is it Effective?
The effectiveness ratings for **LATHYRUS** are as follows:
Insufficient Evidence to Rate Effectiveness for... Any medical use.

How does it work?
There isn't enough information to know how lathyrus might work for any medical use.

Are there safety concerns?

Lathyrus is unsafe when taken by mouth.

Lathyrus is poisonous to nerves. It can cause muscles to become rigid, muscle spasms, weakness, paralysis of leg muscles, weak heartbeat, decreased breathing, seizures, and death.

Do not use lathyrus if: You are pregnant or breast-feeding.

Are there any interactions with medications?

It is not known if lathyrus interacts with any medicines.
Before taking lathyrus, talk with your healthcare professional if you take any medications.

LAURELWOOD

What other names is the product known by?

Alexandrian-laurel, Alexandrinischer Lorbeer, Borneo-mahogany, Calanolide, Calophyllum inophyllum, Caulophyllum Tree, Indian-laurel, Kamani Punna, Mahogany, Palo de Santa Maria, Oleum Caulophyllum, Palo Maria, Punnanga, Undi.

What is it?

Laurelwood is a plant. The nut and other plant parts are used to make medicine.

Is it Effective?

The effectiveness ratings for **LAURELWOOD** are as follows:
Insufficient Evidence to Rate Effectiveness for...HIV/AIDS, sunburn, rashes, burns, psoriasis, scratches, skin blemishes, acne, skin allergies, bedsores, rosacea, hemorrhoids, infant skin care, leprosy, scabies, gonorrhea, vaginal inflammation, chicken pox, and other uses.

How does it work?

Laurelwood contains compounds that seem to have activity against HIV and tuberculosis. However, there isn't enough evidence to know if laurelwood works for medicinal uses in humans.

Are there safety concerns?

Laurelwood is possibly safe when the laurelwood compound (+)-calanolide is used by HIV-negative individuals. It can cause some side effects including dizziness, oily aftertaste, headache, and nausea. There isn't enough reliable information available about the safety of laurelwood for its other uses.

Do not use laurelwood if: You are pregnant or breast-feeding.

Are there any interactions with medications?

It is not known if laurelwood interacts with any medicines.
Before taking laurelwood, talk with your healthcare professional if you take any medications.

LAURIC ACID

What other names is the product known by?

Coconut Oil Extract, N-dodecanoic Acid, N-alkanoic Acid.

What is it?

Lauric acid is a saturated fat.

Is it Effective?

The effectiveness ratings for **LAURIC ACID** are as follows:
Insufficient Evidence to Rate Effectiveness for... Influenza (the flu), common cold, avian flu, bronchitis, herpes simplex virus, cytomegalovirus, HIV/AIDS, preventing maternal HIV transmission, gonorrhea, human papilloma virus (HPV), candida infections, chlamydia, giardia lamblia, and ringworm.

How does it work?

It is not known how lauric acid might work for any medical use. Some research suggests lauric acid might be a safer fatty acid than trans-fats in food preparations.

CONSUMER VERSION

Are there safety concerns?

Lauric acid is safe in amounts found in foods. The safety of lauric acid when used as a medicine is not known.

Are there any interactions with medications?

It is not known if lauric acid interacts with any medicines.
Before taking lauric acid, talk with your healthcare professional if you take any medications.

LAVENDER

What other names is the product known by?

Alhucema, English Lavender, French Lavender, Garden Lavender, Ostokhoddous, Spanish Lavender, Spike Lavender, True Lavender, Lavandula Angustifolia, Lavandula Officinalis, Lavandula Vera, Lavandula Spica, Lavandula Stoechas, Lavandula Latifolia, Lavandula Dentate, Lavandula Pubescens.

What is it?

Lavender is an herb. The flower and the oil of lavender are used to make medicine.

Is it Effective?

The effectiveness ratings for **LAVENDER** are as follows:
Possibly Effective for... Hair loss in a condition called alopecia areata when applied to the scalp in combination with other oils.
Insufficient Evidence to Rate Effectiveness for... Depression, sleeplessness, agitation, loss of appetite, colic, headache, migraine, toothache, acne, nausea, vomiting, cancer, use as a mosquito repellent and insect repellent, and other conditions.

How does it work?

Lavender contains an oil that seems to have sedating effects and might relax certain muscles.

Are there safety concerns?

Lavender seems to be safe for most adults. When taken by mouth, lavender can cause constipation, headache, and increased appetite. Applying lavender to the skin can sometimes cause irritation.

Do not take lavender if: You are pregnant or breast-feeding.

Are there any interactions with medications?

Chloral Hydrate. Chloral hydrate causes sleepiness and drowsiness. Lavender seems to increase the effects of chloral hydrate. Taking lavender along with chloral hydrate might cause too much sleepiness.
Sedative medications (Barbiturates). Lavender might cause sleepiness and drowsiness. Medications that cause sleepiness are called sedatives. Taking lavender along with sedative medications might cause too much sleepiness. Some sedative medications include amobarbital (Amytal), butabarbital (Butisol), mephobarbital (Mebaral), pentobarbital (Nembutal), phenobarbital (Luminal), secobarbital (Seconal), and others.
Sedative medications (CNS depressants). Lavender might cause sleepiness and drowsiness. Medications that cause sleepiness are called sedatives. Taking lavender along with sedative medications might cause too much sleepiness. Some sedative medications include clonazepam (Klonopin), lorazepam (Ativan), phenobarbital (Donnatal), zolpidem (Ambien), and others.

LAVENDER COTTON

What other names is the product known by?

Santolina, Santolina chamaecyparissus.

What is it?

Lavender cotton is a plant. The leaves, stems, flowers, and root bark are used to make medicine.

Is it Effective?

The effectiveness ratings for **LAVENDER COTTON** are as follows:
Insufficient Evidence to Rate Effectiveness for... Digestive disorders, premenstrual syndrome (PMS), worm infestations, jaundice, and other conditions.

How does it work?

There isn't enough information available to know how lavender cotton works.

  Natural Medicines Comprehensive Database Consumer Version (209) 472-2244

Are there safety concerns?

There isn't enough information available to know if lavender cotton is safe. It can cause an allergic reaction in people sensitive to ragweed, daisies, and many other herbs.

Do not use lavender cotton if: You are pregnant or breast-feeding. • You are allergic to marigolds, daisies, or any related herbs.

Are there any interactions with medications?

It is not known if lavender cotton interacts with any medicines.
Before taking lavender cotton, talk with your healthcare professional if you take any medications.

LECITHIN

What other names is the product known by?

Egg Lecithin, Ovolecithin, Soya Lecithin, Soybean Lecithin, Vegilecithin, Vitellin.

What is it?

Lecithin is a fat that is essential in the cells of our body. It can be found in many foods, including soybeans and egg yolks. People use it for medicine.

Is it Effective?

The effectiveness ratings for **LECITHIN** are as follows:
Likely Effective for... Skin inflammation and dry skin, when applied directly to the skin.
Possibly Effective for... Liver disease.
Possibly Ineffective for... Gallbladder disease • High cholesterol.
Likely Ineffective for... Problems with memory such as Dementia and Alzheimer's disease • Movement disorders (extrapyramidal disorders).
Insufficient Evidence to Rate Effectiveness for... Manic-depressive disorder, anxiety, eczema, and other uses.

How does it work?

Lecithin is converted into acetylcholine, a substance that transmits nerve impulses.

Are there safety concerns?

Lecithin seems to be safe for most people. It can cause some side effects including diarrhea, nausea, abdominal pain, or fullness.

Do not use lecithin if: You are pregnant or breast-feeding.

Are there any interactions with medications?

It is not known if lecithin interacts with any medicines.
Before taking lecithin, talk with your healthcare professional if you take any medications.

LEMON

What other names is the product known by?

Citrus limon, Citrus limonum, Limon, Nimbaka, Nimbuka.

What is it?

Lemon is a plant. The fruit and peel are used to make medicine.

Is it Effective?

The effectiveness ratings for **LEMON** are as follows:
Insufficient Evidence to Rate Effectiveness for... Treating scurvy (as a source of vitamin C), increasing resistance against disease, colds, decreasing swelling, and increasing urine.

How does it work?

It is not known how lemon might work for medicinal uses.

Medical professionals should consult the Professional Version at www.NaturalDatabase.com.

Are there safety concerns?

Lemon may be safe when used for medicinal purposes in amounts similar to what is in food. The side effects of higher amounts of lemon are not known.

Do not use lemon in amounts higher than those typically found in foods if: You are pregnant or breast-feeding.

Are there any interactions with medications?

It is not known if lemon interacts with any medicines.
Before taking lemon, talk with your healthcare professional if you take any medications.

LEMON BALM

What other names is the product known by?

Balm, Cure-All, Dropsy Plant, Honey Plant, Melissa, Melissa officinalis, Melissae folium, Melissenblatt, Sweet Balm, Sweet Mary.

What is it?

Lemon balm is a plant. The leaves are used to make medicine.

Is it Effective?

The effectiveness ratings for **LEMON BALM** are as follows:
Possibly Effective for... Alzheimer's disease • Cold sores • Improving sleep, when taken with valerian • Upset stomach (dyspepsia), when a combination of lemon balm and several other herbs is used.
Insufficient Evidence to Rate Effectiveness for... Loss of appetite, stomach and intestinal discomfort with bloating and gas, anxiety, sleeping disorders, spasms, a thyroid condition called Graves' disease, promoting menstrual flow, female discomforts, cramps, headache, toothache, sores, tumors, insect bites, nervous stomach, hysteria, attention deficit-hyperactivity disorder (ADHD), and other conditions.

How does it work?

Lemon balm contains chemicals that seem to have a sedative, calming effect. It might also reduce the growth of some viruses.

Are there safety concerns?

Lemon balm seems to be safe for most people. It can cause nausea, vomiting, abdominal pain, dizziness, and wheezing.

Do not use lemon balm if: You are pregnant or breast-feeding.

Are there any interactions with medications?

Sedative medications (CNS depressants). Lemon balm might cause sleepiness and drowsiness. Medications that cause sleepiness are called sedatives. Taking lemon balm along with sedative medications might cause too much sleepiness. Some sedative medications include clonazepam (Klonopin), lorazepam (Ativan), Phenobarbital (Donnatal), zolpidem (Ambien), and others.

LEMON EUCALYPTUS

What other names is the product known by?

Citron-Scent Gum, Corymbia Citriodora, Eucalyptus Citriodora, Lemon Eucalyptus Oil, Lemon Scented Gum, Oil of Lemon Eucalyptus, OLE, P-menthane Diol, P-menthane-3,8-diol, Para-menthane-3,8-diol, PMD, Quwenling, Spotted Gum, Wild Eucalyptus Citriodora.

What is it?

Lemon eucalyptus is a tree. Oil from the tree leaves is used as a medicine and insect repellent.

Is it Effective?

The effectiveness ratings for **LEMON EUCALYPTUS** are as follows:
Likely Effective for... Preventing mosquito bites when applied to the skin. Lemon eucalyptus oil is an ingredient in some commercial mosquito repellents. It seems to be comparable to other mosquito repellents including some products that contain DEET.
Possibly Effective for... Preventing tick bites.
Insufficient Evidence to Rate Effectiveness for..."Toenail fungus," joint pain, arthritis, and other conditions.

How does it work?
Lemon eucalyptus oil contains a chemical that repels mosquitoes and kills fungus.

Are there safety concerns?
Lemon eucalyptus oil is safe for most adults when applied to the skin as a mosquito repellent. Some people might have a skin reaction to the oil.

Some chest rubs for congestion (Vicks VapoRub) contain lemon eucalyptus oil. These products also contain camphor which can cause seizures and death if eaten.

Do not use lemon eucalyptus if: You are pregnant or breast-feeding.

Are there any interactions with medications?
It is not known if lemon eucalyptus interacts with any medicines.
Before taking lemon eucalyptus, talk with your healthcare professional if you take any medications.

LEMON VERBENA

What other names is the product known by?
Aloysia citrodora, Aloysia triphylla, Herb Louisa, Lemon-Scented Verbena, Lippia citrodora, Lippia triphylla, Louisa, Verbena citrodora, Verbena triphylla, Verveine citronelle, Zappania citrodora.

What is it?
Lemon verbena is a plant. The leaves and the flowering tops are used to make medicine.

Is it Effective?
The effectiveness ratings for **LEMON VERBENA** are as follows:
Insufficient Evidence to Rate Effectiveness for... Digestive disorders, anxiety, sleeplessness (insomnia), asthma, cold, fever, gas (flatulence), colic, diarrhea, indigestion, hemorrhoids, varicose veins, skin conditions, and constipation.

How does it work?
Lemon verbena contains a substance that might kill mites and bacteria.

Are there safety concerns?
Lemon verbena is safe for most people when consumed in amounts found in alcoholic beverages. It also seems to be safe when taken in appropriate amounts as a medicine. It can cause skin irritation (dermatitis) in some people.

Do not use lemon verbena if: You are pregnant or breast-feeding. • You have kidney disease. Large amounts of lemon verbena may irritate the kidneys.

Are there any interactions with medications?
It is not known if lemon verbena interacts with any medicines.
Before taking lemon verbena, talk with your healthcare professional if you take any medications.

LEMONGRASS

What other names is the product known by?
Andropogon citrates, British Indian Lemongrass, Capim-Cidrao, Ceylon Citronella Grass, Citronella, Cochin Lemongrass, Cymbopogon citratus, Cymbopogon flexuosus, Cymbopogon nardis, East Indian Lemongrass, Fever Grass, Guatemala Lemongrass, Lemon Grass, Madagascar Lemongrass, West Indian Lemongrass.

What is it?
Lemongrass is a plant. The leaves and the oil are used to make medicine.

Is it Effective?
The effectiveness ratings for **LEMONGRASS** are as follows:
Insufficient Evidence to Rate Effectiveness for... Stomach and intestinal spasms, stomach ache, high blood pressure, convulsions, pain, vomiting, cough, rheumatism, fever, common cold, exhaustion, headache, use as an antiseptic and astringent, and other uses.

How does it work?

Lemongrass might help prevent the growth of some bacteria and yeast. Lemongrass also contains substances that are thought to relieve pain, reduce fever, stimulate the uterus and menstrual flow, and have antioxidant properties.

Are there safety concerns?

Lemongrass seems to be safe for most people when used in amounts found in foods. It is possibly safe when used for medicinal purposes short term. However, there have been some toxic side effects such as lung problems after inhaling lemongrass and a fatal poisoning after a child swallowed a lemongrass oil-based insect repellent.

Do not use lemongrass if: You are pregnant or breast-feeding.

Are there any interactions with medications?

It is not known if lemongrass interacts with any medicines.
Before taking lemongrass, talk with your healthcare professional if you take any medications.

LENTINAN

What other names is the product known by?

Lenticus edodes, Lentinan edodes, Lentinula edodes, Tricholomopsis edodes.

What is it?

Lentinan is a substance that comes from the shiitake mushroom.

Is it Effective?

The effectiveness ratings for **LENTINAN** are as follows:
Possibly Effective for... Treatment of HIV infection, when administered with the medication didanosine (ddI, Videx) during treatment.
Possibly Ineffective for... Treating breast cancer, stomach cancer, and prostate cancer when administered with other medications during treatment.

How does it work?

Lentinan might increase the effects of certain antiviral and chemotherapy medications. It might also increase the activity of some immune cells.

Are there safety concerns?

There isn't enough information available to know if lentinan is safe. It might cause a decrease in the number of platelets in the blood (thrombocytopenia).

Do not use lentinan if: You are pregnant or breast-feeding.

Are there any interactions with medications?

It is not known if lentinan interacts with any medicines.
Before taking lentinan, talk with your healthcare professional if you take any medications.

LESSER CELANDINE

What other names is the product known by?

Ficaria, Figwort, Pilewort, Ranunculus, Ranunculus ficaria, Smallwort.

What is it?

Lesser celandine is a plant. The above ground parts are used to make medicine. Don't confuse it with greater celandine (Chelidonium majus). Also, don't confuse it with Scrophularia nodosa which is also referred to as figwort or amaranth and bulbous buttercup which are also known as pilewort.

Is it Effective?

The effectiveness ratings for **LESSER CELANDINE** are as follows:
Insufficient Evidence to Rate Effectiveness for... Bleeding wounds and gums, swollen joints, warts, scratches, scurvy, and hemorrhoids.

How does it work?

Lesser celandine contains vitamin C. It also has a drying effect, soothes mucous membranes, and contains substances that cause skin irritation. Some researchers think that lesser celandine might kill or prevent the growth of bacteria and fungus and treat hemorrhoids.

Are there safety concerns?

Lesser celandine is unsafe when used on skin or when taken by mouth. It can cause side effects such as severe irritation of the stomach and intestines; diarrhea; irritation of the urinary tract, mucous membrane, and skin; and skin blisters. Liver damage with the use of lesser celandine has been reported.

Do not use lesser celandine if: You are pregnant or breast-feeding. • You have an infectious or inflammatory gastrointestinal disorder.

Are there any interactions with medications?

It is not known if lesser celandine interacts with any medicines.
Before taking lesser celandine, talk with your healthcare professional if you take any medications.

LEVANT BERRY

What other names is the product known by?

Anamirta cocculus, Anamirta paniculata, Cocculus, Cocculus indicus, Cocculus lacunosus, Cocculus suberosus, Coculus fructus, Fish Berries, Fish Killer, Hockle Elderberry, Indian Berry, Levant Nut, Louseberry, Menispermum cocculus, Menispermum lacunosum, Poisonberry.

What is it?

Levant berry is a fruit. The dried fruit and seed are used to make medicine.

Is it Effective?

The effectiveness ratings for **LEVANT BERRY** are as follows:
Insufficient Evidence to Rate Effectiveness for... Abnormal movements of the eyeball, dizziness, scabies, lice, epilepsy, night sweats, use as a stimulant, and malaria.

How does it work?

Levant berry contains a chemical that stimulates the central nervous system, irritates the stomach and intestines, and stimulates the brain causing changes in breathing. It also slows heart rate and increases blood pressure.

Are there safety concerns?

Levant berry may be unsafe when put on the skin. It is unsafe and poisonous when taken by mouth.

Accidentally taking levant berry requires immediate medical attention. It can cause side effects such as headache, dizziness, nausea, coordination problems, depression, spasms, twitching, increased saliva, vomiting, increased emptying of the bowels, rapid breathing, drowsiness, irregular heartbeat, decreased heart rate, unconsciousness, and death.

Do not use levant berry if: You are pregnant or breast-feeding.

Are there any interactions with medications?

It is not known if levant berry interacts with any medicines.
Before taking levant berry, talk with your healthcare professional if you take any medications.

LICORICE

What other names is the product known by?

Alcacuz, Chinese Licorice, Gan Cao, Gan Zao, Glycyrrhiza, Glycyrrhiza glabra, Glycyrrhiza glabra typica, Glycyrrhiza glabra violacea, Glycyrrhiza glabra glandulifera, Glycyrrhiza uralensis, Isoflavone, Lakritze, Licorice Root, Liquiritiae radix, Liquirizia, Mulhathi, Jethi-Madh, Orozuz, Phytoestrogen, Reglisse, Regliz, Russian Licorice, Spanish Licorice, Subholz, and Sweet Root, Yashtimadhu, Yashti-Madhu, Yashti-Madhuka, Zhi Gan Cao.

What is it?

Licorice is a plant. The root is used to make medicine.

Is it Effective?

The effectiveness ratings for **LICORICE** are as follows:

Possibly Effective for... Upset stomach (dyspepsia), when a combination of licorice and several other herbs is used.
Insufficient Evidence to Rate Effectiveness for... Muscle cramps, arthritis, lupus, infections, hepatitis, infertility, cough, stomach ulcers, prostate cancer, weight loss, atopic dermatitis (eczema), chronic fatigue syndrome (CFS), and other conditions.

How does it work?

The chemicals contained in licorice are thought to decrease swelling, thin mucus secretions, decrease cough and increase the chemicals in our body that heal ulcers.

Are there safety concerns?

Licorice is safe for most people when consumed in amounts found in foods. It seems to also be safe when consumed in larger amounts, short-term. Don't use licorice for more than four weeks without consulting your healthcare professional. Licorice can cause some side effects including absence of a menstrual period in women, increased blood pressure, headache, water and sodium retention, decreased potassium in the blood, and decreased sexual function and libido in men.

Do not take licorice if: You are pregnant or breast-feeding. • You have high blood pressure. • You have heart problems. • You have breast, uterine, or ovarian cancer. • You have endometriosis or uterine fibroids. • You have been told you have low potassium levels.

Are there any interactions with medications?

Digoxin (Lanoxin). Large amounts of licorice can decrease potassium levels in the body. Low potassium levels can increase the side effects of digoxin (Lanoxin).

Estrogens. Licorice seems to change hormone levels in the body. Taking licorice along with estrogen pills might decrease the effects of estrogen pills. Some estrogen pills include conjugated equine estrogens (Premarin), ethinyl estradiol, estradiol, and others.

Ethacrynic Acid (Edecrin). Licorice can cause the body to get rid of potassium. Ethacrynic acid (Edecrin) can also cause the body to get rid of potassium. Taking licorice and ethacrynic acid (Edecrin) together might cause potassium to become too low.

Furosemide (Lasix). Licorice can cause the body to get rid of potassium. Furosemide (Lasix) can also cause the body to get rid of potassium. Taking licorice and furosemide together might cause the potassium levels in your body to go too low.

Medications for high blood pressure (Antihypertensive drugs). Large amounts of licorice seem to increase blood pressure. By increasing blood pressure licorice might decrease the effectiveness of medications for high blood pressure. Some medications for high blood pressure include captopril (Capoten), enalapril (Vasotec), losartan (Cozaar), valsartan (Diovan), diltiazem (Cardizem), amlodipine (Norvasc), hydrochlorothiazide (HydroDiuril), furosemide (Lasix), and many others.

Medications for inflammation (Corticosteroids). Some medications for inflammation can decrease potassium in the body. Licorice might also decrease potassium in the body. Taking licorice along with some medications for inflammation might decrease potassium in the body too much. Some medications for inflammation include dexamethasone (Decadron), hydrocortisone (Cortef), methylprednisolone (Medrol), prednisone (Deltasone), and others.

Medications changed by the liver (Cytochrome P450 2B6 (CYP2B6) substrates). Some medications are changed and broken down by the liver. Licorice might decrease how quickly the liver breaks down some medications. Taking licorice along with some medications that are broken down by the liver can increase the effects and side effects of some medications. Before taking licorice talk to your healthcare provider if you take any medications that are changed by the liver. Some of these medications changed by the liver include ketamine (Ketalar), phenobarbital, orphenadrine (Norflex), secobarbital (Seconal), dexamethasone (Decadron), and others.

Medications changed by the liver (Cytochrome P450 3A4 (CYP3A4) substrates). Some medications are changed and broken down by the liver. Licorice might decrease how quickly the liver breaks down some medications. Taking licorice along with some medications that are broken down by the liver can increase the effects and side effects of some medications. Before taking licorice, talk to your healthcare provider if you are taking any medications that are changed by the liver. Some medications changed by the liver include lovastatin (Mevacor), ketoconazole (Nizoral), itraconazole (Sporanox), fexofenadine (Allegra), triazolam (Halcion), and many others.

Water pills (Diuretic drugs). Large amounts of licorice can decrease potassium levels in the body. "Water pills" can also decrease potassium in the body. Taking licorice along with "water pills" might decrease potassium in the body too much. Some "water pills" that can deplete potassium include chlorothiazide (Diuril), chlorthalidone (Thalitone), furosemide (Lasix), hydrochlorothiazide (HCTZ, HydroDiuril, Microzide), and others.

     Natural Medicines Comprehensive Database Consumer Version   (209) 472-2244

LILY-OF-THE-VALLEY

What other names is the product known by?
Constancy, Convallaria, Convallaria herba, Convallaria majalis, Convall-Lily, Jacob's Ladder, Ladder-To-Heaven, Lily, Lily of the Valley, May Bells, May Lily, Muguet, Our Lady's Tears.

What is it?
Lily-of-the-valley is a plant. The root, rhizome, and dried flower tips are used to make medicine.

Is it Effective?
The effectiveness ratings for **LILY-OF-THE-VALLEY** are as follows:
Insufficient Evidence to Rate Effectiveness for... Heart arrhythmias and other heart problems, urinary tract infections (UTIs), kidney stones, weak contractions in labor, epilepsy, fluid retention, strokes, paralysis, infection of eye (conjunctivitis), and leprosy.

How does it work?
Lily-of-the-valley contains substances that have activity on the heart muscle. It can affect contractions, heart rate, and excitability.

Are there safety concerns?
Lily-of-the-valley seems safe for most people when used under proper medical supervision. It is unsafe when used for self-medication. Accidental ingestion of lily-of-the-valley requires prompt medical attention. It can cause side effects such as nausea, vomiting, abnormal heart rhythm, headache, decreased consciousness and responsiveness, and visual color disturbances.

Do not use lily-of-the-valley if: You are pregnant or breast-feeding. • You have heart disease, without proper medical supervision. • You have a deficiency in potassium.

Are there any interactions with medications?
Antibiotics (Macrolide antibiotics). Lily-of-the-valley can affect the heart. Some antibiotics might increase how much lily-of-the-valley the body absorbs. Taking lily-of-the-valley along with some antibiotics might increase the effects and side effects of lily-of-the-valley. Some antibiotics called macrolide antibiotics include erythromycin, azithromycin, and clarithromycin.
Antibiotics (Tetracycline antibiotics). Taking some antibiotics called tetracycline antibiotics along with lily-of-the-valley might increase the chance of side effects from lily-of-the-valley. Some tetracycline antibiotics include demeclocycline (Declomycin), minocycline (Minocin), and tetracycline (Achromycin).
Calcium supplements. Lily-of-the-valley can stimulate the heart. Calcium might also affect the heart. Taking lily-of-the-valley along with calcium might cause the heart to be too stimulated. Do not take lily-of-the-valley along with calcium supplements.
Digoxin (Lanoxin). Digoxin (Lanoxin) helps the heart beat more strongly. Lily-of-the-valley also seems to affect the heart. Taking lily-of-the-valley along with digoxin can increase the effects of digoxin and increase the risk of side effects. Do not take lily-of-the-valley if you are taking digoxin (Lanoxin) without talking to your healthcare professional.
Medications for inflammation (Corticosteroids). Lily-of-the-valley might affect the heart. Some medications for inflammation can decrease potassium in the body. Low potassium levels can also affect the heart and increase the risk of side effects from lily-of-the-valley. Some medications for inflammation include dexamethasone (Decadron), hydrocortisone (Cortef), methylprednisolone (Medrol), prednisone (Deltasone), and others.
Quinine. Lily-of-the-valley can affect the heart. Quinine can also affect the heart. Taking quinine along with lily-of-the-valley might cause serious heart problems.
Stimulant laxatives. Lily-of-the-valley can affect the heart. The heart uses potassium. Laxatives called stimulant laxatives can decrease potassium levels in the body. Low potassium levels can increase the chance of side effects from lily-of-the-valley. Some stimulant laxatives include bisacodyl (Correctol, Dulcolax), cascara, castor oil (Purge), senna (Senokot), and others.
Water pills (Diuretic drugs). Lily-of-the-valley might affect the heart. "Water pills" can decrease potassium in the body. Low potassium levels can also affect the heart and increase the risk of side effects from lily-of-the-valley. Some "water pills" that can deplete potassium include chlorothiazide (Diuril), chlorthalidone (Thalitone), furosemide (Lasix), hydrochlorothiazide (HCTZ, HydroDiuril, Microzide), and others.

Medical professionals should consult the Professional Version at www.NaturalDatabase.com.

LIME

What other names is the product known by?

Adam's Apple, Bara Nimbu, Bijapura, Citrus Acida, Citrus aurantifolia, Citrus Lima, Citrus Limetta, Citrus Medica, Italian Limetta, Limette, Limonia aurantiifolia, Turanj.

What is it?

Lime is a citrus fruit. The fruit, peel, and oil are used to make medicine.

Is it Effective?

The effectiveness ratings for **LIME** are as follows:

Insufficient Evidence to Rate Effectiveness for... Upset stomach, preventing skin infections, use as a source of vitamin C, and other conditions.

How does it work?

There isn't enough information to know how lime works.

Are there safety concerns?

Lime is safe for most adults when used in amounts found in foods.

Some people are sensitive to lime oil when it is applied directly to the skin. Lime oil can cause the skin to be very sensitive to the sunlight, and might be unsafe when applied directly to the skin. Wear sunblock and protective clothing outside, especially if you are light-skinned.

Do not use lime in medicinal amounts if: You are pregnant or breast-feeding.

Are there any interactions with medications?

Medications that increase sensitivity to sunlight (Photosensitizing drugs). Some medications can increase sensitivity to sunlight. Lime oil might also increase your sensitivity to sunlight. Using lime oil along with medications that increase sensitivity to sunlight could increase the chances of sunburn, and blistering or rashes on areas of skin exposed to sunlight. Be sure to wear sunblock and protective clothing when spending time in the sun. Some drugs that cause photosensitivity include amitriptyline (Elavil), Ciprofloxacin (Cipro), norfloxacin (Noroxin), lomefloxacin (Maxaquin), ofloxacin (Floxin), levofloxacin (Levaquin), sparfloxacin (Zagam), gatifloxacin (Tequin), moxifloxacin (Avelox), trimethoprim/sulfamethoxazole (Septra), tetracycline, methoxsalen (8-methoxypsoralen, 8-MOP, Oxsoralen), and Trioxsalen (Trisoralen).

Medications changed by the liver (Cytochrome P450 3A4 (CYP3A4) substrates). Some medications are changed and broken down by the liver. Lime juice might decrease how quickly the liver breaks down some medications. Drinking lime juice while taking some medications that are broken down by the liver can increase the effects and side effects of these medications. Before taking lime, talk to your healthcare provider if you are taking any medications that are changed by the liver. Some medications changed by the liver include lovastatin (Mevacor), ketoconazole (Nizoral), itraconazole (Sporanox), fexofenadine (Allegra), triazolam (Halcion), and many others.

LIMONENE

What other names is the product known by?

Alpha-Limonene; Dipentene, D-Limonene, L-Limonene, R-Limonene, S-Limonene.

What is it?

Limonene is a chemical found in the peels of citrus fruits and in other plants. It is used to make medicine.

Is it Effective?

The effectiveness ratings for **LIMONENE** are as follows:
Insufficient Evidence to Rate Effectiveness for... Cancer prevention and treatment, weight loss, and bronchitis.

How does it work?

Limonene may block cancer forming chemicals and kill cancer cells. But more research is needed to know if this occurs in humans.

Are there safety concerns?

Limonene appears to be safe for most people when taken by mouth in medicinal amounts for up to one year.
Do not use limonene in medicinal amounts if: You are pregnant or breast-feeding.

Are there any interactions with medications?

Medications that increase the break down of other medications by the liver (Cytochrome P450 2C19 (CYP2C19) inducers). Limonene might be broken down by the liver. Taking limonene along with medications that increase the break down of limonene in the liver might decrease the effects of limonene. Some medications that might increase the breakdown of limonene in the liver include carbamazepine (Tegretol), prednisone (Deltasone), and rifampin (Rifadin, Rimactane).

Medications that decrease the break down of other medications by the liver (Cytochrome P450 2C19 (CYP2C19) inhibitors). Limonene might be broken down by the liver. Taking limonene along with medications that decrease the break down of limonene in the liver might increase the effects and side effects of limonene. Some medications that might decrease the breakdown of limonene in the liver include cimetidine (Tagamet), fluvoxamine (Luvox), omeprazole (Prilosec); ticlopidine (Ticlid), topiramate (Topamax), and others.

Medications changed by the liver (Cytochrome P450 2C9 (CYP2C9) substrates). Some medications are changed and broken down by the liver. Limonene might increase how quickly the liver breaks down some medications. Taking limonene along with some medications that are changed by the liver can lead to a variety of effects and side effects. Before taking limonene talk to your healthcare provider if you take any medications that are changed by the liver. Some of these medications that are changed by the liver include diclofenac (Cataflam, Voltaren), ibuprofen (Motrin), meloxicam (Mobic), and piroxicam (Feldene), amitriptyline (Elavil), warfarin (Coumadin), glipizide (Glucotrol), losartan (Cozaar), and others.

Medications that increase the break down of other medications by the liver (Cytochrome P450 2C9 (CYP2C9) inducers). Limonene might be broken down by the liver. Taking limonene along with medications that increase the break down of limonene in the liver might decrease the effects of limonene. Some medications that might increase the breakdown of limonene in the liver include rifampin (Rifadin, Rimactane) and secobarbital (Seconal).

Medications that decrease the break down of other medications by the liver (Cytochrome P450 2C9 (CYP2C9) inhibitors). Limonene might be broken down by the liver. Taking limonene along with medications that decrease the break down of limonene in the liver might increase the effects and side effects of limonene. Some medications that might decrease the breakdown of limonene in the liver include amiodarone (Cordarone), fluconazole (Diflucan), lovastatin (Mevacor), paroxetine (Paxil), zafirlukast (Accolate), and many others.

LINDEN

What other names is the product known by?

Basswood, European Linden, Hungarian Silver Linden, Lime Blossom, Lime Flower, Lime Tree, Linden Charcoal, Linden Dried Flower, Linden Dried Leaf, Linden Dried Sapwood, Linden Flower, Linden Leaf, Linden Sapwood, Linden Wood, Silver Lime, Silver linden, Tilia argentea, Tilia cordata, Tilia europaea, Tiliae flos, Tiliae folium, Tilia grandifolia, Tiliae lignum, Tilia parvifolia, Tilia platyphyllos, Tilia rubra, Tilia tomentosa, Tilia ulmifolia, Tilia vulgaris.

What is it?

Linden is a tree. The dried flower, leaves, and wood are used for medicine.

Is it Effective?

The effectiveness ratings for **LINDEN** are as follows:
Insufficient Evidence to Rate Effectiveness for... Sleep disorders, headaches including migraines, incontinence, excessive bleeding (hemorrhage), itchy skin, painful swelling of joints (rheumatism), bronchitis, cough, spasms, fluid retention, inducing sweating, and other conditions.

How does it work?

Linden seems to reduce the amount of mucus produced and relieve anxiety. But, more information is needed.

Are there safety concerns?

Linden might be safe when taken by mouth. When used on the skin, linden might cause itching.

Do not take linden if: You are pregnant or breast-feeding. • You have heart trouble.

Are there any interactions with medications?

It is not known if linden interacts with any medicines.
Before taking linden, talk with your healthcare professional if you take any medications.

Medical professionals should consult the Professional Version at www.NaturalDatabase.com.

LIPASE

What other names is the product known by?
Triacylglycerol lipase.

What is it?
Lipase is a digestive enzyme that is found in many plants, animals, bacteria, and molds. People use lipase as a medicine.

Is it Effective?
The effectiveness ratings for **LIPASE** are as follows:
Effective for... Insufficient production of digestive enzymes by the pancreas.
Insufficient Evidence to Rate Effectiveness for... Celiac disease (allergy to gluten in wheat products), Crohn's disease, indigestion, and heartburn.

How does it work?
Lipase seems to work by breaking down fat into smaller pieces making digestion easier.

Are there safety concerns?
Lipase seems to be safe for most people. It can cause some side effects such as nausea, cramping, and diarrhea.

Do not take lipase if: You are pregnant or breast-feeding. • You have cystic fibrosis.

Are there any interactions with medications?
It is not known if lipase interacts with any medicines.
Before taking lipase, talk with your healthcare professional if you take any medications.

LITHIUM

What other names is the product known by?
Lithium Carbonate, Lithium Citrate, Lithium Orotate.

What is it?
Lithium is an element. People use it for medicine.

Is it Effective?
The effectiveness ratings for **LITHIUM** are as follows:
Effective for... Bipolar disorder (manic-depressive disorder).
Likely Effective for... Depression.
Possibly Effective for... Schizophrenia and related mental disorders • Impulsive aggressive behavior • Aggression associated with attention-deficit hyperactivity disorder (ADHD).
Insufficient Evidence to Rate Effectiveness for... Alcohol dependence, blood cell disorders, and other conditions.

How does it work?
Exactly how lithium works is unknown, but it might help mental disorders by increasing the activity of chemical messengers in the brain.

Are there safety concerns?
Lithium seems to be safe for most people when taken orally and appropriately with careful monitoring by a healthcare giver. Lithium can cause nausea, diarrhea, dizziness, muscle weakness, fatigue, and a dazed feeling. These adverse effects often improve with continued use. Fine tremor, frequent urination, and thirst can occur and may persist with continued use. Weight gain and swelling from excess fluid can also occur. Lithium can also cause or make worse skin disorders such as acne, psoriasis, and rashes. The amount of lithium in the body must be carefully controlled and is checked by blood tests.

Do not take lithium without a healthcare giver's advice if: You are pregnant or breast-feeding. • You have thyroid disease. • You have heart disease. • You have kidney disease.

Are there any interactions with medications?
Dextromethorphan (Robitussin DM, and others). Lithium can affect a brain chemical called serotonin. Dextromethorphan (Robitussin DM, others) can also affect serotonin. Taking lithium along with dextromethorphan (Robitussin DM, others) might cause too much serotonin in the brain and serious side effects including heart

problems, shivering, and anxiety could result. Do not take lithium if you are taking dextromethorphan (Robitussin DM, and others).

Medications for high blood pressure (ACE inhibitors). Some medications for high blood pressure can increase lithium levels in the body. Taking lithium along with some medications for high blood pressure might cause too much lithium to be in the body. Some medications for high blood pressure include captopril (Capoten), enalapril (Vasotec), lisinopril (Prinivil, Zestril), ramipril (Altace), and others.

Medications for high blood pressure (Calcium channel blockers). Lithium is commonly used to help fix chemical imbalances in the brain. Some medications for high blood pressure might increase the side effects of lithium, and decrease the amount of lithium in the body. Some medications for high blood pressure include nifedipine (Adalat, Procardia), verapamil (Calan, Isoptin, Verelan), diltiazem (Cardizem), isradipine (DynaCirc), felodipine (Plendil), amlodipine (Norvasc), and others.

Medications for depression (Antidepressant drugs). Lithium increases a brain chemical called serotonin. Some medications for depression also increase the brain chemical serotonin. Taking lithium along with these medications for depression might increase serotonin too much and cause serious side effects including heart problems, shivering, and anxiety. Do not take lithium if you are taking medications for depression. Some of these medications for depression include fluoxetine (Prozac), paroxetine (Paxil), sertraline (Zoloft), amitriptyline (Elavil), clomipramine (Anafranil), imipramine (Tofranil), and others.

Medications for depression (MAOIs). Lithium increases a chemical in the brain. This chemical is called serotonin. Some medications used for depression also increase serotonin. Taking lithium with these medications used for depression might cause there to be too much serotonin. This could cause serious side effects including heart problems, shivering, and anxiety. Some of these medications used for depression include phenelzine (Nardil), tranylcypromine (Parnate), and others.

Medications used to prevent seizures (Anticonvulsants). Medications used to prevent seizures affect chemicals in the brain. Lithium is commonly used to help fix chemical imbalances in the brain. Taking lithium along with some medications used for seizures might increase the side effects of lithium. Some medications used to prevent seizures include phenobarbital, primidone (Mysoline), valproic acid (Depakene), gabapentin (Neurontin), carbamazepine (Tegretol), phenytoin (Dilantin), and others.

Meperidine (Demerol). Lithium increases a chemical in the brain called serotonin. Meperidine (Demerol) can also increase serotonin in the brain. Taking lithium along with meperidine (Demerol) might cause too much serotonin in the brain and serious side effects including heart problems, shivering, and anxiety.

Methyldopa (Aldomet). Taking methyldopa might increase the effects and side effects of lithium. Do not take lithium if you are taking methyldopa unless prescribed by your healthcare professional.

Methylxanthines. Taking methylxanthines can increase how quickly the body gets rid of lithium. This could decrease how well lithium works. Methylxanthines include aminophylline, caffeine, and theophylline.

Muscle relaxants. Lithium might increase how long muscle relaxants work. Taking lithium along with muscle relaxants might increase the effects and side effects of muscle relaxants. Some of these muscle relaxants include carisoprodol (Soma), pipecuronium (Arduan), orphenadrine (Banflex, Disipal), cyclobenzaprine, gallamine (Flaxedil), atracurium (Tracrium), pancuronium (Pavulon), succinylcholine (Anectine), and others.

NSAIDs (Nonsteroidal anti-inflammatory drugs). NSAIDs are anti-inflammatory medications used for decreasing pain and swelling. NSAIDs might increase lithium levels in the body. Taking lithium along with NSAIDs might increase the risk of lithium side effects. Avoid taking lithium supplements and NSAIDs at the same time. Some NSAIDs include ibuprofen (Advil, Motrin, Nuprin, others), indomethacin (Indocin), naproxen (Aleve, Anaprox, Naprelan, Naprosyn), piroxicam (Feldene), aspirin, and others.

Pentazocine (Talwin). Lithium increases a brain chemical called serotonin. Pentazocine (Talwin) also increases serotonin. Taking lithium along with pentazocine (Talwin) might cause too much serotonin in the body. Taking lithium along with pentazocine (Talwin) might cause serious side effects including heart problems, shivering, and anxiety. Do not take lithium supplements if you are taking pentazocine (Talwin).

Phenothiazines. Taking phenothiazines along with lithium might decrease the effectiveness of lithium. Lithium might also decrease the effectiveness of phenothiazines. Some phenothiazines include chlorpromazine (Thorazine), fluphenazine (Prolixin), trifluoperazine (Stelazine), thioridazine (Mellaril), and others.

Tramadol (Ultram). Tramadol (Ultram) can affect a chemical in the brain called serotonin. Lithium can also affect serotonin. Taking lithium along with tramadol (Ultram) might cause too much serotonin in the brain causing confusion, shivering, stiff muscles and other side effects.

Water pills (Loop diuretics). Some "water pills" can increase how much sodium the body gets rid of in the urine. Decreasing sodium in the body can increase lithium levels in the body and increase the effects and side effects of lithium.

Water pills (Thiazide diuretics). Taking lithium with some "water pills" can increase the amount of lithium in the body. This can cause serious side effects. Talk to your healthcare provider if you are taking lithium before taking "water pills." Some types of "water pills" include chlorothiazide (Diuril), hydrochlorothiazide (HydroDIURIL, Esidrix), indapamide (Lozol), metolazone (Zaroxolyn), and chlorthalidone (Hygroton).

Medical professionals should consult the Professional Version at www.NaturalDatabase.com.

LIVER EXTRACT

What other names is the product known by?
Aqueous Liver Extract, Hydrolyzed Liver Extract, Liver, Liver Concentrate, Liver Factors, Liver Fractions, Liver Hydrolysate, Liver Substance.

What is it?
Liver extract is a product that comes from animal liver; most commonly from cattle. Liver extract is used to make medicine.

Is it Effective?
The effectiveness ratings for **LIVER EXTRACT** are as follows:
Insufficient Evidence to Rate Effectiveness for... Improving liver function, preventing liver damage, treating liver diseases, allergies, improving muscle development, improving strength and physical endurance, chronic fatigue syndrome (CFS), removing chemicals from the body (detoxification), chemical addiction recovery, or other uses.

How does it work?
Liver extract contains vitamin B12, folic acid, and iron. In animals, it seems to increase the number of liver cells. It is not known how liver extract might work for medicinal uses in people.

Are there safety concerns?
There isn't enough information to know if liver extract is safe, but since some preparations of liver extract come from animals, there is concern about possible contamination from diseased animals.

Do not take liver extract if: You are pregnant or breast-feeding. • You have problems with too much iron in your body, including a condition called hemochromatosis.

Are there any interactions with medications?
It is not known if liver extract interacts with any medicines.
Before taking liver extract, talk with your healthcare professional if you take any medications.

LIVERWORT

What other names is the product known by?
American Liverleaf, Anemone Acutiloba, Anémone à Lobes Aigus, Anemone Americana, Anémone d'Amérique, Hepatica nobilis var. Acuta, Hepatica Nobilis Var. Obtuse, Hepatici Noblis Herba, Hépatique à Lobes Aigus, Hépatique d'Amérique, Herb Trinity, Kidney Wort, Leberbluemchenkraut, Liverleaf, Liverweed, Liverwort-Leaf, Round-Leaved Hepatica, Round-Lobe Hepatica, Sharp-Lobe Hepatica, Trefoil.

What is it?
Liverwort is a plant. The fresh or dried above ground parts of liverwort are used to make medicine.

Is it Effective?
The effectiveness ratings for **LIVERWORT** are as follows:
Insufficient Evidence to Rate Effectiveness for... Liver diseases and liver conditions such as hepatitis, stomach and digestive discomfort, stimulating appetite, treating gallstones, regulating bowel function, stimulating the pancreas, high cholesterol, varicose veins, stimulating blood circulation, increasing heart blood supply, strengthening nerves, stimulating metabolism, menopausal symptoms, hemorrhoids, and other conditions.

How does it work?
Liverwort might stimulate the central nervous system (CNS).

Are there safety concerns?
Fresh liverwort is unsafe. It can cause many side effects such as diarrhea, stomach irritation, and kidney and urinary tract irritation when taken by mouth. When applied directly to the skin, fresh liverwort can cause irritation, itching, and pus-filled blisters.

It isn't known if dried liverwort is safe or what the side effects might be.

Do not take liverwort if: You are pregnant or breast-feeding.

Are there any interactions with medications?

It is not known if liverwort interacts with any medicines.

Before taking liverwort, talk with your healthcare professional if you take any medications.

LOBELIA

What other names is the product known by?

Asthma Weed, Bladderpod, Emetic Herb, Gagroot, Indian Tobacco, Lobelia inflata, Pukeweed, Vomit Wort, and Wild Tobacco.

What is it?

Lobelia is a plant. The above ground parts are used to make medicine.

Is it Effective?

The effectiveness ratings for **LOBELIA** are as follows:

Likely Ineffective for... Smoking cessation.

Insufficient Evidence to Rate Effectiveness for... Use by mouth for asthma, bronchitis, cough, and other conditions. Use on the skin for muscle soreness, bruises, sprains, insect bites, poison ivy, ringworm, and other conditions.

How does it work?

Lobelia contains chemicals which might thin mucus (phlegm) to make it easier to cough up (expectorate) and help breathing, especially in people with asthma. One chemical in lobelia has actions similar to nicotine.

Are there safety concerns?

Lobelia is considered unsafe for most people when taken by mouth. Side effects include nausea, vomiting, diarrhea, cough, dizziness, tremors, and more serious effects. Overdose may cause many serious toxic effects including sweating, convulsions, fast heartbeat, very low blood pressure, collapse, coma, and possibly death.

Do not take lobelia if: You are pregnant or breast-feeding. • You have heart problems. • You have stomach or intestinal problems including ulcers, Crohn's disease, inflammatory bowel disease, infections, and others.

Are there any interactions with medications?

It is not known if lobelia interacts with any medicines.

Before taking lobelia, talk with your healthcare professional if you take any medications.

LOGWOOD

What other names is the product known by?

Bloodwood, Haematoxylum campechianum, Haematoxylum lignum, Peachwood.

What is it?

Logwood is a plant. People use logwood to make medicine.

Is it Effective?

The effectiveness ratings for **LOGWOOD** are as follows:

Insufficient Evidence to Rate Effectiveness for... Diarrhea, excessive bleeding (hemorrhage), and other conditions.

How does it work?

There isn't enough information to know how logwood might work.

Are there safety concerns?

It is not known if logwood is safe or what the potential side effects might be.

Do not take logwood if: You are pregnant or breast-feeding.

Are there any interactions with medications?

It is not known if logwood interacts with any medicines.

Before taking logwood, talk with your healthcare professional if you take any medications.

LOOSESTRIFE

What other names is the product known by?
Lysimachia vulgaris, Yellow Willowherb.

What is it?
Loosestrife is a plant. It is used to make medicine.

Is it Effective?
The effectiveness ratings for **LOOSESTRIFE** are as follows:
Insufficient Evidence to Rate Effectiveness for... Diarrhea, scurvy, wounds, excessive bleeding (hemorrhage) including nose bleeds and heavy menstrual flow, and other conditions.

How does it work?
There isn't enough information to know how loosestrife might work.

Are there safety concerns?
There isn't enough information to know if loosestrife is safe or what potential side effects might occur.

Are there any interactions with medications?
It is not known if loosestrife interacts with any medicines.
Before taking loosestrife, talk with your healthcare professional if you take any medications.

LORENZO'S OIL

What other names is the product known by?
13-Docosenoic Acid, cis-9-Octadecenoic Acid, Erucic Acid, Glycerol Trierucate Oil, Glycerol Trioleate Oil, Oleic Acid.

What is it?
Lorenzo's oil is a combination of two chemicals called erucic acid and oleic acid. People use Lorenzo's oil as a medicine.

Is it Effective?
The effectiveness ratings for **LORENZO'S OIL** are as follows:
Possibly Effective for... Adrenoleukodystrophy. Lorenzo's oil might help prevent neurological problems in children who have adrenoleukodystrophy, but don't yet have any symptoms. Lorenzo's oil problem does not help children who already have symptoms of adrenoleukodystrophy.
Possibly Ineffective for... Adrenomyeloneuropathy. Lorenzo's oil does not seem to help reduce symptoms of progression of this form of adrenoleukodystrophy.

How does it work?
Adrenoleukodystrophy and adrenomyeloneuropathy are two rare genetic disorders that cause a large buildup of certain chemicals called very-long chain fatty acids. Lorenzo's oil might help prevent some of this buildup. The buildup of these acids is thought to cause many serious problems throughout the brain and body.

Are there safety concerns?
Lorenzo's oil seems to be safe when used under the care of health professionals. There is concern that Lorenzo's oil might cause two blood disorders known as thrombocytopenia (decrease in blood platelets needed for clotting blood) and neutropenia (decrease in white blood cells needed to fight infections). Side effects of Lorenzo's oil can include bruising and bleeding.

Do not take Lorenzo's oil if: You are pregnant or breast-feeding. • You have a blood disorder called thrombocytopenia or neutropenia.

Are there any interactions with medications?
It is not known if Lorenzo's oil interacts with any medicines.
Before taking Lorenzo's oil, talk with your healthcare professional if you take any medications.

LOTUS

What other names is the product known by?
Lian Fang, Lian Xu, Lian Zi, Nelumbo Nucifera, Semen Nelumbinis.

What is it?
Lotus is a plant. The flowers, seed, leaves and parts of the underground stem (rhizome) are used to make medicine.

Is it Effective?
The effectiveness ratings for **LOTUS** are as follows:
Insufficient Evidence to Rate Effectiveness for... Bleeding, digestion problems, diarrhea, and other conditions.

How does it work?
There is not enough information to know how lotus might work.

Are there safety concerns?
There is not enough known about lotus to know if it is safe.

Do not use lotus if: You are pregnant or breast-feeding.

Are there any interactions with medications?
It is not known if lotus interacts with any medicines.
Before taking lotus, talk with your healthcare professional if you take any medications.

LOVAGE

What other names is the product known by?
Angelica levisticum, Hipposelinum levisticum, Lavose, Levistici radix, Levisticum officinale, Ligusticum levisticum, Love Parsley, Maggi Plant, Sea Parsley, Smallage, Smellage.

What is it?
Lovage is a plant. The root and underground stem (rhizome) are used to make medicine.

Is it Effective?
The effectiveness ratings for **LOVAGE** are as follows:
Insufficient Evidence to Rate Effectiveness for... Indigestion, heartburn, intestinal gas, irregular menstrual periods, sore throat, boils, jaundice, gout, migraines, use as "irrigation therapy" for urinary tract inflammation and kidney stones, and other conditions.

How does it work?
The chemicals in lovage might increase water loss through urination, decrease spasms, and help fight infections.

Are there safety concerns?
Lovage is possibly safe for most people. It might increase sensitivity to the sun, especially with long-term use. This might put you at greater risk for rashes from the sun, sunburns, and skin cancer. Wear sunblock and protective clothing outside, especially if you are light-skinned.

Do not take lovage if: You are pregnant or breast-feeding. • You have high blood pressure. • You have kidney problems. • You have heart problems.

Are there any interactions with medications?
Water pills (Diuretic drugs). Lovage seems to work like "water pills" by causing the body to lose water. Taking lovage along with other "water pills" might cause the body to lose too much water. Losing too much water can cause you to be dizzy and your blood pressure to go too low. Some "water pills" include chlorothiazide (Diuril), chlorthalidone (Thalitone), furosemide (Lasix), hydrochlorothiazide (HCTZ, Hydrodiuril, Microzide), and others.

Medical professionals should consult the Professional Version at www.NaturalDatabase.com.

LUFFA

What other names is the product known by?

Angled Loofah, Dishcloth Sponge, Loofa, Loofah, Luffa acutangula, Luffa aegyptiaca, Luffa cylindrical, Luffaschwamm, Sigualuo, Sponge Cucumber, Vegetable Sponge, Water Gourd.

What is it?

Luffa is a plant. The dried fiber from the ripe fruit of luffa is used to make medicine.

Is it Effective?

The effectiveness ratings for **LUFFA** are as follows:

Insufficient Evidence to Rate Effectiveness for... Treating and preventing colds, nasal swelling, sinus problems, removing dead skin, stimulating the skin, shingles infection in the face and eye area, pain, menstrual problems, promoting breast-milk production, and other conditions.

How does it work?

There isn't enough information to know how luffa might work.

Are there safety concerns?

Luffa is safe for most people when applied directly to the skin as a sponge.

There isn't enough information to know if luffa might be safe when taken by mouth as medicine. The potential side effects of luffa are unknown.

Do not take luffa by mouth if: You are pregnant or breast-feeding.

Are there any interactions with medications?

It is not known if luffa interacts with any medicines.
Before taking luffa, talk with your healthcare professional if you take any medications.

LUNGMOSS

What other names is the product known by?

Lungwort, Oak Lungs, Lobaria pulmonaria.

What is it?

Lungmoss is a lichen, a type of fungus. People use lungmoss to make medicine. Be careful not to confuse lungmoss with Pulmonaria officinalis. Both are sometimes called lungwort.

Is it Effective?

The effectiveness ratings for **LUNGMOSS** are as follows:

Insufficient Evidence to Rate Effectiveness for... Bronchitis, asthma, coughs, inflammation, promoting sweating, and other uses.

How does it work?

There isn't enough information to know how lungmoss might work.

Are there safety concerns?

It is not known if lungmoss is safe or what side effects might occur.

Do not use lungmoss if: You are pregnant or breast-feeding.

Are there any interactions with medications?

It is not known if lungmoss interacts with any medicines.
Before taking lungmoss, talk with your healthcare professional if you take any medications.

 (209) 472-2244

LUNGWORT

What other names is the product known by?

Dage of Jerusalem, Lungenkraut, Pulmonaire, Pulmonaire officinale, Pulmonaria, Pulmonariae herba, Pulmonaria officinalis.

What is it?

Lungwort is a plant. People use the above ground parts to make medicine. Be careful not to confuse lungwort and lungmoss. See separate information for lungmoss.

Is it Effective?

The effectiveness ratings for **LUNGWORT** are as follows:
Insufficient Evidence to Rate Effectiveness for... Breathing conditions, stomach and intestinal conditions, kidney and urinary tract conditions, wounds, tuberculosis, and other conditions.

How does it work?

There isn't enough information to know how lungwort might work.

Are there safety concerns?

It is not known if lungwort is safe or what the potential side effects might be.

Do not take lungwort if: You are pregnant or breast-feeding.

Are there any interactions with medications?

It is not known if lungwort interacts with any medicines.
Before taking lungwort, talk with your healthcare professional if you take any medications.

LUTEIN

What other names is the product known by?

Beta,epsilon-carotene-3,3'-diol; Xanthophyll; Zeaxanthin.

What is it?

Lutein is called a carotenoid vitamin. It is related to beta-carotene and vitamin A. Foods rich in lutein include broccoli, spinach, and kale, corn, orange pepper, kiwi fruit, grapes, orange juice, zucchini, and squash.

Is it Effective?

The effectiveness ratings for **LUTEIN** are as follows:
Possibly Effective for... Macular degeneration. Consuming lutein as part of the diet might decrease the risk of getting macular degeneration. There is some information that taking lutein supplements might help decrease symptoms of macular degeneration, but more research is needed • Reducing the risk of developing eye cataracts, as part of the diet. It is not known if supplemental lutein offers the same benefit • Reducing the risk of developing colon and rectal cancer, as part of the diet. It is not known if supplemental lutein offers the same benefit.
Possibly Ineffective for... Reducing the risk of developing type 2 diabetes • Reducing the risk of developing heart disease.
Insufficient Evidence to Rate Effectiveness for... Retinitis pigmentosa, an eye condition that can cause blindness.

How does it work?

Lutein is one of two major carotenoids found as a color pigment in the human eye (macula and retina). It is thought to function as a light filter, protecting the eye tissues from sunlight damage.

Are there safety concerns?

Lutein is safe for most people.

Do not use lutein in amounts greater than those found in foods if: You are pregnant or breast-feeding.

Are there any interactions with medications?

It is not known if lutein interacts with any medicines.
Before taking lutein, talk with your healthcare professional if you take any medications.

LYCIUM

What other names is the product known by?

Chinese Wolfberry, Di Gu Pi, Digupi, Fructus Lycii Berry, Goji, Goji Berry, Goji Juice, Gou Qi Zi, Gouqizi, Lycii Berries, Lycium barbarum, Lycium chinense, Matrimony Vine, Wolfberry.

What is it?

Lycium is a plant. The dried berries and root bark are used to make medicine.

Is it Effective?

The effectiveness ratings for **LYCIUM** are as follows:

Insufficient Evidence to Rate Effectiveness for... Diabetes, high blood pressure, fever, malaria, cancer, blood circulation problems, sexual problems (impotence), dizziness, ringing in the ears (tinnitus), and many other conditions.

How does it work?

Lycium contains chemicals that might help lower blood pressure and blood sugar.

Are there safety concerns?

Lycium seems safe when taken by mouth. It can cause some side effects such as nausea and vomiting.

Do not take lycium if: You are pregnant or breast-feeding. • You have low blood pressure (hypotension).

Are there any interactions with medications?

Medications for high blood pressure (Antihypertensive drugs). Lycium seems to decrease blood pressure. Taking lycium along with medications for high blood pressure might cause your blood pressure to go too low. Some medications for high blood pressure include captopril (Capoten), enalapril (Vasotec), losartan (Cozaar), valsartan (Diovan), diltiazem (Cardizem), Amlodipine (Norvasc), hydrochlorothiazide (HydroDiuril), furosemide (Lasix), and many others.

Medications for diabetes (Antidiabetes drugs). Lycium bark might decrease blood sugar. Diabetes medications are also used to lower blood sugar. Taking lycium bark along with diabetes medications might cause your blood sugar to go too low. Monitor your blood sugar closely. The dose of your diabetes medication might need to be changed. Some medications used for diabetes include glimepiride (Amaryl), glyburide (DiaBeta, Glynase PresTab, Micronase), insulin, pioglitazone (Actos), rosiglitazone (Avandia), chlorpropamide (Diabinese), glipizide (Glucotrol), tolbutamide (Orinase), and others.

Medications changed by the liver (Cytochrome P450 2C9 (CYP2C9) substrates). Some medications are changed and broken down by the liver. Lycium might decrease how quickly the liver breaks down some medications. Taking lycium along with some medications that are broken down by the liver can increase the effects and side effects of some medications. Before taking lycium talk to your healthcare provider if you take any medications that are changed by the liver. Some medications that are changed by the liver include amitriptyline (Elavil), diazepam (Valium), zileuton (Zyflo), celecoxib (Celebrex), diclofenac (Voltaren), fluvastatin (Lescol), glipizide (Glucotrol), ibuprofen (Advil, Motrin), irbesartan (Avapro), losartan (Cozaar), phenytoin (Dilantin), piroxicam (Feldene), tamoxifen (Nolvadex), tolbutamide (Tolinase), torsemide (Demadex), warfarin (Coumadin), and others.

Warfarin (Coumadin). Warfarin (Coumadin) is used to slow blood clotting. Lycium might increase how long warfarin (Coumadin) is in the body, and increase the chances of bruising and bleeding. Be sure to have your blood checked regularly. The dose of your warfarin (Coumadin) might need to be changed.

LYCOPENE

What other names is the product known by?

All-Trans-Lycopene, Psi-Psi-Carotene.

What is it?

Lycopene is a naturally occurring chemical that gives fruits and vegetables a red color. It is present in particularly high amounts in tomatoes and tomato products. People use it to make medicine.

Is it Effective?

The effectiveness ratings for **LYCOPENE** are as follows:

Possibly Effective for... Treating prostate cancer • Preventing prostate cancer, when naturally occurring lycopene is eaten in foods • Preventing lung cancer, when naturally occurring lycopene is eaten in foods • Preventing ovarian cancer, when naturally occurring lycopene is eaten in foods.

Possibly Ineffective for... Preventing an eye disease called age-related maculopathy • Preventing bladder cancer • Preventing colon cancer • Preventing heart disease • Preventing diabetes.
Insufficient Evidence to Rate Effectiveness for... Cancers, exercise-induced asthma, human papilloma virus (HPV) infection, cataracts, and preventing hardening of the arteries (atherosclerosis).

How does it work?
Lycopene is an antioxidant that may help protect cells from damage.

Are there safety concerns?
Lycopene is safe when consumed in amounts found in foods. There isn't enough information to know if lycopene supplements are safe for use.

Do not use lycopene supplements if: You are pregnant or breast-feeding. • You have prostate cancer (without medical advice).

Are there any interactions with medications?
It is not known if lycopene interacts with any medicines.
Before taking lycopene, talk with your healthcare professional if you take any medications.

LYSINE

What other names is the product known by?
L-2,6-diaminohexanoic acid, L-Lysine, Lys, Lysine Hydrochloride, Lysine Monohydrochloride.

What is it?
Lysine is a chemical. People use it to make medicine.

Is it Effective?
The effectiveness ratings for **LYSINE** are as follows:
Possibly Effective for... Reducing recurrences and healing time of cold sores (herpes simplex labialis).
Insufficient Evidence to Rate Effectiveness for... Improving athletic performance.

How does it work?
Lysine seems to prevent the herpes virus from growing.

Are there safety concerns?
Lysine seems safe for most people when taken for up to one year. It can cause side effects such as stomach pain and diarrhea.

Do not take lysine if: You are pregnant or breast-feeding. • You have kidney problems.

Are there any interactions with medications?
Calcium supplements. Lysine can increase how much calcium the body absorbs. Taking calcium along with lysine can increase the amount of calcium in the body. Avoid taking large amounts of calcium and lysine at the same time.

MACA

What other names is the product known by?
Ayak Chichira, Ayuk Willku, Lepidium meyenii, Lepidium peruvianum, Maca Maca, Maino, Maka, Peruvian Ginseng.

What is it?
Maca is a plant. The root of maca is used to make medicine.

Is it Effective?
The effectiveness ratings for **MACA** are as follows:
Possibly Effective for... Enhancing sexual desire in men.
Insufficient Evidence to Rate Effectiveness for... Anemia, leukemia, chronic fatigue syndrome (CFS), enhancing energy and athletic performance, improving memory, depression, female hormone imbalance, menstrual problems, infertility, menopause symptoms, osteoporosis, stomach cancer, tuberculosis, sexual problems, immune system stimulation, AIDS, and other conditions.

Natural Medicines Comprehensive Database Consumer Version

Medical professionals should consult the Professional Version at www.NaturalDatabase.com.

CONSUMER VERSION

Medical professionals should consult the
Professional Version at www.NaturalDatabase.com.

How does it work?

Maca root contains many chemicals, including fatty acids and amino acids. However, there isn't enough information to know how maca might work.

Are there safety concerns?

Maca is safe for most people when taken in amounts found in foods. Maca might also be safe when taken in larger amounts as medicine for up to three months. Maca seems to be well tolerated by most people.

Do not take maca if: You are pregnant or breast-feeding.

Are there any interactions with medications?

It is not known if maca interacts with any medicines.
Before taking maca, talk with your healthcare professional if you take any medications.

MACADAMIA NUT

What other names is the product known by?

Australian nut, Bopple nut, Bush nut, Macadamia integrifolia, Macadamia tetraphylla, Queensland nut.

What is it?

Macadamia nut is a seed. People use it for medicine.

Is it Effective?

The effectiveness ratings for **MACADAMIA NUT** are as follows:
Possibly Effective for... Lowering cholesterol.

How does it work?

Macadamia nuts contain monounsaturated fatty acids (MUFA) and plant substances that might lower cholesterol.

Are there safety concerns?

Macadamia nuts seem to be safe for most people. Rarely, they can cause allergy.

Are there any interactions with medications?

It is not known if macadamia nut interacts with any medicines.
Before taking macadamia nut, talk with your healthcare professional if you take any medications.

MADAGASCAR PERIWINKLE

What other names is the product known by?

Ammocallis rosea, Cape Periwinkle, Catharanthus, Catharanthus roseus, Church-Flower, Lochnera rosea, Magdalena, Myrtle, Old Maid, Periwinkle, Ram-Goat Rose, Red Periwinkle, Vinca rosea.

What is it?

Madagascar periwinkle is a plant. The above ground parts are used to make medicine.

Is it Effective?

The effectiveness ratings for **MADAGASCAR PERIWINKLE** are as follows:
Insufficient Evidence to Rate Effectiveness for... Diabetes, cancer, fluid retention, cough, lung congestion, sore throat, eye irritation, skin infections, and other conditions.

How does it work?

Madagascar periwinkle might alter the immune system, increase the production of urine (diuretic), and lower blood sugar.

Are there safety concerns?

Madagascar periwinkle is UNSAFE when taken by mouth. There isn't enough information to know if it is safe for use on the skin. Madagascar periwinkle can cause side effects such as nausea, vomiting, hair loss, hearing loss, dizziness, bleeding, nerve problems, seizures, liver damage, low blood sugar, and other problems.

Do not use Madagascar periwinkle if: You are pregnant or breast-feeding.

Are there any interactions with medications?
Medications for diabetes (Antidiabetes drugs). Madagascar periwinkle might decrease blood sugar. Diabetes medications are also used to lower blood sugar. Taking Madagascar periwinkle along with diabetes medications might cause your blood sugar to go too low. Monitor your blood sugar closely. The dose of your diabetes medication might need to be changed. Some medications used for diabetes include glimepiride (Amaryl), glyburide (DiaBeta, Glynase PresTab, Micronase), insulin, pioglitazone (Actos), rosiglitazone (Avandia), chlorpropamide (Diabinese), glipizide (Glucotrol), tolbutamide (Orinase), and others.

MADDER

What other names is the product known by?
Dyer's Madder, Farberrote, Garance, Robbia, Rubia, Rubia tinctorum, Rubiae tinctorum radix.

What is it?
Madder is a plant. The root is used to make medicine.

Is it Effective?
The effectiveness ratings for **MADDER** are as follows:
Insufficient Evidence to Rate Effectiveness for... Kidney stones, menstrual problems, urinary problems, and other uses.

How does it work?
The chemicals in madder might help prevent kidney stones.

Are there safety concerns?
Madder is considered unsafe. The chemicals in madder may cause cancer. It can also cause red colored urine, saliva, perspiration, tears, and breast milk.

Do not take madder if: You are pregnant or breast-feeding. It can harm the baby.

Are there any interactions with medications?
It is not known if madder interacts with any medicines.
Before taking madder, talk with your healthcare professional if you take any medications.

MAGNESIUM

What other names is the product known by?
Chelated Magnesium, Magnesia, Epsom Salts, Magnesium Aspartate, Magnesium Carbonate, Magnesium Chloride, Magnesium Citrate, Magnesium Gluconate, Magnesium Glycerophosphate, Magnesium Hydroxide, Magnesium Lactate, Magnesium Orotate, Magnesium Oxide, Magnesium Sulfate, Magnesium Trisilicate, Milk of Magnesia, Mg, atomic number 12.

What is it?
Magnesium is a mineral. Our bodies contain magnesium, about half of which is in our bones. Magnesium is used to make medicine.

Is it Effective?
The effectiveness ratings for **MAGNESIUM** are as follows:
Effective for... Preventing and treating magnesium deficiency, and certain conditions related to magnesium deficiency • Use as a laxative for constipation or preparation of the bowel for surgical or diagnostic procedures • Heartburn or "sour stomach" as an antacid.
Likely Effective for... Conditions that occur during pregnancy called pre-eclampsia or eclampsia • A type of irregular heartbeat called torsades de pointes.
Possibly Effective for... Cluster headaches • Migraine headaches • Asthma attacks, when given intravenously • Premenstrual syndrome (PMS) • Weakened bones (osteoporosis) • Preventing type 2 diabetes in overweight, middle-aged women, when magnesium is obtained from foods. More evidence is needed to know if magnesium helps treat diabetes • Pregnancy-related leg cramps • Irregular heartbeat, arrhythmia • High blood pressure (hypertension) • Diseases of heart valves, mitral valve prolapse • High cholesterol • Chest pain due to artery disease • Kidney stones • Hearing loss in people exposed to loud noise • Fibromyalgia pain, when used with malic acid • Metabolic syndrome (a condition that increases risk for diabetes and heart disease) • Nerve pain caused by cancer • Chronic fatigue syndrome (CFS) • Pain after a hysterectomy • Decreasing the risk of stroke • A lung

Medical professionals should consult the Professional Version at www.NaturalDatabase.com.

disease called Chronic obstructive pulmonary disease (COPD).

Possibly Ineffective for... Helping to restart the heart • Improving energy and endurance during athletic activity • Cerebral palsy, when given in the vein • Heart attack.

Insufficient Evidence to Rate Effectiveness for... Attention deficit-hyperactivity disorder (ADHD), hayfever, anxiety, restless leg syndrome, Lyme disease, multiple sclerosis (MS), premature labor, and other conditions.

How does it work?

Magnesium is required for the proper growth and maintenance of bones. Magnesium is also required for the proper function of nerves, muscles, and many other parts of the body. In the stomach, magnesium helps neutralize stomach acid and move stools through the intestine.

Are there safety concerns?

Magnesium is safe for most people when taken by mouth or when the prescription-only, injectable product is used correctly. In some people, magnesium might cause stomach upset, nausea, vomiting, diarrhea, and other side effects.

Doses less than 350 mg per day are safe for most people. When taken in very large amounts, magnesium might be unsafe. Large doses might cause too much magnesium to build up in the body causing serious side effects including an irregular heartbeat, low blood pressure, confusion, slowed breathing, coma, and death.

Magnesium is safe for pregnant or breast-feeding women when taken by mouth in the amounts recommended. These amounts depend on the age of the woman. Check with your healthcare professional to find out what amounts are right for you.

Do not take magnesium if: You have a heart problem called "heart block." • You have kidney problems such as kidney failure.

Are there any interactions with medications?

Antibiotics (Aminoglycoside antibiotics). Some antibiotics can affect the muscles. These antibiotics are called aminoglycosides. Magnesium can also affect the muscles. Taking these antibiotics and getting a magnesium shot might cause muscle problems. Some aminoglycoside antibiotics include amikacin (Amikin), gentamicin (Garamycin), kanamycin (Kantrex), streptomycin, tobramycin (Nebcin), and others.

Antibiotics (Tetracycline antibiotics). Magnesium can attach to tetracyclines in the stomach. This decreases the amount of tetracyclines that the body can absorb. Taking magnesium along with tetracyclines might decrease the effectiveness of tetracyclines. To avoid this interaction take calcium 2 hours before or 4 hours after taking tetracyclines. Some tetracyclines include demeclocycline (Declomycin), minocycline (Minocin), and tetracycline (Achromycin).

Antibiotics (Quinolone antibiotics). Magnesium might decrease how much antibiotic the body absorbs. Taking magnesium along with some antibiotics might decrease the effectiveness of some antibiotics. To avoid this interaction take magnesium supplements at least 1 hour after antibiotics. Some of these antibiotics that might interact with magnesium include ciprofloxacin (Cipro), enoxacin (Penetrex), norfloxacin (Chibroxin, Noroxin), sparfloxacin (Zagam), trovafloxacin (Trovan), and grepafloxacin (Raxar).

Bisphosphonates. Magnesium can decrease how much bisphosphate the body absorbs. Taking magnesium along with bisphosphates can decrease the effectiveness of bisphosphate. To avoid this interaction take bisphosphonate at least 30 minutes before magnesium or later in the day. Some bisphosphonates include alendronate (Fosamax), etidronate (Didronel), risedronate (Actonel), tiludronate (Skelid), and others.

Medications for high blood pressure (Calcium channel blockers). Magnesium might decrease blood pressure. Taking magnesium with medication for high blood pressure might cause your blood pressure to go too low. Some medications for high blood pressure include nifedipine (Adalat, Procardia), verapamil (Calan, Isoptin, Verelan), diltiazem (Cardizem), isradipine (DynaCirc), felodipine (Plendil), amlodipine (Norvasc), and others.

Muscle relaxants. Magnesium seems to help relax muscles. Taking magnesium along with muscle relaxants can increase the risk of side effects of muscle relaxants. Some muscle relaxants include carisoprodol (Soma), pipecuronium (Arduan), orphenadrine (Banflex, Disipal), cyclobenzaprine, gallamine (Flaxedil), atracurium (Tracrium), pancuronium (Pavulon), succinylcholine (Anectine), and others.

Water pills (Potassium-sparing diuretics). Some "water pills" can increase magnesium levels in the body. Taking some "water pills" along with magnesium might cause too much magnesium to be in the body. Some "water pills" that increase magnesium in the body include amiloride (Midamor), spironolactone (Aldactone), and triamterene (Dyrenium).

Natural Medicines Comprehensive Database Consumer Version
(209) 472-2244

MAGNOLIA

What other names is the product known by?

Beaver Tree, Flos Magnoliae, Ho-No-Ki, Holly Bay, Hou Po, Indian Bark, Japanese whitebark magnolia, Magnolia biondii, Magnolia denudata, Magnolia emargenata, Magnolia fargesii, Magnolia Flower Bud, Magnolia glauca, Magnolia heptaperta, Magnolia hypoleuca, Magnolia officinalis, Magnolia salicifolia, Magnolia sargentiana, Magnolia sprengeri, Magnolia wilsonii, Red Bay, Swamp Laurel, Swamp Sassafras, Sweet Bay, White Bay, White Laurel, Xin Ye Hua.

What is it?

Magnolia is a plant. People use the bark and flower buds to make medicine.

Is it Effective?

The effectiveness ratings for **MAGNOLIA** are as follows:

Insufficient Evidence to Rate Effectiveness for... Anxiety, depression, weight loss, obesity, digestion problems, inflammation, nasal congestion, runny nose, the common cold, headache, facial dark spots, toothaches, weight loss, and other conditions.

How does it work?

Magnolia seems to have anxiety-reducing activity in animals. It might also increase steroid production by the body to treat asthma. All research on magnolia has been in laboratories.

Are there safety concerns?

Magnolia appears to be safe for most people when used short-term. The safety of magnolia use for more than 6 weeks is unknown. In one study, one person experienced heartburn, shaking hands, sexual dysfunction, and thyroid dysfunction. Another person experience fatigue and headache. But it is not known if these side effects were caused by magnolia or some other factor.

Taking large amounts might cause excessive sedation.

Do not take magnolia if: You are pregnant or breast-feeding.

Are there any interactions with medications?

Alcohol. Alcohol can cause sleepiness and drowsiness. Magnolia bark might also cause sleepiness and drowsiness. Taking large amounts of magnolia bark along with alcohol might cause too much sleepiness.

Sedative medications (Barbiturates). Magnolia bark might cause sleepiness and drowsiness. Medications that cause sleepiness are called sedatives. Taking magnolia bark along with sedative medications might cause too much sleepiness. Some sedative medications include amobarbital (Amytal), butabarbital (Butisol), mephobarbital (Mebaral), pentobarbital (Nembutal), phenobarbital (Luminal), secobarbital (Seconal), and others.

Sedative medications (Benzodiazepines). Magnolia bark might cause sleepiness and drowsiness. Drugs that cause sleepiness and drowsiness are called sedative medications. Taking magnolia bark along with sedative medications might cause too much sleepiness. Do not take magnolia bark if you are taking sedative medications. Some of these sedative medications include clonazepam (Klonopin), diazepam (Valium), lorazepam (Ativan), and others.

Sedative medications (CNS depressants). Magnolia bark might cause sleepiness and drowsiness. Medications that cause sleepiness are called sedatives. Taking magnolia bark along with sedative medications might cause too much sleepiness. Some sedative medications include clonazepam (Klonopin), lorazepam (Ativan), phenobarbital (Donnatal), zolpidem (Ambien), and others.

MAIDENHAIR FERN

What other names is the product known by?

Adiantum capillus-veneris, Adiantum pedatum, Five-Finger Fern, Hair of Venus, Maiden Fern, Rock Fern, Venus' Hair.

What is it?

Maidenhair fern is a plant. People use it to make medicine.

Is it Effective?

The effectiveness ratings for **MAIDENHAIR FERN** are as follows:

Insufficient Evidence to Rate Effectiveness for... Bronchitis, coughs, whooping cough, menstrual problems, hair loss, promoting dark hair color, and others.

CONSUMER VERSION

Medical professionals should consult the Professional Version at www.NaturalDatabase.com.

How does it work?
There isn't enough information to know how maidenhair fern might work.

Are there safety concerns?
Maidenhair fern might be safe for most people when taken in amounts found in foods.

There isn't enough information to know if maidenhair fern is safe when taken in amounts larger than found in foods. Large amounts may cause vomiting in some people.

Do not take maidenhair fern if: You are pregnant or breast-feeding.

Are there any interactions with medications?
It is not known if maidenhair fern interacts with any medicines.
Before taking maidenhair fern, talk with your healthcare professional if you take any medications.

MAITAKE MUSHROOM

What other names is the product known by?
Dancing Mushroom, Grifola, Grifola frondosa, Hen Of The Woods, King Of Mushrooms, Maitake, Monkey's Bench, Shelf Fungi.

What is it?
Maitake mushroom is a fungus eaten as food in Asia for thousands of years. People also use it to make medicine.

Is it Effective?
The effectiveness ratings for **MAITAKE MUSHROOM** are as follows:
Insufficient Evidence to Rate Effectiveness for... Cancer, HIV/AIDS, chronic fatigue syndrome, hepatitis, hayfever, diabetes, high blood pressure, high cholesterol, weight loss or control, chemotherapy support, and other uses.

How does it work?
Maitake mushroom contains chemicals which might help fight tumors and stimulate the immune system. There is some evidence that it can lower blood pressure, improve cholesterol levels, lower blood sugar levels, and reduce weight in rats, but this has not been shown for humans yet.

Are there safety concerns?
Maitake mushroom might be safe for most people when used as medicine, but there isn't much information about the potential side effects.

Do not take maitake mushroom if: You are pregnant or breast-feeding.

Are there any interactions with medications?
Medications for diabetes (Antidiabetes drugs). Maitake mushroom might decrease blood sugar. Diabetes medications are also used to lower blood sugar. Taking maitake mushroom along with diabetes medications might cause your blood sugar to go too low. Monitor your blood sugar closely. The dose of your diabetes medication might need to be changed. Some medications used for diabetes include glimepiride (Amaryl), glyburide (DiaBeta, Glynase PresTab, Micronase), insulin, pioglitazone (Actos), rosiglitazone (Avandia), chlorpropamide (Diabinese), glipizide (Glucotrol), tolbutamide (Orinase), and others.

MALABAR NUT

What other names is the product known by?
Adulsa, Arusa, Justicia Adhatoda.

What is it?
Malabar nut is a plant. People use the leaf of the malabar nut to make medicine.

Is it Effective?
The effectiveness ratings for **MALABAR NUT** are as follows:
Insufficient Evidence to Rate Effectiveness for... Coughs, breathing problems, spasms, and other conditions.

How does it work?
There isn't enough information to know how malabar nut might work.

Are there safety concerns?
It is not known if malabar nut is safe or what the potential side effects might be.

Do not take malabar nut if: You are pregnant or breast-feeding.

Are there any interactions with medications?
It is not known if malabar nut interacts with any medicines.
Before taking malabar nut, talk with your healthcare professional if you take any medications.

MALE FERN

What other names is the product known by?
American Aspidium, Bear's Paw, Dryopteris Filix-Mas, European Aspidium, Knotty Brake, Marginal Fern, Shield Fern.

What is it?
Male fern is a plant. People use the above ground parts, leaf and root-like stem of the male fern to make medicine.

Is it Effective?
The effectiveness ratings for **MALE FERN** are as follows:
Insufficient Evidence to Rate Effectiveness for... Nose bleeds, heavy menstrual bleeding, wounds, tumors, and tapeworms.

How does it work?
Male fern contains chemicals which kill intestinal worms such as tapeworms. Once the worms have been killed, saltwater (saline) is taken to flush them from the body.

Are there safety concerns?
Male fern is UNSAFE. It can be a violent poison. Side effects can be serious and include breathing difficulty, nausea, diarrhea, dizziness, headaches, tremors, convulsions, heart and lung failure, eye disorders, muscular weakness, coma, temporary or permanent blindness, and death.

Are there any interactions with medications?
It is not known if male fern interacts with any medicines.
Before taking male fern, talk with your healthcare professional if you take any medications.

MALLOW

What other names is the product known by?
Blue Mallow Flower, Blue Malva, Cheeseflower, Dwarf Mallow, Gul-Khair, High Mallow, Mallow flower, Mallow leaf, Malvae flos, Malvae folium, Malva neglecta, Malva sylvestris, Mauls.

What is it?
Mallow is a plant. People use the flower and leaf to make medicine.

Is it Effective?
The effectiveness ratings for **MALLOW** are as follows:
Insufficient Evidence to Rate Effectiveness for... Wounds, bronchitis, stomach upset, diarrhea, irritation of the mouth and throat, and dry cough.

How does it work?
Mallow flower contains a mucus-like substance that protects and soothes the throat and mouth.

Are there safety concerns?
There is not enough known about mallow to know if it is safe.

Do not take mallow if: You are pregnant or breast-feeding.

Medical professionals should consult the Professional Version at www.NaturalDatabase.com.

Are there any interactions with medications?

It is not known if mallow interacts with any medicines.
Before taking mallow, talk with your healthcare professional if you take any medications.

MANACA

What other names is the product known by?

Brunfelsia hopeana, Pohl, Vegetable Mercury.

What is it?

Manaca is a plant. The root is used to make medicine.

Is it Effective?

The effectiveness ratings for **MANACA** are as follows:
Insufficient Evidence to Rate Effectiveness for... Arthritis, fluid retention, and other conditions.

How does it work?

There isn't enough information to know how manaca works.

Are there safety concerns?

There isn't enough reliable information about the safety of manaca for people. In animals, manaca can cause anxiety, restlessness, increases in heart and breathing rates, drooling, vomiting, muscle spasms, and death.

Do not take manaca if: You are pregnant or breast-feeding.

Are there any interactions with medications?

It is not known if manaca interacts with any medicines.
Before taking manaca, talk with your healthcare professional if you take any medications.

MANGANESE

What other names is the product known by?

Manganese Amino Acid Chelate, Manganese Aminoate, Manganese Ascorbate, Manganese Aspartate Complex, Manganese Chloride, Manganese Chloridetetrahydrate, Manganese Dioxide, Manganese Gluconate, Manganese Sulfate, Manganese Sulfate Monohydrate, Manganese Sulfate Tetrahydrate, Manganum, Mn.

What is it?

Manganese is a mineral. It is found in several foods including nuts, legumes, seeds, tea, whole grains, and leafy green vegetables. People also use manganese as medicine.

Is it Effective?

The effectiveness ratings for **MANGANESE** are as follows:
Effective for... Treating or preventing low manganese levels in the body (manganese deficiency).
Possibly Effective for... Use with calcium, zinc, and copper for osteoporosis (thinning of the bones).
Insufficient Evidence to Rate Effectiveness for... Anemia, premenstrual syndrome (PMS), arthritis (osteoarthritis), and other conditions.

How does it work?

Manganese is an essential nutrient involved in many chemical processes in the body, including metabolism of cholesterol, carbohydrates, and protein. It might also be involved in bone formation.

Are there safety concerns?

Manganese is safe for most adults in amounts up to 11 mg per day. More than 11 mg per day might not be safe. Excess manganese can cause serious side effects, including symptoms resembling Parkinson's disease such as tremors. People who have trouble getting rid of manganese from the body, such as people with liver disease, may get side effects when taking less than 11 mg per day.
Check supplement labels carefully for "hidden" manganese. Some supplements (e.g., Cosamin and Cosamin DS) provide more than 11 mg per day when used according to the directions on the label.

The amount of manganese which is safe for children depends on their age. Discuss the appropriate amount with your healthcare professional before giving manganese to children.

 Natural Medicines Comprehensive Database Consumer Version (209) 472-2244

Do not take manganese if: You have liver problems, without the help of a healthcare professional. Manganese can build up in people with liver problems and cause tremors, mental problems such as psychosis, and other side effects.

Are there any interactions with medications?

Antibiotics (Tetracycline antibiotics). Manganese can attach to tetracyclines in the stomach. This decreases the amount of tetracyclines that can be absorbed. Taking manganese with tetracyclines might decrease the effectiveness of tetracyclines. To avoid this interaction take manganese two hours before or four hours after taking tetracyclines. Some tetracyclines include demeclocycline (Declomycin), minocycline (Minocin), and tetracycline (Achromycin).

Antibiotics (Quinolone antibiotics). Manganese might decrease how much antibiotic the body absorbs. Taking manganese along with some antibiotics might decrease the effectiveness of some antibiotics. To avoid this interaction take manganese supplements at least one hour after antibiotics. Some of these antibiotics that might interact with manganese include ciprofloxacin (Cipro), enoxacin (Penetrex), norfloxacin (Chibroxin, Noroxin), sparfloxacin (Zagam), trovafloxacin (Trovan), and grepafloxacin (Raxar).

MANGOSTEEN

What other names is the product known by?

Amibiasine, Mang Cut, Manggis, Manggistan, Mangosta, Mangostan, Mangostana, Mangostanier, Mangostao, Mangoustanier, Mangouste, Mangostier, Manguita, Meseter, Queen of Fruits, Sementah, Semetah, Xango, Xango Juice.

What is it?

Mangosteen is a tropical fruit. The fruit, fruit juice, rind, and bark are used as a medicine.

Is it Effective?

The effectiveness ratings for **MANGOSTEEN** are as follows:
Insufficient Evidence to Rate Effectiveness for... Dysentery, diarrhea, urinary tract infections (UTI), gonorrhea, thrush, tuberculosis, eczema, menstrual disorders, and other conditions.

How does it work?

The fruit rind contains tannins. These might help for diarrhea. But there is no scientific information about whether mangosteen works for any medical condition.

Are there safety concerns?

There is not enough reliable information to know if mangosteen products are safe for medicinal use.

Do not take mangosteen if: You are pregnant or breast-feeding.

Are there any interactions with medications?

It is not known if mangosteen interacts with any medicines.
Before taking mangosteen, talk with your healthcare provider if you are taking any medications.

MANNA

What other names is the product known by?

Flake Manna, Flowering Ash, Fraxinus ornus, Manna Ash.

What is it?

Manna is a plant. People use the dried sap of manna to make medicine.

Is it Effective?

The effectiveness ratings for **MANNA** are as follows:
Insufficient Evidence to Rate Effectiveness for... Constipation, hemorrhoids, and other rectal conditions.

How does it work?

Manna contains the chemical mannitol which might work a a laxative to help stool move through the intestine.

Are there safety concerns?

Manna appears safe for most people, when used short-term. In some people, manna might cause nausea or gas.

Do not take manna if: You are pregnant or breast-feeding. • You have an intestinal condition called bowel obstruction or ileus.

Are there any interactions with medications?
Digoxin (Lanoxin). Manna is a laxative. Some laxatives can decrease potassium levels in the body. Low potassium levels can increase the risk of side effects of digoxin (Lanoxin).

Water pills (Diuretic drugs). Manna is a laxative. Some laxatives can decrease potassium in the body. "Water pills" can also decrease potassium in the body. Taking manna along with "water pills" might decrease potassium in the body too much. Some "water pills" that can decrease potassium include chlorothiazide (Diuril), chlorthalidone (Thalitone), furosemide (Lasix), hydrochlorothiazide (HCTZ, Hydrodiuril, Microzide), and others.

MARIJUANA

What other names is the product known by?
Anashca, Banji, Bhang, Cannabis, Cannabis sativa, Charas, Esrar, Gaga, Ganga, Grass, Hash, Hashish, Hemp, Kif, Mariguana, Marihuana, Pot, Sawi, Sinsemilla, Weed.

What is it?
Marijuana is an herb. The leaves and flowers are dried to make medicine.

Is it Effective?
The effectiveness ratings for **MARIJUANA** are as follows:
Possibly Effective for... Stimulating appetite in people with AIDS • Treating increased pressure in the eyes (glaucoma) • Treating multiple sclerosis (MS).
Insufficient Evidence to Rate Effectiveness for... Dandruff, hemorrhoids, obesity, asthma, urinary infections, leprosy, preventing rejection after kidney transplants, and other conditions.

How does it work?
Marijuana contains chemicals that work by binding to specific sites in the brain and on the nerves.

Are there safety concerns?
Marijuana seems unsafe when taken by mouth or smoked. Use of marijuana can cause dry mouth, nausea, vomiting, red eyes, heart and blood pressure problems, lung problems, impaired mental functioning, panic reactions, hallucinations, flashbacks, depression, and sexual problems.

Marijuana is classified as an illegal substance. Marijuana does, however, contain dronabinol (Marinol), a substance that is FDA-approved for specific uses.

Do not use marijuana if: You are pregnant or breast-feeding. • You have heart problems or hypertension (high blood pressure). • You have lung problems. • You have seizures (epilepsy). • You have immune system problems.

Are there any interactions with medications?
Disulfiram (Antabuse). Disulfiram (Antabuse) might interact with marijuana. Taking marijuana along with Disulfiram can cause agitation, trouble sleeping, and irritability.

Fluoxetine (Prozac). Taking marijuana with fluoxetine (Prozac) might cause you to feel irritated, nervous, jittery, and excited. Doctors call this hypomania.

Sedative medications (Barbiturates). Marijuana might cause sleepiness and drowsiness. Medications that cause sleepiness are called sedatives. Taking marijuana along with sedative medications might cause too much sleepiness.

Sedative medications (CNS depressants). Marijuana might cause sleepiness and drowsiness. Medications that cause sleepiness are called sedatives. Taking marijuana along with sedative medications might cause too much sleepiness. Some sedative medications include clonazepam (Klonopin), lorazepam (Ativan), phenobarbital (Donnatal), zolpidem (Ambien), and others.

Theophylline. Taking marijuana might decrease the effects of theophylline. But there isn't enough information to know if this is a big concern.

Medical professionals should consult the Professional Version at www.NaturalDatabase.com.

MARJORAM

What other names is the product known by?

Garden Marjoram, Gartenmajoran, Knotted Marjoram, Majoran, Majorana aetheroleum oil, Majorana herb, Majorana hortensis, Majorana majorana, Marjolaine, Mejorana, Origanum majorana, Sweet Marjoram.

What is it?

Marjoram is a plant. The flowers, leaves, and oil are used to make medicine.

Is it Effective?

The effectiveness ratings for **MARJORAM** are as follows:

Insufficient Evidence to Rate Effectiveness for... Coughs, colds, runny nose, stomach cramps, improving appetite and digestion, colic, liver problems, gallstones, headache, improving sleep, diabetes, menstrual (period) problems, menopause symptoms, improving sleep, mental problems, nerve problems, muscle pains, sprains, promoting breast milk, and other conditions.

How does it work?

There isn't enough information to know how marjoram might work.

Are there safety concerns?

Marjoram is possibly safe for most adults when used in medicinal amounts for short periods of time. Avoid skin contact with fresh marjoram. It can cause eye and skin swelling.

Marjoram might not be safe when used long-term. There is some evidence that it could cause cancer.

Do not give marjoram to children in medicinal amounts. It might not be safe for them.

Do not use marjoram if: You are pregnant or breast-feeding. • You are allergic to plants in the Lamiaceae family, such as basil, hyssop, lavender, mint, oregano, and sage.

Are there any interactions with medications?

It is not known if marjoram interacts with any medicines.
Before taking marjoram, talk with your healthcare professional if you take any medications.

MARSH BLAZING STAR

What other names is the product known by?

Backache Root, Blazing-Star, Button Snakeroot, Colic Root, Devil's Bite Prairie-Pine, Gayfeather, Gay-Feather, Liatris spicata, Laciniaria spicata, Liatris callilepis, Serratula spicata.

What is it?

Marsh blazing star is a plant. People use the root to make medicine.

Is it Effective?

The effectiveness ratings for **MARSH BLAZING STAR** are as follows:

Insufficient Evidence to Rate Effectiveness for... Kidney problems, problems with menstruation or "periods," gonorrhea, and fluid retention.

How does it work?

Marsh blazing star contains the chemical coumarin which might improve blood flow.

Are there safety concerns?

There isn't enough reliable information available about the safety of marsh blazing star. It can cause nausea, vomiting, diarrhea, dizziness, inability to sleep (insomnia), and liver damage. When marsh blazing star comes in contact with the skin, it might cause skin irritation and allergic reactions.

Do not use marsh blazing star if: You are pregnant or breast-feeding. • You have an allergy to the Asteraceae/Compositae plant family including ragweed, chrysanthemums, marigolds, daisies, and many others.

Are there any interactions with medications?

It is not known if marsh blazing star interacts with any medicines.
Before taking marsh blazing star, talk with your healthcare professional if you take any medications.

Medical professionals should consult the Professional Version at www.NaturalDatabase.com.

MARSH MARIGOLD

What other names is the product known by?
Bull's Eyes, Caltha palustris, Cowslip, Horse Blobs, Kingcups, Leopard's Foot, Meadow Routs, Palsy Root, Solsequia, Sponsa Solis, Verrucaria, Water Blobs, Water Dragon.

What is it?
Marsh marigold is a plant. People use the above ground parts of the flowering plant to make medicine.

Is it Effective?
The effectiveness ratings for **MARSH MARIGOLD** are as follows:
Insufficient Evidence to Rate Effectiveness for... Pain, cramps, problems related to menstruation or "periods," bronchitis, liver problems, constipation, fluid retention, high cholesterol, low blood sugar, cleaning skin sores, and other conditions.

How does it work?
There isn't enough reliable information to know how marsh marigold works.

Are there safety concerns?
Marsh marigold is UNSAFE. In some people, it can cause diarrhea and severe irritation of the stomach, intestines, bladder, and kidneys. When marsh marigold comes in contact with the skin, it might cause blisters and burns.

Do not use marsh marigold if: You are pregnant or breast-feeding.

Are there any interactions with medications?
It is not known if marsh marigold interacts with any medicines.
Before taking marsh marigold, talk with your healthcare professional if you take any medications.

MARSH TEA

What other names is the product known by?
James' Tea, Ledi palustris herba, Ledum palustre, Marsh Citrus, Moth Herb, Rhododendron tomentosum var. tomentosum, Rhododendron palustre, Romarin Sauvage, Sumpfporst, Swamp Tea, Wild Rosemary.

What is it?
Marsh tea is a plant. People use it to make medicine.

Is it Effective?
The effectiveness ratings for **MARSH TEA** are as follows:
Insufficient Evidence to Rate Effectiveness for... Pain and swelling of the muscles and joints, whooping cough, bronchitis, colds, cough, stimulating milk flow, increasing sweating, fluid retention, abortion, and other conditions.

How does it work?
Marsh tea might help decrease coughing and swelling. It might also affect the uterus.

Are there safety concerns?
Marsh tea is unsafe when taken in large amounts to try to cause abortion. It can cause severe irritation of the stomach and intestines, kidney damage, paralysis, and other serious side effects.

Do not use marsh tea if: You are pregnant or breast-feeding. • You have kidney problems. • You have stomach or intestinal problems such as gastritis or inflammatory bowel disease. • You have urinary tract problems such as kidney or bladder infections.

Are there any interactions with medications?
Sedative medications (CNS depressants). Marsh tea might cause sleepiness and drowsiness. Medications that cause sleepiness are called sedatives. Taking marsh tea along with sedative medications might cause too much sleepiness. Some sedative medications include clonazepam (Klonopin), lorazepam (Ativan), Phenobarbital (Donnatal), zolpidem (Ambien), and others.

MARSHMALLOW

What other names is the product known by?

Alteia, Althaeae folium, , Althaea officinalis, Althaeae radi, Althea, Herba Malvae, Mallards, Mortification Root, Racine De Guimauve, Sweet Weed, Wymote.

What is it?

Marshmallow is a plant. The leaves and the root are used to make medicine.

Is it Effective?

The effectiveness ratings for **MARSHMALLOW** are as follows:

Insufficient Evidence to Rate Effectiveness for... Sores, skin inflammation, burns, wounds, insect bites, chapped skin, diarrhea, constipation, stomach and intestinal ulcers, irritation of the mouth and throat, dry cough, and other conditions.

How does it work?

Marshmallow forms a protective layer on the skin and lining of the digestive tract. It also contains chemicals that might decrease cough and help heal wounds.

Are there safety concerns?

Marshmallow is safe for most people when taken by mouth. In some people, it might cause low blood sugar levels. If you have diabetes, check your blood sugar carefully to avoid dangerously low blood sugar.

Marshmallow might be safe when applied directly to the skin.

Do not take marshmallow if: You are pregnant or breast-feeding.

Are there any interactions with medications?

Medications for diabetes (Antidiabetes drugs). Marshmallow might decrease blood sugar. Diabetes medications are also used to lower blood sugar. Taking marshmallow along with diabetes medications might cause your blood sugar to go too low. Monitor your blood sugar closely. The dose of your diabetes medication might need to be changed. Some medications used for diabetes include glimepiride (Amaryl), glyburide (DiaBeta, Glynase PresTab, Micronase), insulin, pioglitazone (Actos), rosiglitazone (Avandia), chlorpropamide (Diabinese), glipizide (Glucotrol), tolbutamide (Orinase), and others.

Medications taken by mouth (Oral drugs). Marshmallow contains a type of soft fiber called mucilage. Mucilage can decrease how much medicine the body absorbs. Taking marshmallow at the same time you take medications by mouth can decrease the effectiveness of your medication. To prevent this interaction take marshmallow at least one hour after medications you take by mouth.

MARTAGON

What other names is the product known by?

Lilium martagon, Purple Turk's Cap Lily, Turk's Cap.

What is it?

Martagon is a plant. People use the leaf, stem, and flower to make medicine.

Is it Effective?

The effectiveness ratings for **MARTAGON** are as follows:

Insufficient Evidence to Rate Effectiveness for... Skin ulcers, menstrual problems, and other uses.

How does it work?

There isn't enough information to know how martagon might work for the conditions people use it for.

Are there safety concerns?

There isn't enough information to know if martagon might be safe.

Do not use martagon if: You are pregnant or breast-feeding.

Are there any interactions with medications?

It is not known if martagon interacts with any medicines.

Before taking martagon, talk with your healthcare professional if you take any medications.

Natural Medicines Comprehensive Database Consumer Version (209) 472-2244

Medical professionals should consult the Professional Version at www.NaturalDatabase.com.

CONSUMER VERSION

MASTERWORT

What other names is the product known by?

Cow Cabbage, Cow Parsnip, Heracleum lanatum, Heracleum sphondylium, Hogweed, Madnep, Radix Pimpinelle Franconiae, Woolly Parsnip, Youthwort.

What is it?

Masterwort is a plant. People use it to make medicine.

Is it Effective?

The effectiveness ratings for **MASTERWORT** are as follows:
Insufficient Evidence to Rate Effectiveness for... Muscle cramps, stomach disorders, digestion problems, diarrhea, inflammation of the stomach and intestines, and other conditions.

How does it work?

There is not enough information to know how masterwort might work.

Are there safety concerns?

Masterwort might be unsafe. It can cause the skin to burn more easily in the sun, and can also be cancer-causing. Wear protective clothing and sunblock outside, especially if you are light-skinned.

Do not use masterwort if: You are pregnant or breast-feeding. • You spend time in sunlight, use a tanning bed, or use a sunlamp (phototherapy) for certain skin conditions such as psoriasis.

Are there any interactions with medications?

Medications that increase sensitivity to sunlight (Photosensitizing drugs). Some medications can increase sensitivity to sunlight. Masterwort might also increase your sensitivity to sunlight. Taking masterwort along with medication that increase sensitivity to sunlight could increase the chances of sunburn, blistering or rashes on areas of skin exposed to sunlight. Be sure to wear sunblock and protective clothing when spending time in the sun. Some drugs that cause photosensitivity include amitriptyline (Elavil), Ciprofloxacin (Cipro), norfloxacin (Noroxin), lomefloxacin (Maxaquin), ofloxacin (Floxin), levofloxacin (Levaquin), sparfloxacin (Zagam), gatifloxacin (Tequin), moxifloxacin (Avelox), trimethoprim/sulfamethoxazole (Septra), tetracycline, methoxsalen (8-methoxypsoralen, 8-MOP, Oxsoralen), and Trioxsalen (Trisoralen).

MASTIC

What other names is the product known by?

Lentisk, Mastich, Mastix, Pistacia lentiscus.

What is it?

Mastic is a plant. People use the resin to make medicine.

Is it Effective?

The effectiveness ratings for **MASTIC** are as follows:
Insufficient Evidence to Rate Effectiveness for... Stomach and intestinal ulcers, breathing conditions, muscle aches, blood circulation, bacterial and fungal infections, cuts, repelling insects, dental fillings, freshening the breath, and other uses.

How does it work?

Mastic might help reduce stomach acid and have a protective effect on the lining of the stomach and intestine. Mastic also has an aromatic oil which could freshen the breath. In a test tube, mastic seems to fight bacteria and fungi.

Are there safety concerns?

Mastic might be safe for most people. The pollen might cause allergic reactions in some people who are sensitive to mastic and other related herbs. Also, children who take mastic might develop diarrhea.

Do not use mastic if: You are pregnant or breast-feeding.

Are there any interactions with medications?

It is not known if mastic interacts with any medicines.
Before taking mastic, talk with your healthcare professional if you take any medications.

MATE

What other names is the product known by?
Chimarrao, Hervea, Ilex, Ilex paraguariensis, Jesuit's Brazil Tea, Jesuit's Tea, Maté Folium, Paraguay Tea, St. Bartholemew's Tea, Yerba Mate.

What is it?
Mate is a plant. The leaves are used to make medicine.

Is it Effective?
The effectiveness ratings for **MATE** are as follows:
Insufficient Evidence to Rate Effectiveness for... Constipation, depression, urinary tract infections (UTIs), heart conditions, kidney and bladder stones, mental and physical tiredness (fatigue), chronic fatigue syndrome (CFS), fluid retention, headaches, low blood pressure (hypotension), weight loss, and other conditions.

How does it work?
Mate contains caffeine and other chemicals which stimulate the brain, heart, muscles lining blood vessels, and other parts of the body.

Are there safety concerns?
Mate might be safe for most people, when taken for short periods of time. It contains caffeine, which can cause some side effects such as inability to sleep (insomnia), nervousness and restlessness, stomach upset, nausea and vomiting, increased heart rate and breathing, high blood pressure, headache, ringing in the ears, irregular heartbeats, and other side effects.

When taken in large amounts or for long periods of time, mate might be unsafe. It increases the risk of mouth, esophageal, laryngeal, kidney, bladder, and lung cancer. Concurrent smoking and alcohol consumption compounds the risk.

Do not take mate if: You are pregnant or breast-feeding. • You have a heart condition. • You have high blood pressure (hypertension). • You smoke. • You are a heavy alcohol user. • You have anxiety. • You have an eye disease called glaucoma. • You have osteoporosis. • You have a bleeding condition.

Are there any interactions with medications?
Adenosine (Adenocard). Mate contains caffeine. The caffeine in mate might block the affects of adenosine (Adenocard). Adenosine (Adenocard) is often used by doctors to do a test on the heart. This test is called a cardiac stress test. Stop consuming mate or other caffeine-containing products at least 24 hours before a cardiac stress test.
Alcohol. The body breaks down the caffeine in mate to get rid of it. Alcohol can decrease how quickly the body breaks down caffeine. Taking mate along with alcohol might cause too much caffeine in the bloodstream and caffeine side effects including jitteriness, headache, and fast heartbeat.
Amphetamines. Stimulant drugs such as amphetamines speed up the nervous system. By speeding up the nervous system, stimulant medications can make you feel jittery and increase your heart rate. The caffeine in mate might also speed up the nervous system. Taking mate along with stimulant drugs might cause serious problems including increased heart rate and high blood pressure. Avoid taking stimulant drugs along with mate.
Antibiotics (Quinolone antibiotics). The body breaks down caffeine to get rid of it. Some antibiotics might decrease how quickly the body breaks down caffeine. Taking these antibiotics along with mate can increase the risk of side effects including jitteriness, headache, increased heart rate, and other side effects. Some antibiotics that decrease how quickly the body breaks down caffeine include ciprofloxacin (Cipro), enoxacin (Penetrex), norfloxacin (Chibroxin, Noroxin), sparfloxacin (Zagam), trovafloxacin (Trovan), and grepafloxacin (Raxar).
Birth control pills (Contraceptive drugs). The body breaks down the caffeine in mate to get rid of it. Birth control pills can decrease how quickly the body breaks down caffeine. Taking mate along with birth control pills can cause jitteriness, headache, fast heartbeat, and other side effects. Some birth control pills include ethinyl estradiol and levonorgestrel (Triphasil), ethinyl estradiol and norethindrone (Ortho-Novum 1/35, Ortho-Novum 7/7/7), and others.
Cimetidine (Tagamet). Mate contains caffeine. The body breaks down caffeine to get rid of it. Cimetidine (Tagamet) can decrease how quickly your body breaks down caffeine. Taking cimetidine (Tagamet) along with mate might increase the chance of caffeine side effects including jitteriness, headache, fast heartbeat, and others.
Clozapine (Clozaril). The body breaks down clozapine (Clozaril) to get rid of it. The caffeine in mate seems to decrease how quickly the body breaks down clozapine (Clozaril). Taking mate along with clozapine (Clozaril) can increase the effects and side effects of clozapine (Clozaril).
Cocaine. Stimulant drugs such as cocaine speed up the nervous system. By speeding up the nervous system, stimulant medications can make you feel jittery and increase your heart rate. The caffeine in mate might also speed up the nervous system. Taking mate along with stimulant drugs might cause serious problems including increased heart rate and high blood pressure. Avoid taking stimulant drugs along with mate.

Dipyridamole (Persantine). Mate contains caffeine. The caffeine in mate might block the affects of dipyridamole (Persantine). Dipyridamole (Persantine) is often used by doctors to do a test on the heart. This test is called a cardiac stress test. Stop consuming mate or other caffeine-containing products at least 24 hours before a cardiac stress test.

Disulfiram (Antabuse). The body breaks down caffeine to get rid of it. Disulfiram (Antabuse) can decrease how quickly the body gets rid of caffeine. Taking mate (which contains caffeine) along with disulfiram (Antabuse) might increase the effects and side effects of caffeine including jitteriness, hyperactivity, irritability, and others.

Ephedrine. Stimulant drugs speed up the nervous system. Caffeine (contained in mate) and ephedrine are both stimulant drugs. Taking caffeine along with ephedrine might cause too much stimulation and sometimes serious side effects and heart problems. Do not take caffeine-containing products and ephedrine at the same time.

Estrogens. The body breaks down caffeine (contained in mate) to get rid of it. Estrogens can decrease how quickly the body breaks down caffeine. Decreasing the breakdown of caffeine can cause jitteriness, headache, fast heartbeat, and other side effects. If you take estrogens limit your caffeine intake. Some estrogen pills include conjugated equine estrogens (Premarin), ethinyl estradiol, estradiol, and others.

Fluconazole (Diflucan). Mate contains caffeine. The body breaks down caffeine to get rid of it. Fluconazole (Diflucan) might decrease how quickly the body gets rid of caffeine. This could cause caffeine to stay in the body too long and increase the risk of side effects such as nervousness, anxiety, and insomnia.

Fluvoxamine (Luvox). The body breaks down the caffeine in mate to get rid of it. Fluvoxamine (Luvox) can decrease how quickly the body breaks down caffeine. Taking mate along with fluvoxamine (Luvox) might cause too much caffeine in the body, and increase the effects and side effects of mate.

Lithium. Your body naturally gets rid of lithium. The caffeine in mate can increase how quickly your body gets rid of lithium. If you take products that contain caffeine and you take lithium, stop taking caffeine products slowly. Stopping mate too quickly can increase the side effects of lithium.

Medications for depression (MAOIs). The caffeine in mate can stimulate the body. Some medications used for depression can also stimulate the body. Drinking mate and taking some medications for depression might cause too much stimulation to the body and serious side effects including fast heartbeat, high blood pressure, nervousness, and others could occur. Some of these medications used for depression include phenelzine (Nardil), tranylcypromine (Parnate), and others.

Medications for diabetes (Antidiabetes drugs). Mate might increase blood sugar. Diabetes medications are used to lower blood sugar. By increasing blood sugar, mate might decrease the effectiveness of diabetes medications. Monitor your blood sugar closely. The dose of your diabetes medication might need to be changed. Some medications used for diabetes include glimepiride (Amaryl), glyburide (DiaBeta, Glynase PresTab, Micronase), insulin, pioglitazone (Actos), rosiglitazone (Avandia), chlorpropamide (Diabinese), glipizide (Glucotrol), tolbutamide (Orinase), and others.

Medications that slow blood clotting (Anticoagulant / Antiplatelet drugs). Mate contains caffeine. Caffeine might slow blood clotting. Taking mate along with medications that also slow clotting might increase the chances of bruising and bleeding. Some medications that slow blood clotting include aspirin, clopidogrel (Plavix), diclofenac (Voltaren, Cataflam, others), ibuprofen (Advil, Motrin, others), naproxen (Anaprox, Naprosyn, others), dalteparin (Fragmin), enoxaparin (Lovenox), heparin, warfarin (Coumadin), and others.

Mexiletine (Mexitil). Mate contains caffeine. The body breaks down caffeine to get rid of it. Mexiletine (Mexitil) can decrease how quickly the body breaks down caffeine. Taking Mexiletine (Mexitil) along with mate might increase the caffeine effects and side effects of mate.

Nicotine. Stimulant drugs such as nicotine speed up the nervous system. By speeding up the nervous system, stimulant medications can make you feel jittery and increase your heart rate. The caffeine in mate might also speed up the nervous system. Taking mate along with stimulant drugs might cause serious problems including increased heart rate and high blood pressure. Avoid taking stimulant drugs along with mate.

Pentobarbital (Nembutal). The stimulant effects of the caffeine in mate can block the sleep-producing effects of pentobarbital.

Phenylpropanolamine. Mate contains caffeine. Caffeine can stimulate the body. Phenylpropanolamine can also stimulate the body. Taking mate and phenylpropanolamine together might cause too much stimulation and increase heartbeat and blood pressure and cause nervousness.

Riluzole (Rilutek). The body breaks down riluzole (Rilutek) to get rid of it. Taking mate can decrease how fast the body breaks down riluzole (Rilutek) and increase the effects and side effects of riluzole.

Terbinafine (Lamisil). The body breaks down caffeine (contained in mate) to get rid of it. Terbinafine (Lamisil) can decrease how fast the body gets rid of caffeine and increase the risk of side effects including jitteriness, headache, increased heartbeat, and other effects.

Theophylline. Mate contains caffeine. Caffeine works similarly to theophylline. Caffeine can also decrease how quickly the body gets rid of theophylline. Taking mate along with theophylline might increase the effects and side effects of theophylline.

Verapamil (Calan, Covera, Isoptin, Verelan). The body breaks down the caffeine in mate to get rid of it. Verapamil (Calan, Covera, Isoptin, Verelan) can decrease how quickly the body gets rid of caffeine. Drinking mate and taking verapamil (Calan, Covera, Isoptin, Verelan) can increase the risk of side effects for caffeine including jitteriness, headache, and an increased heartbeat.

MEADOWSWEET

What other names is the product known by?
Bridewort, Dolloff, Dropwort, Filipendula, Filipendula ulmaria, Lady Of The Meadow, Meadow Queen, Meadow Sweet, Meadow-Wart, Queen of the Meadow, Spiraeae flos, Spireae herba, Ulmaria.

What is it?
Meadowsweet is a plant. The above ground parts are used to make medicine.

Is it Effective?
The effectiveness ratings for **MEADOWSWEET** are as follows:
Insufficient Evidence to Rate Effectiveness for... Bronchitis, heartburn, upset stomach, ulcers, gout, joint problems, bladder infections, and other conditions.

How does it work?
Meadowsweet contains tannins which might decrease inflammation (swelling) and decrease mucus (phlegm). It also has small amounts of salicylates which are similar to aspirin.

Are there safety concerns?
Meadowsweet, when taken appropriately, is possibly safe for most people. Meadowsweet can cause stomach complaints including nausea. Skin rashes and lung tightness can occur. It might also cause blood in the stool, vomiting, ringing in the ears, kidney problems, and other side effects if taken in large amounts or for long periods of time.

Do not take meadowsweet if: You are pregnant or breast-feeding. • You have asthma. • You are allergic to aspirin.

Are there any interactions with medications?
Aspirin. Meadowsweet contains chemicals similar to aspirin. Taking meadowsweet along with aspirin might increase the effects and side effects of aspirin.
Choline Magnesium Trisalicylate (Trilisate). Meadowsweet contains chemicals that are similar to choline magnesium trisalicylate (Trilisate). Taking meadowsweet along with choline magnesium trisalicylate (Trilisate) might increase the effects and side effects of choline magnesium trisalicylate (Trilisate).
Medications for pain (Narcotic drugs). The body breaks down some medications for pain to get rid of them. Meadowsweet might decrease how fast the body gets rid of some medications for pain. By decreasing how fast the body gets rid of some medications for pain, meadowsweet might increase the effects and side effects of some medications for pain. Some medications for pain include meperidine (Demerol), hydrocodone, morphine, OxyContin, and many others.
Salsalate (Disalcid). Salsalate (Disalcid) is called a salicylate. It's similar to aspirin. Meadowsweet also contains a salicylate similar to aspirin. Taking salsalate with meadowsweet might cause there to be too much salicylates in the body. This might increase the effects and side effects of salicylates.

MEDIUM CHAIN TRIGLYCERIDES (MCT)

What other names is the product known by?
MCTs.

What is it?
Medium chain triglycerides (MCTs) are partially man-made fats. People use MCTs to make medicine.

Is it Effective?
The effectiveness ratings for **MEDIUM CHAIN TRIGLYCERIDES (MCT)** are as follows:
Possibly Effective for... Certain types of seizures in children • Preventing muscle breakdown in critically ill patients.
Possibly Ineffective for... Weight loss associated with AIDS.
Insufficient Evidence to Rate Effectiveness for... Nutritional support of athletic training, decreasing body fat and increasing lean muscle, improving the absorption of calcium and magnesium, chylothorax (a rare lung disorder), and other uses.

How does it work?
Medium chain triglycerides are a fat source for patients who cannot tolerate other types of fats.

Are there safety concerns?

Medium chain triglycerides are safe for most people. They can cause diarrhea, vomiting, irritability, nausea, stomach discomfort, intestinal gas, essential fatty acid deficiency, and other side effects. Taking medium chain triglycerides with food might reduce some side effects.

Do not use medium chain triglycerides if: You have a liver condition. • You have diabetes.

Are there any interactions with medications?

It is not known if medium-chain triglycerides (MCT) interact with any medicines.
Before taking MCT, talk with your healthcare professional if you take any medications.

MELANOTAN-II

What other names is the product known by?

MT-II.

What is it?

Melanotan-II is a synthetic chemical which is similar to a hormone found in people. Be careful not to confuse melanotan-II with melatonin.

Is it Effective?

The effectiveness ratings for **MELANOTAN-II** are as follows:
Possibly Effective for... Use by injection to produce erections in men with erectile problems • Use by injection to produce tanning of the skin.
Insufficient Evidence to Rate Effectiveness for... Prevention of sunlight-induced skin cancers and other conditions.

How does it work?

Melanotan-II is similar to a substance in our bodies, called "melanocyte-stimulating hormone," which increases the production of darkening skin pigments. Melanotan-II might also work in the brain to stimulate erections of the penis.

Are there safety concerns?

Melanotan-II is possibly safe when used under medical supervision for treating erectile dysfunction. There isn't enough information to know whether it is safe for other uses. Adverse effects which may occur with melanotan-II include nausea, stomach cramps, decreased appetite, flushing, tiredness, yawning, darkened skin, spontaneous erections of the penis, and other side effects.

Do not use melanotan-II if: You are pregnant or breast-feeding.

Are there any interactions with medications?

It is not known if melanotan-II interacts with any medicines.
Before taking melanotan-II, talk with your healthcare professional if you take any medications.

MELATONIN

What other names is the product known by?

MEL, MLT, N-acetyl-5-methoxytryptamine, Pineal Hormone.

What is it?

Melatonin is a hormone found naturally in the body. Melatonin used as medicine is usually made synthetically in a laboratory.

Is it Effective?

The effectiveness ratings for **MELATONIN** are as follows:
Likely Effective for... Sleep disorders in blind people • Sleeping problems in children with autism and mental retardation.
Possibly Effective for... Improving alertness in people with jet lag. However, it doesn't seem to be as useful for other jet lag symptoms, such as daytime sleepiness • Insomnia • Improving the effectiveness of certain cancer medications used to fight tumors in the breast, lung, kidney, liver, pancreas, stomach, colon, prostate, and decreasing some side effects of cancer treatment • Decreasing symptoms of a movement disorder called tardive

dyskinesia (TD) • Cluster headaches • Decreasing sunburn when applied to the skin in a cream form before going into the sun • Reducing anxiety before surgery • Helping elderly people sleep after they stop taking a type of drug called benzodiazepines • Helping decrease symptoms in patients who are quitting smoking. • Low blood platelets (Thrombocytopenia).
Possibly Ineffective for... Adjusting sleep schedule in people that do shift work • Chronic fatigue syndrome (CFS).
Likely Ineffective for... Depression.
Insufficient Evidence to Rate Effectiveness for... Ringing in the ears (tinnitus), osteoporosis, irritable bowel syndrome (IBS), epilepsy, birth control, fibromyalgia (an inflammatory condition), aging, menopausal symptoms, sleep problems associated with attention deficit-hyperactivity disorder (ADHD), insomnia caused by medications used for high blood pressure (beta-blockers), headache characterized by sudden sharp pain (idiopathic stabbing headache), migraine, and other conditions.

How does it work?
Melatonin's main job in the body is to regulate night and day cycles or sleep-wake cycles. Darkness causes the body to produce more melatonin, which signals the body to prepare for sleep. Light decreases melatonin production and signals the body to prepare for being awake. Some people who have trouble sleeping have low levels of melatonin. It is thought that adding melatonin from supplements might help them sleep.

Are there safety concerns?
Melatonin is safe for most adults when taken by mouth short-term or applied topically. It can cause some side effects including headache, short-term feelings of depression, daytime sleepiness, dizziness, stomach cramps, and irritability. Do not drive or use machinery for four to five hours after taking melatonin.

Melatonin should not be used in most children. Because of its effects on other hormones, it might interfere with development during adolescence.

Do not take melatonin if: You are pregnant or breast-feeding. • You have high blood pressure. • You have had a seizure. • You have diabetes. • You have cancer. • You have depression.

Are there any interactions with medications?
Birth control pills (Contraceptive drugs). The body makes melatonin. Birth control pills seem to increase how much melatonin the body makes. Taking melatonin along with birth control pills might cause too much melatonin to be in the body. Some birth control pills include ethinyl estradiol and levonorgestrel (Triphasil), ethinyl estradiol and norethindrone (Ortho-Novum 1/35, Ortho-Novum 7/7/7), and others.
Caffeine. Caffeine might decrease melatonin levels in the body. Taking melatonin along with caffeine might decrease the effectiveness of melatonin supplements.
Flumazenil (Romazicon). Flumazenil (Romazicon) might decrease the effects of melatonin. It is not yet clear why this interaction occurs yet. Taking flumazenil (Romazicon) along with melatonin might decrease the effectiveness of melatonin supplements.
Fluvoxamine (Luvox). Taking fluvoxamine (Luvox) can increase the amount of melatonin that the body absorbs. Taking melatonin along with fluvoxamine (Luvox) might increase the effects and side effects of melatonin.
Medications that slow blood clotting (Anticoagulant / Antiplatelet drugs). Melatonin might slow blood clotting. Taking melatonin along with medications that also slow clotting might increase the chances of bruising and bleeding. Some medications that slow blood clotting include aspirin, clopidogrel (Plavix), diclofenac (Voltaren, Cataflam, others), ibuprofen (Advil, Motrin, others), naproxen (Anaprox, Naprosyn, others), dalteparin (Fragmin), enoxaparin (Lovenox), heparin, warfarin (Coumadin), and others.
Medications for diabetes (Antidiabetes drugs). Melatonin might increase blood sugar. Diabetes medications are used to lower blood sugar. By increasing blood sugar, melatonin might decrease the effectiveness of diabetes medications. Monitor your blood sugar closely. The dose of your diabetes medication might need to be changed. Some medications used for diabetes include glimepiride (Amaryl), glyburide (DiaBeta, Glynase PresTab, Micronase), insulin, pioglitazone (Actos), rosiglitazone (Avandia), chlorpropamide (Diabinese), glipizide (Glucotrol), tolbutamide (Orinase), and others.
Medications that decrease the immune system (Immunosuppressants). Melatonin might increase the immune system. Taking melatonin along with medications that decrease the immune system might decrease the effectiveness of medications that decrease the immune system. Some medications that decrease the immune system include azathioprine (Imuran), basiliximab (Simulect), cyclosporine (Neoral, Sandimmune), daclizumab (Zenapax), muromonab-CD3 (OKT3, Orthoclone OKT3), mycophenolate (CellCept), tacrolimus (FK506, Prograf), sirolimus (Rapamune), prednisone (Deltasone, Orasone), corticosteroids (glucocorticoids), and others.
Nifedipine GITS (Procardia XL). Nifedipine GITS (Procardia XL) is used to lower blood pressure. Taking melatonin might decrease the effectiveness of nifedipine GITS for lowering blood pressure.
Sedative medications (CNS depressants). Melatonin might cause sleepiness and drowsiness. Medications that cause sleepiness are called sedatives. Taking melatonin along with sedative medications might cause too much sleepiness. Some sedative medications include clonazepam (Klonopin), lorazepam (Ativan), phenobarbital (Donnatal), zolpidem (Ambien), and others.

Sedative medications (Benzodiazepines). Melatonin might cause sleepiness and drowsiness. Drugs that cause sleepiness and drowsiness are called sedatives. Taking melatonin along with sedative medications might cause too much sleepiness. Some of these sedative medications include clonazepam (Klonopin), diazepam (Valium), lorazepam (Ativan), and others.

Verapamil (Calan, Covera, Isoptin, Verelan). The body breaks down melatonin to get rid of it. Verapamil (Calan, Covera, Isoptin, Verelan) can increase how quickly the body gets rid of melatonin. Taking melatonin along with verapamil (Calan, Covera, Isoptin, Verelan) might decrease the effectiveness of melatonin.

MENTZELIA

What other names is the product known by?
Anguraté, Mentzelia cordifolia.

What is it?
Mentzelia is a plant. The branch tips, stems, and roots are used to make medicine.

Is it Effective?
The effectiveness ratings for **MENTZELIA** are as follows:
Insufficient Evidence to Rate Effectiveness for... Problems of the digestive system, particularly the stomach.

How does it work?
There isn't enough information to know how mentzelia might work.

Are there safety concerns?
There isn't enough information to know if mentzelia might be safe.

Do not use mentzelia if: You are pregnant or breast-feeding.

Are there any interactions with medications?
It is not known if mentzelia interacts with any medicines.
Before taking mentzelia, talk with your healthcare professional if you take any medications.

MERCURY HERB

What other names is the product known by?
Mercurialis annua.

What is it?
Mercury herb is a plant. People use the flowering plant, root, and root-like stem (rhizome) of the plant to make medicine.

Is it Effective?
The effectiveness ratings for **MERCURY HERB** are as follows:
Insufficient Evidence to Rate Effectiveness for... Inflammation with pus; constipation; fluid retention; and for diseases of the stomach, intestines, kidney, bladder, and other parts of the digestive and urinary systems.

How does it work?
The root and stem of mercury herb might work as laxatives to help stool move through the intestine.

Are there safety concerns?
Mercury herb is unsafe when the fresh plant is used. It can cause diarrhea, bladder problems, paralysis, liver and kidney failure, and death. The pollen might also cause allergic reactions, nose irritation, and asthma in some people who are sensitive to mercury herb and other related plants.

Do not use mercury herb if: You are pregnant or breast-feeding.

Are there any interactions with medications?
It is not known if mercury herb interacts with any medicines.
Before taking mercury herb, talk with your healthcare professional if you take any medications.

MESOGLYCAN

What other names is the product known by?

Aortic Glycosaminoglycans, Aortic GAGs, Glycosaminoglycans, Heparinoid Fraction, Heparinoids, Mucopolysaccharide, Sulfomucopolysaccharide.

What is it?

Mesoglycan is a substance obtained from cow lung or blood vessels (aorta), or pig intestine.

Is it Effective?

The effectiveness ratings for **MESOGLYCAN** are as follows:

Possibly Effective for... Treating poor circulation that can lead to varicose veins and other conditions • Treating leg ulcers • Reducing blood levels of certain fats called triglycerides • Reducing pain when walking in people with a disease called peripheral arterial disease • Improving thinking and quality of life in people with limited blood flow to the brain (cerebrovascular disease).

Possibly Ineffective for... Preventing blood clots in the legs and lungs (deep vein thrombosis and pulmonary embolism) • Treating stroke.

Insufficient Evidence to Rate Effectiveness for... Hemorrhoids, atherosclerosis (a type of heart disease), inflammation of blood vessels (vasculitis), and other conditions.

How does it work?

Mesoglycan appears to have effects that improve blood flow and reduce the risk of clotting.

Are there safety concerns?

Mesoglycan seems safe for most adults. It can cause nausea, vomiting, heartburn, headache, diarrhea, and skin reactions.

Because mesoglycan comes from animal products, there is a risk that diseases could be accidentally transmitted from sick animals.

Do not use mesoglycan if: You are pregnant or breast-feeding. • You have an allergy to the blood thinner heparin. • You have a blood-clotting problem.

Are there any interactions with medications?

Medications that slow blood clotting (Anticoagulant / Antiplatelet drugs). Mesoglycan might slow blood clotting. Taking mesoglycan along with medications that also slow clotting might increase the chances of bruising and bleeding. Some medications that slow blood clotting include aspirin, clopidogrel (Plavix), diclofenac (Voltaren, Cataflam, others), ibuprofen (Advil, Motrin, others), naproxen (Anaprox, Naprosyn, others), dalteparin (Fragmin), enoxaparin (Lovenox), heparin, warfarin (Coumadin), and others.

Medications for dissolving blood clots (Thrombolytic drugs). Mesoglycan decreases blood clotting. Taking mesoglycan with medications used for dissolving blood clots might increase the chance of bleeding and bruising. Some medications used for dissolving blood clots include alteplase (Activase), anistreplase (Eminase), reteplase (Retevase), streptokinase (Streptase), and urokinase (Abbokinase).

METHIONINE

What other names is the product known by?

DL-Methionine, L-Methionine, L-2-amino-4-(methylthio)butyric acid.

What is it?

Methionine is called an amino acid, a building block of proteins in our bodies. Methionine is found in meat, fish, and dairy products. Methionine plays an important role in many cell functions.

Is it Effective?

The effectiveness ratings for **METHIONINE** are as follows:

Possibly Effective for... Preventing liver damage in cases of acetaminophen (Tylenol) poisoning.

Insufficient Evidence to Rate Effectiveness for... Preventing cancer; maintaining normal liver function; and treating depression, alcoholism, allergies, asthma, radiation side effects, schizophrenia, drug withdrawal, and Parkinson's disease.

Medical professionals should consult the Professional Version at www.NaturalDatabase.com.

CONSUMER VERSION

How does it work?
In acetaminophen poisoning, methionine prevents the breakdown products of acetaminophen from damaging the liver.

Are there safety concerns?
Methionine seems to be safe for treating acetaminophen poisoning under the supervision of a healthcare professional. It may be unsafe to use methionine to self-medicate if used in amounts larger than those normally found in foods. Methionine can increase blood levels of homocysteine, a chemical that might cause heart disease. Methionine might also promote the growth of some tumors.

Do not use methionine if: You are pregnant or breast-feeding. • You have hardening of the arteries (atherosclerosis). • You have cancer. • You have a genetic disorder called methylenetetrahydrofolate reductase (MTHFR) deficiency.

Are there any interactions with medications?
It is not known if methionine interacts with any medicines.
Before taking methionine, talk with your healthcare professional if you take any medications.

METHOXYLATED FLAVONES

What other names is the product known by?
Citrus Bioflavones, Citrus Bioflavonoids, Citrus Flavones, Citrus Flavonoids, Citrus Polymethoxylated Flavones, Flavonoids, Gardenin D, Heptamethoxyflavones, Hexamethoxyflavones, Methoxyflavones, Methoxylated flavonoids, Nobiletin, Pentamethoxyflavones, PMF, Polymethoxylated Flavones, Sinensetin, Tangeretin, Tetramethoxyflavones.

What is it?
Methoxylated flavones are pigments found in plants.

Is it Effective?
The effectiveness ratings for **METHOXYLATED FLAVONES** are as follows:
Insufficient Evidence to Rate Effectiveness for... Venous insufficiency, varicose veins, heart disease, high cholesterol, cataracts, and cancer.

How does it work?
Methoxylated flavones are natural antioxidants and might also reduce inflammatory (swelling) effects. They might reduce the spread of cancer cells. But more information is needed.

Are there safety concerns?
Methoxylated flavones are a normal component of the diet. They are safe when consumed as part of food. But there is not enough information available to know if taking supplements containing methoxylated flavones are safe.

Are there any interactions with medications?
Medications changed by the liver (Cytochrome P450 1A2 (CYP1A2) substrates). Some medications are changed and broken down by the liver. Methoxylated flavones might increase how quickly the liver breaks down some medications. Taking methoxylated flavones along with some medications that are changed by the liver might decrease the effects of some medications. Before taking methoxylated flavones talk to your healthcare provider if you take any medications that are changed by the liver. Some of these medications that are changed by the liver include clozapine (Clozaril), cyclobenzaprine (Flexeril), fluvoxamine (Luvox), haloperidol (Haldol), imipramine (Tofranil), mexiletine (Mexitil), olanzapine (Zyprexa), pentazocine (Talwin), propranolol (Inderal), tacrine (Cognex), theophylline, zileuton (Zyflo), zolmitriptan (Zomig), and others.
Medications that slow blood clotting (Anticoagulant / Antiplatelet drugs). Some methoxylated flavones might slow blood clotting. Taking methoxylated flavones along with medications that also slow clotting might increase the chances of bruising and bleeding. Some medications that slow blood clotting include aspirin, clopidogrel (Plavix), diclofenac (Voltaren, Cataflam, others), ibuprofen (Advil, Motrin, others), naproxen (Anaprox, Naprosyn, others), dalteparin (Fragmin), enoxaparin (Lovenox), heparin, warfarin (Coumadin), and others.

MEXICAN SCAMMONY ROOT

What other names is the product known by?
Ipomoea, Ipomoea orizabensis, Orizaba Jalap.

What is it?
Mexican scammony is a plant. People use the root of the plant to make medicine.

Is it Effective?
The effectiveness ratings for **MEXICAN SCAMMONY ROOT** are as follows:
Insufficient Evidence to Rate Effectiveness for... Purging stool from the bowel.

How does it work?
Mexican scammony root pushes stool through the intestines by causing a strong laxative effect.

Are there safety concerns?
There is insufficient reliable information available about the safety of Mexican scammony root. It can cause vomiting and intestinal problems.

Do not use Mexican scammony root if: You are pregnant or breast-feeding. • You have stomach, intestine, or other digestive tract problems. • You have a condition called appendicitis, or symptoms of appendicitis such as abdominal pain, nausea, and vomiting.

Are there any interactions with medications?
Digoxin (Lanoxin). Mexican scammony root is a type of laxative called a stimulant laxative. Stimulant laxatives can decrease potassium levels in the body. Low potassium levels can increase the risk of side effects of digoxin (Lanoxin).
Medications taken by mouth (Oral drugs). Mexican scammony root is a laxative. Laxatives can decrease how much medicine your body absorbs. Decreasing how much medicine your body absorbs can decrease the effectiveness of your medication.
Stimulant laxatives. Mexican scammony root is a type of laxative called a stimulant laxative. Stimulant laxatives speed up the bowels. Taking Mexican scammony root along with other stimulant laxatives could speed up the bowels too much and cause dehydration and low minerals in the body. Some stimulant laxatives include bisacodyl (Correctol, Dulcolax), cascara, castor oil (Purge), senna (Senokot), and others.
Water pills (Diuretic drugs). Mexican scammony root is a laxative. Some laxatives can decrease potassium in the body. "Water pills" can also decrease potassium in the body. Taking Mexican scammony root along with "water pills" might decrease potassium in the body too much. Some "water pills" that can decrease potassium include chlorothiazide (Diuril), chlorthalidone (Thalitone), furosemide (Lasix), hydrochlorothiazide (HCTZ, HydroDiuril, Microzide), and others.

MEZEREON

What other names is the product known by?
Camolea, Daphne, Daphne mezereum, Dwarf Bay, Spurge Flax, Spurge Laurel, Spurge Olive, Wild Pepper.

What is it?
Mezereon is a plant. People use the bark of mezereon to make medicine.

Is it Effective?
The effectiveness ratings for **MEZEREON** are as follows:
Insufficient Evidence to Rate Effectiveness for... Headaches, toothaches, joint pains, increasing circulation, and other conditions.

How does it work?
Mezereon might stimulate the skin.

Are there safety concerns?
Mezereon might be unsafe when applied directly to the skin. Skin contact with mezereon can cause red, painful swelling of the skin, blisters, and permanent skin damage (necrosis).
Contact with the eyes can cause severe eye swelling and irritation.

Mezereon is unsafe when taken by mouth. It can cause many serious side effects including redness and swelling of the mouth, upset of the digestive tract, blood in the urine, hallucinations, increased heart rate, spasms, and death.

Do not take mezereon if: You are pregnant or breast-feeding.

Are there any interactions with medications?
It is not known if mezereon interacts with any medicines.
Before taking mezereon, talk with your healthcare professional if you take any medications.

MGN-3

What other names is the product known by?
Biobran, Hemicellulose Complex with Arabinoxylane.

What is it?
MGN-3 is a product made by combining rice bran with chemicals from the shiitake, kawaratake, and suehirotake mushrooms. People use MGN-3 as a medicine.

Is it Effective?
The effectiveness ratings for **MGN-3** are as follows:
Insufficient Evidence to Rate Effectiveness for... Boosting immune function; preventing and treating cancer; treating AIDS, hepatitis, diabetes, or chronic fatigue syndrome; and other immune disorders.

How does it work?
MGN-3 might work by improving the body's natural immune system.

Are there safety concerns?
There is insufficient reliable information available about the safety of MGN-3.

Do not take MGN-3 if: You are pregnant or breast-feeding.

Are there any interactions with medications?
It is not known if MGN-3 interacts with any medicines.
Before taking MGN-3, talk with your healthcare professional if you take any medications.

MILK THISTLE

What other names is the product known by?
Cardui mariae fructus, Cardui mariae herba, Carduus marianum, Carduus marianus, Holy Thistle, Lady's Thistle, Legalon, Marian Thistle, Mariendistel, Mary Thistle, Our Lady's Thistle, Silybin, Silybum, Silybum marianum, Silymarin, St. Mary Thistle.

What is it?
Milk thistle is a plant. The above ground parts and seeds are used to make medicine. The seeds are more commonly used.

Is it Effective?
The effectiveness ratings for **MILK THISTLE** are as follows:
Possibly Effective for... Upset stomach (dyspepsia), when a combination of milk thistle and several other herbs is used.
Insufficient Evidence to Rate Effectiveness for... Gallbladder problems, liver disease (cirrhosis, hepatitis and other liver conditions), liver damage caused by chemicals or poisonous mushrooms, spleen disorders, swelling of the lungs (pleurisy), malaria, menstrual problems, and other conditions.

How does it work?
Milk thistle seed might protect liver cells from toxic chemicals and drugs. It also seems to have antioxidant and anti-inflammatory effects. Milk thistle plant extract might enhance the effects of estrogen.

Are there safety concerns?
Milk thistle is safe for most adults. Milk thistle sometimes causes a laxative effect. Other less common side effects are nausea, diarrhea, indigestion, intestinal gas, bloating, fullness or pain, and loss of appetite. Milk thistle can cause an allergic reaction in people sensitive to plants in the Asteraceae/Compositae family including ragweed,

marigolds, daisies, and other related plants.
Do not take milk thistle if: You are pregnant or breast-feeding. • You are sensitive or allergic to ragweed, marigolds, daisies, and other related plants. • You have a hormone-sensitive condition. Some of these conditions include endometriosis; uterine fibroids; and cancers of the breast, uterus, and ovaries.

Are there any interactions with medications?

Medications changed by the liver (Cytochrome P450 2C9 (CYP2C9) substrates). Some medications are changed and broken down by the liver. Milk thistle might decrease how quickly the liver breaks down some medications. Taking milk thistle along with some medications that are broken down by the liver can increase the effects and side effects of some medications. Before taking milk thistle talk to your healthcare provider if you take any medications that are changed by the liver. Some medications that are changed by the liver include amitriptyline (Elavil), diazepam (Valium), zileuton (Zyflo), celecoxib (Celebrex), diclofenac (Voltaren), fluvastatin (Lescol), glipizide (Glucotrol), ibuprofen (Advil, Motrin), irbesartan (Avapro), losartan (Cozaar), phenytoin (Dilantin), piroxicam (Feldene), tamoxifen (Nolvadex), tolbutamide (Tolinase), torsemide (Demadex), warfarin (Coumadin), and others.

Medications changed by the liver (Cytochrome P450 3A4 (CYP3A4) substrates). Some medications are changed and broken down by the liver. Milk thistle might decrease how quickly the liver breaks down some medications. Taking milk thistle along with some medications that are broken down by the liver can increase the effects and side effects of some medications. Before taking milk thistle, talk to your healthcare provider if you are taking any medications that are changed by the liver. Some medications changed by the liver include lovastatin (Mevacor), ketoconazole (Nizoral), itraconazole (Sporanox), fexofenadine (Allegra), triazolam (Halcion), and many others.

Medications changed by the liver (Glucuronidated Drugs). The body breaks down some medications to get rid of them. The liver helps break down these medications. Taking milk thistle might affect how well the liver breaks down drugs. This could increase or decrease how well some of these medications work. Some of these medications changed by the liver include acetaminophen, atorvastatin (Lipitor), diazepam (Valium), digoxin, entacapone (Comtan), estrogen, irinotecan (Camptosar), lamotrigine (Lamictal), lorazepam (Ativan), lovastatin (Mevacor), meprobamate, morphine, oxazepam (Serax), and others.

Estrogens. Milk thistle might decrease hormones in the body. Milk thistle might help the body break down estrogen pills to get rid of them. Taking milk thistle along with estrogens might decrease the effectiveness of estrogen pills. Milk thistle contains a chemical called silymarin. Silymarin might be the part of milk thistle that helps the body break down estrogens. Some estrogen pills include conjugated equine estrogens (Premarin), ethinyl estradiol, estradiol, and others.

MONEYWORT

What other names is the product known by?

Creeping Jenny, Creeping Joan, Herb Two-Pence, Lysimachia nummularia, Meadow Runagates, Running Jenny, Serpentaria, String Of Sovereigns, Twopenny Grass, Wandering Jenny, Wandering Tailor.

What is it?

Moneywort is a plant. People use it to make medicine.

Is it Effective?

The effectiveness ratings for **MONEYWORT** are as follows:
Insufficient Evidence to Rate Effectiveness for... Skin problems such as eczema, killing bacteria, diarrhea, increasing saliva, cough, and other conditions.

How does it work?

There isn't enough information to know how moneywort might work.

Are there safety concerns?

There isn't enough information to know if moneywort might be safe.

Do not take moneywort if: You are pregnant or breast-feeding.

Are there any interactions with medications?

It is not known if moneywort interacts with any medicines.
Before taking moneywort, talk with your healthcare professional if you take any medications.

MONOLAURIN

What other names is the product known by?
Glycerin Monolaurate, Glycerol Monolaurate, Lauricidin, Lauric Acid Monoglyceride.

What is it?
Monolaurin is a chemical found in breastmilk.

Is it Effective?
The effectiveness ratings for **MONOLAURIN** are as follows:
Insufficient Evidence to Rate Effectiveness for... The common cold, the flu (influenza), herpes, shingles, and other conditions.

How does it work?
Preliminary research suggests monolaurin might have antibacterial and antiviral effects in test tubes. It is not known if monolaurin has these effects when used by people.

Are there safety concerns?
Monolaurin is safe for most people when used in amounts commonly found in foods.

It is not known if monolaurin is safe when used in medicinal amounts.

Do not use monolaurin as medicine if: You are pregnant or breast-feeding.

Are there any interactions with medications?
It is not known if monolaurin interacts with any medicines.
Before taking monolaurin, talk with your healthcare professional if you take any medications.

MORINDA

What other names is the product known by?
Ba Ji Tian, Bois Douleur, Canarywood, Cheese Fruit, Hai Ba Ji, Hog Apple, Indian Mulberry, Luoling, Mengkudu, Menkoedoe, Mora De La India, Morinda citrifolia, Mulberry, Nhau, Noni, Nono, Nonu, Pau-Azeitona, Rotten Cheese Fruit, Ruibarbo Caribe, Tahitian Noni Juice, Ura, Wild Pine.

What is it?
Morinda is a plant. The fruits, leaves, flowers, stems, bark, and roots are used to make medicine.

Is it Effective?
The effectiveness ratings for **MORINDA** are as follows:
Insufficient Evidence to Rate Effectiveness for... Colic, seizures, cough, diabetes, urinary problems, menstrual problems, fever, liver problems, constipation, vaginal discharge, nausea, smallpox, enlarged spleen, kidney disorders, swelling, asthma, bone and joint problems, cancer, eye cataracts, colds, depression, digestion problems, stomach ulcers, heart trouble, high blood pressure, infections, migraine, stroke, pain, reducing signs of aging, and other conditions.

How does it work?
Morinda contains many substances, including potassium. Some of these substances might help repair damaged cells in the body, activate the immune system, and have other activities.

Are there safety concerns?
Morinda seems to be safe when consumed as a food. But there is concern that consuming morinda tea or juice might cause liver damage in some people. There are several reports of liver damage in people who drank morinda tea or juice for several weeks. But it is not known for certain if morinda was the cause.

Do not use morinda if: You are pregnant or breast-feeding. • You have a high potassium level. • You have kidney problems. • You have liver disease.

Are there any interactions with medications?
Medications for high blood pressure (ACE inhibitors). Some medications for high blood pressure can increase potassium levels in the blood. Consuming morinda juice along with these medications for high blood pressure might cause too much potassium in the blood. Some medications for high blood pressure include captopril

Medical professionals should consult the Professional Version at www.NaturalDatabase.com.

(Capoten), enalapril (Vasotec), lisinopril (Prinivil, Zestril), ramipril (Altace), and others.

Medications for high blood pressure (Angiotensin receptor blockers (ARBs)). Some medications for high blood pressure can increase potassium levels in the blood. Consuming morinda juice along with these medications for high blood pressure might cause too much potassium to be in the blood. Some medications for high blood pressure include losartan (Cozaar), valsartan (Diovan), irbesartan (Avapro), candesartan (Atacand), telmisartan (Micardis), eprosartan (Teveten), and others.

Medications that can harm the liver (Hepatotoxic drugs). Morinda might harm the liver. Taking morinda along with medication that might also harm the liver can increase the risk of liver damage. Do not take morinda if you are taking a medication that can harm the liver. Some medications that can harm the liver include acetaminophen (Tylenol and others), amiodarone (Cordarone), carbamazepine (Tegretol), isoniazid (INH), methotrexate (Rheumatrex), methyldopa (Aldomet), fluconazole (Diflucan), itraconazole (Sporanox), erythromycin (Erythrocin, Ilosone, others), phenytoin (Dilantin), lovastatin (Mevacor), pravastatin (Pravachol), simvastatin (Zocor), and many others.

Water pills (Potassium-sparing diuretics). Morinda contains large amounts of potassium. Some "water pills" can also increase potassium levels in the body. Taking some "water pills" along with morinda might cause too much potassium to be in the body. Some "water pills" that increase potassium in the body include amiloride (Midamor), spironolactone (Aldactone), and triamterene (Dyrenium).

MORMON TEA

What other names is the product known by?

Brigham Tea, Desert Tea, Ephedra nevadensis, Gray Ephdra, Nevada Ephedra, Popotillo, Teamster's Tea, Squaw Tea.

What is it?

Mormon tea is made from a plant, ephedra nevadensis. The dried branches are boiled in water to make the tea. People use it as medicine. Be careful not to confuse Mormon tea (ephedra nevadensis) with ephedra (ephedra sinica and other ephedra species).

Is it Effective?

The effectiveness ratings for **MORMON TEA** are as follows:

Insufficient Evidence to Rate Effectiveness for... Colds, kidney problems, sexually transmitted diseases such as syphilis and gonorrhea, and other conditions.

How does it work?

The tannins in Mormon tea have an astringent effect to reduce body secretions such as mucus. There isn't enough information to know how Mormon tea might work for uses such as kidney problems and sexually transmitted diseases.

Are there safety concerns?

There isn't enough information to know if Mormon tea is safe for medicinal uses. Potential side effects include stomach complaints, kidney and liver damage, nose or throat cancer, increased urination, and constipation.

Do not use Mormon tea if: You are pregnant or breast-feeding.

Are there any interactions with medications?

Medications taken by mouth (Oral drugs). Mormon tea absorbs substances in the stomach and intestines. Taking Mormon tea along with medications taken by mouth can decrease how much medicine your body absorbs, and decrease the effectiveness of your medication. To prevent this interaction, take Mormon tea at least one hour after medications you take by mouth.

MOTHERWORT

What other names is the product known by?

Leonuri cardiacae herba, Leonurus, Leonurus cardiaca, Lion's Ear, Lion's Tail, Roman Motherwort, Throw-Wort.

What is it?

Motherwort is a plant. The above ground parts are used to make medicine.

Medical professionals should consult the Professional Version at www.NaturalDatabase.com.

Is it Effective?

The effectiveness ratings for **MOTHERWORT** are as follows:
Insufficient Evidence to Rate Effectiveness for... Heart conditions (fast heart rate, abnormal rhythm), over-active thyroid (hyperthyroidism), itching, shingles, intestinal gas (flatulence), lack of menstrual periods, and other uses.

How does it work?

Motherwort might slow down the heart and thin the blood. It might also stimulate uterine tone and blood flow.

Are there safety concerns?

Motherwort is possibly safe for most people. Side effects include diarrhea, stomach irritation, uterine bleeding, sleepiness, and allergic reactions. Contact with the skin can cause rashes and increased sensitivity to the sun.

Motherwort can interfere with the treatment of heart conditions.

Do not take motherwort if: You are pregnant or breast-feeding. • You have uterine bleeding or unexplained bleeding between menstrual periods.

Are there any interactions with medications?

Sedative medications (CNS depressants). Motherwort might cause sleepiness and drowsiness. Medications that cause sleepiness are called sedatives. Taking motherwort along with sedative medications might cause too much sleepiness. Some sedative medications include clonazepam (Klonopin), lorazepam (Ativan), phenobarbital (Donnatal), zolpidem (Ambien), and others.

MOUNTAIN ASH

What other names is the product known by?

Eberesche, Ebereschenbeeren, European Mountain-Ash, Quickbeam, Rowan Tree, Sorb Apple, Sorbi acupariae fructus, Sorbus aucuparia, Witchen.

What is it?

Mountain ash is a plant. People use the berries to make medicine.

Is it Effective?

The effectiveness ratings for **MOUNTAIN ASH** are as follows:
Insufficient Evidence to Rate Effectiveness for... Kidney diseases, diabetes, arthritis, swelling, vitamin C deficiency, purifying the blood, menstrual problems, diarrhea, lung conditions, and other conditions.

How does it work?

Mountain ash berries contain many chemicals, including vitamin C. There isn't enough information to know how it might work for the conditions for which people use it.

Are there safety concerns?

Fresh mountain ash berries are UNSAFE. Large amounts can cause stomach irritation and pain, vomiting, queasiness, diarrhea, kidney damage, and other side effects.

There isn't enough information to know if the dried or cooked berries might be safe.

Do not take mountain ash if: You are pregnant or breast-feeding.

Are there any interactions with medications?

It is not known if mountain ash interacts with any medicines.
Before taking mountain ash, talk with your healthcare professional if you take any medications.

MOUNTAIN FLAX

What other names is the product known by?

Dwarf Flax, Fairy Flax, Linum catharticum, Mill Mountain, Purging Flax.

What is it?

Mountain flax is a plant. People use the flowering parts to make medicine.

   Natural Medicines Comprehensive Database Consumer Version (209) 472-2244

Is it Effective?
The effectiveness ratings for **MOUNTAIN FLAX** are as follows:
Insufficient Evidence to Rate Effectiveness for... Vomiting, purging stool from the bowel, and other conditions.

How does it work?
Mountain flax might be a laxative which helps stool move through the bowel.

Are there safety concerns?
Mountain flax might be unsafe for some people, especially with long-term use. It can cause some side effects such as vomiting, diarrhea, and stomach and intestinal inflammation.

Do not take mountain flax if: You are pregnant or breast-feeding.

Are there any interactions with medications?
It is not known if mountain flax interacts with any medicines.
Before taking mountain flax, talk with your healthcare professional if you take any medications.

MOUNTAIN LAUREL

What other names is the product known by?
Broad-Leafed Laurel, Calico Bush, Kalmia latifolia, Lambkill, Laurel, Mountain Ivy, Rose Laurel, Sheep Laurel, Spoon Laurel.

What is it?
Mountain laurel is a plant. People use the fresh or dried leaves to make medicine.

Is it Effective?
The effectiveness ratings for **MOUNTAIN LAUREL** are as follows:
Insufficient Evidence to Rate Effectiveness for... Ringworm of the scalp, psoriasis, herpes, syphilis, and other conditions.

How does it work?
Mountain laurel might change how salt is used by cells throughout the body.

Are there safety concerns?
Mountain laurel is unsafe for people to take by mouth. It can cause many side effects such as pain, cold sweats, nausea, vomiting, diarrhea, numbness, dizziness, headache, fever, loss of vision, muscle weakness, serious heart and lung problems, death, and other severe side effects.

There isn't enough information to know if mountain laurel might be safe when applied directly to the skin.

Do not take mountain laurel if: You are pregnant or breast-feeding.

Are there any interactions with medications?
It is not known if mountain laurel interacts with any medicines.
Before taking mountain laurel, talk with your healthcare professional if you take any medications.

MOUSE EAR

What other names is the product known by?
Hawkweed, Pilosella officinarum.

What is it?
Mouse ear is a plant. People use the flowering plant parts to make medicine.

Is it Effective?
The effectiveness ratings for **MOUSE EAR** are as follows:
Insufficient Evidence to Rate Effectiveness for... Asthma, bronchitis, cough, whooping cough, fluid retention, increasing sweating, colic, intestinal gas, wounds, and other conditions.

How does it work?
There isn't enough information to know how mouse ear might work.

Medical professionals should consult the Professional Version at www.NaturalDatabase.com.

CONSUMER VERSION

Medical professionals should consult the Professional Version at www.NaturalDatabase.com.

Are there safety concerns?

There isn't enough information to know if mouse ear might be safe. It can cause an allergic reaction in people sensitive to the Asteraceae/Compositae family of plants including ragweed, marigolds, daisies, and other related plants.

Do not take mouse ear if: You are pregnant or breast-feeding. • You are sensitive or allergic to ragweed, marigolds, daisies, and other related plants.

Are there any interactions with medications?

It is not known if mouse ear interacts with any medicines.

Before taking mouse ear, talk with your healthcare professional if you take any medications.

MSM (METHYLSULFONYLMETHANE)

What other names is the product known by?

Crystalline DMSO, Dimethylsulfone, DMSO2, Methyl Sulfone, Sulfonyl Sulfur.

What is it?

MSM is a chemical found in plants, animals, and humans. It can also be made in a laboratory. People use it as a medicine.

Is it Effective?

The effectiveness ratings for **MSM (METHYLSULFONYLMETHANE)** are as follows:

Possibly Effective for... Osteoarthritis. Taking MSM by mouth seems to modestly reduce some symptoms of arthritis such as pain and joint movement, but it might not reduce other symptoms such as stiffness.

Insufficient Evidence to Rate Effectiveness for... Chronic pain, muscle and bone problems, snoring, allergies, scar tissue, stretch marks, wrinkles, protection against sun/wind burn, eye swelling, dental disease, wounds, cuts, hayfever, asthma, stomach upset, constipation, premenstrual syndrome (PMS), mood elevation, obesity, poor circulation, hypertension, high cholesterol, diabetes mellitus type 2 (NIDDM), and other conditions.

How does it work?

MSM might supply sulfur to make other chemicals in the body.

Are there safety concerns?

MSM appears to be safe for most people when taken by mouth for a month or less. In some people, MSM might cause nausea, diarrhea, bloating, fatigue, headache, insomnia, itching, or worsening of allergy symptoms.

There isn't enough information to know if MSM is safe when applied to the skin, as in creams, lotions, or nose drops.

Are there any interactions with medications?

It is not known if MSM (methylsulfonylmethane) interacts with any medicines.

Before taking MSM, talk with your healthcare professional if you take any medications.

MUGWORT

What other names is the product known by?

Armoise Commune, Artemisia, Artemisia vulgaris, Artemisiae vulgaris herba, Artemisiae vulgaris radix, Carline Thistle, Felon Herb, Gemeiner Beifuss, Hierba de San Juan, Nagadamni, Sailor's Tobacco, St. John's Plant, Wild Wormwood.

What is it?

Mugwort is a plant. The above ground parts and root are used to make medicine.

Is it Effective?

The effectiveness ratings for **MUGWORT** are as follows:

Insufficient Evidence to Rate Effectiveness for... Stomach problems (colic, diarrhea, cramps, constipation, slow digestion, vomiting), epilepsy, irregular menstrual periods, low energy, anxiety, and other uses.

How does it work?

The chemicals in mugwort might stimulate the uterus.

Are there safety concerns?

There isn't enough information to know if mugwort is safe. However, it is known that allergic reactions can happen, especially in people who are sensitive to tobacco, honey, royal jelly, mugwort, celery, wild carrot, or the Asteraceae/Compositae plant family which includes ragweed, chrysanthemums, marigolds, daisies, and other similar plants.

Do not use mugwort if: You are pregnant or breast-feeding. • You are allergic to honey, tobacco, mugwort, celery, wild carrot, ragweed, chrysanthemums, marigolds, daisies, or related plants and plant products.

Are there any interactions with medications?

It is not known if mugwort interacts with any medicines.
Before taking mugwort, talk with your healthcare professional if you take any medications.

MUIRA PUAMA

What other names is the product known by?

Muirapuama, Potency Wood, Ptychopetali lignum, Ptychopetalum olacoides, Ptychopetalum uncinatum.

What is it?

Muira Puama is a plant. The wood and root are used to make medicine.

Is it Effective?

The effectiveness ratings for **MUIRA PUAMA** are as follows:
Insufficient Evidence to Rate Effectiveness for... Sexual disorders, stomach upset, menstrual (period) irregularities, sore joints, or loss of appetite.

How does it work?

The chemicals in muira puama have no known effects on the body.

Are there safety concerns?

It is not known if muira puama is safe or what the potential side effects might be.

Do not take muira puama if: You are pregnant or breast-feeding.

Are there any interactions with medications?

It is not known if muira puama interacts with any medicines.
Before taking muira puama, talk with your healthcare professional if you take any medications.

MULLEIN

What other names is the product known by?

Aaron's Rod, Adam's Flannel, American Mullein, Beggar's Blanket, Blanket Herb, Blanket Leaf, Bouillon Blanc, Candleflower, Candlewick, Clot-Bur, Clown's Lungwort, Cuddy's Lungs, Duffle, European Mullein, Feltwort, Flannelflower, Fluffweed, Hag's Taper, Hare's Beard, Hedge Taper, Higtaper, Jacob's Staff, Longwort, Orange Mullein, Our Lady's Flannel, Rag Paper, Shepherd's Club, Shepherd's Staff, Torches, Torch Weed, Velvet Plant, Verbasci flos, Wild Ice Leaf, Verbascum densiflorum, Verbascum phlomides, Verbascum thapsus, Verbascum thapsiforme, Woolen, Wooly Mullein.

What is it?

Mullein is a plant. The flower is used to make medicine.

Is it Effective?

The effectiveness ratings for **MULLEIN** are as follows:
Insufficient Evidence to Rate Effectiveness for... Use on the skin for wounds, burns, hemorrhoids, bruises, frostbite, and other uses. Use by mouth for earaches, colds, flu, asthma, diarrhea, migraines, gout, tuberculosis, croup, cough, sore throat, inflammation of the airways such as bronchitis, and other conditions.

How does it work?

The chemicals in mullein might have action against the influenza and herpes viruses, and some bacteria that cause respiratory infections.

Are there safety concerns?

There isn't enough information to know if mullein is safe or what the potential side effects might be.

Do not take mullein if: You are pregnant or breast-feeding.

Are there any interactions with medications?

It is not known if mullein interacts with any medicines.
Before taking mullein, talk with your healthcare professional if you take any medications.

MUSK

What other names is the product known by?

Deer Musk, Moschus moschiferus, Tonquin Musk.

What is it?

Musk is a chemical from the musk gland of the male musk deer. The chemical is used to make medicine.

Is it Effective?

The effectiveness ratings for **MUSK** are as follows:
Insufficient Evidence to Rate Effectiveness for... Stroke, coma, nerve problems, convulsions, heart pains, sores, and other conditions.

How does it work?

Musk might decrease inflammation.

Are there safety concerns?

Musk is safe for most people when taken at low concentrations, generally below 0.00001%. It can cause skin irritations in some people who are sensitive to musk.

There isn't enough information to know if musk might be safe when amounts greater than 0.00001% are used.

Do not take musk if: You are pregnant or breast-feeding.

Are there any interactions with medications?

It is not known if musk interacts with any medicines.
Before taking musk, talk with your healthcare professional if you take any medications.

MYRRH

What other names is the product known by?

Abyssinian Myrrh, African Myrrh, Arabian Myrrh, Bal, Balsamodendron Myrrha, Bdellium, Bol, Bola, Commiphora, Commiphora erythraea, Commiphora molmol, Didin, Didthin, Gum Myrrh, Heerabol, Opopanax, Somalien Myrrh, Yemen Myrrh.

What is it?

Myrrh is a sap-like substance from a tree. It is used to make medicine.

Is it Effective?

The effectiveness ratings for **MYRRH** are as follows:
Insufficient Evidence to Rate Effectiveness for... Indigestion, ulcers, colds, cough, asthma, congestion, joint pain, hemorrhoids, bad breath, treating a sore mouth or throat, and other conditions.

How does it work?

Myrrh can help decrease swelling (inflammation) and kill bacteria.

Are there safety concerns?

Myrrh seems safe for most people. It can cause some side effects such as skin rash if applied directly to the skin, and diarrhea if taken by mouth.
Amounts greater than 2-4 grams can cause kidney irritation and heart rate changes.
Do not take myrrh if: You are pregnant or breast-feeding. • You have diabetes. • You have a heart condition. • You have a fever. • You have uterine bleeding.

Are there any interactions with medications?

Medications for diabetes (Antidiabetes drugs). Myrrh might decrease blood sugar. Diabetes medications are also used to lower blood sugar. Taking myrrh along with diabetes medications might cause your blood sugar to go too low. Monitor your blood sugar closely. The dose of your diabetes medication might need to be changed. Some medications used for diabetes include glimepiride (Amaryl), glyburide (DiaBeta, Glynase PresTab, Micronase), insulin, pioglitazone (Actos), rosiglitazone (Avandia), chlorpropamide (Diabinese), glipizide (Glucotrol), tolbutamide (Orinase), and others.

MYRTLE

What other names is the product known by?

Myrti aetherolum, Myrti folium, Myrtus communis.

What is it?

Myrtle is a plant. People use the leaves and branches to make medicine.

Is it Effective?

The effectiveness ratings for **MYRTLE** are as follows:
Insufficient Evidence to Rate Effectiveness for... Lung infections including bronchitis, whooping cough, and tuberculosis; bladder conditions; diarrhea; worms; and other conditions.

How does it work?

Myrtle might help fight against fungus and bacteria.

Are there safety concerns?

The oil of myrtle is unsafe for people, including children, because it can cause asthma-like attacks and lung failure. Myrtle can also cause nausea, vomiting, diarrhea, low blood pressure, blood circulation disorders, and other problems.

There isn't enough information to know if using the leaf and branch of myrtle might be safe.

Do not take myrtle if: You are pregnant or breast-feeding.

Are there any interactions with medications?

It is not known if myrtle interacts with any medicines.
Before taking myrtle, talk with your healthcare professional if you take any medications.

N-ACETYL CYSTEINE

What other names is the product known by?

Acetylcysteine, L-Cysteine, NAC, N-Acetyl-B-Cysteine, N-Acetyl-L-Cysteine.

What is it?

N-acetyl cysteine comes from the amino acid L-cysteine. (Amino acids are the building blocks of proteins).

Is it Effective?

The effectiveness ratings for **N-ACETYL CYSTEINE** are as follows:
Effective for... Acetaminophen (Tylenol) poisoning • Reducing mucus and helping with breathing in various lung conditions • Cystic fibrosis • Helping to prevent crusting in people with a tracheostomy.
Possibly Effective for... Chest pain (angina) • Preventing complications of chronic bronchitis • Preventing complications of lung disease (chronic obstructive pulmonary disease, COPD) • Preventing side effects of ifosfamide (Ifex, used for certain types of cancer) • Preventing kidney problems with dyes used during some X-ray exams • Reducing homocysteine levels (a possible risk factor for heart disease) • Reducing symptoms of the flu • Treating some types of epilepsy (seizures) • Treating a lung disease called fibrosing alveolitis • Preventing problems such as heart attack and stroke in people with serious kidney disease.
Possibly Ineffective for... Preventing side effects of doxorubicin (used for certain types of cancer) • Treating amyotrophic lateral sclerosis (ALS, Lou Gehrig's disease).
Likely Ineffective for... Preventing new tumors in people with head and neck cancer, or lung cancer • Treating Alzheimer's disease • Improving how the body responds to nitroglycerin (Nitrostat) • Treating organ failure.
Insufficient Evidence to Rate Effectiveness for... Carbon monoxide poisoning; allergic reactions to phenytoin (Dilantin); ear infections; hayfever; removing heavy metals such as mercury, lead, and cadmium from the body;

Medical professionals should consult the Professional Version at www.NaturalDatabase.com.

CONSUMER VERSION

chronic fatigue syndrome (CFS); preventing alcoholic liver damage; protecting against environmental pollutants; colon cancer; and other conditions.

How does it work?

N-acetyl cysteine treats acetaminophen (Tylenol) poisoning by binding the poisonous forms of acetaminophen that are formed in the liver. It is also an antioxidant.

Are there safety concerns?

N-acetyl cysteine is safe for most adults, when used as a prescription medication. It can cause nausea, vomiting, and diarrhea or constipation. Rarely, it can cause rashes, fever, headache, drowsiness, low blood pressure, and liver problems. When inhaled (breathed into the lungs), it can also cause swelling in the mouth, runny nose, drowsiness, clamminess, and chest tightness.

N-acetyl cysteine has an unpleasant odor that may make it hard to take.

Do not use N-acetyl cysteine if: You are pregnant or breast-feeding. • You are allergic to acetylcysteine. • You have asthma.

Are there any interactions with medications?

Activated charcoal. Activated charcoal is sometimes used to prevent poisoning in people who take too much acetaminophen and other medications. Activated charcoal can bind up these medications in the stomach and prevent them from being absorbed by the body. Taking N-acetyl cysteine at the same time as activated charcoal might decrease how well it works for preventing poisoning.

Nitroglycerin. Nitroglycerin can dilate blood vessels and increase blood flow. Taking N-acetyl cysteine seems to increase the effects of nitroglycerin. This could cause increased chance of side effects including headache, dizziness, and lightheadedness.

N-ACETYL GLUCOSAMINE

What other names is the product known by?

2-acetamido-2-deoxyglucose, acetylglucosamine, Glucosamine N-Acetyl, N-Acetyl D-Glucosamine, NAG, N-A-G, Poly-NAG.

What is it?

N-acetyl glucosamine is a chemical that comes from the outer shells of shellfish.

Don't confuse N-acetyl glucosamine with other forms such as glucosamine hydrochloride or glucosamine sulfate. They may not have the same effects. Most glucosamine products contain glucosamine sulfate or glucosamine hydrochloride.

Is it Effective?

The effectiveness ratings for **N-ACETYL GLUCOSAMINE** are as follows:
Insufficient Evidence to Rate Effectiveness for... Osteoarthritis, and inflammatory bowel diseases including ulcerative colitis and Crohn's disease.

How does it work?

N-acetyl glucosamine might help protect the lining of the stomach and intestines.

Are there safety concerns?

There isn't enough information available to know if N-acetyl glucosamine is safe.

Some preliminary research suggested that glucosamine might raise blood sugar in people with diabetes. However, glucosamine doesn't seem to significantly affect blood sugar control in people with diabetes. Glucosamine with routine blood sugar monitoring appears to be safe for most people with diabetes.

There is some concern that glucosamine products might cause allergic reactions in people who are sensitive to shellfish. Glucosamine is produced from the shells of shrimp, lobster, and crabs. But allergic reactions in people with shellfish allergy are caused by the meat of shellfish, not the shell. There are no reports of allergic reactions to glucosamine in people who are allergic to shellfish. There is also some information that people with shellfish allergy can safely take glucosamine products.

Do not use N-acetyl glucosamine if: You are pregnant or breast-feeding. • You are allergic to shellfish. • You have asthma.

Are there any interactions with medications?

Medications for cancer (Chemotherapy). There is some concern that N-acetyl glucosamine might decrease the effectiveness of some medications for cancer. But it is too soon to know if this interaction occurs.

Medications for diabetes (Antidiabetes drugs). N-acetyl glucosamine might increase blood sugar in some people. Diabetes medications are used to lower blood sugar. By increasing blood sugar, N-acetyl glucosamine might decrease the effectiveness of diabetes medications. But some people with diabetes can take N-acetyl glucosamine without any blood sugar problems. If you take N-acetyl glucosamine and have diabetes, monitor your blood sugar closely. The dose of your diabetes medication might need to be changed. Some medications used for diabetes include glimepiride (Amaryl), glyburide (DiaBeta, Glynase PresTab, Micronase), insulin, pioglitazone (Actos), rosiglitazone (Avandia), chlorpropamide (Diabinese), glipizide (Glucotrol), tolbutamide (Orinase), and others.

Warfarin (Coumadin). Warfarin (Coumadin) is used to slow blood clotting. There is one report of someone taking very large amounts of glucosamine and chondroitin and having blood that was too "thin." Blood that is too "thin" can cause bruising and bleeding. But there is not enough information to know if this interaction is a big concern or if it can happen with normal amounts of glucosamine and chondroitin.

NADH

What other names is the product known by?

B-DPNH, BNADH, Coenzyme 1, Enada, NAD, Nicotinamide Adenine Dinucleotide Hydrate, Reduced DPN, Reduced Nicotinamide Adenine Dinucleotide.

What is it?

NADH is a form of a chemical called "nicotinamide adenine dinucleotide" which occurs naturally in the body. People use it as medicine.

Is it Effective?

The effectiveness ratings for **NADH** are as follows:

Possibly Ineffective for... Dementia related to Alzheimer's disease and other conditions.

Insufficient Evidence to Rate Effectiveness for... Chronic fatigue syndrome, depression, jet lag, high blood pressure, Parkinson's disease, improving athletic performance, increasing energy, improving memory and concentration, boosting immune function, reducing aging, lowering cholesterol levels, protecting against side effects of the drug zidovudine (AZT) used to treat AIDS, and other uses.

How does it work?

NADH produced by our bodies is involved in making energy in the body. While there is some evidence that suggests NADH supplements might reduce blood pressure, lower cholesterol, help chronic fatigue syndrome by providing energy, and increase nerve signals for people with Parkinson's disease, there isn't enough information to know for sure how or if these supplements work.

Are there safety concerns?

NADH seems safe for most people when used appropriately and short-term, up to 12 weeks. Most people do not experience any side effects when consuming the recommended amount each day, which is 10 mg.

Do not use NADH if: You are pregnant or breast-feeding.

Are there any interactions with medications?

It is not known if NADH interacts with any medicines.

Before taking NADH, talk with your healthcare professional if you take any medications.

NASTURTIUM

What other names is the product known by?

Indian Cress, Tropaeolum majus.

What is it?

Nasturtium is a plant. The above ground parts are used to make medicine.

Is it Effective?

The effectiveness ratings for **NASTURTIUM** are as follows:

Insufficient Evidence to Rate Effectiveness for... Cough, bronchitis, urinary tract infections (UTIs), mild muscle pain, and other conditions.

Medical professionals should consult the Professional Version at www.NaturalDatabase.com.

CONSUMER VERSION

How does it work?

Nasturtium contains vitamin C and might have help fight bacteria, fungi, viruses, and tumors.

Are there safety concerns?

Nasturtium might be safe for adults when applied directly to the skin, in combination with other natural medicines. It can cause skin irritation, especially if used for a long time.

There isn't enough information to know if nasturtium might be safe when taken by mouth. It can cause stomach upset, kidney damage, and other side effects.

Nasturtium is unsafe for children when taken by mouth. There isn't enough information to know if nasturtium might be safe for children when applied directly to the skin.

Do not take nasturtium if: You are pregnant or breast-feeding. • You have kidney disease. • You have stomach or intestinal ulcers.

Are there any interactions with medications?

It is not known if nasturtium interacts with any medicines.
Before taking nasturtium, talk with your healthcare professional if you take any medications.

NATTOKINASE

What other names is the product known by?

BSP, Natto Extract, NK, Fermented Soybeans, Subtilisin NAT.

What is it?

Nattokinase is an enzyme that is found in some fermented soy foods called natto.

Is it Effective?

The effectiveness ratings for **NATTOKINASE** are as follows:
Insufficient Evidence to Rate Effectiveness for... Cardiovascular disease, stroke, angina, deep vein thrombosis (DVT), atherosclerosis, hemorrhoids, venous stasis, varicose veins, peripheral vascular disease, claudication, pain, fibromyalgia, chronic fatigue syndrome, endometriosis, uterine fibroids, muscle spasms, hypertension, infertility, cancer, and beriberi.

How does it work?

Nattokinase decreases the ability of blood to clot. This "thins the blood" and might protect against conditions caused by blood clots such as stroke, heart attack, and others.

Are there safety concerns?

There isn't enough information available to know if nattokinase is safe for most people. Taking two doses of a specific product containing nattokinase (Flite Tabs) seems to be safe. But it is not known if taking more than two doses is safe.

Do not take nattokinase if: You are pregnant or breast-feeding.

Are there any interactions with medications?

Medications that slow blood clotting (Anticoagulant / Antiplatelet drugs). Nattokinase can decrease blood clotting. Taking nattokinase along with medications that also slow clotting might increase the chances of bruising and bleeding. Some medications that slow blood clotting include aspirin, clopidogrel (Plavix), diclofenac (Voltaren, Cataflam, others), ibuprofen (Advil, Motrin, others), naproxen (Anaprox, Naprosyn, others), dalteparin (Fragmin), enoxaparin (Lovenox), heparin, warfarin (Coumadin), and others.

NEEM

What other names is the product known by?

Antelaea azadirachta, Arishta, Arishtha, Azadirachta indica, Bead Tree, Holy Tree, Indian Lilac, Indian Neem, Margosa, Melia azadirachta, Nim, Nimb, Nimba, Persian Lilac, Pride of China.

What is it?

Neem is a tree. The bark, leaves, and seeds are used to make medicine. Less frequently, the root, flower, and fruit are also used.

Is it Effective?

The effectiveness ratings for **NEEM** are as follows:
Insufficient Evidence to Rate Effectiveness for... Ulcers of the stomach and intestine, gum disease (gingivitis), fever, upset stomach, breathing conditions, malaria, worms, head lice, skin conditions and diseases, ulcers, heart disease, diabetes, birth control (contraception), and other conditions.

How does it work?

Neem contains chemicals that might help reduce blood sugar levels, heal ulcers in the digestive tract, prevent conception, and kill bacteria and prevent plaque formation in the mouth.

Are there safety concerns?

Neem appears to be safe for most adults, when taken by mouth for short-term use. When neem is taken in large doses or for long periods of time, it might be unsafe. It might adversely affect the kidneys and liver.

Neem is unsafe for children. Serious side effects in infants and small children can happen within hours after taking neem oil. These serious side effects include vomiting, diarrhea, drowsiness, blood disorders, seizures, loss of consciousness, coma, brain disorders, and death.

Do not take neem if: You are pregnant or breast-feeding. • You are trying to conceive a child. • You have undergone organ transplant. • You have an immune system disease such as multiple sclerosis, lupus erythematosus, or other auto-immune disease. • You have diabetes.

Are there any interactions with medications?

Medications for diabetes (Antidiabetes drugs). Neem might decrease blood sugar. Diabetes medications are also used to lower blood sugar. Taking neem along with diabetes medications might cause your blood sugar to go too low. Monitor your blood sugar closely. The dose of your diabetes medication might need to be changed. Some medications used for diabetes include glimepiride (Amaryl), glyburide (DiaBeta, Glynase PresTab, Micronase), insulin, pioglitazone (Actos), rosiglitazone (Avandia), chlorpropamide (Diabinese), glipizide (Glucotrol), tolbutamide (Orinase), and others.
Medications that decrease the immune system (Immunosuppressants). Neem might increase the immune system. By increasing the immune system, neem might decrease the effectiveness of medications that decrease the immune system. Some medications that decrease the immune system include azathioprine (Imuran), basiliximab (Simulect), cyclosporine (Neoral, Sandimmune), daclizumab (Zenapax), muromonab-CD3 (OKT3, Orthoclone OKT3), mycophenolate (CellCept), tacrolimus (FK506, Prograf), sirolimus (Rapamune), prednisone (Deltasone, Orasone), corticosteroids (glucocorticoids), and others.

NERVE ROOT

What other names is the product known by?

American Valerian, Bleeding Heart, Cypripedium calceolus, Cypripedium parviflorum, Cypripedium pubescens, Lady's Slipper, Moccasin Flower, Monkey Flower, Noah's Ark, Shoe, Slipper Root, Venus' Shoe, Yellows.

What is it?

Nerve root is a plant. People use the root and rhizome (underground stem) to make medicine.

Is it Effective?

The effectiveness ratings for **NERVE ROOT** are as follows:
Insufficient Evidence to Rate Effectiveness for... Menstrual problems, vaginal itching, diarrhea, sleeping disorders, anxiety, and other conditions.

How does it work?

Nerve root might act as an astringent to help shrink blood vessels.

Are there safety concerns?

Nerve root seems to be UNSAFE for most people. It can cause hallucinations, giddiness, restlessness, headache, skin irritation, and other side effects.

Do not take nerve root if: You are pregnant or breast-feeding.

Are there any interactions with medications?

It is not known if nerve root interacts with any medicines.
Before taking nerve root, talk with your healthcare professional if you take any medications.

NEW JERSEY TEA

What other names is the product known by?

Ceanothus americanus, Jersey Tea, Mountain-Sweet, Redroot, Red Root, Walpole Tea, Wild Snowball.

What is it?

New Jersey tea is a plant. People use the root, root bark, and leaf to make medicine.

Is it Effective?

The effectiveness ratings for **NEW JERSEY TEA** are as follows:
Insufficient Evidence to Rate Effectiveness for... Cough, spasms, bleeding, gonorrhea, syphilis, colds, fever, chills, and other conditions.

How does it work?

It is not known how New Jersey tea might work. It might shorten the time it takes for blood to clot.

Are there safety concerns?

New Jersey tea might be safe for most people.

Do not take New Jersey tea if: You are pregnant or breast-feeding.

Are there any interactions with medications?

It is not known if New Jersey tea interacts with any medicines.
Before taking New Jersey tea, talk with your healthcare professional if you take any medications.

NEW ZEALAND GREEN-LIPPED MUSSEL

What other names is the product known by?

NZGLM, Perna canaliculus.

What is it?

New Zealand green-lipped mussel is a shellfish. People use it to make medicine.

Is it Effective?

The effectiveness ratings for **NEW ZEALAND GREEN-LIPPED MUSSEL** are as follows:
Possibly Ineffective for... Rheumatoid arthritis.
Insufficient Evidence to Rate Effectiveness for... Osteoarthritis.

How does it work?

New Zealand green-lipped mussels might contain chemicals that help decrease inflammation.

Are there safety concerns?

New Zealand green-lipped mussel might be safe for most people. It can cause some side effects such as diarrhea, nausea, and intestinal gas. In rare cases, it might cause liver problems.

Do not take New Zealand green-lipped mussel if: You are pregnant or breast-feeding.

Are there any interactions with medications?

It is not known if New Zealand green-lipped mussel interacts with any medicines. Before taking New Zealand green-lipped mussel, talk with your healthcare professional if you take any medications.

NIACIN AND NIACINAMIDE (VITAMIN B3)

What other names is the product known by?
3-Pyridine Carboxamide, Anti-Blacktongue Factor, Antipellagra Factor, B Complex Vitamin, Nicamid, Nicosedine, Nicotinamide, Nicotinic Acid, Nicotinic Acid Amide, Nicotylamidum, Pellagra Preventing Factor, Vitamin PP.

What is it?
Niacin and niacinamide are forms of Vitamin B3. Vitamin B3 is found in many foods including yeast, meat, fish, milk, eggs, green vegetables, beans, and cereal grains. Niacin and niacinamide are also found in many vitamin B complex supplements with other B vitamins.

Is it Effective?
The effectiveness ratings for **NIACIN AND NIACINAMIDE (VITAMIN B3)** are as follows:
Effective for... Treatment and prevention of niacin deficiency, and certain conditions related to niacin deficiency such as pellagra • High cholesterol. Only niacin seems to lower cholesterol, not niacinamide.
Possibly Effective for... Heart disease, including hardening of the arteries (atherosclerosis) • Reducing the risk of a second heart attack in men with heart or circulatory disorders • Diarrhea from an infection called cholera • Diabetes, types 1 and 2 • Prevention of cataracts, an eye condition • Osteoarthritis • Alzheimer's disease. People who consume more niacin in foods and from a multivitamin seem to have a lower risk of getting Alzheimer's disease compared to people who consume less niacin. But there is no evidence that taking a niacin supplement is beneficial for preventing Alzheimer's disease.
Insufficient Evidence to Rate Effectiveness for... Migraine headache, dizziness, depression, motion sickness, alcohol dependence, improving orgasm, acne, attention deficit-hyperactivity disorder (ADHD), and other conditions.

How does it work?
Niacinamide can be made from niacin in the body. Niacin and niacinamide are required for the proper function of fats and sugars in the body and to maintain healthy cells.

Are there safety concerns?
Niacin and niacinamide are safe for most people when taken by mouth. A common minor side effect of niacin is a flushing reaction. This might cause burning, tingling, itching, and redness of the face, arms, and chest, as well as headaches. Starting with small doses of niacin and taking 325 mg of aspirin before each dose of niacin will help reduce the flushing reaction. Usually, this reaction goes away as the body gets used to the medication. Alcohol can make the flushing reaction worse. Avoid large amounts of alcohol while taking niacin.

Other minor side effects of niacin and niacinamide are stomach upset, intestinal gas, dizziness, pain in the mouth, and other problems.

When doses of over 3 grams per day of niacin are taken, more serious side effects can happen. These include liver problems, gout, ulcers of the digestive tract, loss of vision, high blood sugar, irregular heartbeat, and other serious problems. Similar side effects can happen with large doses of niacinamide.

Niacin and niacinamide are also safe for pregnant and breast-feeding women when taken in the recommended amounts. The recommended amount of niacin is 18 mg per day in pregnancy and 19 mg per day while breast-feeding.

Niacin and niacinamide might increase blood sugar. People with diabetes who take niacin or niacinamide should check their blood sugar carefully.

Do not use niacin or niacinamide if you have: Allergies. They can make allergies more severe. • Gallbladder disease. • Gout. • Angina. • Very low blood pressure. • Kidney or liver disease. • Stomach or intestinal ulcers.

Are there any interactions with medications?
Medications used for lowering cholesterol (Statins). Niacin can affect the muscles. Some medications used for lowering cholesterol can also affect the muscles. Taking niacin along with some medications used for lowering high cholesterol might increase the risk of muscle problems. Some medications used for high cholesterol include cerivastatin (Baycol), atorvastatin (Lipitor), lovastatin (Mevacor), pravastatin (Pravachol), simvastatin (Zocor), and others.
Medications used for lowering cholesterol (Resins). Resins used for lowering cholesterol might decrease how much niacin or niacinamide the body absorbs, and reduce the effectiveness of supplements. Take niacin or niacinamide and resins at least 4 hours apart. Resins include cholestyramine (Questran) and colestipol (Colestid).
Medications for diabetes (Antidiabetes drugs). Chronic use of niacin and niacinamide might increase blood

sugar. Diabetes medications are used to lower blood sugar. By increasing blood sugar, niacin and niacinamide might decrease the effectiveness of diabetes medications. Monitor your blood sugar closely. The dose of your diabetes medication might need to be changed. Some medications used for diabetes include glimepiride (Amaryl), glyburide (DiaBeta, Glynase PresTab, Micronase), insulin, pioglitazone (Actos), rosiglitazone (Avandia), metformin (Glucophage), nateglinide (Starlix), repaglinide (Prandin), chlorpropamide (Diabinese), glipizide (Glucotrol), tolbutamide (Orinase), and others.

Clonidine (Catapres). Clonidine and niacin both lower blood pressure. Talk to your doctor before taking niacin supplements with clonidine. Your blood pressure may need monitoring closely to make sure it is not too low, which can cause dizziness and fainting.

Medications for gout. Large doses of niacin might cause gout attacks. The dose of your gout medication might need to be changed. Some medications used for gout include allopurinol (Zyloprim), probenecid, and sulfinpyrazone (Anturane).

Nicotine patch (Transdermal nicotine). Niacin can sometimes cause flushing and dizziness. The nicotine patch can also cause flushing and dizziness. Taking niacin and/or niacinamide (vitamin B3) and using a nicotine patch can increase the possibility of becoming flushed and dizzy.

NIAULI OIL

What other names is the product known by?
Caje Oil, Melaleuca viridiflora, Niauli Aetheroleum.

What is it?
Niauli oil is the oil from the leaves of the Melaleuca viridiflora plant. People use the oil to make medicine. Do not confuse niauli oil with tea tree oil and cajeput oil, which are made from different species of Maleleuca plants.

Is it Effective?
The effectiveness ratings for **NIAULI OIL** are as follows:
Insufficient Evidence to Rate Effectiveness for... Cough and inflammation of the airways.

How does it work?
Niauli oil contains chemicals that might help stimulate blood circulation and kill bacteria and germs.

Are there safety concerns?
Niauli oil might be safe for most adults when taken by mouth. It can cause some side effects such as nausea, vomiting, and diarrhea. It also appears to be safe for most adults when applied directly to the skin.

Niauli oil is unsafe when greater than 10 grams are taken. High amounts can cause low blood pressure, blood circulation problems, and serious breathing problems.

Niauli oil is unsafe for children when applied directly to the skin of the face and in the nose. In some children it might cause asthma-like symptoms and other serious breathing problems.

Do not take niauli oil if: You are pregnant or breast-feeding. • You have a stomach or intestine disease. • You have a liver or gallbladder disease.

Are there any interactions with medications?
It is not known if niauli oil interacts with any medicines.
Before taking niauli oil, talk with your healthcare professional if you take any medications.

NIKKO MAPLE

What other names is the product known by?
Acer nikoense, Megusurinoki.

What is it?
Nikko maple is a tree. The bark is used to make medicine.

Is it Effective?
The effectiveness ratings for **NIKKO MAPLE** are as follows:
Insufficient Evidence to Rate Effectiveness for... Eye conditions and liver disorders.

How does it work?
Preliminary research suggests nikko maple might decrease inflammation. It might also have anti-cancer activity in test tubes.

Are there safety concerns?
It is not known if nikko maple is safe or what the potential side effects might be.

Do not use nikko maple if: You are pregnant or breast-feeding.

Are there any interactions with medications?
It is not known if nikko maple interacts with any medicines.
Before taking nikko maple, talk with your healthcare professional if you take any medications.

NORTHERN PRICKLY ASH

What other names is the product known by?
Angelica Tree, Pepper Wood, Prickly Ash, Toothache Bark, Xanthoxylum, Yellow Wood, Zanthoxylum, Zanthoxylum americanum.

What is it?
Northern prickly ash is a plant. The bark and berry are used to make medicine. Be careful not to confuse northern prickly ash with ash or southern prickly ash.

Is it Effective?
The effectiveness ratings for **NORTHERN PRICKLY ASH** are as follows:
Insufficient Evidence to Rate Effectiveness for... Cramps, joint pain, circulation problems, low blood pressure, fever, swelling, and other conditions.

How does it work?
It is not known how northern prickly ash might work.

Are there safety concerns?
Northern prickly ash might be safe for most people, but the potential side effects are not known.

There isn't enough information to know if the northern prickly ash berry is safe to use as medicine or what the potential side effects might be.

Do not use northern prickly ash if: You are pregnant or breast-feeding. • You have stomach or intestinal problems including ulcers, Crohn's disease, irritable bowel syndrome, infections, or other conditions.

Are there any interactions with medications?
Antacids. Antacids are used to decrease stomach acid. Northern prickly ash may increase stomach acid. By increasing stomach acid, northern prickly ash might decrease the effectiveness of antacids. Some antacids include calcium carbonate (Tums, others), dihydroxyaluminum sodium carbonate (Rolaids, others), magaldrate (Riopan), magnesium sulfate (Bilagog), aluminum hydroxide (Amphojel), and others.
Medications that decrease stomach acid (H2-Blockers). Northern prickly ash might increase stomach acid. By increasing stomach acid, northern prickly ash might decrease the effectiveness of some medications that decrease stomach acid, called H2-Blockers. Some medications that decrease stomach acid include cimetidine (Tagamet), ranitidine (Zantac), nizatidine (Axid), and famotidine (Pepcid).
Medications that decrease stomach acid (Proton pump inhibitors). Northern prickly ash might increase stomach acid. By increasing stomach acid, northern prickly ash might decrease the effectiveness of medications that are used to decrease stomach acid, called proton pump inhibitors. Some medications that decrease stomach acid include omeprazole (Prilosec), lansoprazole (Prevacid), rabeprazole (Aciphex), pantoprazole (Protonix), and esomeprazole (Nexium).

NUTMEG AND MACE

What other names is the product known by?

Jaatipatree, Jatikosha, Jatipatra, Jatipatri, Jatiphala, Jatiphalam, Macis, Muscadier, Muskatbuam, Muskatnuss, Myristica, Myristicae Aril, Myristica Fragrans, Myristica Officinalis, Myristicae Semen, Noix Muscade, Nuez Moscada, Nux Moschata.

What is it?

Nutmeg and mace are plant products. Nutmeg is the shelled, dried seed of the plant Myristica fragrans, and mace is the dried covering of the shell of the seed. Nutmeg and mace are used to make medicine.

Is it Effective?

The effectiveness ratings for **NUTMEG AND MACE** are as follows:

Insufficient Evidence to Rate Effectiveness for... Diarrhea, stomach problems, intestinal gas, cancer, kidney disease, pain, and other conditions. It is also used to produce hallucinations.

How does it work?

Nutmeg and mace contain chemicals that might affect the central nervous system. Nutmeg and mace might also kill bacteria and fungi.

Are there safety concerns?

Nutmeg and mace are UNSAFE in amounts larger than found in foods. Side effects such as thirst, dizziness, nausea, vomiting, feelings of pressure in the chest or stomach, dry mouth, stomach pain, and many other problems might occur in some people. More serious side effects might include hallucinations, miscarriages in pregnant women, seizures, and death.

Are there any interactions with medications?

Medications changed by the liver (Cytochrome P450 1A1 (CYP1A1) substrates). Some medications are changed and broken down by the liver. Nutmeg and mace might increase how quickly the liver breaks down some medications. Taking nutmeg and mace along with some medications that are changed by the liver can lead to a variety of effects and side effects. Before taking nutmeg and mace talk to your healthcare provider if you take any medications that are changed by the liver. Some of these medications that are changed by the liver include chlorzoxazone, theophylline, bufuralol, and others.

Medications changed by the liver (Cytochrome P450 1A2 (CYP1A2) substrates). Some medications are changed and broken down by the liver. Nutmeg and mace might increase how quickly the liver breaks down some medications. Taking nutmeg and mace along with some medications that are changed by the liver can lead to a variety of effects and side effects. Before taking nutmeg and mace talk to your healthcare provider if you take any medications that are changed by the liver. Some of these medications that are changed by the liver include clozapine (Clozaril), cyclobenzaprine (Flexeril), fluvoxamine (Luvox), haloperidol (Haldol), imipramine (Tofranil), mexiletine (Mexitil), olanzapine (Zyprexa), pentazocine (Talwin), propranolol (Inderal), tacrine (Cognex), theophylline, zileuton (Zyflo), zolmitriptan (Zomig), and others.

Medications changed by the liver (Cytochrome P450 2B1 (CYP2B1) substrates). Some medications are changed and broken down by the liver. Nutmeg and mace might increase how quickly the liver breaks down some medications. Taking nutmeg and mace along with some medications that are changed by the liver can lead to a variety of effects and side effects. Before taking nutmeg and mace talk to your healthcare provider if you take any medications that are changed by the liver.

Medications changed by the liver (Cytochrome P450 2B2 (CYP2B2) substrates). Some medications are changed and broken down by the liver. Taking nutmeg and mace along with some medications that are changed by the liver can lead to a variety of effects and side effects. Before taking nutmeg and mace talk to your healthcare provider if you take any medications that are changed by the liver.

Phenobarbital (Luminal). Some medications are changed and broken down by the liver. Taking nutmeg and mace along with some medications that are changed by the liver can lead to a variety of effects and side effects. Before taking nutmeg and mace talk to your healthcare provider if you take any medications that are changed by the liver. The body breaks down phenobarbital (Luminal) to get rid of it. Nutmeg and mace might increase how quickly the body breaks down phenobarbital (Luminal). Taking nutmeg and mace along with phenobarbital (Luminal) might decrease the effectiveness of phenobarbital (Luminal).

Medical professionals should consult the Professional Version at www.NaturalDatabase.com.

NUX VOMICA

What other names is the product known by?
Brechnusssamen, Poison Nut, Quaker Buttons, Shudha Kupilu, Strychni Semen, Strychnos Seed, Strychnos nux-vomica, Vishamushti.

What is it?
Nux vomica is a plant. The seed is used to make medicine.

Is it Effective?
The effectiveness ratings for **NUX VOMICA** are as follows:
Insufficient Evidence to Rate Effectiveness for... Impotence, diseases of the stomach and intestines, heart and blood system disorders, diseases of the eye, nerve disorders, depression, migraine, stimulating the appetite, lung diseases, anemia, and other conditions.

How does it work?
Nux vomica contains strychnine and other chemicals that affect the brain and muscle contractions.

Are there safety concerns?
Nux vomica is UNSAFE. Taking nux vomica for more than a week, or in high amounts of 30 mg or more, can cause severe side effects. Some of these side effects include restlessness, anxiety, dizziness, neck and back stiffness, spasms of jaw and neck muscles, convulsions, seizures, breathing problems, liver failure, death, and other serious problems.

Do not use nux vomica if: You are pregnant or breast-feeding. • You have a liver condition.

Are there any interactions with medications?
It is not known if nux vomica interacts with any medicines.
Before taking nux vomica, talk with your healthcare professional if you take any medications.

OAK bark

What other names is the product known by?
Common Oak, Durmast Oak, Eichenrinde, English Oak, Pedunculate Oak, Quercus alba, Quercus cortex, Quercus petraea, Quercus robur, Sessile Oak, Stave Oak, Stone Oak, Tanner's Bark, Tanner's Oak.

What is it?
Oak bark is the bark from several types of oak trees. The bark is used to make medicine.

Is it Effective?
The effectiveness ratings for **OAK bark** are as follows:
Insufficient Evidence to Rate Effectiveness for... Colds; fever; cough; diarrhea; bronchitis; loss of appetite; improving digestion; inflammation of the skin, mouth, throat, genital, and anal region; and other conditions.

How does it work?
Oak bark contains tannins which might help treat diarrhea and inflammation.

Are there safety concerns?
Oak bark might be safe for most people when taken for up to 3-4 days for diarrhea. Oak bark can cause serious side effects such as stomach and intestinal problems, and kidney and liver damage.

Oak bark might be safe for most people when applied directly to the skin for up to 2-3 weeks. When applied to damaged skin or when taken for longer than 2-3 weeks, oak bark is unsafe.

Do not take oak bark if: You are pregnant or breast-feeding. • You have liver problems. • You have kidney problems. • You have a skin condition called eczema or large areas of skin damage. • You have a heart condition. • You have an infection or a disease with a fever.

Are there any interactions with medications?
It is not known if oak bark interacts with any medicines.
Before taking oak bark, talk with your healthcare professional if you take any medications.

Medical professionals should consult the Professional Version at www.NaturalDatabase.com.

CONSUMER VERSION

OAK MOSS

What other names is the product known by?
Evernia prunastri, Lichen Oak Moss, Tree Moss.

What is it?
Oak moss is the moss from a certain type of oak tree called Evernia prunastri. The moss is used to make medicine.

Is it Effective?
The effectiveness ratings for **OAK MOSS** are as follows:
Insufficient Evidence to Rate Effectiveness for... Intestinal conditions and other conditions.

How does it work?
There is not enough information to know how oak moss works.

Are there safety concerns?
Oak moss might be safe for most people, when taken for short periods of time as a water-based tea. When taken in large amounts, for long periods of time, or as an alcohol extract, oak moss is unsafe. Oak moss contains a toxic chemical. It can cause side effects such as restlessness, vomiting, dizziness, tremors, kidney damage, and convulsions.

Do not take oak moss if: You are pregnant or breast-feeding. • You have kidney problems. • You have a blood disorder called porphyria. • You are allergic to lichens and mosses.

Are there any interactions with medications?
It is not known if oak moss interacts with any medicines.
Before taking oak moss, talk with your healthcare professional if you take any medications.

OATS

What other names is the product known by?
Avena, Avena Fructus, Avena Byzantina, Avena Orientalis, Avena Sativa, Avena Volgensis, Avenae Herba, Avenae Stramentum, Cereal Fiber, Dietary Fiber, Groats, Oat Bran, Oat Fruit, Oat Grain, Oat Herb, Oat Straw, Oatmeal, Oats, Straw, Whole Oat, Whole Oats, Wild Oat Herb.

What is it?
Oat is a plant. People use the above ground parts including the seed (oat), leaves and stem (oat straw), and bran (the outer layer of whole oats) to make medicine.

Is it Effective?
The effectiveness ratings for **OATS** are as follows:
Likely Effective for... Reducing the risk of heart disease, when oat bran is used as part of a diet low in fat and cholesterol • Lowering cholesterol. Consuming oat products such as oatmeal and oat bran when used as part of a diet low in fat and cholesterol can significantly lower cholesterol levels.
Possibly Effective for... Reducing blood sugar levels in people with diabetes when oat bran is used in the diet • Preventing stomach cancer when oats and oat bran are used in the diet.
Possibly Ineffective for... Preventing cancer in the large intestine (colon cancer) when oat bran is used in the diet • Lowering high blood pressure • Reducing the risk of colon cancer.
Insufficient Evidence to Rate Effectiveness for... Blocking fat from being absorbed from the gut, preventing fat redistribution syndrome in people with HIV disease, preventing gallstones, treating irritable bowel syndrome (IBS), diverticulosis, inflammatory bowel disease, constipation, anxiety, stress, nerve disorders, bladder weakness, joint and tendon disorders, gout, kidney conditions, opium and nicotine withdrawal, skin diseases, and other conditions.

How does it work?
Oats might help reduce cholesterol and blood sugar levels and control appetite by causing a feeling of fullness. Oat bran might work by blocking the absorption from the gut of substances that contribute to heart disease, high cholesterol, and diabetes.

Are there safety concerns?
Oat bran is safe for most people. It can cause intestinal gas and bloating. In people who have trouble chewing and swallowing, such as people with poorly fitting dentures or few or no teeth, or who have conditions that interfere

     Natural Medicines Comprehensive Database Consumer Version   (209) 472-2244

with proper functioning of the digestive tract, oat products can cause blockage.
Oats seem to be safe for most people when applied directly to the skin.

Do not use oats if: You have difficulty chewing or swallowing food. • You have a disorder of your digestive tract including the esophagus, stomach, and intestines.

Are there any interactions with medications?

It is not known if oats interact with any medicines.
Before taking oats as medicine, talk with your healthcare professional if you take any medications.

OCTACOSANOL

What other names is the product known by?

1-Octacosanol, Hexacosanol, N-octacosanol, Octacosyl alcohol, Tetracosanol, Triacontanol.

What is it?

Octacosanol is a chemical found in a variety of plant sources, including sugar cane and wheat germ oil.

Is it Effective?

The effectiveness ratings for **OCTACOSANOL** are as follows:
Insufficient Evidence to Rate Effectiveness for... Treating a condition called amyotrophic lateral sclerosis (Lou Gehrig's disease, ALS); improving strength, stamina, and reaction times; herpes infections; skin diseases; Parkinson's disease; high cholesterol levels; hardening of the arteries (atherosclerosis); and other conditions.

How does it work?

Octacosanol might help improve the way our body uses oxygen.

Are there safety concerns?

There is not enough information to know if octacosanol is safe.

Do not take octacosanol if: You are pregnant or breast-feeding. • You have a condition called Parkinson's disease.

Are there any interactions with medications?

Levodopa/Carbidopa (Sinemet). Levodopa/carbidopa (Sinemet) is used for Parkinson's disease. Taking octacosanol along with levodopa/carbidopa (Sinemet) might make Parkinson's disease symptoms worse. Do not take octacosanol if you are taking levodopa/carbidopa (Sinemet).

OLEANDER

What other names is the product known by?

Common Oleander, Nerium Oleander, Oleanderblatter, Oleandri Folium, Rose Bay, Rose Laurel, Thevetia Peruviana, Yellow Oleander.

What is it?

Oleander is a plant. The seeds and leaves are used to make medicine.

Is it Effective?

The effectiveness ratings for **OLEANDER** are as follows:
Insufficient Evidence to Rate Effectiveness for... Heart problems, asthma, seizures, cancer, menstrual problems, skin problems, warts, and many other conditions. It also has been used as a poison.

How does it work?

Oleander contains chemicals called glycosides which can affect the heart. These chemicals can slow the heart rate down.

Are there safety concerns?

Oleander is UNSAFE for anyone. It can cause a burning sensation in the mouth, nausea, vomiting, diarrhea, weakness, headache, stomach pain, serious heart problems, and many other side effects. The oleander leaf, oleander leaf tea, and oleander seeds have led to deadly poisonings. Oleander is particularly unsafe for people with heart conditions and women who are pregnant or breast-feeding.

Medical professionals should consult the Professional Version at www.NaturalDatabase.com.

Are there any interactions with medications?

Antibiotics (Macrolide antibiotics). Oleander can affect the heart. Some antibiotics might increase how much oleander the body absorbs. Increasing how much oleander the body absorbs might increase the effects and side effects of oleander. Some antibiotics called macrolide antibiotics include erythromycin, azithromycin, and clarithromycin.

Antibiotics (Tetracycline antibiotics). Taking some antibiotics called tetracycline antibiotics along with oleander might increase the chance of side effects from oleander. Some tetracycline antibiotics include demeclocycline (Declomycin), minocycline (Minocin), and tetracycline (Achromycin).

Calcium supplements. Oleander can stimulate the heartbeat. Calcium might also affect the heart. Taking oleander along with calcium might cause the heart to be too stimulated. Do not take oleander along with calcium supplements.

Digoxin (Lanoxin). Digoxin (Lanoxin) helps the heart beat more strongly. Oleander also seems to affect the heart. Taking oleander along with digoxin can increase the effects of digoxin and increase the risk of side effects. Do not take oleander if you are taking digoxin (Lanoxin) without talking to your health care professional.

Quinine. Oleander can affect the heart. Quinine can also affect the heart. Taking quinine along with oleander might cause serious heart problems.

Stimulant laxatives. Oleander can affect the heart. The heart uses potassium. Laxatives called stimulant laxatives can decrease potassium levels in the body. Low potassium levels can increase the chance of side effects from taking oleander. Some stimulant laxatives include bisacodyl (Correctol, Dulcolax), cascara, castor oil (Purge), senna (Senokot), and others.

Water pills (Diuretic drugs). Oleander might affect the heart. "Water pills" can decrease potassium in the body. Low potassium levels can also affect the heart and increase the risk of side effects from oleander. Some "water pills" that can deplete potassium include chlorothiazide (Diuril), chlorthalidone (Thalitone), furosemide (Lasix), hydrochlorothiazide (HCTZ, HydroDiuril, Microzide), and others.

OLIVE

What other names is the product known by?

Monounsaturated Fatty Acid, n-9 Fatty Acid, Olea Europaea, Oleae Folium, Olivae Oleum, Olive Leaf, Olive Oil, Olivier, Omega-9, Omega-9 Fatty Acids, Salad Oil, Sweet Oil, Unsaturated Fatty Acid.

What is it?

Olive is a tree. The oil from the fruit and the seeds are used to make medicine.

Is it Effective?

The effectiveness ratings for **OLIVE** are as follows:

Likely Effective for... Use as a mild laxative for constipation.

Possibly Effective for... Lowering cholesterol in people with high cholesterol levels • Lowering blood pressure in people with high blood pressure • Reducing the risk of heart diseases and heart attack • Decreasing the chance of getting serious conditions like breast cancer, colorectal cancer, and rheumatoid arthritis. However, there is no evidence olive oil can help treat these conditions.

Possibly Ineffective for... Softening ear wax • Treating pain associated with ear infections.

Insufficient Evidence to Rate Effectiveness for... Diabetes, gallstones, liver disorders, migraine headache, gas, minor burns, skin conditions, hayfever, lice, infections such as the flu, the common cold, meningitis, Epstein-Barr Virus (EBV), herpes, shingles, HIV/AIDS, chronic fatigue, hepatitis B, pneumonia, tuberculosis, gonorrhea, malaria, urinary tract and surgical infections, and other conditions.

How does it work?

Fatty acids in olive oil seem to decrease cholesterol levels and have anti-inflammatory effects. Olive leaf and olive oil might lower blood pressure.

Are there safety concerns?

Olive is safe for most adults. It can cause upset stomach in some people.

Are there any interactions with medications?

Medications for diabetes (Antidiabetes drugs). Olive and olive oil might decrease blood sugar. Diabetes medications are also used to lower blood sugar. Taking olive oil along with diabetes medications might cause your blood sugar to go too low. Monitor your blood sugar closely. The dose of your diabetes medication might need to be changed. Some medications used for diabetes include glimepiride (Amaryl), glyburide (DiaBeta, Glynase PresTab, Micronase), insulin, pioglitazone (Actos), rosiglitazone (Avandia), chlorpropamide (Diabinese), glipizide (Glucotrol), tolbutamide (Orinase), and others.

Medications for high blood pressure (Antihypertensive drugs). Olive seems to decrease blood pressure. Taking olive along with medications for high blood pressure might cause your blood pressure to go too low. Some medications for high blood pressure include captopril (Capoten), enalapril (Vasotec), losartan (Cozaar), valsartan (Diovan), diltiazem (Cardizem), Amlodipine (Norvasc), hydrochlorothiazide (HydroDIURIL), furosemide (Lasix), and many others.

OMEGA-6 FATTY ACIDS

What other names is the product known by?
N-6, N-6 EFAs, N-6 Essential Fatty Acids, Omega 6, Omega-6 polyunsaturated fatty acids, Omega 6 Oils, Polyunsaturated Fatty Acids, PUFAs.

What is it?
Omega-6 fatty acids are types of fats. These fats can be found in vegetable oils, including corn, evening primrose seed, safflower, and soybean oils; and black currant seed, borage seed, and evening primrose oils.

Is it Effective?
The effectiveness ratings for **OMEGA-6 FATTY ACIDS** are as follows:
Possibly Ineffective for... Improving mental development or growth in infants when arachidonic acid (an omega-6 fatty acid) is used in infant formula.
Insufficient Evidence to Rate Effectiveness for... Reducing the risk of heart disease, lowering bad cholesterol levels, increasing good cholesterol levels, and reducing the risk of cancer.

How does it work?
There isn't enough information available to know how omega-6 fatty acids work.

Are there safety concerns?
There isn't enough information available to know if omega-6 fatty acids are safe to use as medicine. They can cause an increase in the level of triglycerides (a type of cholesterol) in the blood.

Do not use omega-6 fatty acids if: You are pregnant or breast-feeding. • You have high triglycerides (a type of cholesterol).

Are there any interactions with medications?
It is not known if omega-6 fatty acids interact with any medicines.
Before taking omega-6 fatty acids, talk with your healthcare professional if you take any medications.

ONION

What other names is the product known by?
Allii cepae bulbus, Allium cepa, Green Onion, Onions.

What is it?
Onion is a plant. The bulb of the onion is used to make medicine.

Is it Effective?
The effectiveness ratings for **ONION** are as follows:
Insufficient Evidence to Rate Effectiveness for... Asthma, diabetes, upset stomach, fever, colds, cough, bronchitis, high blood pressure (hypertension), infection prevention, swelling (inflammation) of the mouth and throat, wounds, loss of appetite, preventing hardening of the arteries (atherosclerosis), and other conditions.

How does it work?
Onion might help reduce cholesterol levels, a risk factor for hardening of the arteries. There is some evidence that onion might also reduce lung tightness in people with asthma.

Are there safety concerns?
Onion is safe when taken in amounts commonly found in food. It might be safe for most people when taken in larger amounts, up to a maximum of 35 mg of the onion ingredient "diphenylamine" per day.

Onion might lower blood sugar. If you have diabetes, check your blood sugar carefully.

Do not take onion if: You are pregnant or breast-feeding, except in amounts used in foods.

Medical professionals should consult the Professional Version at www.NaturalDatabase.com.

CONSUMER VERSION

Are there any interactions with medications?

Aspirin. Some people are allergic to onions. Aspirin might increase your sensitivity to onions if you are allergic to onions. This has only been reported in one person. But to be on the safe side, if you are allergic to onions do not take aspirin and eat onions.

Medications that slow blood clotting (Anticoagulant / Antiplatelet drugs). Onion might slow blood clotting. Taking onion along with medications that also slow clotting might increase the chances of bruising and bleeding. Some medications that slow blood clotting include aspirin, clopidogrel (Plavix), diclofenac (Voltaren, Cataflam, others), ibuprofen (Advil, Motrin, others), naproxen (Anaprox, Naprosyn, others), dalteparin (Fragmin), enoxaparin (Lovenox), heparin, warfarin (Coumadin), and others.

Medications for diabetes (Antidiabetes drugs). Onion might decrease blood sugar. Diabetes medications are also used to lower blood sugar. Taking onion along with diabetes medications might cause your blood sugar to go too low. Monitor your blood sugar closely. The dose of your diabetes medication might need to be changed. Some medications used for diabetes include glimepiride (Amaryl), glyburide (DiaBeta, Glynase PresTab, Micronase), insulin, pioglitazone (Actos), rosiglitazone (Avandia), chlorpropamide (Diabinese), glipizide (Glucotrol), tolbutamide (Orinase), and others.

OOLONG TEA

What other names is the product known by?

Brown Tea, EGCG, Epigallo Catechin Gallate, Epigallocatechin Gallate, Tea, Tea Oolong.

What is it?

Oolong tea is a product made from the Camellia sinensis plant. The leaves and stems are used to make medicine.

Is it Effective?

The effectiveness ratings for **OOLONG TEA** are as follows:

Likely Effective for... Mental alertness.

Possibly Effective for... Preventing high blood pressure • Reducing the risk of ovarian cancer.

Insufficient Evidence to Rate Effectiveness for... Skin allergies, diabetes, preventing tooth decay, reducing the risk of cancer, promoting weight loss, and other conditions.

How does it work?

Oolong tea contains caffeine. Caffeine works by stimulating the central nervous system (CNS), heart, and muscles. Oolong tea also contains theophylline and theobromine, which are chemicals similar to caffeine.

Are there safety concerns?

Too much oolong tea, more than five cups per day, can cause side effects because of the caffeine. These side effects can range from mild to serious and include headache, nervousness, sleep problems, vomiting, diarrhea, irritability, irregular heartbeat, tremor, heartburn, dizziness, ringing in the ears, convulsions, and confusion.

If you are pregnant or breast-feeding, oolong tea in small amounts is probably not harmful. However, do not drink more than three cups a day of oolong tea. Too much caffeine might cause premature delivery, low birth weight, and harm to the baby.

Caffeine is probably safe in children in amounts commonly found in foods.

Do not take oolong tea if: You have a heart condition. • You have anxiety. • You have an eye disease called glaucoma. • You have osteoporosis. • You have a bleeding condition.

Are there any interactions with medications?

Adenosine (Adenocard). Oolong tea contains caffeine. The caffeine in oolong tea might block the affects of adenosine (Adenocard). Adenosine (Adenocard) is often used by doctors to do a test on the heart. This test is called a cardiac stress test. Stop consuming oolong tea or other caffeine-containing products at least 24 hours before a cardiac stress test.

Alcohol. The body breaks down the caffeine in oolong tea to get rid of it. Alcohol can decrease how quickly the body breaks down caffeine. Taking oolong tea along with alcohol might cause too much caffeine in the bloodstream and caffeine side effects including jitteriness, headache, and fast heartbeat.

Amphetamines. Stimulant drugs such as amphetamines speed up the nervous system. By speeding up the nervous system, stimulant medications can make you feel jittery and increase your heart rate. The caffeine in oolong tea might also speed up the nervous system. Taking oolong tea along with stimulant drugs might cause serious problems including increased heart rate and high blood pressure. Avoid taking stimulant drugs along with oolong tea.

Antibiotics (Quinolone antibiotics). The body breaks down caffeine to get rid of it. Some antibiotics might

Medical professionals should consult the Professional Version at www.NaturalDatabase.com.

decrease how quickly the body breaks down caffeine. Taking these antibiotics along with oolong tea can increase the risk of side effects including jitteriness, headache, increased heart rate, and other side effects. Some antibiotics that decrease how quickly the body breaks down caffeine include ciprofloxacin (Cipro), enoxacin (Penetrex), norfloxacin (Chibroxin, Noroxin), sparfloxacin (Zagam), trovafloxacin (Trovan), and grepafloxacin (Raxar).

Birth control pills (Contraceptive drugs). The body breaks down the caffeine in oolong tea to get rid of it. Birth control pills can decrease how quickly the body breaks down caffeine. Taking oolong tea along with birth control pills can cause jitteriness, headache, fast heartbeat, and other side effects. Some birth control pills include ethinyl estradiol and levonorgestrel (Triphasil), ethinyl estradiol and norethindrone (Ortho-Novum 1/35, Ortho-Novum 7/7/7), and others.

Cimetidine (Tagamet). Oolong tea contains caffeine. The body breaks down caffeine to get rid of it. Cimetidine (Tagamet) can decrease how quickly your body breaks down caffeine. Taking cimetidine (Tagamet) along with oolong tea might increase the chance of caffeine side effects including jitteriness, headache, fast heartbeat, and others.

Clozapine (Clozaril). The body breaks down clozapine (Clozaril) to get rid of it. The caffeine in oolong tea seems to decrease how quickly the body breaks down clozapine (Clozaril). Taking oolong tea along with clozapine (Clozaril) can increase the effects and side effects of clozapine (Clozaril).

Cocaine. Stimulant drugs such as cocaine speed up the nervous system. By speeding up the nervous system, stimulant medications can make you feel jittery and increase your heart rate. The caffeine in oolong tea might also speed up the nervous system. Taking oolong tea along with stimulant drugs might cause serious problems including increased heart rate and high blood pressure. Avoid taking stimulant drugs along with oolong tea.

Dipyridamole (Persantine). Oolong tea contains caffeine. The caffeine in oolong tea might block the affects of dipyridamole (Persantine). Dipyridamole (Persantine) is often used by doctors to do a test on the heart. This test is called a cardiac stress test. Stop consuming oolong tea or other caffeine-containing products at least 24 hours before a cardiac stress test.

Disulfiram (Antabuse). The body breaks down caffeine to get rid of it. Disulfiram (Antabuse) can decrease how quickly the body gets rid of caffeine. Taking oolong tea (which contains caffeine) along with disulfiram (Antabuse) might increase the effects and side effects of caffeine including jitteriness, hyperactivity, irritability, and others.

Ephedrine. Stimulant drugs speed up the nervous system. Caffeine (contained in oolong tea) and ephedrine are both stimulant drugs. Taking caffeine along with ephedrine might cause too much stimulation and sometimes serious side effects and heart problems. Do not take caffeine-containing products and ephedrine at the same time.

Estrogens. The body breaks down the caffeine in oolong tea to get rid of it. Estrogens can decrease how quickly the body breaks down caffeine. Taking oolong tea along with estrogens can cause jitteriness, headache, fast heartbeat, and other side effects. If you take estrogens limit your caffeine intake. Some estrogen pills include conjugated equine estrogens (Premarin), ethinyl estradiol, estradiol, and others.

Fluconazole (Diflucan). Oolong tea contains caffeine. The body breaks down caffeine to get rid of it. Fluconazole (Diflucan) might decrease how quickly the body gets rid of caffeine. Taking oolong tea along with fluconazole (Diflucan) might increase the risk of caffeine side effects such as nervousness, anxiety, and insomnia.

Fluvoxamine (Luvox). The body breaks down the caffeine in oolong tea to get rid of it. Fluvoxamine (Luvox) can decrease how quickly the body breaks down caffeine. Taking oolong tea along with fluvoxamine (Luvox) might cause too much caffeine in the body, and increase the effects and side effects of caffeine.

Lithium. Your body naturally gets rid of lithium. The caffeine in oolong tea can increase how quickly your body gets rid of lithium. If you take products that contain caffeine and you take lithium, stop taking caffeine products slowly. Stopping oolong tea too quickly can increase the side effects of lithium.

Medications that slow blood clotting (Anticoagulant / Antiplatelet drugs). Oolong tea contains caffeine. Caffeine might slow blood clotting. Taking oolong tea along with medications that also slow clotting might increase the chances of bruising and bleeding. Some medications that slow blood clotting include aspirin, clopidogrel (Plavix), diclofenac (Voltaren, Cataflam, others), ibuprofen (Advil, Motrin, others), naproxen (Anaprox, Naprosyn, others), dalteparin (Fragmin), enoxaparin (Lovenox), heparin, warfarin (Coumadin), and others.

Medications for depression (MAOIs). Oolong tea contains caffeine. Caffeine can stimulate the body. Some medications used for depression can also stimulate the body. Taking oolong tea with these medications used for depression might cause serious side effects including fast heartbeat, high blood pressure, nervousness, and others. Some of these medications used for depression include phenelzine (Nardil), tranylcypromine (Parnate), and others.

Medications for diabetes (Antidiabetes drugs). Oolong tea might increase blood sugar. Diabetes medications are used to lower blood sugar. By increasing blood sugar, oolong tea might decrease the effectiveness of diabetes medications. Monitor your blood sugar closely. The dose of your diabetes medication might need to be changed. Some medications used for diabetes include glimepiride (Amaryl), glyburide (DiaBeta, Glynase PresTab, Micronase), insulin, pioglitazone (Actos), rosiglitazone (Avandia), chlorpropamide (Diabinese), glipizide (Glucotrol), tolbutamide (Orinase), and others.

Mexiletine (Mexitil). Oolong tea contains caffeine. The body breaks down caffeine to get rid of it. Mexiletine (Mexitil) can decrease how quickly the body breaks down caffeine. Taking mexiletine (Mexitil) along with oolong tea might increase the caffeine effects and side effects of oolong tea.

Nicotine. Stimulant drugs such as nicotine speed up the nervous system. By speeding up the nervous system, stimulant medications can make you feel jittery and increase your heart rate. The caffeine in oolong tea might also

Medical professionals should consult the Professional Version at www.NaturalDatabase.com.

CONSUMER VERSION

Medical professionals should consult the Professional Version at www.NaturalDatabase.com.

speed up the nervous system. Taking oolong tea along with stimulant drugs might cause serious problems including increased heart rate and high blood pressure. Avoid taking stimulant drugs along with caffeine.

Pentobarbital (Nembutal). The stimulant effects of the caffeine in oolong tea can block the sleep-producing effects of pentobarbital.

Phenylpropanolamine. The caffeine in oolong tea can stimulate the body. Phenylpropanolamine can also stimulate the body. Taking oolong tea along with phenylpropanolamine might cause too much stimulation and increase heartbeat, blood pressure, and cause nervousness.

Riluzole (Rilutek). The body breaks down riluzole (Rilutek) to get rid of it. Taking oolong tea can decrease how fast the body breaks down riluzole (Rilutek) and increase the effects and side effects of riluzole.

Terbinafine (Lamisil). The body breaks down caffeine (contained in oolong tea) to get rid of it. Terbinafine (Lamisil) can decrease how fast the body gets rid of caffeine and increase the risk of side effects including jitteriness, headache, increased heartbeat, and other effects.

Theophylline. Oolong tea contains caffeine. Caffeine works similarly to theophylline. Caffeine can also decrease how quickly the body gets rid of theophylline. Taking oolong tea along with theophylline might increase the effects and side effects of theophylline.

Verapamil (Calan, Covera, Isoptin, Verelan). The body breaks down the caffeine in oolong tea to get rid of it. Verapamil (Calan, Covera, Isoptin, Verelan) can decrease how quickly the body gets rid of caffeine. Taking oolong tea along with verapamil (Calan, Covera, Isoptin, Verelan) can increase the risk of caffeine side effects including jitteriness, headache, and an increased heartbeat.

OPIUM ANTIDOTE

What other names is the product known by?
Combretum, Combretum micranthum, Jungle Weed.

What is it?
Opium antidote is a plant product. The leaf and stem of the plant Combretum micranthum are used to make medicine.

Is it Effective?
The effectiveness ratings for **OPIUM ANTIDOTE** are as follows:
Insufficient Evidence to Rate Effectiveness for... Gallbladder disease, upset stomach, liver disease, and other conditions.

How does it work?
Opium antidote might stimulate bile flow, a substance important in digestion.

Are there safety concerns?
There is insufficient reliable information available about the safety of opium antidote.

Do not take opium antidote if: You are pregnant or breast-feeding.

Are there any interactions with medications?
It is not known if opium antidote interacts with any medicines.
Before taking opium antidote, talk with your healthcare professional if you take any medications.

ORCHIC EXTRACT

What other names is the product known by?
Bovine Orchic Extract, Bovine Testicle Extract, Bull Balls Extract, Orchic Concentrate, Orchic Factors, Orchic Substance.

What is it?
Orchic extract is made from cattle testicles. The extract is used to make medicine.

Is it Effective?
The effectiveness ratings for **ORCHIC EXTRACT** are as follows:
Insufficient Evidence to Rate Effectiveness for... Maintaining healthy testicle function in men and other uses.

How does it work?
Marketers imply that orchic extracts are a good source of testosterone. However, there is currently no evidence to support this claim.

Are there safety concerns?

There is insufficient reliable information available about the safety of orchic extract. However, since orchic extract preparations are made from animals, there is a concern about contamination with diseased animal parts.

Do not take orchic extract if: You are pregnant or breast-feeding.

Are there any interactions with medications?

It is not known if orchic extract interacts with any medicines.
Before taking orchic extract, talk with your healthcare professional if you take any medications.

OREGANO

What other names is the product known by?

Dostenkraut, European Oregano, Labiatae, Lamiaceae, Mountain Mint, Organy, Origanum vulgare, Origani vulgaris herba, Wild Marjoram, Winter Marjoram, Wintersweet.

What is it?

Oregano is a plant. The leaf is used to make medicine.

Is it Effective?

The effectiveness ratings for **OREGANO** are as follows:
Possibly Effective for... Parasites in the intestines.
Insufficient Evidence to Rate Effectiveness for... Asthma, croup, bronchitis, cough, indigestion and bloating, painful menstrual periods, arthritis, headaches, heart conditions, and other conditions.

How does it work?

Oregano contains chemicals that might help reduce cough and spasms. Oregano also might help digestion by increasing bile flow and fighting against some bacteria, viruses, fungi, intestinal worms, and other parasites.

Are there safety concerns?

Oregano is safe for most adults. Mild side effects include stomach upset. Oregano might also cause an allergic reaction in people who have an allergy to plants in the Lamiaceae family.

Oregeno might be safe for pregnant or breast-feeding women in amounts normally found in foods, but larger amounts might not be safe.

Do not take oregano if: You have an allergy to plants in the Lamiaceae family including basil, hyssop, lavender, marjoram, mint, sage, and others.

Are there any interactions with medications?

It is not known if oregano interacts with any medicines.
Before taking oregano, talk with your healthcare professional if you take any medications.

OREGON FIR BALSAM

What other names is the product known by?

Balsam, Balsam Fir Oregon, Balsam Oregon, Coastal Douglas Fir, Douglas Fir, Douglas Spruce, Oregon Balsam, Pseudotsuga douglasii, Pseudotsuga menziesii, Pseudotsuga mucronata, Pseudotsuga taxifolia, Red Fir.

What is it?

Oregon fir balsam is a substance collected from the trunk of the Oregon fir tree. The balsam is used to make medicine.

Is it Effective?

The effectiveness ratings for **OREGON FIR BALSAM** are as follows:
Insufficient Evidence to Rate Effectiveness for... Burns, sores, cuts, heart and chest pain, tumors, and other conditions.

How does it work?

There isn't enough information to know how Oregon fir balsam might work.

Medical professionals should consult the Professional Version at www.NaturalDatabase.com.

Are there safety concerns?

There isn't enough information to know if Oregon fir balsam might be safe.

Do not use Oregon fir balsam if: You are pregnant or breast-feeding.

Are there any interactions with medications?

It is not known if Oregon fir balsam interacts with any medicines.
Before taking Oregon fir balsam, talk with your healthcare professional if you take any medications.

OREGON GRAPE

What other names is the product known by?

Barberry, Berberis aquifolium, Berberis nervosa, Berberis repens, Berberis sonnei, Blue Barberry, Creeping Barberry, Holly Barberry, Holly-Leaved Berberis, Holly Mahonia, Mahonia aquifolium, Mahonia nervosa, Mahonia repens, Mountain-Grape, Oregon Barberry, Oregon-Grape, Oregon Grape-Holly, Scraperoot, Trailing Mahonia, Water-Holly.

What is it?

Oregon grape is a plant. The root and root-like stem (rhizome) are used to make medicine.

Is it Effective?

The effectiveness ratings for **OREGON GRAPE** are as follows:
Possibly Effective for... Psoriasis.
Insufficient Evidence to Rate Effectiveness for... Stomach ulcers, heartburn, stomach upset, and other conditions.

How does it work?

The chemicals in Oregon grape might help fight bacterial and fungal infections. Oregon grape may also slow the production of excessive skin cells in diseases such as psoriasis.

Are there safety concerns?

An Oregon grape cream seems to be safe for most people when applied to the skin. It can cause some side effects such as itching, burning, irritation, and allergic reactions.

There is not enough information to know if Oregon grape is safe when taken by mouth in medicinal amounts.

Oregon grape is unsafe in newborn infants.

Do not use Oregon grape if: You are pregnant or breast-feeding.

Are there any interactions with medications?

Cyclosporin (Neoral, Sandimmune). The body breaks down cyclosporin (Neoral, Sandimmune) to get rid of it. Oregon grape might decrease how fast the body breaks down cyclosporin (Neoral, Sandimmune). This might cause there to be too much cyclosporin (Neoral, Sandimmune) in the body and potentially cause side effects.
Medications changed by the liver (Cytochrome P450 3A4 (CYP3A4) substrates). Some medications are changed and broken down by the liver. Oregon grape might decrease how quickly the liver breaks down some medications. Taking Oregon grape along with some medications that are broken down by the liver can increase the effects and side effects of some medications. Before taking Oregon grape, talk to your healthcare provider if you are taking any medications that are changed by the liver. Some medications changed by the liver include cyclosporin (Neoral, Sandimmune), lovastatin (Mevacor), clarithromycin (Biaxin), indinavir (Crixivan), sildenafil (Viagra), triazolam (Halcion), and many others.

ORIENTAL ARBORVITAE

What other names is the product known by?

Bai Zhi Ren, Biota orientalis, Chinese Arborvitae, Platycladus orientalis, Thuja orientalis.

What is it?

Oriental arborvitae is a plant. The seeds and leafy twigs are used to make medicine.

Medical professionals should consult the Professional Version at www.NaturalDatabase.com.

Is it Effective?
The effectiveness ratings for **ORIENTAL ARBORVITAE** are as follows:
Insufficient Evidence to Rate Effectiveness for... Headache, fever, nausea, pain, nerve disorders, cancer, constipation, seizures, menstrual problems, ejaculation problems, intestinal disorders, excessive bleeding (hemorrhage), inability to sleep (insomnia), burns, and other conditions.

How does it work?
Oriental arborvitae might have some activity against certain types of bacteria.

Are there safety concerns?
Oriental arborvitae might be safe when taken short-term in small amounts. However, it contains a toxic compound called thujone which can cause restlessness, mental changes, vomiting, dizziness, tremors, kidney damage, seizures and other side effects, especially when taken long-term or in large amounts.

Do not take oriental arborvitae if: You are pregnant or breast-feeding. • You have a kidney condition. • You have a condition called porphyria.

Are there any interactions with medications?
It is not known if oriental arborvitae interacts with any medicines.
Before taking oriental arborvitae, talk with your healthcare professional if you take any medications.

ORNITHINE

What other names is the product known by?
L-Ornithine, L-5-aminorvaline, L-2,5-diaminovaleric acid.

What is it?
Ornithine is a chemical called an amino acid. It is made in the body. It can also be made in a laboratory. People use it as a medicine.

Is it Effective?
The effectiveness ratings for **ORNITHINE** are as follows:
Possibly Ineffective for... Improving athletic performance.
Insufficient Evidence to Rate Effectiveness for... Wound healing and other conditions.

How does it work?
It's not known how ornithine might work for medical uses.

Are there safety concerns?
There isn't enough reliable information about the safety of ornithine.

Do not take ornithine if: You are pregnant or breast-feeding.

Are there any interactions with medications?
It is not known if ornithine interacts with any medicines.
Before taking ornithine, talk with your healthcare professional if you take any medications.

ORNITHINE KETOGLUTARATE

What other names is the product known by?
OKG, Ornicetil, Ornithine Alpha Ketoglutarate, L-Ornithine Alpha-Ketoglutarate, L(+)-ornithine alpha-ketoglutarate.

What is it?
Ornithine ketoglutarate is a chemical called an amino acid that is made in the body. It can also be made in a laboratory. People use it as a medicine.

Is it Effective?
The effectiveness ratings for **ORNITHINE KETOGLUTARATE** are as follows:
Possibly Effective for... Wound healing in burn patients.
Possibly Ineffective for... Improving athletic performance.

CONSUMER VERSION

Medical professionals should consult the Professional Version at www.NaturalDatabase.com.

Likely Ineffective for... Treating mental changes caused by liver disease, when given intravenously (IV) by a healthcare professional.

Insufficient Evidence to Rate Effectiveness for... Complications of surgery or long-term feeding by vein and other conditions.

How does it work?

Ornithine ketoglutarate might change the way amino acids, the building blocks of protein, are used in the body. It also increases insulin.

Are there safety concerns?

There isn't enough reliable information about the safety of ornithine ketoglutarate when taken by mouth. It might be safe for most people when given intravenously (IV) by a healthcare professional.

Do not take ornithine ketoglutarate if: You are pregnant or breast-feeding.

Are there any interactions with medications?

It is not known if ornithine ketoglutarate interacts with any medicines.
Before taking ornithine ketoglutarate, talk with your healthcare professional if you take any medications.

ORRIS

What other names is the product known by?

Blue Flag, Daggers, Flag, Flaggon, Flag Lily, Fliggers, Florentine Iris, Gladyne, Iris, Iris florentina, Iris germanica, Iris pallida, Jacob's Sword, Liver Lily, Myrtle Flower, Poison Flag, Rhizoma iridis, Segg, Sheggs, Snake Lily, Water Flag, White Dragon Flower, Wild Iris, Yellow Flag, Yellow Iris.

What is it?

Orris is a plant. The root is used to make medicine.

Is it Effective?

The effectiveness ratings for **ORRIS** are as follows:
Insufficient Evidence to Rate Effectiveness for... Purifying blood, skin diseases, bronchitis, cancer, improving appetite and digestion, inflammation of the spleen, liver and kidney problems, vomiting, constipation, bad breath, teething pain, and other conditions.

How does it work?

Orris contains many chemicals, including some which may loosen lung congestion and make it easier to cough up.

Are there safety concerns?

Orris seems to be safe for most people when taken by mouth. There are no known side effects if the root is carefully peeled and dried. However, the fresh plant juice or root can cause severe irritation of the mouth, stomach pain, vomiting, and bloody diarrhea.

There isn't enough information to know if orris might be safe when applied directly to the skin. However, the fresh plant juice or root can cause severe skin irritation.

Do not take orris if: You are pregnant or breast-feeding.

Are there any interactions with medications?

It is not known if orris interacts with any medicines.
Before taking orris, talk with your healthcare professional if you take any medications.

OSCILLOCOCCINUM

What other names is the product known by?

Anas Barbariae, Anas Moschata, Avian Heart and Liver, Avian Liver Extract, Cairina Moschata, Canard de Barbarie, Duck Liver Extract, Muscovy Duck, Oscillo.

What is it?

Oscillococcinum is a homeopathic product used for the flu (influenza). Homeopathic products are often so diluted that they don't contain any active medicine.

Is it Effective?

The effectiveness ratings for **OSCILLOCOCCINUM** are as follows:
Insufficient Evidence to Rate Effectiveness for... Flu (influenza).

How does it work?

Oscillococcinum is a homeopathic product. Homeopathy is a system of medicine established in the 19th century by a German physician named Samuel Hahnemann. Its basic principles are that "like treats like" and "potentiation through dilution." For example, in homeopathy, influenza would be treated with an extreme dilution of a substance that normally causes influenza when taken in high doses.

A French physician discovered oscillococcinum while investigating the Spanish flu in 1917. But he was mistaken that his "oscillococci" were the cause of the flu.

Practitioners of homeopathy believe that more dilute preparations are more potent. Many homeopathic preparations are so diluted that they contain little or no active ingredient. Therefore, most homeopathic products are not expected to have any pharmacological effects, drug interactions, or other harmful effects. Any beneficial effects are controversial and cannot be explained by current scientific methods.

Dilutions of 1 to 10 are designated by an "X." So a 1X dilution = 1:10; 3X = 1:1000; 6X = 1:1,000,000. Dilutions of 1 to 100 are designated by a "C." So a 1C dilution = 1:100; 3C = 1:1,000,000. Dilutions of 24X or 12C or more contain zero molecules of the original active ingredient. Oscillococcinum is diluted to 200C.

Are there safety concerns?

Oscillococcinum seems to be safe. This is a homeopathic preparation. This means that it does not contain any active ingredient. Most experts believe that it will have no beneficial effect and also no negative side effects.

Are there any interactions with medications?

It is not known if oscillococcinum interacts with any medicines.
Before taking oscillococcinum, talk with your healthcare professional if you take any medications.

OSHA

What other names is the product known by?

Bear Root, Chuchupate, Colorado Cough Root, Indian Parsley, Ligusticum porteri, Mountain Lovage, Porter's Licorice Root, Wild Celery Root.

What is it?

Osha is a plant. The root is used to make medicine.

Is it Effective?

The effectiveness ratings for **OSHA** are as follows:
Insufficient Evidence to Rate Effectiveness for... Sore throat, prevention of skin wound infection, indigestion, bronchitis, cough, common cold, flu, pneumonia, herpes, AIDS/HIV, and other conditions.

How does it work?

Osha contains chemicals that might help fight bacterial and viral infections.

Are there safety concerns?

Osha might be safe for most adults.

Do not take osha if: You are pregnant or breast-feeding.

Are there any interactions with medications?

It is not known if osha interacts with any medicines.
Before taking osha, talk with your healthcare professional if you take any medications.

OSTRICH FERN

What other names is the product known by?

Fiddlehead Fern, Garden Fern, Hardy Fern, Matteuccia struthiopteris, Osmunda struthiopteris.

What is it?

Ostrich fern is a plant. The young shoots of ostrich fern, known as fiddleheads, are used to make medicine.

Medical professionals should consult the Professional Version at www.NaturalDatabase.com.

Is it Effective?

The effectiveness ratings for **OSTRICH FERN** are as follows:
Insufficient Evidence to Rate Effectiveness for... Sore throat, skin wounds, and boils.

How does it work?

There isn't enough information to know how ostrich fern works, although it might have some activity as a laxative.

Are there safety concerns?

Ostrich fern seems to be safe for most people. If it is not properly cooked, it can cause nausea, vomiting, stomach cramps, diarrhea, and headaches. It may also cause severe food poisoning if it is not boiled for at least 10 minutes prior to eating.

Do not take ostrich fern if: You are pregnant or breast-feeding.

Are there any interactions with medications?

It is not known if ostrich fern interacts with any medicines.
Before taking ostrich fern, talk with your healthcare professional if you take any medications.

OSWEGO TEA

What other names is the product known by?

Bee Balm, Blue Balm, High Balm, Low Balm, Monarda, Monarda didyma, Mountain Balm, Mountain Mint, Scarlet Monarda.

What is it?

Oswego tea is made from a plant. People use the tea as medicine. Be careful not to confuse oswego tea with lemon balm as both are called bee balm.

Is it Effective?

The effectiveness ratings for **OSWEGO TEA** are as follows:
Insufficient Evidence to Rate Effectiveness for... Digestion disorders, gas, premenstrual syndrome (PMS), spasms, fluid retention, fever, and other conditions.

How does it work?

There is insufficient reliable information available about how oswego tea works.

Are there safety concerns?

There is insufficient reliable information available about the safety of oswego tea.
Do not take oswego tea if: You are pregnant or breast-feeding.

Are there any interactions with medications?

It is not known if oswego tea interacts with any medicines.
Before taking oswego tea, talk with your healthcare professional if you take any medications.

OX-EYE DAISY

What other names is the product known by?

Butter Daisy, Chrysanthemum leucanthemum, Dun Daisy, Golden Daisy, Goldenseal, Great Ox-Eye, Herb Margaret, Horse Daisy, Horse Gowan, Marguerite, Maudlin Daisy, Maudlinwort, Moon Daisy, Moon Flower, Moon Penny, Poverty Weed, White Daisy, White Weed.

What is it?

Ox-eye daisy is a plant. The above ground flowering parts of the plant are used to make medicine. Though ox-eye daisy is sometimes known as goldenseal, it is unrelated to the plant more commonly called goldenseal (Hydrastis canadensis).

Is it Effective?

The effectiveness ratings for **OX-EYE DAISY** are as follows:
Insufficient Evidence to Rate Effectiveness for... Common cold, cough, bronchitis, fever, mouth and vocal cord swelling (inflammation), liver and gallbladder problems, loss of appetite, reducing spasms, increasing the amount of urine produced (diuretic), skin swelling (inflammation), wounds, and burns.

 Natural Medicines Comprehensive Database Consumer Version (209) 472-2244

How does it work?

There isn't enough information to know how ox-eye daisy might work.

Are there safety concerns?

There isn't enough information to know if ox-eye daisy is safe. Ox-eye daisy can cause allergic reactions. People at the greatest risk of allergic reactions are those who are allergic to plants in the Asteraceae/Compositae family such as ragweed, chrysanthemums, marigolds, daisies, and many other plants.

Do not take ox-eye daisy if: You are pregnant or breast-feeding. • You are allergic to ragweed, marigolds, daisies, and other related plants.

Are there any interactions with medications?

It is not known if ox-eye daisy interacts with any medicines.
Before taking ox-eye daisy, talk with your healthcare professional if you take any medications.

PAGODA TREE

What other names is the product known by?

Chinese Scholartree, Japanese Pagoda-Tree, Sophora japonica, Styphnolobium japonicum.

What is it?

Pagoda is a tree. The seeds are used to make medicine.

Is it Effective?

The effectiveness ratings for **PAGODA TREE** are as follows:
Insufficient Evidence to Rate Effectiveness for... Certain forms of severe diarrhea (dysentery) and other conditions.

How does it work?

There isn't enough information to know how pagoda tree might work.

Are there safety concerns?

The seeds of the pagoda tree seem unsafe for most people. The seeds might cause serious side effects including facial swelling, poisoning, or death.

Do not take pagoda tree seeds if: You are pregnant or breast-feeding.

Are there any interactions with medications?

It is not known if pagoda tree interacts with any medicines.
Before taking pagoda tree, talk with your healthcare professional if you take any medications.

PALM OIL

What other names is the product known by?

African Palm Oil, Crude Palm Oil, Elaeis guineensis, Elaeis melanococca, Main Ja, Oil Palm Tree, Palm Kernel Oil, Palm Oil Carotene, Red Palm Oil.

What is it?

Palm oil is obtained from the oil of the palm tree.

Is it Effective?

The effectiveness ratings for **PALM OIL** are as follows:
Possibly Effective for... Vitamin A deficiency.
Possibly Ineffective for... Decreasing symptoms of malaria.

How does it work?

Palm oil contains saturated and unsaturated fats, vitamin E, and beta-carotene. It might have antioxidant effects.

Are there safety concerns?

Palm oil is safe when consumed in amounts found in foods. It seems to be safe when taken as medicine by children or adults for up to 6 months.

Medical professionals should consult the Professional Version at www.NaturalDatabase.com.

Do not use palm oil in amounts more than those found in foods except on medical advice if: You are pregnant or breast-feeding.

Are there any interactions with medications?
Medications that slow blood clotting (Anticoagulant / Antiplatelet drugs). Palm oil might increase blood clotting. Taking palm oil along with medications that slow clotting might reduce the effectiveness of these medications. Some medications that slow blood clotting include aspirin, clopidogrel (Plavix), diclofenac (Voltaren, Cataflam, others), ibuprofen (Advil, Motrin, others), naproxen (Anaprox, Naprosyn, others), dalteparin (Fragmin), enoxaparin (Lovenox) heparin, warfarin (Coumadin), and others.

PANAX PSEUDOGINSENG

What other names is the product known by?
Chai-Jen-Shen, Field Seven, Himalayan Ginseng, Jia Renshen, Nepal Ginseng, Notoginseng, Panax notoginseng, Panax zingiberensis, Pseudoginseng Root, Samch'il, San Qi, San-Qi Ginseng, San Qui, Sanqi, Sanqi Powder, Sanshichi, Three Seven, Tian Qi, Tienchi, Tienchi Ginseng.

What is it?
Panax pseudoginseng is a plant. The root is used to make medicine. Be careful not to confuse panax pseudoginseng with other forms of ginseng, such as panax ginseng.

Is it Effective?
The effectiveness ratings for **PANAX PSEUDOGINSENG** are as follows:
Insufficient Evidence to Rate Effectiveness for... Bleeding, improving blood flow, pain, swelling, high cholesterol levels, chest pain (angina), high blood pressure, dizziness, sore throat, prostate cancer, and other conditions.

How does it work?
Panax pseudoginseng might relax blood vessels, which would improve blood flow and reduce blood pressure. There isn't enough information to know how panax pseudoginseng might work for prostate cancer and other conditions.

Are there safety concerns?
There isn't enough information to know whether panax pseudoginseng is safe. It can cause some side effects such as dry mouth, flushed skin, nervousness, sleep problems, nausea, and vomiting.

Do not use panax pseudoginseng if: You are pregnant or breast-feeding.

Are there any interactions with medications?
It is not known if panax pseudoginseng interacts with any medicines.
Before taking panax pseudoginseng, talk with your healthcare professional if you take any medications.

PANCREATIN

What other names is the product known by?
Pancreatinum, Pancreatis pulvis.

What is it?
Pancreatin is usually obtained from the pancreas of pigs or cows. It is used as medicine.

Is it Effective?
The effectiveness ratings for **PANCREATIN** are as follows:
Effective for... Pancreatic problems associated with cystic fibrosis, pancreas removal, or an inflamed pancreas (pancreatitis).
Likely Ineffective for... Digestive problems, including intestinal gas, in people without pancreas problems.

How does it work?
Pancreatin contains the enzymes amylase, lipase, and protease, which help to digest food. These digestive enzymes are normally produced by the pancreas.

Medical professionals should consult the Professional Version at www.NaturalDatabase.com.

Are there safety concerns?

Pancreatin is safe for people with pancreas problems who cannot digest food properly. Pancreatin can cause nausea, vomiting, diarrhea, mouth and skin irritation, and allergic reactions. High doses can cause problems such as high blood levels of a substance called uric acid and colon damage.

Do not use pancreatin if: You are pregnant or breast-feeding, unless you have been diagnosed with pancreas problems which makes it essential.

Are there any interactions with medications?

Acarbose (Precose, Prandase). Acarbose (Precose, Prandase) is used to help treat type 2 diabetes. Acarbose (Precose, Prandase) works by decreasing how quickly foods are broken down. Pancreatin seems to help the body break down some foods. By helping the body break down foods pancreatin might decrease the effectiveness of Acarbose (Precose, Prandase).

PANGAMIC ACID

What other names is the product known by?

Calcium Pangamate, Calgam, Di-isopropylamine Dichloroacetate, Vitamin B15.

What is it?

Pangamic acid is a name used for a variety of chemicals. There is no standard formulation. Natural sources for some of the chemicals found in pangamic acid are apricot kernels, rice bran, brewer's yeast, whole brown rice, sesame seeds, and pumpkin seeds.

Is it Effective?

The effectiveness ratings for **PANGAMIC ACID** are as follows:
Possibly Ineffective for... Improving exercise endurance.
Insufficient Evidence to Rate Effectiveness for... Asthma, skin and lung conditions, nerve and joint problems, eczema, alcoholism, fatigue, high cholesterol, and other conditions.

How does it work?

Since there is no standard identity for the chemicals in pangamic acid, how it might work is unknown. Although pangamic acid is also called vitamin B15, there is no research that suggests it is required by the body.

Are there safety concerns?

Pangamic acid is considered unsafe. Chemicals found in some formulations of pangamic acid may cause cancer.

Do not take pangamic acid if: You are pregnant or breast-feeding. • You have kidney stones or other kidney problems.

Are there any interactions with medications?

Digoxin (Lanoxin). Digoxin (Lanoxin) helps the heart beat more strongly. Some types of pangamic acid contain calcium. Calcium might also affect the heart. Taking pangamic acid along with digoxin (Lanoxin) might increase the effects and side effects of digoxin (Lanoxin).

Medications for high blood pressure (Calcium channel blockers). Some medications for high blood pressure affect calcium in the body. These medications are called calcium channel blockers. Taking pangamic acid that contains calcium might decrease the effectiveness of these medications for high blood pressure. Some medications for high blood pressure include nifedipine (Adalat, Procardia), verapamil (Calan, Isoptin, Verelan), diltiazem (Cardizem), isradipine (DynaCirc), felodipine (Plendil), amlodipine (Norvasc), and others.

Water pills (Thiazide Diuretics). Some pangamic acid can contain calcium. Some "water pills" increase the amount of calcium in the body. Taking large amounts of calcium with some "water pills" might cause there to be too much calcium in the body. This could cause serious side effects including kidney problems. Some of these "water pills" include chlorothiazide (Diuril), hydrochlorothiazide (HydroDIURIL, Esidrix), indapamide (Lozol), metolazone (Zaroxolyn), and chlorthalidone (Hygroton).

PANTETHINE

What other names is the product known by?

Bis-pantothenamidoethyl disulfide, D-Pantethine, Pantetina, Pantomin, Pantosin.

What is it?

Pantethine is a dietary supplement that is related to the vitamin B5 (pantothenic acid).

Medical professionals should consult the Professional Version at www.NaturalDatabase.com.

Is it Effective?

The effectiveness ratings for **PANTETHINE** are as follows:

Possibly Effective for... Lowering cholesterol and triglycerides.

Insufficient Evidence to Rate Effectiveness for... Reducing risk of heart and circulatory disease, improving adrenal function, treating cystinosis (a genetic disease), improving athletic performance, and preventing allergy symptoms in people allergic to formaldehyde.

How does it work?

Pantethine might increase the concentrations of chemicals that lower blood cholesterol and triglycerides.

Are there safety concerns?

Pantethine appears to be safe for most people. Pantethine can cause nausea, diarrhea, and stomach discomfort.

Do not take pantethine if: You are pregnant or breast-feeding.

Are there any interactions with medications?

Medications that slow blood clotting (Anticoagulant / Antiplatelet drugs). Pantethine might slow blood clotting. Taking pantethine along with medications that also slow clotting might increase the chances of bruising and bleeding. Some medications that slow blood clotting include aspirin, clopidogrel (Plavix), diclofenac (Voltaren, Cataflam, others), ibuprofen (Advil, Motrin, others), naproxen (Anaprox, Naprosyn, others), dalteparin (Fragmin), enoxaparin (Lovenox), heparin, warfarin (Coumadin), and others.

PANTOTHENIC ACID (VITAMIN B5)

What other names is the product known by?

B Complex Vitamin, Calcii Pantothenas, Calcium Pantothenate, Dexpanthenol, Dexpanthenolum, D-pantothenic Acid, D-Panthenol, D-Pantothenyl Alcohol, Pantothenic Acid, Pantothenol, Pantothenylol, Vitamin B5.

What is it?

Pantothenic acid is a vitamin, also known as vitamin B5. It is widely found in both plants and animals including meat, vegetables, cereal grains, legumes, eggs, and milk.

Is it Effective?

The effectiveness ratings for **PANTOTHENIC ACID (VITAMIN B5)** are as follows:

Effective for... Treating or preventing pantothenic acid deficiency.

Possibly Ineffective for... Treating or preventing skin reactions from radiation therapy.

Insufficient Evidence to Rate Effectiveness for... Skin problems, alcoholism, allergies, attention deficit-hyperactivity disorder (ADHD), rheumatoid arthritis, osteoarthritis, hair loss, asthma, heart problems, carpal tunnel syndrome, lung disorders, colitis, conjunctivitis, convulsions, kidney disorders, dandruff, depression, diabetic problems, enhancing immune function, headache, hyperactivity, low blood pressure, inability to sleep, irritability, multiple sclerosis, muscular dystrophy, muscle cramps, improving athletic performance, and other conditions.

How does it work?

Pantothenic acid is important for our bodies to properly use carbohydrates, proteins, and lipids and for healthy skin.

Are there safety concerns?

Pantothenic acid is safe for most people when used in appropriate amounts. The recommended amount for adults is 5 mg per day. Even larger amounts seem to be safe for some people, but taking larger amounts increases the chance of having side effects such as diarrhea.

Pantothenic acid is safe for pregnant or breast-feeding women when taken in recommended amounts of 6 mg per day, but it is not known if taking more than this amount is safe.

Do not take pantothenic acid if: You have the blood disorder called hemophilia. It can increase the risk of bleeding.
• You have a stomach or intestinal blockage.

Are there any interactions with medications?

It is not known if pantothenic acid (vitamin B5) interacts with any medicines.
Before taking pantothenic acid, talk with your healthcare professional if you take any medications.

PAPAIN

What other names is the product known by?
Carica papaya, Papainum Crudum, Plant Protease Concentrate, Vegetable Pepsin.

What is it?
Papain is taken from the fruit of the papaya tree. Papain is used to make medicine.

Is it Effective?
The effectiveness ratings for **PAPAIN** are as follows:
Possibly Effective for... Herpes zoster (shingles) • Sore throat and throat swelling (pharyngitis).
Insufficient Evidence to Rate Effectiveness for... Digestion problems, diarrhea, hayfever, runny nose, psoriasis, cancer, treating infected wounds, sores, ulcers, intestinal worms, and other conditions.

How does it work?
Papain contains substances called enzymes that help break down proteins.

Are there safety concerns?
Papain seems safe for most adults to use as a medicine. It can cause irritation of the throat and stomach. Skin contact with raw papain can cause irritation and blisters.

Excessive amounts of papain can cause severe throat damage.

Do not use papain if: You are pregnant or breast-feeding. • You are allergic to fig or kiwi fruit. • You have a bleeding disorder.

Are there any interactions with medications?
It is not known if papain interacts with any medicines.
Before taking papain talk with your healthcare professional if you take any medications.

PAPAYA

What other names is the product known by?
Caricae papayae folium, Carica papaya, Chirbhita, Erandachirbhita, Mamaerie, Melonenbaumblaetter, Melon Tree, Papaw, Papayas.

What is it?
Papaya is a plant. The leaves are used to make medicine.

Is it Effective?
The effectiveness ratings for **PAPAYA** are as follows:
Insufficient Evidence to Rate Effectiveness for... Stomach and intestine problems, parasite infections, and other conditions.

How does it work?
The chemicals in papaya might help kill parasites.

Are there safety concerns?
Papaya seems safe for most people when taken in small amounts. It can cause irritation and tears in the throat. Applying papaya to the skin can cause severe irritation and allergic reactions in some people.

Do not take papaya if: You are pregnant or breast-feeding. • You are allergic to a chemical called papain. • You are allergic to latex.

Are there any interactions with medications?
Warfarin (Coumadin). Warfarin (Coumadin) is used to slow blood clotting. Papaya might increase the effects of warfarin (Coumadin) and increase the chances of bruising and bleeding. Be sure to have your blood checked regularly. The dose of your warfarin (Coumadin) might need to be changed.

Medical professionals should consult the Professional Version at www.NaturalDatabase.com.

PARA-AMINOBENZOIC ACID (PABA)

What other names is the product known by?

ABA, Aminobenzoic Acid, Aminobenzoate Potassium, Bacterial Vitamin H1, Ethyl Dihydroxypropyl Aminobenzoate, Glyceryl Paraaminobenzoate, Octyl Diemthyl PABA, Padamate O, P-Aminobenzoic Acid, Vitamin B10, Vitamin Bx, Vitamin H1, 4-Aminobenzoic Acid.

What is it?

Para-aminobenzoic acid (PABA) is a chemical found in the folic acid vitamin and also in several foods including grains, eggs, milk, and meat.

Is it Effective?

The effectiveness ratings for **PARA-AMINOBENZOIC ACID (PABA)** are as follows:
Effective for... Use as a sunscreen, when applied directly to the skin.
Possibly Ineffective for... Treating a condition that causes hardening or thickening of the skin (scleroderma).
Insufficient Evidence to Rate Effectiveness for... Female infertility, arthritis, anemia, constipation, headaches, preventing hair loss, darkening gray hair, and various skin conditions such as vitiligo, pemphigus, dermatomyostis, morphea, Peyronie's disease, and other conditions.

How does it work?

PABA is used as a sunscreen because it can block ultraviolet (UV) radiation to the skin.

Are there safety concerns?

PABA is safe for most people when applied directly to the skin. When taken by mouth, it seems safe if taken correctly. PABA can cause skin irritation and might also stain clothing with a yellow color. Nausea, vomiting, upset stomach, diarrhea, and loss of appetite might sometimes occur.

Taking more than the recommended dose of 12 grams a day can cause serious side effects such as liver, kidney, and blood problems.

When applied directly to the skin, PABA appears safe for children, and also for pregnant and breast-feeding women. Although PABA might be safe for children to take by mouth, serious side effects can occur.

Do not take PABA by mouth if: You are pregnant or breast-feeding. • You have kidney problems.

Are there any interactions with medications?

Antibiotics (Sulfonamide antibiotics). Para-aminobenzoic acid (PABA) can decrease the effectiveness of certain antibiotics called sulfonamides. Some of these antibiotics include sulfamethoxazole (Gantanol), sulfasalazine (Azulfidine), sulfisoxazole (Gantrisin), and trimethoprim/sulfamethoxazole (Bactrim, Septra).
Cortisone (Cortisone Acetate). The body breaks down cortisone to get rid of it. Para-aminobenzoic acid (PABA) might decrease how quickly the body breaks down cortisone. Taking PABA by mouth and getting a cortisone shot might increase the effects and side effects of cortisone.
Dapsone (Avlosulfon). Dapsone (Avlosulfon) is used as an antibiotic. Para-aminobenzoic acid (PABA) might decrease the effectiveness of dapsone (Avlosulfon) for treating infections.

PAREIRA

What other names is the product known by?

Chondrodendron tomentosum, Ice Vine, Pereira Brava, Velvet Leaf.

What is it?

Pareira is a plant. The root is used to make medicine.

Is it Effective?

The effectiveness ratings for **PAREIRA** are as follows:
Insufficient Evidence to Rate Effectiveness for... Fluid retention, promoting the menstrual cycle, and other uses.

How does it work?

There isn't enough information to know how pareira might work.

Are there safety concerns?

There isn't enough information to know if pareira might be safe or what side effects may occur.

Pareira contains tubocurarine, an ingredient in modern anesthetics used to block nerve signals and paralyze muscles. However, very little, if any, of the tubocurarine in pareira gets absorbed into the body when taken by mouth.

Do not use pareira if: You are pregnant or breast-feeding.

Are there any interactions with medications?

It is not known if pareira interacts with any medicines.

Before taking pareira, talk with your healthcare professional if you take any medications.

PARSLEY

What other names is the product known by?

Apium Petroselinum, Carum Petroselinum, Common Parsley, Garden Parsley, Hamburg Parsley, Parsley Fruit, Parsley Oil, Parsley Root, Parsley Seed, Persely, Persil, Petersylinge, Petroselini Fructus, Petroselini Herba, Petrosilini Radix, Rock Parsley, Petroselinum Crispum, Petroselinum Hortense, Petroselinum Sativum.

What is it?

Parsley is an herb. The leaf, seed, and root are used to make medicine. Be careful not to confuse parsley with fool's parsley and parsley piert.

Is it Effective?

The effectiveness ratings for **PARSLEY** are as follows:

Insufficient Evidence to Rate Effectiveness for... Kidney stones, urinary tract infections (UTIs), cracked or chapped skin, bruises, tumors, insect bites, digestive problems, menstrual problems, liver disorders, asthma, cough, fluid retention and swelling (edema), and other conditions.

How does it work?

Parsley might help stimulate the appetite, improve digestion, increase urine production, reduce spasms, and increase menstrual flow.

Are there safety concerns?

Parsley seems to be safe for most adults. In some people, parsley can cause allergic skin reactions. Consuming very large amounts of parsley can cause other side effects like anemia and liver or kidney problems.

Parsley can cause the skin to become extra sensitive to the sun and cause a rash.

Do not take parsley if: You are pregnant or breast-feeding. Small amounts in food are safe, but larger amounts are not. • You have kidney disease. • You have high blood pressure. • You have any swelling or edema.

Are there any interactions with medications?

Aspirin. Some people are allergic to parsley. Aspirin might increase your sensitivity to parsley if you are allergic to parsley. This has only been reported in one person. But to be on the safe side, if you are allergic to parsley do not take aspirin and eat parsley.

Warfarin (Coumadin). Warfarin (Coumadin) is taken to thin the blood and slow blood clotting. Large amounts of parsley leaf might increase blood clotting. Taking parsley along with warfarin might decrease how well warfarin (Coumadin) works to thin the blood.

Water pills (Diuretic drugs). Parsley seems to work like a "water pill" by causing the body to lose water. Taking parsley along with other "water pills" might cause the body to lose too much water. Losing too much water can cause you to be dizzy and your blood pressure to go too low. Some "water pills" include chlorothiazide (Diuril), chlorthalidone (Thalitone), furosemide (Lasix), hydrochlorothiazide (HCTZ, HydroDIURIL, Microzide), and others.

PARSLEY PIERT

What other names is the product known by?

Aphanes arvensis, Field Lady's Mantle, Parsley Breakstone, Parsley Piercestone.

What is it?

Parsley piert is a plant. The above ground parts of the plant are used to make medicine.

Is it Effective?

The effectiveness ratings for **PARSLEY PIERT** are as follows:

Insufficient Evidence to Rate Effectiveness for... Fever, urinary disorders including kidney and bladder stones, fluid retention, and other conditions.

How does it work?

There isn't enough information to know how parsley piert might work.

Are there safety concerns?

There isn't enough information to know if parsley piert might be safe or what side effects may occur.

Do not use parsley piert if: You are pregnant or breast-feeding.

Are there any interactions with medications?

It is not known if parsley piert interacts with any medicines.
Before taking parsley piert, talk with your healthcare professional if you take any medications.

PARSNIP

What other names is the product known by?

Parsnip Herb, Parsnip Root, Pastinaca sativa, Pastinacae herba, Pastinacae Radix.

What is it?

Parsnip is a plant. The above ground parts and root are used to make medicine.

Is it Effective?

The effectiveness ratings for **PARSNIP** are as follows:

Insufficient Evidence to Rate Effectiveness for... Digestion and kidney disorders, fever, pain relief, fluid retention, and other conditions.

How does it work?

There isn't enough information to know how parsnip might work.

Are there safety concerns?

There isn't enough information to know if parsnip is safe to use as medicine.

When used on the skin, parsnip can cause the skin to become extra sensitive to the sun. Wear sunblock and protective clothing outside, especially if you are light-skinned.

Do not use parsnip if: You are pregnant or breast-feeding.

Are there any interactions with medications?

It is not known if parsnip interacts with any medicines.
Before taking parsnip, talk with your healthcare professional if you take any medications.

PASSIONFLOWER

What other names is the product known by?

Apricot Vine, Corona De Cristo, Fleischfarbige, Fleur De La Passion, Flor De Passion, Madre Selva, Maypop, Maypop Passion Flower, Passiflora, Passiflora incarnata, Passiflorae herba, Passiflore, Passiflorina, Passion Vine, Passionaria, Passionblume, Passionflower Herb, Passionsblumenkraut, Purple Passion Flower, Water Lemon, Wild Passion Flower.

What is it?

Passionflower is a plant. The above ground parts are used to make medicine.

Is it Effective?

The effectiveness ratings for **PASSIONFLOWER** are as follows:

Possibly Effective for... Generalized anxiety disorder (GAD), a psychiatric disorder • Relieving symptoms related to narcotic drug withdrawal, when used in combination with a medication called clonidine • A psychiatric disorder known as adjustment disorder with anxious mood when used in a multi-ingredient product (Euphytose, EUP).

 Natural Medicines Comprehensive Database Consumer Version (209) 472-2244

Insufficient Evidence to Rate Effectiveness for... Nervous stomach, burns, insomnia, hemorrhoids, asthma, heart problems, high blood pressure, seizures, and other conditions.

How does it work?
The chemicals in passionflower have calming, sleep inducing, and muscle spasm relieving effects.

Are there safety concerns?
Passionflower seems to be safe for most people when taken by mouth. It can cause some side effects such as dizziness, confusion, irregular muscle action and coordination, altered consciousness, and inflamed blood vessels. It has also been reported to cause nausea, vomiting, drowsiness, a rapid heart rate, and abnormal heart rhythm in one person who took it.

Do not take passionflower if: You are pregnant or breast-feeding.

Are there any interactions with medications?
Sedative medications (CNS depressants). Passionflower might cause sleepiness and drowsiness. Medications that cause sleepiness are called sedatives. Taking passionflower along with sedative medications might cause too much sleepiness. Some sedative medications include pentobarbital (Nembutal), phenobarbital (Luminal), secobarbital (Seconal), clonazepam (Klonopin), lorazepam (Ativan), zolpidem (Ambien), and others.

PATCHOULY OIL

What other names is the product known by?
Agastach Pogostemi, Patchouli, Patchouly, Putcha-Pat, Huo xiang, Pogostemon cablin, Pogostemon heyneanus, Pogostemon patchouly.

What is it?
Patchouly oil is an oil from a plant called Pogostemon cablin. It is used to make medicine.

Is it Effective?
The effectiveness ratings for **PATCHOULY OIL** are as follows:
Insufficient Evidence to Rate Effectiveness for... Colds, headaches, nausea, vomiting, diarrhea, stomach pain, bad breath, tumors, and other conditions.

How does it work?
Patchouly oil might help fight certain kinds of bacterial and fungal infections.

Are there safety concerns?
There isn't enough information to know if patchouly oil is safe when used as a medicine. However, it is safe when taken in amounts commonly found in foods, up to a maximum concentration of 0.0002%.

Do not use patchouly oil if: You are pregnant or breast-feeding.

Are there any interactions with medications?
It is not known if patchouly oil interacts with any medicines.
Before taking patchouly oil, talk with your healthcare professional if you take any medications.

PAU D'ARCO

What other names is the product known by?
Ipe, Ipe Roxo, Ipes, Lapacho, Lapacho Colorado, Lapacho Morado, Purple Lapacho, Red Lapacho, Tabebuia avellanedae, Tabebuia heptaphylla, Tabebuia impetiginosa, Taheebo, Taheebo Tea, Trumpet Bush.

What is it?
Pau d'arco is a tree. The bark and wood are used to make medicine.

Is it Effective?
The effectiveness ratings for **PAU D'ARCO** are as follows:
Insufficient Evidence to Rate Effectiveness for... Yeast infections, common cold, flu, diarrhea, bladder and prostate infections, intestinal worms, cancer, diabetes, ulcers, stomach problems, liver problems, asthma, bronchitis, arthritis-like pain, sexually transmitted diseases (gonorrhea, syphilis), boils, and other conditions.

Medical professionals should consult the Professional Version at www.NaturalDatabase.com.

CONSUMER VERSION

How does it work?
There isn't enough information available to know how pau d'arco works.

Are there safety concerns?
Pau d'arco seems unsafe for use. High doses can cause severe nausea, vomiting, diarrhea, dizziness, and internal bleeding.

Do not use pau d'arco if: You are pregnant or breast-feeding. • You have a bleeding disorder.

Are there any interactions with medications?
Medications that slow blood clotting (Anticoagulant / Antiplatelet drugs). Pau d'arco might slow blood clotting. Taking pau d'arco along with medications that also slow clotting might increase the chances of bruising and bleeding. Some medications that slow blood clotting include aspirin, clopidogrel (Plavix), diclofenac (Voltaren, Cataflam, others), ibuprofen (Advil, Motrin, others), naproxen (Anaprox, Naprosyn, others), dalteparin (Fragmin), enoxaparin (Lovenox), heparin, warfarin (Coumadin), and others.

PEANUT OIL

What other names is the product known by?
Arachis hypogaea, Earth-Nut, Groundnuts, Monkey Nuts.

What is it?
Peanut oil is the oil from the seed, also called the nut, of the peanut plant. Peanut oil is used to make medicine.

Is it Effective?
The effectiveness ratings for **PEANUT OIL** are as follows:
Insufficient Evidence to Rate Effectiveness for... Lowering cholesterol, preventing heart disease, decreasing appetite for weight loss, preventing cancer, arthritis and joint pain, scalp crusting and scaling, dry skin and other skin problems, constipation, and other conditions.

How does it work?
Peanut oil is high in monounsaturated "good" fat, and low in saturated "bad" fat, which is believed to help prevent heart disease and lower cholesterol. However, in animal studies, peanut oil has been shown to clog arteries which would increase the risk for heart disease.

Are there safety concerns?
Peanut oil is safe for most people. The oil can cause serious allergic reactions in people who are allergic to peanuts, soybeans, and related plants.

Peanut oil is also safe for pregnant or breast-feeding women, in amounts found in foods.

Do not use peanut oil if: You are pregnant or breast-feeding, in amounts larger than those found in foods. • You are allergic to peanuts, soybeans, or related plants.

Are there any interactions with medications?
It is not known if peanut oil interacts with any medicines.
Before taking peanut oil, talk with your healthcare professional if you take any medications.

PEAR

What other names is the product known by?
Pyrus communis.

What is it?
Pear is a tree. The fruit is used to make medicine.

Is it Effective?
The effectiveness ratings for **PEAR** are as follows:
Insufficient Evidence to Rate Effectiveness for... Digestion problems, colic, diarrhea, nausea, liver disorders, spasms, tumors, fevers, constipation, fluid retention, and other uses.

How does it work?
Pear fruit contains a substance called pectin which might help reduce diarrhea.

Are there safety concerns?
Pear is safe for most people when the fruit is eaten. There isn't enough information to know if it is safe when used as medicine or what the potential side effects might be.

Are there any interactions with medications?
It is not known if pear interacts with any medicines.
Before taking pear, talk with your healthcare professional if you take any medications.

PECTIN

What other names is the product known by?
Pectinic Acid.

What is it?
Pectin is a fiber found in fruits. Pectin is used to make medicine.

Is it Effective?
The effectiveness ratings for **PECTIN** are as follows:
Possibly Effective for... High cholesterol.
Insufficient Evidence to Rate Effectiveness for... Diarrhea, reducing the risk of colon cancer, diabetes, infection, mouth and throat sores, reducing damage from radiation, heartburn, and other conditions.

How does it work?
Pectin binds substances in the intestine and adds bulk to the stools.

Are there safety concerns?
Pectin appears to be safe for most people when used in medicinal amounts. People who are exposed to pectin dust at work, such as in manufacturing, may develop asthma.

Are there any interactions with medications?
Antibiotics (Tetracycline antibiotics). Pectin might decrease the amount of tetracycline antibiotics that can be absorbed. Taking pectin with tetracycline antibiotics might decrease the effectiveness of tetracyclines. To avoid this interaction take pectin two hours before or four hours after taking tetracycline antibiotics. Some tetracycline antibiotics include demeclocycline (Declomycin), minocycline (Minocin), and tetracycline (Achromycin).
Digoxin (Lanoxin). Pectin is high in fiber. Fiber can decrease the absorption and decrease the effectiveness of digoxin (Lanoxin). As a general rule, any medications taken by mouth should be taken one hour before or four hours after pectin to prevent this interaction.
Lovastatin (Mevacor). Lovastatin (Mevacor) is used to help lower cholesterol. Pectin might decrease how much lovastatin (Mevacor) the body absorbs and decrease the effectiveness of lovastatin (Mevacor). To avoid this interaction take pectin at least one hour after lovastatin (Mevacor).

PELLITORY

What other names is the product known by?
Akarakarabha, Anacyclus pyrethrum.

What is it?
Pellitory is a plant. The root is used to make medicine.

Is it Effective?
The effectiveness ratings for **PELLITORY** are as follows:
Insufficient Evidence to Rate Effectiveness for... Arthritis, improving digestion, toothaches, killing insects, and other uses.

How does it work?
Pellitory might stimulate nerve endings.

Medical professionals should consult the Professional Version at www.NaturalDatabase.com.

CONSUMER VERSION

Are there safety concerns?

There isn't enough information to know if pellitory might be safe. Skin redness and irritation may occur in some people with overuse. Pellitory cause an allergic reaction in people sensitive or allergic to plants in the Asteraceae/Compositae family including ragweed, marigolds, daisies, and many others.

Do not use pellitory if: You are pregnant or breast-feeding. • You are allergic to ragweed, marigolds, daisies, and related plants.

Are there any interactions with medications?

It is not known if pellitory interacts with any medicines.
Before taking pellitory, talk with your healthcare professional if you take any medications.

PELLITORY-OF-THE-WALL

What other names is the product known by?

Lichwort, Parietaria officinalis.

What is it?

Pellitory-of-the-wall is a plant. People use it to make medicine. Be careful not to confuse pellitory-of-the-wall with pellitory, which is a different plant.

Is it Effective?

The effectiveness ratings for **PELLITORY-OF-THE-WALL** are as follows:
Insufficient Evidence to Rate Effectiveness for... Urinary diseases, fluid retention, and other conditions.

How does it work?

There isn't enough information to know how pellitory-of-the-wall might work.

Are there safety concerns?

Pellitory-of-the-wall might be safe for most people, but the potential side effects of pellitory-of-the-wall are not known.

Do not use pellitory-of-the-wall if: You are pregnant or breast-feeding.

Are there any interactions with medications?

It is not known if pellitory-of-the-wall interacts with any medicines.
Before taking pellitory-of-the-wall, talk with your healthcare professional if you take any medications.

PENNYROYAL

What other names is the product known by?

American Pennyroyal, European Pennyroyal, Hedeoma pulegioides, Lurk-In-The-Ditch, Melissa pulegioides, Mentha pulegium, Mosquito Plant, Penny Royal, Pennyroyal Leaf, Pennyroyal Oil, Piliolerial, Pudding Grass, Pulegium, Pulegium vulgare, Run-By-The-Ground, Squaw Balm, Squawmint, Stinking Balm, Tickweed.

What is it?

Pennyroyal is a plant. The oil and leaves are used to make medicine.

Is it Effective?

The effectiveness ratings for **PENNYROYAL** are as follows:
Insufficient Evidence to Rate Effectiveness for... Reducing spasms, intestinal gas, pneumonia, stomach pains, weakness, fluid retention, killing germs, skin diseases, causing abortion (only in amounts that can be fatal to the woman), and other conditions.

How does it work?

There isn't enough information available to know how pennyroyal might work.

Medical professionals should consult the Professional Version at www.NaturalDatabase.com.

  Natural Medicines Comprehensive Database Consumer Version (209) 472-2244

Are there safety concerns?

Pennyroyal is UNSAFE. It can cause side effects such as stomach pain, nausea, vomiting, burning of the throat, fever, confusion, restlessness, seizures, dizziness, vision and hearing problems, high blood pressure, abortion, lung failure, brain damage, kidney and liver damage, death, and other serious side effects.

Do not use pennyroyal if: You are pregnant or breast-feeding. • You have kidney disease.

Are there any interactions with medications?

It is not known if pennyroyal interacts with any medicines.
Before taking pennyroyal, talk with your healthcare professional if you take any medications.

PEONY

What other names is the product known by?

Bai Shao, Chi Shao, Common Peony, Coral Peony, European Peony, Moutan, Mu Dan PI, Paeonia, Paeonia lactiflora, Paeonia mascula; Paeonia obovata; Paeonia officinalis; Paeonia suffruticosa, Paeonia veitchii, Paeoniae Flos, Paeoniae Radix, Peony Flower, Peony Root, Piney, Red Peony, Shakuyaku, Tree Peony, White Peony.

What is it?

Peony is a plant. The root, flower, and seed are used to make medicine.

Is it Effective?

The effectiveness ratings for **PEONY** are as follows:
Insufficient Evidence to Rate Effectiveness for... Muscle cramps, gout, osteoarthritis, breathing problems, cough, skin diseases, hemorrhoids, heart trouble, stomach upset, spasms, nerve problems, migraine headache, chronic fatigue syndrome (CFS), and other conditions.

How does it work?

Peony might block chemicals produced by the body that can cause muscle cramps. It also may prevent blood clotting and act as an antioxidant.

Are there safety concerns?

Peony appears to be safe for short-term use. It can cause stomach upset. It can cause rash when it comes in contact with the skin of sensitive people.

Do not take peony if: You are pregnant or breast-feeding. • You have a bleeding disorder.

Are there any interactions with medications?

Medications that slow blood clotting (Anticoagulant / Antiplatelet drugs). Peony might slow blood clotting. Taking peony along with medications that also slow clotting might increase the chances of bruising and bleeding. Some medications that slow blood clotting include aspirin, clopidogrel (Plavix), diclofenac (Voltaren, Cataflam, others), ibuprofen (Advil, Motrin, others), naproxen (Anaprox, Naprosyn, others), dalteparin (Fragmin), enoxaparin (Lovenox), heparin, warfarin (Coumadin), and others.
Phenytoin (Dilantin). Peony root might decrease the amount of phenytoin in the body. Taking peony root along with phenytoin (Dilantin) might decrease the effectiveness of phenytoin (Dilantin) and increase the risk of seizures.

PEPPERMINT

What other names is the product known by?

Bo He, Brandy Mint, Extract of Mentha Piperita, Extract of Peppermint, Extract of Peppermint Leaves, Lamb Mint, Mentha Lavanduliodora, Mentha Piperita, Menthae Piperitae Aetheroleum, Menta Piperita, Mentha Oil, Mentha Piperita Extract, Mentha Piperita Oil, Menthae Piperitae Folium, Menthe, Menthe Poivree, Mint, Oil of Peppermint, Paparaminta, Peppermint Extract, Peppermint Leaf, Peppermint Leaf Extract, Peppermint Oil.

What is it?

Peppermint is a plant. The leaf and oil are used as medicine.

Is it Effective?

The effectiveness ratings for **PEPPERMINT** are as follows:
Possibly Effective for... Upset stomach (dyspepsia) • Tension headaches when applied topically • Relaxing the colon during exams including barium enemas or radiologic procedures.

Possibly Ineffective for... Nausea following surgery.
Insufficient Evidence to Rate Effectiveness for... Irritable bowel syndrome (IBS), toothaches, itchy skin, infections, morning sickness, nausea and vomiting, painful menstrual periods, bacteria overgrowth in the intestines, lung infections, spasms of the stomach and gallbladder, cough and symptoms of cold, inflammation of mouth and respiratory tract lining, muscle or nerve pain, and other conditions.

How does it work?

Peppermint oil seems to reduce spasms in the digestive tract. When applied to the skin, it can cause surface warmth, which relieves pain beneath the skin.

Are there safety concerns?

Peppermint oil seems to be safe for most people when taken by mouth in small amounts or applied to the skin. It can cause some side effects including heartburn, and allergic reactions including flushing, headache, and mouth sores.

Peppermint oil, when taken by mouth in pills with a special (enteric) coating to prevent contact with the stomach, seems safe for children 8 years of age and older.

Do not take peppermint oil in medicinal amounts if: You are pregnant or breast-feeding.

Are there any interactions with medications?

Antacids. Some peppermint oil products are covered with a special coating. Antacids are used to decrease stomach acid. Low stomach acid can cause the coating of these peppermint oil products to dissolve too quickly. When peppermint oil products dissolve too quickly they can sometimes cause heartburn and nausea. Take antacids at least two hours after coated peppermint oil products. Some antacids include calcium carbonate (Tums, others), dihydroxyaluminum sodium carbonate (Rolaids, others), magaldrate (Riopan), magnesium sulfate (Bilagog), aluminum hydroxide (Amphojel), and others.

Cyclosporine (Neoral, Sandimmune). The body breaks down cyclosporine (Neoral, Sandimmune) to get rid of it. Peppermint oil might decrease how quickly the body breaks down cyclosporine (Neoral, Sandimmune). Taking peppermint oil products along with cyclosporine (Neoral, Sandimmune) might increase the risk of side effects for cyclosporine (Neoral, Sandimmune).

Medications changed by the liver (Cytochrome P450 1A2 (CYP1A2) substrates). Some medications are changed and broken down by the liver. Peppermint oil and leaf might decrease how quickly the liver breaks down some medications. Taking peppermint oil along with some medications that are broken down by the liver can increase the effects and side effects of some medications. Before taking peppermint oil, talk to your healthcare provider if you take any medications that are changed by the liver. Some medications that are changed by the liver include amitriptyline (Elavil), haloperidol (Haldol), ondansetron (Zofran), propranolol (Inderal), theophylline (Theo-Dur, others), verapamil (Calan, Isoptin, others), and others.

Medications changed by the liver (Cytochrome P450 2C19 (CYP2C19) substrates). Some medications are changed and broken down by the liver. Peppermint oil might decrease how quickly the liver breaks down some medications. Taking peppermint oil along with some medications that are broken down by the liver can increase the effects and side effects of some medications. Before taking peppermint oil, talk to your healthcare provider if you take any medications that are changed by the liver. Some medications that are changed by the liver include omeprazole (Prilosec), lansoprazole (Prevacid), and pantoprazole (Protonix); diazepam (Valium); carisoprodol (Soma); nelfinavir (Viracept); and others.

Medications changed by the liver (Cytochrome P450 2C9 (CYP2C9) substrates). Some medications are changed and broken down by the liver. Peppermint oil might decrease how quickly the liver breaks down some medications. Taking peppermint oil along with some medications that are broken down by the liver can increase the effects and side effects of some medications. Before taking peppermint oil, talk to your healthcare provider if you take any medications that are changed by the liver. Some medications that are changed by the liver include diclofenac (Cataflam, Voltaren), ibuprofen (Motrin), meloxicam (Mobic), and piroxicam (Feldene); celecoxib (Celebrex); amitriptyline (Elavil); warfarin (Coumadin); glipizide (Glucotrol); losartan (Cozaar); and others.

Medications changed by the liver (Cytochrome P450 3A4 (CYP3A4) substrates). Some medications are changed and broken down by the liver. Peppermint oil might decrease how quickly the liver breaks down some medications. Taking peppermint oil along with some medications that are broken down by the liver can increase the effects and side effects of some medications. Before taking peppermint oil, talk to your healthcare provider if you are taking any medications that are changed by the liver. Some medications changed by the liver include lovastatin (Mevacor), ketoconazole (Nizoral), itraconazole (Sporanox), fexofenadine (Allegra), triazolam (Halcion), and many others.

Medications that decrease stomach acid (H2-Blockers). Some peppermint oil products are covered with a special coating. Some medications that decrease stomach acid might cause the coating of these peppermint oil products to dissolve too quickly. When peppermint oil products dissolve too quickly they can sometimes cause heartburn and nausea. Take medications that decrease stomach acid at least two hours after coated peppermint oil products. Some medications that decrease stomach acid include cimetidine (Tagamet), ranitidine (Zantac), nizatidine (Axid), and famotidine (Pepcid).

Medications that decrease stomach acid (Proton pump inhibitors). Some peppermint oil products are covered with a special coating. Some medications that decrease stomach acid might cause the coating of these peppermint oil products to dissolve too quickly. When peppermint oil products dissolve too quickly they can sometimes cause heartburn and nausea. Take medications that decrease stomach acid at least two hours after coated peppermint oil products. Some medications that decrease stomach acid include omeprazole (Prilosec), lansoprazole (Prevacid), rabeprazole (Aciphex), pantoprazole (Protonix), and esomeprazole (Nexium).

PERILLA

What other names is the product known by?
Beefsteak Plant, Perilla frutescens, synonyms Dentidia nankinensis, Ocimum frutescens, Perilla arguta, Perilla nankinensis, Perilla ocymoides, Wild Coleus.

What is it?
Perilla is an herb. The leaf and seed are used to make medicine.

Is it Effective?
The effectiveness ratings for **PERILLA** are as follows:
Insufficient Evidence to Rate Effectiveness for... Asthma, nausea, sunstroke, causing sweating, or relieving spasms.

How does it work?
Perilla contains chemicals which might decrease swelling and affect other chemicals which cause asthma symptoms.

Are there safety concerns?
Perilla seems safe for most people when taken by mouth. When put on the skin, perilla can cause an allergic skin reaction and rash.

Do not take perilla if: You are pregnant or breast-feeding.

Are there any interactions with medications?
It is not known if perilla interacts with any medicines.
Before taking perilla, talk with your healthcare professional if you take any medications.

PERIWINKLE

What other names is the product known by?
Common Periwinkle, Earlyflowering, Evergreen, Lesser Periwinkle, Myrtle, Periwinkle, Small Periwinkle, Vinca minor, Vincae minoris herba, Wintergreen.

What is it?
Periwinkle is an herb. The above ground parts are used to make medicine.

Is it Effective?
The effectiveness ratings for **PERIWINKLE** are as follows:
Insufficient Evidence to Rate Effectiveness for... Preventing brain disorders, tonsillitis, sore throat, intestinal swelling (inflammation), toothache, chest pain, wounds, high blood pressure, and other conditions.

How does it work?
Periwinkle can lower blood pressure. It can also help reduce swelling (inflammation) and have a drying (astringent) effect on the tissues.

Are there safety concerns?
Periwinkle is UNSAFE. It can cause side effects such as nausea, vomiting, and other stomach and intestinal symptoms. It can also cause nerve, kidney, and liver damage. Large amounts can cause very low blood pressure.

Do not take periwinkle if: You are pregnant or breast-feeding. • You have low or high blood pressure. • You have trouble with constipation.

Medical professionals should consult the Professional Version at www.NaturalDatabase.com.

CONSUMER VERSION

Are there any interactions with medications?

Medications for high blood pressure (Antihypertensive drugs). Periwinkle seems to decrease blood pressure. Taking periwinkle along with medications for high blood pressure might cause your blood pressure to go too low. Some medications for high blood pressure include captopril (Capoten), enalapril (Vasotec), losartan (Cozaar), valsartan (Diovan), diltiazem (Cardizem), Amlodipine (Norvasc), hydrochlorothiazide (HydroDiuril), furosemide (Lasix), and many others.

PERU BALSAM

What other names is the product known by?

Balsamum Peruvianum, Black Balsam, Indian Balsam, Myroxylon balsamum pereirae, Myroxylon pereirae, Peruvian Balsam.

What is it?

Peru balsam is an herb. The oily sap from the bark is used to make medicine.

Is it Effective?

The effectiveness ratings for **PERU BALSAM** are as follows:
Insufficient Evidence to Rate Effectiveness for... Cancer; intestinal worms; healing wounds, burns, leg ulcers, and bedsores; treating frostbite; and other conditions.

How does it work?

Peru balsam might help prevent bacterial growth, and kill scabies (a parasitic mite). It might also promote skin cell growth.

Are there safety concerns?

Peru balsam applied to the skin seems safe for most people when used for less than one week. It is unsafe to take by mouth because it can damage the kidneys. When applied to the skin, it can cause allergic skin reactions.

Peru balsam might also cause skin to become extra sensitive to the sun. Wear sunblock outside, especially if you are light-skinned.

Do not use Peru balsam if: You are pregnant or breast-feeding. • You have kidney disease.

Are there any interactions with medications?

It is not known if Peru balsam interacts with any medicines.
Before taking Peru balsam, talk with your healthcare professional if you take any medications.

PEYOTE

What other names is the product known by?

Devil's Root, Dumpling Cactus, Lophophora williamsii, Magic Mushrooms, Mescal Buttons, Mescaline, Pellote, Sacred Mushroom.

What is it?

Peyote is a cactus. The above ground parts are used to make medicine.

Is it Effective?

The effectiveness ratings for **PEYOTE** are as follows:
Insufficient Evidence to Rate Effectiveness for... Fever, arthritis-like pain, bone fractures, wounds, and other conditions.

How does it work?

There isn't enough information available to know how peyote works as a medicine.

Are there safety concerns?

Peyote is UNSAFE for use. It can cause nausea and vomiting, anxiety, paranoia, fear, and emotional instability. It can also raise blood pressure, heart, and respiration rate. Changes in vision, drooling, headache, dizziness, and drowsiness may also occur. Although it is rarely fatal, it can cause homicidal, psychotic, or suicidal behavior related to the hallucinations.

Medical professionals should consult the Professional Version at www.NaturalDatabase.com.

     Natural Medicines Comprehensive Database Consumer Version   (209) 472-2244

Peyote is an illegal drug to possess in the US.
Do not take peyote if: You are pregnant or breast-feeding.

Are there any interactions with medications?
Stimulant drugs. Stimulant drugs speed up the nervous system. By speeding up the nervous system, stimulant medications can make you feel jittery and speed up your heartbeat. Peyote might also speed up the nervous system. Taking peyote along with stimulant drugs might cause serious problems including increased heart rate and high blood pressure. Avoid taking stimulant drugs along with peyote. Some stimulant drugs include diethylpropion (Tenuate), epinephrine, phentermine (Ionamin), pseudoephedrine (Sudafed), and many others.

PHEASANT'S EYE

What other names is the product known by?
Adonis herba, Adonis vernalis, False Hellebore, Oxeye, Pheasants Eye, Red Morocco, Rose-A-Rubie, Sweet Vernal, Yellow Pheasants Eye, Yellow Pheasant's Eye.

What is it?
Pheasant's eye is an herb. The above ground parts are used to make medicine.

Is it Effective?
The effectiveness ratings for **PHEASANT'S EYE** are as follows:
Insufficient Evidence to Rate Effectiveness for... Mild heart failure, irregular heart rhythm, cramps, fever, and menstrual disorders.

How does it work?
Pheasant's eye can slow and strengthen the heartbeat, causing it to pump blood more efficiently.

Are there safety concerns?
Pheasant's eye seems safe only if a commercially prepared extract is used under direct medical supervision. It is unsafe for self-use without medical supervision. It can cause side effects such as nausea, vomiting, and irregular heart rhythm.

Do not take pheasant's eye if: You are pregnant or breast-feeding. • You have low blood potassium levels. • You have high blood calcium levels.

Are there any interactions with medications?
Calcium supplements. Pheasant's eye can stimulate the heartbeat. Calcium might also affect the heart. Taking pheasant's eye along with calcium might cause the heart to be too stimulated. Do not take pheasant's eye along with calcium supplements.
Digoxin (Lanoxin). Digoxin (Lanoxin) helps the heart beat more strongly. Pheasant's eye also seems to affect the heart. Taking pheasant's eye along with digoxin can increase the effects of digoxin and increase the risk of side effects. Do not take pheasant's eye if you are taking digoxin (Lanoxin) without talking to your healthcare professional.
Medications for inflammation (Corticosteroids). Pheasant's eye might affect the heart. Some medications for inflammation can decrease potassium in the body. Low potassium levels can also affect the heart and increase the risk of side effects from pheasant's eye. Some medications for inflammation include dexamethasone (Decadron), hydrocortisone (Cortef), methylprednisolone (Medrol), prednisone (Deltasone), and others.
Quinidine. Pheasant's eye can affect the heart. Quinidine can also affect the heart. Taking quinidine along with pheasant's eye might cause serious heart problems.
Stimulant laxatives. Pheasant's eye can affect the heart. The heart uses potassium. Laxatives called stimulant laxatives can decrease potassium levels in the body. Low potassium levels can increase the chance of side effects from taking pheasant's eye. Some stimulant laxatives include bisacodyl (Correctol, Dulcolax), cascara, castor oil (Purge), senna (Senokot), and others.
Water pills (Diuretic drugs). Pheasant's eye might affect the heart. "Water pills" can decrease potassium in the body. Low potassium levels can also affect the heart and increase the risk of side effects from pheasant's eye. Some "water pills" that can deplete potassium include chlorothiazide (Diuril), chlorthalidone (Thalitone), furosemide (Lasix), hydrochlorothiazide (HCTZ, HydroDiuril, Microzide), and others.

Medical professionals should consult the Professional Version at www.NaturalDatabase.com.

Medical professionals should consult the Professional Version at www.NaturalDatabase.com.

PHELLODENDRON

What other names is the product known by?
Amur Cork Bark, Amur Cork Tree, Amur Corktree, Corktree, Huang Bai, Phellodendri Cortex.

What is it?
Phellodendron is a plant. The bark is used to make medicine. Be careful not to confuse phellodendron with the houseplant philodendron.

Is it Effective?
The effectiveness ratings for **PHELLODENDRON** are as follows:
Insufficient Evidence to Rate Effectiveness for... Diarrhea, ulcers, osteoarthritis, weight loss, obesity, diabetes, meningitis, pneumonia, eye infections, tuberculosis, and other conditions.

How does it work?
Chemicals in phellodendron might reduce redness and swelling (inflammation).

Are there safety concerns?
Phellodendron appears to be safe in adults when used short-term. The safety of phellodendron use for more than 6 weeks is unknown. In one study, one person experienced heartburn, shaking hands, sexual dysfunction, and thyroid dysfunction. Another person experience fatigue and headache. But it is not known if these side effects were caused by phellodendron or some other factor.

Phellodendron is unsafe in newborn infants.

Do not use phellodendron if: You are pregnant or breast-feeding.

Are there any interactions with medications?
Cyclosporine (Neoral, Sandimmune). The body breaks down cyclosporine (Neoral, Sandimmune) to get rid of it. Phellodendron might decrease how fast the body breaks down cyclosporine (Neoral, Sandimmune). Taking phellodendron along with cyclosporine (Neoral, Sandimmune) might increase the chance of side effects.
Medications changed by the liver (Cytochrome P450 3A4 (CYP3A4) substrates). Some medications are changed and broken down by the liver. Phellodendron might decrease how quickly the liver breaks down some medications. Taking phellodendron along with some medications that are broken down by the liver can increase the effects and side effects of some medications. Before taking phellodendron, talk to your healthcare provider if you are taking any medications that are changed by the liver. Some medications changed by the liver include cyclosporine (Neoral, Sandimmune), lovastatin (Mevacor), clarithromycin (Biaxin), indinavir (Crixivan), sildenafil (Viagra), triazolam (Halcion), and many others.

PHENYLALANINE

What other names is the product known by?
Alpha-aminohydrocinnamic acid, Beta-phenyl-alanine, DLPA, D-Phenylalanine, DL-Phenylalanine, L-Phenylalanine.

What is it?
Phenylalanine is an amino acid.

Is it Effective?
The effectiveness ratings for **PHENYLALANINE** are as follows:
Possibly Effective for...A skin condition called vitiligo.
Possibly Ineffective for... Pain • Attention deficit-hyperactivity disorder (ADHD).
Insufficient Evidence to Rate Effectiveness for... Depression, arthritis, alcohol withdrawal symptoms, Parkinson's disease, phenylalanine deficiency, and other conditions.

How does it work?
The body uses phenylalanine to make chemical messengers, but it is not clear how phenylalanine might work.

 Natural Medicines Comprehensive Database Consumer Version (209) 472-2244

Are there safety concerns?

Phenylalanine appears to be safe for most people.

Do not take phenylalanine if: You are pregnant or breast-feeding. • You have a psychiatric condition called schizophrenia. • You have a genetic disorder affecting how the body breaks down phenylalanine such as phenylketonuria (PKU) or alkaptonuria.

Are there any interactions with medications?

Levodopa. Levodopa is used for Parkinson's disease. Taking phenylalanine along with levodopa can make Parkinson's disease worse. Do not take phenylalanine if you are taking levodopa.

Medications for depression (MAOIs). Phenylalanine can increase a chemical in the body called tyramine. Large amounts of tyramine can cause high blood pressure. But the body naturally breaks down tyramine to get rid of it. This usually prevents the tyramine from causing high blood pressure. Some medications used for depression stop the body from breaking down tyramine. This can cause there to be too much tyramine and lead to dangerously high blood pressure. Some of these medications used for depression include phenelzine (Nardil), tranylcypromine (Parnate), and others.

Medications for mental conditions (Antipsychotic drugs). Some medications for mental conditions might cause jerky muscle movements. Taking phenylalanine along with some medications for mental conditions might increase the risk of jerky muscle movements. Some medications for mental conditions include chlorpromazine (Thorazine), clozapine (Clozaril), fluphenazine (Prolixin), haloperidol (Haldol), olanzapine (Zyprexa), perphenazine (Trilafon), prochlorperazine (Compazine), quetiapine (Seroquel), risperidone (Risperdal), thioridazine (Mellaril), thiothixene (Navane), and others.

PHOSPHATE SALTS

What other names is the product known by?

Aluminum Phosphate; Calcium Phosphate: Bone Ash, Bone Phosphate, Calcium Orthophosphate, Calcium Phosphate Dibasic Anhydrous, Calcium Phosphate Dibasic Dihydrate, Calcium Phosphate Tribasic, Di-Calcium Phosphate, Dicalcium Phosphate, Dicalcium Phosphates, Neutral Calcium Phosphate, Precipitated Calcium Phosphate, Tertiary Calcium Phosphate, Tricalcium Phosphate, Whitlockite; Potassium Phosphate: Dibasic Potassium Phosphate, Dipotassium Hydrogen Orthophosphate, Dipotassium Monophosphate, Dipotassium Phosphate, Monobasic Potassium Phosphate, Potassium Acid Phosphate, Potassium Biphosphate, Potassium Dihydrogen Orthophosphate; Sodium Phosphate: Anhydrous Sodium Phosphate, Dibasic Sodium Phosphate, Disodium Hydrogen Orthophosphate, Disodium Hydrogen Orthophosphate Dodecahydrate, Disodium Hydrogen Phosphate, Disodium Phosphate, Phosphate of Soda, Sodium Orthophosphate.

What is it?

Phosphate salts refers to many different combinations of the chemical phosphate with salts and minerals. People use them for medicine. Be careful not to confuse phosphate salts with substances such as organophosphates, or with tribasic sodium phosphates and tribasic potassium phosphates, which are very poisonous.

Is it Effective?

The effectiveness ratings for **PHOSPHATE SALTS** are as follows:

Effective for... Low blood phosphate, when sodium and potassium phosphates are used.
Likely Effective for... High blood calcium, when sodium and potassium phosphates are used.
Possibly Effective for... Preventing some types of kidney stones.
Likely Ineffective for... Improving aerobic exercise performance.
Insufficient Evidence to Rate Effectiveness for... Sensitive teeth, heartburn, cleaning out the bowels as a laxative preparation for intestinal tests such as colonoscopy when sodium phosphates are used, and other conditions.

How does it work?

Phosphates are normally absorbed from food and are important chemicals in the body. They are involved in cell structure, energy transport and storage, vitamin function, and numerous other processes essential to health. Phosphate salts can act as laxatives by causing more fluid to be drawn into the intestines and stimulating the gut to push out its contents faster.

Are there safety concerns?

Phosphate salts containing sodium, potassium, aluminum, or calcium appear to be safe for most people when used occasionally or short term. Regular-long-term use can upset the balance of phosphates and other chemicals in the body and should be monitored by a healthcare professional to avoid serious side effects. Phosphate salts can irritate the digestive tract and cause stomach upset, diarrhea, constipation, and other problems.

Medical professionals should consult the Professional Version at www.NaturalDatabase.com.

Phosphate salts from dietary sources are likely safe for pregnant or breast-feeding women when used at the recommended allowances of 1250 mg daily for mothers between 14-18 years of age and 700 mg daily for those over 18 years of age. Other amounts should only be used with the advice and ongoing care of a healthcare professional.

Do not confuse phosphate salts with substances such as organophosphates, or with tribasic sodium phosphates and tribasic potassium phosphates which are very poisonous.

Do not take phosphate salts unless prescribed by a healthcare professional if: You have kidney disease. • You have heart disease. • You have high or low calcium blood levels. • You have high phosphate blood levels. • You have a condition which causes the body to retain fluid (edema), including heart failure, liver problems (cirrhosis), and other conditions.

Are there any interactions with medications?

Antacids. Antacids are used to decrease stomach acid. Many antacids contain aluminum, calcium, or magnesium. The aluminum, calcium, and magnesium in antacids can decrease phosphate absorption. To avoid these interactions take antacids at least two hours after taking phosphate products. Some antacids include calcium carbonate (Tums, others), dihydroxyaluminum sodium carbonate (Rolaids, others), magaldrate (Riopan), magnesium sulfate (Bilagog), aluminum hydroxide (Amphojel), and others.

Cholestyramine (Questran). Cholestyramine (Questran) might decrease how much phosphate the body absorbs. By decreasing how much phosphate the body absorbs, cholestyramine (Questran) might decrease the effectiveness of phosphate supplements. To avoid this interaction take phosphate salts at least one hour before or four hours after taking cholestyramine.

Colestipol (Colestid). Colestipol (Colestid) might decrease how much phosphate the body absorbs. By decreasing how much phosphate the body absorbs, colestipol (Colestid) might decrease the effectiveness of phosphate supplements. To prevent this interaction, take phosphate salts at least one hour before or four hours after taking colestipol.

PHOSPHATIDYLCHOLINE

What other names is the product known by?

Phosphatidyl Choline.

What is it?

Phosphatidylcholine is a chemical contained in eggs, soybeans, and other foods.

Is it Effective?

The effectiveness ratings for **PHOSPHATIDYLCHOLINE** are as follows:

Possibly Effective for... Hepatitis C when used together with regular treatments.

Possibly Ineffective for... Hepatitis A • A movement disorder called tardive dyskinesia • Improving a medical procedure called peritoneal dialysis.

Insufficient Evidence to Rate Effectiveness for... Anxiety, Hepatitis B, eczema, gallbladder disease, manic-depressive illness, circulation disorders of the arms and legs, high cholesterol, premenstrual syndrome (PMS), memory loss, Alzheimer's disease, depressed immunity, preventing aging, and other conditions.

How does it work?

Phosphatidylcholine is a precursor of a brain chemical called acetylcholine. Acetylcholine is important for memory and other bodily functions.

Are there safety concerns?

Phosphatidylcholine appears to be safe for most people. It can sometimes cause excessive sweating. Taking too much can cause stomach upset and diarrhea.

Do not take phosphatidylcholine if: You are pregnant or breast-feeding.

Are there any interactions with medications?

Drying medications (Anticholinergic drugs). Some drying medications are called anticholinergic drugs. Phosphatidylcholine might increase chemicals that can decrease the effects of these drying medications. Some drying medications include atropine, scopolamine, and some medications used for allergies (antihistamines) and for depression (antidepressants).

Medications for Alzheimer's disease (Acetylcholinesterase (AChE) inhibitors). Phosphatidylcholine might increase a chemical in the body called acetylcholine. Medications for Alzheimer's called acetylcholinesterase inhibitors also increase the chemical acetylcholine. Taking phosphatidylcholine along with medications for

Alzheimer's disease might increase effects and side effects of medications for Alzheimer's disease. Some medications called acetylcholinesterase inhibitors include donepezil (Aricept), tacrine (Cognex), rivastigmine (Exelon), and galantamine (Reminyl, Razadyne).

Various medications used for glaucoma, Alzheimer's disease, and other conditions (Cholinergic drugs). Phosphatidylcholine might increase a chemical in the body called acetylcholine. This chemical is similar to some medications used for glaucoma, Alzheimer's disease, and other conditions. Taking phosphatidylcholine with these medications might increase the chance of side effects. Some of these medications used for glaucoma, Alzheimer's disease, and other conditions include pilocarpine (Pilocar and others), and others.

PHOSPHATIDYLSERINE

What other names is the product known by?

BC-PS, Bovine Cortex Phosphatidylserine, Bovine Phosphatidylserine, LECI-PS, Lecithin Phosphatidylserine, PS, PtdSer, Soy-PS, Soy Phosphatidylserine.

What is it?

Phosphatidylserine is a chemical. The body can make phosphatidylserine, but gets most of what it needs from foods. Phosphatidylserine supplements used to be made from cow brains, but now are commonly manufactured from cabbage or soy. People use it for medicine.

Is it Effective?

The effectiveness ratings for **PHOSPHATIDYLSERINE** are as follows:

Possibly Effective for... Alzheimer's disease • Confusion in older people (senile dementia).

Insufficient Evidence to Rate Effectiveness for... Depression, exercise-induced stress, improving athletic performance, improving thinking ability, attention deficit-hyperactivity disorder (ADHD), and other conditions.

How does it work?

Phosphatidylserine is an important chemical with widespread functions in the body. It is part of the cell structure and is key in the maintenance of cellular function, especially in the brain.

Are there safety concerns?

Phosphatidylserine might be safe for most people. Phosphatidylserine can cause insomnia and stomach upset, particularly at doses over 300 mg.

There is some concern that products derived from animal sources could transmit diseases, such as mad cow disease. To date, there aren't any known cases of humans getting animal diseases from supplements, but look for supplements made from plants to be on the safe side.

Do not take phosphatidylserine if: You are pregnant or breast-feeding.

Are there any interactions with medications?

Drying medications (Anticholinergic drugs). Some drying medications are called anticholinergic drugs. Phosphatidylserine might increase chemicals that can decrease the effects of these drying medications. Some drying medications include atropine, scopolamine, and some medications used for allergies (antihistamines) and for depression (antidepressants).

Medications for Alzheimer's disease (Acetylcholinesterase (AChE) inhibitors). Phosphatidylserine might increase a chemical in the body called acetylcholine. Medications for Alzheimer's disease called acetylcholinesterase inhibitors also increase the chemical acetylcholine. Taking phosphatidylserine along with medications for Alzheimer's disease might increase effects and side effects of medications for Alzheimer's disease. Some acetylcholinesterase medications include donepezil (Aricept), tacrine (Cognex), rivastigmine (Exelon), and galantamine (Reminyl, Razadyne).

Various medications used for glaucoma, Alzheimer's disease, and other conditions (Cholinergic drugs). Phosphatidylserine might increase a chemical in the body called acetylcholine. This chemical is similar to some medications used for glaucoma, Alzheimer's disease, and other conditions. Taking phosphatidylserine with these medications might increase the chance of side effects. Some of these medications used for glaucoma, Alzheimer's disease, and other conditions include pilocarpine (Pilocar and others), and others.

Medical professionals should consult the Professional Version at www.NaturalDatabase.com.

PICRORHIZA

What other names is the product known by?

Hu Huang Lian, Katki, Katuka, Katuko, Katurohini, Katvi, Kuru, Kutki, Neopicrorhiza scrophulariiflora, Picrorhiza kurroia, Picrorhiza scrophulariiflora, Xi Zang Hu Huang Lian..

What is it?

Picrorhiza is a plant. People use the root and rhizome (underground stem) for medicine.

Is it Effective?

The effectiveness ratings for **PICRORHIZA** are as follows:

Possibly Effective for... Vitiligo.

Possibly Ineffective for... Asthma.

Insufficient Evidence to Rate Effectiveness for... Acute viral hepatitis, rheumatoid arthritis, and other conditions.

How does it work?

More information is needed to know how picrorhiza might work. Picrorhiza contains chemicals that might stimulate the immune system, kill cancer cells, and relieve inflammation.

Are there safety concerns?

Picrorhiza seems safe for most people, when taken short-term. It can cause vomiting, rash, anorexia, diarrhea, and itching.

Do not take picrorhiza if: You are pregnant or breast-feeding. • You have an immune system disease such as multiple sclerosis (MS), systemic lupus erythematosus (SLE), or other autoimmune diseases.

Are there any interactions with medications?

Medications that decrease the immune system (Immunosuppressants). Picrorhiza might increase the immune system. Taking picrorhiza along with medications that decrease the immune system might decrease the effectiveness of these medications. Some medications that decrease the immune system include azathioprine (Imuran), basiliximab (Simulect), cyclosporine (Neoral, Sandimmune), daclizumab (Zenapax), muromonab-CD3 (OKT3, Orthoclone OKT3), mycophenolate (CellCept), tacrolimus (FK506, Prograf), sirolimus (Rapamune), prednisone (Deltasone, Orasone), corticosteroids (glucocorticoids), and others.

PIMPINELLA

What other names is the product known by?

Bibernellkraut, Burnet Saxifrage, Greater Burnet-Saxifrage, Pimpernell, Pimpinella leaf, Pimpinella magna, Pimpinella major, Pimpinella root, Pimpinella saxifrage, Pimpinellae herba, Pimpinellae radix, Saxifrage.

What is it?

Pimpinella is an herb. The root and above ground parts are used as medicine.

Is it Effective?

The effectiveness ratings for **PIMPINELLA** are as follows:

Insufficient Evidence to Rate Effectiveness for... Respiratory infections, wounds, urinary tract infections (UTIs), bladder and kidney stones, fluid retention, stomach and intestinal disorders, and treating varicose veins.

How does it work?

Pimpinella root is thought to loosen and aid in moving bronchial secretion.

Are there safety concerns?

There isn't enough information available to know if pimpinella is safe.

Do not take pimpinella if: You are pregnant or breast-feeding.

Are there any interactions with medications?

It is not known if pimpinella interacts with any medicines.

Before taking pimpinella, talk with your healthcare professional if you take any medications.

PINE

What other names is the product known by?
Dwarf-Pine, Monteray Pine, Pine Needle Oil, Pine Oils, Pini Atheroleum. Pini Turiones, Pinus radiata, Pinus sylvestris, Pix Liquida, Pumilio Pine, Scotch Fir, Scotch Pine, Swiss Mountain Pine.

What is it?
Pine is a tree. People use the sprouts, needles, and bark to make medicine.

Is it Effective?
The effectiveness ratings for **PINE** are as follows:
Insufficient Evidence to Rate Effectiveness for... Upper and lower respiratory tract swelling (inflammation), mild muscle pain, nerve pain, blood pressure problems, common colds, cough or bronchitis, and fevers.

How does it work?
Pine contains chemicals that might have activity against inflammation. It also has mild antibacterial and antifungal effects.

Are there safety concerns?
There isn't enough information to know if pine is safe or what the potential side effects might be. Pine pollen can cause allergy in sensitive people.

Do not take pine if: You are pregnant or breast-feeding.

Are there any interactions with medications?
It is not known if pine interacts with any medicines.
Before taking pine, talk with your healthcare professional if you take any medications.

PINELLIA TERNATA

What other names is the product known by?
Banha, Ban Xia, P. Ternata, Pinellia ternata tuber, Pinellia tuber, Pinellia tubiferia.

What is it?
Pinellia ternata is a plant. The tuber is used to make medicine.

Is it Effective?
The effectiveness ratings for **PINELLIA TERNATA** are as follows:
Insufficient Evidence to Rate Effectiveness for... Nausea, morning sickness, cough, birth control, influenza (flu), and inflammation.

How does it work?
There isn't enough information available to know how Pinellia ternata might work. Some chemicals in Pinellia ternata might affect the stomach and how fast food moves through it.

Are there safety concerns?
There is some concern that Pinellia ternata might not be safe. It contains a stimulant called ephedrine and might cause serious side effects such as heart attack, stroke, or seizures. Because of these safety concerns, this product is banned in the US.

Do not use Pinellia ternata if: You are pregnant or breast-feeding.

Are there any interactions with medications?
It is not known if Pinellia ternata interacts with any medicines.
Before using Pinellia ternata, talk with your healthcare professional if you take any medications.

PINK ROOT

What other names is the product known by?
American Wormgrass, Carolina Pink, Indian Pink, Maryland Pink, Pinkroot, Spigelia marilandica, Starbloom, Wormgrass.

What is it?
Pink root is an herb. People use the dried root and bulb to make medicine.

Is it Effective?
The effectiveness ratings for **PINK ROOT** are as follows:
Insufficient Evidence to Rate Effectiveness for... Removing intestinal worms.

How does it work?
Pink root has activity against intestinal worms. It is taken along with a strong laxative to remove both the worms and the pink root from the intestines.

Are there safety concerns?
The dried root of pink root seems safe for most people when used short-term along with a strong laxative. The fresh root is UNSAFE for use.

The dried root, which contains potentially poisonous chemicals, can also be unsafe if it is not taken with a strong laxative.

Do not take pink root if: You are pregnant or breast-feeding.

Are there any interactions with medications?
It is not known if pink root interacts with any medicines.
Before taking pink root, talk with your healthcare professional if you take any medications.

PINUS BARK

What other names is the product known by?
Canada Pitch, Canadian Hemlock, Eastern Hemlock, Hemlock Bark, Hemlock Gum, Hemlock Spruce, Hemlocktanne, Pruche de l'Est, Tsuga canadensis.

What is it?
Pinus is a plant. The bark is used as medicine.

Is it Effective?
The effectiveness ratings for **PINUS BARK** are as follows:
Insufficient Evidence to Rate Effectiveness for... Digestive disorders, diarrhea, diseases of the mouth and throat, and scurvy.

How does it work?
Pinus bark contains tannins. Astringent chemicals, such as tannins, can cause the mouth, throat, and digestive tract linings to shrink and form a protective surface coating.

Are there safety concerns?
It is not known if pinus bark is safe or what the potential side effects might be.

Do not take pinus bark if: You are pregnant or breast-feeding.

Are there any interactions with medications?
Medications taken by mouth (Oral drugs). Pinus bark contains a large amount of chemicals called tannins. Tannins absorb substances in the stomach and intestines. Taking pinus bark along with medications taken by mouth can decrease how much medicine your body absorbs, and decrease the effectiveness of your medicine. To prevent this interaction, take pinus bark at least one hour after medications you take by mouth.

PIPSISSEWA

What other names is the product known by?
Bitter Winter, Bitter Wintergreen, Chimaphila, Chimaphila corymbosa, Chimaphila umbellata, Ground Holly, Holly, King's Cure, King's Cureall, Love in Winter, Prince's Pine, Rheumatism Weed, Spotted Wintergreen, Umbellate Wintergreen.

What is it?
Pipsissewa is an herb. The above ground parts are used to make medicine.

Is it Effective?
The effectiveness ratings for **PIPSISSEWA** are as follows:
Insufficient Evidence to Rate Effectiveness for... Urinary tract infections (UTIs), kidney stones, spasms, fluid retention, seizures, anxiety, cancer, ulcerous sores, and blisters.

How does it work?
Pipsissewa might help reduce swelling, have a drying (astringent) effect on the tissues, and kill germs that cause infections in the urinary tract.

Are there safety concerns?
Pipsissewa seems safe for most people when used short-term. Long-term use can cause side effects such as ringing in the ears, vomiting, confusion, and seizures.

Do not take pipsissewa in amounts larger than normal food amounts if: You are pregnant or breast-feeding.

Are there any interactions with medications?
It is not known if pipsissewa interacts with any medicines.
Before taking pipsissewa, talk with your healthcare professional if you take any medications.

PITCHER PLANT

What other names is the product known by?
Eve's Cups, Fly-Catcher, Fly-Trap, Huntsman's Cup, Pitcher Plant, Purple Pitcher Plant, Purple Side-Saddle Flower, Sarapin, Sarracenia purpurea, Side-Saddle Plant, Smallpox Plant, Water-cup.

What is it?
Pitcher plant is a plant. The leaf and root are used as medicine.

Is it Effective?
The effectiveness ratings for **PITCHER PLANT** are as follows:
Insufficient Evidence to Rate Effectiveness for... Digestive disorders, constipation, urinary tract diseases, fluid retention, preventing scar formation, pain, and other conditions.

How does it work?
Pitcher plant contains tannins and other chemicals which are thought to help with some digestive tract problems. There is some evidence that suggests that pitcher plant extract may affect nerves involved in pain sensation.

Are there safety concerns?
A certain pitcher plant extract called Sarapin might be safe when injected by a qualified health professional. It is not safe when injected in areas of inflammation or when injected by an unqualified person. Pitcher plant injections can cause some side effects including feelings of heat or heaviness. It might also worsen symptoms.

There isn't enough information to know if pitcher plant is safe when taken by mouth or what the potential side effects might be.

Do not take pitcher plant if: You are pregnant or breast-feeding.

Are there any interactions with medications?
It is not known if pitcher plant interacts with any medicines.
Before taking pitcher plant, talk with your healthcare professional if you take any medications.

Medical professionals should consult the Professional Version at www.NaturalDatabase.com.

PLEURISY ROOT

What other names is the product known by?

Asclepias tuberosa, Butterfly Weed, Canada Root, Flux Root, Orange Milkweed, Orange Swallow Wort, Pleurisy, Swallow Wort, Tuber Root, White Root, Wind Root.

What is it?

Pleurisy is a plant. The root is used as medicine.

Is it Effective?

The effectiveness ratings for **PLEURISY ROOT** are as follows:

Insufficient Evidence to Rate Effectiveness for... Coughs, pleurisy (lung inflammation), disorders of the uterus, pain, spasms, bronchitis, influenza, easing breathing, promoting sweating, and other conditions.

How does it work?

There isn't enough information to know how pleurisy root might work.

Are there safety concerns?

Pleurisy root does not appear to be safe because it contains a potent chemical that is similar to the prescription drug digoxin (Lanoxin). It might cause serious heart problems. Pleurisy root also can cause side effects such as nausea and vomiting, and skin rash.

Do not take pleurisy root if: You are pregnant or breast-feeding. • You have heart problems.

Are there any interactions with medications?

Digoxin (Lanoxin). Digoxin (Lanoxin) helps the heart beat more strongly. Pleurisy root also seems to affect the heart. Taking pleurisy root along with digoxin can increase the effects of digoxin and increase the risk of side effects. Do not take pleurisy root if you are taking digoxin (Lanoxin) without talking to your healthcare professional.

Estrogens. Large amounts of pleurisy root might have some of the same effects as estrogen. But pleurisy root isn't as strong as estrogen pills. Taking pleurisy root along with estrogen pills might decrease the effects of estrogen pills. Some estrogen pills include conjugated equine estrogens (Premarin), ethinyl estradiol, estradiol, and others.

Water pills (Diuretic drugs). Pleurisy root might affect the heart. "Water pills" can decrease potassium in the body. Low potassium levels can also affect the heart and increase the risk of side effects from pleurisy root. Some "water pills" that can deplete potassium include chlorothiazide (Diuril), chlorthalidone (Thalitone), furosemide (Lasix), hydrochlorothiazide (HCTZ, Hydrodiuril, Microzide), and others.

PODOPHYLLUM

What other names is the product known by?

American Mandrake, Devil's Apple, Duck's Foot, Ground Lemon, Himalayan Mayapple, Hog Apple, Indian Apple, Indian Podophyllum, Mandrake, Mayapple, Podophyllin, Podophyll pelati rhizoma/resina, Podophyllum peltatum, Podophyllum hexandrum, Podophyllum emodi, Raccoon Berry, Umbrella Plant, Vegetable Calomel, Vegetable Mercury, Wild Lemon, and Wild Mandrake.

What is it?

Podophyllum is a plant. The root and underground stem are used to make medicine.

Is it Effective?

The effectiveness ratings for **PODOPHYLLUM** are as follows:

Likely Effective for... Treating human papilloma virus (genital and anal warts).

Insufficient Evidence to Rate Effectiveness for... Raised areas on the tongue and mouth in people with immune system diseases (hairy leukoplakia), liver problems, cancer, and other conditions.

How does it work?

Podophyllum can stop cell duplication and new growth. It can also have laxative effects.

Are there safety concerns?

Podophyllum seems safe for most people when applied to skin with no open areas, under medical supervision. It is highly UNSAFE when taken by mouth. Podophyllum may cause skin irritation, nausea, vomiting, dizziness, headache, spasms, fever, visual changes, low blood pressure, and kidney problems.

 Natural Medicines Comprehensive Database Consumer Version (209) 472-2244

Podophyllum seems safe for most people when applied in low concentrations to small areas with protection of bordering skin, and washed off within four to six hours. Contact with skin should not exceed six hours. Podophyllum is UNSAFE when used in higher concentrations or over large areas of the body. It is absorbed through the skin and can cause the same serious adverse effects as taking podophyllum by mouth.

Do not use podophyllum if: You are pregnant or breast-feeding.

Are there any interactions with medications?
It is not known if podophyllum interacts with any medicines.
Before taking podophyllum, talk with your healthcare professional if you take any medications.

POINSETTIA

What other names is the product known by?
Christmas Flower, Easter Flower, Euphorbia poinsettia, Euphorbia pulcherrima, Lobster Flower Plant, Lobsterplant, Mexican Flame Leaf, Mexican Flameleaf, Paintedleaf, Papagallo Poinsettia pulcherrima.

What is it?
Poinsettia is a flowering plant. The whole plant and its sap are used to make medicine.

Is it Effective?
The effectiveness ratings for **POINSETTIA** are as follows:
Insufficient Evidence to Rate Effectiveness for... Fever, pain, infection, warts, skin disorders, toothache, and other conditions.

How does it work?
There isn't enough information to know how poinsettia works.

Are there safety concerns?
Poinsettia seems UNSAFE. It can cause skin rash; severe eye irritation; and irritation or burns to the mouth, throat, stomach, and intestinal linings.

Do not take poinsettia if: You are pregnant or breast-feeding. • You have a stomach ulcer. • You have an irritable bowel disease. • You have Crohn's disease.

Are there any interactions with medications?
It is not known if poinsettia interacts with any medicines.
Before taking poinsettia, talk with your healthcare professional if you take any medications.

POISON IVY

What other names is the product known by?
Markweed, Poison Vine, Rhus radicans, Rhus Toxicodendron, Three-Leafed Ivy, Toxicodendron pubescens, Toxicodendron quercifolium, Toxicodendron radicans, Toxicodendron toxicarium.

What is it?
Poison ivy is a plant. The leaves are used to make medicine.

Is it Effective?
The effectiveness ratings for **POISON IVY** are as follows:
Insufficient Evidence to Rate Effectiveness for... Pain.

How does it work?
Poison ivy is a severe skin irritant that stimulates the immune system. Re-exposure leads to allergic reactions.

Are there safety concerns?
Poison ivy is unsafe. It can cause severe irritation of the mouth, throat, and lining of the stomach and intestines; nausea; vomiting; colic; diarrhea; dizziness; blood in the urine; fever; and coma. Skin contact can cause redness, swelling, blisters, severe skin destruction, swelling of the eye (cornea), or loss of sight.
Inhaling smoke from the burning plant can result in fever, lung infection, and death.
Do not take poison ivy if: You are pregnant or breast-feeding.

Medical professionals should consult the Professional Version at www.NaturalDatabase.com.

CONSUMER VERSION

Are there any interactions with medications?

It is not known if poison ivy interacts with any medicines.
Before taking poison ivy, talk with your healthcare professional if you take any medications.

POISONOUS BUTTERCUP

What other names is the product known by?

Celery-Leafed Crowfoot, Cursed Crowfoot, Ranunculus sceleratus.

What is it?

Poisonous buttercup is an herb. The above ground parts are used to make medicine.

Is it Effective?

The effectiveness ratings for **POISONOUS BUTTERCUP** are as follows:
Insufficient Evidence to Rate Effectiveness for... Skin diseases, and loss of skin color.

How does it work?

Poisonous buttercup contains a chemical which is extremely irritating to skin and mucous membranes. It causes pain and burning sensations, tongue swelling (inflammation), and an increase in saliva flow.

Are there safety concerns?

Poisonous buttercup is unsafe for use when applied to skin. There isn't enough information to know if it is safe when taken by mouth. Skin contact with fresh or bruised plants can lead to blisters and burns that are difficult to heal. It might also increase the risk of sunburn.

Do not take poisonous buttercup if: You are pregnant or breast-feeding.

Are there any interactions with medications?

It is not known if poisonous buttercup interacts with any medicines.
Before taking poisonous buttercup, talk with your healthcare professional if you take any medications.

POKEWEED

What other names is the product known by?

American Nightshade, American Spinach, Bear's Grape, Branching Phytolacca, Cancer Jalap, Chongras, Coakum, Coakum-Chorngras, Cokan, Crowberry, Fitolaca, Garget, Hierba Carmin, Inkberry, Jalap, Kermesbeere, Phytolacca Berry, Phytolacca americana, Phytolacca decandra, Pigeonberry, Pocan, Poke, Pokeweed berry, Pokeweed root, Raisin d'Amerique, Red-Ink Plant, Red Plant, Red Weed, Scoke, Skoke, Teinturiere, Virginian Poke.

What is it?

Pokeweed is a plant. The berry and root have historically been used as medicine.

Is it Effective?

The effectiveness ratings for **POKEWEED** are as follows:
Insufficient Evidence to Rate Effectiveness for... Arthritis-like pain, tonsillitis, laryngitis, mumps, swelling of the lymph glands, scabies, acne, skin cancers, painful menstruation, tonsillitis, and other conditions.

How does it work?

There isn't enough information available to know how pokeweed works.

Are there safety concerns?

Pokeweed is UNSAFE to use. It can cause nausea, vomiting, cramping, stomach pain, diarrhea, low blood pressure, incontinence, thirst, and other serious side effects.

Pokeweed is UNSAFE for children. Even one berry can be poisonous to a child.

Do not take pokeweed berry if: You are pregnant or breast-feeding.

Are there any interactions with medications?

It is not known if pokeweed interacts with any medicines.

Before taking pokeweed, talk with your healthcare professional if you take any medications.

POLICOSANOL

What other names is the product known by?

Dotriacontanol, Heptacosanol, Hexacosanol, Nonacosanol, Octacosanol, Polycosanol, Tetracosanol, Tetratriacontanol, Triacontanol.

What is it?

Policosanol is a chemical obtained from sugar cane and other sources. People use it for medicine.

Is it Effective?

The effectiveness ratings for **POLICOSANOL** are as follows:

Possibly Effective for... High cholesterol • Intermittent claudication (leg pain when walking and other symptoms).

Insufficient Evidence to Rate Effectiveness for... Increasing blood flow to the heart in people with coronary heart disease, and other conditions.

How does it work?

Policosanol seems to decrease cholesterol production in the liver and to increase the break down of LDL (low-density lipoprotein or "bad") cholesterol. It also decreases the stickiness of particles in the blood known as platelets, which might help reduce blood clots.

Are there safety concerns?

Policosanol appears to be safe for most people when used in doses of 10-80 mg per day for up to two years. It can cause skin redness and rash, migraines, insomnia or drowsiness, irritability, dizziness, upset stomach, increased appetite, trouble urinating, weight loss, nose and gum bleeds, and other side effects.

Do not take policosanol if: You are pregnant or breast-feeding.

Are there any interactions with medications?

Medications that slow blood clotting (Anticoagulant / Antiplatelet drugs). Policosanol might slow blood clotting. Taking policosanol along with medications that also slow clotting might increase the chances of bruising and bleeding. Some medications that slow blood clotting include aspirin, clopidogrel (Plavix), diclofenac (Voltaren, Cataflam, others), ibuprofen (Advil, Motrin, others), naproxen (Anaprox, Naprosyn, others), dalteparin (Fragmin), enoxaparin (Lovenox), heparin, warfarin (Coumadin), and others.

POLYPODIUM LEUCOTOMOS

What other names is the product known by?

Anapsos, Calaguala, Difur, Fern, P. Leucotomos, PL, PLE, Polypodium.

What is it?

Polypodium leucotomos is a fern from Central America. The rhizome is used for medicine.

Is it Effective?

The effectiveness ratings for **POLYPODIUM LEUCOTOMOS** are as follows:

Insufficient Evidence to Rate Effectiveness for... Preventing sunburn, atopic dermatitis (eczema), psoriasis, vitiligo, Alzheimer's disease, skin cancer, and other cancers.

How does it work?

Polypodium leucotomos might have antioxidant effects. Antioxidants might prevent damage caused by excessive sun exposure.

Are there safety concerns?

Polypodium leucotomos seems to be safe when used appropriately for only two days. The safety of long-term use is not known. There is very little information available about potential side effects of Polypodium leucotomos. It may cause upset stomach in some people.

Do not use Polypodium leucotomos if: You are pregnant or breast-feeding.

Medical professionals should consult the Professional Version at www.NaturalDatabase.com.

CONSUMER VERSION

Are there any interactions with medications?

It is not known if Polypodium leucotomos interacts with any medicines.
Before taking Polypodium leucotomos, talk with your healthcare professional if you take any medications.

POMEGRANATE

What other names is the product known by?

Dadima, Fruit of the Dead, Granada, Grenadier, Punica granatum, Roma, Shi Liu Gen Pi, Shi Liu Pi.

What is it?

Pomegranate is a tree. Various parts of the tree and fruit are used to make medicine.

Is it Effective?

The effectiveness ratings for **POMEGRANATE** are as follows:
Possibly Ineffective for... Chronic lung disease (chronic obstructive pulmonary disease, COPD).
Insufficient Evidence to Rate Effectiveness for... High cholesterol (hyperlipidemia), heart disease, intestinal worm infestations, high blood pressure (hypertension), hardening of the arteries (atherosclerosis), gum disease, fungal mouth infections, diarrhea, dysentery, sore throat, hemorrhoids, prostate cancer, and other conditions.

How does it work?

Pomegranate contains a variety of chemicals that might have antioxidant effects. Some preliminary research suggests that chemicals in pomegranate juice might slow the progression of atherosclerosis (hardening of the arteries) and possibly fight cancer cells. But it is not known if pomegranate has these effects when people consume the juice.

Are there safety concerns?

Pomegranate is safe in food amounts for most people. Pomegranate juice appears to be safe for most people when used as a medicine.

Do not take pomegranate if: You are pregnant or breast-feeding. • You have allergies to other plants.

Are there any interactions with medications?

Medications for high blood pressure (ACE inhibitors). Pomegranate juice seems to decrease blood pressure. Taking pomegranate juice along with medications for high blood pressure might cause your blood pressure to be too low. Some medications for high blood pressure include captopril (Capoten), enalapril (Vasotec), lisinopril (Prinivil, Zestril), ramipril (Altace), and others.
Medications for high blood pressure (Antihypertensive drugs). Pomegranate seems to decrease blood pressure. Taking pomegranate along with medications for high blood pressure might cause your blood pressure to go too low. Some medications for high blood pressure include captopril (Capoten), enalapril (Vasotec), losartan (Cozaar), valsartan (Diovan), diltiazem (Cardizem), Amlodipine (Norvasc), hydrochlorothiazide (HydroDIURIL), furosemide (Lasix), and many others.
Medications changed by the liver (Cytochrome P450 2D6 (CYP2D6) substrates). Some medications are changed and broken down by the liver. Pomegranate might decrease how quickly the liver breaks down some medications. Taking pomegranate along with some medications that are changed by the liver can increase the effects and side effects of your medication. Before taking pomegranate talk to your healthcare provider if you take any medications that are changed by the liver. Some medications that are changed by the liver include amitriptyline (Elavil), codeine, desipramine (Norpramin), flecainide (Tambocor), fluoxetine (Prozac), ondansetron (Zofran), tramadol (Ultram), and others.
Medications changed by the liver (Cytochrome P450 3A4 (CYP3A4) substrates). Some medications are changed and broken down by the liver. Drinking pomegranate juice might decrease how quickly the liver breaks down some medications. Drinking pomegranate juice and taking some medications that are broken down by the liver can increase the effects and side effects of some medications. Before consuming pomegranate juice, talk to your healthcare provider if you are taking any medications that are changed by the liver. Some medications changed by the liver include amlodipine (Norvasc), diltiazem (Cardizem), verapamil (Verelan, Calan, others), indinavir (Crixivan), nelfinavir (Viracept), ritonavir (Norvir), saquinavir (Invirase), alfentanil (Alfenta), fentanyl (Sublimaze), midazolam (Versed), ondansetron (Zofran), propranolol (Inderal), and many others.

 Natural Medicines Comprehensive Database Consumer Version (209) 472-2244

POPLAR

What other names is the product known by?
Balm of Gilead, Balsam Poplar Buds, Pappelknospen, Populi Gemma, Populus balsamifera, Populus candicans, Populus tacamahacca.

What is it?
Poplar is an herb. The dried unopened leaf buds are used to make medicine.

Is it Effective?
The effectiveness ratings for **POPLAR** are as follows:
Insufficient Evidence to Rate Effectiveness for... Cough, minor skin injuries, hemorrhoids, frostbite, and sunburn.

How does it work?
There isn't enough information available to know how poplar works.

Are there safety concerns?
Poplar applied to the skin seems safe for most people. It can cause allergic skin reactions in some people.

Do not take poplar if: You are pregnant or breast-feeding. • You are allergic to aspirin or similar medications. • You are allergic to propolis (a honeybee product). • You are allergic to Peru balsam.

Are there any interactions with medications?
It is not known if poplar interacts with any medicines.
Before taking poplar, talk with your healthcare professional if you take any medications.

PORIA MUSHROOM

What other names is the product known by?
China-root, Fu Ling, FuShen, Hoelen, Indian Bread, Matsuhodo, Polyporus, Poria, Poria cocos, Poria Cocos Sclerotium, Sclerotium of Tuckahoe, Sclerotium Poriae Cocos, Tuckahoe, Wolfiporia cocos.

What is it?
Poria mushroom is a fungus. The filaments are used as medicine.

Is it Effective?
The effectiveness ratings for **PORIA MUSHROOM** are as follows:
Insufficient Evidence to Rate Effectiveness for... Amnesia, anxiety, restlessness, fatigue, tension, nervousness, dizziness, difficult or painful urination, fluid retention, insomnia, inflamed spleen, stomach problems, diarrhea, tumors, and coughs.

How does it work?
Poria mushroom contains chemicals that might improve kidney function, lower serum cholesterol, reduce inflammation, and suppress immune function. It might also have antitumor and anti-vomiting effects.

Are there safety concerns?
Poria mushroom appears to be safe for most people. There aren't any known adverse effects of poria mushroom, but it hasn't been well researched by scientists.

Do not take poria mushroom if: You are pregnant or breast-feeding.

Are there any interactions with medications?
It is not known if poria mushroom interacts with any medicines.
Before taking poria mushroom, talk with your healthcare professional if you take any medications.

Medical professionals should consult the Professional Version at www.NaturalDatabase.com.

POTASSIUM

What other names is the product known by?
Atomic number 19, K, Potassium Acetate, Potassium Bicarbonate, Potassium Chloride, Potassium Citrate, Potassium Gluconate, Potassium Glycerophosphate, Potassium Phosphate.

What is it?
Potassium is a mineral. It is found in many foods. It is used to supplement the diet.

Is it Effective?
The effectiveness ratings for **POTASSIUM** are as follows:
Effective for... Low blood potassium (hypokalemia).
Possibly Effective for... High blood pressure • High calcium in the urine (hypercalciuria) • Preventing stroke.
Insufficient Evidence to Rate Effectiveness for... Insulin resistance, heart attack, menopausal symptoms, fatigue and mood swings in early menopause, infant colic, allergies, headaches, acne, alcoholism, Alzheimer's disease, arthritis, blurred vision, cancer, chronic fatigue syndrome, colitis, confusion, constipation, skin problems, fluid retention, fever, gout, insomnia, irritability, Menière's disease, muscle weakness, muscular dystrophy, stress, myasthenia gravis, and many other uses.

How does it work?
Potassium plays a role in many body functions including transmission of nerve signals, muscle contractions, fluid balance, and various chemical reactions.

Are there safety concerns?
Potassium is safe for most people when taken by mouth in amounts of up to 90 mEq of total potassium from the diet and supplements combined. For pregnant or breast-feeding women, safe amounts are obtained from the diet in amounts of 40-80 mEq per day. Potassium can cause stomach upset, nausea, diarrhea, vomiting, intestinal gas, and other side effects.

Too much potassium is dangerous and can cause feelings of burning or tingling, generalized weakness, paralysis, listlessness, dizziness, mental confusion, low blood pressure, irregular heart rhythm, and death.

Do not take potassium if: You have disorders of the digestive tract that might alter the speed food and supplements pass through the body. • You are sensitive to aspirin or tartrazine products.

Are there any interactions with medications?
Medications for high blood pressure (ACE inhibitors). Some medications for high blood pressure can increase potassium levels in the blood. Taking potassium along with some medications for high blood pressure might cause too much potassium in the blood. Some medications for high blood pressure include captopril (Capoten), enalapril (Vasotec), lisinopril (Prinivil, Zestril), ramipril (Altace), and others.
Medications for high blood pressure (Angiotensin receptor blockers (ARBs)). Some medications for high blood pressure can increase potassium levels in the blood. Taking potassium along with some medications for high blood pressure might cause too much potassium to be in the blood. Some medications for high blood pressure include losartan (Cozaar), valsartan (Diovan), irbesartan (Avapro), candesartan (Atacand), telmisartan (Micardis), eprosartan (Teveten), and others.
Water pills (Potassium-sparing diuretics). Some "water pills" can increase potassium levels in the body. Taking some "water pills" along with potassium might cause too much potassium to be in the body. Some "water pills" that increase potassium in the body include amiloride (Midamor), spironolactone (Aldactone), and triamterene (Dyrenium).

POTATO

What other names is the product known by?
Irish Potato, Solanum tuberosum, White Potato.

What is it?
Potato is a plant. The tuber (potato) is used to make medicine.

Is it Effective?
The effectiveness ratings for **POTATO** are as follows:
Insufficient Evidence to Rate Effectiveness for... Stomach disorders, weight loss, arthritis, infections, boils, burns, and other conditions.

How does it work?
Potatoes might have activity as an appetite suppressant to cause weight loss. A chemical in the potato peel might also prevent bacteria from attaching to cells. Potatoes are a source of vitamin C, iron, riboflavin, and carbohydrates.

Are there safety concerns?
Unblemished, ripe potatoes taken as medicine seem safe for most people. Damaged, green potatoes and sprouts contain poisonous chemicals that cannot be destroyed by cooking. These poisonous chemicals can cause headache, flushing, nausea, vomiting, diarrhea, stomach pain, thirst, restlessness, and death.

Do not take potato as medicine if: You are pregnant or breast-feeding. • You have diabetes.

Are there any interactions with medications?
Medications for dissolving blood clots (Thrombolytic Drugs). Potatoes contain a chemical that decreases blood clotting. Taking large amounts of potato with medications used for dissolving blood clots might increase the chance of bleeding and bruising. Some medications used for dissolving blood clots include alteplase (Activase), anistreplase (Eminase), reteplase (Retevase), streptokinase (Streptase), and urokinase (Abbokinase).

POTENTILLA

What other names is the product known by?
Crampweed, Goose Grass, Goose Tansy, Goosewort, Moor Grass, Potentilla anserina, Prince's Feather, Silverweed, Trailing Tansy, Wild Agrimony.

What is it?
Potentilla is an herb. The flower and leaf are used to make medicine.

Is it Effective?
The effectiveness ratings for **POTENTILLA** are as follows:
Insufficient Evidence to Rate Effectiveness for... Premenstrual syndrome (PMS), mild painful menstruation, mouth and throat swelling (inflammation), and diarrhea.

How does it work?
Potentilla contains chemicals called tannins that might help reduce skin inflammation and have a drying (astringent) effect on the tissues.

Are there safety concerns?
Potentilla seems safe for most people. It can cause stomach irritation.

Do not take potentilla if: You are pregnant or breast-feeding.

Are there any interactions with medications?
It is not known if potentilla interacts with any medicines.
Before taking potentilla, talk with your healthcare professional if you take any medications.

PRECATORY BEAN

What other names is the product known by?
Abrus precatorius, Bead Vine, Black-Eyed Susan, Buddhist Rosary Bead, Crab's Eye, Glycine abrus, Indian Bead, Jequirity Bean, Jequirity Seed, Love Bean, Lucky Bean, Ojo De Pajaro, Prayer Beads, Prayer Head, Rosary Pea, Seminole Bead, Weather Plant.

What is it?
Precatory bean is a plant. The seed and other plant parts are used as medicine.

Is it Effective?
The effectiveness ratings for **PRECATORY BEAN** are as follows:
Insufficient Evidence to Rate Effectiveness for... Quickening labor, inducing abortion, preventing pregnancy, pain in terminally ill patients, and eye inflammation.

Medical professionals should consult the Professional Version at www.NaturalDatabase.com.

CONSUMER VERSION

How does it work?

Precatory bean contains abrin, which is toxic and prevents cells from growing or functioning normally. Precatory bean also contains chemicals that might interfere with blood clotting, reduce inflammation, and lessen allergies.

Are there safety concerns?

Precatory bean is UNSAFE because it contains a toxic substance. Symptoms of toxicity include stomach cramping, followed by severe diarrhea and vomiting that can become bloody. Other symptoms include cold sweat, fever, weakness, and a fast heart rate. Symptoms can happen within hours or appear up to several days later. Death can occur after 3-4 days of persistent stomach problems and other symptoms.

Children are particularly sensitive to the effects of precatory bean. Children can die after swallowing just one seed. If exposure to precatory bean is suspected, get immediate medical assistance.

When seeds come in contact with the skin, they can cause inflammation, irritation, and severe eye problems.

While precatory bean isn't safe for anyone to take, some people should be particularly careful to avoid use.

Do not use precatory bean if: You are pregnant or breast-feeding.

Are there any interactions with medications?

It is not known if precatory bean interacts with any medicines.
Before taking precatory bean, talk with your healthcare professional if you take any medications.

PREGNENOLONE

What other names is the product known by?

None.

What is it?

Pregnenolone is a chemical found in our bodies. It can also be made in a laboratory. It is used as a medicine.

Is it Effective?

The effectiveness ratings for **PREGNENOLONE** are as follows:
Insufficient Evidence to Rate Effectiveness for... Slowing or reversing aging, arthritis, depression, endometriosis (abnormal thickening of the lining of uterus), fatigue, and other conditions.

How does it work?

In the body pregnenolone is used to make all steroid hormones. There isn't enough information to know how supplemental pregnenolone works.

Are there safety concerns?

There isn't enough information to know if pregnenolone is safe when taken by mouth. It might cause some steroid-like side effects including overstimulation, insomnia, irritability, anger, anxiety, acne, headache, negative mood changes, facial hair growth, hair loss, and irregular heart rhythm.

Do not take pregnenolone if: You are pregnant or breast-feeding. • You have a hormone-sensitive cancer or other condition.

Are there any interactions with medications?

Estrogens. Pregnenolone is used in the body to make hormones including estrogen. Taking estrogen along with pregnenolone might cause too much estrogen to be in the body. Some estrogen pills include conjugated equine estrogens (Premarin), ethinyl estradiol, estradiol, and others.
Progestin. Progestins are a group of hormones. Taking other hormones along with progesterone pills might cause too much hormones in the body. This could increase the effects and side effects of hormone pills.
Testosterone. The body changes pregnenolone into testosterone. Taking pregnenolone along with a testosterone pill might cause too much testosterone in the body. This might increase the chance of testosterone side effects.

   Natural Medicines Comprehensive Database Consumer Version   (209) 472-2244

PREMORSE

What other names is the product known by?
Devil's Bit, Ofbit, Premorse Scaboius, Scabiosa succisa.

What is it?
Premorse is an herb. The above ground parts are used to make medicine.

Is it Effective?
The effectiveness ratings for **PREMORSE** are as follows:
Insufficient Evidence to Rate Effectiveness for... Colds and coughs.

How does it work?
There isn't enough information available to know how premorse might work.

Are there safety concerns?
There isn't enough information to know if premorse is safe.

Do not take premorse if: You are pregnant or breast-feeding.

Are there any interactions with medications?
It is not known if premorse interacts with any medicines.
Before taking premorse, talk with your healthcare professional if you take any medications.

PRICKLY PEAR CACTUS

What other names is the product known by?
Barbary-fig Cactus, Cactus Flowers, Cactus Fruit, Cactus Pear Fruit, Gracemere-Pear, Indian-fig Prickly Pear Cactus, Opuntia, Nopal, Nopol, OPI, Opuntia ficus indica, Opuntia Fruit, Opuntia fuliginosa, Opuntia hyptiacantha, Opuntia lasciacantha, Opuntia macrocentra, Opuntia megacantha, Opuntia puberula, Opuntia streptacantha, Opuntia velutina, Prickly Pear, Tuna Cardona, Westwood-Pear.

What is it?
Prickly pear cactus is a plant. The leaves, stems, flowers, and fruit are used for medicine.

Is it Effective?
The effectiveness ratings for **PRICKLY PEAR CACTUS** are as follows:
Possibly Effective for... Diabetes. Some forms of prickly pear cactus seem to lower blood sugar levels in people who have diabetes • Hangover. Taking prickly pear cactus before drinking alcohol might reduce some symptoms of hangover the next day.
Insufficient Evidence to Rate Effectiveness for... High blood cholesterol, obesity, colitis, diarrhea, enlarged prostate, and treating infections caused by viruses.

How does it work?
Prickly pear cactus contains fiber and pectin, which can lower blood glucose by decreasing the absorption of sugar in the stomach and intestine. Some researchers think that it might also decrease cholesterol levels, and kill viruses in the body.

Are there safety concerns?
The leaves, stems, flowers, and fruit of the prickly pear cactus appear to be safe for most people when used for a short period of time.

It can cause some side effects including mild diarrhea, nausea, increased amount and frequency of stool, bloating, and headache.

Do not take prickly pear cactus if: You are pregnant or breast-feeding.

Are there any interactions with medications?
Chlorpropamide (Diabinese). Chlorpropamide (Diabinese) is used to decrease blood sugar in people with diabetes. Prickly pear cactus might also decrease blood sugar. Taking prickly pear cactus along with chlorpropamide (Diabinese) might cause your blood sugar to go too low. Monitor your blood sugar closely. The dose of your chlorpropamide (Diabinese) might need to be changed.

Medical professionals should consult the Professional Version at www.NaturalDatabase.com.

PROCAINE

What other names is the product known by?
Gero-Vita, Gerovital, Gerovital-H3, GH-3, KH-3, Procaine Hydrochloride.

What is it?
Procaine is a chemical. People use it for medicine. Be careful not to confuse the procaine used by mouth with the prescription procaine given by injection only under the supervision of a healthcare professional.

Is it Effective?
The effectiveness ratings for **PROCAINE** are as follows:
Effective for... Pain when used as a prescription shot.
Insufficient Evidence to Rate Effectiveness for... Use by mouth for arthritis, hardening of the arteries (cerebral atherosclerosis), dementia, depression, hair loss, high blood pressure, sexual problems, and other conditions.

How does it work?
Procaine works as an anesthetic when injected, but there doesn't seem to be much absorption of procaine when it is taken by mouth. It is unclear how it might work for medicinal uses when taken by mouth.

Are there safety concerns?
It is not known whether procaine is safe when taken by mouth. It can cause some side effects including heartburn, migraines, and a serious condition called systemic lupus erythematosus (SLE). SLE causes a variety of symptoms including joint pain, rashes, lung problems, and many other symptoms.

Do not take procaine if: You are pregnant or breast-feeding. • You have systemic lupus erythematosus (SLE). • You have myasthenia gravis.

Are there any interactions with medications?
Aminosalicylic acid. The body breaks down procaine to get rid of it. Procaine is broken down to a chemical called aminobenzoic acid. Aminobenzoic acid might decrease the effectiveness of aminosalicylic acid. Taking procaine along with aminosalicylic acid might decrease the effectiveness of aminosalicylic acid.
Antibiotics (Sulfonamide antibiotics). The body changes procaine to para-aminobenzoic acid (PABA). PABA can decrease the effectiveness of certain antibiotics called sulfonamides. Some of these antibiotics include sulfamethoxazole (Gantanol), sulfasalazine (Azulfidine), sulfisoxazole (Gantrisin), and trimethoprim/sulfamethoxazole (Bactrim, Septra).
Digoxin (Lanoxin). Digoxin (Lanoxin) helps the heart beat more strongly. Digoxin (Lanoxin) can also control how fast the heart beats. Getting a procaine injection can slow the heartbeat. Taking digoxin with procaine might cause your heartbeat to be too slow.
Muscle relaxants. Procaine is given as a shot to numb pain. Taking procaine with some muscle relaxants can cause the numbing to last too long. Before getting a procaine injection tell your doctor if you are taking any muscle relaxants. Some of these muscle relaxants include atracurium (Tracrium), pancuronium (Pavulon), succinylcholine (Anectine), and others.
Succinylcholine. Procaine is injected and used to numb pain. Taking procaine with succinylcholine can cause the numbing to last too long.

PROGESTERONE

What other names is the product known by?
Corpus Luteum Hormone, Luteal Hormone, Luteohormone, Lutine, NSC-9704, Pregnancy Hormone, Pregnanedione, Progestational Hormone, Progesteronum, 4-Pregnene-3; 20-Dione.

What is it?
Progesterone is a hormone that occurs naturally in the body. It can also be made in a laboratory. People use it for medicine.

Is it Effective?
The effectiveness ratings for **PROGESTERONE** are as follows:
Likely Effective for... Use with estrogen as hormone replacement therapy • Absence of menstrual periods • Infertility when used as a vaginal cream.
Possibly Effective for... Breast pain • Abnormal thickening of the lining of the uterus • Menopausal symptoms • Infertility when used as an injection.
Possibly Ineffective for... Premenstrual syndrome (PMS) • Withdrawal symptoms from drugs such as diazepam

 Natural Medicines Comprehensive Database Consumer Version (209) 472-2244

(Valium), alprazolam (Xanax), temazepam (Restoril), and many others • Preventing bone loss after menopause • Vaginal irritation (vulval lichen sclerosis).

Insufficient Evidence to Rate Effectiveness for... Treating or preventing hormone-mediated allergies, bloating, decreased sex drive, depression, fatigue, headaches, low blood sugar (hypoglycemia), increased blood clotting, irritability, memory loss, miscarriages, thyroid dysfunction, unclear thinking, uterine cancer, uterine fibroids, water retention, weight gain, and other conditions.

How does it work?

Progesterone is a hormone released by the ovaries. Changing progesterone levels can contribute to many of the conditions for which progesterone is used, such as abnormal menstrual periods and menopause. Progesterone may also be beneficial in infertility because it is necessary for implantation of the fertilized egg in the uterus and for maintaining pregnancy.

Are there safety concerns?

Progesterone is safe for most people when used with the advice and care of a healthcare professional. However, it can cause many side effects including stomach upset, changes in appetite, weight gain, fluid retention and swelling (edema), fatigue, acne, drowsiness or insomnia, allergic skin rashes, hives, fever, headache, depression, breast discomfort or enlargement, PMS-like syndrome, altered menstrual cycles, irregular bleeding, and other side effects.

Do not take progesterone without medical supervision if: You are pregnant or breast-feeding. • You have disease of the arteries. • You have breast cancer. • You are or have been depressed. • You have liver disease. • You have vaginal bleeding that is not associated with a menstrual period.

Are there any interactions with medications?

Estrogens. Progesterone and estrogen are both hormones. They are often taken together. Progesterone can decrease some of the side effects of estrogen. But progesterone might also decrease the beneficial effects of estrogen. Taking progesterone along with estrogen might cause breast tenderness. Some estrogen pills include conjugated equine estrogens (Premarin), ethinyl estradiol, estradiol, and others.

PROPIONYL-L-CARNITINE

What other names is the product known by?

L-carnitine Propionyl, LPC, PLC, Propionylcarnitine.

What is it?

Propionyl-L-carnitine is an amino acid (a protein component) that is naturally produced in the body.

Is it Effective?

The effectiveness ratings for **PROPIONYL-L-CARNITINE** are as follows:

Possibly Effective for... Poor circulation that causes leg pain while walking (intermittent claudication) • Chest pain (angina) • Congestive heart failure • A type of heart disease called chronic ischemic heart disease • Treating symptoms of age-related testosterone deficiency ("male menopause") • Erection problems in men with diabetes • Peyronie's disease (an increase in fibrous tissue in the penis).

Insufficient Evidence to Rate Effectiveness for... Chronic fatigue syndrome (CFS), circulatory problems caused by diabetes, and other conditions.

How does it work?

Propionyl-L-carnitine helps the body produce energy. It is important for heart function, muscle movement, and many other body processes. It also seems to help increase circulation.

Are there safety concerns?

Propionyl-L-carnitine is safe for most people. It can cause nausea, vomiting, stomach pain, weakness, and chest pain (angina). It can also cause a "fishy" odor of the urine, breath, and sweat.

Do not take propionyl-L-carnitine if: You are pregnant or breast-feeding. • You have had seizures. • You have thyroid problems.

Are there any interactions with medications?

Acenocoumarol (Sintrom). Acenocoumarol (Sintrom) is used to slow blood clotting. Propionyl-L-carnitine might increase the effects of acenocoumarol (Sintrom). Increasing the effects of acenocoumarol (Sintrom) might slow blood clotting too much and cause bruising and bleeding. The dose of your acenocoumarol (Sintrom) might need to be changed.

Natural Medicines Comprehensive Database Consumer Version   (209) 472-2244

Medical professionals should consult the Professional Version at www.NaturalDatabase.com.

CONSUMER VERSION

Warfarin (Coumadin). Warfarin (Coumadin) is used to slow blood clotting. Propionyl-L-carnitine might increase the effects of warfarin (Coumadin) and increase the chances of bruising and bleeding. Be sure to have your blood checked regularly. The dose of your warfarin (Coumadin) might need to be changed.

Zidovudine (AZT, Retrovir). Zidovudine is used to treat HIV and AIDS infection. Zidovudine decreases how much propionyl-L-carnitine is in muscles and might cause muscle weakness. More information is needed to know if taking propionyl-L-carnitine can decrease muscle weakness due to zidovudine.

PROPOLIS

What other names is the product known by?
Bee Glue, Bee Propolis, Hive Dross, Propolis Balsam, Propolis Resin, Propolis Wax, Russion Penicillin.

What is it?
Propolis is a resin-like material from the buds of poplar and cone-bearing trees. Propolis is rarely available in its pure form. It is usually obtained from beehives and contains bee products. People use it for medicine.

Is it Effective?
The effectiveness ratings for **PROPOLIS** are as follows:
Possibly Effective for... Improving healing and reducing pain and inflammation after mouth surgery • Genital herpes.
Insufficient Evidence to Rate Effectiveness for... Tuberculosis, infections, nose and throat cancer, improving immune response, ulcers, stomach and intestinal disorders, common cold, wounds, inflammation, minor burns, and other conditions.

How does it work?
Propolis seems to have activity against bacteria, viruses, and fungi. It might also have anti-inflammatory effects and help skin heal.

Are there safety concerns?
There isn't enough information to know if propolis is safe. It can cause allergic reactions, particularly in people who are allergic to bees or bee products. Lozenges containing propolis can cause irritation and mouth ulcers.

Do not take propolis if: You are pregnant or breast-feeding. • You are allergic to bees or bee products, poplar or cone-bearing trees, Peru balsam, or aspirin. • You have asthma.

Are there any interactions with medications?
It is not known if propolis interacts with any medicines.
Before taking propolis, talk with your healthcare professional if you take any medications.

PUFF BALL

What other names is the product known by?
Bovista, Deer Balls, Hart's Truffle, Lycoperdon species.

What is it?
Puff ball is a plant. The mushroom cap and spores are used as medicine.

Is it Effective?
The effectiveness ratings for **PUFF BALL** are as follows:
Insufficient Evidence to Rate Effectiveness for... Nosebleeds and skin disorders.

How does it work?
There isn't enough information to know how puff ball might work.

Are there safety concerns?
There isn't enough information to know if puff ball is safe for medicinal use. Inhaling puff ball spores can cause side effects including breathing problems, pneumonia-like symptoms, and chest X-ray changes.

Do not take puff ball if: You are pregnant or breast-feeding.

Are there any interactions with medications?
It is not known if puff ball interacts with any medicines.
Before taking puff ball, talk with your healthcare professional if you take any medications.

PULSATILLA

What other names is the product known by?
Anemone nigricans, Anemone pratensis, Anemone pulsatilla, Anemone serotina, Easter Flower, European Pasqueflower, Meadow Anenome, Meadow Windflower, Pasque Flower, Pasqueflower, Passe Flower, Pulsatilla nigricans, Pulsatilla pratensis, Pulsatilla vulgaris, Wind Flower.

What is it?
Pulsatilla is a plant. The dried above ground parts are used as medicine.

Is it Effective?
The effectiveness ratings for **PULSATILLA** are as follows:
Insufficient Evidence to Rate Effectiveness for... Conditions of the male or female reproductive system, tension headache, hyperactive states, insomnia, boils, skin diseases, asthma and lung disease, earache, migraines, nerve problems, general restlessness, digestive and urinary tract problems, and other conditions.

How does it work?
Pulsatilla might have activity against pain, fever, spasms, and bacteria. It also might act as a sedative.

Are there safety concerns?
Fresh pulsatilla plant is not safe when taken by mouth or applied to the skin. It is a severe irritant anywhere it comes in contact with the body such as the mouth, throat, digestive tract, urinary tract, and skin. It can also cause allergic reactions. Contact with the skin can cause rash, inflammation, and itching. Inhaling the volatile oil can irritate the nose and eyes.

There isn't enough information about the dried plant to know if it is safe or what the side effects might be.

Do not take pulsatilla if: You are pregnant or breast-feeding.

Are there any interactions with medications?
It is not known if pulsatilla interacts with any medicines.
Before taking pulsatilla, talk with your healthcare professional if you take any medications.

PUMPKIN

What other names is the product known by?
Cucurbita galeottii, Cucurbita mammeata, Cucurbita pepo, Cucurbitea peponis semen, Cucumis pepo, Field Pumpkin, Pepo, Pumpkin Seed.

What is it?
Pumpkin is a plant. The seed is used to make medicine.

Is it Effective?
The effectiveness ratings for **PUMPKIN** are as follows:
Possibly Effective for... Benign prostatic hyperplasia (BPH).
Insufficient Evidence to Rate Effectiveness for... Intestinal worms and difficult or painful urination due to benign prostatic hyperplasia (BPH) or bladder irritation.

How does it work?
The chemicals in the pumpkin seed cause an increase in urination (diuretic effect), which helps relieve bladder discomfort.

Are there safety concerns?
Pumpkin is considered safe for most people. It may cause ejaculation problems in some men.

Do not use pumpkin in amounts greater than found in food if: You are pregnant or breast-feeding.

Medical professionals should consult the Professional Version at www.NaturalDatabase.com.

CONSUMER VERSION

Are there any interactions with medications?
It is not known if pumpkin interacts with any medicines.
Before taking pumpkin, talk with your healthcare professional if you take any medications.

PUNCTURE VINE

What other names is the product known by?
Abrojos, Caltrop, Cat's-Head, Common Dubbletjie, Devil's-Thorn, Devil's-Weed, Espigón, Goathead, Gokhru, Gokshura, Nature's Viagra, Tribule terrestre, Tribulis, Tribulis Terrestris, Tribulus, Tribulus terrestris.

What is it?
Puncture vine is a plant. People use the spine-covered fruit as medicine.

Is it Effective?
The effectiveness ratings for **PUNCTURE VINE** are as follows:
Possibly Ineffective for... Enhancing athletic performance.
Insufficient Evidence to Rate Effectiveness for... Chest pain (angina), atopic dermatitis (eczema), problems with erections, anemia, cancer, coughs, intestinal gas (flatulence), and other conditions.

How does it work?
Puncture vine has chemicals that might increase some hormones in animals. However, it doesn't appear to increase male hormones (testosterone) in humans.

Are there safety concerns?
Puncture vine supplements appear to be safe for most people when taken by mouth for a short period of time.

Do not use puncture vine if: You are pregnant or breast-feeding. • You have prostate problems or prostate cancer.

Are there any interactions with medications?
Medications for diabetes (Antidiabetes drugs). Puncture vine might decrease blood sugar. Diabetes medications are also used to lower blood sugar. Taking puncture vine along with diabetes medications might cause your blood sugar to go too low. Monitor your blood sugar closely. The dose of your diabetes medication might need to be changed. Some medications used for diabetes include glimepiride (Amaryl), glyburide (DiaBeta, Glynase PresTab, Micronase), insulin, pioglitazone (Actos), rosiglitazone (Avandia), chlorpropamide (Diabinese), glipizide (Glucotrol), tolbutamide (Orinase), and others.

PURPLE LOOSESTRIFE

What other names is the product known by?
Blooming Sally, Flowering Sally, Long Purples, Loosestrife, Lythrum, Lythrum salicaria, Milk Willow-Herb, Purple Willow-Herb, Rainbow Weed, Salicare, Soldiers, Spiked, Spiked Loosestrife, Willow Sage.

What is it?
Purple loosestrife is a plant. The above ground flowering parts are used as medicine.

Is it Effective?
The effectiveness ratings for **PURPLE LOOSESTRIFE** are as follows:
Insufficient Evidence to Rate Effectiveness for... Diarrhea, intestinal problems, menstrual (period) complaints, inflammation, infection, varicose veins, bleeding gums, hemorrhoids, eczema, and other conditions.

How does it work?
Purple loosestrife contains astringent chemicals called tannins and salicarin. Astringent chemicals might help reduce diarrhea and inflammation. Salicarin may also help fight "bugs," or bacteria, in the intestine.

Are there safety concerns?
It is not known if purple loosestrife is safe or what the side effects might be.
Do not take purple loosestrife if: You are pregnant or breast-feeding.

Are there any interactions with medications?
It is not known if purple loosestrife interacts with any medicines.
Before taking purple loosestrife, talk with your healthcare professional if you take any medications.

Medical professionals should consult the Professional Version at www.NaturalDatabase.com.

PYCNOGENOL

What other names is the product known by?
Condensed Tannins, French Marine Pine Bark Extract, French Maritime Pine Bark Extract, Leucoanthocyanidins, Oligomeric Proanthocyanidins, Pine Bark Extract, Pinus Pinaster, Pinus Maritime, Procyanidin Oligomers, Procyanodolic Oligomers, Pygenol.

What is it?
Pycnogenol is the US registered trademark name for a product derived from the pine bark of a tree known as Pinus pinaster.

Is it Effective?
The effectiveness ratings for **PYCNOGENOL** are as follows:
Possibly Effective for... Circulation problems • Varicose veins • Disease of the retina in the eye • Improved endurance in athletes • High blood pressure • Asthma in children.
Possibly Ineffective for... Attention deficit-hyperactivity disorder (ADHD).
Insufficient Evidence to Rate Effectiveness for... Aging, allergies, heart disease, stroke prevention, muscle soreness, pelvic pain in women, diabetes, arthritis, erectile dysfunction (impotence), and other conditions.

How does it work?
Pycnogenol contains substances that might improve blood flow. It might also stimulate the immune system and have antioxidant effects.

Are there safety concerns?
Pycnogenol might be safe when taken in doses of 120 mg to 450 mg daily for up to three months. Larger doses might not be safe.

Do not take pycnogenol if: You are pregnant or breast-feeding. • You have an immune system disease such as multiple sclerosis, lupus erythematosus, or other auto-immune diseases.

Are there any interactions with medications?
Medications that decrease the immune system (Immunosuppressants). Pycnogenol seems to increase the immune system. By increasing the immune system pycnogenol might decrease the effectiveness of medications that decrease the immune system. Some medications that decrease the immune system include azathioprine (Imuran), basiliximab (Simulect), cyclosporine (Neoral, Sandimmune), daclizumab (Zenapax), muromonab-CD3 (OKT3, Orthoclone OKT3), mycophenolate (CellCept), tacrolimus (FK506, Prograf), sirolimus (Rapamune), prednisone (Deltasone, Orasone), corticosteroids (glucocorticoids), and others.

PYGEUM

What other names is the product known by?
African Plum Tree, Prunus africana, Pygeum africanum.

What is it?
Pygeum is a tree. The bark is used as medicine.

Is it Effective?
The effectiveness ratings for **PYGEUM** are as follows:
Likely Effective for... Low urine flow, nighttime urinating, and other symptoms of an enlarged prostate (benign prostatic hyperplasia or BPH).
Insufficient Evidence to Rate Effectiveness for... Inflammation, kidney disease, malaria, stomachache, fever, madness, sexual dysfunction, and other conditions.

How does it work?
Pygeum contains chemicals that help shrink the prostate to relieve urinary problems such as poor urine flow and nighttime urination in men with enlarged prostates.

Are there safety concerns?
Pygeum appears to be safe for most people. It can cause nausea and abdominal pain.

Do not take pygeum if: You are pregnant or breast-feeding.

Medical professionals should consult the Professional Version at www.NaturalDatabase.com.

Are there any interactions with medications?

It is not known if pygeum interacts with any medicines.

Before taking pygeum, talk with your healthcare professional if you take any medications.

PYRETHRUM

What other names is the product known by?

Chrysanthemum cinerariifolium, Dalmation Insect Flowers, Dalmation Pellitory, Tanacetum cinerariifolium.

What is it?

Pyrethrum is a plant. People use the flower for medicine. Be careful not to confuse pyrethrum with pyrethrin. Pyrethrum is the name of the crude extract obtained from flowers of Chrysanthemum cinerariifolium. Pyrethrin refers to a more refined extract containing several naturally occurring pyrethrins, which are contained in body lice medicines such as A-200 Pyrinate, Barc, Lice-Enz, Licetrol, Pronto, R and C, RID, Tisit, Tisit Blue, and Triple X.

Is it Effective?

The effectiveness ratings for **PYRETHRUM** are as follows:

Effective for... Head lice and crablice infestations.

Ineffective for... Scabies infestation (mites).

How does it work?

The active chemicals, the pyrethrins, are toxic to insect nervous systems.

Are there safety concerns?

Pyrethrum, when less than two grams are applied to the skin, is possibly safe for most people. While pyrethrum has limited toxicity at low doses, it can cause some side effects such as headache, ringing of the ears, nausea, tingling of fingers and toes, breathing problems, and other symptoms of nerve toxicity. Some people might have allergic reactions to pyrethrum. People at the greatest risk of allergic reactions are those who are allergic to plants in the Asteraceae/Compositae family such as ragweed, chrysanthemums, marigolds, daisies, and many other herbs.

Do not use pyrethrum on children less than two years old.

Do not take pyrethrum if: You are pregnant or breast-feeding. • You are allergic to ragweed, chrysanthemums, marigolds, daisies, and other related plants. • You have asthma.

Are there any interactions with medications?

It is not known if pyrethrum interacts with any medicines.

Before taking pyrethrum, talk with your healthcare professional if you take any medications.

PYRIDOXINE (VITAMIN B6)

What other names is the product known by?

Adermine Hydrochloride, B6, B Complex Vitamin, Pyridoxal, Pyridoxamine, Pyridoxine Hydrochloride.

What is it?

Pyridoxine is a vitamin. It can be found in certain foods such as cereals, beans, vegetables, liver, meat, and eggs. It can also be made in a laboratory.

Is it Effective?

The effectiveness ratings for **PYRIDOXINE (VITAMIN B6)** are as follows:

Effective for... Treatment and prevention of pyridoxine deficiency • Treating a type of anemia called sideroblastic anemia • Treating some types of seizures in infants.

Likely Effective for... Reducing elevated blood levels of homocysteine, a substance thought to be involved in heart disease.

Possibly Effective for... Upset stomach and vomiting in pregnancy • Premenstrual syndrome (PMS) • Behavior disorders in children with low levels of a brain chemical called serotonin • Kidney stones • Movement disorders (tardive dyskinesia) in people taking medicines for mental disorders • Reducing lung cancer risk in men who smoke.

Possibly Ineffective for... Autism • Carpal tunnel syndrome • Preventing another stroke • Alzheimer's disease.

Insufficient Evidence to Rate Effectiveness for... Preventing reblockage of blood vessels after angioplasty, boosting the immune system, muscle cramps, eye problems, kidney problems, night leg cramps, arthritis, allergies, asthma, attention deficit-hyperactivity disorder (ADHD), Lyme disease, and other conditions.

How does it work?
Pyridoxine is required for the proper function of sugars, fats, and proteins in the body. It is also required for the proper growth and development of the brain, nerves, skin, and many other parts of the body.

Are there safety concerns?
Pyridoxine is safe for most people. In some people, pyridoxine might cause nausea, vomiting, stomach pain, loss of appetite, headache, tingling, sleepiness, and other side effects. Long-term use of high doses might cause certain brain and nerve problems.

Pyridoxine is also safe for pregnant or breast-feeding women when taken in the amounts recommended. These amounts are 1.9 mg per day for pregnant women and 2.0 mg per day for breast-feeding women.

Are there any interactions with medications?
Amiodarone (Cordarone). Amiodarone (Cordarone) might increase your sensitivity to sunlight. Taking vitamin B6 (pyridoxine) along with amiodarone (Cordarone) might increase the chances of sunburn, blistering, or rashes on areas of skin exposed to sunlight. Be sure to wear sunblock and protective clothing when spending time in the sun.
Levodopa. The body breaks down levodopa to get rid of it. Vitamin B6 (pyridoxine) can increase how quickly the body breaks down and gets rid of levodopa. But this is only a problem if you are taking levodopa alone. Most people take levodopa along with carbidopa (Sinemet). Carbidopa prevents this interaction from occurring. If you are taking levodopa without carbidopa do not take vitamin B6.
Phenytoin (Dilantin). The body breaks down phenytoin (Dilantin) to get rid of it. Pyridoxine (vitamin B6) might increase how quickly the body breaks down phenytoin. Taking pyridoxine (vitamin B6) and taking phenytoin (Dilantin) might decrease the effectiveness of phenytoin (Dilantin) and increase the possibility of seizures. Do not take large doses of pyridoxine (vitamin B6) if you are taking phenytoin (Dilantin).
Phenobarbital (Luminal). The body breaks down phenobarbital (Luminal) to get rid of it. Pyridoxine might increase how quickly the body breaks down phenobarbital (Luminal). This could decrease the effectiveness of phenobarbital (Luminal).

PYRUVATE

What other names is the product known by?
Acetylformic Acid, Alpha-Keto Acid, Alpha-Ketopropionic Acid, Calcium Pyruvate, Creatine Pyruvate, Magnesium Pyruvate, 2-Oxopropanoate, 2-Oxypropanoic Acid, Potassium Pyruvate, Proacemic Acid, Pyruvic Acid, Sodium Pyruvate.

What is it?
Pyruvate is a supplement. It is also produced in the body as a result of breaking down sugar (glucose) for energy.

Is it Effective?
The effectiveness ratings for **PYRUVATE** are as follows:
Possibly Effective for... Aging skin. Pyruvic acid is sometimes applied to the skin as a facial peel.
Insufficient Evidence to Rate Effectiveness for... Weight loss and obesity, improving athletic performance, cataracts, and cancer.

How does it work?
Pyruvate might contribute to weight loss by increasing the breakdown of fat.

Are there safety concerns?
Pyruvate seems to be safe when taken by mouth. Side effects such as stomach upset, gas, bloating, and diarrhea can occur when large amounts are taken.

Pyruvic acid facial peels seem to be safe when applied by a health professional. It can cause severe skin burning and should be applied only to small patches of skin at a time.

Do not use pyruvate if: You are pregnant or breast-feeding. • You have a heart condition called cardiomyopathy.

Are there any interactions with medications?
It is not known if pyruvate interacts with any medicines.
Before taking pyruvate, talk with your healthcare professional if you take any medications.

Medical professionals should consult the Professional Version at www.NaturalDatabase.com.

QUASSIA

What other names is the product known by?

Amargo, Bitter-Ash, Bitter Wood, Bitterwood, Jamaican Quassia, Picrasma, Picrasma excelsa, Quassia amara, Quassia Bark, Ruda, Surinam Quassia, Surinam Wood.

What is it?

Quassia is a plant. The wood is used as medicine.

Is it Effective?

The effectiveness ratings for **QUASSIA** are as follows:
Possibly Effective for... Use on the scalp for head lice.
Insufficient Evidence to Rate Effectiveness for... Appetite loss, indigestion, constipation, fever, intestinal worms, and other conditions.

How does it work?

Quassia contains chemicals that might increase stomach acid and bile secretions, perhaps accounting for appetite stimulant and digestive effects. Other chemicals may have activity against bacteria, fungi, and mosquito larvae.

Are there safety concerns?

Quassia does not appear to be safe for most people when taken by mouth in medicinal amounts. It can cause side effects such as irritation of the mouth, throat, and digestive tract along with nausea and vomiting. Long-term use can cause vision changes and blindness. In very large doses, it could cause abnormal heart function.

It is not known if quassia is safe for use on the skin (including the scalp) or rectally.

Do not take quassia if: You are pregnant or breast-feeding. • You have digestive tract problems or diseases, such as stomach or intestinal ulcers, Crohn's disease, infections, and many other conditions.

Are there any interactions with medications?

Antacids. Antacids are used to decrease stomach acid. Quassia may increase stomach acid. By increasing stomach acid, quassia might decrease the effectiveness of antacids. Some antacids include calcium carbonate (Tums, others), dihydroxyaluminum sodium carbonate (Rolaids, others), magaldrate (Riopan), magnesium sulfate (Bilagog), aluminum hydroxide (Amphojel), and others.
Digoxin (Lanoxin). Quassia is a type of laxative called a stimulant laxative. Stimulant laxatives can decrease potassium levels in the body. Low potassium levels can increase the risk of side effects of digoxin (Lanoxin).
Medications that decrease stomach acid (H2-Blockers). Quassia might increase stomach acid. By increasing stomach acid, quassia might decrease the effectiveness of some medications that decrease stomach acid, called H2-Blockers. Some medications that decrease stomach acid include cimetidine (Tagamet), ranitidine (Zantac), nizatidine (Axid), and famotidine (Pepcid).
Medications that decrease stomach acid (Proton pump inhibitors). Quassia might increase stomach acid. By increasing stomach acid, quassia might decrease the effectiveness of medications that are used to decrease stomach acid, called proton pump inhibitors. Some medications that decrease stomach acid include omeprazole (Prilosec), lansoprazole (Prevacid), rabeprazole (Aciphex), pantoprazole (Protonix), and esomeprazole (Nexium).
Water pills (Diuretic drugs). Quassia is a laxative. Some laxatives can decrease potassium in the body. "Water pills" can also decrease potassium in the body. Taking quassia along with "water pills" might decrease potassium in the body too much. Some "water pills" that can decrease potassium include chlorothiazide (Diuril), chlorthalidone (Thalitone), furosemide (Lasix), hydrochlorothiazide (HCTZ, HydroDiuril, Microzide), and others.

QUEBRACHO

What other names is the product known by?

Aspidosperma quebracho-blanco, Quebracho Blanco, White Quebracho.

What is it?

Quebracho is a plant. The bark is used as medicine. Be careful not to confuse quebracho blanco (white quebracho) with quebracho colorado (red quebracho). Both are known as quebracho.

Is it Effective?

The effectiveness ratings for **QUEBRACHO** are as follows:
Insufficient Evidence to Rate Effectiveness for... Asthma, lung disorders, cough, high blood pressure, spasms, fluid retention, menstrual cramps, fever, increasing sex drive, and other conditions.

How does it work?

There isn't enough information to know how quebracho might work.

Are there safety concerns?

There isn't enough information to know if quebracho is safe in medicinal amounts. It can cause some side effects including drooling, headache, outbreaks of sweating, dizziness, stupor, and sleepiness. In large doses, it can cause nausea and vomiting.

Do not take quebracho if: You are pregnant or breast-feeding.

Are there any interactions with medications?

It is not known if quebracho interacts with any medicines.
Before taking quebracho, talk with your healthcare professional if you take any medications.

QUEEN'S DELIGHT

What other names is the product known by?

Cockup Hat, Marcory, Queens Delight, Queen's Root, Queens Root, Silver Leaf, Stillingia, Stillingia sylvatica, Stillingia tenuis, Yaw Root.

What is it?

Queen's delight is a plant. The root is used as medicine.

Is it Effective?

The effectiveness ratings for **QUEEN'S DELIGHT** are as follows:
Insufficient Evidence to Rate Effectiveness for... Digestive disorders, "blood purification," liver disease, gallbladder disease, skin diseases, constipation, causing vomiting, laryngitis, hemorrhoids, and other conditions.

How does it work?

There isn't enough information to know how queen's delight might work.

Are there safety concerns?

Queen's delight is UNSAFE when used by mouth or on the skin. It contains chemicals that might cause cancer. It might also activate viruses harbored in the body. Queen's delight is very irritating and can cause swelling wherever it comes in contact with the body such as the skin, mouth, throat, and digestive tract. It can also cause vomiting, diarrhea, and nausea. In large amounts, queen's delight may cause a burning sensation of the mouth and throat, painful urination, aches and pains, itching, rash, cough, depression, fatigue, and sweating.

Do not take queen's delight if: You are pregnant or breast-feeding. • You have digestive tract diseases or disorders, including ulcers, Crohn's disease, infections, and other conditions.

Are there any interactions with medications?

It is not known if queen's delight interacts with any medicines.
Before taking queen's delight, talk with your healthcare professional if you take any medications.

QUERCETIN

What other names is the product known by?

Citrus Bioflavonoid, Citrus Bioflavonoids, Meletin, Sophretin.

What is it?

Quercetin is a plant pigment (flavonoid). It is found in many plants and foods, such as red wine, onions, green tea, apples berries, Ginkgo biloba, St. John's Wort, American Elder, and others. People use quercetin in medicines.

Is it Effective?

The effectiveness ratings for **QUERCETIN** are as follows:
Possibly Effective for... Prostate inflammation.
Insufficient Evidence to Rate Effectiveness for... Hardening of the arteries (artherosclerosis), heart disease, high cholesterol, diabetes, cataracts, hayfever (allergic rhinitis), stomach and intestinal ulcers, schizophrenia, inflammation, asthma, gout, viral infections, chronic fatigue syndrome (CFS), preventing cancer, and other conditions.

Medical professionals should consult the Professional Version at www.NaturalDatabase.com.

How does it work?

Quercetin has antioxidant and anti-inflammatory effects which might help reduce prostate inflammation.

Are there safety concerns?

Quercetin appears to be safe for most people when up to 500 mg twice daily are taken by mouth. It is not known if larger amounts might be safe. Quercetin can cause headache and tingling of the arms and legs. Very high doses might cause kidney damage.

Do not take quercetin if: You are pregnant or breast-feeding.

Are there any interactions with medications?

Antibiotics (Quinolone antibiotics). Taking quercetin along with some antibiotics might decrease the effectiveness of some antibiotics. Some scientists think that quercetin might prevent some antibiotics from killing bacteria. But it's too soon to know if this is a big concern. Some of these antibiotics that might interact with quercetin include ciprofloxacin (Cipro), enoxacin (Penetrex), norfloxacin (Chibroxin, Noroxin), sparfloxacin (Zagam), trovafloxacin (Trovan), and grepafloxacin (Raxar).

QUILLAIA

What other names is the product known by?

China Bark, Murillo Bark, Panama Bark, Quillaja, Quillaja saponaria, Soap Tree, Soap Tree Bark, Soapbark.

What is it?

Quillaia is a plant. The inner bark is used as medicine.

Is it Effective?

The effectiveness ratings for **QUILLAIA** are as follows:
Insufficient Evidence to Rate Effectiveness for... Cough, bronchitis, lung ailments, skin sores, athlete's foot, itchy scalp, dandruff, vaginal discharge, and other conditions.

How does it work?

Quillaia contains high concentrations of tannins. Astringent chemicals, such as tannins, can thin mucous to make it easier to cough up. Quillaia also contains a chemical which may help stimulate the immune system.

Are there safety concerns?

Quillaia doesn't appear to be safe when taken by mouth in medicinal doses. Plants such as quillaia that contain high amounts of tannins can cause stomach and intestinal disturbances, and kidney and liver damage. Quillaia also contains chemicals called oxalates that can lower blood calcium levels and cause kidney stones. Quillaia use is also associated with diarrhea, stomach pain, serious breathing problems, convulsions, coma, red blood cell destruction, and kidney failure. It can also irritate and damage the lining of the mouth, throat, and digestive tract.

It is not known if quillaia is safe when used on the skin or in the vagina. If inhaled, the powder can cause sneezing.

While quillaia probably isn't safe for anyone to take, some people should be especially careful to avoid use.

Do not take quillaia if: You are pregnant or breast-feeding. • You have kidney disease. • You have stomach or intestinal disorders or diseases.

Are there any interactions with medications?

Medications taken by mouth (Oral drugs). Quillaia contains a large amount of chemicals called tannins. Tannins absorb substances in the stomach and intestines. Taking quillaia along with medications taken by mouth can decrease how much medicine your body absorbs, and decrease the effectiveness of your medicine. To prevent this interaction, take quillaia at least one hour after medications you take by mouth.
Metformin (Glucophage). Metformin (Glucophage) is used to help decrease blood sugar. Quillaia might decrease how much metformin (Glucophage) the body absorbs. Taking quillaia along with metformin (Glucophage) might decrease the effectiveness of metformin (Glucophage) for lowering blood sugar. Monitor your blood sugar closely. The dose of your metformin (Glucophage) might need to be changed.

QUINCE

What other names is the product known by?
Cognassier, Coing, Cydonia oblongata, Cydonia vulgaris, Marmelo, Membrillo, Pyrus cydonia, Quitte, Quittenbaum.

What is it?
Quince is a plant. The seed is used as medicine.

Is it Effective?
The effectiveness ratings for **QUINCE** are as follows:
Insufficient Evidence to Rate Effectiveness for... Digestive disorders, diarrhea, coughs, stomach and intestinal inflammation, skin injuries, inflammation of the joints, eye discomfort, and other conditions.

How does it work?
There isn't enough information to know how quince might work.

Are there safety concerns?
There isn't enough information to know if quince is safe for medicinal use. The seeds contain cyanide, which suggests that quince seeds might not be safe.

Do not take quince seed if: You are pregnant or breast-feeding.

Are there any interactions with medications?
Medications taken by mouth (Oral drugs). Quince contains a type of soft fiber called mucilage. Mucilage can decrease how much medicine the body absorbs. Taking quince at the same time you take medications by mouth can decrease the effectiveness of your medication. To prevent this interaction take quince at least one hour after medications you take by mouth.

RABDOSIA RUBESCENS

What other names is the product known by?
Bing Ling Cao, Blushred Rabdosia, Dong Ling Cao, Isodon rubescens, Lui Yue Ling, Po Xue Cao, Rubescens, Sui Mi Ya.

What is it?
Rabdosia rubescens is an herb. The whole plant is used to make medicine.

Is it Effective?
The effectiveness ratings for **RABDOSIA RUBESCENS** are as follows:
Insufficient Evidence to Rate Effectiveness for... Cancer, prostate cancer, benign prostatic hyperplasia (BPH), and other conditions.

How does it work?
Preliminary research suggests Rabdosia rubescens might have cancer-fighting effects.

Are there safety concerns?
It is not known if Rabdosia rubescens is safe.

Do not use Rabdosia rubescens if: You are pregnant or breast-feeding.

Are there any interactions with medications?
It is not known if Rabdosia rubescens interacts with any medicines.
Before taking Rabdosia rubescens, talk with your healthcare professional if you take any medications.

Medical professionals should consult the
Professional Version at www.NaturalDatabase.com.

RADISH

What other names is the product known by?
Black Radish, Black Spanish Radish, Long Black Spanish Radish, Radis, Raphani sativi radix, Round Black Spanish Radish, Small Radish, Spanish Radish, Spanish Black Radish, Turnip Radish.

What is it?
Radish is a plant. The root is used as medicine.

Is it Effective?
The effectiveness ratings for **RADISH** are as follows:
Insufficient Evidence to Rate Effectiveness for... Loss of appetite, inflammation of the mouth and throat, tendency towards infections, fever, colds, cough, digestive disorders caused by bile duct problems, inflammation of the airways such as bronchitis, and other conditions.

How does it work?
Radish root may stimulate digestive juices and bile flow. Radish root may also have activity against bacteria and other microorganisms.

Are there safety concerns?
Radish is safe for most people. Large amounts of radish can irritate the digestive tract.

Do not take radish if: You are pregnant or breast-feeding. • You have gallstones.

Are there any interactions with medications?
It is not known if radish interacts with any medicines.
Before taking radish, talk with your healthcare professional if you take any medications.

RED BUSH TEA

What other names is the product known by?
Aspalathus linearis, Aspalathus contaminatus, Borbonia pinifolia, Kaffree Tea, Psoralea linearis, Red Bush, Rooibos Tea.

What is it?
Red bush tea is made from the branches and twigs of a tree.

Is it Effective?
The effectiveness ratings for **RED BUSH TEA** are as follows:
Insufficient Evidence to Rate Effectiveness for... Suppressing HIV infections, preventing cancer, and preventing aging in the brain.

How does it work?
Red bush tea contains chemicals that might help suppress HIV infection, and might also prevent age-related changes in the brain.

Are there safety concerns?
Red bush tea seems safe for most people when consumed as a beverage. There isn't enough information available to know if red bush tea is safe for use as a medicine.

Do not use red bush tea if: You are pregnant or breast-feeding.

Are there any interactions with medications?
It is not known if red bush tea interacts with any medicines.
Before taking red bush tea, talk with your healthcare professional if you take any medications.

RED CLOVER

What other names is the product known by?

Beebread, Cow Clover, Daidzein, Genistein, Isoflavone, Meadow Clover, Phytoestrogen, Purple Clover, Trefoil, Trifolium, Trifolium pretense, Wild Clover.

What is it?

Red clover is a plant. The flower tops are used to make medicine.

Is it Effective?

The effectiveness ratings for **RED CLOVER** are as follows:

Possibly Ineffective for... High cholesterol in women • Menopausal symptoms, hot flashes.

Insufficient Evidence to Rate Effectiveness for... Prevention of osteoporosis in women, prostate gland symptoms (such as increased nighttime urination) in men, cancer prevention, indigestion, lung problems (cough, bronchitis, asthma), cyclical breast pain, sexually transmitted diseases (STDs), premenstrual syndrome (PMS), skin problems (cancerous growths, burns, eczema, psoriasis), and other conditions.

How does it work?

Red clover contains "isoflavones" which are changed in the body to "phytoestrogens" that are similar to the hormone estrogen.

Are there safety concerns?

Red clover seems safe for most people. It can cause rash-like reactions, muscle ache, headache, nausea, and vaginal bleeding (spotting) in some people.

Do not take red clover if: You are pregnant or breast-feeding. • You have a bleeding disorder. • You have breast cancer. • You have uterine cancer. • You have ovarian cancer. • You have endometriosis. • You have uterine fibroids. • You have a condition called protein S deficiency.

Are there any interactions with medications?

Birth control pills (Contraceptive drugs). Some birth control pills contain estrogen. Red clover might have some of the same effects as estrogen. But red clover isn't as strong as the estrogen in birth control pills. Taking red clover along with birth control pills might decrease the effectiveness of birth control pills. If you take birth control pills along with red clover, use an additional form of birth control such as a condom. Some birth control pills include ethinyl estradiol and levonorgestrel (Triphasil), ethinyl estradiol and norethindrone (Ortho-Novum 1/35, Ortho-Novum 7/7/7), and others.

Estrogens. Large amounts of red clover might have some of the same effects as estrogen. But red clover isn't as strong as estrogen pills. Taking red clover along with estrogen pills might decrease the effects of estrogen pills. Some estrogen pills include conjugated equine estrogens (Premarin), ethinyl estradiol, estradiol, and others.

Medications changed by the liver (Cytochrome P450 1A2 (CYP1A2) substrates). Some medications are changed and broken down by the liver. Red clover might decrease how quickly the liver breaks down some medications. Taking red clover along with some medications that are broken down by the liver can increase the effects and side effects of some medications. Before taking red clover, talk to your healthcare provider if you take any medications that are changed by the liver. Some medications that are changed by the liver include amitriptyline (Elavil), haloperidol (Haldol), ondansetron (Zofran), propranolol (Inderal), theophylline (Theo-Dur, others), verapamil (Calan, Isoptin, others), and others.

Medications changed by the liver (Cytochrome P450 2C19 (CYP2C19) substrates). Some medications are changed and broken down by the liver. Red clover might decrease how quickly the liver breaks down some medications. Taking red clover along with some medications that are broken down by the liver can increase the effects and side effects of some medications. Before taking red clover, talk to your healthcare provider if you take any medications that are changed by the liver. Some medications that are changed by the liver include omeprazole (Prilosec), lansoprazole (Prevacid), and pantoprazole (Protonix); diazepam (Valium); carisoprodol (Soma); nelfinavir (Viracept); and others.

Medications changed by the liver (Cytochrome P450 2C9 (CYP2C9) substrates). Some medications are changed and broken down by the liver. Red clover might decrease how quickly the liver breaks down some medications. Taking red clover along with some medications that are broken down by the liver can increase the effects and side effects of some medications. Before taking red clover, talk to your healthcare provider if you take any medications that are changed by the liver. Some medications that are changed by the liver include diclofenac (Cataflam, Voltaren), ibuprofen (Motrin), meloxicam (Mobic), and piroxicam (Feldene); celecoxib (Celebrex); amitriptyline (Elavil); warfarin (Coumadin); glipizide (Glucotrol); losartan (Cozaar); and others.

Medications changed by the liver (Cytochrome P450 3A4 (CYP3A4) substrates). Some medications are changed and broken down by the liver. Red clover might decrease how quickly the liver breaks down some medications. Taking red clover along with some medications that are broken down by the liver can increase the effects and side effects of some medications. Before taking red clover, talk to your healthcare provider if you are

Medical professionals should consult the Professional Version at www.NaturalDatabase.com.

CONSUMER VERSION

taking any medications that are changed by the liver. Some medications changed by the liver include lovastatin (Mevacor), ketoconazole (Nizoral), itraconazole (Sporanox), fexofenadine (Allegra), triazolam (Halcion), and many others.

Medications that slow blood clotting (Anticoagulant / Antiplatelet drugs). Large amounts of red clover might slow blood clotting. Taking red clover along with medications that also slow clotting might increase the chances of bruising and bleeding. Some medications that slow blood clotting include aspirin, clopidogrel (Plavix), diclofenac (Voltaren, Cataflam, others), ibuprofen (Advil, Motrin, others), naproxen (Anaprox, Naprosyn, others), dalteparin (Fragmin), enoxaparin (Lovenox), heparin, warfarin (Coumadin), and others.

Tamoxifen (Nolvadex). Some types of cancer are affected by hormones in the body. Estrogen-sensitive cancers are cancers that are affected by estrogen levels in the body. Tamoxifen (Nolvadex) is used to help treat and prevent these types of cancer. Red clover seems to also affect estrogen levels in the body. By affecting estrogen in the body, red clover might decrease the effectiveness of tamoxifen (Nolvadex). Do not take red clover if you are taking tamoxifen (Nolvadex).

RED MAPLE

What other names is the product known by?
Acer rubrum, Bird's Eye Maple, Sugar Maple, Swamp Maple.

What is it?
Red maple is a tree. The bark is used to make medicine.

Is it Effective?
The effectiveness ratings for **RED MAPLE** are as follows:
Insufficient Evidence to Rate Effectiveness for... Eye conditions or use as a drying agent.

How does it work?
There isn't enough information to know how red maple might work.

Are there safety concerns?
It is not known if red maple is safe or what the potential side effects might be.
Do not use red maple if: You are pregnant or breast-feeding.

Are there any interactions with medications?
It is not known if red maple interacts with any medicines.
Before taking red maple, talk with your healthcare professional if you take any medications.

RED RASPBERRY

What other names is the product known by?
Framboise, Raspberry, Rubi idaei folium, Rubus idaeus, Rubus strigosus.

What is it?
Red raspberry is a plant. The leaves and fruits are used to make medicine.

Is it Effective?
The effectiveness ratings for **RED RASPBERRY** are as follows:
Possibly Ineffective for... Making labor and delivery easier (red raspberry leaf).
Insufficient Evidence to Rate Effectiveness for... Stomach problems, heart problems, lung problems, diabetes, vitamin deficiencies, fluid retention, skin rash, sore throat, and other conditions.

How does it work?
The chemicals in red raspberry might have antioxidant effects and help relax blood vessels.

Are there safety concerns?
Red raspberry fruit seems safe for most people when used as a medicine, or in amounts found in foods.

Red raspberry leaf might be safe for use in medicinal amounts during late pregnancy under the direct supervision of a healthcare provider.

Do not take red raspberry leaf if: You have breast cancer. • You have uterine cancer. • You have ovarian cancer. • You have endometriosis. • You have uterine fibroids.

Are there any interactions with medications?

It is not known if red raspberry interacts with any medicines.
Before taking red raspberry, talk with your healthcare professional if you take any medications.

RED SANDALWOOD

What other names is the product known by?

Pterocarpus santalinus, Red Sanderswood, Red Saunders, Rubywood, Sandalwood Padauk, Santali lignum rubrum, Sappan.

What is it?

Red sandalwood is a plant. The heartwood is used as medicine.

Is it Effective?

The effectiveness ratings for **RED SANDALWOOD** are as follows:
Insufficient Evidence to Rate Effectiveness for... Digestive tract ailments, fluid retention, coughs, and other conditions.

How does it work?

Red sandalwood might increase the loss of body water through the urine (diuretic effect). It might also have astringent effects that may help reduce diarrhea and break up mucus to make it easier to cough up.

Are there safety concerns?

Red sandalwood is possibly safe for most people. The potential side effects aren't known.

Do not take red sandalwood if: You are pregnant or breast-feeding.

Are there any interactions with medications?

It is not known if red sandalwood interacts with any medicines.
Before taking red sandalwood, talk with your healthcare professional if you take any medications.

RED SOAPWORT

What other names is the product known by?

Bouncing-Bet, Saponaria officinalis, Saponariae rubrae radix, Soapwort.

What is it?

Red soapwort is a plant. The root is used as medicine. Be careful not to confuse red soapwort with white soapwort.

Is it Effective?

The effectiveness ratings for **RED SOAPWORT** are as follows:
Insufficient Evidence to Rate Effectiveness for... Inflammation of the airways (bronchitis), poison ivy, acne, psoriasis, eczema, boils, and other conditions.

How does it work?

Red soapwort contains chemicals which may thin mucus and make it easier to cough up.

Are there safety concerns?

Red soapwort is safe for most people when used on the skin. There are no reported side effects when red soapwort is used in soaps and shampoos.

Red soapwort might be safe when taken by mouth. It can cause some side effects including stomach irritation, nausea, and vomiting.

Do not take red soapwort if: You are pregnant or breast-feeding. • You have stomach or intestinal disorders such as ulcers or inflammatory bowl disease.

Are there any interactions with medications?

It is not known if red soapwort interacts with any medicines.
Before taking red soapwort, talk with your healthcare professional if you take any medications.

RED YEAST

What other names is the product known by?

Hong Qu, Monascus, Monascus purpureus, Red Rice Yeast, Red Yeast Rice, Xue Zhi Kang, Zhi Tai.

What is it?

Red yeast is the product of rice fermented with Monascus purpureus yeast. Red yeast supplements are different from red yeast rice sold in Chinese grocery stores. People use red yeast as medicine.

Is it Effective?

The effectiveness ratings for **RED YEAST** are as follows:

Likely Effective for... High cholesterol and triglyceride levels.

Possibly Effective for... High cholesterol and triglyceride levels caused by human immunodeficiency virus (HIV) disease (AIDS).

Insufficient Evidence to Rate Effectiveness for... Indigestion, diarrhea, improving blood circulation, spleen and stomach problems, and other conditions.

How does it work?

Red yeast supplements are manufactured by culturing Monascus purpureus yeast on rice at carefully controlled temperature and growing conditions to increase the concentrations of chemicals that lower blood cholesterol and triglycerides. These chemicals are similar to the prescription drugs known as "statins," including lovastatin (Mevacor) and others.

Are there safety concerns?

Red yeast might be safe for most people when taken by mouth for up to 3 months. There isn't enough information to know if taking it for longer periods is safe. It can cause stomach discomfort, heartburn, intestinal gas, dizziness, and liver function changes.

Rarely, red yeast may cause serious liver disease.

Serious allergic reactions can occur after breathing in red yeast.

Do not give red yeast to children under 18 years old. It might not be safe.

Do not take red yeast if: You are pregnant or breast-feeding. • You have liver disease.

Are there any interactions with medications?

Alcohol. Drinking alcohol might harm the liver. Red yeast might also harm the liver. Taking red yeast along with alcohol might increase the risk of liver damage. Do not drink alcohol if you are taking red yeast.

Cyclosporine (Neoral, Sandimmune). Red yeast might affect the muscles. Cyclosporine (Neoral, Sandimmune) might also affect the muscles. Taking red yeast along with cyclosporine (Neoral, Sandimmune) might cause serious side effects.

Gemfibrozil (Lopid). Gemfibrozil (Lopid) can affect the muscles. Red yeast can also affect the muscles. Taking gemfibrozil along with red yeast might increase the risk of muscle problems.

Levothyroxine. Levothyroxine is used for low thyroid function. Red yeast seems to decrease the thyroid. Taking red yeast along with levothyroxine might decrease the effects of levothyroxine. Some brands that contain levothyroxine include Armour Thyroid, Eltroxin, Estre, Euthyrox, Levo-T, Levothroid, Levoxyl, Synthroid, Unithroid, and others.

Medications used for lowering cholesterol (Statins). Red yeast can help lower cholesterol. Taking red yeast along with other medications used to lower cholesterol might increase the risk of adverse effects. Do not take red yeast if you are already taking medications used for lowering cholesterol. Some medications used for high cholesterol include cerivastatin (Baycol), atorvastatin (Lipitor), lovastatin (Mevacor), pravastatin (Pravachol), simvastatin (Zocor), and others.

Medications that decrease the break down of other medications in the liver (Cytochrome P450 3A4 (CYP3A4) inhibitors). Some medications are changed and broken down by the liver. Some medications might decrease how quickly the liver breaks down red yeast. Taking red yeast along with some medications that decrease the break-down of other medications in the liver can increase the effects and side effects of red yeast. Before taking red yeast, talk to your healthcare provider if you are taking any medications that are changed by the liver. Some medications that might decrease how quickly the liver breaks down red yeast include amiodarone (Cordarone), clarithromycin (Biaxin), diltiazem (Cardizem), erythromycin (E-mycin, Erythrocin), indinavir (Crixivan), ritonavir (Norvir), saquinavir (Fortovase, Invirase), and many others.

Niacin. Niacin can affect the muscles. Red yeast can also affect the muscles. Taking niacin along with red yeast might increase the risk of muscle problems.

RED-SPUR VALERIAN

What other names is the product known by?
Bouncing Bess, Bovis and Soldier, Centranthus ruber, Delicate Bess, Drunken Sailor, Fox's-Brush, Jupiter's Beard, Pretty Betsy, Red Spur Valerian, Red Valerian, Valeriana rubra.

What is it?
Red-spur valerian is a plant. The root is used as medicine.

Is it Effective?
The effectiveness ratings for **RED-SPUR VALERIAN** are as follows:
Insufficient Evidence to Rate Effectiveness for... Use as a sedative.

How does it work?
Red-spur valerian contains a chemical which may have sedative properties.

Are there safety concerns?
There isn't enough information to know if red-spur valerian is safe or what the potential side effects might be.

Do not take red-spur valerian if: You are pregnant or breast-feeding.

Are there any interactions with medications?
It is not known if red-spur valerian interacts with any medicines.
Before taking red-spur valerian, talk with your healthcare professional if you take any medications.

REED HERB

What other names is the product known by?
Common Reed, Ditch Reed, Giant Reed, Phragmites, Phragmites communis, Reed, Roseau Commun, Schilf.

What is it?
Reed herb is a plant. The stem and underground stem (rhizome) are used as medicine.

Is it Effective?
The effectiveness ratings for **REED HERB** are as follows:
Insufficient Evidence to Rate Effectiveness for... Digestive disorders, insect bites, diabetes, leukemia, breast cancer, and other conditions.

How does it work?
Reed herb contains vitamins A and C and some B vitamins. There isn't enough information to know how it might work.

Are there safety concerns?
It is not known if reed herb is safe or what the potential side effects might be.

Do not take reed herb if: You are pregnant or breast-feeding.

Are there any interactions with medications?
It is not known if reed herb interacts with any medicines.
Before taking reed herb, talk with your healthcare professional if you take any medications.

REISHI MUSHROOM

What other names is the product known by?
Ganoderma lucidum, Ling Chih, Ling Zhi, Mannentake, Mushroom Of Immortality, Mushroom of Spiritual Potency, Red Reishi, Reishi, Rei-Shi, Spirit Plant.

What is it?
Reishi mushroom is a fungus. The fruiting body (above ground part) and mycelium (filaments connecting a group of mushrooms) are used as medicine.

Medical professionals should consult the Professional Version at www.NaturalDatabase.com.

CONSUMER VERSION

Medical professionals should consult the Professional Version at www.NaturalDatabase.com.

Is it Effective?

The effectiveness ratings for **REISHI MUSHROOM** are as follows:

Insufficient Evidence to Rate Effectiveness for... Boosting the immune system, high blood pressure, high cholesterol, viral infections, tumors, prostate cancer, inflammatory diseases, heart disease, asthma, bronchitis, stress, kidney disorders, liver disease, HIV disease, altitude sickness, fatigue, chronic fatigue syndrome (CFS), insomnia, stomach ulcers, poisoning, herpes-related pain, shingles, and other conditions.

How does it work?

Reishi mushroom contains chemicals that seem to have a variety of potentially beneficial effects, including activity against tumors (cancer) and beneficial effects on the immune system.

Are there safety concerns?

Reishi mushroom might be safe for most people. It can cause some side effects including dryness of the mouth, throat, and nasal area along with itchiness, stomach upset, nosebleed, and bloody stools. Drinking reishi wine can cause a rash. Breathing in reishi spores can trigger allergies.

Do not take reishi mushroom if: You are pregnant or breast-feeding. • You have low blood pressure. • You have a blood clotting disorder.

Are there any interactions with medications?

Medications that slow blood clotting (Anticoagulant / Antiplatelet drugs). High doses of reishi mushroom might slow blood clotting. Taking reishi mushroom along with medications that also slow clotting might increase the chances of bruising and bleeding. Some medications that slow blood clotting include aspirin, clopidogrel (Plavix), diclofenac (Voltaren, Cataflam, others), ibuprofen (Advil, Motrin, others), naproxen (Anaprox, Naprosyn, others), dalteparin (Fragmin), enoxaparin (Lovenox), heparin, warfarin (Coumadin), and others.

Medications for high blood pressure (Antihypertensive drugs). Reishi mushroom might decrease blood pressure. Taking reishi mushroom along with medications for high blood pressure might cause your blood pressure to go too low. Some medications for high blood pressure include captopril (Capoten), enalapril (Vasotec), losartan (Cozaar), valsartan (Diovan), diltiazem (Cardizem), Amlodipine (Norvasc), hydrochlorothiazide (HydroDIURIL), furosemide (Lasix), and many others.

RESVERATROL

What other names is the product known by?

Cis-Resveratrol, Kojo-Kon, Phytoestrogen, Protykin, Resveratrols, Trans-Resveratrol.

What is it?

Resveratrol is a chemical found in red wine, red grape skins, purple grape juice, mulberries, and in smaller amounts in peanuts. It is used as a medicine.

Is it Effective?

The effectiveness ratings for **RESVERATROL** are as follows:

Insufficient Evidence to Rate Effectiveness for... Hardening of the arteries (atherosclerosis), high cholesterol, and preventing cancer.

How does it work?

Resveratrol might dilate blood vessels and reduce the activity of platelets in blood clotting. Some research suggests that resveratrol has weak estrogen (a female hormone) effects. It may also decrease inflammation.

Are there safety concerns?

There isn't enough information available to know if resveratrol is safe in amounts greater than those typically found in foods.

Do not take resveratrol if: You are pregnant or breast-feeding. • You have breast cancer. • You have uterine cancer. • You have ovarian cancer. • You have endometriosis. • You have uterine fibroids.

Are there any interactions with medications?

Medications that slow blood clotting (Anticoagulant / Antiplatelet drugs). Resveratrol might slow blood clotting. Taking resveratrol along with medications that also slow clotting might increase the chances of bruising and bleeding. Some medications that slow blood clotting include aspirin, clopidogrel (Plavix), diclofenac (Voltaren, Cataflam, others), ibuprofen (Advil, Motrin, others), naproxen (Anaprox, Naprosyn, others), dalteparin (Fragmin), enoxaparin (Lovenox), heparin, warfarin (Coumadin), and others.

562   Natural Medicines Comprehensive Database Consumer Version   (209) 472-2244

Medications changed by the liver (Cytochrome P450 3A4 (CYP3A4) substrates). Some medications are changed and broken down by the liver. Resveratrol might decrease how quickly the liver breaks down some medications. Taking resveratrol along with some medications that are broken down by the liver can increase the effects and side effects of some medications. Before taking resveratrol, talk to your healthcare provider if you are taking any medications that are changed by the liver. Some medications changed by the liver include lovastatin (Mevacor), ketoconazole (Nizoral), itraconazole (Sporanox), fexofenadine (Allegra), triazolam (Halcion), and many others.

RHATANY

What other names is the product known by?
Brazilian Rhatany, Krameria, Krameria argentea, Krameria triandra, Mapato, Peruvian Rhatany, Pumacuchu, Raiz Para Los Dientes, Ratanhiawurzel, Red Rhatany, Rhatanhia, Rhatania, Ratanhiae radix.

What is it?
Rhatany is a plant. The root is used as medicine.

Is it Effective?
The effectiveness ratings for **RHATANY** are as follows:
Insufficient Evidence to Rate Effectiveness for... Intestinal inflammation (enteritis), chest pain (angina), leg ulcers, mild mouth and throat irritation, and other conditions.

How does it work?
Rhatany contains high concentrations of tannins. Astringent chemicals, such as tannins, can reduce inflammation by shrinking tissues and pus.

Are there safety concerns?
Rhatany is possibly safe for most people when taken by mouth for short periods of time. There isn't enough information to know if it is safe for long-term use. It can cause some side effects such as digestive complaints. Rarely, rhatany has caused allergic reactions in the linings of the mouth and throat.

Do not take rhatany if: You are pregnant or breast-feeding.

Are there any interactions with medications?
Medications taken by mouth (Oral drugs). Rhatany contains a large amount of chemicals called tannins. Tannins absorb substances in the stomach and intestines. Taking rhatany along with medications taken by mouth can decrease how much medicine your body absorbs, and decrease the effectiveness of your medicine. To prevent this interaction, take rhatany at least one hour after medications you take by mouth.

RHUBARB

What other names is the product known by?
Chinese Rhubarb, Da Huang, Garden Rhubarb, Himalayan Rhubarb, Indian Rhubarb, Medicinal Rhubarb, Rhei, Rhei radix, Rheum australe, Rheum emodi, Rheum officinale, Rheum palmatum, Rheum tanguticum, Rheum rhabarbarum, Rheum x cultorum, Turkey Rhubarb.

What is it?
Rhubarb is a plant. The root and rhizome (underground stem) are used to make medicine.

Is it Effective?
The effectiveness ratings for **RHUBARB** are as follows:
Possibly Effective for... Cold sores, in combination with sage (Salvia officinalis).
Insufficient Evidence to Rate Effectiveness for... Indigestion, stomach inflammation, hemorrhoids, constipation, diarrhea, or bleeding from the stomach and colon (bowels), and other conditions.

How does it work?
Rhubarb contains several chemicals which might help heal cold sores.

Are there safety concerns?
Rhubarb is SAFE when the root or rhizomes are used in food amounts. It also seems to be safe for most people when taken by mouth for 8 days or less, for medicinal use. It can cause stomach and intestinal pain, watery diarrhea, and uterine contractions. Long-term use can result in muscular weakness, bone loss,

Medical professionals should consult the Professional Version at www.NaturalDatabase.com.

potassium loss, and irregular heart rhythm.
Rhubarb appears to be UNSAFE for children under age 12.

Do not use rhubarb if: You are pregnant or breast-feeding, in amounts greater than those found in food. • You have kidney stones. • You have stomach pain. • You have an intestinal blockage. • You have appendicitis. • You have Crohn's disease. • You have colitis. • You have irritable bowel syndrome (IBS).

Are there any interactions with medications?
Digoxin (Lanoxin). Rhubarb is a type of laxative called a stimulant laxative. Stimulant laxatives can decrease potassium levels in the body. Low potassium levels can increase the risk of side effects of digoxin (Lanoxin).
Medications for inflammation (Corticosteroids). Some medications for inflammation can decrease potassium in the body. Rhubarb is a type of laxative that might also decrease potassium in the body. Taking rhubarb along with some medications for inflammation might decrease potassium in the body too much. Some medications for inflammation include dexamethasone (Decadron), hydrocortisone (Cortef), methylprednisolone (Medrol), prednisone (Deltasone), and others.
Medications taken by mouth (Oral drugs). Rhubarb is a laxative. Laxatives can decrease how much medicine your body absorbs. Decreasing how much medicine your body absorbs can decrease the effectiveness of your medication.
Stimulant laxatives. Rhubarb is a type of laxative called a stimulant laxative. Stimulant laxatives speed up the bowels. Taking rhubarb along with other stimulant laxatives could speed up the bowels too much and cause dehydration and low minerals in the body. Some stimulant laxatives include bisacodyl (Correctol, Dulcolax), cascara, castor oil (Purge), senna (Senokot), and others.
Water pills (Diuretic drugs). Rhubarb is a laxative. Some laxatives can decrease potassium in the body. "Water pills" can also decrease potassium in the body. Taking rhubarb along with "water pills" might decrease potassium in the body too much. Some "water pills" that can decrease potassium include chlorothiazide (Diuril), chlorthalidone (Thalitone), furosemide (Lasix), hydrochlorothiazide (HCTZ, HydroDiuril, Microzide), and others.

RIBOFLAVIN (VITAMIN B2)

What other names is the product known by?
B Complex Vitamin, Flavin, Flavine, Lactoflavin, Riboflavine, Vitamin B-2, Vitamin G.

What is it?
Riboflavin is a B vitamin. It can be found in certain foods such as milk, meat, eggs, nuts, enriched flour, and green vegetables.

Is it Effective?
The effectiveness ratings for **RIBOFLAVIN (VITAMIN B2)** are as follows:
Effective for... Treating and preventing riboflavin deficiency and conditions related to riboflavin deficiency.
Possibly Effective for... Preventing migraine headaches • Preventing cataracts, an eye disorder.
Possibly Ineffective for... Treating migraine headaches.
Insufficient Evidence to Rate Effectiveness for... Acne, muscle cramps, boosting the immune system, aging, maintaining healthy skin and hair, canker sores, memory loss including Alzheimer's disease, lactic acidosis (a serious blood-acid imbalance) in people with acquired immunodeficiency syndrome (AIDS), preventing cervical cancer, and other conditions.

How does it work?
Riboflavin is required for the proper development and function of the skin, lining of the digestive tract, blood cells, and many other parts of the body.

Are there safety concerns?
Riboflavin is safe for most people. In some people, riboflavin can cause the urine to turn a yellow-orange color. When taken in high doses, riboflavin might cause diarrhea, an increase in urine, and other side effects.

Riboflavin is safe for pregnant or breast-feeding women when taken in the amounts recommended. The recommended amounts are 1.4 mg per day for pregnant women and 1.6 mg per day in breast-feeding women.

Are there any interactions with medications?
Drying medications (Anticholinergic drugs). Some drying medications can affect the stomach and intestines. Taking these drying medications with riboflavin (vitamin B2) can increase the amount of riboflavin that is absorbed in the body. But it's not known if this interaction is important.
Medications for depression (Tricyclic antidepressants). Some medications for depression can decrease the amount of riboflavin in the body. This interaction is not a big concern because it only occurs with very large

Medical professionals should consult the Professional Version at www.NaturalDatabase.com.

amounts of some medications for depression.

Phenobarbital (Luminal). Riboflavin is broken down by the body. Phenobarbital might increase how quickly riboflavin is broken down in the body. It is not clear if this interaction is significant.

Probenecid (Benemid). Probenecid (Benemid) can increase how much riboflavin is in the body. This might cause there to be too much riboflavin in the body. But it's not known if this interaction is a big concern.

RIBOSE

What other names is the product known by?
Beta-D-ribofuranose, D-ribose.

What is it?
Ribose is a kind of sugar that is produced by the body. It is used as a medicine.

Is it Effective?
The effectiveness ratings for **RIBOSE** are as follows:

Possibly Effective for... Decreased blood flow through the arteries in the heart (coronary artery disease) • A genetic metabolic disorder called myoadenylate deaminase deficiency (MAD or AMPD deficiency).

Likely Ineffective for... McArdle's disease (a genetic metabolic disorder).

Insufficient Evidence to Rate Effectiveness for... Athletic performance enhancement and other uses.

How does it work?
Ribose is an energy source that the body makes from food. There is some evidence that supplemental ribose might prevent muscle fatigue in people with genetic disorders that prevent sufficient energy production by the body. It might provide extra energy to the heart during exercise in people with heart disease.

Are there safety concerns?
Ribose is possibly safe for most people when taken by mouth for short-term use. However, it can cause some side effects including diarrhea, stomach discomfort, nausea, headache, and low blood sugar.

Do not take ribose if: You are pregnant or breast-feeding. • You have diabetes. • You have low blood sugar (hypoglycemia).

Are there any interactions with medications?
Alcohol. Alcohol might decrease your blood sugar. Ribose might also decrease your blood sugar. Taking ribose along with alcohol might cause your blood sugar to go too low.

Aspirin. Ribose might decrease blood sugar. Large amounts of aspirin might also decrease blood sugar. Taking ribose along with large amounts of aspirin might cause your blood sugar to go too low. But this interaction probably isn't a big concern for most people that take 81 mg of aspirin a day.

Choline Magnesium Trisalicylate (Trilisate). Choline magnesium trisalicylate (Trilisate) might decrease your blood sugar. Ribose might also decrease blood sugar. Taking ribose along with choline magnesium trisalicylate (Trilisate) might cause your blood sugar to be too low. But it is not clear if this interaction is a big concern.

Insulin. Ribose might decrease blood sugar. Insulin is also used to decrease blood sugar. Taking ribose along with insulin might cause your blood sugar to be too low. Monitor your blood sugar closely. The dose of your insulin might need to be changed.

Medications for diabetes (Antidiabetes drugs). Ribose might decrease blood sugar. Diabetes medications are also used to lower blood sugar. Taking ribose along with diabetes medications might cause your blood sugar to go too low. Monitor your blood sugar closely. The dose of your diabetes medication might need to be changed. Some medications used for diabetes include glimepiride (Amaryl), glyburide (DiaBeta, Glynase PresTab, Micronase), insulin, pioglitazone (Actos), rosiglitazone (Avandia), chlorpropamide (Diabinese), glipizide (Glucotrol), tolbutamide (Orinase), and others.

Propranolol (Inderal). Propanolol (Inderal) might decrease blood sugar. Ribose might also decrease blood sugar. Taking ribose along with propanolol (Inderal) might cause your blood sugar to go too low.

Salsalate (Disalcid). Large amounts of salsalate (Disalcid) can cause blood sugar to become low. Taking salsalate along with ribose might cause blood sugar to become too low.

Medical professionals should consult the Professional Version at www.NaturalDatabase.com.

Medical professionals should consult the
Professional Version at www.NaturalDatabase.com.

RICE BRAN

What other names is the product known by?

Dietary Fiber, Oryza sativa, Ricebran Oil, Rice Bran Oil, Stabilized Rice Bran.

What is it?

Rice is a plant. The bran (outer layer of the grain) is used for medicine. Be careful not to confuse rice bran with other forms of bran such as oat and wheat bran.

Is it Effective?

The effectiveness ratings for **RICE BRAN** are as follows:

Possibly Effective for... High cholesterol • Preventing kidney stones in people with high levels of calcium • Allergic skin rash (atopic dermatitis) • Preventing stomach cancer.

Possibly Ineffective for... Preventing cancer of the colon (bowels) or rectum.

Insufficient Evidence to Rate Effectiveness for... Diabetes, high blood pressure, alcoholism, weight loss, AIDS, strengthening the immune system, increasing energy, enhancing athletic performance, improving liver function, preventing heart and blood vessel disease.

How does it work?

Rice bran might help lower cholesterol through its oils, which contain several substances that decrease cholesterol absorption and increase cholesterol elimination. One of the substances in rice bran might decrease calcium absorption, which might help reduce the formation of certain types of kidney stones.

Are there safety concerns?

Rice bran is safe for most people when taken by mouth. Increasing the amount of bran in the diet can cause erratic bowel habits, intestinal gas, and stomach discomfort during the first few weeks.

Rice bran is possibly safe for most people when added to baths. Use of rice bran broth baths can cause itching and skin redness. Rarely, people have experienced rash and itching from rice bran infested with a pest called the straw itch mite.

Do not take rice bran as medicine if: You are pregnant or breast-feeding. • You have a digestive tract problem such as intestinal ulcers, adhesions, conditions that cause narrowing or blockage of the digestive tract, difficulty swallowing, slow digestion, or other stomach or intestinal conditions. • You have low calcium blood levels. • You have low iron levels, or anemia.

Are there any interactions with medications?

Medications taken by mouth (Oral drugs). Rice bran contains a large amount of fiber. Fiber can decrease how much medicine the body absorbs. Taking rice bran along with medicine you take by mouth can decrease the effectiveness of your medication. To prevent this interaction take rice bran at least one hour after medications you take by mouth.

RNA AND DNA

What other names is the product known by?

DNA, DeoxyNucleic Acid, Deoxyribonucleic Acid, Nuclei Acids, Nucleic, Nucleic Acid, Nucleic Acids, Nucleotides, Purines, Pyrimidines, RNA, RNA-DNA, RNA/DNA, Ribonucleic Acid.

What is it?

RNA and DNA are chemical compounds that can be made by the body. They can also be made in a laboratory. The chemical compounds are used as medicine.

Is it Effective?

The effectiveness ratings for **RNA AND DNA** are as follows:

Possibly Effective for... Shortening recovery from surgery or illness.

Possibly Ineffective for... Burn injury recovery.

Insufficient Evidence to Rate Effectiveness for... Alzheimer's disease, improving memory, depression, sagging skin, decreased sex drive, aging, eczema, psoriasis, hives, shingles, and other conditions.

How does it work?

RNA (ribonucleic acid) and DNA (deoxyribonucleic acid) are chemicals called nucleotides that are made by the body. They appear to be essential under conditions of rapid growth such as intestinal development, liver surgery or injury, and also during challenges to the immune system.

Are there safety concerns?

RNA and DNA appear to be safe for most people when taken by mouth or injected under the skin. Injections can cause itching, redness, and swelling at the injection site.

Do not take RNA and DNA as medicine if: You are pregnant or breast-feeding.

Are there any interactions with medications?

It is not known if RNA and DNA interact with any medicines.
Before taking RNA and DNA, talk with your healthcare professional if you take any medications.

ROMAN CHAMOMILE

What other names is the product known by?

Anthemis nobilis, Chamomilla, Chamomile, Chamomillae ramane flos, Chamaemelum nobile, English Chamomile, Fleur De camomille Romaine, Flores Anthemidis, Garden Chamomile, Grosse Kamille, Ground Apple, Low Chamomile, Manzanilla, Romische Kamille, Sweet Chamomile, Whig Plant.

What is it?

Roman chamomile is a plant. The flowerheads are used to make medicine.

Is it Effective?

The effectiveness ratings for **ROMAN CHAMOMILE** are as follows:
Insufficient Evidence to Rate Effectiveness for... Indigestion, nausea, vomiting, painful periods, sore throat, sinusitis, eczema, wounds, sore nipples and gums, liver and gallbladder problems, frostbite, diaper rash, hemorrhoids, and other conditions.

How does it work?

Roman chamomile contains chemicals that can help decrease gas (flatulence), relax muscles, and cause sedation. Depending on the dose it can either relieve or cause nausea.

Are there safety concerns?

Roman chamomile seems safe for most people when used orally for medicinal purposes and in foods. In large amounts it can cause vomiting. It can also cause an allergic reaction in people sensitive to ragweed, marigolds, daisies, or similar herbs.

Do not use Roman chamomile if: You are pregnant or breast-feeding. • You are allergic to ragweed, marigolds, daisies, or similar herbs.

Are there any interactions with medications?

It is not known if Roman chamomile interacts with any medicines.
Before taking Roman chamomile talk to your doctor if you take any medications.

ROSE GERANIUM OIL

What other names is the product known by?

Aetheroleum Pelargonii, Algerian Geranium Oil, Bourbon Geranium Oil, Moroccan Geranium Oil, Oleum Geranii, Pelargonium graveolens, Pelargonium Oil.

What is it?

Rose geranium oil is derived from the leaves and stem of the rose geranium plant. People use it for medicine. Be careful not to confuse rose geranium oil with East Indian or Turkish geranium oil which is derived from a different plant.

Is it Effective?

The effectiveness ratings for **ROSE GERANIUM OIL** are as follows:
Insufficient Evidence to Rate Effectiveness for... Diarrhea, neuropathic pain, and use as an astringent.

Medical professionals should consult the Professional Version at www.NaturalDatabase.com.

How does it work?
There isn't enough information to know how rose geranium oil might work.

Are there safety concerns?
There isn't enough information to know if rose geranium oil is safe in medicinal amounts. Rarely, rose geranium oil causes allergic skin reactions.

Do not take rose geranium oil in medicinal amounts if: You are pregnant or breast-feeding.

Are there any interactions with medications?
It is not known if rose geranium oil interacts with any medicines.
Before taking rose geranium oil, talk with your healthcare professional if you take any medications.

ROSE HIP

What other names is the product known by?
Cynosbatos, Dog Rose, Hip, Hipberry, Hip Fruit, Hip Sweet, Hop Fruit, Rosa de Castillo, Rosae Pseudofructus Cum Semen, Wild Boar Fruit, Rosa Canina, Rosa Alba, Rosa Centifolia, Rosa Damascena, Rosa Gallica, Rosa Rugosa, Rosa Villosa, Rosa Pomifera, Satapatri, Satapatrika.

What is it?
Rose hips are the round portion of the rose flower below the petals. Rose hips contain the seeds of the rose plant. Dried rose hips and the seeds are used to make medicine.

Is it Effective?
The effectiveness ratings for **ROSE HIP** are as follows:
Insufficient Evidence to Rate Effectiveness for... Preventing and treating colds, infections, fever, improving immune function, stomach irritations, diarrhea, arthritis, diabetes, and other conditions.

How does it work?
Some people use rose hip as a source of vitamin C. It is true that fresh rose hip contains vitamin C. But processing and drying of the plant destroys most of the vitamin C.

Are there safety concerns?
Rose hip seems safe for most adults. Rose hip can cause some side effects such as nausea, vomiting, diarrhea, heartburn, stomach cramps, fatigue, headache, inability to sleep, and others. Inhaling rose hip dust can cause an allergic reaction in some people.

Do not take rose hip if: You are pregnant or breast-feeding. • You have diabetes. • You have sickle-cell disease. • You have a condition called glucose-6-phosphate dehydrogenase (G6PD) deficiency. • You have an iron-related disorder such as hemochromatosis, thalassemia, or some types of anemia.

Are there any interactions with medications?
Aspirin. The body breaks down aspirin to get rid of it. Rose hip contains large amounts of vitamin C. Large amounts of vitamin C might decrease the breakdown of aspirin. Taking large amount of rosehip along with aspirin might increase the effects and side effects of aspirin. Do not take large amounts of vitamin C if you take large amounts of aspirin.
Aluminum. Aluminum is found in most antacids. Rose hips contain vitamin C. Vitamin C can increase how much aluminum the body absorbs. But it isn't clear if this interaction is a big concern. Take rose hip two hours before or four hours after antacids.
Choline Magnesium Trisalicylate (Trilisate). Rose hip contains vitamin C. Vitamin C might decrease how quickly the body gets rid of choline magnesium trisalicylate (Trilisate). But it is not clear if this interaction is a big concern.
Estrogens. Rose hip contains a large amount of vitamin C. Vitamin C can increase how much estrogen the body absorbs. Taking rose hip along with estrogen can increase the effects and side effects of estrogens. Some estrogen pills include conjugated equine estrogens (Premarin), ethinyl estradiol, estradiol, and others.
Fluphenazine (Prolixin). Rose hip contains vitamin C. Large amounts of vitamin C might increase how quickly the body gets rid of fluphenazine (Prolixin). Taking rose hip along with fluphenazine (Prolixin) might decrease the effectiveness of fluphenazine (Prolixin).
Salsalate (Disalcid). Rose hip contains vitamin C. Vitamin C might decrease how quickly the body gets rid of salsalate (Disalcid). Taking rose hip along with salsalate (Disalcid) might increase the effects and side effects of salsalate.
Warfarin (Coumadin). Warfarin (Coumadin) is used to slow blood clotting. Rose hip contains vitamin C. Large

amounts of vitamin C might decrease the effectiveness of warfarin (Coumadin). Decreasing the effectiveness of warfarin (Coumadin) might increase the risk of clotting. Be sure to have your blood checked regularly. The dose of your warfarin (Coumadin) might need to be changed.

ROSEMARY

What other names is the product known by?
Compass Plant, Compass Weed, Old Man, Polar Plant, Rosmarinus officinalis, Rusmari.

What is it?
Rosemary is an herb. The leaf is used to make medicine.

Is it Effective?
The effectiveness ratings for **ROSEMARY** are as follows:
Possibly Effective for... Hair loss, in combination with thyme, lavender, and cedarwood.
Possibly Ineffective for... Causing abortions.
Insufficient Evidence to Rate Effectiveness for... Gas (flatulence), indigestion, increasing menstrual flow, gout, cough, headache, liver and gallbladder problems, high blood pressure, toothache, eczema, joint or muscle pain, and other conditions.

How does it work?
Although it's not clear how rosemary works for hair loss, applying it to the scalp irritates the skin and increases blood circulation.

Are there safety concerns?
Rosemary is safe when consumed in amounts found in foods, and seems safe for most people when used as a medicine. The undiluted oil is UNSAFE for use. Taking large amounts of rosemary can cause vomiting, uterine bleeding, kidney irritation, increased sun sensitivity, skin redness, and allergic reactions.

Do not use rosemary as a medicine if: You are pregnant or breast-feeding. • You have a seizure disorder.

Are there any interactions with medications?
It is not known if rosemary interacts with any medicines.
Before taking rosemary, talk with your healthcare professional if you take any medications.

ROSEROOT

What other names is the product known by?
Arctic Root, Golden Root, King's Crown, Lignum rhodium, Rhodiola, Rodia riza, Rhodiola rosea, Rose Root, Rose Root extract, Rosenroot, Sedum rhodiola, Sedum rosea.

What is it?
Roseroot is a plant. The root is used as medicine.

Is it Effective?
The effectiveness ratings for **ROSEROOT** are as follows:
Insufficient Evidence to Rate Effectiveness for... Fatigue, depression, stress-associated heart disorders, high cholesterol, irregular heartbeat, cancer, aging, diabetes, hearing loss, tuberculosis, sexual problems, increasing energy, improving athletic performance, increasing mental ability, and other conditions.

How does it work?
Roseroot extracts might help protect cells from damage, regulate heartbeat, and have the potential for improving learning and memory. However, none of these effects have been studied in humans.

Are there safety concerns?
Roseroot seems to be safe when taken by mouth, short-term, for up to four weeks. The safety of long-term use is not known. The potential side effects of roseroot are not known.
Do not take roseroot if: You are pregnant or breast-feeding.

Are there any interactions with medications?
It is not known if roseroot interacts with any medicines.
Before taking roseroot, talk with your healthcare professional if you take any medications.

Natural Medicines Comprehensive Database Consumer Version

ROSINWEED

What other names is the product known by?

Compass Weed, Pilot Weed, Polar Plant, Silphium laciniatum.

What is it?

Rosinweed is a plant. The root is used as medicine.

Is it Effective?

The effectiveness ratings for **ROSINWEED** are as follows:
Insufficient Evidence to Rate Effectiveness for... Digestive disorders.

How does it work?

Rosinweed root is claimed to reduce edema (excess body water with swelling), cause sweating, and relieve spasms. None of these claims has been tested scientifically.

Are there safety concerns?

It is not known if rosinweed is safe or what the potential side effects might be.

Do not take rosinweed if: You are pregnant or breast-feeding.

Are there any interactions with medications?

It is not known if rosinweed interacts with any medicines.
Before taking rosinweed, talk with your healthcare professional if you take any medications.

ROYAL JELLY

What other names is the product known by?

Apis mellifera, Bee Saliva, Bee Spit, Honey Bee Milk, Honey Bee's Milk.

What is it?

Royal jelly is a milky secretion produced by worker honey bees. Royal jelly is used as medicine.

Is it Effective?

The effectiveness ratings for **ROYAL JELLY** are as follows:
Insufficient Evidence to Rate Effectiveness for... High cholesterol, asthma, hayfever, liver disease, pancreatitis, insomnia, premenstrual syndrome (PMS), stomach ulcers, kidney disease, bone fractures, skin disorders, baldness, boosting immunity, and other conditions.

How does it work?

Some scientific research suggests that royal jelly might have a beneficial effect on cholesterol levels. It also might help decrease symptoms of PMS.

Are there safety concerns?

Royal jelly might be safe for most people. It can cause serious allergic reactions including asthma, swelling of the throat, and death. Rarely, it might cause the colon to bleed, accompanied by stomach pain and bloody diarrhea.

There isn't enough information to know if royal jelly is safe when applied directly to the skin. It has caused inflammation and allergic rash when applied to the scalp.

Do not take royal jelly if: You are pregnant or breast-feeding. • You have inflamed skin (dermatitis). • You have asthma.

Are there any interactions with medications?

Warfarin (Coumadin). Royal jelly might increase the effects of warfarin (Coumadin). Taking royal jelly with warfarin (Coumadin) might result in an increased chance of bruising or bleeding.

Medical professionals should consult the Professional Version at www.NaturalDatabase.com.

RUE

What other names is the product known by?

Common Rue, Garden Rue, German Rue, Herb-of-Grace, Herbygrass, Raute, Ruda, Rue Officinale, Ruta graveolens, Rutae folium, Rutae herba, Ruta graveolens.

What is it?

Rue is a plant. The above ground parts are used to make medicine.

Is it Effective?

The effectiveness ratings for **RUE** are as follows:
Insufficient Evidence to Rate Effectiveness for... Menstrual disorders, indigestion, heart palpitations, nervousness, fever, diarrhea, breathing problems, multiple sclerosis (MS), Bell's palsy, arthritis, sprains, earaches, toothaches, warts, headaches, and other conditions.

How does it work?

The chemicals in rue help decrease muscle contractions and reduce swelling (inflammation).

Are there safety concerns?

Rue is considered safe when consumed in food amounts. It is UNSAFE when used as a medicine. It can cause side effects such as stomach irritation, changes in mood, sleep problems, dizziness, spasms, skin disorders, sensitivity to the sun, and kidney and liver problems.

Do not use rue if: You are pregnant or breast-feeding. • You have kidney problems. • You have liver problems. • You have stomach or intestinal problems. • You have urinary tract problems.

Are there any interactions with medications?

Medications that increase sensitivity to sunlight (Photosensitizing drugs). Some medications can increase sensitivity to sunlight. Rue might also increase your sensitivity to sunlight. Taking rue along with medication that increase sensitivity to sunlight could increase the chances of sunburn, blistering or rashes on areas of skin exposed to sunlight. Be sure to wear sunblock and protective clothing when spending time in the sun. Some drugs that cause photosensitivity include amitriptyline (Elavil), Ciprofloxacin (Cipro), norfloxacin (Noroxin), lomefloxacin (Maxaquin), ofloxacin (Floxin), levofloxacin (Levaquin), sparfloxacin (Zagam), gatifloxacin (Tequin), moxifloxacin (Avelox), trimethoprim/sulfamethoxazole (Septra), tetracycline, methoxsalen (8-methoxypsoralen, 8-MOP, Oxsoralen), and Trioxsalen (Trisoralen).

RUPTUREWORT

What other names is the product known by?

Bruchkraut, Flax weed, Herniaria glabra, Herniaria hirsuta, Herniariae herba, Herniary.

What is it?

Rupturewort is a plant. The above ground parts are used as medicine.

Is it Effective?

The effectiveness ratings for **RUPTUREWORT** are as follows:
Insufficient Evidence to Rate Effectiveness for... Urinary tract disorders, problems with the airways, nerve inflammation, gout, arthritis, rheumatism, fluid retention, "purifying the blood," and other conditions.

How does it work?

Rupturewort contains chemicals that might help stop spasms and promote the loss of water from the body through the urine.

Are there safety concerns?

It is not known if rupturewort is safe or what the potential side effects might be.

Do not take rupturewort if: You are pregnant or breast-feeding.

Are there any interactions with medications?

It is not known if rupturewort interacts with any medicines.
Before taking rupturewort, talk with your healthcare professional if you take any medications.

Medical professionals should consult the Professional Version at www.NaturalDatabase.com.

RUSTY-LEAVED RHODODENDRON

What other names is the product known by?
Rhododendri Ferruginei Folium, Rhododendron ferrugineum, Rosebay, Rust-Red Rhododendron, Rusty Leaved Rhododendron, Snow Rose.

What is it?
Rusty-leaved rhododendron is a plant. The leaves are used as medicine.

Is it Effective?
The effectiveness ratings for **RUSTY-LEAVED RHODODENDRON** are as follows:
Insufficient Evidence to Rate Effectiveness for... Extreme tension of the muscles or arteries (hypertonia), muscle and joint rheumatism, joint disease, hardening of muscles, muscular pain, weak connective tissue, neuralgia, sensitivity to weather change, sciatica, trigeminal neuralgia, migraine, headaches, high blood pressure, rib pain, gout, gall stones, kidney stones, and aging disorders.

How does it work?
Rusty-leaved rhododendron contains chemicals that lower blood pressure. It also contains chemicals that interfere with the electrical activity of nerves, which at low doses might relieve pain associated with some conditions, but at higher doses can result in poisoning.

Are there safety concerns?
Rusty-leaved rhododendron is unsafe. It can cause weakness, dizziness, nausea, vomiting, low blood pressure, slow heartbeat, irregular heartbeat, and blurred vision. Symptoms of poisoning include sweating, impaired consciousness, chills, fainting, shock, seizure, cardiac and respiratory arrest, severe stupor, and possibly death.

Do not take rusty-leaved rhododendron if: You are pregnant or breast-feeding.

Are there any interactions with medications?
It is not known if rusty-leaved rhododendron interacts with any medicines.
Before taking rusty-leaved rhododendron, talk with your healthcare professional if you take any medications.

RUTIN

What other names is the product known by?
Citrus Bioflavonoid, Eldrin, Oxerutin, Quercetin-3-rhamnoglucoside, Quercetin-3-rutinoside, Rutine, Rutinum, Rutosid, Rutoside, Rutosidum, Sclerutin, Sophorin.

What is it?
Rutin is a plant pigment (flavonoid) that is found in fruits and vegetables. Rutin is used to make medicine.

Is it Effective?
The effectiveness ratings for **RUTIN** are as follows:
Possibly Effective for... Osteoarthritis when taken in combination with trypsin and bromelain.
Insufficient Evidence to Rate Effectiveness for... Blood vessel disease, varicose veins, prevention of mouth ulcers associated with cancer treatments, bleeding, and hemorrhoids.

How does it work?
Rutin has chemicals that might offer some protection against cancer.

Are there safety concerns?
Rutin is safe when taken in amounts found in fruits and vegetables; however, it might not be safe in medicinal amounts. It can cause headache, flushing, rashes, or stomach upset.

There is also some concern that rutin might cause stomach blockages or stomach cancer.

Do not take rutin if: You are pregnant or breast-feeding.

Are there any interactions with medications?
It is not known if rutin interacts with any medicines.
Before taking rutin, talk with your healthcare professional if you take any medications.

 Natural Medicines Comprehensive Database Consumer Version (209) 472-2244

RYE GRASS

What other names is the product known by?
Cernilton, Grass Pollen, Grass Pollen Extract, Rye, Rye Grass Pollen, Rye Grass Pollen Extract, Secale cereale.

What is it?
Rye grass is a plant. The rye grass pollen is used to make medicine.

Is it Effective?
The effectiveness ratings for **RYE GRASS** are as follows:
Possibly Effective for... Benign prostatic hyperplasia (enlarged prostate) symptoms including increased urinary frequency, increased nighttime urination, constant feeling of needing to urinate, dribbling, painful urination, and decreased urine flow rate.
Insufficient Evidence to Rate Effectiveness for... Shrinking an enlarged prostate, prostate swelling, and pain.

How does it work?
Rye grass decreases swelling (inflammation) by interfering with certain chemicals. It might also slow down prostate cancer cell growth.

Are there safety concerns?
Rye grass seems safe for most people. It can cause side effects such as stomach swelling (distention), heartburn, and nausea.

Do not take rye grass if: You are pregnant or breast-feeding.

Are there any interactions with medications?
It is not known if rye grass interacts with any medicines.
Before taking rye grass, talk with your healthcare professional if you take any medications.

SACCHAROMYCES BOULARDII

What other names is the product known by?
Brewer's Yeast (Hansen CBS 5926), Hansen CBS 5926, Probiotics, Saccharomyces, Saccharomyces boulardii, Saccharomyces cerevisiae.

What is it?
Saccharomyces boulardii is a yeast. It is used as medicine.

Is it Effective?
The effectiveness ratings for **SACCHAROMYCES BOULARDII** are as follows:
Possibly Effective for... Prevention of diarrhea associated with antibiotics • Prevention of traveler's diarrhea • Diarrhea in infants • HIV-associated diarrhea • Preventing recurring intestinal disease caused by a bacterium called Clostridium difficile • Acne, in combination with other treatments • Reducing side effects of treatment for the ulcer-causing bacterium Helicobacter pylori.
Insufficient Evidence to Rate Effectiveness for... Preventing yeast overgrowth in the digestive tract of patients with cystic fibrosis, urinary tract infections (UTIs), yeast infections, high cholesterol, Lyme disease, hives, fever blisters, canker sores, irritable bowel syndrome (IBS), Crohn's disease, ulcerative colitis, lactose intolerance, and other conditions.

How does it work?
Saccharomyces boulardii is called a "probiotic," a friendly organism that helps to fight off disease causing organisms in the gut such as bacteria and yeast.

Are there safety concerns?
Saccharomyces boulardii is safe for most adults when taken by mouth. It can cause gas in some people. Rarely, it might cause fungal infections that can spread through the bloodstream to the entire body.

Saccharomyces boulardii might be safe for children. However, diarrhea in children should be evaluated by a healthcare professional before using Saccharomyces boulardii.

Do not take Saccharomyces boulardii without medical advice if: You are pregnant or breast-feeding. • You have a weakened immune system or are taking medicines that alter your immune system. • You have a yeast allergy.

Medical professionals should consult the Professional Version at www.NaturalDatabase.com.

CONSUMER VERSION

Are there any interactions with medications?

Medications for fungal infections (Antifungals). Saccharomyces boulardii is a fungus. Medications for fungal infections help reduce fungus in and on the body. Taking Saccharomyces boulardii with medications for fungal infections can reduce the effectiveness of Saccaromyces boulardii. Some medications for fungal infection include fluconazole (Diflucan), terbinafine (Lamisil), itraconazole (Sporanox), and others.

SAFFLOWER

What other names is the product known by?

American Saffron, Bastard Saffron, Benibana Oil, Benibana Flower, Carthamus tinctorius, Dyer's Saffron, Fake Saffron, False Saffron, Hing Hua, Honghua, Zaffer, Zafran.

What is it?

Safflower is a plant. The flower and seed oil are used as medicine.

Is it Effective?

The effectiveness ratings for **SAFFLOWER** are as follows:
Possibly Effective for... Reducing LDL cholesterol.
Insufficient Evidence to Rate Effectiveness for... Fever, tumors, coughs, bronchial conditions, blood circulation disorders, pain, menstrual disorders, chest pain, traumatic injuries, constipation, inducing sweating, causing abortion, and other uses.

How does it work?

The linolenic and linoleic acids in safflower seed oil might help prevent hardening of the arteries, lower cholesterol, and reduce the risk of heart disease. Safflower contains chemicals that may thin the blood to prevent clots, widen blood vessels, lower blood pressure, and stimulate the heart.

Are there safety concerns?

Safflower appears to be safe for most people. It can cause allergic reaction in individuals sensitive to the Asteraceae/Compositae family of plants which includes ragweed, chrysanthemums, marigolds, daisies, and many other plants.

While safflower seed oil is likely safe to take by mouth for pregnant or breast-feeding women, safflower flower is not. Safflower flower can cause abortions and bring on menstrual periods.

Do not take safflower if: You are pregnant or breast-feeding. Safflower seed oil is likely safe, but safflower flower is not. • You are allergic to ragweed, chrysanthemums, marigolds, daisies, and other related plants. • You have stomach or intestinal ulcers. • You have bleeding or clotting disorders.

Are there any interactions with medications?

Medications that slow blood clotting (Anticoagulant / Antiplatelet drugs). Large amounts of safflower might slow blood clotting. Taking safflower along with medications that also slow clotting might increase the chances of bruising and bleeding. Some medications that slow blood clotting include aspirin, clopidogrel (Plavix), diclofenac (Voltaren, Cataflam, others), ibuprofen (Advil, Motrin, others), naproxen (Anaprox, Naprosyn, others), dalteparin (Fragmin), enoxaparin (Lovenox), heparin, warfarin (Coumadin), and others.

SAFFRON

What other names is the product known by?

Autumn Crocus, Azafron, Croci stigma, Crocus sativus, Indian Saffron, Kumkuma, Saffron Crocus, Safran, Spanish Saffron, True Saffron.

What is it?

Saffron is a plant. The stigmas (the thread-like parts) are used to make medicine.

Is it Effective?

The effectiveness ratings for **SAFFRON** are as follows:
Possibly Effective for... Depression.
Insufficient Evidence to Rate Effectiveness for... Asthma, insomnia, cancer, hardening of the arteries due to fatty plaques, cough, stomach gas, premature ejaculation, baldness, pain, and other conditions.

How does it work?
There isn't enough information to know how saffron might work.

Are there safety concerns?
Saffron seems safe for most people when used as a medicine. Some potential side effects include anxiety, drowsiness, change in appetite, and headache. Allergic reactions can occur in some people.

Ingesting large amounts of saffron can cause poisoning including yellow appearance of the skin, eyes, and mucous membranes; vomiting; dizziness; bloody diarrhea; bleeding from the nose, lips, and eyelids; numbness; and other serious side effects.

Do not take saffron if: You are pregnant or breast-feeding. • You are allergic to related plants such as Lolium, Olea, or Salsola. • You have bipolar disorder.

Are there any interactions with medications?
It is not known if saffron interacts with any medicines.
Before taking saffron, talk with your healthcare professional if you take any medications.

SAGE

What other names is the product known by?
Common Sage, Dalmatian Sage, Garden Sage, Meadow Sage, Salvia lavandulaefolia, Salvia officinalis, Sauge, Scarlet Sage, Spanish Sage, True Sage.

What is it?
Sage is an herb. The leaf is used to make medicine.

Is it Effective?
The effectiveness ratings for **SAGE** are as follows:
Possibly Effective for... Alzheimer's disease • Cold sores, when applied as a cream containing sage and rhubarb.
Insufficient Evidence to Rate Effectiveness for... Improving memory, loss of appetite, stomach pain, dry mouth, painful periods, asthma, diarrhea, gas, bloating, indigestion, excessive sweating, and other conditions.

How does it work?
Sage might help chemical imbalances in the brain that cause symptoms of Alzheimer's disease.

Are there safety concerns?
Sage is safe in amounts typically used in foods. Sage appears to be safe for most people when taken short-term by mouth. Some kinds of sage contain a toxic chemical that can cause seizures when taken in large amounts. Sage can cause nausea, vomiting, abdominal pain, dizziness, agitation, and wheezing. In large doses, it can cause seizures and damage to the liver and nervous system.

Do not use sage if: You are pregnant or breast-feeding. • You have epilepsy or a seizure disorder. • You have diabetes.

Are there any interactions with medications?
Medications for diabetes (Antidiabetes drugs). Sage might decrease blood sugar. Diabetes medications are also used to lower blood sugar. Taking sage along with diabetes medications might cause your blood sugar to go too low. Monitor your blood sugar closely. The dose of your diabetes medication might need to be changed. Some medications used for diabetes include glimepiride (Amaryl), glyburide (DiaBeta, Glynase PresTab, Micronase), insulin, pioglitazone (Actos), rosiglitazone (Avandia), chlorpropamide (Diabinese), glipizide (Glucotrol), tolbutamide (Orinase), and others.
Medications used to prevent seizures (Anticonvulsants). Medications used to prevent seizures affect chemicals in the brain. Sage may also affect chemicals in the brain. By affecting chemicals in the brain, sage may decrease the effectiveness of medications used to prevent seizures. Some medications used to prevent seizures include phenobarbital, primidone (Mysoline), valproic acid (Depakene), gabapentin (Neurontin), carbamazepine (Tegretol), phenytoin (Dilantin), and others.
Sedative medications (CNS depressants). Sage might cause sleepiness and drowsiness. Medications that cause sleepiness are called sedatives. Taking sage along with sedative medications might cause too much sleepiness. Some sedative medications include clonazepam (Klonopin), lorazepam (Ativan), phenobarbital (Donnatal), zolpidem (Ambien), and others.

SALACIA

What other names is the product known by?
Chundan, Kathala Hibutu Tea, Ponkoranti, SO, S. Oblonga, Salacia oblonga, Salacia reticulata.

What is it?
Salacia is an herb. The root and stem are used to make medicine.

Is it Effective?
The effectiveness ratings for **SALACIA** are as follows:
Insufficient Evidence to Rate Effectiveness for... Diabetes, weight loss, skin itching, gonorrhea, joint problems, and asthma.

How does it work?
Chemicals in salacia seem to prevent sugars in food from being absorbed by the body.

Are there safety concerns?
Consuming salacia tea with food seems to be safe for most people for up to three months. But there isn't enough information to know if salacia is safe when used for long periods of time.

Do not take salacia if: You are pregnant or breast-feeding.

Are there any interactions with medications?
Medications for diabetes (Antidiabetes drugs). Salacia might decrease blood sugar. Diabetes medications are also used to lower blood sugar. Taking salacia along with diabetes medications might cause your blood sugar to go too low. Monitor your blood sugar closely. The dose of your diabetes medication might need to be changed. Some medications used for diabetes include glimepiride (Amaryl), glyburide (DiaBeta, Glynase PresTab, Micronase), insulin, pioglitazone (Actos), rosiglitazone (Avandia), chlorpropamide (Diabinese), glipizide (Glucotrol), tolbutamide (Orinase), and others.

SALEP

What other names is the product known by?
Cuckoo Flower, Levant Salep, Orchid, Orchis morio, Sahlep, Saloop, Satyrion.

What is it?
Salep is a plant. The tuber (root) is used as medicine.

Is it Effective?
The effectiveness ratings for **SALEP** are as follows:
Insufficient Evidence to Rate Effectiveness for... Diarrhea, heartburn, intestinal gas (flatulence), and indigestion.

How does it work?
Salep contains a mucus-like substance that might help soothe the digestive tract.

Are there safety concerns?
Salep is possibly safe for most people, but the potential side effects aren't known.

Do not take salep if: You are pregnant or breast-feeding.

Are there any interactions with medications?
It is not known if salep interacts with any medicines.
Before taking salep, talk with your healthcare professional if you take any medications.

SAMe

What other names is the product known by?

Ademetionine, Adenosylmethionine, S-Adenosyl-L-Methionine, S-Adenosylmethionine, S-Adenosyl-Methionine, S-Adenosyl Methionine, SAM-e, Sammy.

What is it?

SAMe is a chemical that is found naturally in the body. It can also be made in the laboratory.

Is it Effective?

The effectiveness ratings for **SAMe** are as follows:

Likely Effective for... Osteoarthritis. It works about as well as aspirin and similar drugs, but it can take twice as long to start working. Most people with arthritis need to take SAMe for about a month before they feel better • Depression when given as an injection.

Possibly Effective for... Depression when taken as a pill by mouth • Some types of fibromyalgia when taken as a pill • Liver disease • Some symptoms of AIDS-related nerve problems • Decreased bile flow from the liver to the gallbladder.

Insufficient Evidence to Rate Effectiveness for... Heart disease, anxiety, bursitis, tendonitis, chronic low back pain, improving intelligence, premenstrual syndrome (PMS), premenstrual dysphoric disorder (PMDD), attention deficit-hyperactivity disorder (ADHD), chronic fatigue syndrome (CFS), staying young, multiple sclerosis, spinal cord injury, seizures, migraine headache, and other conditions.

How does it work?

The body uses SAMe to make certain chemicals in the body that play a role in pain, depression, liver disease, and other conditions. People who don't make enough SAMe naturally may be helped by taking SAMe as a supplement.

Are there safety concerns?

SAMe seems to be safe for most people. It can sometimes cause gas, vomiting, diarrhea, constipation, dry mouth, headache, mild insomnia, anorexia, sweating, dizziness, and nervousness, especially at higher doses. It can make some people with depression feel anxious.

Do not use SAMe if: You are pregnant or breast-feeding. • You have bipolar disorder.

Are there any interactions with medications?

Dextromethorphan (Robitussin DM, and others). SAMe can affect a brain chemical called serotonin. Dextromethorphan (Robitussin DM, others) can also affect serotonin. Taking SAMe along with dextromethorphan (Robitussin DM, others) might cause too much serotonin in the brain and serious side effects including heart problems, shivering, and anxiety. Do not take SAMe if you are taking dextromethorphan (Robitussin DM, and others).

Levodopa. Levodopa is used for Parkinson's disease. SAMe can chemically change levodopa in the body and decrease the effectiveness of levodopa. Taking SAMe along with levodopa might make Parkinson's disease symptoms worse. Do not take SAMe if you are taking levodopa.

Medications for depression (Antidepressant drugs). SAMe increases a brain chemical called serotonin. Some medications for depression also increase the brain chemical serotonin. Taking SAMe along with these medications for depression might increase serotonin too much and cause serious side effects including heart problems, shivering, and anxiety. Do not take SAMe if you are taking medications for depression. Some of these medications for depression include fluoxetine (Prozac), paroxetine (Paxil), sertraline (Zoloft), amitriptyline (Elavil), clomipramine (Anafranil), imipramine (Tofranil), and others.

Medications for depression (MAOIs). SAMe increases a chemical in the brain. This chemical is called serotonin. Some medications used for depression also increase serotonin. Taking SAMe along with these medications used for depression might cause too much serotonin in the body, and serious side effects including heart problems, shivering, and anxiety. Some of these medications used for depression include phenelzine (Nardil), tranylcypromine (Parnate), and others.

Meperidine (Demerol). SAMe increases a chemical in the brain called serotonin. Meperidine (Demerol) can also increase serotonin in the brain. Taking SAMe along with meperidine (Demerol) might cause too much serotonin in the brain and serious side effects including heart problems, shivering, and anxiety.

Pentazocine (Talwin). SAMe increases a brain chemical called serotonin. Pentazocine (Talwin) also increases serotonin. Taking SAMe along with pentazocine (Talwin) might cause serious side effects including heart problems, shivering, and anxiety. Do not take SAMe if you are taking pentazocine (Talwin).

Tramadol (Ultram). Tramadol (Ultram) can affect a chemical in the brain called serotonin. SAMe can also affect serotonin. Taking SAMe along with tramadol (Ultram) might cause too much serotonin in the brain and side effects including confusion, shivering, stiff muscles, and other side effects.

Medical professionals should consult the Professional Version at www.NaturalDatabase.com.

SAMPHIRE

What other names is the product known by?
Crest Marine, Crithmum maritimum, Peter's Cress, Pierce-Stone, Sampier, Sea Fennel.

What is it?
Samphire is a plant. The above ground parts are used as medicine.

Is it Effective?
The effectiveness ratings for **SAMPHIRE** are as follows:
Insufficient Evidence to Rate Effectiveness for... Scurvy and other conditions.

How does it work?
Samphire contains vitamin C, which is used to treat and prevent scurvy.

Are there safety concerns?
Samphire is possibly safe for most people, but the potential side effects are not known.

Do not take samphire if: You are pregnant or breast-feeding.

Are there any interactions with medications?
It is not known if samphire interacts with any medicines.
Before taking samphire, talk with your healthcare professional if you take any medications.

SANDY EVERLASTING

What other names is the product known by?
Common Shrubby Everlasting, Eternal Flower, Everlasting, Fleur de Pied de Chat, Goldilocks, Harnblumen, Helichrysum, Helichrysum augustifolium, Helichrysum italicum, Helichrysum oriental, Helichrysum stoechas, Katzenpfotchenbluten, Yellow Chaste Weed.

What is it?
Sandy everlasting is a plant. The dried flowers are used as medicine.

Is it Effective?
The effectiveness ratings for **SANDY EVERLASTING** are as follows:
Insufficient Evidence to Rate Effectiveness for... Liver disorders, gall bladder disease, fluid retention, bronchitis, asthma, whooping cough, psoriasis, burns, rheumatism, headache, migraine, allergies, stomach upset, and other conditions.

How does it work?
Sandy everlasting contains chemicals that might help fight bacteria, reduce inflammation, and increase the production of digestive juices. It might also boost the liver's ability to process harmful toxins.

Are there safety concerns?
Sandy everlasting appears to be safe for most people. But it can cause an allergic reaction in individuals sensitive to the Asteraceae/Compositae plant family which includes ragweed, chrysanthemums, marigolds, daisies, and many other plants.

Do not take sandy everlasting if: You are pregnant or breast-feeding. • You have gall bladder disease such as gallstones or a blockage of bile. • You are allergic to ragweed, chrysanthemums, marigolds, daisies, and other related plants.

Are there any interactions with medications?
It is not known if sandy everlasting interacts with any medicines.
Before taking sandy everlasting, talk with your healthcare professional if you take any medications.

SANGRE DE GRADO

What other names is the product known by?

Blood of the Dragon, Croton lechleri, Drago, Dragon's Blood, Lan-Hiqui, Laniqui, Sangre de Drago, Sangre de Dragon, Sangue de Agua, Sangue de Drago, SP 303, SP-303, Taspine.

What is it?

Sangre de grado is a tree. The tree bark and sap are used to make medicine.

Is it Effective?

The effectiveness ratings for **SANGRE DE GRADO** are as follows:

Possibly Effective for...AIDS-related diarrhea • Traveler's diarrhea • Treatment of herpes lesions (genital and anal) in people with AIDS.

Insufficient Evidence to Rate Effectiveness for... Treating allergic skin reactions, cancer treatment, irritable bowel syndrome (IBS), lung infections, mouth and throat ulcers, stomach and intestinal ulcers, bleeding gums, bone fractures, hemorrhoids, eczema, insect bites and stings, and other conditions.

How does it work?

Sangre de grado appears to help diarrhea by slowing down the intestines. It might also prevent the movement of some viruses into cells.

Are there safety concerns?

Sangre de grado appears to be safe for most people. When applied to the skin, sangre de grado can cause pain, burning, and scarring.

Do not take sangre de grado if: You are pregnant or breast-feeding.

Are there any interactions with medications?

It is not known if sangre de grado interacts with any medicines.
Before taking sangre de grado, talk with your healthcare professional if you take any medications.

SANICLE

What other names is the product known by?

European Sanicle, Poolroot, Sanicula europaea, Saniculae herba, Self-Heal, Wood Sanicle.

What is it?

Sanicle is a plant. The above ground parts are used as medicine. Be careful not to confuse sanicle (sanicula europaea) with prunella vulgaris, both of which are known as self-heal. Also be careful not to confuse sanicula europaea with astrantia major, both of which are known as sanicle.

Is it Effective?

The effectiveness ratings for **SANICLE** are as follows:

Insufficient Evidence to Rate Effectiveness for... Mild respiratory tract mucous membrane inflammation, cough, and bronchitis.

How does it work?

Sanicle seems to thin mucus to make it easier to cough up.

Are there safety concerns?

Sanicle appears to be safe for most people. In large amounts, it may cause some side effects including stomach upset, nausea, and vomiting.

Do not take sanicle if: You are pregnant or breast-feeding. • You have stomach or intestinal disorders, such as ulcers, irritable bowel syndrome, ulcerative colitis, and other digestive tract problems.

Are there any interactions with medications?

It is not known if sanicle interacts with any medicines.
Before taking sanicle, talk with your healthcare professional if you take any medications.

CONSUMER VERSION

Medical professionals should consult the
Professional Version at www.NaturalDatabase.com.

SARSAPARILLA

What other names is the product known by?

Ecudorian Sarsaparilla, Honduras Sarsaparilla, Jamaican Sarsaparilla, Mexican Sarsaparilla, Salsaparilha, Salsepareille, Sarsa, Sarsaparillae radix, Sarsaparillewurzel, Smilax, Smilax aristolochiaefolii, Smilax regelii, Smilax febrifuga, Smilax regelii, Smilax medica.

What is it?

Sarsaparilla is a plant. The root is used to make medicine.

Is it Effective?

The effectiveness ratings for **SARSAPARILLA** are as follows:

Insufficient Evidence to Rate Effectiveness for... Psoriasis, rheumatoid arthritis, kidney problems, fluid retention, digestive problems, syphilis, gonorrhea, and other conditions.

How does it work?

Sarsaparilla can help decrease joint pain and itching, and can also reduce bacteria.

Are there safety concerns?

Sarsaparilla seems safe for most people when used as a medicine. It might cause stomach irritation. High amounts can lead to kidney problems. Exposure to root dust can cause a runny nose and asthma symptoms.

Do not take sarsaparilla if: You are pregnant or breast-feeding. • You have asthma. • You have kidney problems.

Are there any interactions with medications?

Digoxin (Lanoxin). Digoxin (Lanoxin) helps the heart beat more strongly. Sarsaparilla might increase how much digoxin (Lanoxin) the body absorbs. By increasing how much digoxin (Lanoxin) the body absorbs sarsaparilla might increase the effects and side effects of digoxin (Lanoxin).

SASSAFRAS

What other names is the product known by?

Ague Tree, Cinnamon Wood, Common Sassafras, Kuntze Saloop, Laurus albida, Sassafrax, Sassafras albidum, Sassafras variifolium, Saxifrax.

What is it?

Sassafras is a plant. The root bark is used to make medicine.

Is it Effective?

The effectiveness ratings for **SASSAFRAS** are as follows:

Insufficient Evidence to Rate Effectiveness for... Urinary tract problems, gout, arthritis, skin problems, eye swelling, sprains, insect bites and stings, purifying the blood, and other conditions.

How does it work?

There isn't enough information available to know how sassafras works.

Are there safety concerns?

Sassafras seems safe when consumed in foods and beverages if it is "safrole-free." It is unsafe for use as a medicine. Sassafras can cause sweating and hot flashes. High amounts can cause vomiting, high blood pressure, hallucinations, and more severe side effects. It can cause skin rashes when used on the skin.

Sassafras is UNSAFE for children. A few drops of sassafras oil may be deadly.

Do not take sassafras if: You are pregnant or breast-feeding. • You have a urinary condition, such as a urinary tract infection (UTI).

Are there any interactions with medications?

Sedative medications (CNS depressants). Sassafras might cause sleepiness and drowsiness. Medications that cause sleepiness are called sedatives. Taking sassafras along with sedative medications might cause too much sleepiness. Some sedative medications include clonazepam (Klonopin), lorazepam (Ativan), Phenobarbital (Donnatal), zolpidem (Ambien), and others.

SAVIN TOPS

What other names is the product known by?
Juniperus sabina, Sabina, Savin, Savine.

What is it?
Savin tops are the top parts of the savin plant. The branches and leaves are used to make medicine.

Is it Effective?
The effectiveness ratings for **SAVIN TOPS** are as follows:
Insufficient Evidence to Rate Effectiveness for... Some warts called fig warts, causing abortion, and other uses.

How does it work?
Warts, such as genital warts, are caused by viruses. Savin tops contain chemicals the might have activity against some viruses.

Are there safety concerns?
Savin tops are UNSAFE and poisonous. Symptoms of poisoning by savin tops include queasiness, abnormal heart rhythm, spasms, kidney damage, blood in the urine, paralysis, unconsciousness, and death. They can also cause severe irritation of the lungs (pnuemonitis), digestive tract (gastroenteritis), liver (hepatitis), and kidney (nephritis). When applied to the skin, they can cause skin irritation, blisters, and damage from dead cells (necroses).

Do not take savin tops if: You are pregnant or breast-feeding. • You have inflammation of the skin, eyes, nose, mouth, or throat.

Are there any interactions with medications?
It is not known if savin tops interact with any medicines.
Before taking savin tops, talk with your healthcare professional if you take any medications.

SAW PALMETTO

What other names is the product known by?
American Dwarf Palm Tree, Cabbage Palm, Ju-Zhong, Palmier Nain, Sabal, Sabal Fructus, Saw Palmetto Berry.

What is it?
Saw palmetto is a plant. Its fruit is used to make medicine.

Is it Effective?
The effectiveness ratings for **SAW PALMETTO** are as follows:
Likely Effective for... Symptoms of enlarged prostate (benign prostatic hypertrophy [BPH]). Saw palmetto seems to moderately reduce symptoms of BPH. Some evidence suggests that it might work about as well as some prescription medications for some people, but it takes about one or two months of treatment before symptoms improve.
Insufficient Evidence to Rate Effectiveness for... Treating nonbacterial prostatitis/chronic pelvic pain syndrome, increasing breast size, hair growth, colds and coughs, sore throat, asthma, chronic bronchitis, prostate cancer, and migraine headache.

How does it work?
Saw palmetto doesn't shrink the overall size of the prostate, but it seems to shrink the inner lining that puts pressure on the tubes that carry urine.

Are there safety concerns?
Saw palmetto is safe for most people. Side effects are mild and include dizziness, headache, nausea, vomiting, constipation, and diarrhea. Saw palmetto does not appear to cause impotence.

Do not take saw palmetto if: You are pregnant or breast-feeding.

Are there any interactions with medications?
Birth control pills (Contraceptive drugs). Some birth control pills contain estrogen. Saw palmetto might decrease the effects of estrogen in the body. Taking saw palmetto along with birth control pills might decrease the effectiveness of birth control pills. If you take birth control pills along with saw palmetto, use an additional form of birth control such as a condom. Some birth control pills include ethinyl estradiol and levonorgestrel (Triphasil),

CONSUMER VERSION

Medical professionals should consult the Professional Version at www.NaturalDatabase.com.

ethinyl estradiol and norethindrone (Ortho-Novum 1/35, Ortho-Novum 7/7/7), and others.

Estrogens. Saw palmetto seems to decrease estrogen levels in the body. Taking saw palmetto along with estrogen pills might decrease the effectiveness of estrogen pills. Some estrogen pills include conjugated equine estrogens (Premarin), ethinyl estradiol, estradiol, and others.

Medications that slow blood clotting (Anticoagulant / Antiplatelet drugs). Saw palmetto might slow blood clotting. Taking saw palmetto along with medications that also slow clotting might increase the chances of bruising and bleeding. Some medications that slow blood clotting include aspirin, clopidogrel (Plavix), diclofenac (Voltaren, Cataflam, others), ibuprofen (Advil, Motrin, others), naproxen (Anaprox, Naprosyn, others), dalteparin (Fragmin), enoxaparin (Lovenox), heparin, warfarin (Coumadin), and others.

SCARLET PIMPERNEL

What other names is the product known by?

Adder's Eyes, Anagallis arvensis, Poor Man's Weatherglass, Red Chickweed, Red Pimpernel, Shepherd's Barometer.

What is it?

Scarlet pimpernel is a plant. The above ground flowering parts are used as medicine.

Is it Effective?

The effectiveness ratings for **SCARLET PIMPERNEL** are as follows:

Insufficient Evidence to Rate Effectiveness for... Depression, liver disorders, herpes, cancer, kidney disorders, wounds, itching, painful joints, and other conditions.

How does it work?

Scarlet pimpernel contains chemicals that might have activity against some bacteria, fungi, and viruses. It also appears to have estrogen-like effects and might have negative effects on human sperm.

Are there safety concerns?

Scarlet pimpernel appears to be UNSAFE for long-term use when taken by mouth or applied to the skin. Scarlet pimpernel can cause inflammation of the stomach, intestines, and kidneys with long-term use or high doses. There isn't enough information to know if scarlet pimpernel is safe for short-term use.

Do not take scarlet pimpernel if: You are pregnant or breast-feeding. • You are a man or woman trying to conceive a child. • You have hormone-sensitive conditions or cancers such as endometriosis; uterine fibroids; or breast, uterine, or ovarian cancer.

Are there any interactions with medications?

It is not known if scarlet pimpernel interacts with any medicines.
Before taking scarlet pimpernel, talk with your healthcare professional if you take any medications.

SCHISANDRA

What other names is the product known by?

Bac Ngu Vi Tu, Beiwuweizi, Bei Wu Wei Zi, Chinesischer Limonenbaum, Chosen-Gomischi, Five-Flavor-Fruit, Five-Flavor-Seed, Gomishi, Hoku-Gomishi, Kita-Gomishi, Limonnik Kitajskij, Mei Gee, Magnolia Vine, Matsbouza, Nanwuweizi, Ngu Mei Gee, Northern Schisandra, Omicha, Schisandrae, Schisandra Berry, Southern Schisandra, Wuweizi, Wu-Wei-Zi, Western Schisandra, Xiwuweizi.

What is it?

Schisandra is a plant. The fruit is used to make medicine.

Is it Effective?

The effectiveness ratings for **SCHISANDRA** are as follows:

Possibly Effective for... Improving liver function in patients with hepatitis • Improving concentration, coordination, and endurance.

Insufficient Evidence to Rate Effectiveness for... Vision problems, preventing premature aging, preventing motion sickness, diabetes, high blood pressure, and other conditions.

How does it work?

The chemicals in schisandra improve liver function by stimulating enzymes in the liver and promoting liver cell growth.

Medical professionals should consult the Professional Version at www.NaturalDatabase.com.

 Natural Medicines Comprehensive Database Consumer Version (209) 472-2244

Are there safety concerns?

Schisandra fruit is considered safe. It can cause heartburn, upset stomach, decreased appetite, stomach pain, skin rash, and itching.

Do not take schisandra if: You are pregnant or breast-feeding. • You have gastroesophageal reflux disease (GERD). • You have peptic ulcer disease (PUD). • You have epilepsy. • You have high intracranial (brain) pressure.

Are there any interactions with medications?

Medications changed by the liver (Cytochrome P450 3A4 (CYP3A4) substrates). Some medications are changed and broken down by the liver. Schisandra might decrease how quickly the liver breaks down some medications. Taking schisandra along with some medications that are broken down by the liver can increase the effects and side effects of some medications. Before taking schisandra, talk to your healthcare provider if you are taking any medications that are changed by the liver. Some medications changed by the liver include lovastatin (Mevacor), clarithromycin (Biaxin), cyclosporine (Neoral, Sandimmune), diltiazem (Cardizem), estrogens, indinavir (Crixivan), triazolam (Halcion), and many others.

SCHIZONEPETA

What other names is the product known by?

Hairy Sage, Japanese Catnip, Japanese Mint, Jing Jie, Schizonepeta multifida, Schizonepeta tenuifolia, Tenuifolia.

What is it?

Schizonepeta is a plant. The above ground parts are used to make medicine.

Is it Effective?

The effectiveness ratings for **SCHIZONEPETA** are as follows:
Insufficient Evidence to Rate Effectiveness for... Eczema, common cold, fever, sore throat, psoriasis, heavy menstrual bleeding, and others conditions.

How does it work?

Schizonepeta contains chemicals that might help some skin conditions such as eczema.

Are there safety concerns?

Schizonepeta appears to be safe in low doses for most people. In high doses, a chemical in schizonepeta might damage the liver.

Do not use schizonepeta if: You are pregnant or breast-feeding. • You have liver disease.

Are there any interactions with medications?

It is not known if schizonepeta interacts with any medicines.
Before taking schizonepeta, talk with your healthcare professional if you take any medications.

SCOPOLIA

What other names is the product known by?

Belladonna, Belladonna Scopola, Glockenbilsenkraut, Japanese Belladonna, Russian Krainer Tollkraut, Scopola, Scopolia carniolica, Scopoliae Rhizoma.

What is it?

Scopolia is a plant. The root and root-like stem (rhizome) are used as medicine.

Is it Effective?

The effectiveness ratings for **SCOPOLIA** are as follows:
Insufficient Evidence to Rate Effectiveness for... Fluid retention, anxiety, trouble sleeping, pain, liver problems, gall bladder problems, spasms of the digestive tract, and other conditions.

How does it work?

Scopolia contains several chemicals which are similar to prescription medications, including hyoscyamine, atopine, and scopolamine. These chemicals relax muscles lining the digestive and urinary tracts.

Medical professionals should consult the Professional Version at www.NaturalDatabase.com.

CONSUMER VERSION

Are there safety concerns?

Scopolia is UNSAFE. There is only a small difference between a beneficial dose and a poisonous dose, and products vary in concentrations of chemicals. Early symptoms of poisoning include reddened skin, and dry mouth. Other symptoms include high body temperature, vision problems, difficulty urinating, and constipation. Taking large amounts of scopolia can cause restlessness, compulsive speech, and hallucinations, followed by breathing problems, and death.

Do not take scopolia if: You are pregnant or breast-feeding. • You have heart problems such as heart failure or rapid, irregular heartbeat. • You have Down syndrome. • You have a fever. • You have difficulty urinating. • You have narrow-angle glaucoma. • You have hiatal hernia or heartburn (esophageal reflux disease). • You have digestive tract conditions including constipation, stomach ulcers, stomach or intestinal infections, ulcerative colitis, enlarged colon (toxic megacolon), or blockage of the digestive tract.

Are there any interactions with medications?

Drying medications (Anticholinergic drugs). Scopolia contains chemicals that cause a drying effect. It also affects the brain and heart. Drying medications called anticholinergic drugs can also cause these effects. Taking scopolia and drying medications together might cause side effects including dry skin, dizziness, low blood pressure, fast heartbeat, and other serious side effects. Some of these drying medications include atropine, scopolamine, and some medications used for allergies (antihistamines), and for depression (antidepressants).
Medications used for depression (Tricyclic antidepressants). Scopolia contains chemicals that can affect the body. Some of these chemicals have effects similar to some medications used for depression. Taking scopolia might increase the side effects of some medications used for depression. Some of these medicines used for depression include amitriptyline (Elavil), imipramine (Tofranil), and others.
Quinidine. Scopolia can affect the heart. Quinidine can also affect the heart. Taking quinidine along with scopolia might cause serious heart problems.

SCOTCH BROOM

What other names is the product known by?

Bannal, Basam, Besenginaterkraut, Besom, Bizzom, Breeam, Broom Tops, Browme, Brum, Butcher's-Broom, Cytisi Scoparii Flos, Cytisi Scoparii Herba, Cytisus Scoparius, Genet a Balais, Genista andreana, Ginsterkraut, Herbe de Hogweed, Hogweed, Irish Broom Tops, Sarothamnus Scoparius, Sarothamnus Vulgaris, Scoparium, Scoparius, Scotch Broom Herb, Scotch Broom Flower, Spartium Scoparium.

What is it?

Scotch broom is a plant. The flower and above ground parts are used as medicine.

Is it Effective?

The effectiveness ratings for **SCOTCH BROOM** are as follows:
Insufficient Evidence to Rate Effectiveness for... Fluid retention, sore muscles, swelling, low blood pressure, menstrual disorders, heavy bleeding after giving birth, bleeding gums, gout, arthritis-like pain, nerve disorders, gallbladder and kidney stones, spleen disorders, heart disorders, and other conditions.

How does it work?

Scotch broom contains chemicals that might cause an increase in body water loss through the urine and affect heart rhythm.

Are there safety concerns?

Scotch broom is considered to be UNSAFE. It can cause heart and circulation problems. It might also cause side effects such as nausea and diarrhea.

Poisoning can occur with doses greater than 30 grams of scotch broom. Symptoms of poisoning include dizziness, headache, heartbeat changes, leg weakness, sweating, sleepiness, and widening of the pupils.

There isn't enough information to know if scotch broom is safe when applied to the skin.

Do not take scotch broom if: You are pregnant or breast-feeding. • You have high blood pressure. • You have heart disease. • You have kidney disease.

Are there any interactions with medications?

Haloperidol (Haldol). The body breaks down scotch broom to get rid of it. Haloperidol (Haldol) seems to decrease the breakdown of scotch broom. Taking scotch broom along with haloperidol (Haldol) might increase the risk of serious side effects of scotch broom. Do not take scotch broom if you are taking haloperidol (Haldol).

Medications for depression (MAOIs). Scotch broom contains a chemical called tyramine. Large amounts of tyramine can cause high blood pressure. But the body naturally breaks down tyramine to get rid of it. This usually prevents the tyramine from causing high blood pressure. Some medications used for depression called MAOIs stop the body from breaking down tyramine. This can cause there to be too much tyramine and lead to dangerously high blood pressure. Some of these medications used for depression include phenelzine (Nardil), tranylcypromine (Parnate), and others.

Quinidine. The body breaks down scotch broom to get rid of it. Quinidine seems to decrease the breakdown of scotch broom. Taking scotch broom along with quinidine might increase the risk of serious side effects of scotch broom. Do not take scotch broom if you are taking quinidine.

SCOTCH THISTLE

What other names is the product known by?
Onopordum acanthium, Woolly Thistle.

What is it?
Scotch thistle is a plant. It is used as medicine. Be careful not to confuse scotch thistle with similar sounding natural medicines such as milk thistle or scotch pine needle.

Is it Effective?
The effectiveness ratings for **SCOTCH THISTLE** are as follows:
Insufficient Evidence to Rate Effectiveness for... Stimulating the heart.

How does it work?
There isn't enough information to know how scotch thistle might work.

Are there safety concerns?
There isn't enough information to know if scotch thistle is safe. Scotch thistle can cause allergic reactions in individuals sensitive to the Asteraceae/Compositae plant family which includes ragweed, chrysanthemums, marigolds, daisies, and many other plants.

Do not take scotch thistle if: You are pregnant or breast-feeding. • You are allergic to ragweed, chrysanthemums, marigolds, daisies, and other related plants.

Are there any interactions with medications?
It is not known if scotch thistle interacts with any medicines.
Before taking scotch thistle, talk with your healthcare professional if you take any medications.

SCURVY GRASS

What other names is the product known by?
Cochlearia officinalis, Scrubby Grass, Spoonwort.

What is it?
Scurvy grass is an herb. The leaves and flowering parts are used to make medicine.

Is it Effective?
The effectiveness ratings for **SCURVY GRASS** are as follows:
Insufficient Evidence to Rate Effectiveness for... Vitamin C deficiency, gout, arthritis, stomachache, skin irritation, gum disease, and other conditions.

How does it work?
Scurvy grass contains a high concentration of vitamin C. It also has antibacterial and mild laxative effects.

Are there safety concerns?
There isn't enough information available to know if scurvy grass is safe. It can cause stomach and intestinal irritation when large amounts are taken by mouth. It can also irritate the skin when applied directly to the skin.

Do not take scurvy grass if: You are pregnant or breast-feeding.

Medical professionals should consult the Professional Version at www.NaturalDatabase.com.

CONSUMER VERSION

Medical professionals should consult the Professional Version at www.NaturalDatabase.com.

Are there any interactions with medications?

It is not known if scurvy grass interacts with any medicines.

Before taking scurvy grass, talk with your healthcare professional if you take any medications.

SEA BUCKTHORN

What other names is the product known by?

Argasse, Argousier, Buckthorn, Dhar-Bu, Espino Armarillo, Espino Falso, Finbar, Grisset, Hippophae rhamnoides, Meerdorn, Oblepikha, Purging Thorn, Rokitnik, Sallow Thorn, Sanddorn, Sea Buckhorn, Sceitbezien, Seedorn, Star-Bu, Tindved.

What is it?

Sea buckthorn is an herb. The leaves, flowers, and fruits are used to make medicine.

Is it Effective?

The effectiveness ratings for **SEA BUCKTHORN** are as follows:

Insufficient Evidence to Rate Effectiveness for... Arthritis, stomach and intestinal ulcers, gout, high blood pressure, high cholesterol, visual disorders, aging, cough, asthma, angina, cancer, heartburn, sunburn, wounds, pressure ulcers, burns, cuts, acne, dry skin, eczema, and other conditions.

How does it work?

Sea buckthorn contains vitamins A, B1, B2, B6, C, and other active ingredients. It might have some activity against stomach and intestinal ulcers, and heartburn symptoms.

Are there safety concerns?

Sea buckthorn appears to be safe for most people.

Do not take sea buckthorn as a medicine if: You are pregnant or breast-feeding.

Are there any interactions with medications?

Medications that slow blood clotting (Anticoagulant / Antiplatelet drugs). Sea buckthorn might slow blood clotting. Taking sea buckthorn along with medications that also slow clotting might increase the chances of bruising and bleeding. Some medications that slow blood clotting include aspirin, clopidogrel (Plavix), diclofenac (Voltaren, Cataflam, others), ibuprofen (Advil, Motrin, others), naproxen (Anaprox, Naprosyn, others), dalteparin (Fragmin), enoxaparin (Lovenox), heparin, warfarin (Coumadin), and others.

SECRETIN

What other names is the product known by?

Oxykrinin.

What is it?

Secretin is a hormone produced by the digestive tract. It is used as a medicine.

Is it Effective?

The effectiveness ratings for **SECRETIN** are as follows:

Likely Ineffective for... Autism and pervasive developmental disorder (PDD).

Insufficient Evidence to Rate Effectiveness for... Stress ulcers in severe trauma or disease, intestinal ulcers, digestive tract bleeding, pancreatitis, heart failure, and other conditions.

How does it work?

Secretin is a hormone that is produced by the digestive tract. Its primary action is to stimulate release of bicarbonate and water from the pancreas to aid digestion.

Are there safety concerns?

Secretin is available as a prescription product that is used intravenously. These products are safe when used appropriately. It's not known if other secretin products are safe. Common side effects of secretin include flushing of the face, neck, and chest immediately after a dose. Less common potential adverse effects are vomiting, diarrhea, fainting, blood clot, fever, and rapid heartbeat. Some people can have allergic reactions including hives, redness of the skin, and life-threatening allergic reaction (anaphylaxis).

Do not take secretin if: You are pregnant or breast-feeding.

Are there any interactions with medications?
It is not known if secretin interacts with any medicines.
Before taking secretin, talk with your healthcare professional if you take any medications.

SELENIUM

What other names is the product known by?
Atomic number 34, Se, Selenite, Selenium Dioxide, Selenized Yeast, L-Selenomethionine, Selenomethionine.

What is it?
Selenium is a mineral. It is taken into the body in water and foods. People use it for medicine.

Is it Effective?
The effectiveness ratings for **SELENIUM** are as follows:
Possibly Effective for... Protecting against prostate cancer.
Possibly Ineffective for... Preventing heart disease • Protecting against skin cancers • Protecting against lung cancer • Treating rheumatoid arthritis (RA).
Insufficient Evidence to Rate Effectiveness for...HIV/AIDS; hardening of the arteries (atherosclerosis); arthritis (osteoarthritis); rheumatoid arthritis; macular degeneration (eye disease); hayfever; gray hair; mood disorders; abnormal pap smears; infertility; cataracts; chronic fatigue syndrome (CFS); bird flu; preventing miscarriage; protecting against colorectal cancer, esophageal cancer, and overall cancer risk; and other conditions.

How does it work?
Selenium is important for making many body processes work correctly. It seems to increase the action of antioxidant enzymes.

Are there safety concerns?
Selenium is safe for most people when taken by mouth in doses less than 400 mcg per day. Higher doses can cause symptoms of poisoning including nausea, vomiting, nail changes, loss of energy, and irritability. Poisoning from long-term use is similar to arsenic poisoning, with symptoms including hair loss, white horizontal streaking on fingernails, nail inflammation, fatigue, irritability, nausea, vomiting, garlic breath odor, and a metallic taste. Selenium can also cause muscle tenderness, tremor, lightheadedness, facial flushing, blood clotting problems, liver and kidney problems, and other side effects. Some research suggests that long-term use of selenium supplements might slightly increase the risk for skin cancer recurrence. Until more is known, people who have had skin cancer should avoid selenium supplements.

Selenium is safe for pregnant and lactating women up to the tolerable upper intake level of 400 micrograms (mcg) per day. Larger amounts can be harmful.

Do not take selenium if: You are a man with fertility problems. Selenium may decrease the ability of sperm to move, which could reduce fertility. • You have or have had skin cancer.

Are there any interactions with medications?
Medications used for lowering cholesterol (Statins). Taking selenium, beta-carotene, vitamin C, and vitamin E together might decrease the effectiveness of some medications used for lowering cholesterol. It is not known if selenium alone decreases the effectiveness of some medications used for lowering cholesterol. Some medications used for lowering cholesterol include atorvastatin (Lipitor), fluvastatin (Lescol), lovastatin (Mevacor), and pravastatin (Pravachol).
Niacin. Taking selenium along with vitamin E, vitamin C, and beta-carotene might decrease some of the beneficial effects of niacin. Niacin can increase the good cholesterol. Taking beta-carotene along with these other vitamins might decrease the good cholesterol.

SELF-HEAL

What other names is the product known by?
All-Heal, Blue Curls, Brownwort, Carpenter's Herb, Carpenter's Weed, Heal-All, Heart of the Earth, Hercules Woundwort, Hock-Heal, Prunella, Prunella vulgaris, Self Heal, Sicklewort, Siclewort, Slough-Heal, Woundwort.

What is it?
Self-heal is an herb. The above ground parts are used to make medicine.

Medical professionals should consult the Professional Version at www.NaturalDatabase.com.

Is it Effective?

The effectiveness ratings for **SELF-HEAL** are as follows:

Insufficient Evidence to Rate Effectiveness for... Mouth and throat ulcers, stomach upset and irritation, internal bleeding, gynecological disorders, wounds, HIV disease, Crohn's disease, ulcerative colitis, and other conditions.

How does it work?

Self-heal contains vitamins C and K, and thiamine. It also contains chemicals called tannins that might help reduce skin swelling (inflammation) and have a drying (astringent) effect on the tissues.

Are there safety concerns?

Self-heal seems to be safe for most people.

Do not take self-heal if: You are pregnant or breast-feeding.

Are there any interactions with medications?

It is not known if self-heal interacts with any medicines.
Before taking self-heal, talk with your healthcare professional if you take any medications.

SENEGA

What other names is the product known by?

Chinese Senega, Flax, Klapperschlangen, Milkwort, Mountain Polygala, Polygalae radix, Rattlesnake Root, Senaga Snakeroot, Seneca, Seneca Snakeroot, Senega, Senega Snakeroot, Seneka, Snake Root.

What is it?

Senega is a plant. The root is used to make medicine.

Is it Effective?

The effectiveness ratings for **SENEGA** are as follows:

Insufficient Evidence to Rate Effectiveness for... Asthma; emphysema; bronchitis; swelling (inflammation) of the throat, nose, and chest; and other conditions.

How does it work?

The chemicals in senega irritate the stomach lining, which causes larger amounts of lung secretions to be made.

Are there safety concerns?

Senega is considered safe when used short-term. Long-term use can cause stomach irritation, diarrhea, dizziness, nausea, and vomiting.

Do not take senega if: You are pregnant or breast-feeding. • You have a fever. • You have gastroesophageal reflux disease (GERD). • You have an ulcer. • You have ulcerative colitis. • You have Crohn's disease.

Are there any interactions with medications?

It is not known if senega interacts with any medicines.
Before taking senega, talk with your healthcare professional if you take any medications.

SENNA

What other names is the product known by?

Alexandrian Senna, Casse, Cassia acutifolia, Cassia angustifolia, Cassia lanceolata, Cassia senna, Indian Senna, Khartoum Senna, Sena Alejandrina, Séné d'Egypte, Senna alexandrina, Sennae Folium, Sennae Fructus, Tinnevelly Senna, True Senna.

What is it?

Senna is an herb. The leaves and the fruit of the plant are used to make medicine.

Is it Effective?

The effectiveness ratings for **SENNA** are as follows:

Likely Effective for... Constipation.

Insufficient Evidence to Rate Effectiveness for... Hemorrhoids, losing weight, and other conditions.

Medical professionals should consult the Professional Version at www.NaturalDatabase.com.

CONSUMER VERSION

How does it work?
Senna contains many chemicals called sennosides. Sennosides irritate the lining of the bowel, which causes a laxative effect.

Are there safety concerns?
Senna is safe for most adults when used short-term. Senna can cause some side effects including stomach discomfort, cramps, and diarrhea.

Don't use senna for more than two weeks. Longer use can cause abnormal bowel function and might cause dependence on laxatives. Long-term use can also cause low electrolytes which can cause heart function disorders, muscle weakness, liver damage, and other adverse effects.

Do not take senna if: You are pregnant or breast-feeding. • You have a stomach or bowel disorder. • You have hemorrhoids. • You have low electrolytes. • You are dehydrated. • You have diarrhea or loose stools.

Are there any interactions with medications?
Digoxin (Lanoxin). Senna is a type of laxative called a stimulant laxative. Stimulant laxatives can decrease potassium levels in the body. Low potassium levels can increase the risk of side effects of digoxin (Lanoxin).
Water pills (Diuretic drugs). Senna is a laxative. Some laxatives can decrease potassium in the body. "Water pills" can also decrease potassium in the body. Taking senna along with "water pills" might decrease potassium in the body too much. Some "water pills" that can decrease potassium include chlorothiazide (Diuril), chlorthalidone (Thalitone), furosemide (Lasix), hydrochlorothiazide (HCTZ, Hydrodiuril, Microzide), and others.

SERRAPEPTASE

What other names is the product known by?
Butterfly Enzyme, SER, Serratia Peptidase, Serratiopeptidase, Serrato Peptidase, Silk Worm Enzyme, Silkworm Extract.

What is it?
Serrapeptase is a chemical from the silkworm. It is used as a medicine.

Is it Effective?
The effectiveness ratings for **SERRAPEPTASE** are as follows:
Possibly Effective for... Swelling after surgery.
Insufficient Evidence to Rate Effectiveness for... Back pain, osteoarthritis, rheumatoid arthritis, osteoporosis, carpel tunnel syndrome, sinusitis, laryngitis, pharyngitis, diabetes, leg ulcers, migraine headache, tension headache, asthma, empyema, thrombophlebitis, fibromyalgia, fibrocystic breast disease, inflammatory bowel disease (IBD) including ulcerative colitis and Crohn's disease, breast engorgement, heart disease, ear infections, and other conditions.

How does it work?
Serrapeptase helps the body break down protein. This might help decrease inflammation and mucous.

Are there safety concerns?
Serrapeptase seems to be safe for adults when taken by mouth, short-term. The long-term safety of serrapeptase is not known.
Do not use serrapeptase if: You are pregnant or breast-feeding.

Are there any interactions with medications?
It is not known if serrapeptase interacts with any medicines.
Talk with your healthcare professional before taking serrapeptase if you take any medications.

SHARK CARTILAGE

What other names is the product known by?
AE-941, MSI-1256F, Neovastat, Shark Cartilage Powder, Shark Cartilage Extract, Squalus acanthias.

What is it?
Shark cartilage comes from sharks caught in the Pacific Ocean. Cartilage is a substance in the body that provides structure support.

Medical professionals should consult the Professional Version at www.NaturalDatabase.com.

CONSUMER VERSION

Is it Effective?

The effectiveness ratings for **SHARK CARTILAGE** are as follows:
Likely Ineffective for... Some types of cancer such as breast, colorectal, lung, prostate, and brain; and Non-Hodgkin's lymphoma.
Insufficient Evidence to Rate Effectiveness for... Arthritis, eye complications, kidney cancer, wound healing, psoriasis, osteoarthritis, and other conditions.

How does it work?

Shark cartilage might help prevent tumor growth.

Are there safety concerns?

Shark cartilage seems safe for most people. It can cause a bad taste in the mouth, nausea, vomiting, stomach upset, constipation, low blood pressure, dizziness, high blood sugar, high calcium levels, and fatigue. Some products have an unpleasant odor and taste.

Do not take shark cartilage if: You are pregnant or breast-feeding. • You have high calcium levels.

Are there any interactions with medications?

It is not known if shark cartilage interacts with any medicines.
Before taking shark cartilage, talk with your healthcare professional if you take any medications.

SHARK LIVER OIL

What other names is the product known by?

Basking Shark Liver Oil, Cetorhinus maximus, Centroporus squamosus, Deep Sea Shark Liver Oil, Dog Fish Liver Oil, Shark Liver, Shark Oil, Sqaulus acanthias.

What is it?

Shark liver oil is used to make medicine.

Is it Effective?

The effectiveness ratings for **SHARK LIVER OIL** are as follows:
Insufficient Evidence to Rate Effectiveness for... Leukemia and other cancers, side effects of cancer treatment, common cold, flu, skin problems, and other conditions.

How does it work?

Shark liver oil contains chemicals that might have activity against cancer or cancer treatment related side effects.

Are there safety concerns?

There isn't enough information available to know if shark liver oil is safe. It can cause pneumonia in people who accidentally breathe it into the lungs.

Do not take shark liver oil if: You are pregnant or breast-feeding.

Are there any interactions with medications?

It is not known if shark liver oil interacts with any medicines.
Before taking shark liver oil, talk with your healthcare professional if you take any medications.

SHELLAC

What other names is the product known by?

Gommelaque, Lac, Lacca, Laccifer.

What is it?

Shellac is made by the insect Laccifer lacca. It is used in dentistry to make dentures and other dental products, and in pharmaceutical manufacturing as a tablet coating and for other uses.

Is it Effective?

The effectiveness ratings for **SHELLAC** are as follows:
Insufficient Evidence to Rate Effectiveness for... No known medicinal uses.

Medical professionals should consult the Professional Version at www.NaturalDatabase.com.

 Natural Medicines Comprehensive Database Consumer Version (209) 472-2244

How does it work?
Shellac is used for its clear coating properties and as a natural "glue."

Are there safety concerns?
Shellac is safe for most people when taken by mouth in pharmaceutical products. A few people are allergic to shellac. Do not confuse the shellac used in dental and pharmaceutical manufacturing with the varnish-like product from the hardware store. Varnish-like shellac contains methanol (wood alcohol) and is very poisonous.

Do not use shellac if: You are pregnant or breast-feeding.

Are there any interactions with medications?
It is not known if shellac interacts with any medicines.
Before taking shellac, talk with your healthcare professional if you take any medications.

SHEPHERD'S PURSE

What other names is the product known by?
Blind Weed, Bursae Pastoris Herba, Capsella, Caseweed, Cocowort, Lady's Purse, Mother's-Heart, Pepper-And-Salt, Pick-Pocket, Poor Man's Parmacettie, Rattle Pouches, Sanguinary, Shepherd's Heart, Shepherd's Purse Herb, Shepherd's Scrip, Shepherd's Sprout, Shepherds Purse, Shovelweed, St. James' Weed, Thlaspi bursa-pastoris, Toywort, Witches' Pouches.

What is it?
Shepherd's purse is a plant. The above ground parts are used to make medicine.

Is it Effective?
The effectiveness ratings for **SHEPHERD'S PURSE** are as follows:
Insufficient Evidence to Rate Effectiveness for... Headache, heart problems, premenstrual complaints, diarrhea, and other conditions.

How does it work?
Shepherd's purse might decrease bleeding, stimulate muscles, and increase uterine contractions.

Are there safety concerns?
Shepherd's purse is safe when used in small amounts. It can cause drowsiness, changes in blood pressure, thyroid function changes, and heart palpitations.

An overdose of shepherd's purse might cause paralysis, breathing difficulty, and death.

Do not take shepherd's purse if: You are pregnant or breast-feeding. • You have a heart condition. • You have kidney stones. • You have a thyroid problem.

Are there any interactions with medications?
Sedative medications (CNS depressants). Large amounts of shepherd's purse might cause sleepiness and drowsiness. Medications that cause sleepiness are called sedatives. Taking shepherd's purse along with sedative medications might cause too much sleepiness. Some sedative medications include clonazepam (Klonopin), lorazepam (Ativan), phenobarbital (Donnatal), zolpidem (Ambien), and others.
Thyroid hormone. The body naturally produces thyroid hormone. Shepherd's purse might decrease how much thyroid hormone the body produces. Taking shepherd's purse along with thyroid hormone might decrease the effectiveness of thyroid hormone.

SHIITAKE MUSHROOM

What other names is the product known by?
Forest Mushroom, Hua Gu, Lenticus edodes, Lentinan edodes, Lentinula, Lentinula edodes, Tricholomopsis edodes, Lentinus edodes, Pasania Fungus, Shitake, Shiitake, Snake Butter.

What is it?
Shiitake mushroom is a fungus. The extract is used to make medicine.

Medical professionals should consult the Professional Version at www.NaturalDatabase.com.

Is it Effective?

The effectiveness ratings for **SHIITAKE MUSHROOM** are as follows:
Possibly Ineffective for... Prostate cancer.
Insufficient Evidence to Rate Effectiveness for... Reducing high cholesterol and other conditions.

How does it work?

Shiitake mushroom contains chemicals that might help lower cholesterol levels.

Are there safety concerns?

Shiitake mushroom is safe when consumed in food amounts, but it seems unsafe for use as a medicine. It can cause stomach discomfort, blood abnormalities, and skin swelling (inflammation). It might also cause an increased sensitivity to the sun, allergic skin reactions, and breathing problems.

Do not take shiitake mushoom if: You are pregnant or breast-feeding. • You have a blood disorder called eosinophilia.

Are there any interactions with medications?

It is not known if shiitake mushroom interacts with any medicines.
Before taking shiitake mushroom, talk with your healthcare professional if you take any medications.

SILICON

What other names is the product known by?

Orthosilicic Acid, Phytolithic Silica, Silica, Silicium, Silicon Dioxide, Sodium Silicate.

What is it?

Silicon is a mineral. Silicon supplements are used as medicine.

Is it Effective?

The effectiveness ratings for **SILICON** are as follows:
Possibly Effective for... Increasing bone mineral density when obtained from foods.
Insufficient Evidence to Rate Effectiveness for... Heart disease, Alzheimer's disease, sprains and strains, and digestion problems.

How does it work?

A clear biological function for silicon in humans has not been established. There is some evidence, though, that silicon might have a role in bone and collagen formation.

Are there safety concerns?

Silicon seems to be safe in food amounts. Its safety as a medicine is unknown. Kidney stones can occur rarely in people taking silicon-containing antacids for long periods of time.

Do not take silicon in medicinal amounts if: You are pregnant or breast-feeding.

Are there any interactions with medications?

It is not known if silicon interacts with any medicines.
Before taking silicon, talk with your healthcare professional if you take any medications.

SIMARUBA

What other names is the product known by?

Bitter Damson, Dysentery Bark, Mountain Damson, Simaruba amara, Slave Wood, Stave Wood, Sumaroub, Quassia simarouba.

What is it?

Simaruba is a plant. The bark is used as medicine.

Is it Effective?

The effectiveness ratings for **SIMARUBA** are as follows:
Insufficient Evidence to Rate Effectiveness for... Diarrhea, malaria, water retention, fever, stomach upset, causing abortion, and other uses.

How does it work?

Simaruba contains high concentrations of chemicals called tannins. Tannins might help relieve diarrhea.

Are there safety concerns?

It is not known if simaruba is safe. It can cause vomiting when used in large amounts.

Do not take simaruba if: You are pregnant or breast-feeding.

Are there any interactions with medications?

It is not known if simaruba interacts with any medicines.
Before taking simaruba, talk with your healthcare professional if you take any medications.

SITOSTANOL

What other names is the product known by?

Beta-sitostanol, Dihydro-beta-sitosterol, Fucostanol, Phytostanol, Plant Stanol, Stigmastanol, 24-alpha-ethylcholestanol.

What is it?

Sitostanol is a plant product. It is made from vegetable oils or the oil from pine tree wood pulp, and is then combined with canola oil.

Is it Effective?

The effectiveness ratings for **SITOSTANOL** are as follows:
Likely Effective for... Reducing cholesterol levels in adults.
Possibly Effective for... Reducing cholesterol levels in children.

How does it work?

Sitostanol blocks both the cholesterol from food and the cholesterol made by the liver from entering the body.

Are there safety concerns?

Sitostanol is safe for most people. It might cause stomach upset or too much fat in the stool (steatorrhea).

Adults can safely use sitostanol for up to one year, and children can safely use it for up to three months.

Do not take sitostanol if: You are pregnant or breast-feeding.

Are there any interactions with medications?

It is not known if sitostanol interacts with any medicines.
Before taking sitostanol, talk with your healthcare professional if you take any medications.

SKIRRET

What other names is the product known by?

Chervis, Sium sisarum.

What is it?

Skirret is a plant. The root is used as medicine.

Is it Effective?

The effectiveness ratings for **SKIRRET** are as follows:
Insufficient Evidence to Rate Effectiveness for... Digestive disorders, loss of appetite, and chest complaints.

How does it work?

There isn't enough information to know how skirret might work.

Are there safety concerns?

It is not known if skirret is safe or what the potential side effects might be.

Do not take skirret if: You are pregnant or breast-feeding.

Medical professionals should consult the Professional Version at www.NaturalDatabase.com.

Are there any interactions with medications?

It is not known if skirret interacts with any medicines.

Before taking skirret, talk with your healthcare professional if you take any medications.

SKULLCAP

What other names is the product known by?

Blue Pimpernel, Blue Skullcap, Helmet Flower, Hoodwort, Mad-Dog Herb, Mad-Dog Skullcap, Mad-Dog Weed, Mad Weed, Quaker Bonnet, Scutelluria, Scuterlluria lateriflora.

What is it?

Skullcap is a plant. The above ground parts are used to make medicine.

Is it Effective?

The effectiveness ratings for **SKULLCAP** are as follows:

Insufficient Evidence to Rate Effectiveness for... Insomnia, anxiety, seizures, stroke, and other conditions.

How does it work?

The chemicals in skullcap might work by preventing swelling (inflammation).

Are there safety concerns?

There isn't enough information to know if skullcap is safe.

Do not use skullcap if: You are pregnant or breast-feeding.

Are there any interactions with medications?

It is not known if skullcap interacts with any medicines.

Before taking skullcap, talk with your healthcare professional if you take any medications.

SKUNK CABBAGE

What other names is the product known by?

Dracontium, Meadow Cabbage, Polecatweed, Skunkweed, Spathyema Foetida, Swamp Cabbage, Symplocarpus foetidus.

What is it?

Skunk cabbage is a plant. The root and root-like parts are used to make medicine.

Is it Effective?

The effectiveness ratings for **SKUNK CABBAGE** are as follows:

Insufficient Evidence to Rate Effectiveness for... Bronchitis, asthma, whooping cough, and other conditions.

How does it work?

Skunk cabbage contains chemicals that have pain relieving and sedative properties.

Are there safety concerns?

Skunk cabbage seems to be safe for most people. Large amounts can cause nausea, vomiting, diarrhea, headache, dizziness, decreased vision, and stomach cramps.

Do not take skunk cabbage if: You are pregnant or breast-feeding. • You have a history of kidney stones. • You have gastroesophageal reflux disease (GERD). • You have an ulcer. • You have ulcerative colitis. • You have Crohn's disease.

Are there any interactions with medications?

It is not known if skunk cabbage interacts with any medicines.

Before taking skunk cabbage, talk with your healthcare professional if you take any medications.

SLIPPERY ELM

What other names is the product known by?
Indian Elm, Moose Elm, Red Elm, Sweet Elm, Ulmus fulva, Ulmus rubra.

What is it?
Slippery elm is a tree. The inner bark rind is used as medicine.

Is it Effective?
The effectiveness ratings for **SLIPPERY ELM** are as follows:
Possibly Effective for... Sore throat.
Insufficient Evidence to Rate Effectiveness for... Coughs, colic, diarrhea, constipation, hemorrhoids, irritable bowel syndrome (IBS), bladder infection, urinary tract infections, and other conditions.

How does it work?
Slippery elm contains chemicals that can help soothe sore throats. It can also cause mucous secretion which might be helpful for stomach and intestinal problems.

Are there safety concerns?
Slippery elm is safe for most people. It can cause allergic reactions and skin irritation.

The whole bark is unsafe for use in pregnancy because it might cause miscarriage. The inner bark used in throat lozenges appears to be safe for use in pregnancy.

Do not use slippery elm if: You are breast-feeding.

Are there any interactions with medications?
Medications taken by mouth (Oral drugs). Slippery elm contains a type of soft fiber called mucilage. Mucilage can decrease how much medicine the body absorbs. Taking slippery elm at the same time you take medications by mouth can decrease the effectiveness of your medication. To prevent this interaction take slippery elm at least one hour after medications you take by mouth.

SMARTWEED

What other names is the product known by?
Arsesmart, Water Pepper, Polygonum Hydropiper.

What is it?
Smartweed is an herb. The entire plant is used to make medicine.

Is it Effective?
The effectiveness ratings for **SMARTWEED** are as follows:
Insufficient Evidence to Rate Effectiveness for... Bleeding and diarrhea.

How does it work?
Smartweed contains ingredients that are thought to stop bleeding and influence urine elimination.

Are there safety concerns?
It is not known if smartweed is safe. It can cause side effects such as stomach irritation when taken by mouth.

When the fresh plant is handled it can cause skin irritation and inflammation.

Do not use smartweed if: You are pregnant or breast-feeding. • You have ulcers or other stomach conditions.

Are there any interactions with medications?
Warfarin (Coumadin). Smartweed contains large amounts of vitamin K. Vitamin K is used by the body to help blood clot. Warfarin (Coumadin) is used to slow blood clotting. By helping the blood clot, smartweed might decrease the effectiveness of warfarin (Coumadin). Be sure to have your blood checked regularly. The dose of your warfarin (Coumadin) might need to be changed.

Medical professionals should consult the Professional Version at www.NaturalDatabase.com.

SMOOTH ALDER

What other names is the product known by?
Alnus serrulata, Hazel Alder, Tag Alder.

What is it?
Smooth alder is a tree. The bark is used to make medicine.

Is it Effective?
The effectiveness ratings for **SMOOTH ALDER** are as follows:
Insufficient Evidence to Rate Effectiveness for... Sore throat and bleeding of the intestines.

How does it work?
There isn't enough information to know how smooth alder might work.

Are there safety concerns?
It is not known if smooth alder is safe or what the potential side effects might be.

Do not use smooth alder if: You are pregnant or breast-feeding.

Are there any interactions with medications?
It is not known if smooth alder interacts with any medicines.
Before taking smooth alder, talk with your healthcare professional if you take any medications.

SNEEZEWORT

What other names is the product known by?
Achillea ptarmica, Sneezeweed.

What is it?
Sneezewort is a plant. The dried root is used as medicine.

Is it Effective?
The effectiveness ratings for **SNEEZEWORT** are as follows:
Insufficient Evidence to Rate Effectiveness for... Joint and muscular pain, toothache, diarrhea, nausea, vomiting, gas (flatulence), tiredness, urinary tract complaints, loss of appetite, and other complaints.

How does it work?
There isn't enough information to know how sneezewort might work.

Are there safety concerns?
There isn't enough information to know if sneezewort is safe or what the potential side effects might be. Some people get allergic reactions.
Do not use sneezewort if: You are pregnant or breast-feeding.

Are there any interactions with medications?
It is not known if sneezewort interacts with any medicines.
Before taking sneezewort, talk with your healthcare professional if you take any medications.

SOLOMON'S SEAL

What other names is the product known by?
Dropberry, Lady's Seals, Sealroot, Sealwort, St. Mary's Seal, Polygonatum Multiflorum.

What is it?
Solomon's seal is an herb.

Is it Effective?
The effectiveness ratings for **SOLOMON'S SEAL** are as follows:
Insufficient Evidence to Rate Effectiveness for... Lung disorders, inflammation, bruises, boils on the fingers, hemorrhoids, and skin redness.

 (209) 472-2244

How does it work?
Solomon's seal contains chemicals that might decrease blood sugar levels.

Are there safety concerns?
Solomon's seal is safe for most adults when taken for short time periods. It can cause some side effects such as diarrhea, stomach complaints, and nausea when taken for long time periods or in large doses.

Do not use Solomon's seal if: You are pregnant or breast-feeding. • You have diabetes.

Are there any interactions with medications?
Chlorpropamide (Diabinese). Chlorpropamide (Diabinese) is used to decrease blood sugar in people with diabetes. Solomon's seal might also decrease blood sugar. Taking Solomon's seal along with chlorpropamide (Diabinese) might cause your blood sugar to go too low. Monitor your blood sugar closely. The dose of your chlorpropamide (Diabinese) might need to be changed.
Insulin. Solomon's seal might decrease blood sugar. Insulin is also used to decrease blood sugar. Taking Solomon's seal along with insulin might cause your blood sugar to be too low. Monitor your blood sugar closely. The dose of your insulin might need to be changed.
Medications for diabetes (Antidiabetes drugs). Solomon's seal might decrease blood sugar. Diabetes medications are also used to lower blood sugar. Taking Solomon's seal along with diabetes medications might cause your blood sugar to go too low. Monitor your blood sugar closely. The dose of your diabetes medication might need to be changed. Some medications used for diabetes include glimepiride (Amaryl), glyburide (DiaBeta, Glynase PresTab, Micronase), insulin, pioglitazone (Actos), rosiglitazone (Avandia), chlorpropamide (Diabinese), glipizide (Glucotrol), tolbutamide (Orinase), and others.

SORREL

What other names is the product known by?
Acedera Común, Azeda-Brava, Common Sorrel, Field Sorrel, Garden Sorrel, Red Sorrel, Rumex acetosa, Rumex acetosella, Sheep's Sorrel, Sorrel Dock, Sour Dock, Wiesensauerampfer.

What is it?
Sorrel is a plant. People use the above ground parts for medicine. Be careful not to confuse sorrel (Rumex acetosa) with roselle (Hibiscus sabdariffa), which is known as Jamaican sorrel or Guinea sorrel.

Is it Effective?
The effectiveness ratings for **SORREL** are as follows:
Possibly Effective for... Inflamed nasal passage, or "sinusitis," when taken with gentian root, European elder flower, verbena, and cowslip flower (SinuComp, Sinupret).
Insufficient Evidence to Rate Effectiveness for... Fluid retention, infections, and other conditions.

How does it work?
Sorrel contains tannins which have an astringent effect to reduce mucous production.

Are there safety concerns?
Sorrel seems to be safe for most people when used in small amounts as part of a combination product containing gentian root, European elder flower, verbena, and cowslip flower (SinuComp, Sinupret). There isn't enough information to know if sorrel is safe when used in medicinal amounts other than as part of the combination product. The combination product can cause digestive system upset and occasionally allergic skin rash.

When taken in large amounts, sorrel might increase the risk of developing kidney stones.

Do not use sorrel if: You are pregnant or breast-feeding. • You have kidney disease.

Are there any interactions with medications?
It is not known if sorrel interacts with any medicines.
Before taking sorrel, talk with your healthcare professional if you take any medications.

SOUR CHERRY

What other names is the product known by?

Cerezo Acido, Cerisier Acide, English Morello, Ginjeira, Griottier, Guindo, Montmorency Cherry, Morello Cherry, Pie Cherry, Red Cherry, Richmond, Sauerkirsche, Sauerkirschenbaum, Tart Cherry, Prunus Cerasus, Cerasus Vulgaris, Prunus Vulgaris.

What is it?

Sour cherry is a fruit. The fruit and stem of the sour cherry are used to make medicine and food.

Is it Effective?

The effectiveness ratings for **SOUR CHERRY** are as follows:
Insufficient Evidence to Rate Effectiveness for... Arthritis, gout, increasing urination, and improving digestion.

How does it work?

Sour cherry fruit contains ingredients that are thought to reduce inflammation.

Are there safety concerns?

The fruit of the sour cherry is safe for most adults, including pregnant and breast-feeding women, when eaten as food. However, it is not known if sour cherry stems or dietary supplements containing the sour cherry plant are safe. Avoid using products containing sour cherry stems or dietary supplements containing the sour cherry plant.

Are there any interactions with medications?

It is not known if sour cherry interacts with any medicines.
Before taking sour cherry, talk with your healthcare professional if you take any medications.

SOUTH AFRICAN GERANIUM

What other names is the product known by?

African Geranium, EPs 7630, Geranien, Geranium Root, Pelargonien, Pelargonium Root, Pelargonium sidoides, Umckaloabo.

What is it?

South African geranium is a plant. Its roots are used for medicine.

Is it Effective?

The effectiveness ratings for **SOUTH AFRICAN GERANIUM** are as follows:
Possibly Effective for... Bronchitis • Tonsillopharyngitis.
Insufficient Evidence to Rate Effectiveness for... Sinusitis, common cold, tuberculosis, diarrhea, or other conditions.

How does it work?

There is not enough information to know how South African geranium might work for medicinal purposes. Some preliminary research suggests that it might have antibiotic-like effects.

Are there safety concerns?

South African geranium seems to be safe when taken by mouth for seven days or less. There is not enough information to know if it is safe when taken for longer periods of time.
Do not take South African geranium if: You are pregnant or breast-feeding.

Are there any interactions with medications?

There is not enough information to know if South African geranium might interact with medicines.
Before taking South African geranium, talk with your health care professional if you are taking any medications.

SOUTHERN PRICKLY ASH

What other names is the product known by?

Prickly Ash, Prickly Yellow Wood, Sea Ash, Toothache Tree, Xanthoxylum, Zanthoxylum, Zanthoxylum clava-herculis.

What is it?

Southern prickly ash is a plant. The bark and berry are used to make medicine.

Is it Effective?

The effectiveness ratings for **SOUTHERN PRICKLY ASH** are as follows:

Insufficient Evidence to Rate Effectiveness for... Cramps, poor circulation in the legs, Raynaud's syndrome (circulation problems and spasms of the blood vessels in the fingers), joint pain, toothache, fever, sores, ulcers, and cancer.

How does it work?

The chemicals in southern prickly ash are thought to cause sedation, decrease swelling, kill bacteria, inhibits liver enzymes, and increase saliva production.

Are there safety concerns?

The bark of southern prickly ash may be safe when used as a medicine. The safety of the berry is not known. The potential side effects of southern prickly ash are not known.

Do not use southern prickly ash if: You are pregnant or breast-feeding. • You have liver problems.

Are there any interactions with medications?

Antacids. Antacids are used to decrease stomach acid. Southern prickly ash may increase stomach acid. By increasing stomach acid, southern prickly ash might decrease the effectiveness of antacids. Some antacids include calcium carbonate (Tums, others), dihydroxyaluminum sodium carbonate (Rolaids, others), magaldrate (Riopan), magnesium sulfate (Bilagog), aluminum hydroxide (Amphojel), and others.

Medications that decrease stomach acid (H2-Blockers). Southern prickly ash might increase stomach acid. By increasing stomach acid, southern prickly ash might decrease the effectiveness of some medications that decrease stomach acid, called H2-Blockers. Some medications that decrease stomach acid include cimetidine (Tagamet), ranitidine (Zantac), nizatidine (Axid), and famotidine (Pepcid).

Medications that decrease stomach acid (Proton pump inhibitors). Southern prickly ash might increase stomach acid. By increasing stomach acid, southern prickly ash might decrease the effectiveness of medications that are used to decrease stomach acid, called proton pump inhibitors. Some medications that decrease stomach acid include omeprazole (Prilosec), lansoprazole (Prevacid), rabeprazole (Aciphex), pantoprazole (Protonix), and esomeprazole (Nexium).

SOY

What other names is the product known by?

Daidzein, Edamame, Frijol de Soya, Genestein, Genistein, Haba Soya, Isoflavones, Phytoestrogen, Plant Estrogen, Shoyu, Soja, Sojabohne, Soya, Soybean, Soybean Curd, Soy Fiber, Soy Milk, Soy Protein, Touchi, Tofu.

What is it?

Soy comes from soybeans. The beans can be processed into soy protein, which is a powder; soy milk, which is a beverage that may or may not be fortified with extra calcium from the soybeans; or soy fiber, which contains some of the fibrous parts of the bean.

Is it Effective?

The effectiveness ratings for **SOY** are as follows:

Possibly Effective for... High cholesterol • Hot flashes caused by menopause. But it doesn't seem to help for hot flashes in women with breast cancer • Reducing the risk of osteoporosis (weak bones) • Reducing the risk of developing breast cancer • Reducing the duration of diarrhea in infants • Preventing and treating diabetic nerve problems • Providing nutrition to infants who can't digest milk sugars • Reducing protein in the urine of people with kidney disease • Treating diabetes.

Possibly Ineffective for... Reducing muscle soreness caused by exercise • Heart disease.

Insufficient Evidence to Rate Effectiveness for... Preventing thyroid cancer, endometrial cancer, lung cancer, prostate cancer, improving memory, reducing breast pain, weight loss, asthma, high blood pressure, premenstrual syndrome (PMS), and other conditions.

How does it work?

Soy contains "isoflavones" which are changed in the body to "phytoestrogens" which are similar to the hormone estrogen.

Are there safety concerns?

Consuming soy foods such as soy protein is safe. Taking soy dietary supplements also seems to be safe for most people when used short-term. It can cause some mild side effects such as constipation, bloating, and nausea. It can also cause allergic reactions involving rash and itching in some people. Long-term use of high doses of soy dietary supplements might not be safe. There is concern that taking high doses might cause

Medical professionals should consult the Professional Version at www.NaturalDatabase.com.

abnormal tissue growth in the uterus.

Do not take soy in amounts greater than what is normally found in foods if: You are pregnant or breast-feeding. • You have breast cancer or if breast cancer runs in your family. • You have endometrial cancer. • You have kidney disease. • You have a risk of urinary bladder cancer.

Do not use soy in children without medical supervision.

Are there any interactions with medications?

Antibiotic drugs. Antibiotics are used to reduce harmful bacteria in the body. Antibiotics can also reduce friendly bacteria in the intestines. Friendly bacteria in the intestines seem to help increase the effectiveness of soy. By reducing the number of bacteria in intestines antibiotics might decrease the effectiveness of soy. But it is too soon to know if this interaction is a big concern.

Estrogens. Large amounts of soy might have some of the same effects as estrogen. But soy isn't as strong as estrogen pills. Taking soy along with estrogen pills might decrease the effects of estrogen pills. Some estrogen pills include conjugated equine estrogens (Premarin), ethinyl estradiol, estradiol, and others.

Tamoxifen (Nolvadex). Some types of cancer are affected by hormones in the body. Estrogen-sensitive cancers are cancers that are affected by estrogen levels in the body. Tamoxifen (Nolvadex) is used to help treat and prevent these types of cancer. Soy seems to also affect estrogen levels in the body. By affecting estrogen in the body, soy might decrease the effectiveness of tamoxifen (Nolvadex). Do not take soy if you are taking tamoxifen (Nolvadex).

Warfarin (Coumadin). Warfarin (Coumadin) is used to slow blood clotting. Soy has been reported to decrease the effectiveness of warfarin (Coumadin). Decreasing the effectiveness of warfarin (Coumadin) might increase the risk of clotting. It is unclear why this interaction might occur. Be sure to have your blood checked regularly. The dose of your warfarin (Coumadin) might need to be changed.

SOYBEAN OIL

What other names is the product known by?
Glycine Soja, Intralipid, Soybean, Soyca, Travmulsion.

What is it?
Soybean oil is produced from the seeds of the soybean plant.

Is it Effective?
The effectiveness ratings for **SOYBEAN OIL** are as follows:

Effective for... Use as a nutritional supplement in intravenous feedings.

Likely Effective for... Preventing mosquito bites when applied to the skin. Soybean oil is an ingredient in some commercial mosquito repellents. It seems to be comparable to some other mosquito repellents including some products that contain a small amount of DEET.

Possibly Effective for... Lowering cholesterol levels in people with high cholesterol • Osteoarthritis, when a specific processed part of the oil (unsaponifiable fractions) is used in combination with avocado oil.

How does it work?
Soybean oil works to lower cholesterol levels by decreasing cholesterol absorption in the gut. Specific processed parts of soybean oil called unsaponifiables may have a beneficial effect on joints.

Are there safety concerns?
Soybean oil is safe for most adults.

Soybean oil is also safe for pregnant and breast-feeding women, when used as part of the diet. But the safety of soybean oil during pregnancy and breast-feeding is not known when used in amounts greater than those commonly found in foods.

Do not use soybean oil if: You have a peanut or soybean allergy.

Are there any interactions with medications?
Psyllium. Psyllium can decrease the amount of fat the body absorbs from soybean oil. Products containing psyllium include Metamucil, Konsyl, and Perdiem.

SPANISH BROOM

What other names is the product known by?
Genet, Genista Juncea, Spartium Junceum, Weaver's Broom.

What is it?
Spanish broom is an herb. The flowers are used to make medicine.

Is it Effective?
The effectiveness ratings for **SPANISH BROOM** are as follows:
Insufficient Evidence to Rate Effectiveness for... Stimulating bowel movements and increasing urine output.

How does it work?
Spanish broom contains a chemical called sparteine, but it is not known exactly how Spanish broom works.

Are there safety concerns?
Spanish broom seems to be safe when used in amounts found in food, but the safety of using greater amounts is not known.

Do not take Spanish broom if: You are pregnant or breast-feeding.

Are there any interactions with medications?
It is not known if Spanish broom interacts with any medicines.
Before taking Spanish broom, talk with your healthcare professional if you take any medications.

SPANISH ORIGANUM OIL

What other names is the product known by?
Coridothymus Capitatus, Origanum Oil, Satureja Capitata, Sicilian Thyme, Spanish Origanum, Spanish Thyme, Thymus Capitatus.

What is it?
Spanish origanum oil comes from Thymus capitatus and various species of Origanum.

Is it Effective?
The effectiveness ratings for **SPANISH ORIGANUM OIL** are as follows:
Insufficient Evidence to Rate Effectiveness for... Burns and infections.

How does it work?
There isn't enough information to know how Spanish origanum oil might work.

Are there safety concerns?
Spanish origanum oil is safe for most adults when used in amounts found in foods. The safety of using larger amounts is not known.

Do not use Spanish origanum oil in medicinal amounts if: You are pregnant or breast-feeding.

Are there any interactions with medications?
It is not known if Spanish origanum oil interacts with any medicines.
Before taking Spanish origanum oil, talk with your healthcare professional if you take any medications.

SPEARMINT

What other names is the product known by?
Curled Mint, Fish Mint, Garden Mint, Green Mint, Lamb Mint, Mackerel Mint, Our Lady's Mint, Pahari Pudina, Putiha, Sage of Bethlehem, Spire Mint, Yerba Buena, Mentha Spicata, Mentha Viridis.

What is it?
Spearmint is an herb. The leaves and oil are used to make medicine.

Is it Effective?

The effectiveness ratings for **SPEARMINT** are as follows:

Insufficient Evidence to Rate Effectiveness for... Gas (flatulence), indigestion, nausea, sore throat, diarrhea, colds, headaches, toothaches, cramps, cancer, arthritis, muscle pain, and skin conditions.

How does it work?

The oil in spearmint is thought to calm the stomach.

Are there safety concerns?

Spearmint seems to be safe when taken by mouth or applied to the skin.

Do not use spearmint if: You are pregnant or breast-feeding.

Are there any interactions with medications?

It is not known if spearmint interacts with any medicines.
Before taking spearmint, talk with your healthcare professional if you take any medications.

SPINACH

What other names is the product known by?

Spinaciae Folium, Spinacia Oleracea, Spinatblatter.

What is it?

Spinach is a vegetable. The leaves are used for food and to make medicine.

Is it Effective?

The effectiveness ratings for **SPINACH** are as follows:

Insufficient Evidence to Rate Effectiveness for... Gastrointestinal complaints, fatigue, and stimulating growth in children.

How does it work?

Spinach contains vitamins and other nutrients.

Are there safety concerns?

Spinach is safe for most people when used as a food.

Spinach is safe during pregnancy and breast-feeding when used in food amounts, but the safety of spinach supplements in pills is not known.

Do not give spinach to infants less than four months old. It can sometimes cause a blood disorder in young infants.

Do not use spinach if: You have kidney stones.

Are there any interactions with medications?

Medications for diabetes (Antidiabetes drugs). Spinach might decrease blood sugar. Diabetes medications are also used to lower blood sugar. Taking spinach along with diabetes medications might cause your blood sugar to go too low. Monitor your blood sugar closely. The dose of your diabetes medication might need to be changed. Some medications used for diabetes include glimepiride (Amaryl), glyburide (DiaBeta, Glynase PresTab, Micronase), insulin, pioglitazone (Actos), rosiglitazone (Avandia), chlorpropamide (Diabinese), glipizide (Glucotrol), tolbutamide (Orinase), and others.

Warfarin (Coumadin). Spinach contains large amounts of vitamin K. Vitamin K is used by the body to help blood clot. Warfarin (Coumadin) is used to slow blood clotting. By helping the blood clot, spinach might decrease the effectiveness of warfarin (Coumadin). Be sure to have your blood checked regularly. The dose of your warfarin (Coumadin) might need to be changed.

SPINY RESTHARROW

What other names is the product known by?
Cammock, Ground Furze, Hauhechelwurzel, Land Whin, Ononidis Radix, Ononis Spinosa, Petty Whin, Restharrow, Stay Plough, Stinking Tommy, Wild Liquorice.

What is it?
Spiny restharrow is an herb. The root and oil are used to make medicine.

Is it Effective?
The effectiveness ratings for **SPINY RESTHARROW** are as follows:
Insufficient Evidence to Rate Effectiveness for... Gout, joint, or muscle pain; urinary tract infections; and kidney stones.

How does it work?
It is not known how spiny restharrow might work.

Are there safety concerns?
Spiny restharrow seems to be safe.

Do not take spiny restharrow if: You are pregnant or breast-feeding. • You have fluid retention or edema.

Are there any interactions with medications?
It is not known if spiny restharrow interacts with any medicines.
Before taking spiny restharrow, talk with your healthcare professional if you take any medications.

SPLEEN EXTRACT

What other names is the product known by?
Bovine Spleen, Hydrolyzed Spleen Extract, Predigested Spleen Extract, Raw Spleen, Spleen, Spleen Concentrate, Spleen Factors, Spleen Peptides, Spleen Polypeptides, Splenopentin, Tuftsin.

What is it?
Spleen extract is produced from animal spleens.

Is it Effective?
The effectiveness ratings for **SPLEEN EXTRACT** are as follows:
Insufficient Evidence to Rate Effectiveness for... Infections, enhancing immune function, skin conditions, kidney disease, and rheumatoid arthritis.

How does it work?
Spleen extract contains ingredients that are thought to stimulate the immune system.

Are there safety concerns?
It is not known if spleen extract is safe. There is some concern about contamination from sick or diseased animals. Until more is known, don't use products containing spleen extract.

Are there any interactions with medications?
It is not known if spleen extract interacts with any medicines.
Before taking spleen extract, talk with your healthcare professional if you take any medications.

SQUALAMINE

What other names is the product known by?
Spiny Dogfish Shark, Squalus Acanthias.

What is it?
Squalamine is a chemical produced from tissues of the spiny dogfish shark or made synthetically.

Medical professionals should consult the Professional Version at www.NaturalDatabase.com.

Is it Effective?

The effectiveness ratings for **SQUALAMINE** are as follows:

Insufficient Evidence to Rate Effectiveness for... Infections, cancer, and eye conditions in people with diabetes.

How does it work?

Squalamine is thought to prevent growth of bacteria that cause infections and tumors.

Are there safety concerns?

It is not known if squalamine is safe.

Do not take squalamine if: You are pregnant or breast-feeding.

Are there any interactions with medications?

It is not known if squalamine interacts with any medicines.
Before taking squalamine, talk with your healthcare professional if you take any medications.

SQUAWVINE

What other names is the product known by?

Checkerberry, Deerberry, Hive Vine, Mitchella repens, Noon Kie Oo Nah Yeah, One-Berry, Partridgeberry, Running Box, Squaw Berry, Twinberry, Two-Eyed Berry, Winter Clover.

What is it?

Squawvine is an herb. The stem and leaves are used to make medicine.

Is it Effective?

The effectiveness ratings for **SQUAWVINE** are as follows:

Insufficient Evidence to Rate Effectiveness for... Anxiety, depression after childbirth, diarrhea, menstrual disorders, heart or kidney problems, nipple soreness, water retention, and other conditions.

How does it work?

There isn't enough information available to know how squawvine works.

Are there safety concerns?

Squawvine seems safe for most people.

Do not take squawvine if: You are pregnant or breast-feeding.

Are there any interactions with medications?

It is not known if squawvine interacts with any medicines.
Before taking squawvine, talk with your healthcare professional if you take any medications.

SQUILL

What other names is the product known by?

Drimia indica, Drimia maritima, European Squill, Indian Squill, Mediterranean Squill, Red Squill, Sea Onion, Sea Squill Bulb, Scilla, Urginea indica, Urginea maritima, Urginea scilla, White Squill.

What is it?

Squill is a plant. The bulbs of the plant are used to make medicine.

Is it Effective?

The effectiveness ratings for **SQUILL** are as follows:

Insufficient Evidence to Rate Effectiveness for... Abnormal heart rhythm and other heart problems, fluid retention, bronchitis, asthma, whooping cough, thinning mucus, or inducing vomiting.

How does it work?

The chemicals in squill affect the heart. They can also thin mucus secretions in the lungs.

Are there safety concerns?

Squill is unsafe when taken by mouth. It causes stomach irritation, loss of appetite, diarrhea, vomiting, headache, vision changes, depression, confusion, hallucinations, irregular heartbeat, and skin rash. More serious side effects

such as seizures, life-threatening abnormal heart rhythms, and death have occurred.
Do not take squill if: You are pregnant or breast-feeding.

Are there any interactions with medications?

Calcium supplements. Squill can stimulate the heartbeat. Calcium might also affect the heart. Taking squill along with calcium might cause the heart to be too stimulated. Do not take squill along with calcium supplements.

Digoxin (Lanoxin). Digoxin (Lanoxin) helps the heart beat more strongly. Squill also seems to affect the heart. Taking squill along with digoxin can increase the effects of digoxin and increase the risk of side effects. Do not take squill if you are taking digoxin (Lanoxin) without talking to your health care professional.

Medications for inflammation (Corticosteroids). Squill might affect the heart. Some medications for inflammation can decrease potassium in the body. Low potassium levels can also affect the heart and increase the risk of side effects from squill. Some medications for inflammation include dexamethasone (Decadron), hydrocortisone (Cortef), methylprednisolone (Medrol), prednisone (Deltasone), and others.

Quinidine. Squill can affect the heart. Quinidine can also affect the heart. Taking quinidine along with squill might cause serious heart problems.

Stimulant laxatives. Squill can affect the heart. The heart uses potassium. Laxatives called stimulant laxatives can decrease potassium levels in the body. Low potassium levels can increase the chance of side effects squill. Some stimulant laxatives include bisacodyl (Correctol, Dulcolax), cascara, castor oil (Purge), senna (Senokot), and others.

Water pills (Diuretic drugs). Squill might affect the heart. "Water pills" can decrease potassium in the body. Low potassium levels can also affect the heart and increase the risk of side effects from squill. Some "water pills" that can deplete potassium include chlorothiazide (Diuril), chlorthalidone (Thalitone), furosemide (Lasix), hydrochlorothiazide (HCTZ, HydroDiuril, Microzide), and others.

ST. JOHN'S WORT

What other names is the product known by?

Amber, Amber Touch-and-Heal, Demon Chaser, Fuga Daemonum, Goatweed, Hardhay, Hypereikon, Hyperici Herba, Hypericum, Johns Wort, Klamath Weed, Millepertuis, Rosin Rose, Saint Johns Wort, Saint John's Wort, Saynt Johannes Wort, SJW, St Johns Wort, St John's Wort, Tipton Weed.

What is it?

St. John's wort is an herb. Its flowers and leaves are used to make medicine.

Is it Effective?

The effectiveness ratings for **ST. JOHN'S WORT** are as follows:

Likely Effective for... Mild to moderate depression. It might not be as effective for more severe cases of depression.

Possibly Effective for... Somatization disorder.

Possibly Ineffective for... Hepatitis C Virus (HCV) infection • HIV/AIDS • Pain conditions related to diabetes (polyneuropathy).

Insufficient Evidence to Rate Effectiveness for... Stomach upset, bruises, skin conditions, migraine headache, nerve pain, sciatica, excitability, fibromyalgia, chronic fatigue syndrome (CFS), muscle pain, cancer, obsessive compulsive disorder (OCD), seasonal affective disorder (SAD), premenstrual syndrome (PMS), attention deficit-hyperactivity disorder (ADHD), and other conditions.

How does it work?

For a long time, investigators thought a chemical in St. John's wort called hypericin was responsible for its effects against depression. More recent information suggests another chemical, hyperforin, may play a larger role in depression. Hypericin and hyperforin act on chemical messengers in the nervous system that regulate mood.

Are there safety concerns?

St. John's wort is safe for most people when taken by mouth short-term. It can cause some side effects such as insomnia, vivid dreams, restlessness, anxiety, irritability, stomach upset, fatigue, dry mouth, dizziness, headache, skin rash, diarrhea, and tingling.

Do not take St. John's wort for more than two months without medical supervision.

St. John's wort can cause skin to become extra sensitive to the sun. Wear sunblock outside, especially if you are light-skinned.

Do not use St. John's wort if: You are pregnant or breast-feeding. • You are trying to get pregnant or father a child. • You have bipolar disorder. • You have schizophrenia. • You have Alzheimer's disease. • You have major depression.

Are there any interactions with medications?

Aminolevulinic acid. Aminolevulinic acid can make your skin sensitive to the sunlight. St. John's wort might also increase your sensitivity to sunlight. Taking St. John's wort along with aminolevulinic acid might increase the chances of sunburn, blistering or rashes on areas of skin exposed to sunlight. Be sure to wear sunblock and protective clothing when spending time in the sun.

Alprazolam (Xanax). Alprazolam (Xanax) is commonly used for anxiety. The body breaks down alprazolam (Xanax) to get rid of it. St. John's wort can increase how fast the body gets rid of alprazolam (Xanax). Taking St. John's wort along with alprazolam (Xanax) might decrease the effectiveness of alprazolam (Xanax).

Amitriptyline (Elavil). The body breaks down amitriptyline (Elavil) to get rid of it. St. John's wort can increase how quickly the body gets rid of some medications. St. John's wort might decrease the effectiveness of amitriptyline (Elavil) by increasing how quickly the body breaks down amitriptyline (Elavil).

Birth control pills (Contraceptive drugs). Some birth control pills contain estrogen. The body breaks down the estrogen in birth control pills to get rid of it. St. John's wort might increase the break-down of estrogen. Taking St. John's wort along with birth control pills might decrease the effectiveness of birth control pills. If you take birth control pills along with St. John's wort, use an additional form of birth control such as a condom. Some birth control pills include ethinyl estradiol and levonorgestrel (Triphasil), ethinyl estradiol and norethindrone (Ortho-Novum 1/35, Ortho-Novum 7/7/7), and others.

Clopidogrel (Plavix). The body breaks down clopidogrel (Plavix) to a chemical that decreases blood clotting in the body. Taking St. John's wort along with clopidogrel (Plavix) might increase how well the body breaks down clopidogrel (Plavix) and decrease blood clotting too much.

Cyclosporine (Neoral, Sandimmune). The body breaks down cyclosporine (Neoral, Sandimmune) to get rid of it. St. John's wort might increase how quickly the body breaks down cyclosporine (Neoral, Sandimmune). By increasing the breakdown of cyclosporine (Neoral, Sandimmune) St. John's wort might decrease the effectiveness of cyclosporine (Neoral, Sandimmune). Do not take St. John's wort if you are taking cyclosporine (Neoral, Sandimmune).

Dextromethorphan (Robitussin DM, and others). St. John's wort can affect a brain chemical called serotonin. Dextromethorphan (Robitussin DM, others) can also affect serotonin. Taking St. John's wort along with dextromethorphan (Robitussin DM, others) might cause too much serotonin in the brain and serious side effects including heart problems, shivering, and anxiety. Do not take St. John's wort if you are taking dextromethorphan (Robitussin DM, and others).

Digoxin (Lanoxin). Digoxin (Lanoxin) helps the heart beat more strongly. St. John's wort might decrease how much digoxin (Lanoxin) the body absorbs. By decreasing how much digoxin (Lanoxin) the body absorbs St. John's wort might decrease the effects of digoxin (Lanoxin).

Fenfluramine (Pondimin). Fenfluramine (Pondimin) increases a chemical in the brain. This chemical is called serotonin. St. John's wort also increases serotonin. Taking fenfluramine with St. John's wort might cause there to be too much serotonin. This could cause serious side effects including heart problems, shivering, and anxiety.

Fexofenadine (Allegra). The body breaks down fexofenadine (Allegra) to get rid of it. St. John's wort might decrease how quickly the body gets rid of fexofenadine. This could cause fexofenadine (Allegra) to stay in the body too long. This could lead to increased effects and side effects of fexofenadine (Allegra).

Imatinib (Gleevec). The body breaks down imatinib to get rid of it. St. John's wort might increase how quickly the body gets rid of imatinib (Gleevec). Taking St. John's wort along with imatinib (Gleevec) might decrease the effectiveness of imatinib (Gleevec). Do not take St. John's wort if you are taking imatinib (Gleevec).

Irinotecan (Camptosar). Irinotecan (Camptosar) is used to treat cancer. The body breaks down irinotecan (Camptosar) to get rid of it. St. John's wort might increase how fast the body breaks down irinotecan (Camptosar) and decrease the effectiveness of irinotecan (Camptosar).

Medications changed by the liver (Cytochrome P450 1A2 (CYP1A2) substrates). Some medications are changed and broken down by the liver. St. John's wort might increase how quickly the liver breaks down some medications. Taking St. John's wort along with some medications that are changed by the liver can decrease the effectiveness of some medications. Before taking St. John's wort talk to your healthcare provider if you take any medications that are changed by the liver. Some of these medications that are changed by the liver include clozapine (Clozaril), cyclobenzaprine (Flexeril), fluvoxamine (Luvox), haloperidol (Haldol), imipramine (Tofranil), mexiletine (Mexitil), olanzapine (Zyprexa), pentazocine (Talwin), propranolol (Inderal), tacrine (Cognex), zileuton (Zyflo), zolmitriptan (Zomig), and others.

Medications changed by the liver (Cytochrome P450 2C9 (CYP2C9) substrates). Some medications are changed and broken down by the liver. St. John's wort might increase how quickly the liver breaks down some medications. Taking St. John's wort along with some medications that are broken down by the liver can decrease the effectiveness of your medication. Before taking St. John's wort talk to your healthcare provider if you take any medications that are changed by the liver. Some medications that are changed by the liver include amitriptyline (Elavil), diazepam (Valium), zileuton (Zyflo), celecoxib (Celebrex), diclofenac (Voltaren), fluvastatin (Lescol), glipizide (Glucotrol), ibuprofen (Advil, Motrin), irbesartan (Avapro), losartan (Cozaar), phenytoin (Dilantin), piroxicam (Feldene), tamoxifen (Nolvadex), tolbutamide (Tolinase), torsemide (Demadex), warfarin (Coumadin), and others.

Medications changed by the liver (Cytochrome P450 3A4 (CYP3A4) substrates). Some medications are changed and broken down by the liver. St. John's wort might increase how quickly the liver breaks down some

Natural Medicines Comprehensive Database Consumer Version (209) 472-2244

medications. Taking St. John's wort along with some medications that are broken down by the liver can decrease the effectiveness of some medications. Before taking St. John's wort talk to your healthcare provider if you are taking any medications that are changed by the liver. Some medications changed by the liver include lovastatin (Mevacor), ketoconazole (Nizoral), itraconazole (Sporanox), fexofenadine (Allegra), triazolam (Halcion), and many others.

Medications for depression (Antidepressant drugs). St. John's wort increases a brain chemical called serotonin. Some medications for depression also increase the brain chemical serotonin. Taking St. John's wort along with these medications for depression might increase serotonin too much and cause serious side effects including heart problems, shivering, and anxiety. Do not take St. John's wort if you are taking medications for depression. Some of these medications for depression include fluoxetine (Prozac), paroxetine (Paxil), sertraline (Zoloft), amitriptyline (Elavil), clomipramine (Anafranil), imipramine (Tofranil), and others.

Medications for depression (MAOIs). St. John's wort increases a chemical in the brain. This chemical is called serotonin. Some medications used for depression also increase serotonin. Taking St. John's wort with these medications used for depression might cause there to be too much serotonin. This could cause serious side effects including heart problems, shivering, and anxiety. Some of these medications used for depression include phenelzine (Nardil), tranylcypromine (Parnate), and others.

Medications that increase sensitivity to sunlight (Photosensitizing drugs). Some medications can increase sensitivity to sunlight. St. John's Wort might also increase your sensitivity to sunlight. Taking St. John's wort along with medications that increase sensitivity to sunlight could increase the chances of sunburn, blistering or rashes on areas of skin exposed to sunlight. Be sure to wear sunblock and protective clothing when spending time in the sun. Some drugs that cause photosensitivity include amitriptyline (Elavil), Ciprofloxacin (Cipro), norfloxacin (Noroxin), lomefloxacin (Maxaquin), ofloxacin (Floxin), levofloxacin (Levaquin), sparfloxacin (Zagam), gatifloxacin (Tequin), moxifloxacin (Avelox), trimethoprim/sulfamethoxazole (Septra), tetracycline, methoxsalen (8-methoxypsoralen, 8-MOP, Oxsoralen), and Trioxsalen (Trisoralen).

Medications for HIV/AIDS (Nonnucleoside Reverse Transcriptase Inhibitors (NNRTIs)). The body breaks down medications used for HIV/AIDS. St. John's wort can increase how quickly the body breaks down these medications. Taking St. John's wort might decrease how well some medications used for HIV/AIDS work. Some of these medications used for HIV/AIDS include nevirapine (Viramune), delavirdine (Rescriptor), and efavirenz (Sustiva).

Medications for HIV/AIDS (Protease Inhibitors). The body breaks down medications used for HIV/AIDS to get rid of them. Taking St. John's wort might increase how quickly the body breaks down these medications. This could decrease the effectiveness of some medications used for HIV/AIDS. Some of these medications used for HIV/AIDS include amprenavir (Agenerase), nelfinavir (Viracept), ritonavir (Norvir), and saquinavir (Fortovase, Invirase).

Medications for migraine headaches ("Triptans"). Some medications for migraine headaches can affect a chemical in the brain called serotonin. St. John's wort can also affect serotonin. Taking St. John's wort along with some medications for migraine headache might cause too much serotonin in the brain and serious side effects including confusion, shivering, stiff muscles, and other side effects. Some medications for migraine headache include frovatriptan (Frova), naratriptan (Amerge), rizatriptan (Maxalt), sumatriptan (Imitrex), and zolmitriptan (Zomig).

Medications moved by pumps in cells (P-Glycoprotein Substrates). Some medications are moved by pumps in cells. St. John's wort can make these pumps more active and decrease how much of some medications get absorbed by the body. This might decrease the effectiveness of some medications. Some medications that are moved by these pumps include etoposide, paclitaxel, vinblastine, vincristine, vindesine, ketoconazole, itraconazole, amprenavir, indinavir, nelfinavir, saquinavir, cimetidine, ranitidine, diltiazem, verapamil, corticosteroids, erythromycin, cisapride (Propulsid), fexofenadine (Allegra), cyclosporine, loperamide (Imodium), quinidine, and others.

Medications for pain (Narcotic drugs). The body breaks down some medications for pain to get rid of them. St. John's Wort might decrease how fast the body gets rid of some medications for pain. By decreasing how fast the body gets rid of some medications for pain, St. John's wort might increase the effects and side effects of some medications for pain. Some medications for pain include meperidine (Demerol), hydrocodone, morphine, OxyContin, and many others.

Meperidine (Demerol). St. John's wort increases a chemical in the brain called serotonin. Meperidine (Demerol) can also increase serotonin in the brain. Taking St. John's wort along with meperidine (Demerol) might cause too much serotonin in the brain and serious side effects including heart problems, shivering, and anxiety.

Nefazodone (Serzone). Nefazodone can increase a chemical in the brain. This chemical is called serotonin. St. John's wort can also increase serotonin. Taking St. John's wort with nefazodone might cause there to be too much serotonin. This could lead to serious side effects including heart problems, shivering, and restlessness.

Nortriptyline (Pamelor). The body breaks down nortriptyline (Pamelor) to get rid of it. St. John's wort can increase how quickly the body breaks down nortriptyline (Pamelor). This could decrease the effectiveness of nortriptyline (Pamelor).

Paroxetine (Paxil). Paroxetine (Paxil) increases a chemical in the brain. This chemical is called serotonin. St. John's wort also increases serotonin. Taking paroxetine (Paxil) and St. John's wort together might cause there to be too much serotonin. This could lead to serious side effects including heart problems, shivering, and weakness.

Pentazocine (Talwin). St. John's wort increases a brain chemical called serotonin. Pentazocine (Talwin) also increases serotonin. Taking St. John's wort along with pentazocine (Talwin) might increase serotonin too much. This could cause serious side effects including heart problems, shivering, and anxiety. Do not take St. John's wort if you are taking pentazocine (Talwin).

Phenobarbital (Luminal). The body breaks down phenobarbital (Luminal) to get rid of it. St. John's wort might increase how quickly the body breaks down phenobarbital. This could decrease how well phenobarbital works.

Phenprocoumon. The body breaks down phenprocoumon to get rid of it. St. John's wort increases how quickly the body breaks down phenprocoumon. This decreases the effectiveness of phenprocoumon.

Phenytoin (Dilantin). The body breaks down phenytoin (Dilantin) to get rid of it. St. John's wort might increase how quickly the body breaks down phenytoin. Taking St. John's wort and taking phenytoin (Dilantin) might decrease the effectiveness of phenytoin (Dilantin) and increase the possibility of seizures.

Reserpine. St. John's wort can decrease the effects of reserpine.

Sedative medications (Barbiturates). Medications that cause sleepiness and drowsiness are called sedatives. St. John's wort might decrease the effectiveness of sedative medications. It is not clear why this interaction occurs.

Sertraline (Zoloft). Sertraline (Zoloft) can increase a chemical in the brain. This chemical is called serotonin. St. John's wort also increases serotonin. This can cause there to be too much serotonin in the brain. This could lead to serious side effects including heart problems, shivering, and irritability.

Simvastatin (Zocor). The body breaks down simvastatin (Zocor) to get rid of it. St. John's wort increases how quickly the body breaks down simvastatin. This can cause simvastatin to be less effective.

Tacrolimus (Prograf, Protopic). The body breaks down tacrolimus (Prograf, Protopic) to get rid of it. St. John's wort can increase how quickly the body breaks down tacrolimus. This can cause tacrolimus to be less effective.

Theophylline. The body breaks down theophylline to get rid of it. St. John's wort might increase how quickly the body gets rid of theophylline. Taking St. John's wort along with theophylline might decrease the effectiveness of St. John's wort. But it is not clear if this interaction is a big concern.

Tramadol (Ultram). Tramadol (Ultram) can affect a chemical in the brain called serotonin. St. John's wort can also affect serotonin. Taking St. John's wort along with tramadol (Ultram) might cause too much serotonin in the brain and side effects including confusion, shivering, stiff muscles, and other side effects.

Warfarin (Coumadin). Warfarin (Coumadin) is used to slow blood clotting. The body breaks down warfarin (Coumadin) to get rid of it. St. John's wort might increase the breakdown and decrease the effectiveness of warfarin (Coumadin). Decreasing the effectiveness of warfarin (Coumadin) might increase the risk of clotting. Be sure to have your blood checked regularly. The dose of your warfarin (Coumadin) might need to be changed.

STAR ANISE

What other names is the product known by?
Aniseed Stars, Anisi stellati fructus, Badiana, Bajiao, Chinese Anise, Chinese Star Anise, Eight-Horned Anise, Eight Horns, Illicium, Illicium verum.

What is it?
Star anise is an herb. The seed and oil are used to make medicine.

Is it Effective?
The effectiveness ratings for **STAR ANISE** are as follows:
Insufficient Evidence to Rate Effectiveness for... Cough, gas (flatulence), loss of appetite, menstrual disorders, lung swelling (inflammation), upset stomach, and other conditions.

How does it work?
Star anise seeds contain ingredients that might have activity against bacteria, yeast, and fungi. Star anise contains a chemical shikimic acid that is used to make a prescription medicine for preventing and treating the flu. However, there isn't any research showing that star anise has any activity against viruses such as the flu virus.

Are there safety concerns?
Star anise is safe when used as a flavoring in foods. There is not enough information to know if it's safe for use as a medicine. Some ingredients can cause skin problems including swelling, scaling, and blisters when applied to the skin. Star anise should not be given to infants. It can cause severe nervous system problems, including seizures.

The star anise used as medicine is Chinese star anise. Japanese star anise is poisonous and should not be taken. Some Chinese star anise tea products have been contaminated with Japanese star anise. You cannot tell the difference between them just by looking. Unless safety can be assured by chemical analysis, star anise tea should not be used.

Do not take star anise if: You are pregnant or breast-feeding. • You have breast, uterine, or ovarian cancer. • You have uterine problems.

   Natural Medicines Comprehensive Database Consumer Version   (209) 472-2244

Are there any interactions with medications?
It is not known if star anise interacts with any medicines.
Before taking star anise, talk with your healthcare professional if you take any medications.

STAVESACRE

What other names is the product known by?
Delphinium staphisagria, Lousewort.

What is it?
Stavesacre is a plant. The seeds are used to make medicine.

Is it Effective?
The effectiveness ratings for **STAVESACRE** are as follows:
Insufficient Evidence to Rate Effectiveness for... Head lice and nerve pain.

How does it work?
There isn't enough information available to know how stavesacre works.

Are there safety concerns?
Stavesacre is UNSAFE for oral use. The seeds of the plant are poisonous and can cause side effects such as nausea, stomach pain, itching, urination difficulty, and trouble breathing.

It is not known if stavesacre is safe when applied to the skin. It can cause swelling (inflammation), skin redness, and other skin problems.

Do not use stavesacre if: You are pregnant or breast-feeding. • You have stomach problems.

Are there any interactions with medications?
It is not known if stavesacre interacts with any medicines.
Before taking stavesacre, talk with your healthcare professional if you take any medications.

STEVIA

What other names is the product known by?
Azucacaa, Ca-A-Jhei, Ca-A-Yupi, Caa-He-É, Caa'Inhem, Capim Doce, Eira-Caa, Erva Doce, Eupatorium rebaudianum, Kaa Jhee, Mustelia eupatoria, Paraguayan Stevioside, Stevia eupatoria, Stevia purpurea, Stevia rebaudiana, Sweetleaf, Sweet Herb of Paraguay, Sweet Herb, Sweet Leaf of Paraguay, Yerba Dulce.

What is it?
Stevia is a plant. The leaves are used to make medicine.

Is it Effective?
The effectiveness ratings for **STEVIA** are as follows:
Possibly Effective for... High blood pressure.
Insufficient Evidence to Rate Effectiveness for... Preventing pregnancy, diabetes, heartburn, weight loss, water retention, heart problems, and other conditions.

How does it work?
Stevia contains ingredients that are thought to lower blood sugar levels, decrease blood pressure, and increase body water loss through the urine.

Are there safety concerns?
Stevia might be safe for adults when used occasionally as a food sweetener or in medicinal doses. A component of stevia called stevioside can cause bloating, nausea, dizziness, muscle pain, and numbness in some people. It is not known if stevia is safe when used in large amounts for long periods of time. Some research suggests large amounts of a breakdown product of stevia (steviol) might cause kidney damage. Many countries have banned the use of stevia due to concerns about safety; however, stevia is used as a sweetener and flavor enhancer in Japan, Brazil, and other countries.

Stevia might cause an allergic reaction in people who are sensitive to the Asteraceae/Compositae family of plants including ragweed, chrysanthemums, marigolds, daisies, and many other plants.

Do not take stevia if: You are pregnant or breast-feeding. • You have kidney problems.

Are there any interactions with medications?
Medications for diabetes (Antidiabetes drugs). Stevia seems to decrease blood sugar in people with type 2 diabetes. Diabetes medications are also used to lower blood sugar. Taking stevia along with diabetes medications might cause your blood sugar to go too low. Monitor your blood sugar closely. The dose of your diabetes medication might need to be changed. Some medications used for diabetes include glimepiride (Amaryl), glyburide (DiaBeta, Glynase PresTab, Micronase), insulin, pioglitazone (Actos), rosiglitazone (Avandia), chlorpropamide (Diabinese), glipizide (Glucotrol), tolbutamide (Orinase), and others.

Medications for high blood pressure (Antihypertensive drugs). Stevia seems to decrease blood pressure. Taking stevia along with medications for high blood pressure might cause your blood pressure to go too low. Do not take stevia if you are taking medications for high blood pressure. Some medications for high blood pressure include captopril (Capoten), enalapril (Vasotec), losartan (Cozaar), valsartan (Diovan), diltiazem (Cardizem), Amlodipine (Norvasc), hydrochlorothiazide (HydroDiuril), furosemide (Lasix), and many others.

Medications for high blood pressure (Calcium channel blockers). Stevia seems to decrease blood pressure. Taking stevia along with medications for high blood pressure might cause your blood pressure to go too low. Do not take stevia if you are taking medications for high blood pressure. Some medications for high blood pressure include nifedipine (Adalat, Procardia), verapamil (Calan, Isoptin, Verelan), diltiazem (Cardizem), isradipine (DynaCirc), felodipine (Plendil), amlodipine (Norvasc), and others.

STINGING NETTLE

What other names is the product known by?
Common Nettle, Great Stinging Nettle, Nettle, Small Nettle, Urtica, Urtica Dioica, Urtica Urens, Urticae Herba et Folium, Urticae Radix.

What is it?
Stinging nettle is a plant. People use the above ground parts and root as medicine.

Is it Effective?
The effectiveness ratings for **STINGING NETTLE** are as follows:
Possibly Ineffective for... Benign prostatic hyperplasia (BPH) when used as a specific herbal blend.
Insufficient Evidence to Rate Effectiveness for... Allergies, relieving pain from arthritis, water retention, internal bleeding, anemia, poor circulation, diabetes, diarrhea, asthma, cancer, improving wound-healing, and other conditions.

How does it work?
Stinging nettle contains ingredients that might decrease inflammation and increase urine output.

Are there safety concerns?
Stinging nettle seems to be safe. It might cause stomach complaints and sweating. Touching the stinging nettle plant can cause skin irritation.

Do not take stinging nettle if: You are pregnant or breast-feeding. • You have diabetes. • You have a kidney disorder.

Are there any interactions with medications?
Medications for diabetes (Antidiabetes drugs). Stinging nettle above ground parts might decrease blood sugar. Diabetes medications are also used to lower blood sugar. Taking stinging nettle along with diabetes medications might cause your blood sugar to go too low. Monitor your blood sugar closely. The dose of your diabetes medication might need to be changed. Some medications used for diabetes include glimepiride (Amaryl), glyburide (DiaBeta, Glynase PresTab, Micronase), insulin, pioglitazone (Actos), rosiglitazone (Avandia), chlorpropamide (Diabinese), glipizide (Glucotrol), tolbutamide (Orinase), and others.

Medications for high blood pressure (Antihypertensive drugs). Stinging nettle above ground parts seem to decrease blood pressure. Taking stinging nettle along with medications for high blood pressure might cause your blood pressure to go too low. Some medications for high blood pressure include captopril (Capoten), enalapril (Vasotec), losartan (Cozaar), valsartan (Diovan), diltiazem (Cardizem), Amlodipine (Norvasc), hydrochlorothiazide (HydroDiuril), furosemide (Lasix), and many others.

Sedative medications (CNS depressants). Large amounts of stinging nettle above ground parts might cause sleepiness and drowsiness. Medications that cause sleepiness are called sedatives. Taking stinging nettle along with sedative medications might cause too much sleepiness. Some sedative medications include clonazepam (Klonopin), lorazepam (Ativan), phenobarbital (Donnatal), zolpidem (Ambien), and others.

Warfarin (Coumadin). Stinging nettle above ground parts contain large amounts of vitamin K. Vitamin K is used by the body to help blood clot. Warfarin (Coumadin) is used to slow blood clotting. By helping the blood clot, stinging nettle might decrease the effectiveness of warfarin (Coumadin). Be sure to have your blood checked regularly. The dose of your warfarin (Coumadin) might need to be changed.

STONE ROOT

What other names is the product known by?

Citronella, Colinsonia, Collinsonia, Collinsonia Canadensis, Hardback, Hardhack, Heal-all, Horse Balm, Horseweed, Knob Grass, Knob Root, Knobweed, Richleaf, Rich Weed.

What is it?

Stone root is an herb. The root is used to make medicine.

Is it Effective?

The effectiveness ratings for **STONE ROOT** are as follows:

Insufficient Evidence to Rate Effectiveness for... Bladder inflammation, edema, headaches, indigestion, kidney stones, stomach problems, some urinary problems, and water retention.

How does it work?

There isn't enough information available to know how stone root works.

Are there safety concerns?

Stone root seems to be safe. Taking large amounts of stone root can cause some side effects such as dizziness, nausea, painful urination, and stomach irritation.

Do not take stone root if: You are pregnant or breast-feeding.

Are there any interactions with medications?

Water pills (Diuretic drugs). Stone root seems to work like "water pills." Stone root and "water pills" might cause the body to get rid of potassium along with water. Taking stone root along with "water pills" might decrease potassium in the body too much. Some "water pills" that can deplete potassium include chlorothiazide (Diuril), chlorthalidone (Thalitone), furosemide (Lasix), hydrochlorothiazide (HCTZ, Hydrodiuril, Microzide), and others.

STORAX

What other names is the product known by?

American Storax, Balsam Styracis, Balsamum Styrax Liquidus, Copalm, Estoraque Liquido, Gum Tree, Levant Storax, Liquid Amber, Liquid Storax, Liquidambar, Liquidamber Orientalis, Liquidamber Styraciflua, Lu Lu Tong, Opossum Tree, Red Gum, Styrax, Sweet Gum, White Gum.

What is it?

Storax is a tree. Its bark and resin are used to make medicine.

Is it Effective?

The effectiveness ratings for **STORAX** are as follows:

Insufficient Evidence to Rate Effectiveness for... Cancer, colds, coughs, diarrhea, epilepsy, infections from parasites, scabies, sore throats, ulcers, and wound protection.

How does it work?

Storax contains ingredients that might have activity against some bacteria.

Are there safety concerns?

Storax seems to be safe for most people when used appropriately. Moderate amounts of storax can cause some side effects such as diarrhea and rash. Do not take large amounts by mouth or apply large amounts to open wounds. This can cause serious side effects including kidney damage.

Do not use storax if: You are pregnant or breast-feeding.

Medical professionals should consult the Professional Version at www.NaturalDatabase.com.

Are there any interactions with medications?

It is not known if storax interacts with any medicines.
Before taking storax, talk with your healthcare professional if you take any medications.

STRAWBERRY

What other names is the product known by?

Alpine Strawberry, Fragaria Vesca, Fragaria Virginiana, Fragaria Viridis, Fragariae Folium, Mountain Strawberry, Virginian Strawberry, Wild Strawberry, Wood Strawberry.

What is it?

Strawberry is a plant. The leaves and fruit are used to make medicine.

Is it Effective?

The effectiveness ratings for **STRAWBERRY** are as follows:
Insufficient Evidence to Rate Effectiveness for... Arthritis, diarrhea, fever, gout, preventing menstruation, nervous tension, night sweats, rashes, stimulating metabolism, weight loss, water retention, and other conditions.

How does it work?

Strawberry contains chemicals that might have antioxidant effects.

Are there safety concerns?

Strawberry is safe in amounts used as food. There isn't enough information available to know if strawberry is safe for medicinal use.

Do not take strawberry in amounts greater than those found in foods if: You are pregnant or breast-feeding.

Are there any interactions with medications?

It is not known if strawberry interacts with any medicines.
Before taking strawberry, talk with your healthcare professional if you take any medications.

STRONTIUM

What other names is the product known by?

Stable Strontium, Strontium Chloride, Strontium-89 Chloride, Strontium Citrate, Strontium Ranelate.

What is it?

Strontium is an element. It is used as medicine.

Is it Effective?

The effectiveness ratings for **STRONTIUM** are as follows:
Effective for... Bone pain related to cancer. A special prescription form of strontium is given by injection for this use • Sensitive teeth. Strontium chloride is added to some toothpaste for this use.
Possibly Effective for... Treating osteoporosis ("bone thinning") in postmenopausal women. A special form of strontium called strontium ranelate is used. This form of strontium is not used in dietary supplements. It's not known if the strontium contained in dietary supplements is effective for osteoporosis • Treating prostate cancer that is unresponsive to other treatments. A prescription form of strontium is given by injection for this use.
Insufficient Evidence to Rate Effectiveness for... Dental cavities, osteoarthritis, and other conditions. There is also no reliable information that strontium contained in dietary supplements is effective for any condition.

How does it work?

A special form of strontium called strontium ranelate may increase bone formation and prevent bone loss when used in postmenopausal women with osteoporosis. A radioactive form of strontium may kill some cancer cells. These types of strontium are not available in dietary supplements. It's not known if strontium contained in dietary supplements has these effects.

Are there safety concerns?

The forms of prescription strontium are safe when used under the supervision of a healthcare provider. But there's not enough information to know if the form of strontium contained in dietary supplements is safe. It might cause side effects such as stomach pain and diarrhea in some people.
Do not use strontium if: You are pregnant or breast-feeding. • You have kidney problems.

Medical professionals should consult the Professional Version at www.NaturalDatabase.com.

612 Natural Medicines Comprehensive Database Consumer Version (209) 472-2244

Are there any interactions with medications?
It is not known if strontium interacts with any medicines.
Before taking strontium, talk with your healthcare professional if you take any medications.

STROPHANTHUS

What other names is the product known by?
Kombe, Kombe-Strophanthus Seeds, Strophanthus caudatus, Strophanthus divaricatus, Strophanthi Grati Semen, Strophanthus gratus, Strophanthus hispidus, Strophanthi Kombe Semen, Strophanthus kombe, Strophanthus Seeds, Strophanthus wallichii.

What is it?
Strophanthus is an herb. Its seeds are used to make medicine.

Is it Effective?
The effectiveness ratings for **STROPHANTHUS** are as follows:
Insufficient Evidence to Rate Effectiveness for... Artery disease, heart problems, high blood pressure, and stomach problems.

How does it work?
Strophanthus contains ingredients that can stimulate the heart.

Are there safety concerns?
Strophanthus is unsafe for use without the direct supervision of a healthcare provider. It can cause side effects such as nausea, vomiting, headache, disturbance of color vision, and heart problems.

Do not use strophanthus if: You are pregnant or breast-feeding. • You have heart problems, without the direct supervision of a healthcare provider.

Are there any interactions with medications?
Calcium supplements. Strophanthus can stimulate the heartbeat. Calcium might also affect the heart. Taking strophanthus along with calcium might cause the heart to be too stimulated. Do not take strophanthus along with calcium supplements.
Digoxin (Lanoxin). Digoxin (Lanoxin) helps the heart beat more strongly. Strophanthus also seems to affect the heart. Taking strophanthus along with digoxin can increase the effects of digoxin and increase the risk of side effects. Do not take strophanthus if you are taking digoxin (Lanoxin) without talking to your healthcare professional.
Medications for inflammation (Corticosteroids). Strophanthus might affect the heart. Some medications for inflammation can decrease potassium in the body. Low potassium levels can also affect the heart and increase the risk of side effects from strophanthus. Some medications for inflammation include dexamethasone (Decadron), hydrocortisone (Cortef), methylprednisolone (Medrol), prednisone (Deltasone), and others.
Quinidine. Strophanthus can affect the heart. Quinidine can also affect the heart. Taking quinidine along with strophanthus might cause serious heart problems.
Quinine. Strophanthus can affect the heart. Quinine can also affect the heart. Taking quinine along with strophanthus might cause serious heart problems.
Stimulant laxatives. Strophanthus can affect the heart. The heart uses potassium. Laxatives called stimulant laxatives can decrease potassium levels in the body. Low potassium levels can increase the chance of side effects strophanthus. Some stimulant laxatives include bisacodyl (Correctol, Dulcolax), cascara, castor oil (Purge), senna (Senokot), and others.
Water pills (Diuretic drugs). Strophanthus might affect the heart. "Water pills" can decrease potassium in the body. Low potassium levels can also affect the heart and increase the risk of side effects from strophanthus. Some "water pills" that can deplete potassium include chlorothiazide (Diuril), chlorthalidone (Thalitone), furosemide (Lasix), hydrochlorothiazide (HCTZ, HydroDiuril, Microzide), and others.

SULFORAPHANE

What other names is the product known by?
Sulphorafane, sulforafane, SFN, 1-isothiocayanate-4-methyl-sulfonyl butane.

What is it?
Sulforaphane is a chemical found in certain kinds of vegetables such as broccoli, cabbage, and cauliflower.

Medical professionals should consult the Professional Version at www.NaturalDatabase.com.

Is it Effective?

The effectiveness ratings for **SULFORAPHANE** are as follows:
Insufficient Evidence to Rate Effectiveness for... Preventing cancer.

How does it work?

Sulforaphane may increase the death of cancer cells.

Are there safety concerns?

Sulforaphane is safe when used in the amounts found in foods. There isn't enough information available to know if it is safe to take by mouth as a medicine.

Do not use sulforaphane in amounts larger than typically found in foods if: You are pregnant or breast-feeding.

Are there any interactions with medications?

Medications changed by the liver (Cytochrome P450 1A2 (CYP1A2) substrates). Some medications are changed and broken down by the liver. Sulforaphane might decrease how quickly the liver breaks down some medications. Taking sulforaphane along with some medications that are changed by the liver might increase the effects and side effects of some medications. Before taking sulforaphane talk to your healthcare provider if you take any medications that are changed by the liver. Some medications that are changed by the liver include clozapine (Clozaril), cyclobenzaprine (Flexeril), fluvoxamine (Luvox), haloperidol (Haldol), imipramine (Tofranil), mexiletine (Mexitil), olanzapine (Zyprexa), pentazocine (Talwin), propranolol (Inderal), tacrine (Cognex), theophylline, zileuton (Zyflo), zolmitriptan (Zomig), and others.

SUMA

What other names is the product known by?

Brazilian Ginseng, Gomphrena paniculata, Hebanthe eriantha, Hebanthe paniculata, Pfaffia, Pfaffia paniculata.

What is it?

Suma is a plant. The root is used to make medicine.

Is it Effective?

The effectiveness ratings for **SUMA** are as follows:
Insufficient Evidence to Rate Effectiveness for... Improving the immune system, cancer and tumors, diabetes, wounds, and skin problems.

How does it work?

Some researchers think that the chemicals in suma may inhibit some cancers, decrease swelling, and have some pain relieving properties.

Are there safety concerns?

Suma is considered safe for most people when it is taken by mouth for a short period of time. There isn't enough information to know if using suma on the skin is safe.

Suma can cause asthma symptoms if the root powder is inhaled.

Do not take suma if: You are pregnant or breast-feeding.

Are there any interactions with medications?

It is not known if suma interacts with any medicines.
Before taking suma, talk with your healthcare professional if you take any medications.

SUMBUL

What other names is the product known by?

Ferula sumbul, Ferrula, Musk Root.

What is it?

Sumbul is an herb. The root is used to make medicine.

 Natural Medicines Comprehensive Database Consumer Version (209) 472-2244

Is it Effective?
The effectiveness ratings for **SUMBUL** are as follows:
Insufficient Evidence to Rate Effectiveness for... Asthma, bronchitis, causing sleeplessness, and treating muscle spasms.

How does it work?
There isn't enough information available to know how sumbul works.

Are there safety concerns?
There isn't enough information to know if sumbul is safe.

Do not use sumbul if: You are pregnant or breast-feeding.

Are there any interactions with medications?
It is not known if sumbul interacts with any medicines.
Before taking sumbul, talk with your healthcare professional if you take any medications.

SUMMER SAVORY

What other names is the product known by?
Bean Herb, Bohnenkraut, Calamintha hortensis, Satureja hortensis, Savory.

What is it?
Summer savory is a plant. The leaves and stem are used to make medicine.

Is it Effective?
The effectiveness ratings for **SUMMER SAVORY** are as follows:
Insufficient Evidence to Rate Effectiveness for... Appetite stimulant, cough, gas, intestinal cramps, indigestion, diarrhea, nausea, thirst in people with diabetes, sore throat, aphrodisiac, insect bites, and other uses.

How does it work?
The chemicals in summer savory are thought to decrease muscle spasms and kill bacteria and fungus.

Are there safety concerns?
Summer savory seems to be safe for most people when taken by mouth or when the oil is diluted before putting on the skin. The concentrated, undiluted oil is very irritating and should not be used.

Summer savory can cause skin problems.

Do not use summer savory if: You are pregnant or breast-feeding.

Are there any interactions with medications?
It is not known if summer savory interacts with any medicines.
Before taking summer savory, talk with your healthcare professional if you take any medications.

SUNDEW

What other names is the product known by?
Dew Plant, Drosera, Drosera anglica, Drosera intermedia, Drosera longifolia, Drosera ramentacea, Drosera rotundifolia, Lustwort, Red Rot, Round-Leafed Sundew, Youthwort.

What is it?
Sundew is an herb. The dried plant is used to make medicine.

Is it Effective?
The effectiveness ratings for **SUNDEW** are as follows:
Insufficient Evidence to Rate Effectiveness for... Coughs, asthma, bronchitis, cancer, and ulcers.

How does it work?
Sundew seems to help break up chest congestion by thinning mucous and making it easier to cough up (expectorant). It also reduces spasms.

Are there safety concerns?

Sundew seems safe for most people.

Do not take sundew if: You are pregnant or breast-feeding.

Are there any interactions with medications?

It is not known if sundew interacts with any medicines.
Before taking sundew, talk with your healthcare professional if you take any medications.

SUNFLOWER OIL

What other names is the product known by?

Corona Solis, Helianthi Annui Oleum, Helianthus annuus, Marigold of Peru, Sunflower, Sunflower Seed Oil.

What is it?

Sunflower oil is from the seeds of the sunflower. The oil is used to make medicine.

Is it Effective?

The effectiveness ratings for **SUNFLOWER OIL** are as follows:
Insufficient Evidence to Rate Effectiveness for... Arthritis, constipation, skin conditions, wound healing, and lowering low-density lipoprotein (LDL, "bad") cholesterol.

How does it work?

Sunflower oil is used as a source of unsaturated fat in the diet to replace saturated fats.

Are there safety concerns?

Sunflower oil is safe when used in appropriate amounts. A diet high in sunflower oil seems to raise blood sugar after meals in people with type 2 diabetes and might contribute to hardening of the arteries.

Do not take sunflower oil if: You are pregnant or breast-feeding. • You are allergic to ragweed, marigolds, daisies, and related herbs. • You have diabetes.

Are there any interactions with medications?

It is not known if sunflower oil interacts with any medicines.
Before taking sunflower oil, talk with your healthcare professional if you take any medications.

SUPEROXIDE DISMUTASE

What other names is the product known by?

Orgotein, SOD, Super Dioxide Dismutase.

What is it?

Superoxide dismutase is an enzyme found in all living cells. An enzyme is a substance that speeds up certain chemical reactions.

Is it Effective?

The effectiveness ratings for **SUPEROXIDE DISMUTASE** are as follows:
Possibly Effective for... Osteoarthritis and rheumatoid arthritis, when used as an injection • Lung problems in newborn infants, when used as an injection • Treating interstitial cystitis, a kidney condition, when used as an injection.
Likely Ineffective for... Reducing heart damage after a myocardial infarction (MI, heart attack), when used as an injection.
Insufficient Evidence to Rate Effectiveness for... Sports injuries, gout, cancer, helping people tolerate radiation therapy, preventing rejection of kidney transplants, and other conditions.

How does it work?

Superoxide dismutase is an enzyme that helps with the breakdown of poisonous oxygen compounds in cells, and might prevent damage to body tissues.

Are there safety concerns?

Injectable (shot) forms of superoxide dismutase that have been used in clinical studies appear to be safe. There is no evidence that superoxide dismutase products that are taken by mouth are absorbed by the body. Some superoxide dismutase products are obtained from animal sources. There is some concern about contamination from sick or diseased animals. Until more is known, don't use superoxide dismutase products obtained from animals.

Do not use superoxide dismutase if: You are pregnant or breast-feeding.

Are there any interactions with medications?

It is not known if superoxide dismutase interacts with any medicines.
Before taking superoxide dismutase, talk with your healthcare professional if you take any medications.

SWALLOWROOT

What other names is the product known by?

Decalepis hamiltonii, Makali Beru, Nannari.

What is it?

Swallowroot is a plant. The root is used to make medicine.

Is it Effective?

The effectiveness ratings for **SWALLOWROOT** are as follows:
Insufficient Evidence to Rate Effectiveness for... Stimulating appetite.

How does it work?

Preliminary research suggests swallowroot might have antioxidant and antibacterial effects.

Are there safety concerns?

There isn't enough information to know if swallowroot is safe or what the potential side effects might be.

Do not use swallowroot if: You are pregnant or breast-feeding.

Are there any interactions with medications?

Medications that slow blood clotting (Anticoagulant / Antiplatelet drugs). Swallowroot might slow blood clotting. Taking swallowroot along with medications that also slow clotting might increase the chances of bruising and bleeding. Some medications that slow blood clotting include aspirin, clopidogrel (Plavix), diclofenac (Voltaren, Cataflam, others), ibuprofen (Advil, Motrin, others), naproxen (Anaprox, Naprosyn, others), dalteparin (Fragmin), enoxaparin (Lovenox), heparin, warfarin (Coumadin), and others.

SWAMP MILKWEED

What other names is the product known by?

Asclepias incarnata, Rose-Colored Silkweed, Swamp Silkweed.

What is it?

Swamp milkweed is an herb. The root is used to make medicine.

Is it Effective?

The effectiveness ratings for **SWAMP MILKWEED** are as follows:
Insufficient Evidence to Rate Effectiveness for... Digestive disorders.

How does it work?

There isn't enough information available to know how swamp milkweed works.

Are there safety concerns?

Swamp milkweed is UNSAFE to use. It contains chemicals similar to the prescription drug digoxin (Lanoxin) that can cause a dangerously irregular heartbeat. Handling the plant can cause swelling (inflammation) of the skin.

Do not use swamp milkweed if: You are pregnant or breast-feeding. • You have a heart condition.

CONSUMER VERSION

Medical professionals should consult the Professional Version at www.NaturalDatabase.com.

Are there any interactions with medications?

Antibiotics (Macrolide antibiotics). Swamp milkweed can affect the heart. Some antibiotics might increase how much swamp milkweed the body absorbs. Increasing how much swamp milkweed the body absorbs might increase the effects and side effects of swamp milkweed. Some antibiotics called macrolide antibiotics include erythromycin, azithromycin, and clarithromycin.

Antibiotics (Tetracycline antibiotics). Taking tetracycline antibiotics along with swamp milkweed might increase the chance of side effects from swamp milkweed. Some tetracyclines include demeclocycline (Declomycin), minocycline (Minocin), and tetracycline (Achromycin).

Digoxin (Lanoxin). Digoxin (Lanoxin) helps the heart beat more strongly. Swamp milkweed also seems to affect the heart. Taking swamp milkweed along with digoxin can increase the effects of digoxin and increase the risk of side effects. Do not take swamp milkweed if you are taking digoxin (Lanoxin) without talking to your healthcare professional.

Quinine. Swamp milkweed can affect the heart. Quinine can also affect the heart. Taking swamp milkweed along with quinine might cause serious heart problems.

Stimulant laxatives. Swamp milkweed can affect the heart. The heart uses potassium. Laxatives called stimulant laxatives can decrease potassium levels in the body. Low potassium levels can increase the chance of side effects from swamp milkweed. Some stimulant laxatives include bisacodyl (Correctol, Dulcolax), cascara, castor oil (Purge), senna (Senokot), and others.

Water pills (Diuretic drugs). Swamp milkweed might affect the heart. "Water pills" can decrease potassium in the body. Low potassium levels can also affect the heart and increase the risk of side effects from swamp milkweed. Some "water pills" that can deplete potassium include chlorothiazide (Diuril), chlorthalidone (Thalitone), furosemide (Lasix), hydrochlorothiazide (HCTZ, HydroDiuril, Microzide), and others.

SWEET ALMOND

What other names is the product known by?

Almond Oil, Amygdala Dulcis, Expressed Almond Oil, Fixed Almond Oil, Prunus amygdalus dulcis, Sweet Almond Oil.

What is it?

Sweet almond is a plant. Sweet almond oil is prepared by pressing the kernels of both sweet almond and bitter almond. The oil is used to make medicine.

Is it Effective?

The effectiveness ratings for **SWEET ALMOND** are as follows:

Possibly Effective for... Use as a laxative • Relieving chapped and irritated skin.

Insufficient Evidence to Rate Effectiveness for... Treating cancer of the bladder, breast, mouth, spleen, and uterus.

How does it work?

Sweet almond might work as a laxative due to the presence of many fatty acids. When applied to the skin, these same oily ingredients might help chapped skin and irritated mucous membranes.

Are there safety concerns?

Sweet almond is safe for most people when taken by mouth and when applied directly to the skin.

Do not use sweet almond if: You are pregnant or breast-feeding.

Are there any interactions with medications?

It is not known if sweet almond interacts with any medicines.

Before taking sweet almond, talk with your healthcare professional if you take any medications.

SWEET ANNIE

What other names is the product known by?

Annual Mugwort, Annual Wormwood, Artemisia annua, Artemisia, Artemisinin, Chinese Wormwood, Ching-hao, Qing Hao, Qinghaosu, Sweet Wormwood.

What is it?

Sweet Annie is an herb. The above ground parts are used to make medicine.

 (209) 472-2244

Is it Effective?
The effectiveness ratings for **SWEET ANNIE** are as follows:
Insufficient Evidence to Rate Effectiveness for... Malaria, AIDS-related infections, anorexia, arthritis, bacterial and fungal infections, bruises, common cold, constipation, diarrhea, fever, gallbladder disorders, indigestion, jaundice, night-sweats, painful menstruation, psoriasis, scabies, sprains, tuberculosis, and other conditions.

How does it work?
Sweet Annie might help treat malaria. It might deactivate or kill the parasite that causes malaria. Sweet Annie should not be used alone for malaria. Some drugs used for malaria are made from sweet Annie. Using sweet Annie alone might decrease the effects of drugs made from sweet Annie to treat malaria.

Are there safety concerns?
Sweet Annie seems safe for most adults. The tea of sweet Annie might cause upset stomach and vomiting. It might also cause an allergic reaction in some people including a rash and cough.

Do not use sweet Annie if: You are pregnant or breast-feeding. • You are allergic to ragweed, marigolds, daisies, and related herbs.

Are there any interactions with medications?
It is not known if sweet Annie interacts with any medicines.
Before taking sweet Annie, talk with your healthcare professional if you take any medications.

SWEET BAY

What other names is the product known by?
Bay, Bay Laurel, Bay Tree, Daphne, Grecian Laurel, Laurel, Laurus nobilis, Mediterranean Bay, Noble Laurel, Roman Laurel, True Bay.

What is it?
Sweet bay is an herb. The leaves and oil are used to make medicine.

Is it Effective?
The effectiveness ratings for **SWEET BAY** are as follows:
Insufficient Evidence to Rate Effectiveness for... Cancer, dandruff, and relieving gas.

How does it work?
Sweet bay contains ingredients that might cause sleepiness and might act against some bacteria and fungi.

Are there safety concerns?
Sweet bay is safe for most people. It can cause allergic reactions in some people. Use caution when using the whole leaf. It can become lodged in the throat and damage the throat lining.
Do not use sweet bay if: You are pregnant or breast-feeding.

Are there any interactions with medications?
Medications for pain (Narcotic drugs). The body breaks down some medications for pain to get rid of them. Sweet bay might decrease how fast the body gets rid of some medications for pain. By decreasing how fast the body gets rid of some medications for pain, sweet bay might increase the effects and side effects of some medications for pain. Some medications for pain include meperidine (Demerol), hydrocodone, morphine, OxyContin, and many others.
Sedative medications (CNS depressants). Sweet bay might cause sleepiness and drowsiness. Medications that cause sleepiness are called sedatives. Taking sweet bay along with sedative medications might cause too much sleepiness. Some sedative medications include clonazepam (Klonopin), lorazepam (Ativan), phenobarbital (Donnatal), zolpidem (Ambien), and others.

SWEET CHERRY

What other names is the product known by?
Cherry, Prunus avium, Wild Cherry.

What is it?
Sweet cherry is a fruit. The fruit of the sweet cherry is used to make medicine and food.

Medical professionals should consult the Professional Version at www.NaturalDatabase.com.

CONSUMER VERSION

Medical professionals should consult the Professional Version at www.NaturalDatabase.com.

Is it Effective?

The effectiveness ratings for **SWEET CHERRY** are as follows:
Insufficient Evidence to Rate Effectiveness for... Arthritis, gout, preventing cancer, and preventing heart disease.

How does it work?

Sweet cherry contains vitamin C and other components that might act as antioxidants.

Are there safety concerns?

Eating the fruit of the sweet cherry is safe for most adults, including pregnant and breast-feeding women, when consumed as food. It is not known if sweet cherry is safe when used for medicinal purposes. Sweet cherry can occasionally cause allergy in people who are sensitive.

Are there any interactions with medications?

It is not known if sweet cherry interacts with any medicines.
Before taking sweet cherry, talk with your healthcare professional if you take any medications.

SWEET CICELY

What other names is the product known by?

British Myrrh, Myrrhis odorata, Shepherd's Needle, Sweet Bracken, Sweet Chervil, Sweet-Cus, Sweet-Fern, Sweet-Humlock, Sweets, The Roman Plant.

What is it?

Sweet cicely is an herb. It is made into a tea or tonic when used as medicine.

Is it Effective?

The effectiveness ratings for **SWEET CICELY** are as follows:
Insufficient Evidence to Rate Effectiveness for... Asthma, congestion, digestion problems, gout, and urinary tract conditions.

How does it work?

There isn't enough information available to know how sweet cicely works.

Are there safety concerns?

There isn't enough information available to know if sweet cicely is safe.

Do not take sweet cicely if: You are pregnant or breast-feeding.

Are there any interactions with medications?

It is not known if sweet cicely interacts with any medicines.
Before taking sweet cicely, talk with your healthcare professional if you take any medications.

SWEET CLOVER

What other names is the product known by?

Common Melilot, Field Melilot, Hart's Tree, Hay Flower, King's Clover, Melilot, Meliloti herba, Melilotus altissimus, Melilotus officinalis, Sweet Lucerne, Sweet Melilot, Tall Melilot, Wild Laburnum, Yellow Melilot, Yellow Sweet Clover.

What is it?

Sweet clover is an herb. The flowering branches and leaves are used to make medicine.

Is it Effective?

The effectiveness ratings for **SWEET CLOVER** are as follows:
Possibly Effective for... Problems with circulation including leg cramps and swelling • Varicose veins.
Insufficient Evidence to Rate Effectiveness for... Water retention, hemorrhoids, bruises, and other conditions.

How does it work?

Sweet clover contains ingredients that can thin the blood and help wounds heal.

Are there safety concerns?

Sweet clover seems to be safe for most people. It can cause liver damage and bleeding problems when used in large amounts.

Do not use sweet clover if: You are pregnant or breast-feeding. • You have a liver disorder.

Are there any interactions with medications?

Medications that slow blood clotting (Anticoagulant / Antiplatelet drugs). Sweet clover might slow blood clotting. Taking sweet clover along with medications that also slow clotting might increase the chances of bruising and bleeding. Some medications that slow blood clotting include aspirin, clopidogrel (Plavix), diclofenac (Voltaren, Cataflam, others), ibuprofen (Advil, Motrin, others), naproxen (Anaprox, Naprosyn, others), dalteparin (Fragmin), enoxaparin (Lovenox), heparin, warfarin (Coumadin), and others.

Medications that can harm the liver (Hepatotoxic drugs). Large amounts of sweet clover might harm the liver. Taking sweet clover along with medication that can harm the liver can increase the risk of liver damage. Do not take sweet clover if you are taking medications that can harm the liver. Some medications that can harm the liver include acetaminophen (Tylenol and others), amiodarone (Cordarone), carbamazepine (Tegretol), isoniazid (INH), methotrexate (Rheumatrex), methyldopa (Aldomet), fluconazole (Diflucan), itraconazole (Sporanox), erythromycin (Erythrocin, Ilosone, others), phenytoin (Dilantin), lovastatin (Mevacor), pravastatin (Pravachol), simvastatin (Zocor), and many others.

SWEET GALE

What other names is the product known by?

Bayberry, Bog Myrtle, Dutch Myrtle, Myrica gale.

What is it?

Sweet gale is an herb. The leaves, branches, and wax are used to make medicine.

Is it Effective?

The effectiveness ratings for **SWEET GALE** are as follows:
Insufficient Evidence to Rate Effectiveness for... Digestive disorders, intestinal worms, and itching.

How does it work?

Sweet gale contains ingredients that might help reduce skin inflammation and have a drying (astringent) effect on the tissues.

Are there safety concerns?

There isn't enough information available to know if sweet gale is safe. The oil of sweet gale is poisonous.

Do not take sweet gale if: You are pregnant or breast-feeding.

Are there any interactions with medications?

It is not known if sweet gale interacts with any medicines.
Before taking sweet gale, talk with your healthcare professional if you take any medications.

SWEET ORANGE

What other names is the product known by?

Citri Sinensis, Citrus aurantium dulcis, Citrus aurantium var. sinensis, Citrus sinensis, Citrus aurantium var. dulcis, Jaffa Orange, Navel Orange, Pericarpium, Valencia Orange.

What is it?

Sweet orange is a fruit. The peel and juice are used to make medicine.

Is it Effective?

The effectiveness ratings for **SWEET ORANGE** are as follows:
Possibly Effective for... Preventing high blood pressure and stroke • Improving cholesterol levels.
Insufficient Evidence to Rate Effectiveness for... Asthma, colds, coughs, eating disorders, cancerous breast sores, and other conditions.

How does it work?
Sweet orange is a source of vitamin C and potassium.

Are there safety concerns?
Sweet orange seems to be safe for most adults.

In children, taking large amounts of sweet orange peel is unsafe. It can cause colic, convulsions, or death.

Do not take sweet orange if: You are pregnant or breast-feeding.

Are there any interactions with medications?
Antibiotics (Quinolone antibiotics). Calcium-fortified sweet orange juice can reduce the amount of some antibiotics the body absorbs. Reduced absorption of antibiotics can reduce their ability to fight infection. Sweet orange juice without calcium is unlikely to affect quinolone antibiotics. Some quinolone antibiotics include ciprofloxacin (Cipro), enoxacin (Penetrex), gatifloxacin (Tequin), levofloxacin (Levaquin), lomefloxacin (Maxaquin), moxifloxacin (Avelox), norfloxacin (Noroxin), ofloxacin (Floxin), and trovafloxacin (Trovan).
Celiprolol (Celicard). Consuming large amounts of sweet orange juice might decrease how much celiprolol (Celicard) the body absorbs. This might decrease how well celiprolol (Celicard) works. Don't consume large amounts of sweet orange juice if you take celiprolol (Celicard).
Fexofenadine (Allegra). Sweet orange might decrease how much fexofenadine (Allegra) the body absorbs. Taking sweet orange along with fexofenadine (Allegra) might decrease the effectiveness of fexofenadine (Allegra).
Ivermectin. Drinking sweet orange juice might decrease how much ivermectin the body absorbs. Taking sweet orange along with ivermectin might decrease the effectiveness of ivermectin.
Pravastatin (Pravachol). Drinking sweet orange juice might increase how much pravastatin (Pravachol) the body absorbs. Taking pravastatin (Pravachol) with sweet orange juice might increase drug levels in the body and possibly increase the chance of drug side effects.

SWEET SUMACH

What other names is the product known by?
Aromatic Sumac, Fragrant Sumac, Rhus aromatica, Rhus Canadensis, Polecatbush, Skunkbrush, Squawbush.

What is it?
Sweet sumach is a plant. The root bark is used to make medicine.

Is it Effective?
The effectiveness ratings for **SWEET SUMACH** are as follows:
Insufficient Evidence to Rate Effectiveness for... Kidney and bladder problems, and uterine bleeding.

How does it work?
There isn't enough information available to understand how sweet sumach works.

Are there safety concerns?
There isn't enough information available to know if sweet sumach is safe. It can cause an allergic skin rash and irritation in some people.

Do not take sweet sumach if: You are pregnant or breast-feeding.

Are there any interactions with medications?
It is not known if sweet sumach interacts with any medicines.
Before taking sweet sumach, talk with your healthcare professional if you take any medications.

SWEET VERNAL GRASS

What other names is the product known by?
Anthoxanthum odoratum, Grass, Spring Grass.

What is it?
Sweet vernal grass is a plant. The whole plant is used to make medicine.

Natural Medicines Comprehensive Database Consumer Version (209) 472-2244

Is it Effective?

The effectiveness ratings for **SWEET VERNAL GRASS** are as follows:
Insufficient Evidence to Rate Effectiveness for... Headache, nausea, sleeplessness, and urinary problems.

How does it work?

Sweet vernal grass contains ingredients that can thin the blood.

Are there safety concerns?

Sweet vernal grass is UNSAFE. It can cause side effects such as diarrhea, nausea, vomiting, dizziness, headaches, sleeplessness, and liver problems.

Do not take sweet vernal grass if: You are pregnant or breast-feeding. • You have a liver disorder.

Are there any interactions with medications?

Medications that slow blood clotting (Anticoagulant / Antiplatelet drugs). Sweet vernal grass can slow blood clotting. Taking sweet vernal grass along with medications that also slow clotting can increase the chances of bruising and bleeding. Some medications that slow blood clotting include aspirin, clopidogrel (Plavix), diclofenac (Voltaren, Cataflam, others), ibuprofen (Advil, Motrin, others), naproxen (Anaprox, Naprosyn, others), dalteparin (Fragmin), enoxaparin (Lovenox), heparin, warfarin (Coumadin), and others.

SWEET VIOLET

What other names is the product known by?

Banafshah, Garden Violet, Neelapushpa, Neelapuspha, Sweet Violet Herb, Sweet Violet Root, Violae Odoratae Rhizoma, Herba, Violet.

What is it?

Sweet violet is an herb. The root and above ground parts are used to make medicine.

Is it Effective?

The effectiveness ratings for **SWEET VIOLET** are as follows:
Insufficient Evidence to Rate Effectiveness for... Asthma, bronchitis, colds, congestion, cough, depression, flu symptoms, sleeplessness, lung problems, menopausal symptoms, nervousness, stomach problems, urinary problems, and other conditions.

How does it work?

Sweet violet has chemicals that help break up chest congestion by thinning mucous and making it easier to cough up (expectorant).

Are there safety concerns?

There isn't enough information available to know if sweet violet is safe.

Do not use sweet violet if: You are pregnant or breast-feeding.

Are there any interactions with medications?

It is not known if sweet violet interacts with any medicines.
Before taking sweet violet, talk with your healthcare professional if you take any medications.

SWEET WOODRUFF

What other names is the product known by?

Asperula odorata, Galii odorati herba, Galium odorata, Master of the Wood, Waldmeister, Woodruff, Wordward.

What is it?

Sweet woodruff is an herb. The above ground parts are used to make medicine.

Is it Effective?

The effectiveness ratings for **SWEET WOODRUFF** are as follows:
Insufficient Evidence to Rate Effectiveness for... Preventing and treating lung, stomach, liver, gallbladder, and urinary disorders; nervousness; hemorrhoids; sleeplessness; migraines; skin problems; and other conditions.

Medical professionals should consult the Professional Version at www.NaturalDatabase.com.

How does it work?
Sweet woodruff contains ingredients that can help decrease swelling (inflammation) and kill germs.

Are there safety concerns?
Sweet woodruff seems safe when used short-term. It can cause headaches, blackouts, and liver damage when used long-term.

Do not use sweet woodruff if: You are pregnant or breast-feeding.

Are there any interactions with medications?
It is not known if sweet woodruff interacts with any medicines.
Before taking sweet woodruff, talk with your healthcare professional if you take any medications.

TAGETES

What other names is the product known by?
African Marigold, Aztec Marigold, Big Marigold, Chinchilla Enana, Dwarf Marigold, French Marigold, Huacatay, Mexican Marigold, Muster John Henry, Saffron Marigold, Stinking-Roger, Tagetes, Tagetes erecta, Tagetes glandulifera, Tagetes minuta, Tagetes patula.

What is it?
Tagetes is a plant. The above ground parts are used to make medicine.

Is it Effective?
The effectiveness ratings for **TAGETES** are as follows:
Insufficient Evidence to Rate Effectiveness for... Colds, stomach pain, cough, menstrual disorders, mumps, ulcers, and other conditions.

How does it work?
Tagetes contains ingredients that might help decrease swelling (inflammation) and spasms, calm the nerves, and reduce blood pressure.

Are there safety concerns?
There isn't enough information available to know if tagetes is safe. It can cause a skin rash if you touch the plant.

Do not take tagetes if: You are pregnant or breast-feeding. • You are allergic to ragweed, marigolds, daisies, or related herbs.

Are there any interactions with medications?
It is not known if tagetes interacts with any medicines.
Before taking tagetes, talk with your healthcare professional if you take any medications.

TAMARIND

What other names is the product known by?
Imlee, Tamarindo, Tamarindus indica.

What is it?
Tamarind is a fruit. The partially dried fruit is used to make medicine.

Is it Effective?
The effectiveness ratings for **TAMARIND** are as follows:
Insufficient Evidence to Rate Effectiveness for... Constipation, fever, liver and gallbladder disorders, and other conditions.

How does it work?
Tamarind contains ingredients that might have laxative effects and some activity against certain fungi and bacteria.

Are there safety concerns?
Tamarind is safe when used as a food. There isn't enough information available to know if tamarind is safe for use as a medicine.
Do not use tamarind if: You are pregnant or breast-feeding.

Are there any interactions with medications?

Aspirin. Taking tamarind with aspirin might increase how much aspirin the body absorbs. This could increase the amount of aspirin in the body and might increase the chance of aspirin side effects.

Ibuprofen. Taking tamarind with ibuprofen might increase how much ibuprofen the body absorbs. This could increase the amount of ibuprofen in the body and might increase the chance of ibuprofen side effects.

TAMARIX DIOICA

What other names is the product known by?
Saltcedar, Tamarisk, Tamarix.

What is it?
Tamarix dioica is an evergreen shrub.

Is it Effective?
The effectiveness ratings for **TAMARIX DIOICA** are as follows:
Insufficient Evidence to Rate Effectiveness for... Liver conditions, fever, and kidney disorders.

How does it work?
There isn't enough information available to know how Tamarix dioica works.

Are there safety concerns?
There isn't enough information available to know if Tamarix dioica is safe.

Do not take Tamarix dioica if: You are pregnant or breast-feeding.

Are there any interactions with medications?
It is not known if Tamarix dioica interacts with any medicines.
Talk with your health care professional before taking Tamarix dioica if you take any medications.

TANNIC ACID

What other names is the product known by?
None.

What is it?
Tannic acid is a chemical that can be found in oak leaves.

Is it Effective?
The effectiveness ratings for **TANNIC ACID** are as follows:
Possibly Ineffective for... Cold sores and fever blisters • Diaper rash • Minor burn or sunburn • Prickly heat.
Insufficient Evidence to Rate Effectiveness for... Cancer, swollen tonsils, ingrown toenails, poison ivy, thinning gums, sore throat, poison ivy, and other conditions.

How does it work?
Tannic acid contains ingredients that have a protective effect on the skin.

Are there safety concerns?
Tannic acid is safe when used in the amounts found in foods. However, it seems unsafe when applied to the skin or when taken by mouth as a medicine. In large amounts, it can cause side effects such as stomach irritation, nausea, vomiting, and liver damage.

Do not use tannic acid if: You are pregnant or breast-feeding. • You have a kidney or liver disorder. • You have certain skin conditions. • You have a fever or infection. • You have heart problems.

Are there any interactions with medications?
Medications taken by mouth (Oral drugs). Tannic acid absorbs substances in the stomach and intestines. Taking tannic acid along with medications taken by mouth can decrease how much medicine your body absorbs, and decrease the effectiveness of your medication. To prevent this interaction, take tannic acid at least one hour after medications you take by mouth.

Medical professionals should consult the Professional Version at www.NaturalDatabase.com.

Medical professionals should consult the Professional Version at www.NaturalDatabase.com.

TANSY

What other names is the product known by?
Bitter Buttons, Buttons, Chrysanthemi vulgaris flos, Chrysanthemi vulgaris herba, Chrysanthemum vulgare, Daisy, Erva Dos Vermes, Hind Heal, Parsley Fern, Scented Fern, Stinking Willie, Tanaceto,Tanacetum vulgare, Tansy Flower, Tansy Herb.

What is it?
Tansy is a plant. The above ground parts are used to make medicine.

Is it Effective?
The effectiveness ratings for **TANSY** are as follows:
Insufficient Evidence to Rate Effectiveness for... Starting menstrual flow; aborting pregnancy; killing roundworm or threadworm in children; killing bacteria; migraines; seizures; joint pain; improving digestion and appetite; gas, stomach spasms, bloating, and ulcers; fluid retention; calming nerves; kidney problems; and topical use for scabies, itching, bruises, sores, sprains, swelling, freckles, sunburn, toothaches, and as an insect repellent.

How does it work?
The chemicals in tansy increase saliva and blood flow to the tissues in the mouth, stomach, intestines, and pelvic area. Some researches think the chemicals may also have effects on the brain. Tansy extracts may decrease pain, increase bile production, and increase appetite in people with liver and gallbladder problems.

Are there safety concerns?
Tansy is UNSAFE when taken by mouth or applied on the skin.

Tansy can cause restlessness, vomiting, severe diarrhea, stomach pain, dizziness, tremors, kidney or liver damage, bleeding, abortions in pregnant women, seizures, and death. Applying tansy to the skin can cause a severe skin reaction.

Do not take tansy if: You are pregnant or breast-feeding.

Are there any interactions with medications?
Alcohol. Alcohol can cause sleepiness and drowsiness. Tansy might increase the sleepiness and drowsiness caused by alcohol. Do not drink alcohol and take tansy at the same time.

TANSY RAGWORT

What other names is the product known by?
Cankerwort, Common Ragwort, Dog Standard, European Ragwort, Ragweed, Ragwort, Senecio jacobaea, Staggerwort, Stammerwort, St. James' Wort, Stinking Nanny.

What is it?
Tansy ragwort is an herb. The above ground flowering parts are used to make medicine.

Is it Effective?
The effectiveness ratings for **TANSY RAGWORT** are as follows:
Insufficient Evidence to Rate Effectiveness for... Cancer, colic, menstrual problems, spasms, and other conditions.

How does it work?
There isn't enough information available to understand how tansy ragwort works.

Are there safety concerns?
Tansy ragwort is unsafe for use. It may block blood flow in the veins, and cause liver damage or cancer.

Do not take tansy ragwort if: You are pregnant or breast-feeding. • You have an allergy to ragweed, marigolds, or daisies. • You have liver damage.

Are there any interactions with medications?
Medications that increase break down of other medications by the liver (Cytochrome P450 3A4 (CYP3A4) inducers). Tansy ragwort is broken down by the liver. Some chemicals that form when the liver breaks down tansy ragwort can be harmful. Medications that cause the liver to break down tansy ragwort might enhance the toxic

effects of chemicals contained in tansy ragwort. Some of these medicines include carbamazepine (Tegretol), phenobarbital, phenytoin (Dilantin), rifampin, rifabutin (Mycobutin), and others.

TARRAGON

What other names is the product known by?
Artemisia dracunculus, Artemisia glauca, Estragon, Little Dragon, Mugwort.

What is it?
Tarragon is an herb. The above ground parts are used to make medicine.

Is it Effective?
The effectiveness ratings for **TARRAGON** are as follows:
Insufficient Evidence to Rate Effectiveness for... Digestion problems, menstrual problems, toothaches, water retention, and other conditions.

How does it work?
Tarragon is a good source of potassium. It also contains ingredients that work against some bacteria.

Are there safety concerns?
Tarragon seems to be safe when used short-term as a medicine. Long-term use might cause cancer.

Do not use tarragon if: You are pregnant or breast-feeding, in amounts larger than typically found in foods. • You have an allergy to ragweed, marigolds, or daisies.

Are there any interactions with medications?
It is not known if tarragon interacts with any medicines.
Before taking tarragon, talk with your healthcare professional if you take any medications.

TAUMELLOOLCH

What other names is the product known by?
Bearded Darnel, Cheat, Darnel, Drake, Lolium temulentum, Ray-Grass, Tare.

What is it?
Taumelloolch is a plant. The seeds are used to make medicine.

Is it Effective?
The effectiveness ratings for **TAUMELLOOLCH** are as follows:
Insufficient Evidence to Rate Effectiveness for... Cancer, eczema, migraine, nerve pain, nosebleeds, sleeplessness, stomach cramps, movement disorders, toothache, and other conditions.

How does it work?
Taumelloolch contains a chemical that might act as a pain reliever.

Are there safety concerns?
Taumelloolch is UNSAFE for use and is considered a poison. It can cause side effects such as confusion, weakness, dizziness, dilated pupils, headache, confusion, trembling, vision and speech disorders, vomiting, delirium, and death.

Do not use taumelloolch if: You are pregnant or breast-feeding.

Are there any interactions with medications?
It is not known if taumelloolch interacts with any medicines.
Before taking taumelloolch, talk with your healthcare professional if you take any medications.

Medical professionals should consult the Professional Version at www.NaturalDatabase.com.

CONSUMER VERSION

TAURINE

What other names is the product known by?
2-Aminoethane sulfonic acid, Aminoethanesulfonate, L-Taurine.

What is it?
Taurine is a protein found in breast-milk, meat, and fish.

Is it Effective?
The effectiveness ratings for **TAURINE** are as follows:
Possibly Effective for... Congestive heart failure (CHF) • Inflammation of the liver (hepatitis).
Insufficient Evidence to Rate Effectiveness for... High blood pressure, high cholesterol, seizures, improving mental performance, attention deficit-hyperactivity disorder (ADHD), cystic fibrosis, and other conditions.

How does it work?
Taurine might work for heart conditions by helping lower cholesterol and blood pressure.

Are there safety concerns?
Taurine seems safe for short-term use of six weeks or less.

Do not use taurine if: You are pregnant or breast-feeding. • You have a condition called bipolar disorder.

Are there any interactions with medications?
It is not known if taurine interacts with any medicines.
Before taking taurine, talk with your healthcare professional if you take any medications.

TEA TREE OIL

What other names is the product known by?
Australian Tea Tree Oil, Melaleuca alternifolia, Melaleuca Oil, Oleum Melaleucae.

What is it?
Tea tree oil is derived from the leaves of the tea tree (unrelated to the plant used for the beverage tea). It is used to make medicine.

Is it Effective?
The effectiveness ratings for **TEA TREE OIL** are as follows:
Possibly Effective for... Athlete's foot, and fungus infections of the nails • Mild to moderate acne.
Possibly Ineffective for... Cold sores.
Insufficient Evidence to Rate Effectiveness for... Lice; scabies; ringworm; antiseptic for cuts, abrasions, burns, insect bites and stings, and boils; vaginal, mouth, and ear infections; sore throat; cough; and congestion.

How does it work?
The chemicals in tea tree oil may kill bacteria and fungus.

Are there safety concerns?
Tea tree oil is safe for most people when put on the skin.

Tea tree oil can cause skin irritation and swelling when put on the skin. In people with acne, it can sometimes cause skin dryness, itching, stinging, burning, and redness.

Tea tree oil is UNSAFE when taken by mouth. Don't take tea tree oil by mouth. As a general rule never take undiluted essential oils by mouth due to the possibility of serious side effects.

Taking tree tea oil by mouth has caused confusion, inability to walk, unsteadiness, rash, and coma.

Are there any interactions with medications?
It is not known if tea tree oil interacts with any medicines.
Before taking tea tree oil, talk with your healthcare professional if you take any medications.

TEAZLE

What other names is the product known by?
Barber's Brush, Brushes and Combs, Card Thistle, Church Broom, Dipsacus sylvestris, Venus' Basin.

What is it?
Teazle is an herb. The roots are used to make medicine.

Is it Effective?
The effectiveness ratings for **TEAZLE** are as follows:
Insufficient Evidence to Rate Effectiveness for... Arthritis, psoriasis, and small wounds.

How does it work?
There isn't enough information available to know how teazle works.

Are there safety concerns?
There isn't enough information available to know if teazle is safe.

Do not use teazle if: You are pregnant or breast-feeding.

Are there any interactions with medications?
It is not known if teazle interacts with any medicines.
Before taking teazle, talk with your healthcare professional if you take any medications.

TERMINALIA

What other names is the product known by?
Arjuna, Axjun Argun, Bahera, Bala Harade, Balera, Behada, Beleric Myrobalan, Chebulic Myrobalan, Hara, Harada, Haritaki, He Zi, Hirala, Indian Almond, Kalidruma, Karshaphala, Myrobalan, Terminalia arjuna, Terminalia bellirica, Terminalia chebula, Tropical Almond, Vibhitaki.

What is it?
Terminalia is a tree. The bark and fruit are used to make medicine.

Is it Effective?
The effectiveness ratings for **TERMINALIA** are as follows:
Possibly Effective for... Treating chest pain (angina) after a heart attack, when used with conventional medications.
• Treating congestive heart failure (CHF), when used with conventional medications.
Insufficient Evidence to Rate Effectiveness for... Earaches, HIV infection, lung conditions, severe diarrhea, urinary problems, water retention, and other conditions.

How does it work?
Terminalia contains ingredients that help stimulate the heart. It might also help the heart by lowering cholesterol and blood pressure.

Are there safety concerns?
Terminalia seems safe when used short-term, for three months or less.

Do not use terminalia if: You are pregnant or breast-feeding.

Are there any interactions with medications?
It is not known if terminalia interacts with any medicines.
Before taking terminalia, talk with your healthcare professional if you take any medications.

THEANINE

What other names is the product known by?
L-theanine, gamma-glutamylethylamide, 5-N-ethylglutamine.

What is it?
Theanine is an amino acid (a building block for proteins) found in green tea.

Is it Effective?

The effectiveness ratings for **THEANINE** are as follows:

Insufficient Evidence to Rate Effectiveness for... Anxiety, preventing dementia including Alzheimer's disease, treating high blood pressure, or increasing the treatment effects of cancer drugs.

How does it work?

Theanine has a chemical structure very similar to glutamate, a naturally occurring amino acid in the body that helps transmit nerve impulses in the brain. Some of the effects of theanine appear to be similar to glutamate, and some effects seem to block glutamate.

Are there safety concerns?

Theanine seems to be safe when used once per week for three weeks. It's not known if daily use for prolonged periods of time is safe.

Do not use theanine supplements if: You are pregnant or breast-feeding.

Are there any interactions with medications?

Medications for high blood pressure (Antihypertensive drugs). Theanine seems to decrease blood pressure. Taking theanine along with medications for high blood pressure might cause your blood pressure to go too low. Some medications for high blood pressure include captopril (Capoten), enalapril (Vasotec), losartan (Cozaar), valsartan (Diovan), diltiazem (Cardizem), Amlodipine (Norvasc), hydrochlorothiazide (HydroDiuril), furosemide (Lasix), and many others.

Stimulant drugs. Stimulant drugs speed up the nervous system. By speeding up the nervous system stimulant medications can make you feel jittery and speed up your heartbeat. Theanine might work to slow down the nervous system. Taking theanine along with stimulant medications might decrease the effectiveness of stimulant medications. Some stimulant drugs include diethylpropion (Tenuate), epinephrine, phentermine (Ionamin), pseudoephedrine (Sudafed), and many others.

THIAMINE (VITAMIN B1)

What other names is the product known by?

Aneurine Hydrochloride, Antiberiberi Factor, Antiberiberi Vitamin, Antineuritic Factor, Antineuritic Vitamin, B complex Vitamin, Thiamine Chloride, Thiaminium Chloride Hydrochloride, Thiamine Hydrochloride, Vitamin B1.

What is it?

Thiamine is a vitamin, also called vitamin B1. Vitamin B1 is found in many foods including yeast, cereal grains, beans, nuts, and meat. It is often used in combination with other B vitamins, and found in many vitamin B complex formulations.

Is it Effective?

The effectiveness ratings for **THIAMINE (VITAMIN B1)** are as follows:

Effective for... Treatment and prevention of thiamine deficiency, including a specific thiamine deficiency disorder called Wernicke-Korsakoff syndrome • Correcting problems in people with certain types of genetic diseases.

Possibly Effective for... Cataracts.

Insufficient Evidence to Rate Effectiveness for... Poor appetite, ulcerative colitis (UC), chronic diarrhea, stomach problems, brain conditions, AIDS, heart disease, alcoholism, stress, aging, canker sores, improving athletic performance, preventing cervical cancer, and other conditions.

How does it work?

Thiamine is required by our bodies to properly use carbohydrates.

Are there safety concerns?

Thiamine is safe for most adults. Rarely, side effects such as skin irritation or other allergic reactions can happen.

Thiamine is likely safe for pregnant or breast-feeding women when taken in the recommended amount of 1.4 mg daily.

Thiamine might not properly enter the body in some people who have liver problems, drink lots of alcohol, or have other conditions.

Are there any interactions with medications?

It is not known if thiamine (vitamin B1) interacts with any medicines.

Before taking thiamine (vitamin B1), talk with your healthcare professional if you take any medications.

THREONINE

What other names is the product known by?
L-threonine.

What is it?
Threonine is an amino acid.

Is it Effective?
The effectiveness ratings for **THREONINE** are as follows:
Possibly Effective for... Spinal spasticity.
Possibly Ineffective for... Amyotrophic lateral sclerosis. This condition is better known as Lou Gehrig's disease.
Insufficient Evidence to Rate Effectiveness for... Familial spastic paraparesis and multiple sclerosis.

How does it work?
Threonine is changed in the body to a chemical called glycine. Glycine works in the brain to reduce spasticity.

Are there safety concerns?
Threonine seems to be safe when taken by mouth. Some people experience minor side effects such as stomach upset, headache, nausea, and skin rash.

Don't use threonine if: You are pregnant or breast-feeding.

Are there any interactions with medications?
Medications used for Alzheimer's disease (NMDA antagonists). There is some concern that threonine might decrease how well a medication used for Alzheimer's disease works. This medication is called memantine (Namenda).

THUJA

What other names is the product known by?
American Arborvitae, Arborvitae, Cedar Leaf Oil, Eastern Arborvitae, Eastern White Cedar, Hackmatack, Northern White Cedar, Swamp Cedar, Thuga, Thuja, Thuja occidentalis ,Tree of Life, White Cedar.

What is it?
Thuja is a tree. The leaves and leaf oil are used as a medicine.

Is it Effective?
The effectiveness ratings for **THUJA** are as follows:
Insufficient Evidence to Rate Effectiveness for... Stimulating immune function, bronchitis, pneumonia, skin infections, herpes infections, nerve pain, strep throat, abortions, arthritis, joint pain, muscle aches, skin diseases, cancer, warts, and use as an insect repellent.

How does it work?
Thuja contains chemicals that might fight viruses. It also contains a chemical called thujone that can cause brain problems.

Are there safety concerns?
There isn't enough information to know if thuja is safe when used as a medicine. Thuja in large amounts can cause queasiness, vomiting, painful diarrhea, asthma, seizures, and death.

Thuja products can contain a chemical called thujone. Thujone can cause low blood pressure, asthma, seizures, and death.

Do not take thuja if: You are pregnant or breast-feeding. • You have seizures or epilepsy.

Are there any interactions with medications?
Medications used to prevent seizures (Anticonvulsants). Medications used to prevent seizures affect chemicals in the brain. Thuja may also affect chemicals in the brain. By affecting chemicals in the brain, thuja may decrease the effectiveness of medications used to prevent seizures. Some medications used to prevent seizures include phenobarbital, primidone (Mysoline), valproic acid (Depakene), gabapentin (Neurontin), carbamazepine (Tegretol), phenytoin (Dilantin), and others.

Medical professionals should consult the Professional Version at www.NaturalDatabase.com.

Medications that increase the chance of having a seizure (Seizure threshold lowering drugs). Some medications increase the chance of having a seizure. Taking thuja might cause seizures in some people. Taking medications that increase the chance of having a seizure along with thuja might increase the risk of having a seizure. Do not take thuja with medication that increases the chance of having a seizure. Some medications that increase the chance of having a seizure include anesthesia (propofol, others), antiarrhythmics (mexiletine), antibiotics (amphotericin, penicillin, cephalosporins, imipenem), antidepressants (bupropion, others), antihistamines (cyproheptadine, others), immunosuppressants (cyclosporine), narcotics (fentanyl, others), stimulants (methylphenidate), theophylline, and others.

THUNDER GOD VINE

What other names is the product known by?

Huang-T'eng Ken, Lei Gong Teng, Lei-Kung T'eng, Taso-Ho-Hua, Threewingnut, Tripterygium wilfordii, Yellow Vine.

What is it?

Thunder god vine is an herb. Its leaves and root are used to make medicine.

Is it Effective?

The effectiveness ratings for **THUNDER GOD VINE** are as follows:
Possibly Effective for... Rheumatoid arthritis (RA).
Insufficient Evidence to Rate Effectiveness for... Male contraception, menstrual pain, multiple sclerosis (MS), abscesses, boils, lupus erythematosus (SLE), HIV/AIDS, and other conditions.

How does it work?

Thunder god vine might help rheumatoid arthritis (RA) by relieving swelling (inflammation) and by changing the way the immune system responds to the arthritis. Thunder god vine contains chemicals that might decrease male fertility by changing sperm.

Are there safety concerns?

Thunder god vine appears to be safe for most people. It can cause many side effects such as stomach upset, skin reactions, missed menstrual periods, vomiting, diarrhea, and kidney problems.

Do not use thunder god vine if: You are pregnant or breast-feeding. • You have a decreased immune system. • You have osteoporosis.

Are there any interactions with medications?

Medications that decrease the immune system (Immunosuppressants). Large doses of thunder god vine might decrease the immune system. Taking thunder god vine along with other medications that decrease the immune system might decrease the immune system too much. Avoid taking thunder god vine with medications that decrease the immune system. Some medications that decrease the immune system include azathioprine (Imuran), basiliximab (Simulect), cyclosporine (Neoral, Sandimmune), daclizumab (Zenapax), muromonab-CD3 (OKT3, Orthoclone OKT3), mycophenolate (CellCept), tacrolimus (FK506, Prograf), sirolimus (Rapamune), prednisone (Deltasone, Orasone), corticosteroids (glucocorticoids), and others.

THYME

What other names is the product known by?

Common Thyme, French Thyme, Garden Thyme, Red Thyme Oil, Rubbed Thyme, Spanish Thyme, Thyme Aetheroleum, Thymi herba, Thymus vulgaris, Thymus zygis, White Thyme Oil.

What is it?

Thyme is an herb. The flowers, leaves, and oil are used as medicine.

Is it Effective?

The effectiveness ratings for **THYME** are as follows:
Insufficient Evidence to Rate Effectiveness for... Bronchitis, in combination with cowslip; treating hair loss (alopecia areata) when combined with other herbs; improving movement disorders in children when used with other medicines; colic; ear infections; swelling (inflammation) of the tonsils; preventing bedwetting; sore throat; bad breath; bronchitis; and swelling (inflammation) of the lungs and mouth.

How does it work?

Thyme contains chemicals that might help bacterial and fungal infections, and minor irritations. It also might relieve smooth muscle spasms, such as coughing.

Are there safety concerns?

Thyme is safe when consumed in foods and as medicine for short periods of time. It can cause digestive system upset. Thyme oil also seems to be safe when applied to the skin. In some people, applying the oil to the skin can cause irritation.

Do not use thyme if: You are pregnant or breast-feeding. • You are allergic to the herb oregano. People who are allergic to oregano can also be allergic to thyme.

Are there any interactions with medications?

Medications that slow blood clotting (Anticoagulant / Antiplatelet drugs). Thyme might slow blood clotting. Taking thyme along with medications that also slow clotting might increase the chances of bruising and bleeding. Some medications that slow blood clotting include aspirin, clopidogrel (Plavix), diclofenac (Voltaren, Cataflam, others), ibuprofen (Advil, Motrin, others), naproxen (Anaprox, Naprosyn, others), dalteparin (Fragmin), enoxaparin (Lovenox), heparin, warfarin (Coumadin), and others.

THYMUS EXTRACT

What other names is the product known by?

Predigested Thymus Extract, Pure Thymic Extract, Thymomodulin, Thymosin, Thymostimulin, Thymus, Thymus Acid Lysate Derivative, Thymus Complex, Thymus Concentrate, Thymus-Derived Polypeptides, Thymus Factors, Thymus Polypeptides, Thymus Substance.

What is it?

Thymus extract is a chemical that can be man-made or produced from the glands of cows.

Is it Effective?

The effectiveness ratings for **THYMUS EXTRACT** are as follows:
Possibly Effective for... Hayfever • Asthma • Lung infections • Food allergies.
Insufficient Evidence to Rate Effectiveness for...AIDS/HIV, arthritis, cancer, herpes, shingles, and other conditions.

How does it work?

Thymus extract works by improving or boosting the immune system.

Are there safety concerns?

Thymus extract seems to be safe for most people.

Because thymus can come from animals, there is concern about possible contamination with diseased animal parts. Any products made from contaminated or diseased organs might present a human health hazard.

Do not take thymus extract if: You are pregnant or breast-feeding. • You have decreased immune function.

Are there any interactions with medications?

Medications that decrease the immune system (Immunosuppressants). Medications that decrease the immune system can increase your chances of getting sick. Thymus extract is made from animals. There is some concern that products made from animals might contain harmful diseases and cause infections. Taking medications that decrease the immune system along with thymus extract might increase your chances of getting sick. Do not take thymus extract if you are taking medications that decrease the immune system. Some medications that decrease the immune system include azathioprine (Imuran), basiliximab (Simulect), cyclosporine (Neoral, Sandimmune), daclizumab (Zenapax), muromonab-CD3 (OKT3, Orthoclone OKT3), mycophenolate (CellCept), tacrolimus (FK506, Prograf), sirolimus (Rapamune), prednisone (Deltasone, Orasone), corticosteroids (glucocorticoids), and others.

Medical professionals should consult the Professional Version at www.NaturalDatabase.com.

TIRATRICOL

What other names is the product known by?
Triac, triiodothyroacetic acid, 3,3', 5-triiodothyroacetic acid.

What is it?
Tiratricol is a naturally occurring chemical in the body and can also be man-made.

Is it Effective?
The effectiveness ratings for **TIRATRICOL** are as follows:
Likely Effective for... Improving thyroid function.
Possibly Effective for... Treating thyroid cancer when taken with the drug levothyroxine • Thyroid problems in infants.
Likely Ineffective for... Weight loss.
Insufficient Evidence to Rate Effectiveness for... Reducing cellulite.

How does it work?
Tiratricol might work by improving thyroid function. It might also help lower cholesterol and stimulate bone formation.

Are there safety concerns?
Tiratricol is safe when used by a healthcare professional for thyroid problems. It can cause side effects such as severe diarrhea, fatigue, weakness, and weight loss.
Tiratricol can be used during pregnancy for thyroid problems in the fetus, under the direct supervision of a healthcare provider. However, it should not be used for other purposes during pregnancy.

Do not take tiratricol if: You are elderly. • You are breast-feeding. • You have diabetes. • You have a heart problem. • You have high blood pressure. • You have a liver problem.

Are there any interactions with medications?
Cholestyramine (Questran). Cholestyramine (Questran) might decrease how much tiratricol the body absorbs. By decreasing how much tiratricol the body absorbs, cholestyramine (Questran) might decrease the effectiveness of tiratricol supplements. To avoid this interaction take tiratricol at least one hour before or four hours after taking cholestyramine.
Medications that slow blood clotting (Anticoagulant / Antiplatelet drugs). Tiratricol might slow blood clotting. Taking tiratricol along with medications that also slow clotting might increase the chances of bruising and bleeding. Some medications that slow blood clotting include aspirin, clopidogrel (Plavix), diclofenac (Voltaren, Cataflam, others), ibuprofen (Advil, Motrin, others), naproxen (Anaprox, Naprosyn, others), dalteparin (Fragmin), enoxaparin (Lovenox), heparin, warfarin (Coumadin), and others.
Medications for diabetes (Antidiabetes drugs). Large amounts of tiratricol can decrease blood sugar levels. Diabetes medications are also used to lower blood sugar. Taking tiratricol along with diabetes medications might cause your blood sugar to be too low. Monitor your blood sugar closely. The dose of your diabetes medication might need to be changed. Some medications used for diabetes include glimepiride (Amaryl), glyburide (DiaBeta, Glynase PresTab, Micronase), insulin, pioglitazone (Actos), rosiglitazone (Avandia), chlorpropamide (Diabinese), glipizide (Glucotrol), tolbutamide (Orinase), and others.
Stimulant drugs. Stimulant drugs speed up the nervous system. By speeding up the nervous system, stimulant medications can make you feel jittery and speed up your heartbeat. Tiratricol might also speed up the nervous system. Taking tiratricol along with stimulant drugs might cause serious problems including increased heart rate and high blood pressure. Avoid taking stimulant drugs along with tiratricol. Some stimulant drugs include diethylpropion (Tenuate), epinephrine, phentermine (Ionamin), pseudoephedrine (Sudafed), and many others.
Thyroid hormone. Tiratricol works similarly to thyroid hormones. Taking tiratricol along with thyroid hormone pills might increase the chance of side effects from thyroid hormone.

TOLU BALSAM

What other names is the product known by?
Balsam, Balsam Tolu, Balsamum Tolutanum, Myroxylon balsamum, Myroxylon balsamum var. balsamum, Opobalsam, Resina Tolutana, Resin Tolu, Thomas Balsam, Toluifera balsamum, Tolu, Toluiferum Balsamum.

What is it?
Tolu balsam comes from a tree. The sap-like substance is used to make medicine.

Is it Effective?
The effectiveness ratings for **TOLU BALSAM** are as follows:
Insufficient Evidence to Rate Effectiveness for... Bedsores, bronchitis, cancer, cough, cracked nipples, lips, reducing lung swelling (inflammation), and minor skin cuts.

How does it work?
Tolu balsam contains ingredients that help break up congestion. It might also work as a skin protectant.

Are there safety concerns?
Tolu balsam seems safe for use as a medicine. It can cause side effects such as allergic reactions and kidney irritation in some people.

Do not use tolu balsam if: You are pregnant or breast-feeding. • You have a fever. • You have a kidney disorder.

Are there any interactions with medications?
It is not known if tolu balsam interacts with any medicines.
Before taking tolu balsam, talk with your healthcare professional if you take any medications.

TOMATO

What other names is the product known by?
Love Apple, Lycopersicon esculentum.

What is it?
Tomato is a plant. The fruit, leaf, and vine are used to make medicine.

Is it Effective?
The effectiveness ratings for **TOMATO** are as follows:
Possibly Effective for... Reducing the risk of prostate cancer • Reducing the risk of cataracts • Reducing the risk of cardiovascular disease in women.
Possibly Ineffective for... Reducing the risk of bladder cancer • Diabetes. Increasing consumption of tomato or tomato-based products does not seem to decrease the risk of developing type 2 diabetes.
Insufficient Evidence to Rate Effectiveness for... Arthritis, asthma, cancer, high blood pressure, the common cold, chills, and digestive disorders.

How does it work?
Tomatoes are a major dietary source of certain nutrients that can help protect against some cancers. Tomato might also help stimulate the immune system.

Are there safety concerns?
Tomatoes are safe when used as a food. A specific tomato extract (Lyc-O-Mato) might also be safe when used for up to eight weeks.

The tomato leaf is unsafe. In large amounts, tomato leaves can cause poisoning. Symptoms of poisoning may include severe mouth and throat irritation, vomiting, diarrhea, dizziness, headache, mild spasms, and death in severe cases.

Do not use tomato in amounts greater than typically found in foods if: You are pregnant or breast-feeding.

Are there any interactions with medications?
It is not known if tomato interacts with any medicines.
Before taking tomato, talk with your healthcare professional if you take any medications.

TONKA BEAN

What other names is the product known by?
Coumarouna Odorata, Cumaru, Dipteryx odorata, Dutch Tonka, English Tonka, Tonka, Tonka Seed, Tonquin Bean, Torquin Bean.

What is it?
Tonka bean is from a tree. The fruit and seed are used to make medicine.

Medical professionals should consult the
Professional Version at www.NaturalDatabase.com.

Is it Effective?
The effectiveness ratings for **TONKA BEAN** are as follows:
Insufficient Evidence to Rate Effectiveness for... Cough, cramps, earache, mouth sores, nausea, spasms, sore throat, tuberculosis, and other conditions.

How does it work?
Tonka bean contains ingredients that help improve swelling (inflammation) and water retention.

Are there safety concerns?
Tonka bean is UNSAFE. It can cause side effects such as nausea, vomiting, diarrhea, dizziness, sleeplessness, and liver problems.

Do not use tonka bean if: You are pregnant or breast-feeding. • You have liver disease.

Are there any interactions with medications?
Medications that slow blood clotting (Anticoagulant / antiplatelet drugs). Tonka bean might slow blood clotting. Taking tonka bean along with medications that also slow clotting might increase the chances of bruising and bleeding. Some medications that slow blood clotting include aspirin, clopidogrel (Plavix), diclofenac (Voltaren, Cataflam, others), ibuprofen (Advil, Motrin, others), naproxen (Anaprox, Naprosyn, others), dalteparin (Fragmin), enoxaparin (Lovenox), heparin, warfarin (Coumadin), and others.

TORMENTIL

What other names is the product known by?
Biscuits, Bloodroot, Cinquefoil, Earthbank, English Sarsaparilla, Ewe Daisy, Flesh and Blood, Potentilla, Potentilla erecta, Septfoil, Shepherd's Knapperty, Shepherd's Knot, Thormantle, Tormentilla, Tormentillae rhizoma.

What is it?
Tormentil is an herb. The root is used to make medicine.

Is it Effective?
The effectiveness ratings for **TORMENTIL** are as follows:
Insufficient Evidence to Rate Effectiveness for... Bleeding, fever, stomach complaints, diarrhea, and mild swelling (inflammation) of the mouth and throat.

How does it work?
Tormentil contains ingredients called tannins that might help reduce skin inflammation, and have a drying (astringent) effect on the tissues. It might also help to stop bleeding.

Are there safety concerns?
Tormentil seems to be safe for most people. It can cause side effects such as nausea, vomiting, and stomach complaints.

Do not use tormentil if: You are pregnant or breast-feeding.

Are there any interactions with medications?
It is not known if tormentil interacts with any medicines.
Before taking tormentil, talk with your healthcare professional if you take any medications.

TRAGACANTH

What other names is the product known by?
Astragalus gummifera, Goat's Thorn, Green Dragon, Gum Dragon, Gummi Tragacanthae, Gum Tragacanth, Hog Gum, Syrian Tragacanth, Tragacanth Gum.

What is it?
Tragacanth is a plant. The sap-like material (resin) of the plant is used to make medicine.

Is it Effective?
The effectiveness ratings for **TRAGACANTH** are as follows:
Insufficient Evidence to Rate Effectiveness for... Constipation and diarrhea.

 Natural Medicines Comprehensive Database Consumer Version (209) 472-2244

How does it work?
Tragacanth contains ingredients that stimulate the movement of the intestines.

Are there safety concerns?
Tragacanth seems to be safe when used as a medicine. It can block the intestines if you do not drink enough fluid.

Do not take tragacanth if: You are pregnant or breast-feeding. • You are allergic to quillaia bark; breathing problems can occur.

Are there any interactions with medications?
Medications taken by mouth (Oral drugs). Tragacanth is a thick gel. Tragacanth can stick to medications in the stomach and intestines. Taking tragacanth at the same time as medications that you take by mouth can decrease how much medication your body absorbs, and decrease the effectiveness of your medication. To prevent this interaction, take tragacanth at least one hour after medications you take by mouth.

TRAILING ARBUTUS

What other names is the product known by?
Epigaea repens, Gravel Plant, Ground Laurel, Mountain Pink, Water Pink, Winter Pink.

What is it?
Trailing arbutus is an herb. The above ground parts are used to make medicine.

Is it Effective?
The effectiveness ratings for **TRAILING ARBUTUS** are as follows:
Insufficient Evidence to Rate Effectiveness for... Urinary conditions, water retention, and other conditions.

How does it work?
Trailing arbutus contains ingredients that are thought to help kill germs in the urine.

Are there safety concerns?
Trailing arbutus seems to be safe when used short-term. Long-term use can lead to poisoning. Symptoms of poisoning include ringing in the ears, vomiting, confusion, convulsions, and collapse. It may also cause liver damage, weight loss, weakness, loss of hair color, bloody urine, difficulty with urination, and painful urination.

Do not take trailing arbutus if: You are pregnant or breast-feeding.

Are there any interactions with medications?
It is not known if trailing arbutus interacts with any medicines.
Before taking trailing arbutus, talk with your healthcare professional if you take any medications.

TRANSFER FACTOR

What other names is the product known by?
Bovine Dialyzable Leukocyte Extract, Bovine Dialyzable Transfer Factor, Bovine Transfer Factor, Dialyzable Leukocyte Extract, Dialyzable Transfer Factor, DLE, Human Dialyzable Leukocyte Extract, Human Transfer Factor, TF, TFd.

What is it?
Transfer factors are chemicals that are taken from a human or animal that have already developed protection, or immunity, against a certain disease.

Is it Effective?
The effectiveness ratings for **TRANSFER FACTOR** are as follows:
Possibly Effective for... Immunizing children with leukemia against shingles.
Possibly Ineffective for... Chronic fatigue syndrome • Lung cancer • Melanoma (a type of skin cancer) • Treating a disease called amyotrophic lateral sclerosis (Lou Gehrig's disease).
Insufficient Evidence to Rate Effectiveness for...AIDS-related infections, Alzheimer's disease, asthma, autism, diabetes, infertility, muscle weakness, genetic and infectious disease, Hepatitis B, and other conditions.

How does it work?
Transfer factor might boost immunity to specific diseases.

Are there safety concerns?
Transfer factor that has been derived from humans seems to be safe when used for up to two years. Transfer factor that is derived from cows seems to be safe when used short-term, up to three months. It can cause fever in some people. Transfer factor given by injection (shot) can cause swelling and pain where the injection is given.

There is some concern about the possibility of catching "mad cow disease" (bovine spongiform encephalitis, BSE) or other diseases from products that come from animals. "Mad cow disease" has not been transmitted by transfer factor, but it is probably wise to avoid animal products from countries where mad cow disease has been found.

Do not take transfer factor if: You are pregnant or breast-feeding.

Are there any interactions with medications?
It is not known if transfer factor interacts with any medicines.
Before taking transfer factor, talk with your healthcare professional if you take any medications.

TRAVELER'S JOY

What other names is the product known by?
Clematis vitalba, Old Man's Beard.

What is it?
Traveler's joy is an herb. The leaves are used to make medicine.

Is it Effective?
The effectiveness ratings for **TRAVELER'S JOY** are as follows:
Insufficient Evidence to Rate Effectiveness for... Migraine headaches, diseases of the male genitals, and poorly healing wounds.

How does it work?
There isn't enough information available to understand how traveler's joy works.

Are there safety concerns?
Traveler's joy is UNSAFE for any use. It can cause side effects such as severe skin and stomach irritation.

Do not take traveler's joy if: You are pregnant or breast-feeding.

Are there any interactions with medications?
It is not known if traveler's joy interacts with any medicines.
Before taking traveler's joy, talk with your healthcare professional if you take any medications.

TREE OF HEAVEN

What other names is the product known by?
Ailanthus altissima, Ailanthus Glandulosa, Ailanto, A-Lan-Thus, Chinese Sumach, Copal Tree, Heaven Tree, Paradise Tree, Varnish Tree, Vernis de Japon.

What is it?
Tree of heaven is a plant. The dried trunk and root bark are used for medicine.

Is it Effective?
The effectiveness ratings for **TREE OF HEAVEN** are as follows:
Insufficient Evidence to Rate Effectiveness for... Diarrhea, menstrual disorders, asthma, cramps, epilepsy, fast heart rate, gonorrhea, malaria, tapeworms, or use as a tonic.

How does it work?
Some researchers think that chemicals in the bark of tree of heaven may have drying effects, decrease fever, and decrease spasms. Other chemicals found in tree of heaven might kill worms and protozoa and have some effects against cancer cells.

Medical professionals should consult the Professional Version at www.NaturalDatabase.com.

 (209) 472-2244

Are there safety concerns?

It is not known if tree of heaven is safe, but when taken in large amounts, tree of heaven bark can cause queasiness, dizziness, headache, limb tingling, and diarrhea.

Do not use tree of heaven if: You are pregnant or breast-feeding.

Are there any interactions with medications?

It is not known if tree of heaven interacts with any medicines.
Before taking tree of heaven, talk with your healthcare professional if you take any medications.

TREE TURMERIC

What other names is the product known by?

Berberis aristata, Berberis chitria, Berberis coriaria, Chitra, Darhahed, Hint Amberparisi, Indian Lycium, Nepal Barberry Nepalese Barberry, Ophthalmic Barberry.

What is it?

Tree turmeric is a plant. The fruit, stems, leaves, wood, root, and root bark are used to make medicine.

Is it Effective?

The effectiveness ratings for **TREE TURMERIC** are as follows:
Insufficient Evidence to Rate Effectiveness for... Heart failure, burns, trachoma (an eye infection that can cause blindness), and other conditions.

How does it work?

The chemicals in tree turmeric might cause stronger heartbeats. They also might have antibacterial effects.

Are there safety concerns?

There is not enough information to know if tree turmeric is safe in medicinal amounts. Tree turmeric is unsafe in newborn infants.

Do not take tree turmeric if: You are pregnant or breast-feeding.

Are there any interactions with medications?

Cyclosporin (Neoral, Sandimmune). The body breaks down cyclosporin (Neoral, Sandimmune) to get rid of it. Tree turmeric might decrease how fast the body breaks down cyclosporin (Neoral, Sandimmune). This might cause there to be too much cyclosporin (Neoral, Sandimmune) in the body and potentially cause side effects.
Medications changed by the liver (Cytochrome P450 3A4 (CYP3A4) substrates). Some medications are changed and broken down by the liver. Tree turmeric might decrease how quickly the liver breaks down some medications. Taking tree turmeric along with some medications that are broken down by the liver can increase the effects and side effects of some medications. Before taking tree turmeric, talk to your healthcare provider if you are taking any medications that are changed by the liver. Some medications changed by the liver include lovastatin (Mevacor), clarithromycin (Biaxin), indinavir (Crixivan), sildenafil (Viagra), triazolam (Halcion), and many others.

TRONADORA

What other names is the product known by?

Esperanza, Common Yellow Elder, Tecoma stans, Trumpet Bush, Yellow Bells, Yellow Trumpet Bush.

What is it?

Tronadora is an herb. The leaves and stems, and less frequently the roots and flowers, are used to make medicine.

Is it Effective?

The effectiveness ratings for **TRONADORA** are as follows:
Insufficient Evidence to Rate Effectiveness for... Diabetes and digestive disorders.

How does it work?

Tronadora might slightly change the blood sugar level in the body. But it is not known if tronadora increases or decreases blood sugar.

Medical professionals should consult the Professional Version at www.NaturalDatabase.com.

Are there safety concerns?
There isn't enough information available to know if tronadora is safe for use.

Do not use tronadora if: You are pregnant or breast-feeding.

Are there any interactions with medications?
It is not known if tronadora interacts with any medicines.
Before taking tronadora, talk with your healthcare professional if you take any medications.

TRYPSIN

What other names is the product known by?
Proteinase, Proteolytic Enzyme.

What is it?
Trypsin is a protein found in the body. It can also be made from animal sources.

Is it Effective?
The effectiveness ratings for **TRYPSIN** are as follows:
Possibly Effective for... Osteoarthritis • Wound cleansing and healing.
Insufficient Evidence to Rate Effectiveness for... Mouth ulcer cleansing and healing, and other conditions.

How does it work?
Trypsin removes dead skin cells (tissue) and allows healthy tissue to grow.

Are there safety concerns?
Trypsin seems to be safe when used by healthcare professionals. It can cause side effects such as pain and burning.

Do not use trypsin if: You are pregnant or breast-feeding.

Are there any interactions with medications?
It is not known if trypsin interacts with any medicines.
Before taking trypsin, talk with your healthcare professional if you take any medications.

TUNG SEED

What other names is the product known by?
Aleurites cordatus, Aleurites javanicus, Aleurites moluccanus, Aleurites pentaphyllus, Aleurites remyi, Aleurites trilobus, Balucanat, Candleberry, Candleberry Tree, Candlenut, China-Wood Oil, Country Walnut, Indian Walnut, Kukui, Jatropha moluccana, Otaheite Walnut, Tung, Varnish Tree, Vernicia cordata.

What is it?
Tung seed is the seed of a tree. People use the oil and the kernels of tung seed to make medicine.

Is it Effective?
The effectiveness ratings for **TUNG SEED** are as follows:
Insufficient Evidence to Rate Effectiveness for... Asthma, bowel problems such as diarrhea and constipation, and other conditions.

How does it work?
Tung seed contains various substances which might stimulate the bowels and cause sweating. It also contains toxic chemicals, such as cyanide.

Are there safety concerns?
Tung seed is UNSAFE when taken by mouth. It can cause severe stomach pain, violent vomiting, breathing problems, and possibly death.

There isn't enough information to know if tung seed is safe when applied directly to the skin.

Are there any interactions with medications?
It is not known if tung seed interacts with any medicines.
Before taking tung seed, talk with your healthcare professional if you take any medications.

TURKEY CORN

What other names is the product known by?
Bleeding Heart, Dicentra cucullaria, Dutchman's Breeches, Squirrel Corn, Staggerweed.

What is it?
Turkey corn is a plant. The underground stem (tuber) is used to make medicine.

Is it Effective?
The effectiveness ratings for **TURKEY CORN** are as follows:
Insufficient Evidence to Rate Effectiveness for... Digestive and menstrual disorders, urinary tract diseases, and skin rashes.

How does it work?
Turkey corn might help increase body water loss through the urine.

Are there safety concerns?
Turkey corn seems to be UNSAFE. It may cause poisoning.

Do not use turkey corn if: You are pregnant or breast-feeding.

Are there any interactions with medications?
It is not known if turkey corn interacts with any medicines.
Before taking turkey corn, talk with your healthcare professional if you take any medications.

TURMERIC

What other names is the product known by?
Curcuma, Curcuma domestica, Curcuma aromatica, Curcumae longae rhizoma, Curcumin, Haridra, Indian Saffron, Nisha, Rajani, Radix Curcumae, Turmeric Root.

What is it?
Turmeric is a plant. The root is used to make medicine.

Is it Effective?
The effectiveness ratings for **TURMERIC** are as follows:
Possibly Effective for... Upset stomach (dyspepsia).
Insufficient Evidence to Rate Effectiveness for... Jaundice, hepatitis, diarrhea, fibromyalgia, liver and gallbladder problems, headache, menstrual problems, pain, ringworm, bruising, eye infections, skin problems, rheumatoid arthritis (RA), cancer, and other conditions.

How does it work?
The chemicals in turmeric might decrease swelling (inflammation).

Are there safety concerns?
Turmeric seems safe for most people. It can sometimes cause nausea or diarrhea.

Do not take turmeric if: You are pregnant or breast-feeding. • You have gallbladder disease.

Are there any interactions with medications?
Medications that slow blood clotting (Anticoagulant / Antiplatelet drugs). Turmeric might slow blood clotting. Taking turmeric along with medications that also slow clotting might increase the chances of bruising and bleeding. Some medications that slow blood clotting include aspirin, clopidogrel (Plavix), diclofenac (Voltaren, Cataflam, others), ibuprofen (Advil, Motrin, others), naproxen (Anaprox, Naprosyn, others), dalteparin (Fragmin), enoxaparin (Lovenox), heparin, warfarin (Coumadin), and others.

Medical professionals should consult the Professional Version at www.NaturalDatabase.com.

TURPENTINE OIL

What other names is the product known by?
Pinus australis, Pinus palustris, Pinus pinaster, Purified Turpentine Oil, Spirits Of Turpentine, Terebinthinae aetheroleum, Turpentine.

What is it?
Turpentine oil is made from the resin of certain pine trees. It is used as medicine.

Is it Effective?
The effectiveness ratings for **TURPENTINE OIL** are as follows:
Insufficient Evidence to Rate Effectiveness for... Muscle pain, toothaches, use by inhalation for lung problems, use on the skin for joint and nerve pain, and other uses.

How does it work?
Turpentine oil, when inhaled, may help reduce congestion. When used on the skin, turpentine oil may cause warmth and redness which can help relieve pain in the tissue underneath.

Are there safety concerns?
Turpentine oil is possibly safe when used appropriately on the skin or by inhalation in adults. When inhaled, turpentine oil can cause spasms of the airways, particularly in people with asthma and whooping cough. When used on the skin, it can cause skin irritation.

Turpentine oil is unsafe when taken by mouth or used on the skin over large areas. Turpentine oil, when taken by mouth, can cause serious side effects including headache, sleeplessness, coughing, bleeding in the lungs, vomiting, kidney damage, brain damage, coma, and death.

Do not use turpentine oil in children. They are particularly sensitive to the toxicity and can be fatally poisoned.

Do not take turpentine oil if: You are pregnant or breast-feeding. • You have a lung problem, including asthma or whooping cough.

Are there any interactions with medications?
It is not known if turpentine oil interacts with any medicines.
Before taking turpentine oil, talk with your healthcare professional if you take any medications.

TURTLE HEAD

What other names is the product known by?
Balmony, Bitter Herb, Chelone, Chelone glabra, Hummingbird Tree, Salt-rheum Weed, Shellflower, Snakehead, Turtlebloom.

What is it?
Turtle head is a plant. The above ground parts and root are used to make medicine. Be careful not to confuse turtle head (chelone glabra) with red turtle head (chelone oblique).

Is it Effective?
The effectiveness ratings for **TURTLE HEAD** are as follows:
Insufficient Evidence to Rate Effectiveness for... Constipation, purging the bowels, and other uses.

How does it work?
It is not known how turtle head might work.

Are there safety concerns?
Turtle head is possibly safe when taken by mouth, but the potential side effects are not known.

Do not use turtle head if: You are pregnant or breast-feeding.

Are there any interactions with medications?
It is not known if turtle head interacts with any medicines.
Before taking turtle head, talk with your healthcare professional if you take any medications.

Medical professionals should consult the Professional Version at www.NaturalDatabase.com.

TYROSINE

What other names is the product known by?
L-tyrosine, Tyr, Tyrosinum, 2-amino-3-(4-hydroxyphenyl)propionic acid.

What is it?
Tyrosine is an amino acid. The body makes tyrosine from another amino acid called phenylalanine. It can also be found in dairy products, meats, fish, eggs, nuts, beans, oats, and wheat.

Is it Effective?
The effectiveness ratings for **TYROSINE** are as follows:
Effective for... Treating phenylketonuria (PKU), a condition in which people cannot make tyrosine from phenylalanine.
Possibly Effective for... Improving alertness following the loss of sleep.
Possibly Ineffective for... Treating moderate depression • Treating adult attention deficit disorder (ADD) • Treating childhood attention deficit-hyperactivity disorder (ADHD).
Insufficient Evidence to Rate Effectiveness for... Stress, premenstrual syndrome (PMS), Parkinson's disease, chronic fatigue syndrome (CFS), Alzheimer's disease, heart disease, impotence, schizophrenia, wrinkled skin, and other conditions.

How does it work?
The body uses tyrosine to make chemical messengers that are involved in conditions involving the brain such as mental alertness.

Are there safety concerns?
Tyrosine seems safe for most adults, when taken by mouth or applied to the skin. Some people experience side effects such as nausea, headache, fatigue, heartburn, and joint pain.
There isn't enough information available to know if tyrosine is safe for children to use in medicinal amounts.
Do not use tyrosine in medicinal amounts if: You are pregnant or breast-feeding. • You have an overactive thyroid (hyperthyroidism). • You have a condition known as Grave's disease.

Are there any interactions with medications?
Levodopa. Tyrosine might decrease how much levodopa the body absorbs. By decreasing how much levodopa the body absorbs, tyrosine might decrease the effectiveness of levodopa. Do not take tyrosine and levodopa at the same time.
Thyroid hormone. The body naturally produces thyroid hormones. Tyrosine might increase how much thyroid hormone the body produces. Taking tyrosine with thyroid hormone pills might cause there to be too much thyroid hormone. This could increase the effects and side effects of thyroid hormones.

USNEA

What other names is the product known by?
Beard Moss, Old Man's Beard, Sodium Usniate, Tree Moss, Tree's Dandruff, Usnea barbata, Usnea florida, Usnea hirta, Usnea Lichen, Usnea plicata, Usnic Acid, Woman's Long Hair.

What is it?
Usnea is a lichen that grows on trees. The plant body is used to make medicine.

Is it Effective?
The effectiveness ratings for **USNEA** are as follows:
Insufficient Evidence to Rate Effectiveness for... Weight loss, pain, fever, mild inflammation (swelling) of the mouth and throat.

How does it work?
Usnea contains ingredients that are thought to have activity against microbes that might cause infections. It also might decrease inflammation, pain, and fever.

Are there safety concerns?
Usnea is possibly safe when used on the skin, though allergic reactions can occur. The safety of taking usnea by mouth is unknown. A weight loss product containing usnea and other ingredients has been associated with liver damage.
Do not take usnea if: You are pregnant or breast-feeding.

Medical professionals should consult the Professional Version at www.NaturalDatabase.com.

Are there any interactions with medications?

It is not known if usnea interacts with any medicines.
Before taking usnea, talk with your healthcare professional if you take any medications.

UVA URSI

What other names is the product known by?

Arberry, Arbutus uva-ursi, Bearberry, Beargrape, Bearsgrape, Common Bearberry, Hogberry, Kinnikinnik, Manzanita, Mountain Box, Mountain Cranberry, Ptarmigan Berry, Raisan D'Ours, Red Bearberry, Redberry, Rockberry, Sagackhomi, Sandberry, Uvae ursi folium.

What is it?

Uva ursi is a plant. The leaves are used to make medicine.

Is it Effective?

The effectiveness ratings for **UVA URSI** are as follows:
Insufficient Evidence to Rate Effectiveness for... Urinary tract infections, swelling of the bladder and urethra, swelling of the urinary tract, constipation, kidney infections, bronchitis, and other conditions.

How does it work?

Uva ursi can reduce bacteria in the urine. It can also reduce swelling (inflammation), and have a drying (astringent) effect on the tissues.

Are there safety concerns?

Uva ursi seems safe for most adults when used short-term. It can cause nausea, vomiting, stomach discomfort, and a greenish-brown discoloration of the urine. High doses or long-term use can cause liver damage, breathing problems, convulsions, and death.

Severe liver problems can occur if used in children. Avoid use in children.

Do not take uva ursi if: You are pregnant or breast-feeding. • You have a kidney condition. • You have an upset or irritated stomach. • You have a stomach ulcer. • You have Crohn's disease. • You have ulcerative colitis.

Are there any interactions with medications?

It is not known if uva ursi interacts with any medicines.
Before taking uva ursi, talk with your healthcare professional if you take any medications.

UZARA

What other names is the product known by?

Uzarae radix, Xysmalobium undulatum.

What is it?

Uzara is a plant. The root is used to make medicine.

Is it Effective?

The effectiveness ratings for **UZARA** are as follows:
Insufficient Evidence to Rate Effectiveness for... Diarrhea and other conditions.

How does it work?

Uzara contains ingredients that might slow the movement of the contents of the intestines.

Are there safety concerns?

Uzara might be safe when used by mouth for a short time, but the potential side effects are not well known.

Uzara is UNSAFE when used by injection and has caused death.

Do not take uzara if: You are pregnant or breast-feeding. • You have a heart problem. • You have low potassium levels.

Are there any interactions with medications?

Antibiotics (Macrolide antibiotics). Uzara can affect the heart. Some antibiotics might increase how much uzara the body absorbs. Increasing how much uzara the body absorbs might increase the effects and side effects of uzara. Some antibiotics called macrolide antibiotics include erythromycin, azithromycin, and clarithromycin.

Antibiotics (Tetracycline antibiotics). Taking tetracycline antibiotics along with uzara might increase the chance of side effects from uzara. Some tetracycline antibiotics include demeclocycline (Declomycin), minocycline (Minocin), and tetracycline (Achromycin).

Digoxin (Lanoxin). Digoxin (Lanoxin) helps the heart beat more strongly. Uzara also seems to affect the heart. Taking uzara along with digoxin can increase the effects of digoxin and increase the risk of side effects. Do not take uzara if you are taking digoxin (Lanoxin) without talking to your healthcare professional.

Quinine. Uzara can affect the heart. Quinine can also affect the heart. Taking quinine along with uzara might cause serious heart problems.

Stimulant laxatives. Uzara can affect the heart. The heart uses potassium. Laxatives called stimulant laxatives can decrease potassium levels in the body. Low potassium levels can increase the chance of side effects uzara. Some stimulant laxatives include bisacodyl (Correctol, Dulcolax), cascara, castor oil (Purge), senna (Senokot), and others.

Water pills (Diuretic drugs). Uzara might affect the heart. "Water pills" can decrease potassium in the body. Low potassium levels can also affect the heart and increase the risk of side effects from uzara. Some "water pills" that can deplete potassium include chlorothiazide (Diuril), chlorthalidone (Thalitone), furosemide (Lasix), hydrochlorothiazide (HCTZ, HydroDiuril, Microzide), and others.

VALERIAN

What other names is the product known by?

All-Heal, Amantilla, Baldrian, Baldrianwurzel, Belgium Valerian, Common Valerian, Fragrant Valerian, Garden Heliotrope, Garden Valerian, Indian Valerian, Mexican Valerian, Pacific Valerian, Tagara, Valeriana, Valeriana angustifolia, Valeriana Officinalis, Valeriana Rhizome, Valerianae Radix, Valeriane.

What is it?

Valerian is an herb. Medicine is made from the root.

Is it Effective?

The effectiveness ratings for **VALERIAN** are as follows:

Possibly Effective for... Insomnia • Anxiety.

Insufficient Evidence to Rate Effectiveness for... Depression, convulsions, mild tremors, epilepsy, attention-deficit hyperactivity disorder (ADHD), chronic fatigue syndrome (CFS), muscle and joint pain, headache, stomach upset, menstrual pains, menopausal symptoms including hot flashes and anxiety, and other conditions.

How does it work?

Valerian seems to act like a sedative on the brain and nervous system.

Are there safety concerns?

Valerian is safe for most people when used short-term. It can cause some side effects such as headache, excitability, uneasiness, and even insomnia in some people. A few people feel sluggish in the morning after taking valerian, especially at higher doses. The long-term safety of valerian is unknown. To avoid possible side effects when discontinuing valerian after long-term use, it's best to reduce the dose slowly over a week or two before stopping completely.

Do not take valerian if: You are pregnant or breast-feeding.

Are there any interactions with medications?

Alcohol. Alcohol can cause sleepiness and drowsiness. Valerian might also cause sleepiness and drowsiness. Taking large amounts of valerian along with alcohol might cause too much sleepiness.

Alprazolam (Xanax). Valerian can decrease how quickly the liver breaks down alprazolam. Taking valerian with alprazolam might increase the effects and side effects of alprazolam such as drowsiness.

Medications changed by the liver (Cytochrome P450 3A4 (CYP3A4) substrates). Some medications are changed and broken down by the liver. Valerian might decrease how quickly the liver breaks down some medications. Taking valerian along with some medications that are broken down by the liver can increase the effects and side effects of some medications. Before taking valerian, talk to your healthcare provider if you are taking any medications that are changed by the liver. Some medications changed by the liver include lovastatin (Mevacor), ketoconazole (Nizoral), itraconazole (Sporanox), fexofenadine (Allegra), triazolam (Halcion), and many others.

Sedative medications (CNS depressants). Valerian might cause sleepiness and drowsiness. Medications that

Medical professionals should consult the Professional Version at www.NaturalDatabase.com.

cause sleepiness are called sedatives. Taking valerian along with sedative medications might cause too much sleepiness. Taking valerian along with sedative medications used in surgery might cause prolonged sedation. Some sedative medications include pentobarbital (Nembutal), phenobarbital (Luminal), secobarbital (Seconal), thiopental (Pentothal), fentanyl (Duragesic, Sublimaze), morphine, propofol (Diprivan), and others.

Sedative medications (Benzodiazepines). Valerian might cause sleepiness and drowsiness. Drugs that cause sleepiness and drowsiness are called sedatives. Taking valerian along with sedative medications might cause too much sleepiness. Some of these sedative medications include alprazolam (Xanax), clonazepam (Klonopin), diazepam (Valium), lorazepam (Ativan), midazolam (Versed), temazepam (Restoril), triazolam (Halcion), and others.

VANADIUM

What other names is the product known by?
Metavanadate, Orthovanadate, Vanadate, Vanadium Pentoxide, Vanadyl, Vanadyl Sulfate.

What is it?
Vanadium is a mineral. It is used as medicine.

Is it Effective?
The effectiveness ratings for **VANADIUM** are as follows:
Insufficient Evidence to Rate Effectiveness for... Diabetes, heart disease, high cholesterol, water retention (edema), preventing cancer, and other conditions.

How does it work?
There is some evidence that vanadium might act like insulin, or help to increase the effects of insulin.

Are there safety concerns?
Vanadium seems to be safe for most people if less than 1.8 mg per day is taken. At higher doses such as those used to treat diabetes, vanadium frequently causes adverse effects including abdominal discomfort, diarrhea, nausea, and gas. It can also cause some side effects including a greenish tongue, loss of energy, and problems with the nervous system.

Vanadium is unsafe when used in large amounts and for a long time. This increases the risk of serious side effects including kidney damage.

Vanadium might lower blood sugar. People with diabetes should check their blood sugar carefully and watch for signs of low blood sugar (hypoglycemia).

Do not take vanadium if: You are pregnant or breast-feeding. • You have kidney problems.

Are there any interactions with medications?
Medications that slow blood clotting (Anticoagulant / Antiplatelet drugs). Vanadium might slow blood clotting. Taking vanadium along with medications that also slow clotting might increase the chances of bruising and bleeding. Some medications that slow blood clotting include aspirin, clopidogrel (Plavix), diclofenac (Voltaren, Cataflam, others), ibuprofen (Advil, Motrin, others), naproxen (Anaprox, Naprosyn, others), dalteparin (Fragmin), enoxaparin (Lovenox), heparin, warfarin (Coumadin), and others.
Medications for diabetes (Antidiabetes drugs). Vanadium seems to decrease blood sugar in people with type 2 diabetes. Diabetes medications are also used to lower blood sugar. Taking vanadium along with diabetes medications might cause your blood sugar to go too low. Monitor your blood sugar closely. The dose of your diabetes medication might need to be changed. Some medications used for diabetes include glimepiride (Amaryl), glyburide (DiaBeta, Glynase PresTab, Micronase), insulin, pioglitazone (Actos), rosiglitazone (Avandia), chlorpropamide (Diabinese), glipizide (Glucotrol), tolbutamide (Orinase), and others.

VANILLA

What other names is the product known by?
Bourbon Vanilla, Common Vanilla, Madagascar Vanilla, Mexican Vanilla, Réunion Vanilla, Tahitian Vanilla, Tahiti Vanilla, Vanilla planifolia, Vanilla tahitensis.

What is it?
Vanilla is a plant. The fruit is used to make medicine.

Natural Medicines Comprehensive Database Consumer Version (209) 472-2244

Is it Effective?

The effectiveness ratings for **VANILLA** are as follows:

Insufficient Evidence to Rate Effectiveness for... Fever, intestinal gas, and other uses.

How does it work?

Vanilla contains chemicals that are high in flavor and fragrance, but it is not known how it works for medicinal uses.

Are there safety concerns?

Vanilla is safe, but there are some side effects. Skin contact can cause irritation and inflammation. It might also cause headache and insomnia, especially for people who manufacture vanilla.

Vanilla is also safe for pregnant and breast-feeding women when used in amounts found in food. However, there isn't enough information to know if it is safe in medicinal amounts.

Do not use amounts greater than those found in food if: You are pregnant or breast-feeding.

Are there any interactions with medications?

It is not known if vanilla interacts with any medicines.
Before taking vanilla, talk with your healthcare professional if you take any medications.

VERBENA

What other names is the product known by?

Blue Vervain, Common Verbena, Common Vervain, Eisenkraut, Enchanter's Plant, European Vervain, Herb of Grace, Herb of the Cross, Herba Verbenae, Holywort, Juno's Tears, Pigeon's Grass, Pigeonweed, Simpler's Joy, Turkey Grass, Verbenae herba, Verbena officinalis, Vervain, Yerba de Santa Ana.

What is it?

Verbena is a plant. The above ground parts are used to make medicine.

Is it Effective?

The effectiveness ratings for **VERBENA** are as follows:

Possibly Effective for... Treating sinusitis when taken as a combination product containing gentian root, elderflower, cowslip flower, and sorrel.

Insufficient Evidence to Rate Effectiveness for... Sore throat, asthma, whooping cough, chest pain, abscesses, burns, colds, arthritis, itching, and other conditions.

How does it work?

Verbena contains chemicals that might reduce inflammation.

Are there safety concerns?

Verbena seems to be safe for most people when used in small amounts as part of a combination product containing gentian root, elderflower, sorrel, and cowslip flower (SinuComp, Sinupret). There isn't enough information to know if verbena is safe when used in medicinal amounts other than as part of the combination product. The combination product can cause digestive system upset and occasionally allergic skin rash.

Do not take verbena if: You are pregnant or breast-feeding.

Are there any interactions with medications?

It is not known if verbena interacts with any medicines.
Before taking verbena, talk with your healthcare professional if you take any medications.

VERONICA

What other names is the product known by?

Ehrenpreiskraut, Gypsy Weed, Speedwell, Veronicae herba, Veronica Herb, Veronica officinalis.

What is it?

Veronica is a plant. The above ground parts are used to make medicine. Be careful not to confuse veronica (veronica officinalis) with other veronica species such as veronica allionii and veronica chamaedrys.

Is it Effective?

The effectiveness ratings for **VERONICA** are as follows:
Insufficient Evidence to Rate Effectiveness for... Loss of appetite; arthritis; gout; itching; kidney, liver, lung, skin, spleen, stomach, and urinary problems; wound healing; and other conditions.

How does it work?

Veronica may help the stomach lining repair itself.

Are there safety concerns?

Veronica is possibly safe when used as a medicine, but the potential side effects are not known.

Do not take veronica if: You are pregnant or breast-feeding.

Are there any interactions with medications?

It is not known if veronica interacts with any medicines.
Before taking veronica, talk with your healthcare professional if you take any medications.

VETIVER

What other names is the product known by?

Chiendent Odorant, Cuscus, Cuscus Grass, Khas-khas, Khus Khus, Khus-khus Grass, Reshira, Sugandhimula, Ushira, Vétiver, Vetiveria zizanioides, Vetivergras, Zacate Violeta.

What is it?

Vetiver is a plant. The root is used to make medicine.

Is it Effective?

The effectiveness ratings for **VETIVER** are as follows:
Insufficient Evidence to Rate Effectiveness for... Causing abortion, nervous problems, circulation problems, insomnia, lice, muscle relaxation, repelling insects, rheumatism, stress relief, and other conditions.

How does it work?

Vetiver contains an oil which repels insects. It is not known how vetiver might work for medicinal uses.

Are there safety concerns?

Vetiver is possibly safe when used as a medicine, but the potential side effects are not known.

Do not use vetiver if: You are pregnant or breast-feeding.

Are there any interactions with medications?

It is not known if vetiver interacts with any medicines.
Before taking vetiver, talk with your healthcare professional if you take any medications.

VINPOCETINE

What other names is the product known by?

AY-27255, Cavinton, Eburnamenine-14-carboxylic acid, Ethyl Apovincaminate, Ethylapovincaminoate, ethyl ester, RGH-4405, TCV-3b.

What is it?

Vinpocetine is a man-made chemical resembling a substance found in the periwinkle plant. People use it as medicine.

Is it Effective?

The effectiveness ratings for **VINPOCETINE** are as follows:
Possibly Effective for... Diseases, such as Alzheimer's disease, that interfere with thinking.
Insufficient Evidence to Rate Effectiveness for... Prevention of Alzheimer's disease, motion sickness, symptoms of menopause, seizures, stroke, chronic fatigue syndrome (CFS), and other conditions.

How does it work?

It is not known exactly how vinpocetine works, but it seems to have various effects on the brain including increased blood flow.

Are there safety concerns?

Vinpocetine appears to be safe for most people. It can cause some side effects including stomach pain, nausea, sleep disturbances, headache, dizziness, nervousness, and flushing of the face.

Do not use vinpocetine if: You are pregnant or breast-feeding. • You have a blood-clotting disorder.

Are there any interactions with medications?

Medications that slow blood clotting (Anticoagulant / Antiplatelet drugs). Vinpocetine might slow blood clotting. Taking vinpocetine along with medications that also slow clotting might increase the chances of bruising and bleeding. Some medications that slow blood clotting include aspirin, clopidogrel (Plavix), diclofenac (Voltaren, Cataflam, others), ibuprofen (Advil, Motrin, others), naproxen (Anaprox, Naprosyn, others), dalteparin (Fragmin), enoxaparin (Lovenox), heparin, warfarin (Coumadin), and others.

Warfarin (Coumadin). Warfarin (Coumadin) is used to slow blood clotting. Vinpocetine might increase how long warfarin (Coumadin) is in the body, and increase the chances of bruising and bleeding. Be sure to have your blood checked regularly. The dose of your warfarin (Coumadin) might need to be changed.

VITAMIN A

What other names is the product known by?

3-Dehydroretinol, Antixerophthalmic Vitamin, Axeropholum, Dehydroretinol, Oleovitamin A, Retinol Acetate, Retinol Palmitate, Vitamin A1, Vitamin A2, Vitaminum A.

What is it?

Vitamin A is a vitamin. It can be found in many fruits, vegetables, eggs, whole milk, butter, fortified margarine, meat, and oily salt-water fish. It can also be made in a laboratory.

Is it Effective?

The effectiveness ratings for **VITAMIN A** are as follows:

Effective for... Treatment and prevention of vitamin A deficiency.

Possibly Effective for... Reducing complications of diseases such as malaria, HIV, measles, and diarrhea in children with vitamin A deficiency • Reducing problems during pregnancy and after giving birth in underfed (malnourished) women • Breast cancer • Prevention of cataracts • Improving recovery from laser eye surgery when used in combination with vitamin E.

Possibly Ineffective for... Reducing fetal and early infant death in children born to women with nutrition problems • Anemia • Decreasing the risk of HIV transmission during pregnancy, delivery, and breast-feeding • Reducing side effects of chemotherapy in children.

Likely Ineffective for... Reducing the risk of tumors in the head and neck • Treating pneumonia in children living in poor countries.

Insufficient Evidence to Rate Effectiveness for... Lung cancer, ovarian cancer, cervical cancer, esophageal cancer, pancreatic cancer, colorectal cancer, gastric cancer, promoting good vision, age-related macular degeneration (AMD), glaucoma, preventing and speeding recovery from infections, improving immune function, skin conditions other than acne, relieving hayfever symptoms, and other conditions.

How does it work?

Vitamin A is required for the proper development and functioning of our eyes, skin, immune system, and many other parts of our bodies.

Are there safety concerns?

Vitamin A is safe for most people, used in doses less than 10,000 units per day. Some scientific research suggests that lower doses might increase the risk of osteoporosis and hip fracture, particularly in older people. Adults who eat low-fat dairy products, which are fortified with vitamin A, and a lot of fruits and vegetables usually don't need vitamin A supplements or multivitamins that contain vitamin A.

Long-term use of large amounts of vitamin A might cause serious side effects including fatigue, irritability, mental changes, anorexia, stomach discomfort, nausea, vomiting, mild fever, excessive sweating, and many other side effects. In women who have passed menopause, taking too much vitamin A can increase the risk of osteoporosis and hip fracture.

Vitamin A is safe for pregnant or breast-feeding women when taken in recommended amounts. The recommended amount for pregnant and breast-feeding women is less than 10,000 units per day.

Vitamin A is safe for children when taken in the recommended amounts. When amounts greater than those recommended are taken, side effects can include irritability, sleepiness, vomiting, diarrhea, loss of consciousness,

headache, vision problems, peeling skin, increased risk of pneumonia and diarrhea, and other problems. The maximum amounts of vitamin A that are safe for children are based on age:
- Less than 2000 units/day in children up to 3 years old.
- Less than 3000 units/day in children ages 4 to 8 years old.
- Less than 5700 units/day in children ages 9 to 13 years old.
- Less than 9300 units/day in children ages 14 to 18 years old.

Do not take vitamin A if: You drink a lot of alcohol. • You have an uncommon form of high cholesterol called "Type V hyperlipoproteinemia." • You have liver disease.

Are there any interactions with medications?

Antibiotics (Tetracycline antibiotics). Vitamin A can interact with some antibiotics. Taking very large amounts of vitamin A along with some antibiotics can increase the chance of a serious side effect called intracranial hypertension. But taking normal doses of vitamin A along with tetracyclines doesn't seem to cause this problem. Do not take large amounts of vitamin A if you are taking antibiotics. Some of these antibiotics include demeclocycline (Declomycin), minocycline (Minocin), and tetracycline (Achromycin).

Medications that can harm the liver (Hepatotoxic drugs). Taking large amounts of vitamin A might harm the liver. Taking large amounts of vitamin A along with medications that might also harm the liver can increase the risk of liver damage. Do not take large amounts of vitamin A if you are taking a medication that can harm the liver. Some medications that can harm the liver include acetaminophen (Tylenol and others), amiodarone (Cordarone), carbamazepine (Tegretol), isoniazid (INH), methotrexate (Rheumatrex), methyldopa (Aldomet), fluconazole (Diflucan), itraconazole (Sporanox), erythromycin (Erythrocin, Ilosone, others), phenytoin (Dilantin), lovastatin (Mevacor), pravastatin (Pravachol), simvastatin (Zocor), and many others.

Medications for skin conditions (Retinoids). Some medications for skin conditions have vitamin A effects. Taking vitamin A pills and these medications for skin conditions could cause too much vitamin A effects and side effects.

Warfarin (Coumadin). Warfarin (Coumadin) is used to slow blood clotting. Large amounts of Vitamin A can also slow blood clotting. Taking Vitamin A along with warfarin (Coumadin) can increase the chances of bruising and bleeding. Be sure to have your blood checked regularly. The dose of your warfarin (Coumadin) might need to be changed.

VITAMIN B12

What other names is the product known by?

B-12, B Complex Vitamin, Bedumil, Cobamin, Cobalamin, Cyanocobalamin, Cyanocobalaminum, Cycobemin, Hydroxocobalamin, Hydroxocobalaminum, Hydroxocobemine, Idrossocobalamina, Methylcobalamin, Vitadurin.

What is it?

Vitamin B12 is a vitamin. It can be found in foods such as meat, fish, and dairy products. It can also be made in a laboratory.

Is it Effective?

The effectiveness ratings for **VITAMIN B12** are as follows:

Effective for... Treatment and prevention of vitamin B12 deficiency, and diseases caused by low vitamin B12 levels.

Likely Effective for... Reducing a condition related to heart disease called "hyperhomocysteinemia" when taken with folic acid and vitamin B6.

Possibly Effective for... Preventing reblockage of blood vessels after heart artery dilation (balloon angioplasty).

Possibly Ineffective for... Sleep disorders • Preventing another stroke • Alzheimer's disease.

Insufficient Evidence to Rate Effectiveness for... Shaky-leg syndrome, allergies, aging, fatigue or tiredness, chronic fatigue syndrome (CFS), diabetes, heart disease, Lyme disease, immune system problems, memory problems, multiple sclerosis, breast cancer, high cholesterol, lung cancer, preventing cervical cancer, and other conditions.

How does it work?

Vitamin B12 is required for the proper function and development of the brain, nerves, blood cells, and many other parts of the body.

Are there safety concerns?

Vitamin B12 is safe for most people when taken by mouth or when the prescription-only, injectable product is used correctly. In some people, vitamin B12 might cause diarrhea, blood clots, itching, serious allergic reactions, and other side effects.

Vitamin B12 is likely safe for pregnant or breast-feeding women when taken by mouth in the amounts recommended. The recommended amount for pregnant women is 2.6 mcg per day. Breast-feeding women should take no more than 2.8 mcg per day.

Do not take vitamin B12 if: You have high numbers of red blood cells (polycythemia vera) or abnormal red blood cells (megaloblastic anemia). • You have Leber's disease, a hereditary eye disease. • You are allergic or sensitive to cobalt or cobalamin.

Are there any interactions with medications?

Chloramphenicol. Vitamin B12 is important for producing new blood cells. Chloramphenicol might decrease new blood cells. Taking chloramphenicol for a long time might decrease the effects of vitamin B12 on new blood cells. But most people only take chloramphenicol for a short time so this interaction isn't a big problem.

VITAMIN C (ASCORBIC ACID)

What other names is the product known by?

Antiscorbutic Vitamin, Ascorbate, Ascorbyl Palmitate, Calcium Ascorbate, Cevitamic Acid, Iso-Ascorbic Acid, L-Ascorbic Acid, Sodium Ascorbate.

What is it?

Vitamin C is a vitamin. Good sources of vitamin C are fresh fruits and vegetables, especially citrus fruits. It can also be made in a laboratory.

Is it Effective?

The effectiveness ratings for **VITAMIN C (ASCORBIC ACID)** are as follows:

Effective for... Treatment and prevention of vitamin C deficiency, including a condition called "scurvy."

Likely Effective for... Improving the way the body absorbs iron • Treating a disease called tyrosinemia in newborns.

Possibly Effective for... Reducing the risk of certain cancers of the mouth and breast. This only works when fresh fruits and vegetables high in vitamin C are eaten, not with vitamin C supplements. • Treating the common cold. But it is not effective for preventing the common cold. • High blood pressure • Reducing the risk of gallbladder disease • Reducing the risk of bone and cartilage loss • Helping medicines used for chest pain, such as nitroglycerin, to work longer • Flushed looking skin (erythema) • Decreasing lung infections caused by heavy exercise • Reducing the risk in women of a circulatory system disorder called peripheral arterial disease • Preventing "hardening of the arteries" (atherosclerosis) • Preventing kidney problems related to contrast media used during angiography • Treating ulcers in the stomach caused by bacteria called H. pylori • Decreasing protein in the urine of people with type 2 diabetes (albuminuria) • Reducing human immunodeficiency virus (HIV) transmission by mothers to their newborns when taken with vitamins E and B • Treating an eye disease called AMD (age-related macular degeneration) when used with other medicines • Reducing complications after a broken wrist called reflex sympathetic dystrophy • Reducing lead in the blood by eating foods high in vitamin C • Reducing complications of a high risk pregnancy (pre-eclampsia) • Improving physical performance and strength in the elderly • Wrinkled skin.

Possibly Ineffective for... Preventing the common cold • Reducing the risk of stroke • Attention deficit-hyperactivity disorder (ADHD) • Reducing the risk for Alzheimer's disease and other brain diseases causing intellectual loss • Preventing eye disease associated with a medicine called interferon • Treating bronchitis • Reducing skin problems in people being treated for cancer with radiation • Preventing type 2 diabetes.

Insufficient Evidence to Rate Effectiveness for... Wounds, pressure sores, tuberculosis, dental cavities, constipation, acne, hayfever, cystic fibrosis, infertility, diabetes, heart disease, lowering cholesterol, kidney disease, liver disease, esophageal cancer, gastric cancer, pancreatic cancer, mental stress, Lyme disease, chronic fatigue syndrome (CFS), treating and preventing sun-damaged skin when vitamin C is put on the skin, and other conditions.

How does it work?

Vitamin C is required for the proper development and function of many parts of the body. It also plays an important role in maintaining proper immune function.

Are there safety concerns?

Vitamin C is safe for most people when taken by mouth or applied to the skin. In some people, vitamin C might cause nausea, vomiting, heartburn, stomach cramps, headache, and other side effects. The chance of getting these side effects increases the more vitamin C you take. Doses higher than 2000 mg per day might not be safe and may cause a lot of side effects, including kidney stones and severe diarrhea. In people who have had a kidney stone, doses greater than 1000 mg per day greatly increase the risk of kidney stone recurrence.

Vitamin C is likely safe for pregnant or breast-feeding women when taken in the recommended amount of 120 mg per day. Taking too much vitamin C during pregnancy can cause problems for the newborn baby.

Do not take vitamin C in doses greater than those found in basic multivitamins if: You have had a heart attack. • You have had angioplasty, a heart procedure. • You have cancer. • You have diabetes. • You have a blood-iron disorder, including conditions called "thalassemia" and "hemochromatosis." • You have kidney stones, or a history of kidney stones. • You have a metabolic deficiency called "glucose-6-phosphate dehydrogenase deficiency" (G6PDD). • You have a blood disorder called "sickle cell disease."

Are there any interactions with medications?

Acetaminophen (Tylenol, others). The body breaks down acetaminophen (Tylenol, others) to get rid of it. Large amounts of vitamin C can decrease how quickly the body breaks down acetaminophen. It is not clear exactly when or if this interaction is a big concern.

Aluminum. Aluminum is found in most antacids. Vitamin C can increase how much aluminum the body absorbs. But it isn't clear if this interaction is a big concern. Take vitamin C two hours before, or four hours after antacids.

Aspirin. The body breaks down aspirin to get rid of it. Large amounts of vitamin C might decrease the breakdown of aspirin. Decreasing the breakdown of aspirin might increase the effects and side effects of aspirin. Do not take large amounts of vitamin C if you take large amounts of aspirin.

Choline Magnesium Trisalicylate (Trilisate). Vitamin C might decrease how quickly the body gets rid of choline magnesium trisalicylate (Trilisate). But it is not clear if this interaction is a big concern.

Estrogens. The body breaks down estrogens to get rid of them. Vitamin C might decrease how quickly the body gets rid of estrogens. Taking vitamin C along with estrogens might increase the effects and side effects of estrogens.

Fluphenazine (Prolixin). Large amounts of vitamin C might decrease how much fluphenazine (Prolixin) is in the body. Taking vitamin C along with fluphenazine (Prolixin) might decrease the effectiveness of fluphenazine (Prolixin).

Medications used for HIV/AIDS (Protease Inhibitors). Taking large doses of vitamin C might reduce how much of some medications used for HIV/AIDS stays in the body. This could decrease the effectiveness of some medications used for HIV/AIDS. Some of these medications used for HIV/AIDS include amprenavir (Agenerase), nelfinavir (Viracept), ritonavir (Norvir), and saquinavir (Fortovase, Invirase).

Medications for cancer (Chemotherapy). Vitamin C is an antioxidant. There is some concern that antioxidants might decrease the effectiveness of some medications used for cancers. But it is too soon to know if this interaction occurs.

Medications used for lowering cholesterol (Statins). Taking vitamin C, beta-carotene, selenium, and vitamin E together might decrease the effectiveness of some medications used for lowering cholesterol. It is not known if vitamin C alone decreases the effectiveness of some medications used for lowering cholesterol. Some medications used for lowering cholesterol include atorvastatin (Lipitor), fluvastatin (Lescol), lovastatin (Mevacor), and pravastatin (Pravachol).

Niacin. Taking vitamin C along with vitamin E, beta-carotene, and selenium might decrease some of the helpful effects of niacin. Niacin can increase the good cholesterol. Taking vitamin C along with these other vitamins might decrease the effectiveness of niacin for increasing good cholesterol.

Nicardipine (Cardene). Vitamin C is taken up by cells. Taking nicardipine (Cardene) along with vitamin C might decrease how much vitamin C is taken in by cells. The significance of this interaction is not clear.

Nifedipine. Vitamin C is taken up by cells. Taking nifedipine (Adalat, Procardia) along with vitamin C might decrease how much vitamin C is taken in by cells. The significance of this interaction is not clear.

Salsalate (Disalcid). Vitamin C might decrease how quickly the body gets rid of salsalate (Disalcid). Taking vitamin C along with salsalate (Disalcid) might cause too much salsalate (Disalcid) in the body, and increase the effects and side effects of salsalate.

Warfarin (Coumadin). Warfarin (Coumadin) is used to slow blood clotting. Large amounts of vitamin C might decrease the effectiveness of warfarin (Coumadin). Decreasing the effectiveness of warfarin (Coumadin) might increase the risk of clotting. Be sure to have your blood checked regularly. The dose of your warfarin (Coumadin) might need to be changed.

  Natural Medicines Comprehensive Database Consumer Version (209) 472-2244

VITAMIN D

What other names is the product known by?

Activated Ergosterol, Alfacalcidol, Calcifediol, Calciferol, Calcipotriene, Calcipotriol, Calcitriol, Cholecalciferol, Dihydrotachysterol, Ergocalciferol, Ergocalciferolum, Irradiated Ergosterol, Paracalcin, Paricalcitol, viosterol, vitamin D2, vitamin D3.

What is it?

Vitamin D is a vitamin. It can be found in small amounts in many foods such as dairy products, cereals with vitamin D added, and fish. However, skin exposure to the sun provides as much as 80 to 90% of the body's vitamin D. Vitamin D can also be made in the laboratory as medicine.

Is it Effective?

The effectiveness ratings for **VITAMIN D** are as follows:

Effective for... Treating many types of diseases that cause weak and painful bones • High levels of phosphate in the blood due to a disease called Fanconi syndrome • Psoriasis (with a specialized prescription-only form of vitamin D) • Low blood calcium levels because of a low parathyroid thyroid hormone levels. Low blood calcium due to kidney failure (renal osteodystrophy) • Rickets.

Likely Effective for... Reducing bone loss in people taking drugs called corticosteroids • Treating osteoporosis (weak bones) • Preventing falls in older people.

Possibly Effective for... Reducing the risk of multiple sclerosis (MS) • Reducing the risk of rheumatoid arthritis in older women • Bone loss due to hyperparathyroidism • A bone condition called osteogenesis imperfecta.

Possibly Ineffective for... Improving muscle strength in older adults • Preventing bone loss in people with kidney transplants • Preventing bone fractures in frail elderly people when given alone without calcium supplements.

Insufficient Evidence to Rate Effectiveness for...A blood cell disease called myelodysplastic syndrome, a muscle disease called proximal myopathy, cancer including colorectal cancer, bronchitis, asthma, breathing disorders, diabetes, metabolic syndrome, premenstrual syndrome (PMS), and other conditions.

How does it work?

Vitamin D is required for the regulation of the minerals calcium and phosphorus found in the body. It also plays an important role in maintaining the proper bone structure.

Are there safety concerns?

Vitamin D is safe for most people when taken by mouth. Most people do not commonly experience side effects with vitamin D, unless too much is taken. Some side effects of taking too much vitamin D might include weakness, fatigue, sleepiness, headache, loss of appetite, dry mouth, metallic taste, nausea, vomiting, and others. Doses higher than 50 mcg (2000 units) per day might not be safe and may cause excessively high levels of calcium in the blood.

Don't take vitamin D without talking to your healthcare professional if you have the following conditions: Kidney disease. • High levels of calcium in the blood.

Are there any interactions with medications?

Aluminum. Aluminum is found in most antacids. Vitamin D can increase how much aluminum the body absorbs. This interaction might be a problem for people with kidney disease. Take vitamin D two hours before, or four hours after antacids.

Calcipotriene (Dovonex). Calcipotriene is a drug that is similar to vitamin D. Taking vitamin D along with calcipotriene (Dovonex) might increase the effects and side effects of calcipotriene (Dovonex). Avoid taking vitamin D supplements if you are taking calcipotriene (Dovonex).

Cimetidine (Tagamet). The body changes vitamin D into a form that it can use. Cimetidine might decrease how well the body changes vitamin D. This might decrease how well vitamin D works. But this interaction probably isn't important for most people.

Digoxin (Lanoxin). Vitamin D helps your body absorb calcium. Calcium can affect the heart. Digoxin (Lanoxin) is used to help your heart beat stronger. Taking vitamin D along with digoxin (Lanoxin) might increase the effects of digoxin (Lanoxin) and lead to an irregular heartbeat. If you are taking digoxin (Lanoxin), talk to your doctor before taking vitamin D supplements.

Diltiazem (Cardizem, Dilacor, Tiazac). Vitamin D helps your body absorb calcium. Calcium can affect your heart. Diltiazem (Cardizem, Dilacor, Tiazac) can also affect your heart. Taking large amounts of vitamin D along with diltiazem (Cardizem, Dilacor, Tiazac) might decrease the effectiveness of diltiazem.

Heparin. Heparin slows blood clotting and can increase the risk of breaking a bone when used for a long period of time. People taking these medications should eat a diet rich in calcium and vitamin D.

Low molecular weight heparins (LMWHS). Some medications called low molecular weight heparins can increase the risk of breaking a bone when used for a long periods of time. People taking these medications should eat a diet rich in calcium and vitamin D.

Water pills (Thiazide diuretics). Vitamin D helps your body absorb calcium. Some "water pills" increase the amount of calcium in the body. Taking large amounts of vitamin D along with some "water pills" might cause to be too much calcium in the body. This could cause serious side effects including kidney problems. Some of these "water pills" include chlorothiazide (Diuril), hydrochlorothiazide (HydroDIURIL, Esidrix), indapamide (Lozol), metolazone (Zaroxolyn), and chlorthalidone (Hygroton).

Verapamil (Calan, Covera, Isoptin, Verelan). Vitamin D helps your body absorb calcium. Calcium can affect the heart. Verapamil Calan, Covera, Isoptin, Verelan) can also affect the heart. Do not take large amounts of vitamin D if you are taking verapamil (Calan, Covera, Isoptin, Verelan).

VITAMIN E

What other names is the product known by?

All Rac-Alpha-Tocopherol, Alpha-Tocopherol, Alpha Tocopherol Acetate, Alpha Tocopheryl Acetate, d-Alpha-Tocopherol, dl-Alpha-Tocopherol, d-Beta-Tocopherol, d-Delta-Tocopherol, d-Gamma-Tocopherol, Mixed Tocopherols, RRR-Alpha-Tocopherol, Tocopherol, Tocotrienol, Beta-Tocopherol, Delta-Tocopherol, Gamma-Tocopherol, Alpha Tocotrienol, Beta Tocotrienol, Delta Tocotrienol, Gamma Tocotrienol.

What is it?

Vitamin E is a fat-soluble vitamin found in many foods including vegetable oils, cereals, meat, poultry, eggs, fruits, vegetables, and wheat germ oil.

Is it Effective?

The effectiveness ratings for **VITAMIN E** are as follows:

Effective for... Vitamin E deficiency.

Possibly Effective for... Movement disorders called tardive dyskinesia and dyspraxia • Reducing the chance of dying from bladder cancer • Alzheimer's disease. Vitamin E might slow down the worsening of memory loss in people with moderately severe Alzheimer's disease. But vitamin E does not seem to prevent progression from mild memory problems to full-blown Alzheimer's disease • A type of arthritis called rheumatoid arthritis. Taking vitamin E pills with regular treatment seems to help reduce pain. • Male infertility • High blood pressure during pregnancy (pre-eclampsia) • Premenstrual syndrome (PMS) • Preventing Parkinson's disease • Helping to treat kidney problems in children (glomerulosclerosis) • Helping to treat an inherited disorder called G6PD deficiency • Beta-thalassemia • Chemotherapy-related nerve damage. Taking vitamin E before and after treatment with cisplatin chemotherapy might reduce the chance of getting nerve damage. • Preventing dementia in old age • Healing a type of skin sore called granuloma annulare when put on the skin • Improving vision in people with an eye disorder called uveitis • Decreasing sunburn • Reducing the symptoms of a disease called Huntington's chorea • Helping the eyes heal after surgery • Treating a type of eye disease in newborns called retrolental fibroplasia • Decreasing brain and heart bleeding in premature babies • Helping some heart medications called "nitrates" work better • Treating an eye disease called AMD (age-related macular degeneration) when used with other medicines • Improving physical performance and strength in the elderly • Fibrosis caused by radiation.

Possibly Ineffective for... Chest pain (angina) • Hot flashes in people who have had breast cancer • Breast cancer • Hardening of the arteries (atherosclerosis) • Breathing problems in newborns • Lung infections in elderly persons • Heart failure • Treating muscle diseases called Duchenne muscular dystrophy and myotonic dystrophy • High blood pressure • Helping people walk without pain when they have a disease called intermittent claudication • A type of arthritis called osteoarthritis. Vitamin E does not seem to decrease pain or stiffness and does not seem to prevent osteoarthritis from getting worse. • Head and neck cancer • Sores in the mouths of people who smoke • Cancer of the pancreas • Reducing scarring after surgery • Colorectal cancer • An eye condition called retinitis pigmentosa. • Anemia in people having hemodialysis.

Likely Ineffective for... Preventing heart disease. Taking vitamin E supplements does not prevent heart disease. But increasing vitamin E in the diet might be beneficial. • Benign breast disease • Breast cancer • Lung cancer.

Insufficient Evidence to Rate Effectiveness for... Allergies, asthma, skin disorders, cloudy vision in older people (cataracts), diabetes, painful periods in teenage girls, esophageal cancer, gastric cancer, prostate cancer, pharyngeal cancer, chronic fatigue syndrome (CFS), oral cancer, skin cancer, epilepsy, menstrual disorders, high blood fat levels, liver disease, stroke, leg cramps, common cold, and other conditions.

How does it work?

Vitamin E is an important vitamin required for the proper function of many organs in the body. It is also an antioxidant.

Are there safety concerns?

Vitamin E is safe for most healthy people when taken by mouth or applied to the skin. Most people do not experience any side effects when taking the recommended dose each day, which is 15 mg.

If you have a condition such as heart disease or diabetes, don't take doses of 400 IU/day or more. Some research suggests that high doses might increase the chance of death from all causes and possibly

 Natural Medicines Comprehensive Database Consumer Version (209) 472-2244

cause other serious side effects. The higher the dose, the greater the risk of serious side effects.
High doses can also cause nausea, diarrhea, stomach cramps, fatigue, weakness, headache, blurred vision, rash, and bruising and bleeding.

When used in the recommended daily amount vitamin E is considered safe for pregnant and breast-feeding women. However, don't take higher amounts without the advice of your healthcare professional.

Do not use vitamin E if: You have just undergone a procedure called angioplasty. • You have been told you have low levels of vitamin K. • You have an eye condition called retinitis pigmentosa. • You have a blood clotting disorder. • You have head and neck cancer.

Are there any interactions with medications?

Cyclosporine (Neoral, Sandimmune). Taking large amounts of vitamin E along with cyclosporine (Neoral, Sandimmune) might increase how much cyclosporine (Neoral, Sandimmune) the body absorbs. By increasing how much cyclosporine the body absorbs, vitamin E might increase the effects and side effects of cyclosporine (Neoral, Sandimmune).

Medications changed by the liver (Cytochrome P450 3A4 (CYP3A4) substrates). Some medications are changed and broken down by the liver. Vitamin E might increase how quickly the liver breaks down some medications. Taking vitamin E along with some medications that are broken down by the liver can decrease the effectiveness of some medications. Before taking vitamin E talk to your healthcare provider if you are taking any medications that are changed by the liver. Some medications changed by the liver include lovastatin (Mevacor), ketoconazole (Nizoral), itraconazole (Sporanox), fexofenadine (Allegra), triazolam (Halcion), and many others.

Medications that slow blood clotting (Anticoagulant / Antiplatelet drugs). Vitamin E might slow blood clotting. Taking vitamin E along with medications that also slow clotting might increase the chances of bruising and bleeding. Some medications that slow blood clotting include aspirin, clopidogrel (Plavix), diclofenac (Voltaren, Cataflam, others), ibuprofen (Advil, Motrin, others), naproxen (Anaprox, Naprosyn, others), dalteparin (Fragmin), enoxaparin (Lovenox), heparin, warfarin (Coumadin), and others.

Medications for cancer (Chemotherapy). Vitamin E is an antioxidant. There is some concern that antioxidants might decrease the effectiveness of some medications used for cancers. But it is too soon to know if the interaction occurs.

Medications used for lowering cholesterol (Statins). Taking vitamin E, beta-carotene, vitamin C, and selenium together might decrease the effectiveness of some medications used for lowering cholesterol. It is not known if taking vitamin E alone decreases the effectiveness of some medications used for lowering cholesterol. Some medications used for lowering cholesterol include atorvastatin (Lipitor), fluvastatin (Lescol), lovastatin (Mevacor), and pravastatin (Pravachol).

Niacin. Taking vitamin E along with beta-carotene, vitamin C, and selenium might decrease some of the beneficial effects of niacin. Niacin can increase the good cholesterol. Taking vitamin E along with these other vitamins might decrease the good cholesterol.

Warfarin (Coumadin). Warfarin (Coumadin) is used to slow blood clotting. Vitamin E can also slow blood clotting. Taking vitamin E along with warfarin (Coumadin) can increase the chances of bruising and bleeding. Be sure to have your blood checked regularly. The dose of your warfarin (Coumadin) might need to be changed.

VITAMIN K

What other names is the product known by?

4-Amino-2-Methyl-1-Naphthol, Menadiol Acetate, Menadiol Sodium Phosphate, Menadione, Menadione Sodium Bisulfite, Menaquinone, Menatetrenone, Phytonadione, Methylphytyl Naphthoquinone, Phylloquinone, Phytomenadione.

What is it?

Vitamin K is a fat-soluble vitamin found in leafy green vegetables, broccoli, and Brussels sprouts.

Is it Effective?

The effectiveness ratings for **VITAMIN K** are as follows:

Effective for... Treating and preventing vitamin K deficiency • Preventing certain bleeding or blood clotting problems.

Insufficient Evidence to Rate Effectiveness for... Osteoporosis (brittle bones), spider veins, bruises, scars, stretch marks, burns, swelling, and many other conditions.

How does it work?

Vitamin K is an essential vitamin that is required for several body functions such as proper function of the blood clotting process.

Medical professionals should consult the Professional Version at www.NaturalDatabase.com.

CONSUMER VERSION

Medical professionals should consult the
Professional Version at www.NaturalDatabase.com.

Are there safety concerns?

Vitamin K is safe for most people. Most people do not experience any side effects when consuming the recommended amount each day.

When taken in the recommended amount each day, vitamin K is considered safe for pregnant and breast-feeding women but don't use higher amounts without the advice of your healthcare professional.

Don't use vitamin K if: You have severe liver disease. • You have kidney disease and are on dialysis.

Are there any interactions with medications?

Warfarin (Coumadin). Vitamin K is used by the body to help blood clot. Warfarin (Coumadin) is used to slow blood clotting. By helping the blood clot, vitamin K might decrease the effectiveness of warfarin (Coumadin). Be sure to have your blood checked regularly. The dose of your warfarin (Coumadin) might need to be changed.

VITAMIN O

What other names is the product known by?

Liquid Oxygen, Stabilized Liquid Oxygen, Stabilized Oxygen.

What is it?

Vitamin O is a liquid containing chemicals. It is used as medicine. It is not a vitamin.

Is it Effective?

The effectiveness ratings for **VITAMIN O** are as follows:
Insufficient Evidence to Rate Effectiveness for... Arthritis; asthma; constipation; depression; diabetes; dizziness; headaches; increasing energy; improving alertness, concentration, immune function, and memory; irritability; lung disease; menopause; mouth sores; muscle aches and pains; obesity; premenstrual syndrome; sexual problems; and many other uses.

How does it work?

Vitamin O supposedly contains ingredients which release oxygen, but there is little scientific evidence to back this claim.

Are there safety concerns?

It is not known if vitamin O is safe or what the potential side effects might be.

Do not take vitamin O if: You are pregnant or breast-feeding.

Are there any interactions with medications?

It is not known if vitamin O interacts with any medicines.
Before taking vitamin O, talk with your healthcare professional if you take any medications.

WAFER ASH

What other names is the product known by?

Pickaway Anise, Prairie Grub, Ptelea trifoliata, Scubby Trefoil, Stinking Prairie Bush, Swamp Dogwood, Three-Leaved Hop Tree, Wingseed.

What is it?

Wafer ash is a plant. The root bark is used to make medicine.

Is it Effective?

The effectiveness ratings for **WAFER ASH** are as follows:
Insufficient Evidence to Rate Effectiveness for... Loss of appetite, rheumatism, stomach complaints, wound dressings, and other uses.

How does it work?

Wafer ash contains ingredients that are active against certain microbes, such as yeast.

Are there safety concerns?

It is not known if wafer ash is safe. Contact with the skin can cause skin to become extra sensitive to the sun. This might put you at greater risk for sunburns and skin cancer. Avoid sunlight. Wear sunblock and protective clothing outside, especially if you are light-skinned.

Do not take wafer ash if: You are pregnant or breast-feeding.

Are there any interactions with medications?

It is not known if wafer ash interacts with any medicines.
Before taking wafer ash, talk with your healthcare professional if you take any medications.

WAHOO

What other names is the product known by?

Arrowwood, Bitter Ash, Bleeding Heart, Burning Bush, Bursting Heart, Eastern Burning Bush, Euonymus atropurpureus, Fish Wood, Fusanum, Fusoria, Gadrose, Gatten, Gatter, Indian Arrowroot, Indian Arrowwood, Pegwood, Pigwood, Prickwood, Skewerwood, Spindle Tree, Strawberry Bush, Strawberry Tree.

What is it?

Wahoo is a tree. The trunk, root bark, and fruit are used to make medicine.

Is it Effective?

The effectiveness ratings for **WAHOO** are as follows:
Insufficient Evidence to Rate Effectiveness for... Constipation, indigestion, water retention, and other conditions.

How does it work?

Wahoo might stimulate the digestive tract and affect the heart. There isn't enough information to know how it might work for medicinal uses.

Are there safety concerns?

Wahoo is UNSAFE. It is poisonous and even deadly. Symptoms of poisoning include severe upset stomach, bloody diarrhea, fever, shortness of breath, unconsciousness, spasms, and coma.

While wahoo is UNSAFE for anyone to use, some people are especially sensitive to the toxic effects. Be particularly careful not to use wahoo if: You are pregnant or breast-feeding. • You have stomach or intestinal problems. • You have a heart problem.

Are there any interactions with medications?

Antibiotics (Macrolide antibiotics). Wahoo can affect the heart. Some antibiotics might increase how much wahoo the body absorbs. Increasing how much wahoo the body absorbs might increase the effects and side effects of wahoo. Some antibiotics called macrolide antibiotics include erythromycin, azithromycin, and clarithromycin.
Antibiotics (Tetracycline antibiotics). Taking tetracycline antibiotics along with wahoo might increase the chance of side effects from wahoo. Some tetracycline antibiotics include demeclocycline (Declomycin), minocycline (Minocin), and tetracycline (Achromycin).
Digoxin (Lanoxin). Digoxin (Lanoxin) helps the heart beat more strongly. Wahoo also seems to affect the heart. Taking wahoo along with digoxin (Lanoxin) can increase the effects and the side effects from digoxin (Lanoxin). Do not take wahoo if you are taking digoxin (Lanoxin) without talking to your healthcare professional.
Quinine. Wahoo can affect the heart. Quinine can also affect the heart. Taking quinine along with wahoo might cause serious heart problems.
Stimulant laxatives. Wahoo is a type of laxative called a stimulant laxative. Stimulant laxatives speed up the bowels. Taking wahoo along with other stimulant laxatives could speed up the bowels too much and cause dehydration and low minerals in the body. Some stimulant laxatives include bisacodyl (Correctol, Dulcolax), cascara, castor oil (Purge), senna (Senokot) and others.
Water pills (Diuretic drugs). Wahoo might affect the heart. "Water pills" can decrease potassium in the body. Low potassium levels can also affect the heart and increase the risk of side effects from wahoo. Some "water pills" that can deplete potassium include chlorothiazide (Diuril), chlorthalidone (Thalitone), furosemide (Lasix), hydrochlorothiazide (HCTZ, HydroDiuril, Microzide), and others.

Medical professionals should consult the Professional Version at www.NaturalDatabase.com.

WALLFLOWER

What other names is the product known by?
Beeflower, Cheiranthus cheiri, Gillyflower, Giroflier, Handflower, Keiri, Wallstock-Gillofer.

What is it?
Wallflower is a plant. The above ground parts are used to make medicine.

Is it Effective?
The effectiveness ratings for **WALLFLOWER** are as follows:
Insufficient Evidence to Rate Effectiveness for... Heart problems, liver and gallbladder disease, constipation, promoting menstrual periods, and other conditions.

How does it work?
Wallflower contains ingredients that might affect the heart.

Are there safety concerns?
Wallflower seems to be UNSAFE. It might cause side effects including heart problems.
Do not take wallflower if: You are pregnant or breast-feeding. • You have a heart problem.

Are there any interactions with medications?
Calcium supplements. Wallflower can stimulate the heartbeat. Calcium might also affect the heart. Taking wallflower along with calcium might cause the heart to be too stimulated. Do not take wallflower along with calcium supplements.

Digoxin (Lanoxin). Digoxin (Lanoxin) helps the heart beat more strongly. Wallflower also seems to affect the heart. Taking wallflower along with digoxin can increase the effects of digoxin and increase the risk of side effects. Do not take wallflower if you are taking digoxin (Lanoxin) without talking to your healthcare professional.

Medications for inflammation (Corticosteroids). Wallflower might affect the heart. Some medications for inflammation can decrease potassium in the body. Low potassium levels can also affect the heart and increase the risk of side effects from wallflower. Some medications for inflammation include dexamethasone (Decadron), hydrocortisone (Cortef), methylprednisolone (Medrol), prednisone (Deltasone), and others.

Quinidine. Wallflower can affect the heart. Quinidine can also affect the heart. Taking quinidine along with wallflower might cause serious heart problems.

Quinine. Wallflower can affect the heart. Quinine can also affect the heart. Taking quinine along with wallflower might cause serious heart problems.

Stimulant laxatives. Wallflower can affect the heart. The heart uses potassium. Laxatives called stimulant laxatives can decrease potassium levels in the body. Low potassium levels can increase the chance of side effects from wallflower. Some stimulant laxatives include bisacodyl (Correctol, Dulcolax), cascara, castor oil (Purge), senna (Senokot), and others.

Water pills (Diuretic drugs). Wallflower might affect the heart. "Water pills" can decrease potassium in the body. Low potassium levels can also affect the heart and increase the risk of side effects from wallflower. Some "water pills" that can deplete potassium include chlorothiazide (Diuril), chlorthalidone (Thalitone), furosemide (Lasix), hydrochlorothiazide (HCTZ, HydroDiuril, Microzide), and others.

WATER AVENS

What other names is the product known by?
Chocolate Root, Cure All, Geum rivale, Indian Chocolate, Throat Root, Water Chisch, Water Flower.

What is it?
Water avens is a plant. The whole plant is used to make medicine.

Is it Effective?
The effectiveness ratings for **WATER AVENS** are as follows:
Insufficient Evidence to Rate Effectiveness for... Diarrhea, fever, intestinal problems, and other uses.

How does it work?
Water avens contains tannins which can act as astringents. Astringent effects might help reduce diarrhea.

Are there safety concerns?
It is not known if water avens is safe or what the potential side effects might be.
Do not take water avens if: You are pregnant or breast-feeding.

 Natural Medicines Comprehensive Database Consumer Version (209) 472-2244

Are there any interactions with medications?
Medications taken by mouth (Oral drugs). Water avens contains a large amount of chemicals called tannins. Tannins absorb substances in the stomach and intestines. Taking water avens along with medications taken by mouth can decrease how much medicine your body absorbs, and decrease the effectiveness of your medicine. To prevent this interaction, take water avens at least one hour after medications you take by mouth.
Metformin (Glucophage). Metformin (Glucophage) is used to help decrease blood sugar. Water avens might decrease how much metformin (Glucophage) the body absorbs. Taking water avens along with metformin (Glucophage) might decrease the effectiveness of metformin (Glucophage) for lowering blood sugar. Monitor your blood sugar closely. The dose of your metformin (Glucophage) might need to be changed.

WATER DOCK

What other names is the product known by?
Rumex aquaticus.

What is it?
Water dock is a plant. The dried root is used to make medicine.

Is it Effective?
The effectiveness ratings for **WATER DOCK** are as follows:
Insufficient Evidence to Rate Effectiveness for... Constipation, "blood purification," mouth ulcers, skin sores, and cleaning the teeth.

How does it work?
Water dock contains ingredients that are thought to affect the digestive system.

Are there safety concerns?
It is not known if water dock is safe or what the potential side effects might be.

Do not take water dock if: You are pregnant or breast-feeding. • You have a blood disorder. • You have or have had kidney stones or other kidney problems.

Are there any interactions with medications?
It is not known if water dock interacts with any medicines.
Before taking water dock, talk with your healthcare professional if you take any medications.

WATER DROPWORT

What other names is the product known by?
Damoe, Oenanthe javanica, Pak Chi Lawm, Seri, Shelum, Sui-Kan, Water Celery.

What is it?
Water dropwort is an herb. The whole plant is used to make medicine.

Is it Effective?
The effectiveness ratings for **WATER DROPWORT** are as follows:
Insufficient Evidence to Rate Effectiveness for... Liver disease, high blood pressure, diabetes, abdominal pain, food poisoning, and other conditions.

How does it work?
It is not known how water dropwort might work for any medical conditions. Some research suggests water dropwort might prevent liver damage.

Are there safety concerns?
It is not known if water dropwort is safe or what side effects it might cause.

Do not use water dropwort if: You are pregnant or breast-feeding.

Are there any interactions with medications?
It is not known if water dropwort interacts with any medicines.
Before taking water dropwort, talk with your healthcare professional if you take any medications.

Medical professionals should consult the Professional Version at www.NaturalDatabase.com.

CONSUMER VERSION

WATER FENNEL

What other names is the product known by?
Fine Leaf Water Dropwort, Horsebane, Oenanthe aquatica, Water Dropwort, Water Hemlock.

What is it?
Water fennel is a plant. The ripe seeds are used to make medicine.

Is it Effective?
The effectiveness ratings for **WATER FENNEL** are as follows:
Insufficient Evidence to Rate Effectiveness for... Coughs, intestinal gas, water retention, and other conditions.

How does it work?
There isn't enough information to know how water fennel works.

Are there safety concerns?
It is not known if water fennel is safe or what the potential side effects might be.

Do not take water fennel if: You are pregnant or breast-feeding.

Are there any interactions with medications?
It is not known if water fennel interacts with any medicines.
Before taking water fennel, talk with your healthcare professional if you take any medications.

WATER GERMANDER

What other names is the product known by?
Teucrium scordium.

What is it?
Water germander is a plant. The above ground parts are used to make medicine.

Is it Effective?
The effectiveness ratings for **WATER GERMANDER** are as follows:
Insufficient Evidence to Rate Effectiveness for... Asthma, diarrhea, fever, intestinal parasites, hemorrhoids, and inflamed wounds.

How does it work?
There isn't enough information to know how water germander works.

Are there safety concerns?
It is not known if water germander is safe or what the potential side effects might be.

Do not take water germander if: You are pregnant or breast-feeding.

Are there any interactions with medications?
It is not known if water germander interacts with any medicines.
Before taking water germander, talk with your healthcare professional if you take any medications.

WATER HEMLOCK

What other names is the product known by?
Beaver Poison, Brook-Tongue, Carotte a Moreau, Children's Bane, Cicuta bulbifera, Cicuta douglasii, Cicuta maculata, Cicuta occidentalis; Cicuta vagans, Cicuta virosa, Cique Vireuse, Cowbane, Death-of-Man, European Water Hemlock, False Parsley, Fever Root, Mockeel Root, Muskrat Weed, Musquash Root, Poison Parsnip, Snake Weed, Snakeroot, Spotted Cowbane, Spotted Hemlock, Spotted Parsley, Wasser-Schierling, Wild Carrot, Wild Dill, Wild Parsnip.

What is it?
Water hemlock is a plant. The entire plant is used to make medicine. Be careful not to confuse water hemlock with hemlock or hemlock water dropwort.

Is it Effective?

The effectiveness ratings for **WATER HEMLOCK** are as follows:
Insufficient Evidence to Rate Effectiveness for... Migraine headaches, painful menstrual periods, skin inflammation, and worm infestations.

How does it work?

Water hemlock contains ingredients that are poisonous and have many dangerous effects on the body.

Are there safety concerns?

Water hemlock is UNSAFE for anyone to take.

All plant parts are poisonous and can cause death in as little as 15 minutes. Get immediate medical attention if you have taken water hemlock. The first symptoms of water hemlock poisoning are drooling, nausea, vomiting, wheezing sweating, dizziness, stomach pain, flushing, weakness/tiredness (lethargy), delirium, and uncontrollable bowel movements. These are followed by more serious symptoms including trouble breathing, convulsions, heart problems, kidney failure, coma, and death.

Are there any interactions with medications?

It is not known if water hemlock interacts with any medicines.
Before taking water hemlock, talk with your healthcare professional if you take any medications.

WATER PLANTAIN

What other names is the product known by?

Alisma plantago-aquatica, Alisma plantago-aquatica subsp. orientale, synonyms Alisma orientale, Alisma plantago-aquatica var. orientale, Mad-Dog Weed.

What is it?

Water plantain is a plant. The root and underground stem (rhizome) are used to make medicine. Be careful not to confuse water plantain with other plantain species such as buckhorn plantain.

Is it Effective?

The effectiveness ratings for **WATER PLANTAIN** are as follows:
Insufficient Evidence to Rate Effectiveness for... Bladder and urinary tract diseases.

How does it work?

There isn't enough information to know how water plantain works.

Are there safety concerns?

Water plantain may be unsafe and toxic. The fresh rootstock is thought to be poisonous.

Do not take water plantain if: You are pregnant or breast-feeding.

Are there any interactions with medications?

It is not known if water plantain interacts with any medicines.
Before taking water plantain, talk with your healthcare professional if you take any medications.

WATERCRESS

What other names is the product known by?

Agriao, Berro, Berro Di Agua, Brunnenkresse, Crescione Di Fonte, Cresson au Poulet, Cresson D'eau, Cresson De Fontaine, Indian Cress, Mizu-Garashi, Nasilord, Nasturtii herba, Nasturtium officinale, Oranda-Garashi, Scurvy Grass, Selada-Air, Tall Nasturtium, Wasserkresse.

What is it?

Watercress is a plant. The above ground parts are used to make medicine.

Is it Effective?

The effectiveness ratings for **WATERCRESS** are as follows:
Insufficient Evidence to Rate Effectiveness for... Coughs, bronchitis, reducing swelling (inflammation) of the lungs, hair loss, flu, constipation, arthritis, earaches, eczema, scabies, and warts.

Medical professionals should consult the Professional Version at www.NaturalDatabase.com.

CONSUMER VERSION

How does it work?

Watercress may have antibiotic action. It can also increase the amount of urine produced by the body (diuretic).

Are there safety concerns?

Watercress seems safe for most people when used short-term. When used in large amounts or long-term it can cause stomach upset or kidney problems.

Watercress is UNSAFE for use as a medicine in children, especially in those younger than four years old.

Do not use watercress if: You are pregnant or breast-feeding, in amounts larger than in food. • You have a stomach ulcer. • You have an intestinal ulcer. • You have kidney disease.

Are there any interactions with medications?

Chlorzoxazone (Parafon Forte, Paraflex). The body breaks down chlorzoxazone (Parafon Forte, Paraflex) to get rid of it. Watercress might decrease how quickly the body breaks down chlorzoxazone (Parafon Forte, Paraflex). Taking watercress along with chlorzoxazone (Parafon Forte, Paraflex) might increase the effects and side effects of chlorzoxazone (Parafon Forte, Paraflex).

Warfarin (Coumadin). Watercress contains large amounts of vitamin K. Vitamin K is used by the body to help blood clot. Warfarin (Coumadin) is used to slow blood clotting. By helping the blood clot, watercress might decrease the effectiveness of warfarin (Coumadin). Be sure to have your blood checked regularly. The dose of your warfarin (Coumadin) might need to be changed.

WHEAT BRAN

What other names is the product known by?

Bran, Dietary Fiber, Triticum aestrivum.

What is it?

Wheat is a plant. The outer shell of the grain (the bran) is used to make medicine.

Is it Effective?

The effectiveness ratings for **WHEAT BRAN** are as follows:

Possibly Effective for... Constipation • Reducing risk of hemorrhoids • Irritable bowel syndrome (IBS) • Lowering blood pressure • Preventing stomach cancer.

Possibly Ineffective for... Preventing cancer of the colon (bowels) or rectum • Type 2 diabetes.

How does it work?

Wheat bran helps constipation by speeding up the colon and increasing stool output and bowel frequency.

Are there safety concerns?

Wheat bran is safe for most people to use. It may cause gas (flatulence) and stomach discomfort, especially with initial use.

Are there any interactions with medications?

Digoxin (Lanoxin). Wheat bran is high in fiber. Fiber can decrease the absorption and decrease the effectiveness of digoxin (Lanoxin). As a general rule, any medications taken by mouth should be taken one hour before or four hours after wheat bran to prevent this interaction.

WHEATGRASS

What other names is the product known by?

Agropyron repens, Agropyron firmum, Couchgrass, Couch Grass, Cutch, Dog Grass, Dog-grass, Doggrass, Durfa Grass, Elymus repens, Elytrigia repens, Graminis rhizoma, Quack Grass, Quackgrass, Quitch Grass, Scotch Quelch, Triticum firmum, Triticum repens, Twitchgrass, Wheat Grass Witch Grass.

What is it?

Wheatgrass is a kind of grass. The above ground parts, roots, and rhizome are used to make medicine.

Is it Effective?

The effectiveness ratings for **WHEATGRASS** are as follows:

Insufficient Evidence to Rate Effectiveness for... Ulcerative colitis; reducing cholesterol; anemia; diabetes; cancer; high blood pressure; preventing tooth decay; wound healing; preventing infections; removing drugs, metals, toxins, and cancer-causing substances from the body; and other conditions.

How does it work?
Wheatgrass contains chemicals that might have antioxidant and anti-inflammatory (swelling) activity.

Are there safety concerns?
Wheatgrass is safe for most adults in amounts commonly found in foods.

Wheatgrass seems to be safe when used as medicine for up to one month. Wheatgrass can cause nausea, appetite loss, and constipation.

Do not use wheatgrass if: You are pregnant or breast-feeding.

Are there any interactions with medications?
It is not known if wheatgrass interacts with any medicines.
Before taking wheatgrass, talk with your healthcare professional if you take any medications.

WHEY PROTEIN

What other names is the product known by?
Bovine Whey Protein Concentrate.

What is it?
Whey protein is the protein contained in whey, the watery portion of milk that separates from the curds when making cheese.

Is it Effective?
The effectiveness ratings for **WHEY PROTEIN** are as follows:
Possibly Effective for... Reversing weight loss in people with HIV disease (AIDS) • Preventing allergies in infants who have a family history of allergies.
Insufficient Evidence to Rate Effectiveness for... Use as an alternative to milk for people with lactose intolerance, asthma, high cholesterol, cancer, obesity, and other conditions.

How does it work?
Whey protein is a source of protein that might improve the nutrient content of the diet. Whey protein might also have effects on the immune system.

Are there safety concerns?
Whey protein is safe for most adults, including pregnant and breast-feeding women, when used in normal food amounts. High doses can cause increased bowel movements, nausea, thirst, bloating, cramps, reduced appetite, tiredness (fatigue), and headache.

Do not use whey protein if: You are allergic to cow's milk.

Are there any interactions with medications?
Alendronate (Fosamax). Whey protein can decrease how much alendronate (Fosamax) the body absorbs. Taking whey protein and alendronate (Fosamax) at the same time can decrease the effectiveness of alendronate (Fosamax). Don't take whey protein within two hours of taking alendronate (Fosamax).
Antibiotics (Tetracycline antibiotics). Whey protein contains calcium. The calcium in whey protein can attach to tetracyclines in the stomach. This decreases the amount of tetracyclines that can be absorbed. Taking calcium with tetracyclines might decrease the effectiveness of tetracyclines. To avoid this interaction take whey protein two hours before or four hours after taking tetracyclines. Some tetracyclines include demeclocycline (Declomycin), minocycline (Minocin), and tetracycline (Achromycin).
Antibiotics (Quinolone antibiotics). Whey protein might decrease how much antibiotic the body absorbs. Taking whey protein along with some antibiotics might decrease the effectiveness of some antibiotics. To avoid this interaction take whey protein supplements at least one hour after antibiotics. Some of these antibiotics that might interact with whey protein include ciprofloxacin (Cipro), enoxacin (Penetrex), norfloxacin (Chibroxin, Noroxin), sparfloxacin (Zagam), trovafloxacin (Trovan), and grepafloxacin (Raxar).
Levodopa. Whey protein might decrease how much levodopa the body absorbs. By decreasing how much levodopa the body absorbs, whey protein might decrease the effectiveness of levodopa. Do not take whey protein and levodopa at the same time.

WHITE COHOSH

What other names is the product known by?
Actaea alba, Actaea pachypoda, Actaea rubra, Baneberry, Coralberry, Doll's Eye, Snakeberry, White Baneberry.

What is it?
White cohosh is an herb. The whole plant is used to make medicine.

Is it Effective?
The effectiveness ratings for **WHITE COHOSH** are as follows:
Insufficient Evidence to Rate Effectiveness for... Stimulating menstruation (periods), treating female disorders, colds, coughs, stomach problems, and other conditions.

How does it work?
There isn't enough information available to know how white cohosh works.

Are there safety concerns?
Avoid using white cohosh. All parts of the plant are poisonous. It can cause stomach problems, vomiting, bloody diarrhea, headache, heart and blood circulation problems, and delirium.

Avoid skin contact with white cohosh; it can cause swelling and skin blisters.

Do not use white cohosh if: You are pregnant or breast-feeding. • You have stomach or intestinal problems.

Are there any interactions with medications?
It is not known if white cohosh interacts with any medicines.
Before taking white cohosh, talk with your healthcare professional if you take any medications.

WHITE DEAD NETTLE FLOWER

What other names is the product known by?
Archangel, Bee Nettle, Blind Nettle, Deaf Nettle, Dumb Nettle, Lamii Albi Flos, Lamium album, Stingless Nettle, White Archangel.

What is it?
White dead nettle flower is a plant. It is used to make medicine.

Is it Effective?
The effectiveness ratings for **WHITE DEAD NETTLE FLOWER** are as follows:
Insufficient Evidence to Rate Effectiveness for... Swelling (inflammation) of the upper airways, sore throat, skin inflammation, vaginal discharge, and other conditions.

How does it work?
White dead nettle flowers contain chemicals that help reduce swelling and break up mucus.

Are there safety concerns?
White dead nettle flower seems safe for use when taken by mouth.

Do not use white dead nettle flower if: You are pregnant or breast-feeding.

Are there any interactions with medications?
It is not known if white dead nettle flower interacts with any medicines.
Before taking white dead nettle flower, talk with your healthcare professional if you take any medications.

WHITE HELLEBORE

What other names is the product known by?
European Hellebore, European White Hellebore, Langwort, Veratrum album.

What is it?
White hellebore is an herb. The bulb and root are used to make medicine.

Is it Effective?
The effectiveness ratings for **WHITE HELLEBORE** are as follows:
Insufficient Evidence to Rate Effectiveness for... Treating cholera, gout, hypertension, and herpes (cold sores).

How does it work?
There isn't enough information available to know how white hellebore works.

Are there safety concerns?
White hellebore is UNSAFE. All parts of the plant are poisonous. It can cause irritation and burning of the gut, vomiting, slow heart rate, low blood pressure, breathing problems, blindness, paralysis, convulsions, and death.

Avoid skin contact with white hellebore; it can cause skin irritation.

Do not use white hellebore if: You are pregnant or breast-feeding.

Are there any interactions with medications?
It is not known if white hellebore interacts with any medicines.
Before taking white hellebore, talk with your healthcare professional if you take any medications.

WHITE HOREHOUND

What other names is the product known by?
Common Hoarhound, Houndsbane, Marrubii herba, Marrubium, Mastranzo, Marrubium vulgare.

What is it?
White horehound is a plant. The above ground parts are used to make medicine.

Is it Effective?
The effectiveness ratings for **WHITE HOREHOUND** are as follows:
Insufficient Evidence to Rate Effectiveness for... Liver and gallbladder problems, skin damage, ulcers, wounds, constipation, fluid retention, stimulating the appetite, indigestion, bloating, gas (flatulence), coughs and colds, and other conditions.

How does it work?
The chemicals in white horehound can thin mucus secretions, reduce spasms in the stomach and intestines, and decrease swelling (inflammation).

Are there safety concerns?
White horehound is considered safe for most people. Large amounts can cause vomiting. Applying white horehound directly to the skin can cause skin reactions.

Do not use white horehound if: You are pregnant or breast-feeding. • You have a heart condition.

Are there any interactions with medications?
It is not known if white horehound interacts with any medicines.
Before taking white horehound, talk with your healthcare professional if you take any medications.

WHITE LILY

What other names is the product known by?
Baurenlilien, Farmer's Lily, Lilium candidum, Madonna Lily, Meadow Lily, White Pond Lily.

What is it?
White lily is an herb. The root and bulb are used to make medicine.

Is it Effective?
The effectiveness ratings for **WHITE LILY** are as follows:
Insufficient Evidence to Rate Effectiveness for... Gynecological (female) problems, bleeding, coughs, skin ulcers, burns, and boils.

How does it work?
There isn't enough information available to know how white lily works.

Medical professionals should consult the Professional Version at www.NaturalDatabase.com.

Are there safety concerns?

There isn't enough information available to know if white lily is safe.

Do not use white lily if: You are pregnant or breast-feeding.

Are there any interactions with medications?

It is not known if white lily interacts with any medicines.
Before taking white lily, talk with your healthcare professional if you take any medications.

WHITE MUSTARD

What other names is the product known by?

American Yellow Mustard, Brassica Alba, Mustard, Mustard Seed, Sinapis Alba, Sinapis Albae Semen, Weibe Senfsamen, White Mustard Seed, Yellow Mustard.

What is it?

White mustard is an herb. The seeds are used to make medicine.

Is it Effective?

The effectiveness ratings for **WHITE MUSTARD** are as follows:
Insufficient Evidence to Rate Effectiveness for... Coughs and colds; bronchitis; arthritis-like pain; swelling (inflammation) of the mouth, throat, and joints; and other conditions.

How does it work?

There isn't enough information available to know how white mustard works.

Are there safety concerns?

White mustard is safe for most people in the amounts found in foods. It seems safe to use short-term as a medicine for adults. Avoid using white mustard for more than 15-30 minutes, or on a regular basis for more than two weeks. White mustard can cause burns, blisters, and ulcers.

White mustard is unsafe when used to produce vomiting because it can cause irritation and burning of the throat.

Avoid giving white mustard in medicinal amounts to children.

Do not use white mustard in medicinal amounts if: You are pregnant or breast-feeding. • You have kidney problems.

Are there any interactions with medications?

It is not known if white mustard interacts with any medicines.
Before taking white mustard, talk with your healthcare professional if you take any medications.

WHITE SANDALWOOD

What other names is the product known by?

Chandana, East Indian Sandalwood, Oil of Sandalwood, Sanderswood, Santal, Santali Lignum Albi, Santal oil, Santalum album, Tan Xiang, White Sandalwood oil, White Saunders, Yellow Sandalwood, Yellow Saunders.

What is it?

White sandalwood is an evergreen tree. The oil from the wood and the wood are used as medicine.

Is it Effective?

The effectiveness ratings for **WHITE SANDALWOOD** are as follows:
Insufficient Evidence to Rate Effectiveness for... Urinary tract infections (UTIs), common cold, cough, bronchitis, fevers, swelling in the mouth, stomachache, vomiting, pain, heatstroke, liver and gallbladder problems, and other conditions.

How does it work?

White sandalwood might help prevent the growth of fungus and bacteria. It might reduce spasms. But more information is needed.

Medical professionals should consult the Professional Version at www.NaturalDatabase.com.

 Natural Medicines Comprehensive Database Consumer Version (209) 472-2244

Are there safety concerns?

White sandalwood is safe when consumed in the amounts found in foods.

When taken by mouth, white sandalwood can cause itching, nausea, stomach upset, and blood in the urine. Avoid taking white sandalwood for longer than six weeks. Taking it for more than six weeks might cause kidney problems.

Contact with white sandalwood can cause allergic skin reactions in some people.

Do not use white sandalwood in medicinal amounts if: You are pregnant or breast-feeding. • You have kidney disease.

Are there any interactions with medications?

It is not known if white sandalwood interacts with any medicines.
Before taking white sandalwood, talk with your healthcare professional if you take any medications.

WHITE SOAPWORT

What other names is the product known by?

Gypsophila paniculata, Gypsophilae radix, Soapwort.

What is it?

White soapwort is an herb. The root is used to make medicine.

Is it Effective?

The effectiveness ratings for **WHITE SOAPWORT** are as follows:
Insufficient Evidence to Rate Effectiveness for... Cough, bronchitis, swelling (inflammation) of the upper airways and lungs, and skin problems such as eczema.

How does it work?

White soapwort has chemicals that help to break up chest congestion by thinning mucous and making it easier to cough up (expectorant).

Are there safety concerns?

White soapwort seems safe for most adults. It can cause stomach irritation, nausea, and vomiting.

Do not use white soapwort if: You are pregnant or breast-feeding. • You have stomach or intestinal problems.

Are there any interactions with medications?

It is not known if white soapwort interacts with any medicines.
Before taking white soapwort, talk with your healthcare professional if you take any medications.

WILD CARROT

What other names is the product known by?

Beesnest Plant, Bird's Nest Root, Daucus, Daucus carota, Garijara, Queen Anne's Lace, Shikha-Mula.

What is it?

Wild carrot is a plant. The above ground parts and an oil made from the seeds are used to make medicine. Be careful not to confuse wild carrot (which has an inedible white tap root) with the common carrot.

Is it Effective?

The effectiveness ratings for **WILD CARROT** are as follows:
Insufficient Evidence to Rate Effectiveness for... Kidney stones, bladder problems, gout, diarrhea, indigestion, gas, pain in the uterus, heart disease, cancer, kidney problems, use as a nerve tonic, use as a diuretic (water pill), use as an aphrodisiac, inducing menstruation (periods), or treating worms.

How does it work?

Wild carrot contains chemicals which might have effects on blood vessels, muscles, and the heart, but it is not known how wild carrot might work for medicinal uses.

CONSUMER VERSION

Medical professionals should consult the Professional Version at www.NaturalDatabase.com.

Are there safety concerns?

Wild carrot seed oil seems to be safe when taken by mouth for most adults in the amounts used in medicines. There isn't enough information to know whether the above ground parts of wild carrot are safe.

High doses of wild carrot oil can cause kidney damage and nerve problems. Wild carrot can cause skin rash and increase the risk of sunburn when in the sun. Wild carrot can cause allergic reactions in some people. People who are sensitive to birch, celery, or mugwort are more likely to be sensitive to wild carrot.

Avoid skin contact with wild carrot.

Do not use wild carrot if: You are pregnant or breast-feeding. • You are being treated with any type of UV light therapy. • You have kidney problems. • You have allergic reactions to birch, celery, or mugwort.

Are there any interactions with medications?

Estrogens. Large amounts of wild carrot might have some of the same effects as estrogen. But wild carrot isn't as strong as estrogen pills. Taking wild carrot along with estrogen pills might decrease the effects of estrogen pills. Some estrogen pills include conjugated equine estrogens (Premarin), ethinyl estradiol, estradiol, and others.
Medications for high blood pressure (Antihypertensive drugs). Large amounts of wild carrot seem to increase blood pressure. By increasing blood pressure wild carrot might decrease the effectiveness of medications for high blood pressure. Some medications for high blood pressure include captopril (Capoten), enalapril (Vasotec), losartan (Cozaar), valsartan (Diovan), diltiazem (Cardizem), amlodipine (Norvasc), hydrochlorothiazide (HydroDiuril), furosemide (Lasix), and many others.
Medications that increase sensitivity to sunlight (Photosensitizing drugs). Some medications can increase sensitivity to sunlight. Wild carrot might also increase your sensitivity to sunlight. Taking wild carrot along with medications that increase sensitivity to sunlight could increase the chances of sunburn, blistering or rashes on areas of skin exposed to sunlight. Be sure to wear sunblock and protective clothing when spending time in the sun. Some drugs that cause photosensitivity include amitriptyline (Elavil), Ciprofloxacin (Cipro), norfloxacin (Noroxin), lomefloxacin (Maxaquin), ofloxacin (Floxin), levofloxacin (Levaquin), sparfloxacin (Zagam), gatifloxacin (Tequin), moxifloxacin (Avelox), trimethoprim/sulfamethoxazole (Septra), tetracycline, methoxsalen (8-methoxypsoralen, 8-MOP, Oxsoralen), and Trioxsalen (Trisoralen).

WILD CHERRY

What other names is the product known by?

Black Cherry, Black Choke, Choke Cherry, Prunus serotina, Prunus virginiana, Rum Cherry Bark, Virginian Prune, Wild Black Cherry.

What is it?

Wild cherry is a plant. The bark is used to make medicine.

Is it Effective?

The effectiveness ratings for **WILD CHERRY** are as follows:
Insufficient Evidence to Rate Effectiveness for... Cough, colds, bronchitis, diarrhea, and other conditions.

How does it work?

Wild cherry contains chemicals that might help reduce swelling (inflammation) and have a drying (astringent) effect on the tissues.

Are there safety concerns?

Wild cherry seems safe when used in small amounts short-term. Taking large amounts can cause deadly poisonings.

Do not use wild cherry if: You are pregnant or breast-feeding.

Are there any interactions with medications?

Medications changed by the liver (Cytochrome P450 3A4 (CYP3A4) substrates). Some medications are changed and broken down by the liver. Wild cherry might decrease how quickly the liver breaks down some medications. Taking wild cherry along with some medications that are broken down by the liver can increase the effects and side effects of some medications. Before taking wild cherry, talk to your healthcare provider if you are taking any medications that are changed by the liver. Some medications changed by the liver include lovastatin (Mevacor), ketoconazole (Nizoral), itraconazole (Sporanox), fexofenadine (Allegra), triazolam (Halcion), and many others.

 Natural Medicines Comprehensive Database Consumer Version (209) 472-2244

WILD DAISY

What other names is the product known by?
Bellis perennis and Bruisewort.

What is it?
Wild daisy is a plant. The above ground parts are used to make medicine.

Is it Effective?
The effectiveness ratings for **WILD DAISY** are as follows:
Insufficient Evidence to Rate Effectiveness for... Coughs, bronchitis, liver and kidney problems, and swelling when taken by mouth. Wounds and skin diseases when put on the skin.

How does it work?
There isn't enough information to know how wild daisy might work.

Are there safety concerns?
There isn't enough information to know whether wild daisy is safe. But, allergic reactions have occurred in people who are allergic to other plants and herbs in the Asteraceae/Compositae family. Members of this family include ragweed, chrysanthemums, marigolds, and many other herbs.

Do not use wild daisy if: You are pregnant or breast-feeding. • You are allergic to ragweed, chrysanthemums, marigolds, or similar plants.

Are there any interactions with medications?
It is not known if wild daisy interacts with any medicines.
Before taking wild daisy, talk with your healthcare professional if you take any medications.

WILD INDIGO

What other names is the product known by?
American Indigo,Baptisia tinctoria, Baptista, False Indigo, Horsefly Weed, Indigo Broom, Rattlebush, Yellow Broom, Yellow Indigo.

What is it?
Wild indigo is an herb. The root is used to make medicine.

Is it Effective?
The effectiveness ratings for **WILD INDIGO** are as follows:
Insufficient Evidence to Rate Effectiveness for... Diphtheria, influenza ("flu"), malaria, typhoid fever, scarlet fever, sore throats, colds, tonsillitis, swelling of the mouth and throat, fever, or Crohn's disease when taken by mouth. Ulcers, open wounds, or inflamed nipples when put on the skin, or use as a vaginal douche.

How does it work?
There isn't enough information to know how wild indigo works.

Are there safety concerns?
Wild indigo is UNSAFE when taken by mouth or applied to the skin. Large doses can cause vomiting, diarrhea, other intestinal problems, and spasms.

Do not use wild indigo if: You are pregnant or breast-feeding. • You have stomach or intestinal problems.

Are there any interactions with medications?
It is not known if wild indigo interacts with any medicines.
Before taking wild indigo, talk with your healthcare professional if you take any medications.

Medical professionals should consult the Professional Version at www.NaturalDatabase.com.

WILD LETTUCE

What other names is the product known by?
Acrid Lettuce, Bitter Lettuce, German Lactucarium, Green Endive, Lactuca virosa, Lactucarium, Lettuce Opium, Poison Lettuce, Strong-Scented Lettuce.

What is it?
Wild lettuce is a plant. The leaves and latex are used to make medicine.

Is it Effective?
The effectiveness ratings for **WILD LETTUCE** are as follows:
Insufficient Evidence to Rate Effectiveness for... Whooping cough, asthma, urinary tract problems, cough, hardening of the arteries, insomnia, restlessness, painful periods, muscle and joint pain, and use as a topical antiseptic.

How does it work?
Wild lettuce has calming, relaxing, and pain relieving effects.

Are there safety concerns?
Wild lettuce seems safe for most people in small amounts. Applying wild lettuce directly to the skin can cause irritation. Large amounts can cause sweating, fast heartbeat, pupil dilation, dizziness, ringing in the ears, vision changes, sedation, breathing difficulty, and death.

Do not use wild lettuce if: You are pregnant or breast-feeding. • You have prostate enlargement - benign prostatic hyperplasia (BPH). • You have an eye condition called narrow-angle glaucoma.
• You are allergic to ragweed, marigolds, daisies, or related herbs.

Are there any interactions with medications?
Sedative medications (CNS depressants). Wild lettuce might cause sleepiness and drowsiness. Medications that cause sleepiness are called sedatives. Taking wild lettuce along with sedative medications might cause too much sleepiness. Some sedative medications include clonazepam (Klonopin), lorazepam (Ativan), phenobarbital (Donnatal), zolpidem (Ambien), and others.

WILD MINT

What other names is the product known by?
Hairy Mint, Marsh Mint, Mentha aquatica, Water Mint.

What is it?
Wild mint is an herb. The leaves are used to make medicine.

Is it Effective?
The effectiveness ratings for **WILD MINT** are as follows:
Insufficient Evidence to Rate Effectiveness for... Diarrhea, painful menstruation (periods), and other conditions.

How does it work?
There isn't enough information available to know how wild mint works.

Are there safety concerns?
There isn't enough information to know if wild mint is safe.

Do not use wild mint if: You are pregnant or breast-feeding.

Are there any interactions with medications?
It is not known if wild mint interacts with any medicines.
Before taking wild mint, talk with your healthcare professional if you take any medications.

 Natural Medicines Comprehensive Database Consumer Version   (209) 472-2244

WILD RADISH

What other names is the product known by?
Joint-Podded Charlock, Raphanus raphanistrum.

What is it?
Wild radish is an herb. The whole plant, before it flowers, is used to make medicine.

Is it Effective?
The effectiveness ratings for **WILD RADISH** are as follows:
Insufficient Evidence to Rate Effectiveness for... Stomach problems and skin problems.

How does it work?
There isn't enough information available to know how wild radish works.

Are there safety concerns?
There isn't enough information available to know if wild radish is safe. Large amounts can irritate the mouth and all parts of the gut.

Do not use wild radish if: You are pregnant or breast-feeding.

Are there any interactions with medications?
It is not known if wild radish interacts with any medicines.
Before taking wild radish, talk with your healthcare professional if you take any medications.

WILD THYME

What other names is the product known by?
Mother of Thyme, Serpyllum, Shepherd's Thyme, Thymus serpyllum.

What is it?
Wild thyme is an herb. The above ground parts are used to make medicine.

Is it Effective?
The effectiveness ratings for **WILD THYME** are as follows:
Insufficient Evidence to Rate Effectiveness for... Cough, bronchitis, kidney and bladder problems, relieving gas (flatulence), colic, arthritis, and other conditions.

How does it work?
There isn't enough information available to know how wild thyme works.

Are there safety concerns?
Wild thyme is safe in the amounts used in foods, and seems safe for most adults when used as medicine.

Do not use wild thyme if: You are pregnant or breast-feeding, in amounts greater than those typically found in foods. • You have thyroid problems.

Are there any interactions with medications?
It is not known if wild thyme interacts with any medicines.
Before taking wild thyme, talk with your healthcare professional if you take any medications.

WILD YAM

What other names is the product known by?
Atlantic Yam, Barbasco, China Root, Colic Root, Devil's Bones, Dioscorea, Dioscoreae, Dioscorea alata, Dioscorea batatas, Dioscorea japonica, Dioscorea villosa, Dioscorea floribunda, Dioscorea composita, Dioscorea mexicana, Dioscorea macrostachya, Mexican Yam, Mexican Wild Yam, Natural DHEA, Phytoestrogen, Rheumatism Root, Rhizoma Dioscoreae, Wild Mexican Yam, Yuma.

What is it?
Wild yam is a plant. The root and bulb are used to make medicine.

Is it Effective?
The effectiveness ratings for **WILD YAM** are as follows:
Possibly Ineffective for... Hot flashes and night sweats associated with menopause, when wild yam cream is applied to the skin.
Insufficient Evidence to Rate Effectiveness for... Use as a natural alternative to estrogens, postmenopausal vaginal dryness, premenstrual syndrome (PMS), osteoporosis, increasing energy and libido in men and women, gallbladder problems, painful menstruation (periods), or rheumatoid arthritis.

How does it work?
Wild yam contains a chemical that can be made into various steroids, such as estrogen, in the laboratory. However, the body can't change wild yam to estrogen.

Are there safety concerns?
Wild yam seems safe for most adults. Large amounts can cause vomiting.

Do not use wild yam if: You are pregnant or breast-feeding. • You have breast cancer.
• You have cancer of the ovaries or uterus. • You have endometriosis. • You have uterine fibroids.
• You have a condition called protein S deficiency.

Are there any interactions with medications?
It is not known if wild yam interacts with any medicines.
Before taking wild yam, talk with your healthcare professional if you take any medications.

WILLARD WATER

What other names is the product known by?
Biowater, Carbonaceous Activated Water, Catalyst Altered Water, Williard's Water.

What is it?
Willard water is chemically processed water containing ingredients such as rock salt, calcium chloride, and magnesium sulfate.

Is it Effective?
The effectiveness ratings for **WILLARD WATER** are as follows:
Insufficient Evidence to Rate Effectiveness for... Arthritis, acne, anxiety, nervous stomach, hypertension (high blood pressure), ulcers, and hair growth.

How does it work?
There isn't enough information available to understand how Willard water works.

Are there safety concerns?
There isn't enough information available to know if Willard water is safe.

Do not use Willard water if: You are pregnant or breast-feeding.

Are there any interactions with medications?
It is not known if Willard water interacts with any medicines.
Before taking Willard water, talk with your healthcare professional if you take any medications.

WILLOW BARK

What other names is the product known by?
Basket Willow, Bay Willow, Brittle Willow, Crack Willow, Daphne Willow, Knackweide, Laurel Willow, Lorbeerweide, Osier Rouge, Purple Osier, Purple Osier Willow, Purpurweide, Reifweide, Salix alba, Salicis cortex, Salix daphnoides, Salix fragilis, Salix pentandra, Salix purpurea, Silberweide, Violet Willow, Weidenrinde, White Willow, White Willow Bark, Willowbark.

What is it?
Willow bark is the bark from several varieties of the willow tree. The bark is used to make medicine.

Is it Effective?

The effectiveness ratings for **WILLOW BARK** are as follows:

Possibly Effective for... Treating low back pain.

Insufficient Evidence to Rate Effectiveness for... Osteoarthritis ("wear and tear arthritis"), rheumatoid arthritis, weight loss when taken in combination with other herbs, treating fever, joint pain, and headaches.

How does it work?

Willow bark contains a chemical similar to aspirin.

Are there safety concerns?

Willow bark seems to be safe for most people when used for short amounts of time (up to 12 weeks).

It may cause stomach upset and digestive system upset. It can also cause itching, rash, and allergic reactions, particularly in people allergic to aspirin. Do not use in children.

Do not use willow bark if: You are pregnant or breast-feeding. • You are allergic to aspirin. • You have asthma. • You have ulcers. • You have diabetes. • You have gout. • You have hemophilia. • You have hypoprothrombinemia. • You have kidney or liver disease.

Are there any interactions with medications?

Aspirin. Willow bark contains chemicals similar to aspirin. Taking willow bark along with aspirin might increase the effects and side effects of aspirin.

Choline Magnesium Trisalicylate (Trilisate). Willow bark contains chemicals that are similar to choline magnesium trisalicylate (Trilisate). Taking willow bark along with choline magnesium trisalicylate (Trilisate) might increase the effects and side effects of choline magnesium trisalicylate (Trilisate).

Medications that slow blood clotting (Anticoagulant / Antiplatelet drugs). Willow bark might slow blood clotting. Taking willow bark along with medications that also slow clotting might increase the chances of bruising and bleeding. Some medications that slow blood clotting include aspirin, clopidogrel (Plavix), diclofenac (Voltaren, Cataflam, others), ibuprofen (Advil, Motrin, others), naproxen (Anaprox, Naprosyn, others), dalteparin (Fragmin), enoxaparin (Lovenox), heparin, warfarin (Coumadin), and others.

Salsalate (Disalcid). Salsalate (Disalcid) is called a salicylate. It's similar to aspirin. Willow bark also contains a salicylate similar to aspirin. Taking salsalate (Disalcid) along with willow bark might increase the effects and side effects of salsalate (Disalcid).

WINE

What other names is the product known by?

Alcohol, Ethanol, Vitis vinifera, Wine Extract.

What is it?

Wine is an alcoholic beverage prepared by fermenting grapes.

Is it Effective?

The effectiveness ratings for **WINE** are as follows:

Likely Effective for... Preventing cardiovascular (heart and blood circulation) diseases, such as heart attack, stroke, atherosclerosis (hardening of the arteries), and angina (heart pain) • Reducing the risk of dying from cardiovascular disease and other causes.

Possibly Effective for... Reducing the risk of heart attack and other cardiovascular (heart and blood circulation) problems • Reducing the risk of diabetes (type 2) • Reducing the risk of stroke • Reducing the risk of mental decline • Preventing ulcers caused by the bacteria H. pylori.

Insufficient Evidence to Rate Effectiveness for... Reducing the risk of Alzheimer's disease, osteoporosis, and cancer; and treating wounds, ulcers, and anxiety.

How does it work?

Wine contains ethanol (alcohol), which blocks various nerve pathways in the brain. It also contains chemicals that might have beneficial effects on the heart and blood circulation such as antioxidant effects, and preventing blood platelets from forming clots.

Are there safety concerns?

Wine is likely safe for most adults when no more than 2 five-ounce glasses are drunk per day. Avoid higher amounts. Larger amounts can cause flushing, confusion, blackouts, trouble walking, seizures, vomiting, diarrhea, and other serious problems.

Medical professionals should consult the Professional Version at www.NaturalDatabase.com.

CONSUMER VERSION

Long-term use of large amounts of wine causes many serious health problems including dependence, mental problems, heart problems, liver problems, pancreas problems, and certain types of cancer.

Do not use wine if: You are pregnant or breast-feeding. • You have asthma. • You have gout. • You have heart problems such as angina or heart failure. • You have high blood pressure (hypertension). • You have high levels of triglycerides (a type of fat) in your blood. • You have sleeping problems (insomnia). • You have liver problems. • You have pancreas problems (pancreatitis). • You have ulcers or a type of heartburn called gastroesophageal reflux disease (GERD). • You have a disease called porphyria. • You have psychiatric (mental) problems.

Are there any interactions with medications?

Antibiotics (Sulfonamide antibiotics). The alcohol in wine can interact with some antibiotics. This can lead to upset stomach, vomiting, sweating, headache, and an increased heartbeat. Do not drink wine while taking antibiotics. Some antibiotics that interact with wine include sulfamethoxazole (Gantanol), sulfasalazine (Azulfidine), sulfisoxazole (Gantrisin), trimethoprim/sulfamethoxazole (Bactrim, Septra), and others.

Aspirin. Aspirin can sometimes damage the stomach and cause ulcers and bleeding. The alcohol in wine can also damage the stomach. Taking aspirin along with wine might increase the chance of ulcers and bleeding in the stomach. Avoid taking wine and aspirin together.

Chlorpropamide (Diabinese). The body breaks down the alcohol in wine to get rid of it. Chlorpropamide (Diabinese) might decrease how quickly the body breaks down alcohol. Drinking wine and taking chlorpropamide (Diabinese) might cause a headache, vomiting, flushing, and other unpleasant reactions. Don't drink wine if you are taking chlorpropamide (Diabinese).

Cefamandole (Mandol). The alcohol in wine can interact with cefamandole (Mandol). This can lead to upset stomach, vomiting, sweating, headache, and an increased heartbeat. Do not drink wine while taking cefamandole (Mandol).

Cefoperazone (Cefobid). The alcohol in wine can interact with cefoperazone (Cefobid). This can lead to upset stomach, vomiting, sweating, headache, and an increased heartbeat. Do not drink wine while taking cefoperazone (Cefobid).

Cisapride (Propulsid). Cisapride (Propulsid) might decrease how quickly the body gets rid of the alcohol in wine. Taking cisapride (Propulsid) along with wine might increase the effects and side effects of alcohol.

Cyclosporine (Neoral, Sandimmune). Wine might increase how much cyclosporine (Neoral, Sandimmune) the body absorbs. Taking wine along with cyclosporine (Neoral, Sandimmune) might increase the side effects of cyclosporine.

Disulfiram (Antabuse). The body breaks down the alcohol in wine to get rid of it. Disulfiram (Antabuse) decreases how quickly the body breaks down alcohol. Drinking wine and taking disulfiram (Antabuse) can cause a pounding headache, vomiting, flushing, and other unpleasant reactions. Don't drink any alcohol if you are taking disulfiram (Antabuse).

Erythromycin. The body breaks down the alcohol in wine to get rid of it. Erythromycin can decrease how quickly the body gets rid of alcohol. Drinking wine and taking erythromycin might increase the effects and side effects of alcohol.

Felodipine (Plendil). Red wine can change the way the body absorbs and breaks down felodipine. Drinking red wine while taking felodipine for high blood pressure might cause your blood pressure to go too low.

Griseofulvin (Fulvicin). The body breaks down the alcohol in wine to get rid of it. Griseofulvin (Fulvicin) decreases how quickly the body breaks down alcohol. Drinking wine and taking griseofulvin can cause a pounding headache, vomiting, flushing, and other unpleasant reactions. Don't drink any alcohol if you are taking griseofulvin.

Medications that can harm the liver (Hepatotoxic drugs). The alcohol in wine can harm the liver. Drinking wine along with medication that can harm the liver can increase the risk of liver damage. Do not drink wine if you are taking a medication that can harm the liver. Some medications that can harm the liver include acetaminophen (Tylenol and others), amiodarone (Cordarone), carbamazepine (Tegretol), isoniazid (INH), methotrexate (Rheumatrex), methyldopa (Aldomet), fluconazole (Diflucan), itraconazole (Sporanox), erythromycin (Erythrocin, Ilosone, others), phenytoin (Dilantin) , lovastatin (Mevacor), pravastatin (Pravachol), simvastatin (Zocor), and many others.

Medications that decrease stomach acid (H2-Blockers). Some medications that decrease stomach acid might interact with the alcohol in wine. Drinking wine with some medications that decrease stomach acid might increase how much alcohol the body absorbs, and increase the risk of side effects of alcohol. Some medications that decrease stomach acid and might interact with alcohol include cimetidine (Tagamet), ranitidine (Zantac), nizatidine (Axid), and famotidine (Pepcid).

Medications for depression (MAOIs). Wine contains a chemical called tyramine. Large amounts of tyramine can cause high blood pressure. But the body naturally breaks down tyramine to get rid of it. This usually prevents the tyramine from causing high blood pressure. Some medications used for depression stop the body from breaking down tyramine. This can cause there to be too much tyramine and lead to dangerously high blood pressure. Some of these medications used for depression include phenelzine (Nardil), tranylcypromine (Parnate), and others.

Medications for pain (Narcotic drugs). The body breaks down some medications for pain to get rid of them. The alcohol in wine might decrease how quickly the body gets rid of some medications for pain. Taking some medications for pain along with wine might increase the effects and side effects of some medications for pain. Some medications for pain include meperidine (Demerol), hydrocodone, morphine, OxyContin, and many others.

Metformin (Glucophage). Metformin (Glucophage) is broken down by the body in the liver. The alcohol in wine is also broken down in the body by the liver. Drinking wine and taking metformin (Glucophage) might cause serious side effects.

Metronidazole (Flagyl). The alcohol in wine can interact with metronidazole (Flagyl). This can lead to upset stomach, vomiting, sweating, headache, and an increased heartbeat. Do not drink wine while taking metronidazole (Flagyl).

NSAIDs (Nonsteroidal anti-inflammatory drugs). NSAIDs are anti-inflammatory medications used for decreasing pain and swelling. NSAIDs can sometimes damage the stomach and intestines and cause ulcers and bleeding. The alcohol in wine can also damage the stomach and intestines. Taking NSAIDs along with wine might increase the chance of ulcers and bleeding in the stomach and intestines. Avoid taking wine and NSAIDs together. Some NSAIDs include ibuprofen (Advil, Motrin, Nuprin, others), indomethacin (Indocin), naproxen (Aleve, Anaprox, Naprelan, Naprosyn), piroxicam (Feldene), aspirin, and others.

Phenytoin (Dilantin). The body breaks down phenytoin (Dilantin) to get rid of it. The alcohol in wine might increase how quickly the body breaks down phenytoin (Dilantin). Drinking wine and taking phenytoin (Dilantin) might decrease the effectiveness of phenytoin (Dilantin) and increase the possibility of seizures.

Sedative medications (Barbiturates). The alcohol in wine might cause sleepiness and drowsiness. Medications that cause sleepiness and drowsiness are called sedative medications. Taking wine along with sedative medications might cause too much sleepiness. Do not drink wine if you are taking sedative medications.

Sedative medications (Benzodiazepines). The alcohol in wine might cause sleepiness and drowsiness. Medications that cause sleepiness and drowsiness are called sedative medications. Taking wine along with sedative medications might cause too much sleepiness. Do not drink wine if you are taking sedative medications. Some of these sedative medications include clonazepam (Klonopin), diazepam (Valium), lorazepam (Ativan), and others.

Sedative medications (CNS depressants). The alcohol in wine might cause sleepiness and drowsiness. Medications that cause sleepiness and drowsiness are called sedative medications. Drinking wine and taking sedative medications might cause too much sleepiness and other serious side effects. Some sedative medications include clonazepam (Klonopin), lorazepam (Ativan), phenobarbital (Donnatal), zolpidem (Ambien), and others.

Tolbutamide (Orinase). The body breaks down the alcohol in wine to get rid of it. Tolbutamide (Orinase) can decrease how quickly the body breaks down alcohol. Drinking wine and taking tolbutamide (Orinase) can cause pounding headache, vomiting, flushing, and other unpleasant reactions. Don't drink wine if you are taking tolbutamide (Orinase).

Warfarin (Coumadin). Warfarin (Coumadin) is used to slow blood clotting. The alcohol in wine can interact with warfarin (Coumadin). Drinking large amounts of alcohol can change the effectiveness of warfarin (Coumadin). Be sure to have your blood checked regularly. The dose of your warfarin (Coumadin) might need to be changed.

WINTER CHERRY

What other names is the product known by?
Cape Gooseberry, Chinese Lantern, Coqueret, Japanese Lantern, Physalis alkekengi, Strawberry Tomato.

What is it?
Winter Cherry is an herb. The ripened fruit is used to make medicine.

Is it Effective?
The effectiveness ratings for **WINTER CHERRY** are as follows:
Insufficient Evidence to Rate Effectiveness for... Arthritis, gout, and other conditions.

How does it work?
There isn't enough information available to know how winter cherry works.

Are there safety concerns?
There isn't enough information available to know if winter cherry is safe.

Do not use winter cherry if: You are pregnant or breast-feeding.

Are there any interactions with medications?
It is not known if winter cherry interacts with any medicines.
Before taking winter cherry, talk with your healthcare professional if you take any medications.

Medical professionals should consult the Professional Version at www.NaturalDatabase.com.

Medical professionals should consult the Professional Version at www.NaturalDatabase.com.

WINTER SAVORY

What other names is the product known by?
Calamintha Montana, Mountain Savory Oil, Satureja montana, Satureja obovata, Savory.

What is it?
Winter savory is an herb. The leaves and stems are used to make medicine.

Is it Effective?
The effectiveness ratings for **WINTER SAVORY** are as follows:
Insufficient Evidence to Rate Effectiveness for... Indigestion, cramps, diarrhea, nausea, gas (flatulence), sore throat, cough, and other conditions.

How does it work?
Winter savory might work by increasing the production of urine (diuretic) and by opening (dilating) blood vessels.

Are there safety concerns?
Winter savory is safe in the amounts used in foods, but there isn't enough information to know if it is safe for use as a medicine.

Do not use winter savory if: You are pregnant or breast-feeding.

Are there any interactions with medications?
It is not known if winter savory interacts with any medicines.
Before taking winter savory, talk with your healthcare professional if you take any medications.

WINTER'S BARK

What other names is the product known by?
Drimys winteri, Pepper Bark, Wintera, Wintera Aromatica, Winter's Cinnamon.

What is it?
Winter's bark is the bark of a tree. The powdered bark is used to make medicine.

Is it Effective?
The effectiveness ratings for **WINTER'S BARK** are as follows:
Insufficient Evidence to Rate Effectiveness for... Gas (flatulence), colic, stomachache, toothaches, skin irritation, and other conditions.

How does it work?
There isn't enough information available to know how winter's bark works.

Are there safety concerns?
There isn't enough information available to know if winter's bark is safe.

Do not use winter's bark if: You are pregnant or breast-feeding.

Are there any interactions with medications?
It is not known if winter's bark interacts with any medicines.
Before taking winter's bark, talk with your healthcare professional if you take any medications.

WINTERGREEN

What other names is the product known by?
Boxberry, Canada Tea, Checkerberry, Deerberry, Gaultheria Oil, Gaultheria procumbens, Ground Berry, Hilberry, Mountain Tea, Oil of wintergreen, Partridge Berry, Spiceberry, Teaberry, Wax Cluster, Wintergreen leaf, Wintergreen oil.

What is it?
Wintergreen is an herb. The leaves and oil are used to make medicine.

Natural Medicines Comprehensive Database Consumer Version (209) 472-2244

Is it Effective?
The effectiveness ratings for **WINTERGREEN** are as follows:
Insufficient Evidence to Rate Effectiveness for... Headache, minor aches and pains, stomachache, gas (flatulence), fever, kidney problems, asthma, nerve pain, gout, arthritis, menstrual period pains, arthritis-like pain (rheumatism), and other conditions.

How does it work?
Wintergreen leaf contains an aspirin-like chemical that might reduce pain, swelling, and fever.

Are there safety concerns?
Wintergreen is safe in the amounts found in foods, and seems safe for most adults when used as a medicine. The oil is unsafe to take by mouth. Ingesting wintergreen oil or large amounts of wintergreen leaf can cause ringing in the ears, nausea, vomiting, diarrhea, headache, stomach pain, and confusion.

When applied directly to the skin wintergreen oil can cause skin irritation.

Wintergreen leaf and oil can be poisonous for children.

Do not use wintergreen leaf if: You are pregnant or breast-feeding. • You are allergic to aspirin or salicylates. • You have a stomach or intestinal condition.

Are there any interactions with medications?
Aspirin. Wintergreen oil contains a chemical similar to aspirin. Using large amounts of wintergreen oil on your skin and taking aspirin at the same time might increase the risk of side effects. Do not use large amounts of wintergreen oil on your skin and take aspirin at the same time.
Warfarin (Coumadin). Warfarin (Coumadin) is used to slow blood clotting. Wintergreen oil can also slow blood clotting. Taking wintergreen oil along with warfarin (Coumadin) can increase the chances of bruising and bleeding. Be sure to have your blood checked regularly. The dose of your warfarin (Coumadin) might need to be changed.

WITCH HAZEL

What other names is the product known by?
Hamamelis, , Hamamelis virginiana, Hazel, Snapping Tobacco Wood, Spotted Elder, Winter Bloom.

What is it?
Witch hazel is a plant. The leaf, bark, and twigs are used to make medicine.

Is it Effective?
The effectiveness ratings for **WITCH HAZEL** are as follows:
Possibly Effective for... Stopping minor bleeding • Hemorrhoids • Reducing skin irritation.
Insufficient Evidence to Rate Effectiveness for... Diarrhea, vomiting blood, coughing up blood, tuberculosis, colds, fevers, eye inflammation, bruises, varicose veins, and other conditions.

How does it work?
Witch hazel contains chemicals called tannins. When applied directly to the skin, witch hazel might help reduce swelling, help repair broken skin, and fight bacteria.

Are there safety concerns?
Witch hazel is safe for most adults when applied directly to the skin. In some people, it might cause minor skin irritation.

It also seems to be safe for most adults when small doses are taken by mouth. In some people, witch hazel might cause stomach upset when taken by mouth. Large doses might cause liver problems.

Do not take witch hazel by mouth if: You are pregnant or breast-feeding.

Are there any interactions with medications?
It is not known if witch hazel interacts with any medicines.
Before taking witch hazel, talk with your healthcare professional if you take any medications.

Medical professionals should consult the Professional Version at www.NaturalDatabase.com.

CONSUMER VERSION

WOOD ANEMONE

What other names is the product known by?
Anemone nemorosa, Crowfoot, Smell Fox, Wind Flower.

What is it?
Wood anemone is an herb. The above ground parts are used to make medicine.

Is it Effective?
The effectiveness ratings for **WOOD ANEMONE** are as follows:
Insufficient Evidence to Rate Effectiveness for... Stomach pains, delayed menstruation (periods), gout, whooping cough, or asthma.

How does it work?
There isn't enough information to know how wood anemone might work.

Are there safety concerns?
The fresh plant of wood anemone is UNSAFE. There isn't enough information to know if the dried plant is safe.

Wood anemone can cause severe stomach and intestine irritation, diarrhea, and urinary problems. Avoid skin contact with wood anemone because it can cause slow-healing blisters and burns after skin contact.

Do not use wood anemone if : You are pregnant or breast-feeding.

Are there any interactions with medications?
It is not known if wood anemone interacts with any medicines.
Before taking wood anemone, talk with your healthcare professional if you take any medications.

WOOD SAGE

What other names is the product known by?
Ambroise, Garlic Sage, Hind Heal, Large-Leaved Germander, Teucrium scorodonia.

What is it?
Wood sage is an herb. The above ground parts are used to make medicine.

Is it Effective?
The effectiveness ratings for **WOOD SAGE** are as follows:
Insufficient Evidence to Rate Effectiveness for... Stomach and intestine problems, tuberculosis, airway swelling, bronchitis, throat spasms, high blood pressure (hypertension), wound healing, or liver problems.

How does it work?
Wood sage contains chemicals that might decrease spasms and loosen mucus in the chest.

Are there safety concerns?
There isn't enough information to know if wood sage is safe or what the potential side effects might be.

Do not use wood sage if: You are pregnant or breast-feeding.

Are there any interactions with medications?
It is not known if wood sage interacts with any medicines.
Before taking wood sage, talk with your healthcare professional if you take any medications.

WOOD SORREL

What other names is the product known by?
Cuckoo Bread, Cuckowes Meat, Fairy Bells, Green Sauce, Hallelujah, Mountain Sorrel, Oxalis acetosella, Shamrock, Sour Trefoil, Stickwort, Stubwort, Surelle, Three-Leaved Grass, White Sorrel, Wood Sour.

What is it?
Wood sorrel is a plant. The whole flowering plant is used to make medicine.

 Natural Medicines Comprehensive Database Consumer Version (209) 472-2244

Is it Effective?
The effectiveness ratings for **WOOD SORREL** are as follows:
Insufficient Evidence to Rate Effectiveness for... Liver problems, digestion problems, wound healing, scurvy, and gum swelling.

How does it work?
There isn't enough information to know how wood sorrel works.

Are there safety concerns?
Wood sorrel is UNSAFE, especially when used in children or when used in higher doses. Wood sorrel can cause diarrhea, nausea, increased urination, skin reactions, stomach and intestine irritation, swelling of the mouth, tongue and throat, with difficulty in speaking and suffocation, eye damage, and kidney damage. Taking wood sorrel by mouth can lead to crystals forming in the blood and depositing in the kidneys, blood vessels, heart, lungs, and liver.

Wood sorrel can decrease the absorption of the minerals calcium, iron, and zinc.

Do not give wood sorrel to children.

Do not use wood sorrel if: You are pregnant or breast-feeding. • You have had kidney stones. • You have ulcers. • You have blood clotting problems.

Are there any interactions with medications?
It is not known if wood sorrel interacts with any medicines.
Before taking wood sorrel, talk with your healthcare professional if you take any medications.

WOODBINE

What other names is the product known by?
Clematis, Clematis virginiana, Devil's-Darning-Needle, Old Man's Beard, Traveler's Joy, Vine Bower, and Virgin's Bower.

What is it?
Woodbine is an herb. The leaves and flowers are used to make medicine. Avoid confusion with American ivy, gelsemium, or honeysuckle, which are also known as woodbine.

Is it Effective?
The effectiveness ratings for **WOODBINE** are as follows:
Insufficient Evidence to Rate Effectiveness for... Skin sores, cuts, itching, sexually-transmitted diseases, cancer, tumors, fever, kidney problems, ulcers, diuretic (water pill), constipation, or tuberculosis.

How does it work?
There isn't enough information to know how woodbine works.

Are there safety concerns?
Woodbine is UNSAFE when taken by mouth or when put on the skin. The juice of the leaf is very irritating to the mouth, stomach, and intestines.
Do not take woodbine if: You are pregnant or breast-feeding.

Are there any interactions with medications?
It is not known if woodbine interacts with any medicines.
Before taking woodbine, talk with your healthcare professional if you take any medications.

WORMSEED

What other names is the product known by?
Artemisia cina, Levant, Santonica, Sea Wormwood.

What is it?
Wormseed is an herb. The flowers are used to make medicine. Avoid confusing wormseed with chenopodium oil (or wormseed oil), wormwood oil, or wormwood. Avoid confusing wormseed, also referred to as levant, with levant berry.

Natural Medicines Comprehensive Database Consumer Version

CONSUMER VERSION

Medical professionals should consult the Professional Version at www.NaturalDatabase.com.

Medical professionals should consult the
Professional Version at www.NaturalDatabase.com.

Is it Effective?

The effectiveness ratings for **WORMSEED** are as follows:
Insufficient Evidence to Rate Effectiveness for... Treating worm infections.

How does it work?

Wormseed contains a chemical which may kill worms which infest the stomach and intestines.

Are there safety concerns?

Wormseed is UNSAFE when taken by mouth.

Side effects can occur even at low doses, with symptoms such as diarrhea, vision problems, kidney problems, muscle twitching, seizures, and death. Allergic reactions have occurred in people who are allergic to other plants and herbs in the Asteraceae/Compositae family. Members of this family include daisies, ragweed, chrysanthemums, marigolds, and many other herbs.

Do not use wormseed if: You are pregnant or breast-feeding. • You are sensitive to plants such as ragweed, chrysanthemums, marigolds, and daisies.

Are there any interactions with medications?

It is not known if wormseed interacts with any medicines.
Before taking wormseed, talk with your healthcare professional if you take any medications.

WORMWOOD

What other names is the product known by?

Absinth, Absinthe, Absinthii Herba, Absinthites, Absinthium, Ajenjo, Armoise, Artesian Absinthium, Artemisia absinthium, Common Wormwood, Green Ginger, Herba Artemisae, Herbe d'Absinthe, Indhana, Lapsent, Qing Hao, Vilayati Afsanteen, Wermut, Wermutkraut, Wurmkraut.

What is it?

Wormwood is an herb. The above ground plant parts and oil are used for medicine.

Is it Effective?

The effectiveness ratings for **WORMWOOD** are as follows:
Insufficient Evidence to Rate Effectiveness for... Loss of appetite, indigestion, gallbladder disorders, low acid in the stomach, wounds, insect bites, worm infestations, low sexual desire, spasms, and increasing sweating.

How does it work?

Wormwood oil contains the chemical thujone, which excites the central nervous system. However, it can also cause seizures and other adverse effects.

Are there safety concerns?

Wormwood is safe when taken in the amounts commonly found in food and beverages including bitters and vermouth, which are thujone-free. Wormwood containing thujone is UNSAFE when it is taken in large amounts or over a long period of time.

Wormwood can cause restlessness, difficulty sleeping, nightmares, vomiting, stomach cramps, dizziness, tremors, urine retention, kidney damage, and seizures. Other side effects include thirst, restlessness, numbness of arms and legs, paralysis, and death.

Do not use wormwood if: You are pregnant or breast-feeding. • You are allergic to other plants in the Asteraceae/Compositae family, such as daisies, chrysanthemums, or ragweed. • You have a blood disorder known as porphyria. • You have a seizure disorder or epilepsy.

Are there any interactions with medications?

Medications used to prevent seizures (Anticonvulsants). Medications used to prevent seizures affect chemicals in the brain. Wormwood may also affect chemicals in the brain. By affecting chemicals in the brain, wormwood may decrease the effectiveness of medications used to prevent seizures. Some medications used to prevent seizures include phenobarbital, primidone (Mysoline), valproic acid (Depakene), gabapentin (Neurontin), carbamazepine (Tegretol), phenytoin (Dilantin), and others.

XANTHAN GUM

What other names is the product known by?
Corn Sugar Gum, Xanthomonas campestris.

What is it?
Xanthan gum is a sugar-like compound made by mixing aged (fermented) sugars with a certain kind of bacteria. It is used to make medicine.

Is it Effective?
The effectiveness ratings for **XANTHAN GUM** are as follows:
Possibly Effective for... Use as a bulk-forming laxative to treat constipation • Lowering blood sugar in people with diabetes • Lowering cholesterol levels in people with diabetes • Use as a saliva substitute for dry mouth.

How does it work?
Xanthan gum swells in the intestine, which stimulates the digestive tract to push stool through. It also might slow the absorption of sugar from the digestive tract and work like saliva to lubricate and wet the mouth in people who don't produce enough saliva.

Are there safety concerns?
Xanthan gum is safe when up to 15 grams per day are taken. It can cause some side effects such as intestinal gas (flatulence) and bloating.

People who are exposed to xanthan gum powder might experience flu-like symptoms, nose and throat irritation, and lung problems.

Do not take xanthan gum if: You are pregnant or breast-feeding. • You have appendicitis.
• You have a narrowing of your intestines (intestinal stenosis). • You have a blockage in your bowel.

Are there any interactions with medications?
Medications for diabetes (Antidiabetes drugs). Xanthan gum might decrease blood sugar by decreasing the absorption of sugars from food. Diabetes medications are also used to lower blood sugar. Taking xanthan gum with diabetes medications might cause your blood sugar to be too low. Monitor your blood sugar closely. The dose of your diabetes medication might need to be changed. Some medications used for diabetes include glimepiride (Amaryl), glyburide (DiaBeta, Glynase PresTab, Micronase), insulin, pioglitazone (Actos), rosiglitazone (Avandia), chlorpropamide (Diabinese), glipizide (Glucotrol), tolbutamide (Orinase), and others.

XANTHOPARMELIA

What other names is the product known by?
X. scarbosa, Xanthoparmelia scarbosa.

What is it?
Xanthoparmelia is a lichen.

Is it Effective?
The effectiveness ratings for **XANTHOPARMELIA** are as follows:
Insufficient Evidence to Rate Effectiveness for... Sexual dysfunction, erectile dysfunction, increasing sexual desire, and cancer.

How does it work?
There is not enough information available to know how xanthoparmelia might work. It is thought to contain toxic chemicals.

Are there safety concerns?
Xanthoparmelia seems to be unsafe because it contains toxic chemicals. Do not take xanthoparmelia.

Are there any interactions with medications?
It is not known if xanthoparmelia interacts with any medicines.
Before taking xanthoparmelia, talk to your healthcare professional if you take any medications.

XYLITOL

What other names is the product known by?
Birch Sugar, E967, Xylit, Meso-Xylitol, Xylite, and xylo-pentane-1,2,3,4,5-pentol.

What is it?
Xylitol is a naturally occurring alcohol found in most plant material, including many fruits and vegetables. It is extracted from birch wood to make medicine.

Is it Effective?
The effectiveness ratings for **XYLITOL** are as follows:
Likely Effective for... Preventing dental caries (tooth decay).
Possibly Effective for... Reducing episodes of ear infections (otitis media) in preschool children.
Insufficient Evidence to Rate Effectiveness for... Prevention of dry mouth or as a sugar substitute for people with diabetes.

How does it work?
Xylitol tastes sweet but, unlike sugar, it is not converted in the mouth to acids that cause tooth decay. It reduces levels of decay-causing bacteria in saliva and also acts against some bacteria that cause ear infections.

Are there safety concerns?
Xylitol is safe in the amounts found in foods. It seems safe as a medicine for most adults in amounts up to about 50 grams per day. Avoid higher doses. There is some concern that extremely high doses for long periods of time (more than three years) can cause tumors. Xylitol can cause diarrhea and intestinal gas. It is probably safe for children as a medicine in amounts up to 20 grams per day.

Do not use xylitol if: You are pregnant or breast-feeding.

Are there any interactions with medications?
It is not known if xylitol interacts with any medicines.
Before taking xylitol, talk with your healthcare professional if you take any medications.

YARROW

What other names is the product known by?
Achillea, Achillea borealis, Achillea lanulosa, Achillea magna, Achillea millefolium, Band Man's Plaything, Bauchweh, Birangasifa, Birangasipha, Biranjasipha, Bloodwort, Carpenter's Weed, Civan Percemi, Common Yarrow, Devil's Nettle, Devil's Plaything, Erba Da Cartentieri, Erba Da Falegname, Gandana, Gemeine Schafgarbe, Green Arrow, Herbe Aux Charpentiers, Katzenkrat, Milefolio, Millefeuille, Millefolii Flos, Millefolii Herba, Millegoglie, Noble Yarrow, Nosebleed, Old Man's Pepper, Roga Mari, Sanguinary, Soldier's Wound Wort, Staunchweed, Tausendaugbram, Thousand-Leaf, Wound Wort.

What is it?
Yarrow is an herb. The above ground parts are used to make medicine.

Is it Effective?
The effectiveness ratings for **YARROW** are as follows:
Insufficient Evidence to Rate Effectiveness for... Fever, common cold, hayfever, diarrhea, stomach discomfort, bloating, gas, toothache, and other conditions.

How does it work?
Yarrow contains many chemicals that might affect blood pressure and possibly have anti-inflammatory effects.

Are there safety concerns?
Yarrow seems to be safe for most adults. In some people, yarrow might cause drowsiness and increase urination when taken by mouth. When it comes in contact with the skin, yarrow might cause skin irritation.

Do not take yarrow if: You are pregnant or breast-feeding. • You have an allergy to ragweed, chrysanthemums, marigolds, daisies, and many others.

Are there any interactions with medications?

Antacids. Antacids are used to decrease stomach acid. Yarrow may increase stomach acid. By increasing stomach acid, yarrow might decrease the effectiveness of antacids. Some antacids include calcium carbonate (Tums, others), dihydroxyaluminum sodium carbonate (Rolaids, others), magaldrate (Riopan), magnesium sulfate (Bilagog), aluminum hydroxide (Amphojel), and others.

Medications that slow blood clotting (Anticoagulant / Antiplatelet drugs). Large amounts of yarrow might slow blood clotting. Taking yarrow along with medications that also slow clotting might increase the chances of bruising and bleeding. Some medications that slow blood clotting include aspirin, clopidogrel (Plavix), diclofenac (Voltaren, Cataflam, others), ibuprofen (Advil, Motrin, others), naproxen (Anaprox, Naprosyn, others), dalteparin (Fragmin), enoxaparin (Lovenox), heparin, warfarin (Coumadin), and others.

Medications that decrease stomach acid (H2-Blockers). Yarrow might increase stomach acid. By increasing stomach acid, yarrow might decrease the effectiveness of some medications that decrease stomach acid, called H2-Blockers. Some medications that decrease stomach acid include cimetidine (Tagamet), ranitidine (Zantac), nizatidine (Axid), and famotidine (Pepcid).

Medications that decrease stomach acid (Proton pump inhibitors). Yarrow might increase stomach acid. By increasing stomach acid, yarrow might decrease the effectiveness of medications that are used to decrease stomach acid, called proton pump inhibitors. Some medications that decrease stomach acid include omeprazole (Prilosec), lansoprazole (Prevacid), rabeprazole (Aciphex), pantoprazole (Protonix), and esomeprazole (Nexium).

Sedative medications (Barbiturates). Yarrow might cause sleepiness and drowsiness. Medications that cause sleepiness are called sedatives. Taking yarrow along with sedative medications might cause too much sleepiness.

YELLOW DOCK

What other names is the product known by?

Broad-Leaved Dock, Curled Dock, Curly Dock, Field Sorrel, Narrow Dock, Rumex Crispus, Rumex Obstusifolius, Sheep Sorrel, Sour Dock.

What is it?

Yellow dock is an herb. The leaf stalks are used in salads. The root is also used as medicine.

Is it Effective?

The effectiveness ratings for **YELLOW DOCK** are as follows:
Insufficient Evidence to Rate Effectiveness for... Constipation, inflammation of nasal passages and the respiratory tract, bacterial infections, jaundice, scurvy, and other conditions.

How does it work?

Yellow dock contains chemicals called anthraquinones, which work as stimulant laxatives.

Are there safety concerns?

Yellow dock seems to be safe for most adults. Taking too much yellow dock can cause diarrhea, nausea, stomach cramps, excessive urination, skin irritation, and low blood levels of potassium and calcium. People who are allergic to ragweed may also be allergic to yellow dock.

Don't use raw or uncooked yellow dock. It can cause serious side effects including vomiting, heart problems, breathing difficulty, and even death. Also, handling raw yellow dock can cause skin irritation in some people.

Do not take yellow dock if: You are pregnant or breast-feeding. • You have had kidney stones or other kidney disease. • You have a blockage in your digestive tract. • You have stomach or intestinal ulcers. • You have a bleeding disorder.

Are there any interactions with medications?

Digoxin (Lanoxin). Yellow dock is a type of laxative called a stimulant laxative. Stimulant laxatives can decrease potassium levels in the body. Low potassium levels can increase the risk of side effects of digoxin (Lanoxin).

Water pills (Diuretic drugs). Yellow dock is a laxative. Some laxatives can decrease potassium in the body. "Water pills" can also decrease potassium in the body. Taking yellow dock along with "water pills" might decrease potassium in the body too much. Some "water pills" that can decrease potassium include chlorothiazide (Diuril), chlorthalidone (Thalitone), furosemide (Lasix), hydrochlorothiazide (HCTZ, Hydrodiuril, Microzide), and others.

YELLOW LUPIN

What other names is the product known by?
Hasenklee, Lupin Jaune, Lupinus luteus.

What is it?
Yellow lupin is an herb. The above ground parts and seeds are used to make medicine.

Is it Effective?
The effectiveness ratings for **YELLOW LUPIN** are as follows:
Insufficient Evidence to Rate Effectiveness for... Urinary problems, worm infections, use as a diuretic ("water pill") when taken by mouth, and usage on ulcers when put on the skin.

How does it work?
There isn't enough information to know how yellow lupin might work.

Are there safety concerns?
Yellow lupin is UNSAFE when taken by mouth.

Side effects of yellow lupin include vomiting, excessive saliva, swallowing problems, heart problems, paralysis, and breathing problems, which can cause death.

There isn't enough information to know whether yellow lupin is safe when put on the skin.

Do not use yellow lupin if: You are pregnant or breast-feeding.

Are there any interactions with medications?
It is not known if yellow lupin interacts with any medicines.
Before taking yellow lupin, talk with your healthcare professional if you take any medications.

YELLOW TOADFLAX

What other names is the product known by?
Brideweed, Butter and Eggs, Buttered Hayhocks, Calves' Snout, Churnstaff, Devil's Head, Devil's Ribbon, Doggies, Dragon-Bushes, Eggs and Bacon, Eggs and Collops, Flaxweed, Fluelli, Gallwort, Larkspur Lion's Mouth, Linaria vulgaris, Monkey Flower, Pattens and Clogs, Pedlar's Basket, Pennywort, Rabbits, Ramsted, Toadpipe, Wild Snapdragon, Yellow Rod.

What is it?
Yellow toadflax is an herb. The whole plant is used to make medicine.

Is it Effective?
The effectiveness ratings for **YELLOW TOADFLAX** are as follows:
Insufficient Evidence to Rate Effectiveness for... Digestive problems, urinary problems, reducing swelling, use as a diuretic ("water pill"), hemorrhoids, wounds, skin rashes, or other conditions.

How does it work?
There isn't enough information to know how yellow toadflax might work.

Are there safety concerns?
There isn't enough information to know whether yellow toadflax is safe or what the potential side effects might be.

Do not use yellow toadflax if: You are pregnant or breast-feeding.

Are there any interactions with medications?
It is not known if yellow toadflax interacts with any medicines.
Before taking yellow toadflax, talk with your healthcare professional if you take any medications.

YERBA MANSA

What other names is the product known by?
Anemopsis californica, Lizard's Tail, Swamp Root, Yerba Manza.

What is it?
Yerba mansa is an herb. The root and rhizome (underground stem) are used to make medicine.

Is it Effective?
The effectiveness ratings for **YERBA MANSA** are as follows:
Insufficient Evidence to Rate Effectiveness for... Cancer, catarrh, colds, cough, stomach and intestine problems, throat problems, skin problems, pain, constipation, tuberculosis, sexually transmitted diseases, and others.

How does it work?
There isn't enough information to know how yerba mansa might work.

Are there safety concerns?
There isn't enough information to know if yerba mansa is safe or what the potential side effects might be.

Do not use yerba mansa if: You are pregnant or breast-feeding. • You have urinary problems.

Are there any interactions with medications?
Sedative medications (CNS depressants). Yerba mansa might cause sleepiness and drowsiness. Medications that cause sleepiness are called sedatives. Taking yerba mansa along with sedative medications might cause too much sleepiness. Some sedative medications include clonazepam (Klonopin), lorazepam (Ativan), phenobarbital (Donnatal), zolpidem (Ambien), and others.

YERBA SANTA

What other names is the product known by?
Bear's Weed, Consumptive's Weed, Eriodictyon, Eriodictyon californicum, Eriodictyon glutinosum, Gum Bush, Gum Plant, Hierba Santa, Holy Herb, Holy Weed, Mountain Balm, Sacred Herb, Tarweed, Wigandia californicum.

What is it?
Yerba santa is an herb. The leaf is used to make medicine.

Is it Effective?
The effectiveness ratings for **YERBA SANTA** are as follows:
Insufficient Evidence to Rate Effectiveness for... Coughs, colds, reducing fever, tuberculosis, asthma, chronic bronchitis, loosening mucus, spasms, or use as a tonic when taken by mouth. Bruises, sprains, wounds, insect bites, or joint pain when put on the skin.

How does it work?
Yerba santa contains chemicals that are thought to loosen mucus in the chest and may increase urination.

Are there safety concerns?
Yerba santa seems to be safe when taken by mouth for most adults, but the potential side effects are not known.

There isn't enough information to know whether yerba santa is safe when put on the skin.

Do not use yerba santa if: You are pregnant or breast-feeding.

Are there any interactions with medications?
It is not known if yerba santa interacts with any medicines.
Before taking yerba santa, talk with your healthcare professional if you take any medications.

Medical professionals should consult the
Professional Version at www.NaturalDatabase.com.

YEW

What other names is the product known by?
Chinwood, Common Yew, English Yew, Pacific Yew, Taxus bacatta, Taxus brevifolia, Western Yew.

What is it?
Yew is a tree. People use the bark, branch tips, and needles of yew to make medicine. Yew bark is the source of the drug paclitaxel (Taxol), which is a prescription drug for the treatment of breast and ovarian cancer.

Is it Effective?
The effectiveness ratings for **YEW** are as follows:
Insufficient Evidence to Rate Effectiveness for... Menstrual disorders, abortion, intestinal worms, swollen tonsils, seizures, kidney and liver disorders, cancer, and many other conditions.

How does it work?
Yew might affect various parts of the body including nerves, the heart, and muscles.

Are there safety concerns?
Yew is unsafe for people. All parts of the yew plant are considered poisonous. Yew can cause severe stomach problems and can cause the heart rate to slow down dangerously. Signs of poisoning might include nausea, dry mouth, vomiting, stomach pain, dizziness, weakness, nervousness, heart problems, and many others. Death has occurred after taking 50-100 grams of yew needles. Swallowing one berry can be fatal in a child.

Are there any interactions with medications?
It is not known if yew interacts with any medicines.
Before taking yew, talk with your healthcare professional if you take any medications.

YIN CHEN

What other names is the product known by?
Armoise Capillaire, Artemisia capillaris, Artemisia scoparia, Capillary Wormwood, Chiu, In Chen, Inchin-Ko-To, Inchinko, Kawara-Yomogi, Kyunchinho, Rumput Roman, Shih Yin Ch'en, Yin Ch'en, Yin Ch'en Hao, Yin Chen Hao.

What is it?
Yin chen is an herb. The above ground parts are used to make medicine.

Is it Effective?
The effectiveness ratings for **YIN CHEN** are as follows:
Insufficient Evidence to Rate Effectiveness for... Hepatitis, jaundice, gallstones, high cholesterol levels, increasing bile flow from the gallbladder, hepatitis C infections, fever and chills, bitter taste in the mouth, chest tightness, flank pain, dizziness, nausea, loss of appetite, headache, constipation, painful urination, itching, tumors, joint pain, painful periods, malaria, or spasms.

How does it work?
Yin chen is thought to contain chemicals which stimulate bile flow which can help to treat gallstones. The oils in yin chen might also reduce fever, decreases swelling, increase urination, and kill fungus and bacteria.

Are there safety concerns?
Yin chen seems safe for most adults when taken by mouth.

Yin chen can cause nausea, bloating, dizziness, and heart problems. Allergic reactions have occurred in people who are allergic to other plants and herbs in the Asteraceae/Compositae family. Members of this family include daisies, ragweed, chrysanthemums, marigolds, and many other herbs.

Don't attempt to treat liver or gallstone problems without medical advice.

Don't give yin chen to children under 12 years of age.

Do not use yin chen if: You are pregnant or breast-feeding. • You are allergic to plants such as ragweed, chrysanthemums, marigolds, or daisies.

Are there any interactions with medications?

It is not known if yin chen interacts with any medicines.

Before taking yin chen, talk with your healthcare professional if you take any medications.

YLANG YLANG OIL

What other names is the product known by?

Cananga odorata genuina, Canangium odoratum genuina, Ylang Ylang.

What is it?

Ylang ylang oil is made from the flowers of the herb Cangana odorata genuina.

Is it Effective?

The effectiveness ratings for **YLANG YLANG OIL** are as follows:

Insufficient Evidence to Rate Effectiveness for... Head lice, sedative, preventing skin infections, hypotensive, aphrodisiac, and other conditions.

How does it work?

There isn't enough information to know how ylang ylang oil might work.

Are there safety concerns?

Ylang ylang oil seems safe in the amounts found in foods. It also appears to be safe when applied to the scalp in combination with other herbs. There isn't enough information to know if ylang ylang oil taken by mouth is safe or what the potential side effects might be if it is used in amounts higher than what is typically found in foods.

Do not use ylang ylang oil if: You are pregnant or breast-feeding.

Are there any interactions with medications?

It is not known if ylang ylang oil interacts with any medicines.

Before taking ylang ylang oil, talk with your healthcare professional if you take any medications.

YOGURT

What other names is the product known by?

Acidophilus Milk, Bulgarian Yogurt, Live Culture Yogurt, Probiotics, Yoghurt, Yogourt.

What is it?

Yogurt is milk that has been fermented with various bacteria. People use it as medicine.

Is it Effective?

The effectiveness ratings for **YOGURT** are as follows:

Possibly Effective for... Diarrhea in children • Diarrhea associated with antibiotics • Preventing vaginal yeast infections • Lactose intolerance, as an alternative to milk • Treating a bacterial infection that can cause stomach ulcers (Helicobacter pylori), when used in combination with other medicines • High cholesterol levels.

Possibly Ineffective for... Asthma • Diarrhea in malnourished infants and children.

Insufficient Evidence to Rate Effectiveness for... Bacterial vaginosis, preventing urinary tract infections, preventing colorectal cancer, treating peptic ulcers, preventing sunburns, and other conditions.

How does it work?

Yogurt contains bacteria which may help restore the normal bacteria in the digestive tract and vagina. This might help treat diarrhea and vaginal infections.

Are there safety concerns?

Yogurt is likely safe for most adults when taken by mouth. Yogurt is possibly safe when used in the vagina. There aren't many reported side effects, but there have been cases of people getting sick from yogurt contaminated with disease-causing bacteria. Be careful to choose yogurt that has been prepared and stored properly. There is some concern that people with weakened immune systems, such as people with HIV/AIDS or organ transplant recipients, might have an overgrowth of the live bacteria in yogurt, such as lactobacillus, from eating large amounts of yogurt. Lactobacillus in yogurt has caused disease (rarely) in people with weakened immune systems. To be on the safe side, if you have a weakened immune system, avoid eating large amounts of yogurt that contain live bacteria for prolonged periods of time without advice from your healthcare professional.

Are there any interactions with medications?

Antibiotics (Tetracycline antibiotics). Yogurt contains calcium. The calcium in yogurt can attach to tetracyclines in the stomach. This decreases the amount of tetracyclines that can be absorbed. Taking calcium with tetracyclines might decrease the effectiveness of tetracyclines. To avoid this interaction take yogurt two hours before or four hours after taking tetracyclines. Some tetracyclines include demeclocycline (Declomycin), minocycline (Minocin), and tetracycline (Achromycin).

Ciprofloxacin (Cipro). Ciprofloxacin (Cipro) is an antibiotic. Yogurt might decrease how much ciprofloxacin (Cipro) the body absorbs. Taking yogurt along with ciprofloxacin (Cipro) might decrease the effectiveness of ciprofloxacin (Cipro). To avoid this interaction take yogurt at least one hour after ciprofloxacin (Cipro).

Medications that decrease the immune system (Immunosuppressants). Yogurt contains live bacteria and yeast. The immune system usually controls bacteria and yeast in the body to prevent infections. Medications that decrease the immune system can increase your chances of getting sick from bacteria and yeast. Taking yogurt along with medications that decrease the immune system might increase the chances of getting sick. Some medications that decrease the immune system include azathioprine (Imuran), basiliximab (Simulect), cyclosporine (Neoral, Sandimmune), daclizumab (Zenapax), muromonab-CD3 (OKT3, Orthoclone OKT3), mycophenolate (CellCept), tacrolimus (FK506, Prograf), sirolimus (Rapamune), prednisone (Deltasone, Orasone), corticosteroids (glucocorticoids), and others.

YOHIMBE

What other names is the product known by?

Corynanthe johimbi, Corynanthe yohimbi, Johimbi, Pausinystalia yohimbe, Pausinystalia johimbe, Yohimbehe, Yohimbehe cortex.

What is it?

Yohimbe is the name of an evergreen tree that is found in Zaire, Cameroon, and Gabon. The bark of yohimbe is used to make medicine.

Is it Effective?

The effectiveness ratings for **YOHIMBE** are as follows:
Possibly Effective for... Impotence • Sexual dysfunction caused by selective-serotonin reuptake inhibitors (SSRIs).
Insufficient Evidence to Rate Effectiveness for... Sexual excitement, exhaustion, chest pain, diabetic complications, depression, and other conditions.

How does it work?

Yohimbe contains a chemical called yohimbine which can increase blood flow and nerve impulses to the penis or vagina. It also helps counteract the sexual side effects of certain medications used for depression.

Are there safety concerns?

Yohimbe seems to be safe for most adults when used with the supervision of a healthcare professional. In some people, yohimbe might cause nausea, vomiting, inability to sleep, anxiety, high blood pressure, increased heart rate, dizziness, stomach upset, and more.

The chemical yohimbine is considered unsafe for use without a healthcare professional because side effects might occur with improper use. Some of these serious side effects include severe low blood pressure, heart problems, and other serious conditions including death.

Yohimbe is unsafe for children, because children appear to be much more sensitive to the side effects.

Do not take yohimbe if: You are pregnant or breast-feeding. • You have schizophrenia. • You have prostate problems. • You have post-traumatic stress disorder (PTSD). • You have liver disease. • You have kidney disease. • You have high or low blood pressure. • You have chest pain or heart disease. • You have anxiety. • You have depression. • You have diabetes.

Are there any interactions with medications?

Clonidine (Catapres). Clonidine (Catapres) is used to decrease blood pressure. Yohimbe might increase blood pressure. Taking yohimbe along with clonidine (Catapres) might decrease the effectiveness of clonidine (Catapres).
Guanabenz (Wytensin). Yohimbe contains a chemical called yohimbine. Yohimbine can decrease the effectiveness of guanabenz (Wytensin).
Medications for depression (MAOIs). Yohimbe contains a chemical that affects the body. This chemical is called yohimbine. Yohimbine might affect the body in some of the same ways as some medications for depression called MAOIs. Taking yohimbe along with MAOIs might increase the effects and side effects of yohimbe and MAOIs. Some of these medications used for depression include phenelzine (Nardil), tranylcypromine (Parnate), and others.

Medications for depression (Tricyclic antidepressants). Yohimbe can affect the heart. Some medications used for depression called tricyclic antidepressants can also affect the heart. Taking yohimbe along with these medications used for depression might cause heart problems. Don't take yohimbe if you are taking these medications for depression. Some of these tricyclic antidepressants medications used for depression include amitriptyline (Elavil), imipramine (Tofranil), and others.

Medications for high blood pressure (Antihypertensive drugs). Yohimbe seems to increase blood pressure. Taking yohimbe along with some medications for high blood pressure might decrease the effectiveness of medications for high blood pressure. Some medications for high blood pressure include captopril (Capoten), enalapril (Vasotec), losartan (Cozaar), valsartan (Diovan), diltiazem (Cardizem), amlodipine (Norvasc), hydrochlorothiazide (HydroDiuril), furosemide (Lasix), and many others.

Naloxone (Narcan). Yohimbe contains a chemical that can affect the brain. This chemical is called yohimbine. Naloxone (Narcan) also affects the brain. Taking naloxone (Narcan) along with yohimbine might increase the chance of side effects such as anxiety, nervousness, trembling, and hot flashes.

Phenothiazines. Yohimbe contains a chemical called yohimbine. Some medications called phenothiazines have some similar effects to yohimbine. Taking yohimbe along with phenothiazines might increase the effects and side effects of yohimbine. Some phenothiazines include chlorpromazine (Thorazine), fluphenazine (Prolixin), trifluoperazine (Stelazine), thioridazine (Mellaril), and others.

Stimulant drugs. Stimulant drugs speed up the nervous system. By speeding up the nervous system, stimulant medications can make you feel jittery and speed up your heartbeat. Yohimbe might also speed up the nervous system. Taking yohimbe along with stimulant drugs might cause serious problems including increased heart rate and high blood pressure. Avoid taking stimulant drugs along with yohimbe. Some stimulant drugs include diethylpropion (Tenuate), epinephrine, phentermine (Ionamin), pseudoephedrine (Sudafed), and many others.

YUCCA

What other names is the product known by?
Adam's Needle, Aloe Yucca, Bear Grass, Dagger Plant, Joshua Tree, Mohave Yucca, Our-Lord's-Candle, Soapweed, Spanish Bayonet, Yucca aloifolia, Yucca arborescens, Yucca brevifolia, Yucca filamentosa, Yucca glauca, Yucca mohavensis, Yucca schidigera, Yucca whipplei.

What is it?
Yucca is a tree that is used to make medicine. The cooked root is also used as a food.

Is it Effective?
The effectiveness ratings for **YUCCA** are as follows:
Insufficient Evidence to Rate Effectiveness for... Arthritis, migraines, digestive disorders, diabetes, high blood pressure, high cholesterol, high triglycerides, poor blood circulation, skin problems, and other conditions.

How does it work?
Yucca contains chemicals that might help reduce high blood pressure and high cholesterol. It might also reduce arthritis symptoms such as pain, swelling, and stiffness.

Are there safety concerns?
Yucca seems safe when taken short-term. It can cause side effects such as stomach upset, bitter taste, nausea, and vomiting.

Do not take yucca in medicinal amounts if: You are pregnant or breast-feeding.

Are there any interactions with medications?
It is not known if yucca interacts with any medicines.
Before taking yucca, talk with your healthcare professional if you take any medications.

ZEDOARY

What other names is the product known by?
Cedoaria, Cetoal, Curcuma zedoaria, E-Zhu, Indian Arrowroot, Kua, Sati, Shati, Temu Kuning, Temu Putih, Turmeric, Zedoaire, Zedoária, Zedoarie rhizoma, Zitwer, Zitwerwirtzelstock.

What is it?
Zedoary is a plant. The root-like stem (rhizome) is used to make medicine.

Medical professionals should consult the Professional Version at www.NaturalDatabase.com.

Is it Effective?

The effectiveness ratings for **ZEDOARY** are as follows:

Insufficient Evidence to Rate Effectiveness for... Colic, spasms, improving appetite and digestion, inflammation, nervous diseases, and other uses.

How does it work?

Zedoary might increase bile production and flow to improve digestion.

Are there safety concerns?

Zedoary may be safe for most adults, but the potential side effects are not known.

Do not use zedoary if: You are pregnant or breast-feeding. • You have heavy periods.

Are there any interactions with medications?

It is not known if zedoary interacts with any medicines.

Before taking zedoary, talk with your healthcare professional if you take any medications.

ZINC

What other names is the product known by?

Zinc Acetate, Zinc Acexamate, Zinc Aspartate, Zinc Citrate, Zinc Gluconate, Zinc Methionine, Zinc Monomethionine, Zinc Oxide, Zinc Picolinate, Zinc Pyrithione, Zinc Sulfate, Zinc, Zn, atomic number 30.

What is it?

Zinc is a metal. It is called an "essential trace element" because very small amounts of zinc are necessary for human health.

Is it Effective?

The effectiveness ratings for **ZINC** are as follows:

Effective for... Preventing and treating zinc deficiency.

Likely Effective for... Reducing diarrhea in malnourished children, or in children who have low zinc levels • Wilson's disease, a rare genetic disorder.

Possibly Effective for... Decreasing the length of time the common cold lasts, when taken by mouth as a lozenge. However, using zinc as a pill or a nose spray doesn't seem to help prevent colds. • Promoting weight gain and improving depression in people with eating disorders such as anorexia nervosa • Treating hypogeusia, a rare condition where the sense of taste is abnormal • Acne • Treating an inherited disorder called acrodermatitis enteropathica • Leprosy, when used with other medications • Herpes simplex virus, when zinc preparations made for the skin are applied directly to the mouth or genitals • Treating an eye disease called AMD (age-related macular degeneration) when taken with other medicines • Preventing and treating stomach ulcers • Preventing complications related to sickle cell anemia in people who have low zinc levels • Preventing muscle cramps in people who have low zinc levels • Treating leg wounds in people with low zinc levels • As a mouthwash or toothpaste for preventing tarter and gingivitis • Improving healing of burns • Increasing vitamin A levels in under fed children, or in children with low zinc levels • Attention deficit-hyperactivity disorder (ADHD).

Possibly Ineffective for... Raising iron blood levels in pregnant women, when taken with iron and folic acid supplements • Skin conditions including eczema, psoriasis, or hair-loss • Many kinds of arthritis • Preventing or treating cataracts • Malaria in underfed children • Inflammatory bowel disease • "Ringing in the ears" (tinnitus) • AIDS diarrhea-wasting syndrome • Preventing the flu • Increasing birth weight and gestation time in infants born to HIV-infected women.

Insufficient Evidence to Rate Effectiveness for... Alzheimer's disease, wrinkled skin, Crohn's disease, ulcerative colitis, diabetes, treating the common cold when used as a nose spray, Down syndrome, preventing pneumonia in malnourished children, osteoporosis, recurrent ear infections, male sexual problems, preventing cancer, and other conditions.

How does it work?

Zinc is needed for the proper growth and maintenance of the human body. Zinc is needed for immune function, wound healing, blood clotting, thyroid function, and much more.

Are there safety concerns?

Zinc is safe for most adults when applied to the skin or when taken by mouth in amounts not larger than 40 mg per day for adults age 19 and older. Routine zinc supplementation is not recommended without the advice of a healthcare professional. In some people zinc might cause nausea, vomiting, diarrhea, metallic taste, kidney and stomach damage, and other side effects.

High doses above the recommended amounts might cause fever, coughing, stomach pain, fatigue, and many other problems. Taking more than 100 mg of supplemental zinc daily or taking supplemental zinc for 10 or more years doubles the risk of developing prostate cancer. Taking 450 mg or more of zinc daily can cause problems with blood iron. Single doses of 10-30 g of zinc can be fatal.

Some research suggests that zinc nose spray may be UNSAFE. It may cause loss of ability to smell. Until more is known, avoid using zinc nose spray (Zicam, Cold-Eeze).

Zinc is also safe for most pregnant and breast-feeding women when used in the recommended daily amounts (RDA). Pregnant women age 19 to 50 should not take more than 40 mg of zinc per day, pregnant women age 14 to 18 should not take more than 34 mg per day. Breast-feeding women age 19 to 50 should not take more than 40 mg of zinc per day, breast-feeding women age 14 to 18 should not take more than 34 mg per day. Premature births and stillborn infants have been born to women who took 100 mg of zinc three times a day during their third trimester of pregnancy.

Do not take zinc if: You have HIV (human immunodeficiency virus). Zinc might reduce survival time.

Are there any interactions with medications?

Amiloride (Midamor). Amiloride (Midamor) is used as a "water pill" to help remove excess water from the body. Another effect of amiloride (Midamor) is that it can increase the amount of zinc in the body. Taking zinc supplements with amiloride (Midamor) might cause you to have too much zinc in your body.

Antibiotics (Tetracycline antibiotics). Zinc can attach to tetracyclines in the stomach. This decreases the amount of tetracyclines that can be absorbed. Taking zinc with tetracyclines might decrease the effectiveness of tetracyclines. To avoid this interaction take zinc 2 hours before or 4 hours after taking tetracyclines. Some tetracyclines include demeclocycline (Declomycin), minocycline (Minocin), and tetracycline (Achromycin).

Antibiotics (Quinolone antibiotics). Zinc might decrease how much antibiotic the body absorbs. Taking zinc along with some antibiotics might decrease the effectiveness of some antibiotics. To avoid this interaction take zinc supplements at least 1 hour after antibiotics. Some of these antibiotics that might interact with zinc include ciprofloxacin (Cipro), enoxacin (Penetrex), norfloxacin (Chibroxin, Noroxin), sparfloxacin (Zagam), trovafloxacin (Trovan), and grepafloxacin (Raxar).

Cisplatin (Platinol-AQ). Cisplatin (Platinol-AQ) is used to treat cancer. Taking zinc along with EDTA and cisplatin (Platinol-AQ) might increase the effects and side effects of cisplatin (Platinol-AQ).

Penicillamine. Penicillamine is used for Wilson's disease and rheumatoid arthritis. Zinc might decrease how much penicillamine your body absorbs and decrease the effectiveness of penicillamine.

Water pills (Potassium-sparing diuretics). Some "water pills" can increase zinc levels in the body. Taking some "water pills" along with zinc supplements might cause too much zinc to be in the body. Some "water pills" that increase zinc in the body include amiloride (Midamor), spironolactone (Aldactone), and triamterene (Dyrenium).

Water pills (Thiazide diuretics). Some "water pills" can decrease the amount of zinc in the body. This could decrease the effect of zinc supplements. Some of these "water pills" include chlorothiazide (Diuril), hydrochlorothiazide (HydroDiuril, Esidrix), indapamide (Lozol), metolazone (Zaroxolyn), and chlorthalidone (Hygroton).

5-HTP..see 5-HTP
7-ALPHA-HYDROXY-DHEA......................................
.........................see 7-ALPHA-HYDROXY-DHEA
7-KETO-DHEA .... see 7-KETO-DHEA
7-oxo-dehydroepiandrosterone-3-acetate ....
.... see 7-KETO-DHEA
A5MP...see ADENOSINE
Aamalaki....................see INDIAN GOOSEBERRY
Aaron's Rod ....see GOLDENROD,
HOUSELEEK, MULLEIN
ABA ....see PARA-AMINOBENZOIC ACID (PABA)
Abelmoschus moschatus............................ see AMBRETTE
Abelmosk .... see AMBRETTE
A-beta-carotene............................. see BETA-CAROTENE
Abies alba... see FIR
Abies balsamea .... see CANADA BALSAM
Abies excelsa ....see HEMLOCK SPRUCE
Abies gmelinii............ see LARCH ARABINOGALACTAN
Abokado .... see AVOCADO
Abrojos..................................see PUNCTURE VINE
Abrus precatorius ....see PRECATORY BEAN
ABSCESS ROOT..........................see ABSCESS ROOT
Absinthe .... see WORMWOOD
Absinthii Herba................................ see WORMWOOD
Absinthites .... see WORMWOOD
ABUTA .... see ABUTA
Abyssinian Myrrh ....see MYRRH
Abyssinian Tea.................................see KHAT
ACACIA ....see ACACIA
Acacia Catechu .... see CATECHU
Acacia farnesiana .... see CASSIE ABSOLUTE
Acacia senegal ....see ACACIA
Acacia smallii ....see CASSIE ABSOLUTE
Acacia verek ....see ACACIA
ACAI .... see ACAI
Acai Palm .... see ACAI
Acanthopanax senticosus .... see GINSENG, SIBERIAN
ACE .... see ADRENAL EXTRACT
Acedera Común .... see SORREL
Acer nikoense................................ see NIKKO MAPLE
Acer rubrum ....see RED MAPLE
ACEROLA .... see ACEROLA
Acetate Replacing Factor ....see ALPHA-LIPOIC ACID
Acetyl Carnitine .... see ACETYL-L-CARNITINE
Acetylcysteine .... see N-ACETYL CYSTEINE
Acetylformic acid............................ see PYRUVATE
Acetylglucosamine........... see N-ACETYL GLUCOSAMINE
ACETYL-L-CARNITINE ...... see ACETYL-L-CARNITINE
Acetyl-Levocarnitine .... see ACETYL-L-CARNITINE
Ache des Marais................................ see CELERY
Achilee ....see YARROW
Achillea ....see YARROW
Achillea ptarmica .... see SNEEZEWORT
Achiote ....see ANNATTO
Achiotillo ....see ANNATTO
Achweed ....see GOUTWEED
A-chymotrypsin .... see CHYMOTRYPSIN
Acidophilus .... see LACTOBACILLUS
Acidophilus Milk .... see YOGURT
Acidulated Phosphate Fluoride ....see FLUORIDE
ACKEE .... see ACKEE
Ackerkraut......................................see AGRIMONY
ACONITE .... see ACONITE
Aconiti Tuber .... see ACONITE
Aconitum Napellus .... see ACONITE

Aconitum species .... see ACONITE
Acorus americanus ....see CALAMUS
Acorus calamus ....see CALAMUS
Acorus gramineus ....see CALAMUS
Acorus sp ....see CALAMUS
Acrid Crowfoot .... see BUTTERCUP
Acrid Lettuce .... see WILD LETTUCE
Actaea alba .... see WHITE COHOSH
Actaea macrotys ....see BLACK COHOSH
Actaea pachypoda .... see WHITE COHOSH
Actaea racemosa ....see BLACK COHOSH
Actaea rubra .... see WHITE COHOSH
Actinidia chinensis .... see KIWI
ACTIVATED CHARCOAL ....
........................see ACTIVATED CHARCOAL
Active hexose correlated compound ....see AHCC
Activin .... see GRAPE
Acuilee ....see YARROW
Adam's Apple.....................................see LIME
Adam's Flannel .... see MULLEIN
Adam's Needle................................see YUCCA
Adaptogen .... see JIAOGULAN
Adder's Eyes .... see SCARLET PIMPERNEL
Adder's Root ....see ARUM
Adderwort .... see BISTORT
Ademetionine .... see SAMe
Adenine Nucleoside ....see ADENOSINE
Adenine Riboside ....see ADENOSINE
ADENOSINE............................see ADENOSINE
Adenosylcobalamin.....................see DIBENCOZIDE
Adenosylmethionine .... see SAMe
Adermine Hydrochloride ....
.........................see PYRIDOXINE (VITAMIN B6)
Adiantifolia ....see GINKGO
Adiantum capillus-veneris .... see MAIDENHAIR FERN
Adiantum pedatum..................... see MAIDENHAIR FERN
Adiptam ....see BURNING BUSH
Adonis herba .... see PHEASANT'S EYE
Adonis vernalis .... see PHEASANT'S EYE
ADP ....see ADENOSINE
ADRENAL EXTRACT .... see ADRENAL EXTRACT
ADRUE .... see ADRUE
ADT .... see ANDROSTENETRIONE
Adulsa .... see MALABAR NUT
AE-941 ....see SHARK CARTILAGE
Aegle marmelos .... see BAEL
Aegopodium podagraria.......................see GOUTWEED
Aesculus hippocastanum............... see HORSE CHESTNUT
Aetheroleum pelargonii .... see ROSE GERANIUM OIL
Aethusa cynapium...................... see FOOL'S PARSLEY
AFA.........................see BLUE-GREEN ALGAE
Aframomum melegueta .... see GRAINS OF PARADISE
African Chillies........................... see CAPSICUM
African Civet.....................................see CIVET
African Coffee Tree ....see CASTOR
African Cucumber...................... see BITTER MELON
African Geranium .... see SOUTH AFRICAN GERANIUM
African Ginger .... see GINGER
African Marigold .... see TAGETES
African Myrrh ....see MYRRH
African Palm Oil .... see PALM OIL
African Pepper .... see CAPSICUM
African Plum Tree ....see PYGEUM
AFRICAN WILD POTATO.......................................
.........................see AFRICAN WILD POTATO

Natural Medicines Comprehensive Database Consumer Version   (209) 472-2244

AG.................... see LARCH ARABINOGALACTAN
AGA.. see AGA
AGAR .... see AGAR
Agarweed .... see AGAR
Agastach pogostemi ....see PATCHOULY OIL
Agathosma betulina .... see BUCHU
Agathosma crenulata .... see BUCHU
Agathosma serratifolia.................... see BUCHU
Aged Garlic Extract ....see GARLIC
Agnolyt ....see CHASTEBERRY
Agnus-castus ....see CHASTEBERRY
Agracejo .... see EUROPEAN BARBERRY
Agrião .... see WATERCRESS
Agrimonia eupatoria ....see AGRIMONY
Agrimonia odorata ....see AGRIMONY
Agrimonia procera ....see AGRIMONY
Agrimoniae herba.........................see AGRIMONY
AGRIMONY.................................see AGRIMONY
Agromonia ....see AGRIMONY
Agropyron ....see WHEATGRASS
Agropyron firmum ....see WHEATGRASS
Agropyron repens......................see WHEATGRASS
Agrostemma githago .... see CORN COCKLE
Ague .... see ALETRIS
Ague Tree...........................see SASSAFRAS
Agueweed .... see BONESET
AHA................... see ALPHA HYDROXY ACIDS
AHCC ....see AHCC
Ahuacate .... see AVOCADO
Ail ....see GARLIC
Ailanthus altissima.................. see TREE OF HEAVEN
Ailanthus cacodendron............. see TREE OF HEAVEN
Ailanthus giraldii .... see TREE OF HEAVEN
Ailanthus glandulosa................. see TREE OF HEAVEN
Ailanthus vilmoriniana.............. see TREE OF HEAVEN
Ailanto .... see TREE OF HEAVEN
Airelle ....see BILBERRY
Ajagandha .... see ASHWAGANDHA
Ajamoda .... see CELERY
Ajava Seed .... see BISHOP'S WEED
Ajenjo.................................. see WORMWOOD
Ajenuz .... see BLACK SEED
Ajmaline .... see INDIAN SNAKEROOT
Ajo.................................see GARLIC
Ajowan .... see BISHOP'S WEED
Ajowanj .... see BISHOP'S WEED
Ajuga .... see AJUGA NIPPONENSIS
Ajuga .... see BUGLE
Ajuga chamaepitys....................see GROUND PINE
AJUGA NIPPONENSIS............ see AJUGA NIPPONENSIS
Ajuga reptans .... see BUGLE
Ak .... see CALOTROPIS
Akada .... see CALOTROPIS
Akarakarabha ....see PELLITORY
Akee .... see ACKEE
A-ketoglutaric acid........... see ALPHA-KETOGLUTARATE
AKG .... see ALPHA-KETOGLUTARATE
Aki.................................. see ACKEE
Akschota ....see ENGLISH WALNUT
ALA .... see ALPHA-LINOLENIC ACID,
ALPHA-LIPOIC ACID
Alant....................see ELECAMPANE
A-Lan-Thus................. see TREE OF HEAVEN
Alarka.......................... see CALOTROPIS
ALC .... see ACETYL-L-CARNITINE

Alcachofa ....see ARTICHOKE
Alcacuz ....see LICORICE
Alcanna ....see HENNA
Alcar.................... see ACETYL-L-CARNITINE
Alcaucil ....see ARTICHOKE
Alcazuz ....see LICORICE
Alcea rosea ....see HOLLYHOCK
ALCHEMILLA.................................see ALCHEMILLA
Alchemilla alpina .... see ALPINE LADY'S MANTLE
Alchemilla arvensis..................... see PARSLEY PIERT
Alchemilla occidentalis................. see PARSLEY PIERT
Alchemilla vulgaris.................see ALCHEMILLA
Alchemilla xanthochlora..............see ALCHEMILLA
Alchornea castaneifolia .... see IPORURU
Alcohol.................................see BEER, WINE
ALDER BUCKTHORN .... see ALDER BUCKTHORN
Alder Dogwood...................... see ALDER BUCKTHORN
Alehoof .... see GROUND IVY
ALETRIS .... see ALETRIS
Aletris farinosa .... see ALETRIS
Aleurites cordatus .... see TUNG SEED
Aleurites javanicus .... see TUNG SEED
Aleurites moluccanus .... see TUNG SEED
Aleurites pentaphyllus .... see TUNG SEED
Aleurites remyi........................ see TUNG SEED
Aleurites trilobus..................... see TUNG SEED
Alexandrian Senna .... see SENNA
Alexandrian-Laurel ....see LAURELWOOD
Alexandrinische Senna.................. see SENNA
Alexandrinischer Lorbeer ....see LAURELWOOD
Alfacalcidol..............................see VITAMIN D
Alfa-ecdysone .... see ECDYSTERONE
ALFALFA .... see ALFALFA
Algerian Geranium Oil .... see ROSE GERANIUM OIL
ALGIN .... see ALGIN
Alginates .... see ALGIN
Al-Gutub ....see PUNCTURE VINE
Alhandal ....see COLOCYNTH
Alholva ....see FENUGREEK
Alhucema .... see LAVENDER
A-lipoic acid................see ALPHA-LIPOIC ACID
Ali's Walking Stick ....see EURYCOMA LONGIFOLIA
Alisma ....see WATER PLANTAIN
Alisma orientale ....see WATER PLANTAIN
Alisma plantago-aquatica.................see WATER PLANTAIN
Alkanet ....see ALKANNA
ALKANNA .... see ALKANNA
Alkanna lehmanii ....see ALKANNA
Alkanna Radix .... see ALKANNA
Alkanna tinctoria......................see ALKANNA
Alkanna tuberculata ....see ALKANNA
All Rac-Alpha-Tocopherol.................... see VITAMIN E
All-Heal............... see EUROPEAN MISTLETOE,
SELF-HEAL, VALERIAN
Alligator Pear...................... see AVOCADO
Allii cepae bulbus.......................see ONION
Allii sativi bulbus ....see GARLIC
Allium ....see GARLIC
Allium cepa ....see ONION
Allium sativum......................see GARLIC
Allium schoenoprasum .... see CHIVE
Allium sibiricum .... see CHIVE
Allium ursinum .... see BEAR'S GARLIC
Allseed Nine-Joints.................. see KNOTWEED
ALLSPICE................................see ALLSPICE

All-Trans Lycopene..................................see LYCOPENE
Almond oil ....see SWEET ALMOND
Alnus barbata ....see BLACK ALDER
Alnus glutinosa ....see BLACK ALDER
Alnus serrulata ....see SMOOTH ALDER
ALOE...see ALOE
Aloe Vera..see ALOE
Aloe Yucca..see YUCCA
Aloerot ....see ALETRIS
Aloysia citrodora......................see LEMON VERBENA
Aloysia triphylla.......................see LEMON VERBENA
Alpenkraut....................................see HEMP AGRIMONY
ALPHA HYDROXY ACIDS ....
....see ALPHA HYDROXY ACIDS
Alpha KG .... see ALPHA-KETOGLUTARATE
Alpha Tocopherol Acetate...........................see VITAMIN E
Alpha Tocotrienol ....see VITAMIN E
Alpha-amino-4-imidazole propanoic acid .....see HISTIDINE
Alpha-aminohydrocinnamic acid.....see PHENYLALANINE
Alpha-chymotrypsin ....see CHYMOTRYPSIN
Alpha-glycerylphosphorylcholine.............. see ALPHA-GPC
ALPHA-GPC .... see ALPHA-GPC
Alpha-hydroxyethanoic acid................................
....see ALPHA HYDROXY ACIDS
Alpha-keto acid.................................. see PYRUVATE
ALPHA-KETOGLUTARATE ....
....see ALPHA-KETOGLUTARATE
Alpha-ketopropionic acid.........................see PYRUVATE
Alpha-limonene.................................see LIMONENE
ALPHA-LINOLENIC ACID ....
....see ALPHA-LINOLENIC ACID
ALPHA-LIPOIC ACID...............see ALPHA-LIPOIC ACID
Alpha-Tocopherol .... see VITAMIN E
ALPINE CRANBERRY .... see ALPINE CRANBERRY
ALPINE LADY'S MANTLE ....
....see ALPINE LADY'S MANTLE
ALPINE RAGWORT..................see ALPINE RAGWORT
Alpine Strawberry...............................see STRAWBERRY
ALPINIA...see ALPINIA
Alpinia officinarum.............................see ALPINIA
Alquitran de Enebro.............................see CADE OIL
Alraunwurzel........... see EUROPEAN MANDRAKE
Alsine media .... see CHICKWEED
Alstonia Bark ....see FEVER BARK
Alstonia constricta ....see FEVER BARK
Altamisa .... see FEVERFEW
Alteia .... see MARSHMALLOW
Althaea ficifolia................................see HOLLYHOCK
Althaea officinalis .... see MARSHMALLOW
Althaea rosea ....see HOLLYHOCK
Althaea taurinensis...........................see MARSHMALLOW
Althaeae Folium .... see MARSHMALLOW
Althaeae radi .... see MARSHMALLOW
Althea .... see MARSHMALLOW
Althea Rose ....see HOLLYHOCK
Aluminum phosphate ....see PHOSPHATE SALTS
Amachazuru ....see JIAOGULAN
Amalaki....................see INDIAN GOOSEBERRY
Amangura .... see ASHWAGANDHA
Amanita muscaria .... see AGA
Amantilla....................................see VALERIAN
AMARANTH ....see AMARANTH
Amargo .... see QUASSIA
Amazon Acai .... see ACAI
Amber ....see ST. JOHN'S WORT

Amber Touch-and-Heal.................see ST. JOHN'S WORT
Amblabaum...........................see INDIAN GOOSEBERRY
Ambreine.............................. see LABDANUM
Ambretta .... see AMBRETTE
AMBRETTE .... see AMBRETTE
Ambroise..............................see WOOD SAGE
AMERICAN ADDER'S TONGUE............................
.............................see AMERICAN ADDER'S TONGUE
American Angelica.........................see ANGELICA
American Arborvitae .... see THUJA
American Aspen ....see ASPEN
American Aspidium ....see MALE FERN
AMERICAN BITTERSWEET ....
.............................see AMERICAN BITTERSWEET
AMERICAN CHESTNUT .... see AMERICAN CHESTNUT
American Cone Flower ....see ECHINACEA
American Corn Mint .... see JAPANESE MINT
American Cranberry......................... see CRANBERRY
American Dill............................... see DILL
AMERICAN DOGWOOD .... see AMERICAN DOGWOOD
American Dwarf Palm Tree ....see SAW PALMETTO
AMERICAN ELDER .... see AMERICAN ELDER
American Elderberry................... see AMERICAN ELDER
American Ginseng ....see GINSENG, AMERICAN
American Greek Valerian ....see ABSCESS ROOT
AMERICAN HELLEBORE ....
.............................see AMERICAN HELLEBORE
American Indigo ....see WILD INDIGO
American Ipecacuanha......................see INDIAN PHYSIC
AMERICAN IVY .... see AMERICAN IVY
American Liverleaf .... see LIVERWORT
American Mandrake......................... see PODOPHYLLUM
AMERICAN MISTLETOE ....
.............................see AMERICAN MISTLETOE
American Mullein .... see MULLEIN
American Nightshade....................... see POKEWEED
AMERICAN PAWPAW .... see AMERICAN PAWPAW
American Pennyroyal............................ see PENNYROYAL
American Saffron....................see SAFFLOWER
AMERICAN SPIKENARD..................................
.............................see AMERICAN SPIKENARD
American Spinach .... see POKEWEED
American Storax .... see STORAX
American Valerian....................see NERVE ROOT
American Veratrum .... see AMERICAN HELLEBORE
American White Hellebore ....
.............................see AMERICAN HELLEBORE
AMERICAN WHITE POND LILY ....
.............................see AMERICAN WHITE POND LILY
American Woodbine....................... see AMERICAN IVY
American Wormgrass .... see PINK ROOT
American Yellow Mustard .... see WHITE MUSTARD
Amibiasine ....see MANGOSTEEN
Amino Monosaccharide ....
....................see GLUCOSAMINE HYDROCHLORIDE,
....GLUCOSAMINE SULFATE
Aminoacetic Acid.............................. see GLYCINE
Aminobenzoate Potassium..................................
....................see PARA-AMINOBENZOIC ACID (PABA)
Aminobenzoic Acid ....
....................see PARA-AMINOBENZOIC ACID (PABA)
Aminoethanesulfonate ....see TAURINE
Amla....................see INDIAN GOOSEBERRY
Ammi .... see KHELLA
Ammi daucoides .... see KHELLA

Medical professionals should consult the Professional Version at www.NaturalDatabase.com.

Ammi glaucifolium	see BISHOP'S WEED
Ammi majus	see BISHOP'S WEED
Ammi Visnaga	see KHELLA
Ammocallis rosea	see MADAGASCAR PERIWINKLE
Amomum cardamomum	see CARDAMOM
Amomum melegueta	see GRAINS OF PARADISE
Amomum zedoaria	see ZEDOARY
Amomum zingiber	see GINGER
Amoraciae Rusticanae Radix	see HORSERADISH
Amorphophallus konjac	see GLUCOMANNAN
Amorphophallus rivieri	see GLUCOMANNAN
AMP	see ADENOSINE
Amukkirag	see ASHWAGANDHA
Amur Cork	see PHELLODENDRON
Amygdala Amara	see BITTER ALMOND
Amygdala Dulcis	see SWEET ALMOND
Amygdaloside	see APRICOT
Amygdalus armeniaca	see APRICOT
Amygdalus communis	see BITTER ALMOND
Amygdalus dulcis	see BITTER ALMOND
Amyris kataf	see MYRRH
Anabaena species	see BLUE-GREEN ALGAE
Anacardium occidentale	see CASHEW
Anacyclus pyrethrum	see PELLITORY
Anagallis arvensis	see SCARLET PIMPERNEL
Anamirta cocculus	see LEVANT BERRY
Anamirta paniculata	see LEVANT BERRY
Ananas ananas	see BROMELAIN
Ananas comosus	see BROMELAIN
Ananas duckei	see BROMELAIN
Ananas sativus	see BROMELAIN
Anapsos	see POLYPODIUM LEUCOTOMOS
Anas barbaria	see OSCILLOCOCCINUM
Anas barbariae	see OSCILLOCOCCINUM
Anas moschata	see OSCILLOCOCCINUM
Anashca	see MARIJUANA
Anatherum zizanioides	see VETIVER
Anchi Ginseng	see GINSENG, AMERICAN
Anchusa	see ALKANNA
Anchusa bracteolata	see ALKANNA
Anchusa tuberculata	see ALKANNA
Andira araroba	see GOA POWDER
ANDIROBA	see ANDIROBA
Andiroba-Saruba	see ANDIROBA
ANDRACHNE	see ANDRACHNE
Andrachne aspera	see ANDRACHNE
Andrachne cordifolia	see ANDRACHNE
Andrachne phyllanthoides	see ANDRACHNE
Andro	see ANDROSTENEDIONE
Androdiol	see ANDROSTENEDIOL
ANDROGRAPHIS	see ANDROGRAPHIS
Andrographis paniculata	see ANDROGRAPHIS
Andrographolide	see ANDROGRAPHIS
Andropogon citratus	see LEMONGRASS
Andropogon flexuosus	see LEMONGRASS
Andropogon nardus	see CITRONELLA OIL
Andropogon odoratus	see VETIVER
Andropogon sorghum	see BROOM CORN
ANDROSTENEDIOL	see ANDROSTENEDIOL
ANDROSTENEDIONE	see ANDROSTENEDIONE
ANDROSTENETRIONE	see ANDROSTENETRIONE
Anemia californica	see YERBA MANSA
Anémone à Lobes Aigus	see LIVERWORT
Anemone acutiloba	see LIVERWORT
Anemone americana	see LIVERWORT
Anémone d'Amérique	see LIVERWORT
Anemone groenlandica	see GOLDTHREAD
Anemone hepatica	see LIVERWORT
Anemone nemorosa	see WOOD ANEMONE
Anemone nigricans	see PULSATILLA
Anemone pratensis	see PULSATILLA
Anemone pulsatilla	see PULSATILLA
Anemone serotina	see PULSATILLA
Anemopsis californica	see YERBA MANSA
Anethi Fructus	see DILL
Anethum foeniculum	see FENNEL
Anethum graveolens	see DILL
Anethum piperitum	see FENNEL
Anethum sowa	see DILL
Aneurine Hydrochloride	see THIAMINE (VITAMIN B1)
Angel Tulip	see JIMSON WEED
ANGELICA	see ANGELICA, ASHITABA
Angelica acutiloba	see ANGELICA
Angelica archangelica	see ANGELICA
Angelica atropurpurea	see ANGELICA
Angelica curtisi	see ANGELICA
Angelica dahurica	see ANGELICA
Angelica keiskei	see ASHITABA
Angelica levisticum	see LOVAGE
Angelica officinalis	see ANGELICA
Angelica polymorpha var. sinensis	see DONG QUAI
Angelica sinensis	see DONG QUAI
Angelica sylvestris	see ANGELICA
Angelica Tree	see NORTHERN PRICKLY ASH
Angelicae Fructus	see ANGELICA
Angelicae Gigantis Radix	see DONG QUAI
Angelicae Herba	see ANGELICA
Angelicae Radix	see ANGELICA
Angelicin	see BETA-SITOSTEROL
ANGEL'S TRUMPET	see ANGEL'S TRUMPET
Angled Loofah	see LUFFA
ANGOSTURA	see ANGOSTURA
Angostura trifoliata	see ANGOSTURA
Anguraté	see MENTZELIA
Angustura	see ANGOSTURA
Anhydrous aluminum silicates	see COLLOIDAL MINERALS
Anhydrous Caffeine	see CAFFEINE
Anhydrous Sodium Phosphate	see PHOSPHATE SALTS
Aniba duckei	see BOIS DE ROSE OIL
Aniba rosaeodora	see BOIS DE ROSE OIL
Animal Charcoal	see ACTIVATED CHARCOAL
Anis des Vosges	see CARAWAY
ANISE	see ANISE
Aniseed	see ANISE
Aniseed Stars	see STAR ANISE
Anisi Fructus	see ANISE
Anisi Stellati Fructus	see STAR ANISE
Anjye	see ACKEE
ANNATTO	see ANNATTO
Annona cherimola	see GRAVIOLA
Annona macrocarpa	see GRAVIOLA
Annona muricata	see GRAVIOLA
Annona triloba	see AMERICAN PAWPAW
Annotta	see ANNATTO
Annual Mugwort	see SWEET ANNIE
Annual Wormwood	see SWEET ANNIE
Antelaea azadirachta	see NEEM
Antennaria dioica	see CAT'S FOOT
Antennariase Dioicae Flos	see CAT'S FOOT

Anthemis grandiflorum .... see CHRYSANTHEMUM
Anthemis nobilis .... see ROMAN CHAMOMILE
Anthemis pyrethrum .... see PELLITORY
Anthemis stipulacea .... see CHRYSANTHEMUM
Anthoxanthum odoratum ...... see SWEET VERNAL GRASS
Anthriscus cerefolium .... see CHERVIL
Anthriscus longirostris .... see CHERVIL
Antialopecia Factor .... see INOSITOL
Antiberiberi Factor .... see THIAMINE (VITAMIN B1)
Anti-Blacktongue Factor ....
.... see NIACIN AND NIACINAMIDE (VITAMIN B3)
Antineuritic Factor .... see THIAMINE (VITAMIN B1)
Antipellagra Factor ....
.... see NIACIN AND NIACINAMIDE (VITAMIN B3)
Antiscorbutic Vitamin ....
.... see VITAMIN C (ASCORBIC ACID)
Antitumor Angiogenesis Factor ....
.... see BOVINE CARTILAGE
Anti-TAF .... see BOVINE CARTILAGE
Antixerophthalmic Vitamin .... see VITAMIN A
Anurine .... see THIAMINE (VITAMIN B1)
Aonla .... see INDIAN GOOSEBERRY
Aortic GAGs .... see MESOGLYCAN
Aortic Glycosaminoglycans .... see MESOGLYCAN
Aphanes arvensis .... see PARSLEY PIERT
Aphanizomenon flos-aquae .... see BLUE-GREEN ALGAE
Apii Fructus .... see CELERY
Apis cerana .... see BEESWAX
Apis Mellifera .... see BEESWAX, HONEY,
ROYAL JELLY, BEE VENOM
Apis venenum purum .... see BEE VENOM
Apitoxin .... see BEE VENOM
Apium carvi .... see CARAWAY
Apium crispum .... see PARSLEY
Apium graveolens .... see CELERY
Apium petroselinum .... see PARSLEY
Aplotaxis lappa .... see COSTUS
Apocynum cannabinum .... see CANADIAN HEMP
Apothecary Rose .... see ROSE HIP
APPLE .... see APPLE
Apple Acid .... see ALPHA HYDROXY ACIDS
APPLE CIDER VINEGAR ....
.... see APPLE CIDER VINEGAR
APRICOT .... see APRICOT
Apricot Vine .... see PASSIONFLOWER
Aqua Pimentae .... see ALLSPICE
Aqueous Liver Extract .... see LIVER EXTRACT
Aquilegia vulgaris .... see COLUMBINE
Ara-6 .... see LARCH ARABINOGALACTAN
Arabian Myrrh .... see MYRRH
Arabian-Tea .... see KHAT
Arabic Gum .... see ACACIA
Arabinogalactan .... see LARCH ARABINOGALACTAN
Arachis .... see PEANUT OIL
Arachis hypogaea .... see PEANUT OIL
Aralia pseuodoginseng .... see PANAX PSEUDOGINSENG
Aralia racemosa .... see AMERICAN SPIKENARD
Arandano Americano .... see CRANBERRY
Arandano Trepador .... see CRANBERRY
Arañuel .... see BLACK SEED
Araoba .... see GOA POWDER
Arberry .... see UVA URSI
Arborvitae .... see THUJA
Arbre Fricasse .... see ACKEE
Arbutus uva-ursi .... see UVA URSI

Archangel .... see WHITE DEAD NETTLE FLOWER
Archangelica officinalis .... see ANGELICA
Archangle .... see BUGLEWEED
Arctic Root .... see ROSEROOT
Arctium .... see BURDOCK
Arctostaphylos uva-ursi .... see UVA URSI
ARECA .... see ARECA
Areca Catechu .... see ARECA
Areca Nut .... see ARECA
ARENARIA RUBRA .... see ARENARIA RUBRA
Arg .... see L-ARGININE
Argasse .... see SEA BUCKTHORN
Argilla .... see KAOLIN
Arginine .... see L-ARGININE
Arginine Hydrochloride .... see L-ARGININE
Argousier .... see SEA BUCKTHORN
Argyreia nervosa .... see HAWAIIAN BABY WOODROSE
Argyreia speciosa .... see HAWAIIAN BABY WOODROSE
Arisaema cochinchinense .... see PINELLIA TERNATA
Arishta .... see NEEM
Arishtha .... see NEEM
ARISTOLOCHIA .... see ARISTOLOCHIA
Arjuna .... see TERMINALIA
Arka .... see CALOTROPIS
Armeniaca .... see APRICOT
Armeniaca mume .... see JAPANESE APRICOT
Armeniaca vulgaris .... see APRICOT
Armoise .... see WORMWOOD
Armoise capillaire .... see YIN CHEN
Armoise commune .... see MUGWORT
Armoracia lopathifolia .... see HORSERADISH
Armoracia rusticana .... see HORSERADISH
Armstrong .... see KNOTWEED
ARNICA .... see ARNICA
Arnikablüten .... see ARNICA
Arnotta .... see ANNATTO
Aromatic Sumac .... see SWEET SUMACH
ARRACH .... see ARRACH
Arrow Bamboo .... see BAMBOO
Arrow Wood .... see ALDER BUCKTHORN
ARROWROOT .... see ARROWROOT
Arrowwood .... see WAHOO
Arruda bravam .... see JABORANDI
Arruda do Mato .... see JABORANDI
Arryan .... see CHEKEN
Arsesmart .... see SMARTWEED
Artemisia .... see MUGWORT,
SWEET ANNIE, WORMWOOD
Artemisia absinthium .... see WORMWOOD
Artemisia annua .... see SWEET ANNIE
Artemisia capillaris .... see YIN CHEN
Artemisia cina .... see WORMSEED
Artemisia dracunculus .... see TARRAGON
Artemisia glauca .... see TARRAGON
Artemisia scoparia .... see YIN CHEN
Artemisia vulgaris .... see MUGWORT
Artemisinin .... see SWEET ANNIE
Artesian absinthium .... see WORMWOOD
Artetyke .... see COWSLIP
Arthritica .... see COWSLIP
Artichaut commun .... see ARTICHOKE
ARTICHOKE .... see ARTICHOKE
Artischocke .... see ARTICHOKE
ARUM .... see ARUM
Arum dracontium .... see PINELLIA TERNATA

Arum maculatum	see ARUM
Arum ternatum	see PINELLIA TERNATA
Arundinaria japonica	see BAMBOO
Arundo phragmites	see REED HERB
Arundo vulgaris	see REED HERB
Arusa	see MALABAR NUT
ASAFOETIDA	see ASAFOETIDA
Asan	see ASHWAGANDHA
ASARABACCA	see ASARABACCA
Asaroun	see ASARABACCA
Asarum	see ASARABACCA
Asarum europaeum	see ASARABACCA
Asclepias incarnata	see SWAMP MILKWEED
Asclepias procera	see CALOTROPIS
Asclepias tuberosa	see PLEURISY ROOT
Asclepias vincetoxicum	see GERMAN IPECAC
Ascophyllum nodosum	see ALGIN, BLADDERWRACK
Ascorbate	see VITAMIN C (ASCORBIC ACID)
Ascorbic Acid	see VITAMIN C (ASCORBIC ACID)
Ascorbyl Palmitate	see VITAMIN C (ASCORBIC ACID)
Asgand	see ASHWAGANDHA
Asgandh	see ASHWAGANDHA
Asgandha	see ASHWAGANDHA
ASH	see ASH
Ashagandha	see ASHWAGANDHA
Ashangee	see BUGLEWEED
Ashe Juniper	see EASTERN RED CEDAR
ASHITABA	see ASHITABA
ASHWAGANDHA	see ASHWAGANDHA
Ashwanga	see ASHWAGANDHA
Ashweed	see GOUTWEED
Asian Ginseng	see GINSENG, PANAX
Asimina triloba	see AMERICAN PAWPAW
Asoda	see ASHWAGANDHA
Aspalathus contaminatus	see RED BUSH TEA
Aspalathus linearis	see RED BUSH TEA
ASPARAGUS	see ASPARAGUS
Aspartate Chelated Minerals	see ASPARTATES
ASPARTATES	see ASPARTATES
Aspartic Acid	see ASPARTATES
ASPEN	see ASPEN
Asperge	see ASPARAGUS
Asperula odorata	see SWEET WOODRUFF
Aspidosperma quebracho-blanco	see QUEBRACHO
Asplenium scolopendrium	see HARTSTONGUE
Ass Ear	see COMFREY
Assai Palm	see ACAI
Assant	see ASAFOETIDA
Ass's Foot	see COLTSFOOT
ASTAXANTHIN	see ASTAXANTHIN
Aster helenium	see ELECAMPANE
Aster officinalis	see ELECAMPANE
Asthma Weed	see LOBELIA
Asthmaplant	see EUPHORBIA
Astragali	see ASTRAGALUS
ASTRAGALUS	see ASTRAGALUS
Astragalus gummifer	see TRAGACANTH
Astragalus membranaceus	see ASTRAGALUS
Astragalus mongholicus	see ASTRAGALUS
Asundha	see ASHWAGANDHA
Atasi	see FLAXSEED, FLAXSEED OIL
Athenon	see GLYCINE
Athyrium filix-femina	see LADY FERN
ATLANTIC CEDAR	see ATLANTIC CEDAR
Atlantic Cedarwood Oil	see ATLANTIC CEDAR

Atlantic Yam	see WILD YAM
Atlas Cedar	see ATLANTIC CEDAR
Atmagupta	see COWHAGE
ATP	see ADENOSINE
Atractylis lancea	see ATRACTYLODES
Atractylis ovata	see ATRACTYLODES
ATRACTYLODES	see ATRACTYLODES
Atractylodis Radix	see ATRACTYLODES
Atropa acuminata	see BELLADONNA
Atropa belladonna	see BELLADONNA
Aubepine	see HAWTHORN
Auckland costus	see COSTUS
Augentrostkraut	see EYEBRIGHT
August Flower	see GUMWEED
Aurantii pericarpium	see BITTER ORANGE
Australian febrifuge	see FEVER BARK
Australian Fever Bush	see FEVER BARK
Australian Nut	see MACADAMIA NUT
Australian Quinine	see FEVER BARK
Australian Tea Tree Oil	see TEA TREE OIL
AUTUMN CROCUS	see AUTUMN CROCUS, SAFFRON
Autumn Monkshood	see ACONITE
Ava Pepper	see KAVA
Ava Root	see KAVA
Avarada	see ASHWAGANDHA
Avaram	see CASSIA AURICULATA
Avari panchaga choornam	see CASSIA AURICULATA
Aveleira	see HAZELNUT
Avelinier	see HAZELNUT
Avellano	see HAZELNUT
Avena byzantina	see OATS
Avena Fructus	see OATS
Avena orientalis	see OATS
Avena sativa	see OATS
Avena volgensis	see OATS
Avenae herba	see OATS
Avenae stramentum	see OATS
AVENS	see AVENS
Avian Heart and Liver	see OSCILLOCOCCINUM
Avian Liver Extract	see OSCILLOCOCCINUM
AVOCADO	see AVOCADO
AVOCADO SUGAR EXTRACT	see AVOCADO SUGAR EXTRACT
Awa	see KAVA
Axerophtholum	see VITAMIN A
Axjun Argun	see TERMINALIA
AY-27255	see VINPOCETINE
Ayak chichira	see MACA
Ayegreen	see HOUSELEEK
Ayron	see HOUSELEEK
Ayuk Willku	see MACA
Ayurvedic Ginseng	see ASHWAGANDHA
Azadirachta Indica	see NEEM
Azafron	see SAFFRON
Azarum	see ASARABACCA
Azeda-brava	see SORREL
Aztec Marigold	see TAGETES
Azucacaa	see STEVIA
B	see BORON
B Complex Vitamin	see FOLIC ACID, NIACIN AND NIACINAMIDE (VITAMIN B3), PANTOTHENIC ACID (VITAMIN B5), PYRIDOXINE (VITAMIN B6), RIBOFLAVIN (VITAMIN B2), THIAMINE (VITAMIN B1), VITAMIN B12

 Natural Medicines Comprehensive Database Consumer Version (209) 472-2244

B(t) Factor..see L-CARNITINE
B. bifidum ....see BIFIDOBACTERIA
B-12...see VITAMIN B12
B6...........................see PYRIDOXINE (VITAMIN B6)
BA JI TIAN............................see BA JI TIAN, MORINDA
Baby Woodrose ....see HAWAIIAN BABY WOODROSE
Bac Ngu Vi Tu...................................see SCHISANDRA
Bacanta...see CARQUEJA
Baccae..see ELDERBERRY
Baccharis...see CARQUEJA
Bach ....see CALAMUS
Bachelor's Buttons ....see BUTTERCUP,
                            CORNFLOWER, FEVERFEW
Backache Root ....see MARSH BLAZING STAR
Bacopa monnieri .... see BRAHMI
Bacterial Polysaccharide .... see XANTHAN GUM
Bacterial Vitamin H1..
........................see PARA-AMINOBENZOIC ACID (PABA)
Badama ....see BITTER ALMOND
Badiana.....................................see STAR ANISE
Badijamun...................................see JAMBOLAN
BAEL ....see BAEL
Bahama Cascarilla ....see CASCARILLA
Bahera ....see TERMINALIA
Bahia Powder ....see GOA POWDER
Bahira ....see TERMINALIA
Bai Dou Kou ....see CARDAMOM
Bai Gkaprow ....see HOLY BASIL
Bai Guo Ye ....see GINKGO
Bai Qu Cai...................see GREATER CELANDINE
Bai Shao .... see PEONY
Bai Zhi .... see ANGELICA
Bai Zhi Ren ....see ORIENTAL ARBORVITAE
Bai Zhu .... see ATRACTYLODES
Baiguo...see GINKGO
BAIKAL SKULLCAP ....see BAIKAL SKULLCAP
Baises De Sureau .... see ELDERBERRY
Bajiao .... see STAR ANISE
Baked Beans...............................see BEAN POD
Baker's Yeast ....see BREWER'S YEAST
Bal ....see MYRRH
Bala .... see COUNTRY MALLOW
Bala Harade.............................see TERMINALIA
B-alanyl-L-histidine ....see CARNOSINE
Bald-faced Hornet .... see BEE VENOM
Baldrian.................................see VALERIAN
Baldrianwurzel................................see VALERIAN
Balera ....see TERMINALIA
Ballota ....see BLACK HOREHOUND
Ballota nigra.......................see BLACK HOREHOUND
Balm.................................see LEMON BALM
Balm of Gilead..............see CANADA BALSAM, POPLAR
Balm of Gilead Fir ....see HEMLOCK SPRUCE
Balmony .... see TURTLE HEAD
Balsam....... see CANADA BALSAM, COPAIBA BALSAM,
                            OREGON FIR BALSAM,
                            PERU BALSAM, TOLU BALSAM
Balsam Fir.....................................see CANADA BALSAM,
                            HEMLOCK SPRUCE
Balsam Fir Canada........................ see CANADA BALSAM
Balsam Fir Oregon.................see OREGON FIR BALSAM
Balsam of Fir.........................see CANADA BALSAM
Balsam of Peru.............................see PERU BALSAM
Balsam of Tolu .... see TOLU BALSAM
Balsam Pear .... see BITTER MELON

Balsam Peru ....see PERU BALSAM
Balsam Poplar Buds .... see POPLAR
Balsam styracis .... see STORAX
Balsam Tolu .... see TOLU BALSAM
Balsam-apple .... see BITTER MELON
Balsambirne .... see BITTER MELON
Balsamina foemina....................... see JEWELWEED
Balsamo.............................. see BITTER MELON
Balsamodendron myrrha......................see MYRRH
Balsamodendrum habessinicum......................see MYRRH
Balsamodendrum mukul....................see GUGGUL
Balsamodendrum myrrha.....................see MYRRH
Balsamodendrum wightii.....................see GUGGUL
Balsamum peruvianum ....see PERU BALSAM
Balsamum styrax liquidus...................... see STORAX
Balsamum tolutanum .... see TOLU BALSAM
Balsam-weed............................. see JEWELWEED
Balucanat................................. see TUNG SEED
BAMBOO .... see BAMBOO
Ban Lang Gen .... see ISATIS
Ban Xia ....see PINELLIA TERNATA
BANABA ....see BANABA
Banafshah ....see SWEET VIOLET
Band Man's Plaything.........................see YARROW
Baneberry ....see BLACK COHOSH, WHITE COHOSH
Banha ....see PINELLIA TERNATA
Banji .... see MARIJUANA
Banksia abyssinica.............................see KOUSSO
Bannal .... see SCOTCH BROOM
Bantu Tulip...............see AFRICAN WILD POTATO
Baptisia tinctoria ....see WILD INDIGO
Baptista ....see WILD INDIGO
Bara nimbu ....see LIME
Baraka .... see BLACK SEED
Barbados Cherry .... see ACEROLA
Barbary-fig Cactus ....see PRICKLY PEAR CACTUS
Barbasco..................see CANELLA, WILD YAM
Barberry ....see EUROPEAN BARBERRY,
                            OREGON GRAPE
Barberry Matrimony Vine .... see LYCIUM
Barber's Brush .... see TEAZLE
Bardana ....see BURDOCK
Bardanae Radix...............................see BURDOCK
Bardana-minor ....see BURDOCK
Bardane ....see BURDOCK
Bariar .... see COUNTRY MALLOW
Bari-sanuf....................................... see FENNEL
BARLEY ....see BARLEY
Barosma betulina .... see BUCHU
Barosma crenulata.............................. see BUCHU
Barosma serratifolia............................ see BUCHU
Barosmae Folium .... see BUCHU
Barrenwort ....see EPIMEDIUM
Barweed ....see CLIVERS
Basam .... see SCOTCH BROOM
Basidiomycetes Extract......................see AHCC
Basidiomycetes Polysaccharide ....
...........see GENISTEIN COMBINED POLYSACCHARIDE
BASIL ....see BASIL
Basil Thyme .... see CALAMINT
Basilici Herba......................................see BASIL
Basket Willow ....see WILLOW BARK
Basking Shark Liver Oil .... see SHARK LIVER OIL
Bassora tragacanth ....see KARAYA GUM
Basswood.......................................see LINDEN

Bastard Cinnamon	see CASSIA CINNAMON
Bastard Ginseng	see CODONOPSIS
Bastard Mahogany	see ANDIROBA
Bastard Saffron	see SAFFLOWER
Batavia Cassia	see CINNAMON bark
Batavia Cinnamon	see CINNAMON bark
Bauchweh	see YARROW
Baurenlilien	see WHITE LILY
Bay	see SWEET BAY
Bay Laurel	see SWEET BAY
Bay leaf	see SWEET BAY
Bay Tree	see SWEET BAY
Bay Willow	see WILLOW BARK
BAYBERRY	see BAYBERRY, SWEET GALE
BCAA	see BRANCHED-CHAIN AMINO ACIDS
BC-PS	see PHOSPHATIDYLSERINE
BD	see BUTANEDIOL (BD)
Bdellium	see MYRRH
BDO	see BUTANEDIOL (BD)
B-DPNH	see NADH
Bead Tree	see NEEM
Bead Vine	see PRECATORY BEAN
Bean Herb	see SUMMER SAVORY
BEAN POD	see BEAN POD
Bean Trifoil	see LABURNUM
Bear Grass	see YUCCA
Bear Root	see OSHA
Bearberry	see UVA URSI
Bearbind	see GREATER BINDWEED
Beard Moss	see USNEA
Bearded Darnel	see TAUMELLOOLCH
Beargrape	see UVA URSI
BEAR'S GARLIC	see BEAR'S GARLIC
Bear's Grape	see POKEWEED, UVA URSI
Bear's Paw	see MALE FERN
Bear's Weed	see YERBA SANTA
Bear's-Bind	see GREATER BINDWEED
Beaumont Root	see BLACK ROOT
Beaver Poison	see WATER HEMLOCK
Beaver Tree	see MAGNOLIA
Beccabunga	see BROOKLIME
Bedstraw	see CLIVERS
Bedumil	see VITAMIN B12
Bee Balm	see OSWEGO TEA
Bee Glue	see PROPOLIS
Bee Nettle	see WHITE DEAD NETTLE FLOWER
Bee Plant	see BORAGE
BEE POLLEN	see BEE POLLEN
Bee Propolis	see PROPOLIS
Bee saliva	see ROYAL JELLY
Bee spit	see ROYAL JELLY
BEE VENOM	see BEE VENOM
Beebread	see BORAGE, RED CLOVER
Beeflower	see WALLFLOWER
Beefsteak Plant	see PERILLA
BEER	see BEER
Beesnest Plant	see WILD CARROT
BEESWAX	see BEESWAX
BEET	see BEET
Beg Kei	see ASTRAGALUS
Beggar's Blanket	see MULLEIN
Beggar's Buttons	see BURDOCK
Beggarweed	see DODDER, KNOTWEED
Beggary	see FUMITORY
Behada	see TERMINALIA

Bei Chai Hu	see BUPLEURUM
Bei Qi	see ASTRAGALUS
Bei Wu Wei Zi	see SCHISANDRA
Bejunco de Cerca	see ABUTA
Bel	see BAEL
Beleric Myrobalan	see TERMINALIA
Belgium Valerian	see VALERIAN
Belladone	see BELLADONNA
BELLADONNA	see BELLADONNA, SCOPOLIA
Belladonna scopola	see SCOPOLIA
Bellflower	see CODONOPSIS
Bellis Perennis	see WILD DAISY
Benedict's Herb	see AVENS
Bengal Quince	see BAEL
Beni chidori	see JAPANESE APRICOT
Benibana	see SAFFLOWER
Bennet's Root	see AVENS
Benzoe	see BENZOIN
BENZOIN	see BENZOIN
BERBERINE	see BERBERINE
Berberis	see OREGON GRAPE
Berberis aquifolium	see OREGON GRAPE
Berberis aristata	see TREE TURMERIC
Berberis chitria	see TREE TURMERIC
Berberis coriaria	see TREE TURMERIC
Berberis diversifolia	see OREGON GRAPE
Berberis jacquinii	see EUROPEAN BARBERRY
Berberis nervosa	see OREGON GRAPE
Berberis repens	see OREGON GRAPE
Berberis sanguinea	see EUROPEAN BARBERRY
Berberis sonnei	see OREGON GRAPE
Berberis vulgaris	see EUROPEAN BARBERRY
Berberitze	see EUROPEAN BARBERRY
Berberry	see EUROPEAN BARBERRY
Berbis	see EUROPEAN BARBERRY
BERGAMOT OIL	see BERGAMOT OIL
Bergamot Orange	see BERGAMOT OIL
Bergamotto Bigarade Orange	see BERGAMOT OIL
Bergwohlverleih	see ARNICA
Berro	see WATERCRESS
Berro di Agua	see WATERCRESS
Besenginaterkraut	see SCOTCH BROOM
Besom	see SCOTCH BROOM
BETA GLUCANS	see BETA GLUCANS
Beta Glycans	see BETA GLUCANS
Beta sitosterin	see BETA-SITOSTEROL
Beta Tocotrienol	see VITAMIN E
Beta Vulgaris	see BEET
BETA-CAROTENE	see BETA-CAROTENE
Beta-D-fructofuranosidase	see FRUCTO-OLIGOSACCHARIDES
Beta-D-ribofuranose	see RIBOSE
Beta-ecdysone	see ECDYSTERONE
Beta-galactosidase	see LACTASE
Beta-glycan	see BETA GLUCANS
Beta-hydroxy-beta-methylbutyric acid	see HYDROXYMETHYLBUTYRATE (HMB)
Beta-hydroxy-gamma-trimethylammonium butyrate	see L-CARNITINE
Betaine	see BETAINE ANHYDROUS, BETAINE HYDROCHLORIDE
BETAINE ANHYDROUS	see BETAINE ANHYDROUS
Betaine HCl	see BETAINE HYDROCHLORIDE
BETAINE HYDROCHLORIDE	see BETAINE HYDROCHLORIDE

 Natural Medicines Comprehensive Database Consumer Version (209) 472-2244

Beta-phenyl-alanine .... see PHENYLALANINE
Beta-sitostanol.. see SITOSTANOL
BETA-SITOSTEROL .... see BETA-SITOSTEROL
Beta-tocopherol.. see VITAMIN E
Betel Nut .... see ARECA
Betel Quid .... see ARECA
BETH ROOT .... see BETH ROOT
Betonica officinalis .... see BETONY
BETONY .... see BETONY
Betula .... see BIRCH
Betula alba .... see BIRCH
Betula alnus .... see BLACK ALDER
Betula glutinosa .... see BLACK ALDER
Betula pendula .... see BIRCH
Betula pubescens... see BIRCH
Betula verrucosa.. see BIRCH
Betulae Folium .... see BIRCH
BGA .... see BLUE-GREEN ALGAE
Bhang .... see MARIJUANA
BHT (BUTYLATED HYDROXYTOLUENE) ....
.... see BHT (BUTYLATED HYDROXYTOLUENE)
Bhunimba............................... see ANDROGRAPHIS
B-hydroxy B-methylbutyrate monohydrate ....
.... see HYDROXYMETHYLBUTYRATE (HMB)
B-hydroxy-N-trimethyl aminobutyric acid ....
.... see L-CARNITINE
Bi Bo ....see INDIAN LONG PEPPER
Bianco Spino .... see HAWTHORN
Bibernellkraut ....see PIMPINELLA
Bible Frankincense............................ see FRANKINCENSE
Biblical Mint .... see ENGLISH HORSEMINT
Bidara .... see ANDROGRAPHIS
Bidens tripartita........................ see BURR MARIGOLD
BIFIDOBACTERIA .... see BIFIDOBACTERIA
Bifidobacterium.......................... see BIFIDOBACTERIA
Bifidobacterium animalis DN-173 010 ....
.... see BIFIDOBACTERIA
Bifidobacterium bifidum .... see BIFIDOBACTERIA
Bifidobacterium breve.................... see BIFIDOBACTERIA
Bifidobacterium infantis.................. see BIFIDOBACTERIA
Bifidobacterium lactis .... see BIFIDOBACTERIA
Bifidobacterium longum .... see BIFIDOBACTERIA
Bifidobacterium regularis .... see BIFIDOBACTERIA
Bifidum .... see BIFIDOBACTERIA
Big Marigold .... see TAGETES
Bignonia heptaphylla ....see PAU D'ARCO
Bignonia sempervirens............................see GELSEMIUM
Bihara .... see TERMINALIA
Bija.. see ANNATTO
Bijapura ....see LIME
BILBERRY .... see BILBERRY
Biletan...............................see ALPHA-LIPOIC ACID
Bilva .... see BAEL
Bilwa .... see BAEL
Bing Ling Cao..................... see RABDOSIA RUBESCENS
Biobran...see MGN-3
Bioelectrical Minerals.......... see COLLOIDAL MINERALS
Bioflavonoid Concentrate .... see GRAPEFRUIT
Biota orientalis.................... see ORIENTAL ARBORVITAE
BIOTIN .... see BIOTIN
Biowater.............................. see WILLARD WATER
Birangasifa ....see YARROW
Birangasipha ....see YARROW
BIRCH .... see BIRCH
Birch Sugar .... see XYLITOL

Bird Bread............................... see COMMON STONECROP
Bird Pepper .... see CAPSICUM
Birdlime Mistletoe .... see EUROPEAN MISTLETOE
Bird's Eye Maple .... see RED MAPLE
Bird's Foot ....see FENUGREEK
Bird's Nest Root................................... see WILD CARROT
Bird's Tongue .... see ASH, KNOTWEED
Birdweed...see KNOTWEED
Birthroot .... see BETH ROOT
Birthwort .... see ARISTOLOCHIA
Bischofskrautfruchte .... see KHELLA
Biscuits .... see TORMENTIL
Bishop Wort .... see BETONY
Bishop's Elder ....see GOUTWEED
Bishop's Flower .... see BISHOP'S WEED
BISHOP'S WEED .... see BISHOP'S WEED, KHELLA
Bishopsweed ....see GOUTWEED
Bishopswort .... see BETONY, GOUTWEED
Bis-pantothenamidoethyl disulfide ....see PANTETHINE
Bissy Nut................................... see COLA NUT
BISTORT .... see BISTORT
BITTER ALMOND .... see BITTER ALMOND
Bitter Apple...............see BITTER MELON, COLOCYNTH
Bitter Ash ....see WAHOO
Bitter Bark...see CASCARA
Bitter Buttons ....see TANSY
Bitter Candy Tuft .... see CLOWN'S MUSTARD PLANT
Bitter Cucumber.........see BITTER MELON, COLOCYNTH
Bitter Damson ....see SIMARUBA
Bitter Fennel.. see FENNEL
Bitter Gourd .... see BITTER MELON
Bitter Herb .... see CENTAURY, TURTLE HEAD
Bitter Lettuce .... see WILD LETTUCE
BITTER MELON .... see BITTER MELON
BITTER MILKWORT.................see BITTER MILKWORT
Bitter Nightshade .... see BITTERSWEET NIGHTSHADE
BITTER ORANGE........................see BITTER ORANGE
Bitter Redberry...................... see AMERICAN DOGWOOD
Bitter Root.........see CANADIAN HEMP, GENTIAN
Bitter Stick .... see CHIRATA
Bitter Winter .... see PIPSISSEWA
Bitter Wintergreen .... see PIPSISSEWA
Bitter Wood .... see QUASSIA
Bitterbark ....see FEVER BARK
Bittergurke .... see BITTER MELON
Bitterstick .... see CHIRATA
Bittersweet .... see BITTERSWEET NIGHTSHADE
BITTERSWEET NIGHTSHADE ....
.... see BITTERSWEET NIGHTSHADE
Bitterwort ....see GENTIAN
Bixa orellana ....see ANNATTO
Bizzom .... see SCOTCH BROOM
BLACK ALDER...............................see BLACK ALDER
Black Balsam ....see PERU BALSAM
Black Beans ....see BEAN POD
Black Bindweed....................... see BLACK BRYONY
BLACK BRYONY........................... see BLACK BRYONY
Black Caraway ....see BLACK SEED
Black Catechu .... see CATECHU
Black Cherry .... see WILD CHERRY
Black Choke.................................. see WILD CHERRY
BLACK COHOSH..........................see BLACK COHOSH
Black Cumin .... see BLACK SEED
BLACK CURRANT .... see BLACK CURRANT
Black Cutch..................................... see CATECHU

Medical professionals should consult the Professional Version at www.NaturalDatabase.com.

Black Date............ see JUJUBE
Black Dogwood .... see ALDER BUCKTHORN
Black Elder.............see ELDERBERRY, ELDERFLOWER
Black Elderberry .... see ELDERBERRY
Black Ginger.. see GINGER
Black Grape Raisins.. see GRAPE
BLACK HAW ....see BLACK HAW
BLACK HELLEBORE...............see BLACK HELLEBORE
BLACK HOREHOUND...........see BLACK HOREHOUND
BLACK MULBERRY .... see BLACK MULBERRY
BLACK MUSTARD........................see BLACK MUSTARD
BLACK NIGHTSHADE .... see BLACK NIGHTSHADE
BLACK PEPPER AND WHITE PEPPER ....
.... see BLACK PEPPER AND WHITE PEPPER
Black Plum..see JAMBOLAN
BLACK PSYLLIUM .... see BLACK PSYLLIUM
Black Radish ....see RADISH
BLACK RASPBERRY ....see BLACK RASPBERRY
BLACK ROOT................... see BLACK ROOT, COMFREY
Black Sampson.............................see ECHINACEA
BLACK SEED .... see BLACK SEED
Black Snakeroot ....see BLACK COHOSH
Black Spanish Radish ....see RADISH
Black Stinking Horehound.........see BLACK HOREHOUND
Black Susans ....see ECHINACEA
Black Tang ....see BLADDERWRACK
BLACK TEA .... see BLACK TEA
BLACK WALNUT .... see BLACK WALNUT
Black Whortles.................................see BILBERRY
Black-Berried Alder ....see ELDERBERRY,
ELDERFLOWER
BLACKBERRY ....see BLACKBERRY
Blackcap...........................see BLACK RASPBERRY
Blackeye Root .... see BLACK BRYONY
Black-eyed Susan...........................see PRECATORY BEAN
Blackhaw...see BLACK HAW
BLACKTHORN .... see BLACKTHORN
Blackwort...see COMFREY
Bladder Fucus ....see BLADDERWRACK
Bladderpod .... see LOBELIA
BLADDERWORT ....see BLADDERWORT
BLADDERWRACK .... see BLADDERWRACK
Blanc Poivre...
.... see BLACK PEPPER AND WHITE PEPPER
Blanket Herb .... see MULLEIN
Blanket Leaf .... see MULLEIN
Blasentang...................................see BLADDERWRACK
Blatterdock ....see BUTTERBUR
Blazing Star....................see ALETRIS, FALSE UNICORN,
MARSH BLAZING STAR
Bleaberry..see BILBERRY
Bleached Beeswax ....see BEESWAX
Bleeding Heart .... see NERVE ROOT,
TURKEY CORN, WAHOO
Blessed Milk Thistle .... see MILK THISTLE
BLESSED THISTLE....................see BLESSED THISTLE
Blighia sapida.................................... see ACKEE
Blind Nettle............ see WHITE DEAD NETTLE FLOWER
Blind Weed......................see SHEPHERD'S PURSE
Blisterweed .... see BUTTERCUP
Blond Plantago...........................see BLOND PSYLLIUM
BLOND PSYLLIUM..................see BLOND PSYLLIUM
Blood Elder ....see DWARF ELDER
Blood Hilder...............................see DWARF ELDER
Blood of the Dragon....................see SANGRE DE GRADO

Blood Root .... see BLOODROOT
Blood Vine .... see FIREWEED
BLOODROOT .... see BLOODROOT, TORMENTIL
Bloodwood ....see LOGWOOD
Bloodwort ....see BLOODROOT, YARROW
Blooming Sally .... see FIREWEED,
PURPLE LOOSESTRIFE
Blowball... see DANDELION
Blue Balm ....see OSWEGO TEA
Blue Barberry.............................see OREGON GRAPE
Blue Bells ....see ABSCESS ROOT
Blue Cap................................. see CORNFLOWER
Blue Centaury .... see CORNFLOWER
Blue Chamomile .... see GERMAN CHAMOMILE
BLUE COHOSH..............................see BLUE COHOSH
Blue Curls .... see SELF-HEAL
BLUE FLAG................... see BLUE FLAG, ORRIS
Blue Ginseng.................................see BLUE COHOSH
Blue Gum ....see EUCALYPTUS
Blue Mallee ....see EUCALYPTUS
Blue Mallow Flower ....see MALLOW
Blue Malva ....see MALLOW
Blue Monkshood Root .... see ACONITE
Blue Nightshade.......... see BITTERSWEET NIGHTSHADE
Blue Pimpernel.................................see SKULLCAP
Blue Sailors ....see CHICORY
Blue Skullcap.................................see SKULLCAP
Blue Vervain ....see VERBENA
BLUEBERRY ....see BLUEBERRY
Bluebonnet .... see CORNFLOWER
Bluebottle .... see CORNFLOWER
Bluebow .... see CORNFLOWER
Bluebuttons .... see FIELD SCABIOUS
BLUE-GREEN ALGAE .... see BLUE-GREEN ALGAE
Blunt.................................... see MARIJUANA
Blushred Rabdosia .... see RABDOSIA RUBESCENS
BNADH .... see NADH
Bo He .... see PEPPERMINT
Bobbins......................................see ARUM
Bockshornklee.............................see FENUGREEK
Bockshornsame ....see FENUGREEK
Bofareira ....see CASTOR
BOG BILBERRY................... see BOG BILBERRY
Bog Myrtle .... see SWEET GALE
Bog Rhubarb.............................see BUTTERBUR
BOGBEAN .... see BOGBEAN
Bogshorns ....see BUTTERBUR
Bohnenkraut.................see SUMMER SAVORY
Boid d'inde............................. see CHA DE BUGRE
BOIS DE ROSE OIL .... see BOIS DE ROSE OIL
Bois d'ine .... see CHA DE BUGRE
Bois Douleur .... see MORINDA
Bol...see MYRRH
Bola ....see MYRRH
Boldea fragrans ....see BOLDO
Boldine ....see BOLDO
BOLDO ....see BOLDO
Boldo Folium ....see BOLDO
Boldoak Boldea................................see BOLDO
Boldus ....see BOLDO
Boletus versicolor .... see CORIOLUS MUSHROOM
Bolivian Coca .... see COCA
Bolus alba.................................. see KAOLIN
Bombus terrestis ....see BEE VENOM
Bonduc ....see DIVI-DIVI

Bone Meal..see CALCIUM
Bone Phosphate..........................see PHOSPHATE SALTS
BONESET... see BONESET
Bonnet Bellflower .... see CODONOPSIS
Bonplandia trifoliata .... see ANGOSTURA
Bookoo.. see BUCHU
Boor Tree ....see ELDERBERRY, ELDERFLOWER
Bopple Nut.................................... see MACADAMIA NUT
BORAGE .... see BORAGE
Borago.. see BORAGE
Borate..see BORON
Borbonia pinifolia .... see RED BUSH TEA
Borforsin .... see FORSKOLIN
Boric Acid...see BORON
Boric Anhydride...see BORON
Boric Tartrate...see BORON
Borneo-mahogany...............................see LAURELWOOD
BORON...see BORON
Boswellia...........................see INDIAN FRANKINCENSE
Boswellia Carteri .... see FRANKINCENSE
Boswellia Sacra............................... see FRANKINCENSE
Boswellia Serrata ....see INDIAN FRANKINCENSE
Bottle Brush ....see HORSETAIL
Bouillon Blanc .... see MULLEIN
Bouncing Bess .... see RED-SPUR VALERIAN
Bouncing-Bet ....see RED SOAPWORT
Bountry ....see ELDERBERRY, ELDERFLOWER
Bourbon Geranium Oil .... see ROSE GERANIUM OIL
Bourbon Vanilla .... see VANILLA
BOVINE CARTILAGE .... see BOVINE CARTILAGE
Bovine Casein Hydrosylate..............see CASEIN PEPTIDES
Bovine Colostrum .... see COLOSTRUM
Bovine Cortex Phosphatidylserine.......................................
....see PHOSPHATIDYLSERINE
Bovine Dialyzable Leukocyte Extract ....
....see TRANSFER FACTOR
Bovine Dialyzable Transfer Factor ....
....see TRANSFER FACTOR
Bovine Immunoglobulin .... see COLOSTRUM
Bovine Lactoferrin .... see LACTOFERRIN
Bovine Orchic Extract................... see ORCHIC EXTRACT
Bovine Spleen .... see SPLEEN EXTRACT
Bovine Testicle Extract .... see ORCHIC EXTRACT
Bovine Tracheal Cartilage (BTC) ....
.... see BOVINE CARTILAGE
Bovine Transfer Factor.................see TRANSFER FACTOR
Bovine Whey Protein Concentrate.......see WHEY PROTEIN
Bovis and Soldier..................... see RED-SPUR VALERIAN
Bovista ....see PUFF BALL
Bowman's Root......... see BLACK ROOT, INDIAN PHYSIC
Box Holly...................................see BUTCHER'S BROOM
Box Tree.............................. see AMERICAN DOGWOOD
Boxberry ....see WINTERGREEN
BOXWOOD.....see AMERICAN DOGWOOD, BOXWOOD
Brahma-Buti..................................... see GOTU KOLA
Brahma-Manduki .... see GOTU KOLA
BRAHMI................................ see BRAHMI, GOTU KOLA
Brake Root .... see LADY FERN
Bramble..see BLACKBERRY
Bran.. see WHEAT BRAN
BRANCHED-CHAIN AMINO ACIDS................................
.... see BRANCHED-CHAIN AMINO ACIDS
Branching Phytolacca .... see POKEWEED
Brandlattich.................................see COLTSFOOT
Brandy Mint .... see PEPPERMINT

Brassica alba .... see WHITE MUSTARD
Brassica nigra ....see BLACK MUSTARD
Brassica oleracea..............................see CABBAGE
Brauneria Angustifolia ....see ECHINACEA
Brauneria Pallida..................................see ECHINACEA
Brayera anthelmintica ....see KOUSSO
Brazil Powder...................................... see GOA POWDER
Brazil Root .... see IPECAC
Brazilian Cherimoya .... see GRAVIOLA
Brazilian Cocoa................................see GUARANA
Brazilian Diet Pill .... see CHA DE BUGRE
Brazilian Ginseng...................................see SUMA
Brazilian Guava.................................. see GUAVA
Brazilian Ipecac .... see IPECAC
Brazilian Mahogany ....see ANDIROBA
Brazilian Paw Paw .... see GRAVIOLA
Brazilian Red Guava .... see GUAVA
Brazilian Rhatany............................see RHATANY
Brechnusssamen............................see NUX VOMICA
Breeam .... see SCOTCH BROOM
BREWER'S YEAST.....................see BREWER'S YEAST
Brewer's Yeast (Hansen CBS 5926)....................................
.... see SACCHAROMYCES BOULARDII
BRICKELLIA................................see BRICKELLIA
Brickellia arguta................................see BRICKELLIA
Brickellia glutinosa ....see BRICKELLIA
Brickellia veronicaefolia ....see BRICKELLIA
Brideweed ....see YELLOW TOADFLAX
Bridewort ....see MEADOWSWEET
Brigham Tea .... see MORMON TEA
Brindal Berry ....see GARCINIA
Brindle Berry ....see GARCINIA
British Indian Lemongrass..................... see LEMONGRASS
British Myrrh .... see SWEET CICELY
British Tobacco ....see COLTSFOOT
Brittle Willow................................ see WILLOW BARK
Broad-Leafed Laurel.................. see MOUNTAIN LAUREL
Broad-Leaved Dock.................see YELLOW DOCK
Broad-leaved Garlic .... see BEAR'S GARLIC
BROCCOLI .... see BROCCOLI
BROMELAIN................................see BROMELAIN
Bromelainum................................see BROMELAIN
Bromelia ananas..............................see BROMELAIN
Bromelia comosa ....see BROMELAIN
Bromelin ....see BROMELAIN
Brook Mint .... see JAPANESE MINT
BROOKLIME ....see BROOKLIME
Brook-Tongue .... see WATER HEMLOCK
BROOM CORN ....see BROOM CORN
Broom Flower ....see DYER'S BROOM
Broom Tops................................ see SCOTCH BROOM
Browme .... see SCOTCH BROOM
Brown Algae ....see LAMINARIA
Brown Psyllium .... see BLACK PSYLLIUM
BROWN RICE..............................see BROWN RICE
Brown Tea ....see OOLONG TEA
Brownwort .... see SELF-HEAL
Bruchkraut...............................see RUPTUREWORT
Brugmansia suaveolens................ see ANGEL'S TRUMPET
Bruisewort............................ see COMFREY, WILD DAISY
Brum .... see SCOTCH BROOM
Brunfelsia hopeana...............................see MANACA
Brunfelsia uniflora ....see MANACA
Brunnenkresse...............................see WATERCRESS
Brushes and Combs............................... see TEAZLE

Medical professionals should consult the Professional Version at www.NaturalDatabase.com.

BRYONIA	see BRYONIA
Bryoniae Radix	see BRYONIA
BSP	see NATTOKINASE
Bucco	see BUCHU
BUCHU	see BUCHU
Buchweizen	see BUCKWHEAT
Buck Qi	see ASTRAGALUS
Buckbean	see BOGBEAN
Buckels	see COWSLIP
Buckeye	see HORSE CHESTNUT
BUCKHORN PLANTAIN	see BUCKHORN PLANTAIN
Buckthorn	see ALDER BUCKTHORN, CASCARA, EUROPEAN BUCKTHORN, SEA BUCKTHORN
Bucku	see BUCHU
BUCKWHEAT	see BUCKWHEAT
Buckwheat Pollen	see BEE POLLEN
Bud	see MARIJUANA
Buddhist Rosary Bead	see PRECATORY BEAN
Budwood	see AMERICAN DOGWOOD
Buergeria salicifolia	see MAGNOLIA
Bugbane	see AMERICAN HELLEBORE, BLACK COHOSH
BUGLE	see BUGLE, GROUND PINE
BUGLEWEED	see BUGLEWEED
Bugrinho	see CHA DE BUGRE
Bugula	see BUGLE
Bugwort	see BLACK COHOSH
BULBOUS BUTTERCUP	see BULBOUS BUTTERCUP
Bulgarian chlorella	see CHLORELLA
Bulgarian Green Algae	see CHLORELLA
Bulgarian Yogurt	see YOGURT
Bull Balls Extract	see ORCHIC EXTRACT
Bullock's Eye	see HOUSELEEK
Bull's Eyes	see MARSH MARIGOLD
Bullsfoot	see COLTSFOOT
Bullwort	see BISHOP'S WEED
Bumblebee Venom	see BEE VENOM
BUPLEURUM	see BUPLEURUM
Burage	see BORAGE
BURDOCK	see BURDOCK
Burn Plant	see ALOE
Burnet Saxifrage	see BURNING BUSH, PIMPINELLA
BURNING BUSH	see BURNING BUSH, WAHOO
BURR MARIGOLD	see BURR MARIGOLD
Burr Seed	see BURDOCK
Burrage	see BORAGE
Burren Myrtle	see BILBERRY
Burrwort	see BUTTERCUP
Bursae Pastoris Herba	see SHEPHERD'S PURSE
Bursting Heart	see WAHOO
Bush Nut	see MACADAMIA NUT
Bush Tree	see BOXWOOD
BUTANEDIOL (BD)	see BUTANEDIOL (BD)
BUTCHER'S BROOM	see BUTCHER'S BROOM
Butter and Eggs	see YELLOW TOADFLAX
Butter Daisy	see OX-EYE DAISY
Butter Rose	see COWSLIP
BUTTERBUR	see BUTTERBUR
BUTTERCUP	see BUTTERCUP
Butter-Dock	see BUTTERBUR
Buttered Hayhocks	see YELLOW TOADFLAX
Butterfly Dock	see BUTTERBUR
Butterfly Enzyme	see SERRAPEPTASE
Butterfly Weed	see PLEURISY ROOT
Butternussbaum	see BUTTERNUT
BUTTERNUT	see BUTTERNUT
Butterweed	see CANADIAN FLEABANE
Button Snakeroot	see MARSH BLAZING STAR
Buttonhole	see HARTSTONGUE
Buttons	see TANSY
Butua	see ABUTA
Butylated Hydroxytoluene	see BHT (BUTYLATED HYDROXYTOLUENE)
Butylene Glycol	see BUTANEDIOL (BD)
Butyrolactone	see GAMMA BUTYROLACTONE (GBL)
Buxaceae	see BOXWOOD
Buxus	see BOXWOOD
Buxus chinensis	see JOJOBA
Buxus colchica	see BOXWOOD
Buxus hyrcana	see BOXWOOD
Buxus sempervirens	see BOXWOOD
Byaki-jutsu	see ATRACTYLODES
C12 peptide	see CASEIN PEPTIDES
Ca	see CALCIUM
Caa-He-É	see STEVIA
Caa'Inhem	see STEVIA
Ca-A-Jhei	see STEVIA
Ca-A-Yupi	see STEVIA
CABBAGE	see CABBAGE
Cabbage Palm	see ACAI, SAW PALMETTO
Cabra	see CAPERS
Cacalia Amara	see CARQUEJA
Cacalia-Amargosa	see CARQUEJA
Cacao	see COCOA
Cachou	see CATECHU
Caclia Doce	see CARQUEJA
Cacliadoce	see CARQUEJA
Cactus	see HOODIA
Cactus Flowers	see PRICKLY PEAR CACTUS
Cactus Fruit	see PRICKLY PEAR CACTUS
Cactus grandiflorus	see CEREUS
Cactus Pear Fruit	see PRICKLY PEAR CACTUS
CADE OIL	see CADE OIL
Caesalpinia bonduc	see DIVI-DIVI
Caesalpinia bonducella	see DIVI-DIVI
Caesalpinia crista	see DIVI-DIVI
Caesium	see CESIUM
Cafe	see COFFEE
Cafe de Bugre	see CHA DE BUGRE
Cafe do Mato	see CHA DE BUGRE
Cafezinho	see CHA DE BUGRE
CAFFEINE	see CAFFEINE
Caffeine and Sodium Benzoate	see CAFFEINE
Caffeine Anhydrous	see CAFFEINE
Caffeine Citrate	see CAFFEINE
Cairina moschata	see OSCILLOCOCCINUM
Caje Oil	see NIAULI OIL
CAJEPUT OIL	see CAJEPUT OIL
Cajeputi aetheroleum	see CAJEPUT OIL
CALABAR BEAN	see CALABAR BEAN
Calabrese	see BROCCOLI
Calaguala	see POLYPODIUM LEUCOTOMOS
CALAMINT	see CALAMINT
Calamintha hortensis	see SUMMER SAVORY
Calamintha montana	see WINTER SAVORY
Calamintha nepeta	see CALAMINT
CALAMUS	see CALAMUS
Calamus draco	see DRAGON'S BLOOD
Calanolide	see LAURELWOOD
Calcifediol	see VITAMIN D

Calcii pantothenas..
.... see PANTOTHENIC ACID (VITAMIN B5)
Calcipotriene ....see VITAMIN D
Calcitriol ....see VITAMIN D
CALCIUM ....see CALCIUM
Calcium Ascorbate ...... see VITAMIN C (ASCORBIC ACID)
Calcium Carbonate Matrix.................................see CORAL
CALCIUM D-GLUCARATE ....
.... see CALCIUM D-GLUCARATE
Calcium Disodium Edathamil.............................. see EDTA
Calcium Disodium Edetate .... see EDTA
Calcium Disodium EDTA.................................... see EDTA
Calcium Disodium Versenate................................ see EDTA
Calcium Edetate .... see EDTA
Calcium EDTA.. see EDTA
Calcium Glucarate .... see CALCIUM D-GLUCARATE
Calcium Orthophosphate ....see PHOSPHATE SALTS
Calcium Pangamate .... see PANGAMIC ACID
Calcium Pantothenate ....
.... see PANTOTHENIC ACID (VITAMIN B5)
Calcium Phosphate.... see CALCIUM, PHOSPHATE SALTS
Calcium Phosphate Dibasic Anhydrous.......................
....see PHOSPHATE SALTS
Calcium Phosphate Dibasic Dihydrate ....
....see PHOSPHATE SALTS
Calcium Phosphate Tribasic..........see PHOSPHATE SALTS
Calcium Phosphate-Bone Ash........see PHOSPHATE SALTS
Calcium Pyruvate .... see PYRUVATE
CALENDULA ....see CALENDULA
Caley Pea ....see LATHYRUS
Calgam .... see PANGAMIC ACID
Calico Bush............................ see MOUNTAIN LAUREL
California Buckthorn ....see CASCARA
California Fern ....see HEMLOCK
CALIFORNIA POPPY..............see CALIFORNIA POPPY
Callicocca ipecacuanha....................................... see IPECAC
Calluna vulgaris .... see HEATHER
Colomba Root .... see COLOMBO
Calophyllum inophyllum ....see LAURELWOOD
Calophyllum Tree...................................see LAURELWOOD
CALOTROPIS ....see CALOTROPIS
Caltha palustris...........................see MARSH MARIGOLD
Caltrop.....................................see PUNCTURE VINE
Calumba .... see COLOMBO
Calumbo Root .... see COLOMBO
Calves' Snout ....see YELLOW TOADFLAX
Calystegia sepium .... see GREATER BINDWEED
Calzin .... see GRAPE
Camboge .... see GAMBOGE
Cambogia gummi-guta.................................see GARCINIA
Camellia Sinensis....................................see BLACK TEA,
GREEN TEA, OOLONG TEA
Camellia thea .... see BLACK TEA,
GREEN TEA, OOLONG TEA
Camellia theifera...................................... see BLACK TEA,
GREEN TEA, OOLONG TEA
Cammock ....see SPINY RESTHARROW
Camolea ....see MEZEREON
Camomilla............................. see GERMAN CHAMOMILE
Camomille allemande .... see GERMAN CHAMOMILE
CAMPHOR.......................................see CAMPHOR
Camphor of the Poor....................................see GARLIC
Camphora......................................see CAMPHOR
CANADA BALSAM .... see CANADA BALSAM,
HEMLOCK SPRUCE

Canada Pitch ....see PINUS BARK
Canada Root....................................see PLEURISY ROOT
Canada Tea.....................................see WINTERGREEN
Canada Turpentine .... see CANADA BALSAM
Canadian Beaver ....see CASTOREUM
CANADIAN FLEABANE..... see CANADIAN FLEABANE
Canadian Ginseng ....see GINSENG, AMERICAN
Canadian Goldenrod ....see GOLDENROD
Canadian Hemlock...............................see PINUS BARK
CANADIAN HEMP .... see CANADIAN HEMP
Canadian Horseweed.............. see CANADIAN FLEABANE
Canadian Mint......................... see JAPANESE MINT
Canadian Trailing Arbutus ..... see CANADIAN FLEABANE
Canadian-Fleabane................. see CANADIAN FLEABANE
CANAIGRE ....see CANAIGRE
Cananga odorata forma. genuina ....
.... see YLANG YLANG OIL
Cananga odorata forma. macrophylla ....see CANANGA OIL
CANANGA OIL ....see CANANGA OIL
Canard de Barbarie .... see OSCILLOCOCCINUM
Canarium commune .... see ELEMI
Canarium indicum................................... see ELEMI
Canarium luzonicum .... see ELEMI
Canarywood .... see MORINDA
Cancer Jalap .... see POKEWEED
Candleberry..................... see BAYBERRY, TUNG SEED
Candleberry Tree .... see TUNG SEED
Candleflower .... see MULLEIN
Candlenut .... see TUNG SEED
Candlewick .... see MULLEIN
Candytuft..................... see CLOWN'S MUSTARD PLANT
CANELLA ....see CANELLA
Canella alba ....see CANELLA
Canella winteriana ....see CANELLA
Cang Zhu.............................. see ATRACTYLODES
Cankerroot.................................... see GOLDTHREAD
Cankerwort........... see DANDELION, TANSY RAGWORT
Cannabis.. see MARIJUANA
Cannabis sativa .... see MARIJUANA
Cannelier de Ceylan .... see CINNAMON bark
Cannelli Beans ....see BEAN POD
CANTHAXANTHIN....................see CANTHAXANTHIN
Canton Cassia.................. see CASSIA CINNAMON
Cao Ma-Huang.................................see EPHEDRA
Capdockin ....see BUTTERBUR
Cape Aloe ....see ALOE
Cape Gooseberry..................... see WINTER CHERRY
Cape Periwinkle..........see MADAGASCAR PERIWINKLE
CAPERS .... see CAPERS
Capillary Wormwood.....................................see YIN CHEN
Capim Doce .... see STEVIA
Capim-Cidrao............................ see LEMONGRASS
Capparis rupestris................................. see CAPERS
Capparis spinosa .... see CAPERS
Cappero .... see CAPERS
Capsaicin .... see CAPSICUM
Capsella.........................see SHEPHERD'S PURSE
Capsella bursa-pastoris ....see SHEPHERD'S PURSE
CAPSICUM .... see CAPSICUM
Caramuru...see CATUABA
Carapa ....see ANDIROBA
Carapa guianensis ....see ANDIROBA
CARAWAY .... see CARAWAY
Carbenia benedicta.......................see BLESSED THISTLE
Carbon..........................see ACTIVATED CHARCOAL

Carbonaceous Activated Water .... see WILLARD WATER
Carboxyethylgermanium sesquioxide ...... see GERMANIUM
Card Thistle... see TEAZLE
CARDAMOM.....................................see CARDAMOM
Cardamon ....see CARDAMOM
Cardo... see ARTICHOKE
Cardo de Comer .... see ARTICHOKE
Cardo Santo .... see BLESSED THISTLE
Cardomomi Fructus ....see CARDAMOM
Cardon d'Espagne ....see ARTICHOKE
Cardoon..see ARTICHOKE
Cardui mariae Fructus.......................... see MILK THISTLE
Cardui mariae Herba .... see MILK THISTLE
Carduus .... see BLESSED THISTLE
Carduus benedictus ....see BLESSED THISTLE
Carduus marianus............................... see MILK THISTLE
Carex arenaria ....see GERMAN SARSAPARILLA
Carica Papaya............................ see PAPAIN, PAPAYA
Carica peltata .... see PAPAYA
Carica posoposa .... see PAPAYA
Caricae Fructus ....see FIG
Caricae Papayae Folium............................see PAPAYA
Caricis rhizoma ....see GERMAN SARSAPARILLA
Carilla Gourd .... see BITTER MELON
CARLINA....................................... see CARLINA
Carline Thistle...............................see MUGWORT
Carmantina .... see ANDROGRAPHIS
Carnitine................................... see L-CARNITINE
Carnitine Acetyl Ester .... see ACETYL-L-CARNITINE
Carnitor .... see L-CARNITINE
CARNOSINE....................................see CARNOSINE
CAROB...see CAROB
Carolina Pink .... see PINK ROOT
Carolina Vanilla............................see DEERTONGUE
Caroline Jasmine ....see GELSEMIUM
Carony Bark .... see ANGOSTURA
Carophyll Red ....see CANTHAXANTHIN
Carosella .... see FENNEL
Carotenes........................... see BETA-CAROTENE
Carotenoids .... see BETA-CAROTENE
Carotte a Moreau.................. see WATER HEMLOCK
Carpenter's Herb ....see BUGLE, SELF-HEAL
Carpenter's Square .... see FIGWORT
Carpenter's Weed ....see SELF-HEAL, YARROW
Carphephorus odoratissimus...................see DEERTONGUE
CARQUEJA.......................................see CARQUEJA
CARRAGEENAN...................... see CARRAGEENAN
Carrot Weed ....see HEMLOCK
Cartagena Ipecac................................ see IPECAC
Carthamus Tinctorius.......................see SAFFLOWER
Carubinose .... see D-MANNOSE
Carum.......................... see BISHOP'S WEED
Carum carvi.................................... see CARAWAY
Carum petroselinum................................ see PARSLEY
Carum velenovskyi .... see CARAWAY
Carvacrol..................................see OREGANO
Carvi Fructus................................. see CARAWAY
Caryophylli flos .... see CLOVE
Caryophyllus aromaticus .... see CLOVE
Cascabela thevetia..........................see OLEANDER
CASCARA.....................................see CASCARA
Cascara sagrada...............................see CASCARA
CASCARILLA .... see CASCARILLA
CASEIN PEPTIDES.....................see CASEIN PEPTIDES
Casein Protein Hydrosylate...........see CASEIN PEPTIDES

Caseweed ....see SHEPHERD'S PURSE
CASHEW...see CASHEW
Cashou....................................... see CATECHU
Casse .... see SENNA
Cassia acutifolia .... see SENNA
Cassia angustifolia .... see SENNA
Cassia aromaticum .... see CASSIA CINNAMON
CASSIA AURICULATA........... see CASSIA AURICULATA
CASSIA CINNAMON .... see CASSIA CINNAMON
Cassia lanceolata .... see SENNA
Cassia lignea .... see CASSIA CINNAMON
Cassia senna .... see SENNA
CASSIE ABSOLUTE .... see CASSIE ABSOLUTE
Cassis ....see BLACK CURRANT
Castanea americana............... see AMERICAN CHESTNUT
Castanea dentata.................... see AMERICAN CHESTNUT
Castanea sativa .... see EUROPEAN CHESTNUT
Castanea vesca .... see EUROPEAN CHESTNUT
Castanea vulgaris .... see EUROPEAN CHESTNUT
Castaneae Folium................... see EUROPEAN CHESTNUT
Castaño de Indias .... see HORSE CHESTNUT
CASTOR.......................................see CASTOR
Castor canadensis............................see CASTOREUM
Castor Fiber................................see CASTOREUM
Castorbean.....................................see CASTOR
CASTOREUM ....see CASTOREUM
Catalonina Jasmine ....see JASMINE
Catalyst Altered Water ....see WILLARD WATER
Catarrh Root...................................see ALPINIA
Catchfly .... see CANADIAN HEMP
Catchweed.....................................see CLIVERS
CATECHU ....see CATECHU
Catechu nigrum...............................see CATECHU
Caterpillar fungus.......................see CORDYCEPS
Catha edulis....................................see KHAT
Catharanthus ....see MADAGASCAR PERIWINKLE
Catharanthus roseus .....see MADAGASCAR PERIWINKLE
Catmint.................................. see CATNIP
CATNIP...................................... see CATNIP
Catrix.................... see BOVINE CARTILAGE
Catrix-S .... see BOVINE CARTILAGE
CAT'S CLAW ....see CAT'S CLAW
Cat's Ear Flower .... see CAT'S FOOT
CAT'S FOOT ....see CAT'S FOOT
Catsfoot .... see GROUND IVY
Cat's-head ....see PUNCTURE VINE
Cat's-paw .... see GROUND IVY
Catswort .... see CATNIP
CATUABA.....................................see CATUABA
Catuaba casca.................................see CATUABA
Caulophyllum...........................see BLUE COHOSH
Caulophyllum thalictroides...............see BLUE COHOSH
Cavalinha ....see HORSETAIL
Cavinton .... see VINPOCETINE
Cayenne................................. see CAPSICUM
Cayenne Rosewood Oil.................. see BOIS DE ROSE OIL
CDP-choline .... see CITICOLINE
CDS......................... see CHONDROITIN SULFATE
Ce Bai................... see ORIENTAL ARBORVITAE
Ceanothus americanus .... see NEW JERSEY TEA
Ceanothus intermedius................. see NEW JERSEY TEA
Cedar................... see EASTERN RED CEDAR
Cedar Leaf Oil................................ see THUJA
Cedarwood .... see EASTERN RED CEDAR
Cedoaria ....see ZEDOARY

Cedro..see ANDIROBA
Cedrus atlantica....................see ATLANTIC CEDAR
Celandine ....see GREATER CELANDINE
Celastrus edulis..see KHAT
Celastrus scandens ....see AMERICAN BITTERSWEET
Celeriac ....see CELERY
CELERY ....see CELERY
Celery-Leafed Crowfoot .....see POISONOUS BUTTERCUP
Cemphire...see CAMPHOR
Centaurea cyanus ....see CORNFLOWER
Centaurea segetum ....see CORNFLOWER
Centaurium erythraea.........................see CENTAURY
Centaurium minus ....see CENTAURY
Centaurium umbellatum.......................see CENTAURY
CENTAURY ....see CENTAURY
Centella ....see GOTU KOLA
Centella asiatica ....see GOTU KOLA
Centella coriacea ....see GOTU KOLA
Centellase ....see GOTU KOLA
Centinode ....see KNOTWEED
Centranthus ruber.....................see RED-SPUR VALERIAN
Centraria...............................see ICELAND MOSS
Centroporus squamosus ....see SHARK LIVER OIL
Cephaelis acuminata ....see IPECAC
Cephaelis ipecacuanha............................see IPECAC
Cerasee ....see BITTER MELON
Cerasus laurocerasus...........see CHERRY LAUREL WATER
Cerasus vulgaris.............................see SOUR CHERRY
Ceratonia siliqua ....see CAROB
Cerbera thevetia ....see OLEANDER
Cereal Fiber................... see BARLEY, OATS,
RICE BRAN, WHEAT BRAN
CEREUS ....see CEREUS
Cereus grandiflorus ....see CEREUS
Cerezo acido................................see SOUR CHERRY
Cerisier acide................................see SOUR CHERRY
Cernilton ....see RYE GRASS
Cervus elaphus ....see DEER VELVET
Cervus nippon ....see DEER VELVET
CESIUM ....see CESIUM
Cesium Chloride ....see CESIUM
Cesium-137 ....see CESIUM
Cetoal ....see ZEDOARY
Cetorhinus maximus ....see SHARK LIVER OIL
Cetraria islandica ....see ICELAND MOSS
Cetyl Laureate ....see CETYLATED FATTY ACIDS
Cetyl Myristate....................see CETYLATED FATTY ACIDS
Cetyl Myristoleate............see CETYLATED FATTY ACIDS
Cetyl Oleate ....see CETYLATED FATTY ACIDS
Cetyl Palmitate..................see CETYLATED FATTY ACIDS
Cetyl Palmitoleate.............see CETYLATED FATTY ACIDS
CETYLATED FATTY ACIDS...........................
..........................see CETYLATED FATTY ACIDS
Cetylated Monounsaturated Fatty Acids ....
..........................see CETYLATED FATTY ACIDS
Cetylmyristoleate ....see CETYLATED FATTY ACIDS
Cevitamic Acid...........see VITAMIN C (ASCORBIC ACID)
Ceylon Cinnamon ....see CINNAMON bark
Ceylon Citronella ....see CITRONELLA OIL
Ceylon Citronella Grass........................see LEMONGRASS
Ceylonzimt................................see CINNAMON bark
Ceylonzimtbaum ....see CINNAMON bark
CHA DE BUGRE ....see CHA DE BUGRE
Cha de Frade ....see CHA DE BUGRE
Chaat ....see KHAT

Cha-de-Negro-Mina ....see CHA DE BUGRE
Chai-Jen-Shen ....see PANAX PSEUDOGINSENG
Chamaelirium carolianum.................see FALSE UNICORN
Chamaelirium luteum.......................see FALSE UNICORN
Chamaemelum nobile ....see ROMAN CHAMOMILE
Chamaenerion angustifolium.......................see FIREWEED
Chamaesyce hirta.....................................see EUPHORBIA
Chamerion angustifolium.............................see FIREWEED
Chamomile...........................see GERMAN CHAMOMILE,
ROMAN CHAMOMILE
Chamomilla ....see GERMAN CHAMOMILE,
ROMAN CHAMOMILE
Chamomilla recutita..............see GERMAN CHAMOMILE
Chamomillae Ramane Flos.......see ROMAN CHAMOMILE
Champagne of Life ....see KOMBUCHA TEA
CHANCA PIEDRA ....see CHANCA PIEDRA
Chandana.....................see WHITE SANDALWOOD
Chandrika..........see FENUGREEK, INDIAN SNAKEROOT
Chang Zhe ....see ATRACTYLODES
Chanvrin.....................see HEMP AGRIMONY
CHAPARRAL.....................see CHAPARRAL
Charas ....see MARIJUANA
Charcoal ....see ACTIVATED CHARCOAL
Charity....................see JACOB'S LADDER
Charnuska ....see BLACK SEED
Chaste Tree Berry ....see CHASTEBERRY
CHASTEBERRY ....see CHASTEBERRY
CHAULMOOGRA ....see CHAULMOOGRA
Che Qian Zi.....................see BLOND PSYLLIUM
Cheat ....see TAUMELLOOLCH
Chebulic Myrobalan.....................see TERMINALIA
Checkerberry...............see SQUAWVINE, WINTERGREEN
Cheese Fruit ....see MORINDA
Cheese Rennet.....................see LADY'S BEDSTRAW
Cheese Renning ....see LADY'S BEDSTRAW
Cheeseflower.....................see MALLOW
Cheiranthus cheiri ....see WALLFLOWER
CHEKEN ....see CHEKEN
Chelated Boron ....see CHELATED MINERALS
Chelated Calcium ....see CHELATED MINERALS
Chelated Chromium ....see CHELATED MINERALS
Chelated Cobalt.................see CHELATED MINERALS
Chelated Copper ....see CHELATED MINERALS
Chelated Iron ....see CHELATED MINERALS
Chelated Magnesium ....see CHELATED MINERALS,
MAGNESIUM
Chelated Manganese ....see CHELATED MINERALS
CHELATED MINERALS ......see CHELATED MINERALS
Chelated Molybdenum............see CHELATED MINERALS
Chelated Potassium ....see CHELATED MINERALS
Chelated Selenium ....see CHELATED MINERALS
Chelated Trace Minerals ....see CHELATED MINERALS
Chelated Vanadium ....see CHELATED MINERALS
Chelated Zinc.........................see CHELATED MINERALS
Chelidonii Herba....................see GREATER CELANDINE
Chelidonium Majus.................see GREATER CELANDINE
Chelone ....see TURTLE HEAD
Chelone glabra ....see TURTLE HEAD
CHENOPODIUM OIL ....see CHENOPODIUM OIL
Chenopodium vulvaria............................see ARRACH
CHEROKEE ROSEHIP............see CHEROKEE ROSEHIP
Cherry ....see SWEET CHERRY
CHERRY LAUREL WATER..............................
.............................see CHERRY LAUREL WATER
CHERVIL ....see CHERVIL

Medical professionals should consult the
Professional Version at www.NaturalDatabase.com.

Chervis .... see SKIRRET
Chestnut .... see HORSE CHESTNUT
Chi Hu .... see BUPLEURUM
Chi Shao .... see PEONY
CHICKEN COLLAGEN .... see CHICKEN COLLAGEN
Chicken Toe .... see CORAL ROOT
Chickling Vetch .... see LATHYRUS
Chick-Pea .... see LATHYRUS
CHICKWEED................................ see CHICKWEED
CHICORY .... see CHICORY
Chicory Extract .... see INULIN
Chicory Inulin .... see INULIN
Chicory Inulin Hydrolysate.............................
.... see FRUCTO-OLIGOSACCHARIDES
Chiendent Odorant .... see VETIVER
Ch'ih Shen .... see DANSHEN
Child Pick-a-Back .... see CHANCA PIEDRA
Children's Bane .... see WATER HEMLOCK
Chili Pepper .... see CAPSICUM
Chimaphila .... see PIPSISSEWA
Chimarrao ....see MATE
Chimney-Sweeps .... see BUCKHORN PLANTAIN
Chin Cups .... see CUPMOSS
China Bark .... see QUILLAIA
China Clay .... see KAOLIN
China Gooseberry .... see KIWI
China Root .... see ALPINIA, WILD YAM
Chinarinde .... see CINCHONA
China-root .... see PORIA MUSHROOM
China-Wood Oil .... see TUNG SEED
Chinchilla Enana .... see TAGETES
Chinchimani .... see CARQUEJA
Chinese Almond.................................see APRICOT
Chinese Angelica .... see DONG QUAI
Chinese Arborvitae............... see ORIENTAL ARBORVITAE
Chinese Boxthorn............................. see LYCIUM
Chinese Cinnamon .... see CASSIA CINNAMON
CHINESE CLUB MOSS .... see CHINESE CLUB MOSS
Chinese Cornbind............................... see FO-TI
CHINESE CUCUMBER .... see CHINESE CUCUMBER
Chinese Date .... see JUJUBE
Chinese Ephedra .... see EPHEDRA
Chinese Gelatin .... see AGAR
Chinese Ginger...............................see ALPINIA
Chinese Ginseng ....see GINSENG, PANAX
Chinese Goldthread.................... see GOLDTHREAD
Chinese Gooseberry .... see KIWI
Chinese Indigo .... see ISATIS
Chinese Joint-fir .... see EPHEDRA
Chinese Jujube .... see JUJUBE
Chinese Knotweed .... see FO-TI
Chinese Lantern .... see WINTER CHERRY
Chinese Licorice .... see LICORICE
CHINESE MALLOW................. see CHINESE MALLOW
Chinese Mint .... see JAPANESE MINT
Chinese Mint Oil................... see JAPANESE MINT
Chinese Parsley .... see CORIANDER
Chinese Pepper.................. see CHINESE PRICKLY ASH
Chinese Persimmon ....see JAPANESE PERSIMMON
Chinese Plum ....see JAPANESE PERSIMMON
CHINESE PRICKLY ASH .... see CHINESE PRICKLY ASH
Chinese Privet .... see GLOSSY PRIVET
Chinese Rhubarb.............................. see RHUBARB
Chinese Rosehip.................... see CHEROKEE ROSEHIP
Chinese Salvia .... see DANSHEN

Chinese Scholartree .... see PAGODA TREE
Chinese Senega ....see SENEGA
Chinese Skullcap.................see BAIKAL SKULLCAP
Chinese Snake Gourd.............. see CHINESE CUCUMBER
Chinese Star Anise .... see STAR ANISE
Chinese Sumach................... see TREE OF HEAVEN
Chinese Thoroughwax ....see BUPLEURUM
Chinese Vitex ....see CHASTEBERRY
Chinese Wolfberry .... see LYCIUM
Chinese Wormwood................ see SWEET ANNIE
Chinesischer Limonenbaum.................... see SCHISANDRA
Ching-hao ....see SWEET ANNIE
Chinli-Chih .... see BITTER MELON
Chintul .... see ADRUE
Chinwood...................................... see YEW
Chionanthus .... see FRINGETREE
Chionanthus virginicus ....see FRINGETREE
CHIRATA.................................. see CHIRATA
Chirbhita .... see PAPAYA
Chirca Melosa .... see CARQUEJA
Chiretta.................. see ANDROGRAPHIS, CHIRATA
Chisil.................................see BITTER ORANGE
Chitosamine ..... see GLUCOSAMINE HYDROCHLORIDE,
                          GLUCOSAMINE SULFATE
CHITOSAN .... see CHITOSAN
Chitosan Ascorbate .... see CHITOSAN
Chitra.............................see TREE TURMERIC
Chittem Bark ....see CASCARA
Chiu.................................see YIN CHEN
CHIVE .... see CHIVE
CHLORELLA.............................see CHLORELLA
CHLOROPHYLL .... see CHLOROPHYLL
CHLOROPHYLLIN .... see CHLOROPHYLLIN
Chocolate ....see COCOA
Chocolate Root.....................see WATER AVENS
Choke Cherry .... see WILD CHERRY
Cholecalciferol................................see VITAMIN D
CHOLINE ....see CHOLINE
Choline Alphoscerate .... see ALPHA-GPC
Chondrodendron tomentosum................see PAREIRA
CHONDROITIN SULFATE ....
.... see CHONDROITIN SULFATE
Chondrus Crispus.................... see CARRAGEENAN
Chondrus Extract .... see CARRAGEENAN
Chongras .... see POKEWEED
Chop Nut.................see CALABAR BEAN
Chosen-Gomischi.................... see SCHISANDRA
Chota-Chand .... see INDIAN SNAKEROOT
Christe Herbe ....see BLACK HELLEBORE
Christmas Flower .... see POINSETTIA
Christmas Rose ....see BLACK HELLEBORE
Christmas Rose Plant................see BLACK HELLEBORE
Christ's Spear .... see ENGLISH ADDER'S TONGUE
Christ's Thorn .... see HOLLY
CHROMIUM .... see CHROMIUM
Chrysanthemi Vulgaris Flos ....see TANSY
Chrysanthemi Vulgaris Herba ....see TANSY
CHRYSANTHEMUM ....see CHRYSANTHEMUM
Chrysanthemum cinerariifolium ....see PYRETHRUM
Chrysanthemum leucanthemum............see OX-EYE DAISY
Chrysanthemum morifolium........see CHRYSANTHEMUM
Chrysanthemum parthenium .... see FEVERFEW
Chrysanthemum praealtum .... see FEVERFEW
Chrysanthemum sinense ....see CHRYSANTHEMUM
Chrysanthemum stipulaceum........see CHRYSANTHEMUM

Chrysatobine .... see GOA POWDER
CHRYSIN .... see CHRYSIN
Chrysopogon zizanioides .... see VETIVER
Chua ....see AMARANTH
Chuan Dang .... see CODONOPSIS
Chuan Xin Lian .... see ANDROGRAPHIS
Chuan-wu .... see ACONITE
Chuchuhuasha ....see CATUABA
Chuchupate ....see OSHA
Chundan .... see SALACIA
Church Broom.. see TEAZLE
Church-Flower ....see MADAGASCAR PERIWINKLE
Churnstaff ....see YELLOW TOADFLAX
CHYMOTRYPSIN .... see CHYMOTRYPSIN
CI Food Orange 8........................see CANTHAXANTHIN
Ci Wu Jia........................ see GINSENG, SIBERIAN
Cichorii Herba...................................see CHICORY
Cichorii Radix......................................see CHICORY
Cichorium intybus.............................see CHICORY
Cicuta bulbifera.......................... see WATER HEMLOCK
Cicuta californica .... see WATER HEMLOCK
Cicuta douglasii .... see WATER HEMLOCK
Cicuta mackenzieana .... see WATER HEMLOCK
Cicuta maculata........................... see WATER HEMLOCK
Cicuta occidentalis...................... see WATER HEMLOCK
Cicuta vagans .... see WATER HEMLOCK
Cicuta virosa .... see WATER HEMLOCK
Cider Vinegar ....see APPLE CIDER VINEGAR
CIGUATERA ....see CIGUATERA
Cilantro .... see CORIANDER
Cimicifuga racemosa ....see BLACK COHOSH
Cinchol .... see BETA-SITOSTEROL
CINCHONA.................................. see CINCHONA
Cineraria maritima .... see DUSTY MILLER
Cinnamomi cassiae cortex .... see CASSIA CINNAMON
Cinnamomum aromaticum.......... see CASSIA CINNAMON
Cinnamomum camphora............................see CAMPHOR
Cinnamomum cassia .... see CASSIA CINNAMON
Cinnamomum verum .... see CINNAMON bark
Cinnamomum zeylanicum .... see CINNAMON bark
Cinnamon .... see CINNAMON bark
CINNAMON bark .... see CINNAMON bark
Cinnamon Flos........................... see CASSIA CINNAMON
Cinnamon Sedge ....see CALAMUS
Cinnamon Wood ....see SASSAFRAS
Cinquefoil ....see EUROPEAN FIVE-FINGER GRASS,
TORMENTIL
Cique Vireuse .... see WATER HEMLOCK
Cis-capsaicin ....see CAPSICUM
Cis-resveratrol.................................. see RESVERATROL
Cissampelos pareira .... see ABUTA
Ciste .... see LABDANUM
Cistus canadensis ....see FROSTWORT
Cistus creticus .... see LABDANUM
Cistus incanus .... see LABDANUM
Cistus ladanifer .... see LABDANUM
Cistus ladaniferus.............................. see LABDANUM
Cistus polymorphus .... see LABDANUM
Cistus villosus .... see LABDANUM
CITICOLINE .... see CITICOLINE
Citrated Caffeine .... see CAFFEINE
Citri Sinensis....................................... see SWEET ORANGE
Citric Acid........................see ALPHA HYDROXY ACIDS
Citronella.....................see LEMONGRASS, STONE ROOT
CITRONELLA OIL ....see CITRONELLA OIL

Citron-Scent Gum ....see LEMON EUCALYPTUS
Citrullus colocynthis ....see COLOCYNTH
Citrus acida ....see LIME
Citrus amara .... see BITTER ORANGE
Citrus aurantifolia ....see LIME
Citrus aurantium....................see BITTER ORANGE
Citrus aurantium var. bergamia .... see BERGAMOT OIL
Citrus aurantium var. dulcis ..... see SWEET ORANGE
Citrus aurantium var. sinensis .... see SWEET ORANGE
Citrus bergamia .... see BERGAMOT OIL
Citrus bigarradia.............................see BITTER ORANGE
Citrus Bioflavones........see METHOXYLATED FLAVONES
Citrus Bioflavonoids .... see DIOSMIN, HESPERIDIN,
METHOXYLATED FLAVONES,
QUERCETIN, RUTIN
Citrus decumana....................... see GRAPEFRUIT
Citrus Flavones ....see METHOXYLATED FLAVONES
Citrus Flavonoids ....see METHOXYLATED FLAVONES
Citrus Grandis Extract..................... see GRAPEFRUIT
Citrus lima ....see LIME
Citrus limetta var. aromatica ....see LIME
Citrus Limon .... see LEMON
Citrus Limonum .... see LEMON
Citrus macracantha...................... see SWEET ORANGE
Citrus maxima ....see GRAPEFRUIT
Citrus medica var. acida ....see LIME
Citrus paradisi ....see GRAPEFRUIT
Citrus Polymethoxylated Flavones ....
....................................see METHOXYLATED FLAVONES
Citrus Seed Extract ....see GRAPEFRUIT
Citrus Sinensis .... see SWEET ORANGE
Citrus vulgaris..............................see BITTER ORANGE
Civamide .... see CAPSICUM
Civan Percemi ....see YARROW
Cives....................................... see CHIVE
CIVET ....see CIVET
Civettictis civetta.....................................see CIVET
CLA.............see CONJUGATED LINOLEIC ACID
Cladonia pyxidata ....see CUPMOSS
CLA-Free Fatty Acid ....
.......................see CONJUGATED LINOLEIC ACID
Claraiba .... see CHA DE BUGRE
Clarified Honey....................... see HONEY
CLARY SAGE......................................see CLARY SAGE
CLA-Triacylglycerol..
.......................see CONJUGATED LINOLEIC ACID
Claviceps purpurea........................... see ERGOT
Clay Suspension Products..... see COLLOIDAL MINERALS
Clear Eye...see CLARY SAGE
Cleavers..see CLIVERS
Cleaverwort..see CLIVERS
CLEMATIS .... see CLEMATIS, WOODBINE
Clematis recta......................................see CLEMATIS
Clematis virginiana ....see WOODBINE
Clematis vitalba .... see TRAVELER'S JOY
Clerodendranthus spicatus ....see JAVA TEA
Clerodendrum spicatum ....see JAVA TEA
Climbing Knotweed .... see FO-TI
Clinopodium nepeta .... see CALAMINT
CLIVERS...see CLIVERS
Clotbur ....see BURDOCK
Clot-Bur .... see MULLEIN
Clous de Girolfe ....see CLOVE
CLOVE .... see CLOVE
Clove Garlic ....see GARLIC

Clove Pepper...see ALLSPICE
Clovone...see RED CLOVER
Clown's Lungwort................................... see MULLEIN
CLOWN'S MUSTARD PLANT ....
.... see CLOWN'S MUSTARD PLANT
CLUB MOSS ....see CLUB MOSS
Cluster Malva.....................see CHINESE MALLOW
Clustered Wintercherry .... see ASHWAGANDHA
Clutia eluteria............................... see CASCARILLA
CM ....see CETYLATED FATTY ACIDS
CMO ....see CETYLATED FATTY ACIDS
Cnici Benedicti Herba....................see BLESSED THISTLE
Cnicus ....see BLESSED THISTLE
Cnicus benedictus ....see BLESSED THISTLE
Cnidii monnieri fructus.............................see CNIDIUM
CNIDIUM ....see CNIDIUM
Cnidium Monnieri Fructus...........................see CNIDIUM
CO Q10 ....see COENZYME Q-10
Coachweed...see CLIVERS
Coakum-Chorngras .... see POKEWEED
Coastal Douglas Fir................see OREGON FIR BALSAM
Cobalamin.................................see VITAMIN B12
Cobalamin Enzyme.............................see DIBENCOZIDE
Cobamamide ....see DIBENCOZIDE
Cobnut.................................see HAZELNUT
COCA .... see COCA
Cocaine Plant .... see COCA
Cocash Weed........................ see GOLDEN RAGWORT
Coccinia grandis...............................see IVY GOURD
Coccinia indica.................................see IVY GOURD
Coccinia ordifolia.............................see IVY GOURD
Cocculus.............................see LEVANT BERRY
Cocculus palmatus .... see COLOMBO
Cocculus suberosus.........................see LEVANT BERRY
Cochin Ginger.. see GINGER
Cochin Lemongrass .... see LEMONGRASS
Cochlearia armoracia .... see HORSERADISH
Cochlearia officinalis ....see SCURVY GRASS
COCILLANA.............................. see COCILLANA
Cockle .... see CORN COCKLE
Cockle Buttons.................................see BURDOCK
Cocklebur........see AGRIMONY, BURDOCK
Cockspur Rye .... see ERGOT
Cockup Hat .... see QUEEN'S DELIGHT
Cocky Baby.................................see ARUM
Coco Palm .... see COCONUT OIL
COCOA...see COCOA
COCONUT OIL .... see COCONUT OIL
Coconut Oil Extract .... see LAURIC ACID
Coconut Palm.......................... see COCONUT OIL
Cocos nucifera .... see COCONUT OIL
Cocowort.....................see SHEPHERD'S PURSE
Coculus Fructus ....see LEVANT BERRY
COD LIVER OIL.....................see COD LIVER OIL
Cod Liver Oil .... see COD LIVER OIL, FISH OIL
Cod Oil.................................see COD LIVER OIL
Coda cavallina.................................see HORSETAIL
CODONOPSIS ....see CODONOPSIS
Codonopsis tubulosa .... see CODONOPSIS
Coenzyme 1 .... see NADH
Co-enzyme B12 ....see DIBENCOZIDE
COENZYME Q-10 ....see COENZYME Q-10
Coenzyme R .... see BIOTIN
Coffea arabica ....see COFFEE, COFFEE CHARCOAL
Coffea arnoldiana ....see COFFEE

Coffea bukobensis ....see COFFEE
Coffea canephora ....see COFFEE, COFFEE CHARCOAL
Coffea liberica............see COFFEE, COFFEE CHARCOAL
Coffea robusta ....see COFFEE
COFFEE...see COFFEE
COFFEE CHARCOAL...............see COFFEE CHARCOAL
Coffee of the Woods........................... see CHA DE BUGRE
Cognassier.................................. see QUINCE
Coing.................................. see QUINCE
Cokan .... see POKEWEED
Cola acuminata.................................. see COLA NUT
Cola nitida.................................. see COLA NUT
COLA NUT .... see COLA NUT
Colchicum.................................. see AUTUMN CROCUS
Colchicum autumnale .... see AUTUMN CROCUS
Colchicum speciosum .... see AUTUMN CROCUS
Colchicum vernum...................... see AUTUMN CROCUS
Cold Pressed Coconut Oil..................... see COCONUT OIL
Cold-Pressed Grapefruit Oil ....see GRAPEFRUIT
Coleus barbatus.................................. see FORSKOLIN
Coleus forskohlii .... see FORSKOLIN
Colewort.....................see AVENS, CABBAGE
Colforsin .... see FORSKOLIN
Colic Root .... see ALETRIS, ALPINIA,
MARSH BLAZING STAR, WILD YAM
Colinsonia .... see STONE ROOT
Collagen hydrolysate ....see GELATIN
Colle du Japon.................................. see AGAR
Collinsonia canadensis.................see STONE ROOT
COLLOIDAL MINERALS ....
.... see COLLOIDAL MINERALS
COLLOIDAL SILVER ....see COLLOIDAL SILVER
COLOCYNTH.............................see COLOCYNTH
Colocynthidis Fructus ....see COLOCYNTH
Colocynthis vulgaris ....see COLOCYNTH
COLOMBO.............................. see COLOMBO
Colorado Cough Root ....see OSHA
COLOSTRUM ....see COLOSTRUM
Colour Index No. 40850 ....see CANTHAXANTHIN
COLTSFOOT.................................see COLTSFOOT
Coltstail .... see CANADIAN FLEABANE
COLUMBINE.............................see COLUMBINE
Comb Flower ....see ECHINACEA
Combretum ....see OPIUM ANTIDOTE
Combretum micranthum ....see OPIUM ANTIDOTE
Combucha Tea.................................see KOMBUCHA TEA
COMFREY .... see COMFREY
Cominho Negro.................................see BLACK SEED
Commiphora ....see MYRRH
Commiphora mukul ....see GUGGUL
Commiphora wightii ....see GUGGUL
Common Alder.................................. see BLACK ALDER
Common Ash ....see ASH
Common Barberry .... see EUROPEAN BARBERRY
Common Basil .... see BASIL
Common Bean ....see BEAN POD
Common Bearberry............................. see UVA URSI
Common Borage .... see BORAGE
Common Bugloss .... see BORAGE
Common Centaury .... see CENTAURY
Common Cherry Laurel ......see CHERRY LAUREL WATER
Common Chicory Root ....see CHICORY
Common Comfrey .... see COMFREY
Common Condorvine......................... see CONDURANGO
Common Dandelion.................................. see DANDELION

         Natural Medicines Comprehensive Database Consumer Version   (209) 472-2244

Common Dubbletjie..........................see PUNCTURE VINE
Common Elder................................see ELDERFLOWER
Common Elderberry.....................see AMERICAN ELDER
Common Fennel..................................see FENNEL
Common Figwort.............................see FIGWORT
Common Groundsel........................see GROUNDSEL
Common Guelder-Rose.....................see CRAMP BARK
Common Hoarhound...............see WHITE HOREHOUND
Common Hops..................................see HOPS
Common Horsetail........................see HORSETAIL
Common Jasmine............................see JASMINE
Common Juniper.............................see JUNIPER
Common Lavender..........................see LAVENDER
Common Melilot.......................see SWEET CLOVER
Common Nettle.......................see STINGING NETTLE
Common Nightshade ....
...................see BITTERSWEET NIGHTSHADE
Common Oak...............................see OAK bark
Common Oleander.........................see OLEANDER
Common Parsley............................see PARSLEY
Common Peony...............................see PEONY
Common Periwinkle ....see PERIWINKLE
Common Plantain ....see GREAT PLANTAIN
Common Polypod ....see LADY FERN
Common Ragwort....................see TANSY RAGWORT
Common Reed ....see REED HERB
Common Rue ....see RUE
Common Sage ....see SAGE
Common Sandspurry ....see ARENARIA RUBRA
Common Sassafras........................see SASSAFRAS
Common Shrubby Everlasting.............. see IMMORTELLE,
SANDY EVERLASTING
Common Sorrel...............................see SORREL
COMMON STONECROP ......see COMMON STONECROP
Common Thyme ....see THYME
Common Valerian ....see VALERIAN
Common Vanilla ....see VANILLA
Common Verbena.........................see VERBENA
Common Vervain ....see VERBENA
Common Wormwood ....see WORMWOOD
Common Yarrow ....see YARROW
Common Yellow Elder ....see TRONADORA
Common Yew.................................see YEW
Compass Plant..............................see ROSEMARY
Compass Weed.........see ROSEMARY, ROSINWEED
Compound Q...................see CHINESE CUCUMBER
Condamina ....see CARQUEJA
Condensed Tannins ....see PYCNOGENOL
CONDURANGO ....see CONDURANGO
Coneflower..................................see ECHINACEA
Conium...see HEMLOCK
Conium maculata ....see HEMLOCK
CONJUGATED LINOLEIC ACID..........................
...................see CONJUGATED LINOLEIC ACID
Consolida regalis.........................see DELPHINIUM
Consolidae Radix ....see COMFREY
Consound ....see COMFREY
Constancy...................see LILY-OF-THE-VALLEY
Consumptive's Weed......................see YERBA SANTA
Continental Tea ....see LABRADOR TEA
CONTRAYERVA..................... see CONTRAYERVA
Convallaria ....see LILY-OF-THE-VALLEY
Convallaria Herba ....see LILY-OF-THE-VALLEY
Convallaria majalis...............see LILY-OF-THE-VALLEY
Convall-Lily ....see LILY-OF-THE-VALLEY

Convolvulus nervosus ....
...................see HAWAIIAN BABY WOODROSE
Convolvulus orizabensis ....
...................see MEXICAN SCAMMONY ROOT
Convolvulus purga ....see JALAP
Convolvulus speciosus ....
...................see HAWAIIAN BABY WOODROSE
Convolvulus superbus ....
...................see MEXICAN SCAMMONY ROOT
Conyza canadensis .... see CANADIAN FLEABANE
Cool Tankard..................................see BORAGE
COOLWORT ....see COOLWORT
Coon Root ....see BLOODROOT
COPAIBA BALSAM ....see COPAIBA BALSAM
Copaiva ....see COPAIBA BALSAM
Copal Tree................................see TREE OF HEAVEN
Copalm ....see STORAX
COPPER ....see COPPER
Copperose ....see CORN POPPY
Coptide ....see GOLDTHREAD
Coptis chinensis ....see GOLDTHREAD
Coptis chinesis ....see GOLDTHREAD
Coptis deltoidea ....see GOLDTHREAD
Coptis groenlandica ....see GOLDTHREAD
Coptis teeta ....see GOLDTHREAD
Coptis teetoides ....see GOLDTHREAD
Coptis trifolia ....see GOLDTHREAD
Coquelicot................................see CHA DE BUGRE
Coqueret ....see WINTER CHERRY
CORAL ....see CORAL
Coral Calcium ....see CORAL
Coral Peony...................................see PEONY
CORAL ROOT ....see CORAL ROOT
Coralberry ....see WHITE COHOSH
Coralline hydroxyapatite......................see CORAL
Corallorhiza odontorhiza ....see CORAL ROOT
Cordia ecalyculata............see CHA DE BUGRE
Cordia salicifolia ....see CHA DE BUGRE
CORDYCEPS ....see CORDYCEPS
CORIANDER ....see CORIANDER
Coridothymus capitatus ..... see SPANISH ORIGANUM OIL
CORIOLUS MUSHROOM ....
...................see CORIOLUS MUSHROOM
Corktree...................see PHELLODENDRON
CORKWOOD TREE ....see CORKWOOD TREE
Corn Campion ....see CORN COCKLE
CORN COCKLE ....see CORN COCKLE
Corn Horsetail................................see HORSETAIL
Corn Mint..............................see JAPANESE MINT
CORN POPPY ....see CORN POPPY
Corn Rose................see CORN COCKLE, CORN POPPY
CORN SILK..................................see CORN SILK
Corn Sugar Gum ....see XANTHAN GUM
Cornel....................... see AMERICAN DOGWOOD
Cornelian Tree...................... see AMERICAN DOGWOOD
CORNFLOWER ....see CORNFLOWER
Cornmint Oil ....see JAPANESE MINT
Cornsilk................................. see CORN SILK
Cornu cervi parvum ....see DEER VELVET
Cornus florida..................... see AMERICAN DOGWOOD
Corona de Cristo ....see PASSIONFLOWER
Corona solis ....see SUNFLOWER OIL
Corosolic Acid ....see BANABA
Corossol epineux.............................see GRAVIOLA
Corossolier ....see GRAVIOLA

Medical professionals should consult the Professional Version at www.NaturalDatabase.com.

Corpus Luteum Hormone .... see PROGESTERONE
Cortex cinnamomi........................ see CASSIA CINNAMON
CORYDALIS .... see CORYDALIS
Corylus avellana .... see HAZELNUT
Corylus heterophylla .... see HAZELNUT
Corymbia citriodora .... see LEMON EUCALYPTUS
Corynanthe johimbi .... see YOHIMBE
Corynanthe yohimbi .... see YOHIMBE
Cossoo .... see KOUSSO
COSTUS .... see COSTUS
COTTON .... see COTTON
Cotton Dawes ....see CUDWEED
Cotton Weed ....see CUDWEED
Cottonseed Oil ....see GOSSYPOL
Couchgrass .... see WHEATGRASS
Coudrier .... see HAZELNUT
Coughroot .... see BETH ROOT
Coughweed .... see GOLDEN RAGWORT
Coughwort .... see COLTSFOOT
Coumarouna odorata .... see TONKA BEAN
COUNTRY MALLOW .... see COUNTRY MALLOW
Country Walnut .... see TUNG SEED
Covanamilpori .... see INDIAN SNAKEROOT
Cow Cabbage .... see AMERICAN WHITE POND LILY,
                                                     MASTERWORT
Cow Clover ....see RED CLOVER
Cow Grass .... see KNOTWEED
Cow Milk Colostrum .... see COLOSTRUM
Cow Parsnip ....see MASTERWORT
Cowbane .... see WATER HEMLOCK
Cowberry .... see ALPINE CRANBERRY
COWHAGE .... see COWHAGE
Cowitch .... see COWHAGE
COWSLIP .... see COWSLIP, MARSH MARIGOLD
CPS .... see CHONDROITIN SULFATE
Cr .... see CHROMIUM, CREATINE
Cr III .... see CHROMIUM
Cr3+ .... see CHROMIUM
Crab's Eye ....see PRECATORY BEAN
Crabwood ....see ANDIROBA
Crack Willow .... see WILLOW BARK
CRAMP BARK .... see CRAMP BARK
Crampweed .... see POTENTILLA
CRANBERRY .... see CRANBERRY
Cranberry Bush .... see CRAMP BARK
Crape Myrtle .... see BANABA
Crataegi Flos .... see HAWTHORN
Crataegi Folium .... see HAWTHORN
Crataegi Fructus .... see HAWTHORN
Crataegus cuneata .... see HAWTHORN
Crataegus kulingensis .... see HAWTHORN
Crataegus laevigata .... see HAWTHORN
Crataegus monogyna .... see HAWTHORN
Crataegus oxyacantha .... see HAWTHORN
Crataegus pinnatifida .... see HAWTHORN
Crawley Root .... see CORAL ROOT
Crawlgrass ....see KNOTWEED
Creat .... see ANDROGRAPHIS
CREATINE .... see CREATINE
Creatine Monohydrate .... see CREATINE
Creatine Pyruvate .... see CREATINE, PYRUVATE
Creeper .... see AMERICAN IVY
Creeping Barberry .... see OREGON GRAPE
Creeping Charlie .... see GROUND IVY
Creeping Jenny .... see MONEYWORT

Creeping Joan .... see MONEYWORT
Creeping Tom .... see COMMON STONECROP
Creosote Bush ....see CHAPARRAL
Crepe Myrtle .... see BANABA
Crescione di Fonte .... see WATERCRESS
Cresson au Poulet .... see WATERCRESS
Cresson de Fontaine .... see WATERCRESS
Cresson d'Eau .... see WATERCRESS
Crest Marine .... see SAMPHIRE
Crewel .... see COWSLIP
Crithmum maritimum .... see SAMPHIRE
Croci stigma ....see SAFFRON
Crocus .... see AUTUMN CROCUS
Crocus sativus ....see SAFFRON
Crosswort .... see BONESET
Croton eluteria .... see CASCARILLA
Croton lechleri .... see SANGRE DE GRADO
CROTON SEEDS .... see CROTON SEEDS
Croton tiglium .... see CROTON SEEDS
Crow Corn .... see ALETRIS
Crowberry .... see POKEWEED
Crowfoot .... see BULBOUS BUTTERCUP,
                                              WOOD ANEMONE
Crown-of-the-Field .... see CORN COCKLE
Crude Chrysarobin .... see GOA POWDER
Crude Palm Oil .... see PALM OIL
Crystalline DMSO ....
.... see MSM (METHYLSULFONYLMETHANE)
CUBEBS .... see CUBEBS
Cuchi-Cuchi ....see CARQUEJA
Cuckoo Bread........................see WOOD SORREL
Cuckoo Buds .... see BULBOUS BUTTERCUP
Cuckoo Flower .... see SALEP
Cuckoo Pint ....see ARUM
Cuckowes Meat ....see WOOD SORREL
Cucumis colocynthis ....see COLOCYNTH
Cucurbita galeottii .... see PUMPKIN
Cucurbita mammeata .... see PUMPKIN
Cucurbita pepo .... see PUMPKIN
Cucurbitea Peponis Semen .... see PUMPKIN
Cuddy's Lungs .... see MULLEIN
CUDWEED.................... see CAT'S FOOT, CUDWEED
Cuivre .... see COPPER
Cukilanarpak ....see DEVIL'S CLUB
Culveris Root .... see BLACK ROOT
Culvers .... see BLACK ROOT
Culverwort ....see COLUMBINE
Cumaru ....see TONKA BEAN
CUMIN .... see CUMIN
Cumin des Pres .... see CARAWAY
Cuminum cyminum .... see CUMIN
Cuminum odorum .... see CUMIN
Cundeamor .... see BITTER MELON
CUP PLANT ....see CUP PLANT
Cupania sapida .... see ACKEE
CUPMOSS...............................see CUPMOSS
Cup-Puppy ....see CORN POPPY
Cupreol .... see BETA-SITOSTEROL
Cupressus sempervirens................see CYPRESS
Cupric Oxide........................ see COPPER
Curbana ....see CANELLA
Curcuma ....see JAVANESE TURMERIC
Curcuma aromatica ....see TURMERIC
Curcuma domestica....................see TURMERIC
Curcuma longa ....see TURMERIC

Curcuma xanthorrhiza.............. see JAVANESE TURMERIC
Curcuma zedoaria .... see ZEDOARY
Curcumae longae rhizoma .... see TURMERIC
Curcumae xanthorrhizae rhizoma ....
.... see JAVANESE TURMERIC
Curcumin... see TURMERIC
Curdwort .... see LADY'S BEDSTRAW
Cure All .... see WATER AVENS, LEMON BALM
Curled Dock .... see YELLOW DOCK
Curled Mint............................... see SPEARMINT
Curly Dock .... see YELLOW DOCK
Cursed Crowfoot .... see POISONOUS BUTTERCUP
Cuscus .... see VETIVER
Cuscus Grass .... see VETIVER
Cuscuta chinensis..................................... see DODDER
Cuscuta epithymum .... see DODDER
Cuscutae .... see DODDER
Cusparia .... see ANGOSTURA
Cusparia Bark .... see ANGOSTURA
Custard Apple....................... see AMERICAN PAWPAW
Cutch .... see CATECHU, WHEATGRASS
Cutweed .... see BLADDERWRACK
Cyamopsis psoraloides....................... see GUAR GUM
Cyamopsis tetragonoloba.................... see GUAR GUM
Cyani Flos .... see CORNFLOWER
Cyanobacteria .... see BLUE-GREEN ALGAE
Cyanocobalamin .... see VITAMIN B12
CYCLAMEN .... see CYCLAMEN
Cyclohexitol .... see INOSITOL
Cycobemin .... see VITAMIN B12
Cydonia oblongata .... see QUINCE
Cydonia vulgaris .... see QUINCE
Cymbidium odontorhizum .... see CORAL ROOT
Cymbopogon afronardus.............. see CITRONELLA OIL
Cymbopogon citratus .... see LEMONGRASS
Cymbopogon flexuosus .... see LEMONGRASS
Cymbopogon nardus .... see CITRONELLA OIL
Cymbopogon validus .... see CITRONELLA OIL
Cymbopogon winterianus .... see CITRONELLA OIL
Cynanchum vincetoxicum .... see GERMAN IPECAC
Cynara cardunculus........................... see ARTICHOKE
Cynara scolymus............................... see ARTICHOKE
Cynoglossi Herba...................... see HOUND'S TONGUE
Cynoglossi Radix .... see HOUND'S TONGUE
Cynoglossum officinale .... see HOUND'S TONGUE
Cynosbatos .... see ROSE HIP
Cyperus articulatus.................................. see ADRUE
Cyperus corymbosus .... see ADRUE
CYPRESS .... see CYPRESS
Cypress Powder ....see ARUM
CYPRESS SPURGE.................. see CYPRESS SPURGE
Cypripedium .... see NERVE ROOT
Cystadane................. see BETAINE ANHYDROUS
Cyste .... see LABDANUM
Cytidine Diphosphate Choline.................. see CITICOLINE
Cytisus alschingeri..............................see LABURNUM
Cytisus laburnum ....see LABURNUM
Cytisus scoparius .... see SCOTCH BROOM
Da Huang .... see RHUBARB
Da Qing Ye.. see ISATIS
Da Zao .... see JUJUBE
Dade ....see DATE PALM
Dadima ....see POMEGRANATE
Daemonorops draco .... see DRAGON'S BLOOD
DAFFODIL.................................see DAFFODIL

DAG .... see DIACYLGLYCEROL
Dage of Jerusalem...................... see LUNGWORT
Dagger Plant..see YUCCA
Daggers ....see ORRIS
Dahlia Extract ....see INULIN
Dahlia Inulin ....see INULIN
Daidzein .... see KUDZU, RED CLOVER, SOY
Daisy ....see TANSY
Dalmatian Sage .... see SAGE
Dalmation Insect Flowers .... see PYRETHRUM
Dalmation Pellitory............................. see PYRETHRUM
D-alpha-tocopheryl Acetate .... see VITAMIN E
D-alpha-tocopheryl Succinate.................... see VITAMIN E
Dambrose .... see INOSITOL
DAMIANA .... see DAMIANA
Damiana aphrodisiaca.......................... see DAMIANA
Damoe .... see WATER DROPWORT
Dancing Mushroom .... see MAITAKE MUSHROOM
DANDELION .... see DANDELION
Danewort ....see DWARF ELDER
Dang Gui .... see DONG QUAI, ANGELICA
Dangshen .... see CODONOPSIS
DANSHEN................................... see DANSHEN
Daphne .... see MEZEREON, SWEET BAY
Daphne mezereum .... see MEZEREON
Daphne Willow .... see WILLOW BARK
Darhahed .... see TREE TURMERIC
Dark Catechu .... see CATECHU
Darnel .... see TAUMELLOOLCH
Darri ....see BROOM CORN
DATE PALM.............................. see DATE PALM
Datil.................................... see DATE PALM
Dattel .... see DATE PALM
Datter .... see DATE PALM
Dattero .... see DATE PALM
Dattier .... see DATE PALM
Datura .... see JIMSON WEED
Datura inermis.......................... see JIMSON WEED
Datura stramonium...................... see JIMSON WEED
Datura suaveolens .... see ANGEL'S TRUMPET
Datura tatula........................... see JIMSON WEED
Daucus............................... see WILD CARROT
Daucus visagna .... see KHELLA
D-beta-tocopherol .... see VITAMIN E
D-biotin .... see BIOTIN
D-calcium pantothenate ....
.... see PANTOTHENIC ACID (VITAMIN B5)
D-carnitine .... see L-CARNITINE
D-chiro-inositol .... see INOSITOL
D-delta-tocopherol .... see VITAMIN E
Deacetylated Chitosan .... see CHITOSAN
Dead Man's Bells............................. see DIGITALIS
Dead Tongue .... see HEMLOCK WATER DROPWORT
Deadly Nightshade.......................... see BELLADONNA,
                              BITTERSWEET NIGHTSHADE
Deaf Nettle .... see WHITE DEAD NETTLE FLOWER
DEANOL .... see DEANOL
Death-of-Man......................... see WATER HEMLOCK
Decalepis hamiltonii .... see SWALLOWROOT
Deep Sea Shark Liver Oil .... see SHARK LIVER OIL
Deer Antler velvet .... see DEER VELVET
Deer Balls............................. see PUFF BALL
Deer Musk............................... see MUSK
DEER VELVET .... see DEER VELVET
Deerberry .... see SQUAWVINE, WINTERGREEN

Deernut..see JOJOBA
DEERTONGUE.............................see DEERTONGUE
Dehydroepiandrosterone .... see DHEA
Dehydroretinol ....see VITAMIN A
Delicate Bess........................ see RED-SPUR VALERIAN
Delphinii Flos..............................see DELPHINIUM
DELPHINIUM...............................see DELPHINIUM
Delta Tocotrienol............................. see VITAMIN E
Delta-Tocopherol .... see VITAMIN E
Demon Chaser.....................see ST. JOHN'S WORT
Denatured Collagen ....see GELATIN
Dendranthema grandiflorum ....see CHRYSANTHEMUM
Dendranthema morifolium............see CHRYSANTHEMUM
Dentidia nankinensis.............................see PERILLA
DeoxyNucleic Acid........................ see RNA AND DNA
Deoxyribonucleic Acid .... see RNA AND DNA
Derrière-Dos .... see CHANCA PIEDRA
Des Dos .... see CHANCA PIEDRA
Desert Herb ....see EPHEDRA
Desert Tea .... see MORMON TEA
Devil Tree.............................see FEVER BARK
Devil's Apple .... see JIMSON WEED, PODOPHYLLUM
Devil's Bit ....see FEVER BARK, PREMORSE
Devil's Bite ....see AMERICAN HELLEBORE
Devil's Bite Prairie-Pine ....see MARSH BLAZING STAR
Devil's Bones ....see WILD YAM
Devil's Bush............................. see GINSENG, SIBERIAN
Devil's Cherries .... see BELLADONNA
DEVIL'S CLAW ....see DEVIL'S CLAW
DEVIL'S CLUB.............................see DEVIL'S CLUB
Devil's Darning Needle........................see WOODBINE
Devil's Dung ....see ASAFOETIDA
Devil's Eye .... see HENBANE
Devil's Fuge .... see EUROPEAN MISTLETOE
Devil's Guts ....see DODDER
Devil's Head.......................see YELLOW TOADFLAX
Devil's Herb .... see BELLADONNA
Devil's Nettle ....see YARROW
Devil's Plaything...........................see YARROW
Devil's Ribbon ....see YELLOW TOADFLAX
Devil's Root .... see DEVIL'S CLUB, PEYOTE
Devil's Shrub .... see GINSENG, SIBERIAN
Devil's Trumpet ....see ANGEL'S TRUMPET,
                                    JIMSON WEED
Devil's Turnip ....see BRYONIA
Devil's Vine............................ see GREATER BINDWEED
Devil's-bit .... see ALETRIS
Devil's-thorn ....see PUNCTURE VINE
Devil's-weed ....see PUNCTURE VINE
Dew Plant .... see SUNDEW
Dewberry................................see BLACKBERRY
Dexpanthenol ....
..........................see PANTOTHENIC ACID (VITAMIN B5)
Dexpanthenolum ....
..........................see PANTOTHENIC ACID (VITAMIN B5)
D-gamma-tocopherol .... see VITAMIN E
D-glucarate (GA) .... see CALCIUM D-GLUCARATE
D-glucosamine .... see GLUCOSAMINE SULFATE
D-glucosamine HCl .... see GLUCOSAMINE
Hydrochloride DHA..................................
..................see DHA (DOCOSAHEXAENOIC ACID)
DHA (DOCOSAHEXAENOIC ACID) ....
..................see DHA (DOCOSAHEXAENOIC ACID)
Dhanburua.................. see INDIAN SNAKEROOT
Dhanyaka ....see CORIANDER

Dhar-Bu............................see SEA BUCKTHORN
DHEA .... see DHEA
Di Gu Pi ....see LYCIUM
DIACYLGLYCEROL .....see DIACYLGLYCEROL
Dialyzable Leukocyte Extract.......see TRANSFER FACTOR
Dialyzable Transfer Factor............see TRANSFER FACTOR
Dibasic Sodium Phosphate ....see PHOSPHATE SALTS
DIBENCOZIDE................................see DIBENCOZIDE
Dibutylated Hydroxytoluene...............................
.... see BHT (BUTYLATED HYDROXYTOLUENE)
Dicalcium Phosphate ....see CALCIUM,
                                    PHOSPHATE SALTS
Dicentra cucullaria .... see TURKEY CORN
Dictamnus albus......................see BURNING BUSH
Dictamnus caucasicus ....see BURNING BUSH
Dictamnus fraxinellus ....see BURNING BUSH
Dictamo Blanco ....see BURNING BUSH
Didin ....see MYRRH
Didthin ....see MYRRH
Dietary Fiber ....see BARLEY, BLACK PSYLLIUM,
                        BLOND PSYLLIUM, GUAR GUM,
                    LARCH ARABINOGALACTAN, OATS,
                        RICE BRAN, WHEAT BRAN
Difur........................... see POLYPODIUM LEUCOTOMOS
DIGITALIS .... see DIGITALIS
Diglyceride................................see DIACYLGLYCEROL
Digupi .... see LYCIUM
Dihe .... see BLUE-GREEN ALGAE
Dihydro-beta-sitosterol .... see SITOSTANOL
Dihydrotachysterol...........................see VITAMIN D
Dihydroxysuccinic Acid...... see ALPHA HYDROXY ACIDS
DIINDOLYLMETHANE .... see DIINDOLYLMETHANE
DIIODOTHYRONINE .... see DIIODOTHYRONINE
Di-isopropylamine dichloroacetate.... see PANGAMIC ACID
DILL .... see DILL
Dilly .... see DILL
DIM .... see DIINDOLYLMETHANE
Dimethyl Sulfone ....
.... see MSM (METHYLSULFONYLMETHANE)
Dimethylaminoethanol...............................see DEANOL
Dimethylethanolamine ....see DEANOL
DIMETHYLGLYCINE .... see DIMETHYLGLYCINE
Dimethylis sulfoxidum..
.... see DMSO (DIMETHYLSULFOXIDE)
Dimethylsulfone...
.... see MSM (METHYLSULFONYLMETHANE)
Dimethylsulfoxide...
.... see DMSO (DIMETHYLSULFOXIDE)
Dioscorea alata.............................see WILD YAM
Dioscorea batatas ....see WILD YAM
Dioscorea communis........................ see BLACK BRYONY
Dioscorea composita..........................see WILD YAM
Dioscorea floribunda...........................see WILD YAM
Dioscorea hirticaulis ....see WILD YAM
Dioscorea japonica..............................see WILD YAM
Dioscorea macrostachya ....see WILD YAM
Dioscorea mexicana ....see WILD YAM
Dioscorea tepinapensis..........................see WILD YAM
Dioscorea villosa...............................see WILD YAM
Dioscoreae....................................see WILD YAM
Diosma .... see BUCHU
Diosmetin .... see DIOSMIN
DIOSMIN .... see DIOSMIN
Diospyros chinensis ....see JAPANESE PERSIMMON
Diospyros kaki ....see JAPANESE PERSIMMON

Dipentene ....see LIMONENE
Dipotassium Hydrogen Orthophosphate ....
....see PHOSPHATE SALTS
Dipotassium Monophosphate........see PHOSPHATE SALTS
Dipotassium Phosphate ....see PHOSPHATE SALTS
Dipsacus fullonum .... see TEAZLE
Dipsacus sylvestris................................ see TEAZLE
Dipteryx odorata ....see TONKA BEAN
Dishcloth Sponge .... see LUFFA
Disodium Edathamil .... see EDTA
Disodium Edetate .... see EDTA
Disodium EDTA .... see EDTA
Disodium Ethylenediamine Tetraacetic Acid......... see EDTA
Disodium Hydrogen Orthophosphate ....
....see PHOSPHATE SALTS
Disodium Hydrogen Orthophosphate Dodecahydrate ....
....see PHOSPHATE SALTS
Disodium Hydrogen Phosphate ..... see PHOSPHATE SALTS
Disodium Phosphate ....see PHOSPHATE SALTS
Disodium Tetraacetate.......................... see EDTA
Dita Bark.............................see FEVER BARK
Ditch Reed .... see REED HERB
Dittany.............................see BURNING BUSH
Divale .... see BELLADONNA
DIVI-DIVI .... see DIVI-DIVI
Divine Mexican Mint ....see DIVINER'S SAGE
Diviner's Mint ....see DIVINER'S SAGE
DIVINER'S SAGE ....see DIVINER'S SAGE
Divinorin ....see DIVINER'S SAGE
DL Methionine............................ see METHIONINE
DL-alpha-tocopheryl..................... see VITAMIN E
DL-carnitine.............................see L-CARNITINE
DLE............................see TRANSFER FACTOR
D-limonene.............................see LIMONENE
DL-methionine .... see METHIONINE
DLPA ....see PHENYLALANINE
DL-phenylalanine ....see PHENYLALANINE
DL-tocopherol .... see VITAMIN E
DMAE............................... see DEANOL
DMAE Bitartrate............................ see DEANOL
D-mannoheptulose .... see AVOCADO SUGAR EXTRACT
D-MANNOSE.............................. see D-MANNOSE
DMG .... see DIMETHYLGLYCINE
DMSO (DIMETHYLSULFOXIDE) ....
.... see DMSO (DIMETHYLSULFOXIDE)
DMSO2 .... see MSM (METHYLSULFONYLMETHANE)
DNA ....see RNA AND DNA
Docosahexaenoic Acid ....
............see DHA (DOCOSAHEXAENOIC ACID)
Doctor Oje.................................see FICIN
DODDER................................see DODDER
Dodder Of Thyme ....see DODDER
Dog Fish Liver Oil .... see SHARK LIVER OIL
Dog Grass...........................see WHEATGRASS
Dog Parsley .... see FOOL'S PARSLEY
Dog Poison .... see FOOL'S PARSLEY
Dog Rose...............................see ROSE HIP
Dog Standard ....see TANSY RAGWORT
Dog Wood .... see ALDER BUCKTHORN
Dog-banana ....see AMERICAN PAWPAW
Dogbane .... see CANADIAN HEMP
Dog-bur .... see HOUND'S TONGUE
Doggies ....see YELLOW TOADFLAX
Dog's Arrach .... see ARRACH
Dog's Tongue .... see HOUND'S TONGUE

Dog's Tooth Violet .... see AMERICAN ADDER'S TONGUE
Dog-tree .... see AMERICAN DOGWOOD
Dogwood................ see AMERICAN DOGWOOD
Dogwood Bark ....see CASCARA
Dolichos hirsutus .... see KUDZU
Dolichos lobatus .... see KUDZU
Dolichos psoraloides ....see GUAR GUM
Dolichos soja..............see SOY, SOYBEAN OIL
Dolloff ....see MEADOWSWEET
Doll's Eye...................... see WHITE COHOSH
DOLOMITE......................see DOLOMITE
Dolomitic Limestone ....see DOLOMITE
Dong Chong Xia Cao .... see CORDYCEPS
Dong Chong Zia Cao .... see CORDYCEPS
Dong Ling Cao ....see RABDOSIA RUBESCENS
DONG QUAI .... see DONG QUAI
Dongqingzi....................see GLOSSY PRIVET
Donnerkraut ....see HEMP AGRIMONY
Doorweed...................... see KNOTWEED
Dope .... see MARIJUANA
Dorstenia contrayerva .... see CONTRAYERVA
Dostenkraut ....see HEMP AGRIMONY, OREGANO
Dotriacontanol.......................see POLICOSANOL
Douglas Fir................ see OREGON FIR BALSAM
Douglas Spruce .... see OREGON FIR BALSAM
Downy Birch .... see BIRCH
D-pantethine......................see PANTETHINE
D-panthenol....... see PANTOTHENIC ACID (VITAMIN B5)
D-pantothenic Acid ....
.... see PANTOTHENIC ACID (VITAMIN B5)
D-pantothenyl Alcohol ....
.... see PANTOTHENIC ACID (VITAMIN B5)
D-phenylalanine ....see PHENYLALANINE
Dr. Sklenar's Kombucha Mushroom Infusion ....
....................................see KOMBUCHA TEA
Drachenkraut....................see HEMP AGRIMONY
Draconis resina .... see DRAGON'S BLOOD
Dracontium ....see SKUNK CABBAGE
Dracorubin .... see DRAGON'S BLOOD
Drago.................see SANGRE DE GRADO
Dragon Root ....see ARUM
Dragon-bushes ....see YELLOW TOADFLAX
DRAGON'S BLOOD .... see DRAGON'S BLOOD,
                    HERB ROBERT, SANGRE DE GRADO
Dragonwort .... see BISTORT
Drake .... see TAUMELLOOLCH
Draksha .... see GRAPE
Drelip .... see COWSLIP
D-ribose .... see RIBOSE
Dried Persimmon ....see JAPANESE PERSIMMON
Drimia indica .... see SQUILL
Drimia maritima .... see SQUILL
Drimys chilensis.............. see WINTER'S BARK
Drimys winteri .... see WINTER'S BARK
Dromiceius novahollandiae.......................see EMU OIL
Dropberry.......... see SOLOMON'S SEAL
Dropsy Plant.................see LEMON BALM
Dropwort....................see MEADOWSWEET
Drosera .... see SUNDEW
Drosera rotundifolia .... see SUNDEW
Drudenfuss .... see EUROPEAN MISTLETOE
Drug Centaurium .... see CENTAURY
Drunken Sailor .... see RED-SPUR VALERIAN
Dry Ground Cranberry............. see ALPINE CRANBERRY
Dryopteris Filix-mas ....see MALE FERN

D-tocopherol .... see VITAMIN E
Duboisia myoporoides .... see CORKWOOD TREE
Duck Liver Extract .... see OSCILLOCOCCINUM
Duck's Foot .... see PODOPHYLLUM
DUCKWEED .... see DUCKWEED
Dudgeon .... see BOXWOOD
Duffle .... see MULLEIN
Duhat .... see JAMBOLAN
Dukong Anak .... see CHANCA PIEDRA
Dulcamara .... see BITTERSWEET NIGHTSHADE
Dumb Nettle .... see WHITE DEAD NETTLE FLOWER
Dumpling Cactus .... see PEYOTE
Dun Daisy .... see OX-EYE DAISY
Dungkulcha .... see JIAOGULAN
Durfa Grass .... see WHEATGRASS
Durian Benggala .... see GRAVIOLA
Durmast Oak .... see OAK bark
Durri .... see BROOM CORN
DUSTY MILLER .... see DUSTY MILLER
Dutch Agrimony .... see HEMP AGRIMONY
Dutch Eupatoire Commune .... see HEMP AGRIMONY
Dutch Myrtle .... see SWEET GALE
Dutch Rushes .... see HORSETAIL
Dutch Tonka .... see TONKA BEAN
Dutchman's Breeches .... see TURKEY CORN
Dwale .... see BELLADONNA
Dwarf Bay .... see MEZEREON
Dwarf Bilberry .... see BILBERRY
Dwarf Carline .... see CARLINA
DWARF ELDER .... see DWARF ELDER
Dwarf Flax .... see MOUNTAIN FLAX
Dwarf Mallow .... see MALLOW
Dwarf Marigold .... see TAGETES
DWARF PINE NEEDLE .... see DWARF PINE NEEDLE
Dwarf-pine .... see PINE
Dwayberry .... see BELLADONNA
Dyeberry .... see BILBERRY
DYER'S BROOM .... see DYER'S BROOM
Dyer's Bugloss .... see ALKANNA
Dyer's Greenwood .... see DYER'S BROOM
Dyer's Madder .... see MADDER
Dyer's Saffron .... see SAFFLOWER
Dyer's Weed .... see DYER'S BROOM
Dyer's Whin .... see DYER'S BROOM
Dyer's Woad .... see ISATIS
Dysentery Bark .... see SIMARUBA
Dysentery Weed .... see CUDWEED
E Zhu .... see ZEDOARY
E161 .... see CANTHAXANTHIN
E967 .... see XYLITOL
Eagle-vine Bark .... see CONDURANGO
Early Fumitory .... see CORYDALIS
Early Goldenrod .... see GOLDENROD
Earlyflowering .... see PERIWINKLE
Earth Gall .... see AMERICAN HELLEBORE
Earth Smoke .... see FUMITORY
Earthbank .... see TORMENTIL
Earth-nut .... see PEANUT OIL
East India Catarrh Root .... see ALPINIA
East Indian Almond .... see CASHEW
East Indian Balmony .... see CHIRATA
East Indian Lemongrass .... see LEMONGRASS
East Indian Sandalwood .... see WHITE SANDALWOOD
Easter Flower .... see POINSETTIA, PULSATILLA
Easter Giant .... see BISTORT

Easter Mangiant .... see BISTORT
Eastern Arborvitae .... see THUJA
Eastern Burning Bush .... see WAHOO
Eastern Fir .... see CANADA BALSAM
Eastern Hemlock .... see PINUS BARK
Eastern Mistletoe .... see AMERICAN MISTLETOE
EASTERN RED CEDAR .... see EASTERN RED CEDAR
Eastern White Cedar .... see THUJA
Eberesche .... see MOUNTAIN ASH
Ebereschenbeeren .... see MOUNTAIN ASH
Eberwurz .... see CARLINA
Eburnamenine-14-carboxylic Acid .... see VINPOCETINE
Ecdisten .... see ECDYSTERONE
Ecdysone .... see ECDYSTERONE
ECDYSTERONE .... see ECDYSTERONE
ECHINACEA .... see ECHINACEA
Echinacea angustifolia .... see ECHINACEA
Echinacea pallida .... see ECHINACEA
Echinacea purpurea .... see ECHINACEA
Echinaceawurzel .... see ECHINACEA
Echinopanax horridus .... see DEVIL'S CLUB
Echte Kamille .... see GERMAN CHAMOMILE
Ecorce de Quina .... see CINCHONA
Ecuadorian Sarsaparilla .... see SARSAPARILLA
Edamame .... see SOY
Edible Burdock .... see BURDOCK
Edible Date .... see DATE PALM
EDTA .... see EDTA
Egcel .... see HYPERIMMUNE EGG
EGCG .... see GREEN TEA, OOLONG TEA
Egg Extract .... see HYPERIMMUNE EGG
Egg Lecithin .... see LECITHIN
Egg Powder with Immune Components ....
.... see HYPERIMMUNE EGG
Eggs and Bacon .... see YELLOW TOADFLAX
Eggs and Collops .... see YELLOW TOADFLAX
Egyptian Alcee .... see AMBRETTE
Egyptian Privet .... see HENNA
Ehrenpreiskraut .... see VERONICA
Eichenrinde .... see OAK bark
Eicosapentaenoic Acid ....
.... see EPA (EICOSAPENTAENOIC ACID)
Eight Horns .... see STAR ANISE
Eight-horned Anise .... see STAR ANISE
Einbeere .... see HERB PARIS
Eira-caa .... see STEVIA
Eisenkraut .... see VERBENA
Ela .... see CARDAMOM
Elaeis guineensis .... see PALM OIL
Elaeis melanococca .... see PALM OIL
Elder .... see ELDERBERRY
Elder Flower .... see AMERICAN ELDER, ELDERFLOWER
ELDERBERRY ....
.... see AMERICAN ELDER, ELDERBERRY
ELDERFLOWER .... see ELDERFLOWER
Eldrin .... see RUTIN
ELECAMPANE .... see ELECAMPANE
Elemental Copper .... see COPPER
Elemental Iron .... see IRON
ELEMI .... see ELEMI
Elephant Climber .... see HAWAIIAN BABY WOODROSE
Elephant Creeper .... see HAWAIIAN BABY WOODROSE
Elephant's Gall .... see ALOE
Elettaria cardamomum .... see CARDAMOM
Eleuthero Ginseng .... see GINSENG, SIBERIAN

Eleutherococci Radix .... see GINSENG, SIBERIAN
Eleutherococcus .... see GINSENG, SIBERIAN
Eleutherococcus senticosus .... see GINSENG, SIBERIAN
Elfdock .... see ELECAMPANE
Elfwort .... see ELECAMPANE
Elichrysum orientale .... see SANDY EVERLASTING
Elichrysum stoechas .... see SANDY EVERLASTING
Elk Antler Velvet .... see DEER VELVET
ELLAGIC ACID .... see ELLAGIC ACID
Ellanwood .... see ELDERBERRY, ELDERFLOWER
Ellhorn .... see ELDERBERRY, ELDERFLOWER
ELM BARK .... see ELM BARK
Eltroot .... see GOUTWEED
Elymus repens .... see WHEATGRASS
Elytrigia repens .... see WHEATGRASS
Emblic .... see INDIAN GOOSEBERRY
Emblica .... see INDIAN GOOSEBERRY
Emetic Herb .... see LOBELIA
EMU OIL .... see EMU OIL
Enada .... see NADH
Enchanter's Plant .... see VERBENA
Enebro .... see JUNIPER
ENGLISH ADDER'S TONGUE ....
.... see ENGLISH ADDER'S TONGUE
English Alder .... see BLACK ALDER
English Chamomile .... see ROMAN CHAMOMILE
English Cowslip .... see COWSLIP
English Goatweed .... see GOUTWEED
English Green Valerian .... see JACOB'S LADDER
English Hawthorn .... see HAWTHORN
ENGLISH HORSEMINT .... see ENGLISH HORSEMINT
ENGLISH IVY .... see ENGLISH IVY
English Lavender .... see LAVENDER
English Mandrake .... see BRYONIA
English Morello .... see SOUR CHERRY
English Oak .... see OAK bark
English Plantain .... see BUCKHORN PLANTAIN
English Sarsaparilla .... see TORMENTIL
English Tea .... see BLACK TEA
English Tonka .... see TONKA BEAN
ENGLISH WALNUT .... see ENGLISH WALNUT
English Watercress .... see HEDGE MUSTARD
English Yew .... see YEW
Englishman's Foot .... see BLOND PSYLLIUM
Enocianina .... see GRAPE
Enzymatic Polychitosamine Hydrolisat .... see CHITOSAN
EPA (EICOSAPENTAENOIC ACID) ....
.... see EPA (EICOSAPENTAENOIC ACID)
Epazote .... see CHENOPODIUM OIL
EPHEDRA .... see EPHEDRA
Ephedra nevadensis .... see MORMON TEA
Epigaea repens .... see TRAILING ARBUTUS
Epigallo Catechin Gallate .... see GREEN TEA,
OOLONG TEA
Epilobium angustifolium .... see FIREWEED
Epilobium spicatum .... see FIREWEED
EPIMEDIUM .... see EPIMEDIUM
Epine Blanche .... see HAWTHORN
Epine de Mai .... see HAWTHORN
Epine-vinette .... see EUROPEAN BARBERRY
EPO .... see EVENING PRIMROSE OIL
EPs 7630 .... see SOUTH AFRICAN GERANIUM
Epsom Salts .... see MAGNESIUM
Equiseti Herba .... see HORSETAIL
Equisetum arvense .... see HORSETAIL

Equisetum telmateia .... see HORSETAIL
Eranda .... see CASTOR
Erandachirbhita .... see PAPAYA
Erba da Cartentieri .... see YARROW
Erba da Falegname .... see YARROW
Ergocalciferol .... see VITAMIN D
ERGOT .... see ERGOT
Erica vulgaris .... see HEATHER
Eriffe .... see CLIVERS
Erigeron canadensis .... see CANADIAN FLEABANE
Eringo .... see ERYNGO
Eriodictyon .... see YERBA SANTA
Eriodictyon californicum .... see YERBA SANTA
Eriodictyon glutinosum .... see YERBA SANTA
Erva Doce .... see STEVIA
Erva Dos Vermes .... see TANSY
Erva-de-orelha .... see GREAT PLANTAIN
Eryngii Herba .... see ERYNGO
Eryngii Radix .... see ERYNGO
Eryngium campestre .... see ERYNGO
Eryngium maritimum .... see ERYNGO
Eryngium yuccifolium .... see ERYNGO
ERYNGO .... see ERYNGO
Eryngo-leaved Liverwort .... see ICELAND MOSS
Erysimum .... see HEDGE MUSTARD
Erysimum cheiri .... see WALLFLOWER
Erysimum officinale .... see HEDGE MUSTARD
Erythraea centaurium .... see CENTAURY
Erythrina piscipula .... see JAMAICAN DOGWOOD
Erythronium .... see AMERICAN ADDER'S TONGUE
Erythronium americanum ....
.... see AMERICAN ADDER'S TONGUE
Erythroxylum catuaba .... see CATUABA
Erythroxylum coca .... see COCA
Erythroxylum novogranatense .... see COCA
Eschscholzia californica .... see CALIFORNIA POPPY
Escine .... see HORSE CHESTNUT
Esere Nut .... see CALABAR BEAN
Esperanza .... see TRONADORA
Espigón .... see PUNCTURE VINE
Espino armarillo .... see SEA BUCKTHORN
Espino cambrón .... see EUROPEAN BARBERRY
Espino Falso .... see SEA BUCKTHORN
Espresso .... see COFFEE
Esrar .... see MARIJUANA
Essential Fatty Acid .... see ALPHA-LINOLENIC ACID
Estoraque Liquido .... see STORAX
Estragon .... see TARRAGON
Eternal Flower .... see IMMORTELLE,
SANDY EVERLASTING
Ethanol .... see BEER, WINE
Ethyl Apovincaminate .... see VINPOCETINE
Ethyl Dihydroxypropyl Aminobenzoate ....
.... see PARA-AMINOBENZOIC ACID (PABA)
Ethyl Eicosapentaenoic Acid ....
.... see EPA (EICOSAPENTAENOIC ACID)
Ethyl Ester .... see VINPOCETINE
Ethylapovincaminoate .... see VINPOCETINE
Ethylenediamine Tetraacetic Acid .... see EDTA
Eucalypti Folium .... see EUCALYPTUS
EUCALYPTUS .... see EUCALYPTUS
Eucalyptus citriodora .... see LEMON EUCALYPTUS
Euchema species .... see CARRAGEENAN
Eugenia aromatica .... see CLOVE
Eugenia caryophyllata .... see CLOVE

Eugenia caryophyllus.. see CLOVE
Eugenia chequen .... see CHEKEN
Eugenia cumini .... see JAMBOLAN
Eugenia jambolana .... see JAMBOLAN
Eugenia pimenta.. see ALLSPICE
Euonymus atropurpureus .... see WAHOO
Eupatoriadelphus purpureus.................. see GRAVEL ROOT
Eupatorium..................................... see HEMP AGRIMONY
Eupatorium cannabinum .... see HEMP AGRIMONY
Eupatorium perfoliatum .... see BONESET
Eupatorium purpureum .... see GRAVEL ROOT
Eupatorium rebaudianum .... see STEVIA
EUPHORBIA..................................... see EUPHORBIA
Euphorbia cyparissias .... see CYPRESS SPURGE
Euphorbia poinsettia .... see POINSETTIA
Euphorbia pulcherrima .... see POINSETTIA
Euphraisia Eye Bright .... see EYEBRIGHT
Euphrasia officinalis........................... see EYEBRIGHT
Euphrasiae Herba .... see EYEBRIGHT
Eurixor .... see EUROPEAN MISTLETOE
European Alder .... see BLACK ALDER, ELDERBERRY,
ELDERFLOWER
European Angelica .... see ANGELICA
European Ash ....see ASH
European Aspen .... see ASPEN
European Aspidium.............................see MALE FERN
EUROPEAN BARBERRY .... see EUROPEAN BARBERRY
European Beaver .... see CASTOREUM
European Bitter Polygala ....see BITTER MILKWORT
European Black Alder .... see BLACK ALDER
European Black Currant.................. see BLACK CURRANT
EUROPEAN BUCKTHORN ....
.... see EUROPEAN BUCKTHORN
EUROPEAN CHESTNUT .... see EUROPEAN CHESTNUT
European Cranberry.............................. see CRANBERRY
European Cranberry-bush .... see CRAMP BARK
European Dill... see DILL
European Elder Flower .... see ELDERFLOWER
European Elder Fruit......................... see ELDERBERRY
European Elderberry .... see ELDERBERRY
European Filbert..see HAZELNUT
EUROPEAN FIVE-FINGER GRASS...............................
................see EUROPEAN FIVE-FINGER GRASS
European Goldenrod ....see GOLDENROD
European Hazel ....see HAZELNUT
European Hellebore .... see WHITE HELLEBORE
European Hops .... see HOPS
European Linden................................see LINDEN
EUROPEAN MANDRAKE ....
.... see EUROPEAN MANDRAKE
EUROPEAN MISTLETOE ....
.... see EUROPEAN MISTLETOE
European Mountain-ash .... see MOUNTAIN ASH
European Mullein.................................. see MULLEIN
European Oregano ....see OREGANO
European Pasqueflower.......................see PULSATILLA
European Pennyroyal .... see PENNYROYAL
European Peony .... see PEONY
European Ragwort ....see TANSY RAGWORT
European Sanicle ....see SANICLE
European Senega.......................see BITTER MILKWORT
European Squill................................. see SQUILL
European Vervain ....see VERBENA
European Water Hemlock .... see WATER HEMLOCK
European White Hellebore........... see WHITE HELLEBORE

European Wild Pansy ....see HEART'S EASE
Eurphrasia rostkoviana...............................see EYEBRIGHT
EURYCOMA LONGIFOLIA...
................................see EURYCOMA LONGIFOLIA
Euterpe badiocarpa..................................... see ACAI
Euterpe oleracea .... see ACAI
EVENING PRIMROSE OIL ....
.... see EVENING PRIMROSE OIL
Evening Trumpet Flower ....see GELSEMIUM
Evergreen .... see PERIWINKLE
Evergreen Snakeroot ....see BITTER MILKWORT
Everlasting .... see CUDWEED, SANDY EVERLASTING
Everlasting Friendship ....see CLIVERS
Everlasting Pea.................................see LATHYRUS
Evernia prunastri .... see OAK MOSS
Eve's Cups .... see PITCHER PLANT
Ewe Daisy .... see TORMENTIL
Exogonium purga.......................................see JALAP
Expressed Almond Oil ....see SWEET ALMOND
Expressed Grapefruit Oil ....see GRAPEFRUIT
Extra Virgin Olive Oil .... see OLIVE
Extract of Juniper.................................. see JUNIPER
Extract of Mentha Piperita ....see PEPPERMINT
Extract of Peppermint ....see PEPPERMINT
Extrait De Pepins De Raisin .... see GRAPE
Exwort.....................................see BUTTERBUR
Eye Balm....................................... see GOLDENSEAL
Eye Root....................................... see GOLDENSEAL
EYEBRIGHT.................. see CLARY SAGE, EYEBRIGHT
Eyrnigium planum .... see ERYNGO
E-Zhu ....see ZEDOARY
Faba calabarica....................................see CALABAR BEAN
Faex medicinalis ....see BREWER'S YEAST
Fagopyrum esculentum .... see BUCKWHEAT
Fagopyrum sagittatum .... see BUCKWHEAT
Fagopyrum tataricum .... see BUCKWHEAT
Fagopyrum vulgare .... see BUCKWHEAT
Fagus castanea .... see EUROPEAN CHESTNUT
Fagus procera .... see EUROPEAN CHESTNUT
Fairy Bells.................................see WOOD SORREL
Fairy Cap.................................. see DIGITALIS
Fairy Caps .... see COWSLIP
Fairy Finger................................. see DIGITALIS
Fairy Flax.............................see MOUNTAIN FLAX
Fairy Herb ....see JIAOGULAN
Fairywand .... see FALSE UNICORN
Fake Saffron ....see SAFFLOWER
Fall Crocus .... see AUTUMN CROCUS
Fallopia japonica ....see HU ZHANG
False Bittersweet..............see AMERICAN BITTERSWEET
False Box .... see AMERICAN DOGWOOD
False Cinnamon .... see CASSIA CINNAMON
False Coltsfoot ....see ASARABACCA
False Grapes................................ see AMERICAN IVY
False Hellebore .... see AMERICAN HELLEBORE,
PHEASANT'S EYE
False Indigo.................................see WILD INDIGO
False Jacob's Ladder ....see ABSCESS ROOT
False Jasmine ....see GELSEMIUM
False Pareira.................................... see ABUTA
False Parsley .... see WATER HEMLOCK
False Saffron ....see SAFFLOWER
FALSE UNICORN .... see FALSE UNICORN
False Valerian .... see GOLDEN RAGWORT
Farberrote ....see MADDER

              Natural Medicines Comprehensive Database Consumer Version   (209) 472-2244

Färberwaid .... see ISATIS
Farfarae Folium Leaf .... see COLTSFOOT
Farmer's Lily.. see WHITE LILY
Fa-Tha-Lai-Jone .... see ANDROGRAPHIS
Fatsia .... see DEVIL'S CLUB
Fatsia horrida .... see DEVIL'S CLUB
Fe... see IRON
Featherfew... see FEVERFEW
Featherfoil .... see FEVERFEW
Feigen.. see FIG
Feijao macaco .... see COWHAGE
Feldkamille .... see GERMAN CHAMOMILE
Fellen.................. see BITTERSWEET NIGHTSHADE
Fellonwood .... see BITTERSWEET NIGHTSHADE
Felon Herb ....see MUGWORT
Felonwort .... see BITTERSWEET NIGHTSHADE
Feltwort .... see MULLEIN
Female Regulator .... see GOLDEN RAGWORT
Fen Ke .... see KUDZU
Fenge .... see KUDZU
FENNEL .... see FENNEL
Fennel Flower .... see BLACK SEED
FENUGREEK..see FENUGREEK
Fermented Coconut Oil......................... see COCONUT OIL
Fermented Dairy Product..........................see KEFIR
Fermented Genistein ....
...........see GENISTEIN COMBINED POLYSACCHARIDE
Fermented Isoflavone ....
...........see GENISTEIN COMBINED POLYSACCHARIDE
Fermented Milk....................................... see KEFIR
Fermented Soybeans .... see NATTOKINASE
Fern .... see POLYPODIUM LEUCOTOMOS
Ferrous Carbonate Anhydrous ....see IRON
Ferrous Fumarate ....see IRON
Ferrous Gluconate ....see IRON
Ferrous Pyrophosphate..............................see IRON
Ferrous Sulfate ....see IRON
Ferrula.. see SUMBUL
Ferula assa-foetida ....see ASAFOETIDA
Ferula foetida .... see ASAFOETIDA
Ferula galbaniflua .... see GALBANUM
Ferula gummosa .... see GALBANUM
Ferula pseudalliacea................................ see ASAFOETIDA
Ferula rubricaulis ....see ASAFOETIDA
Ferula sumbul....................................... see SUMBUL
Fetid Nightshade .... see HENBANE
Feuille De Luzerne................................... see ALFALFA
Feuilles d'Alchemille.....................see ALCHEMILLA
Feuilles la Fievre .... see CHANCA PIEDRA
FEVER BARK..see FEVER BARK
Fever Grass .... see LEMONGRASS
Fever Plant .... see EVENING PRIMROSE OIL
Fever Root............see CORAL ROOT, WATER HEMLOCK
Fever Tree .... see EUCALYPTUS
Fever Twig.................. see BITTERSWEET NIGHTSHADE
FEVERFEW .... see FEVERFEW
Feverwort .... see BONESET
Ficaria .... see LESSER CELANDINE
FICIN .... see FICIN
Ficus anthelminthica..................................... see FICIN
Ficus carica .... see FIG
Ficus glabrata .... see FICIN
Ficus insipida .... see FICIN
Fiddlehead Fern .... see OSTRICH FERN
Fieberbaumblatter ....see EUCALYPTUS

Fieberrinde.. see CINCHONA
Field Balm... see CATNIP
Field Horsetail.....................................see HORSETAIL
Field Lady's Mantle .... see PARSLEY PIERT
Field Melilot .... see SWEET CLOVER
Field Mint Oil .... see JAPANESE MINT
Field Pansy.......................................see HEART'S EASE
Field Pumpkin .... see PUMPKIN
FIELD SCABIOUS .... see FIELD SCABIOUS
Field Scorpion Grass....................... see FORGET-ME-NOT
Field Seven....................... see PANAX PSEUDOGINSENG
Field Sorrel........ see SORREL, YELLOW DOCK
Fieldhove...see COLTSFOOT
FIG .... see FIG
FIGWORT.............. see FIGWORT, LESSER CELANDINE
Filaginella uliginosa....................................see CUDWEED
Filipendula ....see MEADOWSWEET
Filipendula ulmaria ....see MEADOWSWEET
Filuis Ante Patrem...............................see COLTSFOOT
Finbar .... see SEA BUCKTHORN
Fine Leaf Water Dropwort .... see WATER FENNEL
Finnochio .... see FENNEL
FIR .... see FIR
Fir Needle Oil ....see HEMLOCK SPRUCE
Fir Tree...see HEMLOCK SPRUCE
FIREWEED .... see FIREWEED
Fish Berries ....see LEVANT BERRY
Fish Killer ....see LEVANT BERRY
Fish Mint..see SPEARMINT
FISH OIL .... see COD LIVER OIL, FISH OIL
Fish Oil Fatty Acid...
...........................see DHA (DOCOSAHEXAENOIC ACID),
.................................EPA (EICOSAPENTAENOIC ACID)
Fish Poison Bark....................see JAMAICAN DOGWOOD
Fish Wood ....see WAHOO
Fishfudle ....see JAMAICAN DOGWOOD
Fish-Poison Tree ....see JAMAICAN DOGWOOD
Fitch .... see BLACK SEED
Fitolaca .... see POKEWEED
Five Fingers..........see EUROPEAN FIVE-FINGER GRASS
Five Leaves .... see AMERICAN IVY
Five-Finger Blossom...
.............................see EUROPEAN FIVE-FINGER GRASS
Five-Finger Fern .... see MAIDENHAIR FERN
Five-Fingered Root ....
.... see HEMLOCK WATER DROPWORT
Five-Flavor-Fruit.................................see SCHISANDRA
Fixed Almond Oil.................see SWEET ALMOND
FL-113 .... see IPRIFLAVONE
Flag Lily...see ORRIS
Flaggon ....see ORRIS
Flagroot..see CALAMUS
Flake Manna.. see MANNA
Flame Seedless .... see GRAPE
Flamingo .... see WATER DROPWORT
Flannelflower .... see MULLEIN
Flapperdock.....................................see BUTTERBUR
Flat-Podded Vetch ....see LATHYRUS
Flatspine Prickly Ash .... see CHINESE PRICKLY ASH
Flavin .... see RIBOFLAVIN (VITAMIN B2)
Flavone X .... see CHRYSIN
Flavonoid ....see CHRYSIN, DIOSMIN,
                    HESPERIDIN, QUERCETIN, RUTIN
                    METHOXYLATED FLAVONES
Flax Weed..see RUPTUREWORT

Medical professionals should consult the Professional Version at www.NaturalDatabase.com.

FLAXSEED	see	FLAXSEED
FLAXSEED OIL	see	FLAXSEED OIL
Flaxweed	see	YELLOW TOADFLAX
Flea Wort	see	CANADIAN FLEABANE
Fleaseed	see	BLACK PSYLLIUM
Fleawort	see	BLACK PSYLLIUM
Fleece flower	see	HU ZHANG
Fleischfarbige	see	PASSIONFLOWER
Flesh and Blood	see	TORMENTIL
Fleur de Camomille Romaine	see	ROMAN CHAMOMILE
Fleur de la Passion	see	PASSIONFLOWER
Fleur de Pied de Chat	see	SANDY EVERLASTING
Fleurs d'Arnica	see	ARNICA
Fliggers	see	ORRIS
Flirtwort Midsummer Daisy	see	FEVERFEW
Flor de Passion	see	PASSIONFLOWER
Florence Fennel	see	FENNEL
Florentine Iris	see	ORRIS
Flores anthemidis	see	ROMAN CHAMOMILE
Flores caryophylli	see	CLOVE
Florist's Chrysanthemum	see	CHRYSANTHEMUM
Flos magnoliae	see	MAGNOLIA
Flower Velure	see	COLTSFOOT
Flowering Ammi	see	BISHOP'S WEED
Flowering Ash	see	MANNA
Flowering Sally	see	PURPLE LOOSESTRIFE
Flowering Willow	see	FIREWEED
Flowering Wintergreen	see	BITTER MILKWORT
Flowery Knotweed	see	FO-TI
Fluelli	see	YELLOW TOADFLAX
Fluffweed	see	MULLEIN
FLUORIDE	see	FLUORIDE
Fluorophosphate	see	FLUORIDE
Flux Root	see	PLEURISY ROOT
Fly Agaric	see	AGA
Fly-catcher	see	PITCHER PLANT
Fly-trap	see	CANADIAN HEMP, PITCHER PLANT
Foal's Foot	see	COLTSFOOT
Foalswort	see	COLTSFOOT
Foam Flower	see	COOLWORT
Fodder Beet	see	BEET
Foeniculi antheroleum	see	FENNEL
Foeniculum capillaceum	see	FENNEL
Foeniculum officinale	see	FENNEL
Foeniculum piperitum	see	FENNEL
Foeniculum vulgare	see	FENNEL
Foenugraeci semen	see	FENUGREEK
Foenugreek	see	FENUGREEK
Folacin	see	FOLIC ACID
Folate	see	FOLIC ACID
Folia Vitis Viniferae	see	GRAPE
FOLIC ACID	see	FOLIC ACID
Folium isatidis	see	ISATIS
Food of the Gods	see	ASAFOETIDA
FOOL'S PARSLEY	see	FOOL'S PARSLEY
Fool's-cicely	see	FOOL'S PARSLEY
Forest Mushroom	see	SHIITAKE MUSHROOM
FORGET-ME-NOT	see	FORGET-ME-NOT
Forskohlii	see	FORSKOLIN
FORSKOLIN	see	FORSKOLIN
FORSYTHIA	see	FORSYTHIA
FOS	see	FRUCTO-OLIGOSACCHARIDES
Fossil Tree	see	GINKGO
FO-TI	see	FO-TI
Foxberry	see	ALPINE CRANBERRY
Foxglove	see	DIGITALIS
Fox's Clote	see	BURDOCK
Fox's-brush	see	RED-SPUR VALERIAN
Fragaria collina	see	STRAWBERRY
Fragaria insularis	see	STRAWBERRY
Fragaria vesca	see	STRAWBERRY
Fragaria virginiana	see	STRAWBERRY
Fragaria viridis	see	STRAWBERRY
Fragariae folium	see	STRAWBERRY
Fragrant Agrimony	see	AGRIMONY
Fragrant Sumac	see	SWEET SUMACH
Fragrant Valerian	see	VALERIAN
Framboise	see	RED RASPBERRY
Frangula	see	ALDER BUCKTHORN
Frangula alnus	see	ALDER BUCKTHORN
Frangula purshiana	see	CASCARA
Frangulae Cortex	see	ALDER BUCKTHORN
FRANKINCENSE	see	FRANKINCENSE
Frauenmantelkraut	see	ALCHEMILLA
Fraxinella	see	BURNING BUSH
Fraxinus americana	see	ASH
Fraxinus excelsior	see	ASH
Fraxinus ornus	see	MANNA
Free Base Glycine	see	GLYCINE
French Honeysuckle	see	GOAT'S RUE
French Lavender	see	LAVENDER
French Lilac	see	GOAT'S RUE
French Marigold	see	TAGETES
French Marine Pine Bark Extract	see	PYCNOGENOL
French Psyllium	see	BLACK PSYLLIUM
French Thyme	see	THYME
French Willow	see	FIREWEED
Freshwater Green Algae	see	CHLORELLA
Freshwater Seaweed	see	CHLORELLA
Friar's Cowl	see	ARUM
Frijol de Soya	see	SOY
FRINGETREE	see	FRINGETREE
Frogsfoot	see	BULBOUS BUTTERCUP
Frogwort	see	BULBOUS BUTTERCUP
Frost Plant	see	FROSTWORT
Frostweed	see	FROSTWORT
FROSTWORT	see	FROSTWORT
FRUCTO-OLIGOSACCHARIDES	see	FRUCTO-OLIGOSACCHARIDES, INULIN
Fructus aurantii	see	BITTER ORANGE
Fructus Cortex	see	ENGLISH WALNUT
Fructus Lycii	see	LYCIUM
Fructus Rosae Laevigatae	see	CHEROKEE ROSEHIP
Fruit de Celeri	see	CELERY
Fruit of the Dead	see	POMEGRANATE
Fruits de Khella	see	KHELLA
Fu Ling	see	PORIA MUSHROOM
Fucostanol	see	SITOSTANOL
Fucus	see	BLADDERWRACK
Fucus vesiculosus	see	BLADDERWRACK
Fuga daemonum	see	ST. JOHN'S WORT
Fum	see	ASAFOETIDA
Fumaria officinalis	see	FUMITORY
Fumiterry	see	FUMITORY
FUMITORY	see	FUMITORY
Fumus	see	FUMITORY
Funffing	see	AGRIMONY
Funffingerkraut	see	AGRIMONY
Fungi Extract	see	AHCC

 Natural Medicines Comprehensive Database Consumer Version (209) 472-2244

Fungus japonicus ....see KOMBUCHA TEA
Furze ....see DYER'S BROOM
Fusanum..see WAHOO
FuShen ....see PORIA MUSHROOM
Fusoria...see WAHOO
Fuyu ....see JAPANESE PERSIMMON
Fytic Acid..see IP-6
G Salt .... see GLYCINE
GABA (GAMMA-AMINOBUTYRIC ACID) ....
.............see GABA (GAMMA-AMINOBUTYRIC ACID)
Gadrose ....see WAHOO
GAG ....see CHONDROITIN SULFATE
Gaga .... see MARIJUANA
Gaglee ....see ARUM
Gagroot .... see LOBELIA
Gajabhakshya.................see INDIAN FRANKINCENSE
Galactosaminoglucuronoglycan Sulfate ....
.............................see CHONDROITIN SULFATE
Galanga ....see ALPINIA
Galangal ....see ALPINIA
Galangal Root ....see ALPINIA
Galangin Flavanone .... see CHRYSIN
GALBANUM........................... see GALBANUM
Galega bicolor .... see GOAT'S RUE
Galega officinalis .... see GOAT'S RUE
Galega patula .... see GOAT'S RUE
Galegae Officinalis Herba....................... see GOAT'S RUE
Galeopsidis Herba.................... see HEMPNETTLE
Galeopsis ochroleuca .... see HEMPNETTLE
Galeopsis segetum .... see HEMPNETTLE
Galgant..see ALPINIA
Galii Odorati Herba.............. see SWEET WOODRUFF
Galipea officinalis .... see ANGOSTURA
Galium Aparine ....see CLIVERS
Galium odorata.................. see SWEET WOODRUFF
Galium verum .... see LADY'S BEDSTRAW
Gall Weed...............................see GENTIAN
Gallium ....see CLIVERS
Gallwort ....see YELLOW TOADFLAX
Gambierdiscus toxicus.............................see CIGUATERA
Gambodia .... see GAMBOGE
GAMBOGE .... see GAMBOGE
Gamma Amino Butyric Acid ....
.............see GABA (GAMMA-AMINOBUTYRIC ACID)
GAMMA BUTYROLACTONE (GBL) ....
.... see GAMMA BUTYROLACTONE (GBL)
Gamma Hydrate ....
.................see GAMMA-HYDROXYBUTYRATE (GHB)
Gamma Hydroxybutyrate...............................
.................see GAMMA-HYDROXYBUTYRATE (GHB)
Gamma Hydroxybutyric Acid Lactone ....
.... see GAMMA BUTYROLACTONE (GBL)
GAMMA LINOLENIC ACID ....
..........................see EVENING PRIMROSE OIL,
                    GAMMA LINOLENIC ACID
GAMMA ORYZANOL ....see GAMMA ORYZANOL
Gamma Tocotrienol.......................... see VITAMIN E
Gamma-aminobutyric Acid...............................
.................see GABA (GAMMA-AMINOBUTYRIC ACID)
Gamma-glutamylcysteinylglycine ....see GLUTATHIONE
Gamma-glutamylethylamide....................... see THEANINE
GAMMA-HYDROXYBUTYRATE (GHB)...............................
.................see GAMMA-HYDROXYBUTYRATE (GHB)
Gamma-OH...............................
.................see GAMMA-HYDROXYBUTYRATE (GHB)

Gamma-oryzanol........................see GAMMA ORYZANOL
Gamma-OZ .... see GAMMA ORYZANOL
Gamma-tocopherol .... see VITAMIN E
Gamolenic Acid .... see GAMMA LINOLENIC ACID
Gan Cao ....see LICORICE
Gan Zao......................................see LICORICE
Gandana ....see YARROW
Gandapura ....see AMBRETTE
Gandharva Hasta ....see CASTOR
Ganga .... see MARIJUANA
Gange .... see KUDZU
Ganoderma lucidum.................... see REISHI MUSHROOM
Gao Liang...see ALPINIA
Garacilaria confervoides .... see AGAR
Garance .... see MADDER
GARCINIA............................see GARCINIA
Garcinia hanburyi.......................... see GAMBOGE
Garcinia mangostana..................... see MANGOSTEEN
Garden Angelica............................. see ANGELICA
Garden Artichoke ....see ARTICHOKE
Garden Asparagus .... see ASPARAGUS
Garden Balsam .... see JEWELWEED
Garden Basil..see BASIL
Garden Beet .... see BEET
Garden Burnet...................... see GREATER BURNET
Garden Chamomile .... see ROMAN CHAMOMILE
Garden Chervil.............................. see CHERVIL
GARDEN CRESS...........................see GARDEN CRESS
Garden Fennel............................... see FENNEL
Garden Fern .... see OSTRICH FERN
Garden Heliotrope............................see VALERIAN
Garden Lavender............................ see LAVENDER
Garden Marigold....................... see CALENDULA
Garden Marjoram............................see MARJORAM
Garden Mint ....see SPEARMINT
Garden Nightshade........... see BLACK NIGHTSHADE
Garden Parsley ....see PARSLEY
Garden Pepper.............................see CAPSICUM
Garden Rhubarb .... see RHUBARB
Garden Rue ....see RUE
Garden Sage .... see SAGE
Garden Sorrel .... see SORREL
Garden Thyme .... see THYME
Garden Valerian.............................see VALERIAN
GARDEN VIOLET..
..........................see GARDEN VIOLET, SWEET VIOLET
Gardenin D.................see METHOXYLATED FLAVONES
Gargaut..see ALPINIA
Garget................................... see POKEWEED
Garijara .... see WILD CARROT
GARLIC...see GARLIC
Garlic Sage.................................see WOOD SAGE
Gartenmajoran.................................see MARJORAM
Gas Black .... see ACTIVATED CHARCOAL
Gas Plant ....see BURNING BUSH
Gat...see KHAT
Gatten..see WAHOO
Gatter...see WAHOO
Gattilier ....see CHASTEBERRY
Gaultheria Oil..............................see WINTERGREEN
Gaultheria procumbens ....see WINTERGREEN
Gay-Feather.........................see MARSH BLAZING STAR
GBL................. see GAMMA BUTYROLACTONE (GBL)
GCP...
...........see GENISTEIN COMBINED POLYSACCHARIDE

Natural Medicines Comprehensive Database Consumer Version

Ge Gen	see KUDZU
Ge-132	see GERMANIUM
Gea	see KAVA
Geissrautenkraut	see GOAT'S RUE
GELATIN	see GELATIN
Gelidiella acerosa	see AGAR
Gelidium amanasii	see AGAR
Gelidium cartilagineum	see AGAR
Gelidium crinale	see AGAR
Gelidium divaricatum	see AGAR
Gelidium pacificum	see AGAR
Gelidium vagum	see AGAR
Gelosa	see AGAR
Gelsemii rhizoma	see GELSEMIUM
GELSEMIUM	see GELSEMIUM
Gelsemiumwurzelstock Jessamine	see GELSEMIUM
Gemeine schafgarbe	see YARROW
Gemeiner beifuss	see MUGWORT
Gemeiner wasswedost	see HEMP AGRIMONY
Gemnema melicida	see GYMNEMA
Gemuseartischocke	see ARTICHOKE
General Plantain	see GREAT PLANTAIN
Genet	see SPANISH BROOM
Genet a Balais	see SCOTCH BROOM
Genievre	see JUNIPER
Genista andreana	see SCOTCH BROOM
Genista juncea	see SPANISH BROOM
Genista tinctoria	see DYER'S BROOM
Genistein	see RED CLOVER, SOY
GENISTEIN COMBINED POLYSACCHARIDE	see GENISTEIN COMBINED POLYSACCHARIDE
Genmai	see BROWN RICE
GENTIAN	see GENTIAN
Gentiana acaulis	see GENTIAN
Gentiana chirata	see CHIRATA
Gentiana chirayita	see CHIRATA
Gentiana kochiana	see GENTIAN
Gentiana lutea	see GENTIAN
Gentianae radix	see GENTIAN
Ge-Oxy 132	see GERMANIUM
Geranien	see SOUTH AFRICAN GERANIUM
Geranium robertianum	see HERB ROBERT
Geranium Root	see SOUTH AFRICAN GERANIUM
GERMAN CHAMOMILE	see GERMAN CHAMOMILE
GERMAN IPECAC	see GERMAN IPECAC
German Lactucarium	see WILD LETTUCE
German Rue	see RUE
GERMAN SARSAPARILLA	see GERMAN SARSAPARILLA
GERMANDER	see GERMANDER
GERMANIUM	see GERMANIUM
Germanium Lactate Citrate	see GERMANIUM
Gero-Vita	see PROCAINE
Gerovital	see PROCAINE
Geum	see AVENS
Geum rivale	see WATER AVENS
Geum urbanum	see AVENS
Gewurznelken nagelein	see CLOVE
GH-3	see PROCAINE
GHB	see GAMMA-HYDROXYBUTYRATE (GHB)
Ghoda Asoda	see ASHWAGANDHA
Ghrita-kumari	see ALOE
Gi	see KAVA
Giant Fennel	see ASAFOETIDA
Giant Reed	see REED HERB

Gigartina mamillosa	see CARRAGEENAN
Gillenia trifoliata	see INDIAN PHYSIC
Gill-Go-By-The-Hedge	see GROUND IVY
Gill-Go-Over-The-Ground	see GROUND IVY
Gillyflower	see WALLFLOWER
Ginepro	see JUNIPER
Gingembre	see GINGER
GINGER	see GINGER
Ginjeira	see SOUR CHERRY
GINKGO	see GINKGO
Ginkgo Biloba	see GINKGO
Ginkgo Folium	see GINKGO
Ginseng	see GINSENG, AMERICAN; GINSENG, PANAX; GINSENG, SIBERIAN
Ginseng asiatique	see GINSENG, PANAX
Ginseng Radix Alba	see GINSENG, PANAX
GINSENG, AMERICAN	see GINSENG, AMERICAN
GINSENG, PANAX	see GINSENG, PANAX
GINSENG, SIBERIAN	see GINSENG, SIBERIAN
Ginsterkraut	see SCOTCH BROOM
Giroflier	see WALLFLOWER
GLA	see GAMMA LINOLENIC ACID
Gladdon	see CALAMUS
Gladyne	see ORRIS
Glandular	see ADRENAL EXTRACT
Glechoma hederacea	see GROUND IVY
Glicerol	see GLYCEROL
GLN	see GLUTAMINE
Globe Amaranth	see BUTTERCUP
Globe Artichoke	see ARTICHOKE
Globe Crowfoot	see GLOBE FLOWER
GLOBE FLOWER	see GLOBE FLOWER
Globe Ranunculus	see GLOBE FLOWER
Globe Trollius	see GLOBE FLOWER
Glockenbilsenkraut	see SCOPOLIA
Glossy Buckthorn	see ALDER BUCKTHORN
GLOSSY PRIVET	see GLOSSY PRIVET
Glucerite	see GLYCEROL
GLUCOMANNAN	see GLUCOMANNAN
Gluconolactone	see ALPHA HYDROXY ACIDS
Glucosamine	see GLUCOSAMINE SULFATE
GLUCOSAMINE HYDROCHLORIDE	see GLUCOSAMINE HYDROCHLORIDE
Glucosamine KCL	see GLUCOSAMINE HYDROCHLORIDE
Glucosamine N-acetyl	see N-ACETYL GLUCOSAMINE
GLUCOSAMINE SULFATE	see GLUCOSAMINE SULFATE
Glucose Tolerance Factor-Cr	see CHROMIUM
Glucose-6-phosphate	see GLUCOSAMINE HYDROCHLORIDE, GLUCOSAMINE SULFATE
Glutamate	see GLUTAMINE
Glutamic Acid	see GLUTAMINE
Glutaminate	see GLUTAMINE
GLUTAMINE	see GLUTAMINE
GLUTATHIONE	see GLUTATHIONE
Glycerin	see GLYCEROL
Glycerin Monolaurate	see MONOLAURIN
GLYCEROL	see GLYCEROL
Glycerol Monolaurate	see MONOLAURIN
Glycerol Trierucate Oil	see LORENZO'S OIL
Glycerol Trioleate Oil	see LORENZO'S OIL
Glycerolum	see GLYCEROL
Glycerophosphorylcholine	see ALPHA-GPC

Glyceryl Alcohol..................................see GLYCEROL
Glyceryl Paraaminobenzoate ....
................see PARA-AMINOBENZOIC ACID (PABA)
GLYCINE .... see GLYCINE
Glycine abrus ....see PRECATORY BEAN
Glycine gracilis ....see SOY, SOYBEAN OIL
Glycine hispida ....see SOY, SOYBEAN OIL
Glycine max ....see SOY, SOYBEAN OIL
Glycine soja ....see SOY, SOYBEAN OIL
Glycoaminoglycan ....see HYALURONIC ACID
Glycocoll.. see GLYCINE
Glycolic Acid ....see ALPHA HYDROXY ACIDS
Glycosaminoglycan Polysulphuric Acid Complex ....
.... see BOVINE CARTILAGE
Glycosaminoglycans ....see MESOGLYCAN
Glycosthene................................. see GLYCINE
Glycyrrhiza .... see LICORICE
Glycyrrhiza glabra .... see LICORICE
Glycyrrhiza uralensis .... see LICORICE
Gnaphalium angustifolium...... see SANDY EVERLASTING
Gnaphalium dioicum....................see CAT'S FOOT
Gnaphalium italicum.............. see SANDY EVERLASTING
Gnaphalium orientale............. see SANDY EVERLASTING
Gnaphalium stoechas .... see SANDY EVERLASTING
Gnaphalium uliginosum.....................see CUDWEED
GOA POWDER ....see GOA POWDER
Goat Colostrum.............................see COLOSTRUM
Goathead ....see PUNCTURE VINE
Goatnut................................... see JOJOBA
Goat's Arrach .... see ARRACH
Goat's Leaf...........................see HONEYSUCKLE
Goat's Pod..............................see CAPSICUM
GOAT'S RUE .... see GOAT'S RUE
Goat's Thorn ....see TRAGACANTH
Goatweed ....see ST. JOHN'S WORT
Gobo................................see BURDOCK
God's-Hair ....see HARTSTONGUE
Goji .... see LYCIUM
Gokhru ....see PUNCTURE VINE
Gokshura ....see PUNCTURE VINE
Gold Chain ....see COMMON STONECROP
Gold Cup .... see BUTTERCUP
Gold-Bloom ....see CALENDULA
Goldcup .... see BULBOUS BUTTERCUP
Golden Bell ....see FORSYTHIA
Golden Chain ....see LABURNUM
Golden Daisy ....see OX-EYE DAISY
Golden Groundsel .... see GOLDEN RAGWORT
Golden Moss ....see COMMON STONECROP
GOLDEN RAGWORT .... see GOLDEN RAGWORT
Golden Root......................see ROSEROOT
Golden Senecio .... see GOLDEN RAGWORT
Golden Trumpet ....see CATUABA
GOLDENROD...........................see GOLDENROD
Goldenroot ....see GOLDENSEAL
GOLDENSEAL .... see GOLDENSEAL, OX-EYE DAISY
Goldenthread................................see GOLDTHREAD
Goldilocks ....
.... see IMMORTELLE, SANDY EVERLASTING
Goldsiegel ....see GOLDENSEAL
GOLDTHREAD .... see GOLDTHREAD
Gomishi................................see SCHISANDRA
Gomme arabique ....see ACACIA
Gomme de Senegal ....see ACACIA
Gommelaque ....see SHELLAC

Gomphrena paniculata ....see SUMA
Goniopora species.........................see CORAL
Gonolobus condurango .... see CONDURANGO
Goose Grass .... see CLIVERS, POTENTILLA
Goose Tansy .... see POTENTILLA
Goosebill................................see CLIVERS
Goosefoot .... see ARRACH
Goosewort ....see POTENTILLA
Gorikapuli ....see GARCINIA
Gosling Weed ....see CLIVERS
Gossypium herbaceum.............see COTTON, GOSSYPOL
Gossypium hirsutum ....see COTTON, GOSSYPOL
GOSSYPOL ....see GOSSYPOL
GOTU KOLA............................ see GOTU KOLA
Gou Qi Zi .... see LYCIUM
Goudron de Cade ....see CADE OIL
Gouqizi................................ see LYCIUM
Gout Herb............................see GOUTWEED
Goutberry .... see BLACKBERRY
GOUTWEED ....see GOUTWEED
Goutwort ....see GOUTWEED
GPC .... see ALPHA-GPC
Gracemere-Pear...................see PRICKLY PEAR CACTUS
Graine de Lin ....see FLAXSEED, FLAXSEED OIL
GRAINS OF PARADISE ....see CAPSICUM,
                                    GRAINS OF PARADISE
Graminis rhizoma.....................see WHEATGRASS
Granada ....see POMEGRANATE
Grano turco .... see BUCKWHEAT
Grao-do-Porco.......................see CHA DE BUGRE
GRAPE .... see GRAPE
Grape Bark .... see COCILLANA
GRAPEFRUIT ....see GRAPEFRUIT
Grapple Plant ....see DEVIL'S CLAW
Grass .... see MARIJUANA, SWEET VERNAL GRASS
Grass Myrtle.............................see CALAMUS
Grass Pollen Extract....................see RYE GRASS
Gratiola .... see HEDGE-HYSSOP
Gratiola officinalis .... see HEDGE-HYSSOP
Gravel Plant....................... see TRAILING ARBUTUS
GRAVEL ROOT .... see GRAVEL ROOT
GRAVIOLA .... see GRAVIOLA
Gray Beard Tree ....see FRINGETREE
Gray Ephedra ....see MORMON TEA
Gray Nicker ....see DIVI-DIVI
Greasewood..........................see CHAPARRAL
Great Bur...............................see BURDOCK
Great Burdocks ....see BURDOCK
Great Morel .... see BELLADONNA
Great Ox-Eye ....see OX-EYE DAISY
GREAT PLANTAIN ....see GREAT PLANTAIN
Great Raifort .... see HORSERADISH
Great Stinging Nettle .... see STINGING NETTLE
Great Willowherb ....see FIREWEED
GREATER BINDWEED ....see GREATER BINDWEED
GREATER BURNET...................see GREATER BURNET
Greater Burnet-Saxifrage ....see PIMPINELLA
GREATER CELANDINE.......see GREATER CELANDINE
Greater Plantain ....see GREAT PLANTAIN
Grecian Laurel ....see SWEET BAY
Greek Clover..........................see FENUGREEK
Greek Hay ....see FENUGREEK
Greek Hay Seed ....see FENUGREEK
Greek Oregano ....see GREEK SAGE
GREEK SAGE ....see GREEK SAGE

Green Alga ....see CHLORELLA
Green Algae ....see CHLORELLA
Green Arrow.....................................see YARROW
Green Bean.....................................see BEAN POD
Green Broom..........................see DYER'S BROOM
Green Chili Pepper......................see CAPSICUM
Green Dragon.........................see TRAGACANTH
Green Endive.........................see WILD LETTUCE
Green Ginger............................see WORMWOOD
Green Hellebore ....see AMERICAN HELLEBORE
Green Holy Basil ....see HOLY BASIL
Green Lipped Mussel.....................................
.... see NEW ZEALAND GREEN-LIPPED MUSSEL
Green Mint.................................see SPEARMINT
Green Oil of Charity .....see ENGLISH ADDER'S TONGUE
Green Olive ....see OLIVE
Green Onion...................................see ONION
Green Orange....................see BITTER ORANGE
Green Ozier ....see AMERICAN DOGWOOD
Green Pepper.............................see CAPSICUM
Green Sauce ....see WOOD SORREL
GREEN TEA .... see GREEN TEA
Green Veratrum ....see AMERICAN HELLEBORE
Green Wolf's Foot.......................see BUGLEWEED
Greenweed.............................see DYER'S BROOM
Grenade ....see POMEGRANATE
Grenadier...............................see POMEGRANATE
Griffe du Chat ....see CAT'S CLAW
Griffe du Diable ....see DEVIL'S CLAW
Grifola ....see MAITAKE MUSHROOM
Grifola frondosa...............see MAITAKE MUSHROOM
Grifolan (GRN)..................... see BETA GLUCANS
Grindelia ....see GUMWEED
Grindelia camporum ....see GUMWEED
Grindelia robusta........................see GUMWEED
Grindelia squarrosa ....see GUMWEED
Grindeliae Herba........................see GUMWEED
Griottier...............................see SOUR CHERRY
Grip Grass ....see CLIVERS
Grisset ....see SEA BUCKTHORN
Groats ....see OATS
GroPCho .... see ALPHA-GPC
Groseillier de Ceylan ....see INDIAN GOOSEBERRY
Grosse Kamille......................see ROMAN CHAMOMILE
Grosse Moosbeere .... see CRANBERRY
Ground Apple .... see ROMAN CHAMOMILE
Ground Berry ....see WINTERGREEN
Ground Elder............................see GOUTWEED
Ground Furze ....see SPINY RESTHARROW
Ground Glutton .... see GROUNDSEL
Ground Holly ....see PIPSISSEWA
GROUND IVY .... see GROUND IVY
Ground Laurel ....see TRAILING ARBUTUS
Ground Lemon .... see PODOPHYLLUM
Ground Lily .... see BETH ROOT
GROUND PINE.........................see GROUND PINE
Ground Raspberry ....see GOLDENSEAL
Ground Thistle ....see CARLINA
Groundbread ....see CYCLAMEN
Groundnuts........................see PEANUT OIL
GROUNDSEL .... see GROUNDSEL
Grundy Swallow ....see GOLDEN RAGWORT,
GROUNDSEL
Gua Lou .... see CHINESE CUCUMBER
Gua Luo Ren ....see CHINESE CUCUMBER

Guaiac Heartwood .... see GUAIAC WOOD resin, wood
GUAIAC WOOD resin, wood ....
....see GUAIAC WOOD resin, wood
Guaiacum .... see GUAIAC WOOD resin, wood
Guaiacum guatemalense ... see GUAIAC WOOD resin, wood
Guaiacum officinale .... see GUAIAC WOOD resin, wood
Guaiacum sanctum .... see GUAIAC WOOD resin, wood
Guajaci lignum................ see GUAIAC WOOD resin, wood
Guajava .... see GUAVA
Guanabana .... see GRAVIOLA
Guanavana .... see GRAVIOLA
Guang Fang Ji ....see ARISTOLOCHIA
Guapi ....see COCILLANA
Guar Flour ....see GUAR GUM
GUAR GUM ....see GUAR GUM
GUARANA ....see GUARANA
Guarea guara .... see COCILLANA
Guarea guidonia .... see COCILLANA
Guarea rusbyi .... see COCILLANA
Guarea spiciflora .... see COCILLANA
Guarea trichilioides .... see COCILLANA
Guatemala Lemongrass....................... see LEMONGRASS
GUAVA .... see GUAVA
Gubak .... see ANDROGRAPHIS, ARECA
Guelder Rose........................ see CRAMP BARK
Guflatich ....see COLTSFOOT
Guggal..................................see GUGGUL
GUGGUL...................................see GUGGUL
Guggulipid ....see GUGGUL
Guggulsterone ....see GUGGUL
Gui Zhi .... see CASSIA CINNAMON
Guigai..............................see GINSENG, PANAX
Guilandina bonduc .... see DIVI-DIVI
Guindo...............................see SOUR CHERRY
Guinea Corn ....see BROOM CORN
Guinea Grains .... see GRAINS OF PARADISE
Guinea Rush............................... see ADRUE
Guinea Sorrel .... see HIBISCUS
Gul-khair ....see MALLOW
Gully Gum ....see EUCALYPTUS
Gum Acacia................................see ACACIA
Gum Arabic................................see ACACIA
Gum Benjamin ....see BENZOIN
Gum Benzoin ....see BENZOIN
Gum Bush .... see YERBA SANTA
Gum Camphor.........................see CAMPHOR
Gum Dragon......................... see TRAGACANTH
Gum Guggal.............................see GUGGUL
Gum Guggulu............................see GUGGUL
Gum Ivy ....see ENGLISH IVY
Gum Myrrh ....see MYRRH
Gum Plant ....see COMFREY, YERBA SANTA
Gum Senegal...............................see ACACIA
Gum Tragacanth................... see TRAGACANTH
Gum Tree ....see EUCALYPTUS, STORAX
Gummae Mimosae ....see ACACIA
Gummi Tragacanthae .... see TRAGACANTH
Gummigutta .... see GAMBOGE
GUMWEED...........................see GUMWEED
Gurmar .... see GYMNEMA
Gur-Mar .... see GYMNEMA
Gurmarbooti .... see GYMNEMA
Guru Nut .... see COLA NUT
Gutta cambodia .... see GAMBOGE
Gutta gamba .... see GAMBOGE

Gworo .... see COLA NUT
GYMNEMA .... see GYMNEMA
Gynocardia Oil .... see CHAULMOOGRA
Gynostemma .... see JIAOGULAN
Gynostemma pedatum .... see JIAOGULAN
Gynostemma pentaphyllum .... see JIAOGULAN
Gypsophila paniculata.............. see WHITE SOAPWORT
Gypsophilae Radix .... see WHITE SOAPWORT
Gypsy Flower........................ see HOUND'S TONGUE
Gypsy Weed .... see BUGLEWEED, VERONICA
Gypsy's-Rose .... see FIELD SCABIOUS
Gypsywort................................see BUGLEWEED
Haagdorn .... see HAWTHORN
Haba Soya ....see SOY
Hachiya ....see JAPANESE PERSIMMON
Hackmatack.................................. see THUJA
Haematoxylum campechianum.......... see LOGWOOD
Haematoxylum lignum...................see LOGWOOD
Hagedorn .... see HAWTHORN
Hagenia abyssinica........................see KOUSSO
Hag's Taper .... see MULLEIN
Hai Ba Ji .... see MORINDA
Hair of Venus .... see MAIDENHAIR FERN
Hairy Mint................................ see WILD MINT
Hairy Sage................................ see SCHIZONEPETA
Hallelujah................................see WOOD SORREL
Hallfoot................................see COLTSFOOT
Hamamelis .... see WITCH HAZEL
Hamburg Parsley............................ see PARSLEY
Hanagosho.....................see JAPANESE PERSIMMON
Handflower............................. see WALLFLOWER
Hansen CBS 5926 ....
.... see SACCHAROMYCES BOULARDII
Happy Major .... see BURDOCK
Hara ....see TERMINALIA
Harada ....see TERMINALIA
Haravi .... see CARAWAY
Hardback .... see STONE ROOT
Hardhack .... see STONE ROOT
Hardhay.................see ST. JOHN'S WORT
Hardock ....see BURDOCK
Hardy Fern .... see OSTRICH FERN
Harebur ....see BURDOCK
Hare's Beard........................... see MULLEIN
Hare's Ear Root................... see BUPLEURUM
Haridra ....see TURMERIC
Haritaki ....see TERMINALIA
Harnblumen.............. see SANDY EVERLASTING
HARONGA..............................see HARONGA
Harongablädder Leaf ....see HARONGA
Harongarinde Bark....................see HARONGA
Harpagophyti Radix .... see DEVIL'S CLAW
Harpagophytum procumbens.........see DEVIL'S CLAW
Harthorne .... see HAWTHORN
Hartogia betulin .... see BUCHU
Hart's Tree........................ see SWEET CLOVER
Hart's Truffle Puffball ....see PUFF BALL
Hartshorn......... see EUROPEAN BUCKTHORN
HARTSTONGUE .... see HARTSTONGUE
Harungana madagascariensis ....see HARONGA
Haselnuss .... see HAZELNUT
Haselstrauch............................... see HAZELNUT
Hasenklee................................ see YELLOW LUPIN
Hash .... see MARIJUANA
Hashish................................ see MARIJUANA

Hauhechelwurzel.................see SPINY RESTHARROW
Haw .... see HAWTHORN
HAWAIIAN BABY WOODROSE ....
.... see HAWAIIAN BABY WOODROSE
Hawkweed............................ see MOUSE EAR
HAWTHORN .... see HAWTHORN
Hay Flower.......................... see SWEET CLOVER
Haymaids .... see GROUND IVY
Hayriffe ....see CLIVERS
Hayruff ....see CLIVERS
Hazel .... see HAZELNUT, WITCH HAZEL
Hazel Alder ....see SMOOTH ALDER
HAZELNUT .... see HAZELNUT
Hazelwort ....see ASARABACCA
HCA ....see GARCINIA
He Shou Wu .... see FO-TI, HU ZHANG
He Zi ....see TERMINALIA
Headache ....see CORN POPPY
Headsman.................. see BUCKHORN PLANTAIN
Headwark ....see CORN POPPY
Heal-All......... see FIGWORT, SELF-HEAL, STONE ROOT
Healing Herb .... see COMFREY
Health Inca Tea .... see COCA
Heart of the Earth................... see SELF-HEAL
Heartleaf...................... see COUNTRY MALLOW
HEART'S EASE ....see HEART'S EASE
Heated Oyster Shell-Seaweed Calcium ....see CALCIUM
HEATHER .... see HEATHER
Heaven Tree .... see TREE OF HEAVEN
Heavy Kaolin .... see KAOLIN
Hebanthe eriantha ....see SUMA
Hebanthe paniculata.........................see SUMA
Hedeoma pulegioides........................... see PENNYROYAL
Hedera helix .... see ENGLISH IVY
Hedera senticosa .... see GINSENG, SIBERIAN
Hedera taurica .... see ENGLISH IVY
Hederae Helicis Folium .... see ENGLISH IVY
Hedge Bindweed.............. see GREATER BINDWEED
Hedge Convolvulus .... see GREATER BINDWEED
Hedge Fumitory ....see FUMITORY
Hedge Lily .... see GREATER BINDWEED
HEDGE MUSTARD ....see HEDGE MUSTARD
Hedge Nettles............................. see BETONY
Hedge Taper .... see MULLEIN
Hedge-Burs ....see CLIVERS
Hedgeheriff ....see CLIVERS
Hedgehog..............................see ECHINACEA
HEDGE-HYSSOP .... see HEDGE-HYSSOP
Hedgemaids .... see GROUND IVY
Hedgethorn .... see HAWTHORN
Hediondilla................................see CHAPARRAL
Hedysarum tuberosum .... see KUDZU
Heeng.............................see ASAFOETIDA
Heerabol ....see MYRRH
Hei Zao .... see JUJUBE
Helenium grandiflorum................... see ELECAMPANE
Helianthemum canadense ....see FROSTWORT
Helianthi Annui Oleum .... see SUNFLOWER OIL
Helianthus annuus .... see SUNFLOWER OIL
Helichrysum........................ see SANDY EVERLASTING
Helichrysum angustifolium..... see SANDY EVERLASTING
Helichrysum arenarium........................ see IMMORTELLE
Helichrysum italicum............ see SANDY EVERLASTING
Helichrysum orientale............ see SANDY EVERLASTING
Helichrysum stoechas .... see SANDY EVERLASTING

Natural Medicines Comprehensive Database Consumer Version   (209) 472-2244   **725**

Helixor .... see EUROPEAN MISTLETOE
Helleborus niger........................... see BLACK HELLEBORE
Hellweed ....see DODDER
Helmet Flower ....see SKULLCAP
Helonias .... see FALSE UNICORN
Helonias dioica............................ see FALSE UNICORN
Helonias lutea............................. see FALSE UNICORN
Hemicellulose Complex with Arabinoxylane ......see MGN-3
HEMLOCK...see HEMLOCK
Hemlock Bark .... see PINUS BARK
Hemlock Gum .... see PINUS BARK
HEMLOCK SPRUCE.................see HEMLOCK SPRUCE,
PINUS BARK
HEMLOCK WATER DROPWORT......................
.... see HEMLOCK WATER DROPWORT
Hemlocktanne .... see PINUS BARK
Hemp .... see MARIJUANA
HEMP AGRIMONY ....see HEMP AGRIMONY
Hemp Tree..see CHASTEBERRY
HEMPNETTLE .... see HEMPNETTLE
Hemprichia erythraea............................see MYRRH
Hen Bell .... see HENBANE
Hen Of The Woods................ see MAITAKE MUSHROOM
HENBANE .... see HENBANE
Hendibeh.......................................see CHICORY
HENNA .... see ALKANNA, HENNA
Hennae Folium...................................see HENNA
Henne ....see HENNA
Hens and Chickens........................see HOUSELEEK
HEP-30.. see CHITOSAN
Heparinoid Fraction .... see MESOGLYCAN
Heparinoids .... see MESOGLYCAN
Hepatica nobilis var. acuta .... see LIVERWORT
Hepatica nobilis var. obtusa .... see LIVERWORT
Hepatici Noblis Herba........................ see LIVERWORT
Hépatique à Lobes Aigus .... see LIVERWORT
Hépatique d'Amérique .... see LIVERWORT
Heps .... see ROSE HIP
Heptacosanol.............................see POLICOSANOL
Heptamethoxyflavones................................
................................see METHOXYLATED FLAVONES
Heracleum lanatum .... see MASTERWORT
Heracleum maximum........................... see MASTERWORT
Heracleum montanum........................... see MASTERWORT
Heracleum sphondylium .... see MASTERWORT
Herb Bennet .... see AVENS
Herb Gerard .... see GOUTWEED
Herb Louisa .... see LEMON VERBENA
Herb Margaret.....................see OX-EYE DAISY
Herb of Grace .... see VERBENA
Herb of the Cross .... see VERBENA
HERB PARIS.....................................see HERB PARIS
Herb Perter .... see COWSLIP
HERB ROBERT .... see HERB ROBERT
Herb Trinity................................. see LIVERWORT
Herb Two-Pence .... see MONEYWORT
Herba agrimoniae.............................see AGRIMONY
Herba artemisae .... see WORMWOOD
Herba de la Pastora .... see DAMIANA
Herba de María .... see DIVINER'S SAGE
Herba Dictamni Herba...............see BURNING BUSH
Herba epimedii................................see EPIMEDIUM
Herba eupatoriae ....see AGRIMONY
Herba fumariae................................see FUMITORY
Herba malvae .... see MARSHMALLOW

Herba verbenae .... see VERBENA
Herbal Ecstasy .... see EPHEDRA
Herbe aux Charpentiers........................see YARROW
Herbe d'Absinthe .... see WORMWOOD
Herbe d'Aigremoine .... see AGRIMONY
Herbe de Hogweed......................... see SCOTCH BROOM
Herbe de Sainte Cunegonde............see HEMP AGRIMONY
Herbe de Saint-Guillaume........................see AGRIMONY
Herbe d'Euphraise .... see EYEBRIGHT
Herbe-Chapeau .... see CONTRAYERVA
Herb-of-Grace..see RUE
Herb-of-the-Virgin .... see DIVINER'S SAGE
Herbygrass...see RUE
Hercules Woundwort................................ see SELF-HEAL
Herniaria glabra .... see RUPTUREWORT
Herniaria hirsuta............................. see RUPTUREWORT
Herniariae Herba............................. see RUPTUREWORT
Herniary .... see RUPTUREWORT
Herpestis monniera .... see BRAHMI
Hervea ....see MATE
HESPERIDIN .... see HESPERIDIN
Hexacosanol.............................see POLICOSANOL
Hexacosanol (26-C) .... see OCTACOSANOL
Hexahydroxycyclohexane .... see INOSITOL
Hexamethoxyflavones ....
................see METHOXYLATED FLAVONES
Hexanicotinoyl Inositol..........see INOSITOL NICOTINATE
Hexenbesen .... see EUROPEAN MISTLETOE
HEY .... see HYPERIMMUNE EGG
HIBISCUS .... see HIBISCUS
Hibiscus abelmoschus................................ see AMBRETTE
Hibiscus sabdariffa............................ see HIBISCUS
Hieracium pilosella .... see MOUSE EAR
Hierba carmín............................ see POKEWEED
Hierba de la Virgen .... see DIVINER'S SAGE
Hierba de San Juan.........................see MUGWORT
Hierba Dorada.............................see BRICKELLIA
Hierba Pastel .... see ISATIS
Hierba Santa .... see YERBA SANTA
High Balm ....see OSWEGO TEA
High Bush Cranberry .... see CRAMP BARK
High Mallow .... see MALLOW
High pH Therapy .... see CESIUM
Highbush Blueberry .... see BLUEBERRY
High-bush Cranberry .... see CRAMP BARK
Highwaythorn .... see EUROPEAN BUCKTHORN
Higtaper................................... see MULLEIN
Hilberry.............................see WINTERGREEN
Hillside Blueberry............................. see BLUEBERRY
Himalayan Ginseng............see PANAX PSEUDOGINSENG
Himalayan Mayapple .... see PODOPHYLLUM
Himalayan Rhubarb .... see RHUBARB
Himsra................................... see CAPERS
Hind Heal............................. see TANSY, WOOD SAGE
Hind's Tongue .... see HARTSTONGUE
Hing Hua ....see SAFFLOWER
Hini .... see BLACK ROOT
Hint amberparisi................see TREE TURMERIC
Hip Fruit.............................see ROSE HIP
Hip Sweet................................see ROSE HIP
Hipberry ....see ROSE HIP
Hippocastani Flos........... see HORSE CHESTNUT
Hippophae rhamnoides .... see SEA BUCKTHORN
Hipposelinum levisticum .... see LOVAGE
Hirala................................see TERMINALIA

Hirshklee .... see HEMP AGRIMONY
Hissopo .... see HYSSOP
HISTIDINE .... see HISTIDINE
Hive Dross .... see PROPOLIS
Hive Vine .... see SQUAWVINE
HL-362 .... see FORSKOLIN
Ho Shou Wu .... see FO-TI
Hoarhound .... see BUGLEWEED, WHITE HOREHOUND
Hoary Plantain .... see BUCKHORN PLANTAIN
Hock-Heal .... see SELF-HEAL
Hockle Elderberry .... see LEVANT BERRY
Hoelen .... see PORIA MUSHROOM
Hog Apple .... see MORINDA, PODOPHYLLUM
Hog Bean .... see HENBANE
Hog Gum .... see TRAGACANTH
Hogberry .... see UVA URSI
Hogweed .... see CANADIAN FLEABANE, KNOTWEED,
                        MASTERWORT, SCOTCH BROOM
Hojas de la Pastora .... see DIVINER'S SAGE
Hoku-Gomishi .... see SCHISANDRA
Holcus bicolor .... see BROOM CORN
Holligold .... see CALENDULA
HOLLY .... see HOLLY, PIPSISSEWA
Holly Barberry .... see OREGON GRAPE
Holly Bay .... see MAGNOLIA
Holly Mahonia .... see OREGON GRAPE
HOLLYHOCK .... see HOLLYHOCK
Holly-Leaved Berberis .... see OREGON GRAPE
Holm .... see HOLLY
Holme Chase .... see HOLLY
Holunderbeeren .... see ELDERBERRY
HOLY BASIL .... see HOLY BASIL
Holy Herb .... see YERBA SANTA
Holy Rope .... see HEMP AGRIMONY
Holy Thistle ...... see BLESSED THISTLE, MILK THISTLE
Holy Tree .... see HOLLY, NEEM
Holy Weed .... see YERBA SANTA
Holywort .... see VERBENA
Honduras Sarsaparilla .... see SARSAPARILLA
HONEY .... see HONEY
Honey Bee Milk .... see ROYAL JELLY
Honey Bee Pollen .... see BEE POLLEN
Honey Plant .... see LEMON BALM
Honeybee Pollen .... see BEE POLLEN
Honeybee Venom .... see BEE VENOM
Honeybloom .... see CANADIAN HEMP
HONEYSUCKLE .... see HONEYSUCKLE
Hong Qu .... see RED YEAST
Hong Shen .... see GINSENG, PANAX
Hong Zao .... see JUJUBE
Honghua .... see SAFFLOWER
Honig .... see HONEY
Ho-No-Ki .... see MAGNOLIA
HOODIA .... see HOODIA
Hoodia gordonii .... see HOODIA
Hoodia P57 .... see HOODIA
Hoodwort .... see SKULLCAP
Hop Fruit .... see ROSE HIP
Hop Strobile .... see HOPS
Hopfenzapfen .... see HOPS
HOPS .... see HOPS
Hordeum distychum .... see BARLEY
Hordeum vulgare .... see BARLEY
Horehound .... see WHITE HOREHOUND
Horns of Gold .... see DEER VELVET

Hornseed .... see ERGOT
Horny Goat Weed .... see EPIMEDIUM
Horse Balm .... see STONE ROOT
Horse Blobs .... see MARSH MARIGOLD
HORSE CHESTNUT .... see HORSE CHESTNUT
Horse Daisy .... see OX-EYE DAISY
Horse Gowan .... see OX-EYE DAISY
Horse Herb .... see HORSETAIL
Horse Tongue .... see HARTSTONGUE
Horse Willow .... see HORSETAIL
Horsebane .... see HEMLOCK WATER DROPWORT,
                         WATER FENNEL
Horse-Elder .... see ELECAMPANE
Horsefly Weed .... see WILD INDIGO
Horsefoot .... see COLTSFOOT
Horseheal .... see ELECAMPANE
Horsehoof .... see COLTSFOOT
HORSEMINT .... see HORSEMINT
HORSERADISH .... see HORSERADISH
HORSETAIL .... see HORSETAIL
Horseweed .... see STONE ROOT, CANADIAN FLEABANE
Hot Basil .... see HOLY BASIL
Hot Pepper .... see CAPSICUM
Hou Po .... see MAGNOLIA
Hou Po Hua .... see MAGNOLIA
Houblon .... see HOPS
HOUND'S TONGUE .... see DEERTONGUE,
                         HOUND'S TONGUE
Houndsbane .... see WHITE HOREHOUND
Houndsberry .... see BLACK NIGHTSHADE
Houpu .... see MAGNOLIA
HOUSELEEK .... see HOUSELEEK
HP 200 .... see COWHAGE
Hsia ts'ao tung ch'ung .... see CORDYCEPS
Hsiang-Dan .... see ALOE
Hu Huang Lian .... see PICRORHIZA
Hu Lu Ba .... see FENUGREEK
HU ZHANG .... see HU ZHANG
Hua Gu .... see SHIITAKE MUSHROOM
Huacatay .... see TAGETES
Huang Bai .... see PHELLODENDRON
Huang Ken .... see DANSHEN
Huang Lian .... see GOLDTHREAD
Huang Qi .... see ASTRAGALUS
Huang Qin .... see BAIKAL SKULLCAP
Huang-T'eng Ken .... see THUNDER GOD VINE
Huantli .... see AMARANTH
Huanuco Coca .... see COCA
Huckleberry .... see BILBERRY
Huile de Bourrache .... see BORAGE
Huile d'Onagre .... see EVENING PRIMROSE OIL
Huisache .... see CASSIE ABSOLUTE
Hulm .... see HOLLY
Hulver Bush .... see HOLLY
Hulver Tree .... see HOLLY
Human Dialyzable Leukocyte Extract ....
.... see TRANSFER FACTOR
Human Lactoferrin .... see LACTOFERRIN
Human Transfer Factor .... see TRANSFER FACTOR
Humate .... see HUMIC ACID
HUMIC ACID .... see HUMIC ACID
Humic Shale .... see COLLOIDAL MINERALS
Hummingbird Tree .... see TURTLE HEAD
Humulus Lupulus .... see HOPS
Hungarian Chamomile .... see GERMAN CHAMOMILE

Medical professionals should consult the Professional Version at www.NaturalDatabase.com.

Hungarian Pepper	see CAPSICUM
Hungarian Silver Linden	see LINDEN
Huntsman's Cup	see PITCHER PLANT
Huo Xiang	see PATCHOULY OIL
HupA	see HUPERZINE A
Huperazon	see CHINESE CLUB MOSS
Huperzia serrata	see CHINESE CLUB MOSS
HUPERZINE A	see HUPERZINE A
Hurtleberry	see BILBERRY
Hurtsickle	see CORNFLOWER
Husked Nut	see EUROPEAN CHESTNUT
Hwanggi	see ASTRAGALUS
Hwanggum	see BAIKAL SKULLCAP
Hyaluran	see HYALURONIC ACID
Hyaluronan	see HYALURONIC ACID
Hyaluronate	see HYALURONIC ACID
HYALURONIC ACID	see HYALURONIC ACID
Hydnocarp	see CHAULMOOGRA
Hydnocarpus anthelminthicus	see CHAULMOOGRA
Hydnocarpus kurzii	see CHAULMOOGRA
HYDRANGEA	see HYDRANGEA
Hydrastis canadensis	see GOLDENSEAL
Hydrated Aluminum Silicate	see KAOLIN
HYDRAZINE SULFATE	see HYDRAZINE SULFATE
Hydrocotyle	see GOTU KOLA
Hydrocotyle asiatica	see GOTU KOLA
Hydrogen Fluoride	see FLUORIDE
Hydrolyzed Casein	see CASEIN PEPTIDES
Hydrolyzed Collagen Protein	see GELATIN
Hydrolyzed Gelatin	see GELATIN
Hydrolyzed Liver Extract	see LIVER EXTRACT
Hydrolyzed Soy Protein	see SOY
Hydrolyzed Spleen Extract	see SPLEEN EXTRACT
Hydroxocobalamin	see VITAMIN B12
Hydroxocobalaminum	see VITAMIN B12
Hydroxocobemine	see VITAMIN B12
Hydroxyacetic Acid	see ALPHA HYDROXY ACIDS
Hydroxyapatite	see CALCIUM
Hydroxycaprylic Acid	see ALPHA HYDROXY ACIDS
Hydroxycitrate	see GARCINIA
Hydroxycitric Acid	see GARCINIA
Hydroxydecyl Benzoquinone	see IDEBENONE
Hydroxyecdysterone	see ECDYSTERONE
HYDROXYMETHYLBUTYRATE (HMB)	see HYDROXYMETHYLBUTYRATE (HMB)
Hydroxypropionic Acid	see ALPHA HYDROXY ACIDS
Hydroxysuccinic Acid	see ALPHA HYDROXY ACIDS
Hyoscyami Folium	see HENBANE
Hyoscyamus niger	see HENBANE
Hypereikon	see ST. JOHN'S WORT
Hyperici Herba	see ST. JOHN'S WORT
Hypericum perforatum	see ST. JOHN'S WORT
Hyperimmune Bovine Colostrum	see COLOSTRUM
HYPERIMMUNE EGG	see HYPERIMMUNE EGG
Hyperimmunized Egg Yolk	see HYPERIMMUNE EGG
Hypotensive Peptides	see CASEIN PEPTIDES
Hypoxanthine Riboside	see INOSINE
Hypoxanthosine	see INOSINE
Hypoxis hemerocallidea	see AFRICAN WILD POTATO
Hypoxis Plant	see AFRICAN WILD POTATO
Hypoxis rooperi	see AFRICAN WILD POTATO
Hysope officinale	see HYSSOP
HYSSOP	see HYSSOP
Hyssopus officinalis	see HYSSOP
Iandirova	see ANDIROBA
Iberis amara	see CLOWN'S MUSTARD PLANT
Iberis coronaria	see CLOWN'S MUSTARD PLANT
IBOGA	see IBOGA
Ice Vine	see PAREIRA
Iceland Lichen	see ICELAND MOSS
ICELAND MOSS	see ICELAND MOSS
Ichthyomethia piscipula	see JAMAICAN DOGWOOD
Ici Fructus	see CAPSICUM
Iconyl	see GLYCINE
IDEBENONE	see IDEBENONE
Idrocotyle	see GOTU KOLA
Idrossocobalamina	see VITAMIN B12
Igelkopfwurzel	see ECHINACEA
IGNATIUS BEAN	see IGNATIUS BEAN
IgY	see HYPERIMMUNE EGG
Ilex	see MATE
Ilex aquifolium	see HOLLY
Ilex opaca	see HOLLY
Ilex paraguariensis	see MATE
Ilex vomitoria	see HOLLY
Illicium verum	see STAR ANISE
Imber	see GINGER
Imlee	see TAMARIND
Immortality Herb	see JIAOGULAN
IMMORTELLE	see IMMORTELLE
Immune Egg	see HYPERIMMUNE EGG
Immunoglobulin Egg Extract	see HYPERIMMUNE EGG
Immunoglobulin IgY	see HYPERIMMUNE EGG
Impatiens	see JEWELWEED
In Chen	see YIN CHEN
Inca Tea	see COCA
Inchinko	see YIN CHEN
Inchin-ko-to	see YIN CHEN
Indhana	see WORMWOOD
India Root	see ALPINIA
Indian Almond	see TERMINALIA
Indian Apple	see PODOPHYLLUM
Indian Arrowroot	see WAHOO, ZEDOARY
Indian Arrowwood	see WAHOO
Indian Bael	see BAEL
Indian Balm	see BETH ROOT
Indian Balsam	see PERU BALSAM
Indian Bark	see MAGNOLIA
Indian Basil	see HOLY BASIL
Indian Bdellium-tree	see GUGGUL
Indian Bead	see PRECATORY BEAN
Indian Belladonna	see BELLADONNA
Indian Berry	see LEVANT BERRY
Indian Blackberry	see JAMBOLAN
Indian Bolonong	see CHIRATA
Indian Bread	see PORIA MUSHROOM
Indian Chocolate	see WATER AVENS
Indian Cluster Bean	see GUAR GUM
Indian Corn	see CORN SILK
Indian Cress	see NASTURTIUM, WATERCRESS
Indian Dye	see GOLDENSEAL
Indian Echinacea	see ANDROGRAPHIS
Indian Elm	see SLIPPERY ELM
INDIAN FRANKINCENSE	see INDIAN FRANKINCENSE
Indian Gentian	see CHIRATA
Indian Ginseng	see ASHWAGANDHA
INDIAN GOOSEBERRY	see INDIAN GOOSEBERRY
Indian Guar Plant	see GUAR GUM
Indian Gum	see CUP PLANT

 (209) 472-2244

Indian Head................................see ECHINACEA
Indian Hippo ....see INDIAN PHYSIC
Indian Jointfir..................................see EPHEDRA
Indian Lilac ....see NEEM
INDIAN LONG PEPPER........see INDIAN LONG PEPPER
Indian Lycium ....see TREE TURMERIC
Indian Mulberry ....see BA JI TIAN, MORINDA
Indian Neem ....see NEEM
Indian Olibanum ....see INDIAN FRANKINCENSE
Indian Parsley...................................see OSHA
Indian Pennywort ....see GOTU KOLA
INDIAN PHYSIC ....
.........................see CANADIAN HEMP, INDIAN PHYSIC
Indian Pink ....see PINK ROOT
Indian Plant ....see BLOODROOT, GOLDENSEAL
Indian Plantago ....see BLOND PSYLLIUM
Indian Podophyllum.....................see PODOPHYLLUM
Indian Poke ....see AMERICAN HELLEBORE
Indian Red Paint..........................see BLOODROOT
Indian Rhubarb............................ see RHUBARB
Indian Root.....................see AMERICAN SPIKENARD
Indian Saffron ....see SAFFRON, TURMERIC
Indian Sage...............................see BONESET
Indian Senna .... see SENNA
Indian Shamrock .... see BETH ROOT
INDIAN SNAKEROOT............. see INDIAN SNAKEROOT
Indian Squill .... see SQUILL
Indian Tobacco .... see LOBELIA
Indian Tragacanth.....................see KARAYA GUM
Indian Tumeric ....see GOLDENSEAL
Indian Valerian ....see VALERIAN
Indian Walnut.......................... see TUNG SEED
Indian Water Navelwort ....see GOTU KOLA
Indian-fig Prickly Pear Cactus ....
.............................see PRICKLY PEAR CACTUS
Indian-hemp .... see CANADIAN HEMP
Indian-laurel ....see LAURELWOOD
Indigo .... see ISATIS
Indigo Broom ....see WILD INDIGO
Indigo Woad .... see ISATIS
Indischer Wassernabel.....................see GOTU KOLA
INDOLE-3-CARBINOL........... see INDOLE-3-CARBINOL
Indole-3-methanol..................... see INDOLE-3-CARBINOL
Inkberry .... see POKEWEED
Inorganic Germanium ....see GERMANIUM
Inose .... see INOSITOL
INOSINE.............................. see INOSINE
Inosite................................. see INOSITOL
INOSITOL............................ see INOSITOL
Inositol Hexaniacinate ....see INOSITOL NICOTINATE
Inositol Hexanicotinate ....see INOSITOL NICOTINATE
Inositol Hexaphosphate.............................see IP-6
Inositol Monophosphate............................. see INOSITOL
Inositol Niacinate ....see INOSITOL NICOTINATE
INOSITOL NICOTINATE......see INOSITOL NICOTINATE
Insam ....see GINSENG, PANAX
Intoxicating Long Pepper...........................see KAVA
Intoxicating Pepper ....see KAVA
Intrachol ....see CHOLINE
Intralipid.............................. see SOYBEAN OIL
Inula ....see ELECAMPANE
Inula helenium ....see ELECAMPANE
INULIN...............................see INULIN
Inulin Hydrolysate ....
.... see FRUCTO-OLIGOSACCHARIDES

IODINE................................see IODINE
IP-6....................................see IP-6
Ipe Roxo.........................see PAU D'ARCO
IPECAC ....see IPECAC
Ipecacuanha............................ see IPECAC
Ipomoea....................see MEXICAN SCAMMONY ROOT
Ipomoea purga ....see JALAP
Iporoni .... see IPORURU
Iporuro .... see IPORURU
IPORURU .... see IPORURU
IPRIFLAVONE ....see IPRIFLAVONE
Ipurosa................................ see IPORURU
Ipururo............................... see IPORURU
Iris ....see BLUE FLAG, ORRIS
Iris caroliniana ....see BLUE FLAG
Iris florentina ....see ORRIS
Iris germanica.............................see ORRIS
Iris junonia ....see ORRIS
Iris pallida ....see ORRIS
Iris versicolor ....see BLUE FLAG
Iris virginica ....see BLUE FLAG
Irish Broom Tops .... see SCOTCH BROOM
Irish Moss Extract.................. see CARRAGEENAN
Irish Potato ....see POTATO
IRON ....see IRON
Iron EDTA................................ see EDTA
ISATIS................................ see ISATIS
Isatis indigotica .... see ISATIS
Isatis tinctoria.......................... see ISATIS
Iscador...................... see EUROPEAN MISTLETOE
Ishin .... see ACKEE
Iso-ascorbic Acid ....see VITAMIN C (ASCORBIC ACID)
Isodon rubescens...................see RABDOSIA RUBESCENS
Isoflavone ....see KUDZU, LICORICE,
RED CLOVER, SOY
Isoflavone Combined Polysaccharide ....
...........see GENISTEIN COMBINED POLYSACCHARIDE
Isoinokosterone ....see ECDYSTERONE
Isoleucine ....see BRANCHED-CHAIN AMINO ACIDS
Isorel .... see EUROPEAN MISTLETOE
Ispaghula ....see BLOND PSYLLIUM
Ispagol ....see BLOND PSYLLIUM
Itadori ....see HU ZHANG
Italian Fitch ....see GOAT'S RUE
Italian Jasmine ....see JASMINE
Italian Limetta.............................see LIME
Itchweed ....see AMERICAN HELLEBORE
Ivy ....see AMERICAN IVY, ENGLISH IVY
IVY GOURD ....see IVY GOURD
Ivy-Leafed Cyclamen...................see CYCLAMEN
Jaatipatree .... see NUTMEG AND MACE
JABORANDI ....see JABORANDI
Jaborandi Pepper.....................see INDIAN LONG PEPPER
Jack-Jump-About ....see GOUTWEED
Jack-of-the-Buttery ....see COMMON STONECROP
JACOB'S LADDER .... see JACOB'S LADDER,
LILY-OF-THE-VALLEY
Jacob's Staff...................................... see MULLEIN
Jacob's Sword ....see ORRIS
Jaffa Orange .... see SWEET ORANGE
Jaguar Gum ....see GUAR GUM
Jalanimba .... see BRAHMI
JALAP......................... see JALAP, POKEWEED
Jalapa..............................see JALAP
Jalape...............................see JALAP

Jalnaveri .... see BRAHMI
Jamaica Ginger............................... see GINGER
Jamaica Mignonette ....see HENNA
Jamaica Pepper................................ see ALLSPICE
Jamaica Sorrel .... see HIBISCUS
JAMAICAN DOGWOOD ...... see JAMAICAN DOGWOOD
Jamaican Quassia .... see QUASSIA
Jamaican Sarsaparilla........................ see SARSAPARILLA
Jaman .... see JAMBOLAN
JAMBOLAN .... see JAMBOLAN
Jambolan Plum................................. see JAMBOLAN
Jambolao .... see JAMBOLAN
Jambu .... see JAMBOLAN
Jambul .... see JAMBOLAN
Jamelonguier .... see JAMBOLAN
James' Tea .... see MARSH TEA
Jamestown Weed..............................see JIMSON WEED
Jamguarandi .... see JABORANDI
Jamum .... see JAMBOLAN
Japanese Angelica .... see ANGELICA
JAPANESE APRICOT ....see JAPANESE APRICOT
Japanese Arrowroot........................... see KUDZU
Japanese Ashitaba ....see ASHITABA
Japanese Bamboo.............................see HU ZHANG
Japanese Belladonna ....see SCOPOLIA
Japanese Catnip............................... see SCHIZONEPETA
Japanese Epimedium..........................see EPIMEDIUM
Japanese Flowering Apricot ....see JAPANESE APRICOT
Japanese Ginseng ....see GINSENG, PANAX
Japanese Honeysuckle .... see HONEYSUCKLE
Japanese Isinglas .... see AGAR
Japanese knotweed ....see HU ZHANG
Japanese Lantern.............................. see WINTER CHERRY
JAPANESE MINT ....
.... see JAPANESE MINT, SCHIZONEPETA
Japanese Pagoda Tree .... see PAGODA TREE
JAPANESE PERSIMMON.......................
........................see JAPANESE PERSIMMON
Japanese Silver Apricot.....................see GINKGO
Japanese Tea................................... see GREEN TEA
Japanese Whitebark Magnolia ....see MAGNOLIA
Jarilla... see CHAPARRAL
JASMINE.. see JASMINE
Jasminum grandiflorum .... see JASMINE
Jasminum officinale .... see JASMINE
Jateorhiza columba........................... see COLOMBO
Jateorhiza miersii .... see COLOMBO
Jateorhiza palmata .... see COLOMBO
Jati .... see JASMINE
Jatikosha .... see NUTMEG AND MACE
Jatipatra .... see NUTMEG AND MACE
Jatipatri .... see NUTMEG AND MACE
Jatiphala .... see NUTMEG AND MACE
Jatiphalam .... see NUTMEG AND MACE
Jatropha moluccana...................... see TUNG SEED
Jaundice Berry .... see EUROPEAN BARBERRY
Jaundice Root................................ see GOLDENSEAL
Java..see COFFEE
Java citronella .... see CITRONELLA OIL
Java Coca .... see COCA
Java Dropwort .... see WATER DROPWORT
Java Pepper ....see CUBEBS
Java Plum .... see JAMBOLAN
JAVA TEA ....see JAVA TEA
Java Turmeric ....see JAVANESE TURMERIC

JAVANESE TURMERIC .... see JAVANESE TURMERIC
Jeeraka................................... see CUMIN
Jen-shen................................see GINSENG, PANAX
Jequirity Bean ....see PRECATORY BEAN
Jequirity Seed......................see PRECATORY BEAN
Jersey Tea............................. see NEW JERSEY TEA
Jesuit Tea........................... see CHENOPODIUM OIL
Jesuit's Balsam..................see COPAIBA BALSAM
Jesuit's Bark .... see CINCHONA
Jesuit's Tea ....see MATE
Jethi-madh............................ see LICORICE
Jewel Balsam Weed................ see JEWELWEED
JEWELWEED .... see JEWELWEED
Jew's Harp Plant .... see BETH ROOT
Jew's Myrtle.....................see BUTCHER'S BROOM
Jia Renshen .... see PANAX PSEUDOGINSENG
Jia Yang .... see POPLAR
Jiang .... see GINGER
Jiao Gu Lan .... see JIAOGULAN
JIAOGULAN .... see JIAOGULAN
JIMSON WEED.......................see JIMSON WEED
Jin Yin Hua ....see HONEYSUCKLE
Jing Jie .... see SCHIZONEPETA
Jinsao................................see GINSENG, PANAX
Jintsam ....see GINSENG, PANAX
Jinyingzi ....see CHEROKEE ROSEHIP
Jinyinhua ....see HONEYSUCKLE
Jiro.................................see JAPANESE PERSIMMON
Joe Pye .... see GRAVEL ROOT
Johimbi............................... see YOHIMBE
Johnny-jump-up.....................see HEART'S EASE
Joint .... see MARIJUANA
Joint Fir .... see EPHEDRA
Jointed Flat Sedge .... see ADRUE
Joint-podded Charlock .... see WILD RADISH
JOJOBA .... see JOJOBA
Joshua Tree ....see YUCCA
Joteishi ....see GLOSSY PRIVET
Ju Hua ....see CHRYSANTHEMUM
Juarandi .... see JABORANDI
Jufa .... see HYSSOP
Juglandis ....see ENGLISH WALNUT
Juglandis Folium ....see ENGLISH WALNUT
Juglans ....see ENGLISH WALNUT
Juglans cinerea ....see BUTTERNUT
Juglans nigra .... see BLACK WALNUT
Juglans regia ....see ENGLISH WALNUT
JUJUBE.................................. see JUJUBE
Jujubi .... see JUJUBE
Jumbul ....see JAMBOLAN
Jungle Weed ....see OPIUM ANTIDOTE
Junihitoe .... see AJUGA NIPPONENSIS
JUNIPER............................... see JUNIPER
Juniper Tar........................see CADE OIL
Juniperi Fructus .... see JUNIPER
Juniperus communis................... see JUNIPER
Juniperus oxycedrus.................see CADE OIL
Juniperus sabina .... see SAVIN TOPS
Juniperus virginiana .... see EASTERN RED CEDAR
Juno's Tears ....see VERBENA
Jupiter's Bean............................ see HENBANE
Jupiter's Beard ....see HOUSELEEK,
RED-SPUR VALERIAN
Jupiter's Eye.........................see HOUSELEEK
Jupiter's Nut .... see EUROPEAN CHESTNUT

Justicia adhatoda	see MALABAR NUT
Justicia paniculata	see ANDROGRAPHIS
Jutsu	see ATRACTYLODES
Ju-zhong	see SAW PALMETTO
Kaa Jhee	see STEVIA
Kadaya	see KARAYA GUM
Kadeol	see CADE OIL
Kadira	see KARAYA GUM
Kadsura chinensis	see SCHISANDRA
Kaffree Tea	see RED BUSH TEA
Kairata	see CHIRATA
Kajuputi leucadendra	see CAJEPUT OIL
Kakamachi	see BLACK NIGHTSHADE
Kaki	see JAPANESE PERSIMMON
Kaki Persimmon	see JAPANESE PERSIMMON
Kakkon	see KUDZU
Kalahari Cactus	see HOODIA
Kalahari Diet	see HOODIA
Kalajaji	see BLACK SEED
Kalajira	see BLACK SEED
Kalamegha	see ANDROGRAPHIS
Kale	see CABBAGE
Kalidruma	see TERMINALIA
Kalmia latifolia	see MOUNTAIN LAUREL
Kalmus	see CALAMUS
Kalonji	see BLACK SEED
Kalpa Herbal Tea	see CASSIA AURICULATA
KAMALA	see KAMALA
Kamani Punna	see LAURELWOOD
Kamcela	see KAMALA
Kamillen	see GERMAN CHAMOMILE
Kana	see INDIAN LONG PEPPER
Kanaje Hindi	see ASHWAGANDHA
Kankusta	see GARCINIA
Kankyo	see GINGER
Kansas Snakeroot	see ECHINACEA
Kanshokyo	see GINGER
Kanten Diet	see AGAR
Kanten Jelly	see AGAR
Kanya	see ALOE
Kao	see KAVA
KAOLIN	see KAOLIN
Kapikachchhu	see COWHAGE
Karavella	see BITTER MELON
KARAYA GUM	see KARAYA GUM
Kardone	see ARTICHOKE
Karela	see BITTER MELON
Kargasok Tea	see KOMBUCHA TEA
Kariyat	see ANDROGRAPHIS
Karkade	see HIBISCUS
Karpasa	see COTTON, GOSSYPOL
Karpoora	see CAMPHOR
Karshaphala	see TERMINALIA
Karwiya	see CARAWAY
Kasani	see CHICORY
Kastanienblaetter	see EUROPEAN CHESTNUT
Kasturidana	see AMBRETTE
Kasturilatika	see AMBRETTE
Kat	see KHAT
Kathala Hibutu Tea	see SALACIA
Kathilla	see BITTER MELON
Katila	see KARAYA GUM
Katki	see PICRORHIZA
Katsenpfotchenbluten	see CAT'S FOOT
Katuka	see PICRORHIZA
Katuko	see PICRORHIZA
Katurohini	see PICRORHIZA
Katuvira	see CAPSICUM
Katvi	see PICRORHIZA
Katzenkrat	see YARROW
Katzenpfotchenbluten	see SANDY EVERLASTING
Kaunch	see COWHAGE
KAVA	see KAVA
Kavain	see KAVA
Kavapipar	see KAVA
Kavika Ni India	see JAMBOLAN
Kawa Kawa	see KAVA
Kawa Pepper	see KAVA
Kawanch	see COWHAGE
Kawapfeffer	see KAVA
Kawaratake	see CORIOLUS MUSHROOM
Kawara-yomogi	see YIN CHEN
KEFIR	see KEFIR
Kefir Cheese	see KEFIR
Kefir Grains	see KEFIR
Kefir Yogurt	see KEFIR
Keiri	see WALLFLOWER
Keishi	see CASSIA CINNAMON
Kelp	see BLADDERWRACK, LAMINARIA
Kelp-ware	see BLADDERWRACK
Kemangen	see HOLY BASIL
Kenso	see ASHITABA
Kerala	see BITTER MELON
Kermesbeere	see POKEWEED
Kew	see KAVA
Kew Tree	see GINKGO
Key Flower	see COWSLIP
Key Lime	see LIME
Key of Heaven	see COWSLIP
KH-3	see PROCAINE
Khadira	see CATECHU
Khair	see CATECHU
Khareti	see COUNTRY MALLOW
Kharjura	see DATE PALM
Khartoum Senna	see SENNA
Khas-khas	see VETIVER
KHAT	see KHAT
KHELLA	see KHELLA
Khellin	see KHELLA
Kher	see ACACIA
Khurasani-ajavayan	see HENBANE
Khus Khus	see VETIVER
Kidney Bean	see BEAN POD
Kidney Root	see GRAVEL ROOT
Kidney Wort	see LIVERWORT
Kif	see MARIJUANA
Kijitsu	see BITTER ORANGE
Kiln-Dried Allspice	see ALLSPICE
Kinerase	see KINETIN
Kinetase	see KINETIN
KINETIN	see KINETIN
King of Bitters	see ANDROGRAPHIS
King of Mushrooms	see MAITAKE MUSHROOM
Kingcups	see MARSH MARIGOLD
Kings And Queens	see ARUM
King's Clover	see SWEET CLOVER
King's Crown	see ROSEROOT
King's Cup	see BULBOUS BUTTERCUP
King's Cure	see PIPSISSEWA
King's Cureall	see EVENING PRIMROSE OIL, PIPSISSEWA

Kinnikinnik .... see UVA URSI
Kirata .... see CHIRATA
Kirta .... see ANDROGRAPHIS
Kita-gomishi .... see SCHISANDRA
Kiwach .... see COWHAGE
KIWI .... see KIWI
Klamath Blue/Green Algae .... see BLUE-GREEN ALGAE
Klamath Weed .... see ST. JOHN'S WORT
Klapperschlangen .... see SENEGA
Kleine Kamille .... see GERMAN CHAMOMILE
Knackweide .... see WILLOW BARK
Knautia arvensis .... see FIELD SCABIOUS
Knee Holly .... see BUTCHER'S BROOM
Kneeholm .... see BUTCHER'S BROOM
Knight's Spur .... see DELPHINIUM
Knitback .... see COMFREY
Knitbone .... see COMFREY
Knob Grass .... see STONE ROOT
Knob Root .... see STONE ROOT
Knobweed .... see STONE ROOT
Knotgrass .... see KNOTWEED
Knotted Marjoram .... see MARJORAM
Knotted Wrack .... see BLADDERWRACK
Knotty Brake .... see MALE FERN
KNOTWEED .... see KNOTWEED
Kojo-kon .... see RESVERATROL
Kola Nut .... see COLA NUT
Koloquinthen .... see COLOCYNTH
Kombe .... see STROPHANTHUS
Kombe-strophanthus Seeds .... see STROPHANTHUS
Kombu .... see LAMINARIA
Kombucha Mushroom Tea .... see KOMBUCHA TEA
KOMBUCHA TEA .... see KOMBUCHA TEA
Konjac .... see GLUCOMANNAN
Konjac Mannan .... see GLUCOMANNAN
Kooso .... see KOUSSO
Korean Ginseng .... see GINSENG, PANAX
Korean Panax Ginseng .... see GINSENG, PANAX
Korean Persimmon .... see JAPANESE PERSIMMON
Korean Red Ginseng .... see GINSENG, PANAX
Koriander .... see CORIANDER
Kosho .... see BLACK PEPPER AND WHITE PEPPER
Kosso .... see KOUSSO
KOUSSO .... see KOUSSO
Kovai .... see IVY GOURD
Kraftwurz .... see ARNICA
Krameria .... see RHATANY
Kranbeere .... see CRANBERRY
Krestin .... see CORIOLUS MUSHROOM
Kreteks .... see CLOVE
Kreuzdornbeeren .... see EUROPEAN BUCKTHORN
Krishan Jeeraka .... see CARAWAY
Krishna .... see BLACK PEPPER AND WHITE PEPPER
Krishna Tulsi .... see HOLY BASIL
Krishnajiraka .... see CARAWAY
Kua .... see ZEDOARY
Kuandong Hua .... see COLTSFOOT
KUDZU .... see KUDZU
Kuguazi .... see BITTER MELON
K'u-Kua .... see BITTER MELON
Kukui .... see TUNG SEED
Kullo .... see KARAYA GUM
Kumari .... see ALOE
Kumkuma .... see SAFFRON
Kummel .... see CARAWAY

Kummich .... see CARAWAY
Kunigundendraut .... see HEMP AGRIMONY
Kuntze Saloop .... see SASSAFRAS
Kuru .... see PICRORHIZA
Kus es Salahin .... see KHAT
Kushtha .... see COSTUS
Kustumburi .... see CORIANDER
Kuth .... see COSTUS
Kuthmithi .... see ASHWAGANDHA
Kutki .... see PICRORHIZA
Kwaao Khruea .... see KUDZU
Kwandong Hwa .... see COLTSFOOT
Kwassan .... see KOMBUCHA TEA
Kyunchinho .... see YIN CHEN
L. acidophilus .... see LACTOBACILLUS
L. amylovorus .... see LACTOBACILLUS
L. brevis .... see LACTOBACILLUS
L. bulgaricus .... see LACTOBACILLUS
L. casei .... see LACTOBACILLUS
L. crispatus .... see LACTOBACILLUS
L. delbrueckii .... see LACTOBACILLUS
L. fermentum .... see LACTOBACILLUS
L. gallinarum .... see LACTOBACILLUS
L. johnsonii .... see LACTOBACILLUS
L. johnsonii LC-1 .... see LACTOBACILLUS
L. plantarum .... see LACTOBACILLUS
L. reuteri .... see LACTOBACILLUS
L. salivarius .... see LACTOBACILLUS
L. sporogenes .... see LACTOBACILLUS
La Hembra .... see DIVINER'S SAGE
LABDANUM .... see LABDANUM
LABRADOR TEA .... see LABRADOR TEA
LABURNUM .... see LABURNUM
Laburnum anagyroides .... see LABURNUM
Lac .... see SHELLAC
Lacca .... see SHELLAC
Laccifer lacca .... see SHELLAC
L-acetylcarnitine .... see ACETYL-L-CARNITINE
Laciniaria spicata .... see MARSH BLAZING STAR
LACTASE .... see LACTASE
Lactic Acid .... see ALPHA HYDROXY ACIDS
Lactobacilli .... see LACTOBACILLUS
LACTOBACILLUS .... see LACTOBACILLUS
Lactobacillus acidophilus .... see LACTOBACILLUS
Lactobacillus amylovorus .... see LACTOBACILLUS
Lactobacillus brevis .... see LACTOBACILLUS
Lactobacillus bulgaricus .... see LACTOBACILLUS
Lactobacillus casei .... see LACTOBACILLUS
Lactobacillus crispatus .... see LACTOBACILLUS
Lactobacillus delbrueckii .... see LACTOBACILLUS
Lactobacillus fermentum .... see LACTOBACILLUS
Lactobacillus gallinarum .... see LACTOBACILLUS
Lactobacillus GG .... see LACTOBACILLUS
Lactobacillus johnsonii .... see LACTOBACILLUS
Lactobacillus paracasei .... see LACTOBACILLUS
Lactobacillus plantarum .... see LACTOBACILLUS
Lactobacillus reuteri .... see LACTOBACILLUS
Lactobacillus rhamnosus .... see LACTOBACILLUS
Lactobacillus salivarius .... see LACTOBACILLUS
Lactobacillus sporogenes .... see LACTOBACILLUS
LACTOFERRIN .... see LACTOFERRIN
Lactoflavin .... see RIBOFLAVIN (VITAMIN B2)
Lactuca virosa .... see WILD LETTUCE
Lactucarium .... see WILD LETTUCE
Ladder-to-heaven .... see LILY-OF-THE-VALLEY

Ladies' Delight	see HEART'S EASE
Ladies' Seal	see BRYONIA
Lady Bleeding	see AMARANTH
LADY FERN	see LADY FERN
Lady of the Meadow	see MEADOWSWEET
LADY'S BEDSTRAW	see LADY'S BEDSTRAW
Lady's Mantle	see ALCHEMILLA
Lady's Nightcap	see GREATER BINDWEED
Lady's Purse	see SHEPHERD'S PURSE
Lady's Seals	see SOLOMON'S SEAL
Lady's Slipper	see NERVE ROOT
Lady's Thimble	see DIGITALIS
Lady's Thistle	see MILK THISTLE
Ladysmock	see ARUM
Lady's-seal	see BLACK BRYONY
Laetrile	see APRICOT
Lagerstroemia flos-reginae	see BANABA
Lagerstroemia speciosa	see BANABA
Lai Margose	see BITTER MELON
Lakritze	see LICORICE
L-alpha-glycerylphosphorylcholine	see ALPHA-GPC
Lamb Mint	see PEPPERMINT, SPEARMINT
Lambkill	see MOUNTAIN LAUREL
Lamb's Quarters	see BETH ROOT
Lamb's Tongue	see AMERICAN ADDER'S TONGUE
Lamii Albi Flos	see WHITE DEAD NETTLE FLOWER
LAMINARIA	see LAMINARIA
Laminaria digitata	see ALGIN, LAMINARIA
Laminaria japonica	see LAMINARIA
Lamium album	see WHITE DEAD NETTLE FLOWER
Lamp Black	see ACTIVATED CHARCOAL
Land Whin	see SPINY RESTHARROW
Langer Pfeffer	see INDIAN LONG PEPPER
Languas officinarum	see ALPINIA
Langwort	see BUTTERBUR, WHITE HELLEBORE
Lan-hiqui	see SANGRE DE GRADO
Laniqui	see SANGRE DE GRADO
Lapacho Colorado	see PAU D'ARCO
Lapacho Morado	see PAU D'ARCO
Lappa	see BURDOCK
Lapsent	see WORMWOOD
Laranjeira-do-mato	see CHA DE BUGRE
Larch	see LARCH ARABINOGALACTAN
LARCH ARABINOGALACTAN	
	see LARCH ARABINOGALACTAN
Larch Gum	see LARCH ARABINOGALACTAN
LARCH TURPENTINE	see LARCH TURPENTINE
Large Cranberry	see CRANBERRY
Large Fennel	see FENNEL
Large Indian Civet	see CIVET
Large-Leaved Germander	see WOOD SAGE
L-ARGININE	see L-ARGININE
Larix	see LARCH ARABINOGALACTAN
Larix dahurica	see LARCH ARABINOGALACTAN
Larix decidua	see LARCH TURPENTINE
Larix europaea	see LARCH TURPENTINE
Larix gmelinii	see LARCH ARABINOGALACTAN
Larix occidentalis	see LARCH ARABINOGALACTAN
Lark Heel	see DELPHINIUM
Lark's Claw	see DELPHINIUM
Lark's Toe	see DELPHINIUM
Larkspur	see DELPHINIUM
Larkspur Lion's Mouth	see YELLOW TOADFLAX
Larrea divaricata	see CHAPARRAL
Larrea mexicana	see CHAPARRAL

Larrea tridentata	see CHAPARRAL
Larreastat	see CHAPARRAL
L-ascorbic acid	see VITAMIN C (ASCORBIC ACID), ASPARTATES
Lasuna	see GARLIC
Latakasthuri	see AMBRETTE
Latakasturi	see AMBRETTE
Lathakasthuri	see AMBRETTE
LATHYRUS	see LATHYRUS
Laurel	see MOUNTAIN LAUREL, SWEET BAY
Laurel Camphor	see CAMPHOR
Laurel Willow	see WILLOW BARK
LAURELWOOD	see LAURELWOOD
LAURIC ACID	see LAURIC ACID
Lauric Acid Monoglyceride	see MONOLAURIN
Lauricidin	see MONOLAURIN
Laurocerasus Leaves	see CHERRY LAUREL WATER
Laurocerasus officinalis	see CHERRY LAUREL WATER
Laurocerasus ottinii	see CHERRY LAUREL WATER
Laurocerasus vulgaris	see CHERRY LAUREL WATER
Laurus albida	see SASSAFRAS
Laurus camphora	see CAMPHOR
Laurus cinnamomum	see CINNAMON bark
Laurus nobilis	see SWEET BAY
Laurus persea	see AVOCADO
Laurus winteriana	see CANELLA
Lavandula angustifolia	see LAVENDER
Lavandula dentata	see LAVENDER
Lavandula latifolia	see LAVENDER
Lavandula officinalis	see LAVENDER
Lavandula pubescens	see LAVENDER
Lavandula spica	see LAVENDER
Lavandula stoechas	see LAVENDER
Lavandula vera	see LAVENDER
Lavanga	see CLOVE
LAVENDER	see LAVENDER
LAVENDER COTTON	see LAVENDER COTTON
Lavose	see LOVAGE
Lawsonia alba	see HENNA
Lawsonia inermis	see HENNA
Layor Carang	see AGAR
L-CARNITINE	see L-CARNITINE
L-carnitine Propionyl	see PROPIONYL-L-CARNITINE
L-carnosine	see CARNOSINE
L-cysteine	see N-ACETYL CYSTEINE
Leaves of the Virgin Shepherdess	see DIVINER'S SAGE
Leaves of Tomorrow	see ASHITABA
Leberbluemchenkraut	see LIVERWORT
Leberkraut	see HEMP AGRIMONY
Leche de Higueron	see FICIN
Leche de Oje	see FICIN
LECI-PS	see PHOSPHATIDYLSERINE
LECITHIN	see LECITHIN
Lecithin Phosphatidylserine	
	see PHOSPHATIDYLSERINE
Ledi Palustris Herba	see MARSH TEA
Ledum groenlandicum	see LABRADOR TEA
Ledum latifolium	see LABRADOR TEA
Ledum palustre	see MARSH TEA
Legalon	see MILK THISTLE
Legume	see BEAN POD, CALABAR BEAN, LABURNUM, PRECATORY BEAN, SOY, SOYBEAN OIL, TONKA BEAN
Lei Gong Teng	see THUNDER GOD VINE
Lei-Kung T'eng	see THUNDER GOD VINE

Medical professionals should consult the Professional Version at www.NaturalDatabase.com.

Leimmistel .... see EUROPEAN MISTLETOE
Leinsamen .... see FLAXSEED
Lemna Minor ....see DUCKWEED
LEMON .... see LEMON
LEMON BALM ....see LEMON BALM
LEMON EUCALYPTUS.........see LEMON EUCALYPTUS
Lemon Scented Gum.................see LEMON EUCALYPTUS
LEMON VERBENA ....see LEMON VERBENA
Lemon Walnut ....see BUTTERNUT
LEMONGRASS .... see LEMONGRASS
Lemon-Scented Verbena ....see LEMON VERBENA
Lent Lily...see DAFFODIL
Lenticus edodes... see LENTINAN,
                                        SHIITAKE MUSHROOM
LENTINAN .... see BETA GLUCANS, LENTINAN
Lentinan edodes .... see LENTINAN,
                                        SHIITAKE MUSHROOM
Lentinula .... see SHIITAKE MUSHROOM
Lentinula edodes .... see LENTINAN,
                                        SHIITAKE MUSHROOM
Lentinus edodes ....see SHIITAKE MUSHROOM
Lentisk.. see MASTIC
Leontodon taraxacum...........................see DANDELION
Leontopodium ....see ALCHEMILLA
Leonuri Cardiacae Herba .... see MOTHERWORT
Leonurus .... see MOTHERWORT
Leonurus cardiaca .... see MOTHERWORT
Leopard's Bane .... see ARNICA
Leopard's Foot ....see MARSH MARIGOLD
Lepidium Meyenii.......................................see MACA
Lepidium peruvianum...................................see MACA
Lepidium sativum .... see GARDEN CRESS
Leptandra virginica .... see BLACK ROOT
Lesser calamint .... see CALAMINT
LESSER CELANDINE .... see LESSER CELANDINE
Lesser Centauru .... see CENTAURY
Lesser Dodder ....see DODDER
Lesser Galangal...see ALPINIA
Lesser Hemlock .... see FOOL'S PARSLEY
Lesser Periwinkle..see PERIWINKLE
Lettsomia nervosa ...... see HAWAIIAN BABY WOODROSE
Lettuce Opium .... see WILD LETTUCE
Leucine.............. see BRANCHED-CHAIN AMINO ACIDS
Leucoanthocyanidins .... see PYCNOGENOL
Leucoanthocyanin .... see GRAPE
Levacecarnine .... see ACETYL-L-CARNITINE
Levant..see WORMSEED
LEVANT BERRY ....see LEVANT BERRY
Levant Nut ....see LEVANT BERRY
Levant Salep....................................... see SALEP
Levant Storax .... see STORAX
Levistici Radix ....see LOVAGE
Levisticum officinale ....see LOVAGE
Levocarnitine .... see L-CARNITINE
Levoglutamide .... see GLUTAMINE
Levoglutamine .... see GLUTAMINE
Levo-histidine .... see HISTIDINE
Levure de Biere.........................see BREWER'S YEAST
L-glutamic Acid .... see GLUTAMINE
L-glutamic Acid 5-amide .... see GLUTAMINE
L-glutamine .... see GLUTAMINE
L-glutathione.............................see GLUTATHIONE
L-glycine .... see GLYCINE
L-histidine ....see HISTIDINE
LI 132................................. see HAWTHORN

Lian Fang ....see LOTUS
Lian Qiao ....see FORSYTHIA
Lian Xu ....see LOTUS
Lian Zi...see LOTUS
Liatris .... see DEERTONGUE
Liatris callilepis.............see MARSH BLAZING STAR
Liatris spicata...................see MARSH BLAZING STAR
Lichen islandicus .... see ICELAND MOSS
Lichen Oak Moss .... see OAK MOSS
Lichwort............. see PELLITORY-OF-THE-WALL
LICORICE ....see LICORICE
Lien Chiao ....see FORSYTHIA
Life Everlasting ....see CAT'S FOOT
Life of Man ....see AMERICAN SPIKENARD
Life Root .... see GOLDEN RAGWORT
Life-giving Vine of Peru ....see CAT'S CLAW
Life-of-man ....see AMERICAN SPIKENARD
Light Kaolin .... see KAOLIN
Lignum rhodium ....see ROSEROOT
Ligusticum levisticum...............................see LOVAGE
Ligusticum porteri..see OSHA
Ligustilides .... see DONG QUAI
Ligustro .... see GLOSSY PRIVET
Ligustrum ....see GLOSSY PRIVET
Ligustrum Fruit ....see GLOSSY PRIVET
Ligustrum Lucidum ....see GLOSSY PRIVET
Lilium candidum........................... see WHITE LILY
Lilium martagon...................... see MARTAGON
Lily of the Desert ....see ALOE
LILY-OF-THE-VALLEY ....see LILY-OF-THE-VALLEY
Lima Bean...see BEAN POD
LIME ....see LIME
Lime Flower...see LINDEN
Lime Tree...see LINDEN
Limette ....see LIME
Limon .... see LEMON
LIMONENE...see LIMONENE
Limonia aurantiifolia ....see LIME
Limonnik Kitajskij ....see SCHISANDRA
Linaria vulgaris ....see YELLOW TOADFLAX
LINDEN...see LINDEN
Linden Charcoal..see LINDEN
Ling .... see HEATHER
Ling Chih .... see REISHI MUSHROOM
Ling Zhi .... see REISHI MUSHROOM
Lingen .... see ALPINE CRANBERRY
Lingenberry.............................. see ALPINE CRANBERRY
Lingon .... see ALPINE CRANBERRY
Lingonberry.............................. see ALPINE CRANBERRY
Lingum Vitae.................... see GUAIAC WOOD resin, wood
Lini Semen...see FLAXSEED
Linoleic Acid............see CONJUGATED LINOLEIC ACID,
                    EVENING PRIMROSE OIL, FLAXSEED OIL
Linseed..see FLAXSEED
Linseed Oil................................. see FLAXSEED OIL
Lint Bells .... see FLAXSEED
Linum .... see FLAXSEED
Linum catharticum ....see MOUNTAIN FLAX
Linum crepitans ....see FLAXSEED, FLAXSEED OIL
Linum humile.................see FLAXSEED, FLAXSEED OIL
Linum usitatissimum.......see FLAXSEED, FLAXSEED OIL
Lion's Ear..................................... see MOTHERWORT
Lion's Foot ....see ALCHEMILLA
Lion's Mouth.................................... see DIGITALIS
Lion's Tail .... see MOTHERWORT

Lion's Tooth .... see DANDELION
LIPASE .... see LIPASE
Lipoic Acid .... see ALPHA-LIPOIC ACID
Lipoicin .... see ALPHA-LIPOIC ACID
Lipositol .... see INOSITOL
Lipotropic Factor .... see CHOLINE
Lippia citrodora .... see LEMON VERBENA
Lippia triphylla .... see LEMON VERBENA
Lipstick Tree .... see ANNATTO
Liquid Amber .... see STORAX
Liquid Liver Extract .... see LIVER EXTRACT
Liquid Oxygen .... see VITAMIN O
Liquid Storax .... see STORAX
Liquidambar macrophylla .... see STORAX
Liquidambar orientalis .... see STORAX
Liquidambar styraciflua .... see STORAX
Liquiritiae Radix .... see LICORICE
Liquirizia .... see LICORICE
Liquorice .... see LICORICE
L-isoleucine .... see BRANCHED-CHAIN AMINO ACIDS
LITHIUM .... see LITHIUM
Lithospermum lehmanii .... see ALKANNA
Little Dragon .... see TARRAGON
Little Gourd .... see IVY GOURD
Little Pollom .... see BITTER MILKWORT
Liu Yue Ling .... see RABDOSIA RUBESCENS
Live Culture Yogurt .... see YOGURT
Liveforever .... see HOUSELEEK
Liver .... see LIVER EXTRACT
Liver Concentrate .... see LIVER EXTRACT
LIVER EXTRACT .... see LIVER EXTRACT
Liver Factors .... see LIVER EXTRACT
Liver Fractions .... see LIVER EXTRACT
Liver Hydrolysate .... see LIVER EXTRACT
Liver Lily .... see ORRIS
Liver Oil .... see COD LIVER OIL
Liver Substance .... see LIVER EXTRACT
Liverleaf .... see LIVERWORT
Liverweed .... see LIVERWORT
LIVERWORT .... see LIVERWORT, AGRIMONY
Liverwort-Leaf .... see LIVERWORT
Lizard's Tail .... see YERBA MANSA
Lizzy-run-up-the-hedge .... see GROUND IVY
L-leucine .... see BRANCHED-CHAIN AMINO ACIDS
L-limonene .... see LIMONENE
L-lysine .... see LYSINE
L-methionine .... see METHIONINE
L-methylfolate .... see FOLIC ACID
LNA .... see ALPHA-LINOLENIC ACID
Lobaria pulmonaria .... see LUNGMOSS
LOBELIA .... see LOBELIA
Lobster Flower Plant .... see POINSETTIA
Lobsterplant .... see POINSETTIA
Lochnera rosea .... see MADAGASCAR PERIWINKLE
Locoweed .... see JIMSON WEED
Locust Bean .... see CAROB
Locust Pods .... see CAROB
LOGWOOD .... see LOGWOOD
Lolium temulentum .... see TAUMELLOOLCH
Long Birthwort .... see ARISTOLOCHIA
Long Black Spanish Radish .... see RADISH
Long Pepper .... see INDIAN LONG PEPPER, KAVA
Long Purples .... see PURPLE LOOSESTRIFE
Long-chain Oligosaccharides .... see INULIN
Longjack .... see EURYCOMA LONGIFOLIA

Longwort .... see MULLEIN
Lonicera .... see HONEYSUCKLE
Lonicera aureoreticulata .... see HONEYSUCKLE
Lonicera bournei .... see HONEYSUCKLE
Lonicera caprifolia .... see HONEYSUCKLE
Lonicera japonica .... see HONEYSUCKLE
Lonicera marilandica .... see PINK ROOT
Loofa .... see LUFFA
LOOSESTRIFE .... see LOOSESTRIFE,
                          PURPLE LOOSESTRIFE
Lophophora williamsii .... see PEYOTE
Lorbeerweide .... see WILLOW BARK
Lords and Ladies .... see ARUM
LORENZO'S OIL .... see LORENZO'S OIL
L-ornithine .... see ORNITHINE
L-ornithine Alpha-ketoglutarate ....
.... see ORNITHINE KETOGLUTARATE
LOTUS .... see LOTUS
Louisa .... see LEMON VERBENA
Louisiana Long Pepper .... see CAPSICUM
Louisiana Sport Pepper .... see CAPSICUM
Louro-mole .... see CHA DE BUGRE
Louro-salgueiro .... see CHA DE BUGRE
Louseberry .... see LEVANT BERRY
Lousewort .... see STAVESACRE
LOVAGE .... see LOVAGE
Love Apple .... see TOMATO
Love Bean .... see PRECATORY BEAN
Love in a Mist .... see BLACK SEED
Love in Winter .... see PIPSISSEWA
Love Leaves .... see BURDOCK
Love Parsley .... see LOVAGE
Love-lies-bleeding .... see AMARANTH
Lovely Bleeding .... see AMARANTH
Love-man .... see CLIVERS
Low Balm .... see OSWEGO TEA
Low Chamomile .... see ROMAN CHAMOMILE
Lowbush Blueberry .... see BLUEBERRY
Lowbush Cranberry .... see ALPINE CRANBERRY
LPC .... see PROPIONYL-L-CARNITINE
L-phenylalanine .... see PHENYLALANINE
L-selenomethionine .... see SELENIUM
L-taurine .... see TAURINE
L-theanine .... see THEANINE
L-threonine .... see THREONINE
L-TRYPTOPHAN .... see L-TRYPTOPHAN
L-tyrosine .... see TYROSINE
Lu Lu Tong .... see STORAX
Lu Rong .... see DEER VELVET
Lu Song Guo .... see IGNATIUS BEAN
Lucerne .... see ALFALFA
Lucky Bean .... see PRECATORY BEAN
Luei Gong Gen .... see GOTU KOLA
LUFFA .... see LUFFA
Luffaschwamm .... see LUFFA
Lu-Hui .... see ALOE
Luma chequen .... see CHEKEN
Lungenkraut .... see LUNGWORT
LUNGMOSS .... see LUNGMOSS
LUNGWORT .... see LUNGMOSS, LUNGWORT
Luoling .... see MORINDA
Lupin Jaune .... see YELLOW LUPIN
Lupinus luteus .... see YELLOW LUPIN
Lupuli strobulus .... see HOPS
Lurk-in-the-ditch .... see PENNYROYAL

Lustwort .... see SUNDEW
Luteal Hormone ....see PROGESTERONE
LUTEIN .... see LUTEIN
Luteohormone ....see PROGESTERONE
Lutine ....see PROGESTERONE
L-valine .... see BRANCHED-CHAIN AMINO ACIDS
Lycii Berries...see LYCIUM
LYCIUM .... see LYCIUM
LYCOPENE ....see LYCOPENE
Lycoperdon sp ....see PUFF BALL
Lycopersicon esculentum.............................. see TOMATO
Lycopi Herba......................................see BUGLEWEED
Lycopodium ....see CLUB MOSS
Lycopodium clavatum............................see CLUB MOSS
Lycopus americanus.............................see BUGLEWEED
Lycopus europaeus..............................see BUGLEWEED
Lycopus virginicus..............................see BUGLEWEED
Lyngbya wollei.........................see BLUE-GREEN ALGAE
Lysimachia nummularia .... see MONEYWORT
Lysimachia vulgaris .... see LOOSESTRIFE
LYSINE...see LYSINE
Lythrum salicaria .... see PURPLE LOOSESTRIFE
M Mei Gee .... see SCHISANDRA
Ma Bian Cao .... see VERBENA
Ma Huang.................................... see EPHEDRA
MACA..see MACA
Macadamia integrifolia .... see MACADAMIA NUT
MACADAMIA NUT .... see MACADAMIA NUT
Macadamia tetraphylla................. see MACADAMIA NUT
Macambo................................... see CANELLA
Mace............................ see NUTMEG AND MACE
Macis .... see NUTMEG AND MACE
Mackerel Mint....................................see SPEARMINT
Macochihua .... see IPORURU
Macrocystis Pyrifera .... see ALGIN
Macrotys ....see BLACK COHOSH
Mad Weed ....see SKULLCAP
Madagascar Cinnamon...................... see CINNAMON bark
Madagascar Lemongrass...................... see LEMONGRASS
MADAGASCAR PERIWINKLE ....
.... see MADAGASCAR PERIWINKLE
Madagascar Vanilla .... see VANILLA
Mad-apple ....see JIMSON WEED
MADDER .... see MADDER
Mad-Dog Skullcap ....see SKULLCAP
Mad-Dog Weed ....see WATER PLANTAIN
Madecassol...............................see GOTU KOLA
Madelonitrile...................................see APRICOT
Madhunashini.............................see GYMNEMA
Madhura .... see DILL
Madnep ....see MASTERWORT
Madonna Lily...............................see WHITE LILY
Madre Selva ....see PASSIONFLOWER
Madrepora species ....see CORAL
Madreselva ....see HONEYSUCKLE
Mae-sil-na-moo...................see JAPANESE APRICOT
Magadhi ....see INDIAN LONG PEPPER
Magdalena..................see MADAGASCAR PERIWINKLE
Maggi Plant......................................see LOVAGE
Magic Mushrooms .... see PEYOTE
Magnesia ....see MAGNESIUM
MAGNESIUM ....see MAGNESIUM
Magnesium Pyruvate .... see PYRUVATE
MAGNOLIA.............................see MAGNOLIA
Magnolia Vine............................see SCHISANDRA

Mahajambu .... see JAMBOLAN
Mahogany .... see ANDIROBA, LAURELWOOD
Mahonia aquifolium......................see OREGON GRAPE
Mahonia diversifolia ....see OREGON GRAPE
Mahonia nervosa ....see OREGON GRAPE
Mahonia repens ....see OREGON GRAPE
Mahonia sonnei ....see OREGON GRAPE
Mahuanggen .... see EPHEDRA
Mai Ya ....see BARLEY
Maiden Fern .... see MAIDENHAIR FERN
MAIDENHAIR FERN............... see MAIDENHAIR FERN
Maidenhair Tree ....see GINKGO
Maidis Stigma .... see CORN SILK
Maid's Hair .... see LADY'S BEDSTRAW
Main Ja .... see PALM OIL
Maino ....see MACA
MAITAKE MUSHROOM ...... see MAITAKE MUSHROOM
Maize Pollen ....see BEE POLLEN
Maize Silk .... see CORN SILK
Majoran ....see MARJORAM
Majorana Aetheroleum Oil ....see MARJORAM
Majorana hortensis ....see MARJORAM
Majorana majorana ....see MARJORAM
Maka ....see MACA
Makali Beru .... see SWALLOWROOT
Makombu Thallus ....see LAMINARIA
MALABAR NUT .... see MALABAR NUT
Malabar Tamarind ....see GARCINIA
Malaysian Ginseng.............see EURYCOMA LONGIFOLIA
MALE FERN ....see MALE FERN
Malic Acid............................ see ALPHA HYDROXY ACIDS
Mallaguetta Pepper .... see GRAINS OF PARADISE
Mallards .... see MARSHMALLOW
Mallotus philippensis ....see KAMALA
MALLOW ....see MALLOW
Malohu .... see KAVA
Malpighia glabra .... see ACEROLA
Malpighia punicifolia .... see ACEROLA
Maluk .... see KAVA
Malus sylvestris ....see APPLE, APPLE CIDER VINEGAR
Malva ....see CHINESE MALLOW
Malva Flower .... see HOLLYHOCK
Malva mauritiana ....see MALLOW
Malva neglecta ....see MALLOW
Malva rotundifolia ....see MALLOW
Malva sylvestris ....see MALLOW
Malva verticillata ....see CHINESE MALLOW
Malva-branca .... see COUNTRY MALLOW
Malva-branca-sedosa .... see COUNTRY MALLOW
Malvae Arboreae Flos ....see HOLLYHOCK
Malvae Flos...................................see MALLOW
Malvae Folium ....see MALLOW
Mamaerie .... see PAPAYA
MANACA .... see MANACA
Manchurian Fungus ....see KOMBUCHA TEA
Manchurian Mushroom Tea ....see KOMBUCHA TEA
Mandragora .... see EUROPEAN MANDRAKE
Mandragora officinarum ...... see EUROPEAN MANDRAKE
Mandragora vernalis .... see EUROPEAN MANDRAKE
Mandragore .... see EUROPEAN MANDRAKE
Mandrake .... see EUROPEAN MANDRAKE,
                                                PODOPHYLLUM
Manduk Parani .... see GOTU KOLA
Mandukaparni .... see GOTU KOLA
Mang Cut ....see MANGOSTEEN

Mang Jing Zi......................................see CHASTEBERRY
MANGANESE ....see MANGANESE
Manganum ....see MANGANESE
Mangel ....see BEET
Manggis.......................................see MANGOSTEEN
Manggistan...................................see MANGOSTEEN
Mangold ....see BEET
Mangosta ....see MANGOSTEEN
Mangostan....................................see MANGOSTEEN
Mangostana..................................see MANGOSTEEN
Mangostana cambogia ....see GARCINIA
Mangostanier.................................see MANGOSTEEN
Mangostao....................................see MANGOSTEEN
MANGOSTEEN ....see MANGOSTEEN
Mangostier....................................see MANGOSTEEN
Mangoustanier...............................see MANGOSTEEN
Mangouste....................................see MANGOSTEEN
Manguita......................................see MANGOSTEEN
Manila Elemi...................................... see ELEMI
MANNA .... see MANNA
Mannentake ....see REISHI MUSHROOM
Manno-heptulose.........see AVOCADO SUGAR EXTRACT
Mannose .... see D-MANNOSE
Manzanilla...................... see GERMAN CHAMOMILE,
                              ROMAN CHAMOMILE
Manzanita .... see UVA URSI
Maori Kava ....see KAVA
Mapato ....see RHATANY
Maracuja ....see PASSIONFLOWER
Maranhao Jaborandi...........................see JABORANDI
Maranta .... see ARROWROOT
Marcory.............................see QUEEN'S DELIGHT
Marginal Fern..............................see MALE FERN
Margosa.. see NEEM
Marguerite.............................see OX-EYE DAISY
Marian Thistle .... see MILK THISTLE
Maricha .... see BLACK PEPPER AND WHITE PEPPER
Mariendistel ....see MILK THISTLE
Marienmantel ....see ALCHEMILLA
Marigold....................see CALENDULA, TAGETES
Marigold of Peru .... see SUNFLOWER OIL
Mariguana .... see MARIJUANA
Marihuana .... see MARIJUANA
MARIJUANA .... see MARIJUANA
Marine Oak ....see BLADDERWRACK
Marine Oils .... see FISH OIL
Marjolaine ....see MARJORAM
MARJORAM ....see MARJORAM
Markweed ....see POISON IVY
Marmelo .... see QUINCE
Marron Europeen .... see HORSE CHESTNUT
Marronnier .... see HORSE CHESTNUT
Marrubii Herba.....................see WHITE HOREHOUND
Marrubium ....see WHITE HOREHOUND
Marsdenia cundurango......................see CONDURANGO
Marsdenia reichenbachii ....see CONDURANGO
MARSH BLAZING STAR....see MARSH BLAZING STAR
Marsh Citrus............................... see MARSH TEA
MARSH MARIGOLD.................see MARSH MARIGOLD
Marsh Mint...............................see WILD MINT
Marsh Penny .... see GOTU KOLA
MARSH TEA ....see MARSH TEA
Marsh Trefoil ....see BOGBEAN
MARSHMALLOW ....see MARSHMALLOW
MARTAGON ....see MARTAGON

Mary Jane............................... see MARIJUANA
Mary Thistle .... see MILK THISTLE
Marybud.................................see CALENDULA
Maryland Pink........................... see PINK ROOT
Master of the Wood.....................see SWEET WOODRUFF
MASTERWORT .... see GOUTWEED, MASTERWORT
MASTIC .... see MASTIC
Mastich .... see MASTIC
Mastix .... see MASTIC
Mastranzo .... see WHITE HOREHOUND
MATE.....................................see MATE
Mate de Coca .... see COCA
Maté Folium ....see MATE
Matricaire .... see GERMAN CHAMOMILE
Matricaria chamomilla .... see GERMAN CHAMOMILE
Matricaria eximia .... see FEVERFEW
Matricaria morifolia ....see CHRYSANTHEMUM
Matricaria parthenium..................... see FEVERFEW
Matricaria recutita .... see GERMAN CHAMOMILE
Matricariae Flos .... see GERMAN CHAMOMILE
Matrimony Vine ....see LYCIUM
Matsbouza................................see SCHISANDRA
Matsuhodo .... see PORIA MUSHROOM
Matteuccia struthiopteris.............. see OSTRICH FERN
Matto Grosso Ipecac .... see IPECAC
Maudlin Daisy.......................see OX-EYE DAISY
Maudlinwort.........................see OX-EYE DAISY
Mauls.....................................see MALLOW
May .... see HAWTHORN
May Bells ....see LILY-OF-THE-VALLEY
May Lily.....................see LILY-OF-THE-VALLEY
Mayapple............................ see PODOPHYLLUM
Maybush .... see HAWTHORN
Mayflower ....see COWSLIP
Maypop Passion Flower ....see PASSIONFLOWER
Maythorn .... see HAWTHORN
MCTs ......see MEDIUM CHAIN TRIGLYCERIDES (MCT)
Meadow Anenome ....see PULSATILLA
Meadow Buttercup .... see BUTTERCUP
Meadow Cabbage.................see SKUNK CABBAGE
Meadow Clover ....see RED CLOVER
Meadow Lily ....see WHITE LILY
Meadow Queen .... see MEADOWSWEET
Meadow Routs ....see MARSH MARIGOLD
Meadow Runagates .... see MONEYWORT
Meadow Saffron .... see AUTUMN CROCUS
Meadow Sage .... see SAGE
Meadow Windflower ....see PULSATILLA
Meadowbloom .... see BULBOUS BUTTERCUP,
                                    BUTTERCUP
MEADOWSWEET ....see MEADOWSWEET
Meadow-Wart............................see MEADOWSWEET
Mealy Kudzu............................. see KUDZU
Mechoacán ....see JALAP
Medhika ....see FENUGREEK
Medicago................................ see ALFALFA
Medicago sativa .... see ALFALFA
Medicinal Charcoal..............see ACTIVATED CHARCOAL
Medicinal Rhubarb....................... see RHUBARB
Medicinal Yeast ....see BREWER'S YEAST
Mediterranean Bay .... see SWEET BAY
Mediterranean Oregano ....see OREGANO
Mediterranean Squill........................see SQUILL
MEDIUM CHAIN TRIGLYCERIDES (MCT) ....
...............see MEDIUM CHAIN TRIGLYCERIDES (MCT)

Meerdorn	see SEA BUCKTHORN
Meereiche	see BLADDERWRACK
Meerrettich	see HORSERADISH
Megusurinoki	see NIKKO MAPLE
Mehlbeebaum	see HAWTHORN
Mehndi	see HENNA
Mei	see JAPANESE APRICOT
Meidorn	see HAWTHORN
Mejorana	see MARJORAM
Mel	see HONEY, MELATONIN
Melaleuca alternifolia	see TEA TREE OIL
Melaleuca leucadendra	see CAJEPUT OIL
Melaleuca Oil	see TEA TREE OIL
Melaleuca quinquenervia	see CAJEPUT OIL
Melaleuca viridiflora	see NIAULI OIL
Melampode	see BLACK HELLEBORE
MELANOTAN-II	see MELANOTAN-II
MELATONIN	see MELATONIN
Melegueta Pepper	see GRAINS OF PARADISE
Meletin	see QUERCETIN
Melia azadirachta	see NEEM
Melilot	see SWEET CLOVER
Meliloti herba	see SWEET CLOVER
Melilotus	see SWEET CLOVER
Melilotus altissimus	see SWEET CLOVER
Melilotus arvensis	see SWEET CLOVER
Melilotus macrorrhizus	see SWEET CLOVER
Melilotus officinalis	see SWEET CLOVER
Melilotus vulgaris	see SWEET CLOVER
Melissa	see LEMON BALM
Melissa nepeta	see CALAMINT
Melissa officinalis	see LEMON BALM
Melissa pulegioides	see PENNYROYAL
Melissae Folium	see LEMON BALM
Melissenblatt	see LEMON BALM
Melon Tree	see PAPAYA
Melonenbaumblaetter	see PAPAYA
Membranous Milk Vetch	see ASTRAGALUS
Membrillo	see QUINCE
Memeniran	see CHANCA PIEDRA
Menadiol Acetate (K4)	see VITAMIN K
Menadione (K3)	see VITAMIN K
Menaquinone (K2)	see VITAMIN K
Mendee	see HENNA
Mengkudu	see MORINDA
Menhaden Oil	see FISH OIL
Meniran	see CHANCA PIEDRA
Menispermum cocculus	see LEVANT BERRY
Menispermum columba	see COLOMBO
Menispermum lacunosum	see LEVANT BERRY
Menispermum palmatum	see COLOMBO
Menkoedoe	see MORINDA
Menta de Gato	see CATNIP
Menta piperita	see PEPPERMINT
Mentha aquatica	see WILD MINT
Mentha arvensis aetheroleum	see JAPANESE MINT
Mentha arvensis var. piperascens	see JAPANESE MINT
Mentha cablin	see PATCHOULY OIL
Mentha canadensis	see JAPANESE MINT
Mentha cordifolia	see SPEARMINT
Mentha crispa	see SPEARMINT
Mentha lavanduliodora	see PEPPERMINT
Mentha longifolia	see ENGLISH HORSEMINT
Mentha Oil	see PEPPERMINT
Mentha palustris	see WILD MINT
Mentha piperita	see PEPPERMINT
Mentha pulegium	see PENNYROYAL
Mentha spicata	see SPEARMINT
Mentha sylvestris	see ENGLISH HORSEMINT
Mentha viridis	see SPEARMINT
Menthae piperitae aetheroleum	see PEPPERMINT
Menthae Piperitae Folium	see PEPPERMINT
Menthe	see PEPPERMINT
Menthe poivree	see PEPPERMINT
MENTZELIA	see MENTZELIA
Mentzelia cordifolia	see MENTZELIA
Menyanthes	see BOGBEAN
Menyanthes trifoliata	see BOGBEAN
Merasingi	see GYMNEMA
Mercurialis annua	see MERCURY HERB
MERCURY HERB	see MERCURY HERB
Meruk	see KAVA
Mescal Buttons	see PEYOTE
Mescaline	see PEYOTE
Mesegerak	see JAMBOLAN
Meseter	see MANGOSTEEN
Meshashringi	see GYMNEMA
MESOGLYCAN	see MESOGLYCAN
Meso-inositol	see INOSITOL
Meso-inositol Hexanicotinate	see INOSITOL NICOTINATE
Meso-xylitol	see XYLITOL
Mespilus laevigata	see HAWTHORN
Metavanadate	see VANADIUM
Methi	see FENUGREEK
METHIONINE	see METHIONINE
Methoxyflavones	see METHOXYLATED FLAVONES
METHOXYLATED FLAVONES	see METHOXYLATED FLAVONES
Methyl Sulfone	see MSM (METHYLSULFONYLMETHANE)
Methyl Sulphoxide	see DMSO (DIMETHYLSULFOXIDE)
Methylated Phosphatidylethanolamine	see CHOLINE
Methylcobalamin	see VITAMIN B12
Methylfolate	see FOLIC ACID
Methyl-sulfonyl-methane	see MSM (METHYLSULFONYLMETHANE)
Methylxanthine	see CAFFEINE
Mexican Bamboo	see HU ZHANG
Mexican Chilies	see CAPSICUM
Mexican Damiana	see DAMIANA
Mexican Flame Leaf	see POINSETTIA
Mexican Marigold	see TAGETES
Mexican Sage	see DIVINER'S SAGE
Mexican Sanguinaria	see KNOTWEED
Mexican Sarsaparilla	see SARSAPARILLA
MEXICAN SCAMMONY ROOT	see MEXICAN SCAMMONY ROOT
Mexican Tea	see CHENOPODIUM OIL
Mexican Valerian	see VALERIAN
Mexican Vanilla	see VANILLA
Mexican Wild Yam	see WILD YAM
Mexican Yam	see WILD YAM
Mexico Weed	see CASTOR
MEZEREON	see MEZEREON
MFP	see FLUORIDE
Mg	see MAGNESIUM
MGN-3	see MGN-3
Microalgae	see ASTAXANTHIN

 Natural Medicines Comprehensive Database Consumer Version (209) 472-2244

Microcystis aeruginosa .... see BLUE-GREEN ALGAE
Microcystis wesenbergii .... see BLUE-GREEN ALGAE
Middle Comfrey .... see BUGLE
Middle Confound .... see BUGLE
Miel Blanc .... see HONEY
Mignonette Tree .... see HENNA
Milefolio .... see YARROW
Milfoil .... see YARROW
Milik .... see KAVA
Milium nigricans .... see BROOM CORN
Milk Ipecac .... see BETH ROOT, CANADIAN HEMP
Milk of Magnesia .... see MAGNESIUM
Milk Protein Hydrosylate .... see CASEIN PEPTIDES
MILK THISTLE .... see MILK THISTLE
Milk Vetch .... see ASTRAGALUS
Milk Willow-Herb .... see PURPLE LOOSESTRIFE
Milkweed .... see CANADIAN HEMP
Milkwort .... see SENEGA
Mill Mint .... see CALAMINT
Mill Mountain .... see MOUNTAIN FLAX
Millefeuille .... see YARROW
Millefolii Flos .... see YARROW
Millefolii Herba .... see YARROW
Millefolium .... see YARROW
Millegoglie .... see YARROW
Millepertuis .... see ST. JOHN'S WORT
Mimosa catechu .... see CATECHU
Mimosa farnesiana .... see CASSIE ABSOLUTE
Mimosa senegal .... see ACACIA
Mineral Aspartates .... see ASPARTATES
Mineral-amino Acid Complex ....
.... see CHELATED MINERALS
Minor Centaury .... see CENTAURY
Mint .... see PEPPERMINT
Mint Oil .... see JAPANESE MINT
Minzol .... see JAPANESE MINT
Miraa .... see KHAT
Miracle Grass .... see JIAOGULAN
Miracle Plant .... see ALOE, GYMNEMA
Mirchi .... see CAPSICUM
Mirobalano .... see INDIAN GOOSEBERRY
Mirobalanus embilica .... see INDIAN GOOSEBERRY
Miso .... see SOY
Mistlekraut .... see EUROPEAN MISTLETOE
Mistletein .... see EUROPEAN MISTLETOE
Mistletoe .... see AMERICAN MISTLETOE,
EUROPEAN MISTLETOE
Mitchella repens .... see SQUAWVINE
Mitoquinone .... see COENZYME Q-10
Mitrewort .... see COOLWORT
Mixed Fruit Acid .... see ALPHA HYDROXY ACIDS
Mixed Tocopherols .... see VITAMIN E
Mixed Vespids .... see BEE VENOM
Mizibcoc .... see DAMIANA
Mizu-Garashi .... see WATERCRESS
MLT .... see MELATONIN
Mn .... see MANGANESE
Moccasin Flower .... see NERVE ROOT
Mocha .... see COFFEE
Mockeel Root .... see WATER HEMLOCK
Mohave Yucca .... see YUCCA
Mokko .... see COSTUS
Momordica charantia .... see BITTER MELON
Momordica murcata .... see BITTER MELON
Momordique .... see BITTER MELON

Monarda .... see OSWEGO TEA
Monarda didyma .... see OSWEGO TEA
Monarda lutea .... see HORSEMINT
Monarda punctata .... see HORSEMINT
Monascus .... see RED YEAST
Monascus purpureus .... see RED YEAST
Monazol .... see GLYCINE
MONEYWORT .... see MONEYWORT
Mongolian Ephedra .... see EPHEDRA
Mongolian Larch .... see LARCH ARABINOGALACTAN
Mongolian Larchwood ....
.... see LARCH ARABINOGALACTAN
Mongolian Milk .... see ASTRAGALUS
Moniera cuneifolia .... see BRAHMI
Monkey Flower .... see NERVE ROOT,
YELLOW TOADFLAX
Monkey Nuts .... see PEANUT OIL
Monkey's Bench .... see MAITAKE MUSHROOM
Monk's Pepper .... see CHASTEBERRY
Monkshood .... see ACONITE
Monnier's Snowparsley .... see CNIDIUM
Monobasic Potassium Phosphate ... see PHOSPHATE SALTS
Mono-carboxymethylated Chitosan .... see CHITOSAN
Monofluorophosphate .... see FLUORIDE
Monohydroxysuccinic Acid ....
.... see ALPHA HYDROXY ACIDS
MONOLAURIN .... see MONOLAURIN
Mono-Sulfated Saccharide ....
.... see GLUCOSAMINE SULFATE
Monounsaturated Fatty Acid .... see OLIVE
Monteray Pine .... see PINE
Montmorency Cherry .... see SOUR CHERRY
Moon Daisy .... see OX-EYE DAISY
Moon Flower .... see OX-EYE DAISY
Moon Penny .... see OX-EYE DAISY
Moor Grass .... see POTENTILLA
Moosbeere .... see BOG BILBERRY
Moose Elm .... see SLIPPERY ELM
Moosebeere .... see CRANBERRY
Mora de la India .... see MORINDA
Morella caroliniensis .... see BAYBERRY
Morella cerifera .... see BAYBERRY
Morella pensylvanica .... see BAYBERRY
Morello Cherry .... see SOUR CHERRY
MORINDA .... see BA JI TIAN, MORINDA
Morinda citrifolia .... see MORINDA
Morinda officinalis .... see BA JI TIAN
Morindae Radix .... see BA JI TIAN
MORMON TEA .... see MORMON TEA
Moroccan Geranium Oil .... see ROSE GERANIUM OIL
Mortal .... see BITTERSWEET NIGHTSHADE
Mortification Root .... see MARSHMALLOW
Morus nigra .... see BLACK MULBERRY
Moschus moschiferus (Musk Deer) .... see MUSK
Mosquito Plant .... see PENNYROYAL
Moss Cranberry .... see ALPINE CRANBERRY
Mossberry .... see CRANBERRY
Moth Herb .... see MARSH TEA
Mother of Rye .... see ERGOT
Mother of Thyme .... see WILD THYME
Mother's-heart .... see SHEPHERD'S PURSE
MOTHERWORT .... see MOTHERWORT
MOUNTAIN ASH .... see MOUNTAIN ASH
Mountain Balm .... see CALAMINT,
OSWEGO TEA, YERBA SANTA

Mountain Box .... see UVA URSI
Mountain Cranberry .... see UVA URSI
Mountain Damson ....see SIMARUBA
Mountain Everlasting .... see CAT'S FOOT
MOUNTAIN FLAX ....see MOUNTAIN FLAX
Mountain Geranium .... see HERB ROBERT
Mountain Grape .... see EUROPEAN BARBERRY
Mountain Hydrangea .... see HYDRANGEA
Mountain Ivy .... see MOUNTAIN LAUREL
MOUNTAIN LAUREL .... see MOUNTAIN LAUREL
Mountain Lovage ....see OSHA
Mountain Mint ....see CALAMINT,
OREGANO, OSWEGO TEA
Mountain Pink .... see TRAILING ARBUTUS
Mountain Polygala ....see SENEGA
Mountain Radish .... see HORSERADISH
Mountain Savory Oil .... see WINTER SAVORY
Mountain Sorrel .... see WOOD SORREL
Mountain Strawberry ....see STRAWBERRY
Mountain Tea ....see WINTERGREEN
Mountain Tobacco .... see ARNICA
Mountain-grape ....see OREGON GRAPE
Mountain-sweet .... see NEW JERSEY TEA
Mouse Antialopecia Factor .... see INOSITOL
MOUSE EAR ....see CUDWEED, MOUSE EAR
Mousetail ....see COMMON STONECROP
Mousse d'Irlande .... see CARRAGEENAN
Moutan .... see PEONY
Mouth Root .... see GOLDTHREAD
Mouth-smart ....see BROOKLIME
MSI-1256F ....see SHARK CARTILAGE
MSM (METHYLSULFONYLMETHANE) ....
.... see MSM (METHYLSULFONYLMETHANE)
MT-II ....see MELANOTAN-II
Mu Dan Pi .... see PEONY
Mu Xiang .... see COSTUS
Mucara ....see KARAYA GUM
Mucopolysaccharide .... see MESOGLYCAN
Mucuna .... see COWHAGE
Mudar Bark .... see CALOTROPIS
Muder yercum .... see CALOTROPIS
Mugrela ....see BLACK SEED
Muguet ....see LILY-OF-THE-VALLEY
MUGWORT .... see MUGWORT, TARRAGON
MUIRA PUAMA ....see MUIRA PUAMA
Mukul Myrrh Tree ....see GUGGUL
Mulberry ....see BLACK MULBERRY, MORINDA
Mulhathi ....see LICORICE
MULLEIN .... see MULLEIN
Multiflora preparata .... see FO-TI
Mum ....see CHRYSANTHEMUM
Munchausia speciosa .... see BANABA
Munjariki ....see BASIL
Murillo Bark .... see QUILLAIA
Muscadier .... see NUTMEG AND MACE
Muscatel Sage ....see CLARY SAGE
Muscovy Duck ....see OSCILLOCOCCINUM
Mushroom of Immortality .... see REISHI MUSHROOM
Mushroom of Spiritual Potency ....
.... see REISHI MUSHROOM
MUSK ....see MUSK
Musk Root ....see SUMBUL
Musk Seed .... see AMBRETTE
Muskadana .... see AMBRETTE
Muskat .... see GRAPE
Muskatbuam .... see NUTMEG AND MACE

Muskatnuss .... see NUTMEG AND MACE
Muskmallow ....see AMBRETTE
Muskrat Weed .... see WATER HEMLOCK
Musquash Root .... see WATER HEMLOCK
Mustard ....see BLACK MUSTARD, WHITE MUSTARD
Mustelia eupatoria .... see STEVIA
Muster John Henry .... see TAGETES
Mutton Chops ....see CLIVERS
Muzei Ma Huang ....see EPHEDRA
Myo-Inositol .... see INOSITOL
Myosotis Arvensis .... see FORGET-ME-NOT
Myrica .... see BAYBERRY
Myrica gale .... see SWEET GALE
Myristica .... see NUTMEG AND MACE
Myrobalan ....see TERMINALIA
Myrobalan emblic .... see INDIAN GOOSEBERRY
Myrobalanus bellirica ....see TERMINALIA
Myrobroma fragrans .... see VANILLA
Myrospermum pereirae ....see PERU BALSAM
Myroxylan balsamum .... see TOLU BALSAM
Myroxylan toluiferum .... see TOLU BALSAM
Myroxylon balsamum .... see TOLU BALSAM
Myroxylon pereirae ....see PERU BALSAM
MYRRH ....see MYRRH
Myrrhis odorata .... see SWEET CICELY
Myrti aetherolum .... see MYRTLE
Myrti Folium .... see MYRTLE
Myrtilli Fructus ....see BILBERRY
MYRTLE ....see MADAGASCAR PERIWINKLE,
MYRTLE, PERIWINKLE
Myrtle Flag ....see CALAMUS
Myrtle Flower ....see ORRIS
Myrtle Sedge ....see CALAMUS
Myrtus .... see CHEKEN
Myrtus chequen ....see CHEKEN
Myrtus communis ....see MYRTLE
Myrtus leucadendra ....see CAJEPUT OIL
Mysteria .... see AUTUMN CROCUS
Mystyldene .... see EUROPEAN MISTLETOE
Nabin chanvandi .... see ANDROGRAPHIS
NAC .... see N-ACETYL CYSTEINE
N-ACETYL CYSTEINE .... see N-ACETYL CYSTEINE
N-acetyl D-glucosamine ....
.... see N-ACETYL GLUCOSAMINE
N-ACETYL GLUCOSAMINE ....
.... see N-ACETYL GLUCOSAMINE
N-acetyl-5-methoxytryptamine .... see MELATONIN
N-acetyl-B-cysteine .... see N-ACETYL CYSTEINE
N-acetyl-carnitine .... see ACETYL-L-CARNITINE
N-acetyl-L-carnitine .... see ACETYL-L-CARNITINE
N-acetyl-L-cysteine .... see N-ACETYL CYSTEINE
NAD ....see NADH
NADH ....see NADH
N-A-G .... see N-ACETYL GLUCOSAMINE
Nagadamni ....see MUGWORT
Naked Ladies .... see AUTUMN CROCUS
N-alkanoic Acid .... see LAURIC ACID
N-amidinosarcosine ....see CREATINE
Nan Shanzha .... see HAWTHORN
Nangka Blanda ....see GRAVIOLA
Nangka Londa ....see GRAVIOLA
Nannari ....see SWALLOWROOT
Nanny Bush ....see BLACK HAW
Nanwuweizi ....see SCHISANDRA
Narcissus pseudonarcissus ....see DAFFODIL

Narrow Dock..see YELLOW DOCK
Narrow-leaved Purple Cone Flower...........see ECHINACEA
Nasilord...see WATERCRESS
Nasturtii herba.................................see WATERCRESS
NASTURTIUM....................................see NASTURTIUM
Nasturtium armoracia.........................see HORSERADISH
Nasturtium officinale ....see WATERCRESS
Natto...see SOY
Natto Extract ....see NATTOKINASE
NATTOKINASE ....see NATTOKINASE
Natural DHEA ....see WILD YAM
Nature's Viagra..............................see PUNCTURE VINE
Naughty Man's Cherries ....see BELLADONNA
Navel Orange ....see SWEET ORANGE
Navy Bean..see BEAN POD
N-carboxybutyl Chitosan ....see CHITOSAN
N-dodecanoic Acid.............................see LAURIC ACID
Nebraska Fern ....see HEMLOCK
Neckweed..see BROOKLIME
Nectar of the Gods ....see GARLIC
Neelapushpa.................................see SWEET VIOLET
NEEM .... see NEEM
Nees.. see CASSIA CINNAMON
Neli...see INDIAN GOOSEBERRY
Nelumbo caspica...see LOTUS
Nelumbo komarovii......................................see LOTUS
Nelumbo nelumbo.......................................see LOTUS
Nelumbo nucifera.......................................see LOTUS
Nelumbo speciosum....................................see LOTUS
Neopicrorhiza scrophulariiflora ....see PICRORHIZA
Neovastat...................................see SHARK CARTILAGE
Nepal Ginseng.................. see PANAX PSEUDOGINSENG
Nepalese Barberry......................see TREE TURMERIC
Nepeta cataria .... see CATNIP
Nepeta hederacea .... see GROUND IVY
Nepeta multifida...........................see SCHIZONEPETA
Nerium indicum ....see OLEANDER
Nerium odorum ....see OLEANDER
Nerium Oleander.................................see OLEANDER
Neroli Oil ....see BITTER ORANGE
NERVE ROOT ....see NERVE ROOT
Netchweed...see ARRACH
Nettle .... see STINGING NETTLE
Nettle Seed .... see STINGING NETTLE
Neuromins..........see DHA (DOCOSAHEXAENOIC ACID)
Neustanthus chinensis .... see KUDZU
Neutral Calcium Phosphate...........see PHOSPHATE SALTS
Nevada Ephedra .... see MORMON TEA
NEW JERSEY TEA .... see NEW JERSEY TEA
NEW ZEALAND GREEN-LIPPED MUSSEL....................
.... see NEW ZEALAND GREEN-LIPPED MUSSEL
Ngu Mei Gee....................................see SCHISANDRA
Nhau... see MORINDA
NIACIN AND NIACINAMIDE (VITAMIN B3) ....
.... see NIACIN AND NIACINAMIDE (VITAMIN B3)
Niando... see IPORURU
Niauli aetheroleum.............................see NIAULI OIL
NIAULI OIL .... see NIAULI OIL
Nicamid...
.... see NIACIN AND NIACINAMIDE (VITAMIN B3)
Nicaragua Ipecac................................. see IPECAC
Nichol Seeds .... see DIVI-DIVI
Nicosedine....................................
.... see NIACIN AND NIACINAMIDE (VITAMIN B3)
Nicotinamide....................................
.... see NIACIN AND NIACINAMIDE (VITAMIN B3)

Nicotinamide Adenine Dinucleotide Hydrate........see NADH
Nicotinic Acid ....
.... see NIACIN AND NIACINAMIDE (VITAMIN B3)
Nicotylamidum ....
.... see NIACIN AND NIACINAMIDE (VITAMIN B3)
Nigella sativa....................................see BLACK SEED
Nigelle de Crète ....see BLACK SEED
Night Blooming Cereus ....see CEREUS
Night Willow-Herb .... see EVENING PRIMROSE OIL
Nightshade ....see JIMSON WEED
Nikkar Nuts...see DIVI-DIVI
NIKKO MAPLE ....see NIKKO MAPLE
Nim .... see NEEM
Nimb .... see NEEM
Nimba .... see NEEM
Nimbaka .... see LEMON
Nimbuka .... see LEMON
Nindo...................................... see HONEYSUCKLE
Nine Hooks ....see ALCHEMILLA
Ninety-Knot ....see KNOTWEED
Ning Xia Gou Qi .... see LYCIUM
Ninjin.................................. see GINSENG, PANAX
Nira-brahmi .... see BRAHMI
Niruri .... see CHANCA PIEDRA
Nisha .... see TURMERIC
Niu Bang Zi .... see BURDOCK
N-methylsarcosine .... see DIMETHYLGLYCINE
Noah's Ark .... see NERVE ROOT
Nobiletin .... see METHOXYLATED FLAVONES
Noble Laurel .... see SWEET BAY
Noble Yarrow ....see YARROW
N-octacosanol .... see OCTACOSANOL
No-flush Niacin ....see INOSITOL NICOTINATE
Nogal ....see ENGLISH WALNUT
Nogal americano .... see BLACK WALNUT
Nogal ceniciento ....see BUTTERNUT
Nogueira-preta .... see BLACK WALNUT
Noisetier .... see HAZELNUT
Noix Muscade .... see NUTMEG AND MACE
Nokyong .... see DEER VELVET
Nonacosanol..........................see POLICOSANOL
Noni..................see BA JI TIAN, MORINDA
Nono .... see MORINDA
Nonu .... see MORINDA
Noon Kie Oo Nah Yeah..........................see SQUAWVINE
Nopal...................see PRICKLY PEAR CACTUS
Nopol..................see PRICKLY PEAR CACTUS
North American Ginseng ....see GINSENG, AMERICAN
NORTHERN PRICKLY ASH ....
.... see NORTHERN PRICKLY ASH
Northern Schisandra..............see SCHISANDRA
Northern White Cedar .... see THUJA
Norway Pine....................see HEMLOCK SPRUCE
Norway Spruce.................... see FIR, HEMLOCK SPRUCE
Nosebleed.............................see YARROW
Nostoc ellipsosporum.................see BLUE-GREEN ALGAE
Notoginseng ....see PANAX PSEUDOGINSENG
Noyer Cerdré ....see BUTTERNUT
Noyer Noir .... see BLACK WALNUT
NSC-763 .... see DMSO (DIMETHYLSULFOXIDE)
NSC-9704 ....see PROGESTERONE
Nu Zhen Zi ....see GLOSSY PRIVET
Nucleic Acid............................. see RNA AND DNA
Nucleotides .... see RNA AND DNA
Nuez Moscada .... see NUTMEG AND MACE

Medical professionals should consult the Professional Version at www.NaturalDatabase.com.

NUTMEG AND MACE............. see NUTMEG AND MACE
Nutmeg Flower .... see BLACK SEED
Nux moschata.................... see NUTMEG AND MACE
NUX VOMICA .... see NUX VOMICA
Nuzhenzi .... see GLOSSY PRIVET
Nymphaea maximilianii..
.... see AMERICAN WHITE POND LILY
Nymphaea nelumbo ....see LOTUS
Nymphaea odorata .... see AMERICAN WHITE POND LILY
Nymphaea rosea........ see AMERICAN WHITE POND LILY
NZGLM
.... see NEW ZEALAND GREEN-LIPPED MUSSEL
OAK bark..see OAK bark
Oak Fern................................... see LADY FERN
Oak Lungs..................................... see LUNGMOSS
OAK MOSS .... see OAK MOSS
Oat Bran ....see OATS
Oat Straw ....see OATS
Oatmeal ....see OATS
OATS ....see OATS
Oblepikha............................... see SEA BUCKTHORN
Occidental Ginseng................. see GINSENG, AMERICAN
Ocimum aristatum.............................see JAVA TEA
Ocimum basilicum .... see BASIL
Ocimum frutescens .... see PERILLA
Ocimum sanctum .... see HOLY BASIL
Ocimum tenuiflorum................... see HOLY BASIL
OCTACOSANOL ....
.... see OCTACOSANOL, POLICOSANOL
Octacosyl Alcohol............................. see OCTACOSANOL
Octyl Diemthyl PABA ....
.....................see PARA-AMINOBENZOIC ACID (PABA)
Oderwort .... see BISTORT
Oenanthe aquatica............................see WATER FENNEL
Oenanthe crocata...... see HEMLOCK WATER DROPWORT
Oenanthe javanica .... see WATER DROPWORT
Oenanthe stolonifera .... see WATER DROPWORT
Oenothera biennis .... see EVENING PRIMROSE OIL
Oenothera muricata............. see EVENING PRIMROSE OIL
Oenothera purpurata........... see EVENING PRIMROSE OIL
Oenothera rubricaulis .... see EVENING PRIMROSE OIL
Oenothera suaveolens .... see EVENING PRIMROSE OIL
Ofbit .... see PREMORSE
Ogi .... see ASTRAGALUS
Ogon..................................see BAIKAL SKULLCAP
Oil Nut ....see BUTTERNUT
Oil of Cade ....see CADE OIL
Oil of Clove .... see CLOVE
Oil of Juniper .... see JUNIPER
Oil of Juniper Tar ....see CADE OIL
Oil of Lemon Eucalyptus..........see LEMON EUCALYPTUS
Oil of Melaleuca .... see TEA TREE OIL
Oil of Oregano ....see OREGANO
Oil of Peppermint........................ see PEPPERMINT
Oil of Sandalwood .... see WHITE SANDALWOOD
Oil of Thyme................................... see THYME
Oil of Wintergreen ....see WINTERGREEN
Oil Palm Tree .... see PALM OIL
Oje..see FICIN
Ojo de Pajaro.......................... see PRECATORY BEAN
OKG..................see ORNITHINE KETOGLUTARATE
Okra...................................... see AMBRETTE
Old Maid................... see MADAGASCAR PERIWINKLE
Old Man .... see ROSEMARY
Old Man's Beard .....see FRINGETREE, TRAVELER'S JOY,
USNEA, WOODBINE

Old Man's Night Cap .... see GREATER BINDWEED
Old Man's Pepper ....see YARROW
Old Man's Root.............see AMERICAN SPIKENARD
Old Woman's Broom .... see DAMIANA
OLE.......................see LEMON EUCALYPTUS
Olea europaea..................................... see OLIVE
Oleae Folium .... see OLIVE
OLEANDER ....see OLEANDER
Oleanderblatter..................................see OLEANDER
Oleandri Folium ....see OLEANDER
Oleic Acid ....see LORENZO'S OIL
Oleoresin Capsicum .... see CAPSICUM
Oleovitamin A .... see VITAMIN A
Oleum bergamotte.................... see BERGAMOT OIL
Oleum cadinum ....see CADE OIL
Oleum calophyllum..................see LAURELWOOD
Oleum chaulmoograe .... see CHAULMOOGRA
Oleum geranii...................... see ROSE GERANIUM OIL
Oleum juniperi empyreumaticum ....see CADE OIL
Oleum melaleucae..................... see TEA TREE OIL
Olibanum .... see FRANKINCENSE
Oligofructose............ see FRUCTO-OLIGOSACCHARIDES
Oligomeric Proanthocyanidins........................ see GRAPE,
PYCNOGENOL
Oligomeric Procyanidins .... see GRAPE
Oligosaccharides..... see FRUCTO-OLIGOSACCHARIDES,
INULIN
Olivae oleum .... see OLIVE
OLIVE.. see OLIVE
Omega-3 Fatty Acids .... see ALPHA-LINOLENIC ACID,
COD LIVER OIL,
DHA (DOCOSAHEXAENOIC ACID),
EPA (EICOSAPENTAENOIC ACID),
FISH OIL
Omega-3 Polyunsaturated Fatty Acid ....
.... see ALPHA-LINOLENIC ACID
OMEGA-6 FATTY ACIDS....see OMEGA-6 FATTY ACIDS
Omega-6 Polyunsaturated Fatty Acids.........................
....................................see OMEGA-6 FATTY ACIDS
Omega-9 Fatty Acids .... see OLIVE
Omicha ....see SCHISANDRA
Omum ....see BISHOP'S WEED
Onagra biennis .... see EVENING PRIMROSE OIL
Oneberry ....see HERB PARIS
One-Berry .... see SQUAWVINE
Oneseed Hawthorn.......................... see HAWTHORN
ONION...................................... see ONION
Ononidis Radix .... see SPINY RESTHARROW
Ononis spinosa...................... see SPINY RESTHARROW
Onopordum acanthium.................... see SCOTCH THISTLE
Ontario Ginseng...................... see GINSENG, AMERICAN
OOLONG TEA .... see OOLONG TEA
OPCs .... see GRAPE, PYCNOGENOL
Ophioglossum vulgatum ....
.... see ENGLISH ADDER'S TONGUE
Ophioxylon serpentinum........... see INDIAN SNAKEROOT
Ophthalmic Barberry .... see TREE TURMERIC
OPI ....see PRICKLY PEAR CACTUS
OPIUM ANTIDOTE.................... see OPIUM ANTIDOTE
Oplopanax horridus.................... see DEVIL'S CLUB
Opobalsam .... see TOLU BALSAM
Opopanax ....see MYRRH
Opossum Tree .... see STORAX
Opuntia.................. see PRICKLY PEAR CACTUS
Oraches .... see ARRACH
Oranda-garashi .... see WATERCRESS

     Natural Medicines Comprehensive Database Consumer Version   (209) 472-2244

Orange	see SWEET ORANGE
Orange Milkweed	see PLEURISY ROOT
Orange Mullein	see MULLEIN
Orange Root	see GOLDENSEAL
Orange Swallow Wort	see PLEURISY ROOT
Orchanet	see ALKANNA
Orchic	see ORCHIC EXTRACT
Orchic concentrate	see ORCHIC EXTRACT
ORCHIC EXTRACT	see ORCHIC EXTRACT
Orchic Factors	see ORCHIC EXTRACT
Orchic Substance	see ORCHIC EXTRACT
Orchid	see SALEP
Orchis morio	see SALEP
Ordeal Bean	see CALABAR BEAN
OREGANO	see OREGANO
Oregano de Monte	see BRICKELLIA
Oregano Oil	see OREGANO
Oregon Balsam	see OREGON FIR BALSAM
Oregon Barberry	see OREGON GRAPE
OREGON FIR BALSAM	see OREGON FIR BALSAM
OREGON GRAPE	see EUROPEAN BARBERRY, OREGON GRAPE
Orelha-de-gigante	see BURDOCK
Organic Germanium	see GERMANIUM
Organy	see OREGANO
Orgotein	see SUPEROXIDE DISMUTASE
ORIENTAL ARBORVITAE	see ORIENTAL ARBORVITAE
Oriental Ginseng	see GINSENG, PANAX
Oriental Persimmon	see JAPANESE PERSIMMON
Origan de Marais	see HEMP AGRIMONY
Origani Vulgaris Herba	see OREGANO
Origano	see OREGANO
Origanum	see OREGANO
Origanum majorana	see MARJORAM
Origanum Oil	see SPANISH ORIGANUM OIL
Origanum Vulgare	see OREGANO
Orizaba Jalap	see MEXICAN SCAMMONY ROOT
Ormenis nobilis	see ROMAN CHAMOMILE
Ornicetil	see ORNITHINE KETOGLUTARATE
ORNITHINE	see ORNITHINE
Ornithine Alpha Ketoglutarate	see ORNITHINE KETOGLUTARATE
ORNITHINE KETOGLUTARATE	see ORNITHINE KETOGLUTARATE
Orozuz	see LICORICE
ORRIS	see ORRIS
Orthosilicic Acid	see SILICON
Orthosiphon	see JAVA TEA
Orthosiphonis folium	see JAVA TEA
Orthovanadate	see VANADIUM
Ortie	see STINGING NETTLE
Oryza sativa	see BROWN RICE, RICE BRAN
Oryzanol	see GAMMA ORYZANOL
Oscillo	see OSCILLOCOCCINUM
OSCILLOCOCCINUM	see OSCILLOCOCCINUM
OSHA	see OSHA
Osier	see AMERICAN DOGWOOD
Osier Rouge	see WILLOW BARK
Osmunda struthiopteris	see OSTRICH FERN
Osterick	see BISTORT
Ostokhoddous	see LAVENDER
OSTRICH FERN	see OSTRICH FERN
OSWEGO TEA	see OSWEGO TEA
Otaheite Walnut	see TUNG SEED

Ou-gon	see BAIKAL SKULLCAP
Our Lady's Flannel	see MULLEIN
Our Lady's Keys	see COWSLIP
Our Lady's Mint	see SPEARMINT
Our Lady's Tears	see LILY-OF-THE-VALLEY
Our Lady's Thistle	see MILK THISTLE
Our-Lord's-Candle	see YUCCA
Ovoester	see ASTAXANTHIN
Ovolecithin	see LECITHIN
Owler	see BLACK ALDER
Oxadoddy	see BLACK ROOT
Oxalis acetosella	see WOOD SORREL
Oxalis montana	see WOOD SORREL
Oxerutin	see RUTIN
Oxeye	see PHEASANT'S EYE
OX-EYE DAISY	see OX-EYE DAISY
Oxitriptan	see 5-HTP
Ox's Tongue	see BORAGE
Oxycoccus hagerupii	see CRANBERRY
Oxycoccus macrocarpos	see CRANBERRY
Oxycoccus microcarpus	see CRANBERRY
Oxycoccus palustris	see CRANBERRY
Oxycoccus quadripetalus	see CRANBERRY
Oxykrinin	see SECRETIN
Oyster Shell Calcium	see CALCIUM
P. Leucotomos	see POLYPODIUM LEUCOTOMOS
P. Ternata	see PINELLIA TERNATA
P57	see HOODIA
PABA	see PARA-AMINOBENZOIC ACID (PABA)
Pachyrhizus thunbergianus	see KUDZU
Pacific Kelp	see ALGIN
Pacific Valerian	see VALERIAN
Pacific Yew	see YEW
Padamate O	see PARA-AMINOBENZOIC ACID (PABA)
Padang-cassia	see CINNAMON bark
Paddock-pipes	see HORSETAIL
Paekch'ul	see ATRACTYLODES
Paeonia	see PEONY
Paeoniae Radix	see PEONY
Pagla-ka-dawa	see INDIAN SNAKEROOT
PAGODA TREE	see PAGODA TREE
Pahari pudina	see SPEARMINT
Paigle	see COWSLIP
Paigle Peggle	see COWSLIP
Paintedleaf	see POINSETTIA
Pak Chi Lawm	see WATER DROPWORT
Pakistani Ephedra	see EPHEDRA
Pale Coneflower	see ECHINACEA
Pale Gentian	see GENTIAN
Pale Mara	see FEVER BARK
Pale Psyllium	see BLOND PSYLLIUM
Pali-Mara	see FEVER BARK
Palm Kernel Oil	see PALM OIL
PALM OIL	see PALM OIL
Palm Oil Carotene	see PALM OIL
Palma Christi	see CASTOR
Palmier Nain	see SAW PALMETTO
Palo de Santa Maria	see LAURELWOOD
Palo Maria	see LAURELWOOD
Palsy Root	see MARSH MARIGOLD
Palsywort	see COWSLIP
P-Aminobenzoic Acid	see PARA-AMINOBENZOIC ACID (PABA)
Panama Bark	see QUILLAIA
Panama Ipecac	see IPECAC

Pentaptera arjuna...................................see TERMINALIA
Pentaptera glabra..................................see TERMINALIA
PEONY ....see PEONY
Pepe............... see BLACK PEPPER AND WHITE PEPPER
Pepino Montero...................................see BITTER MELON
Pepo... see PUMPKIN
Pepper Bark...................................... see WINTER'S BARK
Pepper Extract...
.... see BLACK PEPPER AND WHITE PEPPER
Pepper Plant ....
.... see BLACK PEPPER AND WHITE PEPPER
Pepper Wood .... see NORTHERN PRICKLY ASH
Pepper-and-salt ....see SHEPHERD'S PURSE
Peppercorn ..... see BLACK PEPPER AND WHITE PEPPER
PEPPERMINT .... see PEPPERMINT
Pepperrot.................................... see HORSERADISH
Pereira Brava.......................................see PAREIRA
Pericarpium .... see SWEET ORANGE
PERILLA ....see PERILLA
Periploca sylvestris .... see GYMNEMA
PERIWINKLE ....see MADAGASCAR PERIWINKLE,
PERIWINKLE
Perna Canaliculus...
.... see NEW ZEALAND GREEN-LIPPED MUSSEL
Persea americana................................ see AVOCADO
Persea gratissima .... see AVOCADO
Persea leiogyna .... see AVOCADO
Persea persea .... see AVOCADO
Persely .... see PARSLEY
Persian Lilac... see NEEM
Persian Willow .... see FIREWEED
Persil .... see PARSLEY
Persimmon ....see JAPANESE PERSIMMON
Personata..see BURDOCK
PERU BALSAM ....see PERU BALSAM
Peru-apple ....see JIMSON WEED
Peruvian Bark..................................... see CINCHONA
Peruvian Coca .... see COCA
Peruvian Ginseng ....see MACA
Peruvian Rhatany ....see RHATANY
Petasites...see BUTTERBUR
Peter's Cress....................................... see SAMPHIRE
Petersylinge.......................................see PARSLEY
Petite Sirah .... see GRAPE
Petroselini Fructus .... see PARSLEY
Petroselini Herba .... see PARSLEY
Petroselinum crispum........................... see PARSLEY
Petroselinum hortense .... see PARSLEY
Petroselinum sativum........................... see PARSLEY
Petroselinum vulgare .... see PARSLEY
Petrosilini Radix .... see PARSLEY
Pettigree ....see BUTCHER'S BROOM
Petty Morel.............................. see BLACK NIGHTSHADE
Petty Mugget.............................. see LADY'S BEDSTRAW
Petty Mulleins .... see COWSLIP
Petty Whin.............................see SPINY RESTHARROW
Pettymorell.......................... see AMERICAN SPIKENARD
Peucedanum graveolens .... see DILL
Peumus boldus ....see BOLDO
Peumus fragrans...................................see BOLDO
Pewterwort ....see HORSETAIL
PEYOTE .... see PEYOTE
Pfaffia...see SUMA
Pfaffia paniculata ....see SUMA
Pfeffer .... see BLACK PEPPER AND WHITE PEPPER

Pferdefut.. see COLTSFOOT
PGG Glucan .... see BETA GLUCANS
Phaca membranacea............................ see ASTRAGALUS
Phadena ....see JAMBOLAN
Phalaris zizanioides...................................... see VETIVER
Phaseoli Fructus.................................see BEAN POD
Phaseolus max Soja hispida ....see SOY, SOYBEAN OIL
Phaseolus vulgaris................................see BEAN POD
PHEASANT'S EYE .... see PHEASANT'S EYE
Phellodendri cortex ....see PHELLODENDRON
PHELLODENDRON.....................see PHELLODENDRON
PHENYLALANINE ....see PHENYLALANINE
Philanthropium .... see BURDOCK
Phoenix dactylifera ....see DATE PALM
Phoradendron flavescens....... see AMERICAN MISTLETOE
Phoradendron leucarpum ...... see AMERICAN MISTLETOE
Phoradendron macrophyllum.............................
.... see AMERICAN MISTLETOE
Phoradendron serontium .... see AMERICAN MISTLETOE
Phoradendron tomentosum ... see AMERICAN MISTLETOE
Phosphate of Soda.........................see PHOSPHATE SALTS
PHOSPHATE SALTS ....see PHOSPHATE SALTS
PHOSPHATIDYLCHOLINE ....
.... see PHOSPHATIDYLCHOLINE
PHOSPHATIDYLSERINE ....see PHOSPHATIDYLSERINE
Phragmites.. see REED HERB
Phragmites australis .... see REED HERB
Phragmites communis............................ see REED HERB
Phragmites longivalvis .... see REED HERB
Phragmites vulgaris .... see REED HERB
Phyllanthus emblica ....see INDIAN GOOSEBERRY
Phyllanthus niruri .... see CHANCA PIEDRA
Phylloquinone ....see VITAMIN K
Physalis alkekengi.............................see WINTER CHERRY
Physalis somnifera .... see ASHWAGANDHA
Physic Root .... see BLACK ROOT
Physostigma venenosum ....see CALABAR BEAN
Physotigma ....see CALABAR BEAN
Phytic Acid ....see IP-6
Phytoestrogen................................... see ALFALFA; ANISE;
BLACK COHOSH; DONG QUAI;
FENNEL; FLAXSEED; GINSENG, SIBERIAN;
LICORICE; RED CLOVER;
RESVERATROL; SOY; WILD YAM
Phytolacca americana............................... see POKEWEED
Phytolacca Berry .... see POKEWEED
Phytolacca decandra................................. see POKEWEED
Phytolithic Silica...............................see SILICON
Phytomenadione.................................see VITAMIN K
Phytonadione (K1)............................see VITAMIN K
Phytoprogestin ....see OREGANO
Phytostanol .... see SITOSTANOL
Phytosterols................................ see BETA-SITOSTEROL
Pica-pica .... see COWHAGE
Picea abies................................see HEMLOCK SPRUCE
Picea aetheroleum ....see HEMLOCK SPRUCE
Picea excelsa ....see HEMLOCK SPRUCE
Pickaway Anise .... see WAFER ASH
Pickled Ume...............................see JAPANESE APRICOT
Pick-pocket ....see SHEPHERD'S PURSE
Picrasma .... see QUASSIA
PICRORHIZA.............................see PICRORHIZA
Pie Cherry ....see SOUR CHERRY
Pierce-stone .... see SAMPHIRE
Pigeonberry .... see POKEWEED

Medical professionals should consult the Professional Version at www.NaturalDatabase.com.

Pigeon's Grass..................................see VERBENA
Pigeonweed......................................see VERBENA
Pignut ....see JOJOBA
Pigrush ....see KNOTWEED
Pigweed.................... see GOUTWEED, KNOTWEED
Pigwood...see WAHOO
Pilewort........ see AMARANTH, BULBOUS BUTTERCUP, LESSER CELANDINE
Piliolerial ....see PENNYROYAL
Pillbearing Spurge.........................see EUPHORBIA
Pilocarpus microphyllus............................see JABORANDI
Pilosella officinarum .... see MOUSE EAR
Pilot Plant ....see CUP PLANT
Pilot Weed ....see ROSINWEED
Pimela luzonica .... see ELEMI
Pimenta ....see ALLSPICE, BLACK PEPPER AND WHITE PEPPER
Pimenta dioica...............................see ALLSPICE
Pimenta officinalis ....see ALLSPICE
Pimenta-longa ....see INDIAN LONG PEPPER
Pimento .... see ALLSPICE, CAPSICUM
Pimienta .... see BLACK PEPPER AND WHITE PEPPER
Pimpernell ....see PIMPINELLA
PIMPINELLA..............................see PIMPINELLA
Pimpinella anisum...............................see ANISE
Pimpinella magna.........................see PIMPINELLA
Pimpinella major..........................see PIMPINELLA
Pimpinella saxifraga.....................see PIMPINELLA
Pimpinellae Herba........................see PIMPINELLA
Pimpinellae Radix........................see PIMPINELLA
Pin Heads .... see GERMAN CHAMOMILE
Pinag .... see ARECA
PINE..see PINE
Pine Bark Extract .... see PYCNOGENOL
Pine Pollen ....see BEE POLLEN
Pineal Hormone .... see MELATONIN
Pineapple Enzyme.........................see BROMELAIN
PINELLIA TERNATA ....see PINELLIA TERNATA
Piney .... see PEONY
Pini atheroleum ....see PINE
Pini turiones ....see PINE
PINK ROOT .... see PINK ROOT
Pinlag ....see ARECA
Pin-ma Ts'ao .... see DANSHEN
Pinto Bean ....see BEAN POD
Pinus abies ....see HEMLOCK SPRUCE
Pinus australis .... see TURPENTINE OIL
Pinus balsamea........................... see CANADA BALSAM
PINUS BARK .... see PINUS BARK
Pinus larix .... see LARCH TURPENTINE
Pinus maritima .... see PYCNOGENOL
Pinus montana................... see DWARF PINE NEEDLE
Pinus mugo .... see DWARF PINE NEEDLE
Pinus palustris .... see TURPENTINE OIL
Pinus pinaster....... see PYCNOGENOL, TURPENTINE OIL
Pinus pumilio .... see DWARF PINE NEEDLE
Pinus radiata.......................................see PINE
Pinus Sylvestris ....see PINE
Pinus viminalis....................see HEMLOCK SPRUCE
Piper .... see BLACK PEPPER AND WHITE PEPPER
Piper cubeba ....see CUBEBS
Piper longum....................see INDIAN LONG PEPPER
Piper methysticum ....see KAVA
Piper nigrum......................................
.... see BLACK PEPPER AND WHITE PEPPER

Piperine .... see BLACK PEPPER AND WHITE PEPPER
Pipiltzintzintli.................................see DIVINER'S SAGE
Pippali ....see INDIAN LONG PEPPER
Pipperidge ....see EUROPEAN BARBERRY
Piprage ....see EUROPEAN BARBERRY
PIPSISSEWA ....see PIPSISSEWA
Piratancara ....see CATUABA
Piripiri .... see ADRUE
Piscidia communis ....see JAMAICAN DOGWOOD
Piscidia erythrina ....see JAMAICAN DOGWOOD
Piscidia piscipula ....see JAMAICAN DOGWOOD
Pissenlit.....................................see DANDELION
Pistacia lentiscus .... see MASTIC
PITCHER PLANT ....see PITCHER PLANT
Pitirishi.............................see CHANCA PIEDRA
Pituri ....see CORKWOOD TREE
Pix Cadi.......................................see CADE OIL
Pix Juniper ....see CADE OIL
Pix Liquida ....see PINE
Pix Oxycedri ....see CADE OIL
Plague Root......................................see BUTTERBUR
Plant of Immortality...............................see ALOE
Plant Protease Concentrate .... see BROMELAIN, PAPAIN
Plant Stanol .... see SITOSTANOL
Plant Sterols .... see BETA-SITOSTEROL
Plantaginis Lanceolatae Herba.........................
.... see BUCKHORN PLANTAIN
Plantaginis Ovatae Semen...............see BLOND PSYLLIUM
Plantaginis Ovatae Testa ....see BLOND PSYLLIUM
Plantago decumbens.....................see BLOND PSYLLIUM
Plantago fastigiata ....see BLOND PSYLLIUM
Plantago insularis......................see BLOND PSYLLIUM
Plantago ispaghula.....................see BLOND PSYLLIUM
Plantago lanceolata .... see BUCKHORN PLANTAIN
Plantago major .... see GREAT PLANTAIN
Plantago ovata.........................see BLOND PSYLLIUM
Plantago psyllium .... see BLACK PSYLLIUM
Plantain ....see BLACK PSYLLIUM, BUCKHORN PLANTAIN, GREAT PLANTAIN, WATER PLANTAIN
Plant-derived Liquid Minerals ....
.... see COLLOIDAL MINERALS
Platycladus orientalis ....see ORIENTAL ARBORVITAE
PLC .... see PROPIONYL-L-CARNITINE
Plectranthus barbatus .... see FORSKOLIN
Pleurisy ....see PLEURISY ROOT
PLEURISY ROOT ....see PLEURISY ROOT
Plum ....see JAMBOLAN
Plumrocks .... see COWSLIP
PMD.................................see LEMON EUCALYPTUS
P-menthane Diol ....see LEMON EUCALYPTUS
P-menthane-3,8-diol.................see LEMON EUCALYPTUS
PMF ....see METHOXYLATED FLAVONES
Po Xue Cao .... see RABDOSIA RUBESCENS
Pocan.. see POKEWEED
Pockwood.................. see GUAIAC WOOD resin, wood
Podophylli pelati rhizoma/resina .... see PODOPHYLLUM
Podophyllin .... see PODOPHYLLUM
PODOPHYLLUM .... see PODOPHYLLUM
Poet's Jessamine..................................see JASMINE
Pogostemon cablin .... see PATCHOULY OIL
Pogostemon heyneanus.....................see PATCHOULY OIL
Pogostemon patchouly .... see PATCHOULY OIL
Pohl ....see MANACA
POINSETTIA .... see POINSETTIA

Poison Ash .... see FRINGETREE	POMEGRANATE .... see POMEGRANATE
Poison Black Cherries......................... see BELLADONNA	Pomelo .... see GRAPEFRUIT
Poison Flag .... see ORRIS	Pond Lily.................. see AMERICAN WHITE POND LILY
Poison Fool's Parsley .... see HEMLOCK	Ponkoranti .... see SALACIA
POISON IVY .... see POISON IVY	Poogiphalam .... see ANDROGRAPHIS, ARECA
Poison Lettuce.................................... see WILD LETTUCE	Poolroot...see SANICLE
Poison Nut...................................... see NUX VOMICA	Poor Man's Parmacettie ....see SHEPHERD'S PURSE
Poison Parsnip............................ see WATER HEMLOCK	Poor Man's Treacle ....see GARLIC
Poison Tobacco .... see HENBANE	Poor Man's Weatherglass......... see SCARLET PIMPERNEL
Poison Vine ....see POISON IVY	Popinac Absolute .... see CASSIE ABSOLUTE
Poisonberry .... see BLACK NIGHTSHADE,	POPLAR .... see POPLAR
LEVANT BERRY	Popotillo...........................see EPHEDRA, MORMON TEA
Poison-hemlock.....................................see HEMLOCK	Poppy California ....see CALIFORNIA POPPY
POISONOUS BUTTERCUP	Populi Cortex .... see ASPEN
...............................see POISONOUS BUTTERCUP	Populi Folium ....see ASPEN
Poivre .... see BLACK PEPPER AND WHITE PEPPER	Populi Gemma .... see POPLAR
Poivre Long............................see INDIAN LONG PEPPER	Populus balsamifera .... see POPLAR
Poivre Noir..... see BLACK PEPPER AND WHITE PEPPER	Populus canadensis .... see POPLAR
Poke.. see POKEWEED	Populus candicans................................... see POPLAR
Pokeberry .... see POKEWEED	Populus euramericana .... see POPLAR
POKEWEED.. see POKEWEED	Populus marilandica .... see POPLAR
Polar Plant....................................... see CUP PLANT,	Populus serotina .... see POPLAR
ROSEMARY, ROSINWEED	Populus tacamahacca .... see POPLAR
Polecatbush .... see SWEET SUMACH	Populus tremula .... see ASPEN
Polecatweed ....see SKUNK CABBAGE	Populus tremuloides.................................see ASPEN
Polemonium caeruleum .... see JACOB'S LADDER	Porangaba................................ see CHA DE BUGRE
Polemonium reptans.............................see ABSCESS ROOT	Porcelain Clay .... see KAOLIN
Poleo .... see JAPANESE MINT	PORIA MUSHROOM .... see PORIA MUSHROOM
POLICOSANOL ....see POLICOSANOL	Porites species.....................................see CORAL
Poligonum .... see FO-TI	Porteranthus trifoliatus.....................see INDIAN PHYSIC
Poligonum multiflorum .... see FO-TI	Porter's Licorice Root ....see OSHA
Pollen ....see BEE POLLEN	Portland Arrowroot ....see ARUM
Pollen d'Abeille ....see BEE POLLEN	Pot .... see MARIJUANA
Polygala amara.......................see BITTER MILKWORT	Pot Barley..see BARLEY
Polygala glomerata....................................see SENEGA	Pot Marigold .... see CALENDULA
Polygala japonica ....see SENEGA	POTASSIUM .... see POTASSIUM
Polygala reinii ....see SENEGA	Potassium Acetate .... see POTASSIUM
Polygala senega.......................................see SENEGA	Potassium Acid Phosphate ....see PHOSPHATE SALTS
Polygala tenuifolia ....see SENEGA	Potassium Bicarbonate......................... see POTASSIUM
Polygalae Radix ....see SENEGA	Potassium Biphosphate ....see PHOSPHATE SALTS
Polygonatum multiflorum .... see SOLOMON'S SEAL	Potassium Chloride .... see POTASSIUM
Polygoni avicularis herba.......................... see KNOTWEED	Potassium Citrate .... see POTASSIUM
Polygoni multiflora ....see HU ZHANG	Potassium Dihydrogen Orthophosphate ....
Polygonum .... see FO-TI	....see PHOSPHATE SALTS
Polygonum aviculare ....see KNOTWEED	Potassium Gluconate.......................... see POTASSIUM
Polygonum bistorta .... see BISTORT	Potassium Glycerophosphate..................... see POTASSIUM
Polygonum cuspidatum..........................see HU ZHANG	Potassium Iodide...................................see IODINE
Polygonum hydropiper.......................... see SMARTWEED	Potassium Phosphate....................see PHOSPHATE SALTS,
Polygonum multiflorum .... see FO-TI	POTASSIUM
Polygonum tataricum............................. see BUCKWHEAT	Potassium Pyruvate .... see PYRUVATE
Polymethoxylated Flavones	POTATO ....see POTATO
.......................see METHOXYLATED FLAVONES	Potency Wood ....see MUIRA PUAMA
Poly-NAG .... see N-ACETYL GLUCOSAMINE	POTENTILLA .... see POTENTILLA, TORMENTIL
Polypodium .... see POLYPODIUM LEUCOTOMOS	Potentilla anserina .... see POTENTILLA
Polypodium filix-femina .... see LADY FERN	Potentilla erecta...................................... see TORMENTIL
POLYPODIUM LEUCOTOMOS..................................	Potentilla reptans..
.... see POLYPODIUM LEUCOTOMOS	..............................see EUROPEAN FIVE-FINGER GRASS
Polyporus .... see PORIA MUSHROOM	Potentilla tormentilla................................. see TORMENTIL
Polyporus versicolor .... see CORIOLUS MUSHROOM	Potentilla vesca ....see STRAWBERRY
Polysaccharide Krestin.......... see CORIOLUS MUSHROOM	Potentilla virginiana ....see STRAWBERRY
Polysaccharide Peptide .... see CORIOLUS MUSHROOM	Potentilla viridis.................................see STRAWBERRY
Polysaccharide-K .... see CORIOLUS MUSHROOM	Poterium officinale........................ see GREATER BURNET
Polystictus versicolor .... see CORIOLUS MUSHROOM	Poverty Weed ....see OX-EYE DAISY
Polyunsaturated Fatty Acids ....see COD LIVER OIL,	Povidone Iodine ....see IODINE
OMEGA-6 FATTY ACIDS	Prairie Dock ....see CUP PLANT

Natural Medicines Comprehensive Database Consumer Version (209) 472-2244

Prairie Grub...see WAFER ASH
Prasterone... see DHEA
Prayer Beads ....see PRECATORY BEAN
Prayer Head................................see PRECATORY BEAN
Prebiotic ....see FRUCTO-OLIGOSACCHARIDES, INULIN
PRECATORY BEAN....................see PRECATORY BEAN
Precipitated Calcium Phosphate ....see PHOSPHATE SALTS
Predigested Spleen Extract .... see SPLEEN EXTRACT
Predigested Thymus Extract .... see THYMUS EXTRACT
Pregnancy Hormone..........................see PROGESTERONE
Pregnanedione..................................see PROGESTERONE
PREGNENOLONE......................... see PREGNENOLONE
Prele ....see HORSETAIL
PREMORSE .... see PREMORSE
Premorse scaboius .... see PREMORSE
Pretty Betsy .... see RED-SPUR VALERIAN
Prick Madam.......................see COMMON STONECROP
Prickly Ash...................... see NORTHERN PRICKLY ASH,
                                              SOUTHERN PRICKLY ASH
Prickly Eleutherococcus............. see GINSENG, SIBERIAN
PRICKLY PEAR CACTUS ....
......................................see PRICKLY PEAR CACTUS
Prickly Yellow Wood.........see SOUTHERN PRICKLY ASH
Prickwood ....see WAHOO
Pride of China .... see NEEM
Pride-of-India...see BANABA
Prideweed........................... see CANADIAN FLEABANE
Priest's Crown .... see DANDELION
Primrose .... see COWSLIP, EVENING PRIMROSE OIL
Primula...see COWSLIP
Primula elatior.......................................see COWSLIP
Primula officinalis ....see COWSLIP
Primula veris ....see COWSLIP
Prince's Feather............... see AMARANTH, POTENTILLA
Prince's Pine................................... see PIPSISSEWA
Privet.....................................see GLOSSY PRIVET
Proacemic Acid .... see PYRUVATE
Proanthodyn .... see GRAPE
Probiotics ...... see BIFIDOBACTERIA, LACTOBACILLUS,
                        SACCHAROMYCES BOULARDII, YOGURT
PROCAINE...see PROCAINE
Processed Bovine Cartilage .... see BOVINE CARTILAGE
Procyandiol Oligomers .... see PYCNOGENOL
Procyanidin Oligomers .... see PYCNOGENOL
Procyanidolic Oligomers .... see GRAPE, PYCNOGENOL
Progestational Hormone.....................see PROGESTERONE
PROGESTERONE...........................see PROGESTERONE
Progesteronum ....see PROGESTERONE
PROPIONYL-L-CARNITINE......................................
......................................see PROPIONYL-L-CARNITINE
PROPOLIS...................................see PROPOLIS
Proteinase .... see TRYPSIN
Proteolytic Enzyme .... see TRYPSIN
Protykin .... see RESVERATROL
ProVitamin A ....see BETA-CAROTENE
Pruche de l'Est ....see PINUS BARK
Prunella .... see SELF-HEAL
Prunella vulgaris .... see SELF-HEAL
Pruni Spinosae Flos .... see BLACKTHORN
Pruni Spinosae Fructus .... see BLACKTHORN
Prunus africana.....................................see PYGEUM
Prunus amygdalus .... see BITTER ALMOND
Prunus amygdalus dulcis..................see SWEET ALMOND
Prunus armeniaca ....see APRICOT
Prunus avium .... see SWEET CHERRY

Prunus cerasus...................................see SOUR CHERRY
Prunus communis...........................see BITTER ALMOND
Prunus dulcis .... see BITTER ALMOND
Prunus grandifolia............see CHERRY LAUREL WATER
Prunus laurocerasus ....see CHERRY LAUREL WATER
Prunus mume ....see JAPANESE APRICOT
Prunus serotina........................... see WILD CHERRY
Prunus spinosa .... see BLACKTHORN
Prunus virginiana .... see WILD CHERRY
Prunus vulgaris ....see SOUR CHERRY
Pseudoginseng Root...........see PANAX PSEUDOGINSENG
Pseudosasa japonica.. see BAMBOO
Pseudotsuga douglasii ....see OREGON FIR BALSAM
Pseudotsuga menziesii ....see OREGON FIR BALSAM
Pseudotsuga mucronata............see OREGON FIR BALSAM
Pseudotsuga taxifolia ....see OREGON FIR BALSAM
Psidium .... see GUAVA
Psidium guajava .... see GUAVA
Psi-psi-carotene.................................see LYCOPENE
PSK.............................see CORIOLUS MUSHROOM
Psoralea linearis .... see RED BUSH TEA
Psoralea tetragonoloba .... see GUAR GUM
Psoriacin..................... see BOVINE CARTILAGE
Psoriacin-T .... see BOVINE CARTILAGE
PSP...............................see CORIOLUS MUSHROOM
Psychotria ipecacuanha .... see IPECAC
Psyllion .... see BLACK PSYLLIUM
Psyllios .... see BLACK PSYLLIUM
Psyllium afra ....see BLACK PSYLLIUM
Psyllium arenaria ....see BLACK PSYLLIUM
Psyllium indica ....see BLACK PSYLLIUM
Psyllium Seed .... see BLACK PSYLLIUM
Ptarmigan Berry .... see UVA URSI
PtdSer......................see PHOSPHATIDYLSERINE
Ptelea trifoliata .... see WAFER ASH
Pterocarpus santalinus.................. see RED SANDALWOOD
Pteroylglutamic Acid .... see FOLIC ACID
Pteroylmonoglutamic Acid .... see FOLIC ACID
Pteroylpolyglutamate .... see FOLIC ACID
Ptychopetali lignum ....see MUIRA PUAMA
Ptychopetalum olacoides ....see MUIRA PUAMA
Ptychopetalum uncinatum.................see MUIRA PUAMA
Public House Plant.........................see ASARABACCA
Pudding Grass .... see PENNYROYAL
Pudina .... see JAPANESE MINT
Pueraria .... see KUDZU
Puerto Rican Cherry.............................. see ACEROLA
PUFA................. see FISH OIL, OMEGA-6 FATTY ACIDS
PUFF BALL.....................................see PUFF BALL
Puga .... see ARECA
Pukeweed .... see LOBELIA
Pulegium .... see PENNYROYAL
Pulegium vulgare .... see PENNYROYAL
Pulmonaire officinalis ....see LUNGWORT
Pulmonariae Herba..........................see LUNGWORT
PULSATILLA..................................see PULSATILLA
Pumacuchu ....see RHATANY
Pumilio Pine...see PINE
PUMPKIN.................................. see PUMPKIN
PUNCTURE VINE ....see PUNCTURE VINE
Puncture Weed .... see PUNCTURE VINE
Punica granatum..........................see POMEGRANATE
Punk Tree...............................see CAJEPUT OIL
Punnanga..see LAURELWOOD
Pupurweide .... see WILLOW BARK

Pure Thymic Extract .... see THYMUS EXTRACT
Purging Flax...................see MOUNTAIN FLAX
Purging Thorn .... see SEA BUCKTHORN
Purines.. see RNA AND DNA
Purple Boneset .... see GRAVEL ROOT
Purple Clover ....see RED CLOVER
Purple Cockle.............................. see CORN COCKLE
Purple Cone Flower ....see ECHINACEA
Purple Foxglove .... see DIGITALIS
Purple Lapacho ....see PAU D'ARCO
Purple Leptandra .... see BLACK ROOT
PURPLE LOOSESTRIFE ...... see PURPLE LOOSESTRIFE
Purple Medick .... see ALFALFA
Purple Mulberry ....see BLACK MULBERRY
Purple Osier .... see WILLOW BARK
Purple Osier Willow.................... see WILLOW BARK
Purple Passion Flower.....................see PASSIONFLOWER
Purple Pitcher Plant....................see PITCHER PLANT
Purple Rocket.................................... see FIREWEED
Purple Side-saddle Flower ....see PITCHER PLANT
Purple Sprouting Broccoli........................ see BROCCOLI
Purple Turk's Cap Lily............................. see MARTAGON
Purple Willow-Herb .... see PURPLE LOOSESTRIFE
Purpursonnenhutkraut....................see ECHINACEA
Purpursonnenhutwurzel ....see ECHINACEA
Purshiana Bark ....see CASCARA
P'u-T'ao .... see BITTER MELON
Putcha-pat ....see PATCHOULY OIL
Putiha ....see JAPANESE MINT, SPEARMINT
Putikaranja .... see DIVI-DIVI
PYCNOGENOL .... see PYCNOGENOL
Pygenol .... see PYCNOGENOL
PYGEUM....................................see PYGEUM
Pygeum africanum ....see PYGEUM
Pyinma ....see BANABA
PYRETHRUM.............................see PYRETHRUM
Pyrethrum cinerariifolium......................see PYRETHRUM
Pyrethrum parthenium .... see FEVERFEW
Pyridoxal....................see PYRIDOXINE (VITAMIN B6)
Pyridoxal Phosphate........see PYRIDOXINE (VITAMIN B6)
Pyridoxamine ....see PYRIDOXINE (VITAMIN B6)
PYRIDOXINE (VITAMIN B6)................................
.................................see PYRIDOXINE (VITAMIN B6)
Pyrimidines .... see RNA AND DNA
Pyroleum juniperi....................see CADE OIL
Pyroleum oxycedri ....see CADE OIL
Pyrus Asiae-mediae............................ see PEAR
Pyrus aucuparia.................. see MOUNTAIN ASH
Pyrus balansae.................................. see PEAR
Pyrus bourgaeana .... see PEAR
Pyrus communis................................. see PEAR
Pyrus cydonia .... see QUINCE
Pyrus domestica .... see PEAR
Pyrus elata .... see PEAR
Pyrus medvedevii .... see PEAR
PYRUVATE .... see PYRUVATE
Pyruvic Acid................................ see PYRUVATE
Qian Ceng Ta .... see CHINESE CLUB MOSS
Qing Dai..................................... see ISATIS
Qing Hao...............................see SWEET ANNIE
Qinghao..................................see SWEET ANNIE
Qinghaosu ....see SWEET ANNIE
Quack Grass ....see WHEATGRASS
Quaker.......................................see ARUM
Quaker Bonnet ....see SKULLCAP

Quaker Buttons .... see NUX VOMICA
Quaking Aspen.............................. see ASPEN
QUASSIA .... see QUASSIA
Quassia amara .... see QUASSIA
Quassia simarouba ....see SIMARUBA
Quebra Pedra.................... see CHANCA PIEDRA
QUEBRACHO....................see QUEBRACHO
Quebrachol .... see BETA-SITOSTEROL
Queen Anne's Lace .... see WILD CARROT
Queen of Fruits ....see MANGOSTEEN
Queen of the Meadow .... see GRAVEL ROOT,
                                            MEADOWSWEET
Queen's Crape Myrtle ....see BANABA
QUEEN'S DELIGHT .... see QUEEN'S DELIGHT
Queen's Root.....................see QUEEN'S DELIGHT
Queensland Nut...................... see MACADAMIA NUT
QUERCETIN.....................................see QUERCETIN
Quercetin-3-rhamnoglucoside.................. see RUTIN
Quercetin-3-rutinoside .... see RUTIN
Quercus alba..........................see OAK bark
Quercus Cortex ....see OAK bark
Quercus marina .... see BLADDERWRACK
Quercus pedunculata ....see OAK bark
Quercus petraea.........................see OAK bark
Quercus robur.........................see OAK bark
Quercus sessiliflora ....see OAK bark
Quickbeam .... see MOUNTAIN ASH
Quick-in-the-hand .... see JEWELWEED
QUILLAIA .... see QUILLAIA
Quillaja............................... see QUILLAIA
Quillaja saponaria .... see QUILLAIA
Quimotripsina .... see CHYMOTRYPSIN
Quimsa-kuchu ....see CARQUEJA
Quina-de-condamiana ....see CARQUEJA
QUINCE .... see QUINCE
Quing Hao .... see WORMWOOD
Quinina criolla .... see CHANCA PIEDRA
Quinine............................ see CINCHONA
Quinine Créole .... see CHANCA PIEDRA
Quinsu-cucho ....see CARQUEJA
Quitch Grass..........................see WHEATGRASS
Quitte .... see QUINCE
Quittenbaum .... see QUINCE
Qut....................................see KHAT
Qutiba .... see PUNCTURE VINE
Quwenling.................see LEMON EUCALYPTUS
Rabbiteye Blueberry ....see BLUEBERRY
Rabbits ....see YELLOW TOADFLAX
RABDOSIA RUBESCENS ....
..................see RABDOSIA RUBESCENS
Rabo de Gato......................... see HYSSOP
Rabugem .... see CHA DE BUGRE
Raccoon Berry .... see PODOPHYLLUM
Race Ginger .... see GINGER
Racine de Carline Acaule.................see CARLINA
Racine de Guimauve .... see MARSHMALLOW
Racine d'echininacea ....see ECHINACEA
Radicula nasturtium .... see WATERCRESS
Radis ....see RADISH
RADISH...................................see RADISH
Radix Anchusae .... see ALKANNA
Radix Angelicae Gigantis ....see DONG QUAI
Radix Cardopatiae.......................see CARLINA
Radix Chamaeleontis Albae...............see CARLINA
Radix Codonopsis .... see CODONOPSIS

CONSUMER VERSION

Medical professionals should consult the Professional Version at www.NaturalDatabase.com.

Radix Curcumae..see TURMERIC
Radix Ginseng Rubra........................see GINSENG, PANAX
Radix Isatidis .... see ISATIS
Radix Pimpinelle Franconiae.................see MASTERWORT
Radix Polygoni Multiflori ....see FO-TI
Radix Polygoni Shen Min ....see FO-TI
Radix Puerariae .... see KUDZU
Rag Paper .... see MULLEIN
Ragged Cup ....see CUP PLANT
Ragweed..see TANSY RAGWORT
Ragwort..see ALPINE RAGWORT
            GOLDEN RAGWORT, TANSY RAGWORT
Rainbow Water Celery ....see WATER DROPWORT
Rainbow Weed .... see PURPLE LOOSESTRIFE
Raisin d'Amérique .... see POKEWEED
Raisin d'Ours .... see UVA URSI
Raisins.. see GRAPE
Raiz Para Los Dientes.................................see RHATANY
Rajajambu ....see JAMBOLAN
Rajani ....see TURMERIC
Rakta Khakasa .... see CORN POPPY
Rakta-posta .... see CORN POPPY
R-alpha-lipoic Acid.....................see ALPHA-LIPOIC ACID
Rama Tulsi .... see HOLY BASIL
Ramdana ....see AMARANTH
Ram-Goat Rose...........see MADAGASCAR PERIWINKLE
Rami Buah .... see CHANCA PIEDRA
Ramp ....see ARUM
Ramsons .... see BEAR'S GARLIC
Ramsted....................................see YELLOW TOADFLAX
Ramsthorn .... see EUROPEAN BUCKTHORN
Ranawara .... see CASSIA AURICULATA
Ranunculus .... see LESSER CELANDINE
Ranunculus acris .... see BUTTERCUP
Ranunculus acris subsp. friesianus .... see BUTTERCUP
Ranunculus bulbosus .... see BULBOUS BUTTERCUP
Ranunculus ficaria .... see LESSER CELANDINE
Ranunculus friesianus .... see BUTTERCUP
Ranunculus sceleratus.........see POISONOUS BUTTERCUP
Raphani Sativi Radix ....see RADISH
Raphanus raphanistrum.......................... see WILD RADISH
Raphanus sativus....................................see RADISH
Rasna..see ALPINIA
Ratanhiae Radix ....see RHATANY
Ratanhiawurzel ....see RHATANY
Rattle Pouches.....................see SHEPHERD'S PURSE
Rattle Root ....see BLACK COHOSH
Rattle Top ....see BLACK COHOSH
Rattlebush ....see WILD INDIGO
Rattlesnake Root ....see BETH ROOT,
            BLACK COHOSH, SENEGA
Rattlesnake Violet .....see AMERICAN ADDER'S TONGUE
Rattleweed.....................................see BLACK COHOSH
Rauschpfeffer .... see KAVA
Raute ....see RUE
Rauvolfia serpentina................... see INDIAN SNAKEROOT
Rauwolfae Radix....................... see INDIAN SNAKEROOT
Rauwolfia serpentina................... see INDIAN SNAKEROOT
Rauwolfiawurzel .... see INDIAN SNAKEROOT
Raw Liver...................................... see LIVER EXTRACT
Raw Spleen .... see SPLEEN EXTRACT
Ray-Grass................................. see TAUMELLOOLCH
Recombinant Human Lactoferrin .... see LACTOFERRIN
Red American Ginseng ....see CANAIGRE
Red Atractylodes................................ see ATRACTYLODES

Red BaneBerry........................... see WHITE COHOSH
Red Bay..see MAGNOLIA
Red Bearberry .... see UVA URSI
Red Beet... see BEET
Red Berry...............................see GINSENG, AMERICAN
Red Bilberry .... see ALPINE CRANBERRY
RED BUSH TEA ....see RED BUSH TEA
Red Cabbage ....see CABBAGE
Red Cedar................... see EASTERN RED CEDAR
Red Cedarwood.................. see EASTERN RED CEDAR
Red Cherry.............................see SOUR CHERRY
Red Chickweed .... see SCARLET PIMPERNEL
Red Cinchona Bark .... see CINCHONA
RED CLOVER...............................see RED CLOVER
Red Cockscomb ....see AMARANTH
Red Cole .... see HORSERADISH
Red Date.. see JUJUBE
Red Elm ....see SLIPPERY ELM
Red Fir .... see OREGON FIR BALSAM
Red Ginseng..............................see GINSENG, PANAX
Red Globe .... see GRAPE
Red Guava .... see GUAVA
Red Gum ....see EUCALYPTUS, STORAX
Red Holy Basil............................... see HOLY BASIL
Red Indian Paint.................................. see BLOODROOT
Red Juniper .... see EASTERN RED CEDAR
Red Lapacho ....see PAU D'ARCO
Red Legs .... see BISTORT
Red Malaga .... see GRAPE
RED MAPLE................................see RED MAPLE
Red Morocco .... see PHEASANT'S EYE
Red Palm Oil.......................... see PALM OIL
Red Peony .... see PEONY
Red Pepper ....see CAPSICUM
Red Periwinkle............see MADAGASCAR PERIWINKLE
Red Pimpernel .... see SCARLET PIMPERNEL
Red Plant .... see POKEWEED
Red Poppy ....see CORN POPPY
Red Puccoon .... see BLOODROOT
RED RASPBERRY .... see RED RASPBERRY
Red Reishi .... see REISHI MUSHROOM
Red Rhatany.......................................see RHATANY
Red Rice Yeast ....see RED YEAST
Red River Snakeroot .... see ARISTOLOCHIA
Red Robin .... see KNOTWEED
Red Root .... see BLOODROOT, NEW JERSEY TEA
Red Rooted Sage................................ see DANSHEN
Red Rot .... see SUNDEW
Red Sage ....see DANSHEN, GERMAN SARSAPARILLA
RED SANDALWOOD .... see RED SANDALWOOD
Red Sanderswood........................ see RED SANDALWOOD
Red Saunders .... see RED SANDALWOOD
RED SOAPWORT ....see RED SOAPWORT
Red Sorrel .... see SORREL
Red Squill .... see SQUILL
Red Sunflower.................................see ECHINACEA
Red Tea .... see HIBISCUS
Red Thyme Oil.................................. see THYME
Red Valerian .... see RED-SPUR VALERIAN
Red Vine Leaf AS 195................................ see GRAPE
Red Weed .... see POKEWEED
Red Wheatgrass.................see GERMAN SARSAPARILLA
Red Whortleberry.................... see ALPINE CRANBERRY
RED YEAST ....see RED YEAST
Redberries .... see ALPINE CRANBERRY

Redberry..see UVA URSI
Red-Ink Plant .... see POKEWEED
RED-SPUR VALERIAN .... see RED-SPUR VALERIAN
Reduced DPN...see NADH
Reduced Nicotinamide Adenine Dinucleotide.......see NADH
Reed .... see REED HERB
REED HERB .... see REED HERB
Refried Beans.....................................see BEAN POD
Reglisse ....see LICORICE
Regliz ....see LICORICE
Reifweide .... see WILLOW BARK
REISHI MUSHROOM .... see REISHI MUSHROOM
Ren Dong ....see HONEYSUCKLE
Ren Shen ....see GINSENG, AMERICAN
Rengyo .... see FORSYTHIA
Renshen....................................see GINSENG, PANAX
Renxian ....see GINSENG, PANAX
Requia ....see ANDIROBA
Reseda ....see HENNA
Reshira .... see VETIVER
Resin Tolu .... see TOLU BALSAM
Resina Tolutana .... see TOLU BALSAM
Restharrow ....see SPINY RESTHARROW
RESVERATROL .... see RESVERATROL
Retinispora juniperoides ...... see ORIENTAL ARBORVITAE
Retinoids .... see VITAMIN A
Retinol.. see VITAMIN A
Réunion Vanilla .... see VANILLA
Reynoutria japonica ....see HU ZHANG
RGH-4405 .... see VINPOCETINE
Rhamni Cathartica Fructus ....
.... see EUROPEAN BUCKTHORN
Rhamni Purshianae Cortex ....see CASCARA
Rhamnol .... see BETA-SITOSTEROL
Rhamnus cathartica........... see EUROPEAN BUCKTHORN
Rhamnus frangula .... see ALDER BUCKTHORN
Rhamnus purshiana ....see CASCARA
Rhamnus zizyphus .... see JUJUBE
Rhatanhia ....see RHATANY
Rhatania ....see RHATANY
RHATANY ....see RHATANY
Rhei .... see RHUBARB
Rhei Radix .... see RHUBARB
Rheum .... see RHUBARB
Rheum australe.................................. see RHUBARB
Rheum cultorum................................. see RHUBARB
Rheum emodi .... see RHUBARB
Rheum hybridum .... see RHUBARB
Rheum officinale .... see RHUBARB
Rheum palmatum .... see RHUBARB
Rheum rhabarbarum .... see RHUBARB
Rheum rhaponticum .... see RHUBARB
Rheum tanguticum .... see RHUBARB
Rheumatism Root ....see WILD YAM
Rheumatism Weed .... see PIPSISSEWA
Rhizoma dioscoreae..........................see WILD YAM
Rhizoma iridis..see ORRIS
Rhizome di Kava-Kava .... see KAVA
Rhizome Galangae ....see ALPINIA
Rhodiola .... see ROSEROOT
Rhodiola rosea .... see ROSEROOT
Rhododendri Ferruginei Folium ....
.... see RUSTY-LEAVED RHODODENDRON
Rhododendron ferrugineum..........................
.... see RUSTY-LEAVED RHODODENDRON

Rhododendron groenlandicum............see LABRADOR TEA
Rhododendron palustre .... see MARSH TEA
Rhododendron tomentosum var. tomentosum ....
.... see MARSH TEA
Rhoeados Flos...............................see CORN POPPY
RHUBARB .... see RHUBARB
Rhus aromatica.............................see SWEET SUMACH
Rhus cacodendron .... see TREE OF HEAVEN
Rhus canadensis .... see SWEET SUMACH
Rhus radicans ....see POISON IVY
Rhus toxicodendron ....see POISON IVY
Ribes nero ....see BLACK CURRANT
Ribes Nigri Folium ....see BLACK CURRANT
Ribes nigrum...............................see BLACK CURRANT
Ribgrass........................... see BUCKHORN PLANTAIN
RIBOFLAVIN (VITAMIN B2)................................
.... see RIBOFLAVIN (VITAMIN B2)
Ribonucleic Acid.................... see RNA AND DNA
RIBOSE .... see RIBOSE
Ribwort .... see BUCKHORN PLANTAIN
Ribwort Plantain .... see BUCKHORN PLANTAIN
RICE BRAN .... see RICE BRAN
Rich Weed ....see STONE ROOT
Richleaf .... see STONE ROOT
Richmond ....see SOUR CHERRY
Ricin ....see CASTOR
Ricinus communis ....see CASTOR
Ricinus sanguines ....see CASTOR
Ringworm Powder .... see GOA POWDER
Rio Ipecac .... see IPECAC
Ripplegrass .... see BUCKHORN PLANTAIN
Ritterspornblüten.......................see DELPHINIUM
R-Limonene ....see LIMONENE
RNA AND DNA .... see RNA AND DNA
Robbia .... see MADDER
Robin-run-in-the-grass.........................see CLIVERS
Robin-run-in-the-hedge..................... see GROUND IVY
Rock Brake .... see LADY FERN
Rock Cranberry .... see ALPINE CRANBERRY
Rock Fern.................... see MAIDENHAIR FERN
Rock of Polypody .... see LADY FERN
Rock Parsley .... see PARSLEY
Rockberry........................... see UVA URSI
Rockrose .... see LABDANUM
Rock-rose ....see FROSTWORT
Rock-up-hat..............................see ECHINACEA
Rockweed..................... see BLADDERWRACK
Rockwrack .... see BLADDERWRACK
Rodia riza ....see ROSEROOT
Roga mari...............................see YARROW
Rokitnik .... see SEA BUCKTHORN
Rokujo.............................see DEER VELVET
Roma.............................see POMEGRANATE
ROMAN CHAMOMILE .... see ROMAN CHAMOMILE
Roman Cumin .... see CARAWAY
Roman Laurel.......................... see SWEET BAY
Roman Motherwort........................... see MOTHERWORT
Roman-coriander........................... see BLACK SEED
Romarin Sauvage .... see MARSH TEA
Römische Kamille.................. see ROMAN CHAMOMILE
Ronce d'Amerique .... see CRANBERRY
Rooibos Tea............................ see RED BUSH TEA
Root of the Holy Ghost............................ see ANGELICA
Rorippa armoracia............................. see HORSERADISH
Rorippa nasturtium..........................see WATERCRESS

Medical professionals should consult the Professional Version at www.NaturalDatabase.com.

Rosa alba	see ROSE HIP
Rosa camellia	see CHEROKEE ROSEHIP
Rosa canina	see ROSE HIP
Rosa centifolia	see ROSE HIP
Rosa cherokeensi	see CHEROKEE ROSEHIP
Rosa chinensis	see CHEROKEE ROSEHIP
Rosa damascena	see ROSE HIP
Rosa de castillo	see ROSE HIP
Rosa gallica	see ROSE HIP
Rosa indica	see CHEROKEE ROSEHIP
Rosa laevigata	see CHEROKEE ROSEHIP
Rosa lutetiana	see ROSE HIP
Rosa nivea	see CHEROKEE ROSEHIP
Rosa pomifera	see ROSE HIP
Rosa provincialis	see ROSE HIP
Rosa roulettii	see CHEROKEE ROSEHIP
Rosa rugosa	see ROSE HIP
Rosa sinica	see CHEROKEE ROSEHIP
Rosa ternata	see CHEROKEE ROSEHIP
Rosa villosa	see ROSE HIP
Rosae Pseudofructus Cum Semen	see ROSE HIP
Rosary Pea	see PRECATORY BEAN
Rose Apple	see JAMBOLAN
Rose Bay	see OLEANDER
Rose Bay Willow	see FIREWEED
ROSE GERANIUM OIL	see ROSE GERANIUM OIL
ROSE HIP	see ROSE HIP
Rose Laurel	see MOUNTAIN LAUREL, OLEANDER
Rose Mallow	see HOLLYHOCK
Rose Willow	see AMERICAN DOGWOOD
Rose-A-Rubie	see PHEASANT'S EYE
Roseau commun	see REED HERB
Rosebay	see RUSTY-LEAVED RHODODENDRON
Rosebay Willow	see FIREWEED
Rose-colored Silkweed	see SWAMP MILKWEED
Rosehips	see ROSE HIP
Roselle	see HIBISCUS
ROSEMARY	see ROSEMARY
Rosenoble	see FIGWORT
Rosenroot	see ROSEROOT
ROSEROOT	see ROSEROOT
Rosewood oil	see BOIS DE ROSE OIL
Rosin Rose	see ST. JOHN'S WORT
Rosin Weed	see GUMWEED
ROSINWEED	see CUP PLANT, ROSINWEED
Rosmarinus officinalis	see ROSEMARY
Roter Sonnenhut	see ECHINACEA
Roter Wasserhanf	see GRAVEL ROOT
Rotten Cheese Fruit	see MORINDA
Rottlera tinctoria	see KAMALA
Rou Gui	see CASSIA CINNAMON
Roucou	see ANNATTO
Round Black Spanish Radish	see RADISH
Round Buchu	see BUCHU
Round-leafed Sundew	see SUNDEW
Round-leaved Hepatica	see LIVERWORT
Round-lobe Hepatica	see LIVERWORT
Roupellia grata	see STROPHANTHUS
Rowan Tree	see MOUNTAIN ASH
Roxanthin Red 10	see CANTHAXANTHIN
Royal Jasmine	see JASMINE
ROYAL JELLY	see ROYAL JELLY
RRR-alpha-tocopherol	see VITAMIN E
RS-alpha-lipoic Acid	see ALPHA-LIPOIC ACID
Rubbed Thyme	see THYME
Rubescens	see RABDOSIA RUBESCENS
Rubi Fruticosi Folium	see BLACKBERRY
Rubi Fruticosi Radix	see BLACKBERRY
Rubi Idaei Folium	see RED RASPBERRY
Rubia	see MADDER
Rubus	see RED RASPBERRY
Rubus affinis	see BLACKBERRY
Rubus buschii	see RED RASPBERRY
Rubus canadensis	see BLACKBERRY
Rubus fruticosus	see BLACKBERRY
Rubus idaeus	see RED RASPBERRY
Rubus laciniatus	see BLACKBERRY
Rubus millspaughii	see BLACKBERRY
Rubus occidentalis	see BLACK RASPBERRY
Rubus plicatus	see BLACKBERRY
Rubus strigosus	see RED RASPBERRY
Rubywood	see RED SANDALWOOD
Ruda	see QUASSIA, RUE
RUE	see RUE
Rue officinale	see RUE
Ruibarbo caribe	see MORINDA
Rum Cherry Bark	see WILD CHERRY
Rumalon	see BOVINE CARTILAGE
Rumex	see YELLOW DOCK
Rumex acetosa	see SORREL
Rumex acetosella	see SORREL
Rumex aquaticus	see WATER DOCK
Rumex crispus	see YELLOW DOCK
Rumex hymenosepalus	see CANAIGRE
Rumex obtusifolius	see YELLOW DOCK
Rumput Roman	see YIN CHEN
Run-by-the-ground	see PENNYROYAL
Running Box	see SQUAWVINE
Running Jenny	see MONEYWORT
RUPTUREWORT	see RUPTUREWORT
Rusci aculeati	see BUTCHER'S BROOM
Ruscus aculeatus	see BUTCHER'S BROOM
Rusmari	see ROSEMARY
Russian Krainer Tollkraut	see SCOPOLIA
Russian Licorice	see LICORICE
Russian Penicillin	see PROPOLIS
Russian Root	see GINSENG, SIBERIAN
Rust Treacle	see GARLIC
Rust-Red Rhododendron	see RUSTY-LEAVED RHODODENDRON
RUSTY-LEAVED RHODODENDRON	see RUSTY-LEAVED RHODODENDRON
Ruta graveolens	see RUE
Rutae Folium	see RUE
Rutae Herba	see RUE
RUTIN	see RUTIN
Rutine	see RUTIN
Rutinum	see RUTIN
Rutland Beauty	see GREATER BINDWEED
Rutoside	see RUTIN
Rutosidum	see RUTIN
Rye	see RYE GRASS
RYE GRASS	see RYE GRASS
Rye Grass Pollen Extract	see RYE GRASS
Sabal	see SAW PALMETTO
Sabal Fructus	see SAW PALMETTO
Sabal Serrulata	see SAW PALMETTO
Sabina	see SAVIN TOPS
Sabline Rouge	see ARENARIA RUBRA
Sabugueiro	see AMERICAN ELDER

SACCHAROMYCES BOULARDII ....
.... see SACCHAROMYCES BOULARDII
Saccharomyces Cerevisiae............. see BREWER'S YEAST,
SACCHAROMYCES BOULARDII
Sacha Foster .... see CHANCA PIEDRA
Sacred Bark...see CASCARA
Sacred Basil .... see HOLY BASIL
Sacred Herb... see YERBA SANTA
Sacred Mushroom .... see PEYOTE
Sacred Purple Basil .... see HOLY BASIL
S-adenosyl-L-methionine.................................... see SAMe
Sadgrantha...see CALAMUS
Sadi .... see DIVINER'S SAGE
Sadilata.. see ANDROGRAPHIS
SAFFLOWER...see SAFFLOWER
SAFFRON...see SAFFRON
Saffron crocus ....see SAFFRON
Saffron Marigold .... see TAGETES
Safran ....see SAFFRON
Sagackhomi.. see UVA URSI
SAGE .... see SAGE
Sage of Bethlehem ....see SPEARMINT
Sage of the Seers............................... see DIVINER'S SAGE
Sagrada Bark...see CASCARA
Sahlep .... see SALEP
Sailor's Tobacco ....see MUGWORT
Saint Ignatius-beans .... see IGNATIUS BEAN
Sakau.. see KAVA
SALACIA .... see SALACIA
Salad Chervil .... see CHERVIL
Salad Oil.. see OLIVE
Salai Guggal ....see INDIAN FRANKINCENSE
SALEP .... see SALEP
Salicare .... see PURPLE LOOSESTRIFE
Salicis Cortex .... see WILLOW BARK
Salisburia adiantifolia ....see GINKGO
Salix alba .... see WILLOW BARK
Salix daphnoides .... see WILLOW BARK
Salix fragilis .... see WILLOW BARK
Salix pentandra.............................. see WILLOW BARK
Salix Purpurea .... see WILLOW BARK
Sallaki Guggul ....see INDIAN FRANKINCENSE
Sallow Thorn............................... see SEA BUCKTHORN
Salmon Oil .... see FISH OIL
Saloop .... see SALEP
S-alpha-lipoic Acid Thioctacid ....see ALPHA-LIPOIC ACID
Salsaparilha.................................... see SARSAPARILLA
Salsepareille .... see SARSAPARILLA
Salsify .... see COMFREY
Saltcedar................................. see TAMARIX DIOICA
Salt-rheum Weed................................ see TURTLE HEAD
Salvia................................... see DIVINER'S SAGE
Salvia bowleyana .... see DANSHEN
Salvia divinorum............................. see DIVINER'S SAGE
Salvia fruticosa....................................see GREEK SAGE
Salvia lavandulaefolia .... see SAGE
Salvia miltiorrhiza.................................. see DANSHEN
Salvia officinalis... see SAGE
Salvia przewalskii .... see DANSHEN
Salvia Root.................................... see DANSHEN
Salvia Sclarea.....................................see CLARY SAGE
Salvia triloba ....see GREEK SAGE
Salvia yunnanensis................................ see DANSHEN
Salvinorin .... see DIVINER'S SAGE
Sambilata................................... see ANDROGRAPHIS

Sambrani chettu .... see BRAHMI
Sambuci sambucus .... see ELDERBERRY
Sambucus .... see ELDERFLOWER
Sambucus canadensis................... see AMERICAN ELDER
Sambucus ebulus................................see DWARF ELDER
Sambucus nigra ....see ELDERBERRY, ELDERFLOWER
Samch'il .... see PANAX PSEUDOGINSENG
SAMe .... see SAMe
Samento...................................see CAT'S CLAW
Samm al Ferakh .... see ASHWAGANDHA
Sammy .... see SAMe
SAMPHIRE .... see SAMPHIRE
San Qi................... see PANAX PSEUDOGINSENG
San Qui.................. see PANAX PSEUDOGINSENG
Sanchi ....see PANAX PSEUDOGINSENG
Sand Plantain ....see BLOND PSYLLIUM
Sand Sedge....................see GERMAN SARSAPARILLA
Sandalwood Padauk .... see RED SANDALWOOD
Sandberry .... see UVA URSI
Sanddorn .... see SEA BUCKTHORN
Sanderswood .... see WHITE SANDALWOOD
Sandriedgraswurzelstock ...see GERMAN SARSAPARILLA
Sandwort .... see ARENARIA RUBRA
SANDY EVERLASTING ...... see SANDY EVERLASTING
Sang....................see GINSENG, AMERICAN
Sangre de Dragon............see SANGRE DE GRADO
SANGRE DE GRADO .... see SANGRE DE GRADO
Sangree Root .... see ARISTOLOCHIA
Sangrel .... see ARISTOLOCHIA
Sangue de Agua.............see SANGRE DE GRADO
Sangue de Drago ....see SANGRE DE GRADO
Sanguinaria .... see BLOODROOT
Sanguinaria canadensis .... see BLOODROOT
Sanguinary .... see SHEPHERD'S PURSE, YARROW
Sanguis draconis .... see DRAGON'S BLOOD
Sanguisorba .... see GREATER BURNET
Sanguisorba carnea .... see GREATER BURNET
Sanguisorba officinalis................... see GREATER BURNET
Sanguisorba polygama .... see GREATER BURNET
SANICLE..see SANICLE
Sanicula europaea ....see SANICLE
Saniculae Herba ....see SANICLE
Sanqi .... see PANAX PSEUDOGINSENG
San-qi Ginseng.................. see PANAX PSEUDOGINSENG
Sanqi Powder .... see PANAX PSEUDOGINSENG
Sanshichi ....see PANAX PSEUDOGINSENG
Sansho .... see CHINESE PRICKLY ASH
Santa Maria .... see FEVERFEW
Santal Oil .... see WHITE SANDALWOOD
Santali Lignum Albi .... see WHITE SANDALWOOD
Santali lignum rubrum .... see RED SANDALWOOD
Santalum album .... see WHITE SANDALWOOD
Santolina .... see LAVENDER COTTON
Santolina chamaecyparissus........ see LAVENDER COTTON
Santonica...............................see WORMSEED
Sanuf .... see FENNEL
Saponaria officinalis.........................see RED SOAPWORT
Saponariae Rubrae Radix....................see RED SOAPWORT
Sappan...................... see RED SANDALWOOD
Sarapin ....see PITCHER PLANT
Sardian Nut .... see EUROPEAN CHESTNUT
Sarothamnus scoparius...................... see SCOTCH BROOM
Sarothamnus vulgaris...................... see SCOTCH BROOM
Sarpagandha............................ see INDIAN SNAKEROOT
Sarracenia purpurea ....see PITCHER PLANT

Medical professionals should consult the Professional Version at www.NaturalDatabase.com.

Sarrasin	see	BUCKWHEAT
Sarsa	see	SARSAPARILLA
SARSAPARILLA	see	SARSAPARILLA
Sarsaparillae Radix	see	SARSAPARILLA
Sarsaparillewurzel	see	SARSAPARILLA
Sasa japonica	see	BAMBOO
Sasha Foster	see	CHANCA PIEDRA
SASSAFRAS	see	SASSAFRAS
Sassafras albidum	see	SASSAFRAS
Satahva	see	DILL
Satan's Apple	see	EUROPEAN MANDRAKE
Satapatri	see	ROSE HIP
Satapatrika	see	ROSE HIP
Sati	see	ZEDOARY
Sativari	see	ASPARAGUS
Satureja calamintha	see	CALAMINT
Satureja capitata	see	SPANISH ORIGANUM OIL
Satureja hortensis	see	SUMMER SAVORY
Satureja montana	see	WINTER SAVORY
Satureja nepeta	see	CALAMINT
Satureja obovata	see	WINTER SAVORY
Satyrion	see	SALEP
Sauerdorn	see	EUROPEAN BARBERRY
Sauerkirsche	see	SOUR CHERRY
Sauerkirschenbaum	see	SOUR CHERRY
Sauge	see	SAGE
Saussurea costus	see	COSTUS
Saussurea lappa	see	COSTUS
Saussureae Radix	see	COSTUS
SAVIN TOPS	see	SAVIN TOPS
Savine	see	SAVIN TOPS
Savory	see	SUMMER SAVORY, WINTER SAVORY
SAW PALMETTO	see	SAW PALMETTO
Sawi	see	MARIJUANA
Saxifrage	see	PIMPINELLA
Saxifrax	see	SASSAFRAS
Saynt Johannes Wort	see	ST. JOHN'S WORT
Scabiosa arvensis	see	FIELD SCABIOUS
Scabiosa succisa	see	PREMORSE
Scabish	see	EVENING PRIMROSE OIL
Scabwort	see	ELECAMPANE
Scaldweed	see	DODDER
Scaley Dragon's Claw	see	CORAL ROOT
Scandix cerefolium	see	CHERVIL
Scarlet Berry	see	BITTERSWEET NIGHTSHADE
Scarlet Monarda	see	OSWEGO TEA
SCARLET PIMPERNEL	see	SCARLET PIMPERNEL
Scarlet Sage	see	SAGE
Sceau d'Or	see	GOLDENSEAL
Sceitbezien	see	SEA BUCKTHORN
Scented Fern	see	TANSY
SC-FOS	see	FRUCTO-OLIGOSACCHARIDES
Schilf	see	REED HERB
SCHISANDRA	see	SCHISANDRA
SCHIZONEPETA	see	SCHIZONEPETA
Schizophyllan (SPG)	see	BETA GLUCANS
Schmallblaettrige Kegelblumenwurzel	see	ECHINACEA
Schmallblaettriger Sonnenhut	see	ECHINACEA
Schollkraut	see	GREATER CELANDINE
Schwarze Walnuss	see	BLACK WALNUT
Schwarzkümmel	see	BLACK SEED
Schweintang	see	BLADDERWRACK
Scilla	see	SQUILL
Scilla indica	see	SQUILL
Scilla maritima	see	SQUILL
Sclerotium of Tuckahoe	see	PORIA MUSHROOM
Sclerotium Poriae Cocos	see	PORIA MUSHROOM
Sclerutin	see	RUTIN
Scoke	see	POKEWEED
Scolopendrium vulgare	see	HARTSTONGUE
Scoparium	see	SCOTCH BROOM
Scoparius	see	SCOTCH BROOM
Scopola	see	SCOPOLIA
SCOPOLIA	see	SCOPOLIA
Scopolia carniolica	see	SCOPOLIA
Scopoliae Rhizoma	see	SCOPOLIA
Scotch Barley	see	BARLEY
SCOTCH BROOM	see	SCOTCH BROOM
Scotch Fir	see	PINE
Scotch Heather	see	HEATHER
Scotch Mercury	see	DIGITALIS
Scotch Pine	see	PINE
Scotch Quelch	see	WHEATGRASS
SCOTCH THISTLE	see	SCOTCH THISTLE
Scouring Rush	see	HORSETAIL
Scraperoot	see	OREGON GRAPE
Scratchweed	see	CLIVERS
Scrophula Plant	see	FIGWORT
Scrophularia	see	FIGWORT
Scrophularia marilandica	see	FIGWORT
Scrophularia nodosa	see	FIGWORT
Scrubby Grass	see	SCURVY GRASS
Scubby Trefoil	see	WAFER ASH
Scullcap	see	BAIKAL SKULLCAP, SKULLCAP
SCURVY GRASS	see	SCURVY GRASS, WATERCRESS
Scurvy Root	see	ECHINACEA
Scute	see	BAIKAL SKULLCAP
Scutellaria baicalensis	see	BAIKAL SKULLCAP
Scutellaria lateriflora	see	SKULLCAP
Scutellaria macrantha	see	BAIKAL SKULLCAP
Scutelluria	see	SKULLCAP
Se	see	SELENIUM
Sea Ash	see	SOUTHERN PRICKLY ASH
SEA BUCKTHORN	see	SEA BUCKTHORN
Sea Coral	see	CORAL
Sea Fennel	see	SAMPHIRE
Sea Girdles	see	LAMINARIA
Sea Grape	see	EPHEDRA
Sea Holly	see	ERYNGO
Sea Holme	see	ERYNGO
Sea Hulver	see	ERYNGO
Sea Onion	see	SQUILL
Sea Parsley	see	LOVAGE
Sea Sedge	see	GERMAN SARSAPARILLA
Sea Squill Bulb	see	SQUILL
Sea Wormwood	see	WORMSEED
Seagirdle Thallus	see	LAMINARIA
Sealroot	see	SOLOMON'S SEAL
Sealwort	see	SOLOMON'S SEAL
Seaweed	see	CHLORELLA
Seaweed Gelatin	see	AGAR
Seawrack	see	BLADDERWRACK
Secale Cereale	see	RYE GRASS
Secale Cornutum	see	ERGOT
SECRETIN	see	SECRETIN
Sedum acre	see	COMMON STONECROP
Sedum rhodiola	see	ROSEROOT
Sedum rosea	see	ROSEROOT
See Bright	see	CLARY SAGE
Seed on the Leaf	see	CHANCA PIEDRA

Seed-free Bean Pods .... see BEAN POD
Seedorn .... see SEA BUCKTHORN
Segg .... see ORRIS
Sehydrin .... see HYDRAZINE SULFATE
Selada-air .... see WATERCRESS
Selagine .... see HUPERZINE A
Selenicereus grandiflorus .... see CEREUS
Selenite .... see SELENIUM
SELENIUM .... see SELENIUM
Selenized Yeast .... see SELENIUM
Selenomethionine .... see SELENIUM
SELF-HEAL .... see SANICLE, SELF-HEAL
Selinum monnieri .... see CNIDIUM
Selleriefruchte .... see CELERY
Selleriesamen .... see CELERY
Selom .... see WATER DROPWORT
Semen Anisi .... see ANISE
Semen Cumini Pratensis .... see CARAWAY
Semen Nelumbinis .... see LOTUS
Semences de Carvi .... see CARAWAY
Sementah .... see MANGOSTEEN
Semetah .... see MANGOSTEEN
Seminole Bead .... see PRECATORY BEAN
Seminose .... see D-MANNOSE
Sempervivum tectorum .... see HOUSELEEK
Sena alejandrina .... see SENNA
Senaga Snakeroot .... see SENEGA
Séné d'Egypte .... see SENNA
Seneca .... see SENEGA
Seneca Snakeroot .... see SENEGA
Senecio aureus .... see GOLDEN RAGWORT
Senecio cineraria .... see DUSTY MILLER
Senecio Herb .... see ALPINE RAGWORT
Senecio jacobaea .... see TANSY RAGWORT
Senecio nemorensis .... see ALPINE RAGWORT
Senecio Vulgaris .... see GROUNDSEL
SENEGA .... see SENEGA
Senega Snakeroot .... see SENEGA
Senegalia senegal .... see ACACIA
Seneka .... see SENEGA
Sengreen .... see HOUSELEEK
SENNA .... see SENNA
Senna alexandrina .... see SENNA
Senna auriculata .... see CASSIA AURICULATA
Sennae Folium .... see SENNA
Sennae Fructus .... see SENNA
Septfoil .... see TORMENTIL
Serenoa repens .... see SAW PALMETTO
Serenoa serrulata .... see SAW PALMETTO
Seri .... see WATER DROPWORT
Seriphidium cinum .... see WORMSEED
Serpentaria .... see ARISTOLOCHIA, MONEYWORT
Serpentine-Wood .... see INDIAN SNAKEROOT
Serpent's Tongue ...... see AMERICAN ADDER'S TONGUE,
                        ENGLISH ADDER'S TONGUE
Serpyllum .... see WILD THYME
SERRAPEPTASE .... see SERRAPEPTASE
Serratia peptidase .... see SERRAPEPTASE
Serratiopeptidase .... see SERRAPEPTASE
Serratula spicata .... see MARSH BLAZING STAR
Seso Vegetal .... see ACKEE
Sessile Oak .... see OAK bark
Seven Barks .... see HYDRANGEA
Seville Orange .... see BITTER ORANGE
Shaddock Oil .... see GRAPEFRUIT

Shakuyaku .... see PEONY
Shallaki .... see INDIAN FRANKINCENSE
Shallot .... see ONION
Shamrock .... see WOOD SORREL
Shang .... see GINSENG, AMERICAN
Shangzhou Zhiqiao .... see BITTER ORANGE
Shanzha .... see HAWTHORN
SHARK CARTILAGE .... see SHARK CARTILAGE
SHARK LIVER OIL .... see SHARK LIVER OIL
Sharon Fruit .... see JAPANESE PERSIMMON
Sharp-lobe Hepatica .... see LIVERWORT
Shatapuspha .... see FENNEL
Shatavari .... see ASPARAGUS
Shati .... see ZEDOARY
Shatter Stone .... see CHANCA PIEDRA
Shave Grass .... see HORSETAIL
She Chuang Zi .... see CNIDIUM
She Gen Mu .... see INDIAN SNAKEROOT
Sheep Laurel .... see MOUNTAIN LAUREL
Sheep Sorrel .... see YELLOW DOCK
Sheep-lice .... see HOUND'S TONGUE
Sheep's Sorrel .... see SORREL
Sheggs .... see ORRIS
Shelf Fungi .... see MAITAKE MUSHROOM
SHELLAC .... see SHELLAC
Shellflower .... see TURTLE HEAD
Shelum .... see WATER DROPWORT
Shen Jiang .... see GINGER
Shen Min .... see FO-TI
Sheng Shai Shen .... see GINSENG, PANAX
Shepherd's Barometer .... see SCARLET PIMPERNEL
Shepherd's Club .... see MULLEIN
Shepherd's Heart .... see SHEPHERD'S PURSE
Shepherd's Knapperty .... see TORMENTIL
Shepherd's Knot .... see TORMENTIL
Shepherd's Needle .... see SWEET CICELY
SHEPHERD'S PURSE .... see SHEPHERD'S PURSE
Shepherd's Scrip .... see SHEPHERD'S PURSE
Shepherd's Sprout .... see SHEPHERD'S PURSE
Shepherd's Staff .... see MULLEIN
Shepherd's Thyme .... see WILD THYME
Shi Liu Gen Pi .... see POMEGRANATE
Shi Liu Pi .... see POMEGRANATE
Shield Fern .... see MALE FERN
Shigoka .... see GINSENG, SIBERIAN
Shih Yin Ch'en .... see YIN CHEN
SHIITAKE MUSHROOM ...... see SHIITAKE MUSHROOM
Shikha-mula .... see WILD CARROT
Shitake .... see SHIITAKE MUSHROOM
Shivaphala .... see ANDROGRAPHIS, BAEL
Shoe .... see NERVE ROOT
Shoga .... see GINGER
Shokyo .... see GINGER
Shore Cranberry .... see ALPINE CRANBERRY
Short Buchu .... see BUCHU
Short Chain Fructo-oligosaccharides ....
.... see FRUCTO-OLIGOSACCHARIDES
Sho-saiko-to .... see BUPLEURUM
Shou Wu .... see FO-TI
Shou-Wu-Pian .... see FO-TI
Shovelweed .... see SHEPHERD'S PURSE
Shoyu .... see SOY
Shrubby Hare's-ear .... see BUPLEURUM
Shuang Sui Ma Huang .... see EPHEDRA
Shudha Kupilu .... see NUX VOMICA

Shu-wei Ts'ao	see DANSHEN
Shyama tulsi	see HOLY BASIL
Si	see SILICON
Siberian Beaver	see CASTOREUM
Siberian Ginseng	see GINSENG, SIBERIAN
Sicilian Thyme	see SPANISH ORIGANUM OIL
Sickle-leaf Hare's-ear	see BUPLEURUM
Sicklewort	see BUGLE, SELF-HEAL
Siclewort	see SELF-HEAL
Sida cordifolia	see COUNTRY MALLOW
Side-saddle Plant	see PITCHER PLANT
Sigualuo	see LUFFA
Silberdistelwurz	see CARLINA
Silberweide	see WILLOW BARK
Silerkraut	see ALCHEMILLA
Silica	see SILICON
Silicium	see SILICON
SILICON	see SILICON
Silk Worm Enzyme	see SERRAPEPTASE
Silkworm Extract	see SERRAPEPTASE
Silky Cornel	see AMERICAN DOGWOOD
Silky Loofah	see LUFFA
Silky White Mallow	see COUNTRY MALLOW
Silom	see WATER DROPWORT
Silphium laciniatum	see ROSINWEED
Silphium perfoliatum	see CUP PLANT
Silver Birch	see BIRCH
Silver in Suspending Agent	see COLLOIDAL SILVER
Silver Leaf	see QUEEN'S DELIGHT
Silver Lime	see LINDEN
Silver Linden	see LINDEN
Silver Protein	see COLLOIDAL SILVER
Silver Ragwort	see DUSTY MILLER
Silverhull Buckwheat	see BUCKWHEAT
Silver-morning-glory	see HAWAIIAN BABY WOODROSE
Silverweed	see JEWELWEED, POTENTILLA
Silybin	see MILK THISTLE
Silybum	see MILK THISTLE
Silybum marianum	see MILK THISTLE
Silymarin	see MILK THISTLE
SIMARUBA	see SIMARUBA
Simmondsia californica	see JOJOBA
Simmondsia chinensis	see JOJOBA
Simpler's Joy	see VERBENA
Simson	see GROUNDSEL
Sinapis alba	see WHITE MUSTARD
Sinapis nigra	see BLACK MUSTARD
Sine Semine	see BEAN POD
Sinensetin	see METHOXYLATED FLAVONES
Singer's Plant	see HEDGE MUSTARD
Singletary Pea	see LATHYRUS
Sinsemilla	see MARIJUANA
Sisymbrium nasturtium	see WATERCRESS
Sisymbrium officinale	see HEDGE MUSTARD
SITOSTANOL	see SITOSTANOL
Sitosterin	see BETA-SITOSTEROL
Sitosterol	see BETA-SITOSTEROL
Sitosterolins	see BETA-SITOSTEROL
Sium douglasii	see WATER HEMLOCK
Sium sisarum	see SKIRRET
SJW	see ST. JOHN'S WORT
Ska Maria Pastora	see DIVINER'S SAGE
Skewerwood	see WAHOO
SKIRRET	see SKIRRET
Skoke	see POKEWEED
SKULLCAP	see SKULLCAP
SKUNK CABBAGE	see SKUNK CABBAGE
Skunkbrush	see SWEET SUMACH
Skunkweed	see SKUNK CABBAGE
Slave Wood	see SIMARUBA
S-Limonene	see LIMONENE
Slipper Root	see NERVE ROOT
Slipper Weed	see JEWELWEED
SLIPPERY ELM	see SLIPPERY ELM
Slippery Root	see COMFREY
Sloe Berry	see BLACKTHORN
Sloe Flower	see BLACKTHORN
Slough-Heal	see SELF-HEAL
Small Cranberry	see CRANBERRY
Small Hemlock	see FOOL'S PARSLEY
Small Nettle	see STINGING NETTLE
Small Periwinkle	see PERIWINKLE
Small Radish	see RADISH
Small Spikenard	see AMERICAN SPIKENARD
Smallage	see CELERY, LOVAGE
Smallpox Plant	see PITCHER PLANT
Smallwort	see LESSER CELANDINE
SMARTWEED	see SMARTWEED
Smell Fox	see WOOD ANEMONE
Smellage	see LOVAGE
Smilax	see SARSAPARILLA
Smilax aristolochiaefolii	see SARSAPARILLA
Smilax febrifuga	see SARSAPARILLA
Smilax medica	see SARSAPARILLA
Smilax officinalis	see SARSAPARILLA
Smilax ornata	see SARSAPARILLA
Smilax regelii	see SARSAPARILLA
SMOOTH ALDER	see SMOOTH ALDER
Smooth Hydrangea	see HYDRANGEA
Smooth Lawsonia	see HENNA
Smooth Loofah	see LUFFA
Smooth-leaved Elm	see ELM BARK
Smut Rye	see ERGOT
Snake Berry	see BITTERSWEET NIGHTSHADE
Snake Butter	see SHIITAKE MUSHROOM
Snake Leaf	see AMERICAN ADDER'S TONGUE
Snake Lily	see ORRIS
Snake Root	see SENEGA
Snake Weed	see WATER HEMLOCK
Snakeberry	see WHITE COHOSH
Snakebite	see BETH ROOT, BLOODROOT
Snakehead	see TURTLE HEAD
Snakeroot	see ARISTOLOCHIA ASARABACCA, BITTER MILKWORT, BLACK COHOSH, ECHINACEA, WATER HEMLOCK
Snakeweed	see ARISTOLOCHIA, BISTORT, EUPHORBIA
Snap Bean	see BEAN POD
Snapping Tobacco Wood	see WITCH HAZEL
Sneezeweed	see SNEEZEWORT
SNEEZEWORT	see SNEEZEWORT
Snow Rose	see RUSTY-LEAVED RHODODENDRON
Snowball Bush	see CRAMP BARK
Snowdrop Tree	see FRINGETREE
Snowflower	see FRINGETREE
SO	see SALACIA
Soap Tree Bark	see QUILLAIA
Soapbark	see QUILLAIA
Soapweed	see YUCCA

Soapwort ....see RED SOAPWORT, WHITE SOAPWORT
SOD................ see SUPEROXIDE DISMUTASE
Sodium Alginate .... see ALGIN
Sodium Ascorbate ....see VITAMIN C (ASCORBIC ACID)
Sodium Borate ....see BORON
Sodium Edetate .... see EDTA
Sodium Fluoride ....see FLUORIDE
Sodium Gamma-hydroxybutyrate.......................................
.......................see GAMMA-HYDROXYBUTYRATE (GHB)
Sodium Hyaluronate .... see HYALURONIC ACID
Sodium Monofluorophosphate.......................see FLUORIDE
Sodium Orthophosphate.................. see PHOSPHATE SALTS
Sodium Oxybate..
.......................see GAMMA-HYDROXYBUTYRATE (GHB)
Sodium Oxybutyrate ....
.......................see GAMMA-HYDROXYBUTYRATE (GHB)
Sodium Phosphate.........................see PHOSPHATE SALTS
Sodium Pyruvate .... see PYRUVATE
Sodium Silicate ....see SILICON
Sodium Usniate..................................... see USNEA
Sodom-apple .... see CALOTROPIS
Soja ....see SOY
Soja max..see SOY, SOYBEAN OIL
Sojcomponentsabohne ....see SOY
So-jutsu .... see ATRACTYLODES
Solanum dulcamara..... see BITTERSWEET NIGHTSHADE
Solanum nigrum...................... see BLACK NIGHTSHADE
Solanum Tuberosum ....see POTATO
Soldiers .... see PURPLE LOOSESTRIFE
Soldier's Herb .... see BUCKHORN PLANTAIN
Soldier's Wound Wort ....see YARROW
Solidago canadensis...............................see GOLDENROD
Solidago gigantea................................see GOLDENROD
Solidago longifolia..............................see GOLDENROD
Solidago serotina................................see GOLDENROD
Solidago virgaurea ....see GOLDENROD
SOLOMON'S SEAL .... see SOLOMON'S SEAL
Solsequia ....see MARSH MARIGOLD
Soma .... see AGA
Somalien Myrrh ....see MYRRH
Sonnenhutwurzel................................see ECHINACEA
Sophora japonica......................... see PAGODA TREE
Sophorin .... see RUTIN
Sophretin ....see QUERCETIN
Sorb Apple .... see MOUNTAIN ASH
Sorbi Acupariae Fructus.................... see MOUNTAIN ASH
Sorbus aucuparia .... see MOUNTAIN ASH
Sorghum ....see BROOM CORN
Sorghum bicolor................................see BROOM CORN
Sorghum vulgare ....see BROOM CORN
Sorosi .... see BITTER MELON
SORREL .... see SORREL
Sorrel Dock.. see SORREL
Sotapa... see DILL
Soudan Coffee................................... see COLA NUT
SOUR CHERRY ....see SOUR CHERRY
Sour Dock .... see SORREL, YELLOW DOCK
Sour Milk Peptides..................see CASEIN PEPTIDES
Sour Orange ....see BITTER ORANGE
Sour Sop................................. see GRAVIOLA
Sour Trefoil ....see WOOD SORREL
Soursop .... see GRAVIOLA
SOUTH AFRICAN GERANIUM ....
.... see SOUTH AFRICAN GERANIUM
South African Star Grass.......see AFRICAN WILD POTATO

Southern Bayberry .... see BAYBERRY
Southern Black Haw .... see BLACK HAW
Southern Ginseng.......................see JIAOGULAN
SOUTHERN PRICKLY ASH.......................................
......................................see SOUTHERN PRICKLY ASH
Southern Schisandra.............................see SCHISANDRA
Southern Wax Myrtle .... see BAYBERRY
Southernwood Root ....see CARLINA
Sow Berry .... see EUROPEAN BARBERRY
Sowa.. see DILL
Sowbread.................................. see CYCLAMEN
SOY...see SOY
Soy Bean Lecithin.............................. see LECITHIN
Soy Isoflavone Polysaccharide.................................
............see GENISTEIN COMBINED POLYSACCHARIDE
Soy Milk...see SOY
Soy Phosphatidylserine..........see PHOSPHATIDYLSERINE
Soy Protein..see SOY
Soya...see SOY
Soya Oil .... see SOYBEAN OIL
Soybean Curd..................................see SOY
SOYBEAN OIL .... see SOYBEAN OIL
Soyca.................................. see SOYBEAN OIL
Soy-PS........................see PHOSPHATIDYLSERINE
SP-303........................see SANGRE DE GRADO
Spadic.. see COCA
Spanish Bayonet............................see YUCCA
Spanish Black Radish ....see RADISH
SPANISH BROOM.....................see SPANISH BROOM
Spanish Chestnut...................see EUROPEAN CHESTNUT,
HORSE CHESTNUT
Spanish Jasmine.............................see JASMINE
Spanish Lavender .... see LAVENDER
Spanish Licorice............................. see LICORICE
SPANISH ORIGANUM OIL.......................................
.... see SPANISH ORIGANUM OIL
Spanish Pimienta..............................see ALLSPICE
Spanish Psyllium...............see BLACK PSYLLIUM
Spanish Radish.................................see RADISH
Spanish Saffron.................................see SAFFRON
Spanish Sage .... see SAGE
Spanish Thyme................. see SPANISH ORIGANUM OIL,
THYME
Spanish Vetchling.............................see LATHYRUS
Spargelkraut .... see ASPARAGUS
Spargelwurzelstock .... see ASPARAGUS
Sparrow Grass .... see ASPARAGUS
Sparrow Tongue ....see KNOTWEED
Spartium junceum ....see SPANISH BROOM
Spartium scoparium .... see SCOTCH BROOM
Spathyema foetida...........................see SKUNK CABBAGE
SPEARMINT.................................see SPEARMINT
Speckled Jewels .... see JEWELWEED
Speedwell........................ see BROOKLIME, VERONICA
Spergularia rubra................... see ARENARIA RUBRA
Spiceberry ....see WINTERGREEN
Spigelia marilandica....................... see PINK ROOT
Spignet .... see AMERICAN SPIKENARD
Spike Lavender .... see LAVENDER
Spiked Loosestrife .... see PURPLE LOOSESTRIFE
Spikenard ....see AMERICAN SPIKENARD
SPINACH................................see SPINACH
Spinacia inermis.................................see SPINACH
Spinacia oleracea ....see SPINACH
Spinacia spinosa ....see SPINACH

Medical professionals should consult the Professional Version at www.NaturalDatabase.com.

Spinaciae Folium	see SPINACH
Spinatblatter	see SPINACH
Spindle Tree	see WAHOO
Spiny Dogfish Shark	see SQUALAMINE
SPINY RESTHARROW	see SPINY RESTHARROW
Spiraea trifoliata	see INDIAN PHYSIC
Spiraea ulmaria	see MEADOWSWEET
Spiraeae Flos	see MEADOWSWEET
Spire Mint	see SPEARMINT
Spireae Herba	see MEADOWSWEET
Spirit Plant	see REISHI MUSHROOM
Spirits of Turpentine	see TURPENTINE OIL
Spirogermanium	see GERMANIUM
Spirulina	see BLUE-GREEN ALGAE
Spirulina maxima	see BLUE-GREEN ALGAE
Spirulina pacifica	see BLUE-GREEN ALGAE
Spirulina platensis	see BLUE-GREEN ALGAE
Spitzwegerichkraut	see BUCKHORN PLANTAIN
SPLEEN EXTRACT	see SPLEEN EXTRACT
Splenopentin	see SPLEEN EXTRACT
Spogel	see BLOND PSYLLIUM
Sponge Cucumber	see LUFFA
Sponsa Solis	see MARSH MARIGOLD
Spoon Laurel	see MOUNTAIN LAUREL
Spoonwood	see KAMALA
Spoonwort	see SCURVY GRASS
Spotted Cowbane	see WATER HEMLOCK
Spotted Elder	see WITCH HAZEL
Spotted Gum	see LEMON EUCALYPTUS
Spotted Hemlock	see HEMLOCK, WATER HEMLOCK
Spotted Monarda	see HORSEMINT
Spotted Parsley	see WATER HEMLOCK
Spotted Thistle	see BLESSED THISTLE
Spotted Touch-me-not	see JEWELWEED
Spotted Wintergreen	see PIPSISSEWA
Spring Grass	see SWEET VERNAL GRASS
Spruce Fir	see FIR, HEMLOCK SPRUCE
Spumonto	see KOMBUCHA TEA
Spurge Flax	see MEZEREON
Spurge Laurel	see MEZEREON
Spurge Olive	see MEZEREON
Spurred Rye	see ERGOT
SPV-30	see BOXWOOD
SQ-9453	see DMSO (DIMETHYLSULFOXIDE)
SQUALAMINE	see SQUALAMINE
Squalus acanthias	see SHARK CARTILAGE, SHARK LIVER OIL, SQUALAMINE
Squaw Balm	see PENNYROYAL
Squaw Berry	see SQUAWVINE
Squaw Root	see BLACK COHOSH, BLUE COHOSH
Squaw Tea	see MORMON TEA
Squaw Weed	see GOLDEN RAGWORT
Squawbush	see SWEET SUMACH
Squawmint	see PENNYROYAL
SQUAWVINE	see SQUAWVINE
SQUILL	see SQUILL
Squirrel Corn	see CORYDALIS, TURKEY CORN
Sri Lanka Cinnamon	see CINNAMON bark
SSG	see BETA GLUCANS
St. Anthony's Turnip	see BULBOUS BUTTERCUP
St. Barbara's Hedge Mustard	see HEDGE MUSTARD
St. Bartholemew's Tea	see MATE
St. Benedict Thistle	see BLESSED THISTLE
St. James' Tea	see LABRADOR TEA
St. James' Weed	see SHEPHERD'S PURSE
St. James' Wort	see TANSY RAGWORT
St. John's Bread	see CAROB
St. John's Herb	see HEMP AGRIMONY
St. John's Plant	see MUGWORT
ST. JOHN'S WORT	see ST. JOHN'S WORT
St. Josephwort	see BASIL
St. Mary Thistle	see MILK THISTLE
St. Mary's Seal	see SOLOMON'S SEAL
ST-200	see ACETYL-L-CARNITINE
Stabilized Liquid Oxygen	see VITAMIN O
Stabilized Rice Bran	see RICE BRAN
Stable Strontium	see STRONTIUM
Stachys betonica	see BETONY
Stachys officinalis	see BETONY
Staff Vine	see BITTERSWEET NIGHTSHADE
Stag Bush	see BLACK HAW
Staggerweed	see DELPHINIUM, TURKEY CORN
Staggerwort	see TANSY RAGWORT
Stags Horn	see CLUB MOSS
Stammerwort	see TANSY RAGWORT
Standardized Extract of Grapefruit	see GRAPEFRUIT
Stannous Fluoride	see FLUORIDE
STAR ANISE	see STAR ANISE
Star Chickweed	see CHICKWEED
Starbloom	see PINK ROOT
Star-bu	see SEA BUCKTHORN
Starch Blocker	see BEAN POD
Starchwort	see ARUM
Starflower	see BORAGE
Stargrass	see ALETRIS
Starweed	see CHICKWEED
Starwort	see ALETRIS, FALSE UNICORN
Staunchweed	see YARROW
Stave Oak	see OAK bark
Stave Wood	see SIMARUBA
STAVESACRE	see STAVESACRE
Stay Plough	see SPINY RESTHARROW
Stellaria	see ALCHEMILLA
Stellaria Media	see CHICKWEED
Stemless Carlina Root	see CARLINA
Stemless Gentian	see GENTIAN
Sterculia acuminata	see COLA NUT
Sterculia Gum	see KARAYA GUM
Sterculia nitida	see COLA NUT
Sterculia tragacantha	see KARAYA GUM
Sterculia urens	see KARAYA GUM
Sterculia villosa	see KARAYA GUM
Sterinol	see BETA-SITOSTEROL
Sterolins	see BETA-SITOSTEROL
Sterretjie	see AFRICAN WILD POTATO
STEVIA	see STEVIA
Sthula Tvak	see CASSIA CINNAMON
Stick-a-back	see CLIVERS
Stickwort	see AGRIMONY, WOOD SORREL
Stigma Maydis	see CORN SILK
Stigmastanol	see SITOSTANOL
Stillingia	see QUEEN'S DELIGHT
Stillingia sylvatica	see QUEEN'S DELIGHT
Stillingia tenuis	see QUEEN'S DELIGHT
STINGING NETTLE	see STINGING NETTLE
Stingless Nettle	see STINGING NETTLE, WHITE DEAD NETTLE FLOWER
Stinking Arrach	see ARRACH
Stinking Balm	see PENNYROYAL
Stinking Benjamin	see BETH ROOT

Stinking Goosefoot .... see ARRACH
Stinking Motherwort .... see ARRACH
Stinking Nanny .... see TANSY RAGWORT
Stinking Nightshade .... see HENBANE
Stinking Prairie Bush .... see WAFER ASH
Stinking Roger .... see TAGETES
Stinking Rose .... see GARLIC
Stinking Tommy .... see SPINY RESTHARROW
Stinking Willie ....see TANSY
Stinktree .... see TREE OF HEAVEN
Stinkweed .... see JIMSON WEED
Stinkwort .... see JIMSON WEED
Stinky Bob .... see HERB ROBERT
Stizolobium hirsutum .... see COWHAGE
Stone Breaker .... see CHANCA PIEDRA
Stone Oak .... see OAK bark
STONE ROOT .... see STONE ROOT
STORAX .... see STORAX
Storkbill .... see HERB ROBERT
Stractan .... see LARCH ARABINOGALACTAN
Strained Honey .... see HONEY
Stramonium .... see JIMSON WEED
Strangle Tare .... see DODDER
Straw .... see OATS
STRAWBERRY .... see STRAWBERRY
Strawberry Bush .... see WAHOO
Strawberry Tomato .... see WINTER CHERRY
Strawberry Tree .... see WAHOO
String Bean .... see BEAN POD
String of Sovereigns .... see MONEYWORT
Stringy Bark Tree .... see EUCALYPTUS
Strong-scented Lettuce .... see WILD LETTUCE
STRONTIUM .... see STRONTIUM
Strophanthi Grati Semen .... see STROPHANTHUS
Strophanthi Kombe Semen .... see STROPHANTHUS
STROPHANTHUS .... see STROPHANTHUS
Strychni Semen .... see NUX VOMICA
Strychnos ignatii .... see IGNATIUS BEAN
Strychnos Nux-vomica .... see NUX VOMICA
Strychnos Seed .... see NUX VOMICA
Strychnos tieute .... see IGNATIUS BEAN
Stubwort .... see WOOD SORREL
Styphnolobium japonicum .... see PAGODA TREE
Styrax .... see STORAX
Styrax benzoin .... see BENZOIN
Styrax paralleloneurum .... see BENZOIN
Suan Zao Ren .... see JUJUBE
Subholz .... see LICORICE
Subtilisin NAT .... see NATTOKINASE
Succory .... see CHICORY
Sudanese Tea .... see HIBISCUS
Sugandhapatra .... see EUCALYPTUS
Sugandhimula .... see VETIVER
Sugar Maple .... see RED MAPLE
Sugar Pods .... see CAROB
Sugarbeet .... see BEET
Sui Mi Ya .... see RABDOSIA RUBESCENS
Sui-kan .... see WATER DROPWORT
Suikazura .... see HONEYSUCKLE
Sulfated Monosaccharide ....
.... see GLUCOSAMINE SULFATE
Sulfated Saccharide .... see GLUCOSAMINE SULFATE
Sulfomucopolysaccharide .... see MESOGLYCAN
Sulfonyl Sulfur ....
.... see MSM (METHYLSULFONYLMETHANE)
SULFORAPHANE .... see SULFORAPHANE

Sulphated Monosaccharide ....
.... see GLUCOSAMINE SULFATE
Sulphinybismethane ....
.... see DMSO (DIMETHYLSULFOXIDE)
Sultanas .... see GRAPE
SUMA .... see SUMA
Suma .... see ECDYSTERONE, SUMA
Sumaruba .... see SIMARUBA
Sumatra Benzoin .... see BENZOIN
SUMBUL .... see SUMBUL
SUMMER SAVORY .... see SUMMER SAVORY
Sumpfporst .... see MARSH TEA
Sun Drop .... see EVENING PRIMROSE OIL
Sun Rose .... see FROSTWORT
SUNDEW .... see SUNDEW
SUNFLOWER OIL .... see SUNFLOWER OIL
Sunkfield .... see EUROPEAN FIVE-FINGER GRASS
Sunthi .... see GINGER
Supari .... see ANDROGRAPHIS, ARECA
SUPEROXIDE DISMUTASE ....
.... see SUPEROXIDE DISMUTASE
Surasa .... see BASIL
Surelle .... see WOOD SORREL
Surinam Quassia .... see QUASSIA
Surinam Wood .... see QUASSIA
Sushavi .... see BITTER MELON
Svetajiraka .... see CUMIN
Swallow Wort .... see GERMAN IPECAC
SWALLOWROOT .... see SWALLOWROOT
Swallow-wort .... see PLEURISY ROOT
Swamp Cabbage .... see SKUNK CABBAGE
Swamp Cedar .... see THUJA
Swamp Dogwood .... see AMERICAN DOGWOOD,
                                      WAFER ASH
Swamp Laurel .... see MAGNOLIA
Swamp Maple .... see RED MAPLE
SWAMP MILKWEED .... see SWAMP MILKWEED
Swamp Root .... see YERBA MANSA
Swamp Sassafras .... see MAGNOLIA
Swamp Silkweed .... see SWAMP MILKWEED
Swamp Tea .... see MARSH TEA
Sweating Plant .... see BONESET
Sweatroot .... see ABSCESS ROOT
Sweet Acacia .... see CASSIE ABSOLUTE
SWEET ALMOND .... see SWEET ALMOND
SWEET ANNIE .... see SWEET ANNIE
Sweet Balm .... see LEMON BALM
Sweet Bark .... see CASCARILLA
Sweet Basil .... see BASIL
SWEET BAY .... see MAGNOLIA, SWEET BAY
Sweet Bracken .... see SWEET CICELY
Sweet Broom .... see BUTCHER'S BROOM
Sweet Bugle .... see BUGLEWEED
Sweet Calamus .... see CALAMUS
Sweet Cane .... see CALAMUS
Sweet Chamomile .... see ROMAN CHAMOMILE
SWEET CHERRY .... see SWEET CHERRY
Sweet Chervil .... see SWEET CICELY
Sweet Chestnut .... see EUROPEAN CHESTNUT
SWEET CICELY .... see SWEET CICELY
Sweet Cinnamon .... see CALAMUS
SWEET CLOVER .... see SWEET CLOVER
Sweet Cumin .... see ANISE
Sweet Dock .... see BISTORT
Sweet Elder ..... see AMERICAN ELDER, ELDERFLOWER
Sweet Elm .... see SLIPPERY ELM

Medical professionals should consult the Professional Version at www.NaturalDatabase.com.

Sweet False Chamomile.........	see GERMAN CHAMOMILE
Sweet Fennel..	see FENNEL
Sweet Flag......................	see BLUE FLAG, CALAMUS
SWEET GALE................................	see SWEET GALE
Sweet Grass....................................	see CALAMUS
Sweet Gum...................................	see STORAX
Sweet Herb.......................................	see STEVIA
Sweet Herb of Paraguay.......................	see STEVIA
Sweet Leaf of Paraguay	see STEVIA
Sweet Lucerne................................	see SWEET CLOVER
Sweet Mandulin	see HEMP AGRIMONY
Sweet Marjoram..................................	see MARJORAM
Sweet Mary	see LEMON BALM
Sweet Melilot................................	see SWEET CLOVER
Sweet Myrtle....................................	see CALAMUS
Sweet Oil...	see OLIVE
SWEET ORANGE....................	see SWEET ORANGE
Sweet Pea....................................	see LATHYRUS
Sweet Pepper..................................	see CAPSICUM
Sweet Root	see CALAMUS, LICORICE
Sweet Rush...................................	see CALAMUS
Sweet Scented Cactus	see CEREUS
Sweet Sedge...................................	see CALAMUS
Sweet Slumber	see BLOODROOT
SWEET SUMACH	see SWEET SUMACH
Sweet Vernal	see PHEASANT'S EYE
SWEET VERNAL GRASS	
....	see SWEET VERNAL GRASS
SWEET VIOLET	see SWEET VIOLET
Sweet Weed................................	see MARSHMALLOW
Sweet Wood Bark............................	see CASCARILLA
SWEET WOODRUFF	see SWEET WOODRUFF
Sweet Wormwood	see SWEET ANNIE
Sweet-Cus	see SWEET CICELY
Sweet-fern	see SWEET CICELY
Sweethearts	see CLIVERS
Sweet-humlock	see SWEET CICELY
Sweetleaf......................................	see STEVIA
Sweets	see SWEET CICELY
Sweet-smelling Trefoil...........	see HEMP AGRIMONY
Swertia chirata	see CHIRATA
Swertia chirayita	see CHIRATA
Swine Snout	see DANDELION
Swinebread....................................	see CYCLAMEN
Swine's Grass	see KNOTWEED
Swiss Mountain Pine	see PINE
Swynel Grass	see KNOTWEED
Sycocarpus rusbyi	see COCILLANA
Symphytum officinale.....................	see COMFREY
Symplocarpus Foetidus..............	see SKUNK CABBAGE
Synephrine	see BITTER ORANGE
Synkfoyle	see EUROPEAN FIVE-FINGER GRASS
Syrian Tragacanth	see TRAGACANTH
Syringa suspensa............................	see FORSYTHIA
Syzygium aromaticum	see CLOVE
Syzygium cumini	see JAMBOLAN
Syzygium jambolanum	see JAMBOLAN
Syzygium jambos..........................	see JAMBOLAN
Szechuan Peppercorn............	see CHINESE PRICKLY ASH
Szechwan Pepper	see CHINESE PRICKLY ASH
T-2	see DIIODOTHYRONINE
Tabasco Pepper	see CAPSICUM
Tabebuia avellanedae	see PAU D'ARCO
Tabebuia heptaphylla	see PAU D'ARCO
Tabebuia impetiginosa	see PAU D'ARCO
Tabebuia ipe	see PAU D'ARCO
Tabebuia palmeri	see PAU D'ARCO
Tabernanthe iboga	see IBOGA
Table Grapes	see GRAPE
Tag Alder............................	see SMOOTH ALDER
Tagara	see VALERIAN
TAGETES	see TAGETES
Taheebo	see PAU D'ARCO
Taheebo Tea..............................	see PAU D'ARCO
Tahitian Noni Juice	see MORINDA
Tahitian Vanilla	see VANILLA
Tailapatra...................................	see EUCALYPTUS
Tailed Chubebs...............................	see CUBEBS
Tailed Pepper	see CUBEBS
Taja..............................	see CASSIA CINNAMON
Takila...............................	see ANDROGRAPHIS
Talepetrako...............................	see GOTU KOLA
Talewort....................................	see BORAGE
Tall Buttercup............................	see BUTTERCUP
Tall Melilot..............................	see SWEET CLOVER
Tall Nasturtium	see WATERCRESS
Tall Speedwell...........................	see BLACK ROOT
Tall Veronica	see BLACK ROOT
Tallow Shrub	see BAYBERRY
Tamalaka...........................	see CHANCA PIEDRA
TAMARIND	see TAMARIND
Tamarindo	see TAMARIND
Tamarindus indica........................	see TAMARIND
Tamarisk............................	see TAMARIX DIOICA
Tamarix	see TAMARIX DIOICA
TAMARIX DIOICA	see TAMARIX DIOICA
Tame Withy	see FIREWEED
Tamera...................................	see DATE PALM
Tamus......................................	see BRYONIA
Tamus communis	see BLACK BRYONY
Tamus edulis	see BLACK BRYONY
Tan Kue Bai Zhi	see DONG QUAI
Tan Xiang..................	see WHITE SANDALWOOD
Tanaceti parthenii.......................	see FEVERFEW
Tanaceto	see TANSY
Tanacetum boreale............................	see TANSY
Tanacetum cinerariifolium	see PYRETHRUM
Tanacetum parthenium..................	see FEVERFEW
Tanacetum vulgare	see TANSY
Tanchagem	see GREAT PLANTAIN
Tang..............................	see BLADDERWRACK
Tang Kuei	see DONG QUAI
Tangantangan Oil Plant.....................	see CASTOR
Tangeretin	see METHOXYLATED FLAVONES
Tanner's Bark	see OAK bark
Tanner's Cassia	see CASSIA AURICULATA
Tanner's Oak	see OAK bark
TANNIC ACID	see TANNIC ACID
Tan-Shen	see DANSHEN
TANSY......................................	see TANSY
TANSY RAGWORT	see TANSY RAGWORT
Tantusara	see ARECA
Tar Weed	see GUMWEED
Taraktogenos kurzii................	see CHAULMOOGRA
Taraxaci Herba	see DANDELION
Taraxacum..............................	see DANDELION
Taraxacum dens-leonis................	see DANDELION
Taraxacum officinale...................	see DANDELION
Taraxacum Vulgare	see DANDELION
Tare	see TAUMELLOOLCH
Target-leaved Hibiscus..............	see AMBRETTE
TARRAGON..........................	see TARRAGON

Tart Cherry ....see SOUR CHERRY
Tartaric Acid......................see ALPHA HYDROXY ACIDS
Tarweed .... see YERBA SANTA
Tasmanian Blue Gum.............................see EUCALYPTUS
Taso-ho-hua..................... see THUNDER GOD VINE
Taspine .... see SANGRE DE GRADO
Tatuaba ....see CATUABA
TAUMELLOOLCH .... see TAUMELLOOLCH
TAURINE..see TAURINE
Tausendaugbram ....see YARROW
Taxus baccata ....see YEW
Taxus brevifolia...see YEW
TC-80 ....see IPRIFLAVONE
Tchaad ....see KHAT
T'Chai from the Sea....................see KOMBUCHA TEA
TCV-3b .... see VINPOCETINE
Tea .... see BLACK TEA, GREEN TEA
Tea Green .... see GREEN TEA
Tea Oolong...............................see OOLONG TEA
TEA TREE OIL .... see TEA TREE OIL
Teaberry ....see WINTERGREEN
Teamster's Tea................... see EPHEDRA, MORMON TEA
Teasel ....see BONESET, TEAZLE
TEAZLE .... see TEAZLE
Tecoma impetiginosa ....see PAU D'ARCO
Tecoma ipe............................see PAU D'ARCO
Tecoma stans ....see TRONADORA
Tecuitlatl .... see BLUE-GREEN ALGAE
Teinturière .... see POKEWEED
Tela Kucha .... see IVY GOURD
Tempeh..see SOY
Temu Kuning............................see ZEDOARY
Temu Lawak ....see JAVANESE TURMERIC
Temu Lawas ....see JAVANESE TURMERIC
Temu Putih ....see ZEDOARY
Tenuifolia .... see SCHIZONEPETA
Terebinthina laricina .... see LARCH TURPENTINE
Terebinthina veneta .... see LARCH TURPENTINE
Terebinthinae aetheroleum............... see TURPENTINE OIL
TERMINALIA ....see TERMINALIA
Tertiary Calcium Phosphate ....see PHOSPHATE SALTS
Tetracosanol ....see POLICOSANOL
Tetramethoxyflavones ....
.............................see METHOXYLATED FLAVONES
Tetramethylene Glycol................see BUTANEDIOL (BD)
Tetratriacontanol ....see POLICOSANOL
Tetterberry...................................see BRYONIA
Tetterwort...... see BLOODROOT, GREATER CELANDINE
Teucrium chamaedrys .... see GERMANDER,
GROUND PINE
Teucrium scordium ....see WATER GERMANDER
Teucrium scorodonia............................see WOOD SAGE
Tewon Lawa ....see JAVANESE TURMERIC
Texas Cedarwood....................see EASTERN RED CEDAR
Texas Snakeroot .... see ARISTOLOCHIA
Texturized Vegetable Protein ....see SOY
TF..see TRANSFER FACTOR
Thalictroc ....see HEDGE MUSTARD
The Roman Plant...............................see SWEET CICELY
Thea bohea .... see BLACK TEA
Thea bohea ....see GREEN TEA, OOLONG TEA
Thea sinensis......................... see BLACK TEA, GREEN TEA,
OOLONG TEA
Thea viridis .... see BLACK TEA, GREEN TEA,
OOLONG TEA
THEANINE ....see THEANINE

Theobroma ....see COCOA
Theobroma cacao ....see COCOA
Theobroma sativum ....see COCOA
Theobromine ....see COCOA
Thevetia neriifolia ....see OLEANDER
Thevetia peruviana ....see OLEANDER
THIAMINE (VITAMIN B1) ....
.... see THIAMINE (VITAMIN B1)
Thiaminium Chloride Hydrochloride ....
.... see THIAMINE (VITAMIN B1)
Thick-leaved Pennywort .... see GOTU KOLA
Thimbleberry....see BLACK RASPBERRY, BLACKBERRY
Thioctan ....see ALPHA-LIPOIC ACID
Thioctic Acid.........................see ALPHA-LIPOIC ACID
Thlaspi Bursa-pastoris ....see SHEPHERD'S PURSE
Thomas Balsam .... see TOLU BALSAM
Thompson Seedless..................................... see GRAPE
Thormantle .... see TORMENTIL
Thorn-apple ....see JIMSON WEED
Thorny Bearer of Free Berries .... see GINSENG, SIBERIAN
Thorny Burr .... see BURDOCK
Thoroughwax .... see BUPLEURUM
Thoroughwort .... see BONESET, HEMP AGRIMONY
Thor's Beard ....see HOUSELEEK
Thousand-leaf ....see YARROW
Three Seven.......................see PANAX PSEUDOGINSENG
Three-leafed Ivy.....................................see POISON IVY
Three-leafed Nightshade .... see BETH ROOT
Three-leaved Grass ....see WOOD SORREL
Three-leaved Hop Tree............................see WAFER ASH
Three-lobe Sage ....see GREEK SAGE
Threewingnut ....see THUNDER GOD VINE
THREONINE.................................see THREONINE
Throat Root ....see WATER AVENS
Throatwort.............. see DIGITALIS, FIGWORT
Throw-wort .... see MOTHERWORT
THUJA .... see THUJA
Thuja orientalis ....see ORIENTAL ARBORVITAE
THUNDER GOD VINE .... see THUNDER GOD VINE
Thunder Plant.............................see HOUSELEEK
Thwak .... see CINNAMON bark
THYME .... see THYME
Thyme-leave Gratiola .... see BRAHMI
Thymi Herba .... see THYME
Thymomodulin............................ see THYMUS EXTRACT
Thymosin .... see THYMUS EXTRACT
Thymostimulin .... see THYMUS EXTRACT
Thymus .... see THYMUS EXTRACT
Thymus Acid Lysate Derivative.... see THYMUS EXTRACT
Thymus Capitatus .... see SPANISH ORIGANUM OIL
THYMUS EXTRACT .... see THYMUS EXTRACT
Thymus serpyllum ....see WILD THYME
Thymus vulgaris................................... see THYME
Thymus zygis .... see THYME
Thymus-derived Polypeptides....... see THYMUS EXTRACT
Tian Hua Fen............................ see CHINESE CUCUMBER
Tian Qi .... see PANAX PSEUDOGINSENG
Tiarella cordifolia.................................. see COOLWORT
Tickleweed ....see AMERICAN HELLEBORE
Tickweed .... see PENNYROYAL
Tienchi Ginseng ....see PANAX PSEUDOGINSENG
Tiglium .... see CROTON SEEDS
Tilia argentea....................................see LINDEN
Tilia cordata ....see LINDEN
Tilia europaea....................................see LINDEN
Tilia grandifolia.................................see LINDEN

Tilia parvifolia.................................see LINDEN
Tilia platyphyllos............................see LINDEN
Tilia rubra.....................................see LINDEN
Tilia tomentosa...............................see LINDEN
Tilia ulmifolia................................see LINDEN
Tilia vulgaris.................................see LINDEN
Tiliae Flos....................................see LINDEN
Tiliae Folium.................................see LINDEN
Tiliae lignum.................................see LINDEN
Tilki uzumu...........................see HERB PARIS
Tindved .... see SEA BUCKTHORN
Tinnevelly Senna............................ see SENNA
Tipton Weed .... see ST. JOHN'S WORT
TIRATRICOL .... see TIRATRICOL
Tiririca-de-balaio ....see CARQUEJA
TMG.................... see BETAINE ANHYDROUS,
                        BETAINE HYDROCHLORIDE
Toadpipe............ see HORSETAIL, YELLOW TOADFLAX
Tochukaso .... see CORDYCEPS
Tocopherol .... see VITAMIN E
Tocopheryl Acid Succinate .... see VITAMIN E
Tocotrienol .... see VITAMIN E
Tofu.......................................see SOY
Toge-banreisi.......................... see GRAVIOLA
Tohai ....see KHAT
Tohat ....see KHAT
TOLU BALSAM .... see TOLU BALSAM
Toluifera balsamum .... see TOLU BALSAM
Toluifera pereirae.....................see PERU BALSAM
Toluiferum balsamum .... see TOLU BALSAM
Tom Rong .... see GAMBOGE
TOMATO .... see TOMATO
To-nezumimochi ....see GLOSSY PRIVET
Tonga...................................... see KAVA
Tongkat Ali................see EURYCOMA LONGIFOLIA
TONKA BEAN ....see TONKA BEAN
Tonquin Bean ....see TONKA BEAN
Tonquin Musk ....see MUSK
Toothache Bark .... see NORTHERN PRICKLY ASH
Toothache Tree.................see SOUTHERN PRICKLY ASH
Toothpick Ammi .... see KHELLA
Toothpick Plant .... see KHELLA
Torch Weed .... see MULLEIN
Torches .... see MULLEIN
TORMENTIL .... see TORMENTIL
Tormentilla........................... see TORMENTIL
Tormentillae Rhizoma .... see TORMENTIL
Toronja .... see GRAPEFRUIT
Torquin Bean.......................see TONKA BEAN
Touchi ....see SOY
Touch-me-not.... see GINSENG, SIBERIAN; JEWELWEED
Toute Épice ....see BLACK SEED
Toxicodendron altissimum.............. see TREE OF HEAVEN
Toxicodendron pubescens..........................see POISON IVY
Toxicodendron quercifolium..................see POISON IVY
Toxicodendron radicans ....see POISON IVY
Toxicodendron toxicarium ....see POISON IVY
Toywort ....see SHEPHERD'S PURSE
Trackleberry ....see BILBERRY
TRAGACANTH .... see TRAGACANTH
Tragacanth Gum .... see TRAGACANTH
TRAILING ARBUTUS .... see TRAILING ARBUTUS
Trailing Mahonia.....................see OREGON GRAPE
Trailing Swamp Cranberry...................... see CRANBERRY
Trailing Tansy .... see POTENTILLA
Trametes Versicolor..............see CORIOLUS MUSHROOM

Trans-capsaicin .... see CAPSICUM
TRANSFER FACTOR.................see TRANSFER FACTOR
Trans-resveratrol .... see RESVERATROL
TRAVELER'S JOY ....
.... see TRAVELER'S JOY, WOODBINE
Travmulsion .... see SOYBEAN OIL
Tree Moss........................see OAK MOSS, USNEA
TREE OF HEAVEN .... see TREE OF HEAVEN
Tree of Life .... see THUJA
Tree Peony .... see PEONY
TREE TURMERIC ....see TREE TURMERIC
Tree's Dandruff .... see USNEA
Trefoil....................see LIVERWORT, RED CLOVER
Trembling Aspen ....see ASPEN
Tres-espigas ....see CARQUEJA
Triac .... see TIRATRICOL
Triacontanol ....see POLICOSANOL
Triacontanol (30-C)................. see OCTACOSANOL
Triacylglycerol Lipase .... see LIPASE
Tribulus Terrestris ....see PUNCTURE VINE
Tricalcium Phosphate....................see CALCIUM,
                            PHOSPHATE SALTS
Tricholomopsis edodes .... see LENTINAN,
                        SHIITAKE MUSHROOM
Trichosanthes ....see CHINESE CUCUMBER
Trifolium ....see RED CLOVER
Trifolium macrorrhizum .... see SWEET CLOVER
Trifolium officinale .... see SWEET CLOVER
Trifolium pratense ....see RED CLOVER
Trigonella ....see FENUGREEK
Triiodothyroacetic Acid .... see TIRATRICOL
Trilisa odoratissima...................see DEERTONGUE
Trillium erectum .... see BETH ROOT
Trimethyl Chitosan Chloride ....see CHITOSAN
Trimethyl Glycine ....see BETAINE ANHYDROUS,
                        BETAINE HYDROCHLORIDE
Trimethylethanolamine ....see CHOLINE
Trimethylglycine....................see BETAINE ANHYDROUS,
                        BETAINE HYDROCHLORIDE
Trimethylglycine Anhydrous ....
.........................see BETAINE ANHYDROUS
Trimethylglycine Hydrochloride.......................
.... see BETAINE HYDROCHLORIDE
Tripsin .... see TRYPSIN
Tripterygium wilfordii .... see THUNDER GOD VINE
Trisodium Ethylenediamine Tetraacetic Acid......... see EDTA
Triticum.........................see WHEATGRASS
Triticum aestivum .... see WHEAT BRAN
Triticum firmum ....see WHEATGRASS
Triticum repens ....see WHEATGRASS
Trivalent Chromium...................... see CHROMIUM
Troène de Chine.....................see GLOSSY PRIVET
Trollius europaeus....................see GLOBE FLOWER
Trompillo .... see COCILLANA
TRONADORA.......................see TRONADORA
Tropaeolum majus.....................see NASTURTIUM
Tropical Almond ....see TERMINALIA
True Angostura........................see ANGOSTURA
True Bay.............................. see SWEET BAY
True Chamomile .... see GERMAN CHAMOMILE
True Ivy............................ see ENGLISH IVY
True Lavender .... see LAVENDER
True Saffron ....see SAFFRON
True Sage .... see SAGE
True Senna .... see SENNA
True Unicorn Root .... see ALETRIS

    Natural Medicines Comprehensive Database Consumer Version   (209) 472-2244

Trueno .... see GLOSSY PRIVET
Trumpet Bush .... see PAU D'ARCO, TRONADORA
Trumpet Flower .... see GELSEMIUM
Trumpet Weed .... see GRAVEL ROOT
Truxillo Coca .... see COCA
TRYPSIN .... see TRYPSIN
Tryptophan .... see L-TRYPTOPHAN
Tschambucco .... see KOMBUCHA TEA
Tschut .... see KHAT
Tsubo-kusa .... see GOTU KOLA
Tsuga canadensis .... see PINUS BARK
Tsuru-kokemomo .... see CRANBERRY
TTFCA .... see GOTU KOLA
Tu Si Zi .... see DODDER
Tuber Root .... see PLEURISY ROOT
Tuckahoe .... see PORIA MUSHROOM
Tuftsin .... see SPLEEN EXTRACT
Tulasi .... see HOLY BASIL
Tulsi .... see HOLY BASIL
Tumba .... see COLOCYNTH
Tuna Cardona .... see PRICKLY PEAR CACTUS
TUNG SEED .... see TUNG SEED
Tungchian .... see GOTU KOLA
Tun-hoof .... see GROUND IVY
Turangi-ghanda .... see ASHWAGANDHA
Turanj .... see LIME
Turi Hutan .... see CHANCA PIEDRA
Turkey Claw .... see CORAL ROOT
TURKEY CORN .... see TURKEY CORN
Turkey Grass .... see VERBENA
Turkey Rhubarb .... see RHUBARB
Turkey Tail .... see CORIOLUS MUSHROOM
Turk's Cap .... see MARTAGON
TURMERIC .... see TURMERIC, ZEDOARY
Turmeric Root .... see GOLDENSEAL
Turnera diffusa .... see DAMIANA
Turnera microphylla .... see DAMIANA
Turnerae Diffusae Folium .... see DAMIANA
Turnerae Diffusae Herba .... see DAMIANA
Turnhoof .... see GROUND IVY
Turnip Radish .... see RADISH
TURPENTINE OIL .... see TURPENTINE OIL
Turpentine Weed .... see CUP PLANT
TURTLE HEAD .... see TURTLE HEAD
Turtlebloom .... see TURTLE HEAD
Tussilage .... see COLTSFOOT
Tussilago farfara .... see COLTSFOOT
Tussilago hybrida .... see BUTTERBUR
Tvak .... see CINNAMON bark
Twinberry .... see SQUAWVINE
Twitchgrass .... see WHEATGRASS
Two-eyed Berry .... see SQUAWVINE
Twopenny Grass .... see MONEYWORT
Tyosen-azami .... see ARTICHOKE
Type II Collagen .... see CHICKEN COLLAGEN
TYROSINE .... see TYROSINE
Tyrosinum .... see TYROSINE
Tzu Tan-ken .... see DANSHEN
Ubidecarenone .... see COENZYME Q-10
Ubiquinol .... see COENZYME Q-10
Ubiquinone .... see COENZYME Q-10
Udakiryaka .... see DIVI-DIVI
Ugragandha .... see CALAMUS
Ulmus fulva .... see SLIPPERY ELM
Ulmus minor .... see ELM BARK

Ulmus rubra .... see SLIPPERY ELM
Umbellate Wintergreen .... see PIPSISSEWA
Umbrella Leaves .... see BUTTERBUR
Umbrella Plant .... see PODOPHYLLUM
Umckaloabo .... see SOUTH AFRICAN GERANIUM
Ume Brandy .... see JAPANESE APRICOT
Una de Gato .... see CAT'S CLAW
Uncaria guianensis .... see CAT'S CLAW
Uncaria procumbens .... see DEVIL'S CLAW
Uncaria tomentosa .... see CAT'S CLAW
Undi .... see LAURELWOOD
Unsaturated Fatty Acid .... see OLIVE
Untouchable .... see GINSENG, SIBERIAN
Upas .... see COCILLANA
Upright Virgin's Bower .... see CLEMATIS
Upstart .... see AUTUMN CROCUS
Ura .... see MORINDA
Uragoga granatensis .... see IPECAC
Uragoga ipecacuanha .... see IPECAC
Urginea indica .... see SQUILL
Urginea maritima .... see SQUILL
Urginea scilla .... see SQUILL
Urtica .... see STINGING NETTLE
Ushana .... see INDIAN LONG PEPPER
Ushira .... see VETIVER
USNEA .... see USNEA
Ussuri .... see GINSENG, SIBERIAN
Ussurian Thorny Pepperbrush ..... see GINSENG, SIBERIAN
Utricularia Vulgaris .... see BLADDERWORT
Uva de Raposa .... see HERB PARIS
UVA URSI .... see UVA URSI
Uvae ursi Folium .... see UVA URSI
UZARA .... see UZARA
Uzarae Radix .... see UZARA
Vaccinium altomontanum .... see BLUEBERRY
Vaccinium amoenum .... see BLUEBERRY
Vaccinium angustifolium .... see BLUEBERRY
Vaccinium ashei .... see BLUEBERRY
Vaccinium brittonii .... see BLUEBERRY
Vaccinium constablaei .... see BLUEBERRY
Vaccinium corymbosum .... see BLUEBERRY
Vaccinium gaultherioides .... see BOG BILBERRY
Vaccinium hagerupii .... see CRANBERRY
Vaccinium lamarckii .... see BLUEBERRY
Vaccinium macrocarpon .... see CRANBERRY
Vaccinium microcarpum .... see CRANBERRY
Vaccinium myrtillus .... see BILBERRY
Vaccinium occidentale .... see BOG BILBERRY
Vaccinium oxycoccos .... see CRANBERRY
Vaccinium pallidum .... see BLUEBERRY
Vaccinium palustre .... see CRANBERRY
Vaccinium pensylvanicum .... see BLUEBERRY
Vaccinium uliginosum .... see BOG BILBERRY
Vaccinium vacillans .... see BLUEBERRY
Vaccinium virgatum .... see BLUEBERRY
Vaccinium vitis-idaea .... see ALPINE CRANBERRY
Vacha .... see CALAMUS
Valencia Orange .... see SWEET ORANGE
VALERIAN .... see VALERIAN
Valeriana rubra .... see RED-SPUR VALERIAN
Valine .... see BRANCHED-CHAIN AMINO ACIDS
Vanadate .... see VANADIUM
VANADIUM .... see VANADIUM
Vanadyl .... see VANADIUM
Vanatulasi .... see BASIL

Medical professionals should consult the
Professional Version at www.NaturalDatabase.com.

VANILLA .... see VANILLA
Vanilla Leaf.............................. see DEERTONGUE
Vanilla Plant .... see DEERTONGUE
Vanilla trilisa .... see DEERTONGUE
Vanillin .... see VANILLA
Vapor .... see FUMITORY
Varech .... see BLADDERWRACK
Varnish Tree .... see TREE OF HEAVEN, TUNG SEED
Varvara .... see BASIL
Vassoura .... see CARQUEJA
Vatadha .... see BITTER ALMOND
Vataireopsis araroba .... see GOA POWDER
Vathada .... see BITTER ALMOND
Vatya .... see COUNTRY MALLOW
Vayambur .... see CALAMUS
Vegetable Antimony .... see BONESET
Vegetable Calomel .... see PODOPHYLLUM
Vegetable Carbon .... see ACTIVATED CHARCOAL
Vegetable Caterpillar........................ see CORDYCEPS
Vegetable Gelatin .... see AGAR
Vegetable Mercury ....see MANACA, PODOPHYLLUM
Vegetable Pepsin ....see PAPAIN
Vegetable Sponge........................... see LUFFA
Vegetable Sulfur........................see CLUB MOSS
Vegetable Tallow .... see BAYBERRY
Vegetarian Gelatin................................ see AGAR
Vegilecithin ....see LECITHIN
Vellaja .... see BLACK PEPPER AND WHITE PEPPER
Vellorita............................... see AUTUMN CROCUS
Velvet Antler .... see DEER VELVET
Velvet Bean .... see COWHAGE
Velvet Dock .... see ELECAMPANE
Velvet Flower ....see AMARANTH
Velvet Leaf ....see PAREIRA
Velvet Plant .... see MULLEIN
Velvetleaf .... see ABUTA
Venastat .... see HORSE CHESTNUT
Venetian Turpentine .... see LARCH TURPENTINE
Venostasin Retard........................ see HORSE CHESTNUT
Venostat .... see HORSE CHESTNUT
Venus' Basin .... see TEAZLE
Venus' Hair .... see MAIDENHAIR FERN
Venus' Shoe....................... see NERVE ROOT
Veratro Verde..................... see AMERICAN HELLEBORE
Veratrum album .... see WHITE HELLEBORE
Veratrum eschscholtzii ....see AMERICAN HELLEBORE
Veratrum lobelianum.................. see WHITE HELLEBORE
Veratrum luteum...................... see FALSE UNICORN
Veratrum viride ....see AMERICAN HELLEBORE
Verbasci Flos.............................. see MULLEIN
Verbascum densiflorum........................ see MULLEIN
Verbascum phlomides .... see MULLEIN
Verbascum thapiforme .... see MULLEIN
Verbascum thapsus .... see MULLEIN
VERBENA....................................see VERBENA
Verbena triphylla.................see LEMON VERBENA
Verbenae Herba.............................see VERBENA
Vernicia cordata .... see TUNG SEED
Vernis de Japon .... see TREE OF HEAVEN
VERONICA...................................see VERONICA
Veronica beccabunga.....................see BROOKLIME
Veronica virginica .... see BLACK ROOT
Veronicastrum virginicum..................... see BLACK ROOT
Verrucaria....................see MARSH MARIGOLD
Verruguera..................see GREATER CELANDINE

Vervain .... see VERBENA
Verveine Citronelle ....see LEMON VERBENA
Vespula maculata .... see BEE VENOM
VETIVER .... see VETIVER
Vetivergras................................... see VETIVER
Vetiveria zizanioides .... see VETIVER
Vibhitaki......................................see TERMINALIA
Viburnum ....see BLACK HAW
Viburnum alnifolium....................... see HYDRANGEA
Viburnum americanum..................... see HYDRANGEA
Viburnum lentago.......................see BLACK HAW
Viburnum opulus....................... see CRAMP BARK
Viburnum prunifolium.....................see BLACK HAW
Viburnum rufidulum.....................see BLACK HAW
Vidhara.................... see HAWAIIAN BABY WOODROSE
Vilayati afsanteen........................ see WORMWOOD
Vinca Minor .... see PERIWINKLE
Vinca rosea................see MADAGASCAR PERIWINKLE
Vincae Minoris Herba .... see PERIWINKLE
Vincetoxicum hirundinaria.............. see GERMAN IPECAC
Vincetoxicum officinale .... see GERMAN IPECAC
Vine Bower ....see WOODBINE
Vine of Mount Ida..................... see ALPINE CRANBERRY
Vine-of-Sodom.........................see COLOCYNTH
Vinettier................... see EUROPEAN BARBERRY
VINPOCETINE .... see VINPOCETINE
Viola.......................................see HEART'S EASE
Viola odorata....... see GARDEN VIOLET, SWEET VIOLET
Viola Tricolor............................see HEART'S EASE
Violae Odoratae Rhizoma.....................see SWEET VIOLET
Violae Tricoloris Herba.....................see HEART'S EASE
Violet.......................................see SWEET VIOLET
Violet Bloom.............. see BITTERSWEET NIGHTSHADE
Violet Willow .... see WILLOW BARK
Virgin Coconut Oil...................... see COCONUT OIL
Virgin Olive Oil.............................. see OLIVE
Virginia Cedarwood .... see EASTERN RED CEDAR
Virginia Creeper .... see AMERICAN IVY
Virginia Raspberry .... see BLACK RASPBERRY
Virginia Serpentary .... see ARISTOLOCHIA
Virginia Snakeroot .... see ARISTOLOCHIA
Virginia Water Horehound .... see BUGLEWEED
Virginian Poke....................... see POKEWEED
Virginian Prune .... see WILD CHERRY
Virginian Strawberry.....................see STRAWBERRY
Virgin's Bower ....see WOODBINE
Visci .... see EUROPEAN MISTLETOE
Viscum album .... see EUROPEAN MISTLETOE
Viscum flavescens .... see AMERICAN MISTLETOE
Viscum leucarpum .... see AMERICAN MISTLETOE
Vishamushti................................see NUX VOMICA
Vishani .... see GYMNEMA
Visnaga.................................... see KHELLA
Visnagae.................................... see KHELLA
Visnagafruchte .... see KHELLA
Visnagin .... see KHELLA
Vitacarn .... see L-CARNITINE
Vitadurin .... see VITAMIN B12
VITAMIN A .... see VITAMIN A
Vitamin B(t) .... see L-CARNITINE
Vitamin B(t) Acetate .... see ACETYL-L-CARNITINE
Vitamin B1 .... see THIAMINE (VITAMIN B1)
Vitamin B2 .... see RIBOFLAVIN (VITAMIN B2)
Vitamin B3 ....
.... see NIACIN AND NIACINAMIDE (VITAMIN B3)

Vitamin B5 .... see PANTOTHENIC ACID (VITAMIN B5)
Vitamin B6 .... see PYRIDOXINE (VITAMIN B6)
Vitamin B8 .... see INOSITOL
Vitamin B9 .... see FOLIC ACID
Vitamin B10 ....
.... see PARA-AMINOBENZOIC ACID (PABA)
VITAMIN B12 .... see VITAMIN B12
Vitamin B15 .... see PANGAMIC ACID
Vitamin B17 .... see APRICOT
Vitamin Bx ...... see PARA-AMINOBENZOIC ACID (PABA)
VITAMIN C (ASCORBIC ACID) ....
.... see VITAMIN C (ASCORBIC ACID)
VITAMIN D .... see VITAMIN D
VITAMIN E .... see VITAMIN E
Vitamin G .... see RIBOFLAVIN (VITAMIN B2)
Vitamin H .... see BIOTIN,
PARA-AMINOBENZOIC ACID (PABA)
VITAMIN K .... see VITAMIN K
VITAMIN O .... see VITAMIN O
Vitamin PP ....
.... see NIACIN AND NIACINAMIDE (VITAMIN B3)
Vitellin .... see LECITHIN
Vitex .... see CHASTEBERRY
Vitex agnus-castus .... see CHASTEBERRY
Vitex rotundifolia .... see CHASTEBERRY
Vitex trifolia .... see CHASTEBERRY
Viticis Fructus .... see CHASTEBERRY
Vitis pentaphylla .... see JIAOGULAN
Vitis vinifera .... see GRAPE, WINE
Viverra civetta .... see CIVET
Vizra Ufar .... see ANDROGRAPHIS
Vogelknoeterichkraut .... see KNOTWEED
Vogelmistel .... see EUROPEAN MISTLETOE
Volatile Almond Oil .... see BITTER ALMOND
Vomit Wort .... see LOBELIA
Vriddadaru .... see HAWAIIAN BABY WOODROSE
Vrikshamla .... see GARCINIA
Vysorel .... see EUROPEAN MISTLETOE
W Factor .... see BIOTIN
W-3 Fatty Acid ... see DHA (DOCOSAHEXAENOIC ACID),
EPA (EICOSAPENTAENOIC ACID), FISH OIL
Wacholderbeeren .... see JUNIPER
Wacholderteer .... see CADE OIL
WAFER ASH .... see WAFER ASH
WAHOO .... see WAHOO
Wake Robin .... see ARUM, BETH ROOT
Waldmeister .... see SWEET WOODRUFF
Walewort .... see DWARF ELDER
Wall Germander .... see GERMANDER
Wall Ginger .... see COMMON STONECROP
WALLFLOWER ....
.... see CANADIAN HEMP, WALLFLOWER
Wallpepper .... see COMMON STONECROP
Wallstock-gillofer .... see WALLFLOWER
Wallwort .... see COMFREY
Walnussblätter .... see ENGLISH WALNUT
Walnussfrüchtschalen .... see ENGLISH WALNUT
Walnut .... see BLACK WALNUT, ENGLISH WALNUT
Walpole Tea .... see NEW JERSEY TEA
Wandering Jenny .... see MONEYWORT
Wandering Tailor .... see MONEYWORT
Wang Sun .... see HERB PARIS
Warnera .... see GOLDENSEAL
Wartwort .... see CUDWEED
Wasp Venom .... see BEE VENOM

Wasserkresse .... see WATERCRESS
Wasser-schierling .... see WATER HEMLOCK
Wasshanf .... see HEMP AGRIMONY
Wateorhiza palmata .... see COLOMBO
Water Agrimony .... see BURR MARIGOLD
WATER AVENS .... see WATER AVENS
Water Blobs .... see MARSH MARIGOLD
Water Bugle .... see BUGLEWEED
Water Cabbage .... see AMERICAN WHITE POND LILY
Water Celery .... see WATER DROPWORT
Water Chisch .... see WATER AVENS
WATER DOCK .... see WATER DOCK
Water Dragon .... see MARSH MARIGOLD
WATER DROPWORT .... see WATER DROPWORT,
WATER FENNEL
WATER FENNEL .... see WATER FENNEL
Water Flag .... see BLUE FLAG, ORRIS
Water Flower .... see WATER AVENS
WATER GERMANDER .... see WATER GERMANDER
Water Gourd .... see LUFFA
WATER HEMLOCK .... see WATER FENNEL,
WATER HEMLOCK
Water Hoarhound .... see BUGLEWEED
Water Lemon .... see PASSIONFLOWER
Water Lily .... see AMERICAN WHITE POND LILY
Water Maudlin .... see HEMP AGRIMONY
Water Mint .... see WILD MINT
Water Nymph .... see AMERICAN WHITE POND LILY
Water of Pimento .... see ALLSPICE
Water Parsley .... see WATER DROPWORT
Water Pepper .... see SMARTWEED
Water Pimpernel .... see BROOKLIME
Water Pink .... see TRAILING ARBUTUS
WATER PLANTAIN .... see WATER PLANTAIN
Water Purslane .... see BROOKLIME
Water Shamrock .... see BOGBEAN
WATERCRESS .... see WATERCRESS
Water-cup .... see PITCHER PLANT
Waterhemp .... see HEMP AGRIMONY
Water-holly .... see OREGON GRAPE
Waterkres .... see WATERCRESS
Wax Bean .... see BEAN POD
Wax Cluster .... see WINTERGREEN
Wax Dolls .... see FUMITORY
Wax Myrtle .... see BAYBERRY
Waxberry .... see BAYBERRY
Waxwork .... see AMERICAN BITTERSWEET
Waythorn .... see EUROPEAN BUCKTHORN
Weather Plant .... see PRECATORY BEAN
Weaver's Broom .... see SPANISH BROOM
Weed .... see MARIJUANA
Weeping Ash .... see ASH
Weeping Golden Bell .... see FORSYTHIA
Weibe Senfsamen .... see WHITE MUSTARD
Weidenrinde .... see WILLOW BARK
Weissdorn .... see HAWTHORN
Wermut .... see WORMWOOD
Wermutkraut .... see WORMWOOD
West Indian Cherry .... see ACEROLA
West Indian Dogwood .... see JAMAICAN DOGWOOD
West Indian Lemongrass .... see LEMONGRASS
Western Larch .... see LARCH ARABINOGALACTAN
Western Shisandra .... see SCHISANDRA
Western Yew .... see YEW
Western-huckleberry .... see BOG BILBERRY

Westwood-pear	see PRICKLY PEAR CACTUS
Weyl Ash	see GOUTWEED
WHEAT BRAN	see WHEAT BRAN
WHEATGRASS	see WHEATGRASS
WHEY PROTEIN	see WHEY PROTEIN
Whig Plant	see ROMAN CHAMOMILE
White Archangel	see WHITE DEAD NETTLE FLOWER
White Ash	see ASH, GOUTWEED
White Atractylodis	see ATRACTYLODES
White Baneberry	see WHITE COHOSH
White Bay	see MAGNOLIA
White Beeswax	see BEESWAX
White Birch	see BIRCH
White Bole	see KAOLIN
White Bryony	see BRYONIA
White Cabbage	see CABBAGE
White Cedar	see THUJA
White Cinnamon	see CANELLA
WHITE COHOSH	see WHITE COHOSH
White Daisy	see OX-EYE DAISY
WHITE DEAD NETTLE FLOWER	see WHITE DEAD NETTLE FLOWER
White Dragon Flower	see ORRIS
White Fringe	see FRINGETREE
White Ginseng	see GINSENG, PANAX
White Gum	see STORAX
WHITE HELLEBORE	see WHITE HELLEBORE
WHITE HOREHOUND	see WHITE HOREHOUND
White Kidney Bean	see BEAN POD
White Laurel	see MAGNOLIA
WHITE LILY	see WHITE LILY
White Mallow	see COUNTRY MALLOW
WHITE MUSTARD	see WHITE MUSTARD
White Peony	see PEONY
White Pepper	see BLACK PEPPER AND WHITE PEPPER
White Pond Lily	see WHITE LILY
White Potato	see POTATO
White Quebracho	see QUEBRACHO
White Root	see PLEURISY ROOT
White Rot	see GOTU KOLA
WHITE SANDALWOOD	see WHITE SANDALWOOD
White Saunders	see WHITE SANDALWOOD
WHITE SOAPWORT	see WHITE SOAPWORT
White Sorrel	see WOOD SORREL
White Squill	see SQUILL
White Thyme Oil	see THYME
White Walnut	see BUTTERNUT
White Wax	see BEESWAX
White Waxtree	see GLOSSY PRIVET
White Weed	see OX-EYE DAISY
White Willow	see WILLOW BARK
White Wood	see CANELLA
White-faced Hornet	see BEE VENOM
Whitehorn	see HAWTHORN
Whitetube Stargrass	see ALETRIS
Whitlockite	see PHOSPHATE SALTS
Whole Adrenal Extract	see ADRENAL EXTRACT
Whole Oats	see OATS
Whorlywort	see BLACK ROOT
Whortleberry	see BILBERRY
Wickup	see FIREWEED
Wicopy	see FIREWEED
Wiesen-feldkummel	see CARAWAY
Wiesensauerampfer	see SORREL
Wigandia californicum	see YERBA SANTA
Wild Agrimony	see POTENTILLA
Wild Angelica	see ANGELICA
Wild Balsam	see JEWELWEED
Wild Bergamot	see HORSEMINT
Wild Black Cherry	see WILD CHERRY
Wild Boar Fruit	see ROSE HIP
WILD CARROT	see HEMLOCK, WATER HEMLOCK, WILD CARROT
Wild Celandine	see JEWELWEED
Wild Celery Root	see OSHA
Wild Chamomile	see GERMAN CHAMOMILE
WILD CHERRY	see SWEET CHERRY, WILD CHERRY
Wild Chicory	see CHICORY
Wild Cinnamon	see CANELLA
Wild Clover	see RED CLOVER
Wild Coleus	see PERILLA
Wild Cotton	see CANADIAN HEMP
Wild Crane's-bill	see HERB ROBERT
Wild Cucumber	see BITTER MELON
Wild Cumin	see CARAWAY
Wild Curcuma	see GOLDENSEAL
WILD DAISY	see WILD DAISY
Wild Dill	see WATER HEMLOCK
Wild Endive	see DANDELION
Wild Eucalyptus Citriodora	see LEMON EUCALYPTUS
Wild Fennel	see FENNEL
Wild Garlic	see BEAR'S GARLIC
Wild Gentian	see GENTIAN
Wild Germander	see GERMANDER
Wild Ginger	see ASARABACCA
Wild Gourd	see COLOCYNTH
Wild Hops	see BRYONIA
Wild Hydrangea	see HYDRANGEA
Wild Ice Leaf	see MULLEIN
WILD INDIGO	see WILD INDIGO
Wild Iris	see ORRIS
Wild Laburnum	see SWEET CLOVER
Wild Lady's Slipper	see JEWELWEED
Wild Lemon	see PODOPHYLLUM
WILD LETTUCE	see WILD LETTUCE
Wild Liquorice	see SPINY RESTHARROW
Wild Mandrake	see PODOPHYLLUM
Wild Marjoram	see OREGANO
Wild Mexican Yam	see WILD YAM
WILD MINT	see ENGLISH HORSEMINT, WILD MINT
Wild Nard	see ASARABACCA
Wild Nep	see BRYONIA
Wild Oat Herb	see OATS
Wild Pansy	see HEART'S EASE
Wild Parsnip	see ANGELICA, WATER HEMLOCK
Wild Passion Flower	see PASSIONFLOWER
Wild Pea	see LATHYRUS
Wild Pepper	see GINSENG, SIBERIAN; MEZEREON
Wild Pine	see MORINDA
Wild Plum Flower	see BLACKTHORN
WILD RADISH	see WILD RADISH
Wild Red American Ginseng	see CANAIGRE
Wild Red Desert Ginseng	see CANAIGRE
Wild Rosemary	see MARSH TEA
Wild Snapdragon	see YELLOW TOADFLAX
Wild Snowball	see NEW JERSEY TEA
Wild Strawberry	see STRAWBERRY
Wild Sunflower	see ELECAMPANE
WILD THYME	see WILD THYME

     Natural Medicines Comprehensive Database Consumer Version   (209) 472-2244

Wild Tobacco	see LOBELIA
Wild Vanilla	see DEERTONGUE
Wild Vine	see BRYONIA
Wild Woodbine	see AMERICAN IVY
Wild Wormwood	see MUGWORT
WILD YAM	see WILD YAM
WILLARD WATER	see WILLARD WATER
WILLOW BARK	see WILLOW BARK
Willow Herb	see FIREWEED
Willow Sage	see PURPLE LOOSESTRIFE
Willowherb	see FIREWEED
Wind Flower	see PULSATILLA, WOOD ANEMONE
Wind Root	see PLEURISY ROOT
WINE	see WINE
Wine Grapes	see GRAPE
Wineberry	see BILBERRY
Wingseed	see WAFER ASH
Winter Bloom	see WITCH HAZEL
WINTER CHERRY	see ASHWAGANDHA, WINTER CHERRY
Winter Clover	see SQUAWVINE
Winter Marjoram	see OREGANO
Winter Pink	see TRAILING ARBUTUS
WINTER SAVORY	see WINTER SAVORY
Wintera	see WINTER'S BARK
Wintera aromatica	see WINTER'S BARK
Winterana canella	see CANELLA
WINTERGREEN	see PERIWINKLE, WINTERGREEN
Winterlien	see FLAXSEED
WINTER'S BARK	see WINTER'S BARK
Winter's Cinnamon	see WINTER'S BARK
Wintersweet	see OREGANO
Wisconsin Ginseng	see GINSENG, AMERICAN
Witch Grass	see WHEATGRASS
WITCH HAZEL	see WITCH HAZEL
Witch Meal	see CLUB MOSS
Witchen	see MOUNTAIN ASH
Witches' Pouches	see SHEPHERD'S PURSE
Witch's Bells	see DIGITALIS
Withania somnifera	see ASHWAGANDHA
Woad	see ISATIS
Wogon	see BAIKAL SKULLCAP
Wolfberry	see LYCIUM
Wolfiporia Cocos	see PORIA MUSHROOM
Wolf's Bane	see ARNICA
Wolf's Claw	see CLUB MOSS
Wolfsbane	see ACONITE
Wolfstrapp	see BUGLEWEED
Wolly Foxglove	see DIGITALIS
Woman's Long Hair	see USNEA
Wonder Bulb	see AUTUMN CROCUS
Wonder Tree	see CASTOR
WOOD ANEMONE	see WOOD ANEMONE
Wood Betony	see BETONY
Wood Gum	see LARCH ARABINOGALACTAN
WOOD SAGE	see WOOD SAGE
Wood Sanicle	see SANICLE
WOOD SORREL	see WOOD SORREL
Wood Sour	see WOOD SORREL
Wood Spider	see DEVIL'S CLAW
Wood Strawberry	see STRAWBERRY
Wood Sugar	see LARCH ARABINOGALACTAN
Wood Vine	see BRYONIA
Wood Waxen	see DYER'S BROOM
Woodbind	see ENGLISH IVY

WOODBINE	see WOODBINE
Woodbine	see GELSEMIUM, HONEYSUCKLE
Wood-rose	see HAWAIIAN BABY WOODROSE
Woodruff	see SWEET WOODRUFF
Woody	see BITTERSWEET NIGHTSHADE
Woody Climber	see AMERICAN IVY
Woody Nightshade	see BITTERSWEET NIGHTSHADE
Woolen	see MULLEIN
Woolly Morning Glory	see HAWAIIAN BABY WOODROSE
Woolly Parsnip	see MASTERWORT
Woolly Thistle	see SCOTCH THISTLE
Woolmat	see HOUND'S TONGUE
Wooly Mullein	see MULLEIN
Wordward	see SWEET WOODRUFF
Wormgrass	see PINK ROOT
WORMSEED	see WORMSEED
WORMWOOD	see WORMWOOD
Wound Wort	see YARROW
Woundwort	see GOLDENROD, SELF-HEAL
WS 1442	see HAWTHORN
Wu Jia Pi	see GINSENG, SIBERIAN
Wu Ning	see MORINDA
Wu Wei Zi	see SCHISANDRA
Wu-jia	see GINSENG, SIBERIAN
Wu-mei Juice	see JAPANESE APRICOT
Wundkraut	see ARNICA
Wurmkraut	see WORMWOOD
Wurzelstock	see KAVA
Wymote	see MARSHMALLOW
Xango	see MANGOSTEEN
Xango Juice	see MANGOSTEEN
XANTHAN GUM	see XANTHAN GUM
Xanthomonas campestris	see XANTHAN GUM
XANTHOPARMELIA	see XANTHOPARMELIA
Xanthophyll	see LUTEIN
Xanthoxylum	see NORTHERN PRICKLY ASH, SOUTHERN PRICKLY ASH,
Xhoba	see HOODIA
Xi Yang Shen	see GINSENG, AMERICAN
Xi Zang Hu Huang Lian	see PICRORHIZA
Xian Ling Pi	see EPIMEDIUM
Xianxao	see JIAOGULAN
Xiao Chai Hu Tang	see BUPLEURUM
Xin Ye Hua	see MAGNOLIA
Xiwuweizi	see SCHISANDRA
Xue Jie	see DRAGON'S BLOOD
Xue Zhi Kang	see RED YEAST
Xylite	see XYLITOL
XYLITOL	see XYLITOL
Xysmalobium undulatum	see UZARA
Yadake	see BAMBOO
Yagona	see KAVA
Yam	see WILD YAM
Yangona	see KAVA
Yaqona	see KAVA
YARROW	see YARROW
Yashti-madhu	see LICORICE
Yashti-madhuka	see LICORICE
Yavani	see BISHOP'S WEED
Yavatikta	see ANDROGRAPHIS
Yaw Root	see QUEEN'S DELIGHT
Yeast-derived Beta Glucan	see BETA GLUCANS
Yege	see KUDZU
Yellow Astringent	see EPHEDRA

Medical professionals should consult the Professional Version at www.NaturalDatabase.com.

Yellow Bark	see CASCARA
Yellow Beeswax	see BEESWAX
Yellow Beet	see BEET
Yellow Bells	see TRONADORA
Yellow Broom	see WILD INDIGO
Yellow Bugle	see GROUND PINE
Yellow Chaste Weed	see IMMORTELLE, SANDY EVERLASTING
Yellow Cleavers	see LADY'S BEDSTRAW
YELLOW DOCK	see YELLOW DOCK
Yellow Flag	see ORRIS
Yellow Galium	see LADY'S BEDSTRAW
Yellow Gentian	see GENTIAN
Yellow Ginseng	see BLUE COHOSH
Yellow Hornet	see BEE VENOM
Yellow Horse	see EPHEDRA
Yellow Indian Paint	see GOLDENSEAL
Yellow Indigo	see WILD INDIGO
Yellow Iris	see ORRIS
Yellow Jasmine	see GELSEMIUM
Yellow Jessamine Root	see GELSEMIUM
YELLOW LUPIN	see YELLOW LUPIN
Yellow Melilot	see SWEET CLOVER
Yellow Mustard	see WHITE MUSTARD
Yellow Oleander	see OLEANDER
Yellow Paint	see GOLDENSEAL
Yellow Pheasant's Eye	see PHEASANT'S EYE
Yellow Poppy	see CALIFORNIA POPPY
Yellow Puccoon	see GOLDENSEAL
Yellow Rod	see YELLOW TOADFLAX
Yellow Root	see GOLDENSEAL
Yellow Sandalwood	see WHITE SANDALWOOD
Yellow Saunders	see WHITE SANDALWOOD
Yellow Snakeleaf	see AMERICAN ADDER'S TONGUE
Yellow Snowdrop	see AMERICAN ADDER'S TONGUE
Yellow Starwort	see ELECAMPANE
Yellow Sweet Clover	see SWEET CLOVER
YELLOW TOADFLAX	see YELLOW TOADFLAX
Yellow Trumpet Bush	see TRONADORA
Yellow Vine	see THUNDER GOD VINE
Yellow Water Dropwort	see HEMLOCK WATER DROPWORT
Yellow Wax	see BEESWAX
Yellow Willowherb	see LOOSESTRIFE
Yellow Wood	see NORTHERN PRICKLY ASH
Yellowdock	see YELLOW DOCK
Yellow-jacket Venom	see BEE VENOM
Yellowroot	see GOLDTHREAD
Yellows	see BUTTERCUP, NERVE ROOT
Yellowweed	see BUTTERCUP
Yemen Myrrh	see MYRRH
Yerba Buena	see SPEARMINT
Yerba de Maria	see DIVINER'S SAGE
Yerba de Santa Ana	see VERBENA
Yerba dulce	see STEVIA
YERBA MANSA	see YERBA MANSA
Yerba Manza	see YERBA MANSA
Yerba Mate	see MATE
YERBA SANTA	see YERBA SANTA
YEW	see YEW
YIN CHEN	see YIN CHEN
Yin Du Zhang Ya Cai	see CHIRATA
Yin Yang Huo	see EPIMEDIUM
Yinhsing	see GINKGO
YLANG YLANG OIL	see YLANG YLANG OIL

Yoghurt	see YOGURT
Yogourt	see YOGURT
YOGURT	see YOGURT
YOHIMBE	see YOHIMBE
Yohimbehe	see YOHIMBE
Yohimbine	see YOHIMBE
Yojungja	see GLOSSY PRIVET
Yolk Immunoglobulin	see HYPERIMMUNE EGG
Yongona	see KAVA
Youthwort	see MASTERWORT, SUNDEW
Ysop	see HYSSOP
YUCCA	see YUCCA
Yuma	see WILD YAM
Yun Mu Xiang	see COSTUS
Yun-zhi	see CORIOLUS MUSHROOM
Zacate Violeta	see VETIVER
Zaffer	see SAFFLOWER
Zafran	see SAFFLOWER
Zanthoxylum	see NORTHERN PRICKLY ASH, SOUTHERN PRICKLY ASH
Zanthoxylum americanum	see NORTHERN PRICKLY ASH
Zanthoxylum bungeanum	see CHINESE PRICKLY ASH
Zanthoxylum bungei	see CHINESE PRICKLY ASH
Zanthoxylum clava-herculis	see SOUTHERN PRICKLY ASH
Zanthoxylum simulans	see CHINESE PRICKLY ASH
Zanzibar Pepper	see CAPSICUM
Zao	see JUJUBE
Zappania citrodora	see LEMON VERBENA
Zea	see CORN SILK
Zea Mays	see CORN SILK
Zeaxanthin	see LUTEIN
Zedoaire	see ZEDOARY
Zedoária	see ZEDOARY
Zedoarie rhizoma	see ZEDOARY
ZEDOARY	see ZEDOARY
Zergul	see CALENDULA
Zhi Gan Cao	see LICORICE
Zhi Qiao	see BITTER ORANGE
Zhi Shi	see BITTER ORANGE
Zhi Tai	see RED YEAST
Zhihe Shou Wu	see FO-TI
Zhong Mahuang	see EPHEDRA
Zi Shou Wu	see FO-TI
Zibeth	see CIVET
Zimbluten	see CASSIA CINNAMON
Zimbro	see JUNIPER
ZINC	see ZINC
Zingiber officinale	see GINGER
Zingiberis Rhizoma	see GINGER
Zinzeberis	see GINGER
Zira	see CUMIN
Zitter-pappel	see ASPEN
Zitwer	see ZEDOARY
Zitwerwirtzelstock	see ZEDOARY
Ziziphus jujuba	see JUJUBE
Ziziphus sativa	see JUJUBE
Ziziphus spinosa	see JUJUBE
Ziziphus vulgaris	see JUJUBE
Ziziphus zizyphus	see JUJUBE
Zizyphus	see JUJUBE
Zoom	see GUARANA
Zucapsaicin	see CAPSICUM
Zygophyllum tridentatum	see CHAPARRAL
Zyzyphus Jujube	see JUJUBE

Order Additional Books or Subscribe to the Online Version of either *Natural Medicines Comprehensive Database Consumer Version* or *Natural Medicines Comprehensive Database Professional Version.*

Yes, START MY NEW SUBSCRIPTION.

☐ Books

   ☐ *Natural Medicines Comprehensive Database Consumer Version* . . . . $49 ($72 CAN)

   ☐ *Natural Medicines Comprehensive Database Professional Version*. . . . . $92 ($131 CAN)

☐ Online Version:

   ☐ *Natural Medicines Comprehensive Database Consumer Version* . . . . $49 ($72 CAN)

   ☐ *Natural Medicines Comprehensive Database Professional Version*. . . . . $92 ($131 CAN)

☐ **NEW** PDA Version with updates available daily (Professional Version only) . . . . $92 ($131 CAN)

☐ Online + PDA Version - 1 year single-user access (Professional Version only) . . . .$132 ($171 CAN)

Yes, EXTEND MY EXISTING SUBSCRIPTION.

☐ Books

   ☐ *Natural Medicines Comprehensive Database Consumer Version* . . . . $49 ($72 CAN)

   ☐ *Natural Medicines Comprehensive Database Professional Version*. . . . . $92 ($131 CAN)

☐ Online Version:

   ☐ *Natural Medicines Comprehensive Database Consumer Version* . . . . $49 ($72 CAN)

   ☐ *Natural Medicines Comprehensive Database Professional Version*. . . . . $92 ($131 CAN)

☐ **NEW** PDA Version with updates available daily (Professional Version only) . . . . $92 ($131 CAN)

☐ Online + PDA Version - 1 year single-user access (Professional Version only) . . . .$132 ($171 CAN)

For the book only, please add:

In California, add 8% sales tax . . . . $ _____

Shipping in US and Canada. . . . . FREE

Shipping outside of North America. . . . . $24 US

TOTAL . . . .$ _____

Website users will have an opportunity to agree to the license agreement on the website, or get a full refund.

Name _____ Degree _____ Member # (optional) _____

Address _____

City _____ State/Province _____ Zip/Postal Code _____

Email _____ Phone _____

☐ Payment enclosed (please make check payable to *Natural Database*).

☐ Charge my VISA, MasterCard, American Express, or Discover Card.

  Card No. _____ Exp. Date _____

☐ Bill my business or institution with this Purchase Order # _____

NATURAL MEDICINES
COMPREHENSIVE DATABASE
CONSUMER VERSION

For fastest ordering, call (209) 472-2244.
Fax (209) 472-2249 • mail@naturaldatabaseconsumer.com
Visit us online at www.naturaldatabaseconsumer.com
3120 W. March Lane, PO Box 8190, Stockton, CA 95208

You Can Also Get Access to the Online Versions of
www.naturaldatabase.com
www.naturaldatabaseconsumer.com

This book version of *Natural Medicines Comprehensive Database Consumer Version* was current the day it was printed. But a large amount of new information comes in every day. You can get access to the Consumer Version at www.naturaldatabaseconsumer.com or you can get the Professional Version at www.naturaldatabase.com.

These websites give you everything in the book versions, plus lots more. The websites includes functions that allow you to search:
- Interactions, uses, and side effects
- Brand names and ingredients
- Diseases or medical conditions

Or narrow your search further with the *Natural Product Effectiveness Checker, Natural Product/Drug Interaction Checker, Disease/ Medical Condition Checker,* and *Brand Product Finder.*

On the Professional Version, you can click to see all the references that were used to create each monograph, and you can click on any of the thousands of medical reference citations. You can actually read the original medical journal abstract.

When you subscribe to the Professional Version at www.naturaldatabase.com you can also get the latest news emailed to you with *Natural Database eUPDATE and eCE.* Medical professionals who subscribe will also get continuing medical education that is fully accredited for physicians, pharmacists, physician assistants, nurse practitioners, and registered dietitians.

Contact *Natural Medicines Comprehensive Database*:

Phone: 209-472-2244
Fax: 209-472-2249
Email: mail@naturaldatabase.com

Visit us online at www.therapeuticresearch.com

3120 W. March Lane, PO Box 8190, Stockton CA 95208

NATURAL MEDICINES
COMPREHENSIVE DATABASE

For fastest ordering, call (209) 472-2244.
Fax (209) 472-2249 ● mail@naturaldatabase.com
Visit us online at www.therapeuticresearch.com
3120 W. March Lane, PO Box 8190, Stockton, CA 95208

Order Additional Books or Subscribe to the Online Version of either
Natural Medicines Comprehensive Database Consumer Version or
Natural Medicines Comprehensive Database Professional Version.

Yes, START MY NEW SUBSCRIPTION.

- ☐ Books
    - ☐ *Natural Medicines Comprehensive Database Consumer Version* . . . . $49 ($72 CAN)
    - ☐ *Natural Medicines Comprehensive Database Professional Version.* . . . . $92 ($131 CAN)
- ☐ Online Version:
    - ☐ *Natural Medicines Comprehensive Database Consumer Version* . . . . $49 ($72 CAN)
    - ☐ *Natural Medicines Comprehensive Database Professional Version.* . . . . $92 ($131 CAN)
- ☐ **NEW** PDA Version with updates available daily (Professional Version only) . . . . $92 ($131 CAN)
- ☐ Online + PDA Version - 1 year single-user access (Professional Version only) . . . .$132 ($171 CAN)

Yes, EXTEND MY EXISTING SUBSCRIPTION.

- ☐ Books
    - ☐ *Natural Medicines Comprehensive Database Consumer Version* . . . . $49 ($72 CAN)
    - ☐ *Natural Medicines Comprehensive Database Professional Version.* . . . . $92 ($131 CAN)
- ☐ Online Version:
    - ☐ *Natural Medicines Comprehensive Database Consumer Version* . . . . $49 ($72 CAN)
    - ☐ *Natural Medicines Comprehensive Database Professional Version.* . . . . $92 ($131 CAN)
- ☐ **NEW** PDA Version with updates available daily (Professional Version only) . . . . $92 ($131 CAN)
- ☐ Online + PDA Version - 1 year single-user access (Professional Version only) . . . .$132 ($171 CAN)

For the book only, please add:

In California, add 8% sales tax . . . . $ _____

Shipping in US and Canada. . . . . FREE

Shipping outside of North America. . . . . $24 US

TOTAL . . . .$ _____

Website users will have an opportunity to agree to the license agreement on the website, or get a full refund.

Name _____ Degree _____ Member # (optional) _____

Address _____

City _____ State/Province _____ Zip/Postal Code _____

Email _____ Phone _____

- ☐ Payment enclosed (please make check payable to *Natural Database*).
- ☐ Charge my VISA, MasterCard, American Express, or Discover Card.
    Card No. _____ Exp. Date _____
- ☐ Bill my business or institution with this Purchase Order # _____

NATURAL MEDICINES
COMPREHENSIVE DATABASE
CONSUMER VERSION

For fastest ordering, call (209) 472-2244.
Fax (209) 472-2249 • mail@naturaldatabaseconsumer.com
Visit us online at www.naturaldatabaseconsumer.com
3120 W. March Lane, PO Box 8190, Stockton, CA 95208

You Can Also Get Access to the Online Versions of
www.naturaldatabase.com
www.naturaldatabaseconsumer.com

This book version of *Natural Medicines Comprehensive Database Consumer Version* was current the day it was printed. But a large amount of new information comes in every day. You can get access to the Consumer Version at www.naturaldatabaseconsumer.com or you can get the Professional Version at www.naturaldatabase.com.

These websites give you everything in the book versions, plus lots more. The websites includes functions that allow you to search:
- Interactions, uses, and side effects
- Brand names and ingredients
- Diseases or medical conditions

Or narrow your search further with the *Natural Product Effectiveness Checker, Natural Product/Drug Interaction Checker, Disease/ Medical Condition Checker*, and *Brand Product Finder*.

On the Professional Version, you can click to see all the references that were used to create each monograph, and you can click on any of the thousands of medical

reference citations. You can actually read the original medical journal abstract.

When you subscribe to the Professional Version at www.naturaldatabase.com you can also get the latest news emailed to you with *Natural Database eUPDATE and eCE*. Medical professionals who subscribe will also get continuing medical education that is fully accredited for physicians, pharmacists, physician assistants, nurse practitioners, and registered dietitians.

Contact *Natural Medicines Comprehensive Database*:

Phone: 209-472-2244
Fax: 209-472-2249
Email: mail@naturaldatabase.com

Visit us online at
www.therapeuticresearch.com

3120 W. March Lane, PO Box 8190, Stockton CA 95208

NATURAL MEDICINES
COMPREHENSIVE DATABASE

For fastest ordering, call (209) 472-2244.
Fax (209) 472-2249 • mail@naturaldatabase.com
Visit us online at www.therapeuticresearch.com
3120 W. March Lane, PO Box 8190, Stockton, CA 95208

Order Additional Books or Subscribe to the Online Version of either
Natural Medicines Comprehensive Database Consumer Version or
Natural Medicines Comprehensive Database Professional Version.

Yes, START MY NEW SUBSCRIPTION.

☐ Books

  ☐ *Natural Medicines Comprehensive Database Consumer Version* . . . . $49   ($72 CAN)

  ☐ *Natural Medicines Comprehensive Database Professional Version*. . . . . $92 ($131 CAN)

☐ Online Version:

  ☐ *Natural Medicines Comprehensive Database Consumer Version* . . . . $49   ($72 CAN)

  ☐ *Natural Medicines Comprehensive Database Professional Version*. . . . . $92 ($131 CAN)

☐ **NEW** PDA Version with updates available daily (Professional Version only) . . . . $92 ($131 CAN)

☐ Online + PDA Version - 1 year single-user access (Professional Version only) . . . .$132 ($171 CAN)

Yes, EXTEND MY EXISTING SUBSCRIPTION.

☐ Books

  ☐ *Natural Medicines Comprehensive Database Consumer Version* . . . . $49   ($72 CAN)

  ☐ *Natural Medicines Comprehensive Database Professional Version*. . . . . $92 ($131 CAN)

☐ Online Version:

  ☐ *Natural Medicines Comprehensive Database Consumer Version* . . . . $49   ($72 CAN)

  ☐ *Natural Medicines Comprehensive Database Professional Version*. . . . . $92 ($131 CAN)

☐ **NEW** PDA Version with updates available daily (Professional Version only) . . . . $92 ($131 CAN)

☐ Online + PDA Version - 1 year single-user access (Professional Version only) . . . .$132 ($171 CAN)

For the book only, please add:

In California, add 8% sales tax . . . . $ _____

Shipping in US and Canada. . . . . FREE

Shipping outside of North America. . . . . $24 US

TOTAL . . . .$ _____

Website users will have an opportunity to agree to the license agreement on the website, or get a full refund.

Name _____ Degree _____ Member # (optional) _____

Address _____

City _____ State/Province _____ Zip/Postal Code _____

Email _____ Phone _____

☐ Payment enclosed (please make check payable to *Natural Database*).

☐ Charge my VISA, MasterCard, American Express, or Discover Card.

  Card No. _____ Exp. Date _____

☐ Bill my business or institution with this Purchase Order # _____

NATURAL MEDICINES
COMPREHENSIVE DATABASE
CONSUMER VERSION

For fastest ordering, call (209) 472-2244.
Fax (209) 472-2249 ● mail@naturaldatabaseconsumer.com
Visit us online at www.naturaldatabaseconsumer.com
3120 W. March Lane, PO Box 8190, Stockton, CA 95208

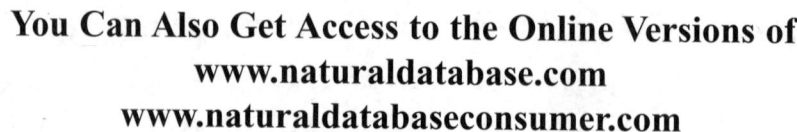

You Can Also Get Access to the Online Versions of
www.naturaldatabase.com
www.naturaldatabaseconsumer.com

This book version of *Natural Medicines Comprehensive Database Consumer Version* was current the day it was printed. But a large amount of new information comes in every day. You can get access to the Consumer Version at www.naturaldatabaseconsumer.com or you can get the Professional Version at www.naturaldatabase.com.

These websites give you everything in the book versions, plus lots more. The websites includes functions that allow you to search:
- Interactions, uses, and side effects
- Brand names and ingredients
- Diseases or medical conditions

Or narrow your search further with the *Natural Product Effectiveness Checker, Natural Product/Drug Interaction Checker, Disease/ Medical Condition Checker*, and *Brand Product Finder*.

On the Professional Version, you can click to see all the references that were used to create each monograph, and you can click on any of the thousands of medical

reference citations. You can actually read the original medical journal abstract.

When you subscribe to the Professional Version at www.naturaldatabase.com you can also get the latest news emailed to you with *Natural Database eUPDATE and eCE*. Medical professionals who subscribe will also get continuing medical education that is fully accredited for physicians, pharmacists, physician assistants, nurse practitioners, and registered dietitians.

Contact *Natural Medicines Comprehensive Database*:

Phone: 209-472-2244
Fax: 209-472-2249
Email: mail@naturaldatabase.com

Visit us online at
www.therapeuticresearch.com

3120 W. March Lane, PO Box 8190, Stockton CA 95208

For fastest ordering, call (209) 472-2244.
Fax (209) 472-2249 ▪ mail@naturaldatabase.com
Visit us online at www.therapeuticresearch.com
3120 W. March Lane, PO Box 8190, Stockton, CA 95208